STREET ATLAS
Greater
Manchester

First published in 1997 by

Philip's, a division of
Octopus Publishing Group Ltd
2–4 Heron Quays, London E14 4JP

Second edition 2001
Third impression 2002

ISBN 0-540-07968-5 (spiral)

© Philip's 2001

Ordnance Survey®

This product includes mapping data licensed
from Ordnance Survey® with the permission of
the Controller of Her Majesty's Stationery Office.
© Crown copyright 2001. All rights reserved.
Licence number 100011710

Printed and bound in Spain
by Cayfosa-Quebecor

Contents

II	**Railways and Metrolink**
III	**Key to map symbols**
IV	**Key to map pages**
VI	**Route planning**
VIII	**Administrative and Postcode Boundaries**
1	**Street maps** at 3½ inches to 1 mile
138	**Street maps of selected areas** at 7 inches to 1 mile
172	**Index** of towns and villages
173	**Index** of streets, hospitals, industrial estates, railway stations, schools, shopping centres and universities

Digital Data

The exceptionally high-quality mapping found in this atlas is available as digital data in TIFF format, which is easily convertible to other bit mapped (raster) image formats.

The index is also available in digital form as a standard database table. It contains all the details found in the printed index together with the National Grid reference for the map square in which each entry is named.

For further information and to discuss your requirements, please contact Philip's on 020 7531 8439 or george.philip@philips-maps.co.uk

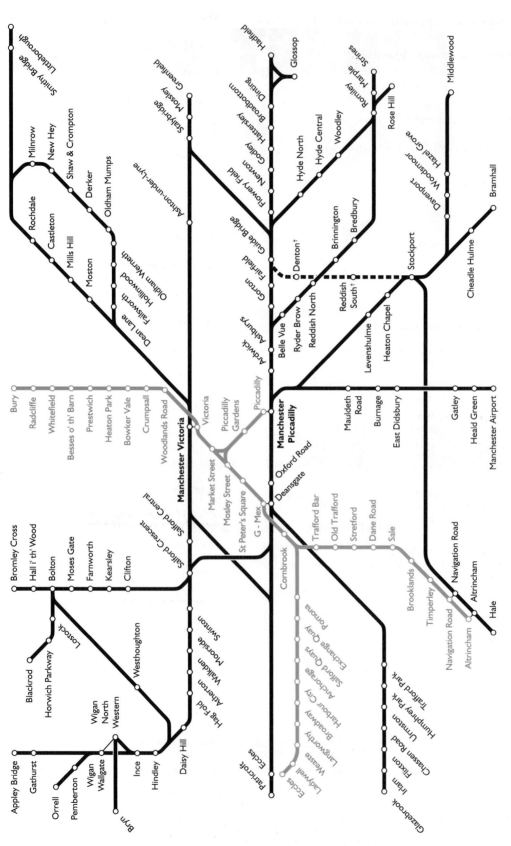

©GMPTE 2000
99/662/02721

KEY

- Rail line in Greater Manchester ticketing area
- Rail line with restricted service
- Metrolink line
- One directional platform (pointing in direction of travel)
- Stations in close proximity
- † Station with restricted service

Motorway with junction number		Railway station	
Primary route - dual carriageway and single		Metrolink	
A road - dual carriageway and single		Private railway station	
B road - dual carriageway and single		Bus, coach station	
Minor road - dual carriageway and single		Ambulance station	
Other minor road - dual carriageway and single		Coastguard station	
Road under construction		Fire station	
Pedestrianised area		Police station	
DY7 Postcode boundaries		Accident and Emergency entrance to hospital	
County and unitary authority boundaries		Hospital	
Railway		Places of worship	
Tramway, miniature railway		Information Centre (open all year)	
Rural track, private road or narrow road in urban area		Parking	
Gate or obstruction to traffic (restrictions may not apply at all times or to all vehicles)		Park and Ride	
Path, bridleway, byway open to all traffic, road used as a public path		Post Office	

The representation in this atlas of a road, track or path is no evidence of the existence of a right of way

84
157
148 Adjoining page indicators
(The colour of the arrow indicates the scale of the page - see scales below)

The map area within the pink band is shown at a larger scale on the page indicated by the red block and arrow

Camping site

Caravan site

Golf course

Picnic site

Prim Sch Important buildings, schools, colleges, universities and hospitals

River Medway Water name

Stream

River or canal - minor and major

Water

Tidal water

Woods

Houses

Allot Gdns	Allotments	Meml	Memorial
Acad	Academy	Mon	Monument
Cemy	Cemetery	Mus	Museum
C Ctr	Civic Centre	Obsy	Observatory
CH	Club House	Pal	Royal Palace
Coll	College	PH	Public House
Crem	Crematorium	Recn Gd	Recreation Ground
Ent	Enterprise	Resr	Reservoir
Ex H	Exhibition Hall	Ret Pk	Retail Park
Ind Est	Industrial Estate	Sch	School
Inst	Institute	Sh Ctr	Shopping Centre
Ct	Law Court	TH	Town Hall/House
L Ctr	Leisure Centre	Trad Est	Trading Estate
LC	Level Crossing	Univ	University
Liby	Library	Wks	Works
Mkt	Market	YH	Youth Hostel

Balls Park Non-Roman antiquity

VILLA Roman antiquity

■ The dark grey border on the inside edge of some pages indicates that mapping does not continue onto the adjacent page

■ The small numbers around the edges of the maps identify the 1 kilometre National Grid lines

The scale of the maps is 5.52 cm to 1 km
3½ inches to 1 mile 1: 18103

0   ¼   ½   ¾   1 mile
0   250m   500m   750m   1 kilometre

The scale of the maps on pages numbered in red is 11.04 cm to 1 km 7 inches to 1 mile 1: 9051.4

0   220 yards   440 yards   660 yards   ½ mile
0   125m   250m   375m   ½ kilometre

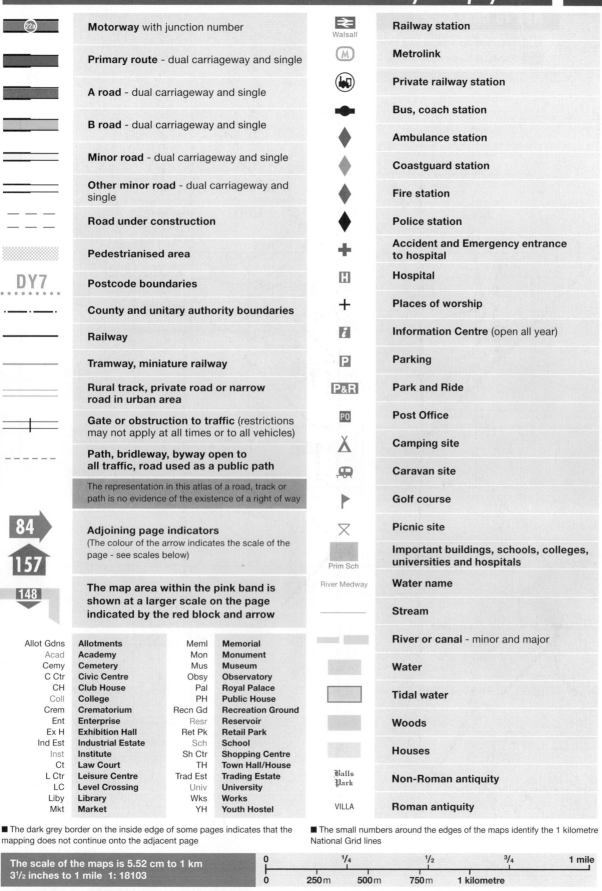

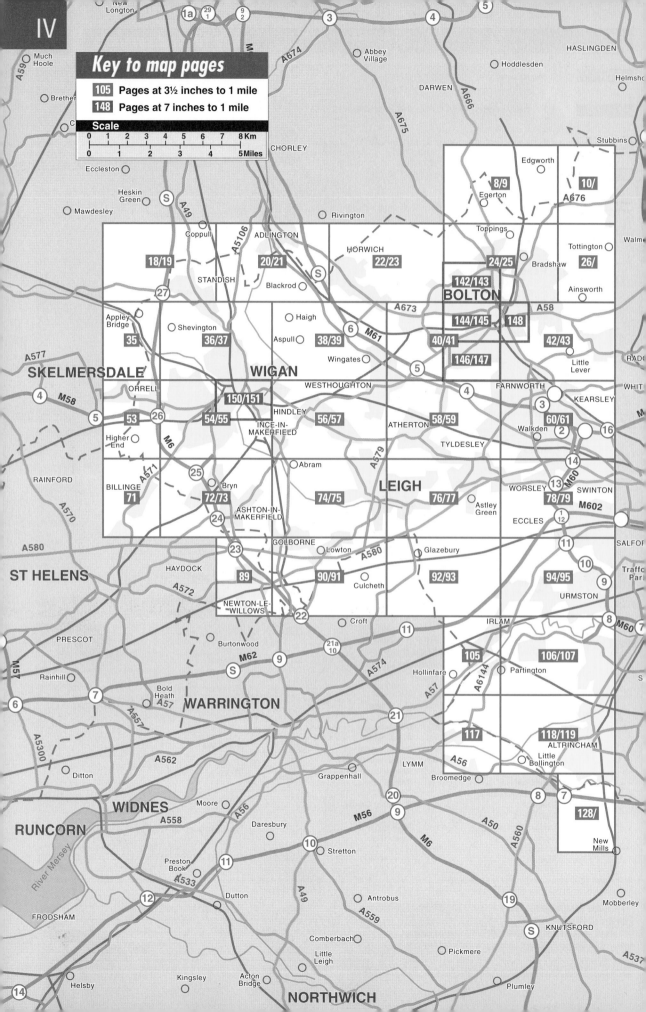

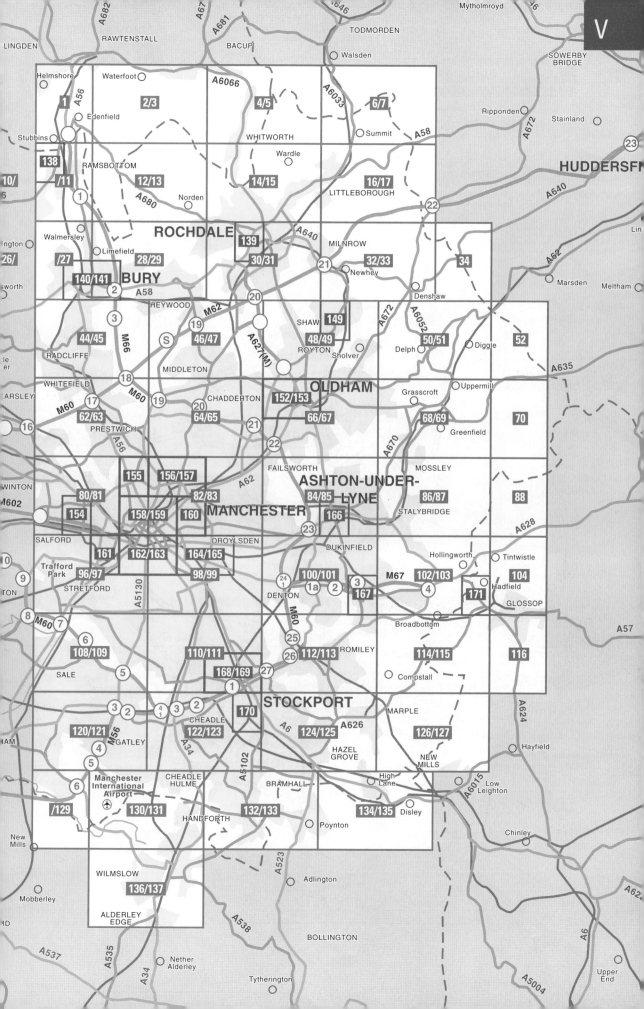

Major administrative and Postcode boundaries

Legend

- County and unitary authority boundaries
- Postcode boundaries
- Area covered by this atlas

Scale

0 5 10 15 km
0 5 10 miles

SD | SE
SJ | SK
SE
SK
SD | SE
SJ | SK

Kirklees
Calderdale
Lancashire
Blackburn with Darwen
Derbyshire
Cheshire
Warrington
Halton
St Helens
Knowsley
Liverpool

Place names and postcodes

Diggle OL3
Denshaw
HD7
HX6
HX7
OL14
Littleborough OL15
OL16 Milnrow
Rochdale OL11
Whitworth OL12
OL13
BB4
BL0
Shaw OL2
Royton
Oldham OL1 OL4
OL9
OL8
OL5 Mossley SK15
Ashton-under-Lyne SK16
Hyde SK14
Romiley SK6
Marple
Disley
SK12
SK22
SK13 Glossop
SK10
Denton M34
OL6
OL7
M35
M40
M11
M12 M13 M18
M19
Stockport SK3 SK1 SK2
Bramhall SK7
SK8 Cheadle
Cheadle Hulme
SK9 Wilmslow
Alderley Edge
M24 Middleton
Heywood OL10
Bury BL9
Ramsbottom
Radcliffe M26
M45
Whitefield M25
Prestwich M8
BL8
BL7
BL2
BL1 Bolton
Horwich BL6
Adlington PR6
PR7
Standish WN6
Orrell WN5
Billinge WN8
Wigan WN1 WN2
Hindley WN3
Ashton-in-Makerfield WN4
Golborne WA3
Newton-le-Willows WA12
WA11
WA1
WA2
Leigh WN7
Tyldesley M46 M29
Atherton M28
Walkden M38
Worsley M27
Kearsley
Farnworth BL4
Little Lever BL3
Westhoughton BL5
Swinton M7
Eccles M30
Salford M6 M5 M3 M4 M1 M2
Stretford M32
Sale M33
Altrincham WA15
Urmston M41
Irlam M44
M31
WA14
WA16
Stockport
Wythenshawe M22 M23
Manchester M14 M15 M16 M21 M20 M90
Trafford
Bury
Rochdale
Oldham
Tameside
Stockport
Salford
Bolton
Wigan

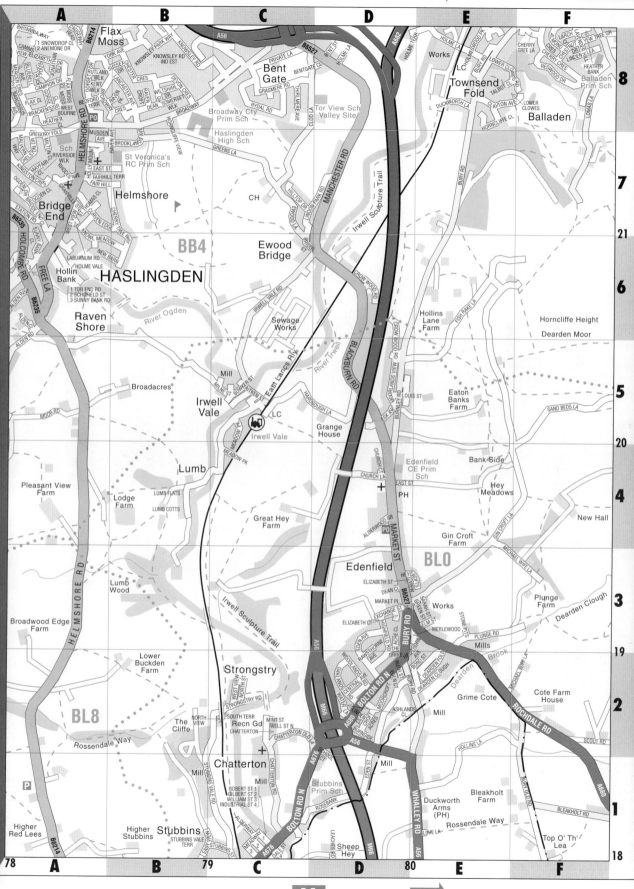

1

F8
1 IVY ST
2 GEORGE'S ROW
3 PILLING ST
4 SPRING GARDENS ST
5 MARKET ST
6 TENTERFIELD ST
7 YARE ST
8 THORNFIELD AVE
9 WOOD LEA BANK
10 INDUSTRIAL COTTS

A
B
C
D
E
F
8
7
21
6
5
20
4
3
19
2
1
18
81
82
83
HARDMAN AVE
Carr Head Farm
NEW BARN LA
Whinberry Naze
Higher Lench
LENCH RD
Irwell Sculpture Trail
A681
Rawtenstall
HOLT MILL RD
FERN LEA ST
WARTH LA
JOE CONNOLLY WAY 1
SCHOFIELD ST 2
BALTIC RD 3
VICTORIA PAR 4
HOLT ST 5
STANSFIELD RD
WEST ST
ST JAMES' ST
CHURCH ST
VICTORIA ST
WILLOW ST
KING ST
DUKE ST
BURNLEY RD E
B6238
BACUP RD
PO
Sch
BOOTH ST
WOOD LEA RD
BARN LA
MOUNT AVE
GLEN RD
IVY COTTS
LENCH ST
MILLAR
STONE ST
ASHWORTH ST
ST JOHN'S ST
TOWNSEND ST
WOLFENDEN GN
BOOTH RD
Bacup & Rawtenstall Gram Sch
A681
River Irwell
RAWTENSTALL
Waterfoot
GREEN BRIDGE N
GREEN BRIDGE S
BRIDGE ST
CARR LA
LUMB HOLES LA
ANDERTON CL
HARDMAN CL
HARDMAN DR
Hugh Mill
TENTERHEADS
COWPE RD
BROOKLAND TERR
SPRING SIDE
SPRING GDNS
BOARSGREAVE LA
Cowpe
BUTTONS ROW
MOOR VIEW
Whitaker Pasture
Lower Mount Pleasant
Higher Mount Pleasant
Cowpe Lowe
BB4
Sand Beds Farm
SAND BEDS LA
Black Hill
Pike Hill
New Hall Close
Dearden Brook
Rossendale Way
Scout Moor Brook
Scout Moor High Level Resr
Scout Moor
Roughs
Rossendale Way
Foe Edge
Tottington Higher End Moor
Moss Top
Scout Fold
Lowes Farm
Whittle Pike
Whittle Hill
Moss
Great Lodge
SCOUT RD
BLO
New Gate
New Gate Brook
Grain Brook
Higher Hill
A680
ROCHDALE RD
Turn
PH
LODGE MILL LA

1

12

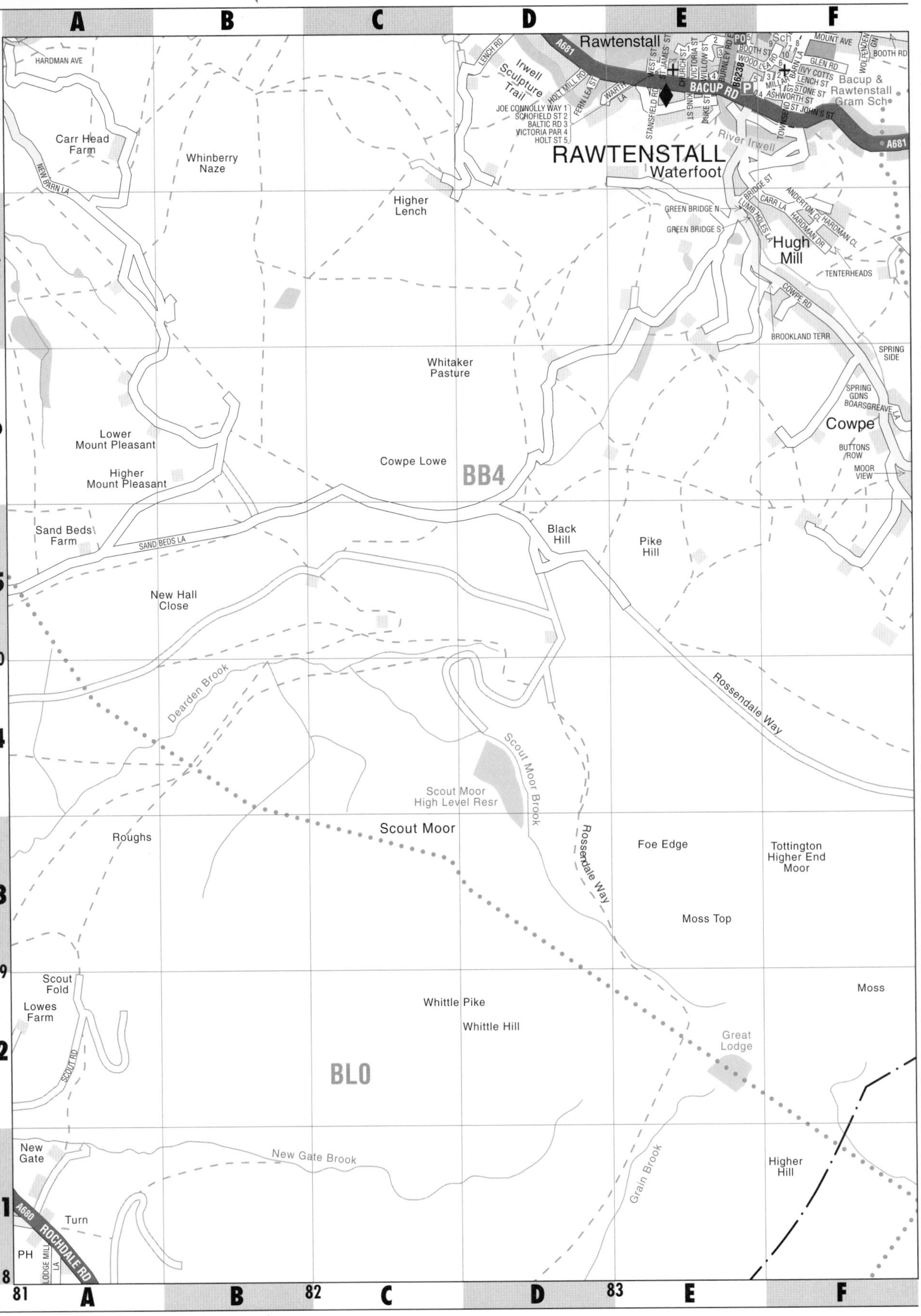

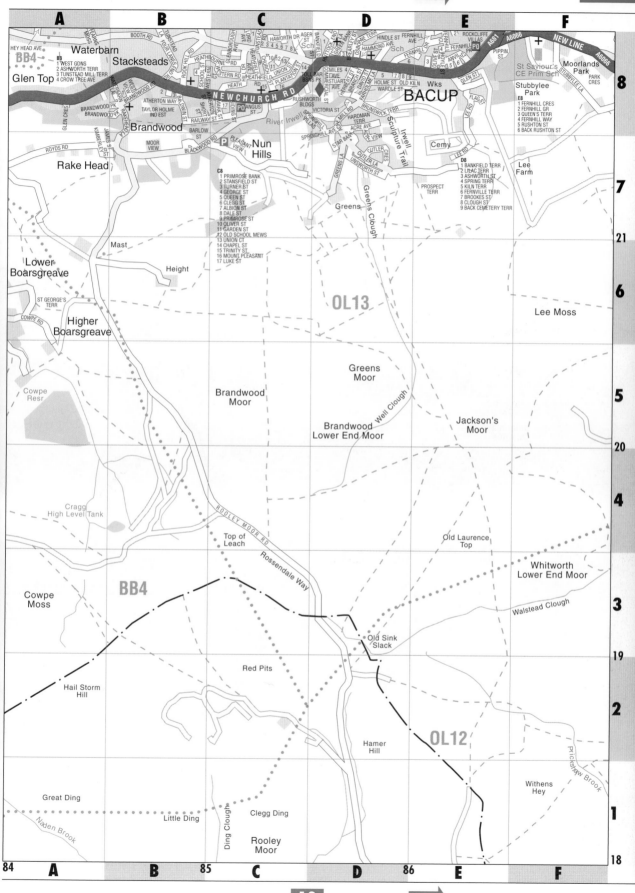

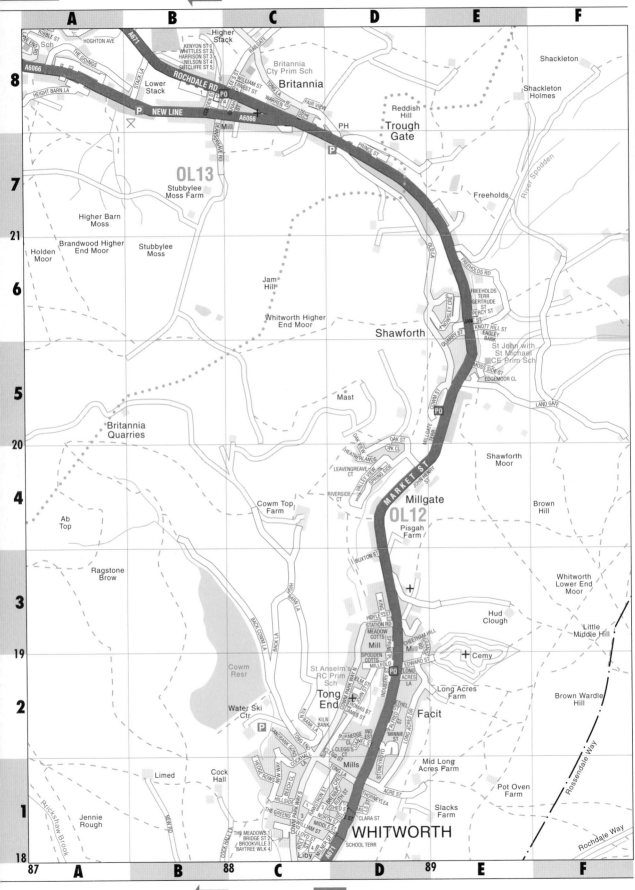

A B C D E F

8
7
21
6
5
20
4
3
19
2
1
18

RIBBLE ST
LANE END RD
HOGHTON AVE
Sch
THE SIDINGS
A671
Higher Stack
KENYON ST 1
WHITTLES ST 2
HARRISON ST 3
NELSON ST 4
SUTCLIFFE ST 5
ST WILLIAM ST
ERNEST ST
RAIL GATE
Britannia Cty Prim Sch
Shackleton
A6066
HEIGHT BARN LA
STACK LA
Lower Stack
ROCHDALE RD
COLLINGE ST
PO
SPRING ST
TONG LA
WARREN ST
Britannia
FAIR VIEW
Shackleton Holmes
P NEW LINE
A6066
Mill
+
PH
Reddish Hill
OL13
DEANSGREAVE RD
P
Prince St
Trough Gate
River Spodden
Stubbylee Moss Farm
Higher Barn Moss
Freeholds
Brandwood Higher End Moor
Stubbylee Moss
Jam Hill
OLD LA
FREEHOLDS RD
Holden Moor
Whitworth Higher End Moor
FREEHOLDS TERR
GERTRUDE ST
PERCY ST
KNOTT HILL ST
EAGLEY BANK
St John with St Michael CE Prim Sch
KINNSLEY CRE
JANE ST
QUARRY ST
Shawforth
MOSS SIDE ST
EDGEMOOR CL
Britannia Quarries
Mast
OAK VIEW
COWM ST
PO
LAND GATE
Shawforth Moor
HEATHERLANDS
OAK ST
2K CL
MILLGATE TERR
LEAVENGREAVE CT
VALLEY VIEW
SPRING SIDE
MARKET ST
JOHN HENRY ST
Brown Hill
Ab Top
Cowm Top Farm
RIVERSIDE CT
Millgate
OL12
Pisgah Farm
Ragstone Brow
BACK COWM LA
HIGH BARN LA
BACK LA
BUXTON ST
+
Whitworth Lower End Moor
Hud Clough
Little Middle Hill
Cowm Resr
KING ST
Hoyle St
STATION RD
MEADOW COTTS
Mill
SPODDEN COTTS
MILLFOLD
SPRING PL
CHEETHAM HILL
Mill
EDWARD ST
PO
LONG ACRES LA
+ Cemy
Brown Wardle Hill
Water Ski Ctr
P
St Anselm's RC Prim Sch
Tong End
+
THOMAS ST
JAMES ST
BURNEDGE CL
CLEGG'S CT
IND EST
MINNIE ST
ETHEL ST
Facit
Long Acres Farm
Rossendale Way
SANDBANK GDNS
TONG END
KILN BANK
COWM PARK WAY N
KILN BANK
Mills
ALFRED ST
STONEY ROYD
LONG ACRES DR
Mid Long Acres Farm
Pot Oven Farm
Limed
Cock Hall
HEDGE ROWS
BEECH CL
NEW WAY
COCKHALL LA
COWM PARK WAY S
RAMSTRONG ST
NORTH ST
MIDDLE ST
CHESS ST
MICHER ST
SHED ST
Mills
THORNEYLEA
ACRE ST
Clara St
Slacks Farm
Prickshaw Brook
Jennie Rough
COCK HALL LA
THE MEADOWS 1
BRIDGE ST 2
BROOKVILLE 3
BAYTREE WLK 4
THE GREENS
HILLSIDE ST
WILLIAM ST
LLOYD ST
NORTH ST
Liby
SCHOOL TERR
WHITWORTH
A671
Rochdale Way

87 A B 88 C D 89 E F

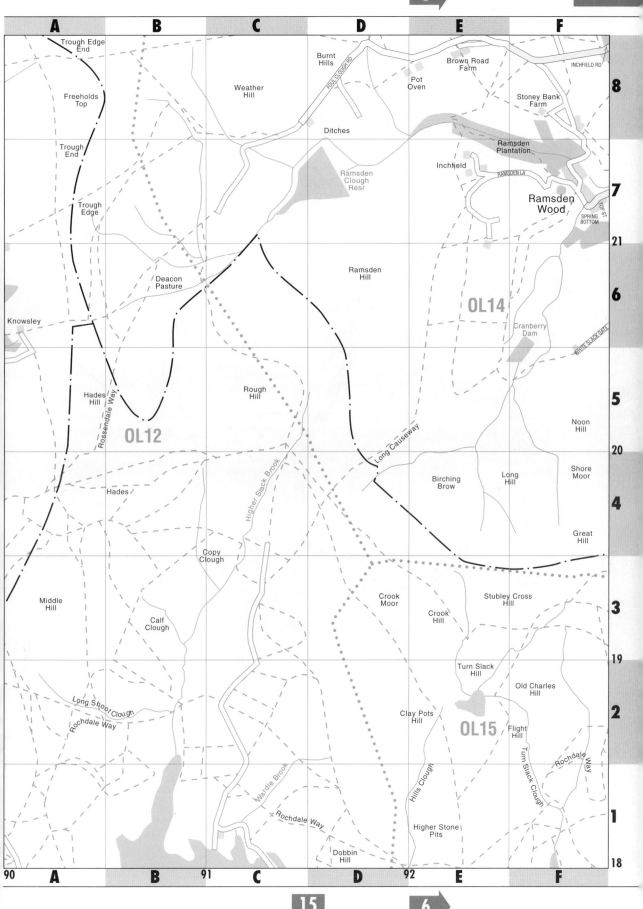

A　B　C　D　E　F

Trough Edge End

Burnt Hills

Brown Road Farm

INCHFIELD RD

Weather Hill

Pot Oven

Stoney Bank Farm

8

Freeholds Top

FOUL CLOUGH RD

Ditches

Inchfield

Ramsden Plantation

RAMSDEN LA

Trough End

Ramsden Clough Resr

Ramsden Wood

7

TOP ST

SPRING BOTTOM

21

Trough Edge

Deacon Pasture

Ramsden Hill

OL14

6

Knowsley

Cranberry Dam

WHITE SLACK GATE

Rossendale Way

Hades Hill

Rough Hill

Noon Hill

5

OL12

Long Causeway

20

Higher Slack Brook

Birching Brow

Long Hill

Shore Moor

Hades

Great Hill

4

Copy Clough

Crook Moor

Stubley Cross Hill

3

Middle Hill

Calf Clough

Crook Hill

Turn Slack Hill

19

Old Charles Hill

Long Shoot Clough

Clay Pots Hill

OL15

Flight Hill

2

Rochdale Way

Rochdale Way

Turn Slack Clough

Wardle Brook

Hills Clough

Rochdale Way

Higher Stone Pits

1

Dobbin Hill

18

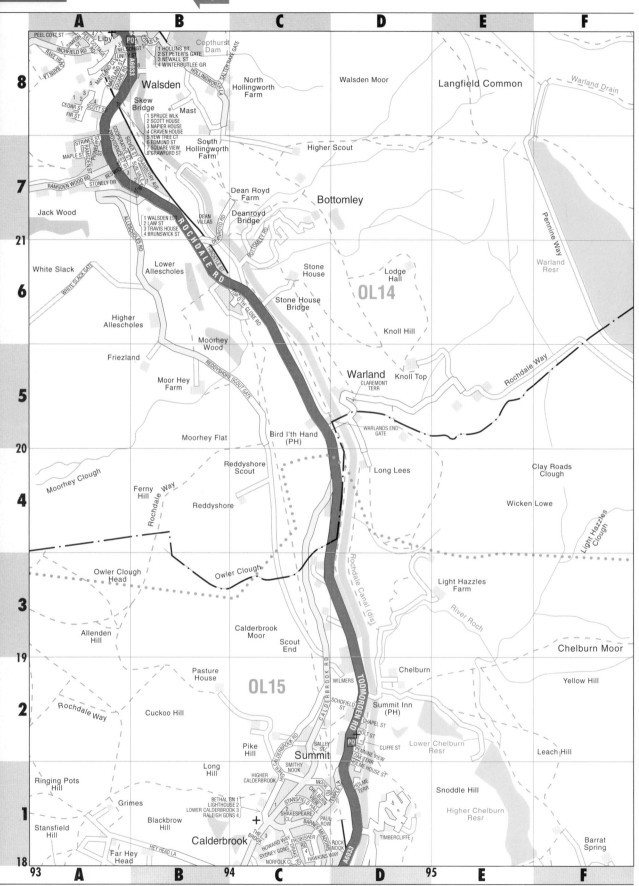

Copthurst
Dam

Walsden Moor

Langfield Common

Warland Drain

Walsden

1 HOLLINS ST
2 ST PETER'S GATE
3 NEWALL ST
4 WINTERBUTLEE GR

North
Hollingworth
Farm

Skew
Bridge

Mast

1 SPRUCE WLK
2 SCOTT HOUSE
3 NAPIER HOUSE
4 CRAVEN HOUSE
5 YEW TREE CT
6 EDMUND ST
7 SQUARE VIEW
8 CRAWFORD ST

South
Hollingworth
Farm

Higher Scout

Jack Wood

Dean Royd
Farm

Deanroyd
Bridge

Bottomley

Pennine Way

1 WALSDEN EST
2 LAW ST
3 TRAVIS HOUSE
4 BRUNSWICK ST

DEAN
VILLAS

Warland
Resr

White Slack

Lower
Allescholes

Stone
House

Lodge
Hall

OL14

Higher
Allescholes

Stone House
Bridge

Knoll Hill

Friezland

Moorhey
Wood

Warland

Knoll Top

Rochdale Way

Moor Hey
Farm

CLAREMONT
TERR

Moorhey Flat

Bird I'th Hand
(PH)

WARLANDS END
GATE

Moorhey Clough

Reddyshore
Scout

Long Lees

Clay Roads
Clough

Ferny
Hill

Rochdale Way

Reddyshore

Wicken Lowe

Light Hazzles Clough

Owler Clough
Head

Owler Clough

Rochdale Canal (dis)

Light Hazzles
Farm

Allenden
Hill

Calderbrook
Moor

Scout
End

River Roch

Chelburn Moor

Rochdale Way

Pasture
House

OL15

WILMERS

Chelburn

Yellow Hill

Cuckoo Hill

SCHOFIELD
ST

Summit Inn
(PH)

CHAPEL ST

Pike
Hill

Long
Hill

SALLEY
ST

HOLT ST

CLIFFE ST

PENNINE VIEW

Lower Chelburn
Resr

Leach Hill

Ringing Pots
Hill

HIGHER
CALDERBROOK

SMITHY
NOOK

Summit

OAK TERR

HOLME HOUSE ST

Snoddle Hill

Grimes

Blackbrow
Hill

BETHAL GN 1
LIGHTHOUSE 2
LOWER CALDERBROOK 3
RALEIGH GDNS 4

STANSFIELD
HALL

SHAKESPEARE
CL

BARNS
MEADOW

PAUL
ROW

HOLME
TERR

TIMBERCLIFFE

Higher Chelburn
Resr

Stansfield
Hill

Calderbrook

THE
BROOK

HOWARD WAY

SYDNEY GDNS

NORFOLK CL

FROBISHER
RD

DRAKE RD

ROCK
NOOK

Barrat
Spring

Far Hey
Head

HEY HEAD LA

HAWKINS ST

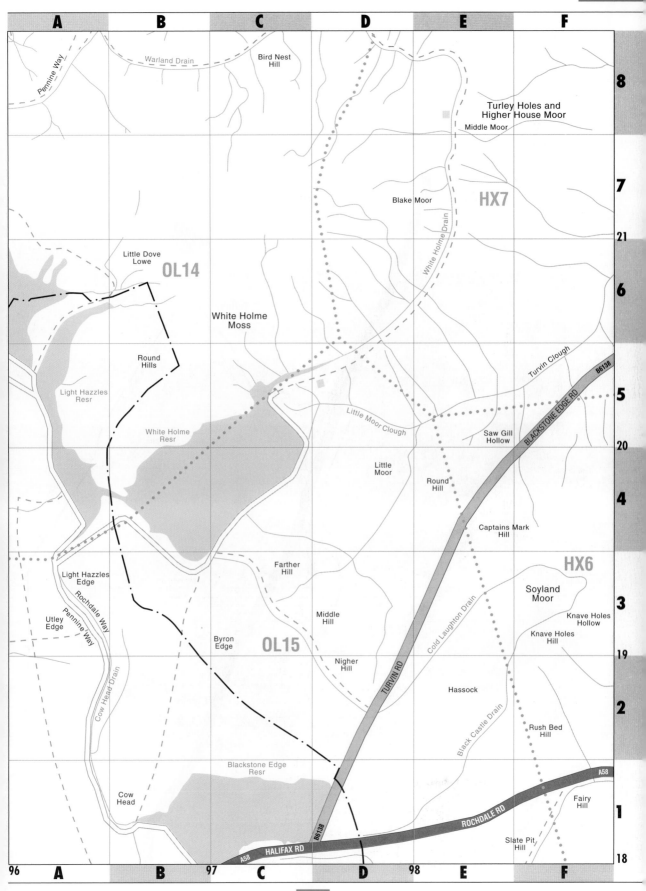

8

Pennine Way

Warland Drain

Bird Nest Hill

Turley Holes and Higher House Moor

Middle Moor

7

Blake Moor

HX7

White Holme Drain

21

Little Dove Lowe

OL14

6

White Holme Moss

Round Hills

Turvin Clough

B6138

Light Hazzles Resr

Little Moor Clough

BLACKSTONE EDGE RD

5

Saw Gill Hollow

White Holme Resr

20

Little Moor

Round Hill

4

Light Hazzles Edge

Captains Mark Hill

Rochdale Way

HX6

Pennine Way

Farther Hill

Soyland Moor

Knave Holes Hollow

3

Utley Edge

Middle Hill

Knave Holes Hill

Cold Laughton Drain

Byron Edge

OL15

19

Cow Head Drain

Nigher Hill

TURVIN RD

Hassock

2

Black Castle Drain

Rush Bed Hill

Blackstone Edge Resr

A58

Cow Head

ROCHDALE RD

Fairy Hill

1

B6138

Slate Pit Hill

A58 HALIFAX RD

18

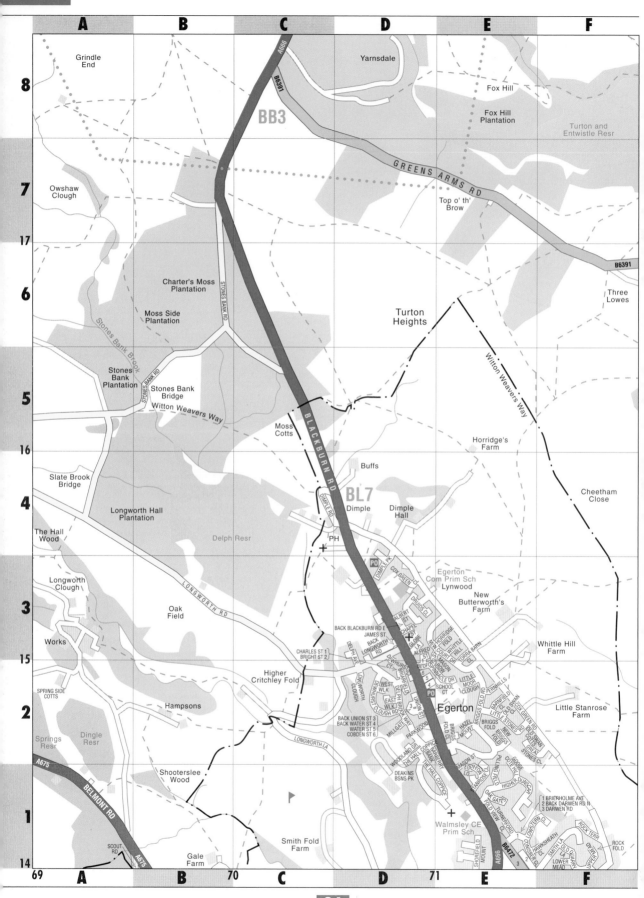

Grindle End

Yarnsdale

Fox Hill

A666

B6391

BB3

Fox Hill Plantation

Turton and Entwistle Resr

8

GREENS ARMS RD

Owshaw Clough

Top o' th' Brow

7

B6391

17

Charter's Moss Plantation

Stones Bank Brook

Stones Bank Rd

Three Lowes

6

Moss Side Plantation

Turton Heights

Witton Weavers Way

Stones Bank Plantation

Stones Bank Rd

Stones Bank Bridge

5

Witton Weavers Way

Moss Cotts

Horridge's Farm

16

Buffs

BLACKBURN RD

Slate Brook Bridge

Cheetham Close

4

Longworth Hall Plantation

Delph Resr

DIMPLE RD

Dimple

Dimple Hall

The Hall Wood

PH

Egerton Com Prim Sch

Lynwood

New Butterworth's Farm

Longworth Clough

LONGWORTH RD

Oak Field

PO

DIMPLE PK

COX GREEN

Whittle Hill Farm

3

Works

ALBERT ST

CHAPEL ST

HORRIDGE FOLD

TORRA BARN

15

BACK BLACKBURN RD E

JAMES ST

BACK LONGWORTH RD

ALFRED ST

CHARLES ST 1

BRIGHT ST 2

DELPH AVE

BEDFORD CT

LITTLE MOOR CLOUGH

Higher Critchley Fold

SCHOOL CT

PO

Egerton

Little Stanrose Farm

2

Hampsons

WEST WLK

EAST WLK

UNION ST

BRIGGS FOLD

BRIGGS FOLD

BARNFIELD CL

LITTLE STONES RD

FOX GREEN RD

DARWEN RD

STONES CL

GREAT CL

Springs Resr

Dingle Resr

BACK UNION ST 3

BACK WATER ST 4

WATER ST 5

COBDEN ST 6

MILLGATE CL

LONGWORTH LA

WOODLAND DR

THE HALL COPPICE

BARBERRY

PILLING FIELD

GORSE RD

Spring Side Cotts

A675

Shooterslee Wood

DEAKINS BSNS PK

THE HALL COPPICE

MASON ST

STANROSE

HIGHER DUNSCAR

1 BRIERHOLME AVE

2 BACK DARWEN RD N

3 DARWEN RD

1

BELMONT RD

A675

OAK GATE

TURNFORD

FOLD VIEW CT

LONGS TERM CL

HAWKSHEATH

SMITH LA

OLD QUARRY

ROCK TERR

ROCK FOLD

UPPER MEAD

SCOUT RD

Gale Farm

Smith Fold Farm

Walmsley CE Prim Sch

SHOREFIELD MOUNT

B6472

A666

LOWER MEAD

14

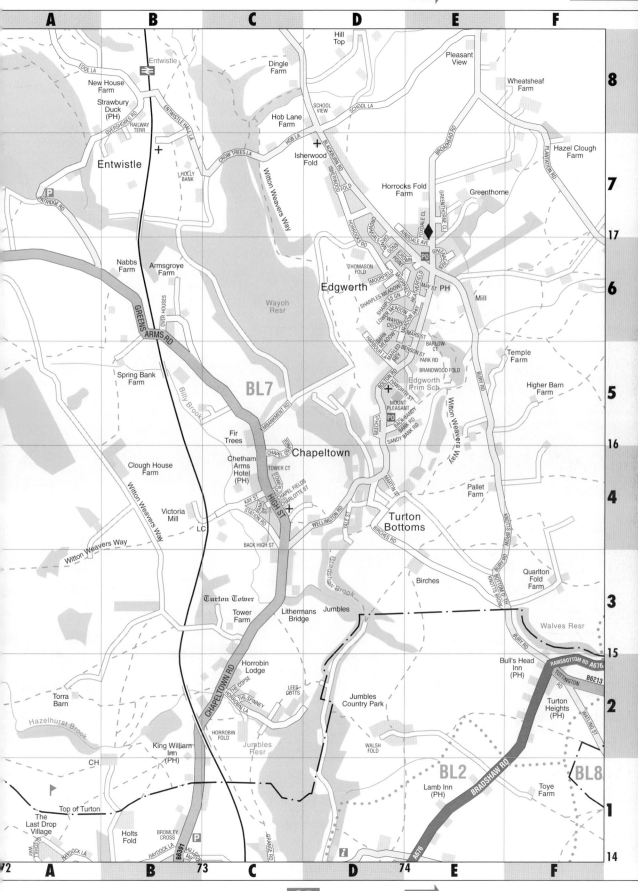

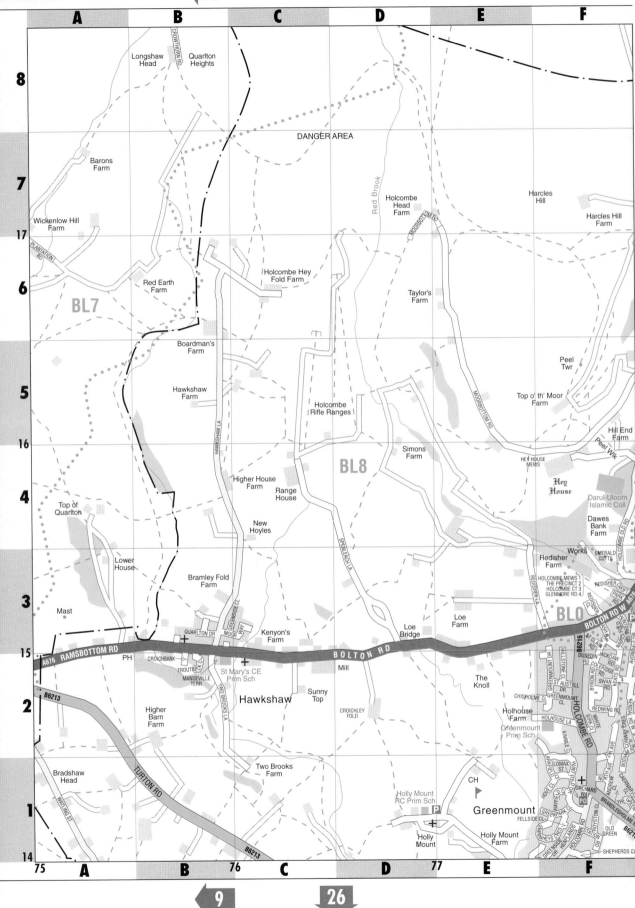

9

A B C D E F

8

9

DANGER AREA

7

Red Brook

Holcombe
Head
Farm

Harcles
Hill

Harcles Hill
Farm

Barons
Farm

Longshaw
Head

Quarlton
Heights

CROWTHORN RD

17

Wickenlow Hill
Farm

MOORBOTTOM RD

6

PLANTATION RD

BL7

Red Earth
Farm

Holcombe Hey
Fold Farm

Taylor's
Farm

Top o' th' Moor
Farm

Peel
Twr

Boardman's
Farm

5

Hawkshaw
Farm

Holcombe
Rifle Ranges

Hill End
Farm

Peel Wlk

16

HAWKSHAW LA

MOORBOTTOM RD

BL8

Simons
Farm

Hey House
Mews

Hey
House

4

Top of
Quarlton

Higher House
Farm

Range
House

Darul-Uloom
Islamic Coll

Dawes
Bank
Farm

New
Hoyles

Lower
House

Bramley Fold
Farm

SPENLEACH LA

Works

Redisher
Farm

Emerald
COTTS

HOLCOMBE OLD RD

3

Mast

GREENSIDE CL

MOOR WAY

Loe
Bridge

Loe
Farm

HOLCOMBE MEWS 1
THE PRECINCT 2
HOLCOMBE CT 3
GLENMORE RD 4.

REDISHER LA

REDISHER CROFT

REISSER RD

BL0

BOLTON RD W

AST

15

A676

RAMSBOTTOM RD

PH

CROICHBANK

QUARLTON DR

Kenyon's
Farm

BOLTON RD

TROUTBE

Mill

The
Knoll

B6215

JACKDAW

DUNEDIN

HILLSTONE CL

ST AUSTELL

COLERIDGE RD

SWAN CL

REDWING RD

BIRCH RD

WHITE

HOLCOMBE RD

2

B6213

MANDEVILLE
TERR

TWO BROOKS LA

St Mary's CE
Prim Sch

Sunny
Top

CROICHLEY
FOLD

Holhouse
Farm

HOLHOUSE LA

CHISHOLME CL

Greenmount
Prim Sch

GREENMOUNT
CL

KIMBLE CL

LOMAX
ST

BODMIN CRES

ROW

CAERNARVON CL

THE CL

Higher
Barn
Farm

Hawkshaw

1

Bradshaw
Head

TURTON RD

Two Brooks
Farm

CH

Holly Mount
RC Prim Sch

P

Greenmount

FELLSIDE CL

ORCHARD
WAY

P

BRANDLESHOLME RD

B621

THE

OLD
GREEN

WAITING ST

B6213

Holly
Mount

Holly Mount
Farm

SHEPHERDS LA

HOVE CL

HAYFIELD CL

GREENPARK RD

GRENEYS CRES

GRENSIDE DR

HEADLANDS

JOHNSTON CL

HOLCOMBE RD

14

75

A

76

B

C

77

D

E

F

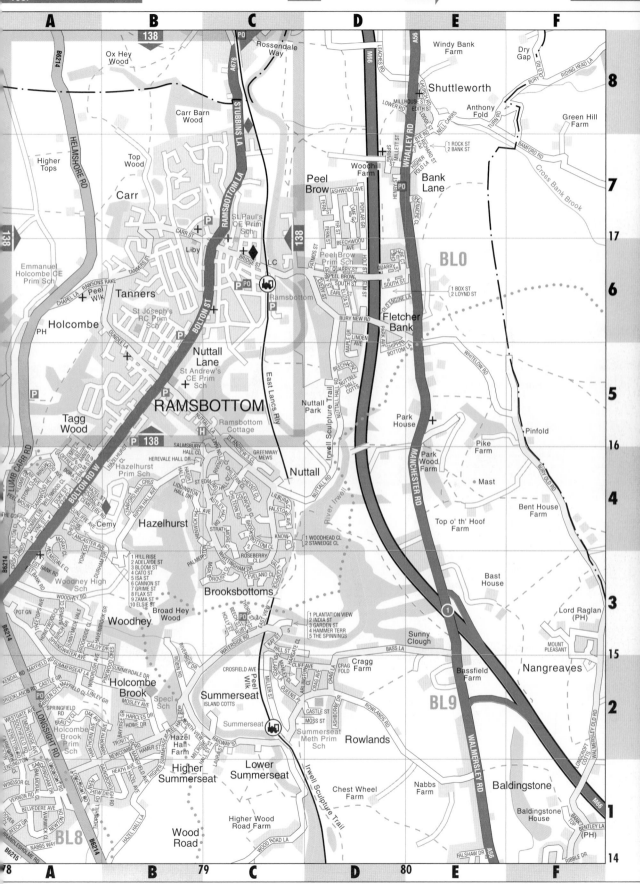

8 Mill
Smithy Carr Farm
Kay Close Farm
Rossendale Way
COAL RD
Fecit Farm
FECIT LA
Turf Moor
Cheesden Pasture
RIDING HEAD LA
A680

7
Moor Side Farm
Rossendale Sch
BLACK LA
MOOR SIDE LA
BLO
Close Nooks Farm
ROCHDALE RD

17
BAMFORD RD
Gate House
Harden Brook
Cheesden Brook

6
Cheesden Bridge
Cheesden
Tom Hill
OL12

5
Harden Moor
Wham Hill
Wham Hill Farm
Lumb Bridge
New Inn (PH)
Owd Betts (PH)
Rochdale Way

16
Throstle Hill
Croston Close
Ashworth Moor
EDENFIELD RD

4
Mam Hill
Ridshaw Farm
Far Buckhurst Brow
Kirkby's
Croston Close Bottoms
Ashworth Moor Resr
CROSTON CLOSE RD

3
Snape Hill
Buckhurst Brow
Buckhurst Rd
Buckhurst Farm
BL9
Closes
Rough Lee
Far Croft Head
A680

15
Whitewall Farm
Sales's Farm
SALES'S LA
Lark Mount
Deeply Vale
Deeply Hill
OL11
Top o' th' Hill Farm
ASHWORTH RD

2
Gindles Farm
DEEPLY VALE LA
Wind Hill
Wind Hill Farm
Bird Fields
Copped Hill Farm
Stand Lees Farm

1
BENTLEY LA
M66
Cob House Farm
Cob House Nab
Copped Hill

14
WHITE CARR LA
Shepherd Hey

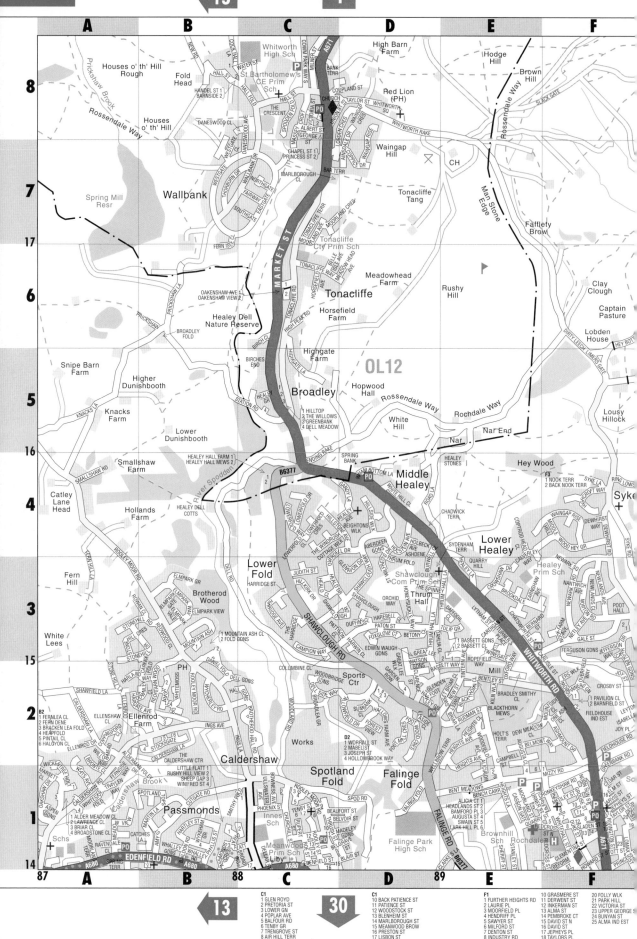

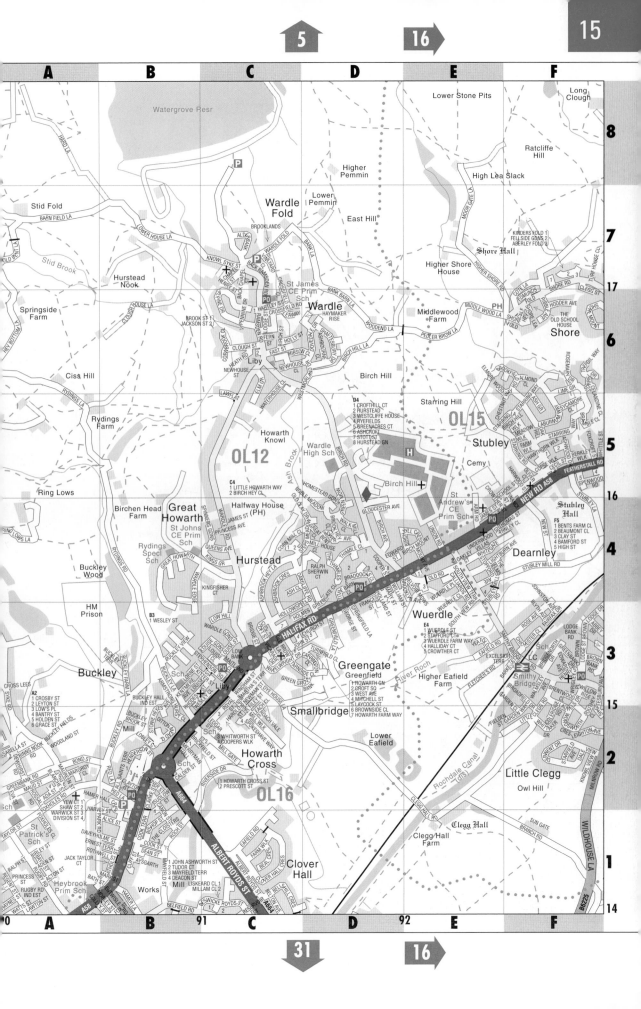

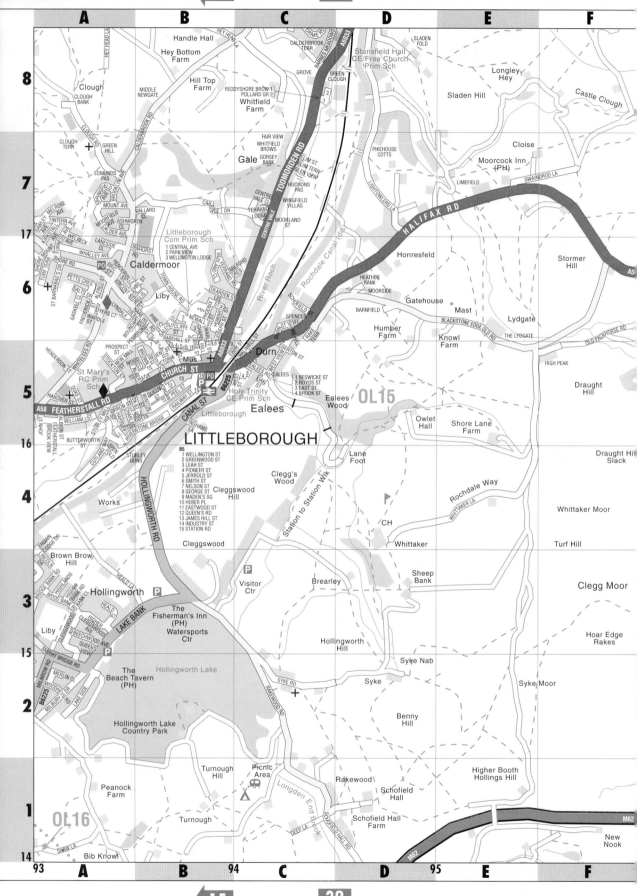

LITTLEBOROUGH

OL15

OL16

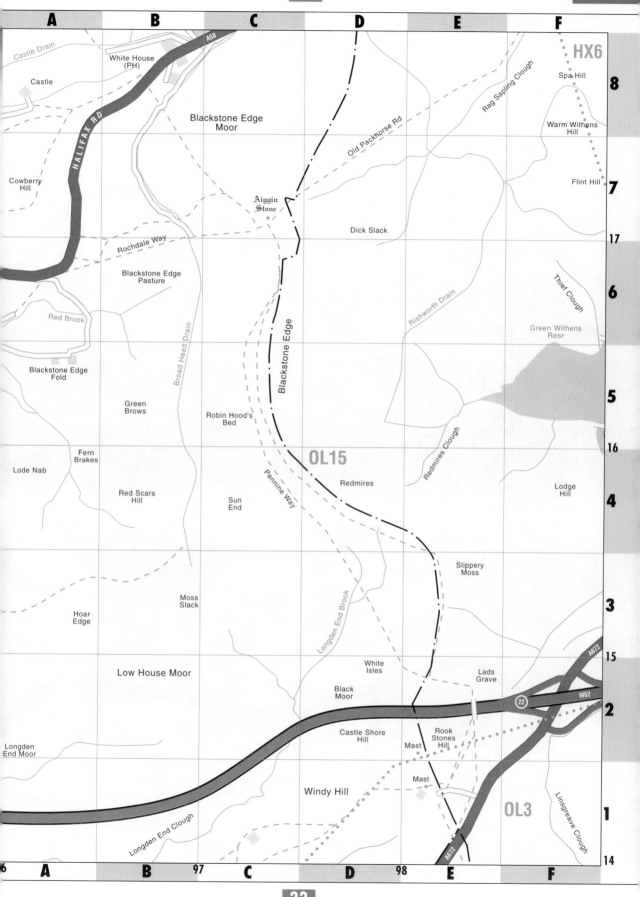

A B C D E F

Castle Drain

White House
(PH)

Spa Hill

8

Castle

Blackstone Edge
Moor

Rag Sapling Clough

Warm Withens
Hill

HALIFAX RD

Old Packhorse Rd

Flint Hill

7

Cowberry
Hill

Aiggin
Stone

17

Rochdale Way

Dick Slack

Blackstone Edge
Pasture

Thief Clough

6

Red Brook

Broad Head Drain

Rishworth Drain

Green Withens
Resr

Blackstone Edge
Fold

Blackstone Edge

5

Green
Brows

Robin Hood's
Bed

Redmires Clough

16

Lode Nab

Fern
Brakes

OL15

Redmires

Lodge
Hill

4

Red Scars
Hill

Sun
End

Pennine Way

Slippery
Moss

3

Hoar
Edge

Moss
Slack

Longden End Brook

White
Isles

Lads
Grave

A672

15

Low House Moor

Black
Moor

22

M62

2

Longden
End Moor

Castle Shore
Hill

Rook
Stones
Hill

Mast

Windy Hill

Mast

OL3

1

Longden End Clough

Linsgreave Clough

14

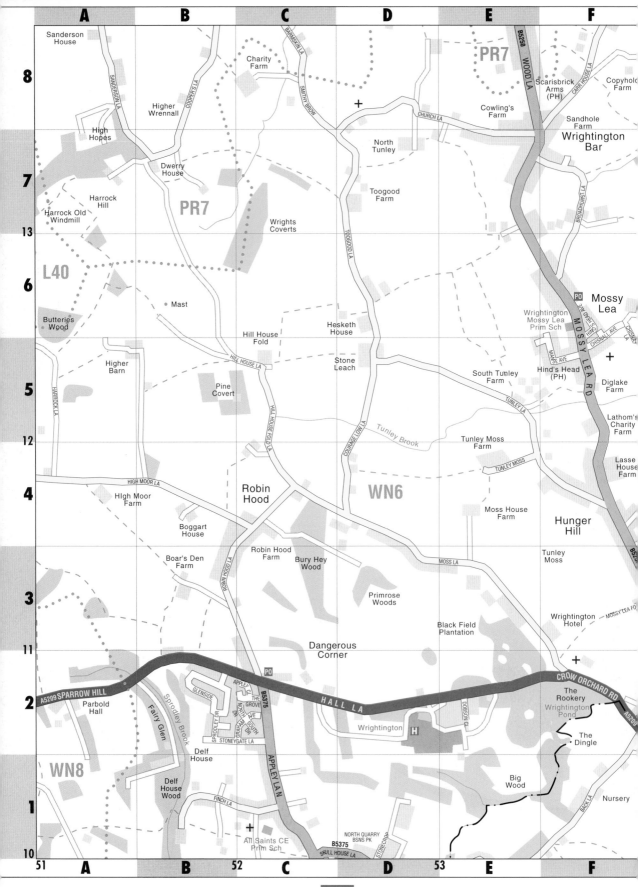

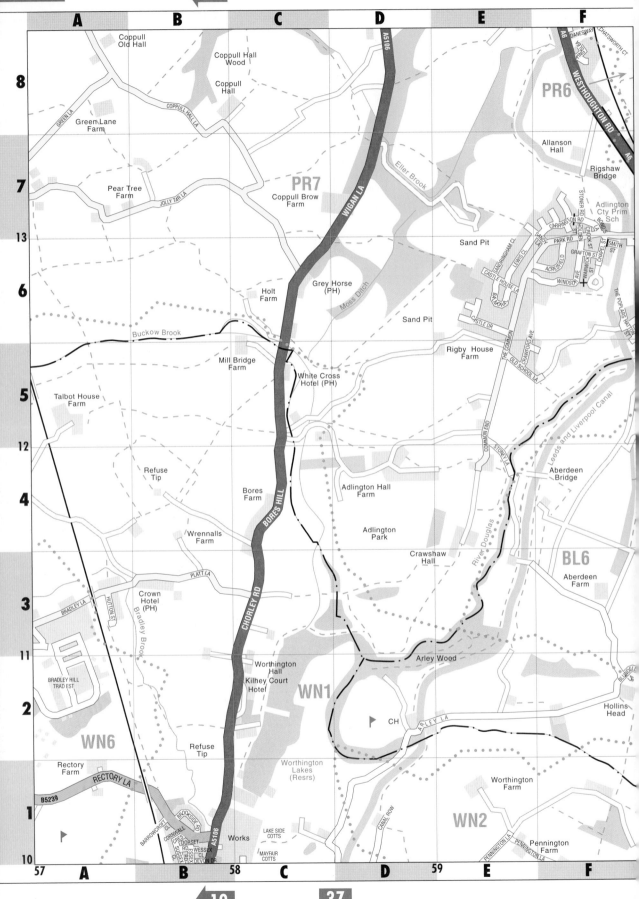

8

7

13

6

5

12

4

11

3

2

1

10

Coppull
Old Hall

Coppull Hall
Wood

Coppull
Hall

Green Lane
Farm

Green La

COPPULL HALL LA

PR7

Pear Tree
Farm

JOLLY TAR LA

Coppull Brow
Farm

WIGAN LA

A5106

Eller Brook

PR6

Allanson
Hall

Rigshaw
Bridge

Adlington
Cty Prim
Sch

STONER RD
HOLDEN
CARRINGTON RD
SANDY
SAND ST
CROOK ST
SMITH
ST

PARK RD

GRAFTON ST
CHAPEL ST

Sand Pit

CASTLE HOUSE LA
SANDRINGHAM CL
LEWIE CL
ACRESFIELD
WARWICK
WINDS
AVE

BALMORAL

CASTLE DR

THE POPLARS

Holt
Farm

Grey Horse
(PH)

Moss Ditch

Sand Pit

Rigby House
Farm

THE COMMON
OLD SCHOOL LA

CRAWFORD

Leeds and Liverpool Canal

Buckow Brook

Mill Bridge
Farm

White Cross
Hotel (PH)

COMMON END
STONY LA

Aberdeen
Bridge

Talbot House
Farm

Refuse
Tip

Bores
Farm

BORES HILL

Adlington Hall
Farm

Adlington
Park

River Douglas

BL6

Aberdeen
Farm

Wrennalls
Farm

PLATT LA

Crawshaw
Hall

BRADLEY LA

HUTTON ST

Crown
Hotel
(PH)

Bradley Brook

CHORLEY RD

Arley Wood

BLACKG

Hollins
Head

BRADLEY HILL
TRAD EST

Worthington
Hall

Kilhey Court
Hotel

WN1

CH

ARLEY LA

WN6

Refuse
Tip

Worthington
Lakes
(Resrs)

Worthington
Farm

Rectory
Farm

RECTORY LA

B5239

BARROWCROFT
CL
CORNWALL
CRES
DORSET
RD
WESSEX
SUSSEX
RD
CL
DEVON DR

A5106

Works

LAKE SIDE
COTTS

MAYFAIR
COTTS

CANAL ROW

WN2

PENNINGTON LA
PENNINGTON LA

Pennington
Farm

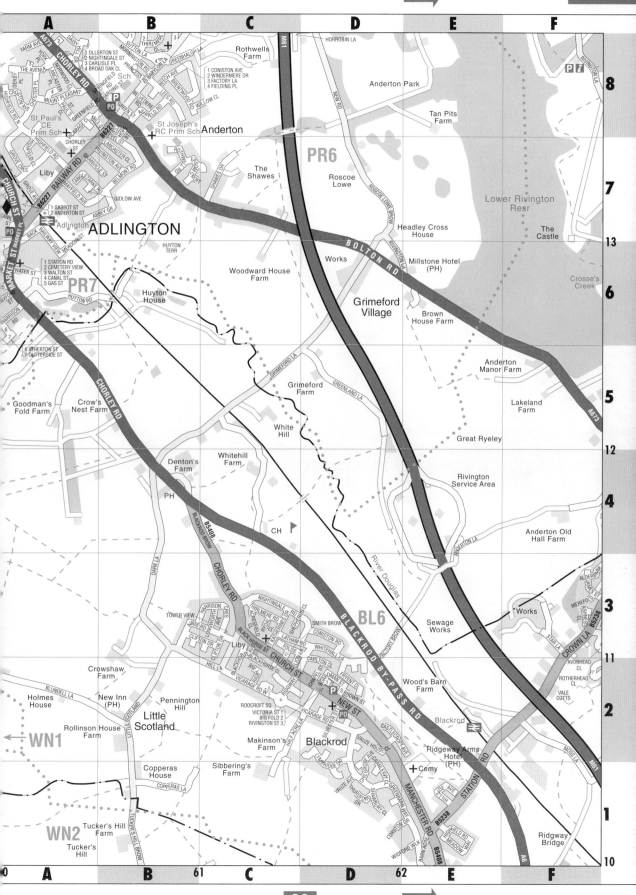

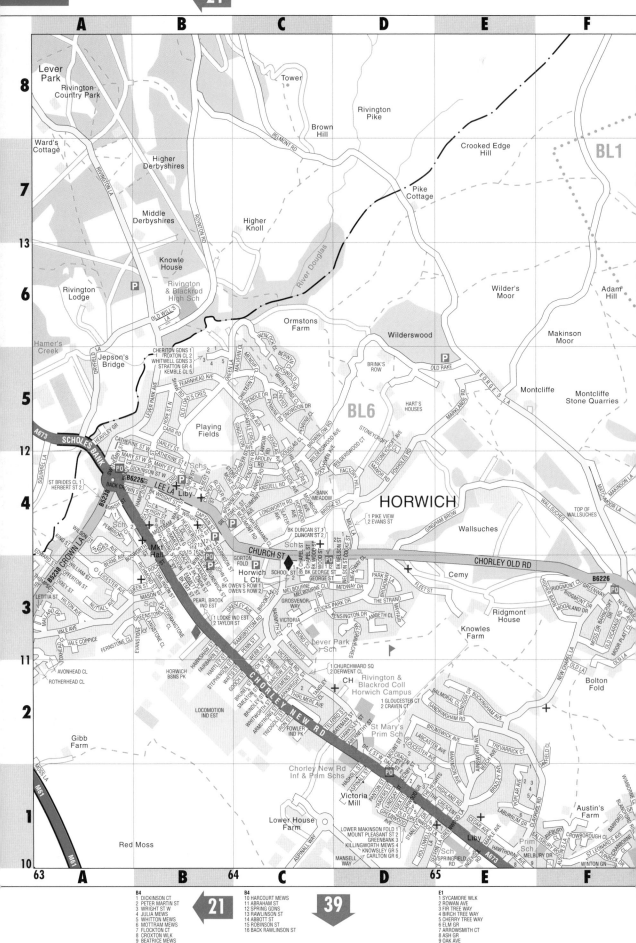

B4
1 DICKINSON CT
2 PETER MARTIN ST
3 WRIGHT ST W
4 JULIA MEWS
5 WHITTON MEWS
6 MOTTRAM MEWS
7 FLOCKTON CT
8 CROXTON WLK
9 BEATRICE MEWS

B4
10 HARCOURT MEWS
11 ABRAHAM ST
12 SPRING GDNS
13 RAWLINSON ST
14 ABBOTT ST
15 ROBINSON ST
16 BACK RAWLINSON ST

E1
1 SYCAMORE WLK
2 ROWAN AVE
3 FIR TREE WAY
4 BIRCH TREE WAY
5 CHERRY TREE WAY
6 ELM GR
7 ARROWSMITH CT
8 ASH GR
9 OAK AVE

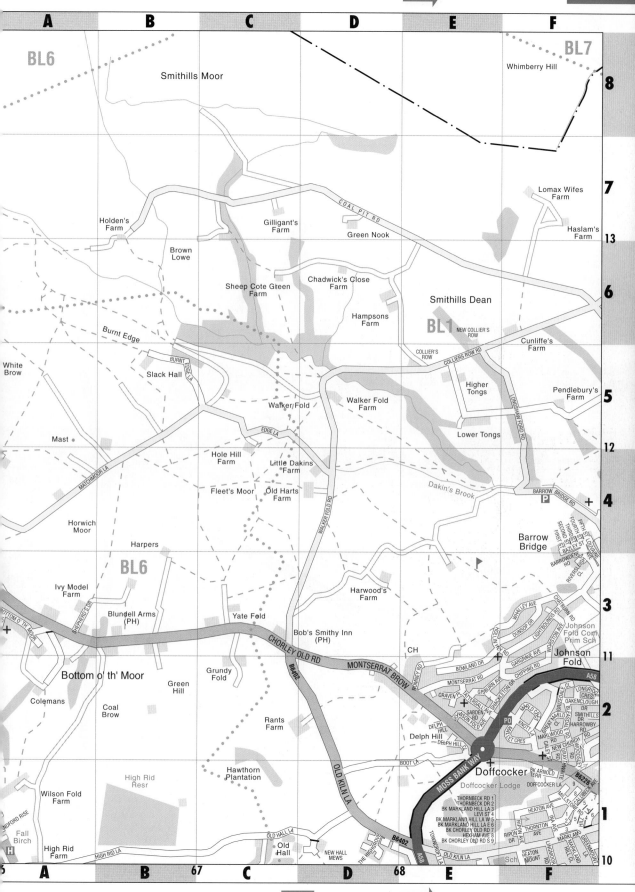

BL6

Smithills Moor

BL7

Whimberry Hill

8

Coal Pit Rd

Holden's Farm

Gilligant's Farm

Green Nook

Lomax Wifes Farm

Haslam's Farm

7

13

Brown Lowe

Sheep Cote Green Farm

Chadwick's Close Farm

Smithills Dean

6

Hampsons Farm

BL1

New Collier's Row

Burnt Edge

Collier's Row

Cunliffe's Farm

White Brow

Slack Hall

BURNT EDGE LA

Colliers Row Rd

Higher Tongs

Pendlebury's Farm

5

Walker Fold

Walker Fold Farm

LONGSHAW FORD RD

Mast

EDGE LA

Lower Tongs

12

Hole Hill Farm

Little Dakins Farm

MATCHMOOR LA

Fleet's Moor

Old Harts Farm

Dakin's Brook

BARROW BRIDGE RD

4

Horwich Moor

WALKER FOLD RD

Harpers

Barrow Bridge

BL6

Harwood's Farm

Ivy Model Farm

SHEPHERD ST DR

Blundell Arms (PH)

Yate Fold

Bob's Smithy Inn (PH)

CH

Johnson Fold Com Prim Sch

WHALLEY AVE

CHATBURN RD

DUNSOP DR

LIGHTBOUNDS RD

WORSTON DR

Johnson Fold

3

11

Bottom o' th' Moor

Green Hill

Grundy Fold

CHORLEY OLD RD

MONTSERRAT BROW

ROMNEY RD

BOWLAND DR

MONTSERRAT RD

GISBURN AVE

SHACKLETON DR

CHIPPING RD

GARGRAVE AVE

A58

Colemans

Coal Brow

Rants Farm

B6402

DELPH FOLD

CRAVEN AVE

PATTERSDALE RD

CHISON RD

SABDEN AVE

Delph Hill

DELPH HILL CL

MARLD CRES

KNOTTA

MARLWOOD

2

Wilson Fold Farm

High Rid Resr

Hawthorn Plantation

OLD KILN LA

BOOT LA

MOSS BANK WAY

PO

Doffcocker

Doffcocker Lodge

BK ARNOLD TERR

DOFFCOCKER LA

B6226

Fall Birch

High Rid Farm

HIGH RID LA

OLD HALL LA

Old Hall

THE MOORSIDE

New Hall Mews

B6402

A58

TOWNCROFT LA

OLD KILN LA

THORNBECK RD 1
THORNBECK DR 2
BK MARKLAND HILL LA 3
LEVI ST 4
BK MARKLAND HILL LA W 5
BK MARKLAND HILL LA E 6
BK CHORLEY OLD RD 7
HEXHAM AVE 8
BK CHORLEY OLD RD S 9

HEATON AVE

RIPON AVE

THORNTON AVE

MILLSTONE RD

HEATON MOUNT

MARKLAND HILL CL

1

H

High Rid Farm

Sch

10

← 23

8

E5
1 BK BELMONT RD
2 DURBAN RD
3 BK HAWARDEN ST
4 BK BLACKBURN RD W
5 BK BELMONT RD E
6 BK BROAD O' TH' LA

F6
1 BK PARK VIEW
2 PARK VIEW
3 PARK ROW
4 KELLETT ST
5 WRENBURY DR
6 BRAMLEY RD

F8
1 BK COX GREEN RD S
2 COX GREEN RD

7 CRUNDALE RD
8 ASHOVER CL
9 SHARPLES HALL
10 LAKENHEATH CL

3 BK COX GREEN RD N
4 BK KING ST
5 KING ST
6 BK MILL ST N
7 BK MILL ST S
8 SMITH LA
9 MILL ST

10 CONNINGSBY CL

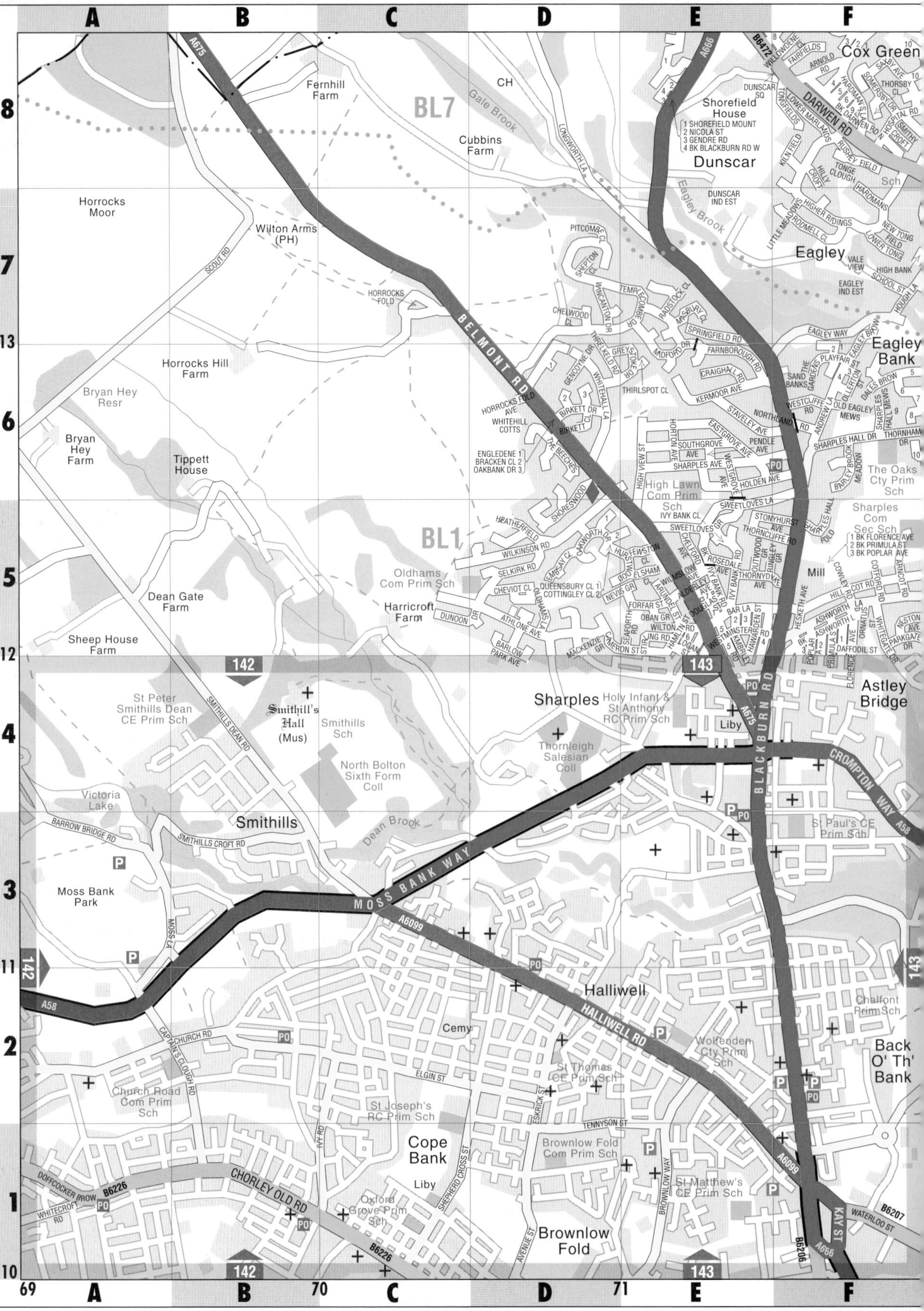

Cox Green

BL7

Gale Brook

CH

Fernhill Farm

Cubbins Farm

Shorefield House
1 SHOREFIELD MOUNT
2 NICOLA ST
3 GENDRE RD
4 BK BLACKBURN RD W

Dunscar

DUNSCAR SQ

DUNSCAR IND EST

Eagley

Horrocks Moor

Wilton Arms (PH)

Horrocks Fold

Eagley Bank

Horrocks Hill Farm

Bryan Hey Resr

Bryan Hey Farm

Tippett House

Horrocks Fold Ave
Whitehill Cotts

ENGLEDENE 1
BRACKEN CL 2
OAKBANK DR 3

The Beeches

High Lawn Com Prim Sch

Sharples Com Sec Sch
1 BK FLORENCE ST
2 BK PRIMULA ST
3 BK POPLAR AVE

The Oaks Cty Prim Sch

Mill

BL1

Dean Gate Farm

Oldhams Com Prim Sch

Harricroft Farm

Sheep House Farm

142

143

Sharples

Holy Infant & St Anthony RC Prim Sch

Astley Bridge

Liby

St Peter Smithills Dean CE Prim Sch

Smithill's Hall (Mus)

Smithills Sch

Thornleigh Salesian Coll

North Bolton Sixth Form Coll

Victoria Lake

Smithills

Dean Brook

MOSS BANK WAY

St Paul's CE Prim Sch

BARROW BRIDGE RD

SMITHILLS CROFT RD

Moss Bank Park

A6099

Halliwell

Chalfont Prim Sch

142

143

A58

Cemy

Wolfenden Cty Prim Sch

Back O' Th' Bank

CAPTAIN'S CLOUGH RD

Church Road Com Prim Sch

ELGIN ST

St Thomas CE Prim Sch

St Joseph's RC Prim Sch

HALLIWELL RD

TENNYSON ST

Cope Bank

Liby

Brownlow Fold Com Prim Sch

St Matthew's CE Prim Sch

DOFFCOCKER BROW

B6226

WHITECROFT RD

CHORLEY OLD RD

Oxford Grove Prim Sch

B6226

Brownlow Fold

BROWNLOW WAY

KAY ST

WATERLOO ST

B6207

A666

B6205

142

143

For full street detail of the highlighted area see pages 142 and 143.

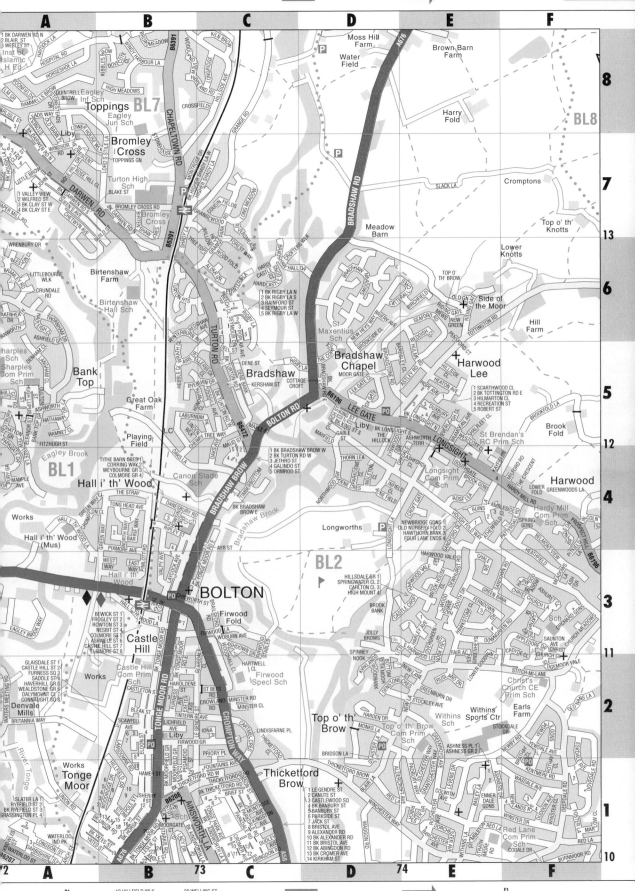

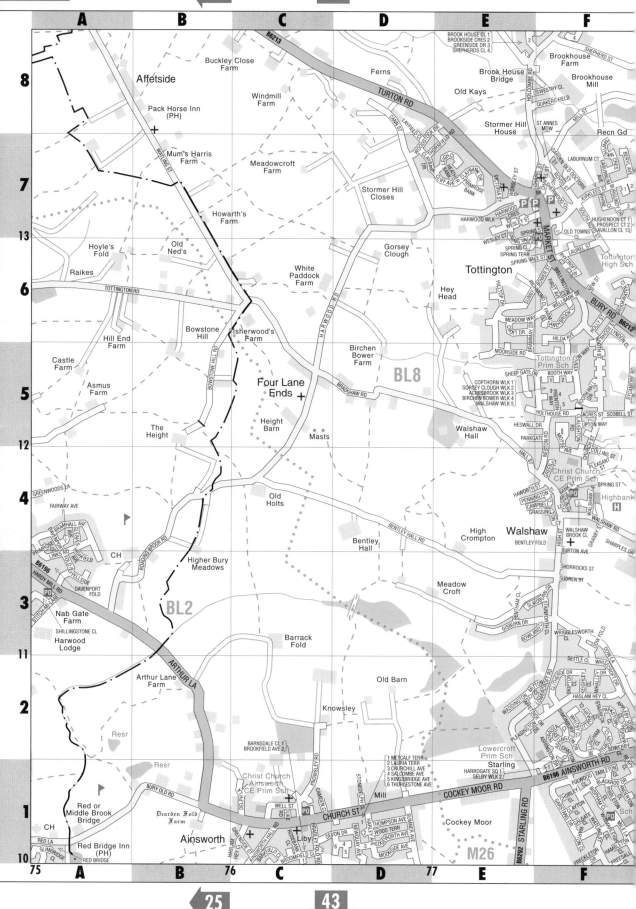

For full street detail of the highlighted area see page 140.

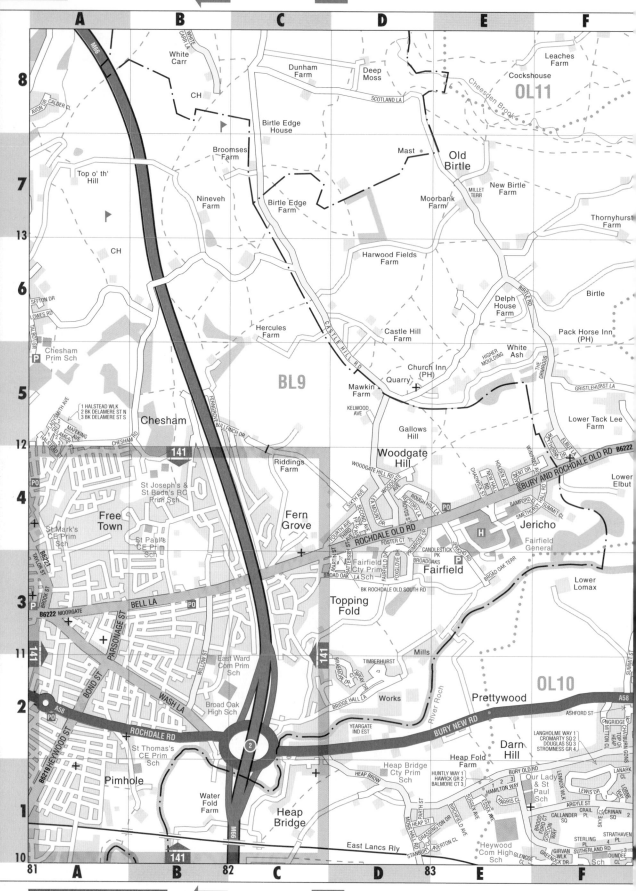

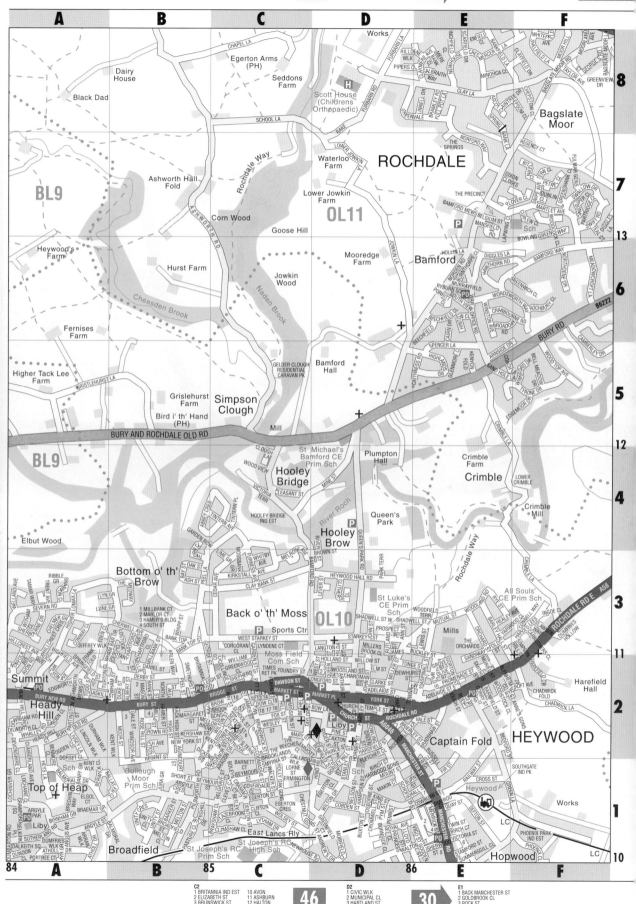

46 30

C2
1 BRITANNIA IND EST
2 ELIZABETH ST
3 BRUNSWICK ST
4 ASHTON ST
5 MOSS ST
6 EARL ST
7 FARNWORTH ST
8 ST JAMES' GR
9 WEST CHURCH ST
10 AVON
11 ASHBURN
12 HALTON
13 HAMMOND
14 KELSEY
15 KENNET
16 WITHERN
17 WAVERLEY
18 WALDEN

D2
1 CIVIC WLK
2 MUNICIPAL CL
3 HARTLAND CT
4 COURT HOUSE WAY
5 UNDSWORTH CT
6 GAS ST
7 SMITH ST
8 GLENDALE CL

E1
1 BACK MANCHESTER ST
2 GOLDBROOK CL
3 ROCK ST
4 GOLDCRAFT CL
5 SPRINGFIELD CL
6 GREGGE ST

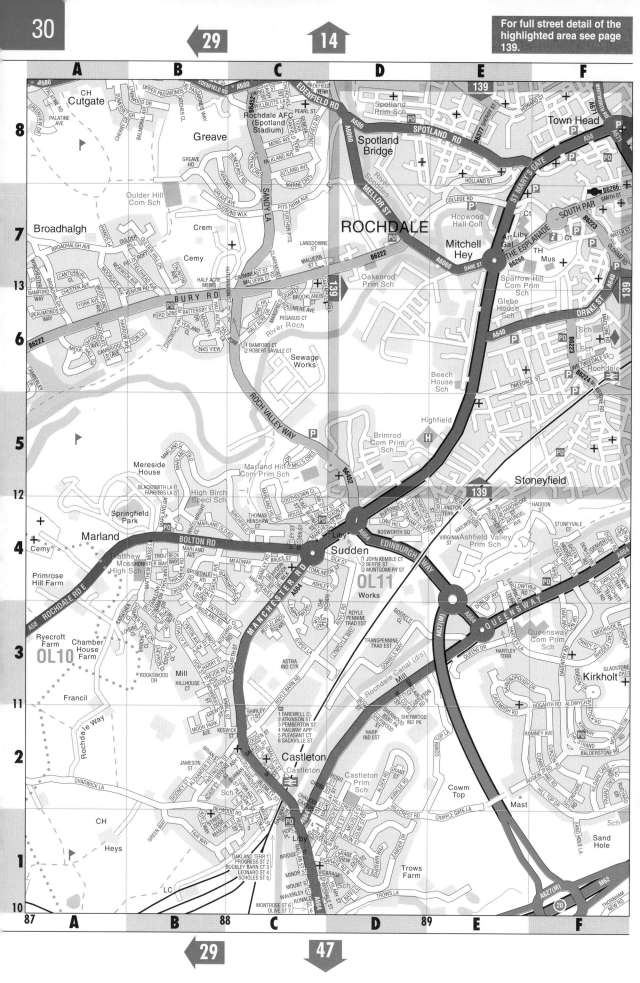

For full street detail of the highlighted area see page 139.

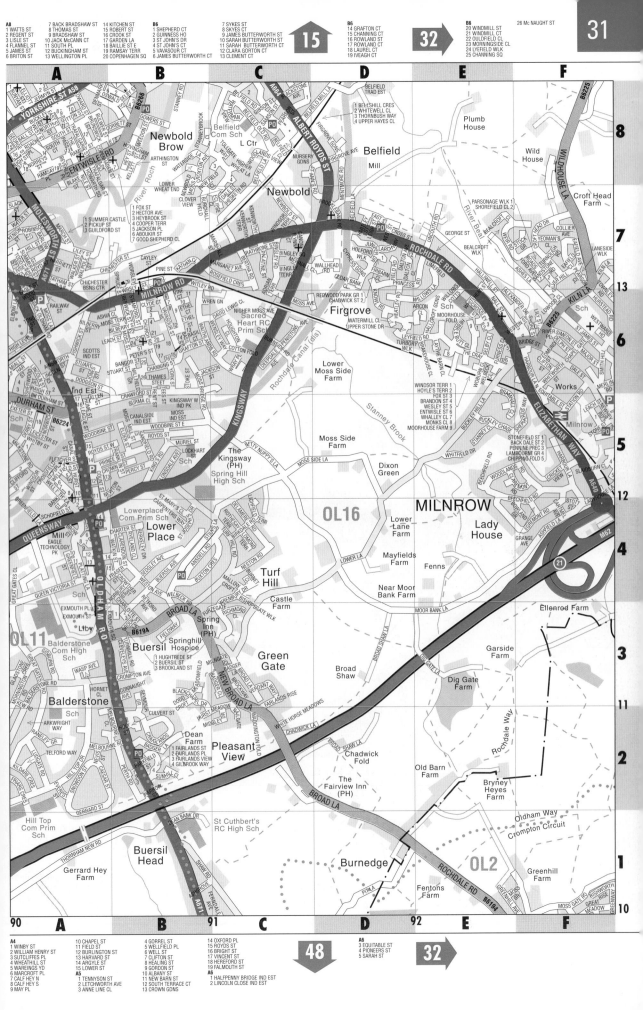

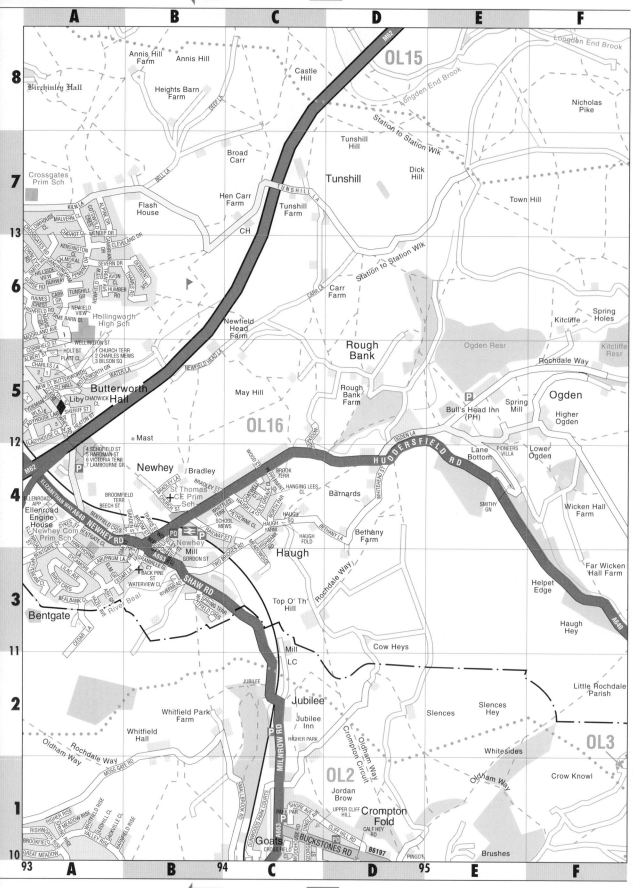

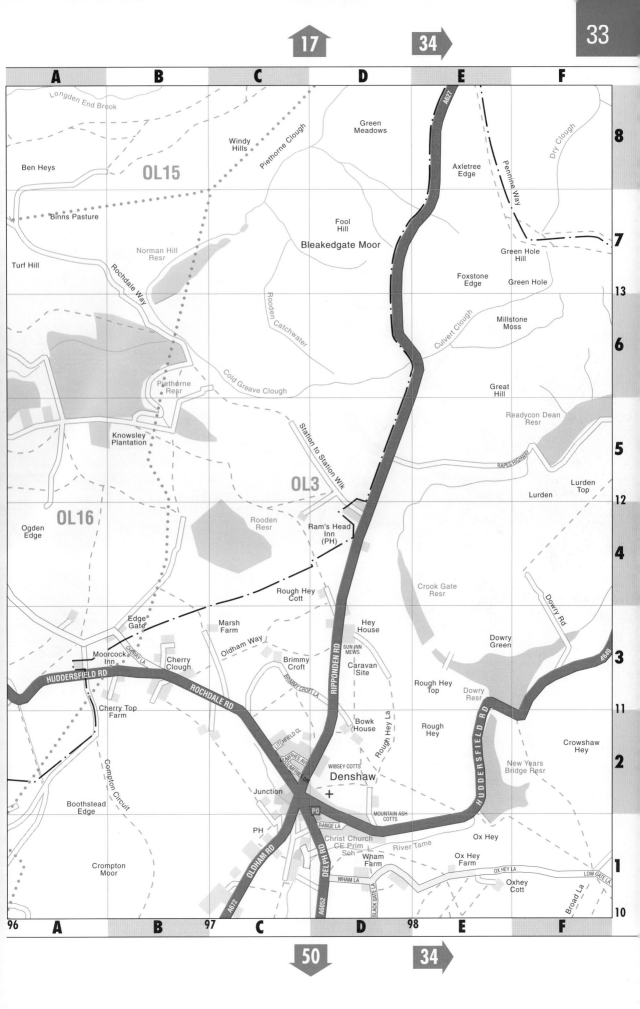

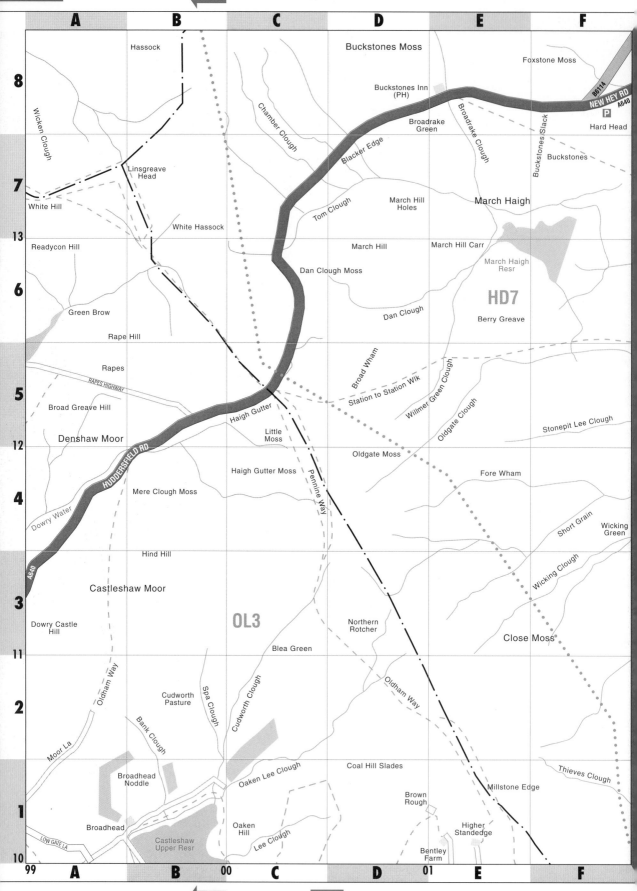

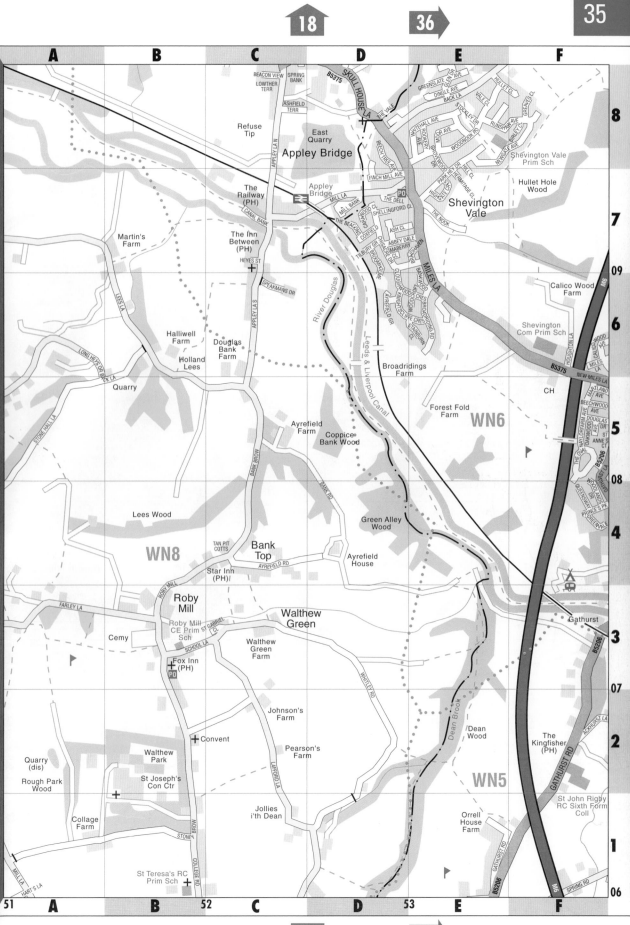

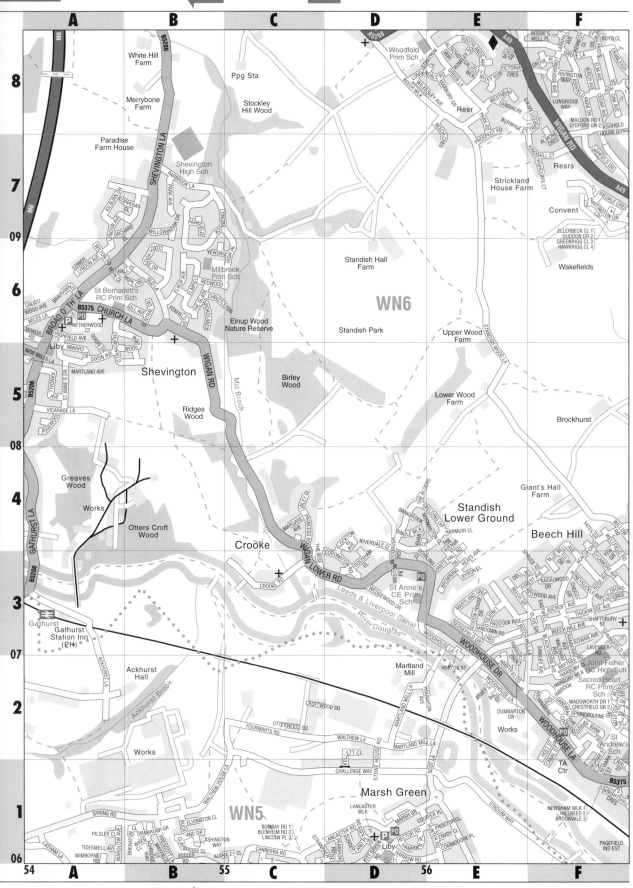

Major labels visible on the map:

Patchcroft Farm, Hampson Green, Red Rock, MEADOW PIT LA, B5239, School Coverts, Winstanleys, Astleys, Home Farm, WN2, CH, Zoo, Haigh Hall, Haigh Upper Plantations, Haigh Country Park, Rothwells Farm, Brock Wood, Haigh Upper Plantations, WN1, Longhurst, Leyland Mill Brow, Haigh Lower Plantations, Marylebone, Bottling Wood, St John the Baptist CE Sch, Boar's Head, Thorn Hill, Mere Oaks Sch, WN6, Cemy, Brimelow Farm, Greenfields, Works, Woodfield Prim Sch, Whitley, Swinley, Wigan, Wheley, Wheley, St Stephen's CE Prim Sch, Gidlow, Springfield, Liby, Wigan & Leigh Coll (Pagefield Bldg), PARK RD, Bull Hey, Water Heyes, Longshoot, CENTRAL PARK WAY, Coll (Linacre Bldg), NORTHWAY

Road labels: CHORLEY RD, WIGAN RD, A5106, A49, RED ROCK LA, RED ROCK BROW, WIGAN LA, MESNES RD, KENYON RD, B5376, B5375, B5238, B5239

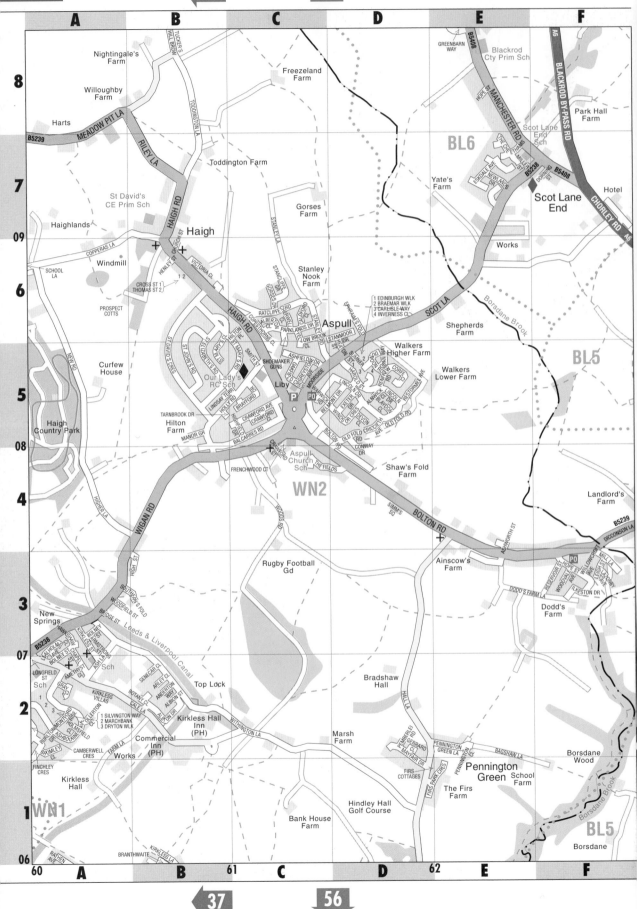

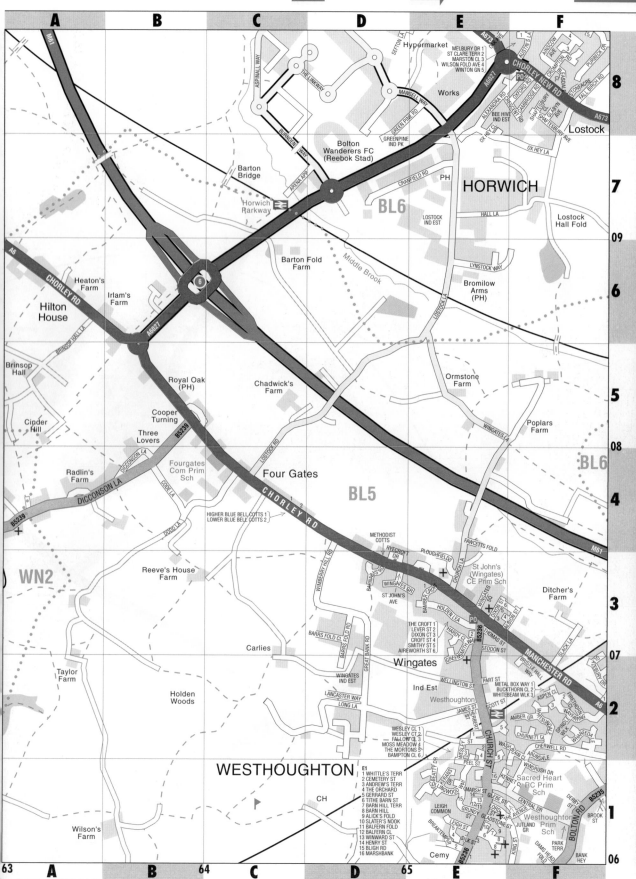

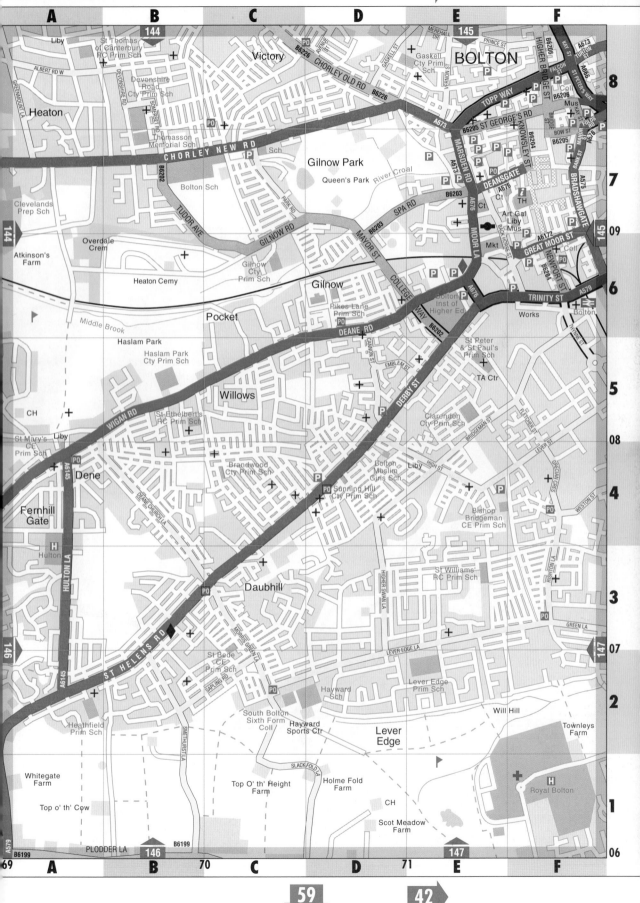

For full street detail of the highlighted area see pages 144, 145, 146 and 147.

24
42

A B C D E F

BOLTON

Heaton

Liby
St Thomas of Canterbury RC Prim Sch
ALBERT RD W
Devonshire Road Cty Prim Sch
DEVONSHIRE RD
SOMERSET RD
GREENMOUNT LA
Thomasson Memorial Sch
PO
Victory
CHORLEY OLD RD
B6226
AVENUE ST
GASKELL ST
Gaskell Cty Prim Sch
MERE HALL DR
PRINCE ST
145
HIGHER BRIDGE ST
B6206
KAY ST
A673
TURTON ST
A666
FALCON ST
ST PETER'S WAY

CHORLEY NEW RD
Sch
Gilnow Park
Queen's Park
River Croal
A673
TOPP WAY
ST GEORGE'S RD
B6205
MARSDEN RD
KNOWSLEY ST
B6206
BRIDGE ST
BOW ST
Mus
FOLDS RD
B6205
B6204

Bolton Sch
B6202
TUDOR AVE
PARK RD
Cleverlands Prep Sch
144
Overdale Crem
GILNOW RD
Gilnow City Prim Sch
MAYOR ST
SPA RD
B6203
B6203
DEANSGATE
A676
PO
Ct
TH
Art Gal Liby Mus
A6172
GREAT MOOR ST
Coll
NEWPORT ST
145
09
Mkt

Atkinson's Farm
Heaton Cemy
Gilnow
COLLEGE WAY
Pikes Lane Prim Sch
Bolton Inst of Higher Ed
A676
Moor La
Works
Bolton
TRINITY ST
A579
6

Middle Brook
Pocket
DEANE RD
B6202
CANNON ST
St Peter & St Paul's Prim Sch
TA Ctr
THYNNE ST

Haslam Park
Haslam Park Cty Prim Sch
EMBLEM ST
DERBY ST
5

Willows
WIGAN RD
St Ethelbert's RC Prim Sch
PO
Brandwood Cty Prim Sch
Bolton Muslim Girls Sch
Liby
HIGH ST
Clarendon Cty Prim Sch
BRIDGEMAN ST
LEVER ST
GRECIAN CRES
08

CH
Liby
St Mary's CE Prim Sch
A6145
Dene
DEANE CHURCH LA
PO
Sonning Hill Cty Prim Sch
WESTON ST
Bishop Bridgeman CE Prim Sch
PO
RISHTON LA
4

Fernhill Gate
HULTON LA
Hulton
H
Daubhill
St Williams' RC Prim Sch
HIGHER SWAN LA
3

ST HELENS RD
MORRIS GREEN LA
St Bede CE Prim Sch
SAPLING RD
LEVER EDGE LA
GREEN LA
PO
147
07

SMETHURST LA
South Bolton Sixth Form Coll
PO
Hayward Sports Ctr
Hayward Sch
SLACK FOLD LA
Lever Edge
Lever Edge Prim Sch
Will Hill
Townleys Farm
2

Heathfield Prim Sch
Whitegate Farm
Top o' th' Cow
Top O' th' Height Farm
Holme Fold Farm
CH
Scot Meadow Farm
Royal Bolton
H
1

B6199
PLODDER LA
146
B6199
147
06

42

← 41 ↑ 25

For full street detail of the highlighted area see page 148.

A B 148 C D E F

8 Mill Hill · Moorgate Prim Sch · Bolton Parish Church CE Prim Sch · BK EMPIRE RD · BK SALISBURY TERR · Breightmet · The Hollies · 1 BOWGREAVE AVE · 2 CHURCHTOWN AVE · 3 WEETON AVE

7 BURY NEW RD · CASTLE ST · BRADFORD ST · Tonge Fold · BK BURY RD E · BK BURY RD S · 3 DORIS AVE · BK LEVER HALL RD · LEVER HALL RD · Liby · Crompton Fold Prim Sch · St Osmund's RC Prim Sch

09 BURY RD · BL2 · Oaken Bottom · GIRTON ST · BK COLENSO RD 1 · COLENSO RD 3 · BRIAR ST 4 · BK OAKENBOTTOM RD N 5 · KINGSFOLD CL

6 Bolton Metropolitan Coll · Springfield · Bolton Inst (Chadwick Campus) · River Tonge · St Stephen & All Martyrs' CE Prim Sch · Leverhulme Park · The Moss City Prim Sch · Playing Fields · CRINAN WAY

5 Rose Hill · TA Ctr · Wheatfield Rd · BRANSCOMBE GDNS · RAMSDEN ST 2 · SNOW HILL RD 3 · GORSES RD · RADCLIFFE RD · Darcy Lever · CROFT SIDE · Crow's Nest Cotts

08 148 · Burnden · RAIKES LA · Burden Ind Est · Raikes Lane Ind Est · Raikes Clough Ind Est · Pilot Ind Est · Moses Gate Country Park · Old Hall Farm · Dove Bank · DOVE BANK

4 BK WESTON ST S · CECILIA ST · BK CECILIA ST · BK RICHELIEU ST · RICHELIEU ST · BK BLACKWOOD S · BLACKWOOD ST · MELVILLE ST · BK MELVILLE ST · PARKFIELD RD · Liby · MANCHESTER RD · ST PETER'S WAY · River Croal · BL3 · FOURTH AVE · FIFTH AVE · SECOND AVE · THIRD AVE · BUTTERMERE · Bowness City Prim Sch

3 WALKER AVE · PATON AVE · WESTBOURNE AVE · Great Lever · St Michael's CE Prim Sch · HARDMAN FOLD · Bull Hill · Little Lever Sch · CHURCH ST · HALL LA

07 LAKESIDE AVE · BISHOP'S RD · BISHOP'S CL · WALLBROOK GR · SHELDON CL · NETHERTON · STARCLIFFE ST · BK LOXHAM ST · LOXHAM ST

2 MINERVA RD · BROAD OAK RD · GLENMORE AVE · WATER'S EDGE · Moses Gate · Moses Gate · BK CORSON ST · CORSON ST · BK FYLDE ST · FYLDE ST E · All Saints' CE Prim Sch · Cemy

1 SPRINGFIELD RD · SILVERDALE RD · Harper Green · Harper Green Sch · BL4 · GREEN BANK 1 · ROSE AVE 2 · GOWER ST · GLADSTONE RD · EGERTON ST · BOLTON RD · Liby · FRANCIS ST · LIMEFIELD AVE · FERN ST · Heathfield · Clammerclough

06 TURTON ST · COLCHESTER RD · RICHMOND RD · LUPIN AVE · ORCHID AVE · DAISY · DIXON DR · GREEN ST · GREENSIDE · GLADSTONE RD · MARKET ST · Farnworth · M26

72 A 73 B C 73 D 74 E F

E8	F8	
1 BK HORNE ST N	1 BK NELSON ST S	7 LINCOLN DR
2 BK DEVON ST N	2 BK DEVON ST S	8 MIDDLESEX ST
3 WALKER ST	3 BK PARKHILLS RD S	
4 BK PARKHILLS RD S	4 BK PARKHILLS RD N	
5 MOSS PL	5 BK NELSON ST N	
	6 NELSON ST	

BL8

Higher Spen Moor

Lower Spen Moor

Brook Bottom Farm

Doffer Fold

Withins Resr

Cemy

Crow Trees Farm

M26

Irwell Sculpture Trail

Florence Nightingale

Elton Resr

Club

Old Hall Farm

Manchester Bolton & Bury Canal (dis)

Hogside LC

Lower Hinds

Bury CE High Sch

Fishpool

The Derby High Sch

St Peter's CE Prim Sch

Redvales

Westmoreland

Works

BL9

Bury FC

Millwood Prim Sch

Sewage Works

A6053

Blackford Bridge

River Roch

River Irwell

WELLINGTON RD

MANCHESTER RD

DUMERS LA

BURY ST

CROSS LA

St Mary's RC Sch

Gorsefield Prim Sch

Coney Green Sch

Radcliffe

RADCLIFFE

A665 WATER ST

A6053

PILKINGTON WAY

NEW RD

RADCLIFFE NEW RD

M45

Lily Hill

New Church Coll

St John's CE Prim Sch

Chapel Field

Chapelfield Prim Sch

St Aiden's CL

St Paul's CT

Chapeltown Rd

Works

Greystoke Cres

Bury Coll (Stand Ctr)

B6198 CHURCH LA

DALES LA

Whitefield

A56

A B C D E F

8
7
09
6
5
08
4
3
07
2
1
06

TOPHAM ST
DURHAM DRI
HIWLAS
DORSET RD
ALFRED ST
WILTSHIRE CL
HAMPSHIRE CL
RUTLAND RD
WILSHIRE RD
River Roch
CORNWALL RD
ULSTER CL
GIGG LA
CHERRY CL
CEMETERY LA
Gigg
Resr
Water
Farm
River Roch

M66

Jackson
Fold

GREENOCK DR
GALLOWAY
DUNBAR GR
East Lancs Rly
HEYWOOD
DISTRIBUTION PK

Goshen
Sports Ctr
PH
THE CROFT
1 BORDEN WAY
2 BEECHWOOD
PILSWORTH WAY

Superstore
3
PILSWORTH RD
Lomax's

Hill Top

THREE LANE
ENDS
PILSWORTH RD
MOSS HALL RD
Three Arrows
Inn
(PH)

Captains
Farm

Brightley Brook

Higher
Barn
OL10

Hollins Brook
CROFT IND EST
1 GAWTHORPE CL
2 WILTON DR
3 HEATON CL
ALNWICK DR
Hollins
Vale
HAWESWATER
CRES
HOLLINS BROOK CL
THE HAGS
Hollins Grundy
Prim Sch
MERE CL

PILSWORTH
COTTS

Meadow
Croft Fold

Broom Hill
Farm

Hollins
PO
STATTER ST
HOWARD HILL
BL9
HOLLINS LA
NORTH AVE
EAST DR
CHANTRY CL
SYKES
AVE
PLANTATION GR
CHAPEL CL
CASTLEBROOK CL
HOLLINS
MEWS
CHURCH CROFT
ST CROSS
ST GEORGE'S
CT
CASTLE RD

Castle
House

Thurston
Fold
Whittle Brook

CH
Sunny
Bank
AJAX DR
Sunny Bank
Prim Sch
1 BLEASDALE CL
2 WENSLEYDALE CL
Cemy
QUEEN ANN CL

Brick
House

Liby
BLOOMFIELD RD
ANFIELD CL
SUNNY BANK RD
Castlebrook
High Sch
PO
POLE LANE
CT
GRIFFE LA

M24
Unsworth
Moss

M62

BORROWDALE
DR
ESKDALE CL
BLUNDELL
CL
MAXWELL ST
HILLSIDE
BRAMHALL
LEEDS
PATTEN
Bury & Whitefield
Prim Sch
Unsworth
Back o' th' Moss
Moss
Side
07

Unsworth
Prim Sch
CHADDERTON DR
MONSALL DR
BLACKLEY CL
BRADLEY DR
KENNEDY DR
Bury Music
Ctr
POLE LA
HILLS LA
CH
The
Hills

Egypt
Farm
M25

All Saints
CE Prim Sch
MELROSE CL
Mersey Drive
Com Sch
IRK
WLK
BOLLIN
WLK
GLAZE
WLK
ALT WLK

Brookvale
Farm

Ribble Drive
Com Prim Sch
PO
ALBERT
HINDBURN CL
GOYT WLK
CALDER WLK
CALDER WAY
ROCH WLK
DOUGLAS WAY
MERSEY SQ
ROCH CRES
YARROW WLK
SPADER WLK
CROAL WLK
DEVESTER WLK
LOSTOCK WLK
M45
EGYPT LA
POLE LA
MODE HILL LA

Same Yet
(PH)
SIMISTER LA

Nursery
CHAPEL WLK
TONGE CL
WENNING CL
M62
18
06

45 29

A B C D E F

8
7
09
6
08
5
4
3
07
2
1
06

OL10

M62
M25
M24

DUMBARTON DR
DUNBLANE DR
ROBIN
ATHOLL DR
PILSWORTH RD

St Andrew's Dr
St Joseph's RC Prim & High Schs

Heywood Distribution Pk

Hares Hill Farm

HARESHILL RD

Higher Fields

Stock Nook

New Gap Farm

Gardner's Arms (PH)

DR70R FOLD LA

Lower Whittle

Birch IND EST

MOSS HALL DR

Birch Service Area

Whittle Fold

WHITTLE LA

White Hart Hotel (PH)

Birch

Top o' th' Hill

Siddal Farm

Siddal Fold

Oakridge Farm

ROCHDALE WAY
OAKEN BANK RD

Mast

Hatters Farm

STOTT LA

The Queen Elizabeth Sch

Dingle Farm

Top of Hebers

HOLLIN LA

A60

Lane End

MIDDLETON RD

A6045

MANCHESTER RD

19

Rochdale Way

1 CASSIDY GDNS
2 BISHOP MARSHALL WAY

LANGLEY LA

Greenhill Farm

Green Lane End

HEYWOOD OLD RD

Rochdale Way

Sports Ctr

The Jolly Butcher Inn (PH)

SIMON LA

Bowlee

Rochdale Way

1 CARROCK WLK
2 HELTON WLK
3 TINSDALE WLK

SIMISTER LA
SIMISTER LA
A6045

RUSCOMBE FOLD 1
RIMINGTON FOLD 2
BISHOPS MDW 3

BENFOLD WLK 1
CLIFTON WLK 2

Furrow Com Prim Sch

Liby

Langley Prim Sch

Langley

St Mary's RC Prim Sch

PO

1 ROSE MOUNT 2 REGENT ST

Middleton Parish Sch

Parkfield Prim Sch

D2
1 LAKELAND CT
2 LONGTHWAITE CL
3 KESWICK CT
4 MILLBECK CT
5 BOWNESS CT

HOPWOOD CT 1
BAKER ST 2
VICTOR ST 3
BARLOW ST 4
CHURCHILL CL 5
LORRAINE CL 6

Siddal Moor Sports Coll

84 A B 85 C D 86 E F

E2
1 DUFTON WLK
2 DUDDON WLK
3 SEASCALE WLK
4 MOWBRAY WLK
5 HAWESWATER MEWS
6 WINSTER DR
7 D'OLIVERA CT
8 DOVEDALE CT
9 ST BEES WLK

F1
1 THROSTLE HALL CT
2 NINIAN CT
3 EXETER CT
4 KID ST
5 WATER ST
6 MARKET ST
7 CHAPEL ST
8 WOOD ST
9 CROSS ST

10 CHISHOLM CT
11 WEAVERS CT
12 GREAT ARBOR WA
13 SCHOLARS WAY

A B C D E F

8 7 09 6 08 5 4 3 07 2 1 06

90 A 91 B C 92 D E F

Areas / Places:

OL11

OL16

Plumpton

Summit

Gravel Hole

Thornham St James' CE Prim Sch

Hanging Chadder

Puckersley Inn (PH)

Narrowgate Farm

Crompton Circuit

Low Crompton

High Crompton

Fir Bank Com Prim Sch

M24

Oozewood Clough

Oozewood

Tandle Hill Country Park

OL2

High Barn Com Prim Sch

Luzley Brook

Hough

Cemy

Thorp

Thorp Com Prim Sch

Milton Street Day Sch

ROYTON

Cinder Hill Farm

Racefield Hamlet

Crofters

Haggate

Royley House

Middleton Rd

Royley

Our Lady's RC Comp Sch

St Anne's CE Prim Sch

Holden Fold

Horton Arms (PH)

OL1

Superstore

Chadderton Hall Com Prim Sch

North Chadderton Sch

OL9

Oldham Athletic AFC (Boundary Pk)

Chadderton Way

Superstore

The Royal Oldham

West Hulme

Long Sight

Oldham Edge

Ind Est

Roads:

A671 OLDHAM RD

ROCHDALE RD

SHAW RD

OLDHAM RD

BROADWAY

A627(M)

MILL BROW

STREET BRIDGE RD

A663

A627

B6195

B6194

B6195

Rochdale Way

Oldham Way

Oozewood Rd

CINDER HILL LA

D4	E4	10 BRADBURY WLK
1 NORTH ST	1 THOMAS HOUSE	
2 HOLLY BANK	2 WESTMORLAND WLK	
3 THROSTLE CT	3 CHARCON WLK	
4 SANDY WLK	4 APPLEBY WLK	
5 CHURCH WLK	5 TROUTBECK WLK	
6 YORK SQ	6 BYRON WLK	
7 CHESTER PL	7 BOWNESS WLK	
8 SPRING GDNS	8 STAVELY WLK	
	9 HORDEN WLK	

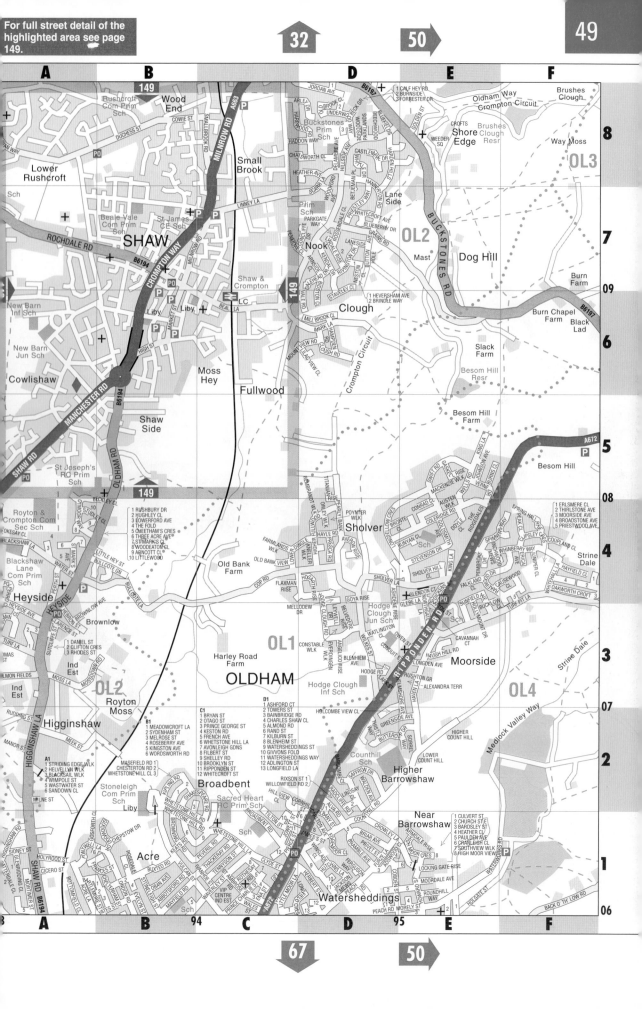

A B C D E F

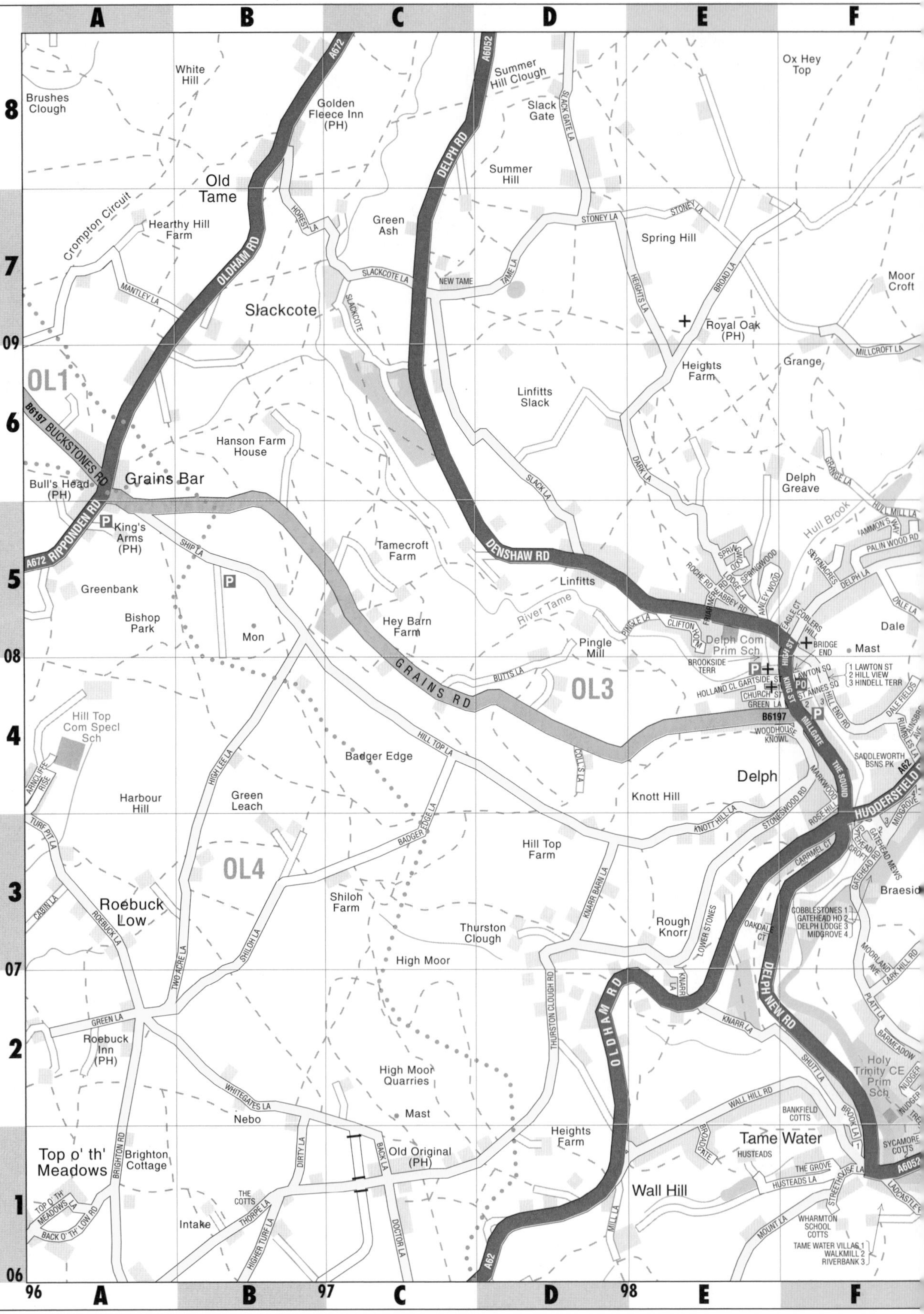

8

Brushes Clough

White Hill

Ox Hey Top

Old Tame

Golden Fleece Inn (PH)

Summer Hill Clough

Slack Gate

7

Hearthy Hill Farm

Green Ash

Summer Hill

Spring Hill

Moor Croft

OLDHAM RD

A672

A6052

DELPH RD

SLACKCOTE LA

NEW TAME

TANE LA

STONEY LA

STONEY LA

HEIGHTS LA

BROAD LA

MANTLEY LA

HORREST LA

SLACKCOTE

Slackcote

09

OL1

Royal Oak (PH)

Grange

Heights Farm

MILLCROFT LA

6

B6197 BUCKSTONES RD

Hanson Farm House

Linfitts Slack

Delph Greave

GRANGE LA

HILL L MILL LA

Bull's Head (PH)

Grains Bar

DARK LA

SLACK LA

Hull Brook

JAMMON...

Greenbank

King's Arms (PH)

P

SHIP LA

Tamecroft Farm

DENSHAW RD

Linfitts

PALIN WOOD RD

DELPH LA

DALE LA

5

A672 RIPPONDEN RD

P

Mon

Hey Barn Farm

River Tame

Pingle Mill

Delph Com Prim Sch

Dale

Mast

08

Bishop Park

GRAINS RD

BUTTS LA

CLIFTON...

BROOKSIDE TERR

1 LAWTON ST
2 HILL VIEW
3 HINDELL TERR

OL3

HOLLAND CL GARTSIDE ST

CHURCH ST

GREEN LA

PO

ST ANNES SQ

DALE FIELDS

4

Hill Top Com Specl Sch

HIGH LEE LA

HILL TOP LA

Knott Hill

B6197

WOODHOUSE KNOWL

WALLGATE

THE SOUND

SADDLEWORTH BSNS PK

HUDDERSFIELD

ARNCLIFFE RISE

Harbour Hill

Badger Edge

COLTS LA

Delph

Braesid...

3

CABUL LA

TURF PIT LA

ROEBUCK LA

Green Leach

OL4

BADGER EDGE LA

Shiloh Farm

KNARR BARN LA

Hill Top Farm

KNOTT HILL LA

Rough Knorr

LOWER STONES

STONESWOOD RD

ROSE HILL

CARRMEL CT

COBBLESTONES 1
GATEHEAD HO 2
DELPH LODGE 3
MIDGROVE 4

GATEHEAD MEWS

Roebuck Low

SHILOH LA

07

GREEN LA

TWO ACRE LA

Thurston Clough

High Moor

THURSTON CLOUGH RD

OLDHAM RD

KNARR LA

DELPH NEW RD

MOORLAND AVE

LARK HILL RD

PLATT LA

2

Roebuck Inn (PH)

BRIGHTON RD

WHITEGATES LA

High Moor Quarries

Mast

SHUTTLA...

Holy Trinity CE Prim Sch

BARMEADOW

1

Top o' th' Meadows

TOP O' TH MEADOWS LA

BACK O' TH' LOW RD

Brighton Cottage

Intake

DIRTY LA

THE COTTS

THORPE LA

HIGHER TURF LA

Nebo

BACK LA

DOCTOR LA

Old Original (PH)

A62

Heights Farm

HUSTEADS

Wall Hill

MILL LA

BRACKEN...

Tame Water

THE GROVE

HUSTEADS LA

STREETHOUSE LA

WHARMTON SCHOOL COTTS

TAME WATER VILLAS 1
WALKMILL 2
RIVERBANK 3

MOUNT LA

BROOK LA

SYCAMORE COTTS

LANCASTER...

A6052

BANKFIELD COTTS

06

96 A B 97 C D 98 E F

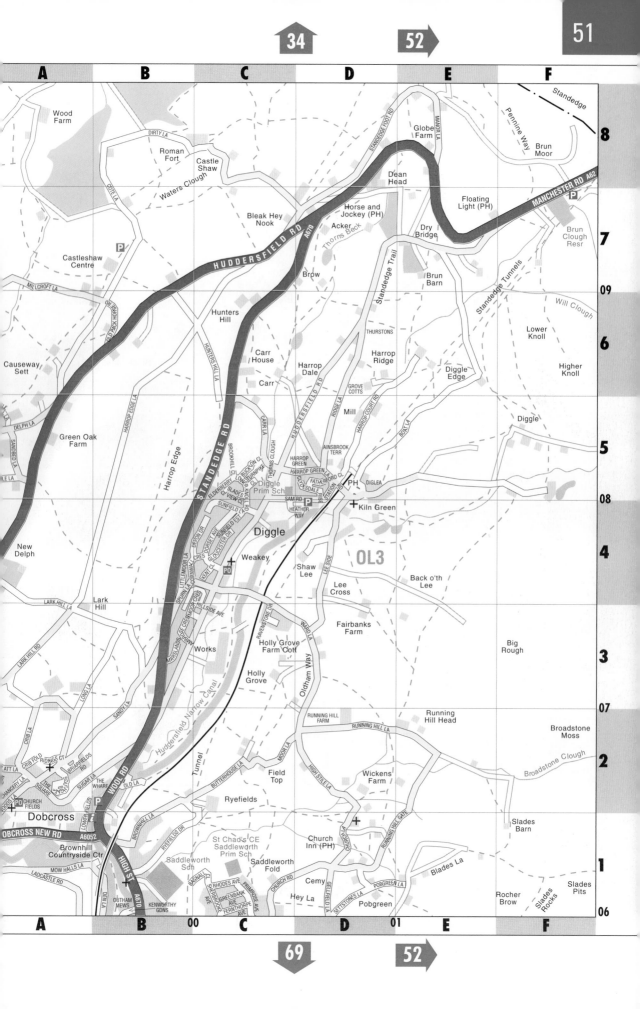

A   B   C   D   E   F

Foul Moss

Standedge Tunnel

MANCHESTER RD

A62

Standedge Trail

Warcock

Redbrook Resr

Warcock Hill

8

Butterly

Butterly Clough

Great Butterly Hill

Little Butterly Hill

Bobus

Swellands Resr

HD7

Round Hill

7

09

Rocher Moss

Blakely Clough

Black Moss Resr

6

Pennine Way

Black Moss

Little Black Moss Resr

Rocher Brow

Rifle Range

Hoar Clough

5

Diggle Resr

Broadhead Brow

Ravenstone Brow

08

Ravenstone Rocks

4

OL3

Wicken Clough

Wicken Clough Moss

Broadhead Moss

3

South Clough

White Moss

Broadstone Moss

07

Broadstone Hill

South Clough Moss

2

Featherbed Moss

Broad Stones

Diggle Rake

Hollin Brown Knoll

1

Near Wain Stones

Far Wain Stones

A6

Boggart Stones

A635

HOLMFIRTH RD

06

02   A   B   03   C   D   04   E   F

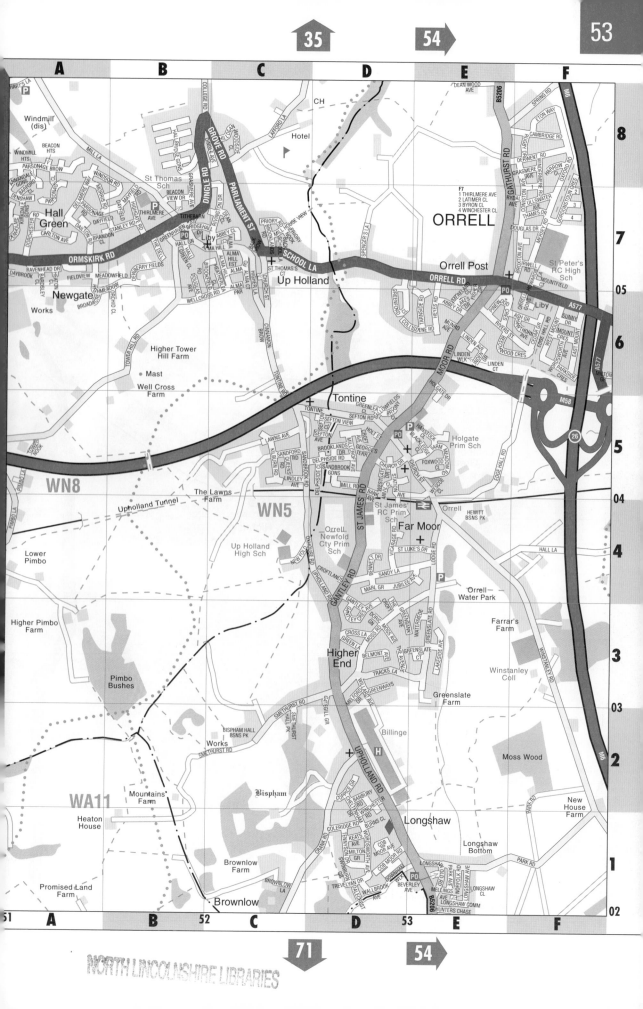

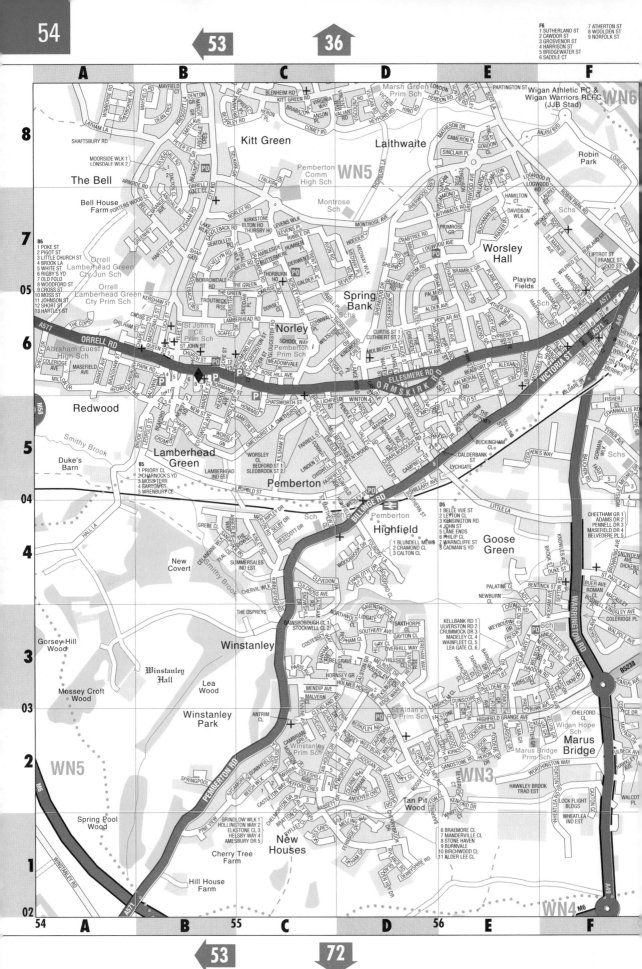

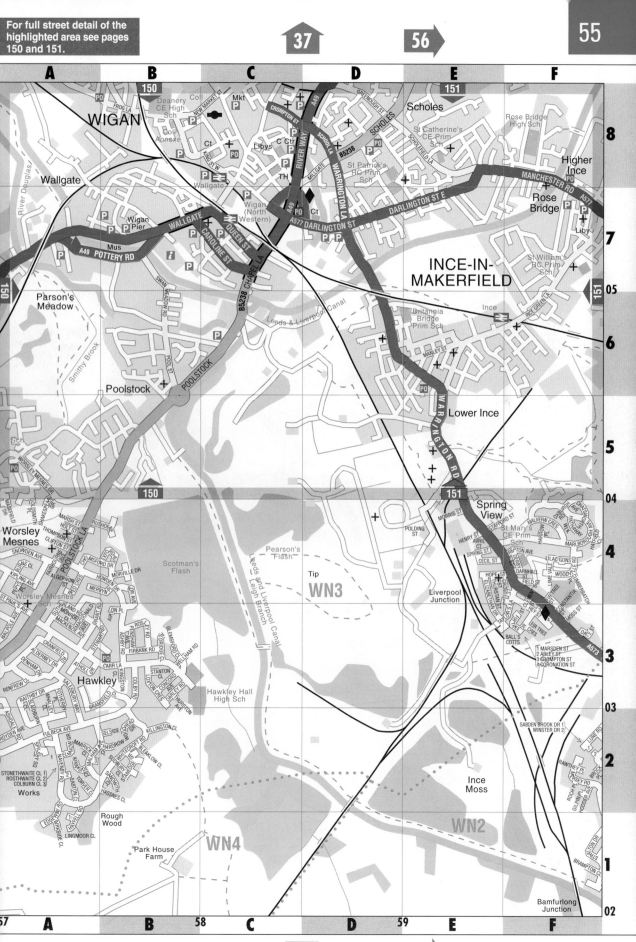

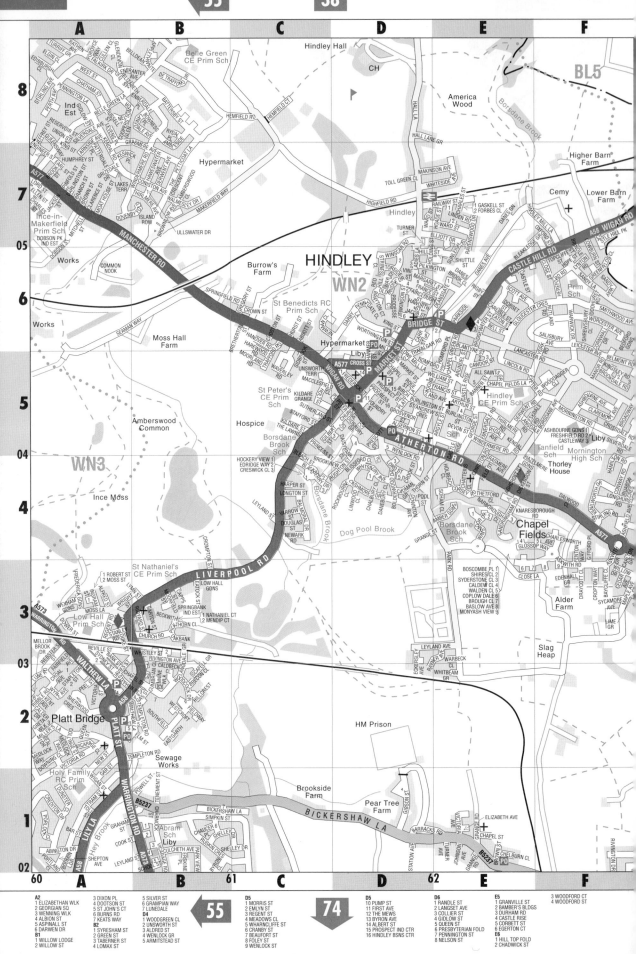

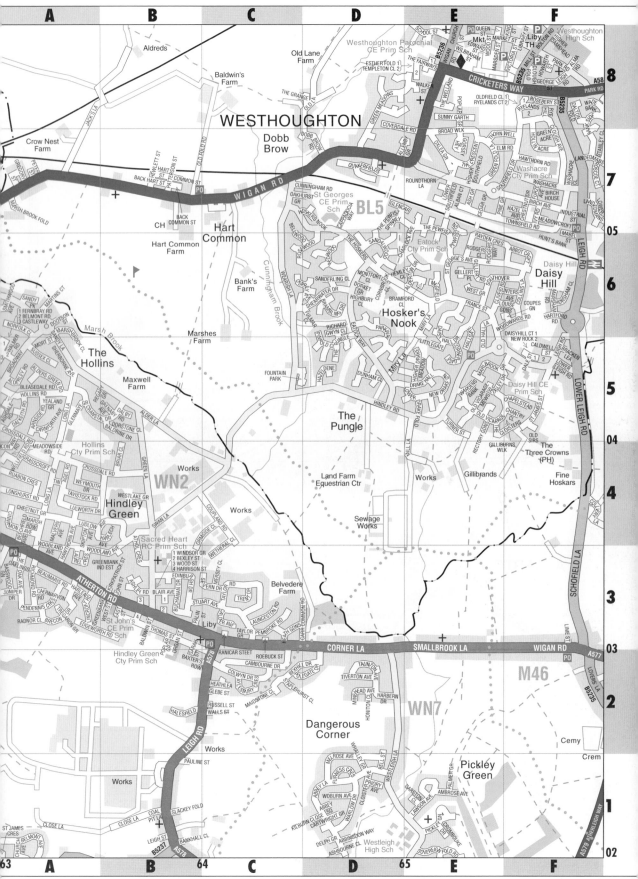

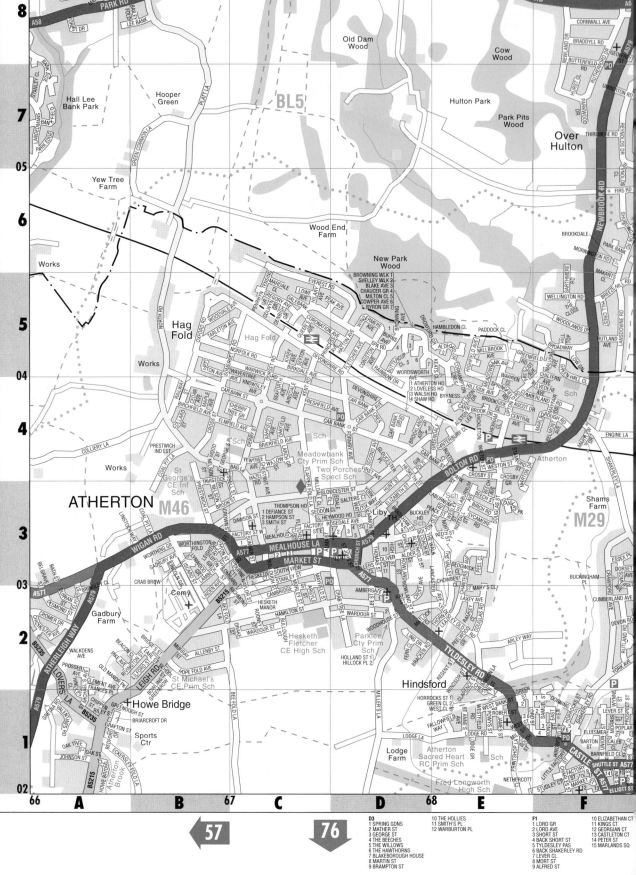

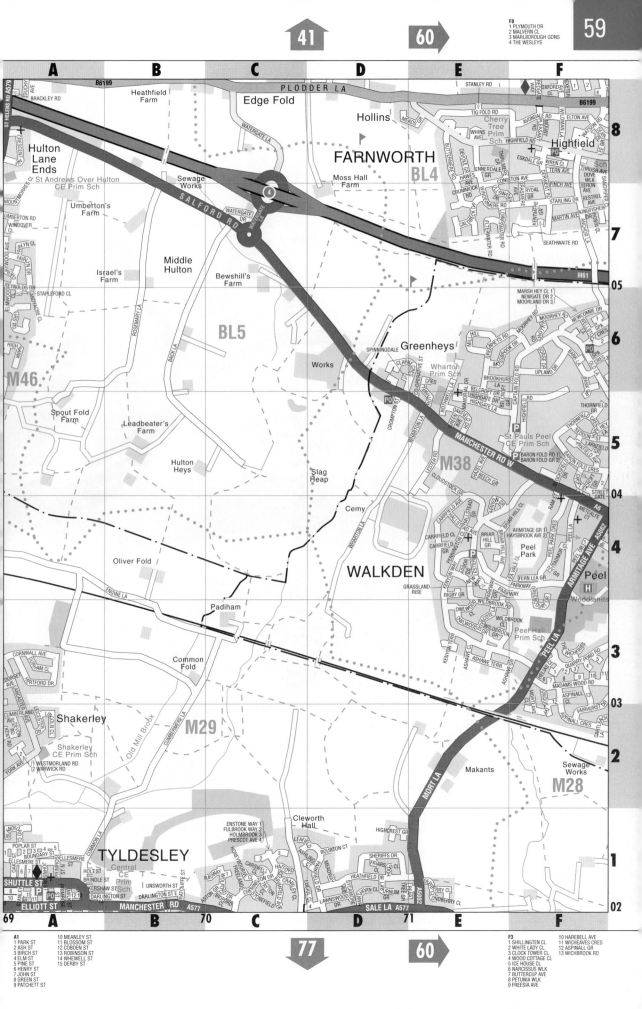

59
42

C8
1 THOMAS GARNET CT
2 PHILIP ARNOLD CT
3 SUTHERLAND ST
4 WESTMINSTER WLK
5 LONSDALE GR
6 KENTFORD GR

C8
7 LIDGATE GR
8 ASHLEY GR
9 ALMOND ST
10 ORMROD ST
11 DIXON GREEN DR

D8
1 JANE BARTER HOUSE
2 BARNES HOUSE
3 ELLESMERE WLK
4 WILCOCKSON HOUSE
5 HESKETH WLK

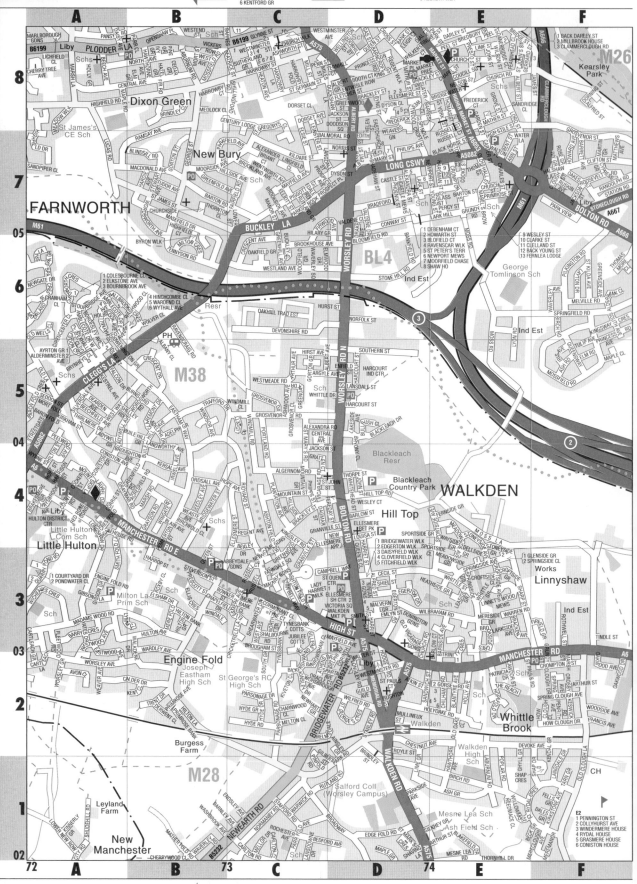

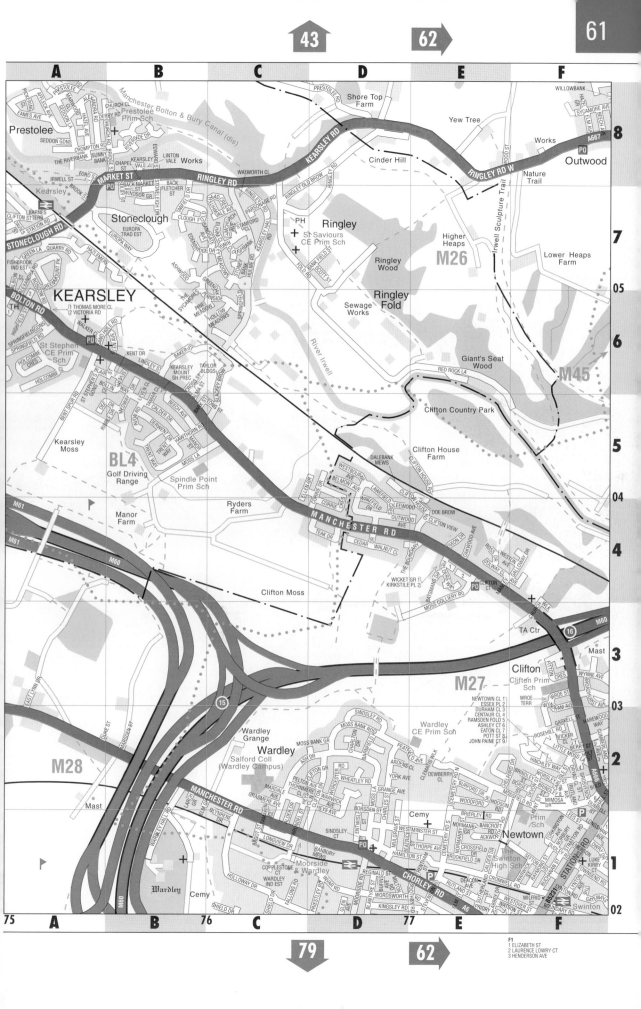

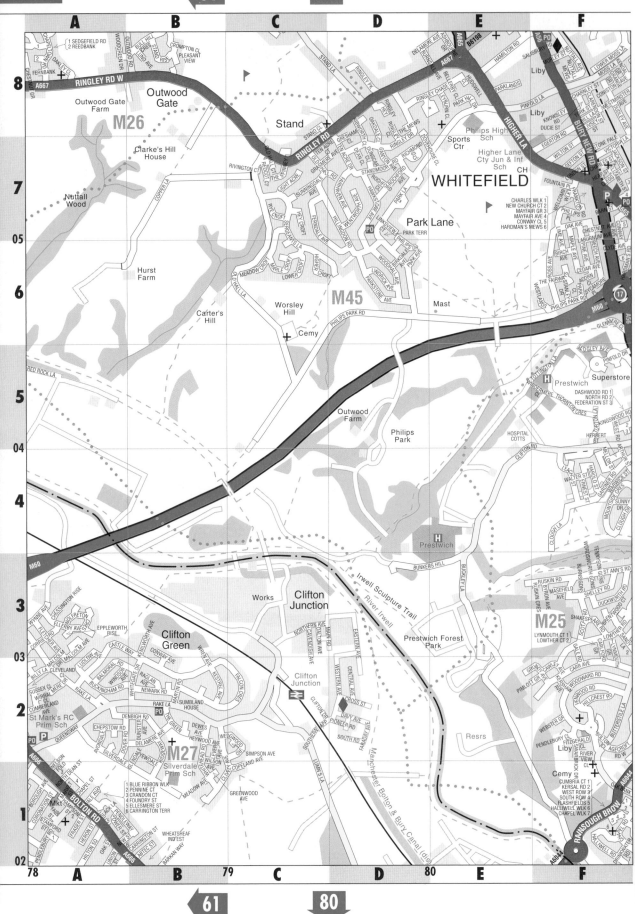

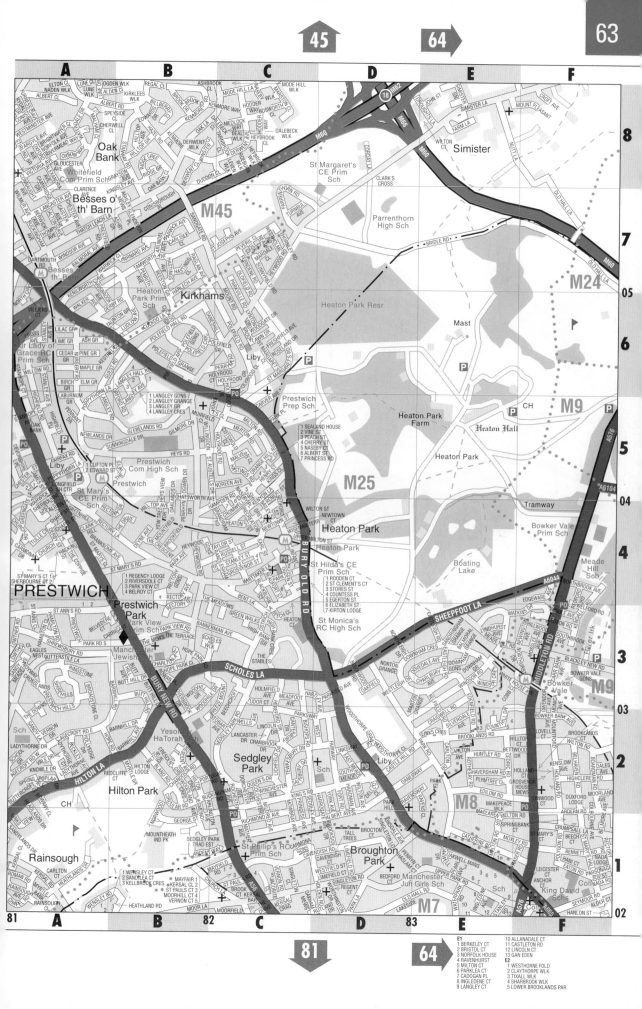

E1
1 BERKELEY CT
2 BRISTOL CT
3 NORFOLK HOUSE
4 RAVENHURST
5 MILTON CT
6 PARKLEA CT
7 CADOGAN PL
8 INGLEDENE CT
9 LANGLEY CT
10 ALLANADALE CT
11 CASTLETON RD
12 LINCOLN CT
13 GAN EDEN
E2
1 WESTHORNE FOLD
2 CLAYTHORPE WLK
3 TIXALL WLK
4 SHARBROOK WLK
5 LOWER BROOKLANDS PAR

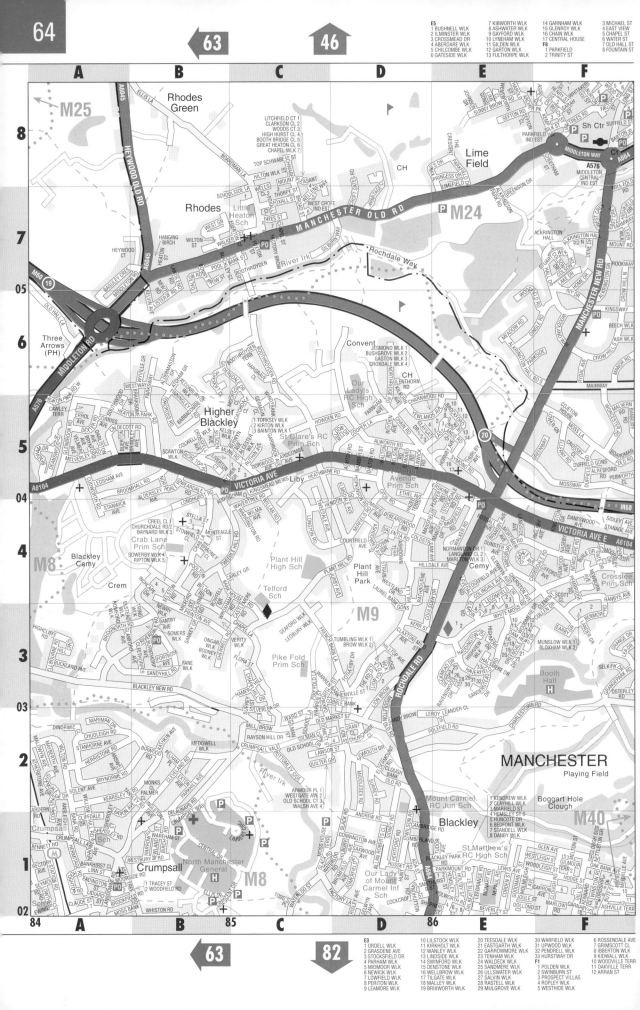

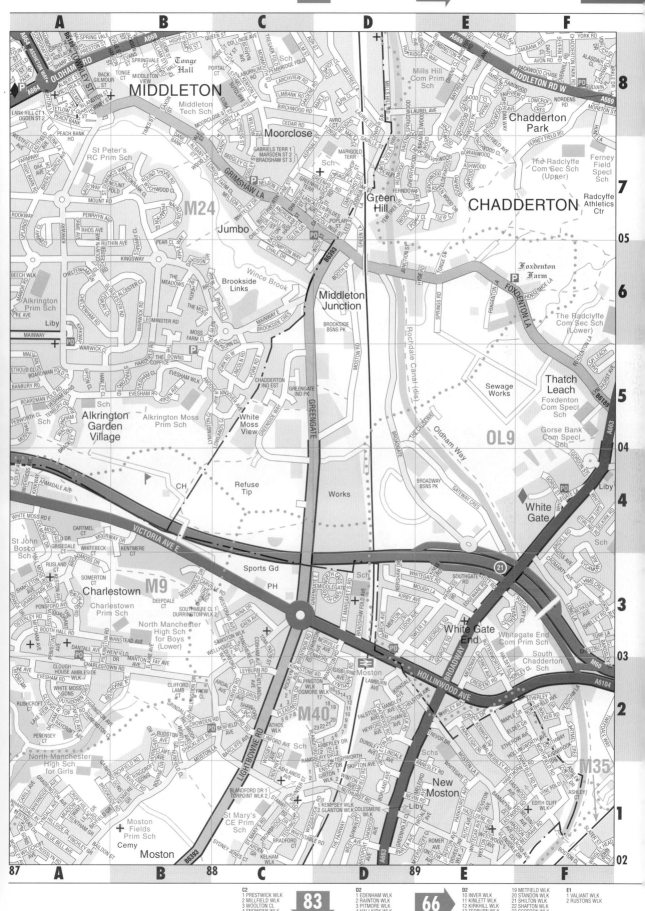

66

For full street detail of the highlighted area see pages 152 and 153.

← **65**   **48**

153

CHADDERTON

Chadderton Cemy

Bare Trees Jun Sch

Eustace Street Com Prim Sch

Busk

Burnley Brow

St Hilda's CE Prim Sch

Cold Hurst

The Parish Church Sch

St Herberts RC Prim Sch

Liby

North Moor

Grange Sch

Blue Coat CE Sch

TA Ctr

MIDDLETON RD

Westwood

Westwood Com Prim Sch

OLDHAM

Oldham Coll

St Mary's Way

Civic Ctr

Mkt

Stock Brook

St Lukes CE Prim Sch

Cowhill

Alder Root

Richmond Jun Sch

Richmond Inf Sch

Bank Top

Pol HQ

YORKSHIRE ST

Liby, Art Gal & Mus

The Radclyffe Sch (Lower)

Christ Church CE Prim Sch

JAMMY LA

Werneth

Freehold Com Prim Sch

St Patricks RC Prim Sch

Nimble Nook

Werneth

Werneth Prep Sch

St Thomas's CE Prim Sch

Werneth Jun & Inf Schs

EAVES LA

Mus

152   **153**

Coppice

Hatthere shaw

OL9

OL8

DRURY LA

Factory Fold

Copster Hill

Hollins

Hollins RD

Hollins Green

Hathershaw Com High Sch Sports Ctr

Hollinwood

M35

Kaskenmoor Sch

The Edge

HOLLINS RD

Holy Rosary RC Prim Sch

Hollinwood

Lime Gate

Cemy Crem

Lime Side

Moss Grove

GREENWOOD ST

St Chads Cres

COAL PIT LA

MARLAND FOLD LA

HILARY AVE

A1
1 DERBY ST
2 WELLINGTON ST
3 PEACE ST
4 CROFT ST
5 CLIFTON VILLAS
6 ROBERT ST

B2
1 MOORFIELD RD
2 PARKFIELD AVE
3 CHELBOURNE DR
4 BARMOUTH WLK
5 NEVIN CL
6 BRECON WLK
7 GEE LA
8 CARDIFF CL
9 PUMP ST

B2
10 ALFORD ST
11 CLOCK ST
C2
1 SCHOOL HOUSE FLATS
2 MILFORD AVE
3 GLENCOE ST
4 BURDER ST
5 FOX PARK RD

← **65**   **84**

D2
1 MALLARD CL
2 SARAH ST
3 CLIVE ST
4 WESTGATE HOUSE
5 CLOUGHGATE HOUSE
6 CLOUGH GATE
7 HIGHGATE HOUSE
8 MOSSGROVE ST

F4
1 SNOWDEN ST
2 WALLACE ST
3 ESTATE ST S
4 DARTMOUTH CL

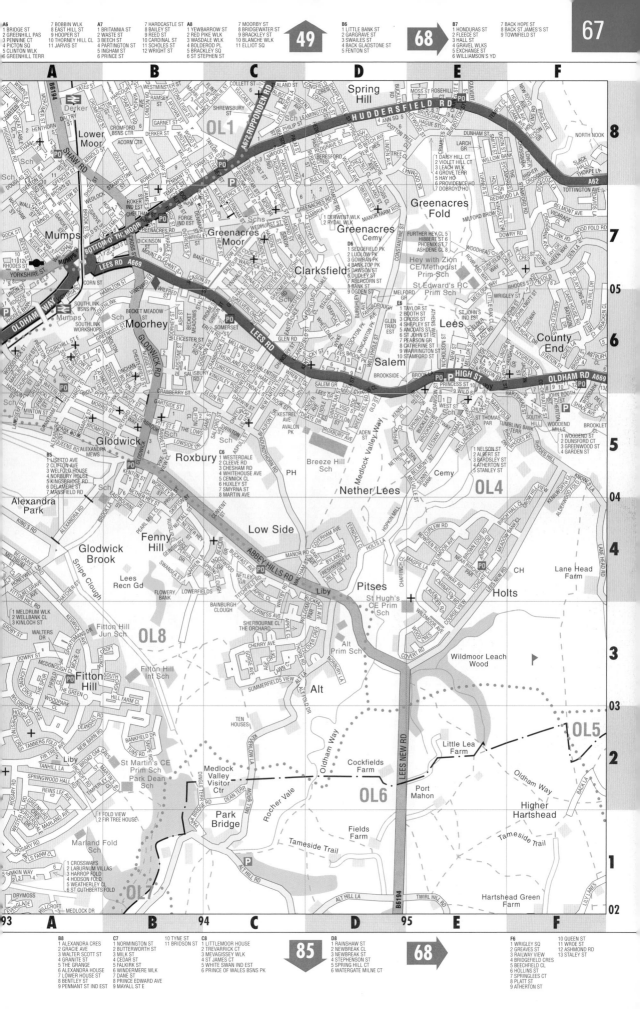

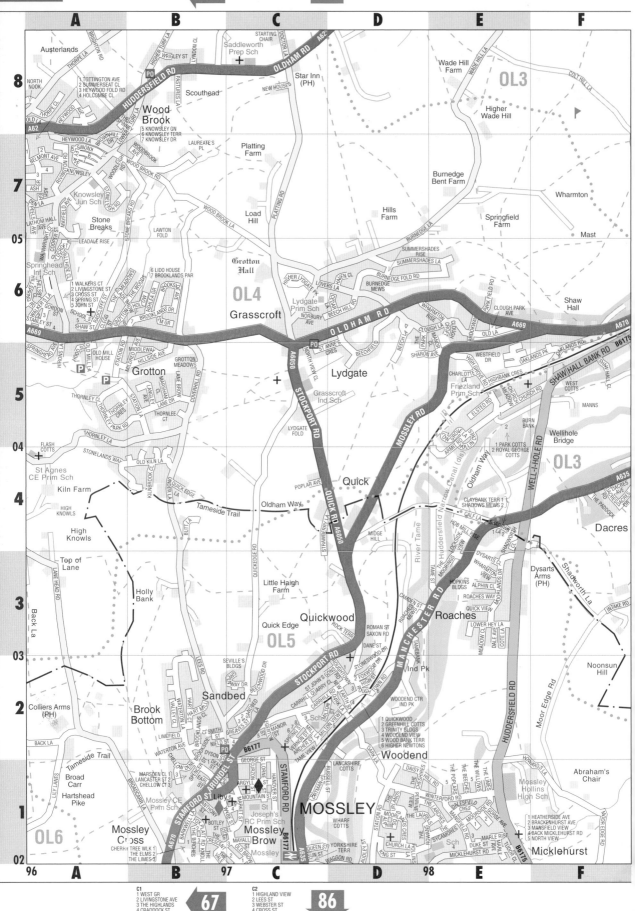

C1
1 WEST GR
2 LIVINGSTONE AVE
3 THE HIGHLANDS
4 CRADDOCK ST
5 CHAPEL CT
6 CHAPEL ST

C2
1 HIGHLAND VIEW
2 LEES ST
3 WEBSTER ST
4 CROSS ST
5 WILD'S SQ
6 SPRING COTTS
7 BACK MILL LA
8 HAWTHORN TERR
9 WOODMEADOW CT

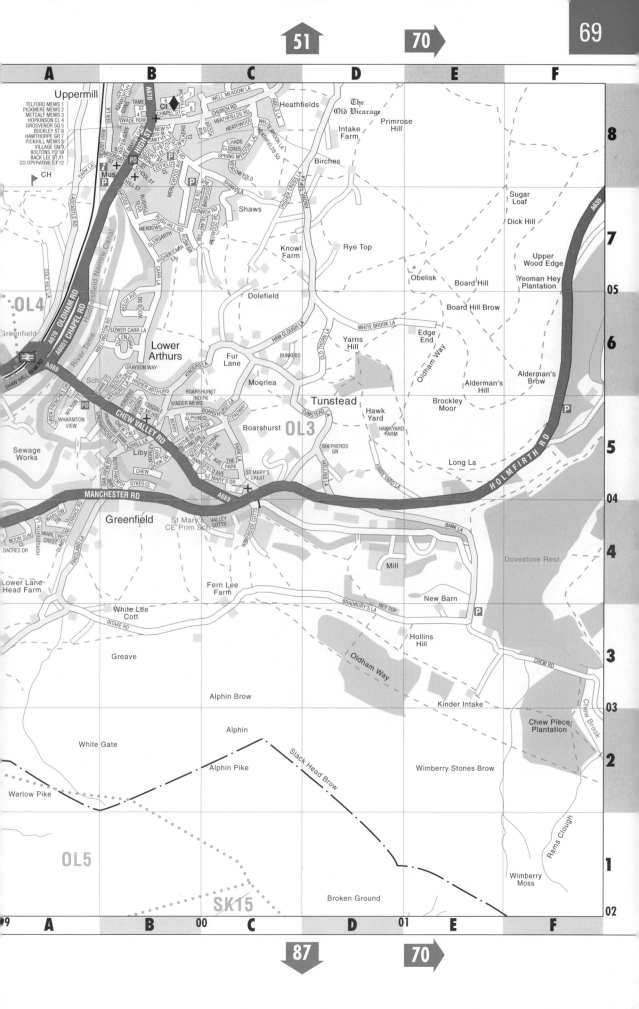

| | 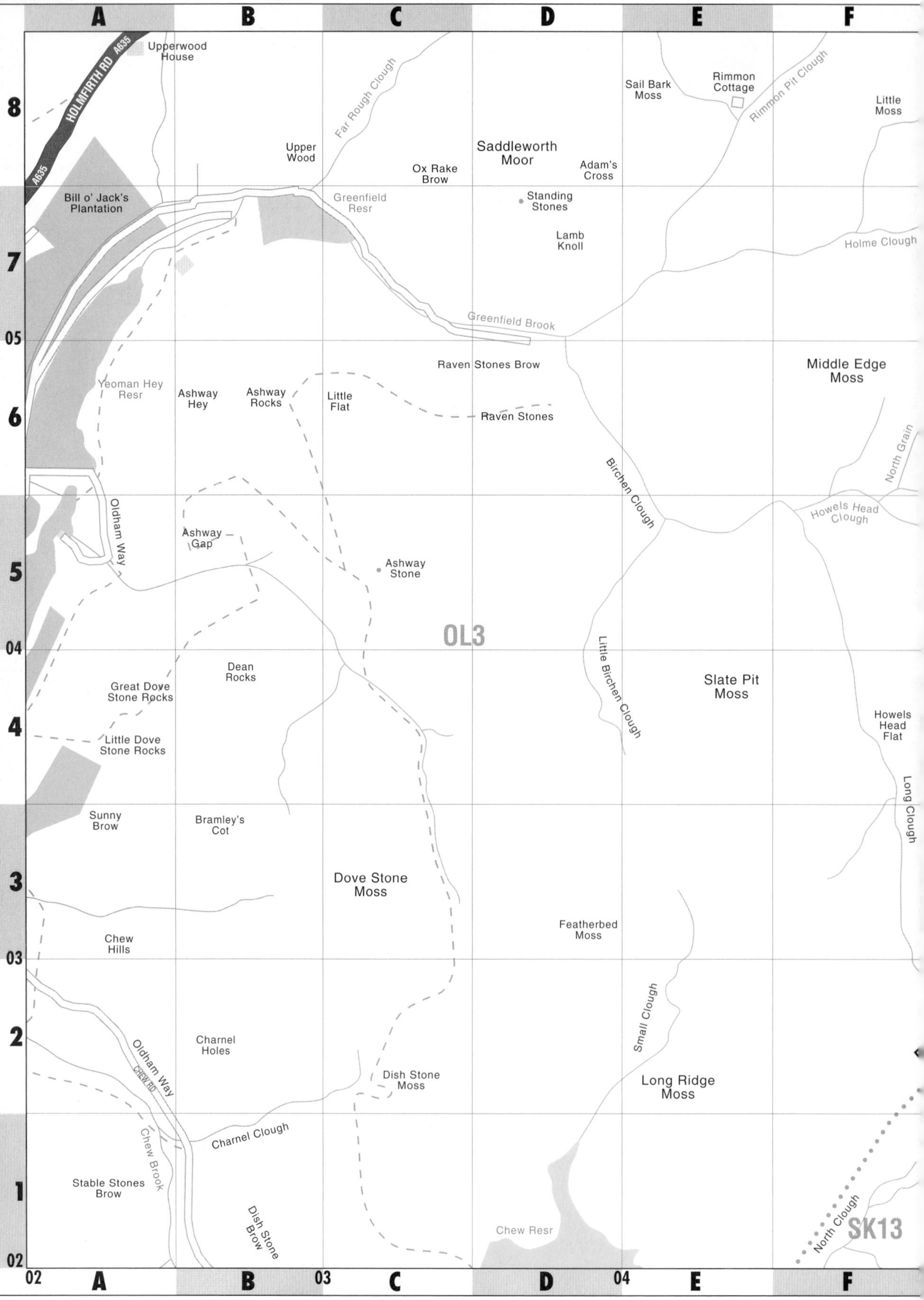 A | B | C | D | E | F |

8

HOLMFIRTH RD A635

Upperwood House

A635

Sail Bark Moss

Rimmon Cottage

Rimmon Pit Clough

Little Moss

Upper Wood

Far Rough Clough

Saddleworth Moor

Ox Rake Brow

Adam's Cross

7

Bill o' Jack's Plantation

Greenfield Resr

Standing Stones

Lamb Knoll

Holme Clough

05

Greenfield Brook

6

Yeoman Hey Resr

Ashway Hey

Ashway Rocks

Little Flat

Raven Stones Brow

Raven Stones

Middle Edge Moss

North Grain

5

Oldham Way

Ashway Gap

Birchen Clough

Howels Head Clough

04

Ashway Stone

OL3

Little Birchen Clough

4

Great Dove Stone Rocks

Dean Rocks

Slate Pit Moss

Howels Head Flat

Little Dove Stone Rocks

Long Clough

3

Sunny Brow

Bramley's Cot

Dove Stone Moss

Chew Hills

Featherbed Moss

03

Small Clough

2

Oldham Way

CHEW RD

Charnel Holes

Dish Stone Moss

Long Ridge Moss

Chew Brook

Charnel Clough

1

Stable Stones Brow

Dish Stone Brow

Chew Resr

North Clough

SK13

02

| 02 | A | | B | 03 | C | | D | 04 | E | | F |

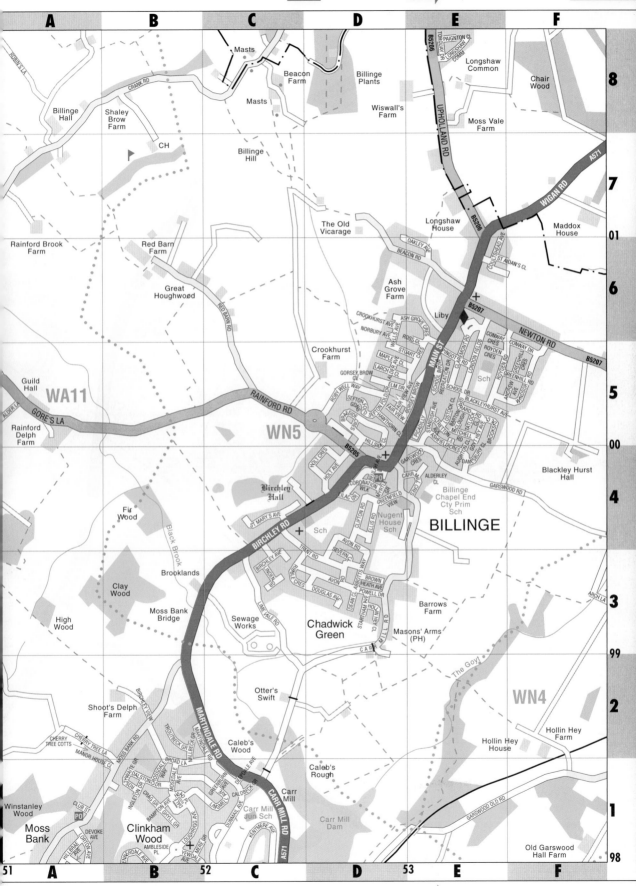

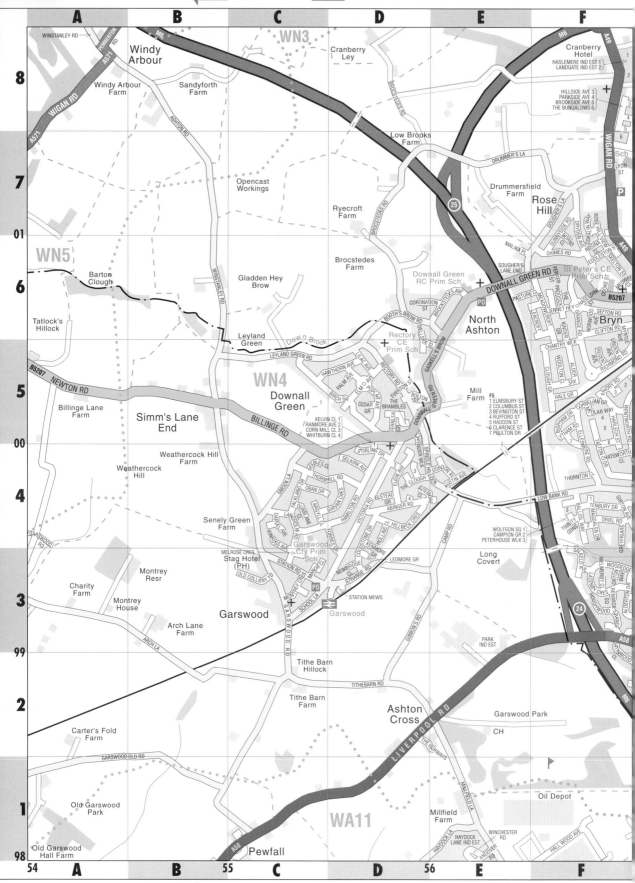

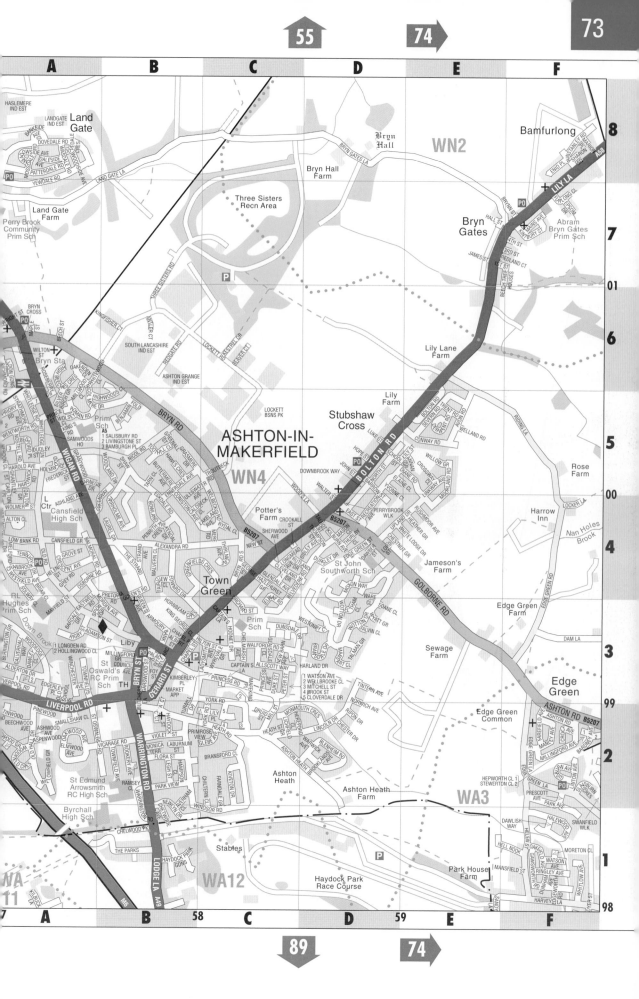

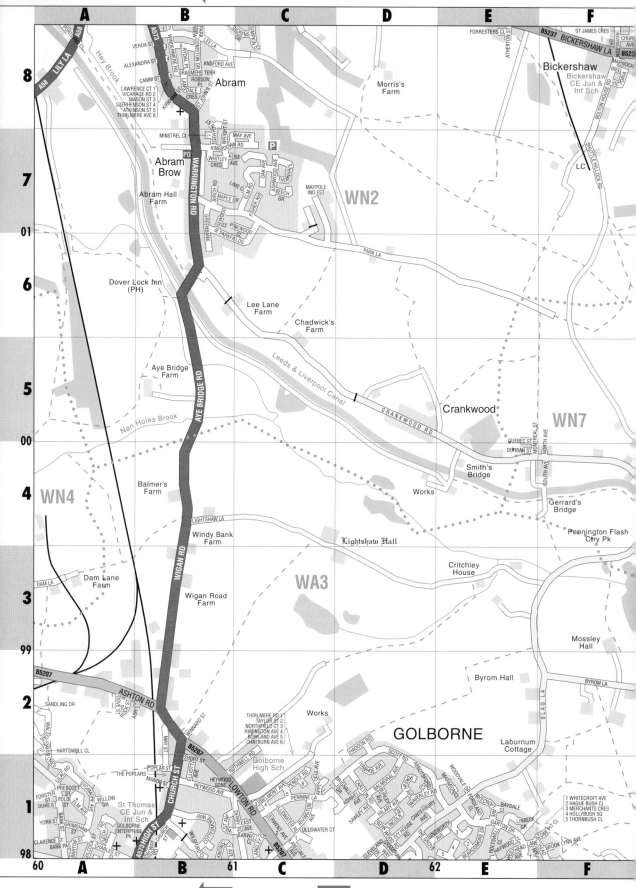

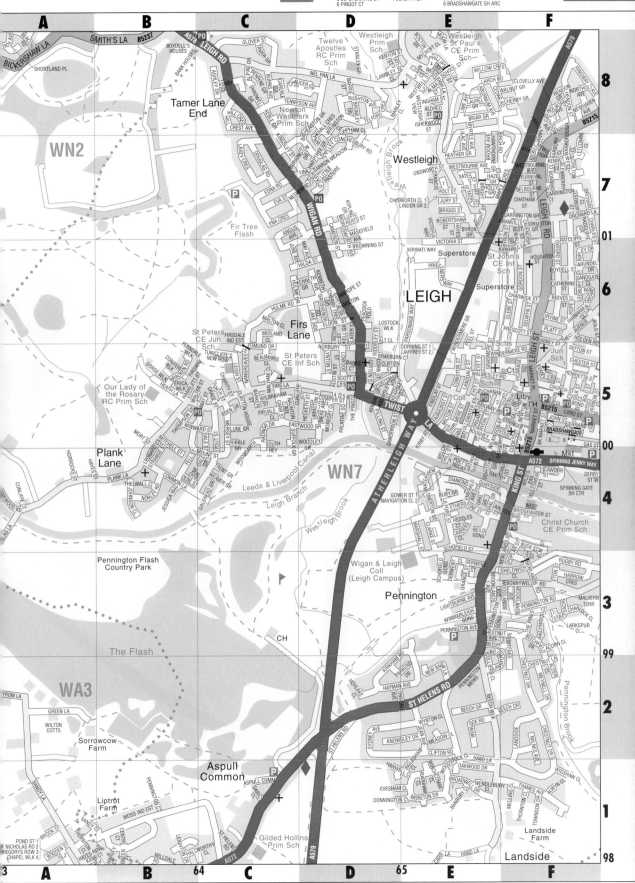

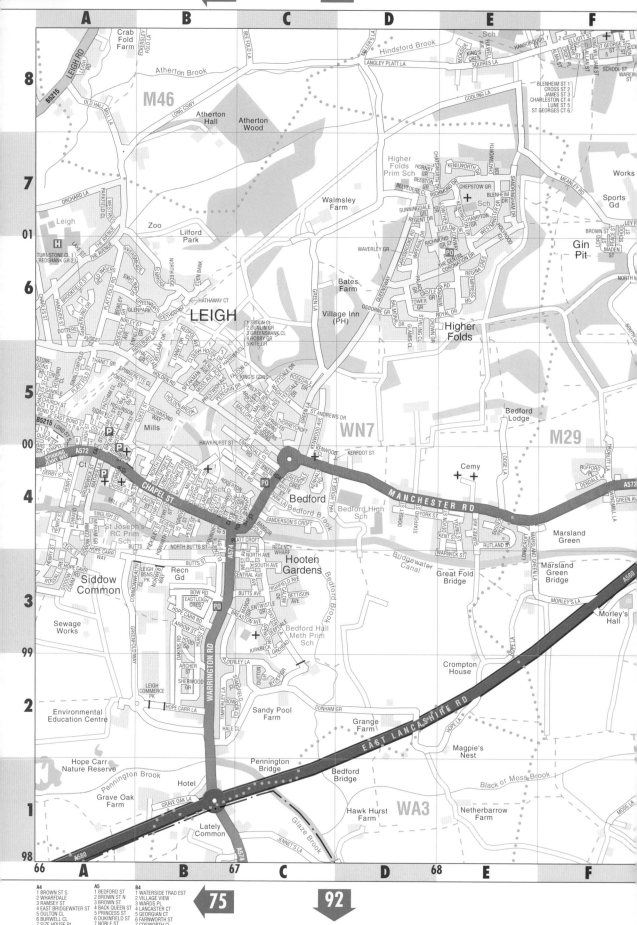

75
58

A4
1 BROWN ST S
2 WHARFDALE
3 RAMSEY ST
4 EAST BRIDGEWATER ST
5 OULTON CL
6 BURWELL CL
7 SIZE HOUSE PL

A5
1 BEDFORD ST
2 BROWN ST N
3 BROWN ST
4 BACK QUEEN ST
5 PRINCESS ST
6 DUKINFIELD ST
7 NOBLE ST
8 WILLIAM ST

B4
1 WATERSIDE TRAD EST
2 VILLAGE VIEW
3 WARDS PL
4 LANCASTER CT
5 GEORGIAN CT
6 FARNWORTH ST
7 COSWORTH ST

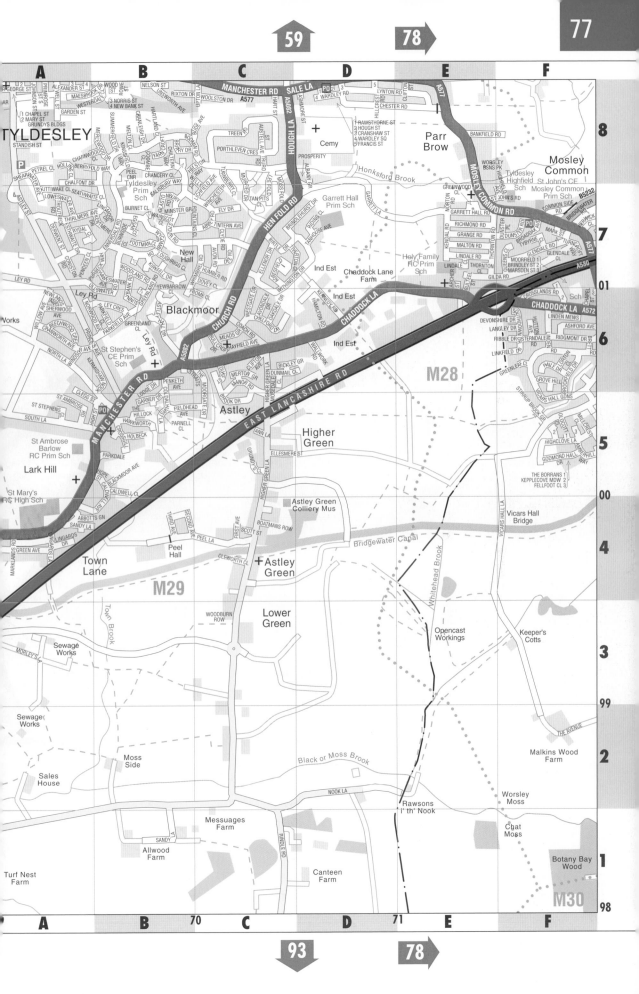

A · B · C · D · E · F

8

TYLDESLEY

MANCHESTER RD · SALE LA · A577

1 CHAPEL ST
2 MARY ST
3 GRUNDYS BLDGS

1 RAWSTHORNE ST
2 HOUGH ST
3 CRANSHAW ST
4 WARDLEY SQ
5 FRANCIS ST

Parr
Brow

BANKFIELD RD

Mosley
Common

Cemy

PROSPERITY

Honksford Brook

Tyldesley
Highfield
Sch

St John's CE

Mosley Common
Prim Sch

B5232

Garrett Hall
Prim Sch

Tyldesley
Prim
Sch

Common Side

7

New
Hall

Ind Est

Chaddock Lane
Farm

Holy Family
RC Prim
Sch

Garrett Hall Rd

Richmond Rd

Grange Rd

Malton Rd

Lindale Rd

Thornton

01

Blackmoor

CHURCH RD

Ind Est

CHADDOCK LA

CHADDOCK LA · A572

6

A5082

St Stephen's
CE Prim
Sch

Ind Est

M28

Devonshire Dr

Langley Dr

Ribble Dr

Linkfield Dr

Ridgmont Dr

Astley

EAST LANCASHIRE RD

Hall Av

Grove Hall

Vicars Hall Gdns

5

MANCHESTER RD

St Ambrose

South La

The
Hillock

Higher
Green

Highclove La

Godmond Hall
Dr

THE BORRANS 1
KEPPLECOVE MDW 2
FELLFOOT CL 3

St Ambrose
Barlow
RC Prim Sch

Astley Green
Colliery Mus

Vicars Hall
Bridge

00

Lark Hill

St Mary's
RC High Sch

Peel
Hall

Astley
Green

Bridgewater Canal

Whitehead Brook

4

Town
Lane

M29

Lower
Green

Opencast
Workings

Keeper's
Cotts

3

Sewage
Works

Town Brook

THE AVENUE

99

Sewage
Works

Moss
Side

Malkins Wood
Farm

2

Sales
House

Black or Moss Brook

Worsley
Moss

Chat
Moss

Messuages
Farm

NOOK LA

Rawsons
i' th' Nook

Botany Bay
Wood

1

Allwood
Farm

Turf Nest
Farm

Canteen
Farm

M30

98

A · 70 · B · C · D · 71 · E · F

61
80

E7
1 BEDFORD AVE
2 PADDISON ST
3 STOCKTON ST
4 THORNFIELD DR
5 ALBERMARLE RD
6 COLLIER ST
7 LINCOLN RD

F7
1 GORSEFIELD DR
2 WAGGONERS CT
3 ROSETTE WLK
4 MAIDEN MEWS
5 LIGHTBOURNE AVE

Roe Green
Hazelhurst
Egerton Park
Broad Oak
Broadoak Park
Moorside
Deans
SWINTON
Light Bourne Green
Dales Brow
Chorlton Fold
Monton
Ellesmere Park
Alder Forest
Westwood Park
Winton
Winton Park
Patricroft
ECCLES
EAST LANCASHIRE RD
WORSLEY RD
PARTINGTON LA
CHORLEY RD
FOLLY LA
ROCKY LA
MONTON RD
HALF EDGE LA
LIVERPOOL RD
BARTON RD
BARTON LA
CHURCH ST
GREEN LA
CANAL BANK
PARRIN LA
Bridgewater Canal
Manchester Ship Canal
M27
M28
M30

B1
1 SARAH ST
2 WINIFRED ST
3 BEECH HOUSE
4 ATHERTON WAY
5 HAMPSON CL
6 GREEN ST

C1
1 WILLOW TREE CT
2 CORNWALL ST
3 CHAPEL ST
4 THOMAS JOHNSON CL
5 ELIZA ANN ST
6 SPOONER RD
7 GREENWATCH CL
8 OLD STATION ST

95

D1
1 ST JOHN ST
2 BRADBURN CL
3 MOORFIELD CL
4 BRADBURN AVE
5 BRADBURN GR
6 DORNING ST
7 WILHAM AVE
8 WADE HOUSE
9 WALKER HOUSE

80

D1
10 O'KANE HOUSE
11 UVEDALE HOUSE
12 PITCAIRN HOUSE
13 DE TRAFFORD HOUSE
14 ELLESMERE ST

E2
1 ABERDEEN
2 MONTROSE
3 DUNDEE
4 PERTH
5 EDINBURGH
6 STERLING
7 BUCKLE HO
8 GARDNER HO

F2
1 CHAPEL WLK
2 THIRKHILL PL
3 KEMBALL
4 NORTHWAY
5 THE MALL
6 SHUTTLE ST
7 SOUTHWAY
8 BOOTHWAY
9 BACK CHAPEL ST
10 COLLEGE CROFT
11 ST MARY'S RD
12 EWOOD
13 CRAUNTON

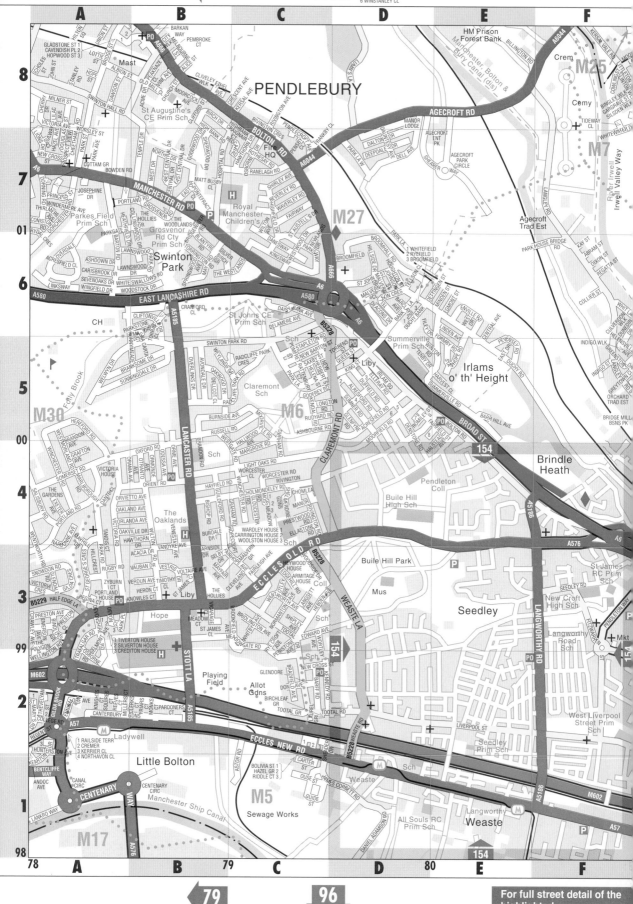

D5
1 RANULPH CT
2 HUNTS RD
3 CROSBY RD
4 PENELOPE RD
5 CHURCHFIELD RD
6 WINSTANLEY CL

7 NORBURY AVE
8 PEACOCK AVE

PENDLEBURY

Swinton Park

Irlams o' th' Height

Brindle Heath

Seedley

Little Bolton

Weaste

Langworthy

For full street detail of the highlighted area see page 154.

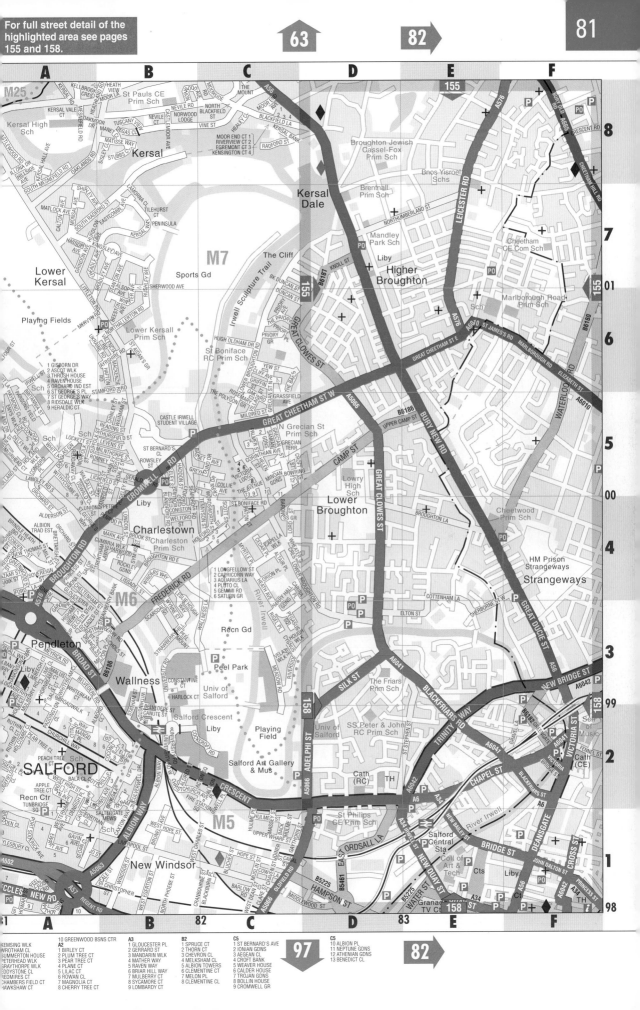

For full street detail of the highlighted area see pages 155 and 158.

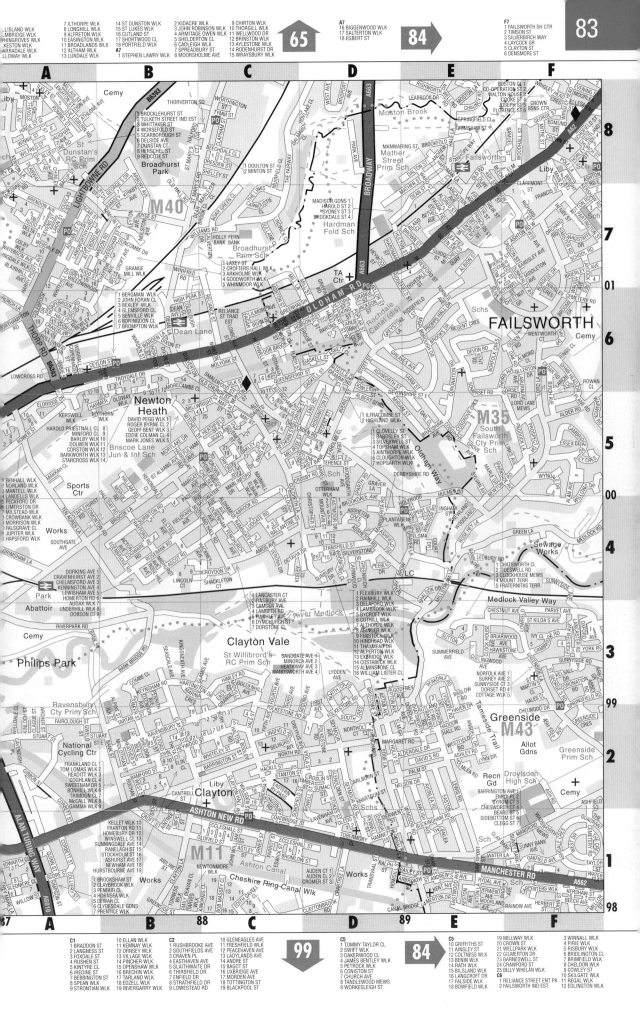

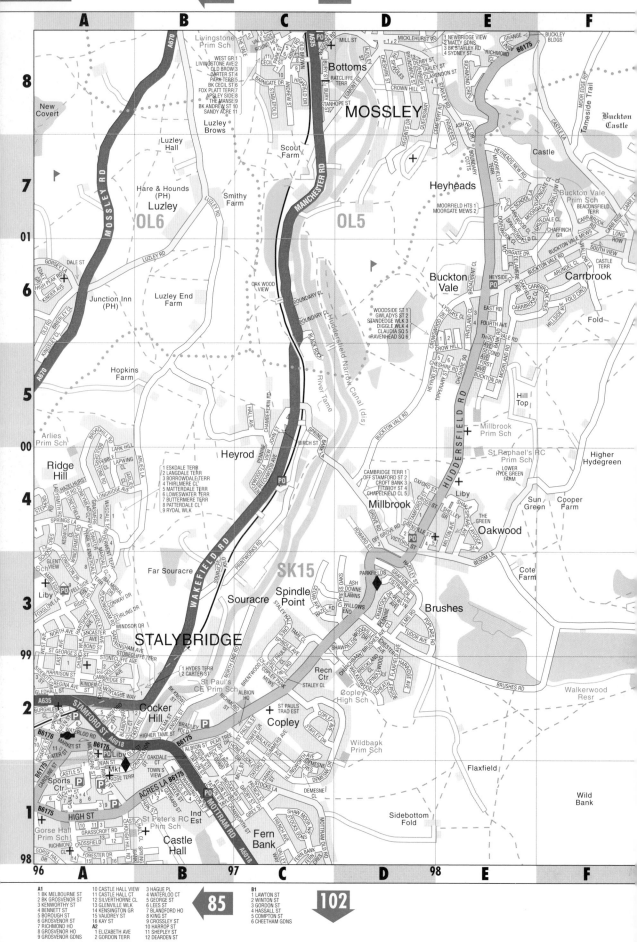

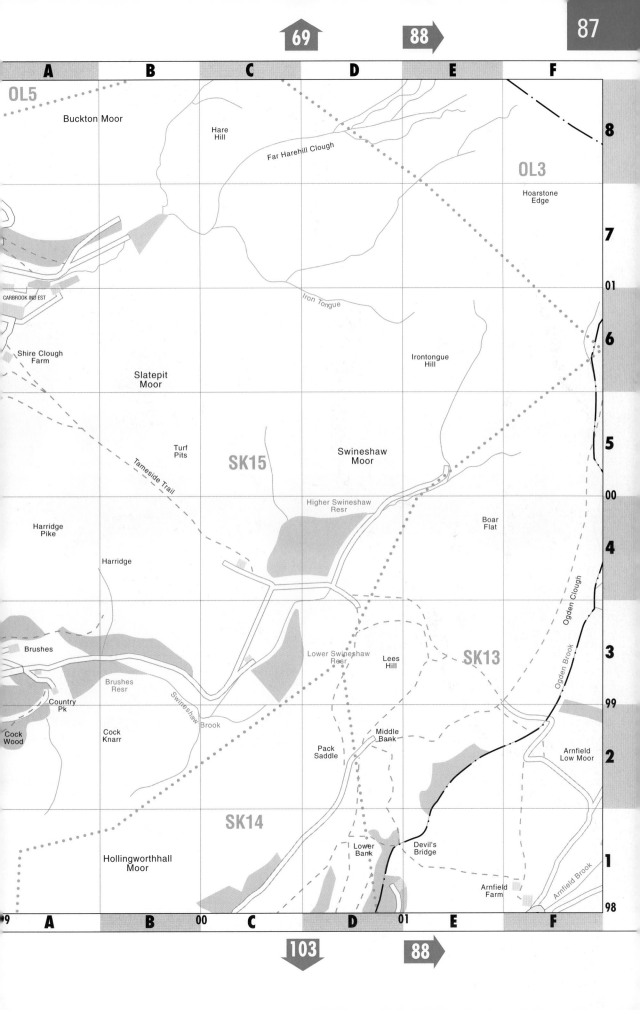

OL5

A   B   C   D   E   F

Buckton Moor

Hare
Hill

Far Harehill Clough

OL3

Hoarstone
Edge

8

7

CARBROOK IND EST

01

Iron Tongue

6

Shire Clough
Farm

Irontongue
Hill

Slatepit
Moor

Turf
Pits

SK15

Swineshaw
Moor

5

Tameside Trail

00

Higher Swineshaw
Resr

Harridge
Pike

Boar
Flat

Harridge

4

Ogden Clough

Brushes

Lower Swineshaw
Resr

Lees
Hill

SK13

3

Ogden Brook

Brushes
Resr

99

Country
Pk

Swineshaw Brook

Cock
Wood

Cock
Knarr

Middle
Bank

Pack
Saddle

Arnfield
Low Moor

2

SK14

Hollingworthhall
Moor

Lower
Bank

Devil's
Bridge

1

Arnfield
Farm

Arnfield Brook

98

'9   A   B   00   C   D   01   E   F

87
70

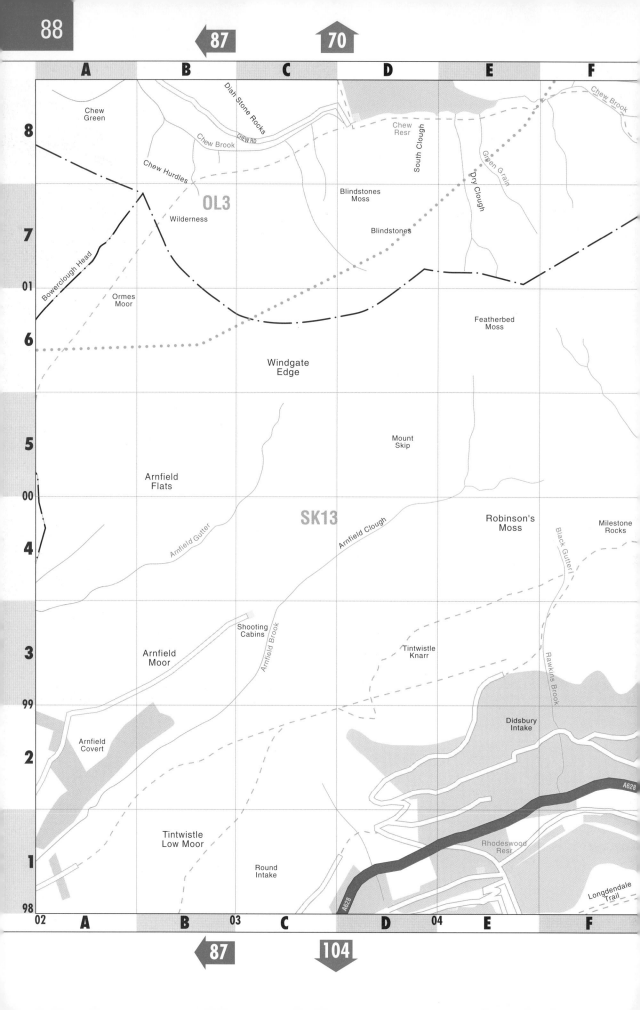

87
104

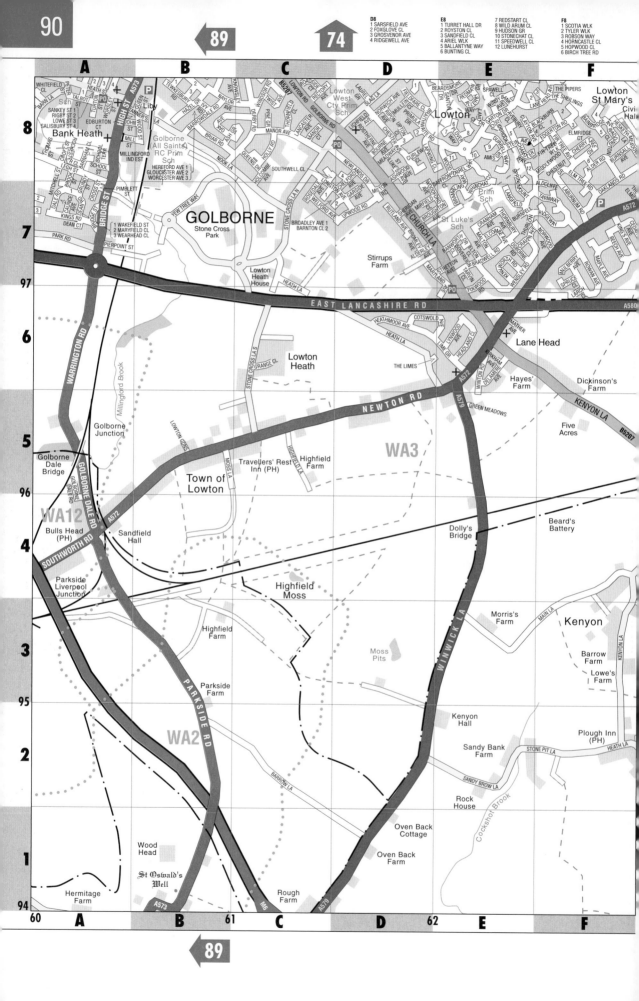

89

74

D8
1 SARSFIELD AVE
2 FOXGLOVE CL
3 GROSVENOR AVE
4 RIDGEWELL AVE

E8
1 TURRET HALL DR
2 ROYSTON CL
3 SANDFIELD CL
4 ARIEL WLK
5 BALLANTYNE WAY
6 BUNTING CL

7 REDSTART CL
8 WILD ARUM CL
9 HUDSON GR
10 STONECHAT CL
11 SPEEDWELL CL
12 LUNEHURST

F8
1 SCOTIA WLK
2 TYLER WLK
3 ROBSON WAY
4 HORNCASTLE CL
5 HOPWOOD CL
6 BIRCH TREE RD

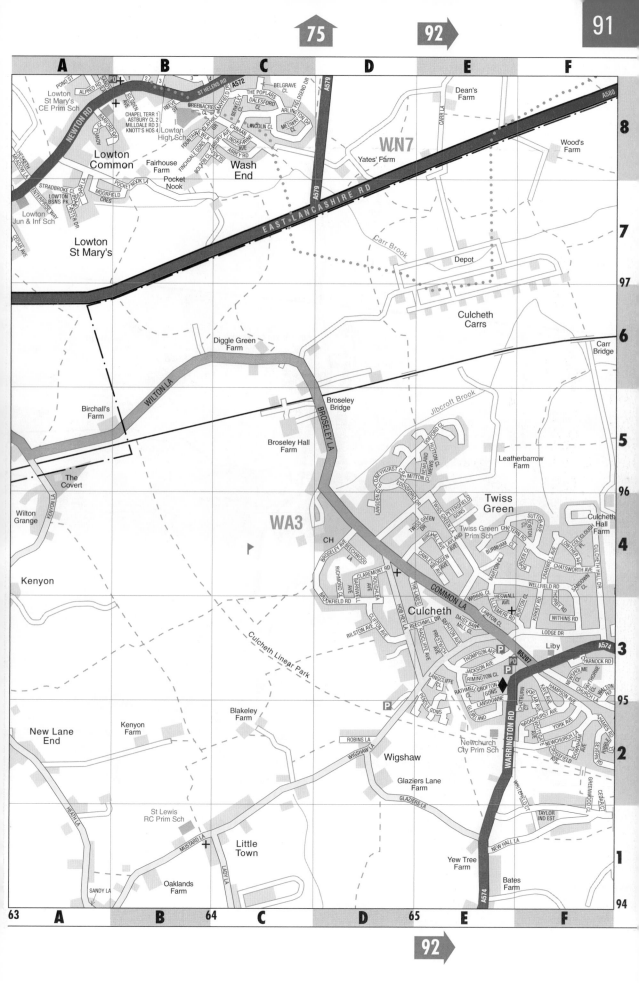

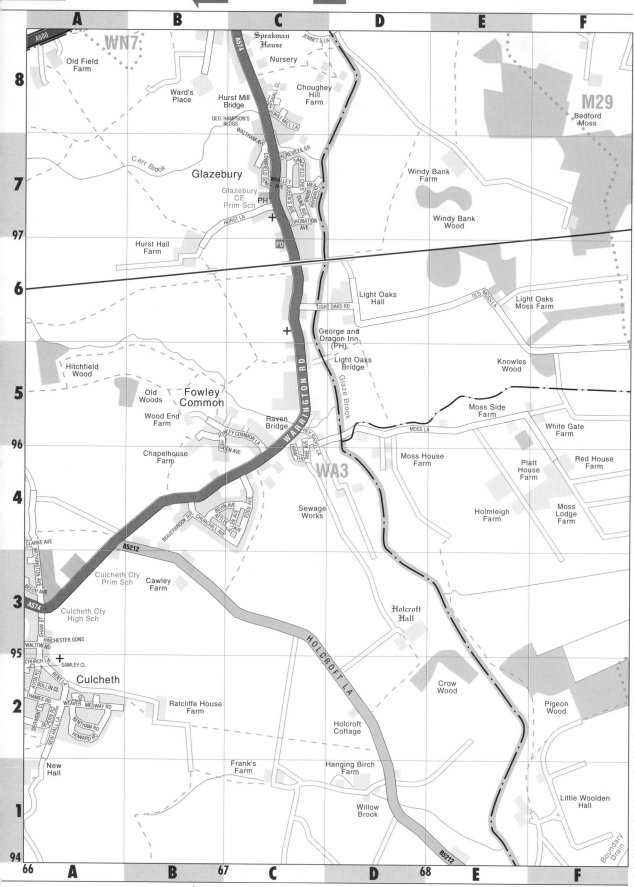

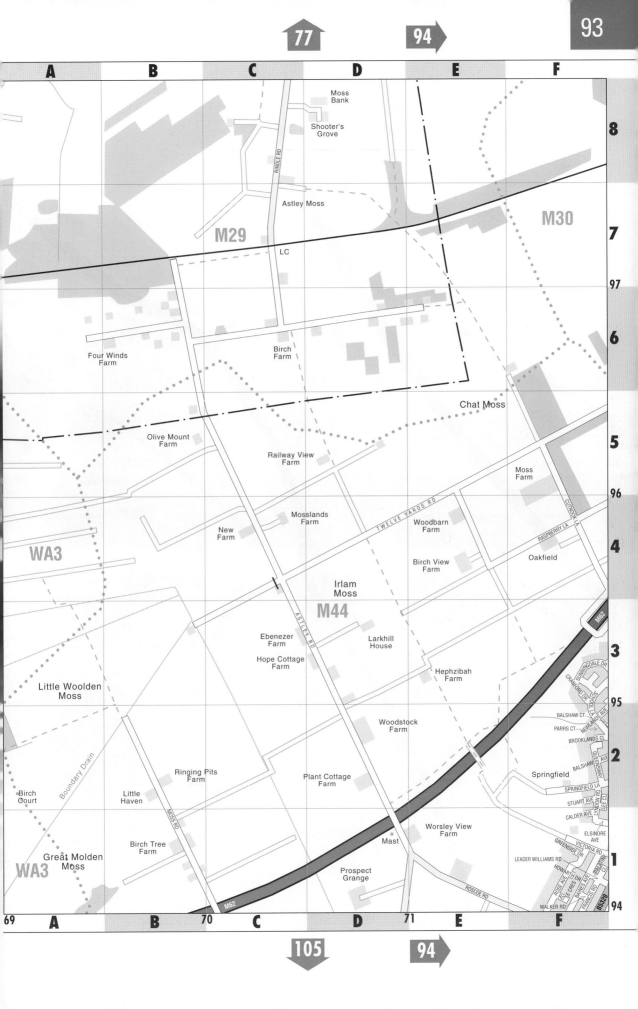

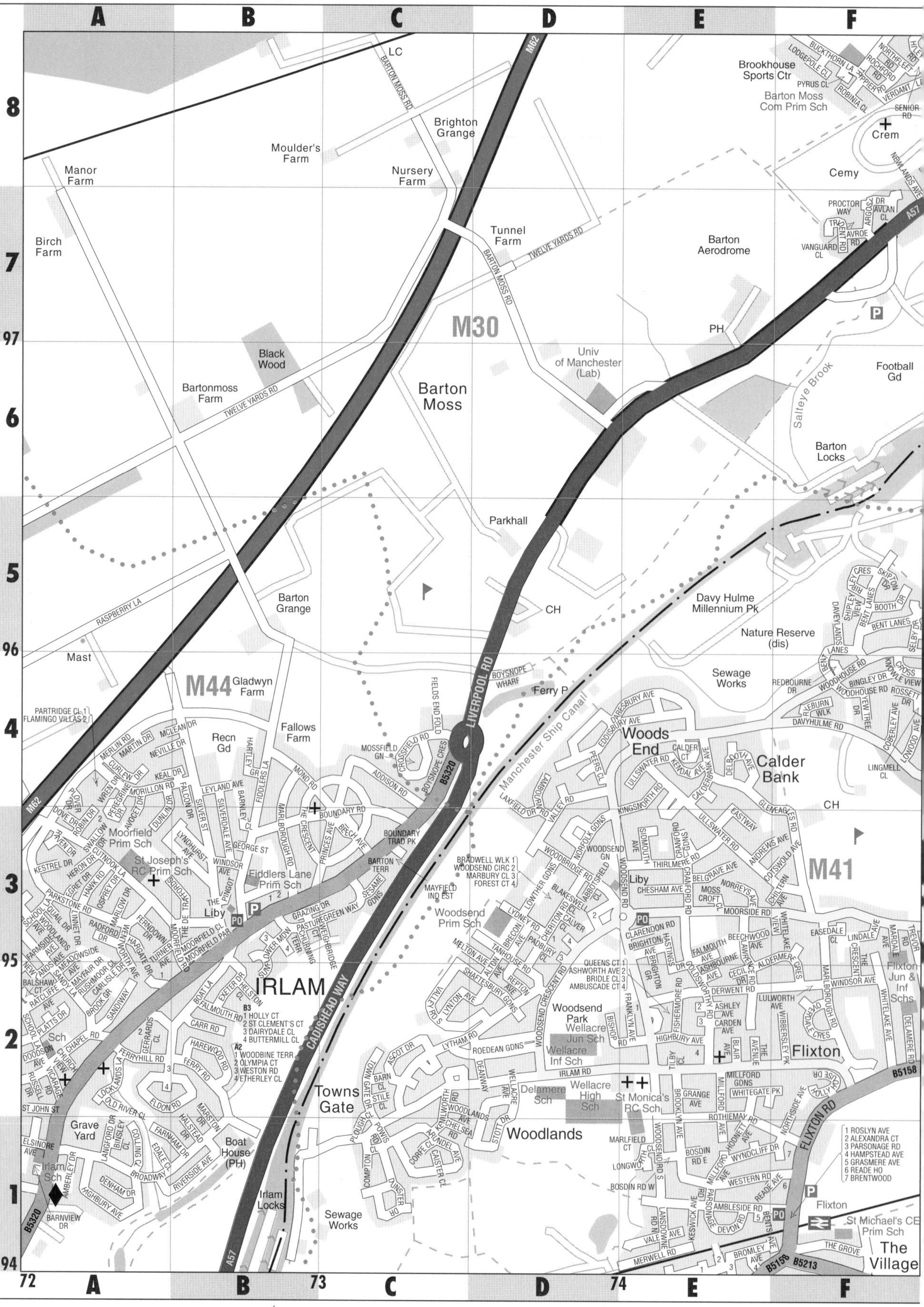

A B C D E F

8

7

97

6

5

96

4

3

95

2

1

94

72 A B 73 C D 74 E F

LC
BARTON MOSS RD
Moulder's Farm
Brighton Grange
Nursery Farm
M62

Manor Farm
Birch Farm

Tunnel Farm
TWELVE YARDS RD
BARTON MOSS RD

Brookhouse Sports Ctr
Barton Moss Com Prim Sch
PYRUS CL
BUCKTHORN LA
LODGEDALE CL
RIBSTER
RICHFORD
NORTHLEF
ROBINIA CL
VERDANT CL
SENIOR RD
Crem
Cemy

PROCTOR WAY
ARGOSY DR
AVLAN DR
AVROE RD
VANGUARD CL
TR
A57

M30

Black Wood

Bartonmoss Farm
TWELVE YARDS RD

Barton Aerodrome
PH

Univ of Manchester (Lab)

Barton Moss

Salteye Brook

Football Gd

Barton Locks

RASPBERRY LA

Barton Grange

Parkhall

CH

Davy Hulme Millennium Pk

Nature Reserve (dis)

Sewage Works

CRES
SKIPTON
SHIPLEY
VIEW LANES
BENT LANES
DAVEYLANDS
BENT
BOOTH
SELBY

Mast

M44 Gladwyn Farm

Fallows Farm
Recn Gd

MOSSFIELD GN
ADDISON RD
CROSSFIELD RD
FIELDS END FOLD
POYSNOPE CRES
B5320
LIVERPOOL RD
BOYSNOPE WHARF
Ferry P

Manchester Ship Canal

Woods End

Calder Bank

REDBOURNE DR
WOODHOUSE RD
BINGLEY DR
ROSSETT
YEW TREE
DAVYHULME RD
LANES
WOODHOUSE RD
KNOWLE DR
CROSS

M41

CH

PARTRIDGE CL 1
FLAMINGO VILLAS 2
M62

MERLIN RD
MARTIN AVE
McLEAN DR
NEVILLE DR
KEAL DR
FALCON DR
HARTLEY
FIDDLERS LA
LEYLAND AVE
BARNLEY
SILVERDALE AVE
BEECH AVE
PRINCES AVE
THE CRESCENT
GEORGE ST
MOND RD
MARLBOROUGH RD
Boundary Rd
Boundary Trad Pk
Barton Terr
LAXFIELD DR
VALLEY RD
KINGSMORTH RD
PIERS RD
PERCY RD
EGBURY AVE
BRADBURY AVE
ASHTON
DELBOW
WOODSEND
EASTWAY
CALDERBANK
GLENEAGG

CLOVER
SWALLOW
DOVE DR
WREN DR
CURLEW DR
PEREGRINE DR
MORILLON DR
WINDSOR AVE
LYNDHURST
Moorfield Prim Sch
St Joseph's RC Prim Sch
Fiddlers Lane Prim Sch
Liby
PO
GRAZING DR
PASTUREGREEN WAY
SCOTT
SCENE GDNS
WOODBRIDGE
MAYFIELD IND EST
BRADWELL WLK 1
WOODSEND CIRC 2
MARBURY CL 3
FOREST CT 4
Woodsend Prim Sch
LYTHER GDNS
CHERITON RD
CALVER
THIRLMERE RD
BELGRAVE AVE
NORREYS AVE
COTSWOLD AVE
CHESTER
SCAFELL
Liby
Chesham Ave
Moss Croft
MOORSIDE RD
EASEDALE
LINDALE
TREVOR

KESTREL DR
HERON DR
HAWK RD
OSPREY DR
PLATTS AVE
FERNDOWN
TURNER DR
MOORFIELD RD
SCENE
BLAKESWELL
LYONET RD
CHEADLE
PADBURY
Woodsend Park
Wellacre Jun Sch
Wellacre Inf Sch
BRIGHTON AVE
CLARENDON RD
HASTINGS RD
FALMOUTH RD
ASHBOURNE RD
BEECHWOOD AVE
WHITEHAVEN
CECIL RD
ASHLEY AVE
ALDERMERE
EASEDALE
FLIXTON

IRLAM

B3
HOLLY CT
ST CLEMENT'S CT
DAIRYDALE CL
BUTTERMILL CL
A2
WOODBINE TERR
OLYMPIA CT
WESTON RD
ETHERLEY CL
CADISHEAD WAY

FALMOUTH CL
EXETER AVE
CARR RD
HAREWOOD CL
FERRY RD
FERRYHILL RD
ASCOT CL
BARN STILE
LYTHAM RD
ROEDEAN GDNS
VALLEY RD
LYNTON AVE
REPTON
MELTON AVE
SHAFTESBURY GDNS
BISHOP AVE
ASHWORTH AVE 1
BRIDLE CL 3
AMBUSCADE CT 4
QUEENS CL 1
IRLAM RD
DERWENT RD
HIGHBURY AVE
CARDEN AVE
FRANKLYN AVE
BLAIR
WIBBERSLEY
Flixton Jun & Inf Schs
THE AVENUE
LULWORTH AVE
MARLBOROUGH RD
WINDSOR AVE
WHITEGATE PK
DELAMERE RD

Sch
CHAPEL RD
GERRARDS CL
WOODSTOCK
OLD RIVER CL
ELDON RD
MARSTON CL
MANOR AVE
Boat House (PH)
Towns Gate
POPLARS
PLOVER CL
POYNTON
PARTINGTON
CHELSEA
CLANDELL
WELLACRE AVE
Woodsend Park
Delamere Sch
Wellacre High Sch
St Monica's RC Sch
MILLFORD GDNS
GRANGE AVE
BROOKLYN AVE
ROTHIEMAY
MILLFORD
NORTHSIDE AVE
FLIXTON RD
B5158

Grave Yard
ELSINORE AVE
LANGFORD RD
AMBER CT DR
DENHAM DR
HIGHBURY AVE
BINGLEY CL
COLUMN RD
EDALE RD
FARNHAM DR
BROADWAY
RIVERSIDE AVE
Irlam Locks
Sewage Works

Woodlands

MARLFIELD
LONGWO
BOSDIN RD E
WYNDCLIFF DR
WESTERN RD
BOSDIN RD W
DEVON
VALE AVE
KESWICK AVE
LANSDOWNE
AMBLESIDE RD
PO
MERWELL RD
BROMLEY AVE
B5156
B5213
THE GROVE
St Michael's CE Prim Sch
The Village
Flixton
1 ROSLYN AVE
2 ALEXANDRA CT
3 PARSONAGE RD
4 HAMPSTEAD AVE
5 GRASMERE AVE
6 READE HO
7 BRENTWOOD

Irlam Sch
BARNVIEW DR
ST JOHN ST
B5320
A57
FLIXTON RD

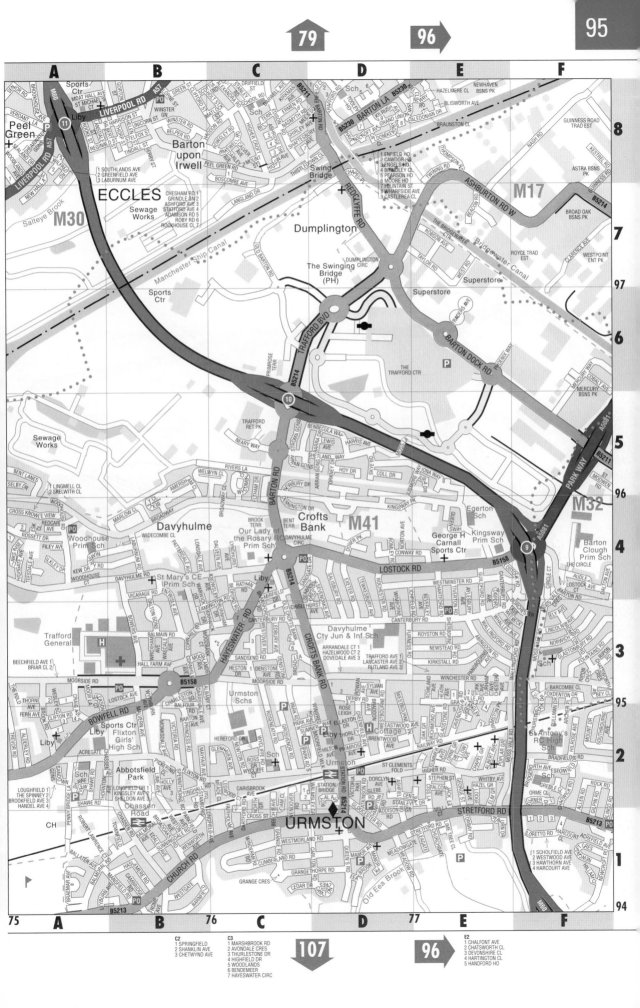

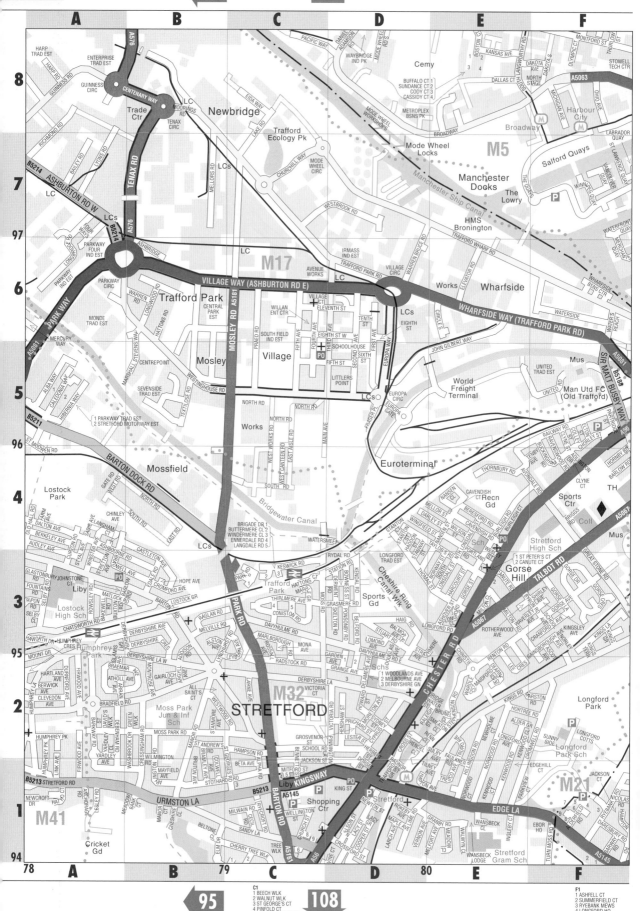

95
80

A B C D E F

8
7
97
6
5
96
4
3
95
1
94

78 A B 79 C D 80 E F

HARP TRAD EST
HARP RD
GUINNESS RD
ENTERPRISE TRAD EST
GUINNESS CIRC
A576
CENTENARY WAY
Trade Ctr
TENAX RD
TENAX CIRC
MOORINGS RD
LC
Newbridge
EIDA WAY
LAKE RD
Trafford Ecology Pk

RICHMOND RD
BAILEY RD
LYONS RD
B5214
ASHBURTON RD W
LC
LCs
A576
B5214
ASHBRIDGE
MELLORS RD
CHURCHILL WAY
MODE WHEEL CIRC
LCs

PACIFIC WAY
WAYBRIDGE IND PK
MODE WHEEL RD
MODE WHEEL WORKSHOPS
Mode Wheel Locks
BOSTON RD
ADAMSON RD
KANSAS AVE
Cemy
BUFFALO CT 1
SUNDANCE CT 2
CODY CT 3
CASSIDY CT 4
METROPLEX BSNS PK
BROADWAY

LANGWORTHY RD
DAKOTA AVE
DAKOTA ST
DALLAS CT
NORTH STAGE
MICHIGAN AVE
OLYMPIC RD
A5063
STOWELL TECH CTR
MONTFORD ST
BARLOW ST
OHIO AVE
Broadway
M
Harbour City
M
LABRADOR QUAY
Salford Quays
P

97
PARKWAY FOUR IND EST
LC
M17
LC
AVENUE WORKS
IRMASS IND EST
TRAFFORD PARK RD
Village CIRC
TRAFFORD WHARF RD
WARREN BRUCE RD
HMS Bronington
Manchester Docks
Manchester Ship Canal
THE QUAYS
The Lowry
WINN
WATERFRONT QUAY
ST LAWRENCE QUAY

PARKWAY CIRC
PARKWAY IND EST
PARK WAY
VILLAGE WAY (ASHBURTON RD E)
Trafford Park
MONDE TRAD EST
MOSLEY RD A5181
CENTRAL PARK EST
PRAED RD
WILLAN ENT CTR
SOUTH FIELD IND EST
Village CT
ELEVENTH ST
TENTH ST
FOURTH AVE
EIGHTH ST W
FIFTH AVE
SCHOOLHOUSE
SIXTH ST
Works
WARREN BRUCE RD
ELEVATOR RD
TRAFFORD WHARF RD
Wharfside
WHARFSIDE WAY (TRAFFORD PARK RD)
WATERSIDE
WATERSIDE
SIR MATT BUSBY WAY
RSBN CTR

MERCURY WAY
A5081
PARK WAY
ALBA WAY
CALEDONIA WAY
HIBERNIA WAY
1 PARKWAY TRAD EST
2 STRETFORD MOTORWAY EST
MARSHALL STEVENS WAY
CENTREPOINT
SEVENSIDE TRAD EST
WESTINGHOUSE RD
TEXTILOSE RD
Mosley
Village
FIFTH ST
LITTLERS POINT
LCs
NORTH RD
NORTH RD
NORTH RD
FIRST AVE
SECOND AVE
EUROPA WAY
FRASER PL
EUROPA CIRC
EURO GATE
JOHN GILBERT WAY
United TRAD EST
UNITED RD
Mus
Man Utd FC (Old Trafford)
A5081
A56
Mus

96
St MODWEN RD
B5211
Lostock Park
Mossfield
BARTON DOCK RD
GATE RD
WEST RD
NORTH RD
SOUTH RD
EAST RD
CHINLEY AVE
Works
WEST WORKS RD
WEST CANTEEN RD
EAST AISLE RD
Euroterminal
World Freight Terminal
Bridgewater Canal
WATERSMEET
NANSEN ST
CAVENDISH CT
Recn Gd
THORNBURY RD
AVONDALE RD
TENBY AVE
RAILWAY RD
CLYNE ST
CHORLEY ST
P
CLYNE ST
TH
Sports Ctr
BRIGGS ST
Coll
A5067
Mus

4
Lostock Park
HALL RD
FIELD RD
DALTON AVE
BERKELEY AVE
AUDLEY AVE
SOUTH RD
LANGHAM RD
WEST RD
CASTLETON AVE
ASHBOURNE AVE
BUXTON AVE
BRIGADE DR 1
BUTTERMERE CL 2
WINDERMERE CL 3
ENNERDALE RD 4
LANGDALE RD 5
LCs
RYDAL AVE
KESWICK AVE
HATTONS CT
MAR 2
DERWENT AVE
STANTON
WINGFIELD ST
DARLEY ST
BERESFORD ST
MELLOR ST
CAVENDISH ST
WILSON ST
Sch
PO
MELLOR ST
DARLEY ST
Stretford High Sch
1 ST PETER'S CT
2 CANUTE CT
Gorse Hill
TALBOT RD
GORSE CRES
GORSE ST
GREAT STONE RD
Mus

3
GLASTONBURY CT
JOHNSTONE CT
FOUNTAINS AVE
RIPON RD
SELBY CL
Liby
Lostock High Sch
CHATSWORTH RD
WINSTER AVE
STRETTON AVE
ROWSLEY AVE
BAKEWELL AVE
DARLEY AVE
EDALE RD
CROMFORD AVE
HOPE AVE
PO
Trafford Park
THIRLMERE AVE
CONISTON RD
BOWNESS RD
GRASMERE RD
SKELTON RD
PONSONBY RD
BELFORD RD
HAIG RD
STRETFORD RD
PARK RD
RAGLAN RD
MELVILLE RD
BARTON RD
LOSTOCK GR
STATION RD
DAVYHULME RD
STAMFORD ST
DERBYSHIRE RD
STUART ST
LOMOND ST
BALTIC ST
NORWAY ST
1 WOODLANDS CT
2 MELBOURNE AVE
3 DERBYSHIRE GN
RENTON RD
ROTHERWOOD AVE
CRAWFORD AVE
SAINSBURY RD
BAINBRIDGE AVE
Kings RD
Kingsley AVE

95
HAWORTH DR
MOUNT DR
HUMPHREY CRES
Humphrey Park
DERBYSHIRE AVE
HUMPHREY CRES
DERBYSHIRE LA W
ADAMS AVE
ADDISON
ALSTON AVE
DERBYSHIRE LA
LEYBOURNE AVE
LEYBO
DAVYHULME RD E
MONA AVE
GARDEN AVE
GRANGE AVE
DERBYSHIRE LA
VICTORIA CT
HOWARD ST
KENDAL RD
PRICHARD ST
GARDEN AVE
STRETFORD RD
DERBYSHIRE RD
KINGSWAY
CHESTER RD
A5067

2
HUMPHREY PK
HARTLAND AVE
BERWICK AVE
CLEVEDON AVE
DURIFORD RD
BRAEMAR AVE
ATHOLL AVE
BARRY
BRADFIELD AVE
BARNWAY
ST DAVID'S
GREEN WLK
DEEBANK RD
WASHBROOK DR
CRESSINGHAM RD
STANMORE AVE
WESTMORE AVE
MANOR AVE
Moss Park Jun & Inf Sch
Moss Park RD
ST ANDREW'S RD
HAMPSON ST
BETA AVE
GROSVENOR ST
SCHOOL RD
LESTER RD
HENSHAW ST
M32
STRETFORD
VICTORIA RD
DERBYSHIRE CT
CROSSLAND RD
KINGS RD
RANTON RD
HEATHFIELD
NEWHOLME CT
LONGFORD AVE
HORTREE RD
KENWOOD RD
SUNNY SIDE
Longford Park
Longford COTTS
Longford Park Sch
EDGEHILL CT
P

B5213 STRETFORD RD
NEWCROFT DR
M41
RICHARD RD
LESLEY RD
MEADOW BANK
MANOR RD
CHESHIRE RD
URMSTON LA
B5213
BARTON RD
A5145
Liby KINGSWAY
King St
Shopping Ctr
WELLINGTON
PO
Stretford
M
EDGE LA
M21
P
JACKSON ST
NICOLAS RD
DARESBURY RD
EBOR HO
INGLEDEN CT
A5145

1
HUMPHREY PK
FIRWOOD AVE
LINK AVE
YARDLEY AVE
MAYFIELD AVE
STOTHARD RD
BRAMLEY AVE
BELTONE
MILWAIN RD
FREEFORD RD
SANDY LA
BARTON RD
A581
TREE WLK
CHERRY TREE WLK
A58
CHURCH ST
KING ST
NEWTON ST
ROKEBY AVE
LILY AVE
GRANBY RD
MAPLE AVE
COPPER LA
LARCH AVE
LACY ST
CROSSFORD ST
MELROSE AVE
WANSBECK CL
MEADOW TOP
LARCH AVE
WANSBECK LODGE
Stretford Gram Sch
Cricket Gd

94
A581

C1
1 BEECH WLK
2 WALNUT WLK
3 ST GEORGE'S CT
4 PINFOLD CT
5 THOMAS GIBBON CL
6 COB HALL RD
7 STRETFORD HO
8 SOUTHWELL CT
9 ST MATHEWS CT

F1
1 ASHFELL CT
2 SUMMERFIELD CT
3 RYEBANK MEWS
4 LONGFORD HO
5 ALDERFIELD HO
6 CRESCENT CT
7 PARK VIEW
8 ALDER EDGE
9 BEECH CT

For full street detail of the highlighted area see pages 161 and 162.

A1
1 SUTTON MANOR
2 MAIDSTONE MEWS
3 SIBSON CT
4 SHANKLIN HO
5 WILBRAHAM REGENCY CT

B2
1 NORTHLEIGH HO
2 TRAFFORD MANS
3 QUEEN'S CT
4 STRATHMORE AVE
5 RAILWAY TERR

81

98

97

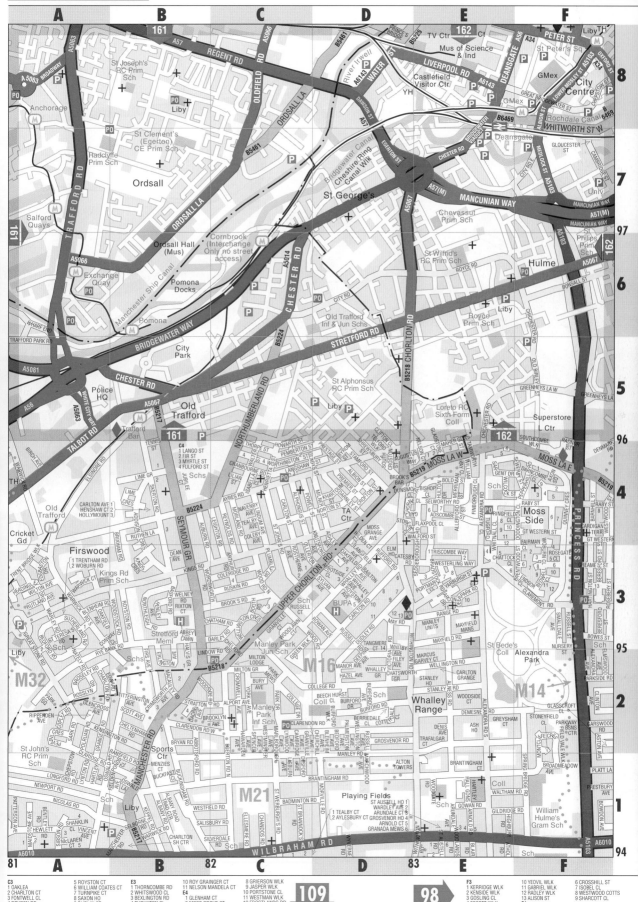

For full street detail of the highlighted area see pages 163 and 164.

MANCHESTER

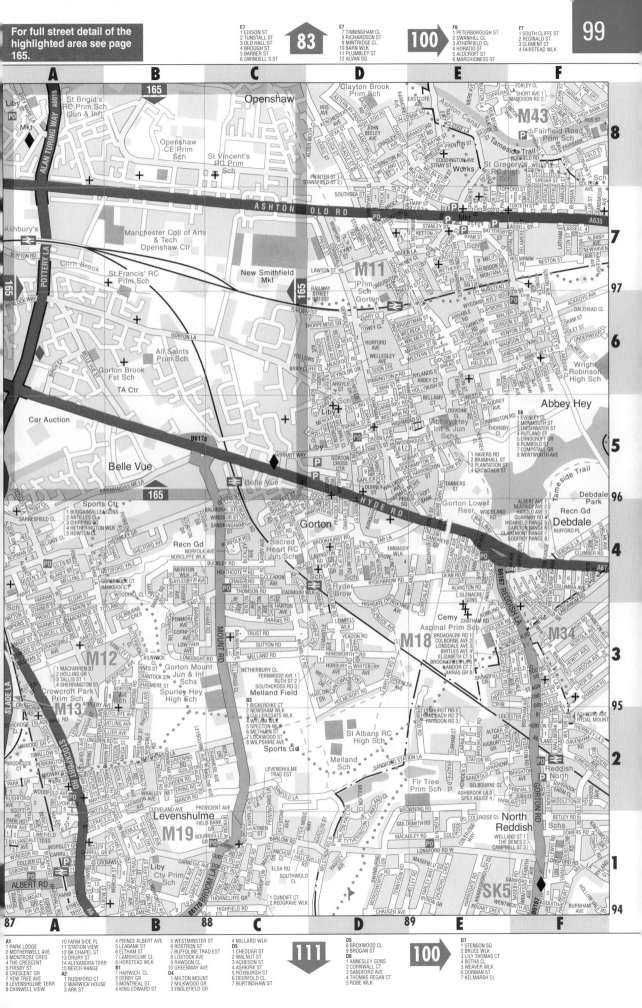

For full street detail of the highlighted area see page 165.

83

E7
1 Edison St
2 Tunstall St
3 Old Hall St
4 Brough St
5 Barber St
6 Swindell's St

100

E7
7 Tinningham Cl
8 Richardson St
9 Mintridge Cl
10 Barn Wlk
11 Plumbley St
12 Alvan Sq

F6
1 Peterborough St
2 Swanhill Cl
3 Atherfield St
4 Horatio St
5 Aldcroft St
6 Marchioness St

F7
1 South Cliffe St
2 Reginald St
3 Clement Ct
4 Fairstead Wlk

A1
1 Park Lodge
2 Motherwell Ave
3 Montrose Cres
4 The Crescent
5 Firsby St
6 Crescent Gr
7 Yew Tree Ave
8 Levenshulme Terr
9 Chinwell View
10 Farm Side Pl
11 Station View
12 BK Chapel St
13 Drury St
14 Alexandra Terr
15 Beech Range

A2
1 Rushford Ct
2 Warwick House
3 Ark St

B1
4 Prince Albert Ave
5 Leabank St
6 Eltham St
7 Lamsholme Cl
8 Horstead Wlk

B2
1 Harwich Ct
2 Derby Gr
3 Montreal St
4 King Edward St

111

B3
5 Westminster St
6 Rostron St
7 Buffoline Trad Est
8 Lostock Ave
9 Greenway Ave

D4
1 Milton Mount
2 Milkwood Gr
3 Englefield Gr

4 Millard Wlk

D5
1 Cheddar St
2 Walnut St
3 Acheson St
4 Roxburgh St
5 Deerfold Cl
7 Burtinshaw St

D5
8 Broxwood Cl
9 Brogan St

D6
1 Annesley Gdns
2 Cornwall Ct
3 Sandford Ave
4 Thomas Regan Ct
5 Robe Wlk

100

D7
1 Stenson Sq
2 Bruce Wlk
3 Lily Thomas Ct
4 Botha Cl
5 Weaver Wlk
6 Dorman St
7 Kelmarsh St

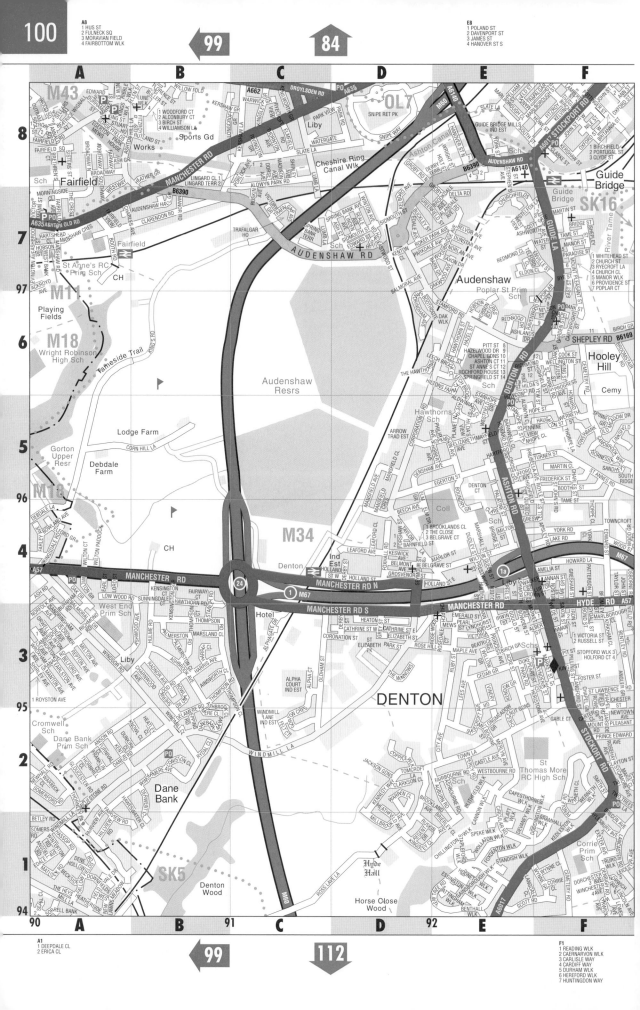

C6
1 VICTORIA MEWS
2 CONSORT CL

D5
1 SPENCER AVE
2 GLENWOOD AVE
3 BENNET MEWS
4 SACK ST

85

D8
1 CONCORD WAY
2 SHEPLEY CL
3 JACKSON AVE
4 REECE CT
5 CLAYTON ST
6 PLOUGH ST

102

E8
1 OLD SCHOOL MEWS
2 OLD CHURCH MEWS
F5
1 GAINSBOROUGH WLK
2 WENTWORTH WLK

F8
1 CLARENCE HO
2 THE ARCADE
3 CLIFF DALE
4 QUARRY HTS

101

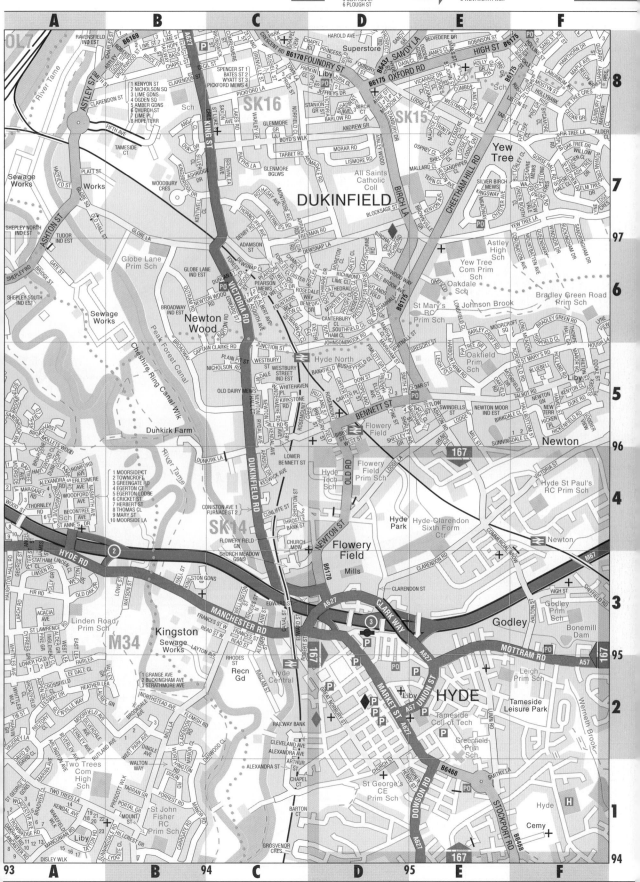

93   94   95   94

A1
1 NORTHAMPTON WAY
2 NEWCASTLE WLK
3 NOTTINGHAM WAY
4 OXFORD WLK
5 MAIDSTONE WLK
6 PEMBROKE WAY
7 SHREWSBURY WAY
8 BOSTON WLK
9 WELSHPOOL WAY

10 IPSWICH WAY
11 CHICHESTER WAY
12 STAFFORD WAY
13 TAUNTON WAY
14 CHELMSFORD WLK
15 GAWSWORTH WAY
16 THORSBY WAY
17 HADDON WAY
18 MORTON TERR

19 ADLINGTON WAY
20 PENSHURST WLK
21 HOLKER WAY
22 ARLEY WAY
23 HAREWOOD WLK

A2
1 WITHY TREE GR
2 WOOD HEY GR
3 GARDEN WLK

113   102

For full street detail of the
highlighted area see page
167.

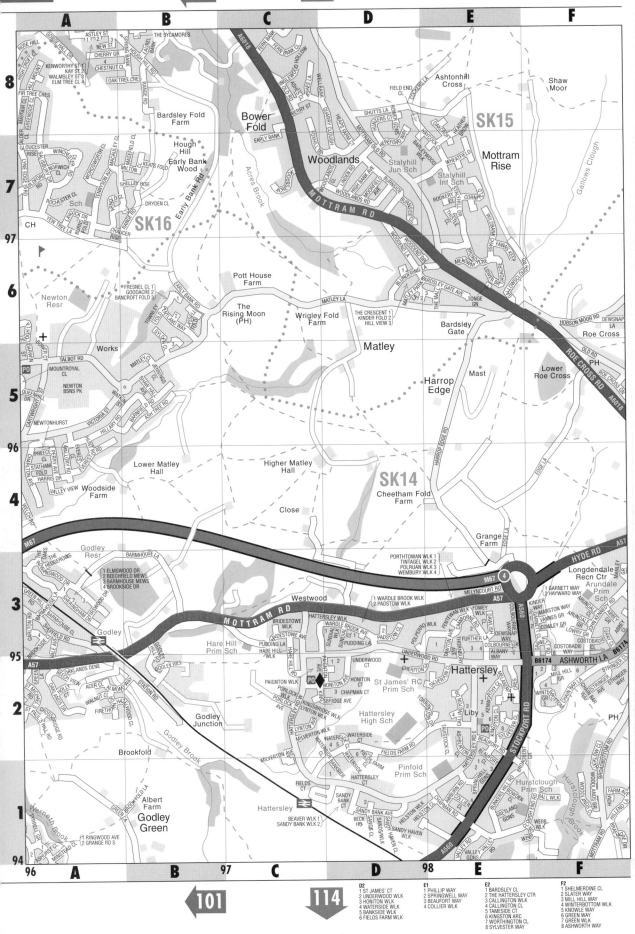

D2
1 ST JAMES' CT
2 UNDERWOOD WLK
3 HONITON WLK
4 WATERSIDE WLK
5 BANKSIDE WLK
6 FIELDS FARM WLK

E1
1 PHILLIP WAY
2 SPRINGWELL WAY
3 BEAUFORT WAY
4 COLLIER WLK

E2
1 BARDSLEY CL
2 THE HATTERSLEY CTR
3 CALLINGTON WLK
4 CALLINGTON CL
5 TAMESIDE CT
6 KINGSTON ARC
7 WORTHINGTON CL
8 SYLVESTER WAY

F2
1 SHELMERDINE CL
2 SLATER WAY
3 MILL HILL WAY
4 WINTERBOTTOM WLK
5 KNOWLE WAY
6 GREEN WAY
7 GREEN WLK
8 ASHWORTH WAY

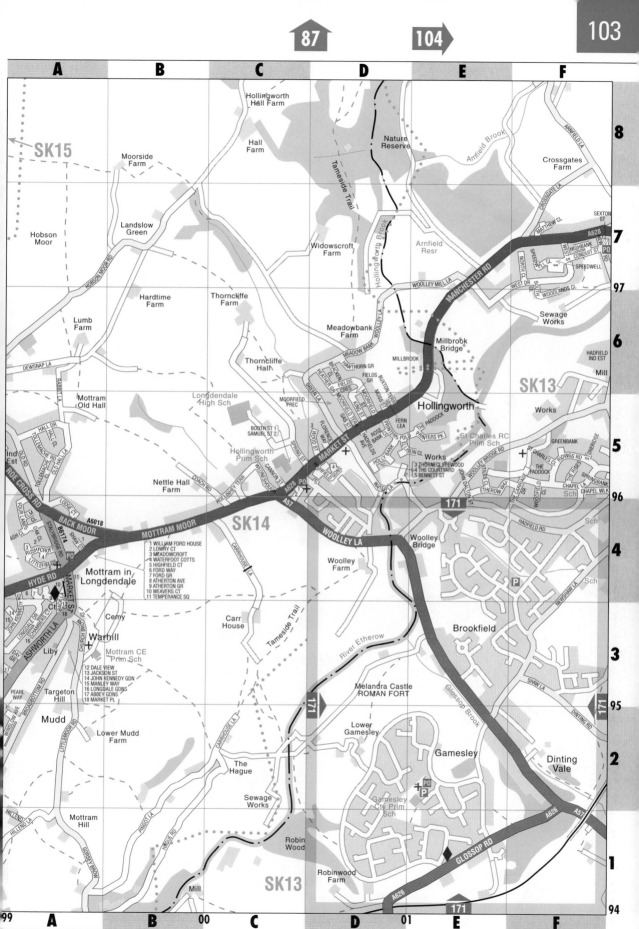

SK15

8

Hobson
Moor

Moorside
Farm

Landslow
Green

Hollingworth
Hall Farm

Hall
Farm

Nature
Reserve

Arnfield Brook

Crossgates
Farm

7
97

Hardtime
Farm

Thorncliffe
Farm

Widowscroft
Farm

Tameside Trail

Hollingworth Brook

Arnfield
Resr

WOOLLEY MILL LA

MANCHESTER RD

SEXTON
ST

A628

PO

MATTHEW CL

HIGHBANK
SPEEDWELL CL

CONDUIT ST
WEST ST

NORTH CL

WEST CL

SOUTH CL

WEST DR

SPEEDWELL

WOODLANDS CL

6

Lumb
Farm

Mottram
Old Hall

DEWSNAP LA

Longdendale
High Sch

Meadowbank
Farm

MEADOW BANK

Thorncliffe
Hall

Millbrook
Bridge

MILLBROOK

Millbrook

Hollingworth

Sewage
Works

HADFIELD
IND EST

Mill

SK13

Works

5
96

RABBIT LA

HALL DR
HALL CL
TOLLEMACHE RD
OLD HALL LA

Ind Est

ROE CROSS RD

BACK MOOR

B6174

A6018

MOTTRAM MOOR

SK14

Nettle Hall
Farm

COACH RD

HOLLINEY TERR

WEDNESCOUGH

BOOTH ST 1
SAMUEL ST 2

Hollingworth
Prim Sch

MOORFIELD
PREC

GREEN LA

BECKENHAM
HEATHER CL
MOORFIELD TERR

FIELDS
CRES

HAWTHORN GR

FIELDS
GR

THE PADDOCK

St Charles RC
Prim Sch

PRINTERS
BANK

PRINTERS PK

FERN
LEA

GREENBANK

ST CHARLES CL
RIDINGS RD

STONERIDGE

THE PADDOCK

CHAPEL CL

THE GLOSSOP
SPRINGBANK

CHAPEL LA

Sch

FLORENCE
ST

WOOD ST

SPRING ST

CANNON ST

A628

PO

MARKET ST

KING ST

GAS ST

BUXTON TERR

MOSS ST

ROSE
HILL

FERN
LEA

THE PADDOCK

PRINTERS
FOLD

ELLISON ST

JOHN DALTON ST

WOOLLEY BRIDGE RD

HADFIELD RD

THE CARRIAGE
DR

ETHEROW WLK

WOODFIELD
CL

171

Sch

96

1 WILLIAM FORD HOUSE
2 LOWRY CT
3 MEADOWCROFT
4 WATERFOOT COTTS
5 HIGHFIELD CT
6 FORD WAY
7 FORD GR
8 ATHERTON AVE
9 ATHERTON GR
10 WEAVERS CT
11 TEMPERANCE SQ

3 THORNECLIFFEWOOD
4 THE COURTYARD
5 BENNETT ST

Works

LOOSE CT

FOUR LANES

OAK CL

ASH CL

STALYBRIDGE RD

SHAW ST

CARRHOUSE LA

Mottram in
Longdendale

Cemy

WOOLLEY LA

Woolley
Farm

Woolley
Bridge

Brookfield

NEWSHAW LA

4

Liby

HYDE RD

MARKET ST

CHURCH BROW RD

Warhill

Mottram CE
Prim Sch

Carr
House

Tameside Trail

River Etherow

P

SHAW LA

3

ASHWORTH LA

PEARL
WAY

Targeton
Hill

WINSLOW AVE

LITTLEMOOR RD

Lower Mudd
Farm

CARRHOUSE LA

The Hague

Melandra Castle
ROMAN FORT

Lower
Gamesley

Glossop Brook

Gamesley

Dinting
Vale

DINTING RD

171

95

12 DALE VIEW
13 JACKSON ST
14 JOHN KENNEDY GDN
15 MANLEY WAY
16 LONGDALE GDNS
17 ABBEY GDNS
18 MARKET PL

Mudd

BROADBOTTOM RD

171

Mottram
Hill

HILLEND LA

GORSEY BROOK

PINGOT LA

HAGUE RD

Sewage
Works

Robin
Wood

PO
P

Gamesley
Cty Prim
Sch

2

Mill

SK13

Robinwood
Farm

GLOSSOP RD

A626

A626

A57

1

99

A

B

00

C

D

01

E

F

94

**For full street detail of the
highlighted area see page
171.**

A B C D E F

M62

Woolden View Farm

Great Woolden Hall Farm

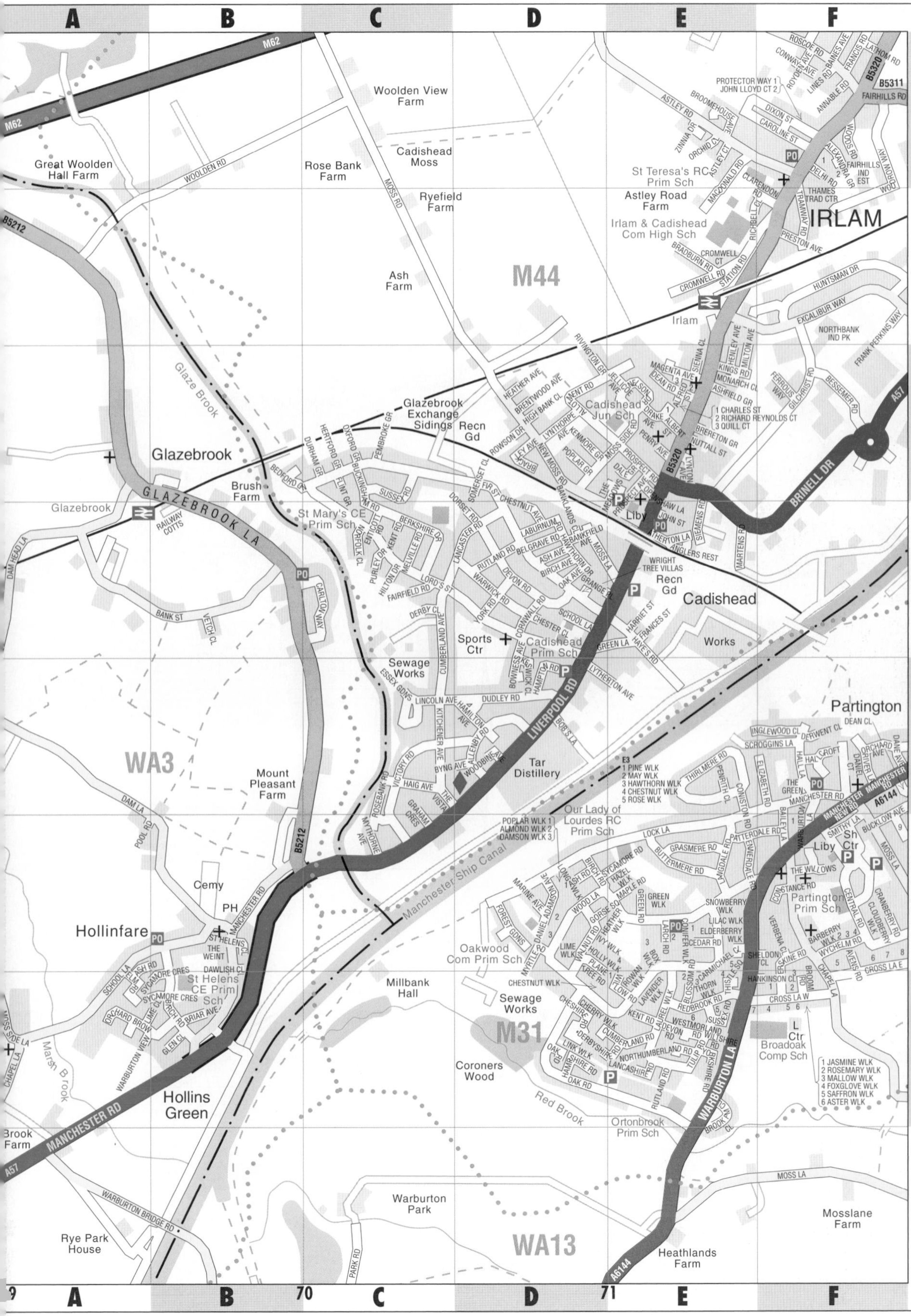

Rose Bank Farm

Cadishead Moss

Ryefield Farm

WOOLDEN RD

MOSS RD

B5212

Ash Farm

M44

8

ROSCOE RD
CONWAY AVE
LINES RD
BAINES AVE
FRANCIS RD
B5320
LATHOM RD
FAIRHILLS RD
B5311

PROTECTOR WAY 1
JOHN LLOYD CT 2
BROOMEHOUSE
ASTLEY RD
ZINNIA CL
ORCHID CL
CAROLINE ST
DIXON ST
DELHI RD
ALEXANDRA DR
FAIRHILLS IND EST

St Teresa's RC Prim Sch

MACDONALD RD
CLARENDON RD
THAMES TRAD CTR

Astley Road Farm

Irlam & Cadishead Com High Sch

CROMWELL CT
BRADBURN RD
CROMWELL RD
STATION RD
RICHBELL CL
PRESTON AVE

IRLAM

7

Glaze Brook

Glazebrook

GLAZEBROOK LA

Brush Farm

Glazebrook

RAILWAY COTTS

Glazebrook Exchange Sidings

Recn Gd

St Mary's CE Prim Sch

Irlam

NORTHBANK IND PK

EXCALIBUR WAY

FRANK PERKINS WAY

HUNTSMAN DR

A57

93

Cadishead Jun Sch

1 CHARLES ST
2 RICHARD REYNOLDS CT
3 QUILL CT

BRINELL DR

6

Liby

Wright Tree Villas

Recn Gd

Cadishead

Works

92

Sports Ctr

Cadishead Prim Sch

Sewage Works

LIVERPOOL RD

Partington

DEAN CL

WA3

Mount Pleasant Farm

B5212

Tar Distillery

E3
1 PINE WLK
2 MAY WLK
3 HAWTHORN WLK
4 CHESTNUT WLK
5 ROSE WLK

SCROGGINS LA

4

Our Lady of Lourdes RC Prim Sch

POPLAR WLK 1
ALMOND WLK 2
DAMSON WLK 3

Manchester Ship Canal

A6144

MANCHESTER RD

Liby

Sh Ctr

Partington Prim Sch

The Willows

91

3

Cemy

PH

MANCHESTER RD

Hollinfare

St Helens the Weint

DAWLISH CL

St Helens CE Prim Sch

Oakwood Com Prim Sch

Millbank Hall

Sewage Works

M31

CHESTNUT WLK

Broadoak Comp Sch

L Ctr

2

E2
1 JASMINE WLK
2 ROSEMARY WLK
3 MALLOW WLK
4 FOXGLOVE WLK
5 SAFFRON WLK
6 ASTER WLK

Coroners Wood

Red Brook

Ortonbrook Prim Sch

WARBURTON LA

WA13

Warburton Park

A6144

Heathlands Farm

Mosslane Farm

90

Brook Farm

A57

MANCHESTER RD

WARBURTON BRIDGE RD

Hollins Green

Rye Park House

PARK RD

1

A B C D E F

E2
1 YEW WLK
2 FORSYTHIA WLK
3 BLACKTHORN WLK
4 THISTLE WLK
5 MAGNOLIA CL
6 LOBELIA WLK
7 IRIS WLK

F3
1 STUART HAMPSON CT
2 ELM CL
3 WINTERGREEN WLK
4 BEECH CL
5 CAMOMILE WLK
6 CHARLOCK WLK
7 WOODRUFF WLK
8 COLUMBINE WLK
9 WORTHINGTON AVE

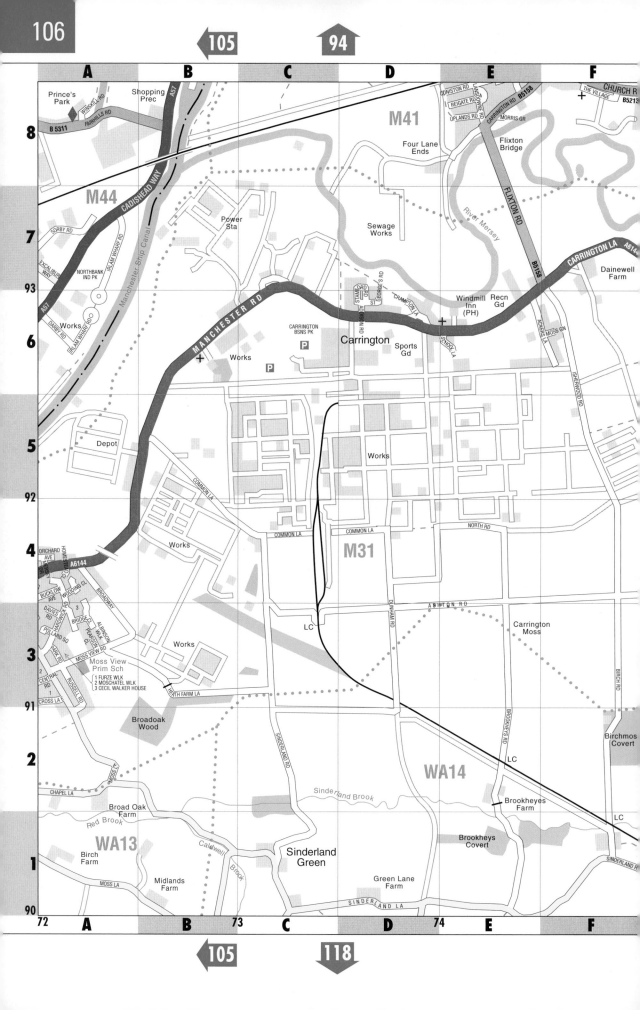

A B C D E F

8

M44

7

93

6

5

92

4

3

91

2

1

90

72 A B 73 C D 74 E F

Prince's Park
Shopping Prec
WINSKILL RD
FAIRHILLS RD
B 5311
SORBY RD
EXCALIBUR WAY
NORTHBANK IND PK
IRLAM WHARF RD
DARBY RD
Works
A57
CADISHEAD WAY
Manchester Ship Canal
MANCHESTER RD
Power Sta
Depot
Works
COMMON LA
ORCHARD AVE
HOMESTEAD CT
MERSEY RD
A6144
BUCKLOW AVE
WOODING CL
BROADWAY
DAVIES RD
NORTHMOOR RD
BRIDGE
ALBINSON WALK
PEARSON
POLLARD SQ
MOSS VIEW RD
PARK RD
CENTRAL RD
RUSSELL RD
CROSS LA
Moss View Prim Sch
1 FURZE WLK
2 MOSCHATEL WLK
3 CECIL WALKER HOUSE
HEATH FARM LA
Works
Works
Broadoak Wood
MOSS LEY
CHAPEL LA
Red Brook
Broad Oak Farm
WA13
Birch Farm
MOSS LA
Midlands Farm
Caldwell Brook
Sinderland Green
SINDERLAND RD
Sinderland Brook
M41
Four Lane Ends
Sewage Works
CONISTON RD
LANSDOWNE RD
REIGATE RD
UPLANDS RD
CARRINGTON RD
B5158
MORRIS GR
THE VILLAGE
CHURCH R
B5213
Flixton Bridge
FLIXTON RD
River Mersey
B5158
CARRINGTON LA
A6144
Dainewell Farm
STAMFORD RD
GEORGE'S RD
ROBIN SON RD
CRAMPTON LA
Carrington
CARRINGTON BSNS PK
P
P
Works
Sports Gd
Windmill Inn (PH)
Recn Gd
SCHOOL LA
ACKERS LA
MOSS GN
ISHERWOOD RD
M31
COMMON LA
COMMON LA
NORTH RD
LC
DUNHAM RD
ASHTON RD
Carrington Moss
BROOKHEYS RD
LC
WA14
BIRCH RD
Birchmos Covert
Brookheyes Farm
Brookheys Covert
LC
Green Lane Farm
SINDERLAND LA
SINDERLAND R

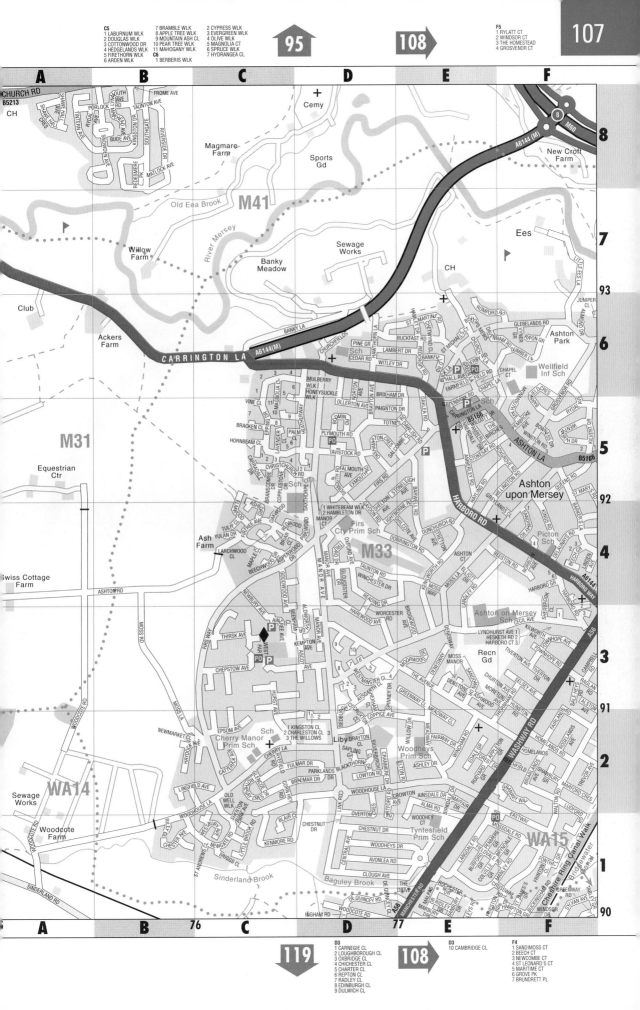

C5	7 BRAMBLE WLK	2 CYPRESS WLK	F5
1 LABURNUM WLK	8 APPLE TREE WLK	3 EVERGREEN WLK	1 RYLATT CT
2 DOUGLAS WLK	9 MOUNTAIN ASH CL	4 OLIVE WLK	2 WINDSOR CT
3 COTTONWOOD DR	10 PEAR TREE WLK	5 MAGNOLIA CT	3 THE HOMESTEAD
4 HEDGELANDS WLK	11 MAHOGANY WLK	6 SPRUCE WLK	4 GROSVENOR CT
5 FIRETHORN WLK	**C6**	7 HYDRANGEA CL	
6 ARDEN WLK	1 BERBERIS WLK		

95 ▶   108 ▶

A | B | C | D | E | F

D3	D3	F4
1 CARNEGIE CL	10 CAMBRIDGE CL	1 SANDIMOSS CT
2 LOUGHBOROUGH CL		2 BEECH CT
3 OXBRIDGE CL		3 NEWCOMBE CT
4 CHICHESTER CL		4 ST LEONARD'S CT
5 CHARTER CL		5 MARITIME CT
6 REPTON CL		6 GROVE PK
7 RADLEY CL		7 BRUNDRETT PL
8 EDINBURGH CL		
9 DULWICH CL		

107
B5
1 WILSON ST
2 PARTINGTON PL
3 ORCHARD PL
4 CURZON RD
5 BENBOW ST

96

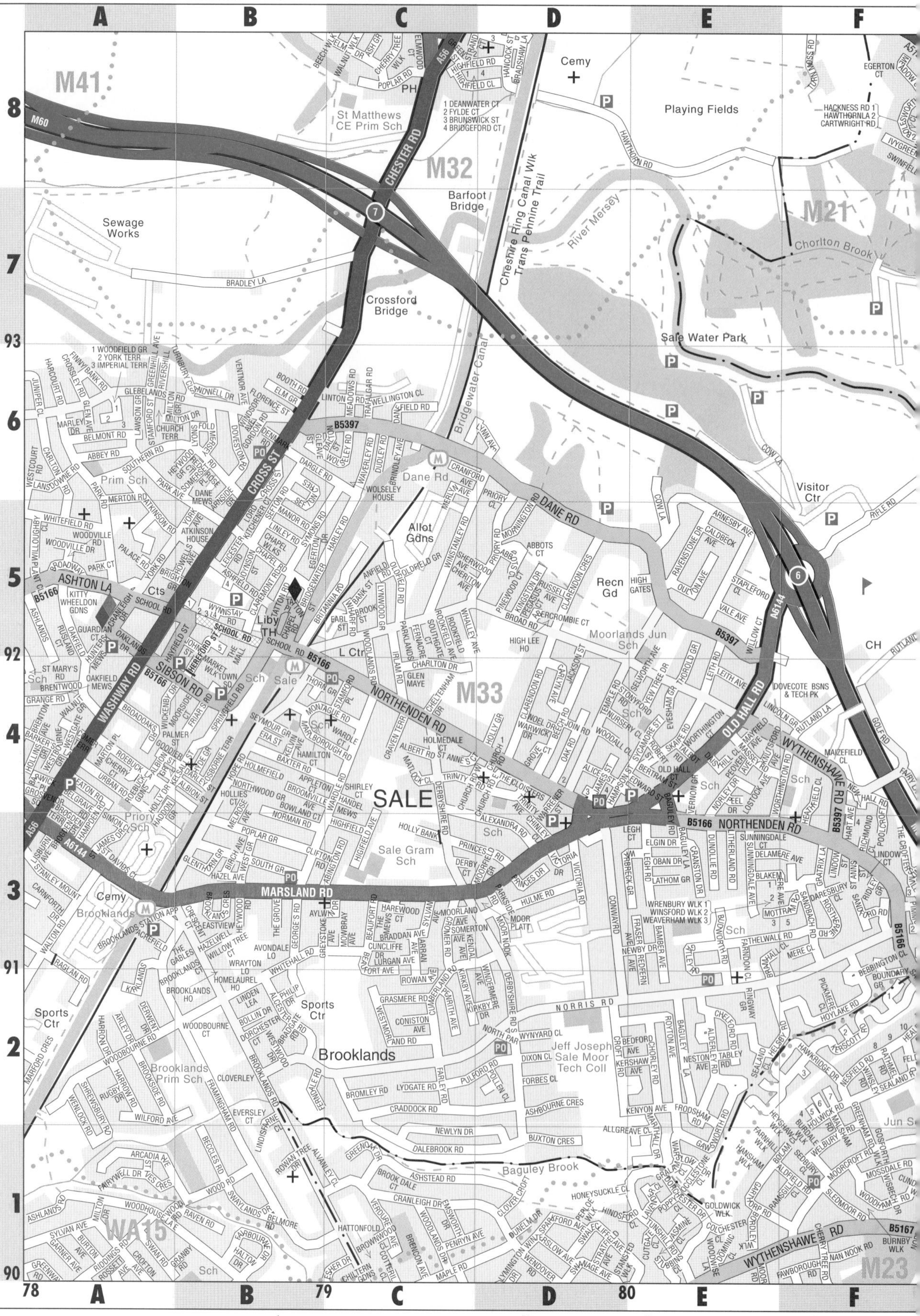

A B C D E F

8
7
93
6
5
92
4
3
91
2
1
90

M41
M60

St Matthews CE Prim Sch
CHESTER RD
M32
Barfoot Bridge
Cemy
Playing Fields
M21
Chorlton Brook
Sewage Works
BRADLEY LA
Crossford Bridge
River Mersey
Cheshire Ring Canal Wlk
Trans Pennine Trail
Sale Water Park
Bridgewater Canal
Visitor Ctr

1 WOODFIELD GR
2 YORK TERR
3 IMPERIAL TERR

B5397
CROSS ST
Prim Sch
Dane Rd
DANE RD
Cranford Ave
PRIORY CL
Wolseley House
Allot Gdns
Recn Gd
High Gates
Moorlands Jun Sch
B5397
A6144
CH

ASHTON LA
B5166
KITTY WHEELDON GDNS
Cts
P
Liby
TH
SIBSON RD
B5166
Sale
P
WASHWAY RD
SCHOOL RD
L Ctr
B5166
NORTHENDEN RD
M33
OLD HALL RD
WYTHENSHAWE RD
B5538
St Mary's Sch
Brentwood
Sale Gram Sch
Old Hall
Sch
SALE
PO
NORTHENDEN RD
B5166

A6144
Priory Pk
St Albert's
Cemy
MARSLAND RD
Sale Moor Tech Coll
Jeff Joseph Dixon Cl
PO
NORRIS RD
PO
Sports Ctr
Brooklands Station App
M
Brooklands
Brooklands Prim Sch
Brooklands
Baguley Brook
PO
Sports Ctr
WA15
M23
WYTHENSHAWE RD
B5167
B5166
Jun Sch

78 A 79 B C 80 D E F

107
D4
1 NORFOLK HO
2 WARWICK HO
3 WILKISON ST
4 HOLLY HEYS

120

F2
1 LANDKEY CL
2 DRAYFORD CL
3 DOWLAND CL
4 NESWICK WLK
5 MELBECKS WLK
6 VAWDREY DR
7 HASELHURST WLK
8 SEDGFIELD WLK
9 MARSETT WLK
10 RIDGEMONT WLK
11 BUCKDEN WLK
12 LINCOLN MINSHULL CL

F3
1 PASTUREFIELD CL
2 CORNFIELD CL
3 THRESHER CL
4 ROSEWOOD GDNS
5 WOODCHURCH WLK

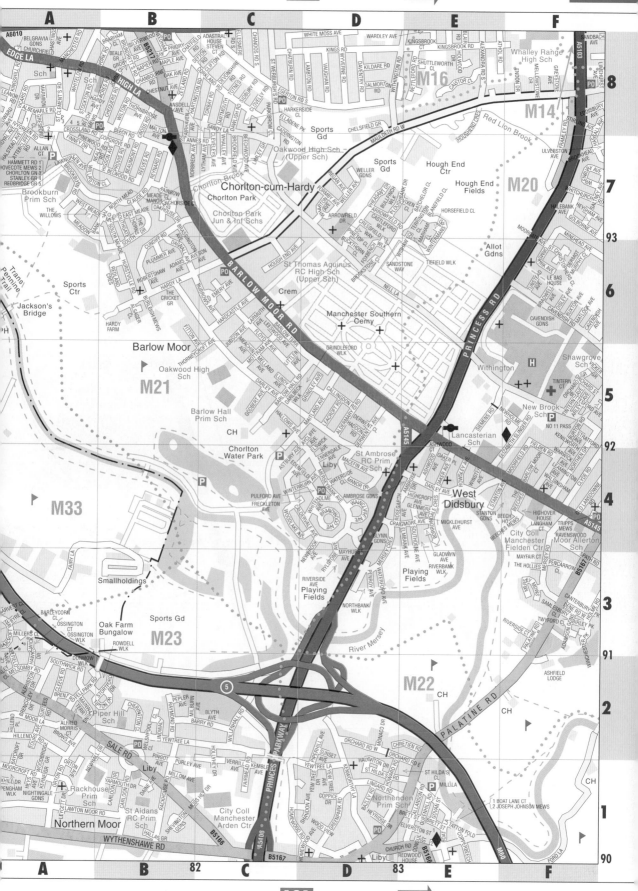

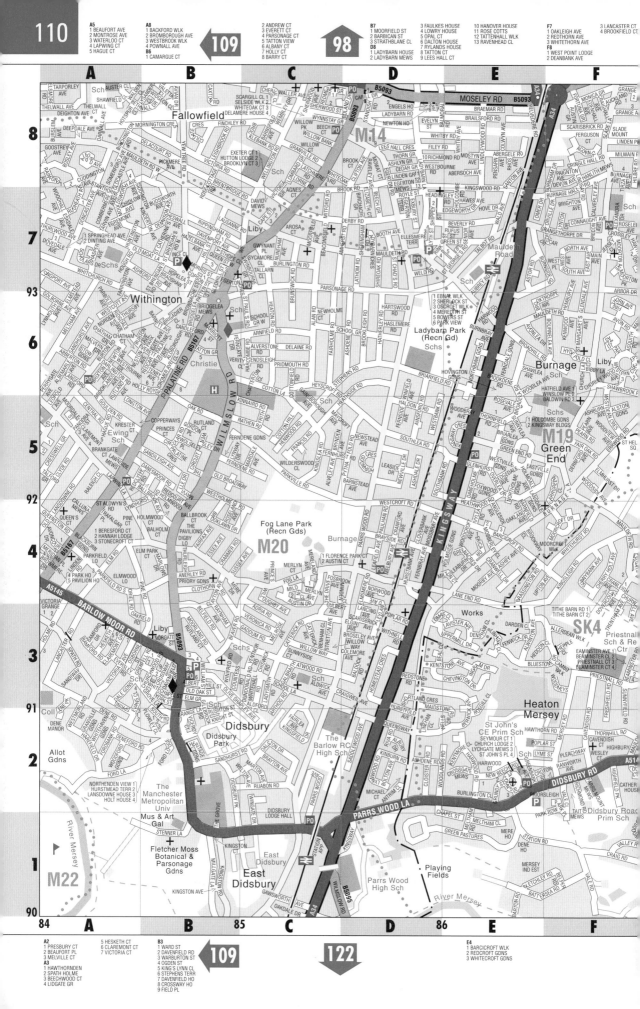

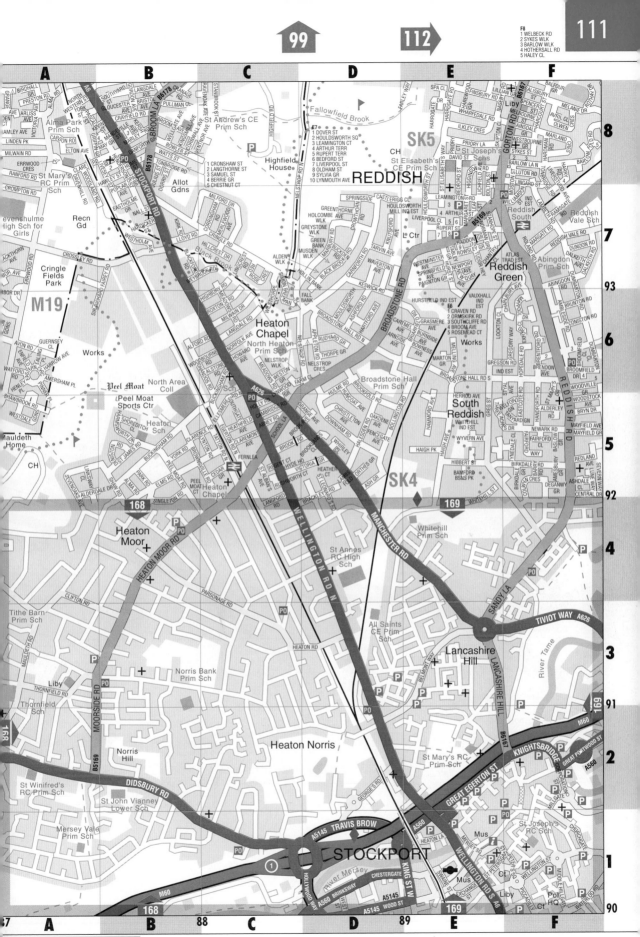

99   112

F8
1 WELBECK RD
2 SYKES WLK
3 BARLOW WLK
4 HOTHERSALL RD
5 HALEY CL

111

For full street detail of the highlighted area see pages 168 and 169.

A B C D E F

8
7
93
6
92
4
3
91
2
1
90

M34

M60

Reddish Vale

Holt Wood

Tameside Trail

Sewage Works

Beight Bridge

Castle Hill

Arden Arms (PH)

Castle Hill Farm

Reddish Vale Country Park

Tame Valley Prim Sch

Arden Hall

Far Cromwell Rd

Cromwell Rd

Stuart Rd

Ind Est

SK5

Hollow Cottage

River Tame

Brinnington

Lincoln Gn

Schs

Castle Hill Sch

Rutland Cres

Lingard La

Horsfield Arms (PH)

The Gate Ctr

Corrie Way

St Mary's CE Prim Sch

CH

Cemy

Brinnington

Brentwood Cl

Huntingdon Cres

Brindale Prim Sch

Hampshire Ho

Gardner Grange

SK6

STOCKPORT RD E

St Bernadette's RC Prim Sch

White Bank Ave

Brindale Rd

Brindale Ho

Crookilley Wood

A560

Whitefield Rd

Bredbury

Midshires Way

St Paul's CE Prim Sch

Crookilley Way

Valley Rd

The Avenue

The Drive

B6104

Bredbury

Works

Arden Park

Stockport Rd W

Arden Prim Sch

Lower Bredbury

A626

M60

B6104

CARRINGTON RD

Portwood

Portwood Ind Est

Pear New Mill Ind Est

Annable Rd

Bredbury Hall Ctry Club

A560

ST MARY'S WAY

Vernon Park

River Goyt

SK1

Mus

Woodbank Meml Park

Sports Gd

Cemy

Middle Farm

Bredbury Green Prim Sch

HALL ST A626

B5465

SK2

Goyt Hall

A B C D E F
90   91   92

A1
1 WATERLOO PK
2 GLENMOOR RD
3 CARNARVON ST
4 CLARE CT
5 MANOR CT
6 PAUL CT
7 RANGE HALL CT

F3
1 AVON BANK
2 WILMCOTE GDNS
3 VERNON VIEW
4 HIGHGATE CTR
5 SILVERDALE
6 HUNTERS CL
7 VICTORIA AVE

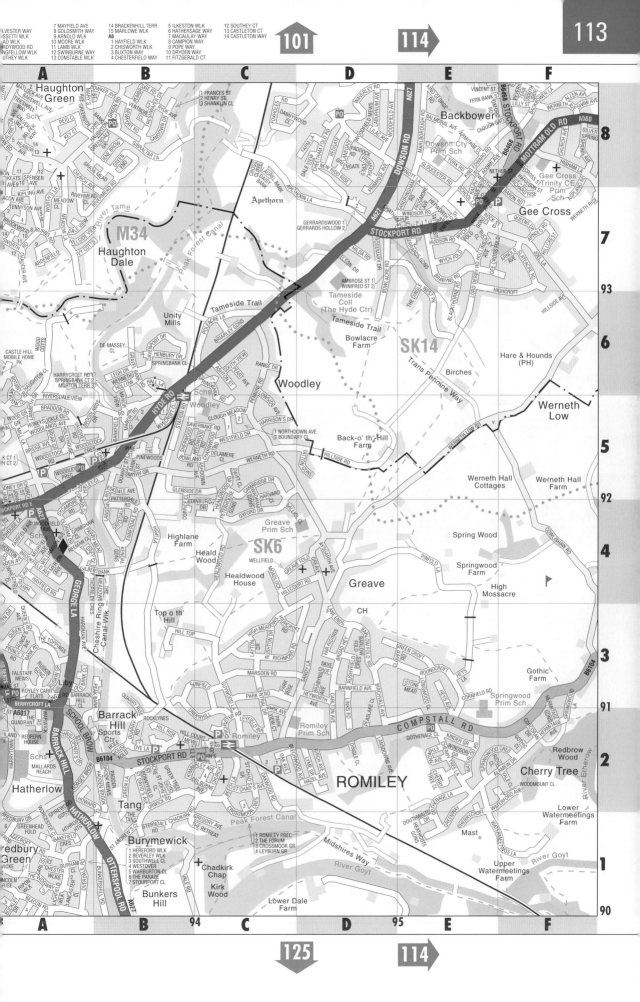

101

114

125

114

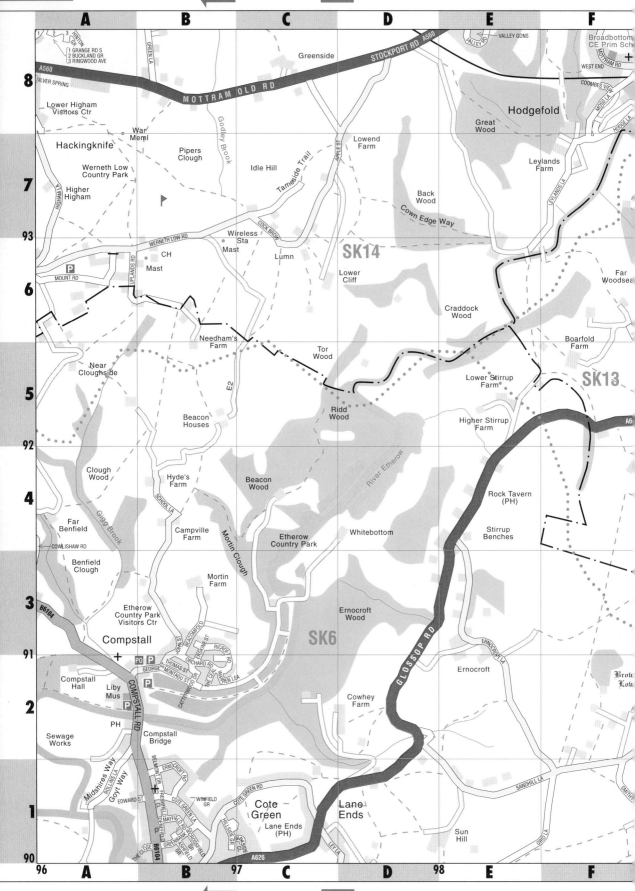

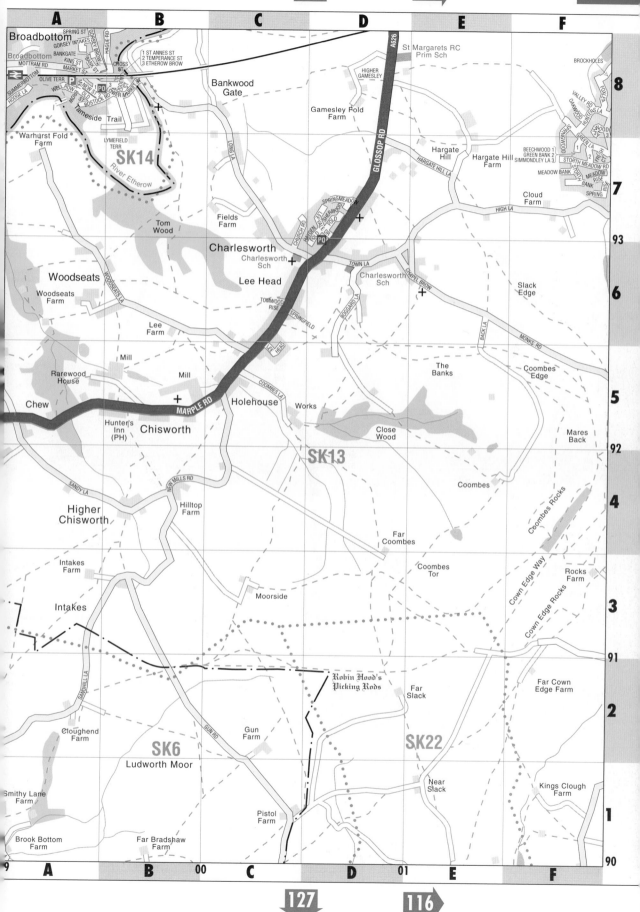

115
104

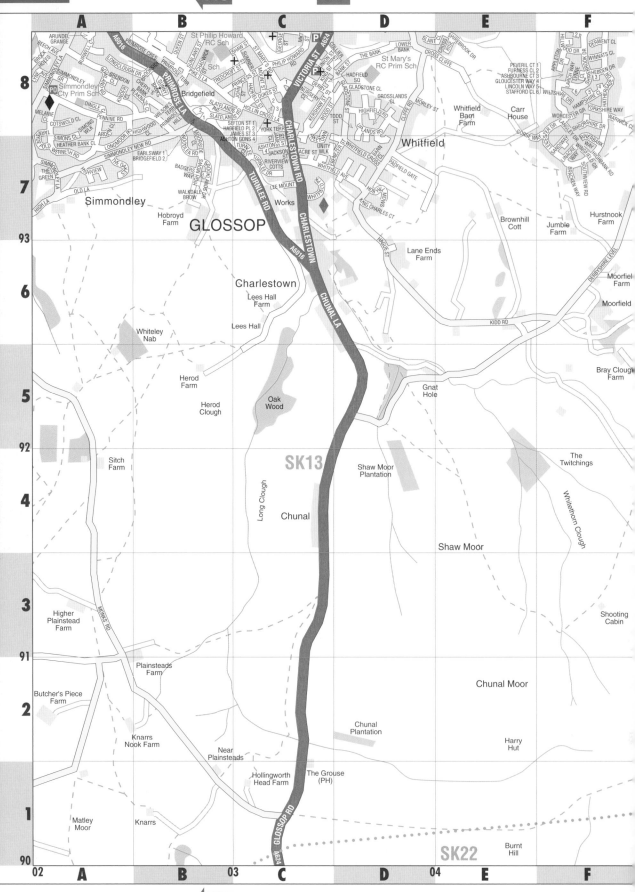

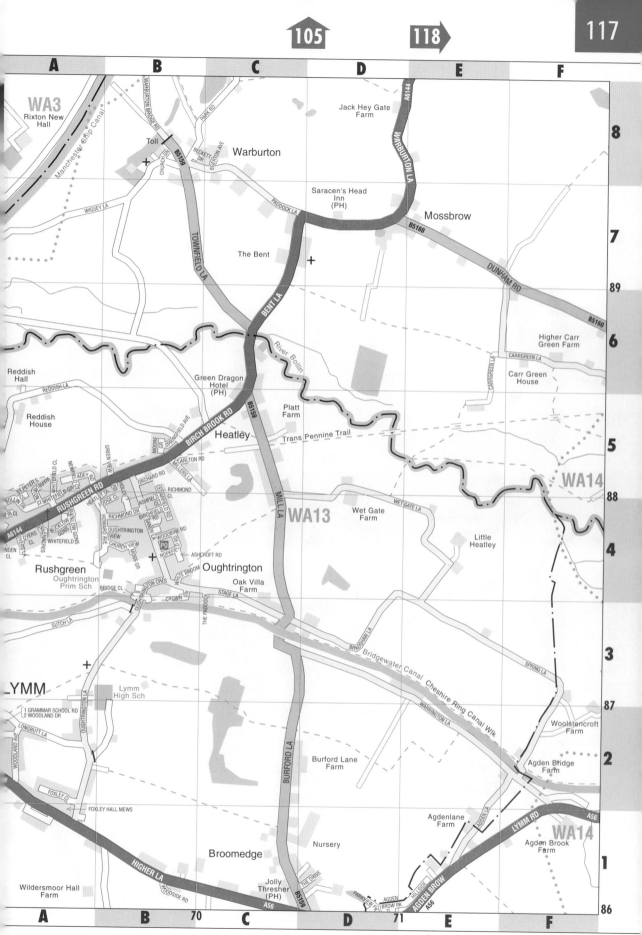

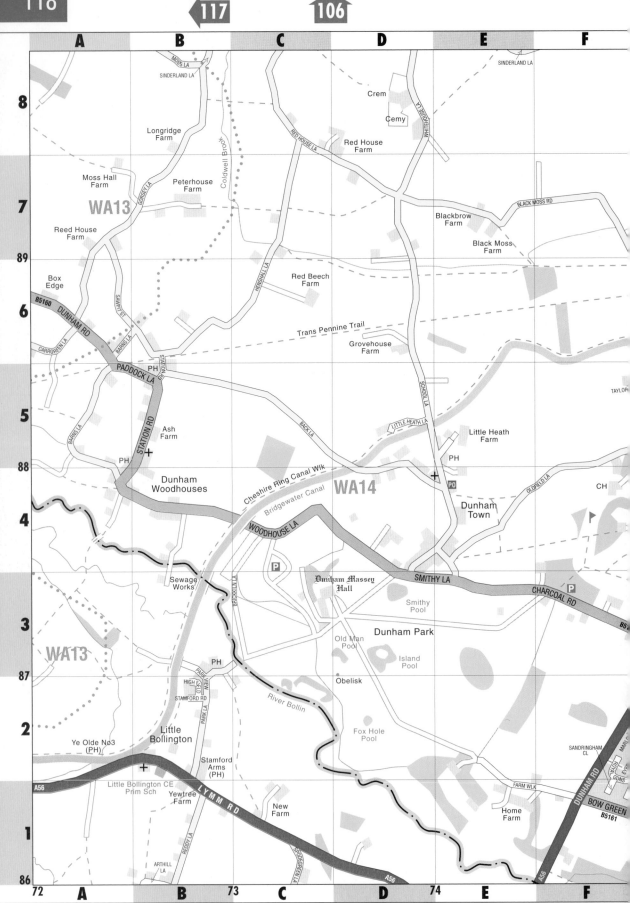

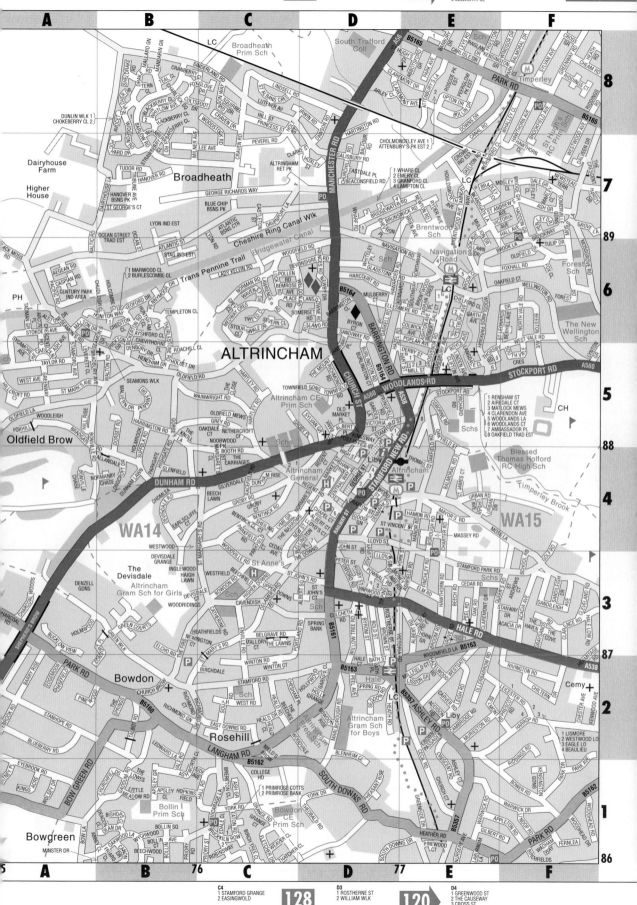

107
D5
1 POLICE ST
2 STAMFORD WAY
3 STAMFORD SQ

120
E6
1 LYNGARTH HO
2 ASTBURY CL
3 THELWALL CL
4 THE WOODS
5 SELWORTH CL

128
C4
1 STAMFORD GRANGE
2 EASINGWOLD

120
D3
1 ROSTHERNE ST
2 WILLIAM WLK

D4
1 GREENWOOD ST
2 THE CAUSEWAY
3 CROSS ST
4 BREWERY ST
5 GRAFTON MALL
6 LLOYD SQ
7 OSBOURNE PL

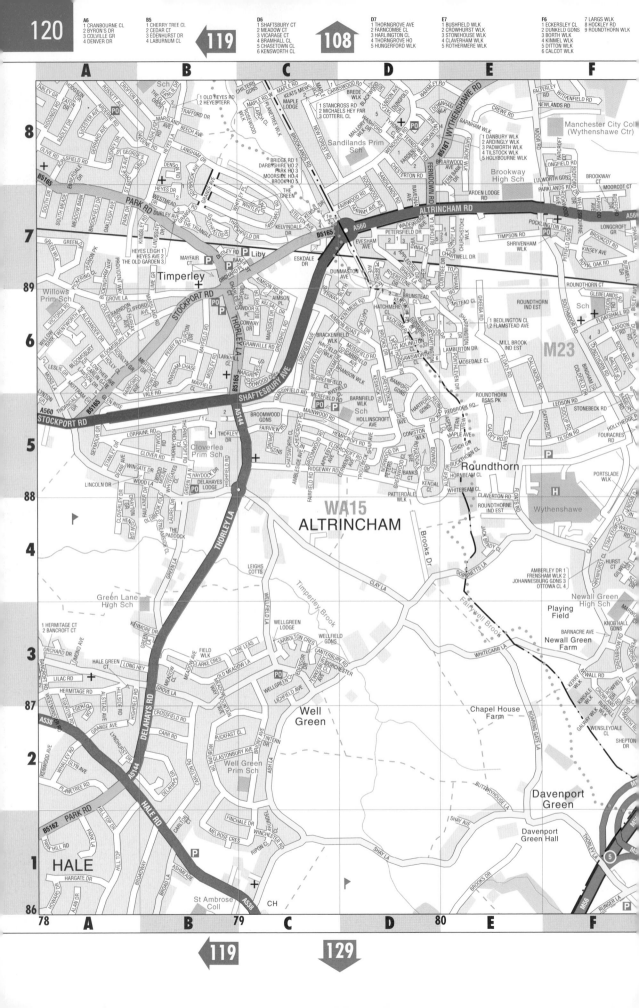

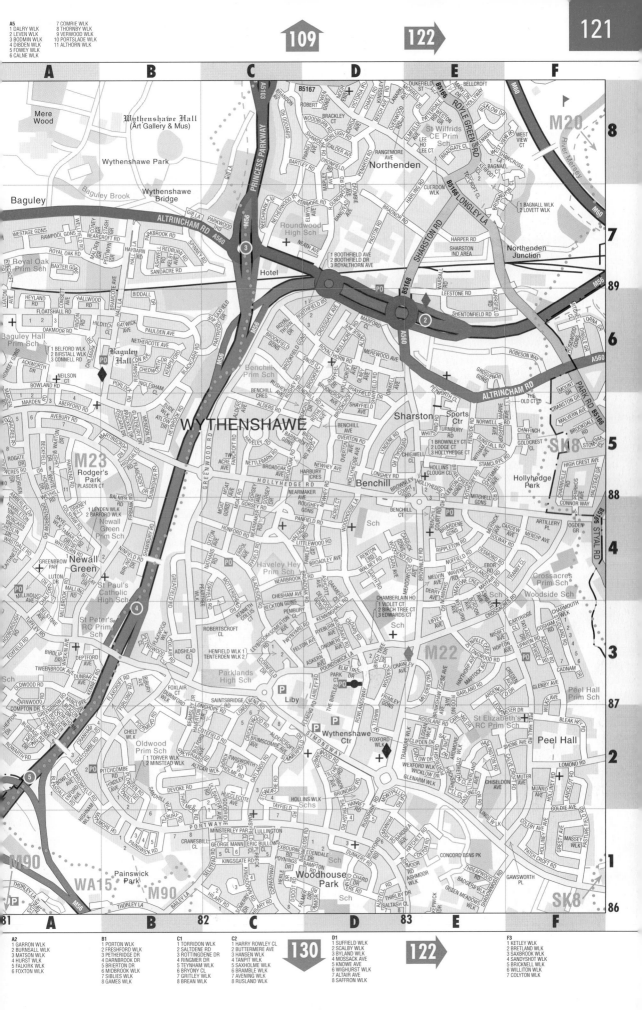

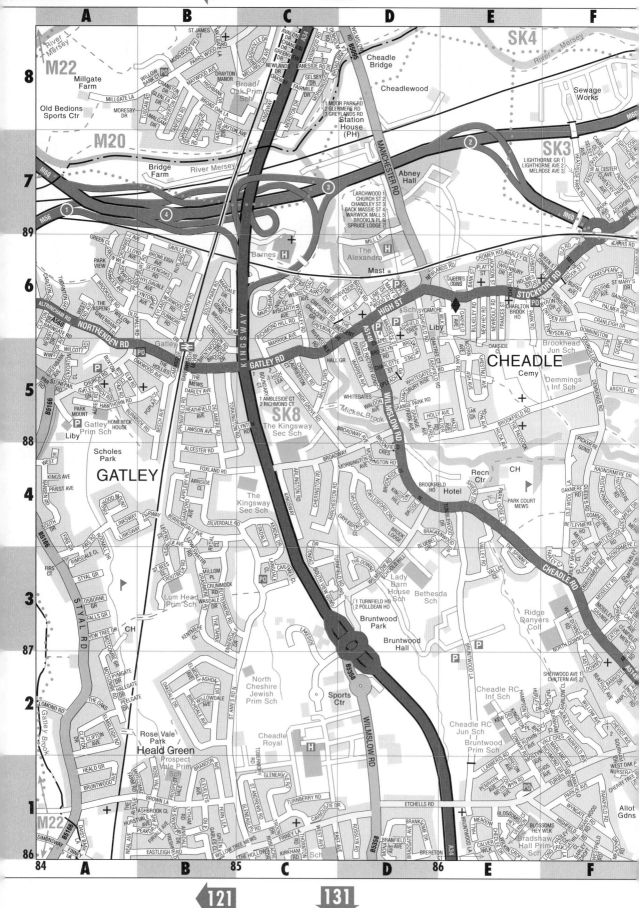

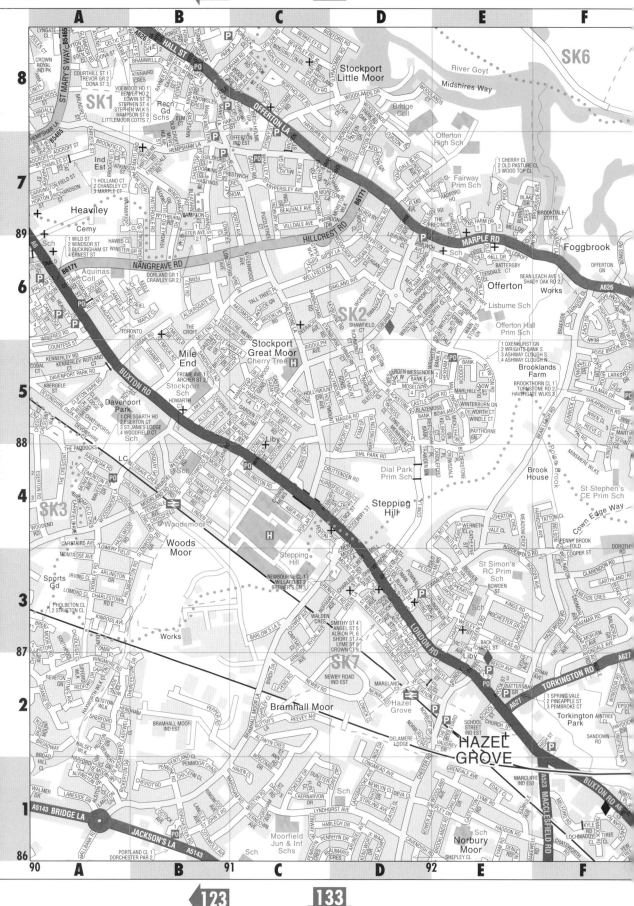

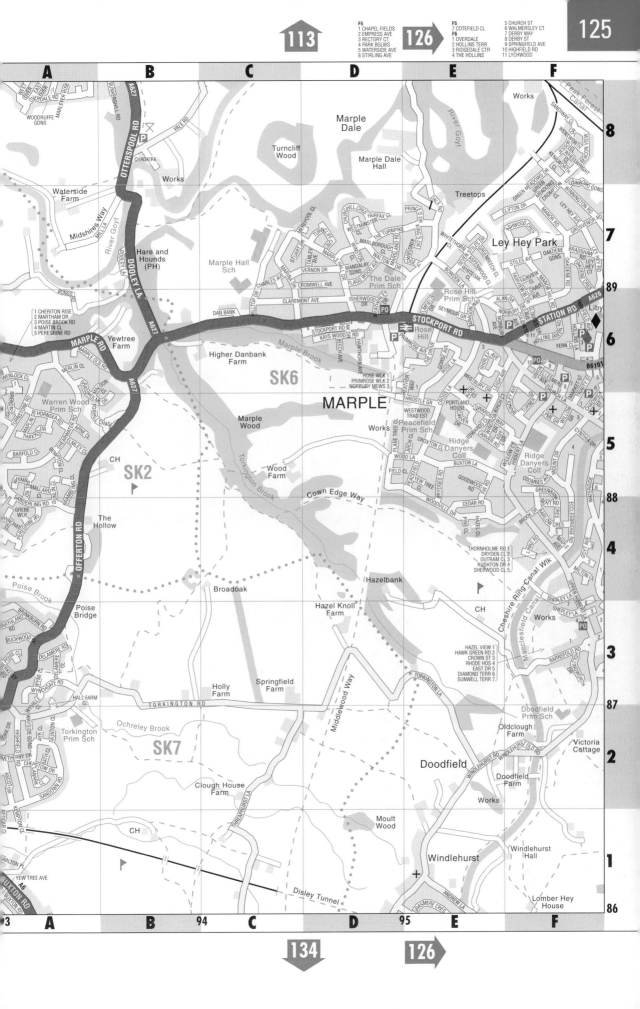

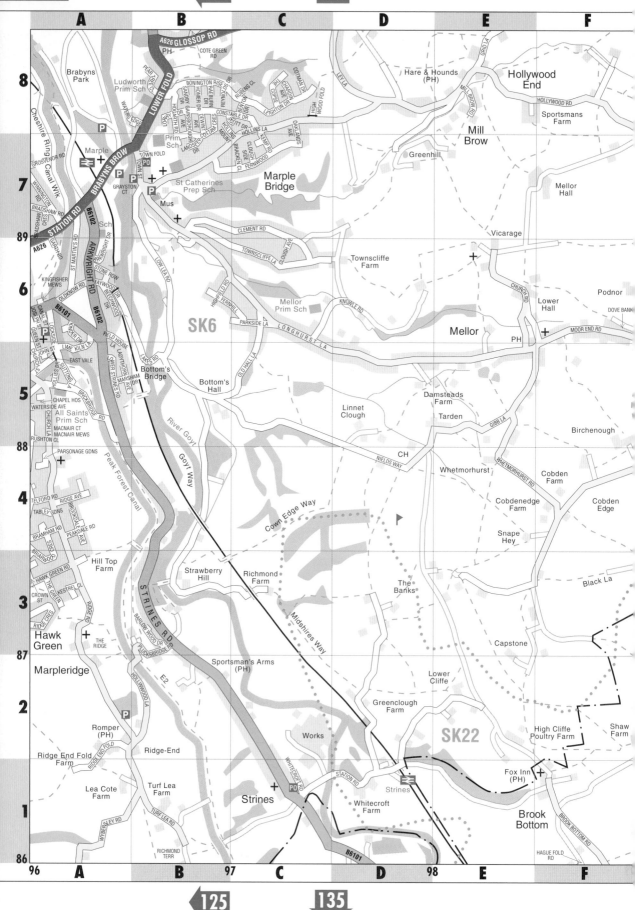

125
114
125
135

A626 GLOSSOP RD
PH
COTE GREEN RD

Brabyns
Park

Ludworth
Prim Sch

LOWER FOLD

BONINGTON RISE

REYNOLDS

RUBENS CL

COTMAN DR

Hare & Hounds
(PH)

Hollywood
End

GRID LA

HOLLYWOOD RD

Sportsmans
Farm

CHEADLE

Prim
Sch

St Catherines
Prep Sch

Mus

Marple
Bridge

Mill
Brow

Greenhill

Mellor
Hall

GROSVENOR RD

WINNINGTON RD

BRADSHAW RD

STATION RD

BRABYNS BROW

TOWN FOLD

TOWN ST

GRAYSTON
CT

STONE ROW

CLEMENT RD

COLUMBA AVE

Vicarage

CHURCH RD

KINGFISHER
MEWS

ARKWRIGHT RD

B6102

OLDKNOW RD

FAYWOOD

BEECHWOOD

LOW LEA RD

HIGH LEA RD

FERNHILL

PARKSIDE LA

Mellor
Prim Sch

KNOWLE RD

LONGHURST LA

Townscliffe
Farm

Lower
Hall

Podnor

DOVE BANK

Mellor

PH

MOOR END RD

SK6

B6101

B6102

LOCKSIDE

FIELD HOUSE LA

LADYTHORN

LOWER STRINES RD

Bottom's
Bridge

LAKES RD

OLD HALL LA

Bottom's
Hall

Linnet
Clough

Damsteads
Farm

Tarden

GIBB LA

Birchenough

CHAPEL HOS

All Saints
Prim Sch

WATERSIDE AVE
CHURCH LA
MACNAIR CT
MACNAIR MEWS

PARSONAGE GDNS

River Goyt

NIELDS WAY

CH

Whetmorhurst

WHETMORHURST LA

Cobden
Farm

Peak Forest Canal

Goyt Way

Cobdenedge
Farm

Cobden
Edge

TELFORD RD
RIDGE AVE
BROOMDALE RD
PEAKDALE AVE

BRAMHAM RD

BRIARWOOD

Hill Top
Farm

Cown Edge Way

Snape
Hey

HAWK GREEN RD

KESTREL CL

THE GREEN

RIDGE RD

STRINES RD

Strawberry
Hill

Richmond
Farm

The
Banks

Black La

Hawk
Green

THE RIDGE

Midshires Way

Capstone

Marpleridge

BARLOW WOOD DR

FLUCKSBRIDGE

HOLLINWOOD LA

E2

Sportsman's Arms
(PH)

Lower
Cliffe

Romper
(PH)

Ridge-End

Greenclough
Farm

SK22

High Cliffe
Poultry Farm

Shaw
Farm

Ridge End Fold
Farm

WYBERSLEY RD

Works

WHITECROFT RD

STATION RD

Strines

Fox Inn
(PH)

BROOK BOTTOM RD

Lea Cote
Farm

Turf Lea
Farm

TURF LEA RD

Strines

PO

Whitecroft
Farm

Brook
Bottom

RICHMOND
TERR

B6101

HAGUE FOLD
RD

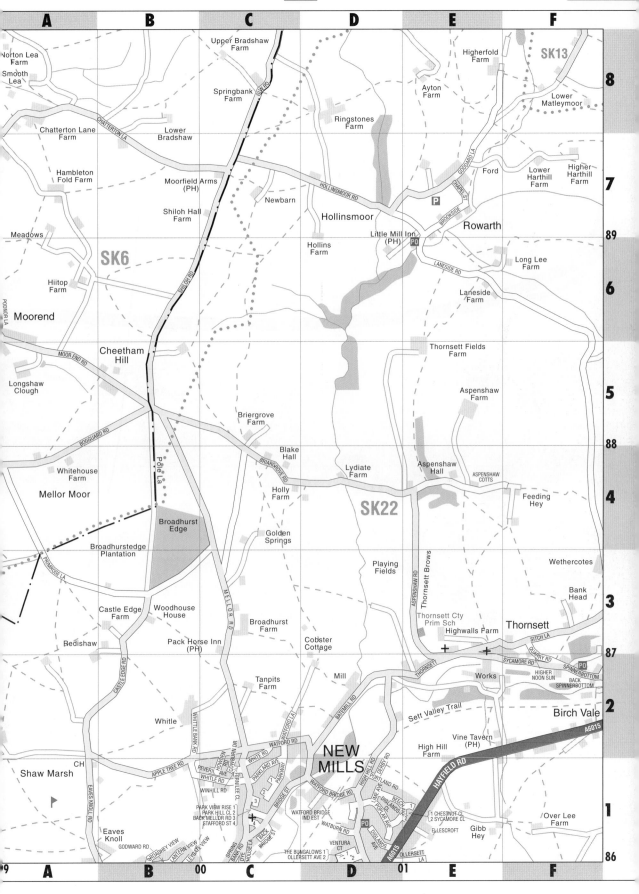

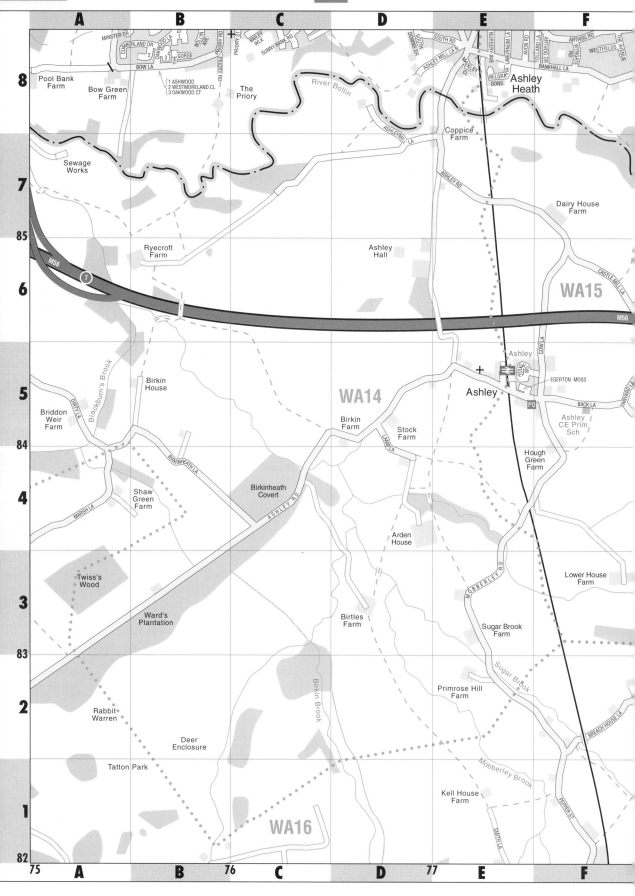

129 121

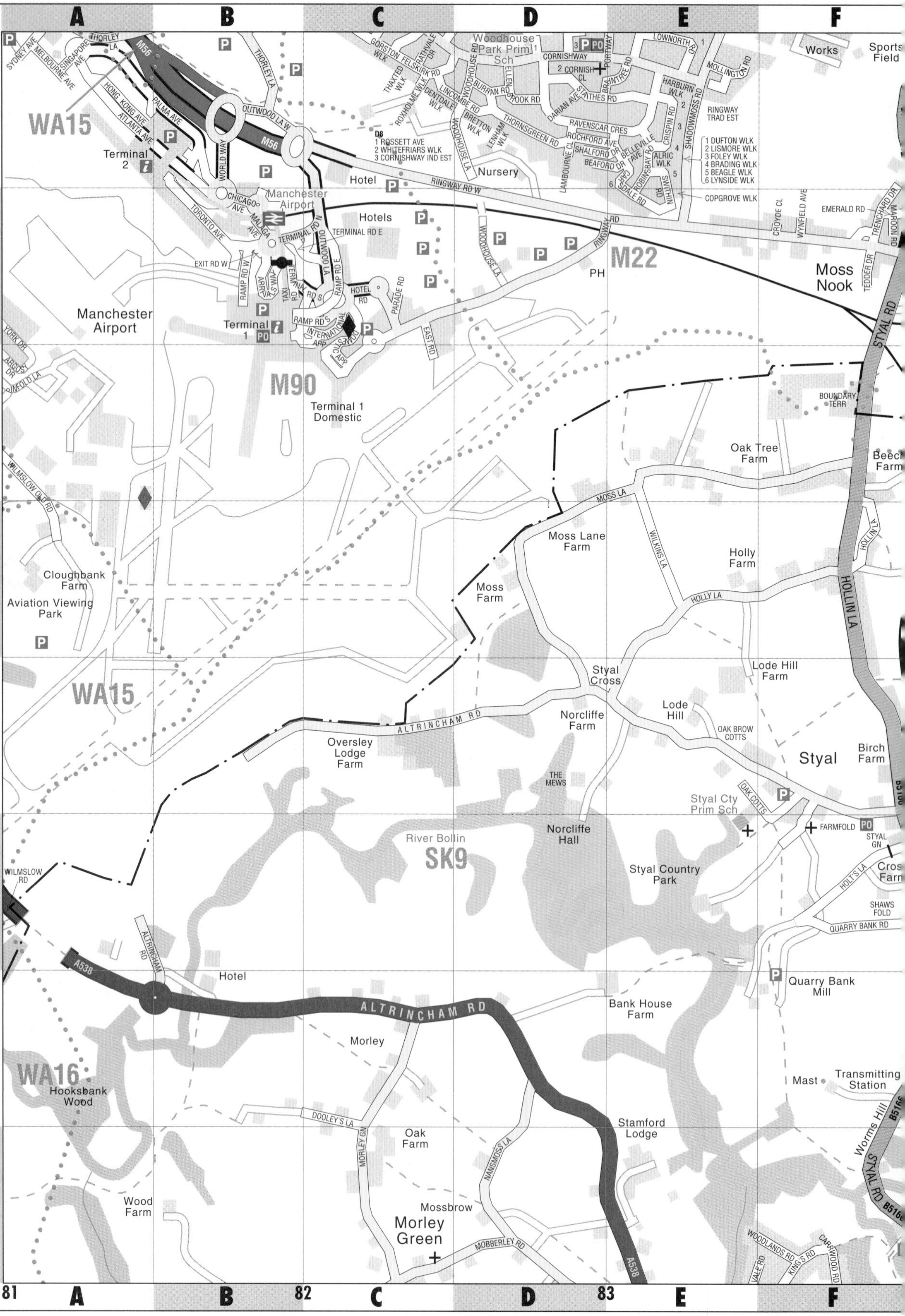

WA15

Manchester Airport

Terminal 2

World Way
Outwood La W
M56
M56

Sydney Ave
Melbourne Ave
Singapore Ave
Thorley La
Palma Ave
Hong Kong Ave
Atlanta Ave
Toronto Ave
Chicago Ave
Malaga Ave
Terminal Rd W
Terminal Rd
Exit Rd W
Ramp Rd W
Ramp Rd S
International App
Taxiway
Parade Rd
East Rd

Terminal 1
PO

Manchester Airport

Ringway Rd W
Hotel
Hotels
Hotel Rd

Woodhouse Park Prim Sch
Cornishway
Cornish Cl
Cornishway Ind Est

Gorston Wlk
Felskirk Rd
Strathvale
Thaxted Wlk
Roxholme Wlk
Burran Wlk
Lincombe Rd
Bretton Wlk
Dentdale Wlk
Johnson Wlk
Ellen Wlk
Thornsgreen Rd
Lenham Wlk
Swithin
Rossett Ave
Whitefriars Wlk
Cornishway Ind Est
DB

Ravenscar Cres
Rochford Ave
Shalford Dr
Beaford Dr
Belleville Ave
Robigsbury Rd
Alric Wlk
Szale Rd

Nursery

Ringway Rd W

Lownorth
Cornishway
Portway
Mollington
Harburn Wlk
Crispin Rd
Shadowmoss Rd
Croyde Cl
Wynfield Ave
Emerald Rd
Trenchard Dr

Works
Sports Field

Ringway Trad Est
1 Dufton Wlk
2 Lismore Wlk
3 Foley Wlk
4 Brading Wlk
5 Beagle Wlk
6 Lynside Wlk
Copgrove Wlk

M22

PH

Moss Nook

Styal Rd

York Rd
Argos Dr
Nicol La
Wilmslow Old Rd

M90

Terminal 1 Domestic

Cloughbank Farm

Aviation Viewing Park
P

WA15

Moss La
Moss Lane Farm
Wilkins La
Holly Farm
Holly La
Oak Tree Farm
Beech Farm
Boundary Terr
Hollin La

Moss Farm

Styal Cross
Norcliffe Farm
Lode Hill
Lode Hill Farm
Oak Brow Cotts
Styal
Birch Farm

Altrincham Rd
Oversley Lodge Farm

The Mews

Norcliffe Hall

Styal Cty Prim Sch
Oak Cotts
Farmfold
PO
Styal Gn
Cross Farm
Holt's La
Shaws Fold

River Bollin
SK9

Styal Country Park
Quarry Bank Rd

Wilmslow Rd

Altrincham Rd
A538
Hotel

Altrincham Rd
Morley

Quarry Bank Mill

Bank House Farm

WA16
Hooksbank Wood
Dooley's La
Oak Farm
Morley Gn
Maxonmoss La
Mobberley Rd

Mast
Transmitting Station

Stamford Lodge

Wood Farm
Mossbrow
Morley Green

A538

Worms Hill
Styal Rd
B5166
Woodlands Rd
Vale Rd
King's Rd
Carwood Rd

129 136

D5
1 TARVIN WAY
2 OVERTON WAY
3 STRETTON WAY
4 BIRTLES WAY
5 PEACOCK WAY
6 KELSALL WAY

D5
7 CUDDINGTON WAY
8 WILLASTON WAY
9 NORBURY WAY
10 PICKMERE CT
11 EASTHAM WAY
12 UPTON WAY

122

132

D5
13 ASTON WAY
14 HOOTON WAY
15 CHRISTLETON WAY
16 CRANAGE WAY
E5
1 SUTTON WAY

2 CHELFORD CT
3 SOMERFORD WAY
4 TATTON CT
5 MARTON WAY
6 NANTWICH WAY
7 HASSALL WAY
8 MARTHALL WAY

D1
1 MILLBROOK GR
2 REDBROOK GR
3 SHELLBROOK GR
4 WADEBROOK GR
5 DINGLEBROOK GR
6 LIME WLK
7 CROWBROOK GR
8 LIME WLK
9 RINGSTEAD DR

10 DEAN ROW CT
11 DRAYTON CL
12 KNIGHTSBRIDGE CL
13 KINGSBURY DR
14 QUEENSBURY CL

137

132

D2
1 TORBROOK GR
2 CLIFFBROOK GR
3 BENSON WLK
4 CARDENBROOK GR
5 TIMBERSBROOK GR
6 LADYBROOK GR
7 FODEN WLK
8 TAME WLK
9 DE TRAFFORD MEWS

D4
1 HILLBRE WAY
2 SEALAND WAY
3 ECCLESTON WAY
4 HELSBY WAY
5 HEATLEY WAY
6 ELWORTH WAY
7 PARKGATE WAY

E1
1 BUDWORTH WLK
2 EDLESTONE GR
3 WOODCOTT GR
4 KETTLESHULME WLK
5 TILSTON WLK
6 SNAPEBROOK GR
7 DAIRYBROOK GR
8 APPLETON WLK
9 MOORSBROOK GR

10 RAINOW WAY
11 PECKFORTON WLK
12 SALTERSBROOK GR
13 PINWOOD CT
14 KINGSTON CT
15 MELROSE CT
16 SEYMOUR HO
17 HAZELDEAN CT

131
123

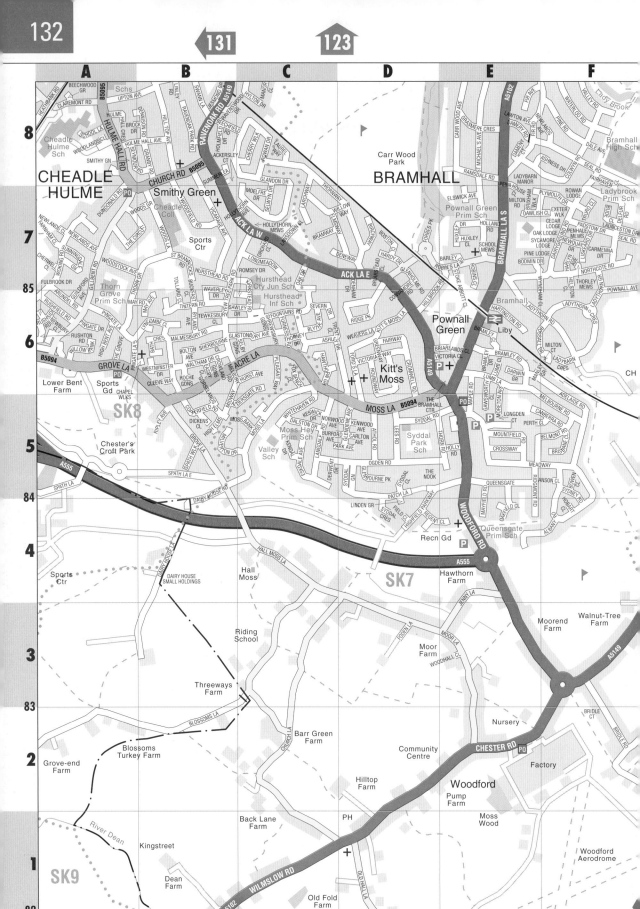

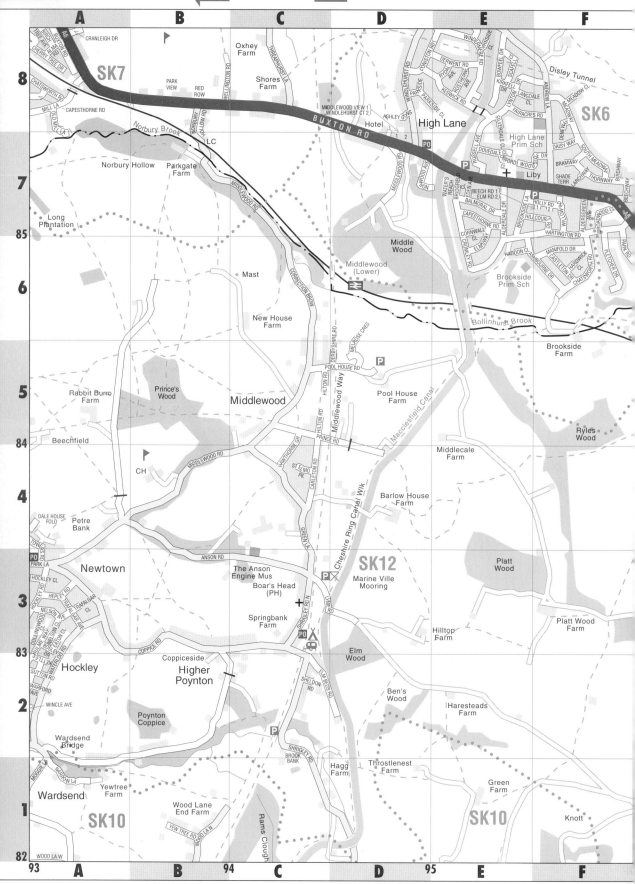

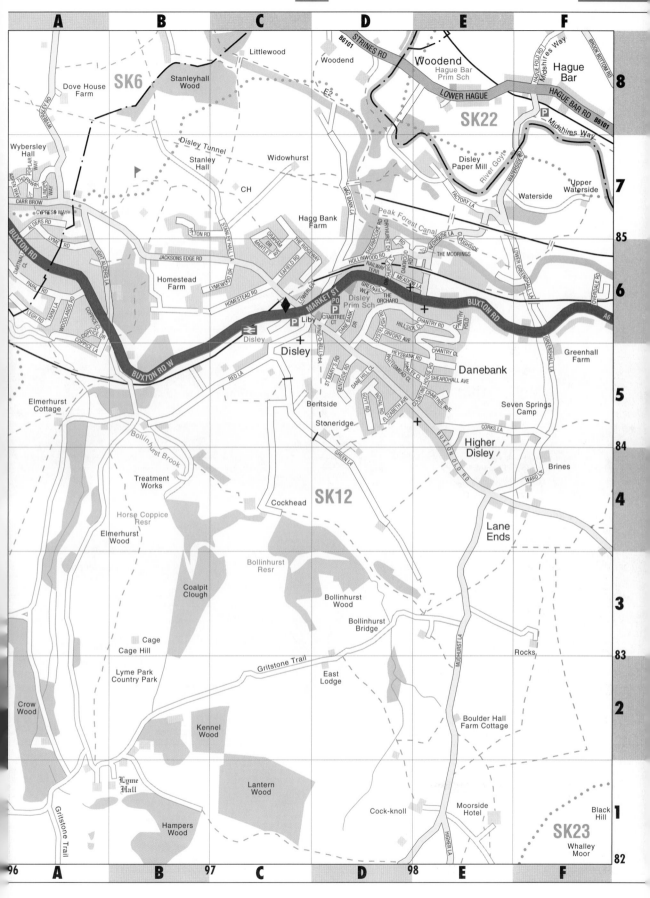

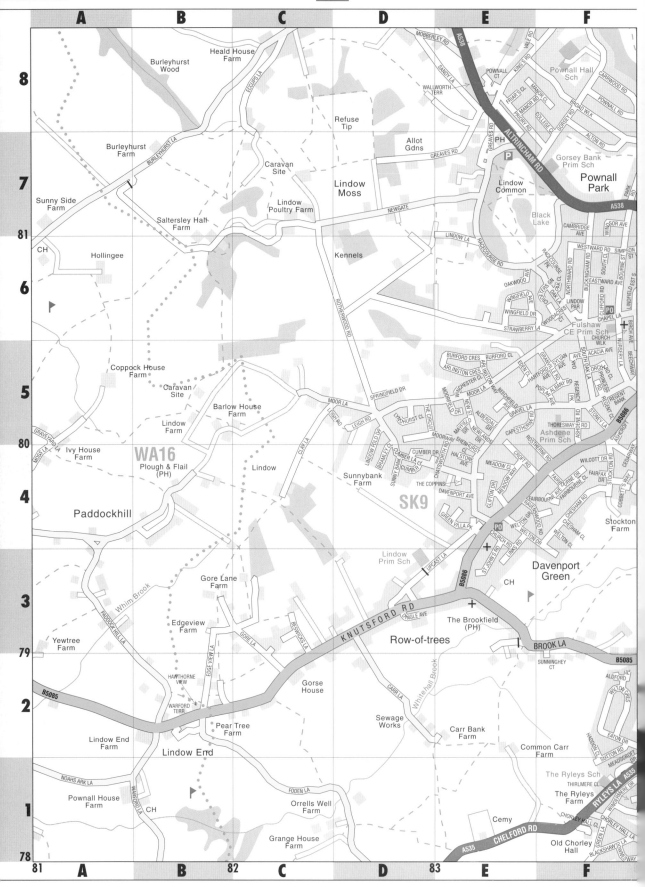

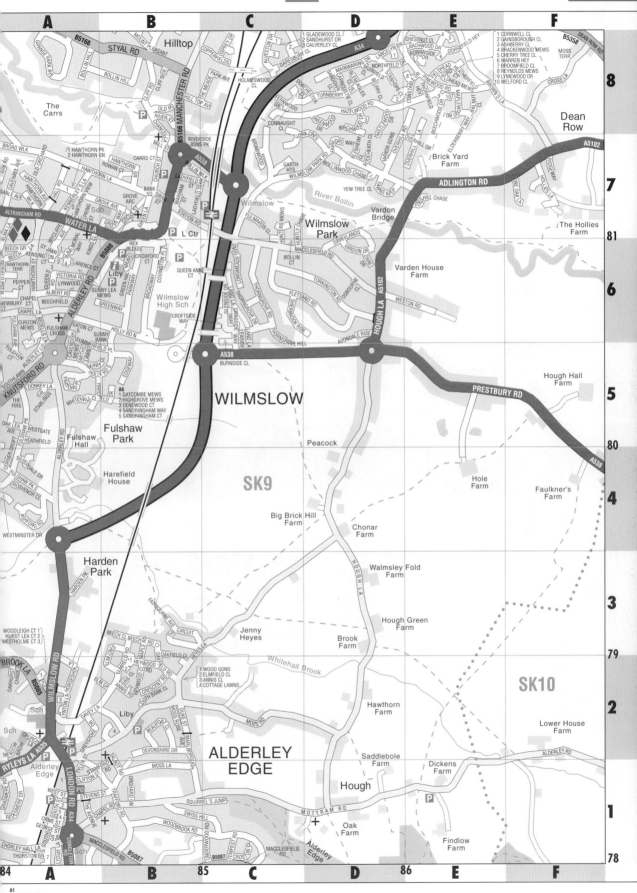

A1
1 THE PARADE
2 BROWN ST
3 GREEN ST
4 MASSEY ST
5 CHAPEL ST
6 HUBERT WORTHINGTON HO
7 CARLISLE ST

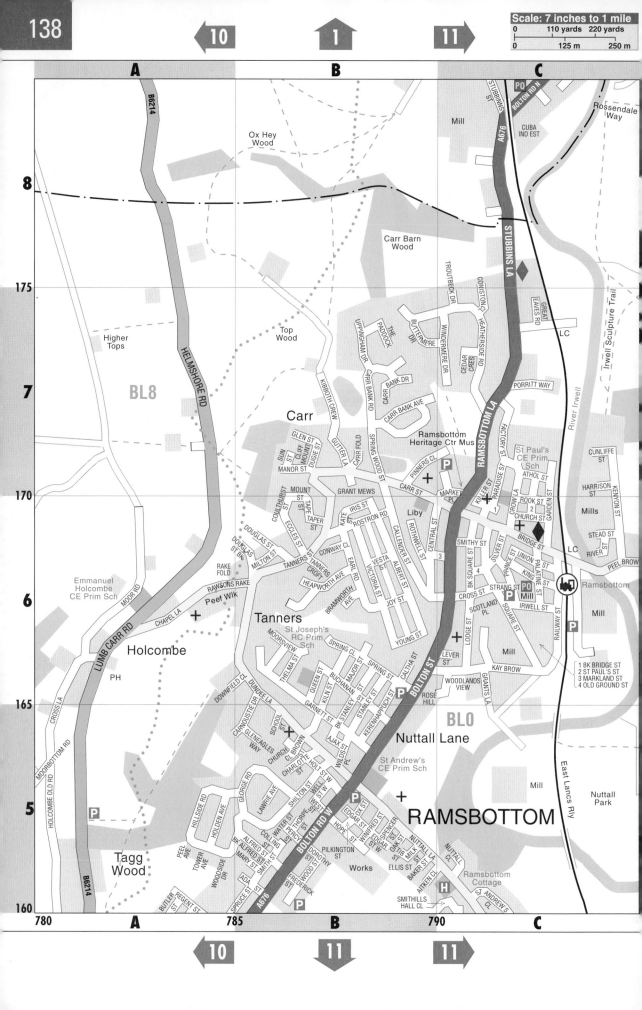

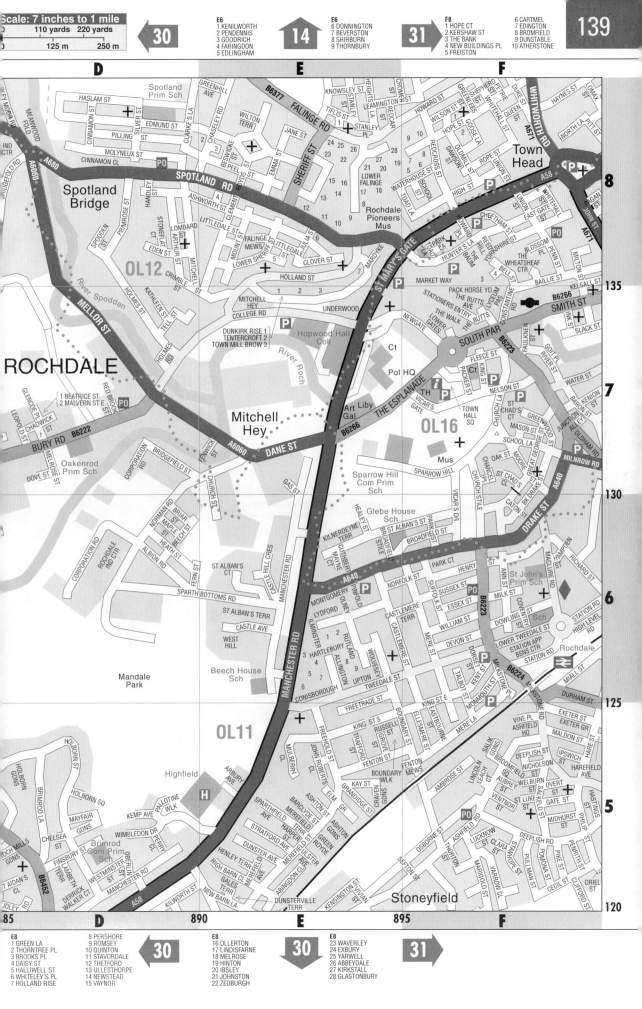

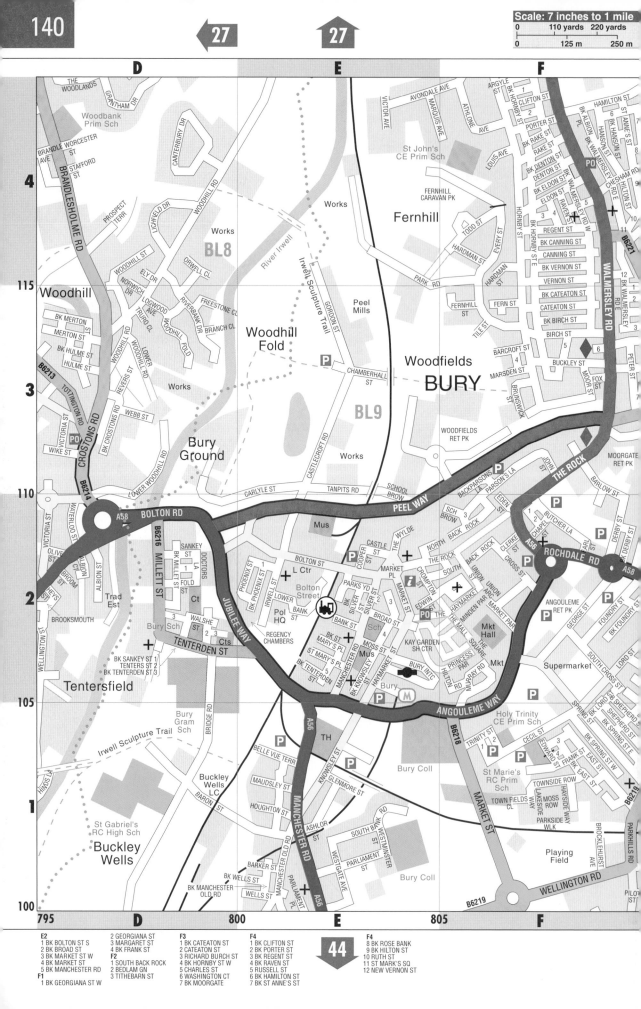

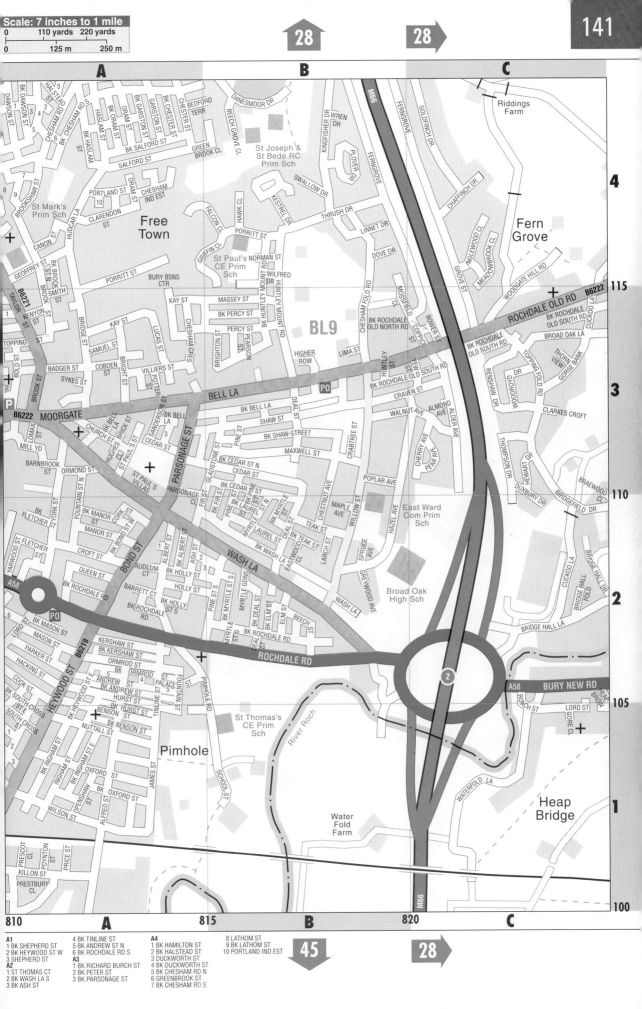

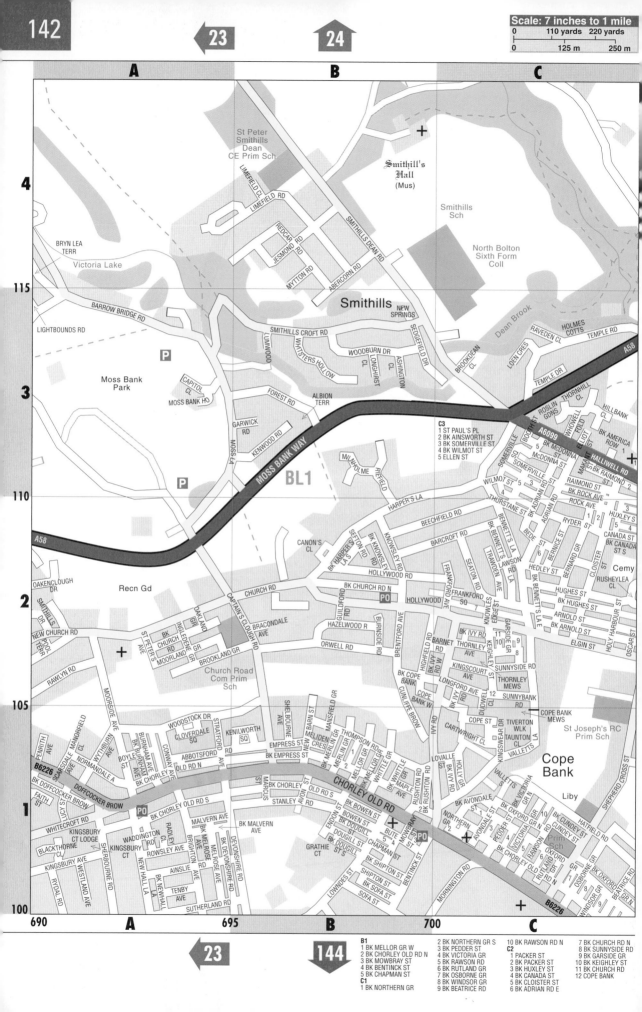

Scale: 7 inches to 1 mile
0 110 yards 220 yards
0 125 m 250 m

D2
1 WORDSWORTH TRAD EST
2 BK ESKRICK ST
3 BK CHAUCER ST
4 BK LYTTON ST
5 MILES ST
6 BK GLEN BOTT ST
7 BK ESKRICK ST E
8 BK FRANCES ST
9 BK GROVE ST
10 BK ST THOMAS ST E
11 BK DARWIN ST

24

D2
12 ST JOSEPH ST
13 BK BOUNDARY ST
14 HALLIWELL ST
15 BK HAYDN ST
16 BK UTTLEY ST
17 BK HALLIWELL RD S
18 BK ST AUGUSTINE ST
19 BK ESKRICK ST S
20 BK CARL ST
21 BK WAPPING ST
22 BK WORDSWORTH ST
23 BK VICKERMAN ST
24 RUSHEY FOLD CT
25 BK AINSWORTH ST

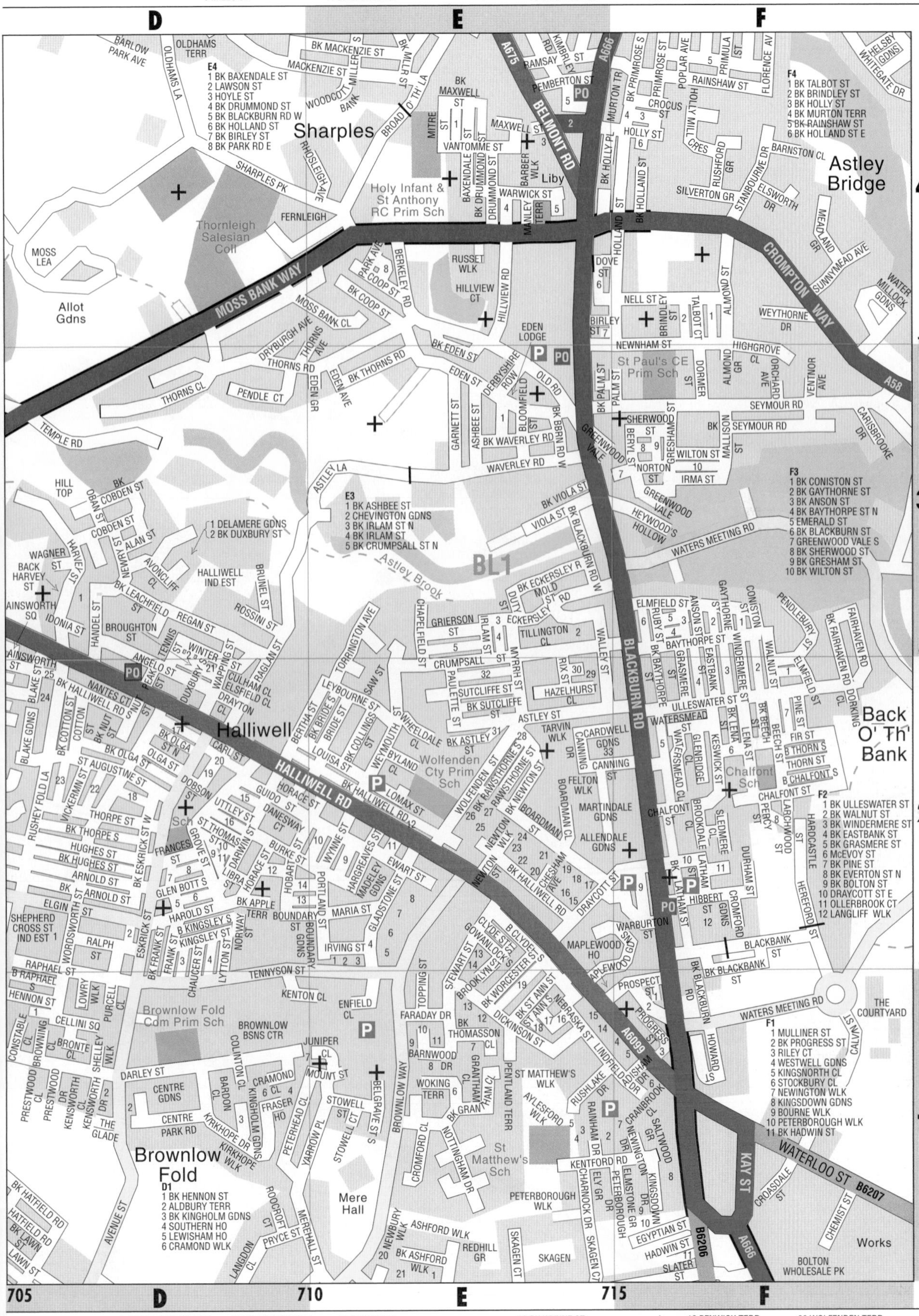

D
E
F
Sharples
Astley Bridge
Halliwell
Back O' Th' Bank
Brownlow Fold
BL1
MOSS BANK WAY
CROMPTON WAY
BELMONT RD
BLACKBURN RD
HALLIWELL RD
WATERLOO ST
KAY ST
A675
A666
A58
A6099
B6207
B6206
Astley Brook
Thornleigh Salesian Coll
Holy Infant & St Anthony RC Prim Sch
St Paul's CE Prim Sch
Wolfenden Cty Prim Sch
Chalfont Sch
Brownlow Fold Cdm Prim Sch
St Matthew's Sch
Mere Hall
Allot Gdns
Works
BOLTON WHOLESALE PK
E4
1 BK BAXENDALE ST
2 LAWSON ST
3 HOYLE ST
4 BK DRUMMOND ST
5 BK BLACKBURN RD W
6 BK HOLLAND ST
7 BK BIRLEY ST
8 BK PARK RD E
F4
1 BK TALBOT ST
2 BK BRINDLEY ST
3 BK HOLLY ST
4 BK MURTON TERR
5 BK RAINSHAW ST
6 BK HOLLAND ST E
E3
1 BK ASHBEE ST
2 CHEVINGTON GDNS
3 BK IRLAM ST N
4 BK IRLAM ST
5 BK CRUMPSALL ST N
1 DELAMERE GDNS
2 BK DUXBURY ST
F3
1 BK CONISTON ST
2 BK GAYTHORNE ST
3 BK ANSON ST
4 BK BAYTHORPE ST N
5 EMERALD ST
6 BK BLACKBURN ST
7 GREENWOOD VALE S
8 BK SHERWOOD ST
9 BK GRESHAM ST
10 BK WILTON ST
F2
1 BK ULLESWATER ST
2 BK WALNUT ST
3 BK WINDERMERE ST
4 BK EASTBANK ST
5 BK GRASMERE ST
6 McEVOY ST
7 BK PINE ST
8 BK EVERTON ST N
9 BK BOLTON ST
10 DRAYCOTT ST E
11 OLLERBROOK CT
12 LANGLIFF WLK
F1
1 MULLINER ST
2 BK PROGRESS ST
3 RILEY CT
4 WESTWELL GDNS
5 KINGSNORTH CL
6 STOCKBURY CL
7 NEWINGTON WLK
8 KINGSDOWN GDNS
9 BOURNE WLK
10 PETERBOROUGH WLK
11 BK HADWIN ST
D1
1 BK HENNON ST
2 ALDBURY TERR
3 BK KINGHOLM GDNS
4 SOUTHERN HO
5 LEWISHAM HO
6 CRAMOND WLK
4
115
3
110
2
105
1
100
705
710
715

E1
1 MIDHURST CL
2 RAINHAM GR
3 WOODCHURCH CL
4 WESTMARSH CL
5 MOUNTFIELD WLK
6 BK WOKING GDNS
7 THOMASSON CL
8 ST MATTHEW'S TERR
9 FOSTER TERR
10 BARNWOOD TERR
11 BARNWOOD CL
12 DICKINSON TERR
13 DICKINSON CL
14 HIGHBROOK GR
15 FERNHURST GR
16 GLENTHORNE ST
17 BK NEVADA ST
18 NEVADA ST
19 WORCESTER ST
20 SHAFTSBURY CL
21 FARNHAM CL
E2
1 IRVING HOUSE
2 KEATS WLK
3 TENNYSON WLK
4 BELGRAVE ST
5 BELGRAVE GDNS
6 GLADSTONE CL
7 LONGTOWN GDNS
8 WHITCHURCH GDNS
9 BK HARGREAVES ST

145

10 BK WYNNE ST
11 BK EWART ST
12 MARSH ST
13 BK STEWART ST
14 BOSTON ST
15 WITNEY CL
16 WATFORD CL
17 WESTWICK TERR

25

18 BENWICK TERR
19 YORK TERR
20 CHESTER WLK
21 HUNTINGDON WLK
22 LANCASTER WLK
23 NEWTON TERR
24 LANCASTER GDNS
25 KEMPSTON GDNS
26 WOLFENDEN TERR
27 TANWORTH WLK
28 CHARLOTTE ST
29 HOLYHURST WLK
30 PINEWOOD CL
31 BK WOLFENDEN ST
32 BK CRUMPSALL ST
33 BK CARDWELL ST

Scale: 7 inches to 1 mile
0   110 yards   220 yards
0   125 m   250 m

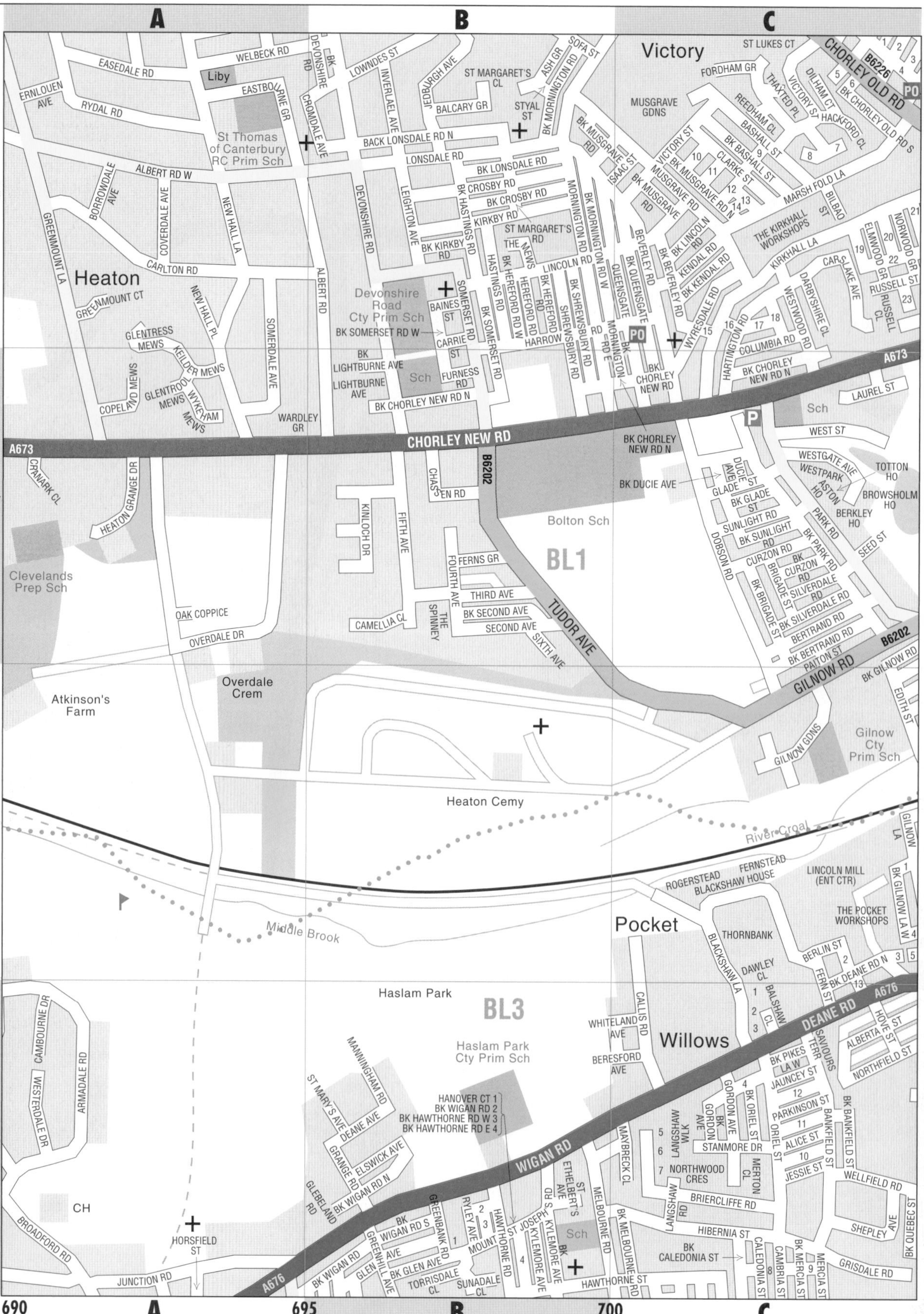

	A	B	C

8

095

7

090

6

085

5

080

690   A   695   B   700   C

Map area labels include: Heaton, Victory, Bolton Sch, BL1, BL3, Haslam Park, Willows, Pocket, Atkinson's Farm, Clevelands Prep Sch, Overdale Crem, Heaton Cemy, Middle Brook, River Croal, Gilnow Cty Prim Sch, St Thomas of Canterbury RC Prim Sch, Devonshire Road Cty Prim Sch, Haslam Park Cty Prim Sch, CHORLEY NEW RD, TUDOR AVE, GILNOW RD, WIGAN RD, DEANE RD, A673, A676, B6202, B6226.

C5
1 TORBAY CL
2 BLACKSHAW ROW
3 LANGLEY DR
4 BK DEANE RD
5 HEARLESDEN CRES
6 NEASDEN GR
7 COLINDALE CL
8 CAMBRIA SQ
9 NORTHUMBRIA ST
10 BK ALICE ST
11 BK PARKINSON ST
12 BK JAUNCEY ST
13 HOVE ST N

C6
1 BK VINE ST
2 BK FERN ST E
3 WASHINGTON ST
4 RYLEY ST
5 BK GILNOW LA

C8
1 BK BATTENBERG RD
2 BATTENBERG RD
3 BK WALDECK ST
4 BK CHORLEY OLD RD N
5 MOORE'S CT
6 TURK ST
7 CAVENHAM GR
8 METFIELD PL
9 MABEL ST
10 BK VICTORY ST E
11 LONGDEN ST
12 BK LONGDEN ST
13 BK CLARKE ST
14 BK MARSH FOLD LA
15 SCORTON ST
16 BK HARTINGTON RD
17 BK COLUMBIA RD
18 BK WESTWOOD RD
19 ELMWOOD GR W
20 BK ELMWOOD GR
21 BK NORWOOD GR
22 BK RUSSELL ST
23 BK RUSSELL CL

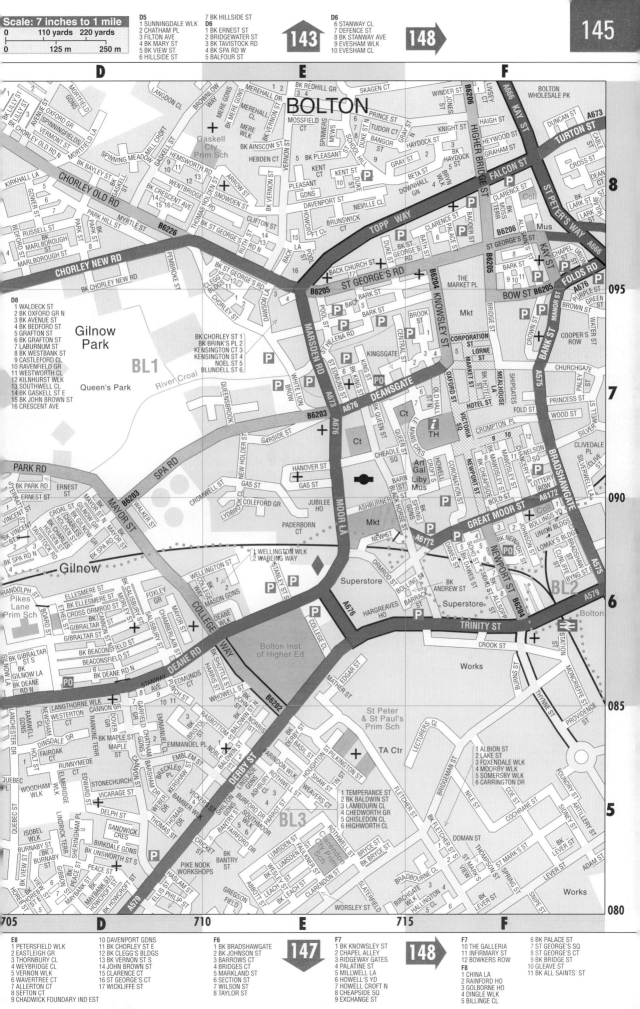

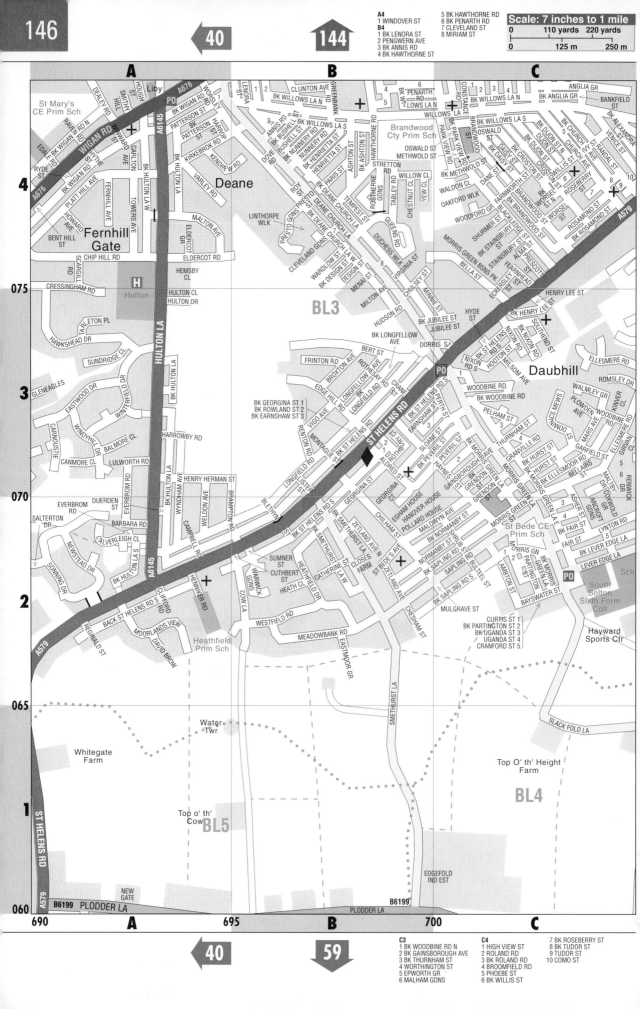

Scale: 7 inches to 1 mile

0 — 110 yards — 220 yards
0 — 125 m — 250 m

145

42

D **E** **F**

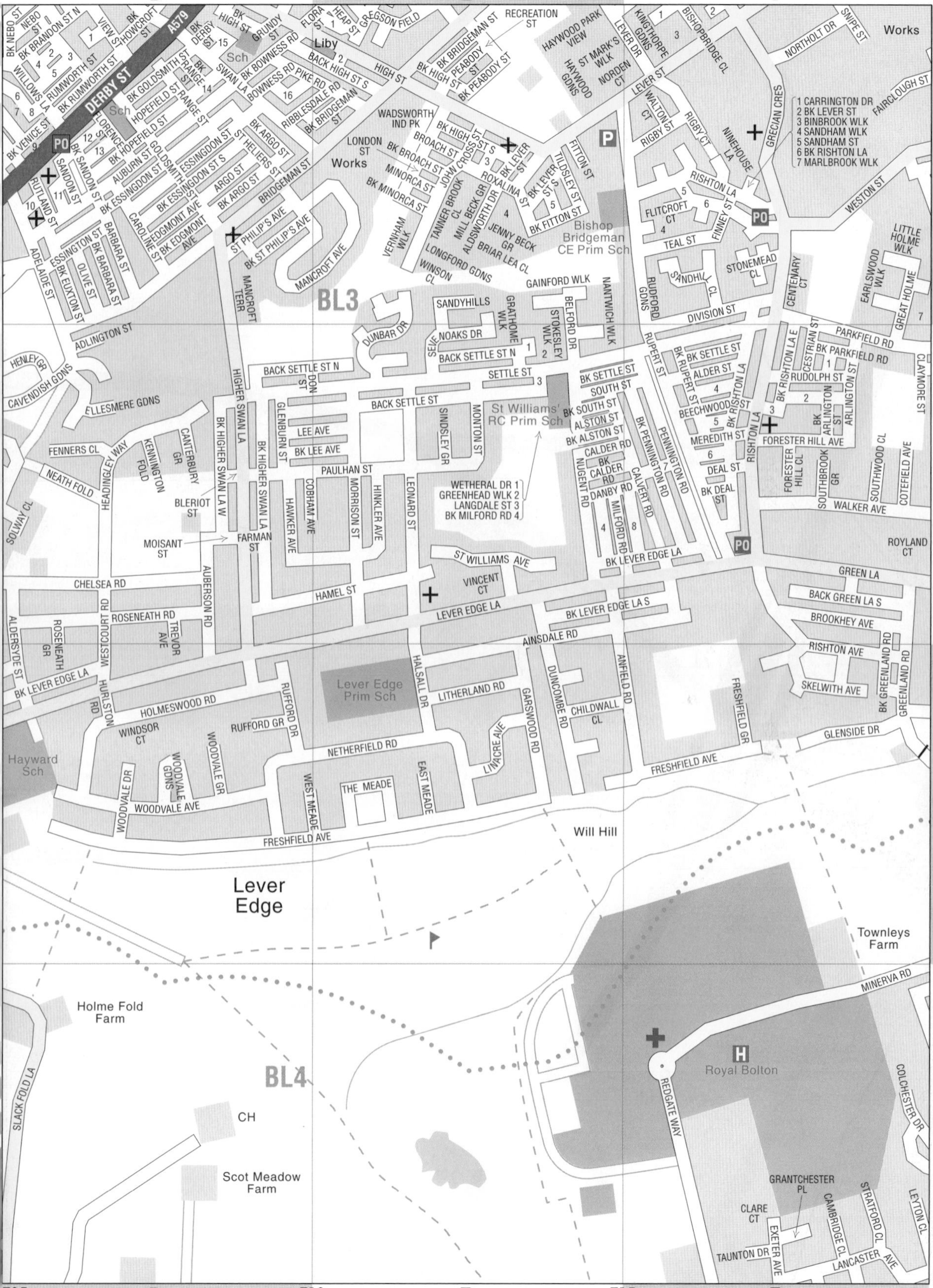

4

075

3

070

2

065

1

060

705 **D** **710** **E** **715** **F** **060**

59

42

BL3

BL4

Lever
Edge

Will Hill

Townleys
Farm

Holme Fold
Farm

Scot Meadow
Farm

Royal Bolton

H

Hayward
Sch

DERBY ST

A579

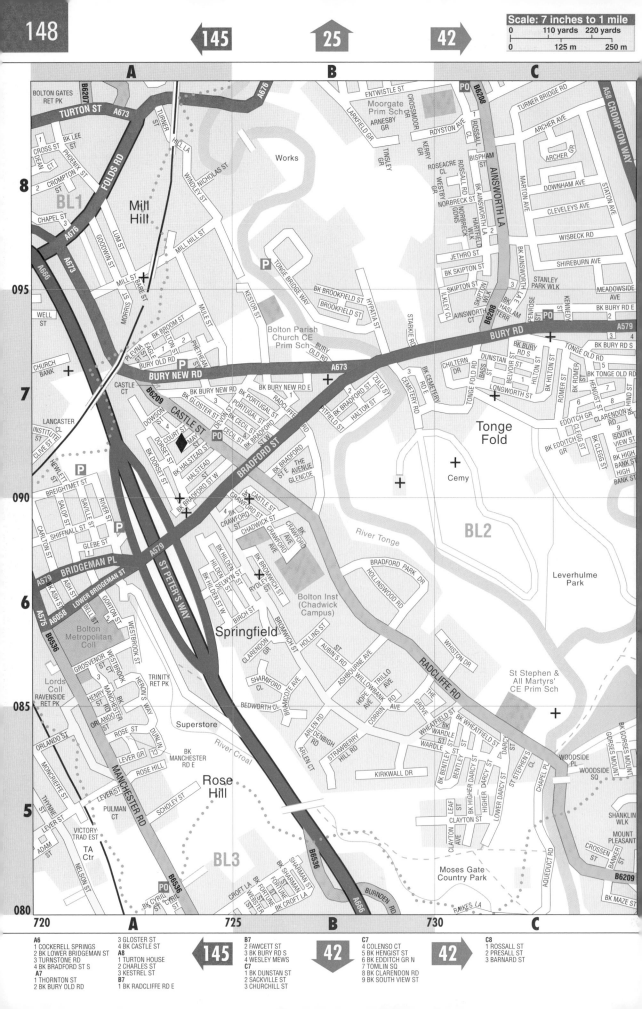

A6
1 COCKERELL SPRINGS
2 BK LOWER BRIDGEMAN ST
3 TURNSTONE RD
4 BK BRADFORD ST S
A7
1 THORNTON ST
2 BK BURY OLD RD

3 GLOSTER ST
4 BK CASTLE ST
A8
1 TURTON HOUSE
2 CHARLES ST
3 KESTREL ST
B7
1 BK RADCLIFFE RD E

B7
2 FAWCETT ST
3 BK BURY RD S
4 WESLEY MEWS
C7
1 BK DUNSTAN ST
2 SACKVILLE ST
3 CHURCHILL ST

C7
4 COLENSO CT
5 BK HENGIST ST
6 BK EDDITCH GR N
7 TOMLIN SQ
8 BK CLARENDON RD
9 BK SOUTH VIEW ST

C8
1 ROSSALL ST
2 PRESALL ST
3 BARNARD ST

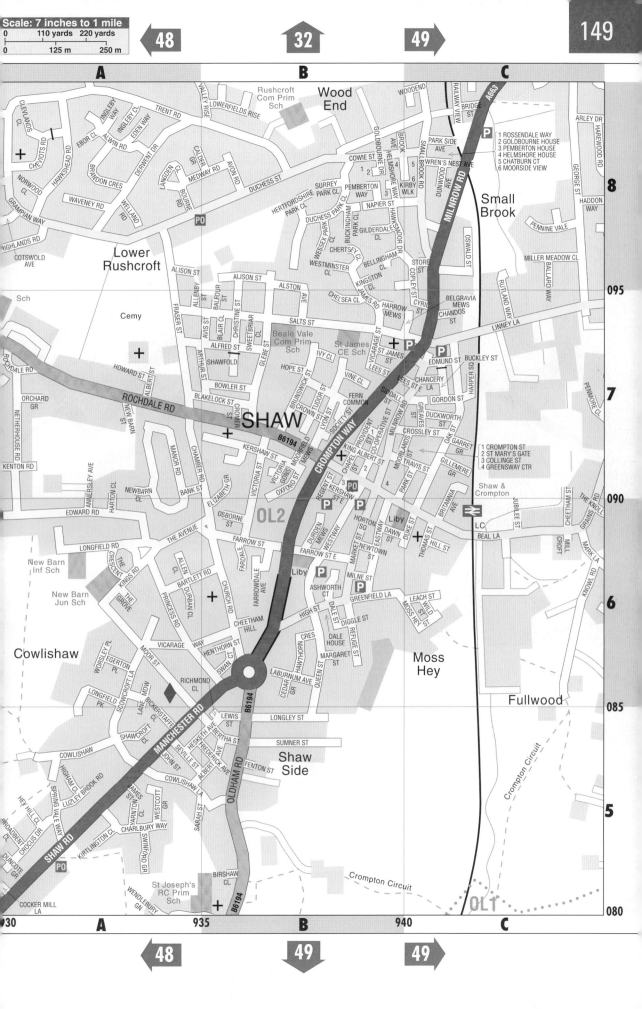

C8
1 HINDLEY WLK
2 WIGAN GALLERY
3 ORRELL ARC
4 LEIGH ARC
5 ROYAL ARC

54

C8
6 ASHTON GALLERY
7 ASPULL ARC
8 ATHERTON SQ
9 GOLBOURNE GALLERY
10 WOODCOCK SQ

37

C8
11 TYDESLEY ARC
12 BILLINGE ARC
13 STANDISH GALLERY
14 CROFTERS' YD
15 MAKINSON ARC

16 BARRACK SQ
17 BRETHERTON ROW
18 ARCADE ST
19 THE GALLERIES

Scale: 7 inches to 1 mile

| 0 | 110 yards | 220 yards |
| 0 | 125 m | 250 m |

A **B** **C**

8

WIGAN

WN6

WN1

Wallgate

Wigan & Leigh Coll (Parsons Walk)

Deanery CE High Sch

Coll Annexe

Mkt

INCE WLK 2 WIGAN SQ

Market St

Marketgate

MARKET PL

055

WALLGATE

Wigan (North Western)

Westbridge Mews

7

River Douglas

Wigan Mus

Wigan Pier

POTTERY RD

CANAL COTTS

Leeds & Liverpool Canal

ACTON'S WLK TRAD CTR

QUEEN ST

CAROLINE ST

CHAPEL LA

B5238

050

WN5

Parson's Meadow

WN3

Poolstock

POOLSTOCK

Leeds & Liverpool Canal Leigh Branch

045

Smithy Brook

POOLSTOCK LA

B5238

5

Sch

PO

Scotman's Flash

Pearson's Flash

040

570 **A** 575 **B** 580 **C**

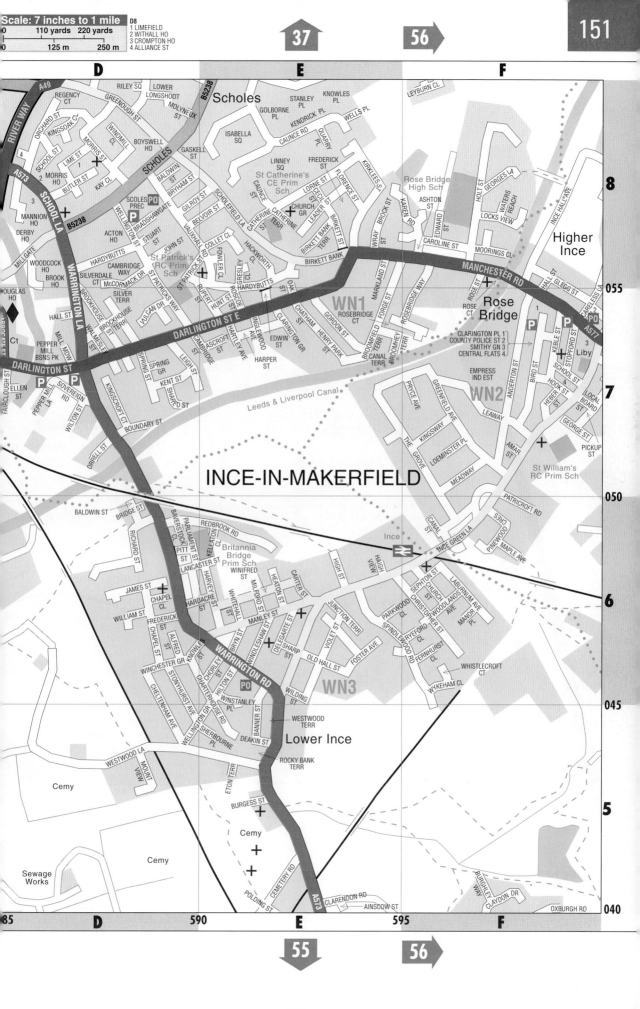

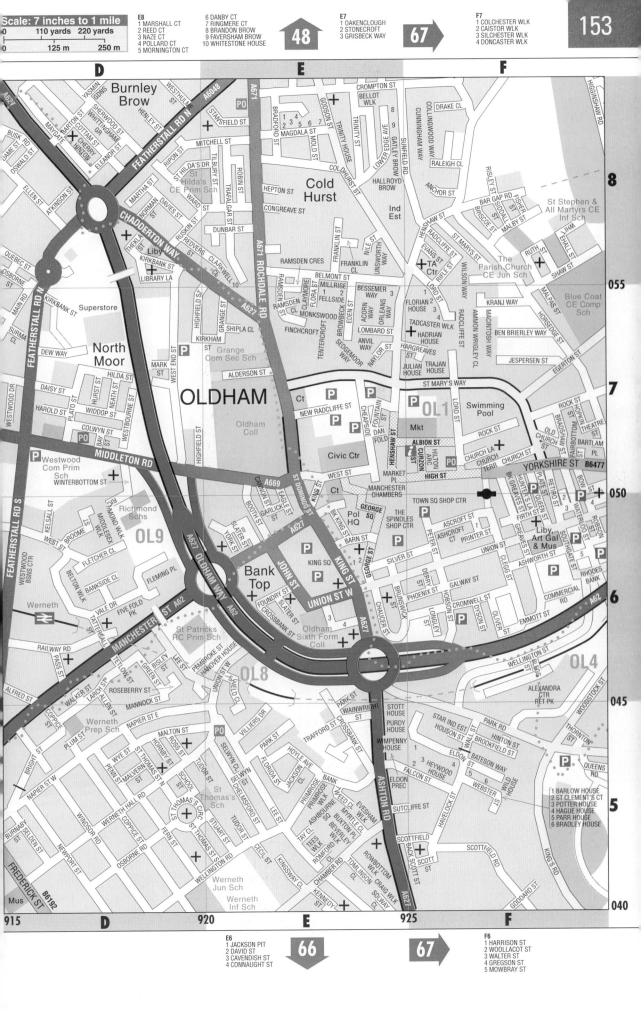

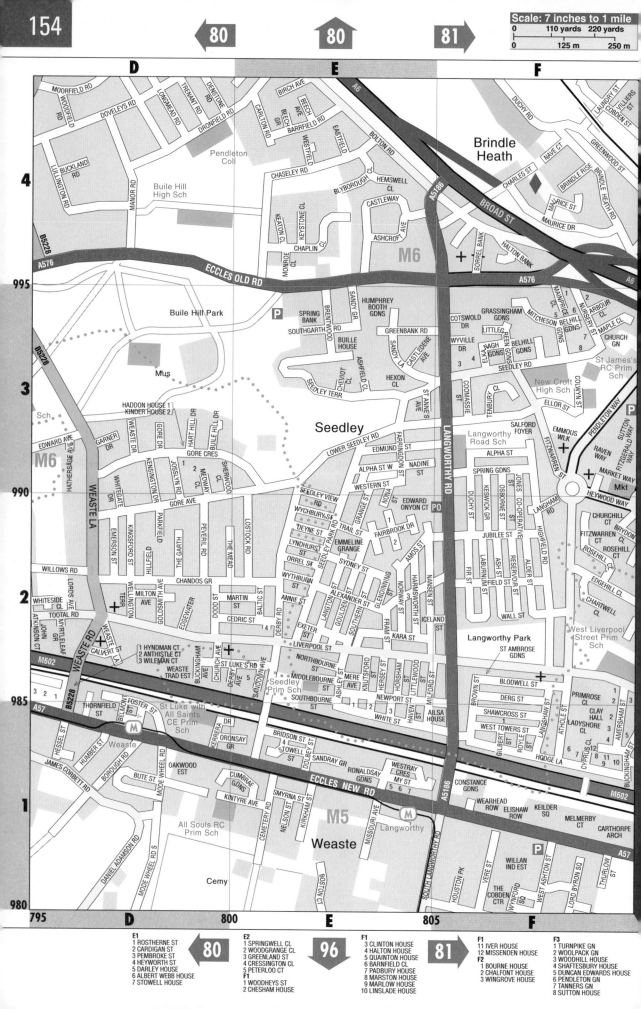

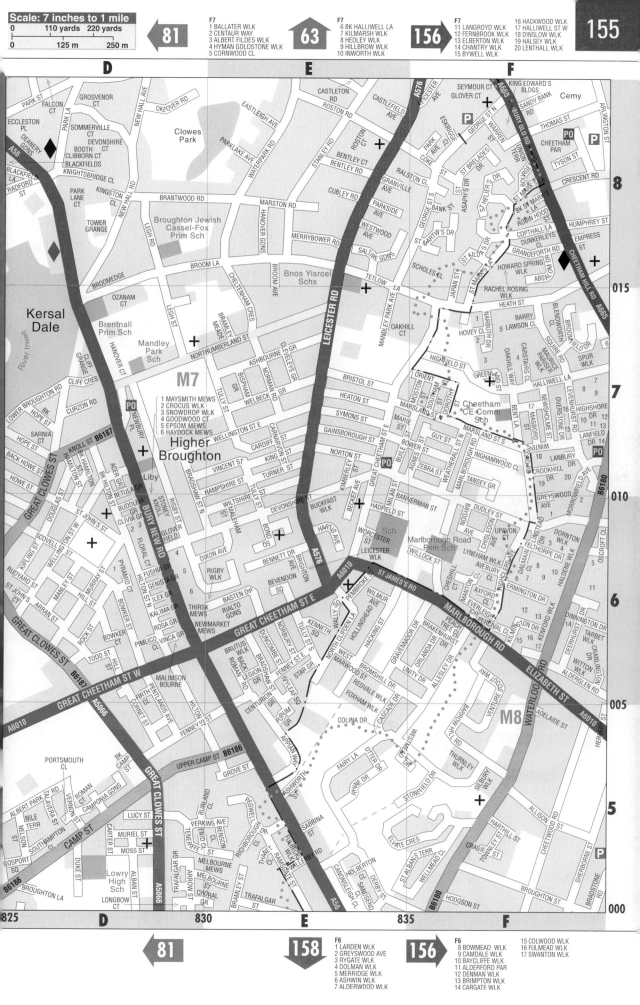

156

← 155

↑ 64

Scale: 7 inches to 1 mile
0 110 yards 220 yards
0 125 m 250 m

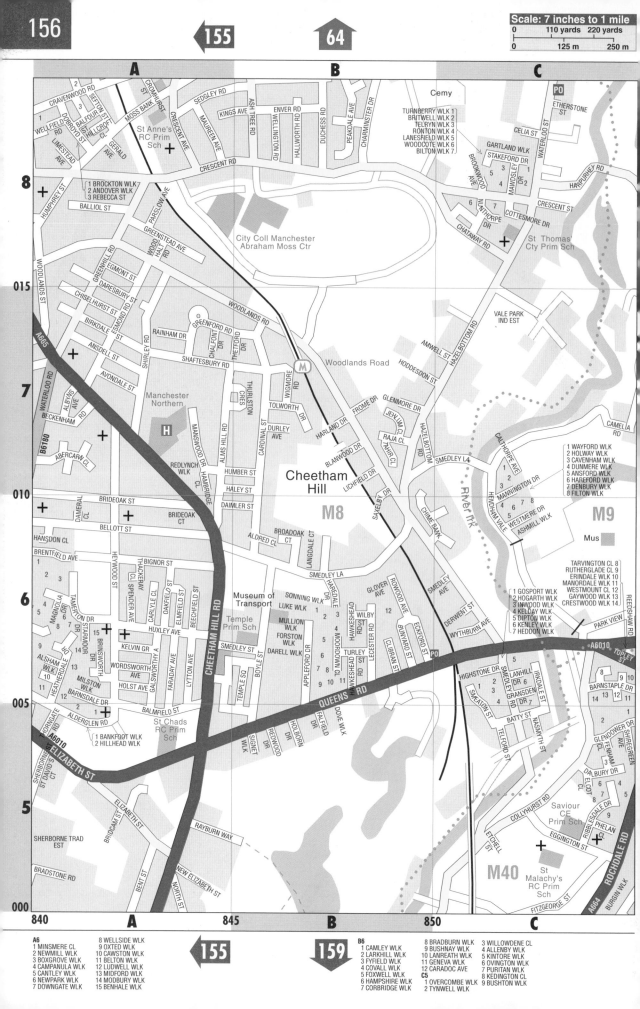

A6
1 MINSMERE CL
2 NEWMILL WLK
3 BOXGROVE WLK
4 CAMPANULA WLK
5 CANTLEY WLK
6 NEWPARK WLK
7 DOWNGATE WLK
8 WELLSIDE WLK
9 OXTED WLK
10 CAWSTON WLK
11 BELTON WLK
12 LUDWELL WLK
13 MIDFORD WLK
14 MODBURY WLK
15 BENHALE WLK

B6
1 CAMLEY WLK
2 LARKHILL WLK
3 FYFIELD WLK
4 COVALL WLK
5 FOXWELL WLK
6 HAMPSHIRE WLK
7 CORBRIDGE WLK
8 BRADBURN WLK
9 BUSHNAY WLK
10 LANREATH WLK
11 GENEVA WLK
12 CARADOC AVE
C5
1 OVERCOMBE WLK
2 TYNWELL WLK
3 WILLOWDENE CL
4 ALLENBY WLK
5 KINTORE WLK
6 OVINGTON WLK
7 PURITAN WLK
8 KEDINGTON CL
9 BUSHTON WLK

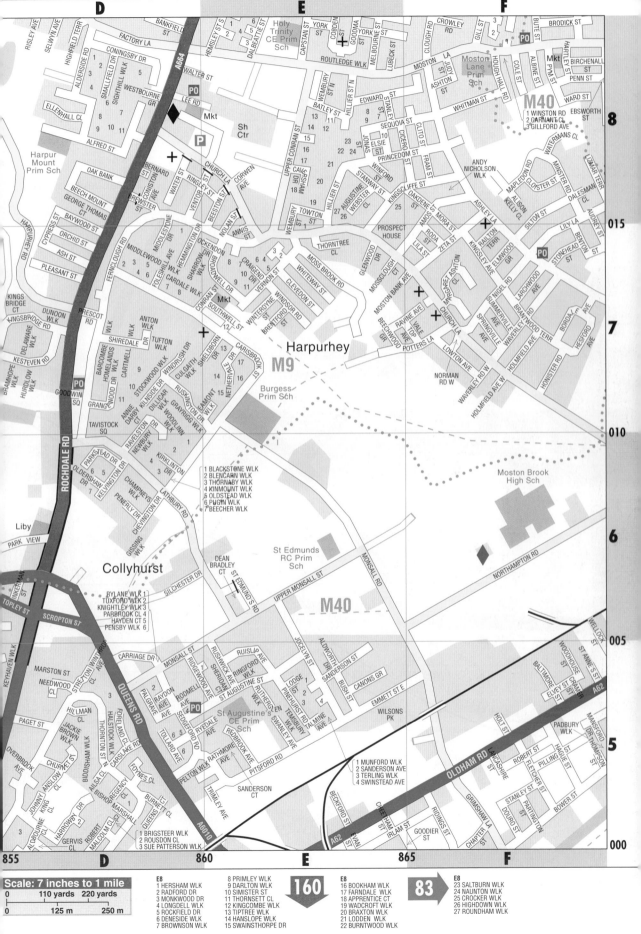

7
BROMWICH DR
CLATFORD WLK
OAKRIDGE WLK
BINDON WLK
WATFIELD WLK
HOLMFOOT WLK

7 LINSLADE WLK
8 SELWOOD WLK
9 PORTWOOD WLK
10 TREMAIN WLK
11 CALDERBROOK WLK

D8
1 MILLPOOL WLK

2 PATHFIELD WLK
3 MURROW WLK
4 DERVILLE WLK
5 SHAPWICK CL
6 HARROWDENE WLK
7 BRENLEY WLK
8 ROXWELL WLK

9 PORTAL WLK
10 HAYGROVE WLK
11 MAYBROOK WLK

E7
1 WILLOW BANK
2 ORPINGTON RD
3 OSBORNE ST

E7
4 ASHGILL WLK
5 GLENPARK WLK
6 DRYGATE WLK
7 BELSYDE WLK
8 NORBET WLK
9 PURTON WLK

E7
10 BANKHALL WLK
11 LOWREY WLK
12 DURHAM ST
13 EVANTON WLK
14 MERTON WLK
15 TRONGATE WLK

16 VIEWFIELD WLK
17 FIRDON WLK

64

83

157

Scale: 7 inches to 1 mile

0   110 yards   220 yards
0   125 m   250 m

E8
1 HERSHAM WLK
2 RADFORD DR
3 MONKWOOD DR
4 LONGDELL WLK
5 ROCKFIELD DR
6 DENESIDE WLK
7 BROWNSON WLK

8 PRIMLEY WLK
9 DARLTON WLK
10 SIMISTER ST
11 THORNSETT CL
12 KINGCOMBE WLK
13 TIPTREE WLK
14 HANSLOPE WLK
15 SWAINSTHORPE DR

160

E8
16 BOOKHAM WLK
17 FARNDALE WLK
18 APPRENTICE CT
19 WADCROFT WLK
20 BRAXTON WLK
21 LODDEN WLK
22 BURNTWOOD WLK

83

E8
23 SALTBURN WLK
24 NAUNTON WLK
25 CROCKER WLK
26 HIGHDOWN WLK
27 ROUNDHAM WLK

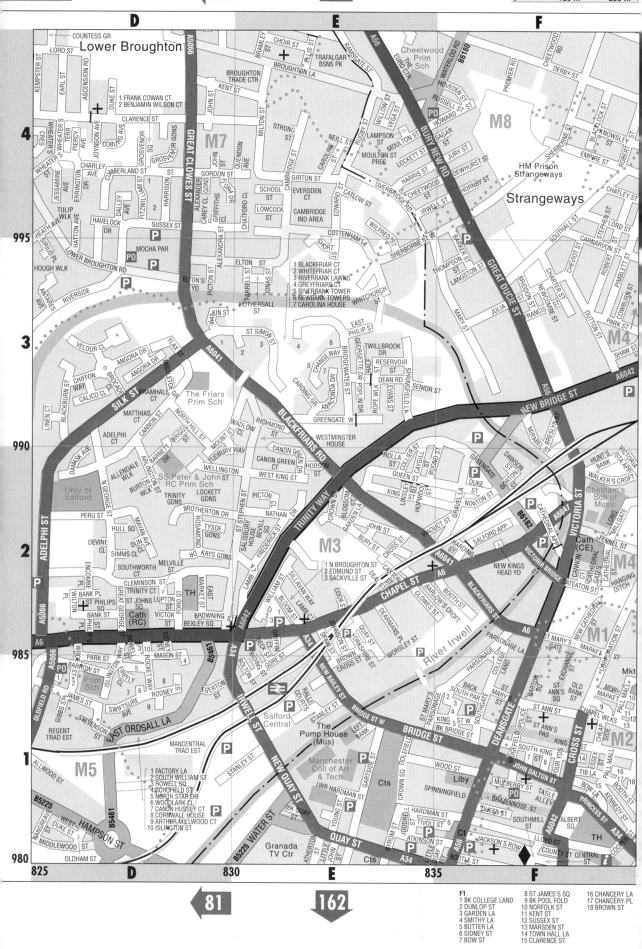

Scale: 7 inches to 1 mile
0   110 yards   220 yards
0   125 m   250 m

D   E   F

COUNTESS GR
Lower Broughton
M7
M8
Strangeways
HM Prison
Strangeways
Cheetwood
Prim Sch

4

995

3

The Friars
Prim Sch

990

Univ of
Salford
M3

2

Cath
(RC)

985

M5

1

M1

M4

River Irwell

Chapel St

Deansgate

Salford
Central

The
Pump House
(Mus)

Manchester
Coll of Art
& Tech

Granada
TV Ctr

Chetham's
Sch of Music
Cath
(CE)

M2

980

825   830   835

1 BLACKFRIAR CT
2 WHITEFRIAR CT
3 RIVERBANK LAWNS
4 GREYFRIARS CT
5 RIVERBANK TOWER
6 NEWBANK TOWERS
7 CAROLINA HOUSE

1 FRANK COWAN CT
2 BENJAMIN WILSON CT

1 N BROUGHTON ST
2 EDMUND ST
3 SACKVILLE ST

1 FACTORY LA
2 SOUTH WILLIAM ST
3 ROWELL SQ
4 SCHOFIELD ST
5 NORTH STAR DR
6 WOODLARK CL
7 CANON HUSSEY CT
8 CORNWALL HOUSE
9 ARTHUR MILLWOOD CT
10 ISLINGTON CT

F1
1 BK COLLEGE LAND
2 DUNLOP ST
3 GARDEN LA
4 SMITHY LA
5 BUTTER LA
6 SIDNEY ST
7 BOW ST
8 ST JAMES'S SQ
9 BK POOL FOLD
10 NORFOLK ST
11 KENT ST
12 SUSSEX ST
13 MARSDEN ST
14 TOWN HALL LA
15 CLARENCE ST
16 CHANCERY LA
17 CHANCERY PL
18 BROWN ST

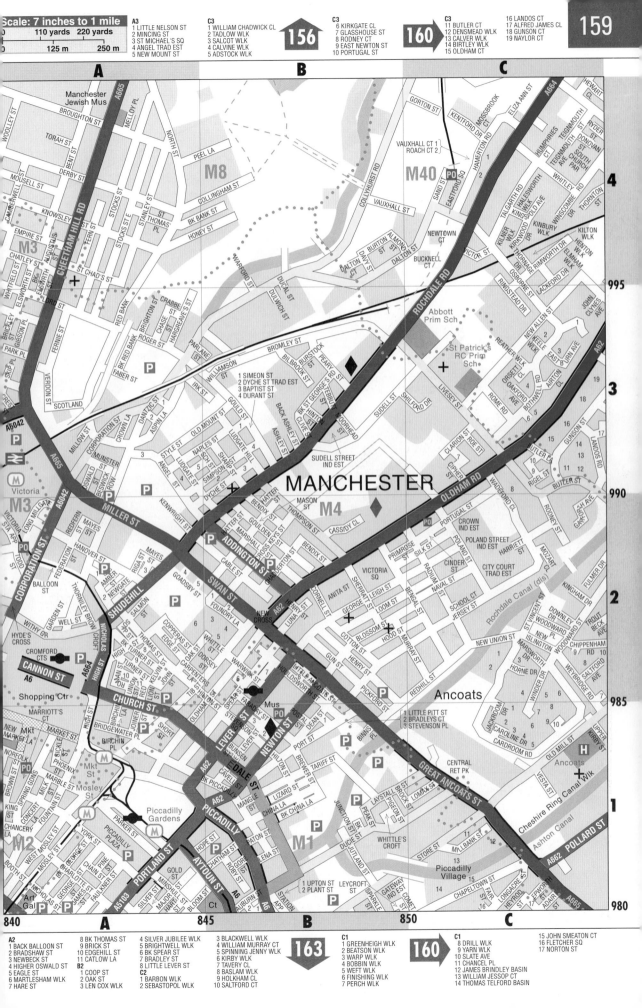

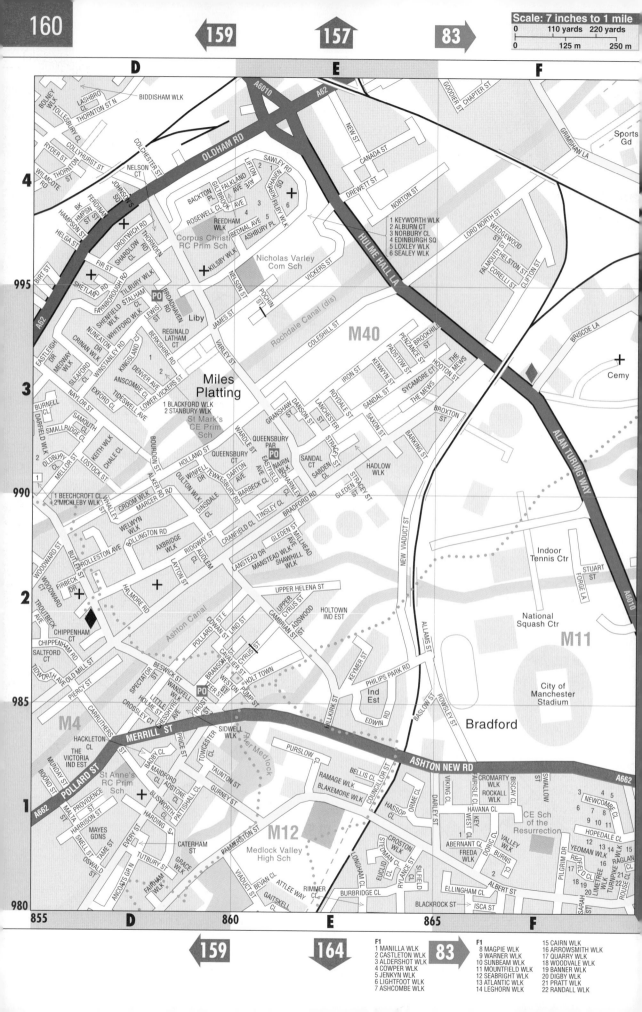

D | E | F

8

M5
ORDSALL LA
B5461
River Irwell
M5
WATER ST
PRINCE'S BRIDGE
B5225
TV Ctr
Mus of Science & Ind
CORONATION ST
OLD MEDLOCK ST
LIVERPOOL RD
Mus
Castlefield Visitor Ctr
RICE ST
GREAT JOHN ST
Ct
ARTILLERY ST
A34
LOWER BYROM ST
ST JOHN ST
CAMP ST
DEANSGATE
A56
PETER ST
St Peter's Sq
TH
Liby
M
MARRON PL
MUSEUM ST
WINDMILL ST
M2
BOOTLE ST
BISHOPS GATE
OXFORD ST
A5103
A34

REGENT RD
A57 A6143
DAWSON ST
NEW ELM RD
POTATO WHARF
M3
WORSLEY ST
A6143
BRIDGEWATER ST
BEAUFORT ST
COLLIER ST
SOUTHERN ST
BYROM ST
City Centre
GMex
Great Bridgewater St
The Bridgewater Hall
ALBION ST
CHEPSTOW ST
MILLING
M1

975
DERWENT IND AREA
D7
1 MEDLOCK HO
2 IRWELL HO
3 EGERTON HO
4 BLANTYRE HO
SLATE WHARF
CASTLE ST
Deansgate
B6469
WHITWORTH ST W
M
TRUMPET ST
Rochdale Canal
M1
B6469
HEWITT ST
LITTLE PETER ST

7
HULME HALL RD
ELLESMERE ST
CATFIELD WLK 5
BRAMFIELD WLK 6
KIMBERLEY WLK 7
WESTCOTT CT 8
THOMAS CT 9
ST GEORGES CT 10
Cheshire Ring Canal Wlk
WORSLEY ST
BALMFORTH ST
ARUNDEL ST
EGERTON ST
A57(M)
BLANTYRE ST
CHESTER RD
A5067
Bridgewater Canal
Bridgewater Viaduct
DEANSGATE
COMMERCIAL ST
JORDAN ST
River Medlock
GILBERT ST 1
CONSTANCE ST 2
ALPHA PL 3
RIVERSIDE MEWS 4
SILVERCROFT ST
GREAT JACKSON ST
CITY RD E
MEDLOCK ST
HULME ST
NEWCASTLE ST
CHESTER ST
Univ
F7
1 GLOUCESTER ST
2 EBENEZER ST
3 NEWCASTLE ST
4 VALERIE WLK
5 CONMERE SQ
A5103

St George's
CLEWORTH WLK
HUME HALL RD
ANNE ST
NUTTALL ST
BRACKLEY AVE
ST GEORGE'S AVE
BARRACK ST
LOWER MOSS LA
KELLING WLK
ANGELA ST
GALGATE CL
MANCUNIAN WAY
HUME ST
BRANN ST
REDHEAD ST
Chevassut Prim Sch
YORK ST
BENTLEY HO
HUMBERSTONE AVE
CLARENDON ST
NEW WELCOME ST
Mancunian Way
CLARENDON ST
LOXFORD CT
LOXFORD ST
A57(M)

970
MALT ST
NANCY ST
MANSON AVE
TATTON ST
ST BROTHERTON CL
QUENBY ST
LANGHOLME CL
STONALL AVE
LEDBURN ST
LEDBURN CT
LORDSMEAD ST
St Wilfrid's RC Prim Sch
ST WILFRIDS ST
SORREL ST
CHEVASSUT ST
MARY FRANCE ST
ELIZA ST
M15
FENN ST
DEARDEN ST
CLAYBURN RD
REILLY ST
DAINTY ST
RASTLE ST
STONELOW CL
EPPING ST
Hulme
BONSALL ST
UPPER MEDLOCK ST

6
PRINCESS CT
CORNBROOK
PO
PK
WELLAND CL
BROWNING ST
CITY RD
SOUTHEND AVE
GRENHAM AVE
NORTHDOWN AVE
SHAWHEATH CL
MOSSHALL CL
9 10
11 12
13 15 16
14 19 20
17 18
21 22 23 24
SHAWGREEN CL
25
26
CHORLTON RD
B5218
UPPER MOSS LA
HORNCHURCH ST
RIBSTON ST
OLD YORK ST
MALLOW ST
ST NICHOLAS RD
STRETFORD RD
Liby
JOHN NASH CRES
ELLIS ST
ORMSGILL CL
POYNTON ST

St Alphonsus RC Prim Sch
VIRGIL ST
LUCY ST
PERCY ST
WEAVER ST
DEAN ST
TRENT CT
WHITE ST
ERSKINE ST
YEW ST
ROYCE RD
WARDE ST
ANCROFT ST
WIZ
John Nash Cres
WARWICK ST
Royce Prim Sch
WILBERFORCE ST
CHESTER RD S
LINGMOOR WLK 1
WASNIDGE WLK 2
OCEAN WLK 3
RAKEHEAD WLK 4
PEATFIELD WLK 5
GREENTHORN WLK 6
BROWNBANK WLK 7
HEBDEN WLK 8
CROWBOROUGH WLK 9
CARVER WLK 10
CAREY WLK 11

965
A5067
TRAFFORD PL
JOHNSON ST
Schs
ESSEX WAY
HYDE ST
HAMILTON ST
CORNBROOK GR
CORNBROOK ST
SCHOOL WLK
CARRIAGE DR
M16
GLOBE CL
CORNBROOK WAY
OXFORD CT
ETON CT
GRAFTON CT
MILLHALL CL
CULMINGTON CL
ELVERDON CL
AVENHAM CL
WINCHAM CL
ABBEYVILLE WLK
RAWKIN CL
CARIB ST
ROLLS CRES
SHEARSBY CL
DENBIGH WLK 1
ALLIOTT WLK 2
WHITEACRE WLK 3
ALANBROOKE WLK 4
ACADEMY WLK 5
WEIR ST
SAM SWIRE ST
HODGATE WLK
Loreto Coll
CARIB ST
GREENHEYS LA W
OLD BIRLEY ST
MYTTON ST
BOSTON ST
Superstore
GREENHEYS LA
ARNOTT CRES
BOTHAM CL
CREDITON CL
WELLHEAD
A5103

5
P
Liby
STAMFORD ST
BELMONT ST
GORDON ST
FAREHAM CT
HAMILTON ST
1 HAMILTON GR
2 CLIFTON GR
RUSHMERE WLK
HIGHMEAD WLK
KERNAN CL
CROSS ST
BLAIR ST
CLIFTON ST
ST BRIDES WAY
DUKE ST
WHITCHURCH DR
MALPAS ST
SHREWSBURY ST
CLIFTON ST
B5218
CLIFFORD ST
TAMWORTH ST
TRAFALGAR GDNS
BOLD ST
DUDLEY CL
RAVEN CT
PICKFORD CT
OSPREY CL
EAGLE CT
FALCON CT
OSPREY CT
MAYER GDNS
CHICHESTER RD S
ST MARY'S RD
PARSONAGE
HERON ST
BLANCHARD ST
ROOK ST
PEREGRINE ST
DENHILL RD
L Ctr

960
825 | D | 830 | E | 835 | F

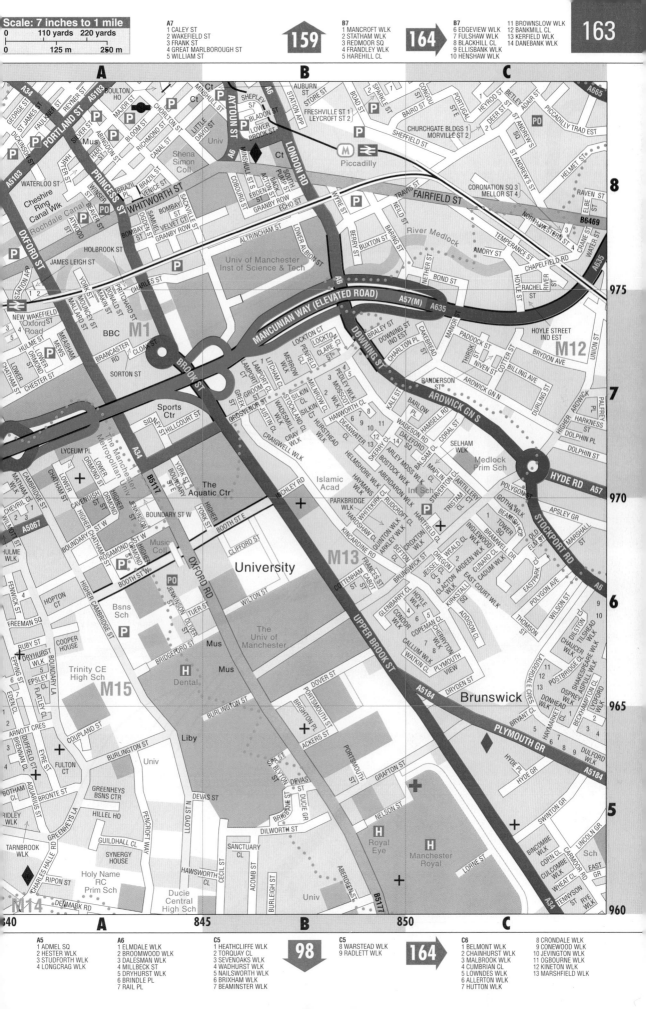

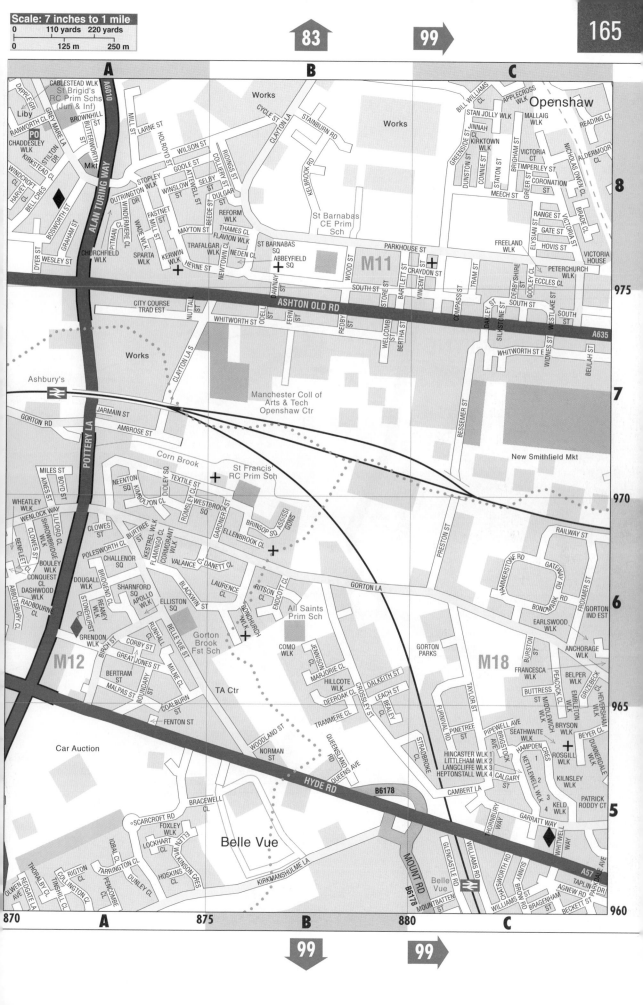

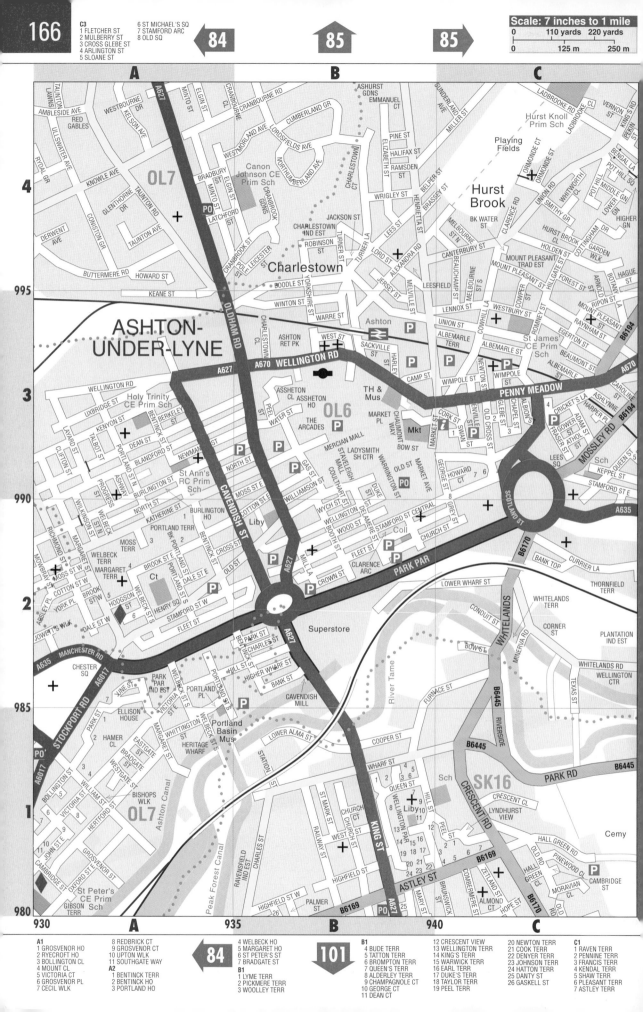

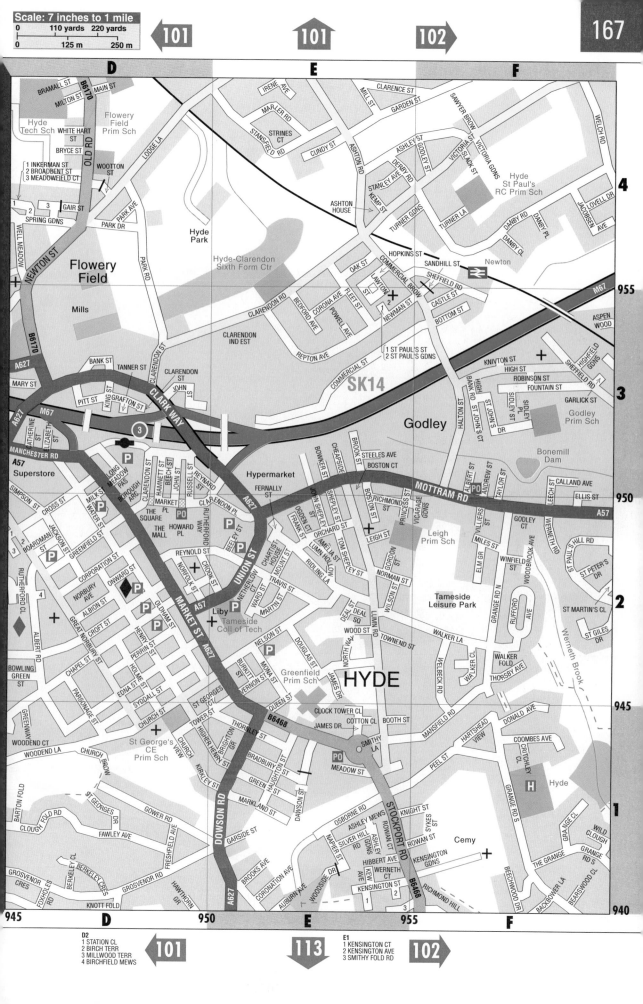

Scale: 7 inches to 1 mile
0   110 yards 220 yards
0   125 m   250 m

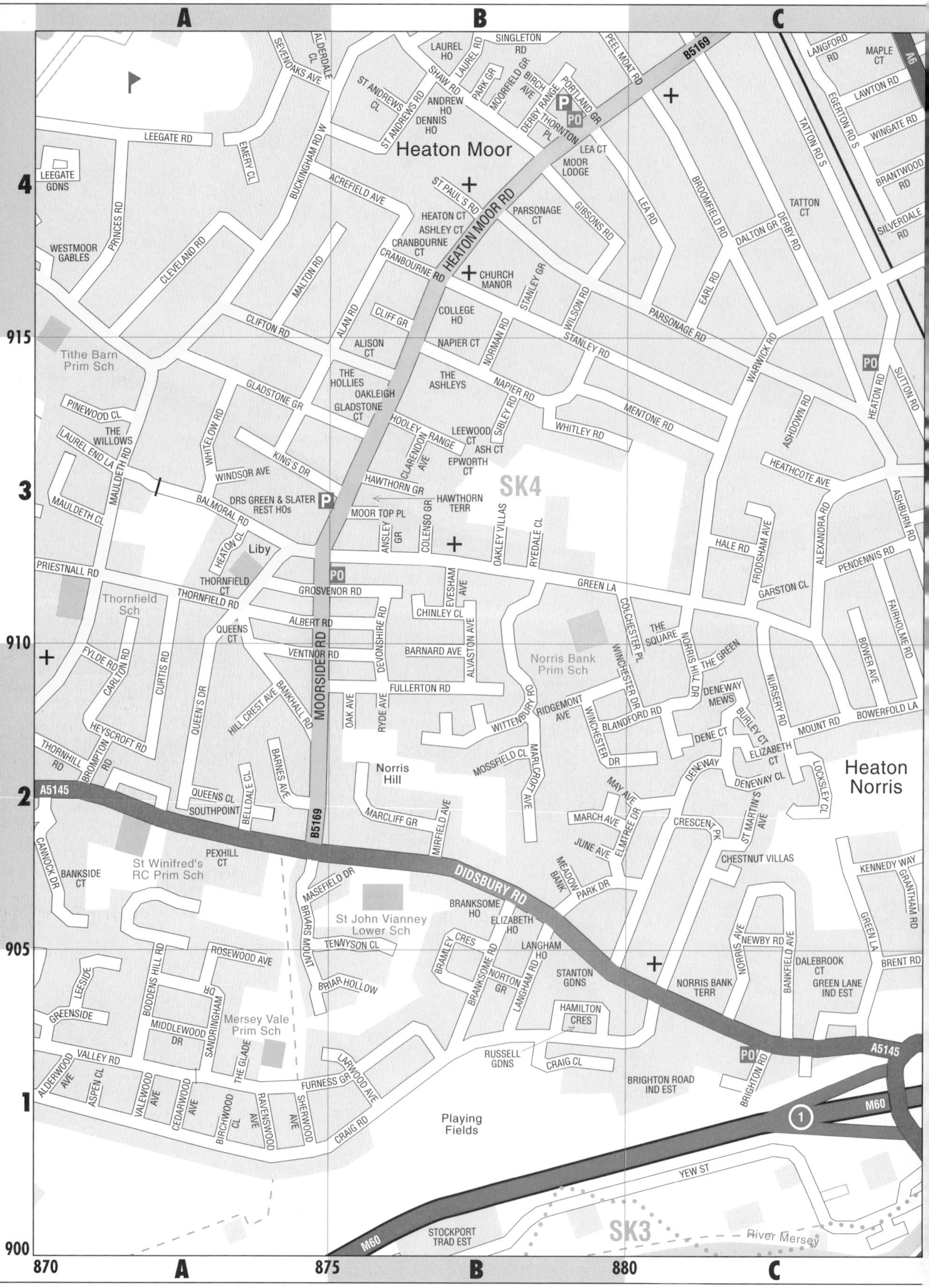

A   B   C

Heaton Moor

SK4

SK3

Heaton Norris

Norris Hill

Tithe Barn Prim Sch

Thornfield Sch

St Winifred's RC Prim Sch

St John Vianney Lower Sch

Mersey Vale Prim Sch

Norris Bank Prim Sch

Playing Fields

River Mersey

M60

A5145

B5169

DIDSBURY RD

MOORSIDE RD

HEATON MOOR RD

Westmoor Gables

Leegate Gdns

Leegate Rd

Sevenoaks Ave

Aldedale Cl

Princes Rd

Cleveland Rd

Clifton Rd

Malton Rd

Alan Rd

Emery Cl

Acrefield Ave

St Andrews Rd

Buckingham Rd W

Shaw Rd

Laurel Ho

Park Gr

Laurel Rd

Singleton Rd

Moorfield Gr

Birch Ave

Derby Range

Portland Gr

Peel Moat Rd

B5169

Langford Rd

Maple Ct

Egerton Rd S

Lawton Rd

Wingate Rd

Brantwood Rd

Silverdale Rd

Tatton Ct

Broomfield Rd

Dalton Rd

Derby Rd

Earl Rd

Parsonage Rd

Warwick Rd

Ashdown Rd

Heaton Rd

Sutton Rd

Alexandra Rd

Heathcote Ave

Garston Cl

Frodsham Rd

Hale Rd

Pendennis Rd

Ashburn Rd

Fairholme Rd

Bower Ave

Bowerfold Ave

Mount Rd

St Paul's Rd

Heaton Ct

Ashley Ct

Cranbourne Ct

Cranbourne Rd

Cliff Gr

College Ho

Alison Ct

Napier Ct

Church Manor

Parsonage Ct

Stanley Gr

Gibsons Rd

Lea Ct

Moor Lodge

Lea Rd

Portland Pl

Thornton Pl

Andrew Ho

Dennis Ho

The Hollies

Oakleigh

Gladstone Ct

The Ashleys

Napier Rd

Sibley Rd

Norman Rd

Stanley Rd

Wilson Rd

Mentone Rd

Whitley Rd

Pinewood Cl

The Willows

Laurel End La

Mauldeth Rd

Whitelow Rd

Gladstone Gr

King's Dr

Windsor Ave

Hooley Range

Clarendon Ave

Leewood Ct

Ash Ct

Epworth Ct

The Ashleys

Hawthorn Gr

Hawthorn Terr

Colenso Gr

Ansley Gr

Oakley Villas

Ryedale Cl

Green La

Priestnall Rd

Mauldeth Cl

Balmoral Rd

Heaton Ct

Liby

Thornfield Ct

Thornfield Rd

DRS Green & Slater Rest Hos

Moor Top Pl

Evesham Ave

Chinley Cl

The Square

Colchester Pl

Winchester Dr

Norris Hill Dr

The Green

Deneway Mews

Burley Ct

Nursery Rd

Fylde Rd

Carlton Rd

Queens Ct

Grosvenor Rd

Albert Rd

Ventnor Rd

Devonshire Rd

Barnard Ave

Alvaston Ave

Fullerton Rd

Ridgemont Ave

Blandford Rd

Dene Ct

Deneway

Elizabeth Ct

Curtis Rd

Queen's Dr

Hill Crest Ave

Bankhall Rd

Oak Ave

Ryde Ave

Mossfield Cl

Wittenbury Rd

Winchester Dr

Deneway Cl

Heyscroft Rd

Thornhill Rd

Brompton Rd

Barnes Ave

Belldale Cl

Norris Hill

Marcliff Gr

Marlcroft Ave

Guy Way

May Ave

Elmtree Dr

March Ave

St Martin's Ave

Crescent Pk

Cooksey Cl

Cannock Dr

Queens Cl

Southpoint

Pexhill Ct

Mirfield Ave

June Ave

Meadow Bank

Park Dr

Chestnut Villas

Bankside Ct

Masefield Dr

Briars Mount

Branksome Ho

Elizabeth Ho

Langham Ho

Stanton Gdns

Kennedy Way

Grantham Rd

Green La

Brent Rd

Rosewood Ave

Tennyson Cl

Bramley Cres

Branksome Rd

Norton Gr

Langham Rd

Hamilton Cres

Newby Rd

Norris Ave

Dalebrook Ct

Green Lane Ind Est

Briar Hollow

Russell Gdns

Craig Cl

Norris Bank Terr

Bankfield Ct

Greenside

Leeside

Boddens Hill Rd

Middlewood Dr

Sandringham Dr

The Glade

Furness Gr

Larwood Ave

Sherwood Ave

Craig Rd

Brighton Road Ind Est

Brighton Rd

Alderwood Ave

Aspen Cl

Valewood Ave

Cedarwood Ave

Birchwood Cl

Ravenswood

Valley Rd

Stockport Trad Est

Yew St

900
905
910
915

1
2
3
4

123
E8
1 CHATHAM HO
2 BOWDON HO
3 PEMBROKE HO
4 PALATINE HO

169
E8
5 LANCASTER HO
6 DURHAM HO
7 FRANCES ST

124
F8
1 LOONIES CT
2 JOULES CT
3 OLD GARDENS ST
4 HOLLINGWORTH CL

5 MOTTRAM ST
6 RATCLIFFE ST
7 GROSVENOR ST

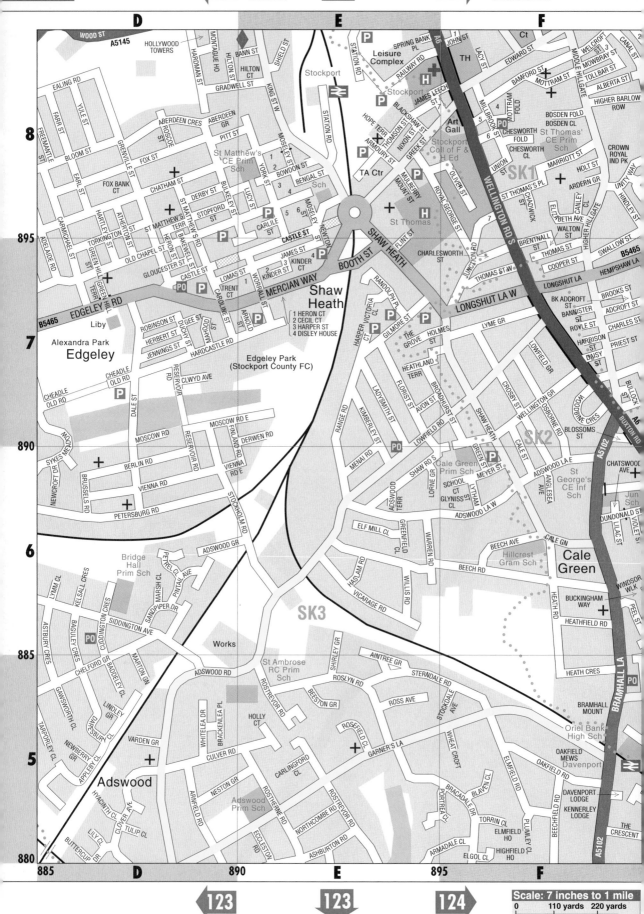

123   123   124

Scale: 7 inches to 1 mile
0   110 yards   220 yards
0   125 m   250 m

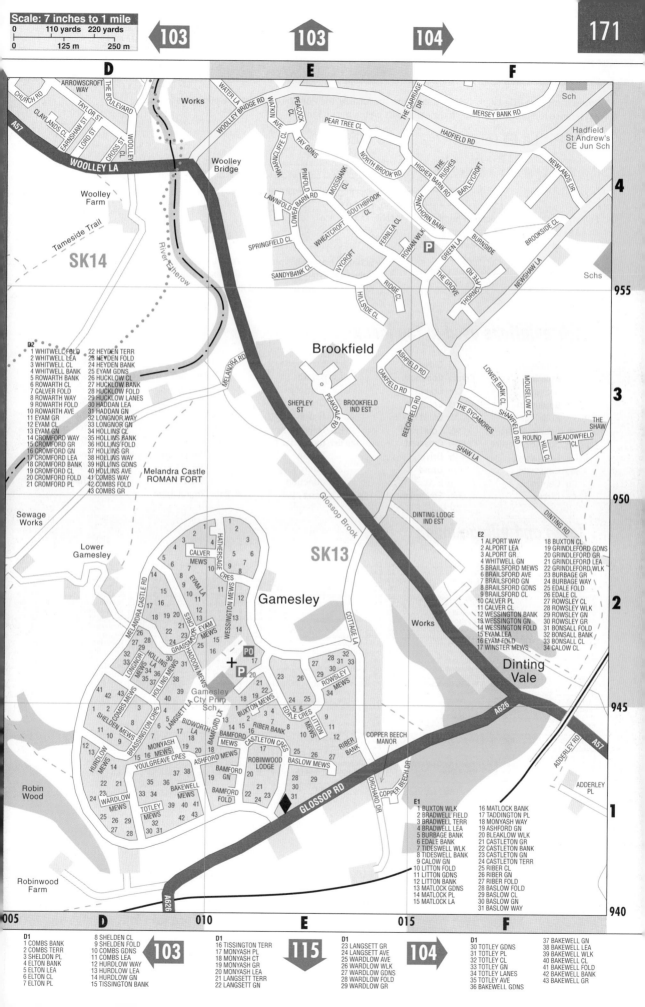

D2
1 WHITWELL FOLD
2 WHITWELL LEA
3 WHITWELL CL
4 WHITWELL BANK
5 ROWARTH BANK
6 ROWARTH CL
7 CALVER FOLD
8 ROWARTH WAY
9 ROWARTH FOLD
10 ROWARTH AVE
11 EYAM GR
12 EYAM CL
13 EYAM GN
14 CROMFORD WAY
15 CROMFORD GR
16 CROMFORD GN
17 CROMFORD LEA
18 CROMFORD BANK
19 CROMFORD CL
20 CROMFORD FOLD
21 CROMFORD PL
22 HEYDEN TERR
23 HEYDEN FOLD
24 HEYDEN BANK
25 EYAM GDNS
26 HUCKLOW CL
27 HUCKLOW BANK
28 HUCKLOW FOLD
29 HUCKLOW LANES
30 HADDAN LEA
31 HADDAN GN
32 LONGNOR WAY
33 LONGNOR GN
34 HOLLINS CL
35 HOLLINS BANK
36 HOLLINS FOLD
37 HOLLINS GR
38 HOLLINS WAY
39 HOLLINS GDNS
40 HOLLINS AVE
41 COMBS WAY
42 COMBS FOLD
43 COMBS GR

E2
1 ALPORT WAY
2 ALPORT LEA
3 ALPORT GR
4 WHITWELL GN
5 BRAILSFORD MEWS
6 BRAILSFORD AVE
7 BRAILSFORD GN
8 BRAILSFORD GDNS
9 BRAILSFORD CL
10 CALVER PL
11 CALVER CL
12 WESSINGTON BANK
13 WESSINGTON GN
14 WESSINGTON FOLD
15 EYAM LEA
16 EYAM FOLD
17 WINSTER MEWS
18 BUXTON CL
19 GRINDLEFORD GDNS
20 GRINDLEFORD GR
21 GRINDLEFORD LEA
22 GRINDLEFORD WLK
23 BURBAGE GR
24 BURBAGE WAY
25 EDALE FOLD
26 EDALE CL
27 ROWSLEY CL
28 ROWSLEY WLK
29 ROWSLEY GN
30 ROWSLEY GR
31 BONSALL FOLD
32 BONSALL BANK
33 BONSALL CL
34 CALOW CL

E1
1 BUXTON WLK
2 BRADWELL FIELD
3 BRADWELL TERR
4 BRADWELL LEA
5 BURBAGE BANK
6 EDALE BANK
7 TIDESWELL WLK
8 TIDESWELL BANK
9 CALOW GN
10 LITTON FOLD
11 LITTON GDNS
12 LITTON BANK
13 MATLOCK GDNS
14 MATLOCK PL
15 MATLOCK LA
16 MATLOCK BANK
17 TADDINGTON PL
18 MONYASH WAY
19 ASHFORD GN
20 BLEAKLOW WLK
21 CASTLETON GR
22 CASTLETON BANK
23 CASTLETON GN
24 CASTLETON TERR
25 RIBER CL
26 RIBER GN
27 RIBER FOLD
28 BASLOW FOLD
29 BASLOW CL
30 BASLOW GN
31 BASLOW WAY

D1
1 COMBS BANK
2 COMBS TERR
3 SHELDON PL
4 ELTON BANK
5 ELTON LEA
6 ELTON CL
7 ELTON PL
8 SHELDEN CL
9 SHELDEN FOLD
10 COMBS GDNS
11 COMBS LEA
12 HURDLOW WAY
13 HURDLOW LEA
14 HURDLOW GN
15 TISSINGTON BANK

D1
16 TISSINGTON TERR
17 MONYASH PL
18 MONYASH CT
19 MONYASH GR
20 MONYASH LEA
21 LANGSETT TERR
22 LANGSETT GN

D1
23 LANGSETT GR
24 LANGSETT AVE
25 WARDLOW GN
26 WARDLOW WLK
27 WARDLOW GDNS
28 WARDLOW FOLD
29 WARDLOW GR

D1
30 TOTLEY GDNS
31 TOTLEY PL
32 TOTLEY CL
33 TOTLEY GN
34 TOTLEY LANES
35 TOTLEY AVE
36 BAKEWELL GDNS
37 BAKEWELL GN
38 BAKEWELL LEA
39 BAKEWELL WLK
40 BAKEWELL CL
41 BAKEWELL FOLD
42 BAKEWELL BANK
43 BAKEWELL GR

Index

Street names are listed alphabetically and show the locality, the Postcode District, the page number and a reference to the square in which the name falls on the map page

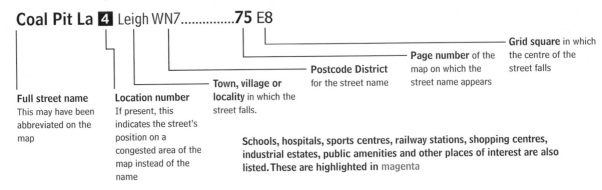

Coal Pit La **4** Leigh WN7..............**75 E8**

- **Full street name**
  This may have been abbreviated on the map
- **Location number**
  If present, this indicates the street's position on a congested area of the map instead of the name
- **Town, village or locality** in which the street falls.
- **Postcode District** for the street name
- **Page number** of the map on which the street name appears
- **Grid square** in which the centre of the street falls

Schools, hospitals, sports centres, railway stations, shopping centres, industrial estates, public amenities and other places of interest are also listed. These are highlighted in magenta

Abbreviations used in the index

App **Approach**	Cl **Close**	Espl **Esplanade**	N **North**	S **South**
Arc **Arcade**	Comm **Common**	Est **Estate**	Orch **Orchard**	Sq **Square**
Ave **Avenue**	Cnr **Corner**	Gdns **Gardens**	Par **Parade**	Strs **Stairs**
Bvd **Boulevard**	Cotts **Cottages**	Gn **Green**	Pk **Park**	Stps **Steps**
Bldgs **Buildings**	Ct **Court**	Gr **Grove**	Pas **Passage**	St **Street, Saint**
Bsns Pk **Business Park**	Ctyd **Courtyard**	Hts **Heights**	Pl **Place**	Terr **Terrace**
Bsns Ctr **Business Centre**	Cres **Crescent**	Ind Est **Industrial**	Prec **Precinct**	Trad **Trading Est**
Bglws **Bungalows**	Dr **Drive**	**Estate**	Prom **Promenade**	Wlk **Walk**
Cswy **Causeway**	Dro **Drove**	Intc **Interchange**	Ret Pk **Retail Park**	W **West**
Ctr **Centre**	E **East**	Junc **Junction**	Rd **Road**	Yd **Yard**
Cir **Circus**	Emb **Embankment**	La **Lane**	Rdbt **Roundabout**	

Town and village index

Abram Brow 74 B7	Culcheth 91 E3	Heywood 29 E2	Oldham 66 E7	Tintwistle 104 A7
Adlington 21 A7	Delph 50 E4	High Lane 134 D8	Orrell 53 E7	Tyldesley 59 B1
Ainsworth 26 B1	Denshaw 33 D2	Hindley 56 D6	Partington 105 F4	Uppermill 69 A8
Alderley Edge 136 C2	Denton 100 D3	Hollinfare 105 A3	Pendlebury 80 C8	Urmston 95 C1
Altrincham 118 C5	Diggle 51 C4	Hollingworth 103 E5	Pennington Green ...38 E1	Walkden 60 D4
Appley Bridge 35 D8	Disley 135 C5	Horwich 22 D4	Platt Bridge 56 A2	Walsden 6 B8
Ashley 128 E5	Downall Green 72 C5	Hyde 101 E2	Poynton 133 E4	Westhoughton 57 C8
Ashton-in-Makerfield ..73 C5	Droylsden 84 B3	Ince-in-Makerfield ...55 E7	Prestwich 63 A4	Whitefield 62 C8
Ashton-under-Lyne ...85 A4	Dukinfield 101 D7	Irlam 105 F7	Radcliffe 44 C3	Whitworth 4 D1
Aspull 38 C6	Eccles 79 E1	Kearsley 61 A7	Ramsbottom 11 B5	Wigan 55 B8
Atherton 58 E2	Edenfield 1 D3	Leigh 75 E6	Rawtenstall 2 E8	Wilmslow 137 C5
Bacup 3 E8	Edgworth 9 D6	Little Bollington ...118 B2	Reddish 111 D8	Windy Arbour 72 B8
Bickershaw 74 F8	Failsworth 83 F6	Little Lever 43 B4	Rochdale 30 D7	Woodford 132 E2
Billinge 71 E4	Farnworth 60 A7	Littleborough 16 B5	Romiley 113 D2	Worsley 78 E6
Blackrod 21 D2	Flixton 94 E2	Longshaw 25 E1	Rowarth 127 E7	Wrightington Bar 18 F7
Bolton 41 E8	Fowley Common 92 B5	Lymm 117 A3	Royton 48 E4	Wythenshawe 121 C5
Boothstown 78 A5	Gamesley 171 E2	Manchester 82 C2	Sale 108 C4	
Bramhall 132 D8	Garswood 72 C3	Marple 125 D5	Salford 81 A2	
Bredbury 112 E4	Gatley 122 A4	Middleton 65 B8	Shaw 49 B7	
Brinnington 112 C5	Glazebury 92 B7	Milnrow 31 E4	Shevington 36 B5	
Broomedge 117 C1	Glossop 104 B1	Moorend 127 A6	Shevington Moor 19 A2	
Bury 27 E3	Golborne 90 B8	Mossley 68 C1	Stalybridge 86 B3	
Carrington 106 D6	Hadfield 104 B5	Mottram-in-	Standish 19 F2	
Chadderton 65 F8	Handforth 131 C4	Longdendale 103 A4	Stockport 111 D1	
Charlesworth 115 C6	Haslingden 1 A6	New Mills 127 D2	Stretford 96 C2	
Cheadle 122 E5	Hattersley 102 E2	Newhey 32 B4	Styal 130 F4	
Coppull 19 E8	Hazel Grove 124 E2	Newton-le-Willows ...89 B2	Swinton 79 F8	

1st–Alb 173

1
1st St WN2 73 E7

3
3rd St WN2 73 E7

4
4th St WN2 73 F7

'
'a' Ct WN4 73 B2

A
Abberley Dr M40 65 D2
Abberley Way WN3 54 B4
Abberton Rd M20 110 A6
Abbey Cl Altrincham WA14 119 B1
Mottram-in-L SK14 102 F3
Orrell WN8 53 C7
Radcliffe M26 43 E5
Urmston M32 95 F3
Abbey Cres OL10 29 B4
Abbey Ct Manchester M18 99 E6
Radcliffe M26 43 E4
Wigan WN5 36 E2
Abbey Dale WN6 35 D7
Abbey Dr Bury BL8 27 A1
Littleborough OL15 15 F3
Orrell WN5 53 E6
Swinton M27 61 E1
Abbey Gdns SK14 103 A3
Abbey Gr Adlington PR6 21 B7
Eccles M30 79 E2
Mottram-in-L SK14 102 F3
Oldham OL9 152 A5
Stockport SK1 124 B8
Abbey Hey Inf
& Jun Schs M18 99 E5
Abbey Hey La M11,M18 99 F6
Abbey Hills Rd OL4,OL8 67 C4
Abbey La WN7 57 D1
Abbey Lawn M16 97 B3
Abbey Rd Cheadle SK8 123 A5
Delph OL3 50 E5
Droylsden M43 83 F3
Failsworth M35 84 B8
Golborne WA3 91 C8
Middleton M24 46 F4
Sale M33 108 A6
Tyldesley M29 77 C7
Abbey Sq WN7 57 D1
Abbey St WN7 75 F6
Abbey Way M26 44 A3
Abbeycourt M30 79 E2
Abbeydale 26 OL12 139 E8
Abbeydale Cl OL6 85 E6
Abbeydale Gdns M28 60 C3
Abbeyfield Sq M11 165 B8
Abbeyfields WN6 36 E2
Abbeyville Wlk M15 162 E5
Abbeyway N WA11 89 A7
Abbeyway S WA11 89 A7
Abbeywood Ave M18 99 E4
Abbingdon Way WN7 57 D1
Abbot Croft BL5 57 F6
Abbot's Fold Rd M28 78 B7
Abbots Cl M33 108 D5
Abbots Ct M33 108 D5
Abbotsbury Cl
Manchester M12 165 A6
Poynton SK12 133 D5
Abbotsfield Cl M41 94 D3
Abbotsford Cl WA3 74 D1
Abbotsford Dr M24 46 D4
Abbotsford Gr WA14 119 E8
Abbotsford Prep Sch M41 95 A2
Abbotsford Rd Bolton BL1 142 A1
Chadderton OL9 65 E8
Manchester M21 97 B1
Oldham OL1 49 B1
Abbotside Cl M16 97 D3
Abbotsleigh Dr SK7 123 F2
Abbott Prim Sch M40 159 C3
Abbott St Bolton BL3 145 E5
Hindley WN2 56 C6
14 Horwich BL6 22 B4
Rochdale OL11 30 B3
Abbotts Gn M29 77 A4
Abbotts Way WN5 71 D3
Abden St M26 44 A3
Abels La OL3 69 C8
Aber Ave SK2 124 C4
Aber Rd SK8 123 A6
Abercarn Cl M8 156 A7
Abercorn Rd BL1 142 B4
Abercorn St 7 OL4 67 D6
Abercrombie Ct M33 108 D5
Aberdare Wlk 4 M9 64 E5
Aberdaron Wlk M13 163 B7
Aberdeen 1 M30 79 E2
Aberdeen Cres SK3 170 D8
Aberdeen Gdns OL12 14 D4
Aberdeen Gr SK3 170 D8
Aberdeen St M13,M15 163 B5
Aberford Rd M23 121 A5
Abergele Rd M14 110 E8
Abergele St SK2 124 A5
Aberley Fold OL15 15 F7
Abernant Cl M11 160 F1
Abernethy St BL6 22 D2
Abersoch Ave M14 110 E8
Abingdon Ave M45 44 F2
Abingdon Cl Oldham OL9 66 B4
Rochdale OL11 139 E5
Whitefield M45 44 F2
Abingdon Prim Sch SK5 111 F7
Abingdon Rd Bolton BL2 25 E6
Reddish SK5 111 F7
Stockport SK7 123 E3
Urmston M41 95 E3
Abingdon St
Ashton-u-L OL6 85 D2
Manchester M1 163 A8
Abinger Rd WN4 72 D4
Abinger Wlk M40 83 D4
Abington Dr WN2 56 A1
Abington Rd M33 108 C3
Abney Grange OL5 86 E8
Abney Rd Mossley OL5 86 C8
Reddish SK4 111 C5
Aboukir St OL16 31 B8
Abraham Guest High Sch
WN5 54 A6
Abraham St 11 BL6 22 B4
Abram Bryn Gates
Prim Sch WN2 73 F7
Abram CE Prim Sch WN2 56 B1
Abram Cl M14 98 A1
Abram St M6 80 F6
Absalom Dr M8 155 F8
Acacia Ave
Altrincham WA15 119 F3
Cheadle SK8 123 A1
Denton M34 101 A3
Swinton M27 79 E6
Wilmslow SK9 136 F5
Acacia Cres WN6 36 F3
Acacia Dr
Altrincham WA15 119 F3
Salford M6 80 B3
Acacia Gr SK5 169 F4
Acacia Rd OL8 66 D1
Acacias Prim Sch M19 110 F7
Academy Wlk M15 162 E5
Acer Cl Hyde SK14 102 A2
Rochdale OL11 13 D1
Acer Gr M7 155 D7
Acheson St 3 M18 99 D5
Ack La E SK7 132 D7
Ack La W SK7,SK8 132 C7
Ackers La M31 106 F6
Ackers St M13 163 B5
Ackersley Ct SK8 132 B8
Ackhurst La WN5 36 A2
Ackroyd Ave M18 99 F6
Ackroyd St M11 99 E7
Ackworth Dr M23 121 A6
Ackworth Rd M27 61 E1
Acme Dr M27 80 B8
Acomb St Manchester M14 98 B4
Manchester M15 163 B5
Acorn Ave Cheadle SK8 122 E5
Hyde SK14 113 E8
Acorn Bsns Ctr SK4 169 D1
Acorn Cl Leigh WN7 75 F3
Manchester M19 110 F8
Whitefield M45 62 F6
Acorn Ctr OL1 67 B8
Acorn St
Newton-le-W WA12 89 D3
Oldham OL4 67 E6
Acorn Way OL1 153 E7
Acre Ave OL13 3 D8
Acre Barn OL2 48 E8
Acre Cl BL0 1 D3
Acre Field BL2 25 D4
Acre La Bramhall SK7,SK8 132 C6
Oldham OL1 49 A1
Acre Mill Rd OL13 3 D8
Acre St Denton M34 100 E3
Glossop SK13 116 C7
Oldham OL9 66 B2
Radcliffe M26 43 E3
Romiley SK6 113 B2
Whitworth OL12 4 D1
Acre Top Rd M9 64 B5
Acre View OL13 3 D7
Acrefield M33 108 A3
Acrefield Ave
Manchester SK4 168 B4
Urmston M41 95 F1
Acregate M41 95 A2
Acres Ct M22 121 D4
Acres La SK15 86 B1
Acres Rd Gatley SK8 122 A5
Manchester M21 109 B8
Acres St BL8 26 F5
Acresbrook SK15 102 C7
Acresbrook Wlk BL8 26 F5
Acresdale BL6 40 C7
Acresfield Adlington PR7 20 F6
Tyldesley M29 77 C7
Acresfield Ave M34 84 C1
Acresfield Cl Blackrod BL6 21 C3
Pendlebury M27 80 A6
Acresfield Rd
Dukinfield SK14 101 F5
Middleton M24 47 C3
Sale WA15 120 A8
Salford M6 80 D5
Walkden M38 60 B4
Acreswood Cl PR7 19 E8
Acreville Gr WA3 92 C7
Acton Ave M40 83 B4
Acton Ho WN1 151 D8
Acton Sq M5 81 B2
Acton St Oldham OL1 67 B8
Rochdale OL12 15 A1
Wigan WN1 37 C1
Acton Terr WN1 37 C1
Acton's Walk Trad Ctr
WN3 150 C7
Ada St Manchester M9 64 D1
Ramsbottom BL0 138 B5
Rochdale OL12 15 A2
Adair St Manchester M1 159 C1
Manchester M1 163 C8
Rochdale OL11 30 B2
Adam Cl SK8 123 B4
Adam St Ashton-u-L OL6 166 C3
Bolton BL3 148 A5
Oldham OL8 66 F2
Adams Ave M21 109 B6
Adams Cl
Newton-le-W WA12 89 D2
Poynton SK12 133 E2
Adams Dr WN3 150 A5
Adamson Gdns M20 109 F3
Adamson Rd M30 95 C8
Adamson St
Ashton-in-M WN4 73 A3
Dukinfield SK16 101 C6
Adamson Wlk 1 M14 98 C3
Adastral Ho M21 109 C8
Adcroft St SK1 170 F7
Adderley Pl SK13 171 F1
Adderley Rd SK13 171 F1
Addingham Cl M9 64 B5
Addington Rd BL3 40 F3
Addington St M4 159 B2
Addison Ave OL6 85 D3
Addison Cl M13 163 C6
Addison Cres M16 97 B4
Addison Dr M24 47 C3
Addison Rd
Altrincham WA15 119 E2
Carrington M31 106 D6
Irlam M44 94 C4
Stretford M32 96 B3
Urmston M41 95 D1
Adelaide Rd Bramhall SK7 132 F5
Stockport SK3 170 D8
Adelaide St Bolton BL3 147 D4
Eccles M30 79 D1
Heywood OL10 29 D2
Manchester M8 155 F5
Middleton M24 65 A8
Ramsbottom BL0 11 A4
Swinton M27 79 D7
Adelaide St E OL10 29 E2
Adelphi Ct M3 158 D3
Adelphi Dr M38 60 B5
Adelphi Gr M38 60 B5
Adelphi St Manchester M3 158 D2
3 Radcliffe M26 43 F5
Standish WN6 19 E2
Aden Cl M12 164 D8
Aden St Oldham OL4 67 D5
Rochdale OL12 15 A1
Adey Rd WA13 117 A5
Adisham Dr BL1 143 F1
Adlington Cl
Altrincham M23,WA15 120 D6
Bury BL8 27 A1
Poynton SK12 133 F2
Adlington Cty Prim Sch
PR7 20 F7
Adlington Dr M32 96 F4
Adlington Pk SK10 133 C1
Adlington Rd SK9 137 E7
Adlington St Bolton BL3 147 D3
Manchester M12 164 D8
12 Oldham OL4 49 D1
Adlington Sta PR6 21 A7
Adlington Way 19 M34 101 A1
Adlington Wlk SK1 169 E1
Adlow Ind Pk M12 164 D8
Admel Sq 1 M15 163 A5
Adria Rd M20 110 C3
Adrian Rd BL1 142 C2
Adrian St M40 83 A7
Adrian Terr OL16 31 C7
Adscombe St M16 97 E4
Adshall Rd SK8 123 A5
Adshead Cl M22 121 B3
Adstock Wlk 5 M40 159 C3
Adstone Cl M4 160 D1
Adswood Cl OL4 49 D1
Adswood Gr SK3 170 D6
Adswood La E SK2 170 F6
Adswood La W SK2,SK3 170 F6
Adswood Old Hall Rd
SK8 123 D4
Adswood Prim Sch SK3 170 E5
Adswood Rd SK3,SK8 170 D5
Adswood St M40 160 E2
Adswood Terr SK3 170 E6
Adwell Cl WA3 91 A8
Aegean Cl 3 M7 81 C5
Aegean Rd WA14 119 A6
Affetside Dr BL8 26 E2
Affleck Ave M26 61 A8
Afghan St OL1 67 B8
Agden Brow WA13 117 E1
Agden Brow Pk WA13 117 D1
Agden La WA13 117 E1
Age Croft OL8 67 C3
Agecroft Ent Pk M27 80 E7
Agecroft Park Circle M27 80 E7
Agecroft Rd
Manchester M25,M27 80 E8
Romiley SK6 113 A1
Agecroft Rd E M25 63 A2
Agecroft Rd W M25 63 A2
Agecroft Trad Est M6 80 F7
Ager St OL13 3 C8
Agincourt St OL10 29 B2
Agnes Cl OL9 66 C4
Agnes Ct M14 110 C7
Agnes St Manchester M19 99 A2
Manchester M7 155 F7
Oldham OL9 152 B6
Agnew Pl M6 81 A4
Agnew Rd M18 165 C5
Aigburth Gr SK5 99 E2
Ailsa Cl M40 157 D5
Ailsa Ho M6 154 F1
Aimson Pl WA15 120 C6
Aimson Road E WA15 120 D6
Aimson Road W WA15 120 C7
Aines St M12 165 A7
Ainley Rd M22 121 D3
Ainley Wood Delph OL3 50 E5
Dukinfield SK16 101 D7
Ainsbrook Ave OL3 50 F4
Ainsbrook Terr OL3 51 D5
Ainscoughs Ct WN7 75 F4
Ainscow Ave BL6 39 F8
Ainscow St WN3 151 E5
Ainsdale Ave Atherton M46 58 C4
Bury BL8 27 B2
Edgworth BL7 9 E6
Manchester M7 63 D1
Ainsdale Cl Bramhall SK7 133 A7
Oldham OL8 66 D4
Ainsdale Cres OL2 48 E2
Ainsdale Dr Gatley SK8 122 B1
Sale M33 107 E2
Whitworth OL12 14 D7
Ainsdale Gr SK5 111 F8
Ainsdale Rd BL3 147 E3
Ainsdale St M12 164 F6
Ainse Rd BL6 21 B3
Ainsford Rd M20 110 D5
Ainsley Gr M28 60 D2
Ainsley St 11 M40 83 C5
Ainslie Rd BL1 142 A1
Ainsty Rd M14 98 A4
Ainsworth Ave BL6 22 E2
Ainsworth Cl M34 100 B3
Ainsworth Ct BL2 148 C7
Ainsworth Hall Rd BL2 43 B8
Ainsworth La BL2 148 C8
Ainsworth Rd Bury BL8 27 B2
Little Lever BL3 43 B4
Radcliffe M26 43 F5
Ainsworth Sq BL1 143 D3
Ainsworth St Bolton BL1 142 C2
Rochdale OL16 31 A6
Ainthorpe Wlk M40 83 D5
Aintree Ave M33 107 C3
Aintree Cl SK7 124 F2
Aintree Dr OL11 29 E8
Aintree Gr SK3 170 E5
Aintree Rd BL3 43 A3
Aintree St M11 83 B1
Aintree Wlk OL9 152 C7
Air Hill Terr 8 OL12 14 C1
Aire Dr BL2 25 B5
Airedale Cl SK8 122 C6
Airedale Ct WA14 119 E5
Aireworth St BL5 39 F3
Airton Cl M40 159 C3
Airton Pl WN3 55 B3
Aitken Cl BL0 138 B5
Aitken St Haslingden BL0 1 C5
Reddish M19 99 C1
Ajax Dr BL9 45 A4
Ajax St Ramsbottom BL0 138 B5
Rochdale OL11 30 B3
Aked Cl M12 164 D6
Akesmoor Dr SK2 124 C6
Alamein Dr SK6 113 F2
Alan Ave M35 83 F5
Alan Dr Altrincham WA15 120 A1
Marple SK6 125 F6
Alan Rd Manchester M20 110 C6
Manchester SK4 168 B4
Alan St BL1 143 D3
Alan Turing Way
Droylsden M11 83 A1
Manchester M10,M40 160 F3
Alanbrooke Wlk M15 162 E5
Alandale Ave M34 100 E7
Alandale Rd SK3 123 C7
Alasdair Cl OL9 65 F8
Alba Cl M30 79 D1
Alba Way M32 96 A5
Alban Ct BL5 57 E7
Alban St M7 155 D5
Albany Ave M11 99 F7
Albany Cl M38 60 B5
Albany Ct
6 Manchester M20 110 B6
Urmston M41 95 B3
Albany Dr BL9 44 F7
Albany Gr M29 77 D8
Albany Rd Bramhall SK7 132 F4
Eccles M30 79 B3
Manchester M21 97 B1
Wilmslow SK9 136 F5
Albany Road Trad Ctr M21 97 B1
Albany St Middleton M24 65 B7
Oldham OL4 49 D1
10 Rochdale OL11 31 A5
Albany Way
Hattersley SK14 102 E2
Salford M6 81 A3
Albemarle Ave M20 110 A6
Albemarle Rd M21 109 A8
Albemarle St
Ashton-u-L OL6 166 C3
Albemarle St *continued*
Manchester M14 98 A4
Albemarle Terr OL6 166 C3
Alberbury Ave M23 120 D7
Albermarle Rd 5 M27 79 E7
Albert Ave Dukinfield SK16 101 C6
Manchester M25 63 D1
Reddish M18 99 F4
Shaw OL2 149 B5
Urmston M41 95 E2
Walkden M28 60 C5
Albert Cl Cheadle SK8 123 A2
Whitefield M45 63 A8
Albert Ct WA14 119 D4
Albert Fildes Wlk 3 M8 155 F7
Albert Gdns M40 83 D5
Albert Gr Farnworth BL4 60 D8
Manchester M12 99 A4
Albert Hill St M20 110 B3
Albert Park Rd M7 155 D5
Albert Pl Altrincham WA14 119 D5
Manchester M13 98 F3
Whitefield M45 45 B1
Albert Rd
Altrincham WA15 119 E3
Cheadle SK8 123 A2
Eccles M30 79 F2
Farnworth BL4 60 D8
Hyde SK14 167 D2
Manchester M19 99 A1
Manchester SK4 168 A3
Sale M33 108 C4
Whitefield M45 63 A8
Wilmslow SK9 137 A6
Albert Rd E WA15 119 E3
Albert Rd W Bolton BL1 144 A8
Bolton BL1 40 F8
Albert Royds St OL12,OL16 15 B2
Albert Sq
Altrincham WA14 119 D3
Manchester M2 158 F1
Stalybridge SK15 85 F1
Albert St Ashton-in-M WN4 73 B3
Bolton BL7 8 D3
Bury BL9 141 A2
Denton M34 100 F3
Droylsden M43 84 B1
Eccles M30 79 F2
Farnworth BL4 60 D7
Farnworth BL4 60 E8
Hadfield SK13 104 A5
Hazel Grove SK7 124 D3
Heywood OL10 29 B2
14 Hindley WN2 56 D5
Horwich BL6 22 B4
Hyde SK14 167 F3
Irlam M44 105 E6
Little Lever BL3 43 B3
Littleborough OL15 16 B5
Manchester M11 160 F1
Middleton M24 65 A8
Milnrow OL16 32 A5
Oldham OL4 67 E5
Oldham OL8 66 B1
Oldham OL9 66 B3
Prestwich M25 63 C4
Ramsbottom BL0 138 B6
Royton OL2 48 D4
Shaw OL2 149 A7
Stockport SK3 169 D1
Whitworth OL12 14 C8
Wigan WN5 54 F6
Albert St W M35 83 D6
Albert Webb Ho 6 M5 154 E1
Alberta St Bolton BL3 144 C5
Stockport SK1 170 F8
Alberton Cl WN2 38 C6
Albine St M40 157 F8
Albinson Wlk M31 106 A3
Albion Cl SK4 169 E3
Albion Ct BL8 140 D2
Albion Dr Aspull WN2 38 B2
Droylsden M43 84 A2
Albion Fold M43 84 A2
Albion Gardens Cl OL2 48 F4
Albion Gdns SK15 86 B1
Albion Gr M33 108 A4
Albion Ho SK15 86 C2
Albion Pl Hazel Grove SK7 124 D3
10 Manchester M7 81 C5
Prestwich M25 63 A4
Albion Rd Manchester M14 98 C1
Rochdale OL11 139 D6
Albion St Ashton-u-L OL6 166 C3
Aspull WN2 38 B2
7 Bacup OL13 3 C8
Bolton BL3 145 F5
Bury BL8 140 D2
Failsworth M35 83 E7
Hyde SK14 167 D2
Kearsley BL4 61 A7
7 Leigh WN7 75 F5
Littleborough OL15 16 A5
Manchester M15 162 F8
Manchester M16 97 D4
Oldham OL1 153 F7
Oldham OL9 152 A7
Pendlebury M27 80 A8
4 Platt Bridge WN2 56 A2
Radcliffe M26 44 B1
Rochdale OL11 30 D1
Sale M33 108 B4
Stalybridge SK15 86 B2
Westhoughton BL5 39 F3
Albion Terr BL1 142 B3

Albion Towers 5 M5 ......81 B2
Albion Trad Est
  Ashton-u-L OL6 ....85 D3
  Salford M6 ....81 A4
Albion Way M5,M6 ......81 B1
Alburn Ct M40 ....160 E4
Albury Dr Manchester M19 110 D2
  Rochdale OL12 ....13 F2
Albury Way WN2 ....37 F2
Albyns Ave M8 ....156 A7
Alcester Ave SK3 .....122 F7
Alcester Cl Bury BL8 ...27 B3
  Middleton M24 ....65 B6
Alcester Rd Gatley SK8 ..122 B4
  Sale M33 ....108 B2
Alcester St OL9 ....66 A3
Alcester Wlk M9 ....64 C5
Alconbury Ct M43 .....100 B8
Alconbury Wlk M9 .....64 C5
Aldborough Cl M20 ....110 B6
Aldbourne Cl M40 ....157 D5
Aldbury Terr 2 BL1 ...143 D1
Aldcliffe M18 ....90 F8
Aldcroft St 5 M18 .....99 F6
Alden Cl Haslingden BB4 ..1 A6
  Whitefield M45 ....63 A8
Alden Rd BB4 ....1 A5
Alden Rise BB4 ....1 A6
Alden Wlk SK4 ....111 D7
Alder Ave Ashton-in-M WN4 .72 F5
  Billinge WN5 ....71 D5
  Bury BL9 ....141 C3
  Poynton SK12 ....133 F3
  Wigan WN5 ....54 D6
Alder Cl Ashton-u-L OL6 ..85 B7
  9 Bury BL8 ....27 C2
  Dukinfield SK16 ......102 A7
  Leigh WN7 ....75 F2
Alder Ct M8 ....63 F4
Alder Dr Altrincham WA15 .120 E5
  Swinton M27 ....61 C1
Alder Edge 8 M21 .....96 F1
Alder Forest Ave M30 ..79 A4
Alder Gr Bolton BL7 ...25 C6
  Denton M34 ....101 A3
  Stockport SK3 ....123 C8
  Stretford M32 ....96 E2
  Oldham OL8 ....66 D2
Alder La Hindley WN2 ...57 B5
  Oldham OL8 ....66 D2
Alder Lee Cl WN3 ......54 D1
Alder Meadow Cl OL12 ..14 A1
Alder Moor Cl M11 .....99 D8
Alder Park Prim Sch M30 .79 A4
Alder Rd Cheadle SK8 ...122 E5
  Failsworth M35 ....83 F5
  Golborne WA3 ....90 F8
  Middleton M24 ....47 C2
  Rochdale OL11 ....30 D2
Alder St Atherton M46 ..58 D3
  Bolton BL3 ....147 F3
  Eccles M30 ....79 A4
  Newton-le-W WA12 .....89 C3
  Salford M6 ....154 F2
Alderbank Horwich BL6 ..21 F3
  Littleborough OL12 ....15 C7
Alderbank Cl BL4 ......60 F6
Aldercroft Ave Bolton BL2 .25 D1
  Wythenshawe M22 .....121 C2
Alderdale Dr
  Droylsden M43 ....83 E2
  High Lane SK6 ....134 E7
  Manchester M34 ....111 A5
Alderdale Gr SK9 ......136 E5
Alderdale Rd SK8 .....123 C4
Alderfield Ho 5 M21 ...96 F1
Alderfield Rd M21 .....96 F1
Alderfold St M46 ......58 D3
Alderford Par 11 M8 ...155 F6
Aldergate Gr OL6 ......85 F5
Alderglen Rd M8 ......156 A5
Alderley Ave Bolton BL1 ..24 E5
  Golborne WA3 ....90 D7
Alderley Cl Billinge WN5 ..71 E5
  Hazel Grove SK7 ......133 F8
  Poynton SK12 ....133 F2
Alderley Dr SK6 ......112 E3
Alderley Edge SK9 ....137 D1
Alderley Edge
  Com Prim Sch SK9 ....137 D3
Alderley Edge Jun Sch
  for Girls SK9 ....137 A1
Alderley Edge Sch
  for Girls SK9 ....137 A2
Alderley Edge Sta SK9 ..137 A2
Alderley La WN7 ....76 B2
Alderley Lo SK9 ......137 A5
Alderley Rd
  Alderley Edge SK10,SK9 .137 F2
  Hindley WN2 ....57 A5
  Reddish SK5 ....111 F5
  Sale M33 ....108 E2
  Urmston M41 ....95 A2
  Wilmslow SK9 ....137 A6
Alderley St OL6 ....85 D5
Alderley Terr 8 SK16 ..166 B1
Alderman Foley Dr OL12 .14 A2
Alderman Kay Sch M24 ..47 A3
Alderman Sq M12 .....164 E8
Aldermary Rd OL9 ....109 D5
Aldermaston Gr M9 ....64 B6
Aldermere Cres M41 ...94 F3
Alderminster Ave M38 ..60 A5
Alderney Dr WN3 ......55 A3
Alders Ave M22 ....121 C6
Alders Ct OL6 ....85 A8

Alders Green Rd WN2 ...57 A5
Alders Rd High Lane SK12 .135 A7
  Wythenshawe M22 .....121 C5
Alders The WN6 ....36 D4
Aldersgate Rd
  Bramhall SK7,SK8 .....132 C5
  Stockport SK2 ....124 B6
Aldersgreen Ave SK6 ..134 F7
Aldershot Wlk 3 M11 ..160 F1
Alderside Rd M9 ......157 D8
Aldersley Ave M9 .....64 B5
Alderson St Oldham OL9 .153 E7
  Salford M6 ....81 A4
Aldersyde St BL3 .....147 D3
Alderton Dr BL5 ......57 E6
Alderue Ave M22 .....121 D6
Alderway BL0 ....1 C1
Alderwood Ave SK4 ...168 A1
Alderwood Fold OL4 ...67 F5
Alderwood Gr BL0 ......1 D4
Alderwood Wlk 7 M8 ..155 F6
Aldfield Rd M23 ......108 F1
Aldford Cl M20 ....110 C3
Aldford Dr M46 ....58 E5
Aldford Gr BL3 ....43 B5
Aldford Pl SK9 ....136 F2
Aldford Way WN6 ......36 E8
Aldham Ave M40 ......83 C4
Aldred Cl M8 ....156 B6
Aldred St Bolton BL3 ..146 B3
  Eccles M30 ....79 C1
  Failsworth M35 ....83 E7
  3 Hindley WN2 ....56 D4
  Leigh WN7 ....75 E8
  Salford M5 ....81 B2
Aldridge Cl WN3 ......55 B3
Aldsworth Dr BL3 ....147 E4
Aldwick Ave M20 .....110 C3
Aldwinians Cl M34 ....106 E5
Aldworth Dr M40 .....157 E5
Aldworth Gr M33 ......107 D3
Aldwych OL11 ....30 F3
Aldwych Ave M14 .....98 B2
Aldwyn Cl M34 ....100 E5
Aldwyn Cres SK7 .....124 C2
Aldwyn Cty Prim Sch M34 84 C1
Aldwyn Park Rd M34 ..100 D3
Alexander Ave M35 ...84 A8
Alexander Briant Ct BL4 .60 C7
Alexander Ct M5 ......161 A8
Alexander Dr
  Altrincham WA15 ......120 A6
  Milnrow OL16 ....31 F6
  Whitefield M45 ....45 A2
Alexander Gdns M7 ...158 D4
Alexander Rd 9 BL2 ...25 C1
  Salford M6 ....154 E2
  Tyldesley M29 ....77 A8
Alexandra Cres
  1 Oldham OL1 ....67 B8
  Wigan WN5 ....54 E6
Alexandra Ct M41 ....94 E1
Alexandra Ctr Ret Pk
  OL4 ....153 F6
Alexandra Dr M19 ....110 F7
Alexandra Gr M44 ....105 F8
Alexandra Ho 6 OL1 ..67 B8
Alexandra Mews OL4 ..67 A5
Alexandra Park Inf Sch
  SK3 ....123 C7
Alexandra Park Prim Sch
  OL8 ....67 A5
Alexandra Rd
  Ashton-in-M WN4 .....73 B4
  Ashton-u-L OL6 ......166 B4
  Dukinfield M34 ....101 A4
  Eccles M30 ....95 C8
  Horwich BL6 ....39 E8
  Kearsley BL4 ....61 A7
  Kearsley M26 ....61 A8
  Manchester M16 ......97 E4
  Manchester SK4 ......168 C3
  Oldham OL8 ....67 A4
  Sale M33 ....108 D3
  Walkden M28 ....60 C5
Alexandra Rd S M16 ..97 E2
Alexandra St Abram WN2 .74 B8
  Ashton-u-L OL6 ......85 D4
  9 Bolton BL3 ....147 D4
  Farnworth BL4 ....60 D7
  Heywood OL10 ....46 E8
  Hyde SK14 ....101 C1
  Manchester M7 ....158 D3
  Oldham OL8 ....67 A5
  Wigan WN5 ....54 F6
Alexandra Terr
  14 Manchester M19 ...99 A1
  Oldham OL4 ....49 E3
Alexandria Dr BL5 ....58 B8
Alf Kaufman Specl Sch
  OL11 ....13 E1
Alford Ave M20 ......110 A8
Alford Cl BL2 ....42 F4
Alford Rd SK4 ....111 C6
Alford St 10 OL9 .....66 B2
Alfred Ave M28 ....79 A7
Alfred James Cl 17 M40 .159 C2
Alfred Morris Ct M23 ..109 A2
Alfred Rd WA3 ....91 A8
Alfred St Ashton-u-L OL6 ..85 D4

Alfred St *continued*
  Bolton BL3 ....42 B4
  Bury BL7 ....8 D3
  Bury BL9 ....141 A1
  Dukinfield SK14 ......101 C3
  Eccles M30 ....79 D3
  Farnworth BL4 ....42 D2
  Ince-in-M WN3 ....151 D6
  Irlam M44 ....105 E6
  Kearsley BL4 ....60 F8
  Littleborough OL15 ...16 A6
  Manchester M9 ....157 D8
  Newton-le-W WA12 ....89 E3
  Oldham OL9 ....152 C6
  Platt Bridge WN2 .....56 A3
  Ramsbottom BL0 ......138 B5
  Shaw OL2 ....149 B7
  9 Tyldesley M29 ......58 F1
  Walkden M28 ....60 D3
  Whitworth OL12 ....4 D2
  Wigan WN1 ....37 B2
Alfreton Ave M34 ....113 A8
Alfreton Rd SK2 .....124 E5
Alfreton Wlk 9 M40 ..83 A6
Alfriston Dr M23 .....109 A2
Alger St 1 OL6 ....85 D4
Algernon Rd M28 .....60 C4
Algernon St Eccles M30 .79 D3
  Hindley WN2 ....56 D5
  Swinton M27 ....79 D8
  Wigan WN3 ....55 A4
Algreave Rd SK3 .....123 A4
Alice Ingham
  RC Prim Sch OL16 ....15 C2
Alice St Bolton BL3 ...144 C5
  Hyde SK14 ....113 E7
  Pendlebury M27 ......80 B8
  Rochdale OL12 ....15 B1
  Sale M33 ....108 D4
Alicia Ct OL12 ....14 E1
Alicia Dr OL12 ....14 E1
Alick's Fold 9 BL5 ....39 E1
Alison Ct SK4 ....168 B3
Alison Kelly Cl M9 ...157 F8
Alison St
  18 Manchester M14 ...97 F3
  2 Manchester M14 ....98 A3
  Shaw OL2 ....149 B8
Alker Rd M40 ....160 D3
Alker St WN5 ....54 F6
Alkrington Cl BL9 ....45 A2
Alkrington Gn M24 ...64 F7
Alkrington Hall M24 ..64 F7
Alkrington Hall Rd N M24 64 F7
Alkrington Hall Rd S M24 64 E6
Alkrington Moss Prim Sch
  M24 ....65 B5
Alkrington Park Rd M24 .64 E7
Alkrington Prim Sch M24 .65 A6
All Saint's CE Prim Sch
  Appley Bridge WN6 ...18 C1
  Marple SK6 ....126 A5
  Rochdale OL12 ....15 A2
  Stockport SK4 ....169 D3
  Whitefield BL9 ....45 A2
All Saints Gr WN2 ....56 E5
All Saints Prim Sch M18 165 B6
All Saints RC Prim Sch
  M33 ....107 D6
All Saints Terr OL12 ..15 B5
All Saints' CE Prim Sch
  BL4 ....42 D2
All Saints' RC Prim Sch
  SK13 ....104 D2
All Saints' Rd SK4 ...169 E4
All Saints' St Bolton BL1 .145 F8
  Failsworth M40 ....83 C5
All Souls RC Prim Sch
  M5 ....154 D1
All Souls' CE Prim Sch
  OL10 ....29 F3
Allams St M11 ....160 E2
Allan Ct M21 ....109 A7
Allan Roberts Cl M9 ..64 D1
Allan St M29 ....76 F8
Allanadale Ct 10 M7 ..63 E1
Allandale WA14 ......119 B4
Allandale Dr OL2 ....48 C5
Allandale Rd M19 ....98 F1
Allanson Rd M22 .....109 E1
Alldis Cl M12 ....164 E5
Alldis St SK2 ....124 B5
Allen Ave
  Fowley Common WA3 ..92 C4
  Hyde SK14 ....113 F8
Allen Cl OL2 ....149 A6
Allen Rd M41 ....95 F2
Allen St Bury BL8 ....27 C3
  Little Lever BL3 ......43 A3
  Oldham OL8 ....153 D6
  Radcliffe M26 ....43 F1
  Rochdale OL16 ....31 A5
Allenby Gr BL5 ....57 D7
Allenby Rd Irlam M44 .105 D4
  Swinton M27 ....79 C6
Allenby St Atherton M46 .58 B2
  Shaw OL2 ....149 A7
Allenby Wlk 4 M40 ..156 C5
Allendale Gdns BL1 ..143 E4
Allendale Wlk M3 ....158 D2
Allerby Way WA3 .....90 E8

Allerdean Wlk SK4 ...110 F3
Allerford St M16 .....97 E4
Allerton Cl BL5 ......40 A1
Allerton Ct 7 BL1 ....145 E8
Allerton Wlk 6 M13 ..163 C6
Allescholes Rd OL14 ..6 B7
Allesley Cl BL5 ....40 A1
Allesley Dr M7 ....155 F6
Allgreave Cl M33 ....108 E1
Alliance St 4 WN1 ...151 D8
Alligin Cl M20 ....152 A8
Allingham St M13 ....98 E4
Allington OL11 ......139 E6
Allington Dr M30 ....79 E4
Alliott Wlk M15 .....162 E5
Allison Gr M30 ....79 B1
Allison St M8 ....155 F5
Allonby Wlk M24 ....46 C2
Allotment Rd M44 ...105 D6
Alloway Wlk 6 M40 ..83 A6
Allscott Way WN4 ...73 C3
Allsopp St BL3 ......145 F6
Allwood St M3 ....158 D1
Alma Cl WN8 ....53 C7
Alma Ct 3 Manchester M15 97 E4
  Orrell WN8 ....53 C7
Alma Gr WN3 ....54 E2
Alma Hill WN8 ....53 C7
Alma Hill Est WN8 ...53 C7
Alma Ind Est 28 OL12 ..14 F1
Alma La SK9 ....137 A7
Alma Par WN8 ....53 C7
Alma Park Prim Sch M19 111 A8
Alma Rd Hazel Grove SK7 .134 A8
  Manchester M19 .....111 A8
  Manchester SK4 ......111 B5
  Orrell WN8 ....53 C7
  Sale M33 ....107 E2
  Westhoughton BL5 ...57 F8
Alma St Atherton M46 ..58 C3
  Bolton BL3 ....146 C4
  Eccles M30 ....79 F1
  Kearsley BL4 ....61 B3
  Leigh WN7 ....75 E8
  Little Lever BL3 ......43 B3
  Newton-le-W WA12 ...89 B3
  Radcliffe M26 ....43 F5
  13 Rochdale OL12 ....14 F1
  Stalybridge SK15 ....86 B2
  Tyldesley M29 ....76 F8
Alminstone Cl M40 ...83 D4
Almond Ave BL9 .....141 C3
Almond Brook Rd WN6 .19 C1
Almond Cl Failsworth M35 .83 F6
  Littleborough OL15 ...15 F6
  Salford M6 ....81 B2
  Stockport SK3 ....123 C8
Almond Cres Rawtenstall BB4 1 F8
  Standish WN6 ....36 F7
Almond Ct SK16 .....166 C1
Almond Dr M33 ......107 F6
Almond Gr Bolton BL1 .143 F4
  Wigan WN5 ....54 E6
Almond Rd 5 OL4 ....49 D1
  9 Farnworth BL4 .....60 C8
  Manchester M40 .....159 D4
Almond Tree Rd SK8 ..123 A1
Almond Way SK14 ....102 A3
Almond Wlk M31 ....105 D3
Alms Hill Rd M8 .....156 A7
Alness Rd M16 ......97 E2
Alnwick Cl WN2 ......38 C5
Alnwick Dr BL9 ......45 A5
Alnwick Rd M9 ....64 D5
Alperton Wlk M40 ...83 D4
Alpha Court Ind Est M34 100 C3
Alpha Cl M34 ....100 C3
Alpha Pl M15 ....162 E5
Alpha Rd M32 ....96 C1
Alpha St Manchester M11 .99 E1
  Salford M6 ....154 F3
Alpha St W M6 ......154 E3
Alphagate Dr M34 ...100 C3
Alphin Cl Oldham OL3 ..69 B5
  Uppermill OL5 ....68 E3
Alphin Sq OL5 ....68 D1
Alphonsus St M16 ...97 C4
Alpine Dr Leigh WN7 ..75 C8
  Littleborough OL12 ...15 C6
  Milnrow OL16 ....32 A7
  Royton OL2 ....48 C3
Alpine Rd Stockport SK1 .112 A1
  Stockport SK1 ....112 A2
Alpine St Droylsden M11 .83 B2
  Newton-le-W WA12 ...89 A3
Alpington Wlk M40 ...65 C2
Alport Ave M16 ......97 C2
Alport Gr 3 SK13 ....171 E2
Alport Lea 2 SK13 ...171 E2
Alport Way 1 SK13 ..171 E2
Alresford Rd Middleton M9 .64 F7
  Salford M6 ....80 D5
Alric Wlk M22 ....130 E8
Alsager Cl M21 ......109 B6
Alsham Wlk M8 ......156 A6
Alsop Ave M7 ....81 B7
Alstead Ave M14 ....120 A3
Alston Ave Sale M33 ..107 F3
  Shaw OL2 ....149 B8
  Stretford M32 ....96 B3
Alston Cl SK7 ....124 A1
Alston Gdns M19 ....110 F5
Alston Lea M46 ......58 E4
Alston Rd Manchester M18 .99 F5
  Wigan WN2 ....37 F5
Alston St Bolton BL3 ..147 E3
  Bury BL8 ....27 C4

Alston Wlk M24 ......46 C2
Alstone Dr WA14 ....119 A6
Alstone Rd SK4 .....111 C6
Alt Cl WN7 ....75 D6
Alt Fold Dr OL8 .....67 C3
Alt Gr OL6 ....85 B6
Alt Hill La OL6,OL7 ..85 C8
Alt Hill Rd OL6 ......67 C1
Alt La OL8 ....67 C3
Alt Prim Sch OL8 ....67 D3
Alt Wlk M45 ....45 C2
Altair Ave 7 M22 ....121 D1
Altair Pl M7 ....81 C4
Altcar Gr SK5 ....99 E2
Altcar Wlk M22 .....121 C2
Altham Cl BL9 ......44 D7
Altham Wlk 12 M40 ..83 A6
Althorn Wlk 11 M23 ..121 A5
Althorpe Wlk M40 ...83 D4
Alton Ave M41 ....94 D2
Alton Cl Ashton-in-M WN4 .73 A4
  Ashton-u-L OL6 ......85 C7
  Whitefield BL9 ....45 A5
Alton Rd SK9 ....136 F7
Alton Sq M11 ....99 E2
Alton St OL8 ....66 F3
Alton Towers M16 ...97 D1
Altrincham CE Prim Sch
  WA14 ....119 D5
Altrincham
  General Hospl WA14 .119 D4
Altrincham Gram Sch
  for Boys WA14 ......119 D2
Altrincham Gram Sch
  for Girls
  Altrincham WA14 ....119 B3
  Altrincham WA14 ....119 C3
Altrincham Prep Sch
  WA14 ....119 D2
Altrincham Priory Hospl
  WA15 ....129 A7
Altrincham Rd
  Altrincham M1 ....163 B8
  Wilmslow SK9 ....130 C2
  Wythenshawe M22 ...121 C5
  Wythenshawe M23 ...121 B7
  Wythenshawe SK9 ...130 C4
Altrincham St M1 ....163 B8
Altrincham Sta WA15 ..119 C4
Altringham Ret Pk WA14 119 C7
Alum Cres BL9 ......45 A3
Alva Rd OL4 ....49 D2
Alvan Sq 1 M11 .....99 E1
Alvanley Cl Sale M33 ..108 C1
  Shevington WN5 .....36 C1
Alvanley Cres SK3 ...123 C6
Alvaston Ave SK4 ...168 B2
Alvaston Rd M18 ....99 E4
Aveley Ave M40 .....110 C5
Alverstone Rd M20 ..110 C6
Alveston Dr SK7 .....137 C8
Alvington Gr SK7 ....124 A1
Alwin Rd OL2 ....149 A8
Alwinton Ave M20 ...110 E3
Alworth Rd M9 ......64 D5
Alwyn Cl WN7 ....75 F1
Alwyn Dr M13 ....98 E4
Alwyn St WN1 ....37 D1
Alwyn Terr WN1 .....37 D1
Amar Rd WN3 ....55 A3
Ambassador Pl WA15 .119 E5
Amber Gdns
  Dukinfield SK16 .....101 B8
  Hindley WN2 ....56 E4
Amber Gr BL5 ....39 F2
Amber St M4 ....159 A2
Ambergate M46 .....58 D2
Ambergate St M11 ..160 E2
Amberhill Way
  Boothstown M28 .....77 F5
  Boothstown M28 .....78 A5
Amberley Cl Bolton BL3 .40 F5
  Wigan WN2 ....37 F2
Amberley Dr
  Altrincham WA15 ....129 B8
  Irlam M44 ....94 A1
  Sale M33 ....107 E5
  Wythenshawe M23 ...121 A4
Amberley Rd M33 ...107 E5
Amberley Wlk OL9 ..152 C7
Amberswood Cl WN2 .56 B7
Amberwood OL9 .....65 E8
Amberwood Dr M23 ..120 D6
Amblecote Dr E M38 ..60 A6
Amblecote Dr W M38 .60 A6
Ambleside Ince-in-M WN2 .56 B7
  Stalybridge SK15 ....86 A3
  Wigan WN5 ....54 C7
Ambleside Ave
  Altrincham WA15 ....120 C5
  Ashton-u-L OL6 ......85 F4
Ambleside Cl Bolton BL2 .25 F4
  Middleton M24 ....46 E1
Ambleside Ct SK8 ...122 C5
Ambleside Pl WA11 ..71 B1
Ambleside Rd
  Reddish SK5 ....111 F6
  Urmston M41 ....94 E1
Ambleside Wlk M9 ..65 A2
Ambrose Ave WN7 ...57 E1
Ambrose Cres OL3 ..51 B3
Ambrose Dr M20 ....109 E4
Ambrose Gdns M20 ..109 E4
Ambrose St Hyde SK14 .113 E7
  Manchester M12 .....165 A2
  Rochdale OL11 ......139 F5
Ambuscade Ct M41 ...94 E2
Ambush St M11 ....99 F7

Amelia St Denton M34 . . . .100 F4
Hyde SK14 . . . . .167 E2
Amersham Cl M41 . . . . . . .95 B5
Amersham Pl M19 . . . . . . .111 A6
Amersham St M5 . . . . . . .154 F1
Amesbury Dr WN3 . . . . . . .54 C2
Amesbury Gr SK5 . . . . . . .111 F5
Amesbury Rd M9 . . . . . . .64 E4
Amethyst Cl WN2 . . . . . . .38 A2
Amherst Rd M14,M20 . . . .110 D7
Amis Gr WA3 . . . . .90 E8
Amlwch Ave SK2 . . . . . . .124 D6
Ammon Wrigley Cl OL1 . . .153 F7
Ammon's Way OL3 . . . . . . .50 F5
Amory St M12 . . . . .163 C8
Amos Ave M40 . . . . .83 C4
Amos St Manchester M9 . . .157 F8
Salford M6 . . . . .154 C2
Ampleforth Gdns M26 . . . .43 C5
Ampney Cl M30 . . . . .79 B1
Amport Wlk 8 M40 . . . . . .65 C2
Amwell St M8 . . . . .156 C7
Amy St Middleton M24 . . . .47 B1
Rochdale OL12 . . . . .14 B1
Anaconda Dr M3 . . . . . . .158 E3
Ancaster Wlk 5 M40 . . . . .65 C2
Anchor Cl M19 . . . . .99 C1
Anchor Ct M8 . . . . .63 F1
Anchor La BL4,M38 . . . . . .59 F7
Anchor St OL1 . . . . .153 F8
Anchorage Quay M5 . . . . .161 A8
Anchorage Rd M32 . . . . . . .96 A1
Anchorage Sta M5 . . . . . .161 A8
Anchorage Wlk M18 . . . . .165 C6
Anchorside Cl M21 . . . . . .109 B7
Ancoats Gr
  Manchester M4 . . . . . . .160 D1
  Manchester M4 . . . . . . .164 D8
Ancoats Gr N M4 . . . . . . .160 D1
Ancoats Hospl M4 . . . . . .159 C1
Ancoats St 5 OL4 . . . . . . .67 E6
Ancroft Gdns BL3 . . . . . .146 C2
Ancroft St M15 . . . . .162 E6
Anderton Cl Bury BL8 . . . . .26 F1
  Rawtenstall BB4 . . . . .2 F7
Anderton Gr OL6 . . . . .85 E5
Anderton La BL6 . . . . .21 E4
Anderton Prim Sch PR6 . . .21 B8
Anderton St Adlington PR7 .21 A7
  Ince-in-M WN2 . . . . . . .151 F7
Anderton Way Aspull WN2 .38 B2
  Handforth SK9 . . . . .131 D3
Andoc Ave M30 . . . . .80 A1
Andover Ave M24 . . . . . . .65 C5
Andover Cres WN3 . . . . . .54 C2
Andover St M30 . . . . .79 C1
Andover Rd WA11 . . . . . . .72 E1
Andover Wlk M8 . . . . . . .156 A8
Andre St 14 M11 . . . . . . .83 C2
Andrew Ave WN5 . . . . . . .71 F5
Andrew Cl Radcliffe M26 . . .44 C1
  Ramsbottom BL8 . . . . . . .10 F1
Andrew Ct 2 M20 . . . . . .110 B6
Andrew Gr SK16 . . . . . . .101 D8
Andrew Ho SK4 . . . . .168 B4
Andrew La Bolton BL1 . . . . .24 F6
  High Lane SK6 . . . . .134 E8
Andrew Rd M9 . . . . .64 D1
Andrew St Ashton-u-L OL6 . .85 D4
  Bury BL9 . . . . .141 A4
  Chadderton OL9 . . . . . . .152 B8
  Droylsden M43 . . . . .84 C4
  Failsworth M35 . . . . .83 E8
  Hyde SK14 . . . . .167 F3
  Middleton M24 . . . . .65 C7
  Mossley OL5 . . . . .86 C8
  Stockport SK4 . . . . .169 D2
Andrew's Terr 3 BL5 . . . . .39 E1
Andrews Ave M41 . . . . . . .94 E3
Andy Nicholson Wlk M9 . .157 F8
Anemone Dr BB4 . . . . .1 A8
Anerley Rd M20 . . . . .110 B4
Anfield Cl BL9 . . . . .45 B3
Anfield Mews SK8 . . . . . . .122 F3
Anfield Rd Bolton BL3 . . . .147 F2
  Cheadle SK8 . . . . .122 F3
  Failsworth M40 . . . . .65 D1
  Sale M33 . . . . .108 C4
Angel Cl M26 . . . . .101 B8
Angel St Dukinfield M34 . .101 A4
  Hazel Grove SK7 . . . . . . .124 D3
  Manchester M4 . . . . . . .159 A4
Angel Trad Est 4 M4 . . . .159 A3
Angela Ave OL1,OL2 . . . . .48 C2
Angela St M15 . . . . .162 D7
Angelico Rise OL1 . . . . . . .49 D3
Angelo St BL1 . . . . .143 D2
Angle St 2 BL3 . . . . .25 B1
Angler Gr M34 . . . . .100 F3
Anglers Rest M44 . . . . . . .105 E5
Anglesea Ave SK2 . . . . . .170 F6
Anglesea Cl OL7 . . . . .85 A6
Anglesey Dr SK12 . . . . . .133 F6
Anglesey Gr SK8 . . . . . . .123 A6
Anglesey Rd OL7 . . . . .84 F6
Anglesey Water SK12 . . . .133 F6
Angleside Ave M19 . . . . . .110 E4
Anglezarke Rd PR6 . . . . . .21 A7
Anglia Gr BL3 . . . . .146 C4
Angora Dr M3 . . . . .158 D3
Angouleme Ret Pk BL9 . . .140 F2
Angouleme Way BL9 . . . . .140 F1
Angus Ave Heywood OL10 . .29 A1
  Leigh WN7 . . . . .75 C7
Angus St 3 OL13 . . . . .3 C8
Aniline St M111 . . . . .83 B1
Anita St M4 . . . . .159 B2
Anjou Bvd WN5 . . . . .54 F8

Ann La M29 . . . . .77 C5
Ann Sq OL4 . . . . .67 D8
Ann St Denton M34 . . . . . .100 E3
  Dukinfield OL7 . . . . .100 F8
  Dukinfield SK14 . . . . . . .101 C3
  Farnworth BL4 . . . . .60 E7
  Heywood OL10 . . . . .29 D3
  Leigh WN7 . . . . .75 E8
  Reddish SK5 . . . . .169 E4
  Rochdale OL11 . . . . .139 F6
Annable Rd Bredbury SK6 .112 D3
  Droylsden M43 . . . . .84 B1
  Irlam M44 . . . . .105 F8
  Manchester M18 . . . . . . .99 E6
Annald Sq M43 . . . . .100 A8
Annan Gr WN4 . . . . .73 E5
Annan St M34 . . . . .100 F4
Annandale Gdns WN8 . . . . .53 A7
Anne Cl 8 OL7 . . . . .85 A6
Anne Line Cl 3 OL11 . . . . .31 A5
Anne Nuttall St M15 . . . .162 D7
Anne St SK16 . . . . .101 D8
Annecy Cl BL8 . . . . .27 B4
Annersley Ave OL2 . . . . . .149 A6
Annesley Cres WN3 . . . . . .54 F3
Annesley Gdns 1 M18 . . . .99 D6
Annesley Rd M40 . . . . .65 E1
Annette Ave WA12 . . . . . . .89 A5
Annie Darby Ct M9 . . . . .157 D7
Annie St Ramsbottom BL0 . .11 A4
  Salford M5,M6 . . . . .154 E2
Annis Cl SK9 . . . . .137 B2
Annis Rd
  Alderley Edge SK9 . . . . .137 B2
  Bolton BL3 . . . . .146 B4
Annis St M9 . . . . .157 E7
Annisdale Cl M30 . . . . .79 B2
Annisfield Ave OL3 . . . . . . .69 C5
Anscombe Cl M40 . . . . . .160 D3
Ansdell Ave M21 . . . . . . .109 C8
Ansdell Dr M43 . . . . .83 E4
Ansdell Rd Horwich BL6 . . .22 C4
  Reddish SK5 . . . . .100 A1
  Rochdale OL16 . . . . .31 B4
  Wigan WN5 . . . . .54 D5
Ansdell St M8 . . . . .156 A7
Ansell Cl M18 . . . . .99 D6
Anselms Ct OL8 . . . . .66 C4
Ansford Ave WN2 . . . . .74 B8
Ansford Wlk M9 . . . . .156 C6
Ansleigh Ave M8 . . . . .64 A1
Ansley Gr SK4 . . . . .168 B3
Anslow Cl M40 . . . . .157 D5
Anson Ave M8 . . . . .79 E6
Anson Cl SK7 . . . . .132 F5
Anson Ct M14 . . . . .98 C3
Anson Engine Mus The
  SK12 . . . . .134 C3
Anson Pl WN5 . . . . .54 C8
Anson Rd Handforth SK9 . .131 E1
  Manchester M14 . . . . . . .98 D3
  Poynton SK12 . . . . .134 B3
  Reddish M34,SK5 . . . . . .100 A2
  Swinton M27 . . . . .79 E6
Anson St Bolton BL1 . . . . .143 F3
  Eccles M30 . . . . .79 B4
  Wigan WN5 . . . . .54 F7
Answell Ave M8 . . . . .64 A2
Antares Ave M7 . . . . .158 D3
Anthistle Ct M5 . . . . .154 D2
Anthony Cl M12 . . . . .164 E7
Anthony St OL5 . . . . .68 B1
Anthorn Rd WN3 . . . . .54 E3
Antilles Cl M12 . . . . .99 A4
Antler Ct WN4 . . . . .73 B6
Anton Wlk M9 . . . . .157 D6
Antrim Cl Manchester M19 .110 D2
  Wigan WN3 . . . . .54 C2
Anvil Cl WN5 . . . . .53 D5
Anvil St OL13 . . . . .3 E8
Anvil Way OL1 . . . . .153 E7
Apethorn La SK14 . . . . . .113 D7
Apollo Ave BL9 . . . . .44 F3
Apollo Wlk M12 . . . . .165 A6
Apperley Grange M30 . . . . .79 E4
Appian Way M7 . . . . .155 E5
Apple Cl M33 . . . . .67 C3
Apple Dell Ave WA3 . . . . . .74 C1
Apple St SK14 . . . . .114 D7
Apple Tree Ct M5 . . . . .81 A2
Apple Tree Rd SK22 . . . . .127 B1
Apple Tree Wlk 8 M33 . . .107 C5
Apple Way M24 . . . . .65 B6
Appleby Ave
  Altrincham WA15 . . . . . .120 C5
  Dukinfield SK14 . . . . . . .101 C5
  Manchester M12 . . . . . . .99 A3
Appleby Cl Bury BL8 . . . . . .26 F2
  Stockport SK3 . . . . .170 D5
Appleby Gdns
  1 Bolton BL3 . . . . .25 B1
  Whitefield M45 . . . . .44 F3
Appleby Lo M14 . . . . .98 D2
Appleby Wlk 4 OL2 . . . . . .48 E4
Applecross Wlk M11 . . . . .165 C8
Appledore Dr
  Altrincham M23 . . . . . . .120 D7
  Bolton BL2 . . . . .25 F3
Appledore Wlk OL9 . . . . .152 B6
Appleford Dr 8 M8 . . . . .156 B6
Applethwaite WN2 . . . . . . .56 B8
Appleton Cl M33 . . . . . . .108 B4
Appleton Dr SK13 . . . . . . .116 F8
Appleton Gr M33 . . . . . . .107 E2
Appleton Rd
  Altrincham WA15 . . . . . .119 F1

Appleton Rd continued
  Reddish SK4 . . . . .111 D6
Appleton St WN3 . . . . . . .150 B8
Appleton Wlk 8 SK9 . . . . .131 E1
Applewood OL9 . . . . .65 E7
Appley Cl WN6 . . . . .18 C2
Appley La N WN6 . . . . .18 C1
Appley La S WN6,WN8 . . . .35 C6
Apprentice Ct 18 M9 . . . . .157 E8
April Cl 1 OL7 . . . . .67 C4
Apsley Cl WA14 . . . . .119 B1
Apsley Gr
  Altrincham WA14 . . . . . .119 B1
  Manchester M12 . . . . . . .163 C6
Apsley Pl OL6 . . . . .166 A2
Apsley Rd M34 . . . . .100 F4
Apsley Side OL5 . . . . .86 C8
Apsley St 3 . . . . .169 F1
Aquarius La M6 . . . . .81 C4
Aquarius St M15 . . . . . . .163 A5
Aqueduct Rd BL3 . . . . . . .148 C5
Aquinas Coll SK2 . . . . . . .124 A6
Aragon Dr OL10 . . . . .29 C2
Aragon Way SK6 . . . . . . .125 E6
Arbor Ave M19 . . . . .110 F6
Arbor Dr M19 . . . . .110 F6
Arbor Gr Droylsden M43 . . .83 F3
  Walkden M38 . . . . .59 E4
Arbory Ave M40 . . . . .83 B7
Arbory Cl WN7 . . . . .76 C5
Arbour Cl Bury BL9 . . . . . . .27 E6
  Salford M6 . . . . .154 F3
Arbour La WN6 . . . . .19 B1
Arbour Rd OL4 . . . . .67 E4
Arbroath St M43 . . . . .83 E1
Arbury Ave Cheadle SK3 . .123 A7
  Rochdale OL11 . . . . .139 C5
Arcade St 18 WN1 . . . . . .150 C8
Arcade The
  Brinnington SK5 . . . . . . .112 C5
  2 Stalybridge SK15 . . . . .101 F8
Arcades The OL6 . . . . . . .166 B3
Arcadia Ave M33 . . . . . . .108 A1
Arch La WN4 . . . . .72 B3
Arch St Bolton BL1 . . . . . .148 A8
  Bolton BL1 . . . . .25 A1
Archer Ave BL2 . . . . .148 C8
Archer Gr BL2 . . . . .148 C8
Archer Pk M24 . . . . .64 E8
Archer Pl M32 . . . . .95 F3
Archer St Boothstown M28 . .77 E7
  Droylsden M11 . . . . .83 A2
  Leigh WN7 . . . . .76 B2
  Mossley OL5 . . . . .68 C2
  Stockport SK2 . . . . .124 C5
Archie St M5 . . . . .161 A7
Arclid Cl SK9 . . . . .131 E1
Arcon Cl OL16 . . . . .31 E6
Arcon Dr M16 . . . . .97 E3
Arcon Pl WA14 . . . . .119 A6
Ardale Ave M40 . . . . .65 C2
Ardcombe Ave M9 . . . . . . .64 C5
Ardeen Wlk M13 . . . . . . .163 C6
Arden Ave M24 . . . . .65 B5
Arden Bsns Ctr SK6 . . . . .112 E6
Arden Cl Ashton-u-L OL6 . . .85 F6
  Bury BL9 . . . . .44 E8
  Gatley SK8 . . . . .131 C7
  Glossop SK13 . . . . .116 A8
Arden Ct SK7 . . . . .123 D1
Arden Gr M40 . . . . .65 C1
Arden Hall SK6 . . . . .112 D7
Arden Ho OL2 . . . . .48 E4
Arden Lodge Rd M23 . . . .120 E7
Arden Rd SK6 . . . . .112 E7
Arden St OL9 . . . . .66 A3
Arden Wlk 6 Sale M33 . . .107 C5
  Stockport SK5 . . . . .169 E1
Ardenfield M34 . . . . .113 A7
Ardenfield Dr M22 . . . . . .121 E3
Ardens Cl M27 . . . . .61 D2
Ardent Way M25 . . . . .63 B1
Ardern Gr SK1 . . . . .170 E8
Ardern Rd M8 . . . . .63 F2
Arderne Rd WA15 . . . . . . .120 A8
Ardingly Wlk M23 . . . . . .120 D8
Ardley Rd BL6 . . . . .22 C4
Ardmore Wlk M22 . . . . . .121 E2
Ardwick Gn N M12 . . . . . .163 C7
Ardwick Gn S M12,M13 . . .163 C7
Ardwick Sta M12 . . . . . . .164 D7
Arena App BL6 . . . . .39 C7
Argo St BL3 . . . . .147 D4
Argosy Dr Eccles M30 . . . . .94 F7
  Wythenshawe M90 . . . . . .129 F7
Argus St OL8 . . . . .66 C2
Argyle Ave Manchester M14 .98 E4
  Walkden M28 . . . . .60 C5
  Whitefield M45 . . . . .63 A8
Argyle Cres OL10 . . . . .29 B1
Argyle Par OL10 . . . . .29 A1
Argyle St Atherton M46 . . . .58 C2
  Bury BL9 . . . . .140 F4
  Droylsden M43 . . . . .84 A1
  Hazel Grove SK7 . . . . . . .124 E2
  Heywood OL10 . . . . .29 A1
  Hindley WN2 . . . . .56 E5
  Manchester M18 . . . . . . .99 D5
  Oldham OL1 . . . . .67 B8
  14 Rochdale OL11,OL16 . .31 A4
  Swinton M27 . . . . .79 E7
  Wigan WN2 . . . . .54 F6
Argyll Ave M32 . . . . .96 B2
Argyll Cl Failsworth M35 . . .84 B5
  Garswood WN4 . . . . .72 C4
Argyll Park Rd M35 . . . . . .84 B7

Argyll Rd Cheadle SK8 . . . .122 F5
  Oldham OL9 . . . . .65 F4
Argyll St Ashton-u-L OL6 . . .85 E3
  Mossley OL5 . . . . .68 C1
Ariel Wlk 4 WA3 . . . . .90 E8
Ark St 3 M19 . . . . .99 A2
Arkendale M35 . . . . .84 C7
Arkholme M28 . . . . .78 A8
Arkholme Wlk M40 . . . . . . .83 B7
Arkle Ave SK8,SK9 . . . . . .131 E4
Arkle Dr OL9 . . . . .65 F8
Arkley Wlk M13 . . . . .163 B6
Arkwright Dr SK6 . . . . . . .126 A6
Arkwright Rd SK6 . . . . . . .126 A6
Arkwright St Horwich BL6 . .22 C2
  Oldham OL9 . . . . .152 C6
Arkwright Way OL11 . . . . . .31 A2
Arlen Ct BL2 . . . . .148 B5
Arlen Rd BL2 . . . . .148 B5
Arlen Way OL10 . . . . .29 B2
Arley Ave Bury BL9 . . . . . . .27 F6
  Manchester M20 . . . . . . .109 F5
Arley Cl Altrincham WA14 . .119 D8
  Aspull WN2 . . . . .38 B2
  Dukinfield SK16 . . . . . . .101 D6
Arley Dr Sale M33 . . . . . .108 A2
  Shaw OL2 . . . . .49 D8
Arley Gr SK3 . . . . .123 D4
Arley La WN1,WN2 . . . . . . .20 D2
Arley Mere Cl SK8 . . . . . .122 F3
Arley Moss Wlk M13 . . . . .163 B7
Arley St Ince-in-M WN3 . . . .55 F4
  Radcliffe M26 . . . . .44 C4
Arley Way Atherton M46 . . .58 E2
  22 Denton M34 . . . . . . .101 A1
Arlies Cl SK15 . . . . .86 A4
Arlies La SK15 . . . . .86 A4
Arlies Prim Sch SK15 . . . . .86 A4
Arlies St SK15 . . . . .85 D4
Arlington Ave Denton M34 .101 A7
  Manchester M25 . . . . . . .63 B2
  Swinton M27 . . . . .79 D6
Arlington Cl BL9 . . . . .11 C2
Arlington Cres SK9 . . . . . .136 E5
Arlington Dr
  Golborne WA3,WN7 . . . . .91 C8
  Poynton SK12 . . . . .133 D3
  Stockport SK2 . . . . .124 A3
Arlington Rd Cheadle SK8 .122 C4
  Stretford M32 . . . . .96 B1
Arlington St
  4 Ashton-u-L OL6 . . . . . .166 C3
  Bolton BL3 . . . . .147 F3
  Manchester M3 . . . . . . .158 D2
  Manchester M8 . . . . . . .155 F8
Arlington Way SK9 . . . . . .136 E5
Arliss Ave M19 . . . . .111 A8
Arm Rd OL15 . . . . .15 E4
Armadale Ave M9 . . . . .65 A4
Armadale Cl SK3 . . . . . . .170 F5
Armadale Rd Bolton BL3 . . .40 E5
  Dukinfield SK16 . . . . . . .101 D7
Armdale Rise OL4 . . . . .49 E1
Armit Rd OL3 . . . . .68 E5
Armitage Ave M38 . . . . . . .59 F4
Armitage CE Prim Sch
  M12 . . . . .164 E6
Armitage Cl Hyde SK14 . . .113 E8
  Middleton M24 . . . . .64 D7
  Oldham OL8 . . . . .66 C3
Armitage Ct M12 . . . . . . .164 F6
Armitage Gr M38 . . . . .59 F4
Armitage Ho M6 . . . . .80 C3
Armitage Owen Wlk 4
  M40 . . . . .83 A7
Armitage Rd WA14 . . . . . .119 D3
Armitage St M30 . . . . .79 D1
Armitstead 5 WN2 . . . . . . .56 D4
Armour Pl M9 . . . . .64 C2
Armoury Bank WN4 . . . . . .73 B3
Armoury St SK3 . . . . .170 E8
Armstrong Hurst Cl OL12 . .15 B2
Armstrong St Aspull WN2 . .38 A3
  Horwich BL6 . . . . .22 C2
Arncliffe Cl 5 BL4 . . . . . . .42 D1
Arncliffe Dr M23 . . . . . . .121 A3
Arncliffe Rise OL4 . . . . .50 A4
Arncot Rd BL1 . . . . .24 F5
Arncott Cl OL2 . . . . .49 A4
Arne Cl SK2 . . . . .125 A5
Arne St OL9 . . . . .152 A5
Arnesby Ave M33 . . . . . . .108 E5
Arnesby Gr BL2 . . . . .148 B8
Arnfield Dr 1 M28 . . . . . . .78 B6
Arnfield La SK13 . . . . . . .103 F8
Arnfield Rd
  Manchester M20 . . . . . . .110 C6
  Stockport SK3 . . . . .170 D5
Arnold Ave Heywood OL10 . .46 F2
  Hyde SK14 . . . . .113 F7
Arnold Cl SK16 . . . . .102 A7
Arnold Ct M16 . . . . .97 E1
Arnold Dr Droylsden M43 . . .84 A1
  Middleton M24 . . . . .47 C3
Arnold Rd Bolton BL7 . . . . .24 F8
  Hyde SK14 . . . . .113 F7
  Manchester M16 . . . . . . .97 E1
Arnold St Ashton-u-L OL6 . .166 C3
  Bolton BL1 . . . . .142 C2
  Oldham OL1 . . . . .67 A8
  Stockport SK3 . . . . .170 E7
Arnold Wlk 9 M34 . . . . . .113 A7
Arnott Cres M15 . . . . .162 F5
Arnside Ave
  Hazel Grove SK7 . . . . . . .124 C2
  Ince-in-M WN2 . . . . .56 A7
  Oldham OL9 . . . . .65 F4
  Reddish SK4 . . . . .111 E6

Arnside Cl Gatley SK8 . . . .122 B4
  High Lane SK6 . . . . .134 E8
  Shaw OL2 . . . . .49 D7
Arnside Dr Dukinfield SK14 .101 C4
  Rochdale OL11 . . . . .29 E5
  Salford M6 . . . . .80 B3
Arnside Gr Bolton BL2 . . . . .42 E8
  Sale M33 . . . . .108 B6
Arnside Rd Hindley WN2 . . .57 A5
  Wigan WN5 . . . . .54 B8
Arnside St M14 . . . . .98 B2
Arosa Ct M20 . . . . .110 C7
Arran Ave Oldham OL8 . . . .66 F3
  Sale M33 . . . . .108 C3
  Stretford M32 . . . . .96 A2
Arran Cl BL3 . . . . .40 E6
Arran Gdns M41 . . . . .95 C5
Arran Gr M26 . . . . .43 E5
Arran Rd SK16 . . . . .101 C7
Arran St 12 Manchester M40 .64 F1
  Manchester M7 . . . . .155 D6
Arran Wlk OL10 . . . . .29 A1
Arrandale Cl M41 . . . . .95 D3
Arras Gr M34 . . . . .99 F3
Arreton Sq M14 . . . . .98 D3
Arrivals Way M90 . . . . . . .130 B7
Arrow St Bolton BL1 . . . . .145 E8
  Leigh WN7 . . . . .76 B3
  Manchester M7 . . . . .155 D5
Arrow Trad Est M4 . . . . . .100 C5
Arrowfield Dr M21 . . . . . .109 D7
Arrowfield Rd M21 . . . . . .109 D7
Arrowhill Rd BL8 . . . . .43 F8
Arrowscroft Way SK14 . . . .171 D4
Arrowsmith Ct 7 BL6 . . . . .22 E1
Arrowsmith Wlk 18 M11 . .160 F1
Arthill La WA14 . . . . .118 B1
Arthington St OL16 . . . . . .31 B8
Arthog Dr WA15 . . . . .128 F3
Arthog Rd
  Altrincham WA15 . . . . . .128 F8
  Manchester M20 . . . . . . .110 C3
Arthur Ave M28 . . . . .60 C5
Arthur La BL2 . . . . .26 B2
Arthur Millwood Ct M3 . . .158 D1
Arthur Rd M16 . . . . .97 C3
Arthur St Bury BL8 . . . . . . .27 C2
  Eccles M30 . . . . .79 C1
  Farnworth BL4 . . . . .60 D8
  Heywood OL10 . . . . .29 D2
  Hindley WN2 . . . . .56 E5
  Hyde SK14 . . . . .101 C1
  Leigh WN7 . . . . .75 E4
  Little Lever BL3 . . . . .43 B3
  Prestwich M25 . . . . .62 F4
  Reddish SK5 . . . . .111 E7
  Rochdale OL12 . . . . .139 D2
  Shaw OL2 . . . . .149 B7
  Swinton M27 . . . . .79 D6
  Walkden M28 . . . . .60 E1
  Walkden M28 . . . . .60 F2
Arthur Terr 4 SK5 . . . . . . .111 E7
Arthurs La OL3 . . . . .69 B6
Artillery Ct M13 . . . . .163 C7
Artillery Pl M22 . . . . .121 F4
Artillery St Bolton BL3 . . . .145 F5
  Manchester M3 . . . . .162 E8
Arundale BL5 . . . . .39 F2
Arundale Ave M16 . . . . . . .97 E1
Arundale Cl SK14 . . . . . . .102 F3
Arundale Ct M16 . . . . .97 E1
Arundale Gr SK14 . . . . . . .102 F3
Arundale Prim Sch SK14 . .102 F3
Arundel Ave
  Hazel Grove SK7 . . . . . . .133 D8
  Prestwich M45 . . . . .63 B7
  Rochdale OL11 . . . . .30 C4
  Urmston M41 . . . . .94 C1
Arundel Cl
  Altrincham WA15 . . . . . .120 C1
  Bury BL8 . . . . .27 C6
  Mossley SK15 . . . . .86 F6
Arundel Dr WN7 . . . . .75 F6
Arundel Gr SK2 . . . . .124 B4
Arundel Grange SK13 . . . .104 A1
Arundel Rd SK8 . . . . .132 A6
Arundel St Ashton-u-L OL6 . .85 E3
  Bolton BL1 . . . . .24 E5
  Glossop SK13 . . . . .104 C1
  Hindley WN2 . . . . .56 E5
  Manchester M15 . . . . . . .162 D7
  Mossley OL5 . . . . .68 B1
  Oldham OL4 . . . . .67 C2
  Rochdale OL11 . . . . .30 E4
  Swinton M27 . . . . .61 C1
  Wigan WN5 . . . . .54 F6
Arundel Wlk OL9 . . . . .152 A6
Asby Cl M24 . . . . .46 D2
Ascension CE Prim Sch
  M7 . . . . .158 D4
Ascension Rd M7 . . . . . . .158 D4
Ascot Ave Sale M33 . . . . . .107 D3
  Stretford M32 . . . . .96 F3
Ascot Cl Oldham OL9 . . . . .152 C2
  Rochdale OL11 . . . . .29 E8
Ascot Dr Atherton M46 . . . .58 E4
  Hazel Grove SK7 . . . . . . .125 A2
  Urmston M41 . . . . .94 C2
Ascot Mdws BL9 . . . . .44 E8
Ascot Par M19 . . . . .110 F6
Ascot Rd Failsworth M40 . . .83 B4
  Little Lever BL3 . . . . .42 F4
Ascot Wlk M6 . . . . .81 A5
Ascroft Ave WN6 . . . . .36 F5
Ascroft St Oldham OL1 . . . .153 F6

Ascroft St continued
Wigan WN1 . . . .**151** E7
Asgard Dr M5 . . . .**161** C8
Asgard Gr M5 . . . .**161** C8
Ash Ave Altrincham WA14 . .**119** A5
Cheadle SK8 . . . .**122** E5
Irlam M44 . . . .**105** D5
Newton-le-W WA12 . . . . . .**89** C2
Ash Cl Appley Bridge WN6 . .**35** D7
Ashton-u-L OL6 . . . .**85** D5
Littleborough OL12 . . . . . .**15** C4
Mottram-in-L SK14 . . . . . .**103** A4
Ash Ct Manchester SK4 . . .**168** B3
Romiley SK6 . . . .**113** A5
Ash Dr M27 . . . .**61** C2
Ash Field Pch M28 . . . . . .**60** E1
Ash Gr Altrincham WA14 . . .**119** C1
Altrincham WA15 . . . .**119** F7
Bolton BL1 . . . .**144** B8
Bolton BL2 . . . .**25** F3
Bury BL8 . . . .**27** A5
Droylsden M43 . . . .**100** A8
Gatley SK8 . . . .**131** B8
Golborne WA3 . . . .**90** B8
Handforth SK9 . . . .**131** C3
8 Horwich BL6 . . . .**22** E1
Littleborough OL15 . . . . . .**15** F5
Manchester M14 . . . .**98** E4
Marple SK6 . . . .**125** E5
Newhey OL16 . . . .**32** A3
Oldham OL4 . . . .**68** A7
Orrell WN5 . . . .**53** F6
Prestwich M25 . . . .**63** A6
Ramsbottom BL0 . . . .**10** F3
Reddish SK4 . . . .**111** D5
Royton OL2 . . . .**48** D6
Stalybridge SK15 . . . .**85** F3
Standish WN6 . . . .**36** F8
Stretford M32 . . . .**108** C8
Swinton M27 . . . .**79** D5
Walkden M28 . . . .**60** E1
Westhoughton BL5 . . . .**57** E7
Ash Grove Cres WN5 . . . . .**71** E6
Ash Hill Dr OL5 . . . .**86** E8
Ash Ho M16 . . . .**97** E4
Ash La Altrincham WA15 . . .**120** C2
Aspull WN2 . . . .**38** A2
Ash Leigh Dr BL1 . . . .**40** E8
Ash Lo SK12 . . . .**133** D4
Ash Rd Coppull PR7 . . . . . .**19** E8
Droylsden M43 . . . .**83** F2
Hollinfare WA3 . . . .**105** A2
Kearsley BL4 . . . .**60** F5
Partington M31 . . . .**105** D3
Poynton SK12 . . . .**133** F3
Reddish M34 . . . .**99** F3
Ash Sq OL4 . . . .**67** D8
Ash St Bolton BL2 . . . .**148** A6
Bury BL9 . . . .**141** A2
Denton M34 . . . .**100** D7
Failsworth M35 . . . .**83** E8
Golborne WA3 . . . .**74** B2
Hazel Grove SK7 . . . .**124** D3
Heywood OL10 . . . .**29** B3
Manchester M9 . . . .**157** D7
Middleton M24 . . . .**65** C8
Oldham OL4 . . . .**67** B6
Rochdale OL11 . . . .**30** C2
Salford M6 . . . .**154** F2
Stockport SK3 . . . .**123** B8
2 Tyldesley M29 . . . .**59** A1
Ash Tree Ave M43 . . . .**83** F2
Ash Tree Dr SK16 . . . .**101** F4
Ash Tree Rd Hyde SK14 . . .**102** B5
Manchester M8 . . . .**64** A1
Ash Wlk Chadderton OL9 . .**152** B8
Middleton M24 . . . .**64** F6
Ashawe Cl M38 . . . .**59** E3
Ashawe Gr M38 . . . .**59** F3
Ashawe Terr M38 . . . .**59** E3
Ashbank Ave BL3 . . . .**40** E6
Ashbee St BL1 . . . .**143** E3
Ashberry Cl SK9 . . . .**137** D8
Ashborne Dr BL9 . . . .**11** D2
Ashbourne Ave Aspull WN2 . .**38** A2
Bolton BL2 . . . .**148** B6
Cheadle SK8 . . . .**122** F6
Hindley WN2 . . . .**56** F5
Middleton M24 . . . .**47** C3
Urmston M41 . . . .**94** E2
Ashbourne Cl Leigh WN7 . . .**57** D1
Littleborough OL12 . . . . . .**15** D6
Ashbourne Cres M33 . . . .**108** D2
Ashbourne Ct SK13 . . . . . .**116** F8
Ashbourne Dr
Ashton-u-L OL6 . . . .**85** D4
High Lane SK6 . . . .**134** F6
Ashbourne Gdns WN2 . . . .**56** F5
Ashbourne Gr
Manchester M7 . . . .**155** E7
Whitefield M45 . . . .**44** D1
Worsley M28 . . . .**78** E8
Ashbourne Rd
Denton M34 . . . .**100** E2
Eccles M30 . . . .**79** E1
Hazel Grove SK7 . . . .**133** F8
Pendlebury M6 . . . .**80** C5
Stretford M32 . . . .**96** A3
Ashbourne Sq OL8 . . . . . .**153** E5
Ashbourne St OL11 . . . . . .**13** C1
Ashbridge M17 . . . .**96** B6
Ashbridge Rd M35 . . . .**84** B6
Ashbrook Ave M34 . . . . . .**100** B3
Ashbrook Cl Gatley SK8 . . .**122** B1
Reddish M34 . . . .**100** B3

Ashbrook Cl continued
Whitefield M45 . . . .**63** B8
Ashbrook Cres OL12 . . . . .**15** C4
Ashbrook Farm Cl SK5 . . . .**99** F3
Ashbrook Hey La OL12 . . . .**15** C4
Ashbrook La SK5 . . . .**99** F2
Ashbrook St M11 . . . .**100** A4
Ashburn **11** OL10 . . . .**29** C2
Ashburn Ave M19 . . . .**110** F5
Ashburn Gr SK4 . . . .**169** D3
Ashburn Rd SK4 . . . .**169** D3
Ashburne Ho M14 . . . .**98** D4
Ashburner St BL1 . . . .**145** E6
Ashburton Cl SK14 . . . . . .**102** E2
Ashburton Rd SK3 . . . . . .**170** E6
Ashburton Rd W M17,M41 . .**95** E7
Ashbury Cl BL3 . . . .**145** E5
Ashbury Pl M40 . . . .**160** E4
Ashbury Prim Sch M11 . .**164** F8
Ashbury's Sta M12 . . . . . .**165** A7
Ashby Ave M19 . . . .**110** E4
Ashby Cl BL3 . . . .**42** C2
Whitefield M45 . . . .**63** B7
Ashby Gr Leigh WN7 . . . . . .**75** C8
Whitefield M45 . . . .**63** B7
Ashby Rd WN3 . . . .**55** B3
Ashcombe Dr Bolton BL2 . . .**43** A6
Radcliffe M26 . . . .**43** D5
Ashcombe Wlk **7** M11 . . .**160** F1
Ashcott Ave M22 . . . .**121** D4
Ashcott Cl BL6 . . . .**40** E5
Ashcroft
6 Littleborough OL12 . . . .**15** D4
Wilmslow SK9 . . . .**136** F5
Ashcroft Ave M6 . . . .**154** E4
Ashcroft Ct OL1 . . . .**153** F6
Ashcroft Rd WA13 . . . .**117** A4
Ashcroft St WN2 . . . .**56** E4
Ashdale Ave BL3 . . . .**40** E5
Ashdale Cl SK5 . . . .**111** F5
Ashdale Cres M43 . . . .**83** F1
Ashdale Dr Gatley SK8 . . . .**122** B2
Manchester M20 . . . .**110** D5
Ashdale Rd Hindley WN2 . . .**57** A5
Wigan WN3 . . . .**55** A2
Ashdene Ashton-u-L OL6 . . .**85** D2
Rochdale OL12 . . . .**14** C4
Ashdene Cl
Oldham OL1,OL9 . . . .**48** C1
Oldham OL4 . . . .**67** F7
Ashdene Cres BL2 . . . .**25** D4
Ashdene Prim Sch SK9 . .**136** F5
Ashdene Rd
Manchester M20 . . . .**110** D6
Manchester SK4 . . . .**110** D2
Wilmslow SK9 . . . .**136** F5
Ashdene Rise OL1 . . . .**49** D4
Ashdown Ave
Manchester M9 . . . .**64** D4
Romiley SK6 . . . .**113** C5
Ashdown Dr Bolton BL2 . . . .**25** C3
Boothstown M28 . . . .**78** A7
Pendlebury M27 . . . .**80** A6
Ashdown Gr M9 . . . .**64** D4
Ashdown Rd SK4 . . . .**168** C3
Ashdown Terr **64** D4
Ashdown Way OL2 . . . .**48** E8
Ashdowne Lawns SK15 . . .**86** D3
Asher St BL3 . . . .**146** C2
Ashes Cl SK15 . . . .**102** C8
Ashes Dr BL2 . . . .**42** F6
Ashes La Glossop SK13 . . .**104** B2
Milnrow OL16 . . . .**31** F7
Oldham OL4 . . . .**67** F6
Stalybridge SK15 . . . .**102** C8
Ashfield Ct **11** M21 . . . .**96** F1
Ashfield M34 . . . .**101** A5
Ashfield Ave Atherton M46 . .**58** C4
Hindley WN2 . . . .**56** F4
Rochdale OL11 . . . .**139** F5
Ashfield Cres Billinge WN5 . .**71** E4
Cheadle SK8 . . . .**122** D6
Oldham OL4 . . . .**67** F6
Ashfield Dr Aspull WN2 . . . .**38** C5
Failsworth M40 . . . .**83** D4
Ashfield Gr Bolton BL1 . . . . .**25** A6
Irlam M44 . . . .**105** E6
Reddish M18,M34 . . . .**99** F4
Romiley SK6 . . . .**114** B1
Stockport SK3 . . . .**123** F4
Ashfield Ho OL11 . . . .**139** F5
Ashfield House Gdns WN6 .**36** F8
Ashfield Lo M20 . . . .**109** F2
Ashfield Park Dr WN6 . . . . .**36** F8
Ashfield Rd Adlington PR6 . .**21** B8
Altrincham WA15 . . . .**119** E3
Cheadle SK8 . . . .**122** D5
Cheadle SK8 . . . .**122** D6
Hadfield SK13 . . . .**171** E3
Manchester M13 . . . .**98** E3
Rochdale OL11 . . . .**139** F5
Sale M33 . . . .**108** B5
Stockport SK3 . . . .**123** F4
Urmston M41 . . . .**95** D2
Ashfield Sq M43 . . . .**83** F2
Ashfield St
Manchester M11 . . . .**160** F2
Oldham OL8 . . . .**66** C3
Ashfield Terr WN6 . . . .**35** C8
Ashfield Valley Prim Sch
OL11 . . . .**30** E4
Ashford M33 . . . .**107** C4
Ashford Ave
Boothstown M28 . . . .**77** F6
Eccles M30 . . . .**95** C8
Reddish SK5 . . . .**99** F2

Ashford Ave continued
Swinton M27 . . . .**79** C7
Ashford Cl Bolton BL2 . . . . .**25** E4
Bury BL8 . . . .**27** B1
Handforth SK9 . . . .**131** C4
Ashford Ct **11** OL4 . . . .**49** D1
Ashford Gr **19** SK13 . . . . .**171** E1
Ashford Mews SK13 . . . . .**171** E1
Ashford Rd
Manchester M20 . . . .**110** B7
Reddish SK4 . . . .**111** D6
Wilmslow SK9 . . . .**137** A4
Ashford Rise WN1 . . . .**37** B4
Ashford St OL10 . . . .**28** F2
Ashford Wlk Bolton BL1 . . .**143** E1
Oldham OL9 . . . .**152** B6
Ashgate Ave M22 . . . .**121** E4
Ashgill Wlk **4** M9 . . . .**157** E7
Ashgrove OL16 . . . .**31** B1
Ashia Cl OL16 . . . .**31** B6
Ashill Wlk M3 . . . .**162** E8
Ashington Cl BL1 . . . .**142** B3
Ashington Dr BL8 . . . .**26** F2
Ashington Way WN5 . . . . . .**36** B1
Ashkirk St **4** M18 . . . .**99** D5
Ashland Ave
Ashton-in-M WN4 . . . .**73** A4
5 Wigan WN1 . . . .**37** C2
Ashlands M33 . . . .**108** A5
Ashlands Ave
Boothstown M28 . . . .**78** A7
Failsworth M40 . . . .**65** C1
Swinton M27 . . . .**79** D6
Ashlands Cl BL0 . . . .**1** D2
Ashlands Dr M34 . . . .**100** E6
Ashlands Rd WA15 . . . . . .**108** A1
Ashlar Dr M12 . . . .**164** E8
Ashlea Gr OL4 . . . .**68** B6
Ashleigh Ave SK13 . . . . . .**104** B3
Ashleigh Cl OL2 . . . .**48** E2
Ashleigh Rd WA15 . . . .**120** B8
Ashley Ave Bolton BL2 . . . . .**42** B8
Manchester M16 . . . .**97** D4
Swinton M27 . . . .**79** D6
Urmston M41 . . . .**94** E2
Ashley CE Prim Sch
WA15 . . . .**128** E5
Ashley Cl OL11 . . . .**30** C4
Ashley Court Dr M40,OL9 . . .**65** F1
Ashley Cres M27 . . . .**79** D7
Ashley Ct Altrincham WA15 .**119** E1
Failsworth M40 . . . .**65** F1
Swinton M27 . . . .**61** F2
Ashley Dr Bramhall SK7 . . .**132** C6
Leigh WN7 . . . .**75** C8
Sale M33 . . . .**107** C2
Swinton M27 . . . .**79** D6
Ashley Gr **8** BL4 . . . .**60** C8
Ashley La M9 . . . .**157** F8
Ashley Mews Hyde SK14 . .**167** E1
Whitefield M45 . . . .**63** B7
Ashley Mill La N WA14 . . .**128** E8
Ashley Rd
Altrincham WA15 . . . .**119** E2
Ashley WA14,WA15 . . . . . .**128** E7
Ashley WA14,WA15,WA16 . .**128** C4
Droylsden M43 . . . .**83** C2
Handforth SK9 . . . .**131** B1
Hindley WN2 . . . .**57** B3
Stockport SK2 . . . .**124** C8
Ashley St Hyde SK14 . . . . .**167** E4
Manchester M4 . . . .**159** B3
Oldham M6 . . . .**152** C7
Salford M6 . . . .**154** E4
Walkden M28 . . . .**60** C5
Ashley St SK4 . . . .**168** B3
Ashleymill La WA14 . . . . . .**128** D7
Ashleys The SK4 . . . .**168** B3
Ashling Ct M29 . . . .**59** D1
Ashlor St BL9 . . . .**140** E1
Ashlyn Gr M14 . . . .**110** D8
Ashlynne OL6 . . . .**166** C3
Ashmeade WA15 . . . .**120** B1
Ashmill Wlk M9 . . . .**156** C6
Ashmond Rd **12** OL4 . . . . . .**67** F6
Ashmoor Rd M22 . . . .**121** E1
Ashmoor Wlk M22 . . . .**121** E1
Ashmore Ave SK3 . . . .**122** F7
Ashmore St M29 . . . .**77** D8
Ashmount Dr OL12 . . . .**14** F2
Ashness Cl BL6 . . . .**21** F3
Ashness Dr Bolton BL2 . . . .**25** E1
Bramhall SK7 . . . .**132** E8
Middleton M24 . . . .**46** D3
Ashness Gr BL2 . . . .**25** E1
Ashness Pl BL2 . . . .**25** E1
Ashover Ave M12 . . . .**164** F6
Ashover Cl **8** BL1 . . . .**24** F6
Ashover St M12 . . . .**164** F6
Ashover St M32 . . . .**96** E3
Ashridge Cl BL6 . . . .**40** C6
Ashridge Dr
Dukinfield SK16 . . . .**101** B7
Eccles M30 . . . .**95** C8
Ashridge Way WN5 . . . .**36** B1
Ashstead Rd M33 . . . .**108** C1
Ashton Ave WA14 . . . .**119** E6
Ashton Cres OL9 . . . .**66** A2
Ashton Ct Denton M34 . . . .**100** F6
Sale M33 . . . .**107** C4
Ashton Field Dr M28 . . . . . .**60** C4
Ashton Gallery **6** WN1 . . .**150** C4
Ashton Gdns
Glossop SK13 . . . .**116** C7
Rochdale OL11 . . . .**139** E5

Ashton Grange Ind Est
WN4 . . . .**73** B6
Ashton Heath WN4 . . . .**73** D2
Ashton Hill La M43 . . . . . .**100** A8
Ashton Ho
Manchester M15 . . . .**162** E8
Hyde SK14 . . . .**167** E4
Ashton La Middleton M24 . . .**65** A8
Sale M33 . . . .**107** F5
Ashton New Rd
Droylsden M11,M43 . . . . . .**83** C1
Manchester M11,M40 . . . .**160** F1
Ashton Nichol Mere
Cty Prim Sch WN4 . . . . . .**73** B5
Ashton Old Rd
Manchester M11 . . . .**99** D7
Manchester M12 . . . .**164** D5
Ashton on Mersey Sch
M33 . . . .**107** F3
Ashton Pl SK7 . . . .**124** F1
Ashton Rd Bredbury SK6 . .**112** E6
Carrington M31,M33 . . . . .**106** C3
Denton M34 . . . .**100** A6
Droylsden M43 . . . .**84** B1
Dukinfield SK14 . . . .**101** E5
Failsworth M35 . . . .**84** C7
Golborne WA3 . . . .**74** A2
Manchester M9 . . . .**64** D5
Newton-le-W WA12 . . . . . .**89** C5
Oldham OL8,OL7 . . . .**66** F3
Windy Arbour M4 &WN5 . . .**72** B8
Ashton Rd E M35 . . . .**84** A7
Ashton Rd W M35 . . . .**83** F7
Ashton Ret Pk OL6 . . . . . .**166** B3
Ashton St Bolton BL3 . . . . .**146** B4
Dukinfield SK16 . . . .**101** A7
Glossop SK13 . . . .**116** C7
4 Heywood OL10 . . . .**29** C2
Little Lever BL3 . . . .**43** B3
Manchester M9 . . . .**157** F8
Oldham OL9 . . . .**66** A3
Rochdale OL11 . . . .**139** E5
Romiley SK6 . . . .**113** C6
Wigan WN1 . . . .**151** E6
Ashton Sta OL6 . . . .**166** B3
Ashton-under-Lyne
Sixth Form Coll OL6 . . . .**85** E3
Ashurst Ave M11 . . . .**83** B2
Ashurst Cl Bolton BL2 . . . . .**25** F3
Hyde SK14 . . . .**102** A1
Ashurst Dr SK3,SK8 . . . . .**123** E6
Ashurst Gdns OL6 . . . .**166** B4
Ashurst Rd
Shevington Moor WN6 . . . . .**19** B2
Wythenshawe M22 . . . . . .**121** F3
Ashville Terr M40 . . . .**64** F1
Ashwater Wlk **8** M9 . . . . . .**64** E5
Ashway OL6 . . . .**166** A3
Ashway Clough N SK2 . . . .**124** D5
Ashway Clough S SK2 . . . .**124** D5
Ashwell Ave WA3 . . . .**74** D1
Ashwell Rd M23 . . . .**121** B7
Ashwell St BL2 . . . .**25** B3
Ashwin Wlk **8** M8 . . . .**155** F6
Ashwood Altrincham WA14 .**128** B8
Chadderton OL9 . . . .**65** C7
Glossop SK13 . . . .**115** F8
Kearsley BL4 . . . .**61** B7
Ashwood Ave
Abram Brow WN2 . . . .**74** C7
Ashton-in-M WN4 . . . .**73** A4
Golborne WA3 . . . .**90** B8
Manchester M20 . . . .**109** E4
Ramsbottom BL0 . . . .**11** D4
Reddish M34 . . . .**100** B3
Sale M33 . . . .**107** C3
Walkden M28 . . . .**60** C5
Ashwood Cres SK6 . . . . . .**125** F7
Ashwood Ct M20 . . . .**109** E4
Ashwood Dr Bury BL8 . . . . .**27** B6
Littleborough OL15 . . . . . .**15** F5
Royton OL2 . . . .**48** C5
Ashwood Rd SK12 . . . .**135** C6
Ashworth Ave Denton M34 .**100** F7
Little Lever BL3 . . . .**43** C3
Urmston M41 . . . .**94** C2
Ashworth Cl
Altrincham WA14 . . . .**119** B1
Littleborough OL15 . . . . . .**16** A7
Oldham OL9 . . . .**66** C4
Royton OL2 . . . .**48** F4
Ashworth Ct
1 Radcliffe M26 . . . .**44** C4
Shaw OL2 . . . .**149** B6
Ashworth La Bolton BL1 . . . .**25** A6
Mottram-in-L SK14 . . . . . .**102** F2
Ashworth Mews OL10 . . . . .**29** A2
Ashworth Rd
Rochdale OL10,OL11 . . . . .**29** B7
Rochdale OL11 . . . .**12** E2
Ashworth St Aspull WN2 . . .**38** E4
3 Bacup OL13 . . . .**3** B8
Bury BL8 . . . .**27** C3
Denton M34 . . . .**100** E4
Failsworth M35 . . . .**83** D6
Farnworth BL4 . . . .**60** C8
Heywood OL10 . . . .**46** B8
Manchester M7,M8 . . . . . .**155** F6
Oldham OL1 . . . .**153** F6
Radcliffe M26 . . . .**44** C4
Rawtenstall BB4 . . . .**2** F5
Rochdale OL12 . . . .**139** E8
Ashworth Terr
2 Bacup OL13 . . . .**3** B8
Bolton BL2 . . . .**25** E4
Ashworth View M5 . . . .**161** B2
Ashworth Way **8** SK14 . . .**102** F2
Asia St **3** BL3 . . . .**42** A3

Askern Ave M22 . . . .**121** D3
Askett Cl M40 . . . .**83** D6
Askrigg Wlk **8** M13 . . . . . .**98** F4
Askwith Dr WN2 . . . .**56** F4
Askwith Rd WN2 . . . .**56** F3
Aspell Cl M24 . . . .**64** F8
Aspen Cl Altrincham WA15 .**120** C5
Stockport SK4 . . . .**168** A1
Westhoughton BL5 . . . .**39** F2
Aspen Gdns OL12 . . . .**14** A1
Aspen Gn M34 . . . .**101** A4
Aspen Way SK6 . . . .**135** A7
Aspen Wood SK14 . . . .**167** F3
Aspen Wood Dr OL9 . . . . . .**65** C7
Aspens The SK8 . . . .**122** A6
Aspenshaw Cotts SK22 . . .**127** A4
Aspenshaw Rd SK22 . . . . .**127** A3
Aspenwood WN4 . . . .**73** A2
Aspenwood Cl SK6 . . . . . .**125** E7
Aspenwood Dr M33 . . . . . .**107** C4
Aspin La M4 . . . .**159** A3
Aspinal Prim Sch M18 . . . . .**99** E3
Aspinall Cl M28 . . . .**59** F3
Aspinall Cres M28 . . . .**59** F3
Aspinall Gr **12** M28 . . . .**59** F3
Aspinall Rd WN6 . . . .**19** B1
Aspinall St Heywood OL10 . . .**29** C2
Horwich BL6 . . . .**22** D1
Manchester M14 . . . .**98** C3
Middleton M24 . . . .**65** C7
5 Platt Bridge WN2 . . . . . .**56** A2
Aspland Rd SK14 . . . .**113** F8
Aspland Way BL6 . . . .**22** C1
Aspull Arc **7** WN1 . . . .**150** C5
Aspull Church Sch WN2 . . .**38** C4
Aspull Comm WN7 . . . .**75** C1
Aspull New Springs
Inf Sch WN2 . . . .**38** A2
Aspull St OL4 . . . .**67** C5
Aspull Wlk M13 . . . .**163** C6
Asquith Ave SK16 . . . .**101** C6
Asquith Rd M19 . . . .**110** F6
Asquith St SK5 . . . .**99** F1
Assheton Ave M34 . . . .**84** C1
Assheton Cl OL6 . . . .**166** B3
Assheton Cres M40 . . . .**83** D4
Assheton Ho OL6 . . . .**166** B3
Assheton Rd
Failsworth M40 . . . .**83** D4
Shaw OL2 . . . .**48** F7
Assheton St
5 Middleton M24 . . . .**47** A1
9 Middleton M24 . . . .**47** A1
Assheton Way M24 . . . .**65** A8
Assisi Gdns M12 . . . .**165** B6
Assumption Rd M24 . . . . . .**46** D3
Astan Ave M43 . . . .**83** D2
Astbury Ave Droylsden M34 .**84** D1
Manchester M21 . . . .**109** C4
Astbury Cl
2 Altrincham WA15 . . . . .**119** C6
Golborne WA3 . . . .**91** B8
Oldham OL4 . . . .**67** F6
Astbury Cres SK3 . . . .**170** D6
Astbury St M26 . . . .**44** B1
Astbury Wlk SK8 . . . .**123** A5
Aster Ave BL4 . . . .**42** A1
Aster Ho OL1 . . . .**48** E1
Aster St OL1 . . . .**48** E1
Aster Wlk M31 . . . .**105** F2
Astley Cl OL2 . . . .**48** F7
Astley Ct M44 . . . .**105** E8
Astley Gdns SK16 . . . .**101** B8
Astley Gr SK15 . . . .**85** F3
Astley Green Colliery Mus
M29 . . . .**77** C4
Astley Hall Dr
Ramsbottom BL0 . . . .**11** C4
Tyldesley M29 . . . .**77** B6
Astley High Sch SK16 . . . .**101** E6
Astley La BL1 . . . .**143** E3
Astley Rd Bolton BL2 . . . . . .**25** E5
Stalybridge SK15 . . . .**85** F2
Astley St Bolton BL1 . . . . . .**143** E2
Droylsden M11 . . . .**83** C1
Dukinfield SK16 . . . .**101** A8
Leigh WN7 . . . .**76** B4
Stockport SK4 . . . .**169** E1
Tyldesley M29 . . . .**77** A7
Astley Terr **7** SK16 . . . . . .**166** C1
Aston Ave M14 . . . .**98** A2
Aston Cl SK3 . . . .**123** C6
Aston Gdns **4** BL4 . . . .**42** D1
Aston Gr M29 . . . .**59** C1
Aston Ho BL1 . . . .**144** C7
Astor Way **13** SK9 . . . .**131** D5
Astor Rd Manchester M19 . .**110** E7
Salford M5 . . . .**80** C1
Astra Bsns Pk M17 . . . .**95** F8
Astra Ind Ctr OL11 . . . .**30** C3
Atcham Gr M9 . . . .**64** D5
Athenian Gdns **12** M5,M7 . .**81** C5
Athens Dr M28 . . . .**60** C2
Athens St SK1 . . . .**124** A8
Athens Way OL4 . . . .**67** E6
Atherfield BL2 . . . .**25** E4
Atherfield Cl **3** M18 . . . .**99** F6
Atherleigh Gr WN7 . . . .**75** F7
Atherleigh Way WN7 . . . . . .**75** E5
Atherley Gr OL9 . . . .**65** C2
Atherstone **10** OL12 . . . . . .**139** F8
Atherstone Ave M8 . . . .**64** A2
Atherton Ave SK14 . . . . . .**103** A4
Atherton Cl M35 . . . .**84** B5
Atherton Gr SK14 . . . .**103** A4

Atherton Green Hall Sch
M46 .....58 F4
Atherton Ho M46 .....58 D4
Atherton La M44 .....105 E5
Atherton Rd WN2 .....56 D5
Atherton Sacred Heart
RC Prim Sch M46 .....58 E1
Atherton Sq 8 WN1 .....150 C8
  Bacup OL13 .....3 C8
  Bickershaw WN2 .....74 E8
  Eccles M30 .....79 B1
  Manchester M3 .....158 A1
  Oldham OL4 .....67 C5
  Oldham OL4 .....67 F5
  9 Oldham OL4 .....67 F6
  Stockport SK3 .....170 D8
  7 Wigan WN5 .....54 F6
Atherton St George's
  Prim Sch M46 .....58 C4
Atherton Sta M46 .....58 E4
Atherton Way Bacup OL13 .....3 B8
  4 Eccles M30 .....79 B1
Athlone Ave Bolton BL1 .....24 D5
  Bury BL9 .....140 F4
  Cheadle SK8 .....123 C5
  Manchester M40 .....83 A8
Athol Cres WN2 .....57 B3
Athol Rd Bramhall SK7 .....132 D5
  Manchester M16 .....109 E8
Athol St Ashton-u-L OL6 .....166 C5
  Eccles M30 .....79 C1
  Ramsbottom BL0 .....138 C7
  Reddish M18 .....99 E5
  Rochdale OL12 .....15 B1
  Stockport SK4 .....169 D3
Athole St M5,M6 .....154 F1
Atholl Ave M32 .....96 A2
Atholl Cl BL3 .....40 F6
Atholl Dr OL10 .....46 A8
Atholl Gr WN3 .....55 A3
Athos Wlk M40 .....65 C2
Atkin St M28 .....60 D2
Atkinson Ave BL3 .....42 B3
Atkinson Ho M33 .....108 B5
Atkinson Rd Sale M33 .....108 A5
  Urmston M41 .....95 D2
Atkinson St Abram WN2 .....74 B8
  Manchester M3 .....158 E1
  Oldham OL9 .....153 D8
  2 Rochdale OL11 .....30 C2
  Stockport SK1 .....124 A7
Atlanta Ave M90 .....130 A8
Atlantic Bsns Ctr WA14 .....119 C7
Atlantic St WA14 .....119 B6
Atlantic Wlk 18 M11 .....160 F1
Atlas St Ashton-u-L OL7 .....85 A6
  Dukinfield SK16 .....101 D8
Atlas Trad Est SK5 .....111 F7
Atlow Dr M23 .....121 B5
Attenbury's La WA14 .....119 E8
Attenbury's Pk Est WA14 119 E8
Attercliffe Rd M21 .....109 A7
Attewell St M11 .....165 A8
Attingham Wlk
  Denton M34 .....100 E1
  Wigan WN3 .....150 A5
Attleboro Rd M40 .....83 A7
Attlee Ave WA3 .....92 C4
Attlee Way M12 .....160 C1
Attwood Rd WA15 .....120 B5
Attwood St M12 .....99 A3
Atwood Rd M20 .....110 C3
Atwood St M1 .....163 A8
Auberson Rd BL3 .....147 D3
Aubrey Rd M14 .....110 E7
Aubrey St Rochdale OL11 .....139 F5
  Salford M5 .....161 A7
Auburn Ave Bredbury SK6 .....112 F4
  Hyde SK14 .....167 E1
Auburn Dr M41 .....95 E1
Auburn Rd Denton M34 .....100 E2
  Manchester M16 .....97 B4
Auburn St Bolton BL3 .....147 D4
  Manchester M1 .....159 B1
  Manchester M1 .....163 B8
Auckland Dr M6 .....81 A5
Auckland Rd M19 .....110 F8
Audax Wlk M40 .....83 B4
Auden Cl M11 .....83 D1
Auden Ct M11 .....83 D1
Audenshaw Hall Gr M34 .....100 B7
Audenshaw Prim Sch
  M34 .....100 D7
Audenshaw Rd
  Ashton-u-L M34 .....100 D7
  Ashton-u-L M34 .....100 E8
Audenshaw Sch M34 .....100 E6
Audenshaw St Stephen's
  CE Prim Sch
  M34 .....100 E8
Audlem Cl M40 .....160 D2
Audlem Wlk SK8 .....123 A6
Audley Ave M32 .....95 F4
Audley Rd M19 .....99 E4
Audley St Ashton-u-L OL6 .....85 E2
  Mossley OL5 .....68 D1
Audlum Ct BL9 .....141 A2
Audrey Ave M18 .....99 E5
Audrey St M9 .....157 F7
Aughton Cl WN5 .....71 E4
Augusta Cl OL12 .....14 E2
Augusta St OL12 .....14 E1
Augustine Webster Cl
  M9 .....157 E8
Augustus St 3 Bolton BL3 .....42 A4
  Manchester M3,M8 .....159 A4

Augustus Way M15 .....97 E4
Austell Rd M22 .....121 D1
Austen Ave BL9 .....44 F6
Austen Rd M30 .....79 D1
Austen Wlk OL11 .....49 E4
Auster Cl M14 .....110 A8
Austin Ave WN4 .....72 E4
Austin Dr M20 .....110 C4
Austin Gr M20 .....110 C4
Austin St WN7 .....75 D5
Austin's La BL6 .....22 F1
Autumn St M13 .....98 C4
Avallon Cl BL8 .....26 F7
Avalon Dr M20 .....122 C8
Avalon Pk OL4 .....67 D6
Avebury Cl Golborne WA3 .....90 E8
  Horwich BL6 .....22 F1
  Manchester M7 .....155 F6
Avebury Rd M23 .....121 A5
Avenham Cl M15 .....162 E5
Avening Wlk 7 M22 .....121 C2
Avens Rd M31 .....105 F3
Avenue St Bolton BL1 .....143 D1
  Stockport SK1 .....169 F2
Avenue The Adlington PR6 .....21 A8
  Alderley Edge SK9 .....137 A1
  Altrincham WA15 .....128 F8
  Bolton BL2 .....148 B7
  Boothstown M28 .....78 B3
  Bredbury SK6 .....112 D4
  Eccles M30 .....79 D1
  Gatley SK8 .....122 A1
  Hadfield SK13 .....104 A4
  Leigh WN7 .....76 A6
  Manchester M7 .....81 C5
  Newton-le-W WA3 .....89 D4
  Orrell WN5 .....53 D3
  Sale M33 .....107 E3
  Shaw OL2 .....149 A6
  Urmston M41 .....94 E2
  Westhoughton BL5 .....39 F1
  Wigan WN1 .....37 D2
  Wigan WN6 .....36 E4
  Worsley M28 .....78 D4
Avenue Works M17 .....96 C6
Averham Cl WN4 .....73 B2
Averhill M28 .....78 B8
Averill St M40 .....83 D5
Averon Rise OL1 .....49 D4
Aveson Ave M21 .....109 B6
Avian Dr M14 .....110 B8
Aviary Rd M28 .....78 F6
Aviary The M28 .....79 A6
Aviemore Cl WN4 .....72 D4
Avis Cl OL2 .....149 B7
Avlan Cl M30 .....94 F7
Avocet Cl Leigh WN7 .....76 A6
  Newton-le-W WA12 .....89 C4
Avocet Dr
  Altrincham WA14 .....119 B8
  Irlam M44 .....94 A4
Avon Bank 1 SK6 .....112 F3
Avon Cl Marple SK6 .....125 E5
  Milnrow OL16 .....32 A6
  Walkden M28 .....60 A2
Avon Ct 3 M15 .....162 D6
Avon Dr BL9 .....28 A8
Avon Gdns M19 .....111 A6
Avon Rd Altrincham WA15 .....128 E8
  Ashton-in-M WN4 .....73 C1
  Billinge WN5 .....71 D3
  Chadderton OL9 .....65 F8
  Culcheth WA3 .....92 A2
  Gatley SK8 .....131 C7
  Heywood OL10 .....29 A2
  Kearsley BL4 .....61 B5
  Manchester M19 .....111 A6
  Shaw OL2 .....149 B8
  Tyldesley M29 .....77 C7
  Wigan WN5 .....54 C7
Avon St Bolton BL1 .....142 B1
  Leigh WN7 .....76 B4
  Oldham OL8 .....66 F4
  Stockport SK3 .....170 E7
Avonbrook Dr OL9 .....65 F2
Avoncliff Cl BL1 .....143 D3
Avoncourt Dr M20 .....110 A4
Avondale
  Ramsbottom BL0 .....10 F3
  Salford M6 .....80 B5
  Tyldesley M29 .....77 C6
Avondale Ave Bury BL9 .....140 F4
  Hazel Grove SK7 .....124 F3
Avondale Cres 2 M41 .....95 C3
Avondale Ct OL11 .....47 D7
Avondale Dr
  Ramsbottom BL0 .....10 F3
  Salford M6 .....80 B5
  Tyldesley M29 .....77 C6
Avondale Lo M33 .....108 B3
Avondale Rd Farnworth 4 59 F8
  Hazel Grove SK7 .....124 F3
  Stockport SK3 .....123 C8
  Stretford M32 .....96 F4
  Whitefield M45 .....44 E1
  Wigan WN1 .....37 C1
Avondale Rise SK9 .....137 D6
Avondale Sch SK3 .....123 B7
Avondale St Bolton BL1 .....142 C1
  Manchester M8 .....156 A4
  Standish WN6 .....19 E2
Avonhead Cl BL6 .....21 F3
Avonlea Dr M19 .....110 E6
Avonlea Rd Droylsden M43 .....83 E2
  Sale M33 .....107 D1
Avonleigh Gdns 7 OL1 .....49 C4
Avril Cl SK5 .....111 F8
Avril Ct WN3 .....55 E4

Avro Cl M14 .....98 B1
Avro Ct M24 .....65 D8
Avro Way M90 .....129 F7
Avroe Rd M30 .....94 F7
Awburn Rd SK14 .....102 E1
Axbridge Wlk M40 .....160 D2
Axford Cl M7 .....155 F6
Axon Sq M16 .....97 F4
Aycliffe Ave M21 .....109 D5
Aycliffe Gr M13 .....98 E3
Aye Bridge Rd WA3 .....74 B5
Aylesbury Ave
  Denton M34 .....100 F1
  Urmston M41 .....95 E3
Aylesbury Cl M5 .....81 A1
Aylesbury Cres WN2 .....57 C2
Aylesbury Gr M21 .....97 C1
Aylesbury Gr M24 .....47 C2
Aylesby Ave M18 .....99 B4
Aylesford Rd M14 .....98 D3
Aylesford Wlk BL1 .....143 E1
Aylestone Wlk 13 M40 .....83 A7
Aylsham Cl SK6 .....112 F4
Aylsham Mews M27 .....79 D5
Aylwin Dr M33 .....108 C3
Ayr Ave OL8 .....66 F3
Ayr Cl SK7 .....125 A2
Ayr Gr OL10 .....29 A1
Ayr St BL2 .....25 C4
Ayrefield Gr WN6 .....35 D6
Ayrefield Rd WN8 .....35 C4
Ayres Rd M16 .....97 C4
Ayrshire Rd M7 .....81 B6
Ayrton Gr M38 .....60 A5
Aysgarth OL16 .....125 D1
Aysgarth Ave Cheadle SK8 .....122 C6
  Droylsden M18 .....99 E5
  Romiley SK6 .....113 D4
Aysgarth Cl M33 .....107 D3
Ayshford OL14 .....119 B6
Ayton Gr M14 .....98 B4
Aytoun St M1 .....159 B1
Azalea Ave M18 .....99 D6

B

Babbacombe Gr M9 .....64 B5
Babbacombe Rd SK2 .....124 C6
Babylon La PR6 .....21 B8
Back Abingdon Rd BL2 .....25 C1
Back Acton St M1 .....163 B8
Back Adrian Rd BL1 .....142 C3
Back Adrian Rd E 6 BL1 .....142 C2
Back Ainscow St BL1 .....145 E8
Back Ainsworth La 2 .....25 C1
Back Ainsworth La E BL1 .....25 C1
Back Ainsworth Rd N
  Bury BL8 .....27 B2
  Bury BL8 .....27 C2
Back Ainsworth Rd S BL8 .....27 C2
Back Ainsworth St
  2 Bolton BL1 .....142 C3
  25 Bolton BL1 .....143 D2
Back Albert St BL9 .....141 A4
Back Albion Pl BL9 .....140 F4
Back Alder St 4 BL3 .....147 F3
Back Alexander Rd 10 BL2 25 C1
Back Alexandra St 4 .....146 C4
Back Alfred St 12 BL3 .....42 A4
Back Alice St
  10 Bolton BL3 .....144 C5
  Little Lever BL3 .....43 B3
Back All Saints' St 11
  BL1 .....147 F8
Back Alston St BL3 .....147 F3
Back America Row BL1 .....142 C3
Back Andrew St
  Bolton BL3 .....145 F6
  Bury BL9 .....141 A2
  BL9 .....141 A2
Back Andrew St N 5
  BL9 .....141 A2
Back Anglia Gr BL3 .....146 C4
Back Annis Rd 3 BL3 .....146 B4
Back Anson St 3 BL1 .....143 F3
Back Apple Terr BL1 .....143 D2
Back Argo St 3 BL3 .....147 D4
Back Argyle St 8 BL9 .....27 F5
Back Arlington St BL3 .....147 F3
Back Arnold St BL1 .....142 C2
Back Arnold Terr BL1 .....23 F1
Back Ash St Bolton BL2 .....148 A6
  3 Bury BL9 .....141 A2
Back Ashbee St 11 BL1 .....145 D8
Back Ashford Wlk BL1 .....143 E1
Back Ashley St M4 .....159 B3
Back Ashton St 3 .....146 B4
Back Ashworth La BL1 .....24 F5
Back Ashworth St 10 BL8 .27 C5
Back Astley St BL1 .....143 E2
Back Auburn St 14 BL3 .....147 D4
Back Augustus St 3 BL3 .....42 A4
Back Augustus St W 1
  BL3 .....42 A4
Back Avenue St 3 BL1 .....145 D8
Back Avondale BL1 .....142 C1
Back Baldwin St BL3 .....145 E5
Back Baldwin St N BL3 .....145 E5
Back Balloon St 1 M4 .....159 A2
Back Banbury St 4 BL2 .....25 C1
Back Bank St M8 .....159 A4
Back Bankfield St BL3 .....144 C5
Back Bantry St BL3 .....145 E5
Back Barbara St BL3 .....147 D4
Back Bark St 3 BL1 .....145 E7
Back Bashall St BL1 .....144 C8

Back Battenberg Rd 1
  BL1 .....144 C8
Back Baxendale St 1
  BL1 .....143 E4
Back Bayley St BL1 .....145 D8
Back Baythorpe St BL1 .....143 F2
Back Baythorpe St N 4
  BL1 .....143 F3
Back Beaconsfield St
  BL3 .....145 D6
Back Beaconsfield Terr
  BL3 .....25 B1
Back Beatrice Rd 9 BL1 .142 C1
Back Bedford St 4 BL1 .145 D8
Back Beech St BL1 .....143 F3
Back Beechwood St 5
  BL3 .....147 F3
Back Belbeck St 3 BL8 .....27 C2
Back Bell La Bury BL9 .....141 A3
  Bury BL9 .....141 B3
Back Belmont Rd 1 BL1 .24 E5
Back Belmont Rd E 5 BL1 24 E5
Back Bennett's La BL1 .....142 C2
Back Bennett's La E BL1 .142 C2
Back Benson St BL9 .....141 A1
Back Bentinck St 4 BL1 .142 B1
Back Bentley St 2 .....148 C5
Back Bertrand Rd BL1 .....144 C7
Back Beverley Rd BL1 .....144 C8
Back Birch St BL9 .....140 F3
Back Birley St 7 BL1 .....142 E4
Back Blackbank St BL1 .....143 F3
Back Blackburn Rd 1 .....142 A1
Back Blackburn Rd E BL7 ..8 D3
Back Blackburn Rd W
  Bolton BL1 .....143 E3
  5 Bolton BL1 .....143 E4
  4 Bolton BL7 .....24 E5
  Bolton BL7 .....24 E8
Back Blackburn St 6
  BL1 .....143 F3
Back Blackwood St 3 BL3 .147 F8
Back Bolton Rd N BL8 .....27 C1
Back Bolton Rd S Bury BL8 27 C1
  Bury BL8 .....27 C2
Back Bolton St 9 BL1 .....143 F3
Back Bolton St S BL9 .....140 E2
Back Bond St W BL1 .....141 A2
Back Boundary St 13 BL1 143 D2
Back Bowen St BL1 .....142 B1
Back Bowness Rd BL3 .....147 D4
Back Bradford Rd
  Bolton BL3 .....42 A3
  18 Bolton BL3 .....42 A4
Back Bradford Rd W 1
  BL3 .....42 A3
Back Bradford St BL2 .....148 B7
Back Bradford St E BL2 .....148 B7
Back Bradford St S 4
  BL2 .....148 A6
Back Bradford St W
  Bolton BL2 .....148 A7
  Bolton BL2 .....148 B7
Back Bradshaw Brow E
  BL2 .....25 C4
Back Bradshaw Brow W
  BL2 .....25 C4
Back Bradshaw Rd E 2 BL2 .25 D5
Back Bradshaw St 7 OL16 31 A8
Back Bradshawgate 1
  BL1 .....145 F6
Back Brandon St 5 BL3 .147 D4
Back Brandon St W 4
  BL3 .....147 F8
Back Brandwood St BL3 .146 C4
Back Bride St BL1 .....143 E2
Back Bridge St
  8 Bolton BL1 .....145 F6
  Manchester M3 .....158 F1
  New Mills SK22 .....127 C1
  Newton-le-W WA12 .....89 B3
  Ramsbottom BL0 .....138 C6
Back Bridgeman St BL3 .147 E4
Back Brierley St BL9 .....44 E8
Back Brierley St S BL9 .....44 E8
Back Brigade St BL1 .....144 C7
Back Brindley St 2 BL1 .143 F3
Back Brink's Pl BL1 .....145 F6
Back Bristol Ave 11 BL2 .....25 C1
Back Bristol St BL3 .....145 D5
Back Broach St BL3 .....147 D4
Back Broad o' th' La 6
  BL1 .....24 E5
Back Broad St 2 BL9 .....140 E2
Back Bromwich St BL2 .....148 B6
Back Brookfield St 12 BL8 .27 C5
Back Broom St BL2 .....148 A7
Back Brow WN8 .....53 C7
Back Bryce St BL3 .....145 E5
Back Burnaby St BL3 .....145 D5
Back Burnham Ave BL1 .142 A1
Back Bury New Rd BL2 .148 A7
Back Bury Old Rd 2 BL2 148 A7
Back Bury Rd BL2 .....42 E7
Back Bury Rd E BL2 .....148 C7
Back Bury Rd S
  3 Bolton BL2 .....148 C7
  Bolton BL2 .....42 F7
Back Bushell St BL3 .....146 B4
Back Byrom St BL3 .....145 E5
Back Byrom St S 10 BL8 .....27 B4

Back Cambridge St OL7 .....84 F1
Back Camp St M7 .....155 D5
Back Canada St
  4 Bolton BL1 .....142 C2
  Horwich BL6 .....22 B3
Back Canada St S BL1 .....142 C2
Back Canning St BL9 .....140 F4
Back Carl St 20 BL1 .....143 D2
Back Carter St 19 BL3 .....42 A4
Back Castle St
  4 Bolton BL2 .....148 A7
  Bolton BL2 .....148 B6
Back Cateaton St 1 BL9 .....140 F3
Back Cecil St BL2 .....148 B7
Back Cecilia St BL3 .....42 A4
Back Cedar St BL3 .....141 B3
Back Cedar St N BL9 .....141 B3
Back Cemetery Rd E BL2 148 B7
Back Cemetery Terr 9
  OL13 .....3 D8
Back Cestrian St 1 BL3 .....147 F3
Back Chalfont St BL1 .....143 F2
Back Chapel St
  9 Eccles M30 .....79 F2
  Hazel Grove SK7 .....124 E3
  Horwich BL6 .....22 C3
  Littleborough OL12 .....15 C7
Back Chapman St 5 BL1 142 B3
Back Charles Holden St
  BL1 .....145 D6
Back Chaucer St 3 BL1 .143 D2
Back Cheapside BL1 .....145 F7
Back Chesham Rd N 6
  BL9 .....141 A4
Back Chesham Rd S 7
  BL9 .....141 A4
Back Chester St BL9 .....141 A4
Back China La M1 .....159 B1
Back Chorley New Rd
  Bolton BL1 .....144 C7
  Bolton BL1 .....145 D8
Back Chorley New Rd N
  Bolton BL1 .....144 B7
  Bolton BL1 .....144 C8
Back Chorley Old Rd
  Bolton BL1 .....142 A1
  2 Bolton BL1 .....142 B1
  Bolton BL1 .....142 C1
  4 Bolton BL1 .....144 C8
Back Chorley Old Rd S
  Bolton BL1 .....142 B1
  Bolton BL1 .....142 B1
  Bolton BL1 .....144 C8
Back Chorley St E 11 BL1 145 E7
Back Church Ave BL3 .....146 C4
Back Church Rd
  Bolton BL1 .....142 A2
  1 Bolton BL1 .....142 C2
Back Church Rd N
  7 Bolton BL1 .....142 B2
Back Church St
  Bolton BL1 .....145 E8
  Little Lever BL3 .....43 A3
Back Clarendon Rd 8
  BL2 .....148 C7
Back Clarke St 18 BL1 .144 C8
Back Clay St E BL7 .....25 A7
Back Clay St W BL7 .....25 A7
Back Clegg St BL2 .....148 C7
Back Clegg's Bldgs 12
  BL1 .....145 E8
Back Clifton St 1 BL9 .140 F4
Back Cloister St 5 BL1 .142 C2
Back Clyde St BL1 .....143 E2
Back Cobden St BL1 .....143 D3
Back Colenso Rd BL2 .....42 D7
Back College Land 1
  M3 .....158 F1
Back College Way BL3 .145 E6
Back Collings St BL1 .....143 E2
Back Columbia Rd 17
  BL1 .....144 C8
Back Common St BL5 .....57 B2
Back Coniston St 1 BL1 143 F3
Back Coop St BL1 .....143 E4
Back Cope Bank BL1 .....142 B2
Back Cornall St BL8 .....27 C3
Back Corson St BL4 .....42 D2
Back Cottam St BL8 .....27 C3
Back Cotton St BL1 .....143 D2
Back Cowm La OL12 .....4 C3
Back Cox Green Rd N 3
  BL7 .....24 F8
Back Cox Green Rd S 1
  BL7 .....24 F8
Back Crawford Ave BL2 148 B6
Back Crawford St BL2 .....148 B6
Back Crescent Ave BL1 .145 D8
Back Crescent Rd BL3 .....42 A4
Back Crescent Rd W BL3 .42 B3
Back Croft La BL3 .....148 B5
Back Cromer Ave BL2 .....25 C1
Back Crosby Rd BL1 .....144 B8
Back Cross La WA12 .....89 B4
Back Croston St BL3 .....146 C4
Back Crostons Rd BL8 .....140 D3
Back Crown St BL6 .....22 A4
Back Crumpsall St 32
  BL1 .....143 E2

Back Crumpsall St N 5
BL1 ....143 E3
Back Cundey St BL1 ....142 C1
Back Curzon Rd BL1 ....144 C7
Back Cyril St BL3 ....148 A5
Back Dale St OL16 ....31 F5
Back Daisy St BL3 ......146 C4
Back Darley St BL4 ......60 E8
Back Darwen Rd N
 Bolton BL7 ....24 F8
 Bolton BL7 ....25 A7
 Bolton BL7 ....25 B7
 Bolton BL7 ....8 E1
Back Darwen Rd S BL7 ...25 A7
Back Darwin St 11 BL1 ..143 D2
Back Dawes St BL3 ......145 F6
Back Deal St Bolton BL3 .147 F3
 Bury BL9 ....141 B2
Back Deane Church La
 BL3 ....146 B4
Back Deane Church La W
 BL3 ....146 B4
Back Deane Rd BL3 ....144 C5
Back Deane Rd N
 Bolton BL3 ....144 C6
 Bolton BL3 ....145 D6
Back Delamere St N BL9 ..28 A5
Back Delamere St S BL9 ..28 A5
Back Denton St BL9 .....140 F4
Back Derby St Bolton BL3 .145 C5
 Bolton BL3 ....147 D4
 Bury BL9 ....140 F2
Back Design St BL3 ......146 B4
Back Devon St N 2 BL3 ..44 E8
Back Devon St S BL3 .....44 F8
Back Devonshire Rd BL1 .142 A1
Back Dijon St BL3 ....146 C4
Back Dijon St N BL3 .....146 C4
Back Dobie St 20 BL3 ....42 A4
Back Doffcocker Brow
 BL1 ....142 A1
Back Dorset St BL2 ......148 A7
Back Dougill St BL1 .....142 B1
Back Dougill St S BL1 ....142 B1
Back Drake St OL16 .....139 F7
Back Drummond St 4
 BL1 ....143 E4
Back Ducie Ave BL1 .....144 C7
Back Duckworth St 4
 BL9 ....141 A4
Back Duncan St
 Horwich BL6 ....22 C3
 Manchester M7 ....81 C7
Back Dunstan St 1 BL2 ..148 C7
Back Durham St OL11 ....31 A5
Back Duxbury St BL1 ....143 D3
Back Earnshaw St BL3 ...146 B3
Back East St BL9 ....140 F1
Back Eastbank St 4 BL3 .143 F2
Back Eckersley Rd BL1 ..143 D3
Back Edditch Gr BL2 ....148 C7
Back Edditch Gr N 6
 BL2 ....148 C7
Back Eden St BL1 ....143 E3
Back Edgmont Ave BL3 ..147 D4
Back Eldon St BL9 ......140 F4
Back Elgin St BL1 ....143 D3
Back Ellesmere Rd BL3 ..146 C3
Back Ellesmere St BL3 ..145 D6
Back Elm St BL9 ....141 B2
Back Elmwood Gr 20 BL3 .144 C8
Back Elmwood Gr W 19
 BL1 ....144 C8
Back Elsworth St M3,M4 ..159 A4
Back Emmett St BL6 ......22 B3
Back Empire Rd BL2 ......42 D7
Back Empress St BL1 ....142 B1
Back Ena St 4 BL3 ....42 A3
Back Ernest St 1 BL1 ...145 D6
Back Eskrick St 2 BL1 ..143 D2
Back Eskrick St E 7 BL1 .143 D2
Back Eskrick St S 15 BL1 .143 D2
Back Eskrick St W BL1 ...143 D2
Back Essingdon St BL3 ..147 D4
Back Essingdon St S BL3 .147 D4
Back Eustace St 2 BL3 ...42 A3
Back Euxton St BL3 .....147 D4
Back Everton St N 6 BL1 .143 F2
Back Ewart St 11 BL1 ...143 E2
Back Fair St BL3 ....146 C2
Back Fairhaven Rd BL1 ..143 F3
Back Fenton St BL8 ......27 C3
Back Fern St E 2 BL3 ....144 C6
Back Fir St BL9 ....141 B2
Back Fitton St BL3 ......147 E4
Back Fletcher St
 Bury BL9 ....141 A2
 Kearsley M26 ....61 B8
Back Fletcher St S BL3 ..145 F5
Back Flora St 1 BL3 .....147 E4
Back Florence Ave BL1 ...24 F5
Back Fortune St BL3 .....148 B5
Back Foundry St BL9 ....140 F2
Back Frances St BL1 ....143 D2
Back Frank St Bolton BL3 .143 D2
 4 Bury BL9 ....140 F1
Back Fylde St BL4 ....42 D2
Back Gainsborough Ave
 BL3 ....146 C3
Back Garside Gr 8 BL1 ..142 C2
Back Garston St BL9 ....141 A4
Back Gaskell St BL1 .....145 D8
Back Gaskell St E 14 BL1 .145 D8
Back Gaythorne St 2
 BL1 ....143 F3

Back George Barton St
 BL2 ....25 B1
Back George St Bolton BL3 42 A4
 Horwich BL6 ....22 C3
 Manchester M1 ....159 A1
Back Georgiana St W 1
 BL9 ....140 F1
Back Georgina St BL3 ...145 D6
Back Gibraltar St BL3 ...145 D6
Back Gibraltar St S BL3 .145 D6
Back Gigg La BL9 ....44 F8
Back Gilmour St M24 .....65 A8
Back Gilnow Gr BL1 .....145 D6
Back Gilnow La
 5 Bolton BL3 ....144 C6
 Bolton BL3 ....145 D6
Back Gilnow La W BL3 ..144 C7
Back Gilnow Rd BL1 .....144 C7
Back Glade St BL1 ....144 C7
Back Gladstone St 4 OL4 .67 B6
Back Glen Ave BL3 .....144 B5
Back Glen Bott St 6 BL1 .143 D2
Back Glenboro Ave BL8 ...27 C2
Back Gloster St BL3 .....148 A7
Back Goldsmith St BL3 ..147 D4
Back Goodlad St 6 BL8 ...27 B4
Back Gordon Ave BL3 ...144 C5
Back Gorses Mount BL2 .148 C5
Back Grafton St 6 BL1 ..145 D8
Back Grantham Cl BL1 ...143 E1
Back Grasmere St 5 BL1 .142 C1
Back Greaves St OL1 ....153 F6
Back Green La BL3 ....42 B3
Back Green La S BL3 ....144 C5
Back Green La M24 ....47 B1
Back Greenhalgh St BL3 ..43 A3
Back Greenland Rd BL3 ..147 F2
Back Gregory Ave BL2 ....42 E8
Back Grendon St BL3 ....146 C3
Back Gresham St 9 BL1 ..143 F3
Back Grove St 8 BL1 ....143 D2
Back Hadwin St 11 BL1 ..143 F1
Back Halliwell St 6 M8 ..155 F7
Back Halliwell Rd BL1 ...143 E2
Back Halliwell Rd S BL1 .143 D2
Back Halstead St
 Bolton BL2 ....148 A7
 2 Bury BL9 ....141 A4
Back Hamilton St
 6 Bury BL9 ....140 F4
 Manchester M7 ....155 D7
Back Hampson St M40 ...160 D4
Back Hanson St BL9 .....140 F4
Back Hargreaves St 9
 BL1 ....143 E2
Back Harper's La S BL1 .142 B2
Back Hart St BL5 ....57 B7
Back Hartington Rd 16
 BL1 ....144 C8
Back Harvey St
 Bolton BL1 ....143 D1
 Bury BL8 ....27 C1
Back Haslam St BL9 .....141 A4
Back Haslam Terr BL2 ...148 C7
Back Hastings Rd BL1 ...144 B8
Back Hatfield Rd BL1 ....143 D1
Back Hawthorne Rd 5
 BL3 ....146 B4
Back Hawthorne Rd E
 BL3 ....144 B5
Back Hawthorne Rd W
 BL3 ....144 B5
Back Hawthorne St 4
 BL3 ....146 B4
Back Haydn St 15 BL1 ...143 D2
Back Haydock St BL1 ....145 F8
Back Hayward St 2 BL8 ..27 C3
Back Hengist St 5 BL2 ..148 C7
Back Hennon St 1 BL1 ..143 D1
Back Henrietta St BL3 ...146 B4
Back Henry Lee St BL3 ..146 C3
Back Hereford Rd BL1 ...144 B8
Back Hereford Rd W BL1 144 B8
Back Heywood St E BL9 .141 A2
Back Heywood St W 2
 BL9 ....141 A1
Back High Bank St BL2 ..148 C7
Back High St Bolton BL3 .147 E4
 Bolton BL3 ....147 E4
 Edgworth BL7 ....9 C4
 Heywood OL10 ....29 B2
Back High St S BL3 ......147 E4
Back High St W 2 BL3 ..147 E4
Back Higher Darcy St
 BL3 ....148 C5
Back Higher Shady La W
 BL7 ....25 B1
Back Higher Swan La
 BL3 ....147 D3
Back Higher Swan La W
 BL3 ....147 D3
Back Hilden St BL2 ......148 A6
Back Hilden St N BL2 ....148 A6
Back Hillside St 7 BL3 ...145 D5
Back Hilton St Bolton BL2 148 C7
 9 Bury BL9 ....140 F4
 Manchester M7 ....155 D7
Back Hind St BL2 ....148 C7
Back Holland St
 6 Bolton BL1 ....143 E4
 Bolton BL1 ....143 F4
Back Holland St E 6
 BL1 ....143 F4
Back Holly Pl BL1 ....143 F4
Back Holly St
 3 Bolton BL1 ....143 F4
 Bury BL9 ....141 A2
Back Holly St S BL9 .....141 A2

Back Hope St
 Manchester M7 ....155 D7
 7 Oldham OL1 ....67 B7
Back Hopefield St BL3 ..147 D4
Back Horbury St BL8 .....27 C2
Back Horeb St E BL3 ....145 D5
Back Hornby St BL9 .....140 F4
Back Hornby St E BL9 ...140 F4
Back Hornby St W 4 BL9 140 F4
Back Horne St N 11 BL9 ...44 E8
Back Horne St S BL9 .....44 E8
Back Horsa St BL2 ....25 B1
Back Horsa St N 17 BL2 ..25 B1
Back Hotel St BL1 ....145 F7
Back Hough La E BL7 .....25 A7
Back Howarden St 8 BL1 .24 E5
Back Howcroft St BL3 ...147 D4
Back Howe St M7 ....155 D7
Back Hughes St BL1 .....142 C2
Back Hulbert St BL8 .....27 C1
Back Hulme St Bury BL8 .140 D3
 Manchester M5 ....81 C1
Back Hulton La
 Bolton BL3 ....146 A3
 Bolton BL3 ....146 A4
Back Hulton La S BL3 ...146 A4
Back Hulton La W BL3 ..146 A4
Back Huntley Mount Rd
 BL9 ....141 B3
Back Hurst St Bolton BL3 .146 C3
 Bury BL9 ....141 A1
Back Huxley St 3 BL1 ...142 C2
Back Ingham St BL3 .....141 A1
Back Ingham St E BL9 ...141 A1
Back Irlam St 4 BL1 .....143 E3
Back Irlam St N 3 BL1 ..143 E3
Back Ivanhoe St 1 BL3 ...42 C2
Back Ivy Bank Rd BL1 ....24 E5
Back Ivy Rd Bolton BL1 ..142 C1
 Bolton BL1 ....142 C2
Back Ivy Rd W BL1 ......142 B2
Back James St BL3 ....43 B3
Back Jauncey St 12 BL3 .144 C5
Back John Brown St 15
 BL1 ....145 D8
Back John Cross St 3
 BL3 ....147 E4
Back John St BL3 ....145 E6
Back Johnson St 2 BL1 .145 F6
Back Jubilee St BL3 .....146 C3
Back Junction St M1 ....159 B1
Back Keighley St 10 BL1 .142 C2
Back Kendal Rd BL1 .....144 C8
Back Kershaw St BL9 ....141 A2
Back King St Bolton BL3 .145 E7
 Oldham OL1 ....153 E6
Back King St N BL7 ....24 F8
Back King St S BL2 ......25 D5
Back Kingholm Gdns 3
 BL1 ....143 D1
Back Kingsley St BL1 ....143 D2
Back Kirkby Rd BL1 .....144 B8
Back Knight St 4 BL8 ....27 C2
Back Knowsley Rd BL1 ..142 B2
Back Knowsley St
 1 Bolton BL1 ....145 F7
 Bury BL9 ....140 E2
Back Kylemore Ave BL3 .147 D4
Back La Altrincham WA15 .129 B4
 Appley Bridge WN6 ......35 E8
 Ashton-u-L OL7 ....84 E5
 Atherton BL5 ....59 B6
 Bolton BL1 ....145 E8
 Charlesworth SK13 ....115 E6
 Mossley OL5,OL6 ....68 A2
 Mottram-in-L SK14 ......103 A4
 Oldham OL4 ....50 C1
 Partington WA14 ....118 C5
 Whitworth OL12 ....4 C3
Back Lark St BL1 ....145 F8
Back Latham St BL1 .....143 F2
Back Lathom St 9 BL9 ..140 A4
Back Laurel St BL9 ......141 B2
Back Lawn St BL1 ....143 D1
Back Leach St BL3 ......145 E5
Back Leachfield St BL1 ..143 D3
Back Lee Ave BL3 ....147 D3
Back Lee St Bolton BL1 ..148 A8
 11 Oldham OL3 ....69 B8
Back Legh St WA12 ......89 A3
Back Lena St BL1 ....143 F2
Back Lenora St 1 BL3 ...146 B4
Back Lever Edge La
 Bolton BL3 ....146 C2
 Bolton BL3 ....147 F3
Back Lever Edge La S
 BL3 ....147 E3
Back Lever Hall Rd BL2 .148 C7
Back Lever St Bolton BL3 .145 F5
 Bolton BL3 ....147 E4
 Bolton BL3 ....43 A4
Back Lever St S BL3 .....147 E4
Back Lightburne Ave BL1 144 B7
Back Lilly St BL1 ....145 D8
Back Lincoln Rd BL1 ....144 C8
Back Lindley St BL3 ......43 B3
Back Linton Ave 2 BL9 ..27 F5
Back Long La BL2 ....43 A3
Back Longden St 12 BL1 .144 C8
Back Longfellow Ave
 BL3 ....146 B3
Back Longfield St BL3 ...146 B3
Back Longsight N BL2 ....25 E5
Back Longsight S BL2 ....25 E5
Back Lonsdale Rd BL1 ...144 B8
Back Lonsdale Rd N BL1 .144 B8
Back Lonsdale St BL8 ....27 C2

Back Lord St Bury BL9 ...140 F2
 Little Lever BL3 ....43 B3
Back Lower Bridgeman
 St 2 ....148 A6
Back Loxham St BL4 .....42 D2
Back Lumsden St BL3 ...145 E5
Back Luton St BL3 ....42 A4
Back Lytton St BL3 ......143 D2
Back Mackenzie St BL1 ..143 E4
Back Malvern Ave
 Bolton BL3 ....142 A1
 5 Bury BL9 ....27 F5
Back Manchester Old Rd
 BL9 ....140 E1
Back Manchester Rd
 Bolton BL2 ....148 A6
 6 Bury BL9 ....140 E2
 11 Farnworth BL3 ....42 C2
Back Manchester Rd E
 BL2 ....148 A5
Back Manchester Rd S
 BL3 ....42 A4
Back Manchester Rd W
 BL3 ....42 B4
Back Manchester St 1
 OL10 ....29 E1
Back Manor St BL9 ......141 A2
Back Maple St BL3 ......145 D5
Back Marion St 2 BL3 ....42 C2
Back Marion St S 4 BL3 ..42 C2
Back Market St
 6 Bury BL9 ....140 E2
 Hindley WN2 ....56 C5
 Kearsley M26 ....61 B8
 Leigh WN7 ....75 F5
 Little Lever BL3 ....43 B3
 Newton-le-W WA12 ....89 A3
Back Market St W BL3 BL9 140 E2
Back Markland Hill La E
 BL1 ....23 F1
Back Markland Hill La W
 BL1 ....23 F1
Back Marlborough St
 BL3 ....145 D8
Back Marsh Fold La 14
 BL1 ....144 C8
Back Mary St 4 BL3 .....145 D5
Back Mason St BL1 ......141 A2
Back Massie St SK8 .....122 D6
Back Mawdsley St BL1 ..145 F7
Back Maxwell St BL1 ....143 E4
Back Maybank St BL3 ...145 D5
Back Mayfield Ave BL3 ..42 B3
Back Mayor St Bolton BL3 145 D6
 4 Bury BL8 ....27 C3
Back Mayor St N BL1 ....145 D6
Back Maze St BL3 ....148 C5
Back McDonna St BL1 ...142 C3
Back McKean St 8 BL3 ....42 A4
Back McKean St N 5 BL3 ..42 A4
Back Melbourne Rd BL3 .144 C5
Back Mellor Gr BL1 ......142 B1
Back Mellor Gr W 1 BL1 .142 B1
Back Mellor Rd SK22 ....127 C1
Back Melrose Ave BL1 ...142 A1
Back Melville St BL3 ......42 A3
Back Mercia St BL3 ......144 C5
Back Mere Gdns BL1 ....145 E8
Back Meredith St 6 BL3 .147 F3
Back Merlin St 7 BL3 ....42 B1
Back Merton St BL8 .....140 D3
Back Mesnes St
 Wigan WN1 ....150 C8
 8 Wigan WN1 ....37 C1
Back Methwold St BL3 ..146 C4
Back Micklehurst Rd OL5 .68 E1
Back Milford St BL3 .....147 E3
Back Mill La 7 OL5 ......68 C2
Back Mill St N BL2 ....24 F8
Back Mill St S 7 BL7 .....24 F8
Back Miller St BL1 ......143 E4
Back Millet St BL9 ......140 D2
Back Milner Ave BL9 .....27 F5
Back Minorca St BL3 ....147 E4
Back Mirey La BL6 ....40 B4
Back Monmouth Ave 7
 BL9 ....27 F5
Back Moor St SK14 ......103 A4
Back Moorfield Gr BL2 ...25 B1
Back Moorgate 7 BL9 ...140 F3
Back Mornington Rd
 BL1 ....144 B8
Back Mornington Rd E
 BL1 ....144 C7
Back Mornington Rd W
 BL1 ....144 B8
Back Morris Green La
 Bolton BL3 ....146 C2
 Bolton BL3 ....146 C3
Back Morris Green La E
 BL3 ....146 C3
Back Moss St 1 BL3 .....146 C2
Back Mostyn Ave 3 BL9 ..27 F5
Back Mowbray St 3 BL1 .142 B1
Back Murton Terr 4 BL1 .143 F4
Back Musgrave Rd
 Bolton BL1 ....144 B8
 Bolton BL1 ....144 C8
Back Musgrave Rd N
 BL1 ....144 B8
Back Myrtle St BL1 ......141 B2
Back Myrtle St S BL9 ....141 B2
Back Nebo St BL3 ....147 D4
Back Nelson St BL6 ......22 C2
Back Nelson St N 5 BL9 ..44 F8
Back Nelson St S 1 BL9 ..44 F8
Back Nevada St 17 BL1 .143 E1

Back New George St 9
 BL8 ....27 C3
Back Newbold St BL8 ....27 C2
Back Newhall Ha BL1 ...142 A1
Back Newport Rd 16 BL3 .42 A4
Back Newport St BL1 ....145 F6
Back Newton St BL1 .....143 E2
Back Nixon Rd BL3 ......146 C3
Back Normanby St BL3 ..146 C2
Back Norris St BL3 ....43 A3
Back Northern Gr 1 BL1 142 C1
Back Northern Gr S 2
 BL1 ....142 C1
Back Nunnery Rd BL3 ...146 B4
Back Nut St BL1 ....143 D2
Back o' th' Low Rd OL4 ..49 F1
Back Oak St M26 ....44 C1
Back Oakenbottom Rd N
 BL2 ....42 D7
Back Olaf St 14 BL2 ......25 B1
Back Oldham Rd OL16 ...31 A4
Back Olga St BL1 ....143 D2
Back Olga St N BL1 .....143 D2
Back Olive Bank 2 BL8 ...27 B4
Back Oram St BL9 ....141 A4
Back Oriel St BL3 ....144 C5
Back Ormrod St BL9 ....141 A2
Back Osborne Gr 7 BL1 .142 C1
Back Owen's Row BL6 ...22 C3
Back Oxford Gr N
 Bolton BL1 ....142 C1
 2 Bolton BL1 ....145 D8
Back Oxford St BL9 .....141 A1
Back Packer St BL1 .....142 C2
Back Palace St 6 BL1 ...145 F8
Back Palm St BL1 ....143 E3
Back Park Rd Bolton BL1 .145 D7
 Bolton BL1 ....145 D7
Back Park Rd E BL1 .....143 E4
Back Park St BL1 ....145 D8
Back Park View 1 BL1 ...24 F6
Back Park View Rd BL3 ..146 C4
Back Parkdale Rd BL2 ...25 C1
Back Parkfield Rd
 Bolton BL3 ....147 F3
 Bolton BL3 ....42 A3
Back Parkhills Rd N 4
 BL9 ....44 F8
Back Parkhills Rd S
 4 Bury BL9 ....44 E8
 3 Bury BL9 ....44 F8
Back Parkinson St 11
 BL3 ....144 C5
Back Parsonage St 3
 BL9 ....141 A3
Back Partington St BL3 ..146 C4
Back Patience St 10 OL12 .14 C1
Back Patterson St BL3 ...146 A4
Back Peabody St BL3 ....147 E4
Back Peace St BL3 ......145 D5
Back Pedder St 3 BL1 ...142 C1
Back Peers St 5 BL8 .....27 C2
Back Penarth Rd 6 BL3 .146 B4
Back Pennington Rd BL3 147 F3
Back Percy St BL9 ....141 B3
Back Peter St 2 BL1 .....141 A3
Back Peveril St BL3 .....146 B3
Back Phoenix St BL9 ....140 E2
Back Piccadilly M1 ......159 B1
Back Pikes La W BL3 ....144 C5
Back Pine St
 7 Bolton BL1 ....143 F2
 Bury BL9 ....141 B2
 Newhey OL16 ....32 B4
Back Pleasant St BL1 ....145 D8
Back Pool Fold 9 M2 ....158 F1
Back Poplar Ave BL1 .....24 F5
Back Porter St 2 BL9 ...140 F4
Back Portugal St BL2 ....148 B7
Back Potter St M26 ....44 D4
Back Preston St BL3 ......42 B4
Back Primrose St BL1 ...143 F4
Back Primula St BL1 .....24 F5
Back Proctor St BL8 .....27 C1
Back Progress St 2 BL1 .143 F1
Back Quay St M3 ....158 E1
Back Quebec St BL3 .....144 C5
Back Queen St Bolton BL1 145 E7
 4 Leigh WN7 ....76 A5
Back Queensgate BL1 ....144 C8
Back Radcliffe Rd E 1
 BL2 ....148 B7
Back Railway View PR7 ..21 A7
Back Raimond St BL1 ....142 C3
Back Rainshaw St 5 BL1 143 F4
Back Rake St BL9 ....140 F4
Back Ramsden St OL12 ..15 C7
Back Range St BL3 ......147 D4
Back Raphael St BL1 ....143 D1
Back Rathbone St WA12 .89 A3
Back Raven St 4 BL9 ....140 F4
Back Rawlinson St 16 BL6 .22 B4
Back Rawson Rd BL1 ....143 D1
Back Rawson Rd N 10
 BL1 ....142 C1
Back Rawsthorne St BL1 143 E2
Back Raymond Ave 6 BL9 27 F5
Back Red Bank M4 ......159 A3
Back Redhill Gr BL1 .....145 E8
Back Regent St 3 BL9 ...140 F4
Back Ribblesdale Rd 18
 BL3 ....147 D4
Back Richard Burch St
 BL9 ....141 A3
Back Richelieu St BL3 ....42 A4
Back Rigby La N BL2 .....25 C6
Back Rigby La S BL2 .....25 C6

Back Rishton La
Bolton BL3 .147 F3
Bolton BL3 .147 F4
Back Rishton La E BL3 .147 F3
Back Rochdale Old North Rd BL9 .141 C3
Back Rochdale Old Rd S BL9 .141 B3
Back Rochdale Old South Rd BL9 .28 D3
Back Rochdale Rd
Bury BL9 .141 A2
Bury BL9 .141 B2
Back Rochdale Rd S 6 BL9 .141 A2
Back Rock Ave BL1 .142 C3
Back Roland Rd 8 BL3 .146 C4
Back Roman Rd M7 .155 E6
Back Romer St BL2 .148 C7
Back Rosamond St BL3 .146 C4
Back Roscow Ave BL2 .42 E8
Back Rose Bank 8 BL9 .140 F4
Back Roseberry St 7 BL3 .146 C4
Back Rowena St BL3 .42 C2
Back Rowland St BL3 .146 B3
Back Roxalina St 5 BL3 .147 E4
Back Royal Ave BL9 .27 F5
Back Rudolph St 2 BL3 .147 F3
Back Rumworth St BL3 .147 D4
Back Rupert St BL3 .147 F3
Back Rushton Rd BL1 .142 B1
Back Rushton St 6 OL13 .3 E8
Back Russell Cl 2 BL1 .144 C8
Back Russell St 22 BL1 .144 C8
Back Rutland Gr 6 BL1 .142 C1
Back Ryefield St BL1 .25 A1
Back Salford WN7 .75 F5
Back Salford St BL9 .141 A4
Back Salisbury St BL3 .145 D6
Back Salisbury Terr BL2 .42 D7
Back Sandon St BL3 .147 D4
Back Sandon St W 11 BL3 .147 D4
Back Sandy Bank Rd BL7 .9 D5
Back Sankey St BL9 .140 D2
Back Sapling Rd BL3 .146 C2
Back Sapling Rd S BL3 .146 C2
Back Scholes St BL8 .27 C3
Back School La WN8 .53 C7
Back Scott St OL8 .153 F5
Back Scowcroft St 22 BL2 .25 B1
Back Second Ave BL1 .144 B7
Back Settle St Bolton BL3 .147 E3
Bolton BL3 .147 F3
Back Settle St N
Bolton BL3 .147 D3
Bolton BL3 .147 E3
Back Seymour Rd BL1 .143 F3
Back Shakerley Rd 6 M29 58 F1
Back Sharman St BL3 .148 B5
Back Shaw-Street BL9 .141 B3
Back Shepherd St 1 BL9 141 A1
Back Sherwood St 8 BL1 .143 F3
Back Shipton St BL1 .142 B1
Back Short St 4 M46 .58 F1
Back Shrewsbury Rd BL1 144 B8
Back Shuttle St BL3 .145 E6
Back Silver St BL9 .140 E2
Back Silverdale Rd BL1 .144 C7
Back Skipton St BL2 .148 C8
Back Smethurst La BL3 .146 B2
Back Smethurst La W BL3 .146 B2
Back Sofa St BL1 .142 B1
Back Soho St BL3 .145 F6
Back Somerset Rd BL1 .144 B8
Back Somerset Rd W BL1 .144 B8
Back Somerville St 3 BL1 .142 C3
Back South Cross St E BL9 .141 A2
Back South Par M3 .158 F1
Back South St BL3 .147 E3
Back South View St 9 BL2 .148 C7
Back Southfield St 1 BL3 .42 B4
Back Spa Rd BL1 .145 D6
Back Spa Rd N BL1 .145 D6
Back Spa Rd W 4 BL1 .145 D6
Back Spear St 6 M1,M4 .159 B2
Back Spinnerbottom SK22 .127 F2
Back Spring Gdns
Bolton BL1 .145 F6
6 Middleton M24 .47 A2
Back Spring St E BL9 .140 F1
Back Spring St W BL9 .140 F1
Back Springfield St 14 BL3 .42 A4
Back Square St BL0 .138 C6
Back St Ann St BL1 .143 E1
Back St Anne's St 7 BL9 140 F4
Back St Augustine St BL1 .143 D2
Back St George's Rd
Bolton BL1 .145 E8
Manchester M4 .159 B3
Back St George's Rd N BL1 .145 E8
Back St Helens Rd
Bolton BL3 .146 B3
10 Bolton BL3 .147 D4
Back St Helens Rd S
Bolton BL3 .146 A2
Bolton BL3 .146 B2
Back St Helens Rd S *continued*
Bolton BL3 .146 B3
Bolton BL3 .146 C3
Back St James's St 8 OL1 67 B7
Back St Mark's La M8 .155 F8
Back St Mary's Pl BL9 .140 E2
Back St Philip's Ave BL3 147 D4
Back St Thomas St E 10 BL1 .143 D2
Back Stainsbury St BL3 .146 C4
Back Stanley St BL0 .138 B5
Back Stanway Ave 8 BL3 .145 D6
Back Stephen St 2 BL8 .27 C2
Back Stewart St 13 BL1 .143 E2
Back Stone St 15 BL2 .25 B1
Back Sunlight Rd BL1 .144 C7
Back Sunning Hill St 12 BL3 .147 D4
Back Sunnyside Rd 8 BL1 .142 C2
Back Sutcliffe St BL1 .143 E2
Back Swan La 15 BL3 .147 D4
Back Talbot St 1 BL1 .143 F4
Back Tavistock Rd 3 BL1 .145 D6
Back Teak St BL9 .141 B2
Back Tenterden St
Bury BL9 .140 D2
Bury BL9 .140 E2
Back Thicketford Rd BL2 .25 C1
Back Thicketford Rd W BL2 .25 B1
Back Thomas St 8 M4 .159 A2
Back Thomasson Cl BL1 .143 E1
Back Thorn St BL1 .143 F2
Back Thorns Rd BL1 .143 E3
Back Thorpe St BL1 .143 D2
Back Thurnham St 3 BL3 .146 C3
Back Tinline St 4 BL9 .141 A2
Back Tonge Moor Rd BL2 .25 B3
Back Tonge Moor Rd E
Bolton BL2 .25 B1
Bolton BL2 .25 B2
Bolton BL2 .25 C3
Back Tonge Old Rd BL2 .148 C7
Back Tottington Rd 5 BL8 .27 B4
Back Tottington Rd E BL2 .25 E5
Back Tottington Rd N BL8 .27 C4
Back Tottington Rd S 1 BL8 .27 C3
Back Tudor St 8 BL3 .146 C4
Back Turner St M4 .159 A2
Back Turton Rd E BL2 .25 C5
Back Turton Rd W BL2 .25 C5
Back Uganda St BL3 .146 C2
Back Ulleswater St 1 BL1 .143 F2
Back Union Rd BL2 .25 B1
Back Union St BL7 .8 D2
Back Unsworth St S BL3 .145 D5
Back Uttley St 16 BL1 .143 D2
Back Venice St BL3 .147 D4
Back Vernon St
Bolton BL1 .145 E8
Bury BL9 .140 F4
Back Vernon St S 13 BL1 .145 E8
Back Vickerman St 23 BL1 .143 D2
Back Victoria Gr 4 BL1 .142 C1
Back Victoria Gr N BL1 .142 C1
Back Victory St E 10 BL1 .144 C8
Back View St 5 BL3 .145 D5
Back Viking St N 11 BL3 .42 A4
Back Vincent St BL1 .145 D6
Back Vine St 1 BL3 .144 C6
Back Viola St BL1 .143 E3
Back Waldeck St 3 BL1 .144 C8
Back Walmersley Rd E
Bury BL9 .140 F3
Bury BL9 .140 F4
4 Bury BL9 .27 F5
Bury BL9 .27 F6
Back Walmersley Rd W
Bury BL9 .140 F4
Bury BL9 .27 F6
Back Walnut St 2 BL1 .143 F2
Back Walshaw Rd N 3 BL8 .27 C3
Back Walshaw Rd S BL8 .27 C3
Back Wapping St 21 BL1 .143 D2
Back Wardle St BL2 .148 C5
Back Wash La BL9 .141 B2
Back Wash La S 2 BL9 .141 A2
Back Water St Bolton BL7 .8 D2
Stockport SK1 .169 F2
Back Waverley Rd BL1 .143 E3
Back Webster St BL3 .148 B5
Back Wellington Rd S BL9 44 F8
Back Wells St BL9 .140 E1
Back Westbank St 8 BL1 .145 D8
Back Westbourne Ave BL3 .42 A3
Back Weston St N 9 BL3 .42 A4
Back Weston St S BL3 .42 A4
Back Westwood Rd 18 BL1 .144 C8
Back Wheatfield St BL2 .148 C5
Back Whittle Gr BL1 .142 B1
Back Whittle St 6 BL8 .27 C3
Back Wigan Rd
Bolton BL3 .144 B5
Bolton BL3 .146 A4
Back Wigan Rd N
Bolton BL3 .144 B5
Back Wigan Rd N *continued*
Bolton BL3 .146 A4
Back Wigan Rd S BL3 .144 B5
Back Willis St 6 BL3 .146 C4
Back Willows La 6 BL3 .147 D4
Back Willows La N
Bolton BL3 .146 B4
Bolton BL3 .146 C4
Back Willows La S
Bolton BL3 .146 B4
Bolton BL3 .146 C4
Back Wilmot St 4 BL1 .142 C3
Back Wilton St 10 BL1 .143 F3
Back Windermere St 3 BL1 .143 F2
Back Windsor Gr 8 BL1 .142 C1
Back Woking Gdns 6 BL1 .143 E1
Back Wolfenden St 31 BL1 .143 E2
Back Wood St Bury BL8 .27 C3
Horwich BL6 .22 C3
Back Woodbine Rd BL3 .146 C3
Back Woodbine Rd N BL3 .146 C3
Back Woodfield St BL3 .42 A3
Back Woodgate St BL3 .42 A3
Back Worcester St BL1 .143 E1
Back Wordsworth St 22 BL1 .143 D2
Back Worsel St N BL3 .146 C4
Back Wright St BL6 .22 B4
Back Wynne St 10 BL1 .143 E2
Back Yates St BL2 .25 B1
Back Young St BL4 .60 E7
Backbower La SK14 .113 F8
Backford Wlk 1 M20 .110 A8
Backparsons La BL9 .140 F3
Backton Pl M40 .160 D4
Baclaw Cl WN1 .37 F1
Bacon Ave M34 .113 A7
Bacup & Rawtenstall Gram Sch BB4 .2 F8
Bacup Rd BB4,OL13 .2 E8
Bacup St M40 .83 A8
Badby Cl M4 .160 D1
Baddeley Cl SK3 .170 D5
Badder St BL1 .145 F8
Baden St M11 .164 E8
Bader Dr OL10 .46 D7
Badger Cl OL16 .31 C3
Badger Edge La OL3,OL4 .50 C3
Badger La Rochdale OL16 .31 B2
Rochdale OL16 .31 C3
Badger St BL9 .141 A3
Badgers Way SK13 .116 B7
Badgers Wlk M22 .121 E1
Badminton Rd M21 .97 C1
Bag La M46 .58 C4
Bagnall Cl Rochdale OL12 .13 F2
Uppermill OL3 .51 C1
Bagnall Ct M22 .121 E8
Bagnall Wlk M22 .121 E8
Bagot St 15 Droylsden M11 .83 C2
Swinton M27 .61 C1
Bagshaw La WN2 .38 E2
Bagshaw St SK14 .101 E5
Bagslate Moor La OL11 .29 F8
Bagslate Moor Rd OL11 .29 F8
Bagstock Ave SK12 .133 E2
Baguley Cres
Middleton M25 .64 A7
Stockport SK3 .170 D6
Baguley Dr BL9 .45 A2
Baguley Hall Prim Sch M23 .121 A6
Baguley La Sale M33 .108 E2
Sale M33 .108 E3
Baguley Rd M33 .108 E4
Baguley St M43 .84 B1
Baildon Rd OL12 .14 B1
Baildon St M40 .65 A1
Bailey Fold BL5 .58 B8
Bailey La Bolton BL2 .25 E1
Partington M31 .105 F3
Wythenshawe M22,M90 .121 B1
Bailey Rd M17 .96 A7
Bailey St Droylsden M43 .83 E1
8 Oldham OL1 .67 A7
Prestwich M25 .63 C4
Bailey Wlk WA14 .128 C8
Bailey's Ct WN1 .150 C8
Baillie St Radcliffe BL9 .44 E5
Rochdale OL16 .139 F8
Baillie St E 18 OL16 .31 A8
Bails The M7 .81 C6
Bain St M27 .79 F7
Bainbridge Ave WA3 .90 F8
Bainbridge Cl M12 .164 D6
Bainbridge Rd 3 OL4 .49 D1
Bainburgh Clough OL8 .67 C4
Baines Ave M44 .93 F1
Baines St BL1 .144 B8
Bainton Wlk M9 .64 C5
Baird St M1 .163 C8
Baitings Row OL12 .13 C2
Baker St Heywood OL10 .46 E8
Kearsley BL4 .61 B6
Middleton M24 .65 B8
Ramsbottom BL0 .138 B5
Sale WA15 .120 C7
Stalybridge SK15 .86 B1
Stockport SK4 .169 E3
Wigan WN3 .150 B6
Bakewell Ave
Ashton-u-L OL6 .85 F6
Denton M34 .113 A8
Bakewell Bank 42 SK13 .171 D1
Bakewell Cl 40 SK13 .171 D1
Bakewell Dr WN6 .37 A4
Bakewell Fold 41 SK13 .171 D1
Bakewell Gdns 36 SK13 .171 D1
Bakewell Gn 37 SK13 .171 D1
Bakewell Gr 43 SK13 .171 D1
Bakewell Lea 38 SK13 .171 D1
Bakewell Mews SK13 .171 D1
Bakewell Rd Droylsden M43 83 E2
Eccles M30 .95 C8
Hazel Grove SK7 .133 E8
Stretford M32 .96 A3
Bakewell St
Manchester M18 .99 C4
Stockport SK3 .170 D7
Bakewell Wlk 39 SK13 .171 D1
Bala Cl M5 .81 A2
Balcarres Ave WN1 .37 E2
Balcarres Rd WN2 .38 C5
Balcary Gr BL1 .144 B8
Balcombe Cl BL8 .27 C7
Balderstone Com High Sch OL11 .31 A3
Balderstone Rd OL11 .31 A3
Baldock Rd M20 .110 D3
Baldrine Dr WN2 .57 B5
Baldwin Rd M19 .110 F6
Baldwin St Bacup OL13 .3 B8
Bolton BL3 .145 E5
Hindley WN2 .57 B3
Ince-in-M WN3 .151 D6
Wigan WN1 .151 D8
Wigan WN5 .54 B6
Bale St M1,M2 .162 F8
Balfern Cl 12 BL5 .39 E1
Balfern Fold 11 BL5 .39 E1
Balfour Gr SK5 .111 F8
Balfour Rd
Altrincham WA14 .119 D7
5 Rochdale OL12 .14 C1
Urmston M41 .95 B3
Balfour St 5 Bolton BL3 .145 D6
Manchester M8 .156 A8
Oldham OL4 .67 C7
Salford M6 .81 A6
Shaw OL2 .149 B7
Balham Wlk M12 .164 F6
Balholm Ct M20 .110 B4
Ball St Rochdale OL16 .31 A8
Shevington WN6 .36 E2
Ball Wlk SK14 .102 F1
Ball's Cotts WN3 .55 F3
Balladen Prim Sch BB4 .1 F8
Ballantine St M40 .83 C4
Ballantyne Way 5 WA3 .90 E8
Ballard Cl OL15 .16 B7
Ballard Way OL2 .149 C8
Ballater Ave M41 .95 A1
Ballater Cl OL10 .29 B1
Ballater Wlk 1 M8 .155 F7
Ballbrook Ave M20 .110 B5
Ballbrook Ct M20 .110 B4
Ballerat St M19 .99 A1
Balliol Cl SK6 .113 C4
Balliol St Manchester M8 .156 A8
Swinton M27 .79 E8
Balliol Way WN4 .72 F4
Balloon St M4 .159 A2
Balm St BL0 .11 A4
Balmain Ave M18 .99 C3
Balmain Rd M41 .95 B3
Balmer Rd M23 .121 B4
Balmfield St M8 .156 A5
Balmforth St M15 .162 D7
Balmoral PR7 .20 E6
Balmoral Ave Cheadle SK8 123 A2
Denton M34 .100 D7
Golborne WA3 .74 D1
Hyde SK14 .113 E8
Little Lever BL3 .43 A3
Rochdale OL11 .30 B8
Royton OL2 .48 F4
Stretford M32 .96 D3
Urmston M41 .95 B1
Whitefield M45 .63 A7
Balmoral Cl Horwich BL6 .22 E2
Milnrow OL16 .32 A6
Ramsbottom BL8 .11 A1
Whitefield BL9 .45 A5
Balmoral Dr Heywood OL10 29 A1
Heywood OL10 .29 B1
High Lane SK6 .134 E7
Hindley WN2 .56 C4
Leigh WN7 .76 D6
Poynton SK12 .133 D3
Reddish M34 .100 A3
Sale WA14 .119 F8
Stalybridge SK15 .86 A3
Balmoral Gr SK7 .124 F3
Balmoral Grange M25 .63 E3
Balmoral Ho M30 .79 C2
Balmoral Rd
Altrincham WA15 .119 E4
Ashton-in-M WN4 .73 A4
Farnworth BL4 .60 D7
Manchester M14 .110 D8
Manchester SK4 .168 A3
Swinton M27 .62 A2
Urmston M41 .95 A1
Wigan WN5 .54 E6
Balmoral St M18 .99 C4
Balmoral Way SK9 .137 A6
Balmore Cl BL3 .146 A3
Balmore Ct OL10 .28 E1
Balniel Wlk WN1 .37 E2
Balsam Cl M13 .163 C7
Balshaw Ave M44 .93 F2
Balshaw Cl BL3 .144 C5
Balshaw Ct M44 .94 A2
Baltic Rd Altrincham WA14 119 A6
Rawtenstall BB4 .2 E8
Baltic St M5 .154 E2
Baltimore St M10,M40 .157 F5
Bamber Ave M33 .108 E3
Bamber Croft BL5 .39 E3
Bamber St M9 .64 D5
Bamber Wlk BL3 .145 D5
Bamber's Bldgs 2 WN2 .56 E5
Bamburgh Cl M26 .43 C5
Bamburgh Dr OL7 .85 A6
Bamburgh Pl 3 WN4 .73 A5
Bamford Ave Denton M34 .112 F8
Middleton M24 .47 A2
Bamford Bsns Pk SK4 .111 E5
Bamford Cl Bury BL9 .28 E4
Gatley SK8 .131 D8
Bamford Ct OL11 .30 C6
Bamford Dr WN2 .37 F2
Bamford Fold SK13 .171 E1
Bamford Gdns WA15 .120 D6
Bamford Gn SK13 .171 E1
Bamford Gr Ashton-u-L OL6 .85 F6
Manchester M20 .110 A3
Bamford La SK13 .171 E1
Bamford Mews
Gamesley SK13 .171 E1
Rochdale OL11 .29 E7
Bamford Pl OL12 .14 E1
Bamford Prim Sch OL11 .29 F7
Bamford Rd Heywood OL10 .29 D3
Manchester M20 .110 A3
Ramsbottom BL0 .12 B6
Bamford St Droylsden M11 .83 B2
4 Littleborough OL15 .15 F5
Oldham OL9 .152 C8
Royton OL2 .48 E3
Stockport SK1 .170 F8
Bamford Way OL11 .29 F6
Bampton Ave WA11 .71 B1
Bampton Cl Stockport SK2 124 B7
Westhoughton BL5 .39 E2
Bampton Rd M22 .121 D1
Bampton Wlk M24 .46 E2
Banastre Dr WA12 .89 F3
Banbury Cl WN7 .75 E1
Banbury Dr WA14 .119 E8
Banbury Mews M27 .61 D1
Banbury Rd
Failsworth M35,M40 .83 E4
Longshaw WN5 .53 D2
Middleton M24 .65 A5
Wythenshawe M23 .120 F5
Banbury St 5 Bolton BL2 .25 C1
Stockport SK1 .169 F1
Bancroft Ave SK8 .123 A1
Bancroft Cl SK6 .112 E3
Bancroft Ct WA15 .120 A3
Bancroft Fold SK14 .102 B5
Bancroft Rd
Altrincham WA15 .120 A3
Swinton M27 .61 E1
Banff Gr OL10 .29 A1
Banff Rd M14 .98 C4
Bangor Fold WN7 .76 C4
Bangor Rd SK8 .122 F6
Bangor St Ashton-u-L OL6 .85 E2
Bolton BL1 .145 E8
Reddish SK5 .169 F4
Rochdale OL16 .31 B6
Banham Ave WN3 .54 C3
Bank Ave WN5 .53 D5
Bank Barn La OL12 .15 D6
Bank Bridge Rd M11,M40 .83 B3
Bank Brow WN8 .35 C5
Bank Cl OL15 .16 A3
Bank Field BL5 .58 A7
Bank Field St M26 .61 D7
Bank Gr M38 .59 F6
Bank Hall BL8 .27 A2
Bank Hey BL5 .39 F1
Bank Hill St OL4 .67 C7
Bank Ho WN2 .75 B8
Bank House Rd M9 .64 C4
Bank La Littleborough OL12 .15 D7
Oldham OL3 .69 E4
Pendlebury M6,M27 .80 D6
Tintwistle SK13 .104 A7
Walkden M38 .59 F6
Bank Mdw BL6 .22 C4
Bank Meadow Prim Sch M12 .164 D8
Bank Pas WA3 .74 A1
Bank Pl Bury BL8 .27 C3
Manchester M3 .158 D2
Bank Rd Appley Bridge WN8 35 D4
Manchester M8 .64 A1
Mossley SK15 .86 E6
Romiley SK6 .113 A3
Bank Side BL5 .58 A7
Bank Sq SK9 .137 B7
Bank St Adlington PR7 .21 A7
Ashton-u-L OL6 .166 B2
Bolton BL1 .145 F7
Bury BL8 .26 F4
Bury BL9 .140 E2
Cheadle SK8 .122 E6
Denton M34 .100 F6
Denton M34 .113 B8
Droylsden M11 .83 B2
Droylsden M43 .99 F8
Edgworth BL7 .9 C4
Failsworth M40 .83 A3
Farnworth BL4 .60 D8

Bank St continued
Glossop SK13 . . . . 116 D8
Golborne WA3 . . . . 74 A1
Heywood OL10 . . . . 29 B2
Hollinrake WA3 . . . . 105 B5
Hyde SK14 . . . . 167 D3
Manchester M3 . . . . 158 D2
Manchester M7 . . . . 155 F8
8 Oldham OL4 . . . . .67 D6
Platt Bridge WN2 . . . . 56 A3
Radcliffe M26 . . . . 44 B2
Ramsbottom BL0 . . . . 11 E7
Rochdale OL11 . . . . 31 A4
Romiley SK6 . . . . 113 B5
Sale M33 . . . . 108 C5
Shaw OL2 . . . . 149 A7
Whitefield M45 . . . . 44 E1
Wigan WN5 . . . . 54 E6
Bank Terr OL12 . . . . 14 C8
Bank The Glossop SK13 . . 116 D8
8 Rochdale OL16 . . . . 139 F8
Bank Top Ashton-u-L OL6 . 166 C2
Bury BL9 . . . . 11 F1
Heywood OL10 . . . . 29 B3
Bank Top Gr BL1 . . . . 25 A5
Bank Top Pk 4 OL4 . . . . . .67 D6
Bank Top St OL10 . . . . 29 B3
Bank Wood BL1 . . . . .40 F7
Bankbottom SK13 . . . . . . 104 A5
Bankbrook WN6 . . . . 36 D4
Banker St BL3 . . . . 148 C5
Bankes Ave WN5 . . . . 54 A6
Bankfield Ainsworth BL2 . . .43 C8
Dukinfield SK14 . . . . 101 D5
Bankfield Ave
Droylsden M43 . . . . 84 A2
Irlam M44 . . . . 105 D5
Manchester M13 . . . . .98 E3
Stockport SK4 . . . . 168 C1
Bankfield Cl BL2 . . . . 26 C1
Bankfield Cotts OL3 . . . . . 50 F2
Bankfield Dr
Boothstown M28 . . . . 78 B7
Oldham OL8 . . . . .67 B2
Bankfield La OL11 . . . . . . 29 E8
Bankfield Mews BL9 . . . . .44 F7
Bankfield Rd Cheadle SK8 . 122 F1
Farnworth BL4 . . . . .60 D6
Romiley SK6 . . . . 113 B5
Sale M33 . . . . 107 E6
Tyldesley M29 . . . . .77 E8
Bankfield St Bacup OL13 . . . .3 D8
Bolton BL3 . . . . 144 C5
Bolton BL3 . . . . 146 C4
Manchester M9 . . . . 157 D8
Reddish SK4 . . . . 169 E3
Bankfield Terr 1 OL13 . . . .3 D8
Bankfield Trad Est SK5 . . 169 E4
Bankfoot Wlk M8 . . . . 156 A5
Bankgate SK14 . . . . 115 A8
Bankhall Cl WN2 . . . . 57 B1
Bankhall La WA14,WA15 . . 128 F8
Bankhall Rd SK4 . . . . 168 A2
Bankhall Wlk 10 M9 . . . . 157 E7
Bankhirst Cl M8 . . . . .64 A1
Bankhouse Rd BL8 . . . . . . .27 C4
Banklands Cl M44 . . . . . . 105 D5
Bankley St M19 . . . . .99 A1
Bankmill Cl 12 M13 . . . . . 163 B7
Banks Croft OL10 . . . . . . .46 D7
Banks Ct Altrincham WA15 120 D5
Leigh WN7 . . . . 75 D5
Banks La SK1 . . . . 124 B8
Banks Lane Inf Sch SK1 . 124 B8
Banks Lane Jun Sch SK1 124 B8
Bankside Altrincham WA15 129 D6
Hattersley SK14 . . . . 102 D1
Bankside Ave
Ashton-in-M WN4 . . . . 73 A8
Oldham OL3 . . . . .69 C7
Radcliffe M26 . . . . 44 D4
Bankside Cl
Handforth SK9 . . . . 131 D1
Oldham OL9 . . . . 153 D6
Romiley SK6 . . . . 114 C1
Bankside Ct
Manchester M12 . . . . .99 A4
Stockport SK4 . . . . 168 A2
Bankside Rd M20 . . . . 122 B7
Bankside Tutorial Unit
M43 . . . . .83 F1
Bankside Wlk 5 SK14 . . . 102 D2
Bankswood Cl SK13 . . . . . 104 A4
Bankwood WN6 . . . . .35 E6
Banky La M33 . . . . 107 D6
Bann St SK3 . . . . 170 E8
Bannatyne Cl M40 . . . . . . .65 E1
Banner Dale Cl M13 . . . . . .98 F4
Banner St Hindley WN2 . . . . 56 E5
Ince-in-M WN3 . . . . 151 E5
Banner Wlk 19 M11 . . . . 160 F1
Bannerman Ave M25 . . . . . .63 C3
Bannerman Rd M43 . . . . . . .84 B1
Bannerman Sq M16 . . . . . .97 F4
Bannerman St M7 . . . . . . 155 E6
Bannister Dr SK8 . . . . . . 122 F2
Bannister St Bolton BL2 . . . .42 E8
Stockport SK1 . . . . 170 F7
Banstead Ave M22 . . . . . . 121 D7
Bantry Ave M9 . . . . .64 B3
Bantry St Bolton BL3 . . . . 145 E5
4 Rochdale OL12 . . . . . . 15 A2
Baptist St M4 . . . . 159 B3
Bar Gap Rd OL1 . . . . 153 F8
Bar La BL1 . . . . 24 E5

Bar St WN2 . . . . 56 A1
Bar Terr OL12 . . . . 14 C7
Barathea Cl OL11 . . . . 30 B3
Barber St 5 Droylsden M11 .99 E7
Hadfield SK13 . . . . 104 B5
Barber Wlk BL1 . . . . 143 E4
Barberry Bank BL7 . . . . . . .8 E2
Barberry Cl WA14 . . . . 119 B7
Barberry Wlk M31 . . . . . . 105 F3
Barbican St 2 M20 . . . . . 110 B7
Barbon Wlk 1 M4 . . . . . . 159 C2
Barbrook Cl WN6 . . . . .19 B2
Barbury Cl WN7 . . . . .75 F7
Barchester Ave BL2 . . . . . 25 E1
Barcheston Rd SK8 . . . . . 122 C4
Barcicroft Rd M19,SK4 . . . 110 E4
Barcicroft Wlk 1 M19 . . . 110 E4
Barclay Rd SK12 . . . . 133 E2
Barclays Ave M6 . . . . .80 D6
Barcliffe Ave M40 . . . . 65 C3
Barclyde St OL11 . . . . 139 E5
Urmston M41 . . . . 92 A5
Barcombe Cl Oldham OL4 . .49 D2
Urmston M41 . . . . 92 A5
Barcombe Wlk M9 . . . . . . 157 D7
Barcroft Rd BL1 . . . . 142 C2
Barcroft St BL9 . . . . 140 F3
Bardale Gr WN4 . . . . 73 A3
Bardell Cl SK12 . . . . 133 D2
Bardney Ave WA3 . . . . .73 F2
Bardon Cl BL1 . . . . 143 D1
Bardon Rd M23 . . . . 120 F6
Bardsea Ave M22 . . . . 121 D1
Bardsley Ave M35 . . . . . . .83 F7
Bardsley Cl Bolton BL2 . . . .25 D5
1 Hattersley SK14 . . . . . 102 E2
Orrell WN8 . . . . 53 A7
Bardsley Gate Ave SK15 . 102 E6
Bardsley St Failsworth M40 .83 D5
Middleton M24 . . . . 47 A1
Oldham OL4 . . . . 49 E1
Oldham OL4 . . . . 67 E5
Oldham OL9 . . . . 65 F3
Stockport SK4 . . . . 169 D3
Bardsley Vale Ave OL8 . . . .85 A8
Bare St BL1 . . . . 148 A8
Bare Trees Jun Sch OL9 . 152 B8
Barehill St OL15 . . . . 16 B6
Barff Rd M5 . . . . .80 C2
Barfold Cl SK2 . . . . 125 A5
Barford Cl WN8 . . . . 53 A7
Barford Dr Golborne WA3 . .91 A8
Handforth SK9 . . . . 131 C1
Barford Gr BL6 . . . . 22 F1
Barford Wlk M23 . . . . 121 B4
Baric Cl M30 . . . . .79 F1
Baring St M1,M12 . . . . . . 163 B8
Bark St Bolton BL1 . . . . . . 145 E7
Bolton BL1 . . . . 145 F8
Kearsley BL4 . . . . 61 B5
Barkan Way M27 . . . . .80 B8
Barke St OL15 . . . . 15 F3
Barker Rd SK6 . . . . 112 F2
Barker St Bury BL9 . . . . . . 140 E1
Heywood OL10 . . . . 29 B1
Leigh WN7 . . . . 75 C5
Manchester M3 . . . . 158 F3
Barker's La M33 . . . . 107 F4
Barking St M40 . . . . 160 E3
Barkway Rd M32 . . . . 96 A3
Barkwell La OL5 . . . . 68 B1
Barkworth Wlk M40 . . . . . .83 B6
Barlborough Rd WN5 . . . . .54 D5
Barlby Wlk M40 . . . . .83 B6
Barlea Ave M40 . . . . .65 D1
Barley Brook Mdw BL1 . . . .24 F6
Barley Brook St WN6 . . . . .37 B1
Barley Croft SK8 . . . . 122 F1
Barley Croft Rd SK14 . . . . 101 E6
Barley Dr SK7 . . . . 132 E7
Barley Hall St OL10 . . . . . 29 E3
Barleycorn Cl M33 . . . . . . 109 A3
Barleycroft St M14 . . . . . 171 F4
Barleyfield Wlk M24 . . . . . 46 F1
Barleywood Wlk SK15 . . . 102 E7
Barlow Cres SK6 . . . . 125 F4
Barlow Ct Edgworth BL7 . . . .9 E5
Walkden M28 . . . . 60 C3
Barlow Fold Bury BL9 . . . . .44 F5
Romiley SK6 . . . . 113 D3
Barlow Fold Cl BL9 . . . . . . .44 F5
Barlow Fold Rd
Reddish SK5 . . . . 111 F8
Romiley SK6 . . . . 113 D3
Barlow Hall Prim Sch
M21 . . . . 109 C5
Barlow Hall Rd M21 . . . . . 109 C5
Barlow Ho OL8 . . . . 153 F5
Barlow La M30 . . . . .79 C2
Barlow La N SK5 . . . . 111 F8
Barlow Moor Cl OL12 . . . . 13 E2
Barlow Moor Ct M20 . . . . . 109 F4
Barlow Moor Rd M21 . . . . 109 C6
Barlow Park Ave BL1 . . . . . .24 D5
Barlow Pl M13 . . . . 163 C7
Barlow RC High Sch The
M20 . . . . 110 C2
Barlow Rd
Altrincham WA14 . . . . 119 B7
Dukinfield SK16 . . . . 101 D8
Handforth SK9 . . . . 131 B1
Manchester M5 . . . . .81 C1
Reddish M19 . . . . .99 C1
Stretford M16,M32 . . . . . . .96 F4
Barlow St Bacup OL13 . . . . .3 B7
Bury BL9 . . . . 140 F3

Barlow St continued
Eccles M30 . . . . .79 D1
Heywood OL10 . . . . .46 E8
Horwich BL6 . . . . .22 C2
Oldham OL4 . . . . .67 A6
Radcliffe M26 . . . . 44 B3
Rochdale OL16 . . . . .31 A7
Walkden M28 . . . . .60 D4
Barlow Terr M21 . . . . 109 C6
Barlow Wlk 3 SK5 . . . . . . 111 F8
Barlow Wood Dr SK6 . . . . 126 B3
Barlow's Croft M3 . . . . . . 158 E2
Barlow's La S SK7 . . . . . . 124 C3
Barmeadow OL3 . . . . .50 F2
Barmhouse Cl SK14 . . . . . 102 A3
Barmhouse La SK14 . . . . . 102 A3
Barmhouse Mews SK14 . 102 A3
Barmouth St M11 . . . . 164 F8
Barmouth Wlk 4 OL8 . . . . .66 B2
Barmskin La WN6 . . . . .18 C8
Barn Acre BL6 . . . . .21 E1
Barn Cl Glossop SK13 . . . . 116 D7
Urmston M41 . . . . 94 C2
Barn Field La OL12 . . . . . . 15 A7
Barn Fold OL4 . . . . .67 E5
Barn Gr M34 . . . . 100 E7
Barn Hill 8 BL5 . . . . 39 E1
Barn Hill Terr 7 BL5 . . . . 39 E1
Barn La WA3 . . . . .89 F8
Barn Mdw BL7 . . . . .9 D5
Barn St Bolton BL1 . . . . . . 145 E7
Oldham OL1 . . . . 153 E6
Whitefield M45 . . . . .62 F7
Barn Way WA12 . . . . 89 B3
Barn Wlk 10 M11 . . . . .99 E7
Barnabys Rd BL5 . . . . 39 D3
Barnacre Ave Bolton BL2 . . 42 F7
Wythenshawe M23 . . . . . . 120 F3
Barnard Ave
Manchester SK4 . . . . 168 B2
Prestwich M45 . . . . .63 B7
Barnard Cl OL7 . . . . 84 F4
Barnard Rd M18 . . . . 99 B3
Barnard St 3 BL2 . . . . . . 148 C8
Barnbrook St BL9 . . . . 141 A4
Barnby St M12 . . . . 99 A3
Barnclose Rd M22 . . . . . . 121 D1
Barncroft Dr BL6 . . . . .22 F3
Barncroft Gdns M22 . . . . . 121 C5
Barncroft Rd BL4 . . . . .60 D8
Barnes Ave SK4 . . . . 168 A2
Barnes Cl Farnworth BL4 . . .60 D8
Ramsbottom BL0 . . . . 11 A3
Barnes Ho 2 BL4 . . . . .60 D8
Barnes Hospl SK8 . . . . . . 122 C6
Barnes Mdws OL15 . . . . . . .6 C1
Barnes St BL4 . . . . .60 B8
Barnes Terr BL4 . . . . .60 B8
Barneswell St 28 M40 . . . .83 C5
Barnett Rd BL1 . . . . 142 C2
Barnett Ave M20 . . . . 110 B6
Barnett Ct OL10 . . . . .29 C1
Barnett Dr M3 . . . . 158 D2
Barnfield
Littleborough OL15 . . . . . . .16 D6
Urmston M41 . . . . 95 B1
Barnfield Cl Bolton BL7 . . . .8 E2
Radcliffe M26 . . . . 43 E3
6 Salford M6 . . . . 154 F1
Tyldesley M29 . . . . 58 F1
Barnfield Cres M33 . . . . . 107 F6
Barnfield Dr
Boothstown M28 . . . . 78 B6
Westhoughton BL5 . . . . . . .40 A1
Barnfield Rd Hyde SK14 . . 102 B5
Manchester M19 . . . . 110 E4
Swinton M27 . . . . .61 D2
Barnfield Rd E SK3 . . . . . 123 F4
Barnfield Rd W SK3 . . . . . 123 D4
Barnfield Rise OL2 . . . . . . .32 A1
Barnfield St Denton M34 . . 100 D4
Heywood OL10 . . . . 29 E2
Rochdale OL12 . . . . 14 F2
Barnfield Wlk WA15 . . . . . 120 C5
Barngate Dr OL5 . . . . .86 C8
Barngate St OL15 . . . . 16 B6
Bargill Gr WN3 . . . . 54 E3
Barnham St WA3 . . . . .90 A8
Barnham Wlk M23 . . . . . . 120 E8
Barnhill Ave M25 . . . . .63 B2
Barnhill Dr M25 . . . . .63 B2
Barnhill Rd M25 . . . . .63 B3
Barnhill St M14 . . . . .97 F4
Barnley Cl M44 . . . . 94 B8
Barns La Partington WA14 . 118 A5
Partington WA14 . . . . 118 A6
Barns Pl WA15 . . . . 129 C8
Barnsdale Cl BL2 . . . . .26 C1
Barnsdale Dr M8 . . . . 156 A6
Barnsfold Ave M14 . . . . . . 110 C8
Barnsfold Rd SK6 . . . . . . 125 F3
Barnside OL12 . . . . 14 B8
Barnside Ave M28 . . . . . . .60 E3
Barnside Cl BL9 . . . . .27 E8
Barnside Way M35 . . . . . . .84 C6
Barnsley St Stockport SK1 124 B8
Wigan WN6 . . . . 37 B2
Barnstaple Dr M40 . . . . . . 156 C6
Barnstead Ave M20 . . . . . 110 D5
Barnston Ave M14 . . . . . . .98 B2
Barnston Cl BL1 . . . . 143 F4
Barnton Cl WA3 . . . . .90 D7
Barnview Dr M44 . . . . 94 B8
Barnway Wlk 7 M40 . . . . . 65 C2
Barnwell Ave WA3 . . . . . . .91 D4
Barnwell Cl M34 . . . . 100 E5

Barnwood Cl 11 BL1 . . . . 143 E1
Barnwood Dr BL1 . . . . 143 E1
Barnwood Rd M23 . . . . . . 121 A3
Barnwood Terr 10 BL1 . . 143 E1
Baron Fold M38 . . . . .60 A5
Baron Fold Cres M38 . . . . .59 F5
Baron Fold Gr M38 . . . . . . .59 F5
Baron Fold Rd M38 . . . . . . .59 F5
Baron Gn SK8 . . . . 131 D7
Baron Rd SK14 . . . . 113 F7
Baron St Bury BL9 . . . . . . 140 D1
Rochdale OL16 . . . . 139 F7
Baron Wlk BL3 . . . . .43 C3
Baroness Gr M7 . . . . .81 C4
Barons Ct M35 . . . . .83 D6
Barr Hill Ave M6 . . . . .80 E5
Barra Dr M41 . . . . 95 D5
Barrack Hill SK6 . . . . 113 A2
Barrack Hill Cl SK6 . . . . . 113 A3
Barrack Hill Prim Sch
SK6 . . . . 113 A2
Barrack Sq 16 WN1 . . . . . 150 C8
Barrack St Bolton BL3 . . . . 145 F6
Manchester M15 . . . . 162 D7
Barracks Rd WN2 . . . . .56 D1
Barracks Yd WN1 . . . . 150 C8
Barrass St M11 . . . . 99 D7
Barratt Gdns M24 . . . . 46 D4
Barrett Ave BL4 . . . . .60 F7
Barrett Ct BL9 . . . . 141 A2
Barrett St OL4 . . . . .67 B5
Barrfield Rd M6 . . . . 154 E4
Barrhill Cl M15 . . . . 162 E6
Barrie St WN7 . . . . .75 D8
Barrie Way BL1 . . . . 25 B4
Barrington Ave
Cheadle SK8 . . . . 123 A1
Droylsden M43 . . . . 83 F1
Barrington Cl
Altrincham WA14 . . . . 119 D6
Wigan WN3 . . . . 54 D2
Barrington Rd WA14 . . . . . 119 D5
Barrington St M11 . . . . . . .83 C2
Barrington Wlk 2 BL2 . . . .25 B1
Barrisdale Cl BL3 . . . . .40 F5
Barron Mdw WN7 . . . . .75 D7
Barrow Bridge Rd
Bolton BL1 . . . . 142 A3
Bolton BL1 . . . . 23 F4
Barrow Hill Rd M8 . . . . . . 155 F5
Barrow La
Altrincham WA14 . . . . 129 B7
Golborne WA2 . . . . .90 C2
Barrow Mdw SK8 . . . . 131 E8
Barrow St Ashton-in-M WN4 73 D5
Manchester M3,M5 . . . . . . 158 D1
Barrowcroft Cl WN1 . . . . . .20 B1
Barrowdale Rd WA3 . . . . . . 90 B3
Barrowdene Ho BL1 . . . . . . 23 F4
Barrowfield Rd M22 . . . . . 121 A2
Barrowfield Wlk 4 M24 . . .47 A1
Barrowfields M24 . . . . 47 A2
Barrows Ct 3 BL1 . . . . . . 145 F6
Barrowshaw Cl M28 . . . . . .60 C2
Barrs Fold Cl BL5 . . . . 39 D3
Barrs Fold Rd BL5 . . . . 39 D3
Barrule Ave SK7 . . . . 124 E1
Barry Cres M28 . . . . .60 A3
Barry Ct 8 M20 . . . . 110 B6
Barry Lawson Cl M8 . . . . . 155 F7
Barry Rd Reddish SK5 . . . . 111 F5
Wythenshawe M23 . . . . . . 109 C2
Barry Rise WA14 . . . . 119 A2
Barry St OL1 . . . . .67 B8
Barsham Dr BL3 . . . . 145 D5
Bartlemore St OL1 . . . . . . .49 B1
Bartlett Rd OL2 . . . . 149 A6
Bartlett St M11 . . . . 165 B8
Bartley Rd M22 . . . . 121 C8
Barton Ave Urmston M41 . . .95 B2
Wigan WN1 . . . . .37 B2
Barton Bsns Pk M30 . . . . . .79 C1
Barton Cl SK9 . . . . 131 D2
Barton Clough WN5 . . . . . .71 E5
Barton Clough Prim Sch
M32 . . . . .95 F4
Barton Ct SK14 . . . . 101 C1
Barton Dock Rd Eccles M41 95 E6
Stretford M32 . . . . .96 B4
Barton Fold SK14 . . . . 167 D1
Barton Hall Ave M30 . . . . . .79 A1
Barton La Eccles M30 . . . . .79 E1
Eccles M30 . . . . 95 D8
Barton Moss
Com Prim Sch M30 . . . . . . 94 F8
Barton Moss Rd M30 . . . . . 94 D7
Barton Rd
Dunkinfield SK14,SK16 . . . 101 C6
Eccles M30 . . . . .79 C1
Farnworth BL4 . . . . .60 B7
Manchester SK4 . . . . 110 E1
Middleton M24 . . . . 64 F8
Pendlebury M27 . . . . .80 A6
Stretford M32 . . . . 96 B3
Stretford M32 . . . . 96 C1
Urmston M41 . . . . 95 C5
Worsley M30 . . . . 78 F5
Barton Sq M2 . . . . 158 F1
Barton St Farnworth BL4 . . .60 E7
Golborne WA3 . . . . .74 A1
Manchester M3 . . . . 162 E8
Oldham OL1 . . . . 153 D8
Platt Bridge WN2 . . . . .56 B3
Tyldesley M29 . . . . 59 F1
4 Wigan WN5 . . . . 54 B5
Barton Terr M44 . . . . 94 C3
Barway Rd M21 . . . . 96 F1

Barwell Cl Golborne WA3 . . 74 C1
Reddish SK5 . . . . 112 A8
Barwell Rd M33 . . . . 107 E5
Barwell Sq 1 BL4 . . . . .42 E2
Barwick Pl M33 . . . . 108 A4
Basechurch Wlk M12 . . . . 164 F6
Basford Rd M16 . . . . .97 B3
Bashall St BL1 . . . . 144 C8
Basil Ct OL16 . . . . 31 B6
Basil St Bolton BL3 . . . . . . 145 E5
Manchester M14 . . . . .98 C3
Rochdale OL16 . . . . .31 B6
Stockport SK4 . . . . 169 E3
Basildon Cl M13 . . . . 164 D5
Baslam Wlk 8 M4 . . . . . . 159 C2
Basle Cl SK7 . . . . 123 E4
Baslow Ave Hindley WN2 . . .56 F3
Manchester M19 . . . . .99 C2
Baslow Cl 25 SK13 . . . . . 171 E1
Baslow Dr Gatley SK8 . . . . 131 C8
Hazel Grove SK7 . . . . 133 F8
Baslow Fold 29 SK13 . . . . 171 E1
Baslow Gn 30 SK13 . . . . . 171 E1
Baslow Gr SK5 . . . . 111 F5
Baslow Mews SK13 . . . . . 171 E1
Baslow Rd Denton M34 . . . 112 F8
Droylsden M43 . . . . 83 E3
Stretford M32 . . . . 96 A3
Baslow St M11 . . . . 160 E2
Baslow Way 51 SK13 . . . . 171 E1
Bass La BL9 . . . . .11 D3
Bass St Bolton BL2 . . . . . . 148 C5
Dukinfield SK16 . . . . 101 B8
Basset Ave M6,M7 . . . . . . .81 C5
Bassett Gr WN3 . . . . .54 C2
Bassett Way OL12 . . . . 14 E2
Basswood Gn WN2 . . . . . . .57 A3
Basten Dr M7 . . . . 155 E6
Batchelor Cl M21 . . . . 109 E7
Bateman St BL6 . . . . .22 D2
Batemill Rd SK22 . . . . 127 C2
Bates Cl OL11 . . . . .30 D1
Bates St Dukinfield SK16 . . 101 C8
Manchester M13 . . . . .98 F4
Bateson Dr OL4 . . . . .67 F6
Bateson St SK1 . . . . 112 A2
Bateson Way OL8 . . . . 153 F5
Bath Cl SK7 . . . . 125 A2
Bath Cres Bramhall SK8 . . 132 B6
Manchester M16 . . . . 161 C5
Bath Pl WA14 . . . . 119 C2
Bath St Altrincham WA14 . 119 D2
Atherton M46 . . . . .58 A3
Bolton BL1 . . . . 145 F8
Oldham OL9 . . . . 152 C5
Rochdale OL12 . . . . .15 B1
Wigan WN2 . . . . .37 F2
Batheaston Gr WN7 . . . . . .75 D8
Batley St M9 . . . . 157 E8
Batridge Rd BL7 . . . . .9 A7
Batsmans Dr M27 . . . . .61 E4
Battenberg Rd 2 BL1 . . . . 144 C8
Battersbay Gr SK7 . . . . . . 124 E2
Battersby Ct SK2 . . . . 124 E6
Battersby St Bury BL9 . . . . 28 D3
Droylsden M11 . . . . .99 E7
Ince-in-M WN2 . . . . .56 B8
Leigh WN7 . . . . 76 B4
Rochdale OL11 . . . . .30 B6
Battersea Rd SK4 . . . . 110 F1
Batty St M8 . . . . 156 C5
Baucher Rd WN3 . . . . .54 F5
Baum The OL16 . . . . 139 F8
Baverstock Cl WN3 . . . . . . 151 E2
Baxendale St BL1 . . . . 143 E4
Baxter Gdns M23 . . . . 121 A2
Baxter Rd M33 . . . . 108 A4
Baxter St Oldham OL8 . . . . .66 B2
Standish WN6 . . . . 19 F1
Baxter's Row WN2 . . . . . . .57 C2
Bay St Heywood OL10 . . . . .29 B3
Oldham OL9 . . . . 153 D7
Rochdale OL12 . . . . .15 A1
Bay Tree Ave M28 . . . . . . .79 A5
Baybutt St M26 . . . . .44 C3
Baycliffe Cl WN2 . . . . .56 F3
Baycliffe Wlk 10 M8 . . . . 155 F6
Baycroft Gr M23 . . . . 109 A1
Baydon Ave M7 . . . . 155 F6
Bayfield Gr M40 . . . . .65 A1
Bayle Cl SK14 . . . . 101 E5
Bayley St SK15 . . . . .85 F1
Bayley Wlk M12 . . . . 164 F6
Bayston Wlk M12 . . . . 164 F6
Bayswater Ave M40 . . . . . .83 C4
Bayswater St BL3 . . . . 146 C2
Baythorpe St BL1 . . . . 143 F3
Baytree
Chadderton OL9 . . . . .65 E8
Dukinfield M34 . . . . 101 A4
Baytree Dr SK6 . . . . 112 F4
Baytree Gr BL0 . . . . .11 B2
Baytree La M24 . . . . .65 D8
Baytree Rd WN6 . . . . .36 F2
Baytree Wlk OL12 . . . . .4 C1
Baywood St M9 . . . . 157 D8
Bazaar St M6 . . . . .81 A4
Bazley Rd M22 . . . . 109 D1
Bazley St BL1 . . . . 23 F4
Beacomfold M46 . . . . 114 B3
Beacon Dr M23 . . . . 121 A2
Beacon Gr OL9 . . . . .67 C4
Beacon Hts WN8 . . . . .53 A8
Beacon Rd Billinge WN5 . . . 71 E6
Eccles M17 . . . . .95 E7

Beacon Rd *continued*
Leigh WN2 75 A8
Romiley SK6 113 A1
Shevington Moor WN6 19 B2
Beacon View
Appley Bridge WN6 35 C8
Marple SK6 125 F8
Beacon View Dr WN8 53 B7
Beacons The WN6 35 D7
Beaconsfield M14 110 C7
Beaconsfield Rd WA14 119 D7
Beaconsfield St BL3 145 D6
Beaconsfield Terr SK15 86 F7
Beadham Dr M9 64 A5
Beaford Cl WN5 54 B5
Beaford Dr M22 130 E8
Beagle Wlk M22 130 E8
Beal Cl SK4 110 D3
Beal Cres OL16 15 C1
Beal Dr WN2 56 A2
Beal La OL2 149 C6
Beal Vale Com Prim Sch OL2 149 B7
Beal Wlk M45 63 C8
Bealbank Cl OL16 32 A3
Bealcroft Cl OL16 31 E7
Bealcroft Wlk OL16 31 E7
Beale Gr M21 109 B8
Bealey Ave BL9 44 E5
Bealey Cl Manchester M18 165 B5
Radcliffe M26 44 D4
Bealey Dr BL9 44 D7
Bealey Hospl M26 44 D4
Bealey Ind Est M26 44 D4
Bealey Row M26 44 C4
Beaminster Ave SK4 110 F3
Beaminster Cl SK4 110 F3
Beaminster Ct SK4 110 F3
Beaminster Rd SK4 110 F3
Beaminster Wlk 7 M13 163 C5
Beamish Cl M12,M13 163 C6
Beamsley Dr M22 121 B2
Bean Leach Ave SK2 124 F6
Bean Leach Dr SK2 124 F6
Bean Leach Rd SK2,SK7 124 F5
Beanfields M28 78 F5
Beard Rd M18 99 C4
Beard St Droylsden M43 83 F1
Royton OL2 48 E3
Beardsmore Dr WA3 74 E1
Beardwood Rd M9 64 D4
Bearswood Cl SK14 167 F1
Beathwaite Dr SK7 123 C1
Beatrice Ave Cheadle SK8 122 F2
Reddish M18 99 F4
Beatrice Mews 9 BL6 22 B4
Beatrice Rd Bolton BL1 142 C1
Swinton M28 79 B7
Beatrice St Denton M34 100 E3
Farnworth BL4 60 C8
Rochdale OL11 139 D7
Swinton M27 61 D1
Beatrice Wignall St M43 100 A8
Beatson Wlk 2 M4 159 C1
Beattock St M15 162 D7
Beatty Dr BL5 39 E1
Beauchamp St OL6 166 C4
Beaufont Dr OL4 67 C5
Beaufort Ave
1 Manchester M20 110 A5
Sale M33 108 C2
Swinton M27 79 D7
Beaufort Chase SK9 131 F1
Beaufort Cl
Alderley Edge SK9 137 B2
Hattersley SK14 102 E2
Beaufort Pl 2 M20 110 A2
Beaufort Rd Ashton-u-L OL6 85 D3
Hattersley SK14 102 E2
Sale M33 108 C3
Stockport SK2 124 D5
Beaufort St Eccles M30 79 B3
7 Hindley WN2 56 D5
Manchester M3 162 E8
Prestwich M25 63 C4
Rochdale OL12 14 C1
Wigan WN5 54 E6
Beaufort Way 3 SK14 102 E1
Beaulieu WA15 119 F2
Beauly Cl BL0 11 A2
Beaumaris Cl Leigh WN7 75 C5
Manchester M12 164 F6
Beaumaris Cres SK7 124 C1
Beaumaris Rd WN2 57 A3
Beaumonds Way OL11 30 A6
Beaumont Ave BL6 22 C4
Beaumont Chase BL3 40 F3
Beaumont Cl 2 OL15 15 F5
Beaumont Com Prim Sch BL3 40 E5
Beaumont Ct Bolton BL1 40 D8
Handforth SK9 131 C5
Beaumont Dr BL3 40 E5
Beaumont Gr WN5 54 B8
Beaumont Hospl BL6 40 C8
Beaumont Rd
Bolton BL1,BL3,BL6 40 E5
Horwich BL6 22 C4
Manchester M21 109 B7
Beaumont St OL6 166 C3
Beauvale Ave SK2 124 C7
Beaver Ct WN4 73 C6
Beaver Dr BL9 45 B4
Beaver Ho SK1 124 B8
Beaver Rd M20 110 B3
Beaver Road Prim Sch M20 110 B3
Beaver St M1 163 A8
Beaver Wlk SK14 102 D1
Beaverbrook Ave WA3 92 B4
Bebbington Cl M33 108 F3
Bebbington St 7 M11 83 C1
Beccles Rd M33 108 B1
Beck Gr Shaw OL2 49 D8
Walkden M28 60 F1
Beck Ho SK14 102 D1
Beck St Droylsden M11 99 E7
Manchester M3 158 E1
Beckenham Cl BL8 27 B1
Beckenham Rd M8 156 A7
Becket Ave M7 155 E6
Becket Mdws OL4 67 B6
Becket Meadow St OL4 67 B6
Beckett Dr WA13 117 B8
Beckett St
Manchester M18 165 C5
Oldham OL4 67 E7
Beckfield Rd M23 121 A5
Beckfoot Dr M13 98 E3
Beckford St M40 157 E5
Beckhampton Cl M13 163 C6
Beckley Ave M25 63 A2
Beckley Cl OL2 49 B4
Beckside Reddish SK5 100 A1
Tyldesley M29 76 E8
Beckton Gdns M22 121 C3
Beckwith WN2 56 B3
Becontree Ave M34 101 A4
Becontree Dr M23 120 E7
Bede St BL1 142 C2
Bedells La SK9 137 A6
Bedfont Wlk M9 64 E1
Bedford Ave Hyde SK14 167 E3
Manchester M16 97 D2
Sale M33 108 D2
Shaw OL2 48 F7
1 Swinton M27 79 E7
Walkden M28 60 C1
Bedford Ct WA15 120 C6
Bedford Dr
Altrincham WA15 120 C6
Atherton M46 58 A1
Bedford Gdns WN2 56 F6
Bedford Gn M44 105 B6
Bedford Hall Meth Prim Sch WN7 76 C3
Bedford High Sch WN7 76 D4
Bedford Pl WN4 73 A5
Bedford Rd Eccles M30 79 E3
Manchester M16 97 A3
Urmston M41 95 C4
Bedford St Bolton BL1 145 D8
Bolton BL7 8 D2
Heywood OL10 29 E2
1 Leigh WN7 76 A5
Prestwich M25 63 C5
6 Reddish SK5 111 E7
Reddish SK5 111 E8
Wigan WN1 37 E1
Wigan WN5 54 C5
Bedford Terr Bury BL9 141 A4
Haslingden BB4 1 A8
Bedlam Gn 2 BL9 140 F2
Bedlington Cl M23 120 E6
Bednal Ave M40 160 E4
Bedwell Cl M16 97 F3
Bedworth Cl BL2 148 B5
Bee Fold La M46 58 C1
Bee Hive Ind Est BL6 39 E8
Beech Ave Adlington PR6 21 B8
Atherton M46 58 E3
Boothstown M28 78 A6
Chadderton OL1,OL9 48 A2
Culcheth WA3 92 A3
Denton M34 100 D4
Droylsden M43 83 F1
Farnworth BL4 60 A8
Gatley SK8 122 B5
Glossop SK13 116 A8
Golborne WA3 90 F7
Hazel Grove SK7 124 E2
Horwich BL6 22 E1
Irlam M44 94 C3
Kearsley BL4 61 B5
Little Lever BL3 43 B2
Marple SK6 125 D6
New Mills SK22 127 D1
Oldham OL3 69 B6
Oldham OL4 67 D8
Radcliffe M26 61 F8
Sale WA15 120 B8
Salford M6 154 E4
Stockport SK2,SK3 170 F6
Urmston M41 95 C2
Whitefield M45 62 F6
Wythenshawe M22 121 D8
Beech Cl
Alderley Edge SK9 137 B3
Bolton BL2 25 C6
Newton-le-W WA12 89 C2
4 Partington M31 105 F3
Prestwich M25 63 C3
Whitworth OL12 4 C1
Beech Cres Leigh WN7 75 F3
Poynton SK12 133 E4
Standish WN6 36 E8
Beech Ct Manchester M14 110 C8
9 Manchester M21 96 F1
Manchester M8 63 F1
2 Sale M33 107 F4
Salford M6 81 A3
Beech Dr WN7 75 F2
Beech Gr Abram Brow WN2 74 C7
Ashton-u-L OL7 84 F1
Leigh WN7 75 E2
Manchester M14 110 D7
Beech Gr *continued*
Ramsbottom BL8 11 A1
Sale M33 107 F4
Salford M6 154 E4
Stalybridge SK15 101 F8
Walkden M38 59 E5
Wigan WN6 36 E3
Wilmslow SK9 137 A6
Beech Grove Cl BL9 141 B4
Beech Hall St WN6 37 A2
Beech Hill Ave WN6 36 F3
Beech Hill La WN6 36 E3
Beech Hill Prim Sch WN6 37 A3
Beech Hill Rd OL4 68 D6
Beech Ho M20 109 F4
Beech Holme Gr SK2 124 C8
Beech House 3 M30 79 B1
Beech House Sch OL11 139 E6
Beech Hurst Cl M16 97 D2
Beech La Romiley SK6 113 C2
Uppermill OL4 68 D5
Wilmslow SK9 137 A6
Beech Lawn WA14 119 C4
Beech Mews
Manchester M21 109 A8
Stockport SK2 124 A5
Beech Mount
Ashton-u-L OL7 85 A6
Manchester M9 157 D8
Beech Range 15 M19 99 A1
Beech Rd
Alderley Edge SK9 137 B3
Altrincham WA15 119 E3
Cheadle SK8 123 B1
Golborne WA3 74 A1
High Lane SK6 134 F7
Manchester M21 109 B7
Sale M33 108 D4
Stockport SK2,SK3 170 F6
Beech St Ashton-in-M WN4 73 A6
Atherton M46 58 E3
Bolton BL1 143 F2
Bury BL9 141 B2
Eccles M30 79 B1
Edgworth BL7 9 D5
Failsworth M35 83 E8
Hyde SK14 167 D3
Middleton M24 64 F8
Newhey OL16 32 B4
3 Oldham OL1 67 A7
Radcliffe M26 44 C1
Ramsbottom BL9 11 C3
Rochdale OL11 139 D6
Swinton M27 79 F7
Beech Street Com Prim Sch M30 79 B1
Beech Tree Ave WN6 35 D8
Beech Tree Ho WN2 73 F7
Beech View SK14 102 A2
Beech Wlk Leigh WN7 75 E2
Middleton M24 65 A6
Standish WN6 36 D8
1 Stretford M32 96 C1
Wigan WN3 54 C2
Beechacre BL0 11 D5
Beechcroft M25 63 C3
Beechcroft Ave BL2 42 E6
Beechcroft Cl M40 160 D3
Beechcroft Gr BL2 42 E6
Beechdale Cl M40 83 C8
Beecher Wlk M9 157 D6
Beeches Mews M20 109 F4
Beeches The
Altrincham WA14 119 C2
4 Atherton M46 58 D3
Bolton BL1 24 D6
Cheadle SK8 123 B1
Eccles M30 79 F3
Heywood OL10 29 C2
Manchester M20 109 F4
Mossley OL5 68 E1
Beechey Sq OL1 67 A7
Beechfield
Altrincham WA14 119 C3
Rochdale OL11 29 E6
Sale M33 107 F2
Uppermill OL4 68 D5
Wilmslow SK9 137 A6
Beechfield Ave
Hindley WN2 57 A4
3 Radcliffe M26 44 C1
Urmston M41 95 A3
Walkden M38 60 A5
Wilmslow SK9 136 E5
Beechfield Cl
5 Oldham OL4 67 F6
Rochdale OL11 29 E6
Beechfield Dr Bury BL9 44 F7
Leigh WN7 75 F3
Beechfield Mews SK14 102 A3
Beechfield Rd
Bolton BL1 142 C2
Cheadle SK8 132 B8
Hadfield SK13 171 F3
Milnrow OL16 31 F4
Stockport SK3 170 F5
Swinton M27 79 D5
Beechfield St M8 156 A6
Beechmill Dr WA3 91 E3
Beechpark Ave M22 121 C7
Beechurst Rd SK8 123 B5
Beechway High Lane SK6 134 F7
Wilmslow SK9 136 F5
Beechwood
Altrincham WA14 119 B1
Glossop SK13 115 F7
Shaw OL2 49 D8
Whitefield BL9 45 A6
Beechwood Ave
Ashton-in-M WN4 73 A2
Littleborough OL15 16 A3
Manchester M21 109 C7
Newton-le-W WA12 89 D4
Ramsbottom BL0 11 D6
Reddish SK5 169 F4
Romiley SK6 113 D2
Shevington WN6 35 F5
Stalybridge SK15 86 C4
Urmston M41 94 E3
Beechwood Cres
Orrell WN5 53 E6
Tyldesley M29 77 A6
Beechwood Ct Bury BL8 27 A5
Coppull PR7 19 F8
3 Manchester M20 110 A3
Beechwood Dr Hyde SK14 167 F1
Marple SK6 126 A6
Mossley OL5 68 C2
Royton OL2 48 C6
Sale M33 107 C4
Swinton M28 79 B6
Wilmslow SK9 137 E8
Beechwood Gr
Cheadle SK8 132 A8
Manchester M9 157 E7
Beechwood La
Culcheth WA3 91 D4
Stalybridge SK15 86 C4
Beechwood Rd
Manchester M25 63 D3
Oldham OL8 66 F2
Beechwood St BL3 147 F3
Beede St M11 165 B8
Beedon Ave BL3 43 A4
Beehive Gn BL5 40 B1
Beehive St OL8 66 F3
Beeley St Hyde SK14 167 E2
Salford M6 81 B5
Beenham Cl M33 107 C3
Beeston Ave
Altrincham WA15 119 F6
Manchester M7 81 B6
Beeston Cl BL1 25 A6
Beeston Gr Leigh WN7 76 D7
Prestwich M45 63 B7
Stockport SK3 170 E5
Beeston Rd Handforth SK9 131 D5
Sale M33 107 F4
Beeston St M9 157 E8
Beeth St M11 99 D7
Beeton Gr M13 98 E4
Beever Prim Sch OL1 67 A8
Beever St Manchester M16 161 C5
Oldham OL1 67 A7
Begley Cl SK6 112 F1
Begonia Ave BL4 42 B1
Begonia Wlk M12 164 F6
Beightons Wlk OL12 14 D4
Beis Yaakov High Sch M7 81 C8
Belbeck St BL8 27 C2
Belbeck St S 8 BL8 27 C2
Belcroft Dr M38 59 E6
Belcroft Gr M38 59 E5
Belding Ave M40 65 F1
Beldon Rd M9 64 B4
Belfairs Cl OL7 85 B7
Belfield Cl OL16 31 C8
Belfield Com Sch OL16 31 C8
Belfield La OL16 31 C8
Belfield Mill La OL16 31 D8
Belfield Old Rd OL16 31 C8
Belfield Rd
Manchester M20 110 B3
Manchester M25 63 E2
Reddish SK5 99 F3
Rochdale OL16 31 C8
Belfield Trad Est OL16 31 D8
Belford Ave M34 100 A3
Belford Dr BL3 147 E3
Belford Rd M32 96 D3
Belford Wlk M23 121 A6
Belfort Dr M5 161 B8
Belfry Cl SK9 137 D8
Belfry Cres WN6 19 F2
Belgate Cl M12 99 A4
Belgium St OL11 29 E7
Belgrave Ave
Failsworth M35 84 B8
Manchester M14 98 E3
Marple SK6 125 F6
Oldham OL8 67 A4
Urmston M41 94 E3
Belgrave Bglws M26 43 F4
Belgrave Cl Golborne WN7 91 C8
Radcliffe M26 44 A4
Wigan WN3 54 D3
Belgrave Cres Eccles M30 79 F2
Horwich BL6 22 D3
Stockport SK2 124 B4
Belgrave Ct Denton M34 100 D4
Oldham OL8 66 F4
Belgrave Dr M26 44 A4
Belgrave Gdns 5 BL1 143 E2
Belgrave Rd
Altrincham WA14 119 C3
Failsworth M40 65 F1
Irlam M44 105 D5
Oldham OL8 66 F4
Sale M33 108 A4
Belgrave St Atherton M46 58 A2
4 Bolton BL1 143 E2
Denton M34 100 D4
Heywood OL10 29 C1
Radcliffe M26 44 A4
Rochdale OL12 14 D1
Belgrave St S BL1 143 E1
Belgravia Gdns
Altrincham WA15 128 E8
Manchester M21 109 A8
Belgravia Mews OL2 149 C7
Belhaven Rd M8 63 F2
Belhill Gdns M6 154 F3
Bell Clough Rd M43 84 B3
Bell Cres M11 164 F8
Bell La Bury BL9 141 B3
Milnrow OL16 32 B7
Wigan WN5 54 B7
Bell Meadow Dr OL11 29 F5
Bell St Bolton BL2 148 A6
Droylsden M43 84 B2
Hindley WN2 56 E6
Leigh WN7 57 D1
Oldham OL1 67 A7
Rochdale OL16 139 F8
Bell Terr M30 95 C8
Bella St BL3 146 C4
Bellairs St BL3 146 C3
Bellamy Ct M18 99 E5
Bellamy Dr WN7 76 B5
Bellcroft M22 121 E8
Belldale Cl SK4 168 A2
Belldean WN2 56 B8
Belle Green CE Prim Sch WN2 56 B8
Belle Green La WN2 56 A8
Belle Isle Ave OL12 14 C6
Belle Vue Ave M12 164 F5
Belle Vue St
Manchester M12 165 A6
1 Wigan WN5 54 D5
Belle Vue Sta M18 165 C5
Belle Vue Terr BL9 140 E1
Bellerby Cl M45 62 E8
Belleville Ave M22 130 E8
Bellew St M11 164 E8
Bellfield Ave Cheadle SK8 123 B1
Oldham OL8 66 F2
Bellingham Ave WN1 37 C2
Bellingham Cl Bury BL8 26 F2
Shaw OL2 149 B8
Bellingham Dr WN1 37 D2
Bellingham Mount WN1 37 D2
Bellis Cl M12 160 E1
Bellot Wlk OL1 153 E8
Bellott St M8 156 A6
Bellpit Cl M28 78 C7
Bells Croft Ave M40 83 B7
Bellshill Cres OL16 15 C1
Bellwood BL5 57 C6
Belmont Ave Atherton M46 58 F4
Denton M34 100 D4
Golborne WA3 74 C1
Kearsley M27 61 D5
Leigh WN2 57 A1
Oldham OL4 67 F7
Orrell WN5 53 D3
Salford M6 80 A2
Belmont Cl SK4 169 E3
Belmont Dr Aspull WN2 38 D5
Bury BL8 27 A1
Romiley SK6 114 B1
Belmont Pl PR7 19 C6
Belmont Rd Adlington PR6 21 B7
Altrincham WA15 119 E2
Bolton BL1,BL7 24 D6
Bramhall SK7 132 F5
Gatley SK8 122 B6
Hindley WN2 56 F5
Horwich BL6 22 C7
Radcliffe M26 44 A1
Sale M33 108 A6
Belmont Sh Ctr SK4 169 E3
Belmont St Eccles M30 79 D3
Manchester M16 162 D5
Oldham OL1 153 E8
Oldham OL4 67 E5
Salford M5 154 D1
Stockport SK4 169 E3
Belmont View BL2 25 F4
Belmont Way Oldham OL9 152 C8
Rochdale OL12 14 E2
Stockport SK4 169 E3
Belmont Wlk 1 M13 163 C6
Belmore Ave M8 63 F1
Belmore Rd M33 108 B1
Belper Rd Eccles M30 95 B8
Manchester SK4 110 F1
Belper St OL6 166 B4
Belper Way M34 113 A8
Belper Wlk M18 165 C6
Belroy Ct M25 63 B3
Belsay Cl OL7 84 F5
Belsay Dr M23 121 A4
Belstone Ave M23 121 A3
Belstone Cl SK7 123 F2
Belsyde Wlk 7 M9 157 E7
Belthorne Ave M9 65 B2
Belton Ave OL16 15 C1
Belton Wlk
11 Manchester M8 156 A6
Oldham OL9 153 D6
Beltone Cl M32 96 B1
Belvedere Ave
Atherton M46 58 F4
Ramsbottom BL8 11 A1
Reddish SK5 99 F2
Belvedere Cl WN7 76 D7
Belvedere Ct M25 63 A3
Belvedere Dr
Bredbury SK6 112 C3
Dukinfield SK15,SK16 101 E8

Belvedere Pl 5 WN3 . . . .54 F5
Belvedere Rd Adlington PR6 21 B8
Ashton-in-M WN4 . . . . . . .73 C4
Manchester M14 . . . .110 E8
Newton-le-W WA12 . . . .89 B5
Salford M6 . . . . .81 A3
Belvedere Rise OL1 . . . .49 D3
Belvedere St M6 . . . . . .81 B2
Belvoir Ave
Hazel Grove SK7 . . . . .133 E8
Manchester M19 . . . . .99 A2
Belvoir Mdws OL16 . . . .15 E4
Belvoir St Bolton BL2 . . . .148 C7
Rochdale OL12 . . . . . .14 C1
Wigan WN1 . . . . . . .151 E8
Belvor Ave M34 . . . . . .100 E7
Belwood Rd M21 . . . . .109 B7
Bembridge Cl M14 . . . .98 C3
Bembridge Ct WN3 . . . .54 E2
Bembridge Dr BL3 . . . .42 D5
Bembridge Rd M34 . . . .113 B8
Bempton Cl SK2 . . . . .125 A5
Bemrose Ave WA14 . . . .119 C6
Bemsley Pl M5 . . . . .161 A8
Ben Brierley Way OL1 . . .153 F7
Ben St M11 . . . . . . .83 B2
Benbecula Way M41 . . . .95 D5
Benbow Ave M12 . . . .164 F5
Benbow St 5 M33 . . . .108 B5
Benbrook Gr SK9 . . . . .131 E2
Bench Carr OL12 . . . . .14 E1
Benchill Ave M22 . . . .121 D5
Benchill Court Rd M22 . .121 E4
Benchill Cres M22 . . . .121 C5
Benchill Ct M22 . . . . .121 E4
Benchill Dr M22 . . . . .121 D5
Benchill Prim Sch M22 . .121 C5
Benchill Rd M22 . . . . .121 D5
Bendall St M11 . . . . . .99 E8
Bendemeer 6 M41 . . . . .95 C3
Bendix St M4 . . . . . .159 B2
Benedict Cl 13 M7 . . . .81 C5
Benedict Dr SK16 . . . .101 D6
Benfield Ave M40 . . . . .65 C2
Benfield St OL10 . . . . .29 D1
Benfleet Cl M12 . . . . .165 A6
Benfold Wlk M24 . . . . .46 D3
Bengairn Cl WN1 . . . . .37 F1
Bengal La OL6 . . . . . .166 C4
Bengal Sq 10 OL6 . . . . .85 D4
Bengal St Leigh WN7 . . .75 F5
Manchester M4 . . . . .159 C2
Stockport SK3 . . . . .170 E8
Benhale Wlk 15 M8 . . . .156 A6
Benham Cl M20 . . . . .110 C3
Benin Wlk 3 M40 . . . . .83 C5
Benjamin Fold WN4 . . . .73 B5
Benjamin Wilson Ct M7 .158 D4
Benmore Ct OL10 . . . . .29 A1
Benmore Rd M9 . . . . . .64 F3
Bennet Mews 3 SK14 . . .101 D5
Bennet St M26 . . . . . .43 D4
Bennett Cl 15 SK3 . . . .123 C8
Bennett Dr Manchester M7 155 E6
Orrell WN5 . . . . .53 D4
Bennett Rd M8 . . . . . .63 F1
Bennett St Ashton-u-L OL7 .84 F1
Dukinfield SK14 . . . . .101 D5
Hollingworth SK14 . . . .103 D5
Manchester M12 . . . .164 E6
4 Stalybridge SK15 . . .86 A1
3 Stockport SK3 . . . .123 C8
Stretford M32 . . . . . .96 C1
Bennett's La BL1 . . . . .142 C2
Benny La M43 . . . . . . .84 D3
Benson Cl M7 . . . . . .155 E5
Benson St Bury BL9 . . . .141 A1
Edgworth BL7 . . . . . . .9 E5
Benson Wlk 3 SK9 . . . .131 D2
Bent Fold Dr BL9 . . . . .45 A1
Bent Hill St Bolton BL3 . .146 A4
Bolton BL3 . . . . .40 F4
Bent La Culcheth WA3 . . .92 A2
Lymm WA13 . . . . . .117 C6
Manchester M8 . . . . .155 F7
Prestwich M25 . . . . . .63 C4
Bent Lanes M41 . . . . . .94 F5
Bent Spur Rd BL4 . . . . .61 A5
Bent St Farnworth BL4 . . .60 E7
Haslingden BB4 . . . . . . .1 D8
Manchester M3,M8 . . . .159 A4
Bent Terr M41 . . . . . . .95 C4
Bentcliffe Way M30 . . . .80 A1
Bentfield Cres OL16 . . . .32 A4
Bentfield Ind Pk OL9 . . .152 B6
Bentgate Cl Haslingden BB4 .1 D8
Newhey OL16 . . . . . .32 A4
Bentgate St OL16 . . . . .32 A4
Benthall Wlk M34 . . . .100 E1
Bentham Cl Bury BL8 . . .26 E3
6 Farnworth BL4 . . . . .42 D1
Bentham Pl WN6 . . . . .19 F2
Bentham Rd Culcheth WA3 .92 A2
Standish WN6 . . . . . .19 F2
Bentinck Cl WA14 . . . .119 C4
Bentinck Ho 2 OL6 . . . .166 A2
Bentinck Rd WA14 . . . .119 C4
Bentinck St
Ashton-u-L OL6 . . . . .166 A2
Bolton BL1 . . . . . . .142 B1
Farnworth BL4 . . . . . .42 C1
Manchester M15 . . . .162 D7
Oldham OL8 . . . . . . .66 F4
9 Rochdale OL12 . . . .14 C1
Wigan WN3 . . . . .54 F4

Bentinck Terr 1 OL6 . . .166 A2
Bentley Ave M24 . . . . .47 D5
Bentley Cl M26 . . . . . .44 D4
Bentley Ct Farnworth BL4 . .42 D1
Manchester M7 . . . . .155 E8
Bentley Fold BL8 . . . . .26 F4
Bentley Ho M15 . . . . .162 E6
Bentley La BL9 . . . . . .12 A1
Bentley Rd Denton M34 . .100 F3
Manchester M21 . . . . .97 A1
Manchester M7 . . . . .155 E8
Bentley St Bolton BL2 . . .148 C5
Farnworth BL4 . . . . . .42 D1
8 Oldham OL1 . . . . . .67 B8
Oldham OL9 . . . . . . .152 C7
Rochdale OL12 . . . . . .14 E2
Bentleys The SK5 . . . . .169 F3
Bentmeadows OL12 . . . .14 E1
Benton Dr SK6 . . . . . .126 C8
Benton St M9 . . . . . .157 F7
Bents Ave Bredbury SK6 . .112 F3
Urmston M41 . . . . . . .94 F1
Bents Farm Cl OL12 . . . .15 F5
Bentside Rd SK12 . . . .135 D5
Benville Wlk M40 . . . . .83 B6
Benwick Terr 18 BL1 . . .143 E2
Benyon St OL4 . . . . . .67 E6
Berberis Wlk 1 M33 . . .107 C6
Beresford Ave BL3 . . . .144 C5
Beresford Cres
Oldham OL4 . . . . .67 D8
Reddish SK5 . . . . . . .99 E3
Beresford Ct M20 . . . .110 A4
Beresford Rd
Manchester M13 . . . . .98 F3
Stretford M32 . . . . . .96 E4
Beresford St
Failsworth M35 . . . . . .83 E7
Manchester M14 . . . . .97 F3
Newhey OL16 . . . . . . .32 B4
Oldham OL4 . . . . .67 D8
8 Wigan WN6 . . . . . .37 A1
Bergman Wlk M40 . . . . .83 B6
Berigan Cl 12 M24 . . . .164 E5
Berisford Cl WA15 . . . .119 E7
Berkeley Ave
Manchester M14 . . . . .98 E4
Oldham OL9 . . . . .65 F3
Stretford M32 . . . . . .96 A4
Wigan WN3 . . . . .54 D2
Berkeley Cl Golborne WN7 .91 C8
Hyde SK14 . . . . .167 D1
Stockport SK3 . . . . . .124 C8
Berkeley Cres Hyde SK14 .167 D1
Little Lever M26 . . . . . .43 C5
Berkeley Ct 1 M7 . . . . .63 E1
8 Oldham OL2 . . . . . .48 D2
Rochdale OL16 . . . . . .31 B4
Berkeley Rd Bolton BL1 . .143 E4
Hazel Grove SK7 . . . .124 F3
Berkeley St OL6 . . . . .166 A3
Berkley Ave M19 . . . . .99 A1
Berkley Ho BL1 . . . . . .144 C7
Berkley St OL15 . . . . . .15 F5
Berkley Wlk OL15 . . . . .15 F5
Berkshire Cl OL9 . . . . .152 B5
Berkshire Ct BL9 . . . . . .44 F7
Berkshire Dr M44 . . . . .105 C5
Berkshire Pl OL9 . . . . .152 C5
Berkshire Rd M40 . . . .160 D3
Berlin Rd SK3 . . . . . .170 D6
Berlin St BL3 . . . . . . .144 C6
Bermondsay St M5 . . . .161 B8
Bernard Gr BL1 . . . . . .142 C2
Bernard St Glossop SK13 .104 C1
Manchester M9 . . . . .157 D8
Rochdale OL12 . . . . . .14 E3
Berne Ave BL6 . . . . . . .22 A3
Berne Cl Oldham OL9 . . .152 C6
Stockport SK7 . . . . . .123 E4
Bernice Ave OL9 . . . . .152 B6
Bernice St BL1 . . . . . .142 C2
Berrie Gr M19 . . . . . .111 B8
Berriedale Cl M16 . . . . .97 D2
Berrington Gr WN4 . . . .73 A3
Berry Brow M40 . . . . . .83 D4
Berry Cl SK9 . . . . . . .137 A5
Berry St Eccles M30 . . . .95 B8
Manchester M1 . . . . .163 B8
Oldham OL3 . . . . .69 B5
Stalybridge SK15 . . . .102 C8
Swinton M27 . . . . . . .61 F2
Berrycroft La SK6 . . . .113 A3
Berryfold Way M29 . . . .77 B8
Bert St BL3 . . . . . . .146 B3
Bertha Rd OL16 . . . . . .31 C7
Bertha St Bolton BL1 . . .143 D2
Manchester M11 . . . .165 B7
Shaw OL2 . . . . .149 B5
Bertie St OL11 . . . . . . .30 D4
Bertram St
Manchester M12 . . . .165 A6
Newton-le-W WA12 . . . .89 A4
Sale M33 . . . . .108 E4
Bertrand Rd BL1 . . . . .144 C7
Berwick Ave
Manchester SK4 . . . . .110 E2
Stretford M41 . . . . . .96 A4
Whitefield M45 . . . . . .63 A7
Berwick Cl Boothstown M28 77 F7
Heywood OL10 . . . . . .29 A1
Berwick Pl WN3 . . . . . .37 E1
Berwick St OL16 . . . . . .31 B6
Berwyn Ave Cheadle SK8 .123 B5
Manchester M9 . . . . . .64 C5
Middleton M24 . . . . . .65 C8
Berwyn Cl BL6 . . . . . . .22 C5

Beryl Ave BL8 . . . . . . .26 F7
Beryl St BL1 . . . . . . .143 F3
Besom La SK15 . . . . . .86 E3
Bessemer Rd M44 . . . .105 F6
Bessemer St M11,M18 . .165 C7
Bessemer Way OL1 . . . .153 E7
Besses o' th' Barn Sta
M45 . . . . .63 A7
Bessie's Well Pl WN6 . . .36 F8
Bessybrook Cl BL6 . . . . .40 C6
Beswick Dr M35 . . . . . .84 A6
Beswick Row M4 . . . . .159 A3
Beswick St
5 Droylsden M43 . . . . .84 B1
Manchester M4 . . . . .160 D2
Oldham OL2 . . . . .48 E2
Walsden OL14 . . . . . . .6 A1
Beswicke Royds St OL16 .15 C1
Beswicke St
Littleborough OL15 . . . .16 C5
Rochdale OL12 . . . . . .139 E8
Beswicks La SK9 . . . . .136 C3
Beta Ave M32 . . . . . . .96 C1
Beta St BL1 . . . . .145 F8
Bethany La OL16 . . . . . .32 D4
Bethel Ave M35 . . . . . .83 E7
Bethel St OL10 . . . . . . .29 C2
Bethersden Rd WN1 . . . .37 B4
Bethesda Sch SK8 . . . .122 D3
Bethesda St OL8 . . . . . .66 F4
Betjeman Pl OL2 . . . . . .49 D8
Betley Rd SK5 . . . . . . .99 F1
Betley St Heywood OL10 . .29 C1
Manchester M1 . . . . .163 C8
Radcliffe M26 . . . . . . .44 C4
Betleymere Rd SK8 . . . .122 F4
Betnor Ave SK1 . . . . . .112 B1
Betony Cl OL12 . . . . . .14 D3
Bettison Ave WN7 . . . . .76 C3
Bettwood Dr M8 . . . . . .63 F2
Betty Nuppy's La OL16 . . .31 C5
Betula Gr M7 . . . . . . .155 D7
Betula Mews OL1 . . . . .13 D1
Beulah Ave WN5 . . . . . .71 D4
Beulah St M18 . . . . . .165 C7
Bevan Cl M12 . . . . . .160 E1
Bevendon Sq M7 . . . . .155 E6
Beveridge St M14 . . . . .98 A3
Beverley Ave Denton M34 .101 A2
Leigh WN7 . . . . .76 A6
Longshaw WN5 . . . . . .53 E1
Urmston M41 . . . . . . .95 E3
Beverley Cl M45 . . . . . .45 B1
Beverley Pl OL16 . . . . . .31 A8
Beverley Rd Bolton BL1 . .144 C8
Little Lever BL3 . . . . . .42 F3
Pendlebury M27 . . . . . .80 C7
Stockport SK2 . . . . . .124 C8
Wigan WN5 . . . . .54 B8
Beverley St M9 . . . . . .64 E1
Beverley Wlk Oldham OL8 .153 E5
Romiley SK6 . . . . . . .113 A1
Beverly Cl OL6 . . . . . . .85 B7
Beverly Rd M14 . . . . .110 E7
Beverston 7 OL11 . . . .139 E6
Bevill Sq M3 . . . . . . .158 E2
Bevin Ave WA3 . . . . . . .92 B4
Bevington St 3 WN4 . . .72 F5
Bevis Gn BL9 . . . . . . .27 F8
Bewerley Cl WN3 . . . .150 B6
Bewick St BL2 . . . . . . .25 B3
Bewley Gr WN7 . . . . . .76 A6
Bewley St OL8 . . . . . . .66 D2
Bewley Wlk M40 . . . . . .83 A6
Bexhill Ave WA15 . . . .119 F6
Bexhill Cl BL3 . . . . . . .43 C3
Bexhill Dr Hindley WN7 . . .57 C2
Manchester M13 . . . . .98 F3
Bexhill Rd SK3 . . . . . .123 E4
Bexhill Wlk OL9 . . . . .152 B6
Bexley Cl Glossop SK13 . .104 C3
Urmston M41 . . . . . . .95 B4
Bexley Dr Bury BL8 . . . .27 B1
Bexley Sq M3 . . . . . .158 D2
Bexley St Hindley WN2 . . .57 B3
Oldham OL9 . . . . . . .152 C5
Bexley Wlk M40 . . . . . .83 B6
Bexlington Rd 8 M16 . . .97 E3
Beyer Cl M18 . . . . . .165 C5
Bibby La M19 . . . . . .110 F6
Bibby St Bury BL9 . . . . .44 F5
Dukinfield SK14 . . . . .101 D5
Bibury Ave M22 . . . . .121 B3
Bickerdike Ave M12 . . . .99 B3
Bickerdike St 1 M12 . . .99 B3
Bickershaw CE Jun
& Inf Sch WN2 . . . . . .74 F8
Bickershaw Dr M28 . . . .60 C2
Bickershaw La
Bickershaw WN2 . . . . .74 F8
Leigh WN2 . . . . .56 D1
Bickerstaffe St OL2 . . . .149 A5
Bickerton Ct OL9 . . . . . .66 B3
Bickerton Dr SK7 . . . . .124 A1
Bickerton Rd WA14 . . . .119 B6
Bickley Gr M29 . . . . . .77 C6
Bickley Wlk 5 M16 . . . .97 F4
Biddall Dr M23 . . . . . .121 B6
Biddisham Wlk M40 . . .157 D5
Biddulph Ave SK2 . . . .124 C5
Bideford Dr
Altrincham M23 . . . . .120 F7
Bolton BL2 . . . . .43 A6
Wythenshawe M23 . . . .120 F8
Bideford Rd Rochdale OL11 .30 B3

Bideford Rd continued
Stockport SK2,SK1 . . . .124 C8
Bidford Cl M29 . . . . . .59 C1
Bidston Ave M14 . . . . .98 B2
Bidston Cl Bury BL8 . . . .27 A2
Shaw OL2 . . . . .49 D6
Bidston Dr SK9 . . . . . .131 E2
Bidworth La SK13 . . . .171 D1
Big Fold BL6 . . . . .21 D2
Biggenwood Wlk 16 M40 .83 A7
Bignor St M8 . . . . . . .156 A6
Bilbao St BL1 . . . . . . .144 C8
Bilberry St Rochdale OL16 .31 A6
Rochdale OL16 . . . . . .31 B6
Bilbrook St M4 . . . . . .159 B3
Bill La M45 . . . . .62 F8
Bill Williams Cl M11 . . .165 C8
Billberry Cl M45 . . . . . .63 B8
Billing Ave M12 . . . . .163 C7
Billinge Arc 12 WN1 . . .150 C8
Billinge Chapel End
Cty Prim Sch WN5 . . . .71 E4
Billinge Cl 5 BL1 . . . . .145 F8
Billinge Hospl WN5 . . . .53 D2
Billinge Rd Garswood WN4 .72 C5
Wigan WN3,WN5 . . . . .54 D4
Wigan WN5 . . . . .54 E6
Billinge St Aidan's
CE Com Prim Sch WN5 . .71 E5
Billington Ave WA12 . . . .89 C5
Billington Rd M27 . . . . .80 E8
Billy La M27 . . . . .62 A2
Billy Meredith Cl 4 M14 .98 A3
Billy Whelan Wlk 25 M40 .83 C5
Bilsland Wlk 18 M40 . . . .83 C5
Bilson Dr SK3 . . . . . .123 B7
Bilson Sq OL16 . . . . . .31 C7
Bilton Wlk M8 . . . . . .156 C8
Binbrook Wlk BL3 . . . .147 E4
Bincombe Wlk M13 . . . .163 C5
Bindloss Ave M30 . . . . .80 A3
Bindon Wlk 4 M9 . . . .157 D7
Bingham Dr M23 . . . . .120 F6
Bingham St M27 . . . . . .79 F8
Bingley Cl M11 . . . . . .164 F8
Bingley Dr M41 . . . . . .94 F4
Bingley Rd OL16 . . . . . .31 C7
Bingley Sq OL16 . . . . . .31 C7
Bingley Terr OL16 . . . . .31 C7
Bingley Wlk M7 . . . . . .80 F8
Binns Nook Rd OL12 . . .15 A2
Binns Pl M4 . . . . . . .159 B1
Binns St SK15 . . . . . . .85 E1
Binsley Cl M4 . . . . . . .94 A1
Binstead Cl M14 . . . . . .98 E3
Birbeck St 2 SK15 . . . . .85 F1
Birch Ave Bury BL8 . . . .27 A5
Chadderton OL1,OL9 . . .48 A2
Failsworth M35 . . . . . .83 F5
Irlam M44 . . . . .105 D5
Littleborough OL12 . . . .15 D4
Manchester M16 . . . . .97 A4
Manchester SK4 . . . . .168 B4
Middleton M24 . . . . . .65 A7
Oldham OL8 . . . . . . .66 D2
Romiley SK6 . . . . . . .113 D2
Sale M33 . . . . .108 B3
Standish WN6 . . . . . . .36 F8
Westhoughton BL5 . . . .57 F7
Whitefield M45 . . . . . .62 F6
Wilmslow SK9 . . . . . .136 F6
Birch Brook Rd WA13 . . .117 C5
Birch Cl OL12 . . . . . . .14 C6
Birch Cres OL16 . . . . . .32 A3
Birch Ct Dukinfield SK16 .101 D8
Heywood OL10 . . . . . .29 E1
Manchester M13 . . . . .98 F4
Marple SK6 . . . . . . .125 E5
Birch Dr Hazel Grove SK7 .124 C2
Oldham OL4 . . . . .67 F4
Pendlebury M27 . . . . . .80 B8
Birch Gn SK13 . . . . . .104 F1
Birch Gr Altrincham WA15 .120 D5
Denton M34 . . . . . . .100 E3
Denton M34 . . . . . . .100 F6
Downall Green WN4 . . . .72 D5
Manchester M14 . . . . .98 D3
Prestwich M25 . . . . . .63 A6
Ramsbottom BL0 . . . . .11 A3
Birch Hall Cl OL4 . . . . . .67 F4
Birch Hall La M13 . . . . .98 E3
Birch Hey Cl 2 OL12 . . .15 C4
Birch Hill Cres OL12 . . . .15 E4
Birch Hill La OL12 . . . . .15 D6
Birch Hill Wlk OL15 . . . .15 F5
Birch Ho BL5 . . . . .57 F7
Birch Ind Est OL10 . . . .46 A5
Birch La Dukinfield SK16 .101 D7
Manchester M13 . . . . .98 F4
Birch Mount OL12 . . . . .15 E4
Birch Polygon M14 . . . . .98 E4
Birch Rd Abram Brow WN2 .74 B7
Atherton M46 . . . . . . .58 E3
Carrington M31,WA14 . .106 F3
Coppull PR7 . . . . .19 E8
Gatley SK8 . . . . .122 A5
Hollinfare WA3 . . . . . .105 B2
Kearsley BL4 . . . . . . .60 F6
Leigh WN7 . . . . .75 F7
Littleborough OL12 . . . .15 D5
Manchester M8 . . . . . .64 B1
Middleton M24 . . . . . .47 C2
Oldham OL3 . . . . .69 C7
Partington M31 . . . . .105 D3
Poynton SK12 . . . . . .133 F2
Swinton M27 . . . . . . .79 D5

Birch Rd continued
Walkden M28 . . . . . . .60 E1
Birch St Ashton-u-L OL7 . .100 F8
Ashton-u-L OL7 . . . . . .84 E1
Bolton BL2 . . . . .148 B6
Bury BL9 . . . . .140 F3
Droylsden M43 . . . . . .100 B8
Heywood OL10 . . . . . .29 C1
Hindley WN2 . . . . . . .56 D5
Littleborough OL12 . . . .15 C6
Manchester M12 . . . .165 A6
Radcliffe M26 . . . . . . .44 E5
Stalybridge SK15 . . . . .86 C5
3 Tyldesley M29 . . . . .59 A1
Wigan WN6 . . . . .37 A1
Birch Terr 2 SK14 . . . .167 D2
Birch Tree Ave SK7 . . . .134 A8
Birch Tree Cl WA14 . . . .119 C5
Birch Tree Ct M22 . . . .121 D3
Birch Tree Dr M22 . . . .121 D3
Birch Tree Rd 6 WA3 . . .90 F8
Birch Tree Way 4 BL6 . . .22 E1
Birch-Lea Cl BL9 . . . . . .44 F7
Birchacre Gr M14 . . . . .110 D7
Birchall Ave WA3 . . . . . .91 E4
Birchall Cl SK16 . . . . . .101 D6
Birchall Gn SK6 . . . . . .113 A5
Birchdale WA14 . . . . . .119 C2
Birchdale Ave SK8 . . . . .122 B2
Birchen Bower Wlk BL8 . .26 F5
Birchenall St M40 . . . .157 E8
Birches End BL7 . . . . . . .9 C4
Birches The Mossley OL5 . .68 B1
Sale M33 . . . . .107 F5
Birchfield Bolton BL2 . . . .25 E6
Dukinfield SK16 . . . . .100 F8
Birchfield Ave
Atherton M46 . . . . . . .58 B4
Heywood BL9 . . . . . . .28 B4
Birchfield Dr
Boothstown M28 . . . . .78 A7
Rochdale OL11 . . . . . .30 C4
Birchfield Gr BL3 . . . . . .40 E4
Birchfield Mews 4 SK14 .167 D2
Birchfield Rd Cheadle SK3 123 A7
Lymm WA13 . . . . . . .117 B4
Birchfields WA15 . . . . .119 F1
Birchfields Ave M13 . . . .98 E3
Birchfields Prim Sch
M14,M19 . . . . .98 E1
Birchfields Rd M13,M14 . .98 E3
Birchfold Cl M38 . . . . . .60 B4
Birchgate Wlk BL3 . . . .145 F5
Birchin La M4 . . . . . . .159 A1
Birchin Pl M4 . . . . . . .159 A1
Birchington Rd M14,M20 .110 A8
Birchinlee Ave OL2 . . . . .48 C3
Birchleaf Gr M5 . . . . . .80 C2
Birchley Ave WN3 . . . . .71 C3
Birchley Rd WA11,WN5 . .71 C4
Birchley St Mary's
RC Prim Sch WN5 . . . . .71 D4
Birchley View WA11 . . . .71 B2
Birchside Ave SK13 . . . .104 B2
Birchvale Ave SK6 . . . . .113 D3
Birchway Bramhall SK7 . .132 D7
High Lane SK6 . . . . . .134 F7
Birchwood OL9 . . . . . . .65 E2
Birchwood Cl Leigh WN7 . .75 F3
Stockport SK4 . . . . . .168 A1
Wigan WN3 . . . . .54 D1
Birchwood Dr SK9 . . . .137 D8
Birchwood Rd M24 . . . . .65 C8
Birchwood Way SK16 . . .101 D8
Bird Hall Ave SK8 . . . . .123 C4
Bird Hall La SK3,SK8 . . .123 B4
Bird Hall Rd SK8 . . . . .123 C5
Bird St M9 . . . . .151 F7
Birdhall Gr M19 . . . . .111 A8
Birdlip Dr M23 . . . . . .121 A3
Birkby Dr M24 . . . . . . .46 E2
Birkdale Ave Atherton M46 .58 C5
Oldham OL2 . . . . .48 E2
Whitefield M45 . . . . . .62 D6
Birkdale Cl Bramhall SK7 .133 A7
Dukinfield SK14 . . . . .101 F5
Heywood OL10 . . . . . .46 D8
Birkdale Dr Bury BL8 . . . .27 B2
Sale M33 . . . . .107 E2
Birkdale Gdns BL3 . . . .145 D5
Birkdale Gr Eccles M30 . . .79 F2
Reddish SK5 . . . . . . .111 F5
Birkdale Rd Reddish SK5 .111 C4
Rochdale OL16 . . . . . .31 C4
Birkdale St M8 . . . . . .156 C6
Birkenhills Dr BL3 . . . . .40 E5
Birkett Bank WN1 . . . . .151 E8
Birkett Bank Terr WN1 . .151 E8
Birkett Cl BL1 . . . . . . .24 D6
Birkett Dr BL1 . . . . . . .24 D6
Birkett St WN1 . . . . . .151 E8
Birkinbrook Cl M45 . . . .45 A1
Birkinheath La WA14 . . .128 B4
Birkleigh Wlk BL2 . . . . .42 E6
Birks Ave OL4 . . . . . . .67 F8
Birks Dr BL8 . . . . .27 B6
Birks La OL14 . . . . .6 B8
Birkside Cl WN3 . . . . . .55 A1
Birkworth Ct SK2 . . . . .124 C6
Birley Cl Altrincham WA15 .119 F7
Appley Bridge WN6 . . . .35 F3
Birley Ct 1 M5 . . . . . .81 A2
Birley Pk M20 . . . . . .109 F3
Birley St Bolton BL1 . . . .143 E4
Bury BL9 . . . . .27 F5
Leigh WN7 . . . . .76 A6

Birley St *continued*
Newton-le-W WA12 89 D4
Rochdale OL12 15 A1
Birling Dr M23 121 B4
Birnham Gr OL10 29 A1
Birshaw Cl OL2 149 B5
Birstall Wlk M23 121 A6
Birt St M40 160 D4
Birtenshaw Cres BL7 25 B7
Birtenshaw Hall Sch BL7 25 B6
Birtle Dr M29 77 C7
Birtle Rd BL9 28 E6
Birtle View Sch OL10 29 C2
Birtles Ave SK5 99 F3
Birtles Cl Cheadle SK8 123 A5
Dukinfield SK16 101 D6
Birtles The M22 121 D3
Birtles Way 4 SK9 131 D5
Birtlespool Rd SK8 122 F4
Birtley Wlk 14 M40 159 C3
Birwood Rd M8 64 B2
Biscay Cl M11 160 F1
Bishop Bilborrow Meml RC Prim Sch M14 97 F3
Bishop Bridgeman CE Prim Sch BL3 147 E4
Bishop Cl M16 97 E4
Bishop Marshall Cl M40 157 D5
Bishop Marshall Way M24 46 D4
Bishop Rd Salford M6 80 B4
Urmston M41 94 D2
Bishop St Middleton M24 65 D7
Rochdale OL16 15 B1
Stockport SK1 112 A1
Bishop's Cl Bolton BL3 42 A2
Cheadle SK8 123 A5
Bishop's Rd BL3 42 A2
Bishopbridge Cl BL3 147 F4
Bishopdale Cl OL2 48 D5
Bishopgate WN1 150 C8
Bishopgate St OL9 152 A5
Bishops Cl
Altrincham WA14 119 B1
Ashton-u-L OL7 85 A5
Bishops Gate M2 162 F8
Bishops Mdw M24 46 D3
Bishops Mews M33 107 E6
Bishops Rd M25 63 C2
Bishops Wlk OL7 166 A1
Bishopsgate Wlk OL16 31 C4
Bishopton Cl M19 99 C1
Bisley Ave M23 120 F6
Bisley St OL8 153 D6
Bismarck St OL4 67 A5
Bispham Ave Bolton BL2 42 F7
Reddish SK5 99 F3
Bispham Cl BL8 26 F1
Bispham Dr WN4 72 F5
Bispham Gr M7 155 E7
Bispham Hall Bsns Pk WN5 53 C2
Bispham St BL2 148 C8
Bittern Cl Poynton SK12 133 A4
Rochdale OL11 29 F7
Bittern Dr M43 84 C3
Bk Adcroft St SK1 170 F7
Bk Alfred St BL0 138 B5
Bk Andrew St OL5 86 C8
Bk Cardwell St 33 BL1 143 E2
Bk Cecil St OL5 86 C8
Bk Chapel St Bury BL8 26 F7
12 Manchester M19 99 A1
Bk Drummond St BL1 143 E4
Bk Grosvenor St 2 SK15 86 A1
Bk Halliwell Rd S 17 BL1 143 D2
Bk Knowl St SK15 86 B2
Bk Melbourne St 1 SK15 86 A1
Bk Nut St BL1 143 D2
Bk Portland St OL6 166 A2
Bk Stayley Rd OL5 86 D8
Bk Water St OL6 166 C4
Black Brook Rd SK4 111 D7
Black Horse St
Blackrod BL6 21 C3
Bolton BL1 145 E6
Farnworth BL4 60 E7
Black La BL0 12 B7
Black Moss Cl M26 43 D3
Black Moss Rd WA14 118 F7
Blackbank St BL1 143 F2
Blackberry Cl WA14 119 B8
Blackberry Dr WN2 56 C4
Blackberry La SK5 112 C7
Blackburn Cl WA3 90 E8
Blackburn Gdns M20 110 A4
Blackburn Pl M5 81 C1
Blackburn Rd Bolton BL1 143 F2
Bolton BL7 8 C4
Edenfield BL0,BB4 1 D5
Blackburn St
Manchester M16 161 C5
Manchester M3 158 D3
Prestwich M25 63 C4
Radcliffe M26 44 A3
Radcliffe M26 44 B2
Blackcap Cl M28 78 B7
Blackcarr Rd M23 121 B6
Blackchapel Dr OL16 31 B3
Blackcroft Cl M27 79 E8
Blackfield La M7 81 C8
Blackfields M7 155 D8
Blackford Ave BL9 44 F4
Blackford Rd M19 111 B7
Blackford Wlk M40 160 D3
Blackfriar Ct M3 158 D3
Blackfriars Rd M3 158 E2
Blackfriars St M3 158 F2
Blackhill Cl 8 M13 163 B7

Blackhorse Ave BL6 21 C2
Blackhorse Cl BL6 21 C3
Blackleach Ctry Pk M28 60 D4
Blackleach Dr M28 60 D5
Blackledge Cl WN5 53 E5
Blackledge St BL3 146 C4
Blackley Cl BL9 45 A2
Blackley New Rd M9,M25 64 B3
Blackley Park Rd M9 64 D1
Blackley St
Manchester M16 161 C5
Middleton M24 64 B7
Blackleyhurst Ave WN5 71 E5
Blacklock St M3,M8 158 F4
Blackmoor Ave M29 77 B5
Blackpits Rd OL11 13 D1
Blackpool St 19 M11 83 C2
Blackrock OL5 86 C6
Blackrock St M11 164 F8
Blackrod Brow BL6 21 B4
Blackrod By-Pass Rd BL6 21 D2
Blackrod Cty Prim Sch BL6 38 E8
Blackrod Dr BL8 26 F1
Blackrod Sta BL6 21 E2
Blacksail Wlk 3 OL1 49 A1
Blackshaw Ho BL3 144 C6
Blackshaw La
Alderley Edge SK9 136 F1
Bolton BL3 144 C6
Royton OL2 49 A4
Blackshaw Lane Com Prim Sch OL2 49 A4
Blackshaw Prim Sch BL2 43 A6
Blackshaw Rd SK13 104 E2
Blackshaw Row 2 BL3 144 C5
Blackshaw St SK3 170 E8
Blacksmith La OL11 30 B4
Blackstock St M13 98 C4
Blackstone Ave OL16 31 C8
Blackstone Edge Old Rd
OL15 16 E6
Blackstone Edge Rd
HX6,HX7 7 F5
Blackstone Rd SK2 124 D5
Blackstone Wlk M9 157 D6
Blackthorn Ave
Manchester M19 111 A7
Wigan WN6 36 F3
Blackthorn Cl OL12 14 E2
Blackthorn Mews OL12 14 E2
Blackthorn Rd OL8 84 C8
Blackthorn Wlk 3 M31 105 E2
Blackthorne Cl BL1 142 A1
Blackthorne Dr M33 107 D2
Blackthorne Rd SK14 113 E7
Blackwell Wlk 3 M4 159 C2
Blackwin St M12 165 A6
Blackwood Dr M23 120 D8
Blackwood Rd OL13 3 B7
Blackwood St BL3 42 A4
Bladen Cl SK8 123 A4
Bladon St M1 163 B8
Blainscough Rd PR7 19 E8
Blair Ave Hindley WN2 57 B3
Urmston M41 94 E2
Walkden M38 60 B4
Blair Cl Hazel Grove SK7 133 C8
Sale M33 107 C1
Shaw OL2 149 B7
Blair La BL2 25 D1
Blair Rd M16 97 E1
Blair St Bolton BL7 25 A8
Kearsley BL4 61 B6
Manchester M16 162 D5
Rochdale OL12 14 D1
Blairhall Ave M40 83 A7
Blairmore Dr BL3 40 E5
Blake Ave M46 58 D5
Blake Cl WN3 150 A5
Blake Dr SK2 124 E7
Blake Gdns BL1 143 D2
Blake St Bolton BL1 143 D2
Bolton BL7 25 A7
Rochdale OL16 31 A8
Blakeborough Ho 7 M46 58 D3
Blakedown Wlk M12 164 E5
Blakefield Dr M28 60 E1
Blakelock St OL2 149 B7
Blakemere Ave M33 108 E3
Blakemore Wlk M12 160 E1
Blakeswell Cl M41 94 D3
Blakey Cl BL3 40 F4
Blakey St M12 99 A4
Blanchard St M15 162 E5
Blanche St OL12 15 A2
Blanche Wlk 10 OL1 67 A8
Bland Cl M35 83 E7
Bland Rd M25 63 B2
Blandford Ave M28 79 A8
Blandford Cl Bury BL8 27 D5
Tyldesley M29 59 A1
Blandford Ct SK15 86 A2
Blandford Dr M40 65 D2
Blandford Ho 7 SK15 86 A2
Blandford Rd Eccles M30 79 B2
Salford M6 81 B4
Stockport SK4 168 C2
Blandford Rise BL6 22 F1
Blandford St
Ashton-u-L OL6 166 A3
Stalybridge SK15 86 A2
Blanefield Cl M21 109 E7
Blantyre Ave M28 60 E2
Blantyre Ho 4 M15 162 D7
Blantyre Rd M27 80 B6
Blantyre St Eccles M30 79 A3
Hindley WN2 56 E6

Blantyre St *continued*
Manchester M15 162 D7
Swinton M27 61 D1
Blanwood Dr M8 156 B7
Blaven Cl SK3 170 F5
Blaydon Cl WN2 38 D5
Blazemoss Bank SK2 124 D5
Bleach St WN2 56 C4
Bleackley St BL8 27 C4
Bleak Hey Rd M22 121 F2
Bleak St BL2 25 B2
Bleakholt Rd BL0 1 F1
Bleakledge Gr WN2 56 F7
Bleakley St 1 M45 44 E1
Bleaklow Cl WN3 55 B2
Bleaklow Wlk 20 SK13 171 E1
Bleasby St OL4 67 C7
Bleasdale Cl Horwich BL6 39 F8
Whitefield BL9 45 A3
Bleasdale Rd Bolton BL1 23 F2
Newton-le-W WA12 89 C4
Wythenshawe M22 121 A2
Bleasdale St OL2 48 E5
Bleasedale Rd WN2 57 A5
Bleasefell Chase M28 78 A5
Bleatarn Rd SK1 124 B7
Bledlow Cl M30 79 E3
Blencarn Wlk M9 157 D6
Blendworth Cl M8 155 F7
Blenheim Ave M16 97 D2
Blenheim Cl
Altrincham WA14 119 D2
6 Hadfield SK13 104 A5
Heywood OL10 29 E2
Poynton SK12 133 F4
Whitefield BL9 45 A5
Wilmslow SK9 137 D7
Blenheim Dr WN7 76 E7
Blenheim Rd
Ashton-in-M WN4 73 D2
Bolton BL2 42 E6
Cheadle SK8 123 B2
Manchester M16 97 A3
Wigan WN5 54 C8
Blenheim St
8 Oldham OL4 49 D1
13 Rochdale OL12 14 C1
Tyldesley M29 76 F8
Blenheim Way OL6 85 E4
Blenhiem Ave OL1 49 D3
Blenmar Cl M26 44 C5
Bleriot St BL3 147 D3
Blessed Thomas Holford RC High Sch WA15 119 E4
Bletchley Cl M13 164 D5
Bletchley Rd SK4 110 E1
Blethyn St BL3 146 B2
Blewberry Cl WN7 75 F7
Bligh Rd 15 BL5 39 E1
Blinco Rd M41 95 F2
Blind La M12 164 D7
Blindsill Rd BL4 60 B7
Blissford Cl WN2 56 D4
Blisworth Ave M30 95 E8
Blisworth Cl M4 160 D1
Blithfield Wlk M34 100 E2
Block La OL9 152 B5
Blocksage St SK16 101 D7
Blodwell St M5,M6 154 F2
Blofield Ct BL4 60 D7
Blomley St OL11 30 C2
Bloom St Manchester M1 163 A8
Manchester M3 158 E2
Ramsbottom BL0 11 A4
Stockport SK3 170 D8
Bloomfield Dr
Boothstown M28 78 A7
Whitefield BL9 45 B3
Bloomfield Rd BL4 60 D6
Bloomfield St BL1 143 E3
Bloomsbury Gr WA15 120 A6
Bloomsbury La WA15 120 A6
Blossom Pl OL16 139 F8
Blossom Rd M31 105 E2
Blossom St
Manchester M3 158 E2
Manchester M4 159 B2
11 Tyldesley M29 59 A1
Blossoms Hey SK8 122 E1
Blossoms Hey Wlk SK8 122 E1
Blossoms La SK7 132 B2
Blossoms St SK2 170 F7
Bloxham Wlk M9 64 F3
Blucher St Ashton-u-L OL7 85 A6
Manchester M12 164 E6
Manchester M5 81 C1
Blue Bell Ave
Manchester M40 65 A1
Wigan WN6 36 F4
Blue Chip Bsns Pk WA14 119 C7
Blue Coat CE Comp Sch OL1 153 F7
Blue Ribbon Wlk M27 62 A1
Bluebell Ave BB4 1 A8
Bluebell Cl SK14 101 F5
Bluebell Dr OL11 30 B3
Bluebell Gr SK8 122 D4
Bluebell Way SK9 131 C1
Blueberry Dr OL2 49 D7
Blueberry Rd WA14 119 A2
Bluefields OL2 49 D8
Bluestone Dr SK4 110 E3
Bluestone Rd
Manchester M40 83 A8
Reddish M34 100 A2
Blundell Cl BL9 45 B3
Blundell La BL6 21 A2

Blundell Mews WN3 54 D4
Blundell St BL1 145 E7
Blundering La SK15 102 D6
Blunn St OL8 66 F4
Blyborough Cl M6 154 E4
Blyth Ave Littleborough OL15 15 F3
Wythenshawe M23 109 C2
Blyth Cl WA15 120 D6
Blythe Ave SK7 132 C6
Blyton St M15 163 B5
Blyton Way M34 112 F8
Bnos Yisroel Schs M7 155 E8
Boad St M1 163 B8
Boar Green Cl M40 83 C7
Board St Ashton-u-L OL6 85 D4
Bolton BL3 145 D6
Boardale Dr M24 46 E1
Boardman Cl BL1 143 E2
Boardman Fold Cl M24 65 A5
Boardman Fold Rd M24 65 A5
Boardman La M24 64 C8
Boardman Rd M8 63 F2
Boardman St Blackrod BL6 21 D2
Bolton BL1 143 E2
Eccles M30 79 E1
Hyde SK14 167 D2
Boars Head Ave WN6 37 A7
Boarsgreave La BB4 2 F6
Boarshaw Clough M24 47 B2
Boarshaw Clough Way M24 47 B2
Boarshaw Com Prim Sch M24 47 B3
Boarshaw Cres M24 47 C3
Boarshaw Ind Est M24 47 B2
Boarshaw La M24 47 D3
Boarshaw Rd M24 47 B2
Boarshurst Ind Pk OL3 69 B6
Boarshurst La OL3 69 C5
Boat La Diggle OL3 51 E5
Irlam M44 94 B2
Wythenshawe M22 109 E1
Boat Lane Ct M22 109 E1
Boatmans Row M29 77 C4
Bob Massey Cl M11 83 C1
Bob's La M44 105 D4
Bobbin Wlk
4 Manchester M4 159 C1
7 Oldham OL1 67 A6
Bodden St WA3 75 A1
Boddens Hill Rd SK4 168 A1
Boddington Rd M30 79 A1
Bodiam Rd BL8 10 F2
Bodley St M11 83 C2
Bodmin Cl OL2 49 A3
Bodmin Cres SK5 112 B5
Bodmin Dr Bramhall SK7 132 E7
Platt Bridge WN2 56 A1
Bodmin Rd Sale M33 107 D5
Tyldesley M29 77 C8
Bodmin Wlk 3 M23 121 A5
Bodney Wlk M9 64 B3
Bogburn La PR7 19 D6
Boggard La SK13 115 D6
Bogguard Rd SK6 127 A5
Bognor Rd SK3 123 E4
Bolam Cl M23 108 F1
Boland Dr M14 110 D8
Bold St Altrincham WA14 119 D3
Bolton BL1 145 F6
Bury BL9 141 A3
Leigh WN7 75 F5
Leigh WN7 75 F6
Manchester M15 162 E5
Manchester M16 97 E4
Swinton M27 61 F2
Wigan WN5 54 E5
Bolderod Pl 4 OL1 67 A8
Bolderstone Pl SK2 124 E4
Bolderwood Dr WN2 56 D4
Bolesworth Cl M21 108 F8
Boleyn Ct OL10 29 C1
Boleyn Wood Ct SK9 131 B1
Bolholt Terr BL8 27 B4
Bolivia St M5 80 C2
Bollin Ave WA14 119 B1
Bollin Cl Culcheth WA3 92 A2
Kearsley BL4 61 B6
Lymm WA13 117 A4
Bollin Cross Sch SK9 131 A2
Bollin Ct Altrincham WA14 119 B1
6 Manchester M15 162 D6
Wilmslow SK9 137 C6
Bollin Dr Altrincham WA14 119 E8
Lymm WA13 117 A4
Sale M33 108 B2
Bollin Hill SK9 137 B8
Bollin Ho 8 M7 81 C5
Bollin Prim Sch WA14 119 B1
Bollin Sq WA14 119 B1
Bollin Way M45 45 C2
Bollin Wlk Reddish SK5 169 F4
Whitefield M45 45 C2
Wilmslow SK9 137 C7
Bolling St BL3 145 F6
Bollings Yd BL1 145 F6
Bollington Cl 3 OL7 166 A1
Bollington Rd
Manchester M40 160 D2
Reddish SK4 111 D5
Bollington St OL7 166 A1
Bollinway WA15 129 A8
Bollinwood Chase SK9 137 D7
Bolney St WN2 38 A3
Bolney Wlk M40 160 D4
Bolshaw Cty Prim Sch SK8 131 B7
Bolshaw Farm La SK8 131 C6

Bolshaw Rd SK8 131 C6
Bolton Ave Bramhall SK8 132 B6
Manchester M19 110 D2
Bolton Cl Golborne WA3 91 B8
Poynton SK12 133 D4
Prestwich M25 62 F2
Bolton Coll BL2 148 A6
Bolton District General Hospl BL4 147 F1
Bolton Gates Ret Pk BL1 148 A8
Bolton House Rd WN2 74 F8
Bolton Inst (Chadwick Campus) BL2 148 B6
Bolton Inst of H Ed BL3 145 E6
Bolton Metropolitan Coll
Bolton BL1 145 F8
Bolton BL2 148 A6
Bolton Muslim Girls Sch BL3 147 D4
Bolton Old Rd M46 58 E3
Bolton Parish Church CE Prim Sch BL2 148 B7
Bolton Rd
Adlington BL6,PR6 21 D6
Ashton-in-M WN2,WN4 73 D5
Aspull WN2 38 D4
Atherton M46 58 E4
Bolton BL2 25 C5
Bolton BL3 40 D2
Bolton BL7 9 D5
Bury BL8 140 D2
Bury BL8 27 C1
Farnworth BL4 42 D2
Kearsley BL4 60 F7
Pendlebury M27 80 C7
Radcliffe M26 43 E3
Ramsbottom BL8 10 D2
Rochdale OL11 30 B4
Salford M6 80 E5
Swinton M27 62 A1
Walkden M28 60 D4
Westhoughton BL5 39 F1
Bolton Rd N BL0 1 D2
Bolton Rd W
Ramsbottom BL0 10 F3
Ramsbottom BL0 11 A4
Bolton Royal Infmy BL1 145 D7
Bolton Sch BL1 144 B7
Bolton Sq WN1 37 E1
Bolton St Bury BL9 140 E2
Downall Green WN4 72 D5
Manchester M3 158 E1
Oldham OL4 67 B6
Radcliffe M26 43 F3
Ramsbottom BL0 138 B6
Reddish SK5 111 E7
Bolton Sta BL3 145 F6
Bolton Street Sta BL9 140 E2
Bolton Wanderers FC (Reebok Stad) BL6 39 D7
Bolton Wholesale Pk
Bolton BL1 143 F1
Bolton BL1 145 F8
Boltons Yd 10 OL3 69 B8
Bombay Rd
Shevington WN5 36 C1
Stockport SK3 123 C7
Bombay St
5 Ashton-u-L OL6 85 D4
Manchester M1 163 A8
Bonar Cl 5 SK3 123 C8
Bonar Rd SK3 123 C8
Boncarn Dr M23 121 A4
Bonchurch Wlk M18 165 B6
Bond Cl BL6 22 C3
Bond Sq M7 155 E6
Bond St Bury BL9 141 A2
Denton M34 100 F3
Edenfield BL0 1 E2
Leigh WN7 75 F5
Manchester M12 163 C8
Rochdale OL12 15 A2
Stalybridge SK15 86 A3
Tyldesley M46 58 F1
Bond's La PR7 20 F7
Bondmark Rd M18 165 C6
Bongs Rd SK2,SK6 125 A6
Bonhill Wlk M11 83 B2
Bonholt Ind Est 11 BL8 27 B4
Bonington Rise SK6 126 B8
Bonis Cres SK2 124 C4
Bonny Brow St M24 64 B7
Bonnyfield SK6 113 B2
Bonnywell Rd WN7 75 F3
Bonsall Bank 32 SK13 171 E2
Bonsall Cl 33 SK13 171 E2
Bonsall Fold 31 SK13 171 E2
Bonsall St M15 162 F6
Bonscale Cres M24 46 E3
Bonville Chase WA14 119 A4
Bonville Rd WA14 119 A4
Boodle St OL6 166 B4
Bookham Wlk 16 M9 157 E8
Boond St Manchester M3 158 E2
Manchester M4 160 D1
Boonfields BL7 25 A8
Boot La BL1 23 E1
Booth Ave M14 110 D7
Booth Bridge Cl M24 64 C7
Booth Cl Bury BL8 27 A5
4 Stalybridge SK15 85 F1
Booth Clibborn Ct M7 155 D8
Booth Ct BL4 60 D8
Booth Dr M41 94 F5
Booth Hall Dr BL8 26 F5

Booth Hall Hospl M9 ....64 F3
Booth Hall Rd M9 ....65 A3
Booth Hill La OL1 ....48 E1
Booth House Trad Est
OL9 ....152 C6
Booth Rd Altrincham WA14 119 C4
Bacup OL13 ....3 B8
Droylsden M34 ....100 A7
Handforth SK9 ....131 A1
Little Lever BL3 ....43 B2
Manchester M16 ....97 C3
Sale M33 ....108 B6
Booth St Ashton-u-L OL6 ..166 B2
Bolton BL1 ....142 C3
Bury BL8 ....26 F5
Denton M34 ....100 F5
Hollingworth SK14 ......103 C5
Hyde SK14 ....167 E1
Manchester M2 ....158 F1
Manchester M3 ....158 F2
Middleton M24 ....65 D6
2 Oldham OL4 ....67 E6
Oldham OL9 ....153 E6
Rawtenstall BB4 ....2 E8
Stalybridge SK15 ....101 F8
Stockport SK3 ....170 E7
Booth St E M13 ....163 B6
Booth St W M13,M15 .....163 A6
Booth Way BL8 ....26 F5
Booth's Brow Rd WN4 ....72 D6
Booth's Hall M28 ....78 B5
Booth's Hall Gr 2 M28 ...78 B6
Booth's Hall Rd M28 .....78 B5
Booth's Hall Way M28 ....78 B6
Boothby Rd M27 ....61 E1
Boothby St SK2 ....124 C4
Boothcote M34 ....100 D6
Boothfield 11 Bury BL8 ...27 C3
Eccles M30 ....79 A3
Boothfield Ave M22 .....121 D6
Boothfield Dr M22 ......121 D6
Boothfield Rd M22 ......121 D6
Boothroyden Cl M24 .....64 C7
Boothroyden Rd M24,M9 ..64 C6
Boothroyden Terr M9 ....64 C6
Boothsbank Ave M28 ....78 B6
Boothshall Paddock M28 ..78 B6
Boothshall Way M28 .....78 A5
Boothstown Dr M28 .....78 A5
Boothstown Meth Sch
M28 ....77 F6
Boothway 8 M30 ....79 F2
Bootle St M2 ....162 F8
Bor WN3 ....55 B4
Bordale Ave M9 ....157 F7
Bordan St M11 ....164 F8
Borden Cl 5 WN2 ....37 F2
Borden Way BL9 ....45 A6
Border Brook La M28 ....78 A6
Bordley Wlk M23 ....108 E1
Bordon Sk3 ....123 B7
Bores Hill WN1 ....20 C4
Boringdon Cl M40 ......83 B6
Borland Ave M40 ....65 D1
Borough Arc SK14 ......167 D2
Borough Ave Radcliffe BL9 .44 D5
Swinton M27 ....62 A1
Borough Rd
Altrincham WA15 ....119 C4
Salford M5 ....154 D1
Borough St 5 SK15 .....86 A1
Borrans The M28 ....77 F5
Borron Rd WA12 ....89 B5
Borron St SK1 ....112 A2
Borrowdale Ave
Bolton BL1 ....144 A8
Gatley SK8 ....122 B4
Borrowdale Cl OL2 .....48 D6
Borrowdale Cres
Ashton-u-L OL7 ....84 F4
Manchester M20 ....109 E4
Borrowdale Dr
Rochdale OL11 ....30 C4
Whitefield BL9 ....45 A3
Borrowdale Rd
Middleton M24 ....46 E2
Stockport SK2 ....124 B6
Wigan WN5 ....54 B7
Borrowdale Terr SK15 ...86 A4
Borsdane Ave WN2 .....56 F5
Borsdane Brook Sch WN2 56 C5
Borsden St M27 ....61 D2
Borth Ave SK2 ....124 C4
Borth Wlk 3 M23 ......120 F6
Borwell St M18 ....99 D5
Boscobel Rd BL3 ....42 B2
Boscombe Ave M30 ....95 C8
Boscombe Dr SK7 ......124 C1
Boscombe Pl WN2 ......56 E4
Boscombe St
Manchester M14 ......98 B2
Reddish SK5 ....99 F2
Boscow Rd BL3 ....43 A2
Bosden Ave SK7 ....124 C2
Stockport SK1 ....170 F8
Bosden Cl Handforth SK9 .131 D5
Stockport SK1 ....170 F8
Bosden Fold SK1 ....170 F8
Bosden Hall Rd SK7 .....124 C3
Bosdenfold Rd SK7 .....124 C3
Bosdin Rd E M41 ....94 E1
Bosdin Rd W M41 ......94 E1
Bosley Ave M20 ....110 A8
Bosley Cl SK9 ....131 D2
Bosley Dr SK12 ....134 A3

Bosley Rd SK3 ....123 A8
Bossall Ave M9 ....64 E4
Bossington Cl SK2 ......124 C8
Bostock Rd SK14 ....115 A8
Bostock Wlk M13 ......163 B7
Boston Ct Bramhall SK7 ..132 D7
Culcheth WA3 ....91 F4
Failsworth M35 ....83 F8
Boston Ct Hyde SK14 ....167 E3
Salford M5 ....96 E8
Boston Gr WN7 ....75 E8
Boston St 14 Bolton BL1 ..143 E2
Hyde SK14 ....167 E2
Manchester M15 ....162 F5
Oldham OL8 ....66 F4
Boston Wlk 8 M34 .....101 A1
Boswell Ave M34 ......84 D1
Boswell Pl WN3 ....54 F3
Boswell Way M24 ......47 E4
Bosworth Cl M45 ......63 C8
Bosworth Sq OL11 .....30 D4
Bosworth St Horwich BL6 ..22 B4
Manchester M11 ....165 A8
Rochdale OL11 ....30 D4
Botanical Ave M16 .....161 A5
Botany Cl Aspull WN2 ...38 B2
Heywood OL10 ....29 B2
Botany La OL6 ....166 C3
Botany Rd Eccles M30 ...79 A4
Romiley SK6 ....113 A6
Botesworth Gn OL16 ...32 A5
Botha Cl 4 M11 ....99 D7
Botham Cl M15 ....162 F5
Bothwell Rd M40 ......159 C3
Botley St OL5 ....68 B1
Bottesford Ave M20 ....109 F5
Bottom o' th' Knotts
Brow 9 E3
Bottom o' th' Moor
Horwich BL6 ....23 A3
Oldham OL1,OL4 ....67 B7
Bottom St SK14 ....167 F3
Bottomfield Cl OL1 .....49 A1
Bottomley Rd OL14 ....6 C6
Bottomley Side M9 .....64 C2
Bougainvillea Gdns M12 ..99 A4
Boughey St WN7 ....75 E5
Boulden Dr BL8 ....27 C5
Boulder Dr M23 ....121 A2
Boulderstone Rd SK15 ..86 A4
Boulevard The
Hazel Grove SK7 ....124 E2
Hollingworth SK14 .....171 D4
Bouley Wlk M12 ....165 A6
Boulton Ho M1 ....163 A8
Boundary Cl Mossley OL5 .86 C6
Romiley SK6 ....113 A6
Boundary Cotts SK15 ...86 C7
Boundary Ct SK8 ......122 C5
Boundary Dr BL2,BL3 ...43 A5
Boundary Gdns
Bolton BL1 ....143 E2
Oldham OL1 ....48 E1
Boundary Gr
Manchester M15 ....163 A6
Shevington Moor WN6 ..19 A3
Boundary Park Rd OL1 ..48 C1
Boundary Rd Cheadle SK8 123 A6
Irlam M44 ....94 C3
Swinton M27 ....61 F1
Boundary St Bolton BL1 ..143 D2
Leigh WN7 ....76 B4
Littleborough OL15 .....16 B6
Manchester M12 ....165 A6
Rochdale OL11 ....139 F5
Tyldesley M29 ....59 A1
Wigan WN1 ....151 D7
Boundary St E M1,M13 ..163 A7
Boundary St W M15 ....163 A6
Boundary Terr SK9 .....130 F6
Boundary The M27 .....61 E4
Boundary Trad Pk M44 ..94 C3
Boundary Wlk OL11 ....139 E5
Boundry Gn M34 ....100 E4
Bourdon St M40 ....160 D3
Bourget St M7 ....155 F8
Bournbrook Ave M38 ...60 A6
Bourne Ave Golborne WA3 .90 D8
Swinton M27 ....79 F7
Bourne Dr M40 ....65 B1
Bourne Ho 1 M6 ......154 F2
Bourne Rd OL2 ....149 A8
Bourne St Oldham OL9 ...66 B2
Stockport SK4 ....169 E4
Wilmslow SK9 ....136 F6
Bourton Cl BL8 ....27 B3
Bourton Dr M29 ....59 D1
Bourton Dr M18 ....99 B4
Bow Green Rd WA14 ...119 A1
Bow La Altrincham WA14 .128 B8
Heywood OL10 ....29 D2
Manchester M2 ....158 F1
Bow Rd WN7 ....76 B3
Bow St Ashton-u-L OL6 ..166 B3
Bolton BL1 ....145 F7
Dukinfield OL6,SK16 ....166 C1
7 Manchester M2 .....158 F1
Oldham OL1 ....153 F7
Rochdale OL11 ....30 D3
Stockport SK3 ....123 C8
Bowden Cl Culcheth WA3 ...91 F4

Bowden Cl continued
Leigh WN7 ....76 C2
Middleton OL10 ....47 D8
Mottram-in-L SK14 .....102 E1
Bowden Rd Glossop SK13 .104 C3
Pendlebury M27 ....80 A7
Bowden St Denton M34 ..100 E3
Hazel Grove SK7 ....124 E3
Bowden Ave M44 ......97 F1
Bowdon CE Aided
Prim Sch WA14 ....119 C1
Bowdon Ho 2 SK3 .....170 E8
Bowdon Prep Sch WA14 119 C2
Bowdon Rd WA14 ......119 C3
Bowdon Rise WA14 ....119 D2
Bowdon St SK3 ....170 E8
Bowen Cl SK7 ....132 F5
Bowen St BL1 ....142 B1
Bower Ave
Hazel Grove SK7 ....124 C1
Littleborough OL12 .....15 D4
Stockport SK4 ....168 C2
Bower Ct SK14 ....102 A5
Bower Gdns SK15 .....102 D8
Bower Gr SK15 ....86 C2
Bower La OL9 ....66 A2
Bower Rd WA15 ....119 F1
Bower St Bury BL9 .....141 C3
Failsworth M40 ....83 A5
Manchester M7 ....155 F7
Oldham OL1 ....67 B8
Reddish SK5 ....99 F2
Sale M33 ....107 C5
Bower Terr M43 ....84 C3
Bowerfield Ave SK7 ....133 D8
Bowerfield Cres SK7 ....133 E8
Bowerfold La SK4 ......169 D2
Bowers Ave M41 ......95 B3
Bowers St M14 ....110 E7
Bowery Ave SK8 ....131 F6
Bowes Cl BL8 ....27 B5
Bowes St M14 ....97 F3
Bowfell Dr SK6 ....134 E8
Bowfell Gr M9 ....64 B4
Bowfell Rd M41 ....95 B2
Bowfield Wlk 18 M40 ...83 C5
Bowgreave Ave BL2 ...42 F7
Bowgreen Wlk 11 M15 ..162 D6
Bowker Ave M34 ......113 B8
Bowker Bank Ave M8 ...63 F2
Bowker Cl OL11 ....13 E1
Bowker St Haslingden BL0 ..1 C5
Hyde SK14 ....167 E3
Manchester M7 ....155 D6
Radcliffe M26 ....44 A3
Walkden M28 ....60 B3
Bowker Vale Gdns M9 ...63 F3
Bowker Vale Prim Sch M8 63 F4
Bowker Vale Sta M8 ....63 F3
Bowkers Row BL1 .....145 F7
Bowlacre Rd SK14 .....113 D7
Bowland Ave
Ashton-in-M WN4 ......73 B4
Golborne WA3 ....74 C1
Reddish M34 ....100 B3
Bowland Cl Ashton-u-L OL6 .85 C7
Bury BL8 ....26 F3
Shaw OL2 ....48 E2
Stockport SK2 ....124 E5
Bowland Ct M33 ....108 B4
Bowland Dr BL1 ....23 E2
Bowland Gr OL16 ......31 F4
Bowland Rd Glossop SK13 116 A8
Reddish M34 ....100 B3
Romiley SK6 ....113 B5
Wythenshawe M23 .....121 A6
Bowler St Manchester M19 111 B8
Shaw OL2 ....149 B7
Bowlers Wlk OL12 .....14 F2
Bowley Ave M22 ....121 A2
Bowling Green Row M46 .58 D3
Bowling Green St
Heywood OL10 ....29 D2
Hyde SK14 ....167 D2
Bowling Green Way OL11 .29 F7
Bowling Rd M18 ....99 E3
Bowlings The WN6 .....37 A2
Bowman Cres SK6 .....85 D3
Bowmead Wlk 6 M8 ...155 F6
Bowmeadow
Grange 2 M12 ....98 F4
Bowmont Cl SK8 ......123 A4
Bowness Ave Cheadle SK8 123 B1
Irlam M44 ....105 D4
Reddish M34 ....111 E6
Rochdale OL12 ....14 C1
Bowness Ct 5 M24 ....46 D2
Bowness Cty Prim Sch
BL3 ....42 F3
Bowness Dr M33 ......107 F5
Bowness Pl WN2 ......56 B8
Bowness Rd
Altrincham WA15 ....120 D5
Ashton-u-L OL7 ....84 F4
Bolton BL3 ....147 D4
Little Lever BL3 ....42 F4
Middleton M24 ....46 D1
Bowness St Droylsden M11 .99 F7
Stretford M32 ....96 D3
Bowness Wlk 7 OL2 ...48 E4
Bowring St M7 ....81 C5
Bowscale Cl 3 M13 ....98 F4
Bowstone Hill Rd BL2,BL8 .26 B5
Box St Littleborough OL15 ..16 A5
Ramsbottom BL0 ....11 D6

Box Wlk M31 ....105 E3
Boxgrove Rd M33 ......107 F5
Boxgrove Wlk 3 M8 ...156 A6
Boxhill Dr M23 ....109 A1
Boxtree Ave M18 ......99 D4
Boyd Cl WN6 ....19 F1
Boyd St M12 ....165 A7
Boyd's Wlk SK16 ......101 C7
Boydell St WN7 ....75 F6
Boydell's Ho WN2 .....75 B8
Boyer St M16 ....161 B5
Boyle St Bolton BL1 ....142 A1
Manchester M8 ....156 B6
Boysnope Cres M30 ....94 C4
Boysnope Wharf M30 ..94 C4
Boyswell Ho WN1 ......151 D8
Brabant Rd SK8 ....123 B2
Brabazon Pl WN5 ......54 C8
Brabham Cl M21 ......109 B8
Brabyns Ave SK6 ......113 D3
Brabyns Brow SK6 .....126 A7
Brabyns Rd SK14 ......113 E7
Brabyns Sch SK6 ......126 B7
Bracadale Dr SK3 ......170 F5
Bracewell Cl M12 .....165 B5
Bracken Ave WN6 .....20 E3
Bracken Cl Bolton BL1 ..24 D6
Droylsden M43 ....84 D2
Heywood OL10 ....46 D8
Hollingworth SK14 .....103 D6
Marple SK6 ....126 C7
Oldham OL4 ....67 C8
Sale M33 ....107 C5
Bracken Dr M23 ....121 B5
Bracken Gr BB4 ....1 A8
Bracken Lea BL5 ......57 F5
Bracken Lea Fold 3 OL12 .14 B2
Bracken Rd Atherton M46 .58 D2
Leigh WN7 ....75 B5
Bracken Way SK13 ....116 F8
Brackenfield Wlk WA15 ..120 D6
Brackenhill Terr 14 M34 ..113 A7
Brackenhurst Ave OL5 ..68 E1
Brackenlea Pl SK3 .....170 D5
Brackenside SK5 ......112 A8
Brackenwood Cl OL1 ...48 C2
Brackenwood Dr SK8 ..122 E4
Brackenwood Mews SK9 137 E8
Brackley Ave Irlam M44 ..105 D6
Manchester M15 ....162 D7
Brackley Ct M22 ......121 D8
Brackley Ct M24 ......65 A5
Brackley Lo M30 ......79 F3
Brackley Rd Atherton BL5 ..59 A8
Eccles M30 ....79 D4
Reddish M34 ....111 D5
Brackley Sq 5 OL1 ....67 A8
Brackley St Farnworth BL4 .60 D4
9 Oldham OL1 ....67 A8
Walkden M28 ....60 C4
Braconade Ave BL1 ....142 B2
Bradbourne Cl BL3 ....145 F5
Bradburn Ave 4 M30 ..79 D1
Bradburn Cl 2 M30 ....79 D1
Bradburn Gr 5 M30 ...79 D1
Bradburn Rd M44 ......105 E7
Bradburn St M30 ......79 D1
Bradburn Wlk 8 M8 ...156 B6
Bradbury Ave WA14 ...119 A5
Bradbury St
Ashton-u-L OL7 ....166 A4
Hyde SK14 ....167 E1
Radcliffe M26 ....44 A2
Bradbury Wlk 10 OL2 ..48 E4
Bradbury's La OL3 ....69 D3
Bradda Mount SK7 ....124 C3
Braddan Ave M33 .....108 C3
Bradden Cl M5 ....81 A1
Braddocks Cl OL12 ....15 D4
Braddon Ave M41 .....95 D2
Braddon Rd SK6 ......113 A5
Braddon St 1 M11 ....83 C1
Braddyll Rd BL5 ......58 F8
Brade Cl M11 ....165 C8
Bradfield Ave M6 .....80 C2
Bradfield Cl SK5 ......99 E2
Bradfield Rd M32,M41 ..96 A2
Bradford Ave BL3 .....42 B3
Bradford Cres 17 BL3 ..42 A4
Bradford Ct M40 ......65 C1
Bradford Park Dr BL2 ..148 B6
Bradford Rd Bolton BL3,BL4 42 A2
Eccles M30 ....79 E4
Manchester M4,M40 ....160 E2
Bradford St Bolton BL2 ..148 B7
Farnworth BL4 ....60 D7
Oldham OL1 ....153 E8
Wigan WN3 ....150 C7
Bradgate Ave SK8 .....122 D1
Bradgate Cl M22 ......121 E8
Bradgate Rd
Altrincham WA14 ......119 A5
Sale M33 ....108 A2
Bradgate St
Ashton-u-L OL7 ....166 A1
7 Ashton-u-L OL7 ....166 A2
Bradgreen Rd M30 ....79 C3
Brading Wlk M22 .....130 E8
Bradlegh Rd WA12 ....89 B1
Bradley Ave M7 ....81 B7
Bradley Cl WA15 ......119 E7
Bradley Dr BL9 ....45 B2
Bradley Fold SK15 .....86 B2
Bradley Fold Cotts BL2 ..43 B6
Bradley Fold Rd
BL2,BL3,BL8,M26 ......43 C7
Bradley Fold Trad Est BL2 .43 C5
Bradley Green Rd SK14 ..101 F6

Bradley Green Road
Prim Sch SK14 ....101 F6
Bradley Hall Trad Est
WN6 ....19 F2
Bradley Hill Trad Est WN6 .20 A2
Bradley Ho OL8 ....153 F6
Bradley La Little Lever BL3 .43 B5
Newhey OL16 ....32 A4
Newton-le-W WA5,WA12 ...89 A1
Sale M32, M33 ....108 B7
Standish WN6 ....19 F2
Bradley Smithy Cl OL12 ..14 E2
Bradley St
7 Manchester M1 .....159 B2
Newhey OL16 ....32 A4
Bradleys Ct M1 ....159 B1
Bradney Cl M9 ....64 B4
Bradnor Rd M22 ......121 D7
Bradshaw Ave
Failsworth M35 ....83 E5
Manchester M20 ....110 B7
Whitefield M45 ....44 E2
Bradshaw Brow BL2 ...25 C4
Bradshaw Cl WN6 .....19 D1
Bradshaw Cres SK6 ...126 A3
Bradshaw Fold Ave M40 .65 D3
Bradshaw Hall Dr BL2 ..25 C6
Bradshaw Hall La
Cheadle SK8 ....131 E8
Gatley SK8 ....131 D8
Bradshaw Hall Prim Sch
SK8 ....122 E1
Bradshaw La Lymm WA13 .117 D3
Stretford M32 ....108 D8
Bradshaw Mdws BL2 ..25 D6
Bury BL8 ....26 D5
Marple SK6 ....113 E7
Bradshaw St Atherton M46 .58 D3
Bolton BL2 ....145 F6
Farnworth BL4 ....60 D7
Heywood OL10 ....29 E2
2 Manchester M4 .....159 A2
Manchester M7 ....155 E6
Middleton M24 ....65 C7
Oldham OL1 ....153 F7
Radcliffe M26 ....43 F3
5 Rochdale OL16 .....31 A8
Wigan WN1 ....37 E2
Wigan WN5 ....54 A6
Bradshaw St N M7 ....155 D7
Bradshawgate
Bolton BL1,BL3 ....145 F7
Leigh WN7 ....75 F5
Wigan WN1 ....151 D8
Bradshawgate Sh Arc 7
WN7 ....75 F5
Bradstock Rd M16 .....97 E3
Bradstone Rd M8 .....156 A5
Bradwell Ave
Manchester M20 ....109 F6
Stretford M32 ....96 A3
Bradwell Dr SK8 ......131 C7
Bradwell Field 2 SK13 ..171 E1
Bradwell Lea 4 SK13 ..171 E1
Bradwell Pl 7 BL2 .....25 B1
Bradwell Rd Golborne WA3 .90 D7
Hazel Grove SK7 ......133 E8
Bradwell Terr 3 SK13 ..171 E1
Bradwell Wlk M41 ....94 D3
Bradwen Ave M8 ......64 A1
Bradwen Cl M34 ......101 A1
Brady St WN3 ....22 A4
Brae Side OL8 ....66 E4
Braeburn Ct WN7 .....75 D5
Braemar Ave Stretford M32 96 A4
Urmston M41 ....95 A1
Braemar Dr M33 ......107 C2
Braemar Gdns BL3 ....40 E5
Braemar Gr 3 OL10 ...29 A1
Braemar La M28 ......78 B6
Braemar Rd
Hazel Grove SK7 ......124 F3
Manchester M14 ......110 E8
Braemar Wlk WN2 ....38 D5
Braemore Cl Shaw OL2 ..48 E8
Wigan WN3 ....54 D2
Braemore Dr Bury BL9 ..28 C3
Mottram-in-L SK14 .....102 F1
Braeside SK2 ....124 F6
Braeside Cres WN5 ....71 D5
Braeside Gr BL3 ....40 F5
Braewood Cl BL9 .....28 D2
Bragenham St M18 ....165 C5
Braidhaven WN6 ......35 A4
Brailsford Ave 6 SK13 ..171 E2
Brailsford Cl 5 SK13 ...171 E2
Brailsford Gdns 8 SK13 171 E2
Brailsford Gn 7 SK13 ..171 E2
Brailsford Mews 5 SK13 171 E2
Brailsford Rd Bolton BL2 ..25 C3
Manchester M14 ......110 E8
Braintree Rd M22 .....130 E8
Braithwaite WN6 ......36 A6
Braithwaite Rd
Golborne WA3 ....90 A4
Middleton M24 ....46 D4
Brakehouse Cl OL16 ...31 E6
Brakenhurst Dr M7 ....155 F6
Brakesmere Gr M28 ...60 A4
Braley St M12 ....163 B7
Bramall Cl BL9 ....45 B2
Bramall Hall (Mus) SK7 .123 E1
Bramall St SK14 ....167 E4
Bramber Way M22 ....152 B6
Bramble Ave Oldham OL4 .49 D1
Salford M5 ....161 C5
Bramble Cl OL15 ......15 F5

Bramble Gr WN5 . . . . .54 E7
Bramble Wlk 7 Sale M33 107 C5
 6 Wythenshawe M22 . . . . .121 C2
Brambles The WN4 . . . . . .72 D5
Bramblewood OL9 . . . . . . .65 E8
Brambling Cl
Droylsden M34 . . . . .84 C2
Hazel Grove SK2 . . . . . . .125 A5
Brambling Dr BL5 . . . . . . .57 D6
Brambling Way WA3 . . . . . .90 E7
Bramcote Ave Bolton BL2 .148 B6
Wythenshawe M23 . . . . . . .121 B6
Bramdean Ave BL2 . . . . . . .25 E5
Bramfield Wlk M15 . . . . . .162 D7
Bramford Cl BL5 . . . . .57 D6
Bramhall Ave BL2 . . . . . . .26 A4
Bramhall Cl
 4 Altrincham WA15 . . . . .120 D6
Dukinfield SK16 . . . . .101 D6
Milnrow OL16 . . . . .31 E5
Sale M33 . . . . .108 E3
Bramhall Ct M3 . . . . .158 D3
Bramhall Ctr The SK7 . . . .132 E6
Bramhall High Sch SK7 . .132 F8
Bramhall La SK2,SK3 . . . .170 F5
Bramhall La S
Bramhall SK7 . . . . .132 E7
Stockport SK3,SK7 . . . . . .123 E2
Bramhall Moor Ind Est
SK7 . . . . .124 B2
Bramhall Moor La SK7 . . .124 C3
Bramhall Mount SK2 . . . .170 F5
Bramhall Park Rd
SK7,SK8 . . . . .123 D1
Bramhall St Bolton BL3 . . .42 B3
Manchester M18 . . . . .99 C5
Bramhall Sta SK7 . . . . . . .132 E6
Bramhall Wlk M34 . . . . . .100 F1
Bramham Rd SK6 . . . . . . .126 A4
Bramhope Wlk M9 . . . . . .157 D7
Bramley Ave
Manchester M19 . . . . .111 A8
Stretford M32 . . . . .96 B1
Bramley Cl Bramhall SK7 .132 E6
Swinton M27 . . . . .79 C6
Wilmslow SK9 . . . . .136 D4
Bramley Cres SK4 . . . . . .168 B1
Bramley Dr Bramhall SK7 .132 E6
Bury BL8 . . . . .27 C6
Bramley Meade M7 . . . . .155 E5
Bramley Rd 6 Bolton BL1 . .24 F6
Bolton BL1 . . . . .25 A6
Bramhall SK7 . . . . .132 E6
Rochdale OL11 . . . . .29 E8
Bramley St M7 . . . . .155 E5
Brammay Dr BL8 . . . . .26 E6
Brampton Cl WN2 . . . . . . .55 F1
Brampton Rd Bolton BL3 .146 A2
Stockport SK7 . . . . .123 F2
Brampton St 9 M46 . . . . . .58 D3
Bramway Bramhall SK7 . . .132 C7
High Lane SK6 . . . . .134 F7
Bramwell Dr M13 . . . . . . .163 C6
Bramwell St SK1 . . . . . . .124 B8
Bramworth Ave BL0 . . . . .138 B6
Brancaster Dr WA3 . . . . . .91 A7
Brancaster Rd M1 . . . . . .163 A4
Branch Cl BL8 . . . . .140 D3
Branch Rd OL15 . . . . .15 F1
Branch St Bacup OL13 . . . . .3 D8
Ince-in-M WN2 . . . . .56 A7
Brancker St BL5 . . . . .40 C1
Brandish Cl M13 . . . . .164 D5
Brandle Ave BL8 . . . . .27 C4
Brandlehow Dr M24 . . . . . .46 C2
Brandlesholme
Cty Prim Sch BL8 . . . . . . .27 C6
Brandlesholme Rd BL8 . . . .27 C5
Brandon Ave Gatley SK8 . .122 B1
Reddish M34 . . . . .99 F3
Salford M30 . . . . .80 A5
Wythenshawe M22 . . . . . .121 C8
Brandon Brow 8 OL1 . . . .153 E8
Brandon Cl Bury BL8 . . . . .27 D5
Handforth SK9 . . . . .131 D2
Orrell WN8 . . . . .53 A7
Brandon Cres OL2 . . . . . .149 A8
Brandon Rd M6 . . . . .80 B5
Brandon St 2 Bolton BL3 .147 D4
Milnrow OL16 . . . . .31 D6
Brandram Rd M25 . . . . . . .63 C4
Brandreth Pl WN6 . . . . . . .19 F1
Brandsby Gdns M5 . . . . . .161 A8
Brandwood Ave M21 . . . . .109 D4
Brandwood Cl M28 . . . . . . .78 B4
Brandwood Cty Prim Sch
BL3 . . . . .146 C4
Brandwood Fold BL7 . . . . . .9 E5
Brandwood Pk OL13 . . . . . .3 B8
Brandwood Rd OL13 . . . . . .3 B8
Brandwood St BL3 . . . . . .146 C4
Branfield Ave SK8 . . . . . .122 D1
Brankgate Ct M20 . . . . . .110 A5
Branksome Ave M25 . . . . . .63 B4
Branksome Dr
Cheadle SK8 . . . . .122 D1
Manchester M9 . . . . .64 B6
Salford M6 . . . . .80 B5
Branksome Ho SK4 . . . . . .168 B1
Branksome Rd SK4 . . . . . .168 B1
Bransby Ave M9 . . . . .64 E4
Branscombe Dr M33 . . . . .107 C5
Bransdale Ave OL2 . . . . . . .48 C4
Bransdale Cl BL3 . . . . .40 F4
Bransdale Dr WN4 . . . . . . .73 D3
Bransfield Cl WN3 . . . . . . .55 B3

Bransford Cl WN4 . . . . . . .73 C2
Bransford Rd
Droylsden M11 . . . . .99 E8
Urmston M41 . . . . .95 C3
Branson St M4,M40 . . . . .160 D2
Branson Wlk WA15 . . . . . .120 C6
Branston Rd M40 . . . . .65 D2
Brantfell Gr BL2 . . . . .42 F8
Branthwaite WN2 . . . . .38 B1
Brantingham Ct M16 . . . . . .97 E1
Brantingham Rd M16,M21 .97 D1
Brantwood Cl OL2 . . . . . . .48 C4
Brantwood Dr BL2 . . . . . . .42 F8
Brantwood Rd
Cheadle SK8 . . . . .122 F1
Manchester M7 . . . . .155 D8
Manchester SK4 . . . . .168 A4
Brantwood Terr M9 . . . . . .157 F7
Branwood Prep Sch M30 . .79 E3
Brassey St Ashton-u-L OL6 .166 B4
Middleton M24 . . . . .47 A1
Brassington Ave
Manchester M21 . . . . .109 B7
Salford M5 . . . . .161 B8
Brassington Cres SK13 . . .171 D1
Brassington Gdns M5 . . . .161 B8
Brassington Rd SK4 . . . . .110 E4
Brathay Cl BL2 . . . . .25 F2
Bratton Cl WN3 . . . . .54 C2
Bratton Wlk M13 . . . . .164 D6
Brattray Dr M24 . . . . .46 E3
Braunston Cl M30 . . . . .95 E8
Braxton Wlk 20 M9 . . . . . .157 E8
Brayton Ave
Manchester M20 . . . . .110 C2
Sale M33 . . . . .107 D5
Brayton Ct WN2 . . . . .56 D6
Brazennose St M2 . . . . . .158 F1
Brazil Pl M1 . . . . .163 A8
Brazil St M1 . . . . .163 A8
Brazley Ave Bolton BL3 . . . .42 B3
Horwich BL6 . . . . .22 E1
Breach House La WA16 . . .129 E1
Bread St M18 . . . . .99 E6
Breaktemper BL5 . . . . .39 E1
Brean Wlk 8 M22 . . . . . . .121 C1
Brearley St OL13 . . . . .3 D8
Breaston Ave WN7 . . . . . . .75 E8
Brechin Way OL10 . . . . . . .29 A1
Brechin Wlk 16 M11 . . . . . .83 C1
Breck Rd M30 . . . . .79 B2
Breckland Cl SK15 . . . . . . .86 D2
Breckland Dr BL1 . . . . .40 D8
Breckles Pl BL3 . . . . .145 D5
Brecon Ave Cheadle SK8 . .122 E1
Denton M34 . . . . .100 F1
Manchester M19 . . . . .110 F7
Urmston M41 . . . . .94 D3
Brecon Cl Platt Bridge WN2 .56 B2
Poynton SK12 . . . . .133 F4
Royton OL2 . . . . .48 C6
Brecon Cres OL6 . . . . .85 B6
Brecon Dr Bury BL9 . . . . . .44 E7
Hindley WN2 . . . . .57 A3
Brecon Wlk 6 OL8 . . . . . . .66 B2
Bredbury Dr BL4 . . . . .60 E8
Bredbury Gn SK6 . . . . . . .113 A1
Bredbury Green
Prim Sch SK6 . . . . .112 F1
Bredbury Hall Ctry Club
SK6 . . . . .112 D2
Bredbury Park Way SK6 . .112 E6
Bredbury Rd M14 . . . . .98 B2
Bredbury St
Dukinfield SK14 . . . . .101 D5
Oldham OL9 . . . . .152 B6
Bredbury Sta SK6 . . . . . . .112 F4
Brede Wlk M23 . . . . .120 D8
Breeze Hill M46 . . . . .58 F5
Breeze Hill Rd
Atherton M46 . . . . .58 F5
Oldham OL4 . . . . .67 D5
Breeze Hill Sch OL4 . . . . .67 D5
Breeze Mount M25 . . . . . . .63 C3
Breightmet Dr BL2 . . . . . . .42 E7
Breightmet Fold La BL2 . . .42 F8
Breightmet St BL2 . . . . . .148 A7
Brellafield Dr OL2 . . . . .48 F8
Brenbar Cres OL12 . . . . . . .4 D1
Brencon Ave M23 . . . . . . .108 C1
Brendall Cl SK2 . . . . .125 A5
Brendon Ave
Manchester M40 . . . . .83 A7
Reddish SK5 . . . . .111 F6
Brendon Cl SK13 . . . . . . .116 A8
Brendon Dr M34 . . . . .84 D1
Brendon Hills OL2 . . . . . . .48 D3
Brenley Wlk 7 M9 . . . . . .157 D8
Brennan Cl M15 . . . . .163 A5
Brennan Ct OL8 . . . . .66 C2
Brennock Cl M11 . . . . . . .164 F8
Brent Cl Little Lever BL3 . . .43 B5
Poynton SK12 . . . . .133 B4
Brent Moor Rd SK7 . . . . . .124 A3
Brentford Ave BL1 . . . . . . .142 B2

Brentford Rd SK5 . . . . . . .111 F6
Brentford St M9 . . . . .157 E7
Brentnall Prim Sch M7 . . .155 D7
Brentnall St SK1 . . . . .170 F7
Brentnor Rd M40 . . . . .65 C3
Brenton Ave M33 . . . . . . .108 A4
Brenton Ct 1 SK8 . . . . . . .131 E8
Brentwood Sale M33 . . . . .108 A4
Salford M6 . . . . .154 E3
Urmston M41 . . . . .94 F1
Wigan WN5 . . . . .54 D5
Brentwood Ave
Altrincham WA14 . . . . . . .119 E7
Irlam M44 . . . . .105 D6
Swinton M28 . . . . .79 B6
Urmston M41 . . . . .95 C3
Brentwood Cl
Brinnington SK5 . . . . .112 D5
Littleborough OL15 . . . . . . .15 F3
Stalybridge SK15 . . . . .86 C2
Brentwood Cres WA14 . . .119 E6
Brentwood Ct M25 . . . . . . .62 F3
Brentwood Dr Eccles M30 . .79 D4
Farnworth BL3,BL4 . . . . . . .42 C2
Gatley SK8 . . . . .122 B5
Brentwood Rd
Adlington PR6 . . . . .21 B8
Swinton M27 . . . . .79 D6
Brentwood Sch WA14 . . . .119 E7
Brentwood St M16 . . . . . . .97 F3
Brereton Cl WA14 . . . . . . .119 C3
Brereton Ct SK8 . . . . .122 E1
Brereton Dr M28 . . . . .78 F7
Brereton Gr Eccles M30 . . .78 F1
Handforth SK9 . . . . .131 E3
Breslyn St M3 . . . . .158 F3
Bretherton Row 17 WN1 . .150 C8
Bretherton St WN2 . . . . . . .56 C3
Brethren's Ct M43 . . . . . . .100 A8
Bretland Gdns SK14 . . . . .102 E1
Bretland Wlk 2 M22 . . . . .121 F3
Brett Rd M22 . . . . .77 F6
Brett St M22 . . . . .109 E1
Brettargh St M6 . . . . .81 A4
Bretton Wlk M22 . . . . . . .130 D8
Brewer St M1 . . . . .159 B1
Brewer's Gn SK7 . . . . . . .124 D3
Brewerton Rd OL4 . . . . . . .67 C6
Brewery La WN7 . . . . .76 A5
Brewery St
 4 Altrincham WA14 . . . . .119 D4
Stockport SK1 . . . . .169 F3
Brewster St
Manchester M9 . . . . .157 D8
 4 Middleton M24 . . . . . . .47 A2
Brian Ave M43 . . . . .84 C3
Brian Rd BL4 . . . . .42 A1
Brian Redhead Ct M15 . . .162 E7
Brian St OL11 . . . . .30 B2
Briar Ave
Hazel Grove SK7 . . . . . . .124 F2
Hollinfare WA3 . . . . .105 B2
Oldham OL4 . . . . .49 D1
Briar Cl Ashton-in-M WN4 . .73 A4
Hindley WN2 . . . . .57 B4
Rochdale OL12 . . . . .14 A1
Sale M33 . . . . .107 C4
Urmston M41 . . . . .95 A3
Briar Cres M22 . . . . .121 E5
Briar Dr Gatley SK8 . . . . . .122 B1
Romiley SK6 . . . . .113 A5
Briar Hill Ave M38 . . . . . . .59 E4
Briar Hill Cl M38 . . . . .59 E4
Briar Hill Gr M38 . . . . .59 E4
Briar Hill Way 4 M6 . . . . . .81 A3
Briar Hollow SK4 . . . . . . .168 B1
Briar Lea Cl BL3 . . . . .147 E4
Briar Rd Golborne WA3 . . . .90 B8
Wigan WN5 . . . . .54 E7
Briar St Bolton BL2 . . . . . . .42 D7
Rochdale OL11 . . . . .139 D6
Briarcroft Dr M46 . . . . .58 A1
Briardene M34 . . . . .101 A4
Briardene Gdns M22 . . . . .121 E4
Briarfield BL7 . . . . .8 D2
Briarfield Rd
Altrincham WA15 . . . . . . .120 C6
Cheadle SK8 . . . . .123 B3
Farnworth BL4 . . . . .42 A1
Manchester M19,M20 . . . .110 D6
Reddish M34 . . . . .111 E6
Worsley M28 . . . . .78 F7
Briarfields Rd OL3 . . . . . . .51 A2
Briargrove Rd SK22 . . . . .127 C4
Briarlands Ave M33 . . . . . .107 F2
Briarlands Cl SK7 . . . . . . .132 D6
Briarlea Gdns M19 . . . . . .110 E5
Briarley Gdns SK6 . . . . . .113 C6
Briarly WN6 . . . . .37 A7
Briarmere Wlk OL9 . . . . . .152 C7
Briars Mount SK4 . . . . . . .168 A2
Briars Pk SK7 . . . . .123 C1
Briary Dr M29 . . . . .77 B8
Brice St SK16 . . . . .101 B8
Brick Ground OL12 . . . . . . .13 C2
Brick Kiln La 7 WN1 . . . . . .37 C1
Brick St Bury BL9 . . . . . . .141 A3
 9 Manchester M4 . . . . . .159 A2
Brickbridge Rd SK6 . . . . . .126 A5

Brickfield St
Hadfield SK13 . . . . .104 B5
Rochdale OL16 . . . . .15 B2
Brickhill La WA15 . . . . . . .129 C3
Brickkiln La WA14 . . . . . . .118 C5
Brickkiln Row WA14 . . . . .119 C1
Brickley St M3,M4 . . . . . .159 A3
Bricknell Wlk 5 M22 . . . . .121 C1
Bridcam St M8 . . . . .156 A5
Briddon St M3 . . . . .158 F3
Bride St BL1 . . . . .143 E2
Brideoak St M8 . . . . .156 A6
Brideoak St M8 . . . . .156 A6
Brideoake St Leigh WN7 . . .76 B4
Oldham OL4 . . . . .67 E8
Bridestowe Ave SK14 . . . .102 C3
Bridestowe Wlk SK14 . . . .102 C3
Bridge Ave SK6 . . . . .113 A5
Bridge Bank Rd OL15 . . . . .16 A3
Bridge Cl Lymm WA13 . . . .117 B4
Partington M31 . . . . .106 A3
 6 Radcliffe M26 . . . . .44 B2
Bridge Coll SK2 . . . . .124 D8
Bridge Dr Cheadle SK8 . . .122 D4
Handforth SK9 . . . . .131 D3
Bridge End Delph OL3 . . . .50 F4
Wigan WN3 . . . . .150 B8
Bridge End Cl BB4 . . . . .1 A7
Bridge Gr WA15 . . . . .119 F7
Bridge Hall Dr BL9 . . . . . .141 C2
Bridge Hall Fold BL9 . . . . .141 C2
Bridge Hall La BL9 . . . . . . .28 D2
Bridge Hall Prim Sch
SK3 . . . . .170 D6
Bridge La SK7 . . . . .123 F1
Bridge Mills Bsns Pk M6 . .80 F5
Bridge Rd Bury BL9 . . . . .140 D1
Sale M23 . . . . .120 C2
Bridge St Aspull WN2 . . . . .38 A3
Bolton BL1 . . . . .145 F7
Bury BL9 . . . . .141 A3
Denton M34 . . . . .100 E4
Droylsden M43 . . . . .99 E8
Dukinfield M34 . . . . .100 F7
Dukinfield SK16 . . . . .101 A6
Farnworth BL4 . . . . .42 E1
Golborne WA3 . . . . .90 A7
Haslingden BB4 . . . . .1 C6
Heywood OL10 . . . . .29 C2
Hindley WN2 . . . . .56 E6
Horwich BL6 . . . . .8 C1
Ince-in-M WN3 . . . . .151 D6
Kearsley M26 . . . . .61 B8
Littleborough OL12 . . . . . . .15 C3
Manchester M3 . . . . .158 F1
Middleton M24 . . . . .65 A8
Milnrow OL16 . . . . .31 F6
New Mills SK22 . . . . .127 C1
Newton-le-W WA12 . . . . . .89 B3
 1 Oldham OL1 . . . . .67 A6
Oldham OL3 . . . . .69 B7
Oldham OL4 . . . . .67 F6
Pendlebury M27 . . . . .80 A8
Ramsbottom BL0 . . . . . . .138 C6
Rawtenstall BB4 . . . . .2 E7
Rochdale OL11 . . . . .30 C1
Shaw OL2 . . . . .149 C8
Stalybridge SK15 . . . . .85 F1
Stockport SK1 . . . . .169 F2
Whitworth OL12 . . . . .4 C1
Wigan WN3 . . . . .150 C7
Bridge St W M3 . . . . .158 E1
Bridge's St M46 . . . . .58 B2
Bridgecrest Ct SK8 . . . . . .123 A4
Bridgefield SK13 . . . . .116 B8
Bridgefield Ave SK9 . . . . .131 C5
Bridgefield Cres 4 OL4 . . .67 F6
Bridgefield Dr BL9 . . . . . . .28 D2
Bridgefield St
Radcliffe M26 . . . . .44 B3
Rochdale OL11 . . . . .139 D7
Stockport SK1 . . . . .169 E2
Bridgefield Wlk 7 M26 . . . .44 B3
Bridgefold Rd OL11 . . . . .139 D8
Bridgefoot Cl M28 . . . . . . .78 A5
Bridgeford Ct M32 . . . . . .108 D8
Bridgeford St M13,M15 . . .163 A6
Bridgehall Dr WN8 . . . . . . .53 B7
Bridgelea Mews M20 . . . . .110 B6
Bridgelea Rd M20 . . . . . . .110 B6
Bridgeman Pl BL2 . . . . . . .148 A6
Bridgeman St Bolton BL3 .145 F5
Farnworth BL4 . . . . .42 D1
Bridgeman Terr WN1 . . . . .37 C1
Bridgemere Cl M26 . . . . . . .43 F5
Bridgend Cl Cheadle SK8 .123 C4
Manchester M12 . . . . .165 A6
Bridgenorth Ave M41 . . . . .95 F2
Bridgenorth Dr OL15 . . . . . .15 F3
Bridges Ave BL9 . . . . .44 F6
Bridges Ct 4 BL3 . . . . . . .145 F6
Bridges Way M34 . . . . . . .112 F7
Bridgewater Cl SK8 . . . . . .131 C5
Bridgewater Ctr The M41 . .95 E7
Bridgewater Hall The
M1 . . . . .162 F8
Bridgewater Ho M15 . . . . .162 D8
Bridgewater Pl M4 . . . . . .159 A1
Bridgewater Rd
Altrincham WA14 . . . . . . .119 D7
Boothstown M28 . . . . .78 A8
Pendlebury M27 . . . . .80 B7
Walkden M28 . . . . .60 D2
Bridgewater Sch M28 . . . . .79 A6
Bridgewater St
 2 Bolton BL1 . . . . .145 D6
Eccles M30 . . . . .79 B2
Farnworth BL4 . . . . .60 E8

Bridgewater St continued
Hindley WN2 . . . . .56 E6
Manchester M3 . . . . .158 E3
Manchester M3 . . . . .162 E8
 8 Oldham OL1 . . . . .67 A8
Sale M33 . . . . .108 B5
Stretford M32 . . . . .96 E2
Walkden M38 . . . . .60 B4
Wigan WN3 . . . . .150 B7
 5 Wigan WN5 . . . . .54 F6
Bridgewater Viaduct
M15,M3 . . . . .162 E7
Bridgewater Way
M15,M16 . . . . .161 B5
Bridgewater Wlk M28 . . . . .60 D3
Bridgfield Cl SK14 . . . . . . .134 E7
Bridgnorth Rd M9 . . . . . . .64 A3
Bridle Cl Droylsden M43 . . .84 A3
Urmston M41 . . . . .94 E2
Bridle Ct SK7 . . . . .132 F2
Bridle Fold M26 . . . . .44 A4
Bridle Rd Prestwich M25 . .63 E7
Woodford SK7,SK10 . . . . .132 F2
Bridle Way 133 A2
Bridlington Ave M6 . . . . . . .80 C3
Bridlington Cl 6 M40 . . . . .83 C6
Bridport Ave M40 . . . . .83 B8
Bridson La BL2 . . . . .25 D2
Bridson St 11 Oldham OL4 . .67 C7
Salford M5 . . . . .154 E1
Brief St BL2 . . . . .25 C1
Briercliffe Cl M18 . . . . .99 D6
Brierfield Ave M46 . . . . . . .58 C4
Brierfield Dr BL9 . . . . .27 E8
Brierholme Ave BL7 . . . . . . .8 E1
Brierley Ave Failsworth M35 84 A7
Whitefield M45 . . . . .44 E2
Brierley Cl Ashton-u-L OL6 . .86 A6
Denton M34 . . . . .100 E1
Brierley Dr M24 . . . . .65 A7
Brierley Rd M27 . . . . .61 E1
Brierley St Bury BL9 . . . . . .44 E8
Heywood OL10 . . . . .29 D2
Oldham OL8 . . . . .66 F3
Oldham OL9 . . . . .152 C8
Stalybridge SK15 . . . . .85 D1
Brierley Wlk OL9 . . . . .152 C8
Brierton Dr 5 M22 . . . . . .121 B1
Brierwood Cl OL1 . . . . .48 E1
Briery Ave BL2 . . . . .25 D6
Brigade Dr M32 . . . . .96 C3
Brigade St BL1 . . . . .144 C7
Brigadier Cl M20 . . . . .110 B6
Brigantine Cl M5 . . . . .161 A8
Briggs Cl M33 . . . . .107 C1
Briggs Fold BL7 . . . . .8 E2
Briggs Fold Cl BL7 . . . . .8 E2
Briggs Fold Rd BL7 . . . . . . .8 E2
Briggs Rd M32 . . . . .96 F4
Briggs St Leigh WN7 . . . . . .75 E7
Manchester M3 . . . . .158 D3
Brigham St M11 . . . . .165 C8
Bright Rd M30 . . . . .79 C2
Bright St 1 Ashton-u-L OL6 .85 D2
Bolton BL2 . . . . .8 D2
Bury BL9 . . . . .141 A3
Droylsden M43 . . . . .84 B1
Leigh WN7 . . . . .75 E7
Oldham OL8 . . . . .153 D5
Oldham OL9 . . . . .66 A4
Radcliffe M26 . . . . .44 C4
 16 Rochdale OL16 . . . . . .31 A5
Brightman St M18 . . . . .99 E6
Brighton Ave Bolton BL1 . .142 A1
Manchester M19 . . . . .110 F7
Manchester M7 . . . . .155 E6
Reddish SK5 . . . . .99 E4
Urmston M41 . . . . .94 E3
Brighton Cl SK8 . . . . .123 C4
Brighton Ct
Manchester M14 . . . . .98 D2
Salford M5 . . . . .161 B7
Brighton Gr Hyde SK14 . . .167 E1
Manchester M14 . . . . .98 D2
Sale M33 . . . . .108 B5
Urmston M41 . . . . .94 E3
Brighton Pl M13 . . . . .163 B6
Brighton Range M18 . . . . . .99 F4
Brighton Rd Oldham OL4 . . .50 A1
Stockport SK4 . . . . .168 C1
Brighton Road Ind Est
SK4 . . . . .168 C1
Brighton St Bury BL9 . . . .141 B3
Manchester M4 . . . . .159 A3
Brightstone Wlk 13 M13 . . .98 E4
Brightwater Cl M45 . . . . . . .63 A8
Brightwell Wlk 5 M4 . . . . .159 B2
Brignall Gr WA3 . . . . .74 D1
Brigsteer Wlk M40 . . . . . .157 D5
Brigstock Ave M18 . . . . . .165 C5
Briksdal Way BL6 . . . . .40 C7
Brimelow St SK6 . . . . .112 D3
Brimfield Ave M29 . . . . . . .59 C1
Brimfield Wlk 7 M40 . . . . . .83 D6
Brimmy Croft La OL3 . . . . .33 C3
Brimpton Wlk 13 M8 . . . . .155 F6
Brimrod Com Prim Sch
OL11 . . . . .139 D5
Brimrod La OL11 . . . . .139 D5
Brimscombe Ave M22 . . . .121 C2
Brindale Ho SK5 . . . . .112 C4
Brindale Prim Sch SK5 . . .112 C4
Brindale Rd SK5 . . . . .112 C4

Brindl Rise M6 154 F4
Brindle Heath Ind Est M6 81 A4
Brindle Heath Rd M6 154 F4
Brindle Pl 6 M15 163 A6
Brindle Rise M6 154 F4
Brindle St Hindley WN2 56 F6
Tyldesley M29 59 A1
Brindle Way OL2 49 D7
Brindlehurst Dr M29 77 D7
Brindley Ave
7 Boothstown M28 78 A6
Manchester M9 64 B5
Marple SK6 125 F5
Sale M33 108 C6
Brindley Cl Atherton M46 58 A2
Eccles M30 95 D8
Farnworth BL4 60 B8
Brindley Gr SK9 131 E2
Brindley Rd M16 161 B5
Brindley St Bolton BL1 143 F4
Boothstown M28 77 F6
Eccles M30 79 B3
Horwich BL6 22 C2
Swinton M27 61 F2
Walkden M28 60 D2
Wigan WN5 54 C5
Brinell Dr M44 105 F6
Brink's Row BL6 22 D5
Brinkburn Rd SK7 125 A3
Brinklow Cl M11 99 E7
Brinks La BL2 43 A6
Brinkshaw Ave M22 121 E2
Brinksway Bolton BL1 40 D7
Stockport SK3 123 C8
Brinksway Trad Est 1
SK3 123 C8
Brinksworth Cl BL2 43 A8
Brinnington Cres SK5 112 B4
Brinnington Rd
Brinnington SK5 112 C4
Stockport SK1 112 A3
Brinnington Rise SK1,SK5 112 B4
Brinnington Sta SK5 112 C6
Brinsop Hall La BL5 39 A6
Brinsop Sq M12 165 B6
Brinston Wlk 12 M40 83 A7
Brinsworth Dr M8 156 A6
Briony Ave WA15 120 C2
Briony Cl OL2 48 E2
Brisbane Cl SK7 132 F5
Brisbane St M13,M15 163 B5
Brisco Wlk M24 46 C2
Briscoe La M40 83 B4
Briscoe Lane
Jun & Inf Sch M40 83 B5
Briscoe St OL1 153 F8
Bristle Hall Way BL5 39 F2
Bristol Ave Ashton-u-L OL6 85 B7
8 Bolton BL2 25 C1
Manchester M19 111 B8
Bristol Cl SK8 131 C7
Bristol Ct 2 M7 63 E1
Bristol St M7 155 E7
Bristowe St M11,M43 83 D3
Britain St BL9 44 F5
Britannia Ave OL2 149 C6
Britannia Bridge
Prim Sch WN3 151 E6
Britannia Cty Prim Sch
OL13 4 C8
Britannia Ind Est 1 OL10 29 C2
Britannia Rd Sale M33 108 C5
Wigan WN5 54 B8
Britannia St Dukinfield OL7 100 F8
Heywood OL10 29 B2
1 Oldham OL1 67 A7
Salford M6 81 A5
Britannia Way Bolton BL1 25 A2
Haslingden BB4 1 A8
Britnall Ave M12 164 F5
Briton St Oldham OL2 48 E2
6 Rochdale OL16 31 A8
Britwell Wlk M8 156 C8
Brixham Ave SK8 131 F7
Brixham Dr M33 107 D6
Brixham Rd M16 97 B4
Brixham Wlk
Bramhall SK7 132 E7
6 Manchester M13 163 C5
Brixton Ave M20 110 A6
Brixworth Wlk 19 M9 64 E3
Broach St BL3 147 E4
Broad Acre OL12 13 E2
Broad Hey SK6 113 D3
Broad Hill Cl SK7 124 A2
Broad Ing OL12 14 C1
Broad La Altrincham WA15 120 B1
Billinge WA11 71 B1
Delph OL3 50 E7
Rochdale OL16 31 B3
Rochdale OL16 31 D2
Broad Lea M41 95 C3
Broad o' th' La Bolton BL1 143 E4
Shevington WN6 36 A6
Broad Oak Bsns Pk M17 95 F7
Broad Oak Cl PR6 21 A8
Broad Oak Cres OL8 67 A2
Broad Oak High Sch BL9 141 B2
Broad Oak La Bury BL9 28 D3
Manchester M20 122 B8
Manchester M20 122 C8
Broad Oak Pk Eccles M30 79 D4
Swinton M28 79 B6
Broad Oak Prim Sch
M20 122 C8
Broad Oak Rd BL3 42 A2
Broad Oak Terr BL9 28 E3
Broad Rd M33 108 D5
Broad Shaw La
Rochdale OL16 31 D2
Rochdale OL16 31 D3
Broad St Bury BL9 140 E2
Middleton M24 64 C7
Salford M6 80 E5
Salford M6 81 A4
Broad Wlk
Westhoughton BL5 57 E7
Wilmslow SK9 136 F8
Broadacre Orrell WN8 53 A6
Shevington Moor WN6 19 B2
Stalybridge SK15 102 E6
Broadacre Rd M18 99 E3
Broadbent Ave
Ashton-u-L OL6 85 C6
Dukinfield SK16 101 D8
Broadbent Cl Mossley SK15 86 E6
Shaw OL2 149 A5
Broadbent Dr BL9 28 E4
Broadbent Fold
Prim Sch SK16 102 A7
Broadbent Gr SK14 102 E1
Broadbent Rd OL1 49 C1
Broadbent St Hyde SK14 167 D4
Swinton M27 79 D7
Broadbottom
CE Prim Sch SK14 114 F8
Broadbottom Rd SK14 103 A3
Broadbottom Sta SK14 115 A8
Broadcarr La OL5 68 B1
Broadfield Cl M34 101 A2
Broadfield Com Prim Sch
OL8 66 F4
Broadfield Dr OL15 15 F3
Broadfield Gr SK5 99 E3
Broadfield Rd
Manchester M14 98 A3
Reddish SK5 99 E3
Broadfield St
Heywood OL10 29 B1
Rochdale OL16 139 F6
Broadfield Stile OL16 139 E6
Broadford Rd BL3 40 F5
Broadgate Bolton BL3 40 F5
Middleton M24,OL9 65 D5
Uppermill OL3 50 E1
Broadgate Mdw M27 79 F6
Broadgreen Gdns 4 BL4 42 D2
Broadhalgh Ave OL11 30 A7
Broadhalgh Rd OL11 30 A6
Broadhaven Rd M40 160 D3
Broadhead Rd BL7 9 E7
Broadhead Wlk M45 45 B1
Broadheath Cl BL5 40 A1
Broadheath Prim Sch
WA14 119 C8
Broadhey View SK22 127 B1
Broadhill Rd
Manchester M19 110 E6
Stalybridge SK15 86 A5
Broadhurst M34 101 A5
Broadhurst Ave
Culcheth WA3 91 F2
Swinton M27 61 F3
Broadhurst Ct 1 BL3 147 D4
Broadhurst Gr OL6 85 C6
Broadhurst La WN6 18 F7
Broadhurst Prim Sch M40 83 C7
Broadhurst St
3 Bolton BL3 147 D4
1 Radcliffe M26 43 F5
Stockport SK3 170 F7
Broadlands WN6 36 B6
Broadlands Rd M28 79 C6
Broadlands Wlk 11 M40 83 A6
Broadlea Gr OL12 14 C2
Broadlea Rd M19 110 E5
Broadley Ave
Golborne WA3 90 C7
Wythenshawe M22 121 D4
Broadley Fold OL12 14 B6
Broadmeadow BL7 25 B8
Broadmeadow Ave M16 97 F1
Broadmoss Dr M9 65 A3
Broadmoss Rd M9 65 A3
Broadoak Ave
Boothstown M28 77 F7
Wythenshawe M22 121 C5
Broadoak Comp Sch
M31 105 F2
Broadoak Cres OL6 85 B5
Broadoak Ct M8 156 B6
Broadoak Dr M22 121 D5
Broadoak Prim Sch
Ashton-u-L OL6 85 C6
Swinton M27 79 C6
Broadoak Rd
Ashton-u-L OL6 85 C6
Rochdale OL11 29 E6
Stockport SK7 123 F2
Wythenshawe M22 121 C5
Wythenshawe M22 121 D4
Broadoaks BL9 28 D3
Broadoaks Rd Sale M33 108 A4
Urmston M41 95 B1
Broadriding Rd WN6 35 E6
Broadstone Ave OL4 49 F4
Broadstone Cl
Prestwich M25 63 A3
Rochdale OL12 14 A1
Broadstone Hall
Prim Sch SK4 111 D6
Broadstone Hall Rd N
SK4 111 D6
Broadstone Hall Rd S
SK4,SK5 111 E6
Broadstone Rd Bolton BL2 25 D5
Reddish SK4,SK5 111 D6
Broadwalk M6 81 A3
Broadway
Altrincham WA15 120 B1
Atherton M46 58 F5
Chadderton OL9 152 A7
Cheadle SK8 122 C4
Droylsden M43 100 A8
Dukinfield SK14,SK16 101 B5
Failsworth M35,M40 83 D8
Failsworth M40,OL9 65 E2
Farnworth BL4 42 A1
Haslingden BB4 1 B8
Hindley WN2 57 A5
Horwich BL6 22 D3
Irlam M44 94 A1
Oldham OL9 48 B1
Partington M31 106 A4
Royton OL1,OL2 48 D2
Sale M33 108 A5
Salford M5 96 E8
Stockport SK2 124 C7
Stockport SK7 123 F2
Urmston M41 95 B4
Walkden M28 60 D1
Wilmslow SK9 137 B6
Broadway Ave SK8 122 D5
Broadway Bsns Pk OL9 65 E4
Broadway Cl M41 95 C5
Broadway Cres BB4 1 A8
Broadway Cty Prim Sch
BB4 1 C8
Broadway Ind Est
Dukinfield SK16 101 B6
Salford M5 161 A8
Broadway N M43 100 A8
Broadway St OL8 66 F4
Broadway Sta M5 96 F8
Broadway The SK6 112 E3
Broadwell Dr Leigh WN7 75 E1
Manchester M9 157 E7
Broadwood BL6 40 C7
Broadwood Cl SK6 134 F7
Brocade Cl M3 158 D3
Broche Cl OL11 30 B3
Brock Ave BL2 42 F7
Brock Cl M11 99 D7
Brock Dr SK8 132 B8
Brock Mill La WN1 37 C4
Brock Pl WN2 55 F2
Brock St Manchester M1 159 B1
Wigan WN1 151 E8
Brockenhurst Dr BL2 25 F3
Brockford Dr M9 64 E5
Brockholes SK13 115 F8
Brockhurst Wlk WN3 150 A5
Brocklebank Rd
Manchester M14 110 C8
Rochdale OL16 31 D7
Brocklehurst Ave BL9 140 F1
Brocklehurst St M9,M40 83 A8
Brockley Ave M14 98 B2
Brockstedes Ave WN4 72 E6
Brockton Wlk M8 156 A8
Brockway OL16 31 C3
Brocstedes Rd WN4 72 D7
Brocton Ct M7 63 D1
Brodick Dr BL2 42 F6
Brodick St M40 157 F8
Brodie Cl M30 79 B2
Brogan St 9 M18 99 D5
Brogden Ave WA3 91 E4
Brogden Dr SK8 122 B5
Brogden Gr M33 108 A3
Brogden Terr M33 108 A1
Bromborough Ave 2
M20 110 A8
Bromfield 8 OL12 139 F8
Bromfield Ave M9 64 D1
Broming St M11 160 F2
Bromleigh Ave SK8 122 B6
Bromley Ave Golborne WA3 90 D7
Royton OL2 48 C6
Urmston M41 94 E1
Bromley Cl WN2 38 A2
Bromley Cres OL6 85 B6
Bromley Cross BL7 9 B1
Bromley Cross Rd BL7 25 B7
Bromley Cross Sta BL7 25 B7
Bromley Dr WN7 75 D8
Bromley Rd M33 108 C2
Bromley St Denton M34 100 F3
Manchester M4,M40 159 B3
Oldham OL9 66 A3
Bromlow St M11 83 C1
Brompton Ave M35 84 B8
Brompton Rd
Manchester M14 98 B2
Manchester SK4 168 A2
Urmston M32 95 F3
Brompton St OL4 67 A5
Brompton Terr 6 SK16 166 B1
Brompton Way SK9 131 E5
Brompton Wlk M40 83 B6
Bromsgrove Ave M30 79 B2
Bromshill Dr M7 155 E6
Bromwich Dr 1 M9 157 D7
Bromwich St BL2 148 B6
Bronington Cl M22 121 E7
Bronte Ave BL9 44 F6
Bronte Cl Bolton BL1 143 D1
Oldham OL1 49 D4
Rochdale OL12 14 A1
Wigan WN3 150 A5
Bronte St M15 163 A5
Bronville Cl OL1 48 C1
Brood Ford Ct OL10 28 F1
Brook Ave
Altrincham WA15 119 E6
Droylsden M43 83 E1
Handforth SK9 131 D4
Manchester M19 99 B2
Oldham OL3 69 C8
Reddish SK4 111 D5
Shaw OL2 149 B8
Swinton M27 79 F7
Brook Bank Bolton BL2 25 D3
Disley SK12 134 C2
Brook Bottom Rd SK22 126 F1
Brook Cl Altrincham WA15 119 E6
Whitefield M45 63 B8
Brook Ct Manchester M14 110 D8
Prestwich M7 63 C1
Brook Dale Ct M33 108 C1
Brook Dr Marple SK6 125 F4
Tyldesley M29 77 C5
Whitefield M45 63 B8
Brook Fm Cl M31 105 E2
Brook Fold La SK14 102 B1
Brook Gdns Bolton BL2 25 E4
Heywood OL10 29 C2
Brook Gr M44 94 A2
Brook Green La M34 99 F3
Brook Hey Cl OL12 15 D4
Brook Ho Sale WA15 120 C7
Wigan WN1 151 D8
Brook House Cl Bolton BL2 25 E3
Bury BL8 26 E8
Brook La Alderley Edge SK9 136 F3
Altrincham WA15 119 F6
Oldham OL4 67 E6
Oldham OL8 67 B4
Rochdale OL16 31 B3
Uppermill OL3 50 F2
Whitefield BL9 45 A4
Wigan WN5 54 B5
Brook Lo SK8 122 D4
Brook Lynn Ave WA3 74 F1
Brook Mdw Glossop SK13 104 E1
Westhoughton BL5 40 A1
Brook Rd Cheadle SK8 122 D6
Manchester M14 110 D7
Reddish SK4 111 C5
Urmston M41 95 A2
Brook St Ashton-in-M WN4 73 C2
Atherton M46 58 B3
Bolton BL1 145 F7
Bury BL9 141 A3
Cheadle SK8 122 F6
Failsworth M35 83 D6
Farnworth BL4 42 E1
2 Glossop SK13 104 C1
Golborne WA3 75 A1
Golborne WA3 90 A8
Hazel Grove SK7 124 E2
Hyde SK14 167 E3
Ince-in-M WN2 56 A7
Kearsley M26 61 A7
Littleborough OL12 15 C6
Littleborough OL15 16 C5
Manchester M1 163 A7
Oldham OL1 67 A7
Oldham OL9 152 B8
Radcliffe M26 44 B3
Royton OL2 48 D3
Sale M33 108 C5
Salford M6 81 B4
Swinton M27 79 D8
Westhoughton BL5 39 F1
Wigan WN3 54 F4
Brook St E OL6 166 A2
Brook St W OL6 166 A2
Brook Terr Manchester M13 98 F3
Newhey OL16 32 C4
Urmston M41 95 C4
Brook The OL15 6 C1
Brook Wlk M34 112 F8
Brook's Bar M16 97 D4
Brook's Pl 3 OL12 139 E8
Brook's Rd M16 97 C3
Brookash Rd M22 131 A8
Brookbank Cl M24 65 B7
Brookbottom Rd M26 43 F6
Brookburn Prim Sch
M21 109 A7
Brookburn Rd M21 109 A7
Brookcot Rd M23 120 F7
Brookcroft Ave M22 121 D5
Brookcroft Rd M22 121 D5
Brookdale Atherton M46 58 F6
Rochdale OL12 14 E3
Brookdale Ave
Denton M34 100 E7
Denton M34 101 B2
Failsworth M40 83 D4
Marple SK6 126 A4
Brookdale Cl Bolton BL1 143 F2
Bredbury SK6 112 F3
Brookdale Cotts SK2 124 F7
Brookdale Rd
Bramhall SK7 123 F1
Hindley WN2 56 F5
Wythenshawe SK8 121 F5
Brookdale Rise SK7 123 F1
Brookdale St M35 83 E7
Brookdean Cl BL1 142 C3
Brookdene Rd
Manchester M19 110 E6
Whitefield BL9 45 A2
Brooke Dr SK9 131 D4
Brooke Way SK9 131 D4
Brookes St 7 Bacup OL13 3 D8
Middleton M24 47 B2
Brookfield Prestwich M25 63 B4
Shaw OL2 32 A1
Brookfield Ave
Ainsworth BL2 26 C1
Ainsworth BL2 43 D8
Altrincham WA15 119 F8
Manchester M21 109 C7
Poynton SK12 133 C3
Romiley SK6 113 A4
Royton OL2 48 D3
Salford M6 80 C3
Stockport SK1 124 A7
Urmston M41 95 A2
Brookfield Cl SK1 124 A7
Brookfield Cres SK8 122 D4
Brookfield Ct 4 M19 110 F8
Brookfield Dr
Altrincham WA15 120 A7
Boothstown M28 77 F6
Littleborough OL15 15 F6
Swinton M27 61 E1
Brookfield Gdns
Wythenshawe M22 121 C6
Wythenshawe M22 121 D6
Brookfield Gr OL6 85 D2
Brookfield Ho SK8 122 D4
Brookfield Ind Est SK13 171 E3
Brookfield Rd Bury BL9 27 E8
Cheadle SK8 122 E5
Culcheth WA3 91 D3
Eccles M30 79 B4
Manchester M8 64 A1
Orrell WN8 53 B7
Shevington Moor WN6 19 B2
Brookfield St Bolton BL2 148 B7
Leigh WN7 76 A6
Newton-le-W WA12 89 B3
Oldham OL8 153 F5
Brookfold M35 83 E8
Brookfold La BL2 25 F5
Brookfold Rd SK4 111 D6
Brookhead Ave M20 109 F7
Brookhead Dr SK8 123 A6
Brookhead Jun Sch SK8 122 F5
Brookhey Ave BL3 147 F3
Brookheys Rd M31,WA14 106 E2
Brookhill Cl OL3 51 C5
Brookhill St M40 160 E3
Brookhouse Ave
Eccles M30 95 A8
Farnworth BL4 60 C6
Brookhouse Sports Ctr
M30 94 F8
Brookhouse St WN1 151 D7
Brookhouse Terr WN1 151 D7
Brookhurst La M38 59 E6
Brookhurst Rd M18 99 D4
Brookland Ave
Denton M34 100 D2
Farnworth BL4 60 C7
Hindley WN2 56 D5
Brookland Gr BL1 142 A2
Brookland Rd WN1 37 B3
Brookland St OL16 31 B3
Brookland Terr BB4 2 F7
Brooklands Horwich BL6 22 C3
Littleborough OL12 15 C7
Brooklands Ave
Ashton-in-M WN4 73 D2
Atherton M46 58 D4
Haslingden BB4 1 B7
Leigh WN7 75 E3
Manchester M20 110 A6
Oldham OL9 152 B5
Brooklands Cl
Denton M34 100 D4
Irlam M44 93 F2
Mossley OL5 68 B2
Reddish SK4 111 D5
Brooklands Cres M33 108 B3
Brooklands Ct
Manchester M8 63 F2
Rochdale OL11 30 C6
Sale M33 108 B3
Brooklands Dr
Droylsden M43 84 C3
Glossop SK13 116 B7
Oldham OL4 68 B6
Orrell WN5 53 D5
Brooklands Ho M33 108 B2
Brooklands Par OL4 68 B6
Brooklands Prim Sch
M33 108 A2
Brooklands Rd
Hazel Grove SK7 124 E1
Manchester M25,M8 63 E2
Orrell WN8 53 C7
Ramsbottom BL0 11 A2
Reddish SK5 99 E2
Sale M23,M33 108 B2
Swinton M27 79 D6
Brooklands St
Middleton M24 47 A1
Royton OL2 48 D5
Brooklands Sta M33 108 A3
Brooklands Station App
M33 108 A3
Brooklands The OL10 29 C2
Brooklawn Dr
Manchester M20 110 B4
Prestwich M25 63 C6
Brookleigh Rd M20 110 D6
Brooklet Cl OL4 67 F5
Brookln Pl SK8 122 D6
Brooklyn Ave
Littleborough OL15 16 A7
Littleborough OL16 15 E4
Manchester M16 97 C2

Brooklyn Ave *continued*
Urmston M41 94 E1
Brooklyn Cres SK8 122 D5
Brooklyn Ct M14 110 C7
Brooklyn Rd Cheadle SK8 122 D5
Stockport SK2 124 C6
Brooklyn St Bolton BL1 143 E1
10 Oldham OL1 49 C1
Brooks Ave
Hazel Grove SK7 124 D3
Hyde SK14 167 E1
Radcliffe M26 43 F6
Brooks Dr
Altrincham M23,WA15 120 D6
Altrincham WA15 129 D8
Failsworth M35 83 E6
Brooks End OL11 13 E1
Brooks Ho 1 WN7 75 E8
Brooks St SK1 170 F7
Brooksbottom Cl BL0 11 C4
Brookshaw St Bury BL9 141 A4
Droylsden M11 83 A1
Brookside Glossop SK13 116 B8
Mossley OL5 68 B2
Oldham OL4 67 D6
Rowarth SK22 127 E7
Wigan WN3 150 A5
Brookside Ave
Ashton-in-M WN4 72 F8
Droylsden M43 84 C3
Farnworth BL4 60 C7
Oldham OL4 68 B6
Poynton SK12 133 E3
Stockport SK2 124 F7
Brookside Bsns Pk M24 65 D6
Brookside Cl Atherton M46 58 E4
Billinge WN5 71 E5
Bolton BL2 25 D5
Cheadle SK8 122 D4
Hadfield SK14 171 F4
Hyde SK14 102 A3
Ramsbottom BL0 11 A3
Brookside Cres Bury BL8 26 E8
Middleton M24 65 C6
Walkden M28 60 E3
Brookside Ct M19 99 A2
Brookside Dr Hyde SK14 102 A3
Manchester M25,M7 63 D1
Brookside La SK6 134 E7
Brookside Miniature Rly
SK12 133 F7
Brookside Prim Sch SK6 134 E6
Brookside Rd Bolton BL2 42 D8
Gatley SK8 122 A6
Manchester M40 65 A1
Sale M33 108 A2
Standish WN1 20 B1
Brookside Terr OL3 50 E4
Brookside Wlk BL8 43 F7
Brooksmouth BL8 140 D2
Brookstone Cl M21 109 D6
Brookthorn Cl SK2 124 F5
Brookthorpe Ave M19 110 E6
Brookthorpe Rd BL8 27 A3
Brookvale 4 WN6 37 A1
Brookview WN2 56 D4
Brookville OL12 4 C1
Brookwater Cl BL8 26 F6
Brookway
Altrincham WA15 119 F7
Oldham OL4 67 E5
Uppermill OL4 68 E6
Brookway Cl M19 110 E4
Brookway Ct M23 120 F7
Brookway High Sch M23 120 E7
Brookwood Ave
Manchester M8 156 C8
Sale M33 107 E3
Brookwood Cl M34 113 A7
Broom Ave Leigh WN7 75 E7
Manchester M19 111 B8
Manchester M7 155 E8
4 Reddish SK5 111 F6
Broom La Manchester M19 111 B8
Manchester M7 155 D8
Broom Rd
Altrincham WA15 119 E3
Partington M31 105 F2
Wigan WN5 54 D7
Broom St Bury BL8 140 D2
Newhey OL16 32 B4
Swinton M27 79 F7
Broom Way BL5 40 A2
Broome Gr M35 83 F6
Broome St OL9 153 D6
Broomedge M7 155 D8
Broomehouse Ave M44 105 E8
Broomfield M6 80 D6
Broomfield Cl
Ainsworth BL2 26 C1
Reddish SK5 111 F6
Wilmslow SK9 137 E8
Broomfield Cres
Middleton M24 46 D1
Stockport SK2,SK3 124 A4
Broomfield Dr
Manchester M8 155 F7
Reddish SK5 111 F6
Broomfield La WA15 119 E3
Broomfield Pl WN6 19 E1
Broomfield Rd
4 Bolton BL3 146 C4
Manchester SK4 168 C4
Standish WN6 19 E2
Broomfield Sq OL11 139 F5
Broomfield Terr
Newhey OL16 32 B4
Wigan WN1 151 E7
Broomfields M34 101 A5
Broomflat Cl WN6 19 E1
Broomgrove La M34 101 A4
Broomhall Rd
Manchester M9 64 B5
Pendlebury M27 80 D6
Broomhey Ave WN1 37 C4
Broomhey Terr WN1 151 E7
Broomhill Dr SK7 123 D1
Broomholme WN6 35 D7
Broomhurst Ave OL8 66 D4
Broomstair Rd M34 100 F6
Broomville Ave M33 108 B4
Broomwood Gdns WA15 120 C5
Broomwood Prim Sch
WA15 120 D5
Broomwood Rd WA15 120 C5
Broomwood Wlk 2 M15 163 A6
Broseley Ave Culcheth WA3 91 D4
Manchester M20 110 D3
Broseley La WA3 91 D5
Broseley Rd M16 97 A2
Broscroft SK13 104 A6
Broscroft Village SK13 104 A6
Brotherdale Cl OL2 48 D5
Brotherod Hall Rd OL12 14 C2
Brotherton Cl M15 162 D6
Brotherton Dr M3 158 D2
Brough Cl WN2 56 E3
Brough St 4 M11 99 E7
Brougham St M28 60 C3
Broughton Ave
Golborne WA3 90 D7
Walkden M38 60 B4
Broughton Cl M24 46 D2
Broughton
Jewish Cassel-Fox
Prim Sch M7 155 D8
Broughton La
Manchester M5,M7 155 D5
Manchester M7,M8 158 E4
Broughton Rd
Reddish SK5 169 F4
Salford M6 81 A4
Broughton Rd E M6 81 B4
Broughton St Bolton BL1 143 D2
Manchester M8 159 A4
Broughton Trade Ctr M7 158 E4
Broughville Dr M20 122 C8
Brow Ave M24 65 C6
Brow St OL11 31 A4
Brow Wlk M9 64 D3
Browbeck OL1 153 E7
Browfield M5 161 B8
Browfield Ave M5 161 B8
Browfield Way OL1 48 E1
Browmere Dr M20 110 A4
Brown Bank Rd OL15 15 F3
Brown Edge Rd OL4 67 E4
Brown Heath Ave WN5 71 D3
Brown La SK8 122 B1
Brown Lodge Dr OL15 15 F3
Brown Lodge St OL15 15 F3
Brown St
2 Alderley Edge SK9 137 A1
Altrincham WA14 119 D3
Blackrod BL6 21 D2
Bolton BL1 145 F7
Chadderton OL9 152 A8
Failsworth M35 83 F7
Heywood OL10 29 D3
Ince-in-M WN2 56 A7
Leigh WN2 56 E1
3 Leigh WN7 76 A5
Littleborough OL15 16 B5
18 Manchester M2 158 F1
Manchester M2 159 A1
Middleton M24 47 A2
Oldham OL1 67 A7
Radcliffe M26 43 F6
Ramsbottom BL0 138 B5
Salford M6 154 F1
Stockport SK1 169 E2
Tyldesley M29 76 F7
Wigan WN3 150 B7
Brown St N 2 WN7 76 A5
Brown St S 1 WN7 76 A4
Brown's La SK9 137 E8
Brownacre St M20 110 B6
Brownbank Wlk M15 162 F5
Browncross St M3 158 E1
Brownhill
Countryside Ctr OL3 51 B1
Brownhill Dr OL4 68 A7
Brownhill La OL3 51 B1
Brownhill Sch OL12 14 E1
Brownhill St M11 165 A8
Brownhills Cl BL8 27 A5
Browning Ave
Atherton M46 58 D5
Droylsden M43 84 A1
Wigan WN3 54 F4
Browning Cl BL1 143 D1
Browning Gr WN6 36 E3
Browning Rd
Middleton M24 47 B2
Oldham OL1 49 B1
Reddish SK5 99 E2
Swinton M27 79 E8
Browning St Leigh WN7 75 D6
Manchester M15 162 D6
Manchester M3 158 D2
Browning Wlk M46 58 D5
Brownlea Ave SK16 101 C7
Brownley Court Rd
M22 121 D5
Brownley Ct M22 121 E5
Brownley Rd M22 121 E4
Brownlow Ave
Ince-in-M WN2 56 B7
Royton OL2 49 A3
Brownlow Bsns Ctr BL1 143 D1
Brownlow Cl SK12 133 E2
Brownlow Fold
Com Prim Sch BL1 143 D1
Brownlow La WN5 53 C1
Brownlow Rd BL6 22 C5
Brownlow Way BL1 143 E1
Brownmere WN6 36 F2
Browns Rd BL2,BL3 43 B6
Brownside Cl OL16 15 C3
Brownslow Wlk 11
M13 163 B7
Brownson Wlk 7 M9 157 E8
Brownsville Rd SK4 111 C5
Brownville Gr SK16 101 E7
Brownwood Ave SK1 112 B1
Brownwood Cl M33 108 C1
Brows Ave M23 109 A2
Browsholm Ho BL1 144 C7
Broxton Ave Bolton BL3 146 B3
Orrell WN5 53 F7
Broxton St M40 160 F3
Broxwood Cl 8 M18 99 D5
Bruce St OL11 30 C4
Bruce Wlk 2 M11 99 D7
Brundage Rd M22 121 D2
Brundrett Pl 7 M33 107 F4
Brundrett St SK1 124 A8
Brundrett's Rd M21 109 B8
Brunel Ave M5 81 B1
Brunel Cl M32 96 E2
Brunel St Bolton BL1 143 D3
Horwich BL6 22 C2
Brunet Wlk M12 164 F6
Brunstead Cl M23 120 D6
Brunswick Ave BL6 22 E2
Brunswick Ct BL1 145 E8
Brunswick Rd
Altrincham WA14 119 D7
Manchester M20 110 C7
Brunswick St Bury BL9 140 F3
Dukinfield SK16 101 C8
3 Heywood OL10 29 C2
Leigh WN7 76 A4
Manchester M13 163 B6
Mossley OL5 86 D8
Oldham OL1 153 E6
Rochdale OL16 31 A8
Shaw OL2 149 B7
Stretford M32 108 D8
Walsden OL14 6 A7
Brunswick Terr OL13 3 D8
Brunt St M14 98 B3
Brunton Rd SK5 111 F6
Bruntwood Ave SK8 122 A1
Bruntwood La
Cheadle SK8 122 E1
Cheadle SK8 122 E2
Bruntwood Prim Sch
SK8 122 E2
Brushes Ave SK15 86 D3
Brushes Rd SK15 86 E2
Brussels Rd SK3 170 D6
Bruton Ave M32 96 B1
Brutus Wlk M7 155 E6
Bryan Rd M21 97 B2
Bryan St 1 OL4 49 C1
Bryant Cl M13 163 C5
Bryant's Acre BL1 40 D7
Bryantsfield BL1 40 D6
Bryce St Bolton BL3 145 E5
Hyde SK14 167 D4
Brydges Rd SK6 125 E5
Brydon Ave M12 163 C7
Brydon Cl Salford M6 154 F2
Salford M6 81 A2
Bryham St WN1 151 D8
Bryn Cross WN4 73 A6
Bryn Dr SK5 111 F5
Bryn Gates La WN2,WN4 73 D8
Bryn Lea Terr BL1 142 A4
Bryn Rd WN4 73 B5
Bryn Rd S WN4 73 C4
Bryn St Ashton-in-M WN4 73 B3
Ince-in-M WN3 151 E6
Bryn Sta WN4 73 A6
Bryn Wlk BL1 145 F8
Bryndale Gr M33 107 F1
Brynden Ave M20 110 C5
Brynford Ave M9 64 A5
Bryngs Dr BL2 25 F4
Brynhall Cl M26 43 E5
Brynheys Cl M38 60 A5
Brynn St WN2 73 F7
Brynorme Rd M8 64 A2
Brynton Rd M13 98 E2
Bryone Dr SK2 124 B5
Bryony Cl Orrell WN5 53 D5
Walkden M28 60 D5
6 Wythenshawe M22 121 C1
Bryson Wlk M18 165 C5
Buchan St M11 83 B2
Buchanan Dr WN2 57 B3
Buchanan Rd WN5 54 E7
Buchanan St Leigh WN7 75 E5
Ramsbottom BL0 138 B5
Swinton M27 61 F1
Buck La M33 107 E6
Buck St WN7 75 F4
Buckden Rd SK4 111 D7
Buckden Wlk 11 M23 108 F2
Buckfast Ave
Ashton-in-M WA11 89 A7
Oldham OL8 67 C4
Oldham OL8 67 D3
Buckfast Cl
Altrincham WA15 120 B2
Bramhall SK8 132 B6
Manchester M21 97 B1
Poynton SK12 133 D5
Buckfast Rd Middleton M24 46 F3
Sale M33 107 E6
Buckfast Wlk M7 155 E6
Buckfield Ave M5 161 B7
Buckhurst Rd
Manchester M19 99 A1
Ramsbottom BL9 12 C3
Buckingham Ave
Denton M34 101 B2
Horwich BL6 22 E2
Salford M6 154 D2
Whitefield M45 63 A7
Buckingham Cl WN5 54 E5
Buckingham Dr Bury BL8 44 B8
Dukinfield SK16 101 F7
Buckingham Park Cl OL2 149 B8
Buckingham Pl M29 58 F3
Buckingham Rd
Cheadle SK8 123 A3
Droylsden M43 83 E1
Irlam M44 105 C6
Manchester M21 97 B1
Manchester M25 63 C2
Manchester SK4 111 B5
Manchester SK4 111 C6
Poynton SK12 133 D3
Sale WA14 107 F1
Stalybridge SK15 86 A3
Stretford M32 96 F4
Swinton M27 62 A2
Wilmslow SK9 136 F6
Buckingham Rd W SK4 168 A4
Buckingham St
12 Rochdale OL16 31 A8
Salford M5 154 F1
Stockport SK2 124 A6
Buckingham Way
Altrincham WA15 120 A7
Stockport SK2 170 F6
Buckland Ave M9 64 A3
Buckland Dr WN5 36 B1
Buckland Gr SK14 114 A8
Buckland Rd M6 154 D4
Buckle Ho 7 M30 79 E2
Buckley Ave M18 99 C4
Buckley Barn Ct OL11 30 C1
Buckley Bldgs OL5 86 E8
Buckley Brook St OL12 15 B2
Buckley Chase OL16 31 E5
Buckley Cl SK14 113 E7
Buckley Dr SK6 113 A1
Buckley Farm La OL12 15 B3
Buckley Fields OL12 15 A2
Buckley Hall Ind Est OL12 15 B3
Buckley Hill La OL16 31 E5
Buckley Ho M46 58 D3
Buckley La Farnworth BL4 60 C7
Prestwich M25 62 E3
Rochdale OL12 15 B3
Buckley Rd
Manchester M18 99 C4
Oldham OL4 67 D8
Rochdale OL12 15 B2
Buckley Sq BL4 60 C6
Buckley St Bury BL9 140 F3
Chadderton OL9 152 A7
Denton M34 100 D7
Droylsden M43 84 A1
Heywood OL10 29 E3
Manchester M11 99 E7
6 Oldham OL3 69 B8
Oldham OL4 67 E5
Radcliffe M26 44 A3
Reddish SK5 99 E2
Rochdale OL16 31 A8
Shaw OL2 149 C7
Stalybridge SK15 101 F8
Wigan WN6 37 B2
Buckley St W WN6 37 A2
Buckley Terr OL12 15 B3
Buckley View OL12 15 B3
Bucklow Ave
Manchester M14 98 B1
Partington M31 105 F4
Bucklow Cl
Mottram-in-L SK14 102 F1
Oldham OL4 49 E4
Bucklow Dr M22 121 E8
Bucklow Gdns WA13 117 A4
Bucklow View WA14 119 A3
Bucknell Ct M40 159 C4
Buckstones
Com Prim Sch OL2 49 D8
Buckstones Rd
Shaw OL1,OL2 49 E7
Shaw OL2 32 D1
Buckthorn Cl
Altrincham WA15 120 E5
Manchester M21 109 D6
Westhoughton BL5 39 F2
Buckthorn La M30 94 F8
Buckton Cl OL3 51 C5
Buckton Dr SK15 86 E5
Buckton Vale Mews SK15 86 F7
Buckton Vale Prim Sch
SK15 86 F7
Buckton Vale Rd
Mossley SK15 86 D5
Mossley SK15 86 F6
Buckwood Cl SK7 125 A3
Buddleia Gr M7 155 D6
Bude Ave Brinnington SK5 112 B5
Tyldesley M29 77 C8
Bude Ave *continued*
Urmston M41 107 B8
Bude Cl SK7 132 F7
Bude Terr 4 SK16 166 B1
Bude Wlk M23 121 B5
Budsworth Ave M20 110 B7
Budworth Gdns 2 M43 84 B1
Budworth Rd M33 108 E3
Budworth Wlk 1 SK9 131 E1
Buer Ave WN3 54 F4
Buersil Ave OL16 31 B4
Buersil St OL16 31 B3
Buerton Ave M9 64 A5
Buffalo Ct M5 96 E8
Buffoline Trad Est 7 M19 99 B1
Bugle St M1 162 E8
Buile Dr M9 64 F4
Buile Hill Ave M38 60 B5
Buile Hill Dr M5 154 D3
Buile Hill Gr M38 60 B5
Buile Hill High Sch M6 154 D4
Buile St M7 155 E7
Buille Ho M6 154 E3
Bulford Ave M22 121 B2
Bulkeley Rd Cheadle SK8 122 E6
Handforth SK9 131 D3
Poynton SK12 133 E3
Bulkeley St SK3 170 D8
Bull Hill Cres M26 62 B8
Bullcote Gn OL2 49 B4
Bullcote La OL1,OL2 49 B4
Bullcroft Dr M29 77 C6
Buller Mews BL8 27 B1
Buller Rd M13 98 F2
Buller St Bury BL8 27 C1
Droylsden M43 100 B8
Farnworth BL3 42 C2
Oldham OL4 67 D8
Bullfinch Dr BL9 28 B5
Bullfinch Wlk M21 109 D7
Bullock St SK1 170 F7
Bullough Moor Prim Sch
OL10 29 B1
Bullough St Atherton M46 58 C2
Atherton M46 58 C3
Bullows Rd M38 59 F6
Bullrush Cl M28 60 D5
Bulteel St Bolton BL3 146 C2
Boothstown M28 77 E7
Eccles M30 79 B3
Wigan WN5 54 D6
Bulwer St OL16 31 A8
Bungalow Rd WA12 89 E1
Bungalows The
Ashton-in-M WN4 72 F7
New Mills SK22 127 D1
Bunkers OL3 69 C6
Bunkers Hill M45 62 D3
Bunkers Hill Rd SK14 102 E1
Bunkershill Rd SK6 113 B1
Bunsen St M1 159 B1
Bunting Cl 6 WA3 90 E8
Bunting Mews M28 78 B8
Bunyan Cl OL1 49 E4
Bunyan St 24 OL12 14 F1
Bunyard St M8 156 B6
BUPA Hospl Manchester
M16 97 D3
Burbage Bank 5 SK13 171 E1
Burbage Gr 23 SK13 171 F2
Burbage Rd M23 121 A2
Burbage Way 24 SK13 171 E2
Burbridge Cl M11 160 E1
Burchall Field OL16 31 B7
Burdale Dr M6 80 B4
Burdale Wlk M23 108 F1
Burder St 4 OL8 66 C2
Burdett Ave OL12 13 F1
Burdett Way M12 164 E5
Burdith Ave M14 98 A2
Burdon Ave M22 121 E3
Burford Ave Bramhall SK7 132 D5
Manchester M16 97 D2
Urmston M41 95 E4
Burford Cl SK9 136 E5
Burford Cres SK9 136 E5
Burford Dr Bolton BL3 145 E5
Manchester M16 97 D2
Swinton M27 61 E2
Burford Gr M33 107 E1
Burford La WA13 117 C2
Burford Rd M16 97 D2
Burford Wlk M16 97 D2
Burgess Ave OL6 85 C5
Burgess Dr M35 83 F7
Burgess Prim Sch M9 157 E7
Burgess St WN3 151 E5
Burghley Ave OL4 67 D6
Burghley Cl Bolton BL3 43 B5
Stalybridge SK15 86 A2
Burghley Dr BL3 43 B5
Burghley Way WN3 151 F5
Burgin Wlk M40 156 C5
Burgundy Dr BL8 26 F7
Burke St BL1 143 D2
Burkhardt Dr WA12 89 E3
Burkitt St SK14 167 E2
Burland Cl M7 155 D5
Burland St WN5 54 F7
Burleigh Cl SK7 124 A1
Burleigh Ct M32 96 E4
Burleigh Mews M21 109 B6
Burleigh Rd M32 96 E4
Burleigh St M15 163 B5
Burlescombe Cl WA14 119 B6

Burley Ave WA3 ....74 D1
Burley Cres WN3 ....54 C2
Burley Ct SK4 ....168 C2
Burleyhurst La SK9,WA16 .136 B7
Burlin Ct 9 M16 ....97 D3
Burlington Ave OL8 ....66 E4
Burlington Cl SK4 ....110 E2
Burlington Ct WA14 ....119 D5
Burlington Dr SK3 ....123 F4
Burlington Gdns SK3 ....123 F4
Burlington Ho OL6 ....166 A3
Burlington Mews SK3 ....123 F4
Burlington Rd
  Altrincham WA14 ....119 D5
  Eccles M30 ....79 E4
  Manchester M20 ....110 C7
Burlington St
  Ashton-u-L OL6,OL7 ....166 A3
  Hindley WN2 ....56 D5
  Hindley WN2 ....56 E5
  Manchester M13,M15 ....163 B5
  Manchester M15 ....163 A5
  12 Rochdale OL11 ....31 A4
Burlton Gr WN2 ....38 A2
Burman St M11,M43 ....99 F7
Burn Bank OL3 ....68 F5
Burnaby St Bolton BL3 ....145 D5
  Oldham OL8 ....153 D5
  Rochdale OL11 ....30 C4
Burnage Ave M19 ....110 F8
Burnage Hall Rd M19 ....110 F7
Burnage High Sch
  for Boys Manchester M19 110 E5
  Manchester M20 ....110 D6
Burnage La M19 ....110 F4
Burnage Range M19 ....99 A1
Burnage Sta M20 ....110 D4
Burnaston Gr WN5 ....54 D5
Burnbray Ave M19 ....110 E6
Burnby Wlk M23 ....108 F1
Burndale Dr BL9 ....45 A3
Burnden Ind Est BL3 ....42 B4
Burnden Rd BL3 ....148 B5
Burnden Way BL6 ....39 C7
Burnedge Cl OL12 ....4 D2
Burnedge Fold Rd OL4 ....68 D6
Burnedge La OL4 ....68 D5
Burnedge Mews OL4 ....68 D6
Burnell Cl M40 ....160 D3
Burnell Ct OL10 ....46 D7
Burneside Cres M24 ....46 E3
Burnet Cl Rochdale OL16 ..31 C4
  Tyldesley M29 ....77 B7
Burnett Ave M5 ....161 B8
Burnett Cl M40 ....157 D5
Burnett Gdns M5 ....161 B8
Burnfell WA3 ....90 E7
Burnfield Rd
  Manchester M18 ....99 D3
  Reddish SK5 ....99 F3
Burnham Ave Bolton BL1 .142 A1
  Reddish SK5 ....99 F1
Burnham Cl Cheadle SK8 .122 F2
  Culcheth WA3 ....91 E4
Burnham Dr
  Manchester M19 ....110 F8
  Urmston M41 ....95 C3
Burnham Gr WN2 ....37 F2
Burnham Rd M34 ....100 A3
Burnham Wlk 3 BL4 ....42 D1
Burnhill Ct M29 ....36 E8
Burnleigh Ct BL5 ....58 F8
Burnley La
  Chadderton OL1,OL9 ....48 A2
  Oldham OL1,OL9 ....48 C1
Burnley Rd Bury BL9 ....27 E8
  Edenfield BL0 ....1 D5
Burnley Rd E BB4 ....2 E8
Burnley St Chadderton OL9 152 B8
  Failsworth M35 ....84 A8
Burnmoor Rd BL2 ....42 F8
Burns Ave Atherton M46 ..58 D5
  Bury BL9 ....44 F6
  Cheadle SK8 ....122 F6
  Leigh WN7 ....75 C8
  Swinton M27 ....61 D1
Burns Cl Ashton-in-M WN4 .72 F6
  Longshaw WN5 ....53 D1
  Manchester M11 ....160 F1
  Oldham OL1 ....49 E5
  Wigan WN3 ....55 A4
Burns Cres SK2 ....124 E7
Burns Fold SK16 ....102 A7
Burns Gdns M25 ....62 F3
Burns Gr M43 ....84 A2
Burns Rd 6 Abram WA2 ..56 B1
  Denton M34 ....113 A4
  Walkden M38 ....60 B5
Burns St Bolton BL3 ....145 F6
  Heywood OL10 ....29 E1
Burnsall Ave Golborne WA3 .90 F8
  Whitefield M45 ....62 D8
Burnsall Gr OL2 ....48 D4
Burnsall Wlk 3 M22 ....121 A2
Burnside Altrincham WA15 129 D7
  Edenfield BL0 ....1 D2
  Hadfield SK14 ....171 F4
  Shaw OL2 ....49 D8
  Stalybridge SK15 ....102 D7
Burnside Ave Reddish SK4 111 E6
  Salford M6 ....80 B5
Burnside Cl Bredbury SK6 .112 F3
  Heywood OL10 ....29 D1
  Radcliffe M26 ....43 F7
  Stalybridge SK15 ....102 D7

Burnside Cl continued
  Tyldesley M29 ....77 B7
  Wilmslow SK9 ....137 C6
Burnside Dr M19 ....110 F7
Burnside Rd Bolton BL1 ..142 B2
  Gatley SK8 ....122 B5
  Rochdale OL16 ....31 C6
Burnt Edge La BL6 ....23 B5
Burnthorp Ave M9 ....64 B3
Burnthorpe Cl OL11 ....29 E6
Burntwood Wlk 22 M9 ..157 E8
Burnvale WN3 ....54 D2
Burran Rd M22 ....130 D8
Burrington Dr WN7 ....75 D7
Burrows Ave M21 ....109 C6
Burrows Yd WN1 ....150 C8
Burrs Cl BL8 ....27 C6
Burrs Ctry Pk BL8 ....27 C6
Burrs Lea Cl BL9 ....27 E6
Burrswood Ave BL9 ....27 F6
Bursar Cl WA12 ....89 D4
Burslem Ave M14 ....110 A8
Burstead St M18 ....99 E7
Burstock St M4 ....159 B3
Burston St M18 ....165 C6
Burtinshaw St 7 M18 ..99 D5
Burton Ave Bury BL8 ....26 F4
  Manchester M20 ....110 B6
  Sale WA15 ....108 A1
Burton Cl WA3 ....91 F3
Burton Dr SK12 ....133 D4
Burton Gr M28 ....79 C8
Burton Rd M20 ....110 A6
Burton St Manchester M40 159 B4
  Middleton M24 ....64 F8
  Oldham OL4 ....67 E5
  Stockport SK4 ....169 E3
Burton Wlk
  Manchester M3 ....158 D2
  Stockport SK4 ....169 E3
Burtree St M12 ....165 A6
Burwell Ave PR7 ....19 D8
Burwell Cl Glossop SK13 ..116 A8
  6 Leigh WN7 ....76 A4
  Rochdale OL12 ....14 D4
Burwell Gr M23 ....120 F7
Bury & Bolton Rd BL8 ....43 E7
Bury & Rochdale Old Rd
  BL9,OL10 ....29 B5
Bury & Whitefield
  Prim Sch BL9 ....45 B3
Bury Art Gall & Mus BL9 .140 E2
Bury Ave M16 ....97 C2
Bury Bsns Ctr BL9 ....141 A4
Bury Catholic Prep Sch
  BL9 ....44 E8
Bury CE High Sch BL9 ..44 D8
Bury Coll BL9 ....140 E1
Bury Coll (Stand Ctr) M45 44 E1
Bury FC (Gigg La) BL9 ..44 F7
Bury General Hospl BL9 .27 F6
Bury Gram Jun Sch BL9 .140 D2
Bury Gram Sch BL9 ....140 D2
Bury Intc BL9 ....140 E2
Bury New Rd
  Bolton BL1,BL2 ....148 A7
  Bolton BL2,BL8 ....43 B7
  Bury BL9 ....141 C2
  Heywood BL9,OL10 ....28 E2
  Manchester M7,M8,M25 .155 B3
  Prestwich M25 ....63 B3
  Ramsbottom BL0 ....11 D6
  Whitefield M45 ....62 F7
Bury Old Rd Ainsworth BL2 .26 B1
  Bolton BL2 ....148 A7
  Bolton BL2 ....148 B7
  Edenfield BL0 ....1 F1
  Heywood BL9,OL10 ....28 E1
  Prestwich M25,M45,M7,M8 .63 C4
  Ramsbottom BL9 ....11 F4
  Rochdale OL11 ....30 B6
Bury Sch of Arts & Crafts
  BL9 ....140 E2
Bury St Heywood OL10 ..29 B2
  Manchester M3 ....158 E2
  Mossley OL5 ....86 C8
  Radcliffe M26 ....44 D4
  Reddish SK5 ....169 F3
Bury Sta BL9 ....140 E2
Bush Moor Wlk M13 ....164 D5
Bush St M40 ....157 E5
Bushell St BL3 ....146 B4
Bushey Dr M23 ....121 A5
Busheyfield Cl SK14 ....101 D5
Bushfield Wlk 1 M23 ....120 E7
Bushgrove Wlk M9 ....64 D5
Bushnay Wlk 9 M8 ....156 B6
Bushnell Wlk 1 M9 ....64 D5
Bushton Wlk 9 M40 ....156 C5
Busk Rd OL9 ....152 C8
Busk Wlk OL9 ....152 C8
Butcher La
  Altrincham M23 ....120 D7
  Bury BL9 ....140 F2
  Royton OL2 ....48 C5
Butchers La WN4 ....73 B3
Bute Ave OL8 ....66 F3
Bute St Bolton BL1 ....142 B1
  Glossop SK13 ....104 B3
  Manchester M40 ....157 F8

Bute St continued
  Manchester M40 ....64 F1
  Salford M5 ....154 D1
Butler Ct 11 M40 ....159 C3
Butler Gn OL9 ....66 A4
Butler La M4,M40 ....159 C3
Butler St
  Manchester M4,M40 ....160 D2
  Ramsbottom BL0 ....138 A5
  Wigan WN1 ....151 D8
Butley St SK7 ....124 E4
Butman St M18 ....99 F6
Butt Hill Ave M25 ....63 B3
Butt Hill Ct M25 ....63 B3
Butt Hill Dr M25 ....63 B3
Butt Hill Rd M25 ....63 B3
Butt La M3 ....68 B4
Butter La 5 M3 ....158 F1
Buttercup Ave 7 M28 ....59 F3
Buttercup Cl M46 ....58 D5
Buttercup Dr Oldham OL4 .49 D2
  Rochdale OL11 ....30 B3
  Stockport SK3 ....170 D5
Butterfield Cl SK8 ....123 B1
Butterfield Rd BL5 ....58 F8
Butterhouse La OL3 ....51 C2
Butterley Cl SK16 ....101 F7
Buttermere Ave
  Ashton-in-M WN4 ....73 B5
  Heywood OL10 ....46 D8
  Swinton M27 ....79 F6
  2 Wythenshawe M22 ..121 C2
Buttermere Cl Bolton BL3 .42 F4
  Stretford M32 ....96 C3
Buttermere Dr
  Altrincham WA15 ....129 D6
  Middleton M24 ....46 E2
  Ramsbottom BL0 ....138 B7
Buttermere Gr OL2 ....48 D7
Buttermere Rd
  Ashton-u-L OL7 ....166 A4
  Farnworth BL4 ....59 E8
  Gatley SK8 ....122 B3
  Oldham OL4 ....67 D8
  Partington M31 ....105 E3
  Wigan WN5 ....54 C6
Buttermere Terr SK15 ..86 A3
Buttermill Cl 4 M44 ....94 B3
Butterstile Prim Sch M25 .63 A2
Butterwick Cl M21 ....109 C8
Butterworth Hall OL16 ..32 A5
Butterworth La M40,OL9 .65 E2
Butterworth St
  Chadderton OL9 ....152 B8
  Littleborough OL15 ....16 A5
  Manchester M11 ....165 A8
  Middleton M24 ....65 C7
  2 Oldham OL4 ....67 C7
  Radcliffe M26 ....44 B4
Butterworth Way OL3 ....69 B5
Butteryhouse La WA15 ..120 E2
Button Hole OL2 ....49 D7
Button La M23 ....109 A2
Button La Jun Sch M23 ..108 F2
Buttons Row BB4 ....2 F6
Buttress St M18 ....165 C6
Butts Ave The WN7 ....76 C3
Butts Cl WN7 ....76 A4
Butts La OL3 ....50 D4
Butts St WN7 ....76 B3
Butts The OL16 ....139 F7
Buxted Rd OL1 ....49 B1
Buxton Ave Ashton-u-L OL6 .85 D7
  Manchester M20 ....109 F6
Buxton Cl Atherton M46 ..58 E4
  18 Gamesley SK13 ....171 E2
Buxton Cres Rochdale OL16 .31 B4
  Sale M33 ....108 D1
Buxton La Droylsden M43 ..83 E1
  Marple SK6 ....125 E5
Buxton Mews SK13 ....171 E2
Buxton Old Rd SK12 ....135 C4
Buxton Pl OL8 ....153 E5
Buxton Rd Disley SK12 ..135 E6
  High Lane SK12,SK6,SK7 ..134 D8
  Stockport SK2 ....124 B5
  Stretford M32 ....96 A3
Buxton Rd W SK12 ....135 B5
Buxton St Bury BL8 ....27 C2
  Gatley SK8 ....122 A5
  Hazel Grove SK7 ....124 D3
  Heywood OL10 ....29 D1
  Manchester M1 ....163 B8
  Whitworth OL12 ....4 D3
Buxton Terr SK14 ....103 D5
Buxton Way 3 M34 ....113 A8
Buxton Wlk 1 SK13 ....171 E1
Bycroft Wlk M40 ....83 D4
Bye Rd BL0 ....11 E8
Bye St M34 ....100 F7
Byfield Rd M22 ....121 C4
Byfleet Cl WN3 ....54 C1
Byland Ave Bramhall SK8 .132 B6
  Oldham OL4 ....67 D4
Byland Cl BL1 ....143 E2
Byland Gdns M26 ....43 E5
Byland Wlk 3 M22 ....121 D1
Bylands Cl SK12 ....133 D4
Bylands Fold SK16 ....101 D6
Byley Rise WN6 ....36 E8
Byng Ave M44 ....105 D4
Byng St Farnworth BL4 ..60 E8
  Heywood OL10 ....46 E8
Byng St E BL2 ....145 F6
Byrchall High Sch WN4 ..73 B1
Byrcland Cl M12 ....164 E8

Byre Cl M23 ....109 A3
Byrness Cl M46 ....58 E4
Byrom Ave M19 ....99 C1
Byrom Cl M43 ....83 F1
Byrom La WA3 ....74 F2
Byrom St Altrincham WA14 119 D3
  9 Bury BL8 ....27 B4
  Manchester M16 ....97 D4
  Manchester M3 ....162 E8
  Salford M5 ....161 A8
Byron Ave Droylsden M43 .84 A2
  18 Hindley WN2 ....56 D5
  Prestwich M25 ....62 F3
  Radcliffe M26 ....43 E4
  Swinton M27 ....79 E8
Byron Cl Abram WN2 ....56 B1
  Wigan WN6 ....36 E3
Byron Cres PR7 ....19 F8
Byron Ct WA14 ....119 D6
Byron Dr SK8 ....122 F6
Byron Gr Atherton M46 ..58 D5
  Leigh WN7 ....75 E7
  Reddish SK5 ....99 E1
Byron Rd Denton M34 ..112 F8
  Middleton M24 ....47 B2
  Ramsbottom BL8 ....10 D2
  Stretford M32 ....96 F3
Byron St Eccles M30 ....79 D2
  Leigh WN7 ....75 F7
  Oldham OL8 ....66 B2
  Royton OL2 ....48 E4
Byron Street
  Com Prim Sch OL2 ..48 E4
Byron Wlk Farnworth BL4 .60 B6
  6 Royton OL2 ....48 E4
Byron's Dr 2 WA15 ....120 A6
Byrth Rd OL8 ....84 F8
Bywell Wlk 19 M8 ....155 F7

[symbol] £

'c' Ct WN4 ....73 B2

C

Cabin La OL4 ....50 A3
Cable St Bolton BL1 ....145 F8
  Manchester M4 ....159 B2
Cablestead Wlk M11 ....165 A8
Cabot Pl SK5 ....169 F4
Cabot St M13 ....163 B6
Caddington Rd M21 ....109 C8
Cadishead Jun Sch M44 .105 E6
Cadishead Prim Sch
  M44 ....105 D5
Cadishead Way M41,M44 ..94 C2
Cadleigh Wlk 6 M40 ....83 A7
Cadman Gr WN2 ....56 D4
Cadman's Yd 8 WN5 ....54 D5
Cadmium Wlk M18 ....99 C4
Cadnam Dr M22 ....121 F3
Cadogan Dr WN3 ....54 D2
Cadogan Pl 7 M7 ....63 E1
Cadogan St M14 ....98 A4
Cadum Wlk M13 ....163 C6
Caen Ave M40 ....65 C3
Caernarvon Cl BL8 ....10 F1
Caernarvon Dr SK7 ....124 C1
Caernarvon Rd WN2 ....57 A3
Caernarvon Way 2 M34 .100 F1
Caesar St OL11 ....31 A2
Cairn Dr Rochdale OL11 ..29 E6
  Salford M6,M7 ....81 C5
Cairn Wlk 18 M11 ....160 F1
Cairngorm Dr BL3 ....40 E5
Cairns Pl OL6 ....85 D5
Cairnwell Rd OL9 ....65 F8
Caister Ave M45 ....63 A7
Caister Cl M41 ....94 C1
Caistor Cl M16 ....109 E8
Caistor St SK1 ....112 B3
Caistor Wlk 2 OL1 ....153 F7
Caithness Cl M23 ....121 A4
Caithness Dr BL3 ....40 E6
Caithness Rd OL11 ....29 E5
Cakebread St M12 ....163 C7
Calbourne Cres M12 ....99 B3
Calcot Wlk 6 M23 ....120 F6
Calcutta Rd SK3 ....123 C7
Caldbeck Ave Bolton BL1 ..23 F1
  Sale M33 ....108 E3
Caldbeck Cl
  Ashton-in-M WN4 ....73 B4
  Platt Bridge WN2 ....56 B2
Caldbeck Dr Farnworth BL4 59 E7
  Middleton M24 ....46 E2
Caldbeck Gr WA11 ....71 C1
Caldecott Rd M9 ....64 A5
Calder Ave Hindley WN2 ..57 C3
  Irlam M44 ....93 F1
  Littleborough OL15 ....16 A7
  Wythenshawe M22 ....121 C4
Calder Cl Bury BL9 ....28 A8
  Poynton SK12 ....133 D2
  Reddish SK5 ....112 A4
Calder Cres M45 ....45 B2
Calder Ct M41 ....94 E4
Calder Dr Kearsley BL4 ..61 B5
  Platt Bridge WN2 ....56 A2
  Swinton M27 ....61 C1
  Walkden M28 ....60 B2
Calder Gr OL2 ....149 B8
Calder Ho 6 M7 ....81 C5
Calder Pl WN5 ....54 C7
Calder Rd BL3 ....147 E3

Calder St Manchester M5 .162 D8
  Rochdale OL16 ....15 B2
Calder Way M45 ....45 B2
Calder Wlk Middleton M24 .46 C2
  Whitefield M45 ....45 B2
Calderbank Ave M41 ....94 E4
Calderbank St WN5 ....54 E5
Calderbrook Dr SK8 ....123 A4
Calderbrook Rd OL15 ....6 C2
Calderbrook Terr OL15 ..16 C8
Calderbrook Way OL4 ..67 B5
Calderbrook Wlk 11 M9 .157 D7
Calderdale Ct OL2 ....48 C5
Caldershaw Ctr The OL12 .14 B2
Caldershaw La OL12 ....14 A2
Caldershaw Prim Sch
  OL12 ....14 A1
Caldershaw Rd OL11,OL12 .14 A1
Caldervale Ave M21 ....109 C6
Calderwood Cl BL8 ....27 A6
Caldew Cl WN2 ....56 E4
Caldey Rd M23 ....120 E5
Caldford Cl WN2 ....38 C6
Caldon Cl M30 ....95 D8
Caldwell Ave M29 ....77 B4
Caldwell Cl M29 ....77 B5
Caldwell St BL5 ....57 F5
Caldy Dr BL9 ....11 A3
Caldy Rd Handforth SK9 .131 D3
  Salford M6 ....154 D4
Cale Gn SK2 ....170 E5
Cale Green Prim Sch
  SK3 ....170 F6
Cale La WN2 ....38 B2
Cale St SK2 ....170 F6
Caleb Cl M29 ....58 F1
Caledon Ave M40 ....83 A8
Caledonia St Bolton BL3 .144 B5
  3 Radcliffe M26 ....44 C4
Caledonia Way M32 ....96 A5
Caledonian Dr M30 ....95 E8
Caley St Bolton BL1 ....23 F2
  1 Manchester M1 ....163 A7
Calf Hey OL15 ....15 F6
Calf Hey Cl M26 ....43 D3
Calf Hey N 7 OL11 ....31 A4
Calf Hey Rd OL2 ....49 D8
Calf Hey S 8 OL11 ....31 A4
Calf La OL3,OL5 ....68 E4
Calgarth Dr M24 ....46 D3
Calgary St M18 ....165 C5
Calico Cl M3 ....158 D3
Calico Wood Ave WN6 ..35 F6
Callaghan Wlk OL10 ....29 C1
Calland Ave SK14 ....167 F3
Callander Ct WN5 ....54 E8
Callander Sq OL10 ....28 F1
Callender St BL0 ....138 B6
Calliards Rd OL16 ....15 C4
Callingdon Rd M21 ....109 D5
Callington Cl 4 SK14 ..102 E2
Callington Dr SK14 ....102 E2
Callington Wlk 3 SK14 .102 E2
Callis Rd BL3 ....144 C5
Callum Wlk M13 ....163 C6
Calluna Mews M20 ....110 A4
Calne Wlk 6 M23 ....121 A5
Calow Cl 32 SK13 ....171 E2
Calow Dr WN7 ....76 C3
Calow Gn 9 SK13 ....171 E1
Caltha St BL0 ....138 B6
Calthorpe Ave M9 ....156 C7
Calton Ave M7 ....81 A7
Calve Croft Rd M22 ....121 F2
Calveley Wlk WN6 ....36 E8
Calver Ave M30 ....95 C8
Calver Cl
  11 Gamesley SK13 ......171 E2
  Urmston M41 ....94 D3
Calver Fold 7 SK13 ....171 E2
Calver Hey Cl BL5 ....40 C2
Calver Mews SK13 ....171 E2
Calver Pl 10 SK13 ....171 E2
Calver Wlk Cheadle SK8 .122 E1
  Denton M34 ....113 A8
  18 Manchester M40 ....159 C3
Calverhall Way WN4 ....73 A3
Calverleigh Cl BL3 ....146 A2
Calverley Ave M19 ....110 F7
Calverley Cl SK9 ....137 C8
Calverley Way OL12 ....14 E4
Calverly Rd SK8 ....123 A5
Calvert Rd BL3 ....147 F3
Calvert St M5 ....154 D2
Calverton Dr M40 ....83 C7
Calvin St BL1 ....143 F1
Calvine Wlk 4 M40 ....159 C3
Camargue Ct 1 M20 ....110 B6
Cambeck Cl M45 ....45 B1
Cambeck Wlk M45 ....45 A1
Cambell Rd M30 ....79 B2
Camberley Cl SK7 ....133 A7
Camberley Dr OL11 ....29 F5
Camberly Dr OL11 ....29 F6
Cambert La
  Manchester M18 ....165 C5
  Manchester M18 ....99 D5
Camberwell Cres WN2 ..37 F1
Camberwell Dr OL7 ....85 A7
Camberwell St
  Manchester M3,M8 ....159 A4
  Oldham OL8 ....66 E4
Camberwell Way OL2 ..48 C4
Cambo Wlk M9 ....110 F3
Camborne Rd SK14 ....102 E3
Camborne St M14 ....98 B3
Cambourne Dr Bolton BL3 144 A5
  Hindley WN2 ....57 C2

Cambrai Cres M30 ... 79 A4
Cambria Sq 8 BL3 ... 144 C5
Cambria St Bolton BL3 ... 144 C5
Oldham OL4 ... 67 D7
Cambrian Cres WN3 ... 54 C2
Cambrian Dr Milnrow OL16 ... 32 A6
Royton OL2 ... 48 C3
Cambrian Rd SK3 ... 123 C8
Cambrian St M11,M40 ... 160 E2
Cambridge Ave
Manchester M16 ... 97 C2
Rochdale OL11 ... 30 A6
Wilmslow SK9 ... 136 F7
Cambridge Cl
Farnworth BL4 ... 147 F1
10 Sale M33 ... 107 D3
Cambridge Dr
Little Lever BL3 ... 43 B4
Reddish M34 ... 100 A3
Romiley SK6 ... 113 C5
Cambridge Gr Eccles M30 ... 79 F2
Whitefield M45 ... 63 A7
Cambridge Ind Area M7 ... 158 E4
Cambridge Rd
Altrincham WA15 ... 119 E2
Droylsden M43 ... 83 F3
Failsworth M35 ... 83 F5
Gatley SK8 ... 122 B5
Horwich BL6 ... 39 F8
Manchester M9 ... 64 D1
Orrell WN5 ... 53 F8
Reddish SK4 ... 111 C5
Urmston M41 ... 95 B1
Cambridge St
Ashton-u-L OL7 ... 84 F1
Atherton M46 ... 58 C2
Dukinfield SK16 ... 166 C1
Manchester M1,M15 ... 162 F7
Manchester M7,M8 ... 158 E4
Oldham OL9 ... 66 C4
Stalybridge SK15 ... 86 A2
Stockport SK2 ... 124 A6
Wigan WN1 ... 151 D7
Cambridge Terr SK15 ... 86 D4
Cambridge Way WN1 ... 151 D8
Camdale Wlk 9 M8 ... 155 F6
Camden Ave M40 ... 83 C4
Camden Cl BL2 ... 26 C1
Camden St OL5 ... 68 D3
Camelia Rd M9 ... 156 C7
Camellia Cl BL1 ... 144 B7
Cameron Ct OL2 ... 48 D6
Cameron Pl WN5 ... 54 E8
Cameron St Bolton BL1 ... 143 D4
Bury BL8 ... 27 C2
Leigh WN7 ... 75 D7
Manchester M1,M15 ... 162 F8
Camley Wlk 1 M8 ... 156 B6
Camm St WN2 ... 74 B8
Camms View BB4 ... 1 A8
Camomile Wlk 5 M31 ... 105 F3
Camp Rd WN4 ... 72 E4
Camp St Ashton-u-L OL6 ... 166 B3
Bury BL8 ... 27 C3
Manchester M3 ... 162 E8
Manchester M5,M7 ... 155 D5
Campania St OL2 ... 48 E2
Campanula Wlk 4 M8 ... 156 A6
Campbell Cl BL8 ... 26 F4
Campbell Ct BL4 ... 42 C2
Campbell Rd Bolton BL3 ... 146 A2
Manchester M13 ... 98 F2
Sale M33 ... 107 F3
Swinton M27 ... 79 E6
Campbell St Farnworth BL4 ... 42 B1
Reddish SK5 ... 99 F1
Rochdale OL12 ... 14 E2
Wigan WN5 ... 54 D5
Campbell Way M28 ... 60 D3
Campbell Wlk 5 BL4 ... 42 C2
Campden Way SK9 ... 131 D4
Campion Dr BB4 ... 1 A8
Campion Gr WN4 ... 72 F4
Campion Way
8 Denton M34 ... 113 A8
Rochdale OL12 ... 14 C3
Campion Wlk M11 ... 164 F8
Camponia Gdns M7 ... 155 D5
Camrose Wlk M13 ... 164 D5
Cams Acre Cl M26 ... 43 E3
Cams La M26 ... 43 E2
Cams Lane Prim Sch M26 ... 43 F3
Canaan WA3 ... 91 C8
Canada St Bolton BL1 ... 142 C2
Horwich BL6 ... 22 B3
Manchester M40 ... 160 E4
Stockport SK2 ... 124 A6
Canal Bank
Appley Bridge WN6 ... 35 C7
Eccles M30 ... 79 C3
Canal Bridge La M43 ... 83 E1
Canal Circ M30 ... 80 A1
Canal Cotts WN3 ... 150 B7
Canal Rd WA14 ... 119 E8
Canal Row WN2 ... 20 D1
Canal Side M30 ... 79 C3
Canal St Adlington PR7 ... 21 A6
Droylsden M43 ... 84 A1
Dukinfield SK14 ... 101 C3
Heywood OL10 ... 46 F8
Leigh WN7 ... 75 F4
Littleborough OL15 ... 16 B5
Manchester M1 ... 163 A8
Manchester M5 ... 81 C1
Marple SK6 ... 126 A6
Oldham OL9 ... 66 B3
Rochdale OL11 ... 31 A5
Shevington WN6 ... 36 F2
Canal St *continued*
Stalybridge SK15 ... 86 A1
Stockport SK1 ... 170 F8
Wigan WN2 ... 151 F6
Canal Terr WN1 ... 151 E7
Canalside Ind Est OL16 ... 31 B5
Canberra Rd Bramhall SK7 ... 132 F5
Shevington WN5 ... 36 C1
Canberra St M11 ... 83 C2
Candahar St BL3 ... 42 A3
Candleford Pl SK2 ... 124 E4
Candleford Rd M20 ... 110 B6
Candlestick Pk BL9 ... 28 D4
Canisp Cl OL9 ... 48 A1
Canley Cl SK1 ... 170 F8
Canmore Cl BL3 ... 146 A3
Cann St BL8 ... 26 D8
Cannel Fold M28 ... 78 B7
Canning Dr BL1 ... 143 E2
Canning St Bolton BL1 ... 143 F2
Bury BL9 ... 140 F4
Stockport SK4 ... 169 E2
Cannock Dr SK4 ... 168 A2
Cannon Ct M4 ... 158 F2
Cannon Gr BL3 ... 145 D5
Cannon St Atherton M46 ... 58 D3
Bolton BL3 ... 145 D5
Eccles M30 ... 79 E1
Hollingworth SK14 ... 103 C5
Manchester M3 ... 158 D3
Manchester M4 ... 159 A2
Oldham OL9 ... 153 E7
Radcliffe M26 ... 43 F5
Ramsbottom BL0 ... 11 A4
Cannon St N BL3 ... 145 D6
Cannon Wlk M34 ... 100 E2
Canon Burrows
CE Prim Sch OL7 ... 85 A5
Canon Cl WN6 ... 19 F2
Canon Dr WA14 ... 119 B1
Canon Flynn Ct OL16 ... 31 C7
Canon Green Ct M3 ... 158 E2
Canon Green Dr M3 ... 158 E2
Canon Hussey Ct M3 ... 158 D1
Canon Johnson
CE Prim Sch OL7 ... 166 B4
Canon Slade Sch BL2 ... 25 C4
Canon St Bury BL9 ... 141 A4
Rochdale OL16 ... 15 B2
Canon Tighe Ct OL9 ... 152 A7
Canon Williamson
CE High Sch M30 ... 78 F1
Canon's Cl BL1 ... 142 B2
Canons Gr M40 ... 157 E5
Canonsleigh Cl M8 ... 155 E5
Canonsway M27 ... 79 E8
Cansfield Gr WN4 ... 73 A4
Cansfield High Sch WN4 ... 73 A4
Canterbury Ave WA3 ... 74 D1
Canterbury Cl
Atherton M46 ... 58 E4
Dukinfield SK16 ... 101 D6
Rochdale OL11 ... 30 A7
Canterbury Cres M24 ... 47 D2
Canterbury Dr Bury BL8 ... 140 D4
Manchester M25 ... 63 C2
Canterbury Gdns M30,M5 ... 80 B2
Canterbury Gr BL3 ... 147 D3
Canterbury Pk M20 ... 109 F3
Canterbury Rd
Altrincham WA15 ... 120 C3
Stockport SK1 ... 112 B1
Urmston M41 ... 95 D3
Canterbury St OL6 ... 166 C4
Canterfield Cl M43 ... 84 D2
Cantley Wlk 5 M8 ... 156 A6
Cantrell St M11 ... 83 B2
Canute Ct M32 ... 96 E3
Canute Rd M32 ... 96 E3
Canute St 2 Bolton BL2 ... 25 C1
Radcliffe M26 ... 43 E3
Salford M6 ... 81 B2
Cape St M14 ... 110 C7
Capella Wlk M7 ... 81 C4
Capenhurst Cl
Poynton SK12 ... 133 F4
Sale M23 ... 120 F4
Capesthorne Cl SK7 ... 133 F8
Capesthorne Dr OL2 ... 48 F7
Capesthorne Rd
Altrincham WA15 ... 120 D6
Dukinfield SK16 ... 101 D6
Hazel Grove SK7 ... 133 F8
High Lane SK6 ... 134 E7
Wilmslow SK9 ... 136 E5
Capesthorne Wlk M34 ... 100 E2
Capital Quay M5 ... 161 A7
Capital Rd M11 ... 99 F7
Capitol Cl BL1 ... 142 A3
Cappadocia Way BL5 ... 57 D7
Capps St WN2 ... 56 B3
Capricorn Way M6 ... 81 C4
Capstan St M9 ... 157 E8
Captain Clarke Rd SK14 ... 101 C5
Captain Fold Rd M38 ... 59 F6
Captain Lees Gdns BL5 ... 58 A8
Captain Lees Rd BL5 ... 40 A1
Captain St BL6 ... 22 B4
Captain's Clough Rd BL1 ... 142 B2
Captain's La WN4 ... 73 C3
Capton Cl SK7 ... 124 A2
Car Bank Ave M46 ... 58 D4
Car Bank Cres M46 ... 58 D4
Car Bank Sq M46 ... 58 D4
Car Bank St M46 ... 58 D4
Car St WN2 ... 56 A2
Caradoc Ave 12 M8 ... 156 B6
Carawood Cl WN6 ... 35 D7
Carberry Rd M18 ... 99 D5
Cardale Wlk M9 ... 157 D7
Carden Ave Swinton M27 ... 79 D7
Urmston M41 ... 94 E2
Cardenbrook Gr 4 SK9 ... 131 D2
Carder Cl M27 ... 79 F7
Carders Cl WN7 ... 75 E4
Cardew Ave M22 ... 121 F4
Cardiff Cl 8 OL8 ... 66 B2
Cardiff St M7 ... 155 E7
Cardiff Wlk 4 M34 ... 100 F1
Cardigan Dr BL9 ... 44 E7
Cardigan Rd OL8 ... 66 B2
Cardigan St Radcliffe M26 ... 43 F6
Rochdale OL12 ... 14 E3
Royton OL2 ... 48 E4
2 Salford M6 ... 154 E1
Cardigan Terr M14 ... 97 F4
Cardinal Langley
RC High Sch M24 ... 47 B4
Cardinal Mews M24 ... 46 D2
Cardinal St
Manchester M8 ... 156 B7
10 Oldham OL1 ... 67 A7
Carding Gr M3 ... 158 E3
Cardroom Rd M4 ... 159 C1
Cardus St M19 ... 99 A1
Cardwell Gdns BL1 ... 143 E2
Cardwell Rd M30 ... 79 A1
Cardwell St OL8 ... 66 F3
Careless La WN2 ... 151 F8
Carey Cl Manchester M7 ... 158 D4
Wigan WN3 ... 54 D2
Carey Wlk M15 ... 162 F5
Carfax Fold OL12 ... 14 B2
Carfax St M18 ... 99 D5
Cargate Wlk 14 M8 ... 155 F6
Carib St M15 ... 162 F5
Carill Ave M40 ... 65 A1
Carill Dr M14 ... 110 D8
Carina Pl M7 ... 81 C4
Cariocca Ent Pk M12 ... 164 D6
Carisbrook Ave
Prestwich M25,M45 ... 63 A6
Urmston M41 ... 95 C2
Carisbrook Dr M27 ... 80 A6
Carisbrook St M9 ... 157 E7
Carisbrooke Ave SK7 ... 124 D1
Carisbrooke Dr BL1 ... 143 F3
Carisbrooke Rd WN7 ... 76 D6
Carl St BL1 ... 143 D2
Carlburn St M11 ... 83 D2
Carleton Rd SK12 ... 134 C4
Carley Gr M9 ... 64 B4
Carlford Gr M25 ... 62 F3
Carlile St SK3 ... 170 E8
Carlin Gate WA15 ... 120 A6
Carling Dr M22 ... 121 E2
Carlingford Cl SK3 ... 170 E5
Carlisle Cl Little Lever BL3 ... 43 A2
Prestwich M45 ... 63 B7
Romiley SK6 ... 113 A1
Carlisle Cres OL6 ... 85 C7
Carlisle Dr Irlam M44 ... 94 A2
Sale WA14 ... 119 E8
Carlisle Pl PR6 ... 21 A8
Carlisle St
7 Alderley Edge SK9 ... 137 A1
Bolton BL7 ... 25 A8
Hindley WN2 ... 56 E6
Oldham OL9 ... 152 C5
Oldham OL9 ... 66 C4
Rochdale OL12 ... 14 E3
Swinton M27 ... 61 F2
Wigan WN5 ... 54 D6
Carlisle Way Aspull WN2 ... 38 D5
3 Denton M34 ... 100 F1
Carloon Dr M23 ... 109 B1
Carloon Rd M23 ... 109 B1
Carlow Dr M22 ... 121 E2
Carlton Ave Bolton BL3 ... 146 A4
Bramhall SK7 ... 132 D5
Cheadle SK8 ... 122 F3
Handforth SK9 ... 131 C2
Manchester M14 ... 98 B3
Manchester M16 ... 97 B4
Manchester M25 ... 63 E2
Oldham OL4 ... 49 D1
Orrell WN8 ... 53 A7
Romiley SK6 ... 113 D2
Whitefield M45 ... 44 D1
Carlton Cl Ashton-in-M WN4 ... 73 A5
Blackrod BL6 ... 21 D2
Bolton BL2 ... 25 E3
Walkden M28 ... 60 C1
Carlton Cres
Stockport SK1 ... 112 A2
Urmston M41 ... 95 D1
Carlton Ct
Altrincham WA15 ... 120 B1
Manchester M25 ... 63 A1
Carlton Dr Gatley SK8 ... 122 A6
Manchester M25,M8 ... 63 E2
Carlton Gdns BL4 ... 42 D1
Carlton Gr Hindley WN2 ... 56 F4
Horwich BL6 ... 22 D1
Carlton Grange M16 ... 97 E2
Carlton Mans 4 M16 ... 97 D3
Carlton Pl Farnworth BL4 ... 42 D1
Hazel Grove SK7 ... 125 A1
Carlton Range M18,M34 ... 99 F4
Carlton Rd
Altrincham WA15 ... 120 B2
Ashton-u-L OL6 ... 85 C5
Bolton BL1 ... 144 A8
Golborne WA3 ... 74 D1
Hyde SK14 ... 102 A3
Lymm WA13 ... 117 B5
Carlton Rd *continued*
Manchester M16 ... 97 D3
Manchester SK4 ... 168 A2
Sale M33 ... 108 A6
Salford M6 ... 154 E4
Urmston M41 ... 95 D1
Walkden M28 ... 60 C1
Carlton St Bolton BL2 ... 148 A6
Bury BL9 ... 44 F8
Eccles M30 ... 79 D3
Farnworth BL4 ... 42 D1
Manchester M16 ... 97 C4
Wigan WN3 ... 150 B6
Carlton Way Irlam M44 ... 105 C5
Oldham OL1,OL2 ... 48 D2
Carlyle Cl M8 ... 156 A6
Carlyle Gr WN7 ... 75 C8
Carlyle St BL9 ... 140 E2
Carlyn Ave M33 ... 108 D4
Carmel Ave M5 ... 161 C8
Carmel Cl M5 ... 161 C8
Carmenna Dr SK7 ... 132 F7
Carmichael Cl M31 ... 105 E3
Carmichael St SK3 ... 170 D8
Carmine Fold M24 ... 46 F2
Carmona Dr M25 ... 63 A4
Carmona Gdns M25,M7 ... 63 C1
Carmoor Rd M13 ... 163 C5
Carna Rd SK5 ... 99 E2
Carnaby St M9 ... 64 F1
Carnarvon St
Manchester M3 ... 158 F3
Manchester M7 ... 155 E7
Oldham OL8 ... 66 B2
3 Stockport SK1 ... 112 A1
Carnation Rd
Farnworth BL4 ... 42 A1
Oldham OL4 ... 67 E4
Carnegie Ave M19 ... 99 B1
Carnegie Cl 1 M33 ... 107 D3
Carnegie Dr WN4 ... 73 A5
Carnforth Ave Hindley WN2 ... 57 A5
Middleton OL11 ... 47 D7
Oldham OL9 ... 152 A6
Carnforth Dr
Ramsbottom BL0,BL8 ... 11 A2
Sale M33 ... 108 A3
Carnforth Rd Cheadle SK8 ... 123 C4
Reddish SK4 ... 111 D7
Carnforth Sq OL11 ... 47 D7
Carnforth St M14 ... 98 B3
Carnoustie BL3 ... 146 A3
Carnoustie Cl
Failsworth M40 ... 83 C7
Wilmslow SK9 ... 137 D8
Carnoustie Dr Gatley SK8 ... 122 C1
Ramsbottom BL0 ... 138 B5
Carnwood Cl M40 ... 83 D4
Carolina Ho M3 ... 158 E3
Caroline Dr M4 ... 159 C1
Caroline St
Ashton-u-L OL6 ... 166 C3
Bolton BL3 ... 147 D4
Irlam M44 ... 105 F8
Manchester M7 ... 158 E4
Stalybridge SK15 ... 86 A1
Stockport SK3 ... 170 D7
Wigan WN1 ... 151 F8
Wigan WN3 ... 150 C7
Carpenters La M4 ... 159 A2
Carpenters Way OL16 ... 31 B4
Carpenters Wlk M43 ... 83 F1
Carr Ave M25 ... 62 F2
Carr Bank Ave
Manchester M9 ... 63 F3
Ramsbottom BL0 ... 138 B7
Carr Bank Dr BL0 ... 138 B7
Carr Bank Rd BL0 ... 138 B7
Carr Brook Dr M46 ... 58 E4
Carr Brow SK6 ... 135 A7
Carr Cl SK1 ... 124 B8
Carr Common Rd WN2 ... 57 D3
Carr Fold BL0 ... 138 B7
Carr Gr OL16 ... 32 A6
Carr House La WN6 ... 18 F8
Carr House Rd OL4 ... 67 F6
Carr La Alderley Edge SK9 ... 136 D2
Diggle OL3 ... 51 C5
Golborne WA3 ... 91 A7
Leigh WA3,WN7 ... 91 E8
Mossley SK15 ... 86 F7
Newhey OL16 ... 32 C6
Oldham OL3 ... 69 B7
Rawtenstall BB4 ... 2 F7
Wigan WN3 ... 55 B3
Carr Mill Cres WN5 ... 71 E4
Carr Mill Jun Sch WA11 ... 71 C1
Carr Mill Mews SK9 ... 131 B1
Carr Mill Rd WA11,WN5 ... 71 D3
Carr Rd Altrincham WA15 ... 120 B2
Horwich BL6 ... 22 B5
Irlam M44 ... 94 B2
Carr Rise SK15 ... 86 F7
Carr St Ashton-u-L OL6 ... 85 D5
Hindley WN2 ... 56 D6
Leigh WN7 ... 75 C5
Ramsbottom BL0 ... 138 B7
Swinton M27 ... 79 D7
Carr Wood Ave SK7 ... 132 E8
Carr Wood Rd SK7 ... 123 E1
Carradale Dr M33 ... 107 C5
Carradale Wlk 5 M40 ... 83 A6
Carradon Dr WN6 ... 19 E1
Carrbrook Cl SK15 ... 86 E6
Carrbrook Cres SK15 ... 86 F6
Carrbrook Dr OL1 ... 48 E1
Carrbrook Ind Est SK15 ... 87 A6
Carrbrook Rd SK15 ... 86 F7
Carrbrook Terr 6 M26 ... 44 C4
Carrfield Ave
Altrincham WA15 ... 120 D6
Stockport SK3 ... 124 A4
Walkden M38 ... 59 E4
Carrfield Cl M38 ... 59 E4
Carrfield Gr M38 ... 59 E4
Carrgate Rd M34 ... 101 B1
Carrgreen Cl M19 ... 110 F5
Carrgreen La WA13 ... 117 F6
Carrhill Quarry Cl OL5 ... 68 C2
Carrhill Rd OL5 ... 68 C2
Carrhouse La
Hollingworth SK14 ... 103 C4
Mottram-in-L SK14 ... 103 C2
Carriage Dr
Littleborough OL15 ... 16 B7
Manchester M40 ... 157 D5
Carriage Dr The SK13 ... 103 F5
Carriage St M15 ... 162 D5
Carriages The WA14 ... 119 C4
Carrick Gdns
Middleton M24 ... 46 F4
Wythenshawe M22 ... 121 D4
Carrie St BL1 ... 144 B8
Carrigart M25 ... 63 B3
Carrill Gr M19 ... 99 A1
Carrill Gr E M19 ... 99 A1
Carrington Bsns Pk M31 ... 106 C6
Carrington Cl OL16 ... 15 D3
Carrington Dr BL3 ... 145 F5
Carrington Field St
SK1,SK2 ... 124 A7
Carrington Gr WN7 ... 75 F7
Carrington Ho M6 ... 80 C4
Carrington La
Sale M31,M33 ... 107 C6
Sale M33 ... 107 E5
Carrington Rd
Adlington PR7 ... 20 F7
Flixton M41 ... 106 E8
Manchester M14 ... 98 C1
Stockport SK1 ... 112 B3
Carrington St Leigh WN7 ... 75 F7
Oldham OL9 ... 66 B3
Swinton M27 ... 62 B1
Carrington Terr M27 ... 62 A1
Carrmel Ct OL3 ... 50 F3
Carrock Wlk M24 ... 46 B1
Carron Ave M9 ... 64 F1
Carron Gr BL2 ... 42 F7
Carrs Ave SK3,SK8 ... 123 A6
Carrs Ct SK9 ... 137 B7
Carrs Rd SK8 ... 122 F6
Carrsfield Rd M22 ... 121 E6
Carrslea Cl M26 ... 43 E5
Carrsvale Ave M41 ... 95 B3
Carrswood Rd M23 ... 120 D8
Carruthers Cl OL10 ... 29 F3
Carruthers St M4 ... 160 D1
Carrwood WA15 ... 129 B7
Carrwood Hey BL0 ... 11 A4
Carrwood Rd SK9 ... 136 F8
Carsdale Rd M22 ... 130 E8
Carslake Ave BL1 ... 144 C8
Carslake Rd M40 ... 157 D5
Carson Rd M19 ... 111 A8
Carstairs Ave SK2 ... 124 A4
Carstairs Cl M8 ... 155 F7
Carswell Cl M29 ... 59 C1
Carter Cl M34 ... 100 F2
Carter Pl SK14 ... 101 D5
Carter St Bolton BL3 ... 42 A4
Dukinfield SK14 ... 101 D5
Farnworth BL4 ... 60 E7
Ince-in-M WN3 ... 151 E6
Manchester M7 ... 155 D5
Mossley OL5 ... 86 C8
Salford M5 ... 80 C1
Stalybridge SK15 ... 86 B2
Carthage St OL8 ... 66 F4
Carthorpe Arch M5 ... 154 F1
Cartleach Gr M28 ... 60 A2
Cartleach La M28 ... 60 A2
Cartmel 6 OL12 ... 139 F8
Cartmel Ave Milnrow OL16 ... 31 F4
Reddish SK4 ... 111 E6
Wigan WN1 ... 37 B3
Cartmel Cl Bolton BL3 ... 40 D2
Gatley SK8 ... 122 C3
Hazel Grove SK7 ... 124 C3
Oldham OL8 ... 66 D3
Whitefield BL9 ... 45 A3
Cartmel Cres Bolton BL2 ... 25 C2
Failsworth OL9 ... 65 F2
Cartmel Ct M9 ... 65 A4
Cartmel Dr WA15 ... 120 D6
Cartmel Gr M28 ... 79 B7
Cartmel Wlk
Manchester M9 ... 157 D7
Middleton M24 ... 46 F2
Cartridge Cl M22 ... 121 F3
Cartridge St OL10 ... 29 C2
Cartwright Cl BL1 ... 142 C1
Cartwright Gr WN7 ... 57 D1
Cartwright Rd M21 ... 108 F8
Cartwright St Denton M34 ... 100 F6
Dukinfield SK14 ... 102 A5
Carver Ave M25 ... 63 C5
Carver Cl M16 ... 161 B5
Carver Dr SK6 ... 125 E5
Carver Rd
Altrincham WA15 ... 119 E2
Marple SK6 ... 125 E5
Carver St M16 ... 161 B5

Carver Wlk M15 162 F5
Carville Rd M9 65 B3
Carwood Gr BL6 22 D1
Cascade Dr M7 155 E5
Cash Gate Ct OL8 66 D3
Cashmere Rd SK3 123 C7
Cashmore Dr WN2 56 D4
Cashmore Wlk M12 164 E6
Caspian Rd WA14 119 A6
Cass Ave M5 161 A8
Cassandra Ct M5 161 C8
Cassidy Cl M4 159 B2
Cassidy Ct M5 96 E8
Cassidy Gdns M24 46 D4
Casson Gate OL12 14 E1
Casson St M35 83 F7
Casterton Way M28 78 A5
Castle Ave Denton M34 100 E2
Rochdale OL11 139 E6
Castle Cl M43 84 B2
Castle Cres BL6 22 C5
Castle Croft BL2 25 E3
Castle Ct Ashton-u-L OL6 85 B7
Bolton BL2 148 A7
Castle Dr PR7 20 E6
Castle Edge Rd SK22 127 B2
Castle Farm Dr SK2 124 B5
Castle Farm La SK2 124 C5
Castle Gr Leigh WN7 76 D6
Ramsbottom BL0 11 A2
Castle Hall Cl SK15 86 B1
Castle Hall Ct 11 SK15 86 A1
Castle Hall View 10 SK15 86 A1
Castle Hill Glossop SK13 104 E2
Newton-le-W WA12 89 E4
Castle Hill Com Prim Sch BL2 25 B2
Castle Hill Cres OL11 139 E6
Castle Hill Mobile Home Pk SK6 113 A6
Castle Hill Pk WN2 56 F7
Castle Hill Rd Bury BL9 28 D5
Hindley WN2 56 E6
Manchester M25 63 D2
Castle Hill Sch SK5 112 C6
Castle Hill St Bolton BL2 25 B2
Bolton BL2 25 B3
Castle Hill St Philip's CE Prim Sch WN2 56 F6
Castle House La PR7 20 E6
Castle Irwell Student Village M6,M7 81 B5
Castle L Ctr BL9 140 E2
Castle La OL5,SK15 86 F8
Castle Mews BL4 60 D7
Castle Mill La WA15 129 B5
Castle Rd BL9 45 C4
Castle Rise 4 WN2 56 E5
Castle Shaw Rd SK2 124 E5
Castle St Bolton BL2 148 A7
Bury BL9 140 E2
Eccles M30 79 F2
Farnworth BL4 60 D7
Hadfield SK13 104 A4
Hindley WN2 56 E6
Hyde SK14 167 F3
Manchester M3 162 E8
Middleton M24 65 D7
Ramsbottom BL9 11 D2
Stalybridge SK15 86 A1
Stockport SK3 170 D7
Stockport SK3 170 E8
Tyldesley M29 58 F1
Castle Terr SK15 86 F6
Castle Way M27 62 A3
Castle Wlk OL6 85 B7
Castle Yd SK1 169 F2
Castlebrook Cl BL9 45 B4
Castlebrook High Sch BL9 45 C3
Castlecroft Ave BL6 21 D2
Castlecroft Rd BL9 140 E3
Castledene Ave M6 154 E3
Castlefield Ave M7 155 E8
Castlefield Visitor Ctr M3 162 E8
Castleford Cl 9 BL1 145 D8
Castleford St OL1 48 C1
Castleford Wlk M21 109 D7
Castlemere Dr OL2 49 D8
Castlemere Rd M9 64 C3
Castlemere St OL11 139 E6
Castlemere Terr OL11 139 F6
Castlemill St OL1 67 B7
Castlemoor Ave M7 81 B8
Castlerea Cl M30 95 D8
Castlerigg Cl SK4 111 D7
Castlerigg Dr
Middleton M24 46 C2
Royton OL2 48 C6
Castleton Ave M32 96 B3
Castleton Bank 22 SK13 171 E1
Castleton Cres SK13 171 E1
Castleton Ct
13 Denton M34 113 A8
13 Tyldesley M29 58 F1
Castleton Dr SK6 134 F6
Castleton Gn 23 SK13 171 E1
Castleton Gr Ashton-u-L OL6 85 F6
21 Gamesley SK13 171 E1
Castleton Prim Sch OL11 30 D2
Castleton Rd
Hazel Grove SK7 124 E1
Manchester M7 155 E8
11 Manchester M7 63 E1
Royton OL16,OL2 48 D8
Castleton Rd S OL11 30 D3
Castleton St
Altrincham WA14 119 C7
Bolton BL2 25 B2
Oldham OL9 152 C6
Castleton Sta OL11 30 C2
Castleton Terr 24 SK13 171 E1
Castleton Way
14 Denton M34 113 A8
Wigan WN3 54 C2
Castleton Wlk 2 M11 160 F1
Castleway
Altrincham WA15 129 C7
Hindley WN2 56 F5
Hindley WN2 57 A5
Rochdale OL11 30 B1
Salford M6 154 E4
Castlewood Gdns SK2 124 C5
Castlewood Rd M7 81 A8
Castlewood Sq 3 BL2 25 C1
Catchdale Cl M9 64 C5
Catches Cl OL11 30 B8
Catches La OL11 14 B1
Cateaton St 2 Bury BL9 140 F3
Manchester M3,M4 158 F2
Caterham St M4 160 D1
Catesby Rd M16 97 D3
Catfield Wlk M15 162 D7
Catford Rd M23 120 F5
Cathedral App M3 158 F2
Cathedral Cl SK16 101 D6
Cathedral Gates M4 158 F2
Cathedral Rd OL9 48 A1
Cathedral St M4 158 F2
Catherine Ho SK4 110 F2
Catherine Rd
Altrincham WA14 119 C3
Manchester M8 63 E1
Romiley SK6 112 F2
Swinton M27 79 C7
Catherine St Bolton BL3 146 B2
Bury BL9 44 E6
Eccles M30 79 B3
Hazel Grove SK7 124 E3
Hyde SK14 167 D3
Leigh WN7 75 F6
Manchester M11 99 E7
8 Oldham OL4 67 E6
Wigan WN1 151 E8
Catherine St E BL6 22 B4
Catherine St W BL6 22 B5
Catherine Terr WN1 151 E8
Catherine Way WA12 89 B2
Catherston Cl 7 M16 97 E3
Cathrine St E M34 100 D3
Cathrine St W M34 100 D3
Catlow La 11 M4 159 A2
Catlow St M7 158 E4
Cato St BL0 11 A4
Caton Cl BL9 44 E8
Caton St OL16 139 F6
Catterall Cres BL2 25 E6
Catterick Ave
Manchester M20 110 C3
Sale M33 107 C2
Catterick Dr BL3 43 A3
Catterick Rd M20 110 C3
Catterwood Dr SK6 114 B2
Cattlin Way OL8 66 C2
Caunce Ave
Ashton-in-M WA12 89 C1
Golborne WA3 90 A7
Caunce Rd WN1 151 E8
Caunce St WN1 151 E8
Causeway Head BB4 1 A8
Causeway The
2 Altrincham WA14 119 D4
Oldham OL9 65 E5
Causewood Cl OL4 49 E4
Causey Dr M24 46 D3
Cavalier St M40 160 D2
Cavan Cl SK3 122 F7
Cavanagh Cl M13 164 D6
Cavannah Ct OL1 49 E3
Cavell St M1 159 B1
Cavell Way M5 81 A1
Cavendish Ave
Manchester M20 109 F6
Swinton M27 62 C3
Cavendish Ct
Manchester M7 63 D1
Manchester SK4 110 F2
Stretford M32 96 E4
Cavendish Dr WN3 54 D2
Cavendish Gdns
Bolton BL3 147 D3
Manchester M20 109 F6
Cavendish Gr M30 79 E3
Cavendish Mews SK9 137 A6
Cavendish Mill OL6 166 B2
Cavendish Pl
Droylsden M11 83 A2
Pendlebury M27 80 A8
Cavendish Rd
Altrincham WA14 119 C3
Eccles M30 79 E4
Hazel Grove SK7 133 E8
Manchester M20 109 F6
Manchester M25,M7 63 D1
Manchester SK4 110 F2
Rochdale OL11 30 E3
Stretford M32 96 E4
Swinton M28 79 B6
Urmston M41 95 E2
Cavendish Road Prim Sch M20 110 A5
Cavendish St
Ashton-u-L OL6 166 A2
Cavendish St *continued*
Leigh WN7 75 F7
Manchester M15 163 A6
3 Oldham OL8 153 E6
Cavendish Way OL1 48 C2
Cavenham Gr 7 BL1 144 C8
Cavenham Wlk M9 156 C7
Caversham Dr M9 157 E8
Cawdor Ave BL4 42 B2
Cawdor Ct BL4 42 C2
Cawdor Ho M30 95 D8
Cawdor Pl WA15 120 C6
Cawdor Rd M14 98 C1
Cawdor St Eccles M30 79 C1
Farnworth BL4 42 C1
Hindley WN2 56 E5
Leigh WN7 75 F4
Manchester M15 162 D7
Swinton M27 79 D8
Walkden M28 60 E2
2 Wigan WN5 54 F6
Cawdor Wlk 6 BL4 42 C2
Cawley Ave Culcheth WA3 91 E4
Prestwich M25 62 F2
Cawley Terr M9 64 A5
Cawood Sq SK5 112 C6
Cawston Wlk 10 M8 156 A6
Caxton Cl WN3 54 F2
Caxton Rd M14 110 B8
Caxton St Heywood OL10 29 D2
Manchester M3 158 E2
Rochdale OL11 30 C1
Caxton Way M5,M6 81 B1
Caygill St M3 158 E2
Cayley St OL16 31 B7
Caythorpe St M14 98 A3
Cayton St M12 99 A3
CE Sch of the Resurrection M11 160 F1
Ceal The SK6 114 B2
Cecil Ave Sale M33 107 F3
Wigan WN6 37 A2
Cecil Ct SK3 170 E7
Cecil Dr M41 94 E2
Cecil Gr M18 99 D5
Cecil Rd Altrincham WA15 119 E2
Eccles M30 79 E1
Manchester M9 64 D5
Stretford M32 96 C1
Cecil St Ashton-u-L OL7 166 A1
Ashton-u-L OL7 84 F1
Bolton BL2 148 B7
Bury BL9 140 F1
Dukinfield SK16 101 C8
Ince-in-M WN3 55 E4
Leigh WN7 76 A4
Littleborough OL15 15 F5
Manchester M15 163 B5
Mossley OL5 86 C8
Oldham OL8 153 E5
Rochdale OL11 139 F5
Royton OL2 48 C4
Stalybridge SK15 86 B1
Walkden M28 60 D3
Wigan WN1 151 E8
Cecil Walker Ho M31 106 A3
Cecil Wlk 7 OL7 166 A1
Cecilia St BL3 42 A4
Cedar Ave
Altrincham WA14 119 C4
Ashton-u-L OL6 85 D5
Atherton M46 58 B4
Golborne WA3 90 F7
Golborne WA3 91 A7
Hazel Grove SK7 124 E2
Heywood OL10 29 C3
Hindley WN2 56 F3
Horwich BL6 22 E1
Little Lever BL3 43 B2
Stalybridge SK15 86 C3
Standish WN6 36 F8
Whitefield M45 62 F6
Cedar Bank Cl OL16 31 D7
Cedar Cl Glossop SK13 104 B2
Poynton SK12 133 E3
Cedar Cres
Newton-le-W WA12 89 D2
Oldham OL9 152 B8
Ramsbottom BL0 138 C7
Cedar Ct
2 Altrincham WA15 120 B5
Culcheth WA3 91 F1
Manchester M14 98 C1
Cedar Dr Droylsden M43 84 C2
Kearsley M27 61 D4
Urmston M41 95 C1
Wigan WN1 37 D2
Cedar Gr Denton M34 100 E3
Downall Green WN4 72 D5
Farnworth BL4 60 B8
Manchester M14 110 D8
Manchester SK4 111 C5
Orrell WN5 53 F6
Prestwich M25 63 A6
Royton OL2 48 D6
Shaw OL2 149 B6
Stalybridge SK16 101 F8
Westhoughton BL5 57 E7
Cedar Ho 11 M14 98 E4
Cedar La Newhey OL16 32 A3
Uppermill OL4 68 D6
Cedar Lo SK7 132 F7
Cedar Mews OL7 85 B5
Cedar Pl M7 81 C4
Cedar Rd Altrincham WA15 119 E3
Failsworth M35 83 F6
Gatley SK8 122 A5
Leigh WN7 75 E8
Cedar Rd *continued*
Marple SK6 125 E4
Middleton M24 65 C8
Partington M31 105 E3
Sale M33 107 D6
Stockport SK2 124 B4
Cedar St Ashton-u-L OL6 85 D4
Bury BL9 141 A3
Bury BL9 141 B3
Dukinfield SK14 101 E5
Newton-le-W WA12 89 C2
4 Oldham OL4 67 C7
Rochdale OL12 14 F1
Walsden OL14 6 A8
Cedarfield Rd WA13 117 B4
Cedars Rd M22 121 D3
Cedarway SK9 136 F5
Cedarwood Ave SK4 168 A1
Cedric Rd Manchester M8 63 E2
Oldham OL4 67 C7
Cedric St M5 154 E2
Celandine Cl OL15 15 F6
Celandine Wlk WN3 54 B4
Celia St M8 156 C8
Cellini Sq BL1 143 D1
Celtic St SK1 124 A8
Cemetery La BL9 45 A7
Cemetery Rd Bolton BL2 148 B7
Bolton BL3,BL4 42 F1
Denton M34 100 F1
Denton M34 100 F6
Droylsden M43 83 F1
Failsworth M35 83 F6
Glossop SK13 104 C4
Ince-in-M WN3 151 E5
Mossley OL5 86 E8
Radcliffe M26 43 F4
Ramsbottom BL0 11 A4
Royton OL2 48 C5
Salford M5 154 E1
Cemetery Rd N M27 61 E2
Cemetery Rd S M27 61 E1
Cemetery St Middleton M24 47 A1
2 Westhoughton BL5 39 E1
Cemetery View PR7 21 A6
Cennick Cl 5 OL4 67 C6
Centaur Cl M27 61 F2
Centaur Way 2 M8 155 F7
Centenary Circ M5 80 B1
Centenary Ct BL3 147 F4
Centenary Way Eccles M17 96 B8
Eccles M5 80 A1
Central Ave Atherton M46 58 E4
Bury BL9 44 D7
Eccles M41 95 E6
Edenfield BL0 1 D2
Farnworth BL4 60 B8
Leigh WN7 76 C3
Littleborough OL15 16 B6
Manchester M19 99 A1
Oldham OL3 69 B5
Pendlebury M6 80 E6
Sale M33 107 D1
Swinton M27 62 D2
Walkden M28 60 C5
Central CE Prim Sch M29 59 A1
Central Dr Bury BL9 27 F8
Gatley SK8 131 D8
Manchester M8 64 B1
Pendlebury M27 80 B7
Reddish SK5 111 F5
Romiley SK6 113 C3
Shevington WN6 36 B6
Stockport SK7 123 D2
Urmston M41 95 E2
Westhoughton BL5 39 F1
Central Flats WN2 151 F7
Central Ho 17 M9 64 E5
Central Park Est M17 96 B6
Central Park Way WN1 37 D1
Central Prim Sch
Denton M34 100 E3
Leigh WN7 75 F5
Central Rd
Manchester M20 110 A5
Partington M31 105 F3
Central Ret Pk M4 159 C1
Central St Bolton BL1 145 E7
Manchester M2 158 F1
Ramsbottom BL0 138 C6
Central Store 6 SK13 104 C1
Central Way
Altrincham WA14 119 D4
Newton-le-W WA12 89 E2
Centre Ct WN7 75 B1
Centre Gdns BL1 143 D1
Centre Park Rd BL1 143 D1
Centre The WN7 76 E6
Centre Vale OL15 16 C7
Centre Vale Cl OL15 16 C7
Centrepoint M17 96 B5
Centurion Gr M7 155 E6
Century Lo BL4 60 C8
Century Park Ind Area WA14 119 A6
Century St M3 162 E8
Cestrian St BL3 147 F3
Ceylon St Failsworth M40 83 A6
Oldham OL4 67 D5
Chadderton Dr BL9 45 A2
Chadderton Hall Com Prim Sch OL9 48 A2
Chadderton Hall Rd OL1,OL9 47 F1
Chadderton Ind Est M24 65 C5
Chadderton Park Rd OL9 47 F1
Chadderton Prec OL9 152 B7
Chadderton St M4 159 B2
Chadderton Way
Oldham OL1,OL9 153 D8
Oldham OL1,OL9 48 C1
Chaddesley Wlk M11 165 A8
Chaddock La
Boothstown M28 77 F6
Tyldesley M28,M29 77 D6
Chaddock Level The M28 78 A5
Chadkirk SK6 125 B8
Chadkirk Chap SK6 113 C1
Chadkirk Rd SK6 113 B1
Chadvil Rd SK8 122 C5
Chadwell Rd SK2 124 E7
Chadwick Cl
Handforth SK9 131 C1
12 Manchester M14 98 B3
Milnrow OL16 32 A5
Chadwick Fold Bury BL9 27 F7
Heywood OL10 29 F2
Chadwick Foundary Ind Est 9 BL1 145 E8
Chadwick Hall Rd OL11 30 B6
Chadwick La
Rochdale OL10,OL11 30 A2
Rochdale OL16 31 C2
Chadwick Rd Eccles M30 79 E2
Urmston M41 95 F2
Chadwick St Ashton-u-L OL6 85 E2
Bolton BL2 148 B6
Bury BL9 28 E4
Glossop SK13 116 B8
2 Hindley WN2 56 E6
Leigh WN7 75 F6
Little Lever BL3 43 B3
Marple SK6 125 F5
Milnrow OL16 31 D7
Rochdale OL11 139 D7
Stockport SK1 170 F8
Swinton M27 79 F8
Wigan WN3 150 B6
Chadwick Terr OL12 14 D4
Chaffinch Cl Droylsden M43 84 C3
Oldham OL4 67 D4
Wythenshawe M22 121 F5
Chaffinch Dr BL9 141 C4
Chaffinch Gr SK15 86 E7
Chain Bar La SK14 102 F2
Chain Bar Way SK14 102 F2
Chain Rd M9 64 D5
Chain St M1 159 A1
Chain Wlk 16 M9 64 E5
Chainhurst Wlk 2 M13 163 C6
Chalbury Cl WN2 56 D4
Chalcombe Grange 1 M12 98 F4
Chale Cl M40 160 D3
Chale Dr M24 65 C6
Chale Gn BL2 25 E3
Chalfont Ave 1 M41 95 E2
Chalfont Cty Prim Sch BL1 143 F2
Chalfont Dr
Manchester M8 156 A7
Tyldesley M29 77 A8
Walkden M28 78 E8
Chalfont Ho 2 M6 154 F2
Chalfont St BL1 143 F2
Chalford Rd M23 121 A4
Challenge Way WN5 36 D1
Challenor Sq M12 165 A6
Challum Dr OL9 152 A8
Chamber Hall Cl OL8 66 D4
Chamber House Dr OL11 30 B3
Chamber House Farm OL11 30 A3
Chamber Rd Oldham OL8 66 D4
Shaw OL2 149 A7
Chamberhall St BL9 140 E3
Chamberlain Ho M22 121 E4
Chamberlain Rd SK15 86 C5
Chamberlain St BL3 145 D6
Chambers Ct SK14 103 A3
Chambers Field Ct
Salford M5 161 A8
8 Salford M5 81 A1
Champagnole Ct 9 SK16 166 B1
Champneys Wlk M9 157 D6
Chancel Ave M5 161 C8
Chancel Cl SK16 101 C6
Chancel La SK9 137 B8
Chancel Mews SK1 112 A1
Chancel Pl
11 Manchester M1 159 C1
Rochdale OL16 139 F7
Chancellor La M12 164 D7
Chancery Cl M29 77 B8
Chancery La Bolton BL1 145 F7
16 Manchester M3 158 F1
Shaw OL2 149 C7
Uppermill OL3 51 A2
Chancery Pl 17 M3 158 F1
Chancery St Oldham OL4 67 C6
Oldham OL9 152 C8
Chancery Wlk OL9 152 C8
Chandler Way WA3 90 E8
Chandlers Row M28 79 A5
Chandley Ct SK1 124 A7
Chandley St SK8 122 D6
Chandos Gr M5 154 D2
Chandos Rd
Manchester M21 97 C1
Manchester M25 63 B2
Manchester SK4 111 C6
Chandos Rd S M21 109 C8
Chandos St OL2 149 C7
Change Way M3 158 E3
Channing Ct 15 OL16 31 B6
Channing Sq 25 OL16 31 B6

Channing St OL16 . . . . .31 B6
Chanters Ave M46 . . . . .58 E3
Chanters The M28 . . . . .78 C7
Chantlers Ave BL8 . . . . .27 A1
Chantlers Prim Sch BL8 . .27 A2
Chantry Cl Disley SK12 . . .135 E5
Reddish SK5 . . . . .111 E7
Westhoughton BL5 . . . . .57 F5
Chantry Fold SK12 . . . . . .135 E6
Chantry Rd SK12 . . . . .135 E6
Chantry Wlk
Ashton-in-M WN4 . . . . .72 F5
■14 Manchester M8 . . . . . . .155 F7
Chapel Alley ■2 BL1 . . . . . .145 F7
Chapel Brow
Charlesworth SK13 . . . . . . .115 C6
Tintwistle SK13 . . . . .104 A7
Chapel Cl Dukinfield SK16 .101 D8
Ince-in-M WN3 . . . . .151 D6
Whitefield BL9 . . . . .45 B4
Chapel Croft OL2 . . . . .48 D4
Chapel Ct
Altrincham WA14 . . . . .119 D4
Hyde SK14 . . . . .101 C1
■5 Mossley OL5 . . . . .68 C1
Sale M33 . . . . .107 E6
Wilmslow SK9 . . . . .137 A6
Chapel Dr
Altrincham WA15 . . . . .129 C7
Ashton-u-L OL6 . . . . .85 E5
Chapel Field Rd M34 . . . . .100 F3
Chapel Fields Edgworth BL7 .9 C4
■1 Marple SK6 . . . . .125 F5
Chapel Fields La WN2 . . . .56 E5
Chapel Gate OL16 . . . . .31 F6
Chapel Gdns M34 . . . . .100 F3
Chapel Gn M34 . . . . .100 F3
Chapel Gr M41 . . . . .95 E2
Chapel Grange BL7 . . . . .9 C4
Chapel Green Rd WN2 . . . .56 E5
Chapel Hill OL15 . . . . .16 B5
Chapel Hos SK6 . . . . .126 A5
Chapel La
Altrincham WA15 . . . . .129 C7
Coppull PR7 . . . . .19 E8
Hadfield SK13 . . . . .103 F5
Hollinfare WA3 . . . . .105 A2
Manchester M9 . . . . .64 C3
Partington M31 . . . . .105 F2
Ramsbottom BL8 . . . . .138 A6
Rochdale OL11 . . . . .29 C8
Royton OL2 . . . . .48 D4
Sale M33 . . . . .107 E6
Wigan WN1,WN3 . . . . .150 C7
Wilmslow SK9 . . . . .137 A6
Chapel Mdw M28 . . . . .78 B7
Chapel Pl Ashton-in-M WN4 .73 B3
Bolton BL2,BL3 . . . . .148 C5
Eccles M41 . . . . .95 D4
Chapel Rd
Alderley Edge SK9 . . . . . . .137 A1
Irlam M44 . . . . .94 A2
Manchester M25 . . . . .63 A1
Oldham OL3 . . . . .69 A6
Oldham OL8 . . . . .67 B5
Sale M33 . . . . .108 B5
Swinton M27 . . . . .79 C7
Wythenshawe M23 . . . . . . .121 D8
Chapel St Adlington PR7 . . .20 F6
■6 Alderley Edge SK9 . . . . .137 A1
Ashton-in-M WN4 . . . . .73 B3
Ashton-u-L OL6 . . . . .166 C3
Aspull WN2 . . . . .38 A2
Atherton M46 . . . . .58 D3
■14 Bacup OL13 . . . . .3 C8
Blackrod BL6 . . . . .21 D2
Bolton BL1 . . . . .145 F8
Bolton BL7 . . . . .8 D3
Boothstown M28 . . . . .77 F6
Bury BL8 . . . . .26 F7
Bury BL9 . . . . .140 F2
Cheadle SK8 . . . . .122 D5
Denton M34 . . . . .100 F6
Droylsden M43 . . . . .84 B1
Dukinfield SK16 . . . . .101 B8
■3 Eccles M30 . . . . .79 C1
Farnworth BL4 . . . . .60 E8
Glossop SK13 . . . . .104 C1
Hazel Grove SK7 . . . . .124 E3
Heywood OL10 . . . . .29 D2
Hindley WN2 . . . . .56 D5
Horwich BL6 . . . . .22 C3
Hyde SK14 . . . . .167 D2
Ince-in-M WN3 . . . . .151 D6
Kearsley M26 . . . . .61 B8
Leigh WN2 . . . . .56 E1
Leigh WN7 . . . . .76 B4
Little Lever BL3 . . . . .43 B3
Littleborough OL12 . . . . . . .15 C7
Littleborough OL15 . . . . .6 D2
Manchester M19 . . . . .99 B1
Manchester M3 . . . . .158 E2
Manchester SK4 . . . . .110 D2
■7 Middleton M24 . . . . .46 F1
■6 Mossley OL5 . . . . .68 C1
Newton-le-W WA12 . . . . . . .89 B3
Oldham OL3 . . . . .69 B8
Oldham OL4 . . . . .67 E6
Platt Bridge WN2 . . . . .56 B2
Prestwich M25 . . . . .63 A4
■10 Rochdale OL11 . . . . . . .31 A4
Romiley SK6 . . . . .113 B6
Rowarth SK22 . . . . .127 E7
Royton OL2 . . . . .48 D4
Shaw OL2 . . . . .149 B7
Stalybridge SK15 . . . . .86 A2
Swinton M27 . . . . .62 A1
Tyldesley M29 . . . . .77 A8

Chapel St continued
Whitworth OL12 . . . . .14 C8
Wigan WN3 . . . . .150 C2
Wigan WN5 . . . . .54 B5
Wigan WN5 . . . . .54 B6
Chapel Street Prim Sch
M19 . . . . .99 B1
Chapel Terr WA3 . . . . .91 B8
Chapel View SK16 . . . . . . .101 C8
Chapel Way PR7 . . . . .19 F8
Chapel Wlk ■1 Eccles M30 . .79 F2
Golborne WN7 . . . . .75 B1
Hadfield SK13 . . . . .103 F5
Manchester M25 . . . . .62 F1
Middleton M24 . . . . .64 C7
Whitefield M45 . . . . .45 B1
Chapel Wlks Bramhall SK8 132 B6
Manchester M2 . . . . .158 F1
Sale M33 . . . . .108 B5
Chapelfield M26 . . . . .44 C1
Chapelfield Cl SK15 . . . . . . .86 D4
Chapelfield Dr M28 . . . . . . .60 B3
Chapelfield Prim Sch M26 44 C1
Chapelfield Rd M12 . . . . . .163 C8
Chapelfield St BL1 . . . . . . .143 E3
Chapelhill Dr M9 . . . . .64 C3
Chapelstead BL5 . . . . .57 F5
Chapeltown Rd
Edgworth BL7 . . . . .9 C2
Radcliffe M26 . . . . .62 A8
Chapeltown St M1 . . . . . . .159 C1
Chapelway Gdns OL2 . . . . .48 D6
Chaplin Cl M6 . . . . .154 E4
Chapman Ct SK14 . . . . . . .102 D2
Chapman Mews M18 . . . . . .99 D5
Chapman Rd SK14 . . . . . . .102 E1
Chapman St Bolton BL1 . . .142 B1
Manchester M18 . . . . .99 D5
Chappell Rd M43 . . . . .84 A2
Chapter St M40 . . . . .160 F4
Charcoal Rd WA14 . . . . . . .118 F3
Charcoal Woods WA14 . . . .118 F4
Charcon Wlk ■3 OL2 . . . . .48 E4
Chard Dr M22 . . . . .121 D1
Chard St M26 . . . . .44 A3
Chardin Ave SK6 . . . . .126 C8
Charges St OL7 . . . . .84 F1
Chariot St M11 . . . . .99 D8
Charity St WN7 . . . . .75 C5
Charlbury Ave
Manchester M25 . . . . .63 E3
Reddish SK5 . . . . .111 F6
Charlbury Way OL2 . . . . . .149 A5
Charlecote Rd SK12 . . . . . .133 F4
Charles Ave
Droylsden M34 . . . . .100 A4
Marple SK6 . . . . .125 C7
Charles Barry Cres M15 .162 E6
Charles Ct WA15 . . . . .120 B6
Charles Halle Rd M15 . . . .163 A5
Charles Holden St BL1 . . .145 D8
Charles La Glossop SK13 . .104 E3
Milnrow OL16 . . . . .32 A5
Charles Mews OL16 . . . . . .32 A5
Charles Morris Cl M35 . . . .84 B8
Charles Morris Ho M35 . . .84 A7
Charles Shaw Cl ■4 OL4 . . .49 D1
Charles St Ashton-u-L OL7 .166 B3
■2 Bolton BL1 . . . . .148 A8
Bolton BL1 . . . . .8 D2
■5 Bury BL9 . . . . .140 F3
Denton M34 . . . . .100 F5
Droylsden M43 . . . . .83 E1
Dukinfield SK16 . . . . .166 B1
■3 Farnworth BL4 . . . . .42 E1
Glossop SK13 . . . . .104 C1
Golborne WA3 . . . . .74 A1
Hazel Grove SK7 . . . . .124 D3
Heywood OL10 . . . . .46 E8
Hindley WN2 . . . . .56 E7
Ince-in-M WN2 . . . . .56 A7
Irlam M44 . . . . .105 E6
Leigh WN7 . . . . .76 A5
Leigh WN7 . . . . .76 A6
Littleborough OL15 . . . . . . .16 A5
Manchester M1 . . . . .163 A8
Oldham OL9 . . . . .152 C6
Royton OL2 . . . . .48 D4
Salford M6 . . . . .154 F4
Stockport SK1 . . . . .124 A7
Swinton M27 . . . . .61 D2
Tyldesley M29 . . . . .58 F1
Whitefield M45 . . . . .62 F7
■2 Wigan WN1 . . . . .37 C1
Charles Whittaker St ■2
OL12 . . . . .13 F1
Charles Wlk M45 . . . . .62 F7
Charleston Cl M33 . . . . . . .107 D2
Charleston Ct SK15 . . . . . . .86 D4
Charleston Prim Sch M6 . .81 B4
Charleston Sq M41 . . . . . . .95 B3
Charleston St OL6 . . . . .66 F4
Charlestown SK13 . . . . . . .116 C7
Charlestown Cl OL6 . . . . . .166 B3
Charlestown Ct OL6 . . . . . .166 B4
Charlestown Ind Est OL6 166 B4
Charlestown Prim Sch
M9 . . . . .65 B3
Charlestown Rd
Glossop SK13 . . . . .116 C7
Manchester M9 . . . . .64 D2
Charlestown Rd E SK2 . . .124 A3
Charlestown Rd W SK3 . . .123 F3
Charlesworth Ave
Bolton BL3 . . . . .42 B3
Denton M34 . . . . .112 F4
Hindley WN2 . . . . .56 F4

Charlesworth Sch
Charlesworth SK13 . . . . . . .115 C6
Charlesworth SK13 . . . . . . .115 D6
Charlesworth St
Manchester M11 . . . . .164 F8
Stockport SK1,SK3 . . . . . . .170 F7
Charley Ave M7 . . . . .158 D4
Charlock Ave BL5 . . . . .57 E6
Charlock Cl WN7 . . . . .75 F3
Charlock Sq WA14 . . . . . . .119 B8
Charlock Wlk ■6 M31 . . . .105 F3
Charlotte La OL4 . . . . .68 E5
Charlotte St ■28 Bolton BL1 143 E2
Cheadle SK8 . . . . .122 D5
Edgworth BL7 . . . . .9 C4
Manchester M1,M2 . . . . . . .159 A1
Ramsbottom BL0 . . . . .138 B5
Rochdale OL16 . . . . .31 B3
Stockport SK1 . . . . .112 B3
Charlton Ave Eccles M30 . . .79 D1
Hyde SK14 . . . . .102 A4
Prestwich M25 . . . . .63 B3
Charlton Brook Ho SK8 . .122 E6
Charlton Ct ■2 M16 . . . . . . .97 C3
Charlton Dr Sale M33 . . . . .108 C4
Swinton M27 . . . . .61 D2
Charlton Pl M12 . . . . .163 B7
Charlton Rd M19 . . . . .99 B1
Charlton Sh Ctr M21 . . . . .97 B1
Charminster Dr M8 . . . . . .156 B8
Charmouth Wlk M22 . . . . .121 F3
Charnley Cl M40 . . . . .160 E3
Charnley St M45 . . . . .62 F8
Charnock Dr BL1 . . . . .143 E1
Charnock Rd WA3 . . . . .91 F3
Charnock St WN2 . . . . .56 B1
Charnock's Yd ■2 WN5 . . .54 B5
Charnville Rd SK8 . . . . . . .121 F5
Charnwood Ave M34 . . . . .100 B3
Charnwood Cl
Ashton-u-L OL6 . . . . .85 C7
Shaw OL2 . . . . .48 E8
Tyldesley M29 . . . . .77 B8
Walkden M28 . . . . .60 C2
Charnwood Cres SK7 . . . .133 D8
Charnwood Rd
Manchester M9 . . . . .64 D5
Romiley SK6 . . . . .113 C5
Charter Ave M26 . . . . .44 C2
Charter Cl ■5 M33 . . . . . . .107 D3
Charter Ho M30 . . . . .79 F1
Charter Rd WA15 . . . . .119 E4
Charter St Manchester M3 .158 F3
Oldham OL1 . . . . .67 A8
Rochdale OL16 . . . . .31 B4
Charterhouse Rd WN3 . . .151 E6
Chartist Ho SK14 . . . . .167 E2
Chartwell Cl M5,M6 . . . . . .154 F2
Chartwell Dr M23 . . . . . . .120 E7
Chase St M4 . . . . .159 A3
Chase The M28 . . . . .79 A5
Chasefield WA14 . . . . .119 A2
Chaseley Rd
Rochdale OL12 . . . . .139 E8
Salford M6 . . . . .154 E4
Chasetown Cl ■5 M23 . . . .120 D6
Chassen Ave M41 . . . . .95 B2
Chassen Rd Bolton BL1 . . .144 B7
Urmston M41 . . . . .95 B1
Chassen Road Sta M41 . . .95 B1
Chataway Rd M8 . . . . .156 C8
Chatburn Ave
Golborne WA3 . . . . .74 C1
Middleton M24 . . . . .47 D8
Chatburn Ct Culcheth WA3 .91 F2
Shaw OL2 . . . . .149 C8
Chatburn Gdns OL10 . . . . .28 F2
Chatburn Rd Bolton BL1 . . .23 F3
Manchester M21 . . . . .109 C8
Chatburn Sq OL11 . . . . . . .47 D8
Chatcombe Rd M22 . . . . . .121 A2
Chatfield Rd M21 . . . . .109 B8
Chatford Cl M7 . . . . .158 E4
Chatham Ct M20 . . . . .110 A3
Chatham Gdns BL3 . . . . . .145 D5
Chatham Gr M20 . . . . .110 A6
Chatham Ho ■1 SK3 . . . . .170 E8
Chatham Pl ■2 BL3 . . . . . .145 D5
Chatham Rd
Manchester M16 . . . . .97 C3
Reddish M18 . . . . .99 E3
Chatham St Hyde SK14 . . .113 E4
Ince-in-M WN2 . . . . .56 A8
Leigh WN7 . . . . .75 F7
Manchester M1 . . . . .159 B1
Stockport SK3 . . . . .170 D8
Wigan WN1 . . . . .151 E7
Chatley Rd M30 . . . . .78 F1
Chatley St M3,M4 . . . . . . .159 A4
Chatswood Ave SK2 . . . . .170 F6
Chatsworth Ave
Culcheth WA3 . . . . .91 F4
Ince-in-M WN3 . . . . .55 F4
Prestwich M25 . . . . .63 B4
Chatsworth Cl
Altrincham WA15 . . . . .120 C5
Ashton-in-M WN4 . . . . .72 C4
Droylsden M43 . . . . .83 E3
Shaw OL2 . . . . .49 D8
■2 Urmston M41 . . . . .95 E2
Chatsworth Ct
Adlington PR7 . . . . .20 E8
Stockport SK2 . . . . .124 A5
Chatsworth Dr Leigh WN7 .76 D7
Leigh WN7 . . . . .76 D7

Chatsworth Gr
Little Lever BL3 . . . . .43 A4
Manchester M16 . . . . .97 C2
Chatsworth Rd
Droylsden M43 . . . . .83 E2
Eccles M30 . . . . .79 F4
Hazel Grove SK7 . . . . .133 F8
High Lane SK6 . . . . .134 F6
Manchester M18 . . . . .165 C5
Radcliffe M26 . . . . .43 D5
Stretford M32 . . . . .96 A3
Swinton M27 . . . . .79 C5
Wilmslow SK9 . . . . .136 E4
Chatsworth St Oldham OL4 .67 C5
Rochdale OL16 . . . . .14 E3
Wigan WN5 . . . . .54 C5
Chatteris Cl WN3 . . . . .54 C2
Chatterton BL0 . . . . .1 C2
Chatterton Cl M20 . . . . . . .110 C6
Chatterton La SK6 . . . . . . .127 B6
Chatterton Old La BL0 . . . . .1 C1
Chatterton Rd BL0 . . . . .1 C1
Chattock Cl M16 . . . . .97 E3
Chatton Cl BL8 . . . . .26 F2
Chatwell Ct OL16 . . . . .32 C4
Chatwood Rd M40 . . . . .65 D2
Chaucer Ave Denton M34 . .113 A7
Droylsden M43 . . . . .84 A1
Radcliffe M26 . . . . .43 E4
Reddish SK5 . . . . .99 D1
Chaucer Gr Atherton M46 . .58 D5
Leigh WN7 . . . . .75 D8
Chaucer Mews SK1 . . . . . .112 B1
Chaucer Pl Abram WN2 . . . .56 B1
Wigan WN1 . . . . .37 C3
Chaucer Rd M24 . . . . .47 B2
Chaucer Rise SK16 . . . . . .102 A7
Chaucer St Bolton BL1 . . . .143 D2
Oldham OL1 . . . . .153 E6
Rochdale OL11 . . . . .30 C2
Royton OL2 . . . . .48 E5
Chaucer Wlk M13 . . . . . . .163 C6
Chaumont Way OL6 . . . . . .166 B3
Chauncy Rd M40 . . . . .83 E8
Chaytor Ave M40 . . . . .83 B7
Cheadle Ave M7 . . . . .81 A7
Cheadle Coll SK8 . . . . .132 B7
Cheadle Heath Jun
& Inf Sch SK3 . . . . .123 A7
Cheadle Hulme Sch SK8 .132 A8
Cheadle Hulme Sta SK8 . .123 D7
Cheadle Old Rd SK3 . . . . .123 C7
Cheadle Prim Sch SK8 . . .122 D6
Cheadle RC Inf Sch SK8 . .122 E2
Cheadle RC Jun Sch SK8 .122 E2
Cheadle Rd SK8 . . . . .122 F3
Cheadle Royal Hospl
SK8 . . . . .122 C2
Cheadle Sq BL1 . . . . .145 E7
Cheadle St M11 . . . . .99 D8
Cheadle Wood SK8 . . . . . . .131 E8
Cheam Rd WA15 . . . . .119 F8
Cheap Side M24 . . . . .47 A2
Cheapside Hyde SK14 . . . .167 E3
Manchester M2 . . . . .158 F1
Oldham OL1 . . . . .153 E7
Cheapside Sq ■8 BL1 . . . .145 F7
Cheddar St ■1 M18 . . . . . . .99 D5
Chedlee Dr SK8 . . . . .131 E8
Chedlin Dr M23 . . . . .121 A3
Chedworth Cres M38 . . . . .60 A6
Chedworth Dr M23 . . . . . .121 B6
Chedworth Gr BL3 . . . . . . .145 E5
Cheeryble St M11,M43 . . . .99 F7
Cheesden Wlk M45 . . . . . . .45 C1
Cheetham Ave M24 . . . . . . .47 B1
Cheetham CE Com Sch
M8 . . . . .155 F7
Cheetham Fold Rd SK14 . .113 D8
Cheetham Gdns ■6 SK15 . .86 B1
Cheetham Gr ■1 WN3 . . . . .54 F5
Cheetham Hill Shaw OL2 . .149 B6
Whitworth OL12 . . . . .4 D3
Cheetham Hill Rd
Dukinfield SK15,SK16 . . . .101 E7
Manchester M4,M8 . . . . . . .159 A3
Manchester M8 . . . . .156 A6
Cheetham Par M8 . . . . . . .155 F8
Cheetham Pl SK6 . . . . .112 F4
Cheetham Rd M27 . . . . . . .80 A7
Cheetham St
Failsworth M35 . . . . .84 A8
Manchester M40 . . . . .157 E5
Middleton M24 . . . . .64 F8
Oldham OL1 . . . . .67 B7
Radcliffe M26 . . . . .44 C4
Rochdale OL16 . . . . .139 F8
Shaw OL2 . . . . .149 C6
Cheetham's Cres OL2 . . . . .49 A4
Cheethams The BL6 . . . . . .38 E7
Cheetwood Prim Sch M8 158 A4
Cheetwood Rd M8 . . . . . . .155 F5
Cheetwood St M8 . . . . . . .158 A4
Chelbourne Dr ■3 OL8 . . . .66 B2
Chelburn Cl Leigh WN2 . . . .56 E1
Stockport SK2 . . . . .124 D5
Chelburn View OL15 . . . . . . .6 C1
Cheldon Wlk ■8 M40 . . . . .83 C6
Chelford Ave Bolton BL1 . . .24 E5
Golborne WA3 . . . . .90 D8
Chelford Cl
Altrincham WA15 . . . . .119 E6
Manchester M13 . . . . .164 D5
Middleton M24 . . . . .47 C2
Wigan WN3 . . . . .54 F2
Chelford Ct ■2 SK9 . . . . . .131 E5
Chelford Dr Swinton M27 . .61 E2
Tyldesley M29 . . . . .77 C6

Cha–Che 191

Chelford Gr SK3 . . . . .170 D5
Chelford Rd
Alderley Edge SK9 . . . . . . .136 E1
Handforth SK9 . . . . .131 D5
Manchester M16 . . . . .97 C3
Sale M33 . . . . .108 E2
Chell St K3 . . . . .98 F4
Chellow Ct OL5 . . . . .68 B1
Chellow Dene OL5 . . . . .68 B1
Chelmarsh Ave WN4 . . . . . .73 C3
Chelmer Cl BL5 . . . . .40 A1
Chelmer Gr OL10 . . . . .29 A3
Chelmorton Gr WN3 . . . . . .54 C2
Chelmsford Ave M40 . . . . . .83 B4
Chelmsford Dr WN3 . . . . . .55 A4
Chelmsford Mews WN1 . . .37 C2
Chelmsford Rd SK3 . . . . . .123 C8
Chelmsford St OL8 . . . . . . .153 E5
Chelmsford Wlk ■14 M34 .101 A1
Chelsea Ave M26 . . . . .43 D4
Chelsea Cl OL2 . . . . .149 B7
Chelsea Rd Bolton BL3 . . . .147 D3
Failsworth M40 . . . . .83 C5
Urmston M41 . . . . .94 C1
Chelsea St Bury BL9 . . . . . .44 F4
Rochdale OL11 . . . . .139 D5
Chelsfield Gr M21 . . . . . . .109 D8
Chelston Ave M40 . . . . .65 D2
Chelston Dr Gatley SK8 . . .131 C6
Haslingden BB4 . . . . .1 A7
Chelt Wlk M22 . . . . .121 B2
Cheltenham Ave Bury BL9 .151 D5
Cheltenham Cres M7 . . . . .155 E7
Cheltenham Dr
Longshaw WN5 . . . . .53 D2
Newton-le-W WA12 . . . . . . .89 C5
Sale M33 . . . . .108 C4
Cheltenham Gn M24 . . . . . .65 A6
Cheltenham Rd
Cheadle SK3 . . . . .123 A7
Manchester M21 . . . . .97 B2
Middleton M24 . . . . .65 A6
Cheltenham St Oldham OL1 49 B1
Rochdale OL11 . . . . .30 D4
Salford M6 . . . . .81 A4
■3 Wigan WN2 . . . . .37 F2
Chelwood Cl BL1 . . . . .24 D7
Chelwood Dr M43 . . . . .83 F2
Chelwood Pk WA12 . . . . . . .73 B1
Chelworth Manor SK7 . . . .123 C1
Chemical St WA12 . . . . .89 B3
Chemist St BL1 . . . . .143 F1
Chendre Rd M9 . . . . .65 B3
Cheney Cl M11 . . . . .99 D7
Chepstow Ave M33 . . . . . .107 C3
Chepstow Cl OL11 . . . . . . .29 F8
Chepstow Dr
Hazel Grove SK7 . . . . .125 A2
Oldham OL1 . . . . .49 B1
Chepstow Gr WN7 . . . . .76 D7
Chepstow Rd
Manchester M21 . . . . .97 A1
Swinton M27 . . . . .62 D3
Chepstow St M1,M2 . . . . . .162 F8
Chepstow St S M1 . . . . . . .162 F8
Chequers Rd M21 . . . . . . .109 B8
Chequers St WN1 . . . . .150 B8
Cherington Cl
Handforth SK9 . . . . .131 F3
Wythenshawe M23 . . . . . . .109 B2
Cherington Dr M29 . . . . . . .59 C1
Cherington Rd SK8 . . . . . .122 C4
Cheriton Ave M33 . . . . . . .108 C5
Cheriton Cl SK14 . . . . .102 D2
Cheriton Dr BL2 . . . . .42 E6
Cheriton Gdns BL6 . . . . . . .22 B5
Cheriton Rd M41 . . . . .94 D3
Cheriton Rise SK2 . . . . . . .125 A6
Cherrington Dr OL11 . . . . .47 D8
Cherry Ave
Ashton-u-L OL6 . . . . .85 B6
Bury BL9 . . . . .141 C3
Oldham OL8 . . . . .67 C3
Cherry Cl Bury BL9 . . . . . . .45 A7
Stockport SK2 . . . . .124 E7
Cherry Cres BB4 . . . . .1 F8
Cherry Ct M33 . . . . .108 A4
Cherry Dr M27 . . . . .80 A8
Cherry Gr Leigh WN7 . . . . . .75 F8
Rochdale OL11 . . . . .30 A8
Royton OL2 . . . . .48 C6
Stalybridge SK15 . . . . .102 A8
Wigan WN6 . . . . .36 F3
Cherry Hall Dr OL2 . . . . . . .48 E7
Cherry Hinton OL1 . . . . . . .153 D8
Cherry Holt Ave SK4 . . . . .110 F4
Cherry La
Denshaw OL16,OL3 . . . . . . .33 B3
Sale M33 . . . . .107 C3
Cherry Manor Prim Sch
M33 . . . . .107 C2
Cherry Orchard SK7 . . . . .123 D1
Cherry St M25 . . . . .63 C5
Cherry Tree Ave
Farnworth BL4 . . . . .60 A8
Poynton SK12 . . . . .133 F3
Cherry Tree Cl
■1 Altrincham WA15 . . . . .120 B5
Romiley SK6 . . . . .113 C2
Wilmslow SK9 . . . . .137 E8
Cherry Tree Cotts WA11 . . .71 A2
Cherry Tree Ct
■8 Salford M6 . . . . .81 A2
Standish WN6 . . . . .19 D2
Cherry Tree Dr SK7 . . . . . .134 A8

Cherry Tree Gr
Atherton M46 .....58 C4
Leigh WN7 .....75 D6
Cherry Tree Hospl SK2 .124 C5
Cherry Tree Jun Sch SK6 113 E2
Cherry Tree La
Billinge WA11 .....71 A2
Bury BL8 .....27 C1
Rawtenstall BB4 .....1 F8
Romiley SK6 .....113 E2
Stockport SK2 .....124 C5
Cherry Tree Prim Sch BL4 .59 E8
Cherry Tree Rd
Cheadle SK8 .....123 A1
Golborne WA3 .....90 F8
Wythenshawe M23 .....108 F1
Cherry Tree Way
Bolton BL2 .....25 C5
Haslingden BB4 .....1 B7
5 Horwich BL6 .....22 E1
Cherry Tree Wlk
Mossley OL5 .....68 B1
Stretford M32 .....96 C1
Cherry Wlk Cheadle SK8 .132 C8
Partington M31 .....105 C2
Cherrybrook Dr WN3 .....54 D1
Cherryton Wlk M13 .....163 C6
Cherrycroft SK6 .....113 E1
Cherrywood OL9 .....65 D7
Cherrywood Ave BL5 .....59 A7
Cherrywood Cl M28 .....60 B1
Chertsey Cl Droylsden M18 .99 E5
Shaw OL2 .....149 B8
Chervil Cl M14 .....110 C8
Chervil Wlk WN3 .....54 C4
Cherwell Ave OL10 .....29 E3
Cherwell Cl Aspull WN2 .....38 C6
Cheadle SK8 .....132 A7
Oldham OL8 .....66 C1
Whitefield M45 .....63 A8
Cherwell Rd BL5 .....39 F2
Cheryl's Bank SK13 .....116 B8
Chesham Ave Bolton BL1 .143 E2
Middleton OL11 .....47 D7
Urmston M41 .....94 E3
Wythenshawe M22 .....121 C4
Chesham Cl Hadfield SK13 104 B5
Wilmslow SK9 .....136 F4
Chesham Cres BL9 .....141 A3
Chesham Fold Rd BL9 .141 B4
Chesham Ho **2** M5 .....154 F1
Chesham Ind Est BL9 .....141 A4
Chesham Pl WA14 .....119 C2
Chesham Prim Sch BL9 .....28 A5
Chesham Rd Bury BL9 .....28 A5
Eccles M30 .....95 C8
3 Oldham OL4 .....67 C6
Wilmslow SK9 .....136 F4
Chesham St BL3 .....146 B2
Cheshill Ct M7 .....155 F6
Cheshire Cl
Newton-le-W WA12 .....89 E3
Stretford M32 .....96 B1
Cheshire Ct BL0 .....11 D6
Cheshire Gdns M14 .....98 A1
Cheshire Rd Mossley SK15 .86 E5
Partington M31 .....105 D2
Cheshire Sq SK15 .....86 E5
Cheshire St OL5 .....68 D1
Cheshires The OL5 .....68 D1
Chesney Ave OL9 .....65 E2
Chesshyre Ave M4 .....160 D1
Chessington Rise M27 .....62 A3
Chester Ave
Altrincham WA15 .....119 F2
Dukinfield SK16 .....101 E7
Golborne WA3 .....90 D8
Little Lever BL3 .....43 B4
Rochdale OL11 .....30 A6
Sale M33 .....107 B1
Stalybridge SK15 .....86 D3
Urmston M41 .....95 E3
Whitefield M45 .....63 A7
Chester Cl Handforth SK9 .131 E2
Irlam M44 .....105 D5
Little Lever BL3 .....43 B4
Chester Cres BB4 .....1 B8
Chester Dr
Ashton-in-M WN4 .....73 D2
Ramsbottom BL0 .....11 A4
Chester Pl Adlington PR6 ..21 A8
7 Royton OL2 .....48 D4
Chester Rd
Hazel Grove SK7,SK12 ....124 D1
Manchester M15,M16 .....161 B5
Manchester M15,M16 .....161 C6
Poynton SK12 .....133 A4
Stretford M16,M32 .....96 E3
Tyldesley M29 .....77 D8
Woodford SK7 .....132 E2
Chester Sq OL7 .....166 A2
Chester St Bury BL9 .....141 A4
Denton M34 .....100 F2
Leigh WN7 .....75 F5
Manchester M1 .....163 A4
Manchester M1,M15 .....162 F7
Oldham OL9 .....152 C5
Prestwich M25 .....63 A5
Stockport SK3 .....169 D1
Swinton M27 .....79 F7
Tyldesley M46 .....58 E1
Chester Wlk **20** BL1 .....143 E2
Chester Wlks SK6 .....113 A1
Chesterfield Gr OL6 .....85 D3
Chesterfield St OL4 .....67 B6

Chesterfield Way **4** M34 .113 A8
Chestergate SK1,SK3,SK4 .169 E1
Chesterton Cl WN3 .....150 A5
Chesterton Dr BL3 .....40 E5
Chesterton Gr M43 .....84 A2
Chesterton Rd Oldham OL1 .49 B2
Sale M23 .....120 D8
Chestnut Ave Atherton M46 58 C4
Bury M26 .....27 A5
Bury BL9 .....141 B2
Cheadle SK8 .....122 E5
Droylsden M43 .....83 E3
Irlam M44 .....105 D5
Leigh WN7 .....75 F3
Manchester M21 .....109 B8
Walkden M28 .....60 D2
Whitefield M45 .....62 F1
Chestnut Cl Bolton BL3 ....146 B4
New Mills SK22 .....127 C1
Oldham OL4 .....67 D8
Stalybridge SK15 .....102 A8
Wilmslow SK9 .....137 E8
Chestnut Cres OL8 .....67 A2
Chestnut Ct
Manchester M19 .....111 B8
Stockport SK7 .....123 D2
Chestnut Dr Leigh WN7 .....75 F2
Poynton SK12 .....133 F3
Rawtenstall BB4 .....1 F8
Sale M33 .....107 D1
Westhoughton BL5 .....57 F7
Chestnut Dr S WN7 .....75 F1
Chestnut Fold M26 .....44 A4
Chestnut Gdns
Denton M34 .....100 E2
Heywood OL10 .....29 C1
Chestnut Gr
Ashton-in-M WN4 .....73 D4
Failsworth M35 .....83 F6
Golborne WA3 .....90 F8
Hindley WN2 .....57 A4
Radcliffe M26 .....62 A8
Chestnut La WN7 .....75 F2
Chestnut Rd Eccles M30 .....79 A4
Wigan WN1 .....37 E2
Chestnut St OL9 .....66 A3
Chestnut Villas SK4 .....168 C2
Chestnut Way OL15 .....15 F6
Chestnut Wlk
Partington M31 .....105 D2
4 Partington M31 .....105 E3
Chesworth Ct SK1 .....170 F8
Chesworth M43 .....83 F1
Chesworth Fold SK1 .....170 F8
Chetham Cl M5 .....161 B7
Chetham's Sch of Music M4 .....158 F2
Chetwode Ave WN4 .....73 B1
Chetwyn Ave Bolton BL7 ...25 A7
Royton OL2 .....48 C4
Chetwynd Ave **3** M41 .....95 C2
Chetwynd Cl M33 .....107 E6
Chevassut Prim Sch M15 162 E7
Chevassut St M15 .....162 E6
Chevin Gdns SK7 .....133 A7
Chevington Dr
Manchester M9 .....157 D6
Manchester M9 .....110 E3
Chevington Gdns **2** BL1 .143 E3
Cheviot Ave Cheadle SK8 ..122 F2
Oldham OL8 .....66 E3
Royton OL2 .....48 C3
Cheviot Cl Bolton BL1 .....24 D5
Bury BL8 .....27 A3
Horwich BL6 .....22 C5
Middleton M24 .....65 D8
Milnrow OL16 .....32 A7
Oldham OL9 .....152 A5
Ramsbottom BL0 .....11 C4
Salford M6 .....154 E3
Stockport SK4 .....169 D3
Wigan WN3 .....54 C2
Cheviot Ct OL8 .....66 E4
Cheviot Rd SK7 .....124 B1
Cheviot St M3 .....158 F3
Cheviots Rd OL2 .....149 A8
Chevithorne Cl WA14 .....119 B8
Chevril Cl M15 .....163 A6
Chevron Cl Rochdale OL11 ..30 B3
3 Salford M5,M6 .....81 B2
Chevron Pl WA14 .....119 D7
Chew Brook Dr OL3 .....69 B5
Chew Moor La BL5,BL6 ....40 A2
Chew Rd OL3 .....70 A2
Chew Vale Dukinfield SK16 .101 F7
Oldham OL3 .....69 B5
Chew Valley Rd OL3 .....69 B5
Chicago Ave M90 .....130 B7
Chichester Ave M46 .....58 A2
Chichester Cl
Littleborough OL15 .....15 F3
4 Sale M33 .....107 D3
Chichester Cres OL9 .....48 A1
Chichester Rd
Manchester M15 .....162 F5
Romiley SK6 .....113 C2
Chichester Rd S M15 .....162 E5
Chichester St OL16 .....31 B7
Chichester Way **11** M34 ..101 A1
Chidlow Ave M20 .....110 A7
Chidwall Rd M22 .....121 B2
Chief St OL4 .....67 A6
Chiffon Way M3 .....158 D3
Chigwell Cl M22 .....121 E5
Chilcombe Wlk **5** M9 ....64 E5
Chilcote Ave M33 .....107 E4
Childwall Cl BL3 .....147 E2

Chilgrove Ave BL6 .....21 D1
Chilham Rd Eccles M30 .....79 F4
Walkden M28 .....60 E2
Chilham St Bolton BL3 ....146 B2
Swinton M27 .....79 E6
Wigan WN5 .....54 B6
Chillingham Dr WN7 .....76 C4
Chillington Wlk M34 .....100 E1
Chiltern Ave Atherton M46 .58 F5
Cheadle SK8 .....122 F2
Urmston M41 .....94 F3
Chiltern Cl
Ashton-in-M WN4 .....73 C2
Horwich BL6 .....22 C5
Ramsbottom BL0 .....11 C4
Shaw OL2 .....48 F8
Stockport SK7 .....124 B1
Walkden M28 .....78 E8
Chiltern Dr
Altrincham WA15 .....119 F2
Bolton BL2 .....148 C7
Bury BL8 .....27 B4
Royton OL2 .....48 C4
Stockport SK2 .....124 B4
Swinton M27 .....79 F6
Wigan WN3 .....54 D2
Chiltern Gdns M33 .....108 C1
Chiltern Rd Culcheth WA3 ..91 E4
Ramsbottom BL0 .....11 C4
Chiltern Way M29 .....77 B8
Chilton Ave OL9 .....152 A6
Chilton Cl WN7 .....75 F7
Chilton Dr M24 .....65 C7
Chilworth St M14 .....98 B2
Chime Bank M8 .....156 B6
Chimes Rd WN4 .....72 F6
China La **1** Bolton BL1 ....145 F8
Manchester M1 .....159 B1
Chingford Wlk **5** M13 .....98 F4
Chinley Ave
Manchester M40 .....83 A8
Stretford M32 .....96 A4
Chinley Cl Manchester SK4 168 B3
Sale M33 .....108 D3
Stockport SK7 .....123 E3
Chinley St M6 .....81 B5
Chinnor Cl WN7 .....75 F7
Chinwell View **3** M19 .....99 A1
Chip Hill Rd BL3 .....146 A4
Chippendale Pl OL6 .....85 E5
Chippenham Ct M4 .....160 D2
Chippenham Rd M4 .....160 D2
Chipping Fold OL16 .....31 F5
Chipping Rd BL1 .....23 F2
Chipping Sq M12 .....99 A4
Chipstead Ave M12 .....164 E5
Chirmside St **8** BL8 .....27 B1
Chirton Wlk **9** M40 .....83 A7
Chisacre Dr WN6 .....35 D7
Chiseldon Ave M22 .....121 E2
Chiselhurst St M8 .....156 A7
Chisholm Cl WN6 .....19 B2
Chisholm Ct **10** M24 .....46 F1
Chisholm St M11 .....99 D7
Chisholme Cl BL8 .....10 F7
Chisledon Ave M7 .....155 F6
Chisledon Cl BL3 .....145 E5
Chislehurst Ave M41 .....95 D3
Chislehurst Cl BL8 .....27 B1
Chisnall Ave WN6 .....18 F6
Chisnall La Coppull PR7 ....19 C6
Wrightington Bar WN6 .....19 A5
Chiswell St WN5 .....54 C5
Chiswick Dr BL3 .....43 B5
Chiswick Rd M20 .....110 C3
Chisworth Cl Leigh WN7 ...75 E7
Stockport SK7 .....123 E3
Chisworth St BL2 .....25 B3
Chisworth Wlk **2** M34 .....113 A8
Choir St M7 .....158 E4
Chokeberry Cl WA14 .....119 B8
Cholmley Dr WA12 .....89 E2
Cholmondeley Ave WA14 119 E8
Cholmondeley Rd M6 .....80 C4
Chomlea WA14 .....119 B4
Chomlea Manor M6 .....80 C4
Choral Gr M7 .....155 D5
Chorley Cl BL8 .....26 F1
Chorley Hall Cl SK9 .....136 F1
Chorley Hall La SK9 .....137 A1
Chorley New Rd
Bolton BL1,BL6 .....40 C7
Horwich BL6 .....22 C2
Chorley New Rd Inf Sch BL6 .....22 D2
Chorley New Rd Prim Sch BL6 .....22 D2
Chorley Old Rd
Bolton BL1 .....142 B1
Bolton BL1,BL6 .....23 C3
Chorley Rd
Adlington BL6,PR7 .....21 B5
Adlington PR6 .....21 A8
Sale M33 .....108 E2
Standish WN1 .....20 C3
Swinton M27 .....79 F8
Westhoughton BL5,BL6 .....39 C4
Chorley St Adlington PR6 ...21 B8
Bolton BL1 .....145 E7
Ince-in-M WN3 .....151 E6
Stretford M32 .....96 F5
Chorley Wood Ave M19 ..110 F6
Chorlton CE Prim Sch M21 .....109 A8
Chorlton Dr SK8 .....122 E6
Chorlton Fold M30 .....79 D4

Chorlton Gn M21 .....109 A8
Chorlton Gr SK1 .....124 B7
Chorlton Park Jun & Inf Schs 109 C6
Chorlton Rd M15,M16 .....162 D6
Chorlton St
Manchester M1 .....163 A8
Manchester M16 .....161 C5
Chorlton Water Park 109 C4
Chowbent Cl M46 .....58 E3
Chowbent Prim Sch M46 .58 D3
Chretien Rd M22 .....109 E2
Christ Church (Patricroft) CE Prim Sch M30 .....79 D2
Christ Church Ainsworth CE Prim Sch BL2 .....26 C1
Christ Church CE Prim Sch Bury BL8 ...26 F4
Denshaw OL3 .....33 D1
Leigh WN7 .....75 F4
Oldham OL9 .....152 A6
Christ Church Cl BL2 .....25 F2
Christ Church La BL2 .....25 F3
Christ the King RC Prim Sch Failsworth M40 .83 C5
Walkden M28 .....60 E2
Christ's Church CE Prim Sch BL2 .....25 F2
Christchurch Ave M5 .....81 B2
Christchurch Ct OL9 .....152 C5
Christchurch Rd M33 .....107 C5
Christie Hospl & Holt Radium Inst M20 ...110 B6
Christie Rd M32 .....96 C3
Christie St SK1 .....124 A7
Christine St OL2 .....149 B7
Christleton WN6 .....36 B6
Christleton Ave SK4 .....111 D5
Christleton Way **15** SK9 .131 E5
Christopher Acre OL11 ....13 E1
Christopher St
Failsworth M40 .....83 D4
Ince-in-M WN3 .....151 F6
Salford M5 .....81 B1
Chronnell Dr BL2 .....42 E8
Chudleigh Cl
Altrincham WA14 .....119 B6
Stockport SK7 .....124 A1
Chudleigh Rd M8 .....64 A2
Chulsey Gate La BL6 .....40 A4
Chulsey St BL3 .....146 B4
Chunal La SK13 .....116 C6
Church Ave
Bickershaw WN2 .....74 F8
Bolton BL3 .....146 C4
Denton M34 .....113 A8
7 Failsworth M40 .....83 C5
Handforth SK9 .....131 A2
Hyde SK14 .....113 F8
Leigh WN2 .....75 A8
Middleton OL11 .....47 D6
Salford M6 .....154 D2
Church Bank BL1 .....148 A7
Church Brow
Altrincham WA14 .....119 B2
Hyde SK14 .....167 D1
Mottram-in-L SK14 .....103 A3
Church Cl Dukinfield M34 .100 F7
Glossop SK13 .....104 E2
Handforth SK9 .....131 D3
Kearsley M26 .....61 B8
Ramsbottom BL0 .....138 B5
Church Croft BL9 .....45 C4
Church Ct
Altrincham WA15 .....119 E1
Dukinfield SK16 .....166 B1
Edenfield BL0 .....1 D4
Church Dr
Newton-le-W WA12 .....89 C1
Orrell WN5 .....53 D5
Prestwich M25 .....63 A4
Church Fields OL3 .....51 A2
Church Fold PR7 .....19 E5
Church Gn Lymm WA13 ...117 B8
Radcliffe M26 .....44 D4
Salford M6 .....154 F3
Church Gr SK7 .....124 E2
Church La
Alderley Edge SK9 .....137 A2
Culcheth WA3 .....91 F3
Edenfield BL0 .....1 D4
Golborne WA3 .....90 D7
Manchester M19 .....110 F6
Manchester M25,M7 .....63 C1
Manchester M40 .....83 A6
Manchester M40,M9 .....157 F7
Manchester M9 .....157 E8
Marple SK6 .....125 F5
Mossley OL5 .....68 D1
Oldham OL1 .....153 F7
Prestwich M25 .....63 A4
Rochdale OL16 .....139 F7
Romiley SK6 .....113 C2
Sale M33 .....107 C6
Shevington WN6 .....36 A6
Uppermill OL3 .....51 D1
Westhoughton BL5 .....39 E4
Whitefield M45 .....44 E1
Woodford SK7 .....132 C2
Wrightington Bar WN6 .....18 D8
Church Lo SK4 .....110 E2
Church Manor SK4 .....168 B4
Church Mdw
Dukinfield SK14 .....101 C3
Whitefield M45 .....45 C4
Church Mdws Bolton BL2 ..25 F3

Church Mdws continued
Uppermill OL3 .....68 E5
Church Meadow Gdns SK14 .....101 C3
Church Mews Denton M34 100 E3
1 Radcliffe M26 .....44 C1
Church Pl OL10 .....29 D2
Church Rd Bolton BL1 ....142 B8
Charlesworth SK13 .....115 C7
Cheadle SK8 .....132 B8
Eccles M30 .....79 F2
Farnworth BL4 .....60 E8
Gatley SK8 .....122 A5
Handforth SK9 .....131 D3
Hollingworth SK14 .....171 D4
Kearsley M26 .....61 A8
Middleton M24 .....65 D7
Moorend SK6 .....126 E6
Oldham OL3 .....69 C8
Platt Bridge WN2 .....56 B3
Ramsbottom BL0 .....11 E8
Rochdale OL16 .....31 B6
Sale M33 .....108 D4
Shaw OL2 .....149 B6
Stockport SK4 .....169 E2
Tyldesley M29 .....77 C6
Uppermill OL3 .....68 E5
Urmston M41 .....95 D1
Walkden M28 .....60 D3
Wilmslow SK9 .....136 E4
Wythenshawe M22 .....109 E1
Church Rd E M33 .....108 D4
Church Rd W M33 .....108 D4
Church Road Com Prim Sch BL1 ...142 B2
Church St Adlington PR7 ...21 A7
Ainsworth BL2 .....26 D1
Altrincham WA14 .....119 D5
Ashton-u-L OL6 .....166 B2
Aspull WN2 .....38 B6
Atherton M46 .....58 D3
Bacup OL13 .....3 C8
Blackrod BL6 .....21 C2
Bolton BL2 .....25 D5
Bury BL8 .....26 F5
Bury BL9 .....141 A3
Cheadle SK8 .....122 D6
Delph OL3 .....50 E4
Droylsden M43 .....84 B1
Dukinfield M34 .....100 F7
Dukinfield SK16 .....166 B1
Eccles M30 .....79 F2
Failsworth M35 .....83 F8
Farnworth BL4 .....60 E8
Glossop SK13 .....104 D2
Golborne WA3 .....74 B1
Hadfield SK13 .....104 A4
Heywood OL10 .....29 D2
Hindley WN2 .....56 D5
Horwich BL6 .....22 C3
Hyde SK14 .....167 D1
Ince-in-M WN3 .....151 F6
Leigh WN7 .....75 F5
Little Lever BL3 .....42 F3
Littleborough OL15 .....16 B5
Littleborough OL16 .....15 D3
Manchester M4 .....159 A2
5 Marple SK6 .....125 F6
Marple SK6 .....126 A5
Middleton M24 .....47 A2
Newhey OL16 .....32 B4
Newton-le-W WA12 .....89 E4
Oldham OL1 .....153 F7
Oldham OL4 .....67 E8
Orrell WN5 .....53 D5
Orrell WN8 .....53 C7
Pendlebury M27 .....80 B8
Radcliffe M26 .....44 C3
Rawtenstall BB4 .....2 E8
Rochdale OL12 .....139 E7
Romiley SK6 .....113 A5
Royton OL2 .....48 D4
Stalybridge SK15 .....86 A2
Standish WN6 .....19 E1
Stockport SK4 .....169 E3
Stretford M32 .....96 C1
Swinton M27 .....79 E8
Tintwistle SK13 .....104 A7
Westhoughton BL5 .....39 E2
Whitworth OL12 .....14 C8
Wigan WN1 .....150 C8
Wigan WN5 .....54 B6
Wilmslow SK9 .....137 B7
Church St E Oldham OL4 ...67 E8
Church St S SK13 .....104 E2
Church St W M26 .....44 B3
Church Stile OL16 .....139 F7
Church Street Ind Est **3** M24 .....47 A2
Church Terr
Handforth SK9 .....131 D4
Milnrow OL16 .....32 A5
Oldham OL1 .....153 F7
Sale M33 .....108 A6
Church View
Handforth SK9 .....131 A2
Hyde SK14 .....167 D1
Irlam M44 .....94 A2
Lymm WA13 .....117 B4
Rochdale OL12 .....14 C2
Church Wlk Farnworth BL4 .60 C8
Kearsley M27 .....61 F4
5 Royton OL2 .....48 D4
Stalybridge SK15 .....86 A3
Wilmslow SK9 .....136 F6
Churchbank SK15 .....86 D2

Churchdale Rd M9 . . . . .64 B4
Churchfield
 Manchester M21 . . . . .109 A8
 Shevington WN6 . . . . .36 A5
Churchfield Cl OL10 . . . . . . .43 F1
Churchfield Rd 5 M6 . . . . . .80 C5
Churchfield Wlk M11 . . . . . .165 A8
Churchfields
 Altrincham WA14 . . . . .119 B1
 Denton M34 . . . . .100 E4
 Sale M33 . . . . .107 D6
Churchgate Bolton BL1 . . . .145 F7
 Stockport SK1 . . . . .169 F1
 Urmston M41 . . . . .95 E1
Churchgate Bldgs M1 . . . .163 C8
Churchill Ave
 Ainsworth BL2 . . . . .26 D1
 Fowley Common WA3 . . . . .92 B4
 Manchester M16 . . . . .97 D2
Churchill Cl OL10 . . . . .46 E8
Churchill Cres
 Marple SK6 . . . . .125 D7
 Reddish SK5 . . . . .99 E1
Churchill Ct M6 . . . . .154 F2
Churchill Dr BL3,M26 . . . . .43 C3
Churchill Pl M30 . . . . .79 C4
Churchill Rd WA14 . . . . . . .119 D7
Churchill St 3 Bolton BL2 .148 C7
 Oldham OL4 . . . . .67 A6
 Rochdale OL11,OL12 . . . . .14 C1
 Stockport SK4 . . . . .169 D3
Churchill St E OL4 . . . . . . .67 A6
Churchill Way
 Salford M5,M6 . . . . .81 A4
 Stretford M17 . . . . .96 C7
Churchlands La WN6 . . . . . .19 F1
Churchley Cl SK3 . . . . .123 A6
Churchley Rd SK3 . . . . . . .123 A7
Churchside BL4 . . . . .60 B7
Churchside Cl M9 . . . . .64 D2
Churchston Ave SK7 . . . . . .124 A2
Churchtown Ave BL2 . . . . . .42 F7
Churchward Sq BL6 . . . . . . .22 C2
Churchwood Rd M20 . . . . .110 B3
Churnet St M40 . . . . .157 D5
Churnett Cl BL5 . . . . .39 F2
Churning Terr M44 . . . . .94 B3
Churston Ave M9 . . . . .64 E4
Churton Ave
 Manchester M14 . . . . .98 B2
 Sale M33 . . . . .107 F3
Churton Gr WN6 . . . . .19 B2
Churton Rd M18 . . . . .99 C3
Churwell Ave SK4 . . . . .110 F4
Cicero St Manchester M9 . .157 F8
 Oldham OL1 . . . . .49 A1
Cinder Hill La M24,OL1,OL2 48 A3
Cinder St M4 . . . . .159 C2
Cinnabar Dr M24 . . . . .46 F2
Cinnamon Ave M27 . . . . . . .57 A4
Cinnamon Brow WN8 . . . . .53 C6
Cinnamon Cl OL12 . . . . . . .139 D8
Cinnamon St OL12 . . . . . . .139 D8
Cipher St M4 . . . . .159 C3
Circle Ct M41 . . . . .95 F4
Circle S M17 . . . . .96 E6
Circle The M32 . . . . .95 F4
Circuit The
 Alderley Edge SK9 . . . . . . .137 B3
 Bramhall SK8 . . . . .132 A4
 Manchester M20 . . . . .110 B5
 Stockport SK3 . . . . .123 C6
 Wilmslow SK9 . . . . .136 D5
Circular Rd Denton M34 . . .100 E1
 Manchester M20 . . . . .110 B5
 Manchester M25 . . . . .63 B2
Cirencester Cl M38 . . . . . . .60 A6
Ciss La M41 . . . . .95 E2
Citrus Way M6 . . . . .81 A2
City Ave M34 . . . . .100 E2
City Coll Manchester
 Abraham Moss Ctr M8 .156 B4
City Coll Manchester
 Arden Ctr M23 . . . . .109 C1
City Coll Manchester
 Fielden Ctr M20 . . . . .109 F4
City Course Trad Est
 M11 . . . . .165 A7
City Court Trad Est M4 .159 C2
City Rd Boothstown M28 . . .78 A8
 Manchester M15 . . . . .162 D6
 Wigan WN5 . . . . .54 B7
City Rd E M15 . . . . .162 F7
City Wlk M27 . . . . .80 B8
Civic Wlk 1 OL10 . . . . .29 D2
Clacton Wlk M13 . . . . .163 C6
Clague St M11 . . . . .83 A2
Claife Ave M40 . . . . .65 B2
Clammerclough Rd BL4 . . . .60 F8
Clandon Ave M30 . . . . .79 B1
Clanwood Cl WN3 . . . . .54 E2
Clap Gate La WN3 . . . . .54 E3
Clapgate SK6 . . . . .112 F1
Clapgate Rd OL11 . . . . .13 E1
Clapham St M40 . . . . .83 C8
Clara Gorton Ct 12 OL16 . .31 B6
Clara St Oldham OL9 . . . . . .66 C4
 Rochdale OL11 . . . . .139 F5
 Whitworth OL12 . . . . .4 D1
Clare Ave SK9 . . . . .131 C4
Clare Cl BL8 . . . . .27 D5
Clare Rd Manchester M19 . .111 A8
 Reddish SK5 . . . . .169 F4
Clare St Denton M34 . . . . .100 E4
 Manchester M1 . . . . .163 B7

Clare St continued
 Manchester M5 . . . . .81 C1
Clarebank BL1 . . . . .40 F7
Claremont Ave
 Altrincham WA14 . . . . .119 E8
 Hindley WN2 . . . . .56 F5
 Manchester M20 . . . . .110 A5
 Manchester SK4 . . . . .111 C5
 Marple SK6 . . . . .125 C6
Claremont Dr
 Altrincham WA14 . . . . .119 E8
 Walkden M38 . . . . .60 B5
Claremont Gdns OL6 . . . . . .85 E5
Claremont Rd
 Altrincham WA15 . . . . .119 E3
 Cheadle SK8 . . . . .132 A8
 Culcheth WA3 . . . . .91 D4
 Manchester M14 . . . . .98 B3
 Manchester M16 . . . . .97 F3
 Milnrow OL16 . . . . .31 F5
 Rochdale OL11 . . . . .30 C7
 Sale M33 . . . . .108 B5
 Salford M6 . . . . .80 D5
 Stockport SK2 . . . . .124 B4
Claremont Road Inf Sch
 M14 . . . . .98 A3
Claremont Sch M6 . . . . . . .80 C5
Claremont St
 Failsworth M35 . . . . .83 F8
 Oldham OL8 . . . . .66 F2
 Oldham OL9 . . . . .48 C1
Claremont Terr OL14 . . . . . .6 D5
Clarence Ave Eccles M17 . . .95 F7
 Oldham OL8 . . . . .66 D4
 Whitefield M45 . . . . .63 A7
Clarence Ct 15 Bolton BL1 .145 E8
 Newton-le-W M12 . . . . .89 A4
 Wilmslow SK9 . . . . .137 A6
Clarence Ho 1 SK15 . . . . .101 F8
Clarence Rd
 Altrincham WA15 . . . . .119 F3
 Ashton-u-L OL6 . . . . .166 C4
 Manchester M13 . . . . .98 E4
 Manchester SK4 . . . . .111 C5
 Swinton M27 . . . . .79 C7
Clarence St
 6 Ashton-in-M WN4 . . . . .72 F5
 Bolton BL1 . . . . .145 E8
 Farnworth BL4 . . . . .42 E1
 Golborne WA3 . . . . .74 A1
 Hyde SK14 . . . . .167 E4
 Ince-in-M WN2 . . . . .56 A7
 Leigh WN7 . . . . .76 B4
 15 Manchester M3 . . . . . .158 F1
 Manchester M7 . . . . .158 D4
 Rochdale OL12 . . . . .14 D2
 Royton OL2 . . . . .49 A3
 Stalybridge SK15,SK16 . . .85 E1
 Tyldesley M46 . . . . .58 E2
Clarence Yd WN1 . . . . .150 C8
Clarendon Ave
 Altrincham WA15 . . . . .119 E5
 Manchester SK4 . . . . .168 B3
 Sale M33 . . . . .108 D5
Clarendon Cres Eccles M30 79 F3
 Sale M33 . . . . .108 D5
Clarendon Cty Prim Sch
 BL3 . . . . .145 E5
Clarendon Fields
 Prim Sch SK16 . . . . .101 B8
Clarendon Gr BL2 . . . . . . .148 B6
Clarendon Ind Est SK14 . .167 E3
Clarendon Pl SK14 . . . . . . .167 E4
Clarendon Rd Bolton BL2 . .148 C7
 Denton M34 . . . . .101 B2
 Droylsden M34 . . . . .100 B7
 Eccles M30 . . . . .79 F3
 Hazel Grove SK7 . . . . .124 F3
 Hyde SK14 . . . . .167 E3
 Ince-in-M WN3 . . . . .151 E5
 Irlam M44 . . . . .105 F7
 Manchester M16 . . . . .97 D2
 Sale M33 . . . . .108 D4
 Swinton M27 . . . . .79 F8
 Urmston M41 . . . . .94 E3
Clarendon Rd W M41 . . . . . .97 B2
Clarendon Recn Ctr M5 . .81 A2
Clarendon Road Prim Sch
 M30 . . . . .79 F3
Clarendon St
 Bolton BL3 . . . . .145 E5
 Bury BL9 . . . . .141 A4
 Dukinfield SK16 . . . . .101 A8
 Dukinfield SK16 . . . . .101 B8
 Hyde SK14 . . . . .167 D3
 Manchester M15 . . . . .162 F6
 Manchester M15 . . . . .162 F7
 Mossley OL5 . . . . .86 D8
 Reddish SK5 . . . . .169 F3
 Rochdale OL16 . . . . .31 B4
 Whitefield M45 . . . . .62 F1
Claribel St M11 . . . . .164 E8
Claridge Rd M21 . . . . .97 A1
Clarington Gr WN1 . . . . . . .151 E7
Clarington Pl WN2 . . . . . . .151 F7
Clarion St M4 . . . . .159 C3
Clark Ave M18 . . . . .99 E5
Clark Way SK14 . . . . .167 D3
Clark's Cross M25 . . . . .63 D8
Clark's Hill M25 . . . . .63 A4
Clarke Ave Culcheth WA3 . . .92 A4
 Salford M5 . . . . .161 B7
Clarke Brow M24 . . . . .47 A1

Clarke Cres . . . .
 Altrincham WA15 . . . . .120 B3
 Walkden M38 . . . . .59 E6
Clarke St Altrincham WA14 119 D7
 Bolton BL1 . . . . .144 C8
 Dukinfield OL7 . . . . .100 F8
 Farnworth BL4 . . . . .60 E7
 Heywood OL10 . . . . .29 D2
 Leigh WN7 . . . . .75 E4
 Rochdale OL16 . . . . .15 B2
Clarke's La OL12 . . . . .139 D8
Clarkes Croft BL9 . . . . .141 C3
Clarkethorn Terr SK5 . . . . .169 E3
Clarksfield Jun & Inf Sch
 OL4 . . . . .67 C6
Clarksfield Rd OL4 . . . . . . .67 C6
Clarksfield St OL4 . . . . .67 C6
Clarkson Cl Denton M34 . .100 D2
 Middleton M24 . . . . .64 C7
Clarkwell Cl OL1 . . . . .153 E8
Clatford Wlk 2 M9 . . . . . .157 D7
Claude Ave M27 . . . . .79 D8
Claude Rd M21 . . . . .109 B7
Claude St Eccles M30 . . . . .79 B3
 Manchester M8 . . . . .64 A1
 Swinton M27 . . . . .79 D8
 Wigan WN5 . . . . .54 D6
Claudia St SK15 . . . . .86 E5
Claughton Ave Bolton BL2 . .42 F7
 Walkden M28 . . . . .78 C8
Claughton Rd BL8 . . . . .26 F5
Claverham Wlk 4 M23 . . . .120 E7
Claverton Rd M23 . . . . .120 E5
Claxton Ave M9 . . . . .64 D3
Clay Bank M9 . . . . .83 F1
Clay Bank St OL10 . . . . .29 C3
Clay Hall M5 . . . . .154 F1
Clay La Altrincham WA15 . .120 D4
 Handforth SK9 . . . . .131 C5
 Rochdale OL11 . . . . .29 E8
 Wilmslow SK9 . . . . .136 C4
 Wythenshawe M23 . . . . . .120 F4
Clay St Bolton BL7 . . . . .25 A7
 3 Littleborough OL15 . . . .15 F5
 Oldham OL8 . . . . .66 E4
Claybank Dr Bury BL8 . . . . .26 D7
 Bury BL8 . . . . .26 E7
Claybank Terr OL5 . . . . .68 E4
Claybar Dr M30 . . . . .79 E3
Claybridge Cl WN5 . . . . . . .36 B1
Claybrook Wlk M11 . . . . . . .83 A1
Clayburn Rd M15 . . . . .162 E6
Claycourt Ave M30 . . . . . . .79 B4
Claydon Dr Ince-in-M WN3 151 F5
 Little Lever BL3,M26 . . . . .43 C5
Clayfield Dr OL11 . . . . .29 E8
Claygate Dr M9 . . . . .64 D5
Clayhill Gr WA3 . . . . .91 B8
Clayhill Wlk M9 . . . . .64 E1
Claylands Cl SK14 . . . . . . .171 D4
Claymere Ave OL11 . . . . . . .29 E8
Claymore OL1 . . . . .153 E7
Claymore St Bolton BL3 . . .147 F3
 Droylsden M18 . . . . .99 E6
Claypool Prim Sch BL6 . .22 F1
Claypool Rd BL6 . . . . .22 E1
Claythorpe Wlk 2 M8 . . . . .63 E2
Clayton Ave Bolton BL3 . . .148 C5
 Golborne WA3 . . . . .90 E8
 Manchester M20 . . . . .110 B4
 Rawtenstall BB4 . . . . .1 E8
Clayton Brook Prim Sch
 M11 . . . . .99 D8
Clayton Cl Bury BL8 . . . . . . .26 F1
 Manchester M15 . . . . .162 E5
Clayton Hall Rd M11 . . . . . .83 C2
Clayton Ho M7 . . . . .75 C5
Clayton La M11 . . . . .83 B1
Clayton La S M11,M12 . . . .165 A7
Clayton St Bolton BL3 . . . .148 C5
 Denton M34 . . . . .100 F2
 Droylsden M34 . . . . .83 B2
 5 Dukinfield SK16 . . . . . .101 D8
 5 Failsworth M35 . . . . . . .83 F7
 Oldham OL9 . . . . .66 A3
 Rochdale OL16 . . . . .15 B2
 Wigan WN3 . . . . .150 B7
Claytonbrook Rd M11 . . . .83 D1
Claytons Cl OL4 . . . . .67 F7
Cleabarrow Dr M28 . . . . . . .78 A5
Cleadon Ave M18 . . . . .99 C4
Cleadon Dr S BL8 . . . . .27 C5
Cleavley St M30 . . . . .79 B2
Clee Ave M13 . . . . .98 F2
Cleethorpes Ave M9 . . . . . .64 B3
Cleeve Rd 2 Oldham OL4 . .67 C6
 Wythenshawe M23 . . . . . .109 A4
Cleeve Way M8 . . . . .132 B6
Clegg Hall Rd OL15,OL16 . .15 E1
Clegg Pl 2 OL6 . . . . .85 D4
Clegg St 6 Bacup OL13 . . . .3 C8
 Bolton BL2 . . . . .148 C7
 Bredbury SK6 . . . . .112 F3
 Droylsden M43 . . . . .83 F1
 Littleborough OL15 . . . . . . .15 F7
 Milnrow OL16 . . . . .32 A5
 Oldham OL4 . . . . .153 F6
 Oldham OL4 . . . . .68 A6
 Shaw OL2 . . . . .48 F8
 Tyldesley M46 . . . . .77 A5
 Whitefield M45 . . . . .62 F7
 Whitworth OL12 . . . . .4 C2
Clegg's Bldgs BL1 . . . . . . .145 E8
Clegg's Ct OL12 . . . . .4 C2
Clegg's La M38 . . . . .60 A5
Cleggswood Ave OL15 . . . .16 A3
Clelland St BL4 . . . . .60 E7
Clematis Wlk M27 . . . . .61 E2

Clement Ave M46 . . . . .58 A2
Clement Ct
 Manchester M11 . . . . .99 F7
 13 Rochdale OL16 . . . . . . .31 B6
Clement Rd SK6 . . . . .126 C7
Clement Royds St OL12 . . .139 E8
Clement Scott Cl M9 . . . . . .64 F4
Clement St Oldham OL9 . . . .66 B3
 Stockport SK4 . . . . .169 E3
Clementina St OL12 . . . . . .14 F1
Clementine Cl M6 . . . . .81 B2
Clementine Ct M6 . . . . .81 B2
Cleminson St M3 . . . . .158 D2
Clemshaw Cl OL10 . . . . .29 C1
Clerewood Ave SK8 . . . . . .131 B7
Clerke St BL9 . . . . .140 F2
Clerks Ct M5 . . . . .80 B2
Clevedon Ave M41 . . . . .96 A2
Clevedon Dr WN3 . . . . .54 D4
Clevedon Rd OL9 . . . . .48 B1
Clevedon St M9 . . . . .157 E7
Cleveland Ave Hyde SK14 . .101 C2
 Manchester M19 . . . . .99 B2
 Salford M6 . . . . .80 C3
 Wigan WN3 . . . . .54 C3
Cleveland Cl
 Ramsbottom BL0 . . . . .11 C3
 Swinton M27 . . . . .62 A2
Cleveland Dr
 Ashton-in-M WN4 . . . . .73 C4
 Golborne WA3 . . . . .74 D1
 Milnrow OL16 . . . . .32 A6
Cleveland Gdns BL3 . . . . . .146 B4
Cleveland Gr OL2 . . . . .48 C3
Cleveland Rd
 Altrincham WA15 . . . . .119 F3
 Manchester M8 . . . . .64 B2
 Manchester SK4 . . . . .168 A4
Cleveland St 7 BL3 . . . . . .146 B4
Cleveleys Ave Bolton BL2 . .148 C8
 Bury BL9 . . . . .44 E7
 Gatley SK8 . . . . .122 B1
 Manchester M21 . . . . .109 C7
 Rochdale OL16 . . . . .31 B3
Cleveleys Gr M7 . . . . .155 E7
Cleves Ct OL10 . . . . .29 C1
Clevlands Cl OL2 . . . . .149 A8
Cleworth Rd M24 . . . . .46 F2
Cleworth St M15 . . . . .162 D7
Cleworth Wlk M15 . . . . . . .162 D7
Clibran St M8 . . . . .156 B6
Clifden Dr M22 . . . . .121 E2
Cliff Ave Bury BL8 . . . . .26 E7
 Ramsbottom BL0 . . . . .11 C2
 Salford M7 . . . . .81 B1
Cliff Cres M7 . . . . .155 D7
Cliff Dale 3 SK15 . . . . .101 F8
Cliff Gr SK4 . . . . .168 B4
Cliff Grange M7 . . . . .155 D7
Cliff Hill Rd OL2 . . . . .32 D1
Cliff Mount BL0 . . . . .138 B7
Cliff Rd Bury BL9 . . . . .44 F5
 Wilmslow SK9 . . . . .137 B8
Cliff Side SK9 . . . . .137 B8
Cliff St OL16 . . . . .15 B1
Cliffbrook Gr 2 SK9 . . . . . .131 D2
Cliffdale Dr M8 . . . . .64 A1
Cliffe Rd SK13 . . . . .116 D8
Cliffe St OL15 . . . . .6 D2
Cliffmere Cl SK8 . . . . .122 F3
Clifford Ave
 Altrincham WA15 . . . . .120 B6
 Denton M34 . . . . .100 E5
Clifford Ct M15 . . . . .162 E5
Clifford Lamb Ct M9 . . . . . .65 B2
Clifford Rd Bolton BL3 . . . .146 A4
 Poynton SK12 . . . . .133 D3
 Wilmslow SK9 . . . . .136 F6
Clifford St Eccles M30 . . . . .95 B8
 Leigh WN7 . . . . .76 B4
 Manchester M13 . . . . .163 B6
 Pendlebury M27 . . . . .80 B8
 Rochdale OL11 . . . . .139 F5
 Rochdale OL11 . . . . .31 A5
Clifton Ave
 Altrincham WA15 . . . . .119 E5
 Culcheth WA3 . . . . .91 D3
 Eccles M30 . . . . .79 D3
 Gatley SK8 . . . . .122 A2
 Manchester M14 . . . . .110 D8
 2 Oldham OL4 . . . . .67 B5
 Oldham OL4 . . . . .67 B5
Clifton Cl Heywood OL10 . . .29 C1
 Manchester M16 . . . . .162 D5
 Oldham OL4 . . . . .67 B5
Clifton Cres Royton OL2 . . .49 A3
 Wigan WN1 . . . . .37 C2
Clifton Ct 5 Farnworth BL4 .42 B2
 Swinton M27 . . . . .61 F3
Clifton Ctry Pk M27 . . . . . .61 E5
Clifton Dr Blackrod BL6 . . . .21 C3
 Gatley SK8 . . . . .122 A2
 Gatley SK8 . . . . .122 A6
 Marple SK6 . . . . .125 F7
 Swinton M27 . . . . .61 D2
 Swinton M27 . . . . .62 C2
 Wilmslow SK9 . . . . .136 E4
Clifton Gr
 Manchester M16 . . . . .162 D5
 Swinton M27 . . . . .61 D2
Clifton Holm OL3 . . . . .50 E5
Clifton House Rd M27 . . . . .61 E4
Clifton Junction Sta M27 .62 C2
Clifton Lo SK2 . . . . .124 A5
Clifton Park Rd SK2 . . . . . .124 A5
Clifton Pl M25 . . . . .63 A5

Clifton Prim Sch M27 . . . . .61 F3
Clifton Rd Ashton-in-M WN4 .72 F6
 Billinge WN5 . . . . .71 D4
 Eccles M30 . . . . .79 D3
 Leigh WN7 . . . . .75 E2
 Manchester M21 . . . . .109 C8
 Manchester M34 . . . . .168 A4
 Middleton OL11 . . . . .47 D6
 Prestwich M25 . . . . .62 F4
 Sale M33 . . . . .108 B3
 Urmston M41 . . . . .95 A2
Clifton St
 Alderley Edge SK9 . . . . . . .137 A1
 Ashton-u-L OL6 . . . . .166 A3
 Bolton BL1 . . . . .145 E8
 Bury BL9 . . . . .140 F4
 Failsworth M35 . . . . .66 A1
 Farnworth BL4 . . . . .42 B2
 Kearsley BL4 . . . . .60 F7
 Leigh WN7 . . . . .75 D5
 Manchester M19 . . . . .162 D5
 Manchester M40 . . . . .160 F4
 Milnrow OL16 . . . . .31 F6
 7 Rochdale OL11 . . . . .31 A5
 Tyldesley M29 . . . . .77 E8
 4 Wigan WN1 . . . . .37 C1
 Wigan WN3 . . . . .55 A4
Clifton View 6 . . . . .61 E4
Clifton Villas 5 M35 . . . . . .66 A1
Clifton Wlk M34 . . . . .46 D3
Cliftonmill Mdw WA3 . . . . . .89 F8
Cliftonmill Dr M6,M27 . . . . .80 B6
Cliftonville Rd OL16 . . . . . . .48 C8
Clinton Ave M14 . . . . .98 A2
Clinton Gdns M14 . . . . .98 A2
Clinton Ho 3 M5 . . . . .154 F1
Clinton St 8 OL6 . . . . .85 D4
Clinton Wlk 5 OL4 . . . . .67 A6
Clippers Quay M5 . . . . .161 A6
Clipsley Cres OL4 . . . . .49 F4
Cliston Wlk SK7 . . . . .124 E1
Clitheroe Cl OL10 . . . . .29 D3
Clitheroe Dr BL8 . . . . .26 F2
Clitheroe Rd M13 . . . . .98 F3
Clito St M9 . . . . .157 F8
Clive Ave M45 . . . . .44 E1
Clive Rd Failsworth M35 . . .83 E6
 Westhoughton BL5 . . . . . . .57 E6
Clive St Ashton-u-L OL7 . . .85 A5
 Bolton BL2 . . . . .148 A7
 Manchester M4 . . . . .159 B3
 8 Oldham OL8 . . . . .66 D2
Clivedale Pl BL1 . . . . .145 F7
Cliveley Wlk M27 . . . . .80 B8
Clively Ave M27 . . . . .62 C1
Clivewood Wlk M12 . . . . . .164 E6
Clivia Gr M7 . . . . .155 D6
Cloak St M1 . . . . .163 A7
Clock House Ave M43 . . . . .83 E3
Clock St 11 OL9 . . . . .66 B2
Clock Tower Cl
 Hyde SK14 . . . . .167 E1
 3 Manchester M28 . . . . . .59 F3
Clockhouse Mews M43 . . .83 E3
Clod La 7 . . . . .1 C8
Cloister Ave WN7 . . . . .57 F7
Cloister Cl SK16 . . . . .101 C6
Cloister Rd SK4 . . . . .110 D2
Cloister St Bury BL1 . . . . . .142 C1
Cloister The M15 . . . . .157 F8
Cloisters The Cheadle SK8 123 A5
 Rochdale OL16 . . . . .15 B1
 Sale M33 . . . . .108 D4
 Westhoughton BL5 . . . . . . .57 E5
Clondberry Cl M29 . . . . .59 E1
Close La Hindley WN2 . . . . .56 E3
 Leigh WN7 . . . . .57 A1
Close St WN2 . . . . .56 F6
Close The
 Altrincham WA14 . . . . .119 C5
 Atherton M46 . . . . .58 F5
 Bolton BL2 . . . . .25 B3
 Bury BL8 . . . . .27 C5
 Denton M34 . . . . .100 D4
 Middleton M24 . . . . .47 B3
 Newton-le-W WA12 . . . . . .89 E1
 Romiley SK6 . . . . .114 B1
 Stalybridge SK15 . . . . .85 F4
Closebrook Rd WN5 . . . . . . .54 D6
Closes Farm BL3 . . . . .146 B2
Clothorn Rd M20 . . . . .110 B4
Cloudberry Wlk M31 . . . . . .105 F3
Cloudstock Gr M38 . . . . . . .59 E5
Clough Ave Handforth SK9 131 B2
 Marple SK6 . . . . .126 C6
 Sale M33 . . . . .107 D1
 Westhoughton BL5 . . . . . . .57 F7
Clough Bank
 Littleborough OL15 . . . . . . .16 A8
 Manchester M9 . . . . .64 D2
Clough Croft OL4 . . . . .68 E6
Clough Dr M25 . . . . .62 F4
Clough End Rd SK14 . . . . .102 F1
Clough Fold Kearsley M26 . .61 B7
 Westhoughton BL5 . . . . . . .57 F8
Clough Fold Rd SK14 . . . .167 D1
Clough Gate Hyde SK14 . . .113 F8
 6 Oldham OL8 . . . . .66 D2
Clough Gr Ashton-in-M WN4 .72 F5
 Whitefield M45 . . . . .44 D2
Clough Ho M9 . . . . .65 A2
Clough House Dr WN7 . . . . .76 B5
Clough House La OL12 . . . .15 B6
Clough La Heywood OL10 . .29 C4
 Prestwich M25 . . . . .62 F4

Clough La continued
Uppermill OL4 . . . .**68** E6
Clough Mdw Bolton BL1 . .**40** D6
Romiley SK6 . . . .**113** C5
Clough Meadow Rd M26 .**43** E3
Clough Park Ave OL4 . . . .**68** E6
Clough Rd Droylsden M43 .**84** B2
Failsworth M35 . . . .**84** A6
Littleborough OL15 . . . .**16** A7
Manchester M9 . . . .**64** F1
Middleton M24 . . . .**47** A2
Shaw OL2 . . . .**49** D6
Clough Side Marple SK6 .**126** C7
Oldham M9 . . . .**64** F1
Clough St ⑧ Bacup OL13 . . .**3** D8
Failsworth M40 . . . .**83** C4
Kearsley BL4 . . . .**60** F7
Littleborough OL12 . . . .**15** C6
Middleton M24 . . . .**47** B2
Radcliffe M26 . . . .**44** C1
Clough Terr OL15 . . . .**16** A7
Clough The
Brinnington SK5 . . . .**112** B6
Garswood WN4 . . . .**72** D4
Clough Top Rd M9 . . . . . .**65** A2
Clough Wlk SK5 . . . .**112** B6
Cloughbank M26 . . . .**61** C7
Cloughfield Ave M5 . . . . .**161** B8
Cloughgate Ho ⑤ OL8 . . . .**66** D2
Cloughs Ave OL9 . . . .**65** D8
Cloughside SK12 . . . .**135** E6
Cloughton Wlk M40 . . . . . .**83** D5
Cloughwood Cres M35 . . . .**35** D6
Clovelly Ave Leigh WN7 . . .**75** F8
Oldham OL2 . . . .**66** C2
Clovelly Rd
Manchester M21 . . . .**109** C8
Stockport SK2 . . . .**124** C4
Swinton M27 . . . .**79** C6
Clovelly St Failsworth M40 .**83** D5
Rochdale OL12 . . . .**30** B3
Clover Ave SK3 . . . .**170** D5
Clover Cres OL8 . . . .**67** C3
Clover Croft M33 . . . .**108** D1
Clover Hall Cres OL16 . . . .**15** C1
Clover Rd
Altrincham WA15 . . . .**120** B5
Romiley SK6 . . . .**113** E3
Clover St Rochdale OL12 .**139** E8
Wigan WN6 . . . .**37** B2
Clover View OL16 . . . .**31** C7
Cloverbank Ave M19 . . . .**110** D4
Cloverdale DrWN4 . . . .**73** C2
Cloverdale Sq BL1 . . . . . .**142** A1
Cloverfield Wlk M28 . . . . .**60** D3
Cloverlea Prim Sch
WA15 . . . .**120** B5
Cloverley M33 . . . .**108** B2
Cloverley Dr WA15 . . . . . .**120** A4
Clowes St Manchester M12 **164** F6
Manchester M3 . . . .**158** B2
Oldham OL9 . . . .**66** B2
Club St Billinge WA11 . . . . .**71** A1
Droylsden M11 . . . .**99** F7
Clumber Cl SK12 . . . .**133** E3
Clumber Rd Poynton SK12 **133** E3
Reddish M18,M34 . . . .**99** F4
Clunton Ave BL3 . . . .**146** B4
Clutha Rd SK3 . . . .**123** F4
Clwyd Ave SK3 . . . .**170** D7
Clyde Ave M45 . . . .**62** F6
Clyde Ct OL16 . . . .**31** B6
Clyde Rd Manchester M20 .**110** A5
Radcliffe M26 . . . .**43** F5
Stockport SK3 . . . .**123** C2
Tyldesley M29 . . . .**77** C7
Clyde St Bolton BL1 . . . . .**143** E2
Dukinfield OL7 . . . .**100** F8
Leigh WN7 . . . .**76** B4
Oldham OL1 . . . .**49** C1
Clyde Terr OL16 . . . .**43** F5
Clydesdale Gdns M11 . . . . .**83** A1
Clydesdale Rise OL3 . . . . . .**51** D5
Clydesdale St OL8 . . . .**66** E4
Clyne Ct M32 . . . .**96** F4
Clyne St M32 . . . .**96** F5
Clysbarton Ct SK7 . . . . . .**123** D1
Co-operation St M35 . . . . .**83** F8
Co-operative St
Hazel Grove SK7 . . . .**124** E3
⑤ Leigh WN7 . . . .**75** D5
⑫ Oldham OL3 . . . .**69** B8
Oldham OL4 . . . .**67** F5
⑧ Radcliffe M26 . . . .**44** A4
Salford M6 . . . .**154** F2
Shaw OL2 . . . .**149** B7
Walkden M38 . . . .**59** E5
Coach House Dr WN6 . . . . .**36** B6
Coach La OL11 . . . .**29** C5
Coach Rd
Hollingworth SK14 . . . .**103** D4
Tyldesley M29 . . . .**77** C6
Coach St M46 . . . .**58** D4
Coal Pit La Atherton M46 . .**58** B4
Atherton M46 . . . .**58** B4
Leigh WN2 . . . .**57** B1
④ Leigh WN7 . . . .**75** E8
Oldham OL4 . . . .**66** E1
Oldham OL8 . . . .**84** D8
Coal Pit Rd BL1 . . . .**23** D7
Coal Rd BL0 . . . .**12** C8
Coalbrook Wlk M12 . . . . .**164** E8
Coalburn St M12 . . . .**165** A6
Coalshaw Green Rd OL9 . .**66** A3
Coatbridge St M11 . . . .**83** C1

Cob Hall Rd ⑥ M32 . . . .**96** C1
Cob Moor Ave WN5 . . . .**53** D1
Cob Moor Rd WN5 . . . .**53** D1
Cobal Ct SK2 . . . .**124** A5
Cobalt Ave M41 . . . .**95** F6
Cobb Cl M8 . . . .**63** E3
Cobbett's Way SK9 . . . . . .**136** F4
Cobble Bank M9 . . . .**64** D3
Cobblestones OL3 . . . .**50** F3
Cobden Ctr The M6 . . . . . .**154** F1
Cobden St
② Ashton-u-L OL6 . . . .**85** D2
Bacup OL13 . . . .**4** B8
Bolton BL1 . . . .**143** D3
Bolton BL7 . . . .**8** D2
Bury BL9 . . . .**141** A3
Heywood OL10 . . . .**29** D1
Manchester M9 . . . .**64** E1
Newton-le-W WA12 . . . .**89** D4
Oldham OL4 . . . .**49** D1
Oldham OL9 . . . .**152** B7
Radcliffe M26 . . . .**43** F6
⑫ Tyldesley M29 . . . .**59** A1
Coberley Ave M41 . . . .**94** F4
Cobham Ave Bolton BL3 . .**147** D3
Manchester M40 . . . .**65** C2
Coblers Hill OL3 . . . .**50** F5
Cobourg St M1 . . . .**163** B8
Coburg Ave M7 . . . .**158** D4
Cochrane Ave M12 . . . . . .**164** E5
Cochrane St BL3 . . . .**145** F5
Cock Brow SK14 . . . .**114** C7
Cock Clod St M26 . . . .**44** C3
Cock Hall La OL12 . . . .**14** C8
Cockcroft Rd M6 . . . .**81** B2
Cockcroft St M9 . . . .**64** E1
Cocker Hill SK15 . . . .**86** B2
Cocker Mill La Royton OL2 . .**48** F5
Shaw OL2 . . . .**149** A5
Cocker St M38 . . . .**60** A4
Cockerell Springs ① BL2 **148** A6
Cockers La SK15 . . . .**102** D8
Cockey Moor Rd BL2,BL8 . .**26** E1
Cockhall La OL12 . . . .**4** C1
Coconut Gr M6 . . . .**81** B2
Codale Dr BL2 . . . .**25** F1
Coddington Ave M11 . . . . . .**99** E8
Code La BL5 . . . .**39** B4
Cody Ct M5 . . . .**96** E8
Coe St BL3 . . . .**145** F5
Coghlan Cl M11 . . . .**83** B2
Coin St OL2 . . . .**48** E4
Cojeton Ho M9 . . . .**64** F5
Coke St M7 . . . .**155** F8
Colborne Ave Eccles M30 . .**79** B2
Reddish SK5 . . . .**99** F3
Romiley SK6 . . . .**113** C2
Colbourne Ave M8 . . . .**63** F1
Colbourne Gr SK14 . . . . . .**102** E3
Colbourne Way SK14 . . . . .**102** E3
Colburn Cl WN3 . . . .**55** A2
Colby Rd WN3 . . . .**55** B3
Colby Wlk M40 . . . .**83** A7
Colchester Ave Bolton BL2 .**42** E8
Manchester M25 . . . .**63** C2
Colchester Cl M23 . . . .**108** E1
Colchester Dr BL4 . . . .**42** A1
Colchester Pl SK4 . . . .**168** C3
Colchester St M40 . . . . . .**160** D4
Colchester Wlk ① OL1 . . .**153** F7
Colclough Cl M40 . . . .**83** B6
Cold Greave Cl OL16 . . . . . .**32** C4
Coldalhurst La M29 . . . .**77** B5
Coldfield Dr M23 . . . .**120** F6
Coldhurst St OL1 . . . .**153** E8
Coldstone Dr WN4 . . . .**72** D4
Coldstream Ave M9 . . . . . .**64** D4
Cole Ave WA12 . . . .**89** C4
Cole St M40 . . . .**157** F8
Colebrook Dr M40 . . . .**83** A6
Colebrook Rd WA15 . . . . .**120** A6
Coleby Ave
Manchester M16 . . . .**97** C4
Wythenshawe M22 . . . .**121** F4
Coleclough Pl WA3 . . . .**91** A4
Coledale Dr M24 . . . .**46** C2
Coleford Gr BL1 . . . .**145** E6
Colemore Ave M20 . . . . . .**110** D3
Colenso Ct ④ BL2 . . . .**148** C3
Colenso Gr SK4 . . . .**168** B3
Colenso Rd BL2 . . . .**42** D7
Colenso St OL8 . . . .**66** D3
Coleport Cl SK8 . . . .**123** A1
Coleridge Ave
Middleton M24 . . . .**47** C3
Radcliffe M26 . . . .**43** E4
Wigan WN5 . . . .**54** A6
Coleridge Cl SK5 . . . .**99** E1
Coleridge Pl WN3 . . . .**54** F3
Coleridge Rd
Littleborough OL15 . . . .**15** F2
Longshaw WN5 . . . .**53** D1
Manchester M16 . . . .**97** C3
Oldham OL1 . . . .**49** E4
Ramsbottom BL8 . . . .**10** E2
Reddish SK5 . . . .**99** E1
Coleridge Way SK5 . . . .**99** E1
Colerne Way WN3 . . . .**54** D2
Colesbourne Cl M38 . . . .**60** A6
Coleshill Rise WN3 . . . .**54** C2
Coleshill St M40 . . . .**83** B4
Colesmere Wlk M40 . . . . . .**65** D1
Colgate Cres M14 . . . .**110** B8
Colgate La M5 . . . .**161** A6
Colgrove Ave M40 . . . .**65** C2
Colin Rd SK4 . . . .**169** E4
Colin St WN1 . . . .**37** D1

Colina Dr M7 . . . .**155** E5
Colindale Ave M9 . . . .**64** E4
Colindale Dr ⑦ BL3 . . . . .**144** C5
Colinwood Cl BL9 . . . .**44** F3
Coll Dr M41 . . . .**95** D5
Coll's La OL3 . . . .**50** D4
Collard St M46 . . . .**58** B4
College Ave Droylsden M43 .**99** F8
Oldham OL8 . . . .**66** E4
Wigan WN1 . . . .**150** C8
College Cl Bolton BL3 . . . .**145** E6
Stockport SK2 . . . .**124** A6
Wilmslow SK9 . . . .**136** F8
College Croft ⑩ M30 . . . . .**79** F2
College Dr M16 . . . .**97** C2
College Ho
Altrincham WA14 . . . .**119** C1
Manchester SK4 . . . .**168** B4
College Land M3 . . . .**158** F1
College Rd Manchester M16 **97** D2
Oldham OL8 . . . .**66** E4
Orrell WN8 . . . .**35** B1
Orrell WN8 . . . .**53** B8
Rochdale OL12 . . . .**139** E7
Salford M30 . . . .**80** A2
College St WN7 . . . .**76** A5
College Way BL3 . . . .**145** E6
Collen Cres BL8 . . . .**27** C6
Collett Cl WN1 . . . .**151** E8
Collett St OL1 . . . .**67** C8
Colley St Rochdale OL16 . . .**15** B1
Stretford M32 . . . .**96** F5
Collie Ave M6,M7 . . . .**81** C5
Collier Ave OL16 . . . .**31** F7
Collier Cl SK14 . . . .**102** E1
Collier Ct M19 . . . .**99** A1
Collier Hill OL8 . . . .**66** D3
Collier Hill Ave OL8 . . . . . .**66** C3
Collier St Glossop SK13 . .**116** C8
③ Hindley WN2 . . . .**56** D6
Manchester M3 . . . .**158** E2
Manchester M3 . . . .**162** E8
Manchester M6 . . . .**80** F6
⑥ Swinton M27 . . . .**79** E7
Collier Wlk ④ SK14 . . . . .**102** E1
Collier's Row BL1 . . . .**23** E5
Colliers Cl WN7 . . . .**75** E2
Colliers Row Rd BL1 . . . . . .**23** E5
Colliery La M46 . . . .**58** A4
Colliery St Droylsden M11 . .**83** A1
Manchester M11 . . . .**165** B8
Collin Ave M18 . . . .**99** C4
Colling Cl M44 . . . .**94** A1
Colling St BL0 . . . .**138** B5
Collingburn Ave M5 . . . . . .**161** B7
Collingburn Ct M5 . . . .**161** B7
Collinge Ave M24 . . . .**65** C8
Collinge St Bury BL8 . . . . . .**27** B4
Heywood OL10 . . . .**29** C2
Middleton M23 . . . .**65** D7
Platt Bridge WN2 . . . .**56** A2
Shaw OL2 . . . .**149** B7
Collingham St M8 . . . .**159** B4
Collings St BL1 . . . .**143** E2
Collington Cl M12 . . . .**165** A5
Collingwood Ave M43 . . . .**83** E3
Collingwood Cl SK12 . . . . .**134** A3
Collingwood Dr M27 . . . . . .**80** B7
Collingwood Rd
Manchester M19 . . . .**98** C1
Newton-le-W WA12 . . . .**89** B3
Collingwood St
Middleton OL11 . . . .**47** D8
Standish WN6 . . . .**19** E1
Collingwood Way
Oldham OL1 . . . .**153** F8
Westhoughton BL5 . . . .**39** E1
Collins La BL5 . . . .**57** F6
Collins St BL8 . . . .**26** F4
Collisdene Rd WN5 . . . .**53** B6
Collop Dr OL10 . . . .**46** E7
Collyhurst Ave ② M28 . . . .**60** C8
Collyhurst Rd M40 . . . . . .**156** C5
Collyhurst St M40 . . . .**160** D4
Colman Gdns M5 . . . .**161** B7
Colmore Dr M9 . . . .**65** A4
Colmore Gr BL2 . . . .**25** D3
Colmore St BL2 . . . .**25** B3
Colnbrook WN6 . . . .**19** B1
Colne St OL11 . . . .**30** D1
Colonial Rd SK2 . . . .**124** A6
Colshaw Cl E M26 . . . .**43** F4
Colshaw Cl S M26 . . . .**43** F4
Colshaw Dr SK9 . . . .**131** D2
Colshaw Rd M23 . . . .**121** A4
Colshaw Wlk SK9 . . . .**131** D1
Colson Dr M24 . . . .**64** F7
Colsterdale Cl OL2 . . . .**48** E5
Colt Hill La Oldham OL3 . . . .**69** A6
Uppermill OL3 . . . .**68** D7
Coltishall Ho SK8 . . . .**123** A5
Coltness Wlk ⑫ M40 . . . . . .**83** C5
Coltsfoot Dr WA14 . . . .**119** B8
Columbia Ave M18,M34 . . . .**99** F4
Columbia Rd BL1 . . . .**144** C8
Columbia St OL8 . . . .**66** F4
Columbine Cl OL12 . . . .**14** C3
Columbine St M11 . . . .**99** D7
Columbine Wlk ⑧ M31 . . .**105** F3
Columbus St ⑦ WN4 . . . . . .**72** F5
Colville Dr BL8 . . . .**27** B1
Colville Gr
③ Altrincham WA15 . . . . . .**120** A4
Sale M33 . . . .**107** E1
Colville Rd OL1 . . . .**48** D1
Colwell Ave M32 . . . .**96** B1
Colwell Wlk M9 . . . .**64** B5

Colwick Ave WA14 . . . . . .**119** E6
Colwith Ave BL2 . . . .**25** E1
Colwood Wlk ⑬ M8 . . . . . .**155** F6
Colwyn Ave
Manchester M14 . . . .**110** E8
Middleton M24 . . . .**65** A6
Colwyn Cres SK5 . . . .**111** F5
Colwyn Dr WN2 . . . .**57** C2
Colwyn Gr M46 . . . .**58** C5
Colwyn Rd Bramhall SK7 . .**132** F8
Cheadle SK8 . . . .**122** E1
Swinton M27 . . . .**79** C6
Colwyn St Ashton-u-L OL7 . .**85** A6
Oldham OL9 . . . .**153** D7
Rochdale OL11 . . . .**30** B2
Salford M6 . . . .**154** F3
Colyton Wlk ⑦ M22 . . . . . .**121** F3
Combe Cl M11 . . . .**83** B3
Combermere Ave M20 . . . .**110** A7
Combermere Cl SK8 . . . . .**122** F4
Combermere St SK16 . . . .**166** C1
Combs Bank ① SK13 . . . . .**171** D1
Combs Fold ㊷ SK13 . . . . .**171** D2
Combs Gdns ㊺ SK13 . . . . .**171** D2
Combs Gr ㊸ SK13 . . . .**171** D2
Combs Lea ⑪ SK13 . . . . . .**171** D1
Combs Mews SK13 . . . . . .**171** D1
Combs Terr ② SK13 . . . . .**171** D1
Combs Way ㊶ SK13 . . . . .**171** D2
Comer Terr M33 . . . .**108** A4
Comet Rd WN5 . . . .**54** C8
Comet St M1 . . . .**159** B1
Commercial Ave SK8 . . . . .**131** F5
Commercial Brow SK14 . .**167** E4
Commercial Rd
Hazel Grove SK7 . . . .**124** E3
Oldham OL1 . . . .**153** F6
Commercial St Bacup OL13 . .**3** D8
Hyde SK14 . . . .**167** E3
Manchester M15 . . . .**162** F7
Oldham OL9 . . . .**152** C6
Commodore Pl WN5 . . . . . .**36** E1
Common End PR7 . . . .**20** E5
Common La Culcheth WA3 . .**91** E4
Leigh WN7 . . . .**75** B4
Partington M31 . . . .**106** B5
Partington M31 . . . .**106** A4
Tyldesley M29 . . . .**59** A1
Common Nook WN2 . . . . . .**56** B1
Common Side Rd M28 . . . . .**77** F7
Common St BL5 . . . .**57** B7
Common The PR7 . . . .**20** E5
Commonwealth Cl WN7 . . .**76** B3
Como St BL3 . . . .**146** C4
Como Wlk M18 . . . .**165** B6
Compass St M11 . . . .**165** C7
Compstall Ave M14 . . . .**98** B1
Compstall Gr ⑦ M18 . . . . . .**99** E6
Compstall Rd SK6 . . . .**113** E2
Compton Cl M41 . . . .**94** C1
Compton Dr M23 . . . .**121** A2
Compton St ⑤ SK15 . . . . . .**86** B1
Compton Way
Middleton M24 . . . .**65** C6
Shaw OL2 . . . .**149** B6
Comrie Wlk ⑦ M23 . . . . . .**121** A5
Comus St M5 . . . .**161** C8
Concert La M2 . . . .**159** A1
Concord Ave WN3 . . . .**55** B3
Concord Bsns Pk M22 . . . . **121** E2
Concord Pl M6 . . . .**81** A5
Concord Way ① SK16 . . . .**166** C1
Condor Cl M43 . . . .**84** C3
Condor Pl M6 . . . .**81** A5
Condor Wlk M13 . . . .**163** B6
Conduit St Ashton-u-L OL6 **166** C2
Oldham OL1 . . . .**49** E3
Tintwistle SK13 . . . .**103** F7
Conewood Wlk ⑨ M13 . . .**163** C6
Coney Gr M23 . . . .**121** A7
Coney Green High Sch
M26 . . . .**44** B4
Coneymead SK15 . . . .**86** A4
Congham Rd ⑥ SK3 . . . . .**123** C8
Congleton Ave M14 . . . .**98** A2
Congleton Rd SK9 . . . .**137** A1
Congou St M1 . . . .**163** B8
Congreave St OL1 . . . .**153** E8
Congresbury Rd WN7 . . . . .**75** D7
Conifer Wlk Leigh WN7 . . . .**75** B5
Partington M31 . . . .**105** E3
Coningsby Dr M9 . . . .**157** D8
Conisber Cl BL7 . . . .**8** E1
Conisborough OL11 . . . . . .**139** E6
Conisborough Pl M45 . . . . .**63** B7
Coniston Ave Adlington PR6 **21** B8
Ashton-in-M WN4 . . . .**73** B4
Atherton M46 . . . .**58** D5
Dukinfield SK14 . . . .**101** C4
Farnworth BL4 . . . .**59** F8
Ince-in-M WN2 . . . .**56** B7
Manchester M9 . . . .**157** D8
Oldham OL8 . . . .**66** D4
Orrell WN5 . . . .**53** F7
Sale M33 . . . .**108** C2
Walkden M38 . . . .**60** A4
Whitefield M45 . . . .**62** F8
Wigan WN1 . . . .**37** C3
Coniston Cl
Chadderton OL9 . . . .**152** A7
Little Lever BL3 . . . .**43** A4
Ramsbottom BL0 . . . .**138** C7
Reddish M34 . . . .**100** B3
Coniston Dr Abram WN2 . . .**74** B8
Bury BL9 . . . .**44** E7
Handforth SK9 . . . .**131** C4
Middleton M24 . . . .**46** F2
Stalybridge SK15 . . . .**86** A3

Coniston Gr
Ashton-u-L OL7 . . . .**166** A4
Heywood OL10 . . . .**46** D8
Royton OL2 . . . .**48** D6
Walkden M38 . . . .**60** A4
Coniston Ho ⑥ M28 . . . . . .**60** C7
Coniston Park Dr WN6 . . . .**37** A6
Coniston Rd Blackrod BL6 . .**21** C5
Flixton M41 . . . .**106** E8
Gatley SK8 . . . .**122** B5
High Lane SK6 . . . .**134** D8
Hindley WN2 . . . .**56** E4
Partington M31 . . . .**105** E4
Reddish SK5 . . . .**111** F6
Stretford M32 . . . .**96** C3
Swinton M27 . . . .**79** F7
Tyldesley M29 . . . .**77** A7
Coniston St Bolton BL1 . . .**143** F3
⑥ Failsworth M40 . . . .**83** C5
Leigh WN7 . . . .**75** E5
Salford M6 . . . .**81** B4
Coniston Wlk WA15 . . . . . .**120** D5
Conmere Sq ⑤ M15 . . . . . .**162** F7
Connaught Ave
Manchester M19 . . . .**110** F7
Rochdale OL16 . . . .**31** B3
Whitefield M45 . . . .**63** A7
Connaught Cl SK9 . . . .**137** C8
Connaught Dr WA12 . . . . . .**89** C2
Connaught Sq BL2 . . . .**25** B2
Connaught St Bury BL8 . . . .**27** B1
④ Oldham OL8 . . . .**153** E6
Connel Cl BL2 . . . .**42** F4
Connell Rd M23 . . . .**121** A4
Connell Way OL10 . . . .**29** F3
Connery Cres OL6 . . . .**85** D6
Connie St M11 . . . .**165** C8
Conningsby Cl ⑩ BL7 . . . . .**24** C7
Connington Ave M9 . . . .**64** D1
Connington Cl OL2 . . . .**48** C4
Connor Way SK8 . . . .**121** F4
Conquest Cl M12 . . . .**165** A6
Conrad Cl Oldham OL1 . . . . .**49** C4
Wigan WN3 . . . .**150** A5
Conran St M9 . . . .**157** E7
Consett Ave M23 . . . .**121** A6
Consort Ave OL2 . . . .**48** C6
Consort Cl ② SK16 . . . . . .**101** C4
Consort Pl WA14 . . . .**119** B3
Constable Cl BL1 . . . .**143** D1
Constable Dr Marple SK6 . .**126** B8
Wilmslow SK9 . . . .**137** E8
Constable St M18 . . . .**99** E6
Constable Wlk ⑬ M34 . . . .**113** A7
Constance Gdns M5 . . . . . .**154** F1
Constance Rd Bolton BL3 . .**146** C4
Partington M31 . . . .**105** F3
Constance St M15 . . . .**162** E7
Constantia St WN3 . . . .**55** F3
Constantine Ct M6 . . . .**81** B3
Constantine Rd OL16 . . . . .**139** F7
Constantine St OL4 . . . .**67** D7
Consul St M22 . . . .**109** E1
Convamore Rd SK7 . . . . . .**132** C2
Convent St OL8 . . . .**67** C4
Conway Ave Bolton BL1 . . .**142** A1
Irlam M44 . . . .**105** F8
Swinton M27 . . . .**62** B3
Whitefield M45 . . . .**62** F7
Conway Cl Heywood OL10 . . .**29** A3
Leigh WN7 . . . .**76** E2
Manchester M16 . . . .**97** A3
Middleton M24 . . . .**65** A7
Ramsbottom BL0 . . . .**138** B6
Whitefield M45 . . . .**62** F7
Conway Cres Billinge WN5 . .**71** E5
Ramsbottom BL8 . . . .**10** F2
Conway Dr
Altrincham WA15 . . . .**120** C6
Aspull WN2 . . . .**38** D5
Billinge WN5 . . . .**71** F5
Bury BL9 . . . .**28** D2
Hazel Grove SK7 . . . .**124** C1
Newton-le-W WA12 . . . .**89** E3
Stalybridge SK15 . . . .**86** A3
Conway Gr OL9 . . . .**47** F1
Conway Rd
Ashton-in-M WN4 . . . .**73** C5
Cheadle SK8 . . . .**122** E2
Hindley WN2 . . . .**56** F4
Sale M33 . . . .**108** D3
Urmston M41 . . . .**95** D4
Conway St Farnworth BL4 . .**60** E7
Reddish SK5 . . . .**169** E4
Wigan WN5 . . . .**54** C5
Conyngham Rd M14 . . . . . .**98** D3
Cook St Abram WN2 . . . .**56** B1
Bury BL9 . . . .**141** A2
Denton M34 . . . .**100** F6
Eccles M30 . . . .**79** C2
Leigh WN7 . . . .**75** F5
Manchester M3 . . . .**158** E2
Oldham OL4 . . . .**67** C7
Rochdale OL16 . . . .**15** B1
Stockport SK3 . . . .**169** E1
Cook Terr
㉑ Dukinfield SK16 . . . . . .**166** B1
Rochdale OL16 . . . .**15** B1
Cooke St Ashton-in-M WN4 . .**72** F1
Denton M34 . . . .**100** F3
Dukinfield SK14 . . . .**101** F5
Failsworth M35 . . . .**83** F8
Farnworth BL4 . . . .**60** E7
Hazel Grove SK7 . . . .**124** D3
Horwich BL6 . . . .**22** D4
Cooling La M29,WN7 . . . . . .**76** E3
Coomassie St
Heywood OL10 . . . .**29** C1

Coomassie St *continued*
Radcliffe M26 44 A3
Salford M6 154 F3
Coombe Cl M29 77 B8
Coombes Ave Hyde SK14 167 F1
Marple SK6 125 F5
Coombes La SK13 115 C5
Coombes St SK2 124 B5
Coombes View SK14 114 F8
Coop St Bolton BL1 143 E4
1 Manchester M4 159 B2
Wigan WN1 37 D1
Cooper Fold M24 47 A4
Cooper Ho M15 163 A6
Cooper La Manchester M9 64 D5
Middleton M24 46 F3
Cooper St Bury BL9 140 E2
Dukinfield SK16 166 B1
Glossop SK13 104 B1
Hazel Grove SK7 124 F3
Horwich BL6 22 B4
Littleborough OL12 15 D4
Manchester M2 158 F1
Oldham OL4 68 A7
Stockport SK1 170 F7
Stretford M32 96 D1
Cooper Terr OL16 31 B8
Cooper's Fold SK8 131 F6
Cooper's La PR7 18 B8
Cooper's Row BL1 145 F7
Cooperative St OL14 6 A7
Coopers Glen WN2 56 A8
Coopers Row WN1 150 C8
Coopers Wlk OL16 15 C2
Cop Rd OL1 49 C4
Copage Dr SK6 113 A4
Cope Bank 12 BL1 142 C2
Cope Bank Mews BL1 142 C1
Cope Bank W BL1 142 B2
Cope Cl M11 99 E7
Cope St BL1 142 C1
Copeland Ave M27 62 C1
Copeland Cl M24 46 C1
Copeland Dr WN6 19 F1
Copeland Mews BL1 144 A7
Copeland St SK14 101 D5
Copeman Cl M13 163 C6
Copenhagen Sq 20 OL16 31 A8
Copenhagen St
Failsworth M40 83 A6
Rochdale OL16 31 A8
Copesthorne Cl WN2 38 C6
Copgrove Rd M21 109 B7
Copgrove Wlk M22 130 E7
Copley Ave SK15 86 C2
Copley High Sch SK15 86 D2
Copley Park Mews SK15 86 C2
Copley Rd M21 97 A2
Copley St OL2 149 C8
Coplow Dale WN2 56 E3
Copper Beech Dr SK13 171 E1
Copper Beech Manor SK13 171 E1
Copper La M45 62 B7
Copperas Cl WN6 36 B7
Copperas La Aspull WN2 38 A6
Blackrod BL6 21 B1
Droylsden M43 99 E8
Copperas St M4 159 A2
Copperbeech M22 109 E1
Copperbeech Dr WN6 37 B7
Copperfield WN1 37 C2
Copperfield Rd
Bramhall SK8 132 B5
Poynton SK12 133 D2
Copperfields Bolton BL6 40 B3
Poynton SK12 133 D2
Wilmslow SK9 137 C8
Copperways M20 110 B5
Coppice Ave M33 107 D2
Coppice Cl
High Lane SK12 135 A6
Romiley SK6 113 B4
Coppice Dr
High Lane SK12 135 A6
Longshaw WN5 53 D2
Whitworth OL12 14 D7
Wigan WN3 54 F2
Wythenshawe M22 109 D1
Coppice Inf Sch OL8 66 E4
Coppice Jun Sch OL8 66 E4
Coppice La SK12 135 A5
Coppice Rd SK12 134 B3
Coppice St Bury BL9 141 C3
Oldham OL8 153 D5
Coppice The
Altrincham WA15 129 B8
Bolton BL2 25 D5
Middleton M24 65 B5
Prestwich M25 63 A4
Ramsbottom BL0 11 A4
Swinton M28 79 C5
Worsley M28 78 F8
Coppice Way SK9 131 E3
Coppice Wlk M34 100 D2
Copping St M12 164 F6
Coppingford Cl OL12 14 A2
Coppins The SK9 136 E4
Coppleridge Dr M8 64 A2
Copplestone Ct M27 61 C1
Copplestone Dr M33 107 C5
Coppull Cross Rds PR7 19 F7
Coppull Hall La PR7 20 B8
Coppull La WN1 37 D2
Coppull Moor La PR7 19 E6
Copse Ave M22 121 E3
Copse Dr BL9 27 F6
Copse The
Altrincham WA15 129 D7
Edgworth BL7 9 C2
Marple SK6 126 C8
Newton-le-W WA12 89 B4
Wigan WN5 54 A6
Copse Wlk OL15 15 F5
Copson St M20 110 B7
Copster Ave OL8 66 E3
Copster Hill Rd OL8 66 E4
Copster Pl OL8 66 E3
Copthall La M8 155 F8
Copthorn Wlk BL8 26 F5
Copthorne Cl OL10 46 D8
Copthorne Cres M13 98 E3
Copthorne Dr BL2 42 E6
Coptrod Head Cl OL12 14 E4
Coral Ave SK8 123 A1
Coral Gr WN7 75 E4
Coral Rd SK8 123 A1
Coral St Manchester M13 163 C7
Wigan WN6 37 A3
Coralin Way WN4 72 F7
Coram St M18 99 F6
Corbar Rd SK2 124 B5
Corbett Ct 5 WN2 56 E5
Corbett St Droylsden M11 83 A1
Rochdale OL16 31 B8
Corbridge Wlk 7 M8 156 B6
Corby St M12 165 A6
Corcoran Cl OL10 29 C3
Corcoran Dr SK6 113 F2
Corda Ave M22 121 D8
Corday La M25 63 D8
Cordingley Ave M43 99 F8
Cordova Ave M34 99 F3
Corelli St M40 160 F4
Corfe Cl Aspull WN2 38 D5
Urmston M41 94 C1
Corfe Cres SK7 124 D1
Corhampton Cres M46 58 E5
Corinth Wlk M28 60 D2
Corinthian Ave M7 81 C5
Cork St Ashton-u-L OL6 166 C3
Bury BL9 141 A2
Manchester M12 164 D8
Corkland Cl OL6 85 E2
Corkland Rd M21 109 C8
Corkland St OL6 85 E2
Corks La SK12 135 E5
Corley Ave SK3 122 F7
Cormallen Gr M35 84 A7
Cormorant Cl M28 60 C3
Cormorant Wlk M12 165 A6
Corn Cl M13 163 C5
Corn Hey Rd M33 107 C2
Corn Hill La M34 100 B5
Corn Mill Cl
Garswood WN4 72 D4
Rochdale OL12 15 C4
Corn St Failsworth M35 83 C6
Glossop SK13 104 D1
Leigh WN7 75 D5
Oldham OL4 67 A7
Cornall St BL8 27 C3
Cornbrook Cl
Littleborough OL12 15 C6
Westhoughton BL5 57 D6
Cornbrook Ct M15 162 D6
Cornbrook Gr M16 162 D5
Cornbrook Park Rd M15 161 C6
Cornbrook Rd M15 161 C7
Cornbrook Sta M15 161 C6
Cornbrook St M16 162 D5
Cornbrook Way M16 162 D5
Cornelian Gr WN4 72 F5
Cornell St M4 159 B2
Corner Croft SK9 137 A4
Corner Ct SK8 122 F6
Corner La WN7 57 D3
Corner St OL6 166 C2
Cornergate BL5 57 E5
Cornet St M7 155 D5
Cornfield SK15 102 E7
Cornfield Cl Bury BL9 27 F7
2 Sale M33 108 F3
Cornfield Dr M22 121 C3
Cornfield Rd SK6 113 E3
Cornfield St OL16 32 A5
Cornford Ave M18 99 B3
Cornhill Ave M41 95 B3
Cornhill Rd M41 95 B3
Cornhill St OL1 49 D2
Cornish Cl M22 130 D8
Cornish Way OL2 49 A4
Cornishway M22 130 D8
Cornishway Ind Est 3 M22 130 D8
Cornlea Dr M28 78 C7
Cornwall Ave Atherton BL5 58 F8
Manchester M19 111 B8
Tyldesley M29 59 A3
Cornwall Cl SK6 134 E7
Cornwall Cres
Brinnington SK5 112 C6
Diggle OL3 51 B4
Standish WN1 20 B1
Cornwall Ct 2 M18 99 D6
Cornwall Dr Bury BL9 45 A8
Hindley WN2 56 F6
Cornwall Ho M3 158 D1
Cornwall Pl WN5 54 C6
Cornwall Rd Droylsden M43 84 A3
Gatley SK8 131 B8
Irlam M44 105 D5
Cornwall St 2 Eccles M30 79 C1
Manchester M11,M18 99 D7
Oldham OL9 152 B5
Cornwallis Rd WN3 150 A5
Cornwell Cl SK9 137 D8
Cornwood Cl 5 M8 155 F7
Corona Ave Hyde SK14 167 E3
Oldham OL8 66 E3
Coronation Ave
Atherton M46 58 C5
Dukinfield SK16 101 F6
Glazebury WA3 92 C7
Heywood OL10 46 E8
Hyde SK14 167 E1
Coronation Dr
Ashton-in-M WA11 89 A7
Leigh WN7 76 E6
Newton-le-W WA12 89 E1
Coronation Gdns M26 43 E4
Coronation Rd
Ashton-u-L OL6 85 C6
Droylsden M43 83 F3
Failsworth M35 83 E6
Radcliffe M26 43 E4
Wigan WN6 36 D3
Coronation Sq
Little Lever BL3 43 B3
Manchester M1,M12 163 C8
Coronation St Bolton BL1 145 F7
Denton M34 100 D3
Downall Green WN4 72 D6
Ince-in-M WN3 55 F3
Manchester M11 165 C8
Manchester M3 162 E8
Reddish SK5 169 E4
Salford M5 161 B8
Swinton M27 62 A1
Wigan WN3 150 B6
Coronation Wlk
Billinge WN5 71 D4
Radcliffe M26 43 E5
Corporation Rd
Denton M34 100 D5
Eccles M30 79 F1
Rochdale OL11 139 D6
Rochdale OL11 139 D7
Corporation St Bolton BL1 145 F7
Hyde SK14 167 D2
Manchester M4 159 A2
Middleton M24 65 A8
Stalybridge SK15 86 A1
Stockport SK1 169 F2
Wigan WN3 150 B6
Corpus Christi RC Inf & Jun Sch OL9 66 B4
Corpus Christi RC Prim Sch M40 160 D4
Corran Cl M30 79 B2
Corranstone Cl BL6 22 B3
Correction Brow SK12 134 C6
Corrie Cl M34 100 F1
Corrie Cres BL4 61 D4
Corrie Dr M26 61 D5
Corrie Prim Sch M34 100 F1
Corrie Rd M27 62 A3
Corrie St M38 60 A4
Corrie Way SK6 112 F5
Corrigan St M18 99 E6
Corrin Rd BL2 148 B5
Corring Way BL1 25 B4
Corringham Rd M19 111 C7
Corriss Ave M9 64 A5
Corry St OL10 29 E2
Corsey Rd WN2 56 E4
Corsock Dr WN1 37 E1
Corson St BL4 42 D2
Corston Gr BL6 21 D1
Corston Wlk M40 83 B6
Corwen Ave M9 157 E8
Corwen Cl OL8 66 B2
Cosgrove Cres M35 83 E5
Cosgrove Rd M35 83 E5
Cosham Rd M22 121 F3
Costabeck Wlk M40 83 D4
Costessey Way WN3 54 C3
Costobadie Cl SK14 102 F3
Costobadie Way SK14 102 F3
Cosworth Cl 7 WN7 76 B4
Cotaline Cl OL11 30 B3
Cote Green La SK6 114 B1
Cote Green Rd SK6 114 C1
Cote La Delph OL3 51 B7
Littleborough OL15 15 F6
Uppermill OL5 68 E3
Cotefield Ave BL3 147 F3
Cotefield Cl 7 SK6 125 F5
Cotefield Rd M22 121 C2
Cotford Rd BL1 24 F5
Cotman Dr SK6 126 C8
Cotswold Ave Golborne WA3 90 D6
Hazel Grove SK7 124 B1
Oldham OL9 152 A5
Shaw OL2 149 A8
Shaw OL2 48 F8
Urmston M41 94 F3
Wigan WN5 54 B5
Cotswold Cl Glossop SK13 116 A8
Prestwich M25 63 C5
Ramsbottom BL0 11 C4
Cotswold Cres Bury BL8 27 B3
Milnrow OL16 32 A7
Cotswold Dr Horwich BL6 22 C5
Royton OL2 48 B3
Salford M6 154 F3
Cotswold Rd SK4 169 D3
Cottage Croft BL2 25 D5
Cottage Gdns SK6 112 D3
Cottage Hospl M41 95 D2
Cottage La SK13 171 E2
Cottage Lawns SK9 137 B2
Cottage Wlk Droylsden M43 83 F3
Cottage Wlk *continued*
Rochdale OL12 14 C4
Cottam Cres SK6 126 B7
Cottam Gr M27 80 A7
Cottam St Bury BL8 27 C3
Oldham OL1 153 D8
Cottenham La M3,M7 158 E4
Cottenham St M13 163 B6
Cotter St M12 163 C7
Cotterdale Cl M16 97 D2
Cotteril Cl M23 120 C8
Cotterill St M5,M6 81 B2
Cottesmore Dr M8 156 C8
Cottesmore Gdns WA15 129 C8
Cottesmore Way WA3 74 B1
Cottingham Dr OL6 166 C4
Cottingham Rd M12 164 E6
Cottingley Cl BL1 24 D5
Cotton Cl SK14 167 E1
Cotton Fold OL16 31 C6
Cotton Hill M20 110 C5
Cotton La M20 110 C6
Cotton Mill Cres OL9 66 B4
Cotton St Bolton BL1 143 D2
Leigh WN7 75 D5
Manchester M4 159 B2
Cotton St E OL6 166 B2
Cotton St W OL6 166 A2
Cotton Tree Cl OL4 67 E8
Cotton Tree St SK4 169 E1
Cottonfield Rd M20 110 C6
Cottonwood Dr 3 M33 107 C5
Cottrell Rd WA15 129 D7
Cotts The OL4 50 B1
Coucill Sq BL4 60 E8
Coulsden Dr M9 64 D3
Coulthart St OL6 166 B3
Coulthurst St BL0 138 B6
Coultshead Ave WN5 71 E6
Council Ave WN4 73 B3
Councillor La SK8 123 A4
Councillor St M12 160 E1
Count St OL16 31 A5
Countess Ave SK8 131 E5
Countess Gr M7 158 D4
Countess La M26 43 D4
Countess Pl M25 63 C4
Countess Rd M20 110 B3
Countess St Ashton-u-L OL6 85 D2
Stockport SK2 124 A5
Counthill Com Sec Sch OL4 49 D2
Counthill Dr M8 63 E2
Counthill Rd OL4 49 D1
Counting House Rd SK12 135 E5
County Ave OL6 85 E4
County Police St WN2 151 F7
County Rd M28 60 A4
County St Manchester M2 158 F1
Oldham OL8 66 C2
Coupes Gn BL5 57 F6
Coupland Cl OL4 49 F4
Coupland Rd WN2 57 C4
Coupland St
Manchester M15 163 A5
Whitworth OL12 14 C8
Courage Low La WN6 18 D5
Courier Pl WN5 36 E1
Courier St M18 99 F6
Course View OL4 67 E3
Court Dr M40 83 E4
Court House Way 4 OL10 29 D2
Court St Bolton BL2 148 A7
Oldham OL3 69 B8
Courtfield Ave M9 64 D4
Courthill St SK1 124 A8
Courtney Gn SK9 131 D2
Courtney Pl WA14 119 A1
Courtyard Dr M28 60 A3
Courtyard The Bolton BL1 143 F1
Hollingworth SK14 103 D5
Newton-le-W WA12 89 E4
Cousin Fields BL7 25 C7
Covall Wlk 4 M8 156 B6
Cove The WA15 119 F3
Covell Rd SK12 133 D5
Covent Gdns SK1 169 F1
Coventry Ave SK3 122 F7
Coventry Gr OL9 48 A1
Coventry Rd M26 43 F5
Coventry St OL11 139 F6
Coverdale Ave Bolton BL1 144 A8
Royton OL2 48 C5
Coverdale Cl OL10 29 C1
Coverdale Cres M12 164 E6
Coverdale Rd BL5 57 D8
Coverham Ave OL4 67 D4
Coverhill Rd OL4 68 B5
Covert Rd Oldham OL4 67 D3
Wythenshawe M22 121 E5
Coverts The WN6 36 F2
Covington Pl SK9 137 B6
Cow La Ashley WA15 128 F6
Bolton BL3 146 B2
Failsworth M35 83 E7
Manchester M5 81 C1
Oldham OL4 67 C7
Sale M33 108 E5
Stockport SK2,SK7 124 D4
Cow Lees BL5 40 A1
Cowan St M40 160 D2
Cowbrook Ave SK13 104 F1
Cowburn Dr SK22 127 C1
Cowburn St Heywood OL10 29 E1
Hindley WN2 56 F6
1 Leigh WN7 75 D5
Manchester M3 158 F3
Cowdals Rd BL6 40 B4
Cowesby St M14 98 A3
Cowhill La OL6 166 C3
Cowie St OL2 149 B8
Cowley Gr SK14 102 F3
Cowley Rd BL1 24 F5
Cowley St 9 M40 83 C6
Cowling St Manchester M7 80 F8
Oldham OL8 66 F4
Wigan WN3 150 B6
Cowlishaw OL2 149 A5
Cowlishaw La OL2 149 A5
Cowlishaw Rd SK14,SK6 113 F4
Cowm Park Way N OL12 4 D2
Cowm Park Way S OL12 4 C1
Cowm St OL12 4 E5
Cowm Top La OL11 30 E2
Cowpe Rd BB4 2 F7
Cowper Ave M46 58 D5
Cowper St Ashton-u-L OL6 166 C3
Leigh WN7 75 D5
Middleton M24 65 D8
Cowper Wlk 4 M11 160 F1
Cox Green Cl BL7 8 D3
Cox Green Rd
2 Bolton BL7 24 F8
Bolton BL7 8 E2
Cox Way M46 58 D3
Coxfield WN6 35 D7
Coxton Rd M22 121 E1
Coxwold Gr BL3 146 C2
Crab Brow M46 58 B3
Crab La M9 64 B4
Crab Lane Prim Sch M9 64 B4
Crab Tree La M46 58 D2
Crabbe St M4 159 A3
Crabtree Ave
Altrincham WA15 129 D7
Disley SK12 135 E5
Crabtree Ct SK12 135 D6
Crabtree La M11 83 D1
Crabtree Rd Oldham OL1 67 B8
Wigan WN5 54 D7
Crabtree St BL9 141 B3
Craddock Rd M33 108 C2
Craddock St 4 OL5 68 C1
Cradley Ave M11 99 D8
Crag Ave BL9 11 D2
Crag Fold BL9 11 D2
Crag Gr WA11 71 B1
Crag La BL9 11 D2
Cragg Rd OL1 48 A2
Cragie St M8 155 F5
Cragside Way SK9 137 C6
Craig Ave Bury BL8 27 B1
Urmston M41 95 A3
Craig Cl SK4 168 B1
Craig Rd Manchester M18 99 C4
Stockport SK4 168 B1
Craig Wlk OL8 153 E5
Craigend Dr M9 157 E7
Craighall Ave M19 110 F8
Craighall Rd BL1 24 E6
Craiglands OL16 31 B2
Craigmore Ave M20 109 E4
Craignair Ct M27 80 C7
Craigslands Ave M40 83 A6
Craigweil Ave M20 110 D3
Craigwell Rd M25 63 E2
Craigwell Wlk M13 163 B7
Crail Pl OL10 28 F1
Cramer St M10,M40 157 F5
Crammond Cl M40 83 D6
Cramond Cl BL1 143 D1
Cramond Wlk 6 BL1 143 D1
Crampton Dr WA15 129 C8
Crampton La M31 106 D6
Cranage Rd M19 111 B8
Cranage Way 16 SK9 131 D5
Cranark Cl BL1 144 A7
Cranberry Ave Walsden OL14 6 B7
Wigan WN6 36 F3
Cranberry Cl WA14 119 B8
Cranberry Rd M31 105 F3
Cranberry St OL4 67 B6
Cranborne Cl Horwich BL6 22 F1
Standish WN6 19 D1
Cranbourne Ave SK8 123 B2
Cranbourne Cl
1 Altrincham WA15 120 A6
Ashton-u-L OL7 166 A4
Cranbourne Ct SK4 168 B4
Cranbourne Rd
Ashton-u-L OL7 166 B4
Manchester M16 97 C4
Manchester M21 109 B8
Manchester SK4 168 B4
Rochdale OL11 29 E6
Cranbourne St M5 81 C1
Cranbourne Terr OL6 85 B5
Cranbrook Ave WN4 73 A4
Cranbrook Cl BL1 143 F1
Cranbrook Dr M25 63 C2
Cranbrook Gdns OL7 166 B4
Cranbrook Rd Eccles M30 79 B4
Reddish M18 99 F3
Cranbrook St
Ashton-u-L OL7 166 B4
Oldham OL4 67 C6
Radcliffe M26 44 C5
Cranbrook Way WN1 37 B4
Cranbrook Wlk OL9 152 A6
Cranby St 6 WN2 56 D5
Crandon Ct M27 62 A1
Crandon Dr M20 122 C8
Crane St Bolton BL3 146 B3

Crane St continued
Coppull PR7 . . . .**19** D6
Manchester M12 . . . .**163** C8
Cranesbill Cl M22 . . . .**121** C1
Cranfield Cl M40 . . . .**160** D2
Cranfield Rd Horwich BL6 . . .**39** E7
Wigan WN3 . . . .**55** A3
Cranford Ave
Manchester M20 . . . .**110** D4
Sale M33 . . . .**108** C6
Stretford M32 . . . .**96** F3
Whitefield M45 . . . .**44** E2
Cranford Cl Salford M27 . . .**80** B6
Whitefield M45 . . . .**44** E2
Cranford Dr M44 . . . .**93** F3
Cranford Gdns
Marple SK6 . . . .**125** F8
Urmston M41 . . . .**94** E3
Cranford Ho M30 . . . .**79** F3
Cranford Rd
Handforth SK9 . . . .**131** A1
Urmston M41 . . . .**94** E3
Cranford St BL3 . . . .**146** C2
Cranham Ave WA3 . . . .**90** E7
Cranham Cl Bury BL8 . . . . . .**27** B3
Walkden M38 . . . .**60** A6
Cranham Rd M22 . . . .**121** A2
Crank Rd WA11,WN5 . . . . . .**71** B8
Crankwood Rd WN2,WN7 . .**74** D5
Cranleigh WN6 . . . .**37** A8
Cranleigh Ave SK4 . . . .**110** F4
Cranleigh Cl Blackrod BL6 . .**21** D1
Oldham OL1 . . . .**49** E1
Cranleigh Dr Cheadle SK8 .**122** F6
Hazel Grove SK7 . . . .**134** A8
Sale M23, M33 . . . .**108** C1
Sale M33 . . . .**108** A5
Tyldesley M29 . . . .**77** B8
Walkden M28 . . . .**78** E8
Cranlington Dr M8 . . . .**155** F6
Cranmer Ct OL10 . . . .**29** C1
Cranmer Rd M20 . . . .**110** B4
Cranmere Ave M19 . . . .**99** C2
Cranmere Dr M33 . . . .**107** D2
Cranshaw St M29 . . . .**77** D8
Cranstal Dr WN2 . . . .**57** A5
Cranston Dr
Manchester M20 . . . .**122** B8
Sale M33 . . . .**108** C3
Cranston Gr SK8 . . . .**121** F5
Cranswick St ∎ M14 . . . . . .**98** A3
Stalybridge SK15 . . . .**86** D3
Crantock Dr Gatley SK8 . . .**131** C8
Crantock St M12 . . . .**99** B3
Cranwell Ave WA3 . . . .**91** F4
Cranwell Dr M19 . . . .**110** E4
Cranworth Ave M29 . . . .**77** A6
Cranworth St SK15 . . . .**86** B1
Craston Rd M13 . . . .**98** E2
Craunton ⊞ M30 . . . .**79** F2
Craven Ave Golborne WA3 . .**90** E7
Salford M5 . . . .**161** B8
Craven Ct BL6 . . . .**22** D2
Craven Dr
Altrincham WA14 . . . .**119** C8
Salford M5 . . . .**161** A7
Craven Gdns OL11 . . . .**139** E5
Craven Ho OL14 . . . .**6** A8
Craven Pl Bolton BL1 . . . . . .**23** E2
∎ Droylsden M11 . . . .**83** C2
Craven Rd
Altrincham WA14 . . . .**119** C7
∎ Reddish SK5 . . . .**111** F6
Craven St Ashton-u-L OL6 . .**85** D5
Bury BL9 . . . .**141** C3
Manchester M5 . . . .**81** C1
Oldham OL1 . . . .**48** E1
Craven St E BL6 . . . .**22** D2
Craven Terr M33 . . . .**108** C4
Cravenhurst Ave M40 . . . . .**83** B4
Cravenwood Prim Sch M8 64 A1
Cravenwood Rd M8 . . . . . .**156** A8
Crawford Ave
Adlington PR7 . . . .**20** E5
Aspull WN2 . . . .**38** C5
Bolton BL2 . . . .**148** B6
Tyldesley M29 . . . .**58** F2
Worsley M28 . . . .**79** A8
Crawford Cl WN2 . . . .**38** C5
Crawford Sq OL10 . . . .**29** A1
Crawford St Ashton-u-L OL6 **85** D2
Aspull WN2 . . . .**38** C4
Bolton BL2 . . . .**148** B6
Eccles M30 . . . .**79** D3
⊠ Failsworth M40 . . . .**83** C5
Rochdale OL16 . . . .**31** B6
Walsden OL14 . . . .**6** B8
Wigan WN1 . . . .**150** C8
Crawley Ave Salford M30 . . .**80** A3
Wythenshawe M22 . . . .**121** E3
Crawley Cl M29 . . . .**59** C1
Crawley Gr SK2 . . . .**124** B6
Crawley Way OL9 . . . .**152** A6
Cray The OL16 . . . .**31** E6
Cray Wlk M13 . . . .**163** B7
Craydon St M11 . . . .**165** C8
Crayfield Rd M19 . . . .**111** B8
Crayford Rd M40 . . . .**83** B4
Creaton Way M24 . . . .**46** D4
Creden Ave M22 . . . .**121** F3
Crediton Cl
Altrincham WA14 . . . .**119** B6
Manchester M15 . . . .**162** F5
Crediton Dr Bolton BL2 . . . .**43** A7
Platt Bridge WN2 . . . .**56** A1

Crediton Ho M6 . . . .**80** A3
Creel Cl M9 . . . .**64** B4
Cremer M30 . . . .**80** A2
Cresbury St M12 . . . .**164** D8
Crescent M5 . . . .**81** C2
Crescent Ave
Ashton-in-M WN4 . . . .**73** A4
Atherton BL5 . . . .**59** A8
⊞ Bolton BL1 . . . .**145** D8
Farnworth BL4 . . . .**60** C6
Manchester M25 . . . .**63** B4
Manchester M8 . . . .**156** A8
Pendlebury M27 . . . .**80** B8
Crescent Cl
Dukinfield SK16 . . . .**166** C1
Stockport SK3 . . . .**124** A5
Crescent Ct
⊡ Manchester M21 . . . .**96** F1
Sale M33 . . . .**108** B3
Crescent Dr Manchester M8 **64** B1
Walkden M38 . . . .**60** B5
Crescent Gr Cheadle SK8 . .**122** C6
⊡ Manchester M19 . . . .**99** A1
Manchester M25 . . . .**63** B2
Crescent Pk SK4 . . . .**168** C2
Crescent Range M14 . . . . . .**98** C3
Crescent Rd
Alderley Edge SK9 . . . .**137** B2
Altrincham WA14 . . . .**119** A6
Altrincham WA15 . . . .**119** E1
Bolton BL3 . . . .**42** B3
Cheadle SK8 . . . .**122** C6
Dukinfield SK16 . . . .**166** C1
Failsworth OL9 . . . .**65** E2
Horwich BL6 . . . .**39** F8
Kearsley BL4 . . . .**60** F6
Manchester M8 . . . .**156** A8
Rochdale OL11 . . . .**30** B4
Stockport SK1 . . . .**112** B3
Crescent St M8 . . . .**156** C8
Crescent The
Altrincham WA14 . . . .**119** A5
Altrincham WA15 . . . .**119** F7
Bolton BL2 . . . .**25** F4
Bolton BL7 . . . .**25** A7
Bredbury SK6 . . . .**112** D4
Cheadle SK8 . . . .**122** D6
Droylsden M43 . . . .**83** F1
Eccles M28 . . . .**79** A5
Horwich BL6 . . . .**22** E1
Ince-in-M WN2 . . . .**56** B7
Irlam M44 . . . .**94** B3
Little Lever BL3 . . . .**43** B2
⊠ Manchester M19 . . . .**99** A1
Middleton M24 . . . .**64** E8
Mossley OL5 . . . .**68** B1
Prestwich M25 . . . .**63** B4
Radcliffe M26 . . . .**43** D5
Shaw OL2 . . . .**149** A6
Stalybridge SK15 . . . .**102** D6
Stockport SK3 . . . .**124** A4
Urmston M41 . . . .**94** F3
Westhoughton BL5 . . . .**57** E7
Whitworth OL12 . . . .**14** C8
Wigan WN5 . . . .**54** D6
Crescent View ⊡ SK16 . . . .**166** B1
Crescent Way SK3 . . . .**124** A5
Cresgarth Ho SK3 . . . .**124** A4
Cressell Pk WN6 . . . .**19** B1
Cressfield Way M21 . . . . . .**109** D7
Cressingham Rd
Bolton BL3 . . . .**146** A4
Stretford M32 . . . .**96** B2
Cressington Cl ⊠ M5 . . . . .**154** E2
Cresswell Gr M20 . . . .**110** A5
Crest Lo SK7 . . . .**123** F2
Crest St M4 . . . .**159** A3
Crest The M43 . . . .**100** A4
Crestfield Gr WN6 . . . .**36** F2
Crestfold M38 . . . .**60** A4
Crestwood Ave WN3 . . . . . .**54** F3
Crestwood Wlk M40 . . . . . .**156** C6
Creswick Cl WN2 . . . .**56** C4
Crete St OL8 . . . .**66** F4
Crewe Rd M23 . . . .**120** E8
Crib Fold OL3 . . . .**51** A2
Crib La OL3 . . . .**51** A2
Criccieth Ave WN2 . . . .**38** D5
Criccieth Rd SK3 . . . .**123** A7
Criccieth St ⊠ M16 . . . .**97** F4
Cricket Gr The M21 . . . . . .**109** B6
Cricket St Bolton BL3 . . . . .**145** D5
Dukinfield M34 . . . .**101** A4
Wigan WN6 . . . .**150** B8
Cricket View OL16 . . . .**31** F5
Cricket's La OL6 . . . .**85** D3
Cricketers Way BL5 . . . .**57** F8
Cricketfield La M28 . . . .**60** C3
Cricklewood Rd M22 . . . . . .**121** C2
Crimble La OL10,OL11 . . . . .**29** F3
Crimble St OL12 . . . .**139** D8
Crimbles St OL4 . . . .**67** E8
Crime La OL8 . . . .**84** D7
Crimsworth Ave M16 . . . . . .**97** B2
Crinan Sq OL10 . . . .**28** F1
Crinan Way BL2 . . . .**42** F6
Crinan Wlk M40 . . . .**160** D3
Cringle Ave M19 . . . .**110** F8
Cringle Barrow Cl M28 . . . .**78** A5
Cringle Cl BL3 . . . .**40** F1
Cringle Dr SK8 . . . .**122** C3
Cringle Hall Rd M19 . . . . . .**110** F8
Cringle Rd M19 . . . .**111** C7
Cringleford Wlk M12 . . . . . .**164** F5
Crippen St M46 . . . .**58** A1
Cripple Gate M9 . . . .**19** A2
Cripple Gate La OL11 . . . . . .**30** E1
Crispin Rd M22 . . . .**130** E8
Critchley Cl SK14 . . . .**167** F1

Criterion St SK5 . . . .**99** F2
Croal Ave WN2 . . . .**56** A2
Croal St BL1 . . . .**145** D6
Croasdale Dr OL2 . . . .**48** E5
Croasdale St BL1 . . . .**143** F1
Crocker Wlk ⊠ M9 . . . .**157** E8
Crocus Dr OL2 . . . .**149** A5
Crocus St BL1 . . . .**143** F4
Crocus Wlk M7 . . . .**155** D6
Croft Acres BL0 . . . .**1** D2
Croft Ave Atherton M46 . . . . .**58** D2
Golborne WA3 . . . .**73** F2
Middleton M25 . . . .**63** F8
Orrell WN5 . . . .**53** D5
Croft Bank Manchester M18 **99** E5
∎ Manchester M7 . . . .**81** C5
Stalybridge SK15 . . . .**86** D4
Croft Brow OL8 . . . .**66** E2
Croft Cl WA15 . . . .**129** C6
Croft Gate BL2 . . . .**25** E4
Croft Gates Rd M24 . . . .**64** D7
Croft Gr M38 . . . .**59** F5
Croft Head OL2 . . . .**48** D4
Croft Head Dr OL16 . . . .**31** F7
Croft Hill Rd M40 . . . .**65** A1
Croft Ind Est BL9 . . . . .45 A5
Croft La Bolton BL3 . . . .**148** B5
Radcliffe M26 . . . .**44** C4
Whitefield BL9 . . . .**45** A5
Croft Manor SK13 . . . .**104** E1
Croft Pl M29 . . . .**76** F8
Croft Rd Cheadle SK8 . . . . .**123** B2
Sale M33 . . . .**108** D2
Wilmslow SK9 . . . .**136** E4
Croft Side BL3 . . . .**42** E5
Croft Sq OL12 . . . .**15** C3
Croft St Bolton BL3 . . . .**42** B4
Bury BL9 . . . .**141** A2
Droylsden M11 . . . .**83** B1
∎ Failsworth M35 . . . .**66** A1
Golborne WA3 . . . .**90** A8
Hyde SK14 . . . .**167** D2
Littleborough OL12 . . . .**15** C3
Manchester M5,M7 . . . .**81** C5
Stalybridge SK15 . . . .**86** B2
Walkden M38 . . . .**59** F5
Westhoughton BL5 . . . .**39** E3
Whitefield BL9 . . . .**45** A6
Croft The Hadfield SK13 . . .**104** A6
Oldham OL8 . . . .**66** E2
Orrell WN5 . . . .**53** D3
Stockport SK2 . . . .**124** B6
Westhoughton BL5 . . . .**39** E3
Crofters Brook M26 . . . .**44** C4
Crofters Gn SK9 . . . .**136** F6
Crofters Hall Wlk M40 . . . . .**83** B7
Crofters The M33 . . . .**108** F3
Crofters Wlk BL2 . . . .**25** C6
Crofters'Yd ⊞ M1 . . . .**150** C8
Crofthill Ct ∎ OL12 . . . .**15** D4
Croftlands Orrell WN5 . . . . .**53** D4
Ramsbottom BL0 . . . .**11** A3
Croftlands Rd M22 . . . .**121** E4
Croftleigh Cl M45 . . . .**44** E2
Crofton Ave WA15 . . . .**120** A8
Crofton Gdns WA3 . . . .**91** E3
Crofton St Manchester M14 **98** B3
Manchester M16 . . . .**97** D4
Oldham OL8 . . . .**66** F5
Crofts OL2 . . . .**49** E8
Crofts Bank Rd M41 . . . .**95** D3
Croftside Ave M28 . . . .**60** E3
Croftside Cl M28 . . . .**60** E3
Croftside Gr M28 . . . .**60** E3
Croftside Way SK9 . . . .**137** C6
Croftwood Sq WN5 . . . .**36** C2
Croichbank BL8 . . . .**10** D2
Croichley Fold BL8 . . . .**10** D2
Cromar Rd SK7 . . . .**124** F3
Cromarty Ave OL9 . . . .**65** F3
Cromarty Sq OL10 . . . .**28** F1
Cromarty Wlk M11 . . . .**160** F1
Crombie Ave M22 . . . .**121** D7
Crombouke Dr WN7 . . . .**57** E1
Crombouke Fold M28 . . . . . .**78** B7
Cromdale Ave Bolton BL1 . .**144** B8
Hazel Grove SK7 . . . .**124** F3
Cromedale Cres WN6 . . . . . .**37** A7
Cromer Ave Bolton BL2 . . . . .**25** C1
Manchester M20 . . . .**110** B6
Reddish M34 . . . .**100** A3
Cromer Ind Est M24 . . . . . . .47 B1
Cromer Rd Bury BL8 . . . .**27** D5
Cheadle SK8 . . . .**122** E6
Sale M33 . . . .**108** C3
Wigan WN3 . . . .**54** E3
Cromer St Droylsden M11 . . .**83** D1
Middleton M24 . . . .**47** B1
Rochdale OL12 . . . .**139** E8
Shaw OL2 . . . .**149** B7
Stockport SK1 . . . .**112** A2
Cromford Ave M32 . . . .**96** B3
Cromford Bank ⊞ SK13 . . .**171** D2
Cromford Bsns Ctr OL1 . . . .67 B8
Cromford Cl Bolton BL1 . . . .**143** E1
⊞ Gamesley SK13 . . . .**171** D2
Cromford Cts **159** A2
Cromford Dr WN5 . . . .**54** B5
Cromford Fold ⊠ SK13 . . . .**171** D2
Cromford Gdns BL1 . . . . . .**143** F2
Cromford Grn ⊞ SK13 . . . .**171** D2
Cromford Gr ⊞ SK13 . . . . .**171** D2
Cromford Lea ⊡ SK13 . . . .**171** D2
Cromford Pl ⊡ SK13 . . . . .**171** D2
Cromford St OL1 . . . .**67** A8

Cromford Way ⊞ SK13 . . . .**171** D2
Cromhurst St M8 . . . .**156** A8
Cromley Rd High Lane SK6 **134** C6
Stockport SK2 . . . .**124** A3
Crompton Ave Bolton BL2 . . .**42** D8
Rochdale OL16 . . . .**31** B3
Crompton Cl Bolton BL1 . . . .**25** A4
Marple SK6 . . . .**125** F7
Radcliffe M26 . . . .**62** B8
Crompton Ct BL3 . . . .**43** C3
Crompton Fold Prim Sch
BL2 . . . . .42 E7
Crompton Ho ⊡ WN1 . . . .**151** D8
Crompton House Sch OL2 .48 F7
Crompton Pl Bolton BL1 . . .**145** F7
Radcliffe M26 . . . .**44** B3
Crompton Rd Horwich BL6 . .**39** F8
Kearsley M26 . . . .**61** A8
Manchester M19 . . . .**111** A7
Crompton St
Ashton-u-L OL6 . . . .**85** E4
Bolton BL1 . . . .**148** A8
Bury BL9 . . . .**140** E2
Farnworth BL4 . . . .**60** E7
Ince-in-M WN3 . . . .**55** F3
Oldham OL1 . . . .**153** E8
Oldham OL9 . . . .**152** C7
Platt Bridge WN2 . . . .**56** B3
Royton OL2 . . . .**48** D3
Royton OL2 . . . .**48** D3
Shaw OL2 . . . .**149** B7
Swinton M27 . . . .**79** E8
Walkden M28 . . . .**60** F2
Walkden M38 . . . .**59** D5
Wigan WN1 . . . .**150** C8
Crompton Vale BL2 . . . .**42** D8
Crompton Way Bolton BL2 . .**25** C2
Shaw OL2 . . . .**149** A7
Cromwell Ave Gatley SK8 . .**122** A6
Manchester M16 . . . .**97** C2
Marple SK6 . . . .**125** D7
Cromwell Cl WA12 . . . .**89** A4
Cromwell Ct M44 . . . .**105** E7
Cromwell Gr
Manchester M19 . . . .**99** B1
⊞ Manchester M7 . . . .**81** C5
Cromwell Range M14 . . . . . .**98** D2
Cromwell Rd
Bramhall SK7 . . . .**132** D6
Bredbury SK6 . . . .**112** D6
Eccles M30 . . . .**79** D2
Irlam M44 . . . .**105** E7
Prestwich M25 . . . .**63** C4
Royton OL2 . . . .**48** C6
Salford M6 . . . .**81** B5
Stretford M32 . . . .**96** F2
Swinton M27 . . . .**61** E1
Whitefield M45 . . . .**44** D2
Cromwell Sch SK5 . . . . . . .100 A2
Cromwell St Bolton BL1 . . .**145** E7
Heywood OL10 . . . .**29** D1
Oldham OL1 . . . .**153** F6
Stockport SK4 . . . .**169** D3
Crondale Wlk ⊠ M13 . . . . .**163** C6
Crondall St M14 . . . .**98** A3
Cronkeyshaw Rd OL12 . . . . .**14** F1
Cronshaw St M19 . . . .**111** B8
Crook St Adlington PR7 . . . . .**20** F7
Bolton BL3 . . . .**145** F6
Hindley WN2 . . . .**56** D4
Hyde SK14 . . . .**167** E2
⊞ Radcliffe M26 . . . .**44** B3
⊞ Rochdale OL16 . . . .**31** A8
Wigan WN1 . . . .**150** B8
Crookall St WN4 . . . .**73** C4
Crooke Rd WN6 . . . .**36** C3
Crookhill Dr M8 . . . .**155** F7
Crookhurst Ave WN5 . . . . . .**71** D6
Crookilley Way SK1,SK6 . . .**112** C4
Croom Wlk M40 . . . .**160** D2
Cropton Way WN2 . . . .**56** F3
Crosby Ave M28 . . . .**60** F2
Crosby Gr M46 . . . .**58** E4
Crosby Rd Bolton BL1 . . . . .**144** B8
Failsworth M40 . . . .**83** D5
Radcliffe BL8 . . . .**43** E7
⊡ Salford M6 . . . .**80** D5
Crosby St Atherton M46 . . . . .**58** A4
∎ Rochdale OL12 . . . .**15** A2
Stockport SK2 . . . .**170** F7
Crosfield Ave BL9 . . . .**11** C2
Crosfield Gr M18 . . . .**99** D4
Cross Ave M25 . . . .**63** A6
Cross Cliffe Glossop SK13 .**116** E8
Hyde SK14 . . . .**113** C8
Cross Field Cl OL2 . . . .**32** C1
Cross Glebe St ⊞ OL6 . . . .**166** C3
Cross Gr WA15 . . . .**119** F8
Cross Keys St M4 . . . .**159** B2
Cross Knowle View M41 . . . .**95** A4
Cross La Droylsden M43 . . . .**84** D4
Manchester M18 . . . .**99** D5
Marple SK6 . . . .**125** E6
Newton-le-W WA12 . . . .**89** A4
Orrell WN5 . . . .**53** D3
Radcliffe M26 . . . .**44** C4
Ramsbottom BL8 . . . .**138** A6
Salford M5,M6 . . . .**81** C4
Wilmslow SK9 . . . .**137** F8
Cross La E M31 . . . .**105** F3
Cross La W M31 . . . .**105** F2
Cross Lees OL2 . . . .**15** A3
Cross Ormrod St BL3 . . . . .**145** D6
Cross Rd Gatley SK8 . . . . . .**131** B7
Manchester M21 . . . .**109** B8
Cross Rise SK13 . . . .**116** C8
Cross St
⊡ Altrincham WA14 . . . . . .**119** D4

Cross St continued
Ashton-u-L OL6 . . . .**166** A2
Aspull WN2 . . . .**38** B6
Atherton M46 . . . .**58** B4
Bolton BL1 . . . .**145** F8
Bolton BL7 . . . .**25** A7
Bury BL9 . . . .**140** F2
Denton M34 . . . .**100** E5
Farnworth BL4 . . . .**60** D8
⊡ Glossop SK13 . . . .**104** C1
Golborne WA3 . . . .**90** A7
Hadfield SK13 . . . .**104** A4
Heywood OL10 . . . .**29** E1
Hindley WN2 . . . .**56** D5
Hollingworth SK14 . . . .**171** D4
Hyde SK14 . . . .**167** D2
Ince-in-M WN3 . . . .**55** E4
Kearsley BL4 . . . .**61** B6
Leigh WN7 . . . .**76** A4
Little Lever BL3 . . . .**43** B3
Manchester M1,M2,M4 . . .**158** F1
Manchester M16 . . . .**162** D5
Manchester M3 . . . .**158** E2
⊞ Middleton M24 . . . .**46** F1
Middleton M25 . . . .**64** B8
Milnrow OL16 . . . .**31** D7
⊠ Mossley OL5 . . . .**68** C2
Mottram-in-L SK14 . . . .**115** B8
Oldham OL4 . . . .**67** B7
⊡ Oldham OL4 . . . .**67** E6
Oldham OL4 . . . .**68** A6
Radcliffe M26 . . . .**44** B3
Ramsbottom BL0 . . . .**138** C6
Rochdale OL11 . . . .**30** C2
Sale M32, M33 . . . .**108** B6
Stalybridge SK15 . . . .**86** D4
Standish WN6 . . . .**19** E1
Stretford M32 . . . .**96** D2
Swinton M28 . . . .**79** C7
Tyldesley M29 . . . .**76** F8
Urmston M41 . . . .**95** C1
Whitefield M45 . . . .**44** E1
Wigan WN3 . . . .**150** C7
Cross The ⊡ SK13 . . . .**104** A5
Crossacres Cty Prim Sch
M22 . . . . .121 E4
Crossacres Prim Sch
M22 . . . . .121 F4
Crossacres Rd M22 . . . . . .**121** E3
Crossbank Ave OL4 . . . .**67** F7
Crossbank Cl M13 . . . .**164** D5
Crossbank St Oldham OL8 .**153** E5
Oldham OL8 . . . .**153** E6
Crossbank Way M24 . . . . . .**46** F1
Crossbridge Rd SK14 . . . . .**102** A2
Crossby Cl M9 . . . .**64** F5
Crosscliffe ⊡ M16 . . . .**97** F4
Crossdale Rd Bolton BL2 . . .**42** F8
Hindley WN2 . . . .**57** A5
Manchester M9 . . . .**64** F4
Crossdale Way WA11 . . . . . .**71** B1
Crossefield Rd SK8 . . . . . .**123** A3
Crossen St BL3 . . . .**148** C5
Crossfell Ave M9 . . . .**64** B5
Crossfield Ave WA3 . . . .**91** F2
Crossfield Cl Denton M34 . .**101** A2
Littleborough OL12 . . . .**15** C6
Stalybridge SK15 . . . .**86** A1
Crossfield Dr Radcliffe M26 **43** D3
Swinton M27 . . . .**61** E1
Worsley M28 . . . .**78** F7
Crossfield Gr Romiley SK6 **114** B3
Stockport SK2 . . . .**124** B4
Crossfield Pl OL11 . . . .**31** A5
Crossfield Rd
Altrincham WA15 . . . .**120** B2
Handforth SK9 . . . .**131** D4
Irlam M30,M44 . . . .**94** C4
Littleborough OL12 . . . .**15** C6
Crossfield St BL9 . . . .**44** F4
Crossfields BL7 . . . .**25** C8
Crossford Dr BL3 . . . .**40** E4
Crossford St M32 . . . .**96** D1
Crossgate Ave M22 . . . .**121** D6
Crossgate La SK13 . . . .**103** F7
Crossgate Mews SK4 . . . . .**110** E2
Crossgates Prim Sch OL16 32 A7
Crossgates Rd SK13 . . . .**32** A7
Crossgill M29 . . . .**77** B5
Crosshill St ⊡ M16 . . . .**97** F4
Crosshill Wlk BL3 . . . .**40** E5
Crossings The WA12 . . . .**89** C3
Crossland Rd
Droylsden M43 . . . .**84** B2
Manchester M21 . . . .**109** A8
Crosslands M25 . . . .**63** A3
Crosslands Cl SK13 . . . . . .**116** D8
Crosslands Rd M28 . . . .**77** F6
Crosslee Cty Prim Sch M9 64 F4
Crossley Cres OL6 . . . .**85** E6
Crossley Rd
Manchester M19,SK4 . . . . .**111** A7
Sale M33 . . . .**108** A6
Crossley St Little Lever BL3 . .**43** A4
Manchester M18 . . . .**165** B6
Milnrow OL16 . . . .**31** E6
Oldham OL2 . . . .**48** E2
Shaw OL2 . . . .**149** C7
⊠ Stalybridge SK15 . . . . . .**86** A2
Crossmead Dr ⊡ M9 . . . . . .**64** E5
Crossmoor Cres SK6 . . . . .**113** C1
Crossmoor Dr BL2 . . . .**148** B8
Crossmoor Gr SK6 . . . .**113** C2
Crosswaite Rd SK2 . . . .**124** E6
Crossway Bramhall SK7 . . . .**132** E5
Manchester M20 . . . .**110** B3

Crossway continued
Stockport SK2 . . . . .124 A4
Crossway Cl WN4 . . . . .73 E5
Crossway Ho 8 M20 . . . . .110 B3
Crossway Rd M33 . . . . .107 F1
Crossways Bramhall SK7 . . .123 C1
Oldham OL8 . . . . .67 A1
Croston Ave PR6 . . . . .21 A8
Croston Cl SK9 . . . . .137 C1
Croston Close Rd
BL9,OL12 . . . . .12 C4
Croston St Bolton BL3 . . . .146 C4
Hindley WN2 . . . . .56 C6
Croston Wlk M11 . . . . .160 E1
Crostons Rd BL8 . . . . .140 D3
Croton St SK4 . . . . .110 E2
Croughton Cl M11 . . . . .99 D7
Crow Hill SK15 . . . . .86 E5
Crow Hill N M24 . . . . .64 F7
Crow Hill S M24 . . . . .64 F6
Crow Hill View OL4 . . . . . . .67 F5
Crow La BL0 . . . . .138 C6
Crow La E WA12 . . . . .89 C4
Crow La W WA12 . . . . .89 A4
Crow Orchard Rd WN6 . . . . .19 A1
Crow Tree Ave 4 OL13 . . . . .3 B8
Crow Trees La BL7 . . . . .9 C7
Crow Wood Rd
Edenfield BB4 . . . . .1 D6
Golborne WA3 . . . . .74 D1
Crow's Nest BL3 . . . . .42 F5
Crow's Nest Cotts BL3 . . . . .42 F5
Crowbank Wlk M40 . . . . . . .83 A5
Crowborough Cl BL6 . . . . . . .22 F1
Crowborough Wlk M15 . . . .162 F5
Crowbrook Gr 7 SK9 . . . . .131 D1
Crowcroft Park Prim Sch
M12 .99 A3
Crowcroft Rd M12,M13 . . . . .99 A3
Crowden Rd M40 . . . . .65 B2
Crowhill Rd OL7 . . . . .84 F4
Crowhurst Dr WN1 . . . . .37 B3
Crowhurst Wlk 2 M23 . . . .120 E7
Crowland Gdns SK8 . . . . . .132 B6
Crowland Rd Bolton BL2 . . . .25 C2
Wythenshawe M23 . . . . .120 F3
Crowley La OL4 . . . . .49 D1
Crowley Rd
Altrincham WA15 . . . . .120 B6
Manchester M9 . . . . .157 F8
Crown Bsns Ctr M35 . . . . . . .83 F8
Crown Ct SK7 . . . . .124 D3
Crown Fields Cl WA12 . . . . .89 B5
Crown Gdns Edgworth BL7 . . .9 D6
Newton-le-W WA12 . . . . .89 B4
13 Rochdale OL16 . . . . .31 A5
Crown Gn WA13 . . . . .117 A3
Crown Gr WN7 . . . . .76 D6
Crown Hill OL5 . . . . .86 D8
Crown Ind Est
Altrincham WA14 . . . . .119 E7
Manchester M4 . . . . .159 C2
Crown La Horwich BL6 . . . . . .22 A4
Manchester M4 . . . . .159 A3
Crown Mews SK2 . . . . .124 C4
Crown Park Dr WA12 . . . . . .89 B5
Crown Pasages WA15 . . . . .119 E2
Crown Point BL7 . . . . .9 D6
Crown Point Ave M40 . . . . . .83 C5
Crown Rd OL10 . . . . .29 A2
Crown Royal Ind Pk SK1 . .124 A8
Crown Sq M3 . . . . .158 E1
Crown St Ashton-u-L OL6 . . .166 B2
Atherton M46 . . . . .58 B3
Bolton BL1 . . . . .145 F7
Bredbury SK6 . . . . .112 F4
Denton M34 . . . . .100 E4
Failsworth M35 . . . . .83 F8
20 Failsworth M40 . . . . . . .83 C5
Hindley WN2 . . . . .56 C6
Manchester M15 . . . . .162 E7
Manchester M3 . . . . .158 E2
Marple SK6 . . . . .125 F3
Newton-le-W WA12 . . . . .89 A3
Rochdale OL16 . . . . .31 B5
Shaw OL2 . . . . .149 B7
Wigan WN3 . . . . .150 B6
Crowndale BL7 . . . . .9 D7
Crowneast St OL11 . . . . . . .30 C7
Crownhill Rd M43 . . . . .84 D4
Crowsdale Pl SK2 . . . . .124 E4
Crowshaw Dr OL12 . . . . .14 E3
Crowswood Dr SK15 . . . . . . .86 D6
Crowther Ave M5 . . . . .161 A8
Crowther Ct 5 OL15 . . . . . .15 E4
Crowther St
Littleborough OL15 . . . . .15 E4
Manchester M18 . . . . .99 E5
Rochdale OL16 . . . . .31 B4
Crowthorn Dr M23 . . . . . . .121 A2
Crowthorn Rd
Ashton-u-L OL7 . . . . .84 F1
Edgworth BL7 . . . . .10 B8
Reddish SK4 . . . . .111 D7
Crowton Ave M33 . . . . .107 D2
Croxdale Cl OL7 . . . . .84 E5
Croxdale Wlk M9 . . . . .64 D5
Croxton Ave OL16 . . . . .31 B8
Croxton Cl Marple SK6 . . . .125 E5
Sale M33 . . . . .107 D2
Croxton Wlk
8 Horwich BL6 . . . . .22 B4
Manchester M13 . . . . .163 C6
Croyde Cl Bolton BL2 . . . . . . .25 F3
Wythenshawe M22 . . . . .130 F7
Croydon Ave Leigh WN7 . . . .75 F8
Middleton OL11 . . . . .47 D8
Royton OL2 . . . . .48 C6

Croydon Ct M5 . . . . .161 B8
Croydon Dr M40 . . . . .83 C4
Croydon Sq OL11 . . . . .47 D8
Crummock Cl BL3 . . . . .42 F3
Crummock Dr
Middleton M24 . . . . .46 E3
Wigan WN3 . . . . .54 F3
Crummock Rd
Farnworth BL4 . . . . .59 E7
Gatley SK8 . . . . .122 B3
Crumpsall La M8 . . . . .64 A1
Crumpsall Lane Prim Sch
M8 .64 A1
Crumpsall St BL1 . . . . .143 E3
Crumpsall Sta M8 . . . . .64 A1
Crumpsall Vale M9 . . . . .64 C2
Crumpsall Way M8 . . . . .64 B1
Crundale Way 7 BL1 . . . . . .24 F6
Cruttenden Rd SK2 . . . . . . .124 D4
Cryer St M43 . . . . .84 C4
Cuba Ind Est BL0 . . . . .138 C8
Cubley Rd M7 . . . . .155 E8
Cuckoo Gr M25 . . . . .63 B6
Cuckoo La Bury BL9 . . . . . .141 C2
Bury BL9 . . . . .141 C3
Prestwich M25 . . . . .63 B6
Cuddington Ave M20 . . . . . .110 A8
Cuddington Cres SK3 . . . . . .170 D6
Cuddington Way 7 SK9 . . .131 D5
Cudworth Rd M9 . . . . .64 A5
Cuerden Wlk M22 . . . . .121 E8
Cuerdon Wlk M6 . . . . .80 F6
Culand St M12 . . . . .164 E6
Culbert Ave M20 . . . . .110 C3
Culbeth Ct SK6 . . . . .125 F6
Culcheth Ave WN2 . . . . .56 B1
Culcheth Cty High Sch
WA3 . . . . .92 A3
Culcheth Cty Prim Sch
WA3 . . . . .92 A3
Culcheth Hall Dr WA3 . . . . . .91 F4
Culcheth Hall Prep Sch
WA14 . . . . .119 D3
Culcheth La M40 . . . . .83 C4
Culcheth Rd WA14 . . . . . . .119 D3
Culcombe Wlk M13 . . . . . . .163 C5
Culcross Ave WN3 . . . . .54 C4
Culford Cl M12 . . . . .164 E5
Culgaith Wlk M9 . . . . .157 D7
Culham Cl BL1 . . . . .143 D2
Cullen Cl WN2 . . . . .56 A8
Cullen Gr M9 . . . . .64 F3
Cullercoats Wlk 3 M12 . . . .99 B3
Culmere Rd M22 . . . . .121 D1
Culmington Cl M15 . . . . . . .162 E5
Culross Ave Bolton BL3 . . . . .40 E6
Failsworth M40 . . . . .65 E1
Culver Rd SK3 . . . . .170 D5
Culvercliffe Wlk M3 . . . . . . .162 E8
Culverdon Wlk M6 . . . . .80 F6
Culvert St Oldham OL4 . . . . . .67 E8
Rochdale OL16 . . . . .31 B2
Wigan WN6 . . . . .37 A3
Culverwell Dr M5,M6 . . . . . .81 B2
Culzean Cl WN7 . . . . .76 C4
Cumber Cl SK9 . . . . .136 D4
Cumber Dr SK9 . . . . .136 D4
Cumber La SK9 . . . . .136 D4
Cumberbatch Pl WN3 . . . . . .55 F4
Cumberland Ave
Brinnington SK5 . . . . .112 C4
Dukinfield SK16 . . . . .101 E8
Heywood OL10 . . . . .29 A2
Irlam M44 . . . . .105 C5
Swinton M27 . . . . .61 F2
Tyldesley M29 . . . . .58 F2
Cumberland Cl BL9 . . . . .44 E6
Cumberland Dr
Altrincham WA14 . . . . .128 B8
Oldham OL1,OL2 . . . . .48 D2
Cumberland Gr OL7 . . . . . . .166 B4
Cumberland Rd
Atherton M46 . . . . .58 F4
Manchester M9 . . . . .64 D1
Partington M31 . . . . .105 E2
Rochdale OL11 . . . . .30 F2
Sale M33 . . . . .108 C2
Urmston M41 . . . . .95 C4
Cumberland St
Manchester M7 . . . . .158 D4
3 Stalybridge SK15 . . . . . .85 F2
2 Wigan WN1 . . . . .37 E1
Cumbermere La M29 . . . . . .59 B2
Cumbrae Gdns M5 . . . . . . .154 E1
Cumbrae Rd M19 . . . . .99 C1
Cumbria Ct M25 . . . . .62 F1
Cumbria Wlk M6 . . . . .81 B4
Cumbrian Cl
4 Manchester M13 . . . . . .163 C6
Platt Bridge WN2 . . . . .56 B2
Shaw OL2 . . . . .48 F8
Cummings St OL8 . . . . .66 C2
Cunard Cl M13 . . . . .163 C6
Cuncliffe Dr Sale M33 . . . . .108 C3
Shaw OL2 . . . . .49 D7
Cundall Wlk M23 . . . . .108 F1
Cundey St BL1 . . . . .142 C1
Cundiff Ct M19 . . . . .99 C1
Cundiff Rd M21 . . . . .109 B6
Cundy St SK14 . . . . .167 E4
Cunliffe Ave
Newton-le-W WA12 . . . . .89 B5
Ramsbottom BL0 . . . . .11 A4
Cunliffe Brow BL1 . . . . .142 B1
Cunliffe Ct WN7 . . . . .75 A4
Cunliffe St Bolton BL2 . . . . .145 F6
Dukinfield SK14 . . . . .101 C4
Leigh WN7 . . . . .75 C5

Cunliffe St continued
Radcliffe M26 . . . . .44 C3
Ramsbottom BL0 . . . . .138 C7
Stockport SK3 . . . . .123 C8
Cunningham Dr
Gatley M22 . . . . .131 A8
Whitefield M45 . . . . .45 B2
Cunningham Rd BL5 . . . . . . .57 D7
Cunningham Way OL1 . . . . .153 F8
Curate Ct SK1 . . . . .112 A1
Curate St SK1 . . . . .112 A1
Curlew Cl OL11 . . . . .29 F7
Curlew Dr M44 . . . . .94 A4
Curlew Rd OL4 . . . . .67 E4
Curlew Wlk M12 . . . . .164 E5
Currier La OL6 . . . . .85 D2
Curteis St SL6 . . . . .22 B4
Curtels Cl M28 . . . . .79 C7
Curtis Gr SK13 . . . . .104 A5
Curtis Rd Manchester SK4 . .168 A2
Reddish M19 . . . . .99 C1
Curtis St Bolton BL3 . . . . . .146 C4
Wigan WN5 . . . . .54 D6
Curven Edge M41 . . . . .1 A7
Curzon Ave M14 . . . . .98 E4
Curzon Dr WA15 . . . . .120 B6
Curzon Gn SK2 . . . . .124 D7
Curzon Mews SK9 . . . . .137 A5
Curzon Rd Ashton-u-L OL6 . . .85 C4
Bolton BL1 . . . . .144 C7
Gatley SK8 . . . . .131 B7
Manchester M7 . . . . .155 D7
Poynton SK12 . . . . .133 E2
Rochdale OL11 . . . . .30 F2
Stockport SK2 . . . . .124 D7
Stretford M32 . . . . .96 A4
Curzon St Mossley OL5 . . . . .68 C1
Oldham OL1 . . . . .153 F7
Cut La OL12 . . . . .13 F1
Cutgate Cl M23 . . . . .108 E1
Cutgate Rd OL12 . . . . .14 B1
Cuthbert Ave M19 . . . . .99 B2
Cuthbert Mayne Ct OL16 . .139 E6
Cuthbert Rd SK8 . . . . .122 E6
Cuthbert St Bolton BL3 . . . .146 B2
Wigan WN5 . . . . .54 D6
Cuthill Wlk M40 . . . . .83 D4
Cutland Cl 16 M40 . . . . .83 A6
Cutland Way OL15 . . . . .16 A4
Cutler Cres OL13 . . . . .3 D7
Cutler Hill Rd M35 . . . . .84 C7
Cutnook La M44 . . . . .94 A3
Cutter Cl M5 . . . . .161 A8
Cycle St M11 . . . . .165 B8
Cyclone St M11 . . . . .164 F8
Cygnet St WN3 . . . . .150 B6
Cygnus Ave M7 . . . . .81 C3
Cymbal Ct SK5 . . . . .169 F3
Cynthia Dr SK6 . . . . .125 F5
Cypress Ave OL9 . . . . .152 B8
Cypress Cl SK3 . . . . .123 C8
Cypress Gdns OL16 . . . . .31 D7
Cypress Gr Denton M34 . . . .101 A3
Kearsley BL4 . . . . .60 F7
Cypress Ho 10 M14 . . . . . . .98 E4
Cypress Oaks SK15 . . . . . . .86 D3
Cypress Rd Droylsden M43 . . .84 A3
Eccles M30 . . . . .79 A4
Oldham OL4 . . . . .67 D8
Wigan WN5 . . . . .54 E6
Cypress St Manchester M9 . .157 D7
Middleton M24 . . . . .65 C8
Cypress Way SK6 . . . . .135 A7
Cypress Wlk 2 M33 . . . . . .107 C6
Cyprus Cl Oldham OL4 . . . . . .67 D6
Salford M5 . . . . .154 F1
Cyprus St M32 . . . . .96 D2
Cyril St Bolton BL3 . . . . . . .148 A5
Manchester M14 . . . . .98 B3
Shaw OL2 . . . . .149 C7
Cyrus St M40 . . . . .160 E2

D

D'Olivera Ct 7 M24 . . . . . . .46 E2
Daccamill Dr M27 . . . . .79 F6
Dacre Ave M16 . . . . .97 B2
Dacre Cl M24 . . . . .46 B1
Dacre Rd OL11 . . . . .30 F4
Dacres Ave OL3 . . . . .68 F4
Dacres Dr OL3 . . . . .68 F4
Dacres Rd OL3 . . . . .68 F4
Daffodil Cl Haslingden BB4 . . .1 A8
Rochdale OL12 . . . . .14 E3
Daffodil Rd BL4 . . . . .42 A1
Daffodil St BL1 . . . . .24 F5
Dagenham Rd M14 . . . . .98 C4
Dagmar St M28 . . . . .60 C4
Dagnall Ave M21 . . . . .109 B6
Dahlia Cl OL12 . . . . .14 D3
Dailton Rd WN8 . . . . .53 A7
Daimler St M8 . . . . .156 B6
Dain Cl SK16 . . . . .101 D8
Daine Ave M23 . . . . .109 B1
Dainton St M12 . . . . .164 D7
Daintry Cl M15 . . . . .162 F6
Daintry Rd OL9 . . . . .152 C7
Dairy House La SK7 . . . . . .132 C4
Dairy House Rd SK7 . . . . . .132 B5
Dairy House
Small Holdings SK7 . . . . .132 B4
Dairy St OL9 . . . . .152 B7
Dairydale Cl 8 M44 . . . . . . .94 B3
Dairyground Rd SK7 . . . . . .132 F7
Dairyhouse La WA14 . . . . . .119 B7

Daisy Ave Farnworth BL4 . . . .42 A1
Manchester M13 . . . . .98 E4
Newton-le-W WA12 . . . . .89 C4
Daisy Bank Failsworth M40 . .83 D5
Hyde SK14 . . . . .113 C8
Daisy Bank Ave M6,M27 . . . .80 C6
Daisy Bank La SK8 . . . . . . .122 A1
Daisy Bank Mill Cl WA3 . . . .91 E3
Daisy Bank Rd M14 . . . . . . .98 D4
Daisy Hall Dr BL5 . . . . .57 E5
Daisy Hill CE Prim Sch
BL5 .57 F5
Daisy Hill Ct OL4 . . . . .67 E8
Daisy Hill Dr PR6 . . . . .21 A8
Daisy Hill Rd OL5 . . . . .68 D1
Daisy Hill Sta BL5 . . . . .57 F6
Daisy Mews SK9 . . . . .137 A5
Daisy Nook Ctry Pk OL8 . . .84 E6
Daisy Rd WN5 . . . . .54 E6
Daisy St Bolton BL3 . . . . . . .146 C4
6 Bury BL8 . . . . .27 C2
Oldham OL9 . . . . .152 A8
Oldham OL9 . . . . .153 D7
4 Rochdale OL12 . . . . . . .139 E8
Stockport SK1,SK2 . . . . .170 F7
Daisy Way SK6 . . . . .134 F7
Daisyfield Cl WN2 . . . . .56 D5
Daisyfield Ct BL8 . . . . .27 C1
Daisyfield Wlk M28 . . . . .60 D3
Daisyhill Cl M33 . . . . .108 E4
Daisyhill Ct BL5 . . . . .57 F5
Dak Wlk M14 . . . . .100 E6
Dakerwood Cl 3 M40 . . . . . .83 C5
Dakins Rd M17 . . . . .76 B3
Dakley St M11 . . . . .165 C7
Dakota Ave M5 . . . . .96 F8
Dakota S M5 . . . . .96 F8
Dalbeatie Rise WN1 . . . . . . .37 F1
Dalbeattie St M9 . . . . .64 E1
Dalberg St M12 . . . . .164 D1
Dalbury Dr M40 . . . . .156 C5
Dalby Ave M27 . . . . .79 E7
Dalby Gr SK1 . . . . .112 A1
Dalby Rd WN2 . . . . .57 B5
Dale Ave Bramhall SK7 . . . .132 F8
Eccles M30 . . . . .79 C3
Uppermill OL5 . . . . .68 E3
Dale Brook Ave SK16 . . . . .101 C6
Dale Fields OL3 . . . . .50 F4
Dale Gr Altrincham WA15 . . .119 F7
Ashton-u-L OL7 . . . . .85 A5
Irlam M44 . . . . .105 E6
Leigh WN7 . . . . .75 C4
Dale Grove Sch OL7 . . . . . . .85 A5
Dale Ho OL2 . . . . .149 B6
Dale House Fold SK12 . . . . .134 A4
Dale Ind Est M26 . . . . .44 A2
Dale La OL3 . . . . .50 F5
Dale Lee BL5 . . . . .58 A8
Dale Prim Sch The SK6 . . .125 D7
Dale Rd Golborne WA3 . . . . . .90 A7
Marple SK6 . . . . .125 E7
Middleton M24 . . . . .47 B2
Dale Sq OL2 . . . . .48 F4
Dale St Ashton-u-L OL6 . . . . . .86 A6
8 Bacup OL13 . . . . .3 C8
Bury BL8 . . . . .27 C4
Farnworth BL4 . . . . .42 E1
Ince-in-M WN3 . . . . .55 F3
Leigh WN7 . . . . .75 C5
Manchester M1 . . . . .159 B1
Middleton M24 . . . . .65 B7
Milnrow OL16 . . . . .31 F6
Ramsbottom BL0 . . . . .1 C1
Rochdale OL16 . . . . .31 C7
Shaw OL2 . . . . .149 B6
Stalybridge SK15 . . . . .85 F1
Stockport SK3 . . . . .170 D7
Swinton M27 . . . . .79 E6
Westhoughton BL5 . . . . .57 F5
Whitefield M45 . . . . .44 E1
Dale St E Ashton-u-L OL6 . . .166 A2
Horwich BL6 . . . . .22 D2
Dale St W Ashton-u-L OL6 . .166 A2
Horwich BL6 . . . . .22 D2
Dale View Denton M34 . . . . .113 A7
Hyde SK14 . . . . .113 D8
Littleborough OL15 . . . . .15 F2
Mottram-in-L SK14 . . . . .103 A3
Newton-le-W WA12 . . . . .89 E4
Dalebank M46 . . . . .58 C5
Dalebank Mews M27 . . . . . . .61 D5
Dalebeck Cl M45 . . . . .63 C8
Dalebeck Wlk M45 . . . . .63 C8
Dalebrook Ct SK4 . . . . .168 C1
Dalebrook Rd M33 . . . . .108 C1
Dalecrest WN5 . . . . .53 D1
Daleford Sq M13 . . . . .163 C7
Dalegarth Ave BL1 . . . . .40 C7
Dalehead Cl M18 . . . . .99 F6
Dalehead Dr OL2 . . . . .49 D7
Dalehead Gr WN7 . . . . .75 C4
Dalehead Pl WA11 . . . . .71 B1
Dales Ave Manchester M8 . . .155 F6
Whitefield M45 . . . . .44 D1
Dales Brow Bolton BL1 . . . . .24 F6
Swinton M27 . . . . .79 E6
Dales Brow Ave OL7 . . . . . . .85 A5
Dales Gr M28 . . . . .60 F1
Dales La M45 . . . . .44 E1
Dales Park Dr M27 . . . . .79 D6
Dalesbrook Cl BL3 . . . . .43 A4
Dalesfield Cres OL5 . . . . . . .68 E1
Dalesford Cl WN7 . . . . .91 C8
Daleside Ave WN4 . . . . .73 A8
Dalesman Cl M9 . . . . .157 F8
Dalesman Wlk 3 M15 . . . . .163 A6

Daleswood Ave M45 . . . . . . .44 D1
Dalham Ave M9 . . . . .65 A2
Dalkeith Ave SK5 . . . . .111 F7
Dalkeith Gr BL3 . . . . .40 F5
Dalkeith Rd Hindley WN2 . . . .57 A5
Reddish SK5 . . . . .111 F7
Dalkeith Sq OL10 . . . . .29 A1
Dalkeith St M18 . . . . .165 B6
Dallas Ct M5 . . . . .96 E8
Dalley Ave M7 . . . . .158 D4
Dallimore Rd M23 . . . . .120 E6
Dalmahoy Cl M40 . . . . .83 C8
Dalmain Cl M8 . . . . .155 F6
Dalmeny Terr OL11 . . . . .30 F4
Dalmorton Rd M21 . . . . .109 D8
Dalny St M19 . . . . .99 B1
Dalry Wlk 1 M23 . . . . .121 A5
Dalrybrook Gr 9 SK9 . . . . .131 E1
Dalston Ave M35 . . . . .84 B8
Dalston Dr Billinge WA11 . . . .71 A5
Bramhall SK7 . . . . .132 C5
Manchester M20 . . . . .110 C2
Dalston Gr WN3 . . . . .54 D3
Dalton Ave Manchester M14 . .98 A2
Milnrow OL16 . . . . .31 D7
Stretford M32 . . . . .96 A4
Swinton M27 . . . . .62 C3
Whitefield M45 . . . . .63 A7
Dalton Cl Milnrow OL16 . . . . .31 D7
Ramsbottom BL0 . . . . .11 A4
Wigan WN5 . . . . .54 B7
Dalton Ct M40 . . . . .159 B4
Dalton Dr Pendlebury M27 . . .80 D7
Wigan WN3 . . . . .54 E4
Dalton Fold BL5 . . . . .57 F8
Dalton Gdns M41 . . . . .95 B3
Dalton Gr Ashton-in-M WN4 . .73 A4
Manchester SK4 . . . . .168 C4
Dalton Ho 6 M14 . . . . .110 D8
Dalton Rd Manchester M9 . . . .64 D5
Middleton M24 . . . . .64 D1
Dalton St Bury BL8 . . . . .27 B2
Chadderton OL9 . . . . .152 B7
Eccles M30 . . . . .79 D3
Failsworth M35 . . . . .83 E8
Manchester M4,M40 . . . . . . .159 B4
Oldham OL1 . . . . .67 B7
Sale M33 . . . . .108 C6
Daltry St OL1 . . . . .67 A8
Dalveen Ave M41 . . . . .95 C4
Dalveen Dr WA15 . . . . .119 F7
Dalwood Cl WN2 . . . . .56 F4
Dalymount Cl BL2 . . . . .25 B2
Dam Head Dr M9 . . . . .64 C3
Dam Head La WA3 . . . . . . .105 A5
Dam La Ashton-in-M WA3 . . . .73 F3
Hollinfare WA3 . . . . .105 A4
Damask Ave M3 . . . . .158 D2
Dame Hollow SK8 . . . . .131 C6
Dame St OL9 . . . . .153 D8
Dameny Ct SK7 . . . . .132 E8
Dameral Cl M8 . . . . .156 A6
Damery Rd SK7 . . . . .132 E8
Damian Dr WA12 . . . . .89 A5
Damien St M12 . . . . .99 B2
Dams Head Fold BL5 . . . . . .39 F1
Damson Wlk M31 . . . . .105 D3
Dan Bank SK6 . . . . .125 C6
Dan Fold OL1 . . . . .153 E7
Danbury Wlk M23 . . . . .120 D8
Danby Cl SK14 . . . . .167 F4
Danby Ct 6 OL1 . . . . .153 E8
Danby Pl SK14 . . . . .167 F4
Danby Rd Bolton BL3 . . . . . .147 E3
Hyde SK14 . . . . .167 F4
Danby Wlk M9 . . . . .64 E1
Dane Ave Cheadle SK3 . . . . .123 A8
Partington M31 . . . . .105 A4
Dane Bank M24 . . . . .65 B7
Dane Bank Dr SK12 . . . . . . .135 D6
Dane Bank Prim Sch
SK5 . . . . .100 A2
Dane Cl SK7 . . . . .123 D3
Dane Dr SK9 . . . . .137 D6
Dane Hill Cl SK12 . . . . .135 D5
Dane Mews M33 . . . . .108 A4
Dane Rd Reddish M34 . . . . .100 A2
Sale M33 . . . . .108 D5
Dane Road Sta M33 . . . . . .108 C4
Dane St Bolton BL3 . . . . . . .146 C4
Manchester M11 . . . . .99 E7
Mossley OL5 . . . . .68 D3
7 Oldham OL4 . . . . .67 C7
Rochdale OL11 . . . . .139 E7
Dane Wlk SK5 . . . . .169 F4
Danebank Mews M34 . . . . .100 B2
Danebank Wlk 14 M13 . . . .163 B7
Danebridge Cl BL4 . . . . .60 E8
Danebury Cl WN2 . . . . .56 D5
Danecroft Cl M13 . . . . .164 D5
Danefield Ct SK8 . . . . .131 C6
Danefield Rd M33 . . . . .108 C6
Daneholme Rd M19 . . . . . . .110 E5
Danes Ave WN2 . . . . .56 E6
Danes Brook Cl WN2 . . . . . .56 E6
Danes Gn WN2 . . . . .56 E7
Danes Rd M14 . . . . .98 D2
Danesbury Pl BL1 . . . . .25 A4
Danesbury Rd BL2 . . . . .25 B4
Danesbury Rise SK8 . . . . . .122 D5
Daneshill M25 . . . . .63 B6
Danesmoor Dr BL9 . . . . . . .141 B4
Danesmoor Rd M20 . . . . . . .110 B5
Danesway Adlington PR7 . . . .20 F8
Manchester M25 . . . . .63 D2

Danesway *continued*
Pendlebury M27 . . . .**80** C6
Wigan WN1 . . . .**37** B3
Danesway Ct BL1 . . . .**143** D2
Daneswood Ave
Manchester M9 . . . .**64** F4
Whitworth OL12 . . . .**14** C8
Danett Cl M12 . . . .**165** B6
Danforth Gr M19 . . . .**111** B8
Daniel Adamson Ave
M31 . . . .**105** D3
Daniel Adamson Rd M5 .**154** D1
Daniel Ct M31 . . . .**105** F4
Daniel Fold OL12 . . . .**14** B2
Daniel St Hazel Grove SK7 .**124** C2
Heywood OL10 . . . .**29** B2
Oldham OL1 . . . .**67** C8
Royton OL2 . . . .**49** A3
Whitworth OL12 . . . .**4** D2
Daniel's La SK1 . . . .**169** F2
Danisher La OL8 . . . .**84** F8
Dannywood Cl SK14 . . . . .**113** C8
Danson St M40 . . . .**160** E3
Dantall Ave M9 . . . .**65** A3
Dante Cl M6,M30 . . . .**80** A4
Danty St M4 . . . .**159** A3
Dantzic St M4 . . . .**159** A3
Danwood Cl M34 . . . .**101** B1
Dapple St M11 . . . .**165** A8
Darbishire St BL1 . . . .**25** A1
Darby La WN2 . . . .**56** D6
Darby Rd M44 . . . .**106** A6
Darbyshire Cl BL1 . . . .**144** C8
Darbyshire Ho WA15 . . . . .**120** C7
Darbyshire St M26 . . . .**44** A3
Darbyshire Wlk 1 M26 . . .**44** B3
Darcy St BL2 . . . .**148** C5
Darcy Wlk M14 . . . .**98** A4
Darden Cl SK4 . . . .**110** E3
Darell Wlk M8 . . . .**156** B6
Daresbury Ave
Altrincham WA15 . . . .**119** E5
Urmston M41 . . . .**94** E4
Daresbury Cl Sale M33 . . .**108** F3
Stockport SK3 . . . .**170** D5
Wilmslow SK9 . . . .**137** C8
Daresbury Rd M21 . . . .**96** F1
Daresbury St M8 . . . .**156** A7
Darfield Wlk M40 . . . .**160** D3
Dargai St M11 . . . .**83** D1
Dargle Rd M33 . . . .**108** B6
Darian Ave M22 . . . .**130** D8
Daric Cl WN7 . . . .**75** C1
Dark La Blackrod BL6 . . . . . .**21** B3
Delph OL3 . . . .**50** E6
Manchester M12 . . . .**164** D8
Mossley OL5 . . . .**68** D2
Oldham OL3 . . . .**69** A8
Darlbeck Wlk M21 . . . .**109** C5
Darley Ave Eccles M30 . . . .**95** C8
Farnworth BL4 . . . .**42** E1
Gatley SK8 . . . .**122** B6
Manchester M21 . . . .**109** C5
Darley Gr BL4 . . . .**42** E1
Darley Ho 5 M5 . . . .**154** E1
Darley Rd Hazel Grove SK7 .**133** F7
Manchester M16 . . . .**97** C3
Rochdale OL11 . . . .**30** F4
Wigan WN3 . . . .**55** B3
Darley St Bolton BL1 . . . . .**143** D1
Farnworth BL4 . . . .**60** E8
Horwich BL6 . . . .**22** B5
Manchester M11 . . . .**160** F1
Sale M33 . . . .**108** B4
Stretford M32 . . . .**96** E4
Darley Terr 7 BL1 . . . .**143** D1
Darlington Cl BL8 . . . .**27** B5
Darlington Rd
Manchester M20 . . . .**110** A6
Rochdale OL11 . . . .**30** F3
Darlington St
Ince-in-M WN2 . . . .**56** A7
Tyldesley M29 . . . .**59** A1
Wigan WN1 . . . .**151** D7
Darlington St E
Tyldesley M29 . . . .**59** B1
Wigan WN1 . . . .**151** E7
Darliston Ave M9 . . . .**64** A5
Darlton Wlk 6 M9 . . . . . .**157** E8
Darnall Ave M14 . . . .**110** A8
Darnbrook Dr 4 M22 . . . .**121** B1
Darncombe Cl M16 . . . .**97** F4
Darnhall St WN3 . . . .**55** F4
Darnhill Cty Prim Sch
OL10 . . . .**28** F1
Darnley Ave M28 . . . .**60** C1
Darnley St M16 . . . .**97** D4
Darnton Gdns OL6 . . . .**85** E3
Darnton Rd OL6,SK15 . . . . .**85** E3
Darran Ave WN3 . . . .**54** F3
Darras Rd M18 . . . .**99** C3
Dart Cl OL9 . . . .**65** F8
Dartford Ave
Brinnington SK5 . . . .**112** B6
Eccles M30 . . . .**79** B2
Dartford Cl M12 . . . .**164** D6
Dartford Rd M41 . . . .**95** C1
Dartington Cl
Altrincham M23 . . . .**120** D6
Stockport SK7 . . . .**123** F2
Dartmouth Cl 4 OL8 . . . . .**66** F4
Dartmouth Cres SK5 . . . . .**112** C5
Dartmouth Rd
Manchester M21 . . . .**109** C8

Dartmouth Rd *continued*
Whitefield M45 . . . .**63** A7
Dartnall Cl SK12 . . . .**135** A6
Darton Ave M40 . . . .**160** E3
Darul-Uloom Islamic Coll
BL8 . . . .**10** F4
Darvel Ave WN4 . . . .**72** C4
Darvel Cl BL2 . . . .**42** F6
Darwell Ave M30 . . . .**95** C8
Darwen Dr 8 WN2 . . . .**56** A2
Darwen Rd BL7 . . . .**25** A7
Darwen St M16 . . . .**161** C5
Darwin Gr SK7 . . . .**132** E6
Darwin St Bolton BL1 . . . . .**143** D2
Dukinfield SK14 . . . .**102** A5
Oldham OL4 . . . .**67** C5
Dashwood Rd M25 . . . .**62** F5
Dashwood Wlk M12 . . . . . .**165** A6
Datchett Terr OL11 . . . .**30** F4
Dauntesy Ave M27 . . . .**80** D7
Davehall Ave SK9 . . . .**137** A7
Davenfield Gr M20 . . . .**110** B3
Davenfield Ho 7 M20 . . . .**110** B3
Davenfield Rd 2 M20 . . . .**110** B3
Davenham Rd
Handforth SK9 . . . .**131** D4
Reddish SK5 . . . .**99** F2
Sale M33 . . . .**107** F6
Davenhill Rd M19 . . . .**111** A8
Davenport Ave
Manchester M20 . . . .**110** B7
Radcliffe M26 . . . .**43** F6
Wilmslow SK9 . . . .**136** E4
Davenport Dr SK6 . . . .**113** B6
Davenport Fold BL2 . . . .**26** A3
Davenport Fold Rd BL2 . . .**26** A4
Davenport Gdns 10 BL1 . .**145** E8
Davenport La WA14 . . . . . .**119** C7
Davenport Lo SK3 . . . .**170** F5
Davenport Park Rd SK2 . .**124** A5
Davenport Rd SK7 . . . .**124** D2
Davenport St Bolton BL1 . .**145** E8
2 Denton M34 . . . .**100** E8
Droylsden M43 . . . .**83** C1
Davenport Sta SK3 . . . . .**170** F5
Daventry Rd
Manchester M21 . . . .**109** D8
Rochdale OL11 . . . .**30** F3
Davey La SK9 . . . .**137** B2
Daveyhulme St OL12 . . . . . .**15** B1
Daveylands Urmston M41 . . .**94** F5
Wilmslow SK9 . . . .**137** D7
David Brow BL3 . . . .**146** A2
David Cl M34 . . . .**101** A1
David Lewis Cl OL16 . . . . . .**31** C6
David Mews M14 . . . .**110** C7
David Pegg Wlk M40 . . . . .**83** B5
David St Bacup OL13 . . . .**3** D8
Bury BL8 . . . .**27** C4
Denton M34 . . . .**101** A2
2 Oldham OL1 . . . .**153** E6
Reddish SK5 . . . .**111** E8
16 Rochdale OL16 . . . .**14** F1
David St N 15 OL12 . . . . . .**14** F1
David's Farm Cl M24 . . . . .**65** C7
David's Rd M43 . . . .**83** E2
Davids La OL4 . . . .**67** F7
Davidson Dr M24 . . . .**65** B6
Davidson Wlk WN5 . . . .**54** E7
Davies Ave Gatley SK8 . . . .**131** B6
Newton-le-W WA12 . . . .**89** C4
Davies Rd Bredbury SK6 . . .**112** D3
Partington M31 . . . .**106** A3
Davies Sq M14 . . . .**98** A4
Davies St Ashton-u-L OL7 . . .**84** F1
Kearsley BL4 . . . .**61** A7
Oldham OL1 . . . .**153** D8
Platt Bridge WN2 . . . .**56** A2
Davis St M30 . . . .**79** F1
Davy Ave M27 . . . .**62** D2
Davy St M40 . . . .**159** B4
Davyhulme Circ M41 . . . . . .**95** C4
Davyhulme
Cty Jun & Inf Sch M41 . .**95** B4
Davyhulme Rd
Stretford M32 . . . .**96** C3
Urmston M41 . . . .**94** F4
Urmston M41 . . . .**95** B4
Davyhulme Rd E M32 . . . . .**96** D3
Daw Bank SK3 . . . .**169** E1
Dawber St WN4 . . . .**73** D4
Dawes St BL3 . . . .**145** F6
Dawley Cl Ashton-in-M WN4 .**73** A3
Bolton BL3 . . . .**144** C5
Dawlish Ave
Brinnington SK5 . . . .**112** C5
Chadderton OL9 . . . .**47** F4
Cheadle SK8 . . . .**131** F7
Droylsden M43 . . . .**83** E1
Dawlish Cl Bramhall SK7 . .**132** E7
Hattersley SK14 . . . .**102** E3
Hollinfare WA3 . . . .**105** B3
Dawlish Rd
Manchester M21 . . . .**109** C8
Sale M33 . . . .**107** C5
Dawlish Way WA3 . . . .**73** F1
Dawn St OL2 . . . .**149** B6
Dawnay St M11 . . . .**165** B7
Dawson Ave WN6 . . . .**37** A3
Dawson La BL1 . . . .**145** E7
Dawson Rd
Altrincham WA14 . . . .**119** D8
Gatley SK8 . . . .**131** D8
Dawson St Atherton M46 . . .**58** C3
Bury BL9 . . . .**141** A4
Heywood OL10 . . . .**29** C2
Hyde SK14 . . . .**167** E1
Manchester M3 . . . .**158** F2

Dawson St *continued*
Manchester M3,M15 . . . . . .**162** D8
5 Oldham OL4 . . . .**67** D6
Pendlebury M27 . . . .**80** A8
Rochdale OL12 . . . .**139** F8
Stockport SK1 . . . .**112** B3
Day Dr M35 . . . .**83** F6
Day Gr SK14 . . . .**103** A3
Dayfield WN8 . . . .**53** B7
Daylesford Cl SK8 . . . .**122** D4
Daylesford Cres SK8 . . . . .**122** D4
Daylesford Rd SK8 . . . . . .**122** D4
De La Salle Coll M6 . . . . . .**80** C3
De Lacy Dr BL2 . . . .**25** B1
De Quincey Cl WA14 . . . . .**107** D1
De Quincey Rd WA14 . . . . .**107** D1
De Trafford Dr WN2 . . . .**56** B8
De Trafford Mews 9
SK9 . . . .**131** D2
De Traffords The M44 . . . . .**94** B3
De-Massey Cl SK6 . . . .**113** B6
Deacon Ave M27 . . . .**61** E1
Deacon Cl WA14 . . . .**119** B1
Deacons Cl SK1 . . . .**112** A1
Deacons Cres BL8 . . . .**27** A5
Deacons Dr M6 . . . .**80** D6
Deakin St WN3 . . . .**151** E5
Deakins Bsns Pk BL7 . . . . . .**8** D1
Deal Ave SK5 . . . .**112** B6
Deal Cl M40 . . . .**83** D5
Deal Sq SK14 . . . .**167** E2
Deal St Bolton BL3 . . . .**147** F3
Bury BL9 . . . .**141** B2
Hyde SK14 . . . .**167** C2
Manchester M3 . . . .**158** E2
Dealey Rd BL3 . . . .**146** A4
Dean Ave Failsworth M40 . . .**83** B6
Manchester M16 . . . .**97** B3
Dean Bank Dr OL16 . . . .**31** B1
Dean Bradley St M40 . . . .**157** E6
Dean Brook Cl M40 . . . .**83** B7
Dean Cl Billinge WN5 . . . . . .**71** D3
Edenfield BL0 . . . .**1** D3
Farnworth BL4 . . . .**59** F8
Handforth SK9 . . . .**131** C1
Whitefield M45 . . . .**62** D7
Dean Cres WN5 . . . .**54** B8
Dean Ct Bolton BL1 . . . .**148** A8
11 Dukinfield SK16 . . . .**166** B1
Golborne WA3 . . . .**90** A7
Manchester M15 . . . .**162** D6
Rochdale OL11 . . . .**30** F4
Dean Dr Altrincham WA14 . .**119** B1
Wilmslow SK9 . . . .**131** D2
Dean La Failsworth M40 . . . .**83** B6
Hazel Grove SK7 . . . .**133** E8
Dean Lane Sta M40 . . . . . .**83** B6
Dean Mdw WA12 . . . .**89** C4
Dean Moor Rd SK7 . . . . . .**124** A1
Dean Rd Golborne WA3 . . . .**90** A7
Handforth SK9 . . . .**131** E3
Irlam M44 . . . .**105** E6
Manchester M3 . . . .**158** E3
Reddish M18 . . . .**99** E4
Dean Row Ct 10 SK9 . . . .**131** D1
Dean Row Cty Jun Sch
SK9 . . . .**131** E1
Dean Row Rd SK9 . . . .**137** F8
Dean St Ashton-u-L OL6 . . .**166** A3
Failsworth M35 . . . .**83** E7
Manchester M1 . . . .**159** B1
Mossley OL5 . . . .**68** B1
Radcliffe M26 . . . .**43** F3
Rochdale OL16 . . . .**15** B1
Stalybridge SK15 . . . .**86** A1
Dean Terr OL6 . . . .**67** C2
Dean Villas OL14 . . . .**6** D7
Dean Wlk M24 . . . .**46** D2
Dean Wood Ave WN5 . . . . .**53** E8
Deanbank Ave 2 M19 . . . .**110** F8
Deane Ave
Altrincham WA15 . . . .**120** A5
Bolton BL3 . . . .**144** B5
Cheadle SK8 . . . .**122** F5
Deane Church La BL3 . . . .**146** B4
Deane Com Sec Sch The
BL3 . . . .**40** F4
Deane Rd BL3 . . . .**145** D6
Deane Wlk BL3 . . . .**145** E6
Deanery CE High Sch
WN1 . . . .**150** B8
Deanery Gdns M7 . . . .**155** D8
Deanery Way SK1 . . . .**169** F2
Deanroyd Rd OL14 . . . .**6** B7
Deans Prim Sch The M27 .**79** E8
Deanscourt Ave M27 . . . . . .**79** E8
Deansgate Bolton BL1 . . . .**145** E7
Hindley WN2 . . . .**56** E6
Manchester M1,M2,M3 . . . .**158** F1
Manchester M15,M3 . . . . . .**162** E1
Radcliffe M26 . . . .**44** B3
Deansgate La
WA14,WA15 . . . .**119** E7
Deansgate Sta M3 . . . . . .**162** E8
Deansgreave Rd OL13 . . . . . .**4** B7
Deanshut Rd OL8 . . . .**67** A2
Deansway M27 . . . .**79** E8
Deanswood Dr M9 . . . .**64** A5
Deanwater Cl M13 . . . .**163** B7
Deanwater Ct Gatley SK8 . .**131** D7

Deanwater Ct *continued*
Stretford M32 . . . .**108** C8
Deanway Handforth SK9 . .**131** C1
Manchester M40 . . . .**83** A8
Urmston M41 . . . .**94** D2
Deanway Trad Est SK9 . . .**131** D3
Dearden Ave M38 . . . .**60** A5
Dearden Clough BL0 . . . .**1** E2
Dearden Fold BL0 . . . .**1** E2
Dearden St Little Lever BL3 .**43** A4
Littleborough OL15 . . . .**16** B6
Manchester M15 . . . .**162** E6
12 Stalybridge SK15 . . . . . .**86** A2
Deardens Fold BL8 . . . .**27** C1
Deardens St BL8 . . . .**27** C1
Dearmans Pl M3 . . . .**158** E2
Dearne Dr M32 . . . .**96** E2
Dearnley Cl OL15 . . . .**15** E4
Debdale La
Reddish M18,M34 . . . .**99** F4
Tyldesley M29 . . . .**76** F4
Deben Cl WN6 . . . .**19** D1
Debenham Ave M40 . . . . . .**83** C4
Debenham Ct BL4 . . . .**60** D7
Debenham Rd M32 . . . .**96** A2
Dee Ave WA15 . . . .**120** D5
Dee Dr BL4 . . . .**61** B5
Dee Rd M29 . . . .**77** C2
Deep La Littleborough OL15 . .**16** C1
Milnrow OL15,OL16 . . . .**32** B8
Deepcar St M19 . . . .**99** A2
Deepdale Leigh WN7 . . . . . .**76** C3
Oldham OL4 . . . .**67** D6
Deepdale Ave
Billinge WA11 . . . .**71** C1
Manchester M14 . . . .**110** A8
Rochdale OL16 . . . .**31** C6
Royton OL2 . . . .**48** C8
Deepdale Cl 1 SK5 . . . . . .**100** A1
Deepdale Ct M9 . . . .**65** B3
Deepdale Dr M27 . . . .**80** D7
Deepdale Rd BL2 . . . .**25** F1
Deepdene St M12 . . . .**164** F6
Deeping Ave M16 . . . .**97** D2
Deeplish Com Prim Sch
OL11 . . . .**31** A5
Deeplish Rd OL11 . . . .**139** F5
Deeplish St OL11 . . . .**139** F5
Deeply Vale La BL9 . . . .**12** C2
Deer St M1 . . . .**163** D8
Deeracre Ave SK2 . . . .**124** C6
Deerfold Cl 6 M18 . . . .**99** D5
Deerhurst Dr M8 . . . .**155** F6
Deeroak Cl M18 . . . .**165** B6
Deerpark Rd M16 . . . .**97** E3
Defence St 7 BL3 . . . .**145** D6
Defiance St M46 . . . .**58** C3
Deganwy Gr SK5 . . . .**111** F5
Degas Cl M7 . . . .**81** B8
Deighton Ave M14 . . . .**110** A8
Delacourt Rd M14 . . . .**110** B8
Delafield Ave M12 . . . .**99** A2
Delaford Ave M28 . . . .**78** E7
Delaford Cl SK3 . . . .**123** E4
Delaford Wlk M40 . . . .**83** D4
Delahayes Lo WA15 . . . . . .**120** B5
Delahays Dr WA15 . . . .**120** B2
Delahays Range M18,M34 .**99** F4
Delahays Rd WA15 . . . .**120** B2
Delaine Rd M20 . . . .**110** C6
Delamer Rd WA14 . . . .**119** C3
Delamere Ave
Golborne WA3 . . . .**90** E6
Sale M33 . . . .**108** E3
Salford M6 . . . .**80** C6
Shaw OL2 . . . .**49** D8
Stretford M32 . . . .**96** D2
Swinton M27 . . . .**62** B2
Whitefield M45 . . . .**62** B2
Delamere Cl
Hazel Grove SK7 . . . .**125** A3
Mossley SK15 . . . .**86** C6
Romiley SK6 . . . .**113** C5
Delamere Gdns BL1 . . . . . .**143** D3
Delamere Ho M14 . . . .**110** C8
Delamere Lo 5 SK7 . . . . .**124** D2
Delamere Rd Gatley SK8 . .**122** B5
Handforth SK9 . . . .**131** E4
Hazel Grove SK7 . . . .**125** A3
Manchester M19 . . . .**99** B1
Reddish M34 . . . .**100** B2
Rochdale OL16 . . . .**31** C4
Stockport SK2 . . . .**124** B4
Urmston M41 . . . .**94** F2
Delamere Sch M41 . . . .**94** D2
Delamere St
Ashton-u-L OL6 . . . .**166** B2
Bury BL9 . . . .**28** A5
Droylsden M11 . . . .**99** F7
6 Oldham OL8 . . . .**67** B5
Delamere Way WN8 . . . .**53** A7
Delaunays Rd
Manchester M8 . . . .**64** B2
Sale M33 . . . .**107** F4
Delaware Wlk M9 . . . .**157** D7
Delbooth Ave M41 . . . .**94** E4
Delegarte St WN3 . . . .**151** E6
Delfhaven Ct WN6 . . . .**37** A7
Delft Wlk M6 . . . .**81** A5
Delfur Rd SK7 . . . .**132** F7
Delhi Rd M44 . . . .**105** F8
Dell Ave Pendlebury M27 . . .**80** D7
Wigan WN6 . . . .**36** E3
Dell Cl OL4 . . . .**67** D7
Dell Gdns OL12 . . . .**14** B2
Dell Mdw OL12 . . . .**14** C5
Dell Rd OL12 . . . .**14** B3
Dell Side SK6 . . . .**112** C1

Dell Side Way OL12 . . . . . .**14** C2
Dell St BL2 . . . .**25** C5
Dellar St Appley Bridge WN6 .**35** D7
Orrell WN8 . . . .**53** B7
Dellar St OL12 . . . .**14** C1
Dellcot Cl Manchester M25 .**63** D2
Salford M6 . . . .**80** B5
Dellcot La M28 . . . .**78** F5
Dellhide Cl OL4 . . . .**68** A6
Dellside Cl WN4 . . . .**72** D5
Dellside Gr M28 . . . .**60** E3
Delph Ave BL7 . . . .**8** D3
Delph Brook Way BL7 . . . . . .**8** D2
Delph Com Prim Sch OL3 .**50** E5
Delph Gr WN7 . . . .**57** D1
Delph Hill BL1 . . . .**23** E2
Delph Hill Cl BL1 . . . .**23** E2
Delph La Ainsworth BL2 . . . .**26** C1
Delph OL3 . . . .**50** F5
Delph Lodge OL3 . . . .**50** F3
Delph New Rd OL3 . . . .**50** E2
Delph Rd OL3 . . . .**50** C8
Delph St Bolton BL3 . . . . . .**145** D5
Milnrow OL16 . . . .**31** F6
Wigan WN6 . . . .**37** B3
Delphi Ave M28 . . . .**60** D2
Delphside Cl WN5 . . . .**53** D5
Delphside Rd WN5 . . . .**53** D5
Delside Ave M40 . . . .**83** A8
Delta Cl OL2 . . . .**48** D2
Delta Rd M34 . . . .**100** E7
Delta Wlk M40 . . . .**83** A4
Delvino Wlk M14 . . . .**98** A4
Delwood Gdns M22 . . . . . .**121** D3
Demesne Cl SK15 . . . .**86** C1
Demesne Cres SK15 . . . . . .**86** C1
Demesne Dr SK15 . . . .**86** C1
Demesne Rd M16 . . . .**97** E2
Demmings Inf Sch SK8 . . .**122** F5
Demmings Rd SK8 . . . .**122** F5
Dempsey Dr M45 . . . .**45** B2
Den Hill Dr OL4 . . . .**67** F6
Den La Oldham OL3 . . . .**69** B8
Oldham OL4 . . . .**67** F7
Denbigh Cl SK7 . . . .**133** C8
Denbigh Dr OL2 . . . .**48** F6
Denbigh Gr M46 . . . .**58** C5
Denbigh Pl M5 . . . .**81** A2
Denbigh Rd Bolton BL2 . . .**148** B5
Denton M34 . . . .**100** F1
Swinton M27 . . . .**62** B2
Denbigh St Mossley OL5 . . .**86** D8
Oldham OL8 . . . .**66** F3
Stockport SK4 . . . .**169** D3
Denbigh Wlk M15 . . . .**162** E6
Denbury Dr WA14 . . . .**119** B5
Denbury Gn SK7 . . . .**124** A1
Denbury Wlk M9 . . . .**156** C6
Denby La SK4 . . . .**169** D4
Denby Rd SK16 . . . .**101** C7
Denbydale Way OL2 . . . .**48** C4
Dencombe St M12,M13 . . . .**98** F4
Dene Bank BL2 . . . .**25** C5
Dene Brow M34 . . . .**113** B8
Dene Ct SK4 . . . .**168** C2
Dene Dr M24 . . . .**64** F7
Dene Gr WN7 . . . .**75** B4
Dene Ho SK4 . . . .**110** E1
Dene Hollow SK5 . . . .**100** A1
Dene Manor M20 . . . .**110** A2
Dene Pk M20 . . . .**110** A2
Dene Rd M20 . . . .**110** A2
Dene Rd W M20 . . . .**109** F3
Dene St Bolton BL2 . . . .**25** C5
Leigh WN7 . . . .**75** B4
Denefield Cl SK6 . . . .**114** B1
Denefield Pl M30 . . . .**79** F3
Deneford Rd M20 . . . .**110** A2
Denehurst Rd OL11 . . . .**30** C8
Denehurst St M12 . . . .**164** F6
Denes The SK5 . . . .**99** F1
Deneside Cres SK7 . . . . . .**124** F3
Deneside Wlk 6 M9 . . . . .**157** D7
Denesway M33 . . . .**107** E3
Deneway Bramhall SK7 . . . .**132** C7
High Lane SK6 . . . .**134** F8
Stockport SK4 . . . .**168** C2
Deneway Cl SK4 . . . .**168** C2
Deneway Mews SK4 . . . . . .**168** C2
Denewell Cl M13 . . . .**164** D6
Denewood Ct 3 SK9 . . . . .**137** A6
Denford Cl WN3 . . . .**54** F1
Denham Cl BL1 . . . .**25** A5
Denham Dr Bramhall SK7 . .**132** D7
Irlam M44 . . . .**94** A1
Wigan WN3 . . . .**55** A3
Denham St
Manchester M13 . . . .**98** D4
Radcliffe M26 . . . .**43** F6
Denhill Rd M15 . . . .**162** F5
Denholm Rd M20 . . . .**122** C8
Denholme WN8 . . . .**53** A7
Denholme Rd OL11 . . . .**30** F4
Denhurst Rd OL15 . . . .**16** B6
Denis Ave M16 . . . .**97** E2
Denison Ct 7 M14 . . . .**98** C3
Denison Rd
Hazel Grove SK7 . . . .**133** C8
Manchester M14 . . . .**98** D3
Denison St M14 . . . .**98** D3
Deniston Rd SK4 . . . .**111** B5
Denman Wlk 12 M8 . . . . . .**155** F6
Denmark Rd
Manchester M14,M15 . . . . . .**98** A4
Sale M33 . . . .**108** B6
Denmark St
Altrincham WA14 . . . .**119** C4
Oldham OL4 . . . .**67** B7

Denmark St *continued*
Oldham OL9 152 C8
Rochdale OL16 31 A8
Denmark Way OL9 152 C8
Denmore Rd M40 65 D3
Dennington Dr M41 95 C4
Dennis Ho SK4 168 B4
Dennison Ave M20 110 B7
Dennison Rd SK8 132 B8
Denshaw Ave M34 100 D5
Denshaw Cl M19 110 E3
Denshaw Rd OL3 50 D5
Densmead Wlk 12 M40 159 C3
Densmore St 6 M35 83 F7
Denson Rd WA15 120 B8
Denstone Ave Eccles M30 79 E3
Sale M33 107 E3
Urmston M41 95 C3
Denstone Cres BL2 25 D2
Denstone Rd Reddish SK5 99 F1
Salford M6 80 D5
Urmston M41 95 C3
Denstone Wlk 15 M9 64 E3
Dent Cl SK5 112 C6
Dental Hospl M13,M15 163 A6
Dentdale Cl BL1 40 D6
Dentdale Wlk M22 130 C8
Denton Ct M34 100 E5
Denton Gr WN5 54 B8
Denton La OL9 152 A5
Denton Rd Denton M34 100 E6
Little Lever BL3 43 B6
Denton St Bury BL9 140 F4
Heywood OL10 29 C1
7 Rochdale OL12 14 F1
Denton Sta M34 100 C4
Denton West End Prim Sch M34 100 A3
Denver Ave M40 160 D3
Denver Dr 4 WA15 120 A6
Denver Rd OL11 30 F4
Denville Cres M22 121 E3
Denyer Terr 22 SK16 166 B1
Depleach Rd SK8 122 D5
Deptford Ave M23 121 A3
Deramore Cl OL6 85 E3
Deramore St M14 98 B3
Derby Ave M5 154 E2
Derby Cl Irlam M44 105 C5
Newton-le-W WA12 89 B3
Derby Ct Oldham OL9 152 C5
Sale M33 108 C3
Derby Gr 2 M19 99 B1
Derby High Sch The BL9 44 D8
Derby Ho WN1 151 D8
Derby Pl PR6 21 A8
Derby Range SK4 168 B4
Derby Rd Ashton-u-L OL6 85 D3
Golborne WA3 90 C8
Hyde SK14 167 E4
Kearsley M26 61 A8
Manchester M14,M20 110 D7
Manchester SK4 168 C4
New Mills SK22 127 D1
Prestwich M25,M45 63 A6
Sale M33 107 E6
Salford M5,M6 154 E2
Urmston M41 95 D3
Derby St Altrincham WA14 119 E5
Ashton-u-L OL7 85 A5
Atherton M46 58 C4
Bolton BL3 145 E5
Bury BL9 140 F2
Denton M34 100 D3
Denton M34 100 D4
1 Failsworth M35 66 A1
Glossop SK13 116 C8
Heywood OL10 29 B2
Horwich BL6 22 D1
Ince-in-M WN3 55 F4
Leigh WN7 76 A4
Manchester M8 158 F4
8 Marple SK6 125 F6
Mossley OL5 86 D8
Newton-le-W WA12 89 B3
Oldham OL9 152 C5
Oldham OL9 66 B4
Prestwich M25 63 A4
Ramsbottom BL0 11 D6
Rochdale OL11 31 A5
Stockport SK3 170 D8
15 Tyldesley M29 59 A1
Westhoughton BL5 39 F1
Derby St W WN7 75 F4
Derby Terr M34 100 E8
Derby Way 7 SK6 125 F6
Derbyshire Ave M32 96 B3
Derbyshire Cres M32 96 B3
Derbyshire Gn M32 96 D2
Derbyshire Gr M32 96 B3
Derbyshire La M32 96 C2
Derbyshire La W M32 96 B2
Derbyshire Level SK13 116 F6
Derbyshire Rd
Failsworth M40 83 D4
High Lane SK12 134 D5
Partington M31 105 E2
Sale M33 108 C4
Wigan WN3 54 D1
Derbyshire Rd S M33 108 D2
Derbyshire Row BL1 143 E3
Derbyshire St M11 165 C7
Dereham Cl BL8 27 D5
Dereham Way WN3 54 D3
Derg St M6 154 F1
Derker St OL1 67 B8
Derker Sta OL1 67 A8
Dermot Murphy Cl M20 109 F6
Dernford Ave M19 110 F5
Derngate Dr WN6 37 A7
Derrick Walker Ct OL11 139 D5
Derry Ave M22 121 E4
Derry St OL1 153 F6
Derville Wlk 4 M9 157 D8
Derwen Rd SK3 170 E7
Derwent Ave
Altrincham WA15 120 D5
Ashton-u-L OL7 166 A4
Droylsden M43 83 E1
Golborne WA3 74 C1
Heywood OL10 46 D8
Ince-in-M WN2 56 B7
Manchester M21 109 D5
Milnrow OL16 32 B6
Whitefield M45 63 C8
Derwent Cl Culcheth WA3 92 A2
Glossop SK13 116 F8
Horwich BL6 22 C2
Leigh WN7 75 E3
Little Lever BL3 42 F4
Manchester M21 109 D5
Partington M31 105 F4
Reddish M34 100 B2
Walkden M28 60 B2
Whitefield M45 63 B8
Derwent Dr Bramhall SK7 132 C5
Bury BL9 44 D7
Chadderton OL9 152 A7
Handforth SK9 131 C5
Kearsley BL4 61 B5
Littleborough OL15 15 F2
Sale M33 108 A2
Shaw OL2 149 A8
Derwent Ind Area M5 162 D8
Derwent Pl WN5 54 C7
Derwent Rd
Ashton-in-M WN4 73 E5
Farnworth BL4 59 F7
High Lane SK6 134 E8
Hindley WN2 56 E5
Middleton M24 46 E3
Orrell WN5 53 F8
Stretford M32 96 D3
Urmston M41 94 E2
Derwent St Droylsden M43 83 D1
Leigh WN7 75 E3
Manchester M8 156 C6
11 Rochdale OL12 14 F1
Salford M5 161 C8
Tyldesley M29 77 A7
Derwent Terr SK15 86 A4
Derwent Wlk Oldham OL4 67 D7
Whitefield M45 63 B8
Desford Ave M16,M21 97 C1
Design St BL3 146 B4
Desmond Rd M22 121 E4
Desmond St M46 58 A2
Dettingen St M6 80 D6
Deva Cl Hazel Grove SK7 124 D1
Poynton SK12 133 B4
Deva Ct M16 161 C5
Deva Sq OL9 152 C5
Devaney Wlk M34 100 E1
Devas St M13,M15 163 B5
Deverill Ave M18 99 F4
Devine Cl Manchester M3 158 D2
Royton OL2 48 D6
Devisdale Grange WA14 119 B3
Devisdale Rd WA14 119 B4
Devoke Ave Billinge WA11 71 A1
Walkden M28 60 F2
Devoke Gr BL4 59 E8
Devoke Rd M22 121 B2
Devon Ave
Manchester M19 110 F8
Whitefield M45 44 E1
Devon Cl Aspull WN2 38 D5
Brinnington SK5 112 C4
Little Lever BL3 43 B4
Salford M6 80 A3
Shaw OL2 48 F7
Wigan WN5 54 C6
Devon Cres BB4 1 B8
Devon Dr Ainsworth BL2 26 D1
Diggle OL3 51 C4
Standish WN1 20 B1
Devon Mews 2 M45 44 E1
Devon Rd Droylsden M43 84 A3
Failsworth M35 83 E6
Irlam M44 105 D5
Partington M31 105 E2
Tyldesley M29 59 A2
Urmston M41 94 E1
Devon St Bolton BL2 148 A7
Bury BL9 44 F8
Farnworth BL4 42 D2
Hindley WN2 56 E5
Leigh WN7 76 E4
Oldham OL9 66 C4
Rochdale OL11 139 F6
Swinton M27 61 F2
Devon Way OL8 66 C2
Devonport Cres OL2 48 F4
Devonshire Cl
Heywood OL10 29 A1
3 Urmston M41 95 E2
Devonshire Ct
Manchester M7 155 D8
Stockport SK2 124 A5
Devonshire Dr
Alderley Edge SK9 137 B2
Boothstown M28 77 F6
Devonshire Gdns WA12 89 C2
Devonshire Park Rd SK2 124 A5
Devonshire Pl
Atherton M46 58 D4
Devonshire Pl *continued*
Prestwich M25 63 A5
Devonshire Rd
Altrincham WA14 119 D6
Atherton M46 58 C5
Bolton BL1 144 B8
Eccles M30 79 E2
Hazel Grove SK7 133 F8
Manchester M21 109 C8
Manchester SK4 168 B3
Rochdale OL11 30 F2
Salford M6 80 A3
Walkden M28 60 C6
Devonshire Road Cty Prim Sch BL1 144 B8
Devonshire St
Manchester M12 164 D6
Manchester M7 155 E6
Devonshire St E M35 83 E5
Devonshire St N M12 164 D7
Devonshire St S M13 164 D5
Dew Meadow Cl OL12 14 E2
Dew Way OL9 153 D7
Dewar Cl M11 83 A1
Dewberry Cl Swinton M27 61 E2
Tyldesley M29 59 E1
Dewberry Fields WN8 53 B7
Dewes Ave M27 62 B2
Dewey St M11 99 D7
Dewhirst Rd OL12 14 F4
Dewhirst Way OL12 14 F4
Dewhurst Clough Rd BL7 8 D2
Dewhurst Ct BL7 8 D3
Dewhurst Rd BL2 25 E3
Dewhurst St Heywood OL10 29 E2
Manchester M8 158 F4
Dewint Ave SK6 126 B8
Dewsnap Cl SK16 101 C6
Dewsnap La
Dukinfield SK16 101 D6
Mottram-in-L SK14 103 A6
Dewsnap Way SK14 102 E2
Dexter Rd M9 64 A5
Deyne Ave Manchester M14 98 C4
Prestwich M25 63 B4
Deyne St M5,M6 154 E2
Dial Ct BL4 60 D8
Dial Park Prim Sch SK2 124 D4
Dial Park Rd SK2 124 D4
Dial Rd Altrincham WA15 129 C8
Stockport SK2 124 C5
Dialstone La SK1,SK2 124 C6
Diamond Cl 9 OL6 85 D4
Diamond St
8 Ashton-u-L OL6 85 D4
Leigh WN7 75 E4
Stockport SK2 124 A6
Wigan WN6 37 A3
Diamond Terr SK6 125 F3
Diane Rd WN4 73 E5
Dibden Wlk 4 M23 121 A5
Dicconson Cres 6 WN1 37 C1
Dicconson La Aspull BL5 39 B4
Aspull BL5,WN2 39 A4
Dicconson St WN1 37 C1
Dicconson Terr WN1 37 C1
Dicken Gn OL11 30 F4
Dicken Green La OL11 30 F4
Dickens Cl SK8 132 B5
Dickens Dr WN2 74 C8
Dickens La SK12 133 E2
Dickens Pl WN3 54 F4
Dickens Rd Coppull PR7 19 E8
Eccles M30 79 D1
Dickens St Heywood OL10 29 B2
Oldham OL1 49 E4
Dickenson Rd M13,M14 98 E3
Dickenson St WN2 56 E4
Dickinson Cl 13 BL1 143 E1
Dickinson Ct 1 BL6 22 B4
Dickinson St Bolton BL1 143 E1
Manchester M1 163 A8
Oldham OL4 67 B7
Dickinson St W BL6 22 B4
Dickinson Terr 12 BL1 143 E1
Dickson St W BL6 22 A4
Didcot Rd M22 121 C1
Didley Sq M12 165 A7
Didsbury CE Prim Sch M20 110 B3
Didsbury Gr WN2 56 D5
Didsbury Lodge Hall M20 110 C1
Didsbury Pk M20 110 B2
Didsbury Rd SK4 168 B2
Didsbury Road Prim Sch SK4 110 F2
Dig Gate La OL16 31 E3
Digby Lo M20 110 B4
Digby Rd OL11 30 F4
Digby Wlk 20 M11 160 F1
Diggle Prim Sch OL3 51 C5
Diggle St Shaw OL2 149 B6
Wigan WN6 37 A1
Diggle Wlk SK15 86 E6
Diggles La OL11 29 F6
Diglands Ave SK22 127 D1
Diglands Cl SK22 127 D1
Diglea OL3 51 D5
Dijon St BL3 146 C4
Dilham Ct BL1 144 C8
Dillicar Wlk M9 157 D7
Dillmass Wlk 19 M15 162 D6
Dillon Dr M12 164 E5
Dilston Cl M13 163 C6
Dilworth Cl OL10 29 A2
Dilworth Ct SK2 124 E5
Dilworth St M13,M15 163 B5
Dimple Pk BL7 8 D3
Dimple Rd BL7 8 C4
Dingle Ave
Alderley Edge SK9 136 D3
Appley Bridge WN6 35 E8
Denton M34 101 B2
Orrell WN8 53 C8
Shaw OL2 32 C1
Dingle Bank Rd SK7 123 D1
Dingle Cl Glossop SK13 116 A8
Romiley SK6 113 D2
Dingle Dr M43 84 B3
Dingle Gr SK8 121 F6
Dingle Rd Middleton M24 64 F6
Orrell WN8 53 B7
Dingle Terr OL6 67 B2
Dingle The Bramhall SK7 123 C1
Hyde SK14 113 E7
Dingle Wlk 4 Bolton BL1 145 F8
Wigan WN6 36 D4
Dinglebrook Gr 5 SK9 131 D1
Dinglewood SK7 123 C1
Dinmor Rd M22 121 D1
Dinmore Ct SK2 124 D5
Dinnington Dr M8 155 F6
Dinorwic Cl M8 64 A2
Dinsdale Cl M40 160 D2
Dinsdale Dr BL3 145 D5
Dinslow Wlk 18 M8 155 F7
Dinting Ave M20 110 A7
Dinting CE Prim Sch SK13 104 A1
Dinting La SK13 104 A1
Dinting Lane Trad Est SK13 104 A1
Dinting Lodge Ind Est SK13 171 F2
Dinting Rd SK13 104 B2
Dinting Sta SK13 104 A2
Dinting Vale SK13 104 A1
Dinton St M15 161 C7
Dipton Wlk M8 156 C6
Dirty La Ashley WA14 128 A5
Delph OL3 51 B8
Oldham OL4 50 B1
Dirty Leech OL12 14 F6
Disley Ave M20 109 F6
Disley Cty Prim Sch SK12 135 D6
Disley Ho SK3 170 E7
Disley St OL11 30 C4
Disley Sta SK12 135 C6
Disley Wlk M34 101 A1
Distaff Rd SK12 133 B4
District CE Prim Sch The WA12 89 A4
Ditton Mead Cl OL12 15 B2
Ditton Wlk 5 M23 120 F6
Division St Bolton BL3 147 F4
Rochdale OL12 15 B2
Dixey St BL6 22 A3
Dixon Ave Manchester M7 155 E6
Newton-le-W WA12 89 C5
Shevington WN6 36 A5
Dixon Cl Ashton-in-M WA11 89 A8
Sale M33 108 D2
Dixon Closes OL11 29 E7
Dixon Ct Cheadle SK8 122 D5
Westhoughton BL5 39 E3
Dixon Dr Kearsley M27 61 E4
Shevington WN6 36 A5
Dixon Green Dr 11 BL4 60 C8
Dixon Pl 3 WN2 56 B1
Dixon Rd M34 101 B1
Dixon St 12 Ashton-u-L OL6 85 D4
Failsworth M40 83 B6
Horwich BL6 22 B3
Irlam M44 105 F8
Manchester M6 80 F6
Middleton M24 47 A2
Oldham OL4 67 E8
Rochdale OL11 30 D4
Westhoughton BL5 39 E3
Dob Brook Cl M35,M40 83 C6
Dobb Brow Rd BL5 57 D7
Dobb Hedge Cl WA15 129 C6
Dobbin Dr OL11 30 F3
Dobbinetts La M23,WA15 120 E4
Dobcross Cl M13 99 A2
Dobcross New Rd OL3 51 A1
Dobhill St BL4 60 D8
Dobroyd Ho OL4 67 E8
Dobroyd St M8 156 A8
Dobson Cl
Appley Bridge WN6 18 E2
Manchester M13 164 D6
Dobson Ct M40 83 B4
Dobson Pk Ind Est WN2 56 A7
Dobson Rd BL1 144 C7
Dobson St Bolton BL1 143 D2
Ince-in-M WN2 56 A6
Doctor Fold La OL10 46 C5
Doctor La OL4 50 C1
Doctors La BL9 140 D2
Dodd Croft OL16 31 B3
Dodd La BL5 39 B4
Dodd St M5 154 D2
Dodd's Farm La WN2 38 E3
Doddington Cl M16 97 F4
Doddington La M5 161 A8
Doddington Wlk M34 100 E1
Dodge Fold SK2 124 E6
Dodge Hill SK4 169 E2
Dodgson St OL16 31 A6
Dodhurst Rd WN2 56 F6
Doe Brow M27 61 E4
Doe Hey Gr BL4 42 B2
Doe Hey Rd BL3 42 B2
Doefield Ave M28 78 C8
Doeford Cl WA3 91 E5
Doffcocker Brow BL1 142 A1
Doffcocker La BL1 23 F2
Dogford Rd OL2 48 D5
Dolbey St M5 154 E1
Dolefield M3 158 E1
Dollond St M9 64 E1
Dolman Wlk 4 M8 155 F6
Dolphin Pl M12 163 C7
Dolphin St M12 163 C7
Dolwen Wlk M40 83 B6
Doman St BL3 145 F5
Dombey Rd SK12 133 D2
Domestic App M90 130 C6
Domett St M9 64 C2
Dominic Cl M23 108 E1
Don Ave M6 80 C2
Don St Bolton BL3 147 D3
Middleton M24 47 C1
Dona St SK1 124 A8
Donald Ave SK14 167 F1
Donald St M1 163 A7
Doncaster Ave M20 110 A7
Doncaster Cl BL3 42 F3
Doncaster Wlk 4 OL1 153 F7
Donhead Wlk M13 163 C6
Donington Gdns M28 60 D3
Donkey La SK9 137 A5
Donleigh St M35 83 D6
Donnington 6 OL11 139 E6
Donnington Ave SK8 122 F6
Donnington Cl WN7 75 E1
Donnington Rd
Droylsden M18 99 E5
Little Lever M26 43 C5
Donnison St M12 164 F6
Donovan St M40 159 C4
Doodfield Prim Sch SK6 125 F2
Doodson Ave M44 94 A2
Doodson Sq BL4 60 D8
Dooley La SK2,SK6 125 B7
Dooley's La SK9 130 C2
Dootson St 4 Abram WN2 56 B1
Hindley WN2 57 A6
Dora St BL0 11 A4
Dorac Ave SK8 131 C7
Dorchester Ave Bolton BL2 25 E1
Denton M34 100 F1
Manchester M25 63 C2
Urmston M41 95 F3
Dorchester Cl
Altrincham WA15 120 C3
Wilmslow SK9 137 D8
Dorchester Ct
Bramhall SK8 123 B1
Sale M33 108 B2
Dorchester Dr Oldham OL2 48 E2
Sale M23, M33 108 E1
Dorchester Gr OL10 46 D8
Dorchester Par SK7 124 B1
Dorchester Rd
Hazel Grove SK7 124 B1
Orrell WN8 53 A7
Swinton M27 79 F6
Dorclyn Ave M41 95 D2
Dorfield Cl SK6 112 E3
Doric Ave SK6 112 D2
Doric Cl M11 160 F1
Doric Gn WN5 53 D3
Doris Ave BL2 42 D7
Doris Rd SK3 123 C8
Doris St M24 47 A2
Dorket Gr BL5 57 D6
Dorking Ave M40 83 B4
Dorking Cl Bolton BL1 143 F2
Stockport SK1,SK2 124 B7
Dorlan Ave M18 99 F4
Dorland Gr SK2 124 B7
Dorman St 6 M11 99 D7
Dormer St BL1 143 F3
Dorney St M18 99 D5
Dorning Rd M27 80 A7
Dorning St Blackrod BL6 38 F7
Bury BL8 27 B4
6 Eccles M30 79 D1
Kearsley BL4 60 F8
Leigh WN7 75 E5
Tyldesley M29 58 F1
Wigan WN1 150 B8
Dornton Wlk M8 155 F6
Dorothy Gr WN7 75 E4
Dorothy Rd SK7 124 F3
Dorothy St Manchester M8 155 F7
Ramsbottom BL0 138 B5
Dorrian Mews BL1 40 F7
Dorrington Rd
Cheadle SK3 123 A7
Sale M33 107 E4
Dorris St Bolton BL3 146 C3
Manchester M19 111 B8
Dorrit Cl SK12 133 E2
Dorset Ave Bramhall SK7 123 D1
Brinnington SK5 112 C5
Cheadle SK8 123 C5
Diggle OL3 51 C4
Droylsden M34 100 C8
Farnworth BL4 60 C8
Manchester M14 98 A2
Shaw OL2 48 F7
Tyldesley M29 59 A3
Dorset Cl Farnworth BL4 60 C8
Heywood OL10 29 A1
Wigan WN5 54 C6
Dorset Dr Bury BL9 45 A8

Dorset Dr continued
Haslingden BB4 . . . . .1 A8
Dorset Rd
Altrincham WA14 . . . . .119 B5
Atherton M46 . . . . .58 C5
Droylsden M43 . . . . .83 F3
Failsworth M35 . . . . .83 F6
Irlam M44 . . . . .105 D5
Reddish M19 . . . . .99 C1
Standish WN1 . . . . .20 B1
Dorset St Ashton-u-L OL6 . .85 D2
Bolton BL2 . . . . .148 A7
Hindley WN2 . . . . .56 E6
Leigh WN7 . . . . .76 D4
Oldham OL9 . . . . .152 C5
Rochdale OL11 . . . . .139 F6
Stretford M32 . . . . .96 D1
Swinton M27 . . . . .61 F2
Dorsey St M4 . . . . .159 B2
Dorstone Cl Failsworth M40 83 C4
Hindley WN2 . . . . .57 B5
Dorwood Ave M9 . . . . .64 C5
Dotterel Cl WN7 . . . . .76 A6
Dougall Wlk M12 . . . . . . .165 A6
Doughty Ave M30 . . . . .79 F3
Dougill St BL1 . . . . .142 B1
Douglas Ave Billinge WN5 . .71 D3
Bury BL8 . . . . .27 B2
Horwich BL6 . . . . .22 C5
Orrell WN5 . . . . .53 B7
Stretford M32 . . . . .96 D3
Douglas Bank Dr WN6 . . . .36 F2
Douglas Cl Horwich BL6 . . .22 C5
Whitefield M45 . . . . .45 C2
Douglas Dr Orrell WN5 . . . .53 F7
Shevington WN6 . . . . .35 F5
Douglas Gn M6 . . . . .81 A5
Douglas Pk M46 . . . . .58 E3
Douglas Rd Atherton M46 . .58 E2
Hazel Grove SK7 . . . . .124 E3
Leigh WN7 . . . . .75 C7
Shevington Moor WN6 . . . . . .19 B2
Stockport SK3 . . . . .123 E4
Swinton M28 . . . . .79 C7
Wigan WN1 . . . . .37 D1
Douglas Sq OL10 . . . . .28 F1
Douglas St Ashton-u-L OL6 .85 D3
Atherton M46 . . . . .58 E3
Bolton BL1 . . . . .24 E5
Failsworth M35 . . . . .84 A7
Hindley WN2 . . . . .56 C4
Hyde SK14 . . . . .167 E2
Manchester M40 . . . . .83 A7
Manchester M7 . . . . .155 D6
Oldham OL1 . . . . .67 A8
Pendlebury M27 . . . . .80 A7
Ramsbottom BL0 . . . . .138 B6
Wigan WN5 . . . . .150 A7
Douglas St Back BL0 . . . .138 B6
Douglas Way M45 . . . . .45 C1
Douglas Wlk 2 Sale M33 .107 C5
Whitefield M45 . . . . .45 C2
Doulton St M40 . . . . .83 C8
Dounby Ave M30 . . . . .79 B3
Douro St M10,M40 . . . . . . .157 F5
Douthwaite Dr SK6 . . . . . .113 E1
Dove Bank SK6 . . . . .126 F6
Dove Bank Rd BL3 . . . . . . .43 A4
Dove Dr Bury BL9 . . . . . . .141 B4
Irlam M44 . . . . .94 A3
Dove Rd BL3 . . . . .146 B4
Dove St Bolton BL1 . . . . . .143 E4
Golborne WA3 . . . . .74 A2
Oldham OL4 . . . . .67 C6
Rochdale OL11 . . . . .139 D7
Dove Wlk Farnworth BL4 . .59 F8
Manchester M8 . . . . .156 B5
Dovebrook Cl SK15 . . . . . . .86 E7
Dovecote M43 . . . . .84 D3
Dovecote Bsns & Tech Pk
M33 . . . . .108 F4
Dovecote Cl BL7 . . . . .25 B8
Dovecote La Oldham OL4 . .67 F8
Walkden M28 . . . . .59 E3
Dovecote Mews M21 . . . .109 A8
Dovedale Ave
Droylsden M43 . . . . .83 E2
Eccles M30 . . . . .79 E3
Manchester M20 . . . . .110 A4
Manchester M25 . . . . .63 E3
Urmston M41 . . . . .95 D3
Dovedale Cl SK6 . . . . .134 E7
Dovedale Cres WN4 . . . . . .73 A8
Dovedale Ct Glossop SK13 104 F1
8 Middleton M24 . . . . .46 E2
Dovedale Dr
Littleborough OL12 . . . . .15 D6
Standish WN6 . . . . .19 E2
Dovedale Rd
Ashton-in-M WN4 . . . . .73 A8
Bolton BL2 . . . . .25 F1
Stockport SK2 . . . . .124 D7
Dovedale St M35 . . . . .83 E7
Dovehouse Cl M45 . . . . . . .62 D7
Doveleys Rd M6 . . . . .154 D4
Dovenby Fold WN2 . . . . . . .56 B7
Dover Cl BL8 . . . . .11 A1
Dover Gr BL3 . . . . .145 D5
Dover Pk M41 . . . . .95 D4
Dover Rd M27 . . . . .62 A2
Dover St Eccles M30 . . . . . .79 B2
Farnworth BL4 . . . . .42 D2
Manchester M13 . . . . .163 B6
Oldham OL9 . . . . .152 C5

Dover St continued
1 Reddish SK5 . . . . .111 E7
Rochdale OL16 . . . . .15 B2
Dovercourt Ave SK4 . . . . .110 F4
Doveston Rd M33 . . . . . . .108 B6
Dovestone Cres SK16 . . . .101 F7
Dovestone Wlk M40 . . . . . .65 C1
Dovey Cl M29 . . . . .77 C7
Dow Fold BL8 . . . . .26 F3
Dow La BL8 . . . . .26 F3
Dow St SK14 . . . . .101 D5
Dower St M40 . . . . .56 A3
Dowland Cl 3 M23 . . . . . .108 F2
Dowling Cl WN6 . . . . .36 D3
Dowling St OL11 . . . . .139 F6
Downall Green
RC Jun Sch WN4 . . . . .72 E6
Downall Green
RC Prim Sch WN4 . . . . .72 E6
Downall Green Rd WN4 . . .72 E6
Downbrook Way WN4 . . . . .73 D5
Downesway SK9 . . . . .136 F1
Downfield Cl BL0 . . . . .138 B6
Downfields SK5 . . . . .100 A1
Downgate Wlk 7 M8 . . . . .156 A6
Downgreen Rd BL2 . . . . . . .25 E3
Downhall Gn BL1 . . . . .145 F8
Downham Ave Bolton BL2 148 C8
Culcheth WA3 . . . . .91 F2
Downham Chase WA15 . .120 B6
Downham Cl OL1 . . . . .48 D2
Downham Cres M25 . . . . . .63 E3
Downham Gdns M25 . . . . . .63 E3
Downham Gr M25 . . . . .63 E3
Downham Rd
Heywood OL10 . . . . .29 A2
Reddish SK4 . . . . .111 D5
Downham Wlk
Longshaw WN5 . . . . .53 D1
Sale M33 . . . . .120 E8
Downhill Cl OL1 . . . . .48 E1
Downing Cl Ashton-u-L OL7 .84 F6
Platt Bridge WN2 . . . . .56 A2
Downing St Ashton-u-L OL7 .84 F5
5 Leigh WN7 . . . . .75 F5
Manchester M1,M12,M13 . .163 B7
Downing Street Ind Est
M12 . . . . .163 B7
Downley Cl OL12 . . . . .14 B2
Downley Dr M4 . . . . .159 C2
Downs Dr WA14 . . . . .119 E8
Downs The
Altrincham WA14 . . . . .119 D3
Cheadle SK8 . . . . .122 D3
Middleton M24 . . . . .65 B5
Prestwich M25 . . . . .63 A2
Wigan WN3 . . . . .54 C4
Downshaw Rd OL7 . . . . . . .85 A6
Downton Ave WN2 . . . . . . .56 D4
Dowry Rd OL4 . . . . .67 F7
Dowry St BL3 . . . . .146 B4
Dowson Cty Prim Sch
SK14 . . . . .113 E8
Dowson Rd SK14 . . . . .113 E8
Dowson St BL2 . . . . .148 A7
Doyle Ave SK6 . . . . .112 D3
Doyle Cl OL1 . . . . .49 E4
Doyle Rd BL3 . . . . .40 E2
Drake Ave Farnworth BL4 . .60 D7
Irlam M44 . . . . .105 E6
Drake Cl OL1 . . . . .153 F8
Drake Ct SK5 . . . . .169 E4
Drake Hall BL5 . . . . .57 E5
Drake Rd Altrincham WA14 119 B8
Littleborough OL15 . . . . .6 C1
Rochdale OL11,OL16 . . . . .139 F6
Drake St Atherton M46 . . . .58 C2
Rochdale OL11,OL16 . . . . .139 F6
Draycott Cl WN2 . . . . .56 F3
Draycott St BL3 . . . . .143 E2
Draycott St E 10 BL1 . . . .143 F2
Drayfields M43 . . . . .84 D2
Drayford Cl 2 M23 . . . . . .108 F2
Drayton Ave SK8 . . . . .131 B7
Drayton Cl Bolton BL1 . . . .143 D2
Sale M33 . . . . .107 D2
11 Handforth SK9 . . . . .131 D1
Drayton Gr WA15 . . . . .120 A5
Drayton Manor M20 . . . . .122 B8
Drayton Wlk M16 . . . . .162 D5
Dresden St M40 . . . . .83 C8
Drewett St M40 . . . . .160 E4
Dreyfus Ave M11 . . . . .83 D2
Dreyfus St M40 . . . . .160 E3
Driffield St Eccles M30 . . . .95 C8
Manchester M14 . . . . .98 A3
Drill Wlk 8 M4 . . . . .159 C1
Drinkwater Rd M25 . . . . . . .62 F1
Driscoll St 1 M13 . . . . .98 F3
Drive The
Altrincham WA15 . . . . .129 D8
Bredbury SK6 . . . . .112 D3
Brinnington SK5 . . . . .112 C4
Broomedge WA13 . . . . .117 D1
Bury BL9 . . . . .27 F5
Cheadle SK8 . . . . .123 C4
Edenfield BL0 . . . . .1 D3
Leigh WN7 . . . . .75 F3
Manchester M20 . . . . .110 C4
Manchester M7 . . . . .63 C1
Marple SK6 . . . . .125 E6
Prestwich M25 . . . . .63 B4
Sale M33 . . . . .107 E1
Droitwich Rd M40 . . . . . . .160 D4
Dronfield Rd Salford M6 . .154 D4
Wythenshawe M22 . . . . .121 D8
Droughts La M25 . . . . .63 E8
Drovers Wlk SK13 . . . . . . .104 D1
Droxford Ct SK9 . . . . .137 B6

Droxford Gr M46 . . . . .58 E5
Droylsden High Sch M43 . .83 F2
Droylsden Rd
Droylsden M34 . . . . .100 D8
Droylsden M34 . . . . .84 C1
Failsworth M40 . . . . .83 D5
Drs Green & Slater
Rest Hos SK4 . . . . .168 A3
Druid St WN4 . . . . .73 C2
Druids Cl BL7 . . . . .8 D3
Drummer's La WN4 . . . . . .72 E7
Drummond Sq WN5 . . . . . .54 E7
Drummond St BL1 . . . . . . .143 E4
Drummond Way WN7 . . . . .76 B5
Drury La OL9 . . . . .66 B3
Drury St 8 M19 . . . . .99 A1
Dryad Cl M27 . . . . .61 F2
Drybrook Cl M13 . . . . .164 E5
Dryburgh Ave BL1 . . . . . . .143 D4
Dryclough Wlk OL2 . . . . . .48 E3
Dryden Ave
Ashton-in-M WN4 . . . . .72 F6
Cheadle SK8 . . . . .122 F6
Swinton M27 . . . . .79 D7
Dryden Cl Dukinfield SK16 .102 B7
Marple SK6 . . . . .125 F4
Wigan WN3 . . . . .150 A5
Dryden Rd 4 M16 . . . . .97 C3
Dryden St M13 . . . . .163 C6
Dryden Way 10 M34 . . . . .113 A8
Dryfield La BL6 . . . . .22 A5
Drygate Wlk 6 M9 . . . . . .157 E7
Dryhurst Dr SK12 . . . . . . .135 D6
Dryhurst La SK12 . . . . . . .135 D6
Dryhurst Wlk M15 . . . . . . .163 A6
Drymoss OL8 . . . . .67 A1
Dryton Wlk WN2 . . . . .38 A2
Drywood Ave M28 . . . . .79 A5
Ducal St M4 . . . . .159 B4
Duchess Park Cl OL2 . . . . .48 F8
Duchess Rd M8 . . . . .156 B8
Duchess St OL2 . . . . .149 B8
Duchess Wlk BL3 . . . . . . .146 B4
Duchy Ave Atherton BL5 . . .59 A8
Walkden M28 . . . . .78 D8
Duchy Bank M6 . . . . .80 D6
Duchy Rd M6 . . . . .80 E5
Duchy St Salford M6 . . . . .154 F3
Stockport SK3 . . . . .170 D7
Ducie Ave BL1 . . . . .144 C7
Ducie Gr M13 . . . . .163 B5
Ducie High Sch M15 . . . . . .98 B4
Ducie St Manchester M1 . .159 B1
Oldham OL8 . . . . .66 F2
Radcliffe M26 . . . . .43 F5
Whitefield M45 . . . . .62 F8
Duckshaw La BL4 . . . . .60 D8
Duckworth La BB4 . . . . .1 E8
Duckworth Rd M25 . . . . . . .62 F3
Duckworth St
3 Bury BL9 . . . . .141 A4
Shaw OL2 . . . . .149 C7
Duddon Ave BL2 . . . . .25 F1
Duddon Cl M45 . . . . .63 C8
Duddon Dr WN6 . . . . .36 F7
Duddon Wlk 2 M24 . . . . . .46 E2
Dudley Ave Bolton BL2 . . . .25 C1
Whitefield M45 . . . . .62 F8
Dudley Cl M15 . . . . .162 E5
Dudley Ct 10 M16 . . . . .97 D3
Dudley Rd Irlam M44 . . . . .105 D4
Manchester M16 . . . . .97 D3
Sale M33 . . . . .108 C6
Sale WA15 . . . . .120 B7
Swinton M27 . . . . .61 F1
Dudley St Ashton-in-M WN4 .73 A5
Denton M34 . . . . .100 E4
Eccles M30 . . . . .79 C4
Manchester M7,M8 . . . . . . .155 F6
6 Oldham OL4 . . . . .67 D6
Dudlow Wlk 24 M15 . . . . .162 D6
Dudwell Cl BL1 . . . . .142 C2
Duerden St BL3 . . . . .146 A2
Duffield St M15 . . . . .163 A5
Duffield Gdns M9 . . . . .64 F5
Duffield Rd Middleton M9 . .64 F5
Salford M6 . . . . .80 D5
Duffins Cl OL12 . . . . .14 D3
Dufton Wlk
1 Middleton M24 . . . . .46 E2
Wythenshawe M22 . . . . .130 E8
Dugdale Ave M9 . . . . .64 E4
Dugie St BL0 . . . . .138 B7
Duke Ave Cheadle SK8 . . .131 F6
Glazebury WA3 . . . . .92 C7
Duke Ct M16 . . . . .162 D5
Duke of Norfolk's CE
Prim Sch Glossop SK13 .104 D1
Glossop SK13 . . . . .104 D1
Duke Pl M3 . . . . .162 E8
Duke Rd Ainsworth BL2 . . . .26 C1
Dukinfield SK14 . . . . .101 F5
Duke St Alderley Edge SK9 .137 B2
Ashton-in-M WN4 . . . . .73 C3
Ashton-u-L OL6 . . . . .166 B3
Bolton BL1 . . . . .145 E8
Denton M34 . . . . .100 E3
Eccles M30 . . . . .79 C4
Failsworth M35 . . . . .84 A8
Golborne WA3 . . . . .74 A1
Heywood OL10 . . . . .29 B2
Leigh WN7 . . . . .76 A4
Littleborough OL15 . . . . .16 A5
Manchester M3 . . . . .162 E8
Manchester M3 . . . . .162 E8
Manchester M7 . . . . .155 D5
Manchester M7 . . . . .158 D4
Mossley OL5 . . . . .68 E1

Duke St continued
Newton-le-W WA12 . . . . .89 B3
Platt Bridge WN2 . . . . .56 A3
Radcliffe M26 . . . . .44 B2
Ramsbottom BL0 . . . . .11 A4
Rawtenstall BB4 . . . . .2 E8
Rochdale OL12 . . . . .14 F1
Shaw OL2 . . . . .149 C6
Stalybridge SK15 . . . . .85 F1
Stockport SK1 . . . . .169 F1
Tyldesley M29 . . . . .77 C6
Walkden M28 . . . . .61 A2
Walkden M38 . . . . .60 A5
Wigan WN1 . . . . .37 C2
Wigan WN3 . . . . .54 F4
Duke St N BL1 . . . . .145 E8
Duke's Terr 17 SK16 . . . . .166 B1
Dukefield St M22 . . . . .121 E8
Dukes Ave BL3 . . . . .43 A4
Dukes Platting OL6 . . . . . . .85 F5
Dukes St SK13 . . . . .116 C8
Dukes Wharf M28 . . . . .78 F5
Dukesgate Cty Prim Sch
M38 . . . . .60 A5
Dukinfield Rd SK14 . . . . . .101 C4
Dukinfield St 6 WN7 . . . . . .76 A5
Dulford Wlk M13 . . . . .163 C5
Dulgar St M11 . . . . .165 B8
Dulverton Gdns BL3 . . . . . .43 B3
Dulverton St M40 . . . . .83 B6
Dulwich Cl 9 M33 . . . . . . .107 D3
Dulwich St M4 . . . . .159 B3
Dumbarton Cl SK5 . . . . . .111 F6
Dumbarton Dr OL10 . . . . . .46 A8
Dumbarton Gn WN6 . . . . . .36 C7
Dumbarton Rd
Heywood OL10 . . . . .29 A1
Reddish SK5 . . . . .111 F6
Dumber La M33 . . . . .107 F6
Dumbell St M27 . . . . .61 F2
Dumers Cl M26 . . . . .44 D4
Dumers La BL9,M26 . . . . . .44 E5
Dumfries Ave OL3 . . . . .33 C2
Dumfries Dr OL3 . . . . .33 C2
Dumfries Hollow OL10 . . . .29 F3
Dumfries Wlk OL10 . . . . . . .29 A1
Dumplington Circ M41 . . . .77 F7
Dun Cl M3 . . . . .158 D2
Dunbar Ave M23 . . . . .121 A3
Dunbar Dr BL3 . . . . .147 E3
Dunbar Gr OL10 . . . . .45 F8
Dunbar St OL1 . . . . .153 E8
Dunblane Ave Bolton BL3 . .40 E5
Stockport SK4 . . . . .169 D2
Dunblane Cl WN4 . . . . .72 C4
Dunblane Gr OL10 . . . . .46 A8
Duncan Ave WA12 . . . . .89 C5
Duncan Edwards Ho 5
M6 . . . . .154 F3
Duncan Pl WN5 . . . . .54 E7
Duncan Rd M13 . . . . .98 F3
Duncan St Bolton BL1 . . . .145 F8
Dukinfield SK16 . . . . .101 C6
Horwich BL6 . . . . .22 C5
Manchester M7 . . . . .81 C6
Salford M5 . . . . .161 C8
Dunchurch Cl BL6 . . . . .40 D6
Dunchurch Rd M33 . . . . . .107 E4
Duncombe Cl SK7 . . . . . . .124 A3
Duncombe Dr M40 . . . . . . .83 B7
Duncombe Rd BL3 . . . . . . .147 E7
Duncombe St M7 . . . . .155 E6
Duncote Gr OL2 . . . . .149 A5
Dundee 3 M30 . . . . .79 C2
Dundee Cl OL10 . . . . .28 F1
Dundee La BL0 . . . . .138 B6
Dundonald Rd
Cheadle SK8 . . . . .132 A7
Manchester M20 . . . . .110 C3
Dundonald St SK2 . . . . . . .170 F6
Dundraw Cl M24 . . . . .46 B1
Dundrennan Cl SK12 . . . . .133 D5
Dunecroft M34 . . . . .101 A4
Dunedin Dr M6 . . . . .80 F6
Dunedin Rd BL8 . . . . .10 F2
Dunelm Dr M33 . . . . .108 D1
Dunham Ave WA3 . . . . .73 F1
Dunham Cl BL5 . . . . .57 D5
Dunham Gr WN7 . . . . .76 C2
Dunham Lawn WA14 . . . . .119 B4
Dunham Massey Hall
WA14 . . . . .118 D3
Dunham Pk WA14 . . . . . . .118 D3
Dunham Rd
Altrincham WA14 . . . . .118 F1
Altrincham WA14 . . . . .119 B4
Dukinfield SK16 . . . . .101 D6
Partington M31 . . . . .106 D3
Partington WA13 . . . . .117 E7
Dunham Rise WA14 . . . . . .119 C4
Dunham St OL4 . . . . .67 E8
Dunkeld Gdns 2 M23 . . . .120 F6
Dunkeld Rd M23 . . . . .120 F6
Dunkerley Ave M35 . . . . . . .83 F7
Dunkerley St
Ashton-u-L OL7 . . . . .85 A5
Oldham OL4 . . . . .67 C7
Royton OL2 . . . . .48 D4
Dunkerleys Cl M8 . . . . . . .155 F8
Dunkery Rd M22 . . . . .121 D1
Dunkirk Cl M34 . . . . .100 A2
Dunkirk La SK14 . . . . .101 B4
Dunkirk Rd M45 . . . . .44 F1
Dunkirk Rise OL12 . . . . . .139 E7
Dunkirk St M43 . . . . .84 B1
Dunley Cl M12 . . . . .165 A5
Dunlin Ave WA12 . . . . .89 C4
Dunlin Cl Bolton BL2 . . . . .148 A5

Dunlin Cl continued
Hazel Grove SK2 . . . . .125 A3
Poynton SK12 . . . . .133 A4
Rochdale OL11 . . . . .29 F7
Dunlin Dr M44 . . . . .94 A3
Dunlin Gr WN7 . . . . .76 B5
Dunlin Wlk WA14 . . . . .119 B8
Dunlop Cl OL11 . . . . .30 E4
Dunlop St 2 M3 . . . . .158 F1
Dunmail Ave WA11 . . . . . . .71 C1
Dunmail Cl M29 . . . . .77 C6
Dunmail Dr M24 . . . . .46 E3
Dunmaston Ave M23 . . . . .120 D7
Dunmere Wlk M9 . . . . .156 C6
Dunmore Rd SK8 . . . . .122 B6
Dunmow Ct SK2 . . . . .124 E5
Dunmow Wlk M23 . . . . . . .109 A2
Dunne La SK13 . . . . .104 E2
Dunnerdale Wlk M18 . . . . .165 C5
Dunnisher Rd M23 . . . . . . .121 B5
Dunnock Cl SK2 . . . . .124 F5
Dunollie Rd M33 . . . . .108 E3
Dunoon Cl OL10 . . . . .29 A1
Dunoon Dr BL1 . . . . .24 C5
Dunoon Rd Aspull WN2 . . . .38 D5
Reddish SK5 . . . . .111 F7
Dunoon Wlk M9 . . . . .157 D7
Dunrobin Cl OL10 . . . . .46 A8
Dunscar Cl M45 . . . . .62 D7
Dunscar Ind Est BL7 . . . . . .24 E7
Dunscar Sq BL7 . . . . .24 F8
Dunscore Rd WN3 . . . . .54 E3
Dunsdale Dr WN4 . . . . .73 C3
Dunsfold Dr M23 . . . . .120 D8
Dunsford Ct OL4 . . . . .67 F5
Dunsley Ave M40 . . . . .65 D2
Dunsmore Cl M16 . . . . .97 E4
Dunsop Dr BL1 . . . . .23 F3
Dunstable 9 OL12 . . . . . . .139 F8
Dunstable St M19 . . . . .99 B1
Dunstall Rd M22 . . . . .121 E5
Dunstan Ct M40 . . . . .83 A8
Dunstan St BL2 . . . . .148 C3
Dunstar Ave M34 . . . . .100 E3
Dunster Ave
Brinnington SK5 . . . . .112 C5
Manchester M9 . . . . .64 E4
Rochdale OL11 . . . . .139 E5
Swinton M27 . . . . .62 B2
Dunster Cl
Hazel Grove SK7 . . . . .124 C1
Platt Bridge WN2 . . . . .56 A1
Dunster Dr M41 . . . . .94 C1
Dunster Pl M28 . . . . .77 F7
Dunster Rd M28 . . . . .77 F7
Dunsters Ave BL8 . . . . .27 C5
Dunsterville Terr OL11 . . .139 E5
Dunston St M11 . . . . .165 C8
Dunton Gn SK5 . . . . .112 B6
Dunton Towers SK5 . . . . . .112 B6
Dunvegan Rd SK7 . . . . . . .124 F1
Dunwood Ave OL2 . . . . . . .149 C8
Dunwoods Park
Courts OL2 . . . . .32 C1
Dunworth St M14 . . . . .98 B3
Durant St M4 . . . . .159 B3
Durban Cl OL2 . . . . .149 A6
Durban Rd 2 BL1 . . . . .24 E5
Durban St Ashton-u-L OL7 . .84 C1
Atherton M46 . . . . .58 A2
Golborne WN2,WN7 . . . . .74 C4
Oldham OL8 . . . . .66 C3
Rochdale OL11 . . . . .30 C2
Durden Mews OL2 . . . . . . .149 B6
Durham Ave M41 . . . . .95 E3
Durham Cl
Dukinfield SK16 . . . . .101 C6
Little Lever BL3 . . . . .43 B4
Romiley SK6 . . . . .113 A1
Swinton M27 . . . . .61 F2
Tyldesley M29 . . . . .59 A3
Durham Cres M35 . . . . .84 A6
Durham Dr Ashton-u-L OL6 . .85 D8
Bury BL9 . . . . .45 A8
Ramsbottom BL0 . . . . .11 B3
Durham Gr M44 . . . . .105 C6
Durham Ho 6 SK3 . . . . . . .170 E4
Durham Rd Handforth SK9 131 D5
3 Hindley WN2 . . . . .56 E5
Salford M6 . . . . .80 C4
Durham St Bolton BL1 . . . .143 F2
Droylsden M43 . . . . .100 A8
12 Manchester M9 . . . . .157 F7
Oldham OL9 . . . . .66 C4
Radcliffe M26 . . . . .44 C5
Reddish SK5 . . . . .99 E2
Rochdale OL11 . . . . .31 A5
Wigan WN1 . . . . .37 E1
Durham Wlk
5 Denton M34 . . . . .100 F1
Heywood OL10 . . . . .29 A2
Durley Ave Manchester M8 156 B7
Sale M33 . . . . .120 B7
Durling St M12 . . . . .163 C7
Durn St OL15 . . . . .16 C6
Durnford Ave M41 . . . . .96 A4
Durnford Cl OL12 . . . . .13 D2
Durnford St M24 . . . . .46 F1
Durnford Wlk M22 . . . . . . .121 B3
Durrell Way M43 . . . . .90 E8
Durrington Wlk M40 . . . . . .65 C3
Dursley Dr WN4 . . . . .73 D4
Dutton Gr WN7 . . . . .76 C2
Dutton St M3 . . . . .158 F3
Duty St BL1 . . . . .143 E4
Duxbury Ave Bolton BL2 . . .25 E5
Little Lever BL3 . . . . .43 A5
Duxbury Dr BL9 . . . . .141 C2

Duxbury St BL1 ....143 D2
Duxford Lo M8 ....63 F2
Duxford Wlk M40 ....65 C3
Dyche St M4 ....159 B3
Dyche Street Trad Est
M4 ....159 B3
Dye House La
New Mills SK22 ....127 C1
Rochdale OL16 ....15 C3
Dye La SK6 ....113 B2
Dyer St Golborne WA3 ....73 F1
Manchester M11 ....165 A8
Salford M5 ....161 C7
Dyers Cl WA13 ....117 A4
Dyers Ct OL15 ....16 A6
Dyers La WA13 ....117 A4
Dymchurch Ave M26 .....61 C7
Dymchurch St M40 ......83 C4
Dysart St 4 Ashton-u-L OL6 .85 D2
Stockport SK2 ....124 B5
Dysarts Cl OL15 ....68 E3
Dyserth Gr SK5 ....169 F4
Dyson Cl BL4 ....60 D8
Dyson Gr OL4 ....67 F8
Dyson St Farnworth BL4 ...60 D7
Mossley OL5 ....68 B2
Oldham OL1 ....153 F6
Dystelegh Rd SK12 ....135 D6

E

Eades St M6 ....81 A3
Eadington St M8 ....64 A1
Eafield Ave OL16 ....31 F7
Eafield Cl OL16 ....31 F7
Eafield Rd
Littleborough OL15 .....15 E3
Rochdale OL16 ....15 C1
Eagar St M40 ....83 C6
Eagle Ct Delph OL3 .....50 F5
Salford M15 ....162 E5
Eagle Dr M6 ....81 A5
Eagle St Bolton BL2 ....148 A7
5 Manchester M4 .....159 A2
Oldham OL9 ....153 E6
Rochdale OL16 ....31 A6
Eagle Tech Pk OL11 .....31 A4
Eagles Nest M25 ....63 A3
Eagley Bank OL12 ....4 E6
Eagley Brook Way BL1 ...25 A3
Eagley Brow BL1 ....24 F7
Eagley Dr BL8 ....27 A1
Eagley Ind Est BL7 .....24 F7
Eagley Inf Sch BL7 .....25 A8
Eagley Jun Sch BL7 .....25 B8
Eagley Way BL1,BL7 ....24 F7
Ealees OL15 ....16 C5
Ealees Rd OL15 ....16 C5
Ealing Ave M14 ....98 C2
Ealing Pl M19 ....111 A6
Ealing Rd SK3 ....170 D8
Eames Ave M26 ....61 A8
Eamont Wlk M9 ....157 D7
Earby Gr M9 ....64 F3
Earl Rd Handforth SK8,SK9 131 E5
Manchester SK4 ....168 C4
Ramsbottom BL0 ......138 B6
Earl St Atherton M46 ....58 B2
Bury BL9 ....140 F2
6 Heywood OL10 ....29 C2
Ince-in-M WN2 ....56 A4
Leigh WN7 ....76 A4
Manchester M7 ....158 D4
Middleton OL11 ....47 D8
Mossley OL5 ....68 B1
Prestwich M25 ....63 C4
Ramsbottom BL0 ......11 D6
Reddish M34 ....100 A4
Sale M33 ....108 C5
Stockport SK3 ....170 D8
Wigan WN1 ....37 D1
Earl Terr 16 SK16 .....166 B1
Earl Wlk M12 ....164 F5
Earl's Lo M35 ....83 D6
Earle Rd SK7 ....123 E3
Earle St Ashton-u-L OL7 ..84 F2
Newton-le-W WA12 .....89 A3
Earlesdon Cres M38 ....60 A5
Earlestown Dist
CE Jun Sch WA12 .....89 A3
Earlestown Sta WA12 ...89 B3
Earls Way M35 ....83 D6
Earlscliffe Ct WA14 ...119 B4
Earlston Ave M34 ......100 A3
Earlsway SK13 ....116 B8
Earlswood Rd OL8 ......66 E3
Earlswood Wlk Bolton BL1 147 F4
Manchester M18 ......165 C6
Early Bank SK14 ....102 C7
Early Bank Rd SK14,SK16 .102 B6
Earnshaw Ave
Rochdale OL7 ....14 E3
Stockport SK1 ....112 B1
Earnshaw Cl OL7 ....84 A8
Earnshaw St Bolton BL3 146 B3
Hollingworth SK14 ....171 D4
Easby Cl Bramhall SK8 ..132 B6
Poynton SK12 ....133 D4
Easby Rd M24 ....46 F3
Easedale Cl M41 ....94 F3
Easedale Rd BL1 ....144 A8
Easington Wlk 10 M40 ...83 A6
Easingwold 7 WA14 ....119 D4
East Aisle Rd M17,M32 ..96 C5
East Ave Gatley SK8 ...131 D8
Golborne WA3 ....74 C1
Leigh WN7 ....76 C3

East Ave continued
Manchester M19 ....110 F7
Stalybridge SK15 ....86 A3
Whitefield M45 ....44 E2
East Bond St WN7 ......76 A5
East Bridgewater St 4
WN7 ....76 A4
East Central Dr M27 ....80 B7
East Court Wlk M13 ...163 C6
East Cres M24 ....64 F7
East Crompton
St George's CE Prim Sch
OL2 ....49 D7
East Didsbury Sta M20 .110 C1
East Downs Rd
Altrincham WA14 ......119 C2
Cheadle SK8 ....122 F2
East Dr Marple SK6 ....125 F3
Pendlebury M27 ....80 B7
Salford M6 ....80 E5
Whitefield BL9 ....45 B4
East Gate St OL16 ....139 F8
East Gr M13 ....164 D5
East Grange M11 ....83 C3
East Hill St 8 OL1 .....67 A6
East Lancashire Rd
Leigh WA3,WN7 ....76 B1
Newton-le-W
WA11,WA12,WA3 ......89 C7
Pendlebury M6,M27 ....80 B6
Swinton M27,M28 ......79 D7
Tyldesley M28,M29 .....77 C5
Worsley M28 ....78 D7
East Lancashire Rly BL0 138 C5
East Lancs Rly Bury BL8 .27 D6
Heywood OL10 ....29 C1
East Lea M34 ....101 A2
East Lynn Dr M28 ......61 A2
East Market St M3 ....158 D2
East Meade Bolton BL3 .147 E2
Manchester M21 ......109 B7
Manchester M25 ....63 D2
Swinton M27 ....79 E6
East Moor M28 ....78 A7
East Mount WN5 ....53 F6
East Newton St M4 ....159 C3
East Ordsall La M3,M5 .158 D1
East Over SK6 ....125 A8
East Park Cl M13 .....163 C6
East Philip St M3 ....158 E3
East Rd Eccles M41 ....95 F6
Manchester M12 ....99 A3
Manchester M18 ....99 B4
Mossley SK15 ....86 E6
Stretford M32 ....96 B4
Wythenshawe M90 ....130 C7
East St Ashton-in-M WN4 .73 D4
3 Ashton-u-L OL6 ......85 D4
Bury BL9 ....140 F1
Dukinfield M34 ....100 F7
Edenfield BL0 ....1 D4
Haslingden BB4 ....1 A7
Hindley WN2 ....57 B3
Littleborough OL12 .....15 C6
Littleborough OL15 .....16 C5
Milnrow OL16 ....31 D7
Radcliffe M26 ....44 B3
Rochdale OL16 ....31 A8
Tyldesley M46 ....58 F1
East Union St M16 ....161 C6
East Vale SK6 ....126 A5
East View 4 Middleton M24 .64 F8
Ramsbottom BL0 ....1 C1
Ramsbottom BL9 ....11 C3
East Ward Com Prim Sch
BL9 ....141 B2
East Way BL1 ....25 B3
East Wlk BL7 ....8 D2
Eastbank St BL1 ......143 F2
Eastbourne Gr BL1 ...144 B4
Eastbourne St Oldham OL8 .67 B4
Rochdale OL11 ....139 F5
Eastbrook Ave 2 M26 ..44 C4
Eastburn Ave M40 ....159 C3
Eastchurch Cl BL4 .....60 D7
Eastcombe Ave M7 .....81 B7
Eastcote Ave M11 ......99 E8
Eastcote Rd SK5 ......111 F5
Eastcote Wlk 5 BL4 ....42 E1
Eastdale Pl WA14 ....119 D7
Easterdale OL4 ....67 C6
Eastern Ave M27 ....62 D3
Eastern By-Pass
Droylsden M43 ....83 C2
Manchester M11 ....99 D8
Eastern Circ M19 .....111 A6
Eastfield M6 ....154 E4
Eastfield Ave
Manchester M40 ......160 A8
Middleton M24 ....65 A7
Eastfields M26 ....43 E5
Eastford Sq M40 .....159 C4
Eastgarth M19 ....56 B2
Eastgarth Wlk 21 M9 ...64 D2
Eastgate OL12 ....14 C7
Eastgate St OL7 ......166 A1
Eastgrove Ave BL1 .....24 E6
Eastham Ave Bury BL9 ...27 C6
Gatley SK8 ....131 D7
Eastham Way
11 Handforth SK9 .....131 D5
Walkden M38 ....60 B5
Easthaven Ave 4 M11 ..83 C2
Eastholme Dr M19 ....111 B7
Easthope Cl M20 ......110 B7
Eastlands Rd M9 ....64 E5
Eastleigh Ave M7 ....155 E8
Eastleigh Cres WN7 ....76 B3

Eastleigh Dr M40 .....160 D3
Eastleigh Gr 2 BL1 ...145 E8
Eastleigh Rd Gatley SK8 .122 B1
Manchester M25 ....63 E3
Eastmoor Dr M40 ......83 D4
Eastmoor Gr BL3 .....146 B2
Eastnor Cl M15 ....162 D6
Easton Cl Middleton M24 .65 C7
Wigan WN3 ....55 A2
Easton Dr SK8 ....123 A5
Easton Rd M43 ....83 E1
Eastpark Cl M13 .....163 C6
Eastview M33 ....108 B3
Eastville Gdns M19 ...110 E5
Eastward Ave SK9 ....136 F6
Eastway Middleton M24 ..46 F1
Sale M33 ....107 F1
Shaw OL2 ....149 B6
Urmston M41 ....94 E3
Eastwell
Ashton-in-M WN4 ......73 A3
Wigan WN6 ....36 F3
Eastwood M14 ....98 C1
Eastwood Ave
Droylsden M43 ....83 E1
Failsworth M40 ....65 F1
Newton-le-W WA12 ....89 F3
Urmston M41 ....95 D2
Walkden M28 ....60 A2
Eastwood Cl BL9 .....141 B2
Eastwood Dr BL3 .....146 A3
Eastwood Gr WN7 .....75 D5
Eastwood Rd M40 ......65 E1
Eastwood St Denton M34 .100 D7
11 Littleborough OL15 ..16 B5
Eastwood Terr BL1 .....40 E8
Eatock Cty Prim Sch BL5 .57 E6
Eatock St WN2 ....56 B3
Eatock Way BL5 ....57 D6
Eaton Cl Cheadle SK8 ..122 F3
Dukinfield SK16 ......101 C6
Poynton SK12 ....134 A3
Swinton M27 ....61 F2
Eaton Ct SK9 ....137 A6
Eaton Dr Alderley Edge SK9 136 F2
Ashton-u-L OL7 ....84 F4
Sale WA15 ....120 A8
Eaton Rd Altrincham WA14 119 C1
Manchester M8 ....63 F1
Sale M33 ....108 A4
Eaton St WN2 ....56 E6
Eaves Knoll Rd SK22 ...127 A1
Eaves La OL9 ....152 A5
Ebbdale Cl SK1 ....124 A8
Ebberstone St M14 .....98 A2
Ebden St M1 ....163 B8
Ebenezer St Glossop SK13 116 D7
2 Manchester M15 ...162 F7
Ebnal Wlk M14 ....110 D7
Ebor Cl OL2 ....149 A8
Ebor Ho M21 ....96 F1
Ebor Rd M22 ....121 E4
Ebor St OL15 ....16 B5
Ebsworth St
Manchester M40 ......157 F8
Manchester M40 ....83 A8
Ebury St M26 ....43 F3
Eccles Cl M11 ....165 C8
Eccles Coll M30 ....79 F4
Eccles New Rd M5 .....80 C2
Eccles Old Rd M6,M30 ..80 C3
Eccles Rd Swinton M27 ..79 F6
Wigan WN5 ....36 B1
Eccles St BL0 ....138 B6
Eccles Sta M30 ....79 F2
Ecclesbridge Rd SK6 ..125 F4
Eccleshall St M11 ......83 C1
Eccleston Ave
28 Bolton BL2 ....25 B1
Manchester M14 ....98 B1
Swinton M27 ....79 D7
Eccleston Cl BL8 ....27 A1
Eccleston Pl M7 ......155 D8
Eccleston Rd SK3 .....123 E4
Eccleston St
Failsworth M35 ....84 A8
Wigan WN1 ....37 C1
Eccleston Way 3 SK9 ..131 D4
Eccups La SK9 ....136 C8
Echo St M1 ....163 B8
Eckersley Ave WN2 .....56 D3
Eckersley Cl 1 M23 ...120 F6
Eckersley Fold La M46 ..58 A1
Eckersley Rd BL1 .....143 E3
Eckersley St Bolton BL3 .146 C4
Wigan WN1 ....37 E1
Eckford St M8 ....156 B6
Eclipse Cl OL16 ....31 C7
Edale Ave Denton M34 ..100 D7
Denton M34 ....112 F4
Manchester M40 ....83 A8
Reddish SK5 ....100 A1
Urmston M41 ....95 B1
Edale Bank M13 ......171 E1
Edale Cl Altrincham WA14 .119 C1
Atherton M46 ....58 C3
28 Gamesley SK13 ....171 E2
Gatley SK8 ....131 D7
Hazel Grove SK7 ......124 E1
Edale Cres SK13 ......171 E1
Edale Dr WN6 ....19 E2
Edale Fold 25 SK13 ...171 E2
Edale Gr Ashton-u-L OL6 .86 A6
Sale M33 ....107 E2
Edale Rd Bolton BL3 ...146 A4
Farnworth BL4 ....60 C7

Edale Rd continued
Leigh WN7 ....76 C4
Stretford M32 ....96 B3
Edale St M6 ....81 B5
Edbrook Wlk M13 ....164 D5
Edburton Ct WA3 ......90 A8
Eddie Colman Cl M40 ...83 B5
Eddisbury Ave
Manchester M20 ......109 F8
Urmston M41 ....94 D4
Eddisford Dr WA3 .....91 D4
Eddystone Cl 6 M5 ....81 A1
Eden Ave Bolton BL1 ..143 E3
Edenfield BL0 ....1 D3
Fowley Common WA3 ...92 C4
High Lane SK6 ....134 E2
Eden Bank WN7 ....76 B6
Eden Cl Heywood OL10 ..29 A3
Manchester M15 ......163 A6
Stockport SK1 ....124 A8
Wilmslow SK9 ....136 E5
Eden Ct M19 ....111 A8
Eden Gr Bolton BL1 ...143 E3
Leigh WN7 ....75 C5
Eden Lo BL1 ....143 E3
Eden Pl SK8 ....122 D6
Eden St Bolton BL1 ...143 E3
Bury BL9 ....140 F2
Edenfield BL0 ....1 D1
Oldham OL1 ....153 E7
Rochdale OL12 ....139 D8
Eden Way OL2 ....149 A8
Edenbridge Dr M26 ....61 B7
Edenbridge Rd
Cheadle SK8 ....123 B4
Failsworth M40 ....83 B4
Edendale Dr M22 .....121 D1
Edenfield Ave M21 ....109 D4
Edenfield CE Prim Sch BL0 1 D4
Edenfield La M28 ......78 F4
Edenfield Rd
Manchester M25,M8 ...63 E2
Rochdale OL11,OL12 ...13 C2
Rochdale OL11,OL12 ...14 C1
Edenhall Ave M19 ....110 F8
Edenhall Gr M27 ....56 F3
Edenhurst 3 WA15 ...120 B5
Edenhurst Rd SK2 ....124 B6
Edensor Cl WN6 ....37 A4
Edensor Dr WA15 ....120 C3
Edenvale M28 ....78 A7
Edgar St Bolton BL3 ..145 E6
Ramsbottom BL0 ......138 B3
Rochdale OL16 ....15 C2
Edgar St W BL0 ......138 B5
Edgbaston Dr M16 .....97 A3
Edge Fold Cres M28 ...78 D8
Edge Fold Rd M28 .....60 D1
Edge Gn M28 ....78 C8
Edge Green La WA3 ....73 F2
Edge Green Rd WA3,WN4 .73 F2
Edge Green St WN4 ....73 D4
Edge Hall Rd WN5 .....53 E5
Edge Hill Ave OL2 .....48 E5
Edge Hill Rd Bolton BL3 146 B3
Oldham OL2 ....48 E3
Edge La Bacup OL13 .....4 C8
Bolton BL1,BL6 ....23 C5
Droylsden M11,M43 ....83 D2
Edgworth BL7 ....9 A8
Stalybridge SK14 .....102 F4
Stretford M21,M32 .....96 E1
Edge Lane Rd OL1 .....67 A8
Edge Lane St OL2 .....48 E4
Edge St M4 ....159 A2
Edge View OL1 ....47 E1
Edge View La SK9 ....136 B2
Edge Ware Gr WN3 .....54 D3
Edgedale Ave M19 ....110 E5
Edgefield Ave M9 ......64 E4
Edgefold Ind Est BL4 .146 B1
Edgehill Chase SK9 ...137 E7
Edgehill Cl M5 ....154 F7
Edgehill Ct M32 ....96 E1
Edgehill Rd M6 ....80 C3
Edgehill St 10 M4 ....159 A2
Edgeley Fold SK3 ....123 C7
Edgeley Park
(Stockport County FC)
SK3 ....170 E7
Edgeley Rd Stockport SK3 123 B7
Urmston M41 ....107 A8
Edgemoor WA14 ......119 C2
Edgemoor Cl Oldham OL4 .49 D1
Radcliffe M26 ....43 E5
Whitworth OL12 ....1 C1
Edgemoor Dr OL11 .....29 F5
Edgerley Pl WN4 ......73 A3
Edgerton Rd WA3 ......90 F8
Edgerton Wlk M28 .....60 D3
Edgeview Wlk 6 M11 ...83 C1
Edgeware Ave M25,M8 ..63 F4
Edgeware Rd Eccles M30 .79 A4
Failsworth M40 ....65 E3
Edgewater M5 ....154 D2
Edgeway SK9 ....137 B5
Edgeway Rd WN3 ......55 A1
Edgewood WN6 ....36 A5
Edgeworth Dr Bury BL8 ..27 A1
Manchester M14 ......110 E7
Edgeworth Rd
Golborne WA3 ....73 F1
Hindley WN2 ....57 A3

Edgmont Ave BL3 .....147 D4
Edgware Rd M40 ....83 B4
Edgworth Cl OL10 ......29 A2
Edgworth Prim Sch BL7 ..9 D5
Edilom Rd M8 ....63 E2
Edinburgh 8 M30 ......79 E2
Edinburgh Cl Cheadle SK8 122 F6
Ince-in-M WN2 ....56 A8
8 Sale M33 ....107 D3
Edinburgh Dr Hindley WN2 .57 B3
Romiley SK6 ....113 C4
Wigan WN5 ....54 D5
Edinburgh Rd BL3 .....43 A2
Edinburgh Sq M40 ...160 E4
Edinburgh Way OL11 ...30 C4
Edinburgh Wlk WN2 ....38 D5
Edington 7 OL12 .....139 F8
Edison Rd M30 ....95 C8
Edison St 1 M11 ......99 E7
Edith Ave M14 ....98 A3
Edith Cavell Cl M11 ...83 C1
Edith Cliff Wlk M40 ...65 F1
Edith St Bolton BL1 ..144 C6
Farnworth BL4 ....60 D7
Oldham OL8 ....66 F3
Ramsbottom BL0 ......11 E8
Wigan WN3 ....150 B7
Edleston Gr 2 SK9 ...131 E1
Edlin Cl M12 ....164 E5
Edlingham 6 OL11 ...139 E6
Edlington Wlk 12 M40 ..83 C6
Edmonds St M24 ......47 B1
Edmonton Rd
Failsworth M40 ....83 A4
Stockport SK2,SK3 ...124 A4
Edmund Cl SK4 ......169 E4
Edmund Dr WN7 ....75 C5
Edmund Potter Hospl BL1 40 F7
Edmund St Droylsden M43 .84 A1
Failsworth M35 ....83 B8
Manchester M3 ......158 E2
Milnrow OL16 ....31 E7
8 Radcliffe M26 ......44 C4
Rochdale OL12 ....139 D8
Salford M6 ....154 E3
Shaw OL2 ....149 C7
Walsden OL14 ....6 A4
Edmunds Ct BL3 .....145 D6
Edmunds Fold OL15 ....15 F6
Edna Rd WN7 ....75 C7
Edna St SK14 ....167 D2
Edridge Way WN2 ......56 C4
Edson Rd M9 ....63 F3
Edward Ave Bredbury SK6 .112 E4
Littleborough OL15 ....15 F3
Manchester M21 ......109 A8
Salford M5,M6 ....80 C3
Edward Charlton Rd
M16,M21 ....97 A2
Edward Dr WN4 ....73 B4
Edward Mews OL9 ...152 C5
Edward Onyon Ct M5 .154 E2
Edward Rd Manchester M9 .64 D5
Shaw OL2 ....149 A6
Edward St Ashton-u-L OL6 .85 E2
Bolton BL3 ....145 D5
Bury BL9 ....140 F1
Chadderton OL9 ......152 A6
Denton M34 ....100 D7
Denton M34 ....100 A8
Droylsden M43 ....100 A8
Dukinfield SK14 ......101 C3
Dukinfield SK16 ......101 C6
Farnworth BL4 ....42 B2
Glossop SK13 ....104 C1
Horwich BL6 ....22 A3
Kearsley M26 ....61 B8
Leigh WN7 ....76 A4
Littleborough OL12 ....15 D4
Manchester M7 ......158 E4
Manchester M9 ......157 E8
Middleton M24 ....47 A1
Oldham OL9 ....152 C5
Prestwich M25 ....63 A5
Radcliffe M26 ....44 B2
Rochdale OL16 ....31 A8
Romiley SK6 ....114 B3
Sale M33 ....108 E4
Stockport SK1 ....170 F8
Westhoughton BL5 .....57 E8
Whitworth OL12 ....4 D2
Wigan WN1 ....151 F8
Wigan WN1 ....37 C2
Edward Sutcliffe Cl M14 .98 A2
Edwards Cl SK6 ......125 E5
Edwards Ct M22 .....121 C2
Edwards Dr M45 ....63 B8
Edwards Way SK6 ....125 E5
Edwin Rd M11 ....160 E1
Edwin St Bury BL9 ....140 E2
Stockport SK1 ....124 B8
Edwin Waugh Gdns OL12 .14 D3
Edzell Wlk 18 M11 ....83 C1
Eeasbrook M45 ....95 C1
Egbert St 18 M40 ......83 A7
Egerton Ave WA13 ....117 C8
Egerton Cl OL10 ....29 D1
Egerton Com Prim Sch BL7 8 D3
Egerton Cres
Heywood OL10 ....29 B7
Manchester M20 ......110 B7
Egerton Ct Dukinfield M34 101 A4
6 Hindley WN2 ....56 E5
Manchester M14 ....98 C4

Egerton Ct continued
Stockport SK3 . . . .**124** A4
Stretford M21 . . . .**108** F8
Egerton Dr
Altrincham WA15 . . . .**120** A3
Sale M33 . . . .**108** B5
Egerton Gr M28 . . . .**60** D3
Egerton Ho 3 M15 . . . . . .**162** D7
Egerton Lo Bolton BL7 . . . . . .**8** E1
Denton M34 . . . .**101** A4
Egerton Mews
Droylsden M43 . . . .**100** A8
Manchester M14 . . . .**110** D8
Egerton Moss WA15 . . . . .**128** E5
Egerton Park Arts Coll
M34 . . . .**100** E4
Egerton Pk M28 . . . .**79** B7
Egerton Pl OL2 . . . .**149** A6
Egerton Rd
Altrincham WA15 . . . .**120** A2
Eccles M30 . . . .**79** D4
Handforth SK9 . . . .**131** B1
Manchester M14 . . . .**110** D8
Stockport SK3 . . . .**124** A4
Walkden M28 . . . .**60** D3
Whitefield M45 . . . .**62** F7
Egerton Rd N
Manchester M16,M21 . . . . . .**97** C1
Manchester SK4 . . . .**111** C5
Egerton Rd S
Manchester M14 . . . .**109** C8
Manchester SK4 . . . .**168** C4
Egerton Sch M41 . . . .**95** E4
Egerton St
Abram Brow WN2 . . . .**74** B7
Ashton-u-L OL6 . . . .**166** C3
Denton M34 . . . .**100** E5
Droylsden M43 . . . .**84** B1
Eccles M30 . . . .**79** B2
Farnworth BL4 . . . .**42** C1
Heywood OL10 . . . .**29** C1
Littleborough OL15 . . . .**16** C5
Manchester M15 . . . .**162** D7
Manchester M3 . . . .**158** D1
Middleton M24 . . . .**64** C7
Mossley OL5 . . . .**68** C2
Oldham OL1 . . . .**67** A8
Prestwich M25 . . . .**63** C4
Egerton Terr M14 . . . .**110** D7
Eggar Cl M29 . . . .**77** B7
Eggington St M40 . . . .**156** C5
Egham Ct BL2 . . . .**25** E1
Egham Ho BL3 . . . .**146** B2
Egmont Manchester M8 **156** A8
Mossley OL5 . . . .**86** D8
Pendlebury M6 . . . .**80** E6
Egmont Ave M20 . . . .**110** A7
Egremont Cl M45 . . . .**45** A1
Egremont Ct M7 . . . .**81** C8
Egremont Gr 2 SK3 . . . . .**123** B8
Egremont Rd OL16 . . . .**31** F4
Egret Dr M44 . . . .**94** A3
Egypt La M45 . . . .**45** D1
Egyptian St BL1 . . . .**143** F1
Ehlinger Ave SK13 . . . . . .**104** A5
Eida Way M17 . . . .**96** C8
Eight Acre M45 . . . .**62** C7
Eighth Ave OL8 . . . .**66** D1
Eighth St M17 . . . .**96** D6
Eighth St W M17 . . . .**96** D6
Eileen Gr M14 . . . .**98** C2
Eileen Gr W M14 . . . .**98** B2
Elaine Ave M9 . . . .**65** B2
Elaine Cl WN4 . . . .**73** D5
Elbain Wlk M40 . . . .**83** C5
Elbe St M12 . . . .**163** C8
Elberton Wlk 13 M8 . . . . .**155** F7
Elbow La OL11 . . . .**31** A6
Elbow St M19 . . . .**99** A1
Elbut La BL9 . . . .**28** F5
Elcho Rd WA14 . . . .**119** B3
Elcombe Ave WA3 . . . .**90** E7
Elcot Cl M40 . . . .**156** C5
Elder Cl SK2 . . . .**124** D8
Elder Gr M40 . . . .**65** F2
Elder Rd OL4 . . . .**67** E6
Elder St OL16 . . . .**31** B5
Elderberry Cl Diggle OL3 . . .**51** C5
Wigan WN1 . . . .**37** B4
Elderberry Way SK9 . . . . .**137** E8
Elderberry Wlk M31 . . . . .**105** E3
Eldercot Gr BL3 . . . .**146** A4
Eldercot Rd BL3 . . . .**146** A4
Eldercroft Rd WA15 . . . . .**120** D5
Elderfield Dr SK6 . . . .**112** F4
Eldermount Rd M9 . . . .**64** D2
Elderwood OL9 . . . .**65** E7
Eldon Cl M34 . . . .**100** E7
Eldon Gdns WN4 . . . .**73** A6
Eldon Pl M30 . . . .**79** C1
Eldon Prec OL8 . . . .**153** E5
Eldon Rd Irlam M44 . . . .**94** A2
Stockport SK3 . . . .**123** C7
Eldon St Bolton BL2 . . . .**25** B2
Bury BL9 . . . .**140** F4
Leigh WN7 . . . .**75** D6
Oldham OL8 . . . .**153** F5
Eldridge Dr M40 . . . .**83** A5
Eleanor Rd
Manchester M21 . . . .**109** A8
Oldham OL2 . . . .**48** E3
Eleanor St Bolton BL1 . . . . .**25** A5
Oldham OL1 . . . .**153** D8
Wigan WN3 . . . .**150** A2
Electo St M11 . . . .**99** E7

Elevator Rd M17 . . . .**96** E6
Eleventh St M17 . . . .**96** D6
Elf Mill Cl SK3 . . . .**170** E6
Elford Gr M18 . . . .**100** A4
Elgar St M12 . . . .**99** A4
Manchester M20 . . . .**110** D3
Elgin Ave Garswood WN4 . . .**72** C4
Manchester M20 . . . .**110** D3
Elgin Cl WN2 . . . .**56** A8
Elgin Dr M33 . . . .**108** E3
Elgin Rd Dukinfield SK16 . . .**101** C6
Oldham OL4 . . . .**67** C5
Elgin St Ashton-u-L OL7 . . .**166** A4
Bolton BL1 . . . .**142** C2
Stalybridge SK15 . . . .**86** B1
Elgol Cl SK3 . . . .**170** F5
Elgol Ct OL10 . . . .**29** A1
Elgol Dr BL3 . . . .**40** E6
Elham Cl M26 . . . .**61** C7
Eli St OL9 . . . .**66** A3
Elim Cl OL15 . . . .**16** C7
Elim Terr OL15 . . . .**16** C7
Eliot Dr WN3 . . . .**150** A5
Eliot Rd M30 . . . .**79** D1
Elishaw Row M5 . . . .**154** F1
Eliza Ann St 5 Eccles M30 . .**79** C1
Manchester M40 . . . .**159** C4
Eliza St Manchester M15 . . .**162** E6
Ramsbottom BL0 . . . .**11** D6
Elizabeth Ave Denton M34 **100** E5
Disley SK12 . . . .**135** D5
Leigh WN2 . . . .**56** E1
Oldham OL9 . . . .**66** A3
Royton OL2 . . . .**48** D3
1 Stalybridge SK15 . . . .**86** A2
Stockport SK1 . . . .**170** F8
Elizabeth Ct Edenfield BL0 . . .**1** D3
Manchester M14 . . . .**110** D7
Reddish M18 . . . .**99** F3
Stockport SK4 . . . .**168** C2
Elizabeth Dr BB4 . . . .**1** A8
Elizabeth Gr OL2 . . . .**149** B7
Elizabeth Ho SK4 . . . .**168** B2
Elizabeth Rd M31 . . . .**105** E4
Elizabeth Slinger Rd
M20 . . . .**109** F5
Elizabeth St
Ashton-u-L OL6 . . . .**166** B4
Atherton M46 . . . .**58** D3
Denton M34 . . . .**100** D3
Edenfield BL0 . . . .**1** D3
2 Heywood OL10 . . . .**29** C2
Hyde SK14 . . . .**167** D3
Ince-in-M WN2 . . . .**56** B8
Leigh WN7 . . . .**76** B3
Manchester M8 . . . .**155** F6
Manchester M8 . . . .**156** A5
Prestwich M25 . . . .**63** C4
3 Radcliffe M26 . . . .**44** A3
Rochdale OL11 . . . .**30** C3
1 Swinton M27 . . . .**61** F1
Whitefield M45 . . . .**62** F7
Elizabethan Ct 10 M29 . . . .**58** F1
Elizabethan Dr WN3 . . . . . .**55** E4
Elizabethan Way OL16 . . . . .**31** F5
Elizabethan Wlk 1 WN2 . . .**56** A2
Elkanagh Gdns M6 . . . . . .**154** F3
Elkstone Ave M38 . . . .**60** A6
Elkstone Cl WN3 . . . .**54** C2
Elkwood Cl WN1 . . . .**37** B4
Elladene Pk M21 . . . .**109** C8
Ellan Wlk 10 M11 . . . .**83** C1
Ellanby Cl M14 . . . .**98** B3
Elland Cl BL9 . . . .**45** B2
Ellaston Dr M41 . . . .**95** D2
Ellastone Rd M6 . . . .**80** C4
Ellbourne Rd M9 . . . .**64** A3
Ellen Brook Rd M22 . . . . . .**130** D8
Ellen Gr BL4 . . . .**61** C5
Ellen St 5 Bolton BL1 . . . . .**142** C3
Droylsden M43 . . . .**100** B8
Oldham OL9 . . . .**153** D8
Ince-in-M WN2 . . . .**56** A7
Stockport SK4 . . . .**169** D3
Wigan WN1 . . . .**151** D7
Ellen Wilkinson Cres
M12 . . . .**165** A5
Ellen Wilkinson
High Sch M12 . . . .**164** D6
Ellenbrook Cl M12 . . . .**165** B6
Ellenbrook Prim Sch M28 .**78** C8
Ellenbrook Rd M28 . . . .**78** B7
Ellendale Grange M28 . . . . .**78** B8
Ellenhall Cl M9 . . . .**157** D8
Ellenor Dr M29 . . . .**77** C7
Ellenroad App OL16 . . . . . .**32** A4
Ellenroad Engine Ho OL16 **32** A4
Ellenroad St OL16 . . . .**32** A4
Ellenrod Dr OL12 . . . .**14** A2
Ellenrod La OL12 . . . .**14** A2
Ellenshaw Cl OL12 . . . .**14** A2
Elleray Cl BL3 . . . .**43** C3
Elleray Rd Middleton M9 . . .**64** F5
Salford M6 . . . .**80** D5
Ellerbeck Cl Bolton BL2 . . . .**25** C5
Standish WN6 . . . .**36** F7
Ellerbeck Cres M28 . . . .**78** C8
Ellerby Ave M27 . . . .**62** A3
Ellerscroft SK22 . . . .**127** E1
Ellesmere Ave
Ashton-u-L OL6 . . . .**85** C7
Eccles M30 . . . .**79** C4
Marple SK6 . . . .**125** F6
Walkden M28 . . . .**60** C3
Ellesmere Cl SK16 . . . .**101** E8
Ellesmere Dr SK8 . . . .**123** A5
Ellesmere Gdns BL3 . . . . .**147** D3
Ellesmere Rd
Altrincham WA14 . . . .**119** E6

Ellesmere Rd continued
Ashton-in-M WN4 . . . .**72** F4
Bolton BL3 . . . .**146** C3
Cheadle SK3 . . . .**123** A7
Culcheth WA3 . . . .**91** E3
Eccles M30 . . . .**79** E3
Manchester M21 . . . .**97** C1
Wigan WN5 . . . .**54** D6
Ellesmere Rd N SK4 . . . . .**111** C5
Ellesmere Rd S SK4 . . . . .**111** C5
Ellesmere Ret Pk M28 . . . . .**60** D4
Ellesmere Sh Ctr M28 . . . . .**60** D4
Ellesmere St Bolton BL3 . . .**145** D6
14 Eccles M30 . . . .**79** D1
Failsworth M35 . . . .**83** F8
Farnworth BL4 . . . .**60** D8
Leigh WN7 . . . .**75** F4
Manchester M15 . . . .**162** D7
Swinton M27 . . . .**62** A1
Swinton M27 . . . .**79** D7
Tyldesley M29 . . . .**59** A1
Tyldesley M29 . . . .**77** C5
Walkden M38 . . . .**60** C4
Ellesmere Terr M14 . . . . . .**110** D7
Ellesmere Wlk 3 BL4 . . . . .**60** D8
Ellingham Cl M11 . . . .**160** F1
Elliot Sq OL1 . . . .**67** A8
Elliot St Bolton BL1 . . . .**142** C3
Oldham OL4 . . . .**67** E6
Elliot Wlk M40 . . . .**47** C3
Elliott Ave Dukinfield SK14 .**101** D5
Golborne WA3 . . . .**74** B1
Elliott Dr Hindley WN2 . . . . .**56** E7
Sale M33 . . . .**107** E4
Elliott St Farnworth BL4 . . . .**60** C4
Rochdale OL12 . . . .**31** A8
Tyldesley M29 . . . .**76** F8
Ellis Cres M28 . . . .**60** B3
Ellis Dr M8 . . . .**64** B1
Ellis Fold OL12 . . . .**13** E2
Ellis La M24 . . . .**64** B8
Ellis Rd WN5 . . . .**71** D4
Ellis St Bolton BL3 . . . .**145** D5
Bury BL8 . . . .**27** B2
Hyde SK14 . . . .**167** F2
Manchester M15 . . . .**162** E6
Manchester M7 . . . .**158** E4
Ramsbottom BL0 . . . .**138** B5
Wigan WN1 . . . .**37** E1
Ellisbank Wlk 9 M13 . . . . .**163** B7
Ellisland Wlk 1 M40 . . . . . .**83** A6
Ellison Cl SK14 . . . .**103** D5
Ellison Ho OL7 . . . .**166** A1
Ellison St SK13 . . . .**104** D1
Elliston Sq M12 . . . .**165** A6
Ellor St Salford M5 . . . .**81** B2
Salford M6 . . . .**154** F3
Ellwood Rd SK1 . . . .**112** B1
Elm Ave Downall Green WN4 **72** D5
Golborne WA3 . . . .**74** A1
Newton-le-W WA12 . . . .**89** C2
Radcliffe M26 . . . .**61** F8
Standish WN6 . . . .**36** F8
Wigan WN5 . . . .**54** E6
Elm Beds Rd SK12 . . . .**134** C2
Elm Cl Mottram-in-L SK14 . .**103** A4
2 Partington M31 . . . .**105** F3
Poynton SK12 . . . .**133** F3
Elm Cres
Alderley Edge SK9 . . . .**137** B3
Swinton M28 . . . .**79** A7
Elm Croft WN1 . . . .**37** B4
Elm Ct SK1 . . . .**124** B8
Elm Dr Billinge WN5 . . . .**71** D5
Bramhall SK7 . . . .**132** C7
Denton M34 . . . .**100** D4
Stretford M32 . . . .**96** A4
Elm Gr Alderley Edge SK9 . . .**137** B2
Ashton-u-L OL6 . . . .**85** C5
Bolton BL7 . . . .**25** A8
Denton M34 . . . .**100** D5
Droylsden M43 . . . .**83** D2
Farnworth BL4 . . . .**60** B8
Glossop SK13 . . . .**104** C2
Handforth SK9 . . . .**131** C3
6 Horwich BL6 . . . .**22** E1
Hyde SK14 . . . .**167** F2
Littleborough OL12 . . . .**15** C6
Manchester M20 . . . .**110** B3
Newhey OL16 . . . .**32** A3
Oldham OL4 . . . .**67** E8
Prestwich M25 . . . .**63** A6
Sale M33 . . . .**108** B6
Swinton M27 . . . .**61** B2
Urmston M41 . . . .**95** E2
Elm Ho M16 . . . .**97** D3
Elm Park Ct M20 . . . .**110** B4
Elm Rd Abram Brow WN2 . . .**74** C7
Altrincham WA15 . . . .**119** E3
Gatley SK8 . . . .**122** A5
High Lane SK6 . . . .**134** F7
Hollinfare WA3 . . . .**105** A2
Kearsley BL4 . . . .**60** F5
Little Lever BL3 . . . .**43** B2
Manchester M20 . . . .**110** A4
Oldham OL3 . . . .**66** D2
Westhoughton BL5 . . . .**57** F7
Elm Rd S SK3 . . . .**123** A7
Elm St Bredbury SK6 . . . . . .**112** F4
Bury BL9 . . . .**141** D3
Eccles M30 . . . .**79** D1
Edenfield BL0 . . . .**1** E3
Failsworth M35 . . . .**83** F8
Farnworth BL4 . . . .**42** E1
Heywood OL10 . . . .**29** D2
Leigh WN7 . . . .**75** F3
Middleton M24 . . . .**65** C8

Elm St continued
Platt Bridge WN2 . . . .**56** A2
Ramsbottom BL0 . . . .**11** D6
Rochdale OL12 . . . .**14** F1
Swinton M27 . . . .**61** C1
Whitworth OL12 . . . .**4** D2
Elm Tree Cl Failsworth M35 .**84** B7
Stalybridge SK15 . . . .**102** A8
Elm Tree Dr
Dukinfield SK16 . . . .**101** F7
Wythenshawe M22 . . . .**121** E3
Elm Tree Rd Bredbury SK6 **112** C3
Golborne WA3 . . . .**90** F8
Elm Wood Prim Sch M24 .**65** C8
Elmbank Ave M20 . . . .**109** E4
Elmbank Rd M24 . . . .**65** C8
Elmbridge Wlk
Bolton BL3 . . . .**145** D5
2 Manchester M40 . . . .**83** A6
Elmdale Ave SK8 . . . .**122** B2
Elmdale Wlk 1 M15 . . . . . .**163** A6
Elmfield WN6 . . . .**36** B6
Elmfield Ave Atherton M46 . .**58** C4
Wythenshawe M22 . . . .**121** E8
Elmfield Cl SK9 . . . .**137** B2
Elmfield Dr SK6 . . . .**125** E6
Elmfield Ho SK3 . . . .**170** E6
Elmfield Rd
Alderley Edge SK9 . . . .**137** B2
Droylsden M34 . . . .**100** C8
Stockport SK3 . . . .**170** F5
Wigan WN1 . . . .**37** B5
Elmfield St Bolton BL1 . . . .**143** F2
Manchester M8 . . . .**156** A6
Elmgate Gr M19 . . . .**99** A1
Elmham Wlk M40 . . . .**159** C4
Elmhow Gr WN3 . . . .**55** A2
Elmhurst Dr M19 . . . .**110** F5
Elmley Cl SK2 . . . .**125** A5
Elmore Wood OL15 . . . .**15** E4
Elmpark Gate OL12 . . . .**14** B3
Elmpark Gr OL12 . . . .**14** B3
Elmpark Vale OL12 . . . .**14** B3
Elmpark View OL12 . . . .**14** B3
Elmpark Way OL12 . . . .**14** B3
Elmridge WN7 . . . .**76** B6
Elmridge Ct WA3 . . . .**90** F8
Elmridge Dr WN3 . . . .**129** C8
Elmridge Prim Sch
WA15 . . . .**129** C8
Elms Bank
Com High Sch M45 . . . . .**44** F2
Elms Cl M45 . . . .**44** F2
Elms Farm 3 M45 . . . .**44** F2
Elms Rd Manchester SK4 . . .**111** B5
Stalybridge SK15 . . . .**86** D3
Whitefield M45 . . . .**44** F2
Elms St M45 . . . .**44** F2
Elms The Golborne WA3 . . . .**90** F7
Littleborough OL15 . . . .**15** E4
Mossley OL5 . . . .**68** B1
4 Whitefield M45 . . . .**44** F2
Elmsbury St 1 WN4 . . . .**72** F5
Elmscott Wlk M13 . . . .**164** D5
Elmsdale Ave M9 . . . .**64** D5
Elmsfield Ave OL11 . . . .**13** E1
Elmsleigh Ct M30 . . . .**79** F3
Elmsleigh Rd SK8 . . . .**122** A2
Elmsmere Rd M20 . . . .**110** D4
Elmstead Ave M20 . . . .**110** A6
Elmsted Cl SK8 . . . .**123** B3
Elmstone Gr BL1 . . . .**143** F1
Elmsway Altrincham WA15 . .**129** B8
Bramhall SK7 . . . .**132** C7
High Lane SK6 . . . .**134** E6
Elmswood Ave M14 . . . .**97** F2
Elmswood Dr SK14 . . . .**102** A3
Elmsworth Ave M19 . . . .**99** B1
Elmton Rd M9 . . . .**64** E3
Elmtree Dr SK4 . . . .**168** C2
Elmwood M33 . . . .**107** C4
Elmwood Ave WN4 . . . .**73** A2
Elmwood Cl BL5 . . . .**59** A6
Elmwood Ct M32 . . . .**108** C2
Elmwood Dr OL2 . . . .**48** C5
Elmwood Gr Bolton BL1 . . .**144** C8
Farnworth BL4 . . . .**60** C4
Manchester M9 . . . .**157** F7
Elmwood Lo M20 . . . .**110** A4
Elnup Ave WN6 . . . .**36** B6
Elnup Wood
Nature Reserve WN6 . . . .**36** C6
Elsa Rd M19 . . . .**99** C1
Elsdon Dr Atherton M46 . . . .**58** E4
Manchester M18 . . . .**99** D6
Elsdon Gdns 8 BL2 . . . .**25** B1
Elsdon Rd M13 . . . .**98** F2
Elsfield Cl BL1 . . . .**143** D2
Elsham Cl BL1 . . . .**24** E5
Elsham Dr M28 . . . .**60** B3
Elsham Gdns M18 . . . .**99** B4
Elsie St Farnworth BL4 . . . . .**60** C7
Manchester M9 . . . .**157** F8
Ramsbottom BL0 . . . .**11** A4
Elsinore Ave M44 . . . .**94** A1
Elsinore Cl M35 . . . .**84** B7
Elsinore Rd M16 . . . .**97** C4
Elsinore St BL2 . . . .**25** B3
Elsma Rd M40 . . . .**83** E4
Elsmore Rd M14 . . . .**110** A8
Elson Dr SK14 . . . .**113** D7
Elson St BL8 . . . .**27** B4
Elstead Gr WN4 . . . .**72** D4
Elstead Wlk M9 . . . .**64** A3
Elsted Rd OL3 . . . .**68** E5
Elston Ave WA12 . . . .**89** C3
Elstree Av M40 . . . .**83** B4

Elswick Ave Bolton BL3 . . .**144** B5
Bramhall SK7 . . . .**132** E7
Manchester M21 . . . .**109** D4
Elsworth Dr BL1 . . . .**143** F4
Elsworth St M3 . . . .**159** A4
Elterwater Cl BL8 . . . .**27** B4
Elterwater Rd BL4 . . . .**59** E7
Eltham Ave SK2 . . . .**124** C5
Eltham Cl WN4 . . . .**73** B3
Eltham Dr M41 . . . .**95** C5
Eltham St 6 M19 . . . .**99** A2
Elton Ave Farnworth BL4 . . . .**59** F8
Manchester M19 . . . .**111** A4
Elton Bank 4 SK13 . . . . . .**171** D1
Elton Brook Cl BL8 . . . .**27** C3
Elton Cl 6 Gamesley SK13 .**171** D1
Golborne WA3 . . . .**90** E7
Handforth SK9 . . . .**131** E1
Whitefield M45 . . . .**63** A8
Elton Com Prim Sch BL8 . .**27** C4
Elton Dr SK7 . . . .**133** D8
Elton High Sch The BL8 . . .**27** A4
Elton House WN5 . . . .**54** C7
Elton Lea 3 SK13 . . . .**171** D1
Elton Pl 7 SK13 . . . .**171** D1
Elton Rd M33 . . . .**107** E2
Elton St Bolton BL2 . . . .**148** A4
Manchester M7 . . . .**158** E3
Rochdale OL11 . . . .**30** C1
Stretford M32 . . . .**96** F5
Elton Vale Rd BL8 . . . .**27** B2
Elton's Yd M7 . . . .**158** D3
Elvate Cres M8 . . . .**155** F5
Elverdon Cl M15 . . . .**162** E4
Elverston St M22 . . . .**109** E1
Elverston Way OL9 . . . .**152** C8
Elvey St M10,M40 . . . .**157** F5
Elvington Cl WN5 . . . .**36** B1
Elvington Cres 1 M28 . . . . .**78** C8
Elvira Cl M35 . . . .**84** B7
Elway Rd WN4 . . . .**73** C4
Elwick Cl 8 M16 . . . .**97** F3
Elworth Way 6 SK9 . . . . . .**131** D4
Elworthy Gr WN1 . . . .**37** E2
Elwyn Ave M22 . . . .**121** D7
Ely Ave M32 . . . .**95** F3
Ely Cl M28 . . . .**78** B8
Ely Cres M35 . . . .**83** F5
Ely Dr Bury BL8 . . . .**140** D4
Tyldesley M29 . . . .**77** C7
Ely Gr BL1 . . . .**143** E1
Ely St OL9 . . . .**152** B5
Elysian St M11 . . . .**165** C6
Embankment Rd BL7 . . . .**9** C5
Embassy Wlk M18 . . . .**99** D4
Ember St M11 . . . .**83** D2
Emblem St BL3 . . . .**145** D5
Embleton Cl BL2 . . . .**25** E1
Embleton Wlk M18 . . . .**165** C6
Embsay Cl BL1 . . . .**24** D5
Emerald Ave WN7 . . . .**75** E4
Emerald Cotts BL8 . . . .**10** F3
Emerald Rd M22 . . . .**130** F7
Emerald St 5 Bolton BL1 . . .**143** F3
Denton M34 . . . .**100** E3
Wigan WN6 . . . .**37** A3
Emerson Ave M30 . . . .**80** A3
Emerson Dr M24 . . . .**46** F1
Emerson St Salford M5 . . . .**154** D2
Swinton M27 . . . .**61** F1
Emery Ave M21 . . . .**109** C6
Emery Cl Altrincham WA14 .**119** D7
Manchester SK4 . . . .**168** A4
Emily Beavan Cl M11 . . . . . .**83** B1
Emily Pl M43 . . . .**83** F1
Emley St M19 . . . .**99** B1
Emlyn Gr SK8 . . . .**123** A6
Emlyn St Farnworth BL4 . . . .**42** C1
2 Hindley WN2 . . . .**56** D5
Swinton M27 . . . .**79** D8
Walkden M28 . . . .**60** D3
Emma St Oldham OL8 . . . . .**153** E5
Rochdale OL12 . . . .**139** E8
Emmanuel Cl BL3 . . . .**145** D5
Emmanuel Ct OL6 . . . .**166** B4
Emmanuel Holcombe
CE Prim Sch BL8 . . . .**138** A6
Emmanuel Pl BL3 . . . .**145** D5
Emmeline Grange M6 . . . .**154** E2
Emmett St E M40 . . . .**157** E5
Emmett St OL10 . . . .**29** C2
Emmott St OL1 . . . .**153** F6
Emmous Wlk M6 . . . .**154** F3
Empire Rd Bolton BL2 . . . . . .**42** E7
Dukinfield SK16 . . . .**101** C6
Empire St M3,M8 . . . .**158** F4
Empress Ave 2 SK6 . . . . . .**125** F5
Empress Bsns Ctr M16 . . .**161** C6
Empress Ct M15 . . . .**161** C6
Empress Dr Leigh WN7 . . . . .**76** E6
Reddish SK4 . . . .**169** D4
Empress Ind Est M16 . . . . .**151** F7
Empress St Bolton BL1 . . . .**142** B1
Manchester M16 . . . .**161** C6
Manchester M8 . . . .**155** F8
Emsworth Cl BL2 . . . .**25** B1
Emsworth Dr M33 . . . .**108** C1
Ena Cres WN7 . . . .**75** C7
Ena St Bolton BL3 . . . .**42** A3
Oldham OL1 . . . .**49** C1
Enbridge St M5 . . . .**161** A8
Encombe Pl M3 . . . .**158** F2
Endcott Cl M18 . . . .**165** B6
Enderby Rd M40 . . . .**65** C1
Ending Rake OL12 . . . .**14** C4
Endon Dr M21 . . . .**109** E8
Endon St BL1 . . . .**142** B1

Endsleigh Gdns ◼1◾ WN7 . . .75 F5
Endsleigh Rd M20 . . . . . . .110 C6
Endsley Ave M28 . . . . .60 C1
Endsor Cl M16 . . . . .97 F3
Energy St M40 . . . . .160 E3
Enfield Ave
 Manchester M19 . . . . . . .111 A6
 Oldham OL8 . . . . .66 B3
Enfield Cl Bolton BL1 . . . . .143 E1
 Bury BL9 . . . . .44 F5
 Eccles M30 . . . . .95 D8
 Rochdale OL11 . . . . .29 E8
Enfield Dr ◼7◾ M11 . . . . . . .83 C2
Enfield Gr WN7 . . . . .76 B6
Enfield Ho M30 . . . . .95 D8
Enfield Rd Eccles M30 . . . . .79 D4
 Swinton M27 . . . . .79 E6
Enfield St Hyde SK14 . . . . .113 E7
 Walkden M28 . . . . .60 D5
 Wigan WN5 . . . . .54 C5
Enford Ave M22 . . . . .121 A2
Engell Cl M8 . . . . .155 F6
Engels Ho Eccles M30 . . . . .95 D8
 Manchester M14 . . . . . . .110 D8
Engine Fold Rd M28 . . . . . .60 A3
Engine La M29 . . . . .59 B4
Engine St OL9 . . . . .66 B4
Engineer St WN2 . . . . .56 A7
Engledene BL1 . . . . .24 D6
Englefield Gr ◼3◾ M18 . . . . .99 D4
English Martyrs Sch M41 .95 C2
English St WN7 . . . . .76 A4
Enid Cl M7 . . . . .155 D5
Enid Pl WN2 . . . . .73 F8
Ennerdale Ave
 Ashton-in-M WN4 . . . . . . .73 B5
 Billinge WA11 . . . . .71 B1
 ◼4◾ Bolton BL2 . . . . .25 F1
 Manchester M21 . . . . . . .109 D4
 Royton OL2 . . . . .48 C7
 Swinton M27 . . . . .79 F6
Ennerdale Cl BL3 . . . . .42 F3
Ennerdale Dr Gatley SK8 . .122 B3
 Sale M33 . . . . .107 E5
 Sale WA15 . . . . .120 A8
 Whitefield BL9 . . . . .45 A2
Ennerdale Gdns BL2 . . . . . .25 E1
Ennerdale Gr
 Ashton-u-L OL7 . . . . .84 F5
 Farnworth BL4 . . . . .59 E8
Ennerdale Rd Hindley WN2 .56 E5
 Leigh WN7 . . . . .76 C4
 Middleton M24 . . . . .46 F2
 Partington M31 . . . . .105 E3
 Rochdale OL11 . . . . .30 B4
 Romiley SK6 . . . . .113 B4
 Stockport SK1 . . . . .124 B7
 Stretford M32 . . . . .96 C3
 Tyldesley M29 . . . . .77 B7
Ennerdale Terr SK15 . . . . . .86 A3
Ennis Cl M23 . . . . .120 E5
Ennismore Ave M5,M30 . . . .80 A2
Enstone Dr M40 . . . . .65 D1
Enstone Way M27 . . . . .59 C1
Enterprise Trad Est M31 .96 A8
Enterprise Way WA3 . . . . . .91 A7
Enticott Rd M44 . . . . .105 C5
Entwisle Ave M41 . . . . .95 B4
Entwisle Rd OL16 . . . . .31 A8
Entwisle Row BL4 . . . . .60 D8
Entwisle St
 ◼1◾ Farnworth BL4 . . . . . .42 E1
 Milnrow OL16 . . . . .31 E6
 Swinton M27 . . . . .61 D1
Entwistle Gr WN7 . . . . .76 C3
Entwistle Hall La BL7 . . . . . .9 B8
Entwistle St BL2 . . . . .148 B8
Entwistle Sta BL7 . . . . .9 B8
Enver Rd M8 . . . . .156 B8
Enville Rd
 Altrincham WA14 . . . . . . .119 C3
 Manchester M40 . . . . .65 B1
 Pendlebury M6 . . . . .80 E6
Enville St Ashton-u-L OL6 . .166 C3
 Denton M34 . . . . .100 F7
 Manchester M9 . . . . .64 D3
Envoy Cl WN5 . . . . .36 E1
Enys Wlk M6 . . . . .81 A5
Ephraim's Fold WN2 . . . . . .38 D6
Epping Cl Ashton-u-L OL6 . .85 C7
 Chadderton OL9 . . . . .65 E8
Epping Dr M33 . . . . .107 C5
Epping Rd M34 . . . . .100 B2
Epping St Manchester M15 .162 F6
 Manchester M15 . . . . . . .163 A6
Epping Wlk M15 . . . . .163 A5
Eppleworth Rise M27 . . . . . .62 A3
Epsley Cl M15 . . . . .163 A6
Epsom Ave
 Handforth SK8,SK9 . . . . . .131 E4
 Manchester M19 . . . . . . .110 F6
 Sale M33 . . . . .107 C2
Epsom Cl Hazel Grove SK7 .124 F2
 Rochdale OL11 . . . . .29 F8
Epsom Croft PR6 . . . . .21 B7
Epsom Dr WN2 . . . . .73 F7
Epsom Mews M7 . . . . .155 D6
Epsom Wlk OL9 . . . . .152 C7
Epworth Ct SK4 . . . . .168 B3
Epworth Gr ◼5◾ BL3 . . . . .146 C3
Epworth St M1 . . . . .163 A6
Equitable St Milnrow OL16 . .31 F5
 Oldham OL4 . . . . .67 D8
 ◼3◾ Rochdale OL11 . . . . .31 A6
Era St Bolton BL2 . . . . .42 E7
 Sale M33 . . . . .108 E4
Ercall Ave M12 . . . . .164 E6

Eric Brook Cl ◼8◾ M14 . . . .98 A3
Eric Bullows Cl M22 . . . . . .121 C1
Eric St Littleborough OL15 . .16 A6
 Oldham OL4 . . . . .67 C6
Erica Ave OL4 . . . . .49 F4
Erica Cl ◼2◾ SK5 . . . . .100 A1
Erica Dr M19 . . . . .110 E4
Erica Wlk WN7 . . . . .75 B5
Erin St M11 . . . . .99 E7
Erindale Wlk M40 . . . . .156 C6
Erith Cl SK5 . . . . .112 B6
Erith Rd OL4 . . . . .67 C6
Erlesmere Ave M34 . . . . . . .101 A4
Erlesmere Cl OL4 . . . . .49 F4
Erlington Ave M16 . . . . .97 E3
Ermen Rd M30 . . . . .95 C8
Ermington Ct OL10 . . . . .29 C1
Ermington Dr M8 . . . . .155 F6
Erneley Cl M12 . . . . .99 B3
Ernest St Bacup OL13 . . . . . .4 C8
 Bolton BL1 . . . . .145 D7
 Cheadle SK8 . . . . .122 C6
 Prestwich M25 . . . . .62 F4
 Stockport SK2 . . . . .124 A6
Ernest Terr OL12 . . . . .15 B1
Ernlouen Ave M8 . . . . .144 A8
Ernocroft Gr ◼5◾ M18 . . . . .99 E6
Ernocroft La SK6 . . . . .114 E3
Ernocroft Rd SK6 . . . . .114 B1
Erradale Cres WN3 . . . . . . .54 D2
Erringdon Cl SK2 . . . . .124 E6
Errington Cl BL3 . . . . .40 F5
Errington Dr M7 . . . . .158 D4
Errol Ave Manchester M9 . . .64 D3
 Wythenshawe M22 . . . . . .121 C4
Errwood Cres M19 . . . . . . .111 A8
Errwood Rd M19 . . . . .111 A7
Erskine Cl BL3 . . . . .40 E5
Erskine Pl WN2 . . . . .56 B1
Erskine Rd Manchester M9 . .64 C1
 Partington M31 . . . . .105 E4
Erskine St
 Manchester M15 . . . . . . .162 D6
 Romiley M6 . . . . .114 B3
Erwin St M40 . . . . .83 B6
Eryngo St SK1 . . . . .112 A1
Esher Dr M23,M33 . . . . . . .108 C1
Esk Ave BL0 . . . . .1 D5
Esk Cl M41 . . . . .95 A4
Eskdale SK8 . . . . .122 C4
Eskdale Ave Blackrod BL6 . . .38 E7
 Bolton BL2 . . . . .25 F2
 Bramhall SK7 . . . . .132 C5
 Manchester M20 . . . . . . .110 A4
 Oldham OL3 . . . . .69 B5
 Oldham OL8 . . . . .66 D4
 Rochdale OL11 . . . . .30 B4
 Romiley SK6 . . . . .113 B4
 Royton OL2 . . . . .48 D7
 Wigan WN1 . . . . .37 B3
Eskdale Cl BL9 . . . . .45 A3
Eskdale Dr
 Altrincham WA15 . . . . . . .120 C7
 Middleton M24 . . . . .46 F3
Eskdale Gr BL4 . . . . .59 F8
Eskdale Ho ◼3◾ M13 . . . . . .98 E4
Eskdale Mews OL3 . . . . .69 B5
Eskdale Rd
 Ashton-in-M WN4 . . . . . . .73 B4
 Hindley WN2 . . . . .56 E5
Eskdale Terr SK15 . . . . .86 A4
Eskrick St BL1 . . . . .143 D2
Eskrigge Cl M7 . . . . .155 F8
Esmond Rd M8 . . . . .156 A7
Esmont Dr M24 . . . . .46 E3
Esplanade The OL16 . . . . . .139 E7
Essex Ave Droylsden M43 . . .84 A3
 Heywood BL9 . . . . .28 E1
 Manchester M20 . . . . . . .110 A4
 Stockport SK3 . . . . .123 B8
Essex Cl Failsworth M35 . . . .83 F5
 Shaw OL2 . . . . .48 F7
Essex Dr BL9 . . . . .45 A8
Essex Gdns M44 . . . . .105 C4
Essex Pl Swinton M27 . . . . .61 F2
 Tyldesley M29 . . . . .58 F3
Essex Rd Brinnington SK5 . .112 C5
 Reddish M18 . . . . .99 F4
 Standish WN1 . . . . .37 B8
Essex St Horwich BL6 . . . . . .22 D1
 Manchester M2 . . . . .158 F1
 Rochdale OL11 . . . . .139 F6
 Wigan WN1 . . . . .37 C1
Essex Way M15,M16 . . . . . .162 D5
Essingdon St BL3 . . . . .147 D4
Essington Wlk M34 . . . . . . .100 E1
Est Bank Rd BL0 . . . . .11 A3
Estate Cl OL8 . . . . .66 D4
Estate St S OL8 . . . . .66 F4
Estcourt Sch OL8 . . . . .66 D4
Esther Fold BL5 . . . . .57 E8
Esther St OL4 . . . . .67 D7
Esthwaite Dr M29 . . . . .77 A7
Eston St M13 . . . . .98 D4
Estonfield Dr M41 . . . . .95 F2
Eswick St M11 . . . . .83 C1
Etchell St M40 . . . . .156 C6
Etchells Prim Sch SK8 . . . .122 C1
Etchells St SK1 . . . . .169 F1
Ethel Ave Manchester M9 . . .64 D5
 Pendlebury M27 . . . . .80 D4
Ethel Ct OL16 . . . . .31 B6
Ethel St Bolton BL3 . . . . . . .145 D6
 Oldham OL8 . . . . .66 F3
 Rochdale OL16 . . . . .31 B6
 Whitworth OL12 . . . . .4 D2

Ethel Terr M19 . . . . .99 A1
Etherley Cl ◼4◾ M44 . . . . . .94 A2
Etherow Ave
 Failsworth M40 . . . . .65 F2
 Romiley SK6 . . . . .113 C2
Etherow Brow SK14 . . . . . .115 B8
Etherow Ctry Pk SK6 . . . . .114 C4
Etherow Ctry Pk
 Visitors Ctr SK6 . . . . . . .114 B3
Etherow Way SK13 . . . . . . .103 E5
Etherstone St Leigh WN7 . . .75 E4
Eton Ave OL8 . . . . .66 E3
Eton Cl Manchester M16 . . . .162 D7
 Rochdale OL11 . . . . .30 B6
 Stockport M16 . . . . .162 D5
Eton Hill Ind Est M26 . . . . .44 C5
Eton Hill Rd M26 . . . . .44 C5
Eton St WN7 . . . . .75 F3
Eton Terr WN3 . . . . .151 E5
Eton Way N M26 . . . . .44 C5
Eton Way S M26 . . . . .44 D5
Etruria Cl M13 . . . . .164 E5
Ettington Cl BL8 . . . . .27 A3
Ettrick Cl M11 . . . . .99 D7
Euclid Cl M11 . . . . .160 E1
Euro Ctr The M8 . . . . .158 E4
Europa Bsns Pk SK3 . . . . . .123 B6
Europa Gate M17 . . . . .96 D5
Europa Trad Est M26 . . . . . .61 B7
Europa Way Cheadle SK3 . .123 B6
 Kearsley M26 . . . . .61 B7
 Stretford M17 . . . . .96 B5
Euroterminal M17,M32 . . . .96 D4
Eustace St Bolton BL3 . . . . .42 A3
 Oldham OL9 . . . . .152 C8
Eustace Street
 Com Prim Sch OL9 . . . . .152 C8
Euston Ave M9 . . . . .65 A3
Euxton Cl BL8 . . . . .27 A1
Eva Rd SK3 . . . . .123 A7
Eva St Leigh WN7 . . . . .75 C7
 Manchester M14 . . . . .98 C3
 Rochdale OL12 . . . . .15 A2
Evans Rd M30 . . . . .79 A1
Evans St Ashton-u-L OL6 . . .85 D3
 Horwich BL6 . . . . .22 D4
 Leigh WN7 . . . . .75 F5
 Manchester M3 . . . . .158 E3
 Middleton M24 . . . . .65 B8
 Oldham OL1 . . . . .153 F8
Evanston Cl BL6 . . . . .22 B3
Evanton Wlk ◼19◾ M9 . . . .157 E7
Eve St OL8 . . . . .66 F2
Evelyn St Manchester M14 . .110 D8
 Oldham OL4 . . . . .49 B1
Evening St M35 . . . . .83 F8
Evenley Cl ◼1◾ M18 . . . . . . .99 E6
Everard Cl M28 . . . . .78 C8
Everard St ◼5◾ M5 . . . . . .161 C7
Everbrom Rd BL3 . . . . .146 A3
Everdingen Wlk OL1 . . . . . . .49 D3
Everest Ave OL7 . . . . .85 B5
Everest Cl SK14 . . . . .102 A4
Everest Pl ◼4◾ WN7 . . . . . .37 C2
Everest Rd Atherton M46 . . .58 C5
 Hyde SK14 . . . . .102 A4
Everest St OL11 . . . . .31 A2
Everett Ct ◼3◾ M20 . . . . . .110 B6
Everett Rd M20 . . . . .110 B6
Everglade OL8 . . . . .67 A1
Evergreen Wlk M33 . . . . . . .107 C6
Everleigh Cl BL2 . . . . .25 C4
Everleigh Dr M7 . . . . .155 F6
Eversden Ct M7 . . . . .158 E4
Eversley Ct M33 . . . . .108 B2
Eversley Rd M20 . . . . .110 A4
Everton Rd Oldham OL8 . . . .66 D3
 Reddish SK5 . . . . .99 F2
Everton St
 Downall Green WN4 . . . . . .72 D5
 Swinton M27 . . . . .79 E8
Every St Bury BL9 . . . . .140 F4
 Manchester M4 . . . . .160 D1
 Ramsbottom BL0 . . . . .11 D6
Evesham Ave
 Altrincham M23 . . . . .120 D7
 ◼4◾ Hadfield SK13 . . . . . .104 A5
 Manchester SK4 . . . . . . .168 B3
Evesham Cl ◼10◾ Bolton BL3 .145 E1
 Leigh WN7 . . . . .75 E1
 Middleton M24 . . . . .65 B5
Evesham Dr
 Farnworth BL3,BL4 . . . . . .42 B2
 Wigan WN5 . . . . .71 D5
Evesham Gdns M24 . . . . . . .65 A5
Evesham Gr Ashton-u-L OL6 .85 C7
 Sale M33 . . . . .108 E4
Evesham Rd Cheadle SK8 . .123 A4
 Manchester M9 . . . . .65 A2
 Middleton M24 . . . . .65 B5
Evesham Wlk
 ◼9◾ Bolton BL3 . . . . .145 D6
 Middleton M24 . . . . .65 B5
 Oldham OL8 . . . . .153 D6
Eveside Cl SK8 . . . . .123 B4
Evington Ave M11 . . . . .100 A1
Ewan St M18 . . . . .99 D6
Eward St M8 . . . . .64 A1
Ewart Ave M5 . . . . .161 C1
Ewart St BL1 . . . . .143 E2
Ewhurst Ave M27 . . . . .79 D6
Ewing Cl M8 . . . . .64 A1
Ewing Sch M20 . . . . .110 A5

Ewood ◼12◾ Eccles M30 . . . .79 F2
 Oldham M30 . . . . .85 A8
Ewood Dr BL8 . . . . .44 A8
Ewood La BB4 . . . . .1 C7
Exbourne Rd M22 . . . . .121 C1
Exbridge Wlk M40 . . . . .83 D4
Exbury ◼24◾ OL12 . . . . . . .139 E8
Exbury St M14 . . . . .110 D7
Excalibur Way M44 . . . . . . .105 F7
Excelsior Terr OL15 . . . . . . .15 C3
Exchange Quay M5 . . . . . . .161 A6
Exchange Quay Sta M5 . . . .161 A6
Exchange St ◼9◾ Bolton BL1 .145 F7
 Edenfield BL0 . . . . .1 D3
 Manchester M2 . . . . .158 F1
 ◼5◾ Oldham OL4 . . . . . . .67 B7
 Stockport SK3 . . . . .169 E1
Exeter Ave Bolton BL2 . . . . .25 B2
 Denton M34 . . . . .100 F1
 Farnworth BL4 . . . . .59 F8
 Radcliffe M26 . . . . .43 E5
 Salford M30 . . . . .80 A4
Exeter Cl Cheadle SK8 . . . .131 F8
 Dukinfield SK16 . . . . .101 D6
Exeter Ct Manchester M14 . .110 C7
 ◼3◾ Manchester M41 . . . .46 F1
Exeter Dr Ashton-u-L OL6 . . .85 D7
 Aspull WN2 . . . . .38 D5
 Irlam M44 . . . . .94 B2
Exeter Gr OL11 . . . . .139 F5
Exeter Rd Brinnington SK5 . .112 C5
 Hindley WN2 . . . . .56 C5
 Urmston M41 . . . . .95 D4
Exeter St Rochdale OL11 . . .139 F5
 Salford M6 . . . . .154 E2
Exeter Wlk SK7 . . . . .132 F7
Exford Ave WN3 . . . . .55 B8
Exford Cl Manchester M40 . .160 D3
 Reddish SK5 . . . . .111 F6
Exford Dr BL2 . . . . .43 A6
Exhall Cl M38 . . . . .60 A6
Exit Rd W M90 . . . . .130 B7
Exmoor Cl OL6 . . . . .85 C7
Exmouth Ave SK5 . . . . .112 C5
Exmouth Pl OL11 . . . . .31 A4
Exmouth Rd M33 . . . . .107 D5
Exmouth Sq OL11 . . . . .31 A3
Exmouth St OL11 . . . . .31 A3
Exmouth Wlk ◼7◾ M16 . . . .97 F3
Eyam Cl ◼12◾ SK13 . . . . . .171 D2
Eyam Fold ◼16◾ SK13 . . . .171 E2
Eyam Gdns ◼25◾ SK13 . . .171 D2
Eyam Gn ◼13◾ SK13 . . . . .171 D2
Eyam Gr
 ◼11◾ Gamesley SK13 . . . .171 D2
 Stockport SK2 . . . . .124 D5
Eyam La SK13 . . . . .171 D2
Eyam Lea SK13 . . . . .171 E2
Eyam Mews SK13 . . . . .171 D2
Eyam Rd SK7 . . . . .124 E1
Eyebrook Rd WA14 . . . . . . .119 A2
Eyet St WN7 . . . . .75 E5
Eynford Ave SK5 . . . . .112 B6
Eyre St M15 . . . . .163 A5

F

Faber St M4 . . . . .159 A3
Factory Brow Blackrod BL6 . .21 D3
 Middleton M24 . . . . .64 C7
Factory Hill BL6 . . . . .22 D4
Factory La Adlington PR6 . . .21 B8
 Disley SK12 . . . . .135 E7
 Manchester M3 . . . . .158 D1
 Manchester M9 . . . . .64 D1
Factory St Middleton M24 . . .64 F8
 Radcliffe M26 . . . . .44 B3
 Ramsbottom BL0 . . . . .138 C2
 Tyldesley M29 . . . . .58 F1
Factory St E M46 . . . . .58 C3
Factory St W M46 . . . . .58 C3
Faggy La WN3 . . . . .150 C7
Failsworth Ind Est M40 .83 C6
Failsworth Rd M35 . . . . .84 C7
Failsworth Sch M35 . . . . . . .84 A7
Failsworth Sch (Lower)
 M35 . . . . .83 F7
Failsworth Sh Ctr ◼1◾ M35 .83 F7
Failsworth Sta M35 . . . . . . .83 E8
Fair Acres BL2 . . . . .25 E3
Fair Hill BB4 . . . . .1 A7
Fair Oak Rd M19 . . . . .110 F5
Fair St Bolton BL3 . . . . .146 C2
 Manchester M1 . . . . .159 C1
 Swinton M27 . . . . .62 A1
Fair View Bacup OL13 . . . . . .4 C8
 Billinge WN5 . . . . .71 D5
 Littleborough OL15 . . . . . .16 C7
Fair View WN5 . . . . .71 D5
Fair Way OL11 . . . . .30 B1
Faircres WN6 . . . . .19 B1
Faircres Rd SK6 . . . . .134 E8
Fairbairn St BL6 . . . . .22 B3
Fairbank M43 . . . . .99 F8
Fairbank Ave M14 . . . . .98 A4
Fairbank Dr M24 . . . . .46 D2
Fairbottom St OL1 . . . . .153 F7
Fairbottom Wlk ◼4◾ M43 . .100 A8
Fairbourne Ave
 Wigan WN3 . . . . .55 A4
 Wilmslow SK9 . . . . .136 F4
 Wilmslow SK9 . . . . .137 B3
Fairbourne Dr Sale WA15 . .108 B1
 Wilmslow SK9 . . . . .136 F4
Fairbourne Rd
 Denton M34 . . . . .100 E2

End–Fai 203

Fairbourne Rd continued
 Reddish M19 . . . . .99 C1
Fairbrook Dr M6 . . . . .154 E2
Fairbrother St M5 . . . . .161 C3
Fairclough St Bolton BL3 . . . .42 A4
 Droylsden M11 . . . . .83 A2
 Hindley WN2 . . . . .56 D6
 Newton-le-W WA12 . . . . . .89 B3
 Wigan WN1 . . . . .151 D7
Fairfax Ave
 Altrincham WA15 . . . . . . .120 A6
 Manchester M20 . . . . . . .110 B4
 Rochdale SK6 . . . . .125 D7
Fairfax Dr
 Littleborough OL15 . . . . . .15 F3
 Wilmslow SK9 . . . . .136 F4
Fairfax Rd M25 . . . . .63 A5
Fairfield OL6 . . . . .85 C8
Fairfield Ave Cheadle SK8 . .122 F2
 Droylsden M43 . . . . .100 A4
 Platt Bridge WN2 . . . . .56 A3
 Romiley SK6 . . . . .113 A4
 Wigan WN5 . . . . .54 D5
Fairfield Ct M14 . . . . .98 D4
Fairfield Cty Prim Sch
 BL9 . . . . .28 D3
Fairfield Dr BL9 . . . . .28 D3
Fairfield General Hospl
 BL9 . . . . .28 E4
Fairfield High Sch
 for Girls M43 . . . . .100 A8
Fairfield Ho M43 . . . . .84 A1
Fairfield Rd
 Altrincham WA15 . . . . . . .120 C5
 Droylsden M11,M43 . . . . . .99 F8
 Farnworth BL4 . . . . .60 C7
 Irlam M44 . . . . .105 C5
 Middleton M24 . . . . .46 E1
Fairfield Road Prim Sch
 M43 . . . . .99 F8
Fairfield Sq M43 . . . . .100 A8
Fairfield St
 Manchester M1,M12 . . . . .163 C8
 Salford M6 . . . . .80 E5
 Wigan WN5 . . . . .54 D5
Fairfield Sta M34 . . . . .100 A7
Fairfield View M34 . . . . .100 A8
Fairfields Bolton BL7 . . . . . .24 F8
 Oldham OL8 . . . . .66 E2
Fairford Cl SK5 . . . . .111 F5
Fairford Dr BL3 . . . . .145 E6
Fairford Way Reddish SK5 . .111 F5
 Wilmslow SK9 . . . . .137 D2
Fairham Wlk M12 . . . . .160 D1
Fairhaven Ave
 Manchester M21 . . . . . . .109 B8
 Westhoughton BL5 . . . . . . .58 B8
 Whitefield M45 . . . . .62 D7
Fairhaven Cl SK7 . . . . .132 F8
Fairhaven Rd BL1 . . . . .143 F3
Fairhaven St M12 . . . . .164 F6
Fairhill Terr BB4 . . . . .1 A7
Fairhills Ind Est M44 . . . . .105 A4
Fairhills Rd M44 . . . . .106 A8
Fairholme Ave
 Ashton-in-M WN4 . . . . . . .73 B4
 Urmston M41 . . . . .95 C1
Fairholme Rd
 Manchester M20 . . . . . . .110 C6
 Manchester SK4 . . . . . . .168 A3
Fairhope Ave M6 . . . . .80 C3
Fairhurst Ave WN6 . . . . .19 D3
Fairhurst Dr M28 . . . . .59 F2
Fairhurst St Leigh WN7 . . . .75 E5
 Wigan WN3 . . . . .150 B3
Fairisle Cl M11 . . . . .160 F1
Fairlands Pl OL11 . . . . .31 B2
Fairlands Rd Bury BL9 . . . . . .27 F6
 Sale M33 . . . . .107 F2
Fairlands St OL11 . . . . .31 B2
Fairlands View OL11 . . . . . . .31 B2
Fairlawn SK4 . . . . .169 D3
Fairlawn Cl M14 . . . . .98 A4
Fairlea M34 . . . . .101 A2
Fairlea Ave M20 . . . . .110 C2
Fairlee Ave M34 . . . . .84 C1
Fairleigh Ave M6 . . . . .80 C3
Fairless Rd M30 . . . . .79 D1
Fairlie Ave BL3 . . . . .40 F5
Fairlie Dr WA15 . . . . .120 B8
Fairlyn Cl BL5 . . . . .59 A7
Fairlyn Dr BL5 . . . . .59 A7
Fairman Cl M16 . . . . .97 E3
Fairmead Rd M23 . . . . .109 C1
Fairmile Dr M20 . . . . .122 C8
Fairmount Ave BL2 . . . . .42 E8
Fairmount Rd M27 . . . . .79 C6
Fairoak Ct BL3 . . . . .145 D5
Fairstead Wlk ◼4◾ M11 . . . .99 F7
Fairthorne Grange OL7 . . .84 F1
Fairview Ave
 Manchester M19 . . . . .98 F2
 Reddish M34 . . . . .100 A1
Fairview Cl
 Ashton-in-M WN4 . . . . . . .73 B4
 Chadderton OL9 . . . . .65 F8
 Marple SK6 . . . . .125 F7
 Rochdale OL12 . . . . .13 C2
Fairview Dr SK6 . . . . .125 F7
Fairview Rd
 Altrincham WA15 . . . . . . .120 C5
 Reddish M34 . . . . .100 A1
Fairway Bramhall SK7 . . . . .132 C6
 Droylsden M43 . . . . .100 A8
 Gatley SK8 . . . . .122 B4

Fairway continued
  Manchester M25 . . . .**63** D3
  Milnrow OL16 . . . .**32** A6
  Pendlebury M27 . . . .**80** C7
  Whitworth OL12 . . . .**14** C7
Fairway Ave Bolton BL2 . . .**26** A4
  Sale M23 . . . .**120** D7
Fairway Cres OL2 . . . .**48** D6
Fairway Ct M34 . . . .**100** B4
Fairway Dr M33 . . . .**107** E2
Fairway Prim Sch SK2 . . .**124** E7
Fairway Rd Oldham OL4 . . .**67** E4
  Whitefield BL9 . . . .**45** A3
Fairway The Failsworth M40 **83** C8
  Stockport SK2 . . . .**124** D7
Fairways BL2 . . . .**22** C3
Fairways Cl SK13 . . . .**104** F1
Fairways The
  Garswood WN4 . . . .**72** D2
  Westhoughton BL5 . . . .**57** E8
  Whitefield M45 . . . .**62** F6
Fairwood Rd M23 . . . .**120** D7
Fairy La Manchester M7,M8 **155** E5
  Wythenshawe M23 . . . .**109** A3
Fairy St BL8 . . . .**27** C2
Fairywell Cl SK9 . . . .**131** D1
Fairywell Dr M33 . . . .**108** A1
Fairywell Rd WA15 . . . . . .**120** C7
Faith St Bolton BL1 . . . .**142** A1
  Leigh WN7 . . . .**75** C5
Falcon Ave M41 . . . .**95** E2
Falcon Bsns Ctr OL9 . . . . .**152** C8
Falcon Cl Bury BL9 . . . .**141** B4
  Leigh WN7 . . . .**76** B5
  Rochdale OL12 . . . .**13** C2
Falcon Cres M27 . . . .**62** C2
Falcon Ct Manchester M15 **162** E5
  Manchester M7 . . . .**155** D8
Falcon Dr Irlam M44 . . . . . .**94** B4
  Middleton M24 . . . .**46** E3
  Oldham OL9 . . . .**152** C8
  Walkden M38 . . . .**60** A5
Falcon St Bolton BL1 . . . . .**145** F8
  Oldham OL8 . . . .**153** F5
Falconers Gn WN3 . . . .**150** B5
Falconwood Chase M28 . .**78** C6
Falconwood Cl WN6 . . . . .**37** A1
Falfield Dr M8 . . . .**156** B5
Falinge Fold OL12 . . . .**14** D1
Falinge Mews OL12 . . . . .**139** E8
Falinge Park High Sch
  OL12 . . . .**14** D1
Falinge Rd OL12 . . . .**14** E1
  Ince-in-M WN2 . . . .**56** A8
Falkirk Dr Bolton BL2 . . . .**42** F6
Falkirk Gr WN5 . . . .**54** C8
Falkirk St OL4 . . . .**67** C7
Falkirk Wlk M23 . . . .**121** A2
Falkland Ave
  Manchester M40 . . . .**160** D4
  Rochdale OL11 . . . .**30** C8
Falkland Cl OL4 . . . .**49** E4
Falkland Dr WN4 . . . .**72** C4
Falkland Ho M14 . . . .**98** C1
Falkland Rd BL2 . . . .**43** A7
Fall Bank SK4 . . . .**111** D6
Fall Birch Hospl BL6 . . . . .**23** A1
Fall Birch Rd BL6 . . . .**39** F8
Fallons Rd M28 . . . .**61** C1
Fallow Cl BL5 . . . .**39** E2
Fallow Fields Dr SK5 . . . .**100** A1
Fallowfield Ave M5 . . . . . .**161** B7
Fallowfield Dr OL12 . . . . . .**14** D2
Fallowfield Sh Ctr M14 . .**98** E1
Fallowfield Way M46 . . . . .**58** E1
Fallows The OL9 . . . .**152** A5
Falls Gr SK8 . . . .**122** A3
Falmer Cl BL8 . . . .**27** C6
Falmer Dr M22 . . . .**121** D1
Falmer St M18 . . . .**99** F6
Falmouth Ave Sale M33 . . .**107** D5
  Urmston M41 . . . .**94** E3
Falmouth Cres SK5 . . . . . .**112** C5
Falmouth Rd M44 . . . .**94** B2
Falmouth St
  Manchester M40 . . . .**160** F4
  Oldham OL8 . . . .**66** F4
  Rochdale OL11 . . . .**31** A5
Falsgrave Cl M40 . . . .**83** A5
Falshaw Dr BL9 . . . .**11** E1
Falside Wlk M40 . . . .**83** C5
Falston Ave M40 . . . .**65** D2
Falstone Cl WN3 . . . .**54** E2
Falterley Rd M23 . . . .**120** F8
Fancroft Rd M22 . . . .**121** C5
Fane Wlk M9 . . . .**64** B3
Far Cromwell Rd SK6 . . . .**112** D7
Far Hey Cl M26 . . . .**43** E3
Far La M18 . . . .**99** D4
Far Ridings SK6 . . . .**113** C5
Far Woodseats La SK14 . .**114** F5
Faraday Ave
  Manchester M8 . . . .**156** A6
  Swinton M27 . . . .**62** D2
Faraday Dr BL1 . . . .**143** E1
Faraday Rd WN6 . . . .**150** A8
Faraday St M1 . . . .**159** B1
Farcroft Ave M26 . . . .**44** C6
Farcroft Cl M23 . . . .**120** F8
Fardale OL2 . . . .**149** B6
Farden Dr M23 . . . .**120** D8
Fardon Cl WN3 . . . .**54** F3
Farefield Ave WA3 . . . .**73** F2

Fareham Ct M16 . . . .**162** D5
Farewell Cl OL11 . . . .**30** C2
Farholme OL1 . . . .**48** C2
Faringdon OL11 . . . .**139** E6
Faringdon Wlk BL3 . . . . . .**145** E5
Farland Pl BL3 . . . .**40** F5
Farlands Dr M20 . . . .**122** B7
Farlands Rise OL16 . . . .**31** C3
Farleigh Cl BL5 . . . .**40** A2
Farley Ave M18 . . . .**100** A4
Farley Ct SK8 . . . .**122** F3
Farley La WN8 . . . .**35** A3
Farley Rd M33 . . . .**108** C2
Farley Way SK5 . . . .**99** E1
Farm Ave Adlington PR6 . . . .**21** A8
  Stretford M32 . . . .**96** A4
Farm Cl Bury BL8 . . . .**26** F6
  Reddish SK4 . . . .**111** C6
Farm La Aspull WN2 . . . .**38** A2
  High Lane SK12 . . . .**135** A6
  Hyde SK14 . . . .**113** D8
  Middleton M25 . . . .**63** E8
  Worsley M28 . . . .**78** F5
Farm Meadow Rd WN5 . . .**53** E5
Farm Rd OL8 . . . .**84** C8
Farm Side Pl M19 . . . .**99** A1
Farm St Failsworth M35 . . .**83** B6
  Heywood OL10 . . . .**46** E8
  Oldham OL1,OL9 . . . .**48** B1
Farm Way WA12 . . . .**89** E1
Farm Wlk
  Altrincham WA14 . . . .**118** C1
  Littleborough OL15 . . . .**15** F5
  Rochdale OL16 . . . .**15** C1
Farm Yd M19 . . . .**99** A1
Farman St BL3 . . . .**147** D3
Farmer St SK4 . . . .**169** E3
Farmers Cl M33 . . . .**109** A3
Farmfield M33 . . . .**107** E6
Farmfold SK9 . . . .**130** F3
Farmlands Wlk OL1 . . . . . .**49** C4
Farmside Ave M44 . . . .**94** A3
Farmstead Ct M35 . . . .**84** C6
Farmway M24 . . . .**65** A7
Farn Ave SK5 . . . .**99** F2
Farnborough Ave OL4 . . . .**67** D6
Farnborough Rd
  Bolton BL1 . . . .**24** E6
  Manchester M40 . . . .**160** D3
Farncombe Cl M23 . . . . . .**120** D7
Farndale Gr WN4 . . . .**73** C2
Farndale Sq M38 . . . .**60** C3
Farndale Wlk M9 . . . .**157** E8
Farndon Ave SK7 . . . .**124** F4
Farndon Cl M33 . . . .**108** E3
Farndon Dr WA15 . . . .**120** A6
Farndon Rd SK5 . . . .**99** E2
Farnham Ave M9 . . . .**64** D5
Farnham Cl Bolton BL1 . . .**143** E1
  Cheadle SK8 . . . .**132** A7
  Leigh WN7 . . . .**75** F6
Farnham Dr M44 . . . .**94** B1
Farnhill Wlk M23 . . . .**108** C1
Farnley Cl OL12 . . . .**13** F2
Farnsfield WN1 . . . .**37** F1
Farnsworth Ave OL7 . . . . .**85** B5
Farnworth Cl OL7 . . . .**85** B5
Farnworth Dr M14 . . . .**98** C2
Farnworth St Bolton BL3 . .**146** C4
  Heywood OL10 . . . .**29** C2
  Leigh WN7 . . . .**76** B4
Farnworth Sta BL4 . . . .**42** E1
Farr Cl WN3 . . . .**54** F5
Farr St SK3 . . . .**170** D6
Farrand Rd OL8 . . . .**66** B2
Farrant Rd M12 . . . .**99** A4
Farrar Rd M43 . . . .**99** F8
Farrell St Manchester M7 .**158** E3
  Wigan WN5 . . . .**54** C5
Farrer Rd M13 . . . .**98** F3
Farrier's Croft WN6 . . . . . .**36** E3
Farriers La OL11 . . . .**30** B4
Farringdon Dr M26 . . . .**43** E4
Farringdon St M6 . . . .**154** E3
Farrington Ave M20 . . . . .**110** A7
Farrow Dr M30 . . . .**79** B4
Farrow St OL2 . . . .**149** B6
Farrow St E OL2 . . . .**149** B6
Farrowdale Ave OL2 . . . . .**149** B6
Farwood Cl M16 . . . .**161** C5
Fastnet St M11 . . . .**165** A8
Fatherford Cl OL3 . . . .**51** D5
Faulkenhurst Mews OL1 .**48** C1
Faulkenhurst St OL1,OL9 .**48** C1
Faulkes Ho M14 . . . .**110** D8
Faulkner Dr WA15 . . . .**120** B5
Faulkner Rd M32 . . . .**96** E2
Faulkner St Bolton BL3 . . .**145** E5
  Manchester M1 . . . .**163** A4
  Rochdale OL16 . . . .**139** F7
Fauvel Pl SK13 . . . .**104** C1
Fauvel Rd SK13 . . . .**104** C2
Faversham Brow OL1 . . . .**153** E8
Faversham St M40 . . . .**83** B7
Fawborough Rd M23 . . . . .**108** F1
Fawcett St BL2 . . . .**148** B7
Fawcetts Fold BL5 . . . .**39** E4
Fawley Ave SK14 . . . .**167** D1
Fawley Gr M22 . . . .**121** D4
Fawns Keep
  Stalybridge SK15 . . . .**102** E6
  Wilmslow SK9 . . . .**137** D7
Fay Ave M9 . . . .**65** B2
Fay Gdns SK13 . . . .**171** E4
Faywood Dr SK6 . . . .**126** A6
Fearn St OL10 . . . .**29** C2
Fearney Side BL3 . . . .**42** F3

Fearnham Cl WN7 . . . .**75** E1
Fearnhead Ave BL6 . . . .**22** B5
Fearnhead Cl BL4 . . . .**60** E8
Fearnhead St BL3 . . . .**146** C4
Fearnley Way WA12 . . . . . .**89** C1
Fearns Moss OL13 . . . .**3** A8
Featherstall Brook View
  OL15 . . . .**16** A5
Featherstall Ho OL9 . . . . .**152** C5
Featherstall Rd OL15 . . . . .**16** A5
Featherstall Rd N
  OL1,OL9 . . . .**153** D8
Featherstall Rd S OL9 . . .**153** D6
Fecit St BL2 . . . .**12** C8
Federation St
  Manchester M4 . . . .**159** A2
  Prestwich M25 . . . .**62** F5
Feldom Rd M23 . . . .**108** F2
Fell St Bury BL8 . . . .**27** C2
  Leigh WN7 . . . .**75** B4
Fellbridge Cl BL5 . . . .**40** B1
Fellbrigg Cl M18 . . . .**99** C3
Fellfoot Cl M28 . . . .**77** F5
Felling Wlk M14 . . . .**98** B3
Fellpark Rd M23 . . . .**109** A2
Fells Gr M28 . . . .**60** F1
Fellside Bolton BL2 . . . .**26** A3
  Oldham OL1 . . . .**153** E7
  Wigan WN1 . . . .**37** D2
Fellside Cl BL8 . . . .**10** F1
Fellside Gdns OL15 . . . . . .**15** F7
Fellside Gn SK15 . . . .**86** A3
Felltop Dr SK5 . . . .**112** A8
Felskirk Rd M22 . . . .**130** C8
Felsted BL1 . . . .**40** B1
Felt Cl M34 . . . .**100** C2
Felthorpe Dr M8 . . . .**155** F6
Felton Ave M22 . . . .**121** D3
Felton Cl BL9 . . . .**45** A5
Felton Wlk BL1 . . . .**143** E2
Fence St SK2 . . . .**124** D4
Fencegate Ave SK4 . . . . . .**111** D5
Fenchurch Ave M40 . . . . . .**83** C4
Fencot Dr M12 . . . .**99** A4
Fenella St M13 . . . .**98** E4
Fenham Cl M40 . . . .**156** C5
Fenmore Ave M18 . . . .**99** B3
Fenn St M15 . . . .**162** B6
Fennel St M3,M4 . . . .**158** F2
Fenners Cl BL3 . . . .**147** D3
Fenney St M7 . . . .**155** D5
Fenney St E M7 . . . .**155** E6
Fenside Rd M22 . . . .**121** E6
Fenstock Wlk M40 . . . .**83** D4
Fentewan Wlk SK14 . . . . .**102** E3
Fenton Ave SK2,SK7 . . . . .**124** D4
Fenton Mews OL11 . . . .**139** E6
Fenton St Bury BL8 . . . .**27** C3
  Manchester M12 . . . .**165** A5
  Oldham OL4 . . . .**67** B6
  Rochdale OL11 . . . .**139** E5
  Shaw OL2 . . . .**149** B5
Fenton Way WN2 . . . .**56** F4
Fenwick Cl SK4 . . . .**110** E3
Fenwick St
  Manchester M15 . . . .**163** A6
  Rochdale OL12 . . . .**139** E7
Ferdinand St M40 . . . .**160** D4
Fereday St M28 . . . .**60** D4
Ferguson Ct M19 . . . .**110** F8
Ferguson Gdns OL12 . . . . .**14** F3
Ferguson Rise WN5 . . . . . .**54** E8
Ferguson Way OL4 . . . .**49** D1
Fern Ave
  Newton-le-W WA12 . . . .**89** D2
  Urmston M41 . . . .**95** A2
Fern Bank Failsworth M40 .**83** C7
  Stalybridge SK15 . . . .**86** C1
Fern Bank Cl SK15 . . . .**102** C8
Fern Bank Dr M23 . . . .**120** E8
Fern Bank St SK14 . . . . . .**113** E8
Fern Clough BL1 . . . .**40** F7
Fern Common OL2 . . . . . .**149** B7
Fern Cres SK15 . . . .**86** C1
Fern Dene OL12 . . . .**14** B2
Fern Hill La OL12 . . . .**14** A3
Fern Isle Cl OL12 . . . .**14** B6
Fern Lea Gatley SK8 . . . . . .**122** B1
  Hollingworth SK14 . . . .**103** D5
Fern Lea Gr M38 . . . .**59** F4
Fern Lea St BB4 . . . .**2** D8
Fern St Bolton BL3 . . . .**144** C6
  Bury BL9 . . . .**140** F3
  Chadderton OL9 . . . .**152** A8
  Farnworth BL4 . . . .**42** E1
  Littleborough OL12 . . . .**15** C6
  Manchester M11 . . . .**165** B7
  Oldham OL4,M8 . . . .**159** A4
  Oldham OL8 . . . .**153** D5
  Ramsbottom BL0 . . . .**11** D7
  Rochdale OL11 . . . .**139** D6
Fern View WA15 . . . .**120** C5
Fernacre M33 . . . .**108** C5
Fernally St SK14 . . . .**167** E2
Fernbank M26 . . . .**62** A8
Fernbray Ave M19 . . . .**110** D4
Fernbray Rd WN2 . . . .**57** A2
Fernbrook Cl M13 . . . .**164** D5
Fernbrook Wlk M8 . . . .**155** F7
Fernclough Rd M9 . . . .**157** D7
Ferndale Ave Royton OL16 .**48** C8
  Stockport SK2 . . . .**124** B4
  Whitefield M45 . . . .**62** C7

Ferndale Cl OL4 . . . .**67** D4
Ferndale Gdns M19 . . . . .**110** E6
Ferndale Rd M33 . . . .**108** B2
Ferndene Gdns M20 . . . . .**110** B5
Ferndene Rd
  Manchester M20 . . . .**110** B5
  Prestwich M25,M45 . . . .**63** C7
Ferndown Ave
  Chadderton OL9 . . . .**65** E7
  Hazel Grove SK7 . . . .**124** C1
Ferndown Dr M44 . . . .**94** A3
Ferndown Rd Bolton BL2 . .**25** E3
  Sale M23 . . . .**120** D8
Ferney Field
  Com Specl Sch OL9 . . . . .**65** F7
Ferney Field Rd OL9 . . . . . .**65** F7
Ferngate Dr M20 . . . .**110** B6
Ferngrove BL9 . . . .**28** B5
Fernhill SK6 . . . .**126** B6
Fernhill Ave Bacup OL13 . . . .**3** E8
  Bolton BL3 . . . .**146** A4
Fernhill Caravan Pk BL9 .**140** F4
Fernhill Cl Bacup OL13 . . . . .**3** E8
  Glossop SK13 . . . .**104** D3
Fernhill Cres OL13 . . . .**3** E8
Fernhill Dr Bacup OL13 . . . . .**3** E8
  Manchester M18 . . . .**99** B4
Fernhill Gr OL13 . . . .**3** E8
Fernhill Pk OL13 . . . .**3** E8
Fernhill St BL9 . . . .**140** F3
Fernhill Way OL13 . . . .**3** E8
Fernhills BL7 . . . .**8** E2
Fernholme Ct OL8 . . . .**66** C4
Fernhurst Cl WN3 . . . .**151** F6
Fernhurst Gr BL1 . . . .**143** E1
Fernhurst Rd M20 . . . .**110** C5
Fernhurst St OL1,OL9 . . . . .**48** C1
Fernie St M4 . . . .**159** A3
Fernlea Cl SK22 . . . .**127** C1
Fernlea Altrincham WA15 . . .**119** F1
  Manchester SK4 . . . .**111** C5
Fernlea Ave OL1 . . . .**48** C5
Fernlea Cl Hadfield SK13 . .**171** E4
  Rochdale OL12 . . . .**14** B2
Fernlea Cres M27 . . . .**79** E7
Fernlea Gr WN4 . . . .**72** D5
Fernlea Lo BL4 . . . .**60** E7
Fernleaf St M14 . . . .**98** A4
Fernleigh BL1 . . . .**143** E4
Fernleigh Ave M19 . . . .**99** C1
Fernleigh Dr M16 . . . .**162** D5
Fernley Ave M34 . . . .**101** A2
Fernley Rd SK2 . . . .**124** B6
Ferns Gr BL1 . . . .**144** B7
Fernside M26 . . . .**61** C6
Fernside Ave M20 . . . .**110** D5
Fernside Gr Walkden M28 . .**60** E4
  Wigan WN3 . . . .**54** D1
Fernside Way OL12 . . . .**14** A1
Fernstead BL3 . . . .**144** C6
Fernstone Cl BL6 . . . .**22** A3
Fernthorpe Ave OL3 . . . . . .**51** C1
Fernview Dr BL0 . . . .**11** A1
Fernville Terr OL13 . . . .**3** D8
Fernwood SK6 . . . .**126** C7
Fernwood Ave M18 . . . .**99** D3
Fernwood Gr SK9 . . . .**137** C8
Ferrand Lodge OL15 . . . . . .**16** B6
Ferrand Rd OL15 . . . .**16** B6
Ferrer St WN4 . . . .**72** F6
Ferring Wlk OL9 . . . .**152** B6
Ferris St M11 . . . .**99** D8
Ferrous Way M44 . . . .**105** F6
Ferry Rd M44 . . . .**94** B2
Ferry St M11 . . . .**164** E8
Ferryhill Rd M44 . . . .**94** A2
Fettler Cl M27 . . . .**79** F7
Fewston Cl BL1 . . . .**24** E5
Fiddlers La M44 . . . .**94** B4
Fiddlers Lane Prim Sch
  M44 . . . .**94** B3
Field Bank Gr M19 . . . .**99** C1
Field Cl Bramhall SK7 . . . . .**132** D4
  Marple SK6 . . . .**125** D5
Field End Cl SK15 . . . .**102** D8
Field House La SK6 . . . . . .**126** A6
Field La OL6 . . . .**85** D5
Field Pl M20 . . . .**110** B3
Field Rd Milnrow OL16 . . . . .**31** D7
  Sale M33 . . . .**107** E6
Field St Droylsden M43 . . . . .**99** F8
  Dukinfield SK14 . . . .**101** D5
  Failsworth M35 . . . .**83** E7
  Hindley WN2 . . . .**56** E4
  Ince-in-M WN3 . . . .**55** F4
  Manchester M18 . . . .**99** E6
  Rochdale OL11 . . . .**31** A4
  Romiley SK6 . . . .**113** A3
  Salford M6 . . . .**154** F2
  Wigan WN6 . . . .**150** B8
Field Vale Dr SK5 . . . .**100** A1
Field Wlk M16 . . . .**97** F2
Field Wlk WA15 . . . .**120** B3
Fieldbrook Wlk BL5 . . . . . .**40** A1
Fieldcroft OL11 . . . .**30** B7
Fielden Ave M21 . . . .**97** B1
Fielden Rd M20 . . . .**109** F4
Fielden St OL15 . . . .**15** E2
Fielders Way M27 . . . .**61** E4
Fieldfare Ave M40 . . . .**83** B4
Fieldfare Way OL7 . . . .**85** B5
Fieldhead Ave Bury BL8 . . .**27** A2
  Rochdale OL11 . . . .**30** B7
  Tyldesley M29 . . . .**77** B5
Fieldhead Mews SK9 . . . .**137** E8
Fieldhead Rd SK9 . . . .**137** E8
Fieldhouse Ind Est OL12 . .**14** F2

Fieldhouse Rd OL12 . . . . . .**14** F2
Fielding Ave SK12 . . . .**133** E2
Fielding Pl PR6 . . . .**21** B8
Fielding St Eccles M30 . . . . .**79** C1
  Middleton M24 . . . .**47** A2
Fields Cres SK14 . . . .**103** D6
Fields Ct SK14 . . . .**102** C1
Fields End Fold M30 . . . . . .**94** C4
Fields Farm Cl SK14 . . . . .**102** D2
Fields Farm Rd SK14 . . . . .**102** D2
Fields Farm Wlk SK14 . . .**102** D2
Fields Gr SK14 . . . .**103** D5
Fields New Rd OL9 . . . .**152** B5
Fields The WN2 . . . .**38** C4
Fieldsend Dr WN7 . . . .**91** C8
Fieldsway OL8 . . . .**66** E2
Fieldvale Rd M33 . . . .**107** E1
Fieldview WN8 . . . .**53** A7
Fieldway Platt Bridge WN2 . .**56** B2
  Rochdale OL16 . . . .**31** B3
Fife Ave OL9 . . . .**66** A4
Fifield Cl OL8 . . . .**67** A3
Fifth Ave Bolton BL1 . . . . . .**144** B7
  Bury BL9 . . . .**28** D4
  Droylsden M11 . . . .**83** C2
  Dukinfield SK16 . . . .**101** A8
  Little Lever BL3 . . . .**42** F4
  Oldham OL8 . . . .**66** C2
  Stretford M17 . . . .**96** C6
Fifth St Bolton BL1 . . . .**23** F4
  Stretford M17 . . . .**96** D5
Filbert St OL1 . . . .**49** C1
Filby Wlk M40 . . . .**160** E4
Fildes St M24 . . . .**65** D7
Filey Ave Manchester M16 . .**97** D2
  Urmston M41 . . . .**95** A4
Filey Dr M6 . . . .**80** D6
Filey Rd Manchester M14 . .**110** D8
  Stockport SK2 . . . .**124** C7
Filey St OL16 . . . .**15** C3
Filton Ave BL3 . . . .**145** D5
Filton Wlk M9 . . . .**156** C6
Finance St OL15 . . . .**15** C2
Finborough Cl M16 . . . .**97** E4
Finch Ave BL4 . . . .**59** F7
Finch La WN6 . . . .**18** B1
Finch Mill Ave WN6 . . . . . .**35** D7
Finchale Dr WA15 . . . .**120** C1
Finchcroft OL1 . . . .**153** E7
Finchdale Gdns WA3 . . . . .**91** B8
Finchley Ave M40 . . . .**83** C4
Finchley Cres WN2 . . . .**38** A2
Finchley Gr M40 . . . .**65** A1
Finchley Rd
  Altrincham WA15 . . . .**119** E3
  Manchester M14 . . . .**110** B8
Findlay Cl WA12 . . . .**89** C2
Findlay St WN7 . . . .**75** E5
Findon Rd M23 . . . .**121** A6
Finger Post BL3 . . . .**43** A4
Finghall Rd M41 . . . .**95** B2
Finishing Wlk M4 . . . .**159** C1
Finlan Rd M24 . . . .**47** E5
Finland Rd SK3 . . . .**170** D8
Finlay Ct WN5 . . . .**54** E8
Finlay St BL4 . . . .**60** D8
Finney Cl SK9 . . . .**131** C2
Finney Dr Handforth SK9 . .**131** C2
  Manchester M21 . . . .**109** A6
Finney La SK8 . . . .**122** C1
Finney St BL3 . . . .**147** F4
Finningley Rd M9 . . . .**64** B5
Finny Bank Rd M33 . . . . . .**108** A6
Finsbury Ave M40 . . . .**83** C4
Finsbury Rd SK5 . . . .**111** E8
Finstock Cl M30 . . . .**79** B1
Finsbury St OL11 . . . .**139** D5
Fintry Gr M30 . . . .**79** D1
Fir Ave SK7 . . . .**132** E8
Fir Bank Com Prim Sch
  OL2 . . . .**48** D7
Fir Bank Rd OL2 . . . .**48** D6
Fir Cl SK12 . . . .**133** E3
Fir Gr Manchester M19 . . . . .**99** A1
  Oldham OL9 . . . .**152** B8
  Wigan WN6 . . . .**37** A3
Fir La OL2 . . . .**48** D6
Fir Rd Bramhall SK7 . . . .**132** E4
  Denton M34 . . . .**101** A3
  Farnworth BL4 . . . .**60** B8
  Marple SK6 . . . .**125** E5
  Swinton M27 . . . .**79** E6
Fir St Bolton BL1 . . . .**143** F2
  Bury BL9 . . . .**141** A2
  Eccles M30 . . . .**79** D1
  Failsworth M35 . . . .**83** E7
  Heywood OL10 . . . .**29** E1
  Irlam M44 . . . .**105** D6
  Manchester M16 . . . .**97** C4
  Manchester M40 . . . .**160** D4
  Radcliffe M26 . . . .**44** B2
  Ramsbottom BL0 . . . .**11** D7
  Royton OL2 . . . .**48** D5
  Salford M6 . . . .**154** F2
  Stockport SK4 . . . .**169** E2
  Walsden OL14 . . . .**6** A1
Fir Tree Ave
  Boothstown M28 . . . .**78** C8
  Golborne WA3 . . . .**90** F8
  Oldham OL8 . . . .**67** A2
Fir Tree Cl SK16 . . . .**101** E8
Fir Tree Cres
  Ince-in-M WN3 . . . .**55** F5
  Stalybridge SK16 . . . .**101** F8
Fir Tree Dr
  Dukinfield SK14 . . . .**101** E5
  Ince-in-M WN3 . . . .**55** F3
Fir Tree Ho OL8 . . . .**67** A2

Fir Tree La SK16 . . . . .101 F8
Fir Tree Prim Sch SK5 . . . . . .99 E2
Fir Tree St WN3 . . . . .55 F4
Fir Tree Way 3 BL6 . . . . . . .22 E1
Fir Tree Wlk WA3 . . . . .90 F8
Firbank Rd Wigan WN3 . . . .55 B3
Wythenshawe M23 . . . . . .121 B4
Firbarn Cl OL16 . . . . .31 D7
Firbeck Dr M4 . . . . .160 D2
Fircroft WN6 . . . . .19 A2
Fircroft Ct 6 SK3 . . . . . . .123 F4
Fircroft Rd OL8 . . . . .67 A2
Firdale Ave M40 . . . . .65 E1
Firdale Wlk OL9 . . . . .152 C7
Firdon Wlk 17 M9 . . . . . . .157 F7
Fire Station Sq M5 . . . . . . .81 C2
Firecrest M28 . . . . .78 B8
Firefly Cl M3 . . . . .158 D1
Firethorn Ave M19 . . . . . .110 F6
Firethorn Cl BL5 . . . . .39 F2
Firethorn Dr SK14 . . . . . . .102 A2
Firethorn Wlk 5 M33 . . . . .107 C5
Firfield Gr M28 . . . . .60 F3
Firgrove Ave OL16 . . . . . . .31 D8
Firgrove Gdns OL16 . . . . . .31 D8
Firs Ashton-u-l OL6 . . . . . .85 B5
Failsworth M35 . . . . .83 E7
Manchester M16 . . . . .97 B2
Firs Cotts WN2 . . . . .38 D1
Firs Ct SK8 . . . . .122 A3
Firs Cty Prim Sch M33 . . . .107 D4
Firs Gr SK8 . . . . .122 A4
Firs La WN7 . . . . .75 C5
Firs Park Cres WN2 . . . . . .38 C1
Firs Rd Atherton BL5 . . . . . .59 A6
Gatley SK8 . . . . .122 A4
Sale M33 . . . . .107 D5
Firs The Altrincham WA14 . .119 B3
Manchester M14 . . . . .98 D1
Wilmslow SK9 . . . . .137 A5
Firs Way M33 . . . . .107 C3
Firsby Ave SK6 . . . . .112 F4
Firsby St 5 M19 . . . . .99 A1
Firsdale Ind Est WN7 . . . . .75 C6
First Ave Atherton M46 . . . . .58 D4
Bury BL8 . . . . .26 F6
Droylsden M11 . . . . .83 D2
11 Hindley WN2 . . . . .56 D5
Little Lever BL3 . . . . .43 A4
Mossley SK15 . . . . .86 E6
Oldham OL8 . . . . .66 D2
Poynton SK12 . . . . .133 D1
Stretford M17 . . . . .96 D6
Swinton M27 . . . . .79 D5
Tyldesley M29 . . . . .77 C4
Wigan WN6 . . . . .37 A2
First St BL1 . . . . .23 F4
Firsway WN7 . . . . .75 B5
Firswood Dr Hyde SK14 . .102 A3
Royton OL2 . . . . .48 C6
Swinton M27 . . . . .79 E6
Firswood Mount SK8 . . . . .122 A4
Firth Cl M7 . . . . .155 D6
Firth St OL1 . . . . .153 F6
Firtree Ave M33 . . . . .107 C4
Firvale Ave SK8 . . . . .122 B1
Firvale Cl WN7 . . . . .75 C5
Firwood Ave Farnworth BL4 .60 C7
Stretford M41 . . . . .96 A4
Firwood Cl SK2 . . . . .124 C8
Firwood Cres M26 . . . . . . .44 B1
Firwood Gr
Ashton-in-M WN4 . . . . . .73 A4
Bolton BL2 . . . . .25 B2
Firwood La BL2 . . . . .25 C3
Firwood Pk OL9 . . . . .65 E8
Firwood Specl Sch BL2 . . . .25 C2
Firwood Stables BL2 . . . . . .25 C3
Fish Rake La BL0,BB4 . . . . . .1 E6
Fishbourne Sq 8 M14 . . . . .98 C3
Fishbrook Ind Est BL4 . . . . .61 A7
Fisher Ave M34 . . . . .74 C7
Fisher Cl WN3 . . . . .54 F5
Fisher Dr WN5 . . . . .53 E7
Fisher St OL1 . . . . .153 F8
Fisherfield OL12 . . . . .13 F1
Fishermore Rd M41 . . . . . .94 E2
Fishpool Inf Sch BL9 . . . . . .44 F8
Fishwick St OL16 . . . . .31 A6
Fistral Ave SK8 . . . . .131 C8
Fistral Cres SK15 . . . . .86 D3
Fitchfield Wlk M28 . . . . . . .60 D3
Fitton Ave M21 . . . . .109 B6
Fitton Cres M27 . . . . .61 F3
Fitton Hill Inf Sch OL8 . . . . .67 B3
Fitton Hill Jun Sch OL8 . . . .67 A3
Fitton St Bolton BL3 . . . . . .147 E4
Rochdale OL16 . . . . .31 A6
Royton OL2 . . . . .48 F4
Shaw OL2 . . . . .48 F7
Fitzadam St WN1 . . . . . . .150 B8
Fitzalan St SK13 . . . . .104 C1
Fitzgeorge St M40 . . . . . .156 C5
Fitzgerald Cl M25 . . . . .62 F2
Fitzgerald Ct 11 M34 . . . . .113 A8
Fitzgerald Way M6 . . . . . .154 F3
Fitzhugh St BL1 . . . . .25 A5
Fitzroy St Ashton-u-L OL7 . .100 F8
Droylsden M43 . . . . .100 B8
Stalybridge SK15 . . . . . . .86 D4
Fitzwarren Ct M6 . . . . . . .154 F2
Fitzwarren St M6 . . . . . . .154 F3
Fitzwilliam St M7 . . . . . . .158 D4
Five Fold Pk OL9 . . . . . . .153 D6
Five Quarters M26 . . . . . . .43 E5
Fiveways M43 . . . . .84 A2
Fiveways Par SK7 . . . . . . .133 E8

Flag St OL13 . . . . .3 E8
Flagcroft Dr M23 . . . . . . .121 B5
Flagg Wood Ave SK6 . . . .125 D7
Flagship Ave M5 . . . . .161 B8
Flamborough Wlk 17 M14 . .98 B3
Flamingo Cl M12 . . . . . . .165 A6
Flamingo Villas M44 . . . . . .94 A3
Flamstead Ave M23 . . . . .120 E6
Flannel St 4 OL12,OL16 . . . .31 A8
Flapper Fold La M46 . . . . . .58 C3
Flash St M40 . . . . .83 C6
Flash Cotts OL4 . . . . .68 A4
Flash St M40 . . . . .83 C6
Flashfields M25 . . . . .62 F1
Flatley Cl M15 . . . . .163 A5
Flavion Wlk M11 . . . . .165 B8
Flax Cl BB4 . . . . .1 A8
Flax Moss Cl BB4 . . . . .1 A8
Flax St Manchester M3 . . . .158 D3
Ramsbottom BL0 . . . . . . .11 A4
Flaxcroft Rd M22 . . . . . . .121 B3
Flaxfield Ave SK15 . . . . . . .86 D2
Flaxman Rise OL1 . . . . . . .49 C4
Flaxpool Cl M16 . . . . .97 E4
Flaxwood Wlk M22 . . . . . .121 B3
Fleece St 2 Oldham OL4 . . .67 B7
Rochdale OL16 . . . . .139 F7
Fleeson St M14 . . . . .98 E3
Fleet St Ashton-u-L OL6 . . .166 B2
Droylsden M18 . . . . .99 F6
Horwich BL6 . . . . .22 D3
Hyde SK14 . . . . .167 E3
Oldham OL4 . . . . .67 C7
Wigan WN5 . . . . .54 B6
Fleetwood Rd M28 . . . . . . .60 A3
Fleming Pl OL9 . . . . .153 D6
Fleming Rd M22 . . . . .121 D2
Flemish Rd M34 . . . . .101 B2
Fletcher Ave Atherton M46 . .58 D5
Standish WN6 . . . . .19 F1
Fletcher Cl Heywood OL10 . .29 D2
Oldham OL9 . . . . .153 D6
Fletcher Dr
Altrincham WA14 . . . . . .119 C1
High Lane SK12 . . . . . . .134 F6
Fletcher Fold Rd BL9 . . . . .44 F6
Fletcher Moss Botanical
& Parsonage Gdns
M20 . . . . .110 B1
Fletcher Moss Mus
& Art Gal M20 . . . . . . .110 B1
Fletcher Sq 18 M1 . . . . . . .159 C1
Fletcher St
1 Ashton-u-L OL6 . . . . .166 C1
Atherton M46 . . . . .58 C3
Bolton BL3 . . . . .145 E5
Bury BL9 . . . . .141 A2
Farnworth BL4 . . . . .60 D8
Little Lever BL3 . . . . .43 B3
Manchester M10,M40 . . . .157 F5
Radcliffe M26 . . . . .44 C4
Rochdale OL11 . . . . .31 A5
Stockport SK1 . . . . .169 F1
Fletcher's Rd OL15 . . . . . . .15 E3
Fletsand Rd SK9 . . . . . . .137 D6
Flexbury Wlk M40 . . . . . . .83 D4
Flint Cl Droylsden M11 . . . . .83 B2
Hazel Grove SK7 . . . . . .124 C1
Flint Gr M44 . . . . .105 C6
Flint St Droylsden M43 . . . . .84 B2
Oldham OL1 . . . . .67 C8
Stockport SK3 . . . . .170 E7
Flitcroft Ct BL3 . . . . .147 F4
Flixton Girls' High Sch
M41 . . . . .95 A2
Flixton Inf Sch M41 . . . . . . .94 F3
Flixton Jun Sch M41 . . . . . .94 F2
Flixton Rd Flixton M31 . . . .106 E2
Urmston M41 . . . . .94 F1
Urmston M41 . . . . .95 B2
Flixton Sta M41 . . . . .94 F1
Flixton Wlk M13 . . . . .164 D5
Floats Rd Altrincham M23 . .120 E4
Altrincham M23 . . . . . . .120 E6
Floatshall Rd M23 . . . . . .121 A6
Flockton Ave WN6 . . . . . . .36 D4
Flockton Ct 7 BL6 . . . . . . .22 B4
Flora Dr M7 . . . . .158 D4
Flora St
Ashton-in-M WN4 . . . . . .73 B2
Bolton BL3 . . . . .147 E4
Manchester M9 . . . . .64 C3
Oldham OL1 . . . . .153 E7
Floral Ct M7 . . . . .155 D6
Florence Ave BL1 . . . . .24 F5
Florence Ct SK3 . . . . .123 B6
Florence Nightingale
Hosp1 BL8 . . . . .27 C1
Florence Park Ct M20 . . . .110 C4
Florence St Bolton BL3 . . . .147 D4
Droylsden M43 . . . . .100 B8
Eccles M30 . . . . .79 B1
Failsworth M35 . . . . .83 F8
Sale M33 . . . . .108 B6
Stockport SK4 . . . . .169 E2
Wigan WN1 . . . . .151 E8
Florence Way SK14 . . . . . .103 D5
Florian Ho OL1 . . . . .153 F7
Florida St OL8 . . . . .153 E5
Florist St SK3 . . . . .170 E7
Flowery Bank OL8 . . . . . . .67 B4
Flowery Field OL8 . . . . . . .124 A3
Flowery Field Gn SK14 . . . .101 C4
Flowery Field Prim Sch
SK14 . . . . .167 D4
Flowery Field Sta SK14 . . . .101 D5
Floyd Ave M21 . . . . .109 C5
Floyer Rd M9 . . . . .64 E5

Foden La
Alderley Edge SK9 . . . . . .136 C1
Woodford SK7 . . . . .132 D3
Foden Wlk 7 SK9 . . . . . . .131 D2
Fog La M19,M20 . . . . .110 C4
Fold Ave M43 . . . . .84 B2
Fold Cres SK15 . . . . .86 F6
Fold Gdns OL12 . . . . .14 B4
Fold Gn OL9 . . . . .152 A6
Fold Mews SK7 . . . . .124 C3
Fold Rd M26 . . . . .61 C7
Fold St Bolton BL1 . . . . . . .145 F7
Bury BL9 . . . . .140 D2
Golborne WA3 . . . . .74 A1
Heywood OL10 . . . . .29 E3
Manchester M40 . . . . .83 A8
Fold The Manchester M9 . . . .64 D3
Royton OL2 . . . . .49 A4
Urmston M41 . . . . .95 A3
Fold View Bolton BL7 . . . . . .8 E1
Oldham OL8 . . . . .67 A2
Folds BL6 . . . . .21 C3
Folds Rd BL1,BL2 . . . . . . .148 A8
Foleshill Ave M9 . . . . .157 D7
Foley Gdns OL10 . . . . .46 E7
Foley St 8 WN2 . . . . .56 D5
Foley Wlk M22 . . . . .130 E8
Foliage Cres SK5 . . . . .112 B5
Foliage Gdns SK5 . . . . . . .112 C5
Foliage Rd SK5 . . . . .112 B4
Folkestone Rd M11 . . . . . . .83 D1
Folkestone Rd E M11 . . . . . .83 D1
Folkestone Rd W M11 . . . . .83 D2
Follows St M18 . . . . .99 D6
Folly La M27 . . . . .79 D6
Folly Wlk 20 OL12 . . . . . . .14 F1
Fonthill Gr M33 . . . . .107 C3
Fontwell Cl
3 Manchester M16 . . . . . .97 C3
Standish WN6 . . . . .19 F1
Fontwell La OL1 . . . . .49 A1
Fontwell Rd BL3 . . . . .43 A2
Fontwell Wlk 6 M40 . . . . . .65 D2
Foot Mill Cres OL12 . . . . . .14 D2
Foot Wood Cres OL12 . . . . .14 D2
Footman Cl M29 . . . . .77 B7
Forber Cres M18 . . . . .99 D3
Forbes Cl Sale M33 . . . . . .108 D2
Stockport SK1 . . . . .124 B8
Forbes Pk SK7 . . . . .132 C5
Forbes Rd SK1 . . . . .112 B1
Forbes St SK6 . . . . .112 F4
Ford Gr SK14 . . . . .103 A4
Ford La Manchester M20 . . .110 A2
Salford M6 . . . . .81 A4
Wythenshawe M20,M22 . . .109 F1
Ford Lo M20 . . . . .110 B2
Ford St Dukinfield SK16 . . . .101 C6
Kearsley M26 . . . . .61 A8
Manchester M12 . . . . . . .164 D7
Stockport SK3 . . . . .169 D1
Ford Way M34 . . . . .103 A4
Ford's La SK7 . . . . .132 D6
Fordbank Rd M20 . . . . . . .110 A2
Fordham Gr BL1 . . . . .144 C8
Fordland Cl WA3 . . . . .74 E1
Fordoe La OL12 . . . . .13 C4
Fordyce Way WN2 . . . . . . .56 A8
Foreland Cl M40 . . . . .157 D5
Forest Ave WN6 . . . . .36 F3
Forest Cl SK16 . . . . .101 C6
Forest Ct M41 . . . . .94 F4
Forest Dr Altrincham WA15 .119 F6
Sale M33 . . . . .107 E2
Shevington Moor WN6 . . . .19 A2
Westhoughton BL5 . . . . . .58 A8
Forest Gdns M31 . . . . . . .105 D3
Forest Range M19 . . . . . . .99 A1
Forest Rd BL1 . . . . .142 B3
Forest Sch WA15 . . . . . . .119 F6
Forest St Ashton-u-L OL6 . .166 C4
Eccles M30 . . . . .79 A4
Oldham OL8 . . . . .66 F2
Forest View OL12 . . . . . . .14 D2
Forest Way SK6 . . . . .25 C6
Forester Dr SK15 . . . . .86 A3
Forester Hill Ave
Bolton BL3 . . . . .147 F3
Bolton BL3 . . . . .42 A3
Forester Hill Cl BL3 . . . . . .147 F3
Forfar St BL1 . . . . .24 E5
Forge Ind Est OL4 . . . . . . .67 B7
Forge La M11 . . . . .160 F7
Forge St Oldham OL4 . . . . .67 B7
Wigan WN1 . . . . .151 E7
Formby Ave Atherton M46 . .58 D4
Manchester M21 . . . . . . .109 D7
Formby Dr SK8 . . . . .131 B8
Formby Rd M6 . . . . .80 E5
Forres Gr WN4 . . . . .72 F4
Forrest Rd M34 . . . . .101 B1
Forrester Dr OL2 . . . . .49 D8
Forrester St M28 . . . . .79 A8
Forresters Cl WN2 . . . . . . .74 E8
Forshaw Ave M18 . . . . .99 F6
Forshaw St M34 . . . . .100 D4
Forster St WA3 . . . . .74 A1
Forston Wlk M8 . . . . .156 B6
Forsyth St OL12 . . . . .13 E2
Forsythia Wlk 2 M31 . . . . .105 E2
Fort Rd M25 . . . . .63 D2
Fortescue Rd SK2 . . . . . . .124 D7
Forth Pl M26 . . . . .43 F5
Forth Rd M26 . . . . .43 F5
Forton Ave BL2 . . . . .42 E7
Forton Rd WN3 . . . . .54 F2

Fortran Cl M5 . . . . .81 A1
Fortrose Ave M9 . . . . .64 B3
Fortuna Gr M19 . . . . .110 F8
Fortune St BL3 . . . . .148 B5
Fortyacre Dr SK6 . . . . . . .112 C3
Forum Gr M7 . . . . .155 F5
Forum The M6 . . . . .113 C2
Fosbrook Ave M20 . . . . . .110 C4
Foscarn Dr M23 . . . . .121 B5
Fossgill Ave BL2 . . . . .25 C5
Foster Ave WN3 . . . . .151 E6
Foster Ct BL3 . . . . .28 D4
Foster La BL2 . . . . .25 F1
Foster St Denton M34 . . . .100 F3
Oldham OL4 . . . . .67 C7
Radcliffe M26 . . . . .43 F3
Salford M5 . . . . .154 D1
6 Wigan WN6 . . . . .37 A1
Foster Terr 9 BL1 . . . . . . .143 E1
Fosters Bldgs WN6 . . . . . .150 B8
Fotherby Dr M9 . . . . .64 D3
Fotherby Pl WN3 . . . . .55 A3
Foul Clough Rd OL14 . . . . . .5 D7
Foulds Ave BL8 . . . . .27 B2
Foundry La
Manchester M4 . . . . .159 B3
Wigan WN3 . . . . .54 D4
Foundry St Bolton BL3 . . . .145 F5
Bury BL9 . . . . .140 D2
Dukinfield SK16 . . . . .101 D8
Heywood OL10 . . . . .29 C2
Hindley WN2 . . . . .56 D5
Leigh WN7 . . . . .76 B4
Little Lever BL3 . . . . .43 A3
Newton-le-W WA12 . . . . . .89 B3
Oldham OL3 . . . . .153 E6
4 Radcliffe M26 . . . . .44 A3
Swinton M27 . . . . .62 A1
Fountain Ave WA15 . . . . . .120 C5
Fountain Park BL5 . . . . .57 C5
Fountain Pl Poynton SK12 . .133 D4
Whitefield M45 . . . . .62 F7
Fountain St Ashton-u-L OL6 .85 E4
Bury BL8 . . . . .28 A4
Bury BL9 . . . . .141 A2
Eccles M30 . . . . .95 D8
Hyde SK14 . . . . .113 C5
Manchester M2 . . . . .159 A1
Middleton M24 . . . . .65 A8
Oldham OL1 . . . . .153 E7
Fountain St N BL9 . . . . . . .141 A3
Fountains Ave BL2 . . . . .25 C5
Fountains Cl M29 . . . . .77 C7
Fountains Rd
Bramhall SK7,SK8 . . . . . .132 C6
Urmston M32 . . . . .95 F3
Fountains Wlk
Dukinfield SK16 . . . . .101 C6
Golborne WA3 . . . . .91 B8
Oldham OL9 . . . . .152 A5
Four Lane Ends BL2 . . . . . . .25 E4
Four Lanes SK14 . . . . .103 A4
Four Lanes End Rd OL13 . . . .3 B8
Four Lanes Way OL11 . . . . .13 C2
Four Yards M2 . . . . .158 F1
Fouracres Rd M23 . . . . . . .121 A5
Fourgates Com Prim Sch
BL5 . . . . .39 C4
Fourmarts Rd WN5 . . . . . . .36 C2
Fourteen Meadows Rd
WN3 . . . . .150 B6
Fourth Ave Bolton BL1 . . . .144 B7
Bolton BL3 . . . . .42 F4
Bury BL9 . . . . .28 A4
Droylsden M11 . . . . .83 C3
Mossley SK15 . . . . .86 E6
Oldham OL8 . . . . .66 C1
Oldham OL8 . . . . .152 A5
Stretford M17 . . . . .96 C6
Swinton M27 . . . . .79 D5
Fourth St BL1 . . . . .23 F3
Fourways M17 . . . . .96 A6
Fowey Wlk
5 Hattersley SK14 . . . . . .102 E3
Wythenshawe M23 . . . . . .121 A5
Fowler Ave M18 . . . . .99 F7
Fowler Cl WN1 . . . . .151 E6
Fowler Ind Pk BL6 . . . . .22 C2
Fowler St OL8 . . . . .66 C3
Fowley Common La WA3 . . .92 C5
Fownhope Ave M33 . . . . . .107 F3
Fownhope Rd M33 . . . . . . .107 F3
Fox Bank Cl SK7,SK8 . . . . .132 C6
Fox Cl WA15 . . . . .119 F6
Fox Hill OL2 . . . . .48 D8
Fox Hill Rd OL11 . . . . .47 D8
Fox Park Rd 5 OL8 . . . . . . .66 C2
Fox Platt Rd OL5 . . . . .68 B1
Fox Platt Terr OL5 . . . . .86 C8
Fox St Bury BL9 . . . . .140 F3
Eccles M30 . . . . .79 F2
Heywood OL10 . . . . .29 C2
Horwich BL6 . . . . .22 C2
Milnrow OL16 . . . . .31 E6
Oldham OL8 . . . . .15 B1
Stockport SK3 . . . . .170 D8
Foxall Cl M24 . . . . .64 C7
Foxall St M24 . . . . .64 C7
Foxbank St M13 . . . . .98 E4
Foxbench Wlk M21 . . . . . .109 D6
Foxcroft OL15 . . . . .15 C5
Foxdale Cl BL7 . . . . .9 E7
Foxdale St 3 M11 . . . . .83 C1
Foxdene Gr WN3 . . . . .54 E2
Foxdenton Com Specl Sch
OL9 . . . . .65 F5

Foxdenton Dr M32 . . . . . . .95 F3
Foxdenton La M24,OL9 . . . . .65 F6
Foxdenton Wlk M34 . . . . .100 E1
Foxendale Wlk BL3 . . . . . .145 F5
Foxfield Cl BL8 . . . . .27 B5
Foxfield Dr OL8 . . . . .66 C1
Foxfield Gr WN6 . . . . .36 B6
Foxfield Rd M23 . . . . .121 A3
Foxford Wlk M22 . . . . .121 E2
Foxglove Cl
2 Golborne WA3 . . . . . . .90 D8
Standish WN6 . . . . .19 D2
Foxglove Ct OL12 . . . . .14 D3
Foxglove Dr
Altrincham WA14 . . . . . .119 C8
Bury BL9 . . . . .28 D3
Foxglove La SK15 . . . . .86 A3
Foxglove Wlk M31 . . . . . . .105 F2
Foxhall Rd
Altrincham WA15 . . . . . .119 F6
Denton M34 . . . . .100 D4
Foxham Wlk M7 . . . . .155 E6
Foxhill WA14 . . . . .119 A5
Foxhill Chase SK2 . . . . . . .125 A5
Foxhill Dr SK15 . . . . .102 C7
Foxhill Rd M30 . . . . .78 F1
Foxholes Cl OL12 . . . . .15 A1
Foxholes Rd Horwich BL6 . . .22 D4
Hyde SK14 . . . . .113 C8
Rochdale OL12 . . . . .15 A2
Foxlair Ct M22 . . . . .121 B3
Foxlair Rd M22 . . . . .121 B3
Foxland Rd SK8 . . . . .122 B4
Foxlea SK13 . . . . .115 A8
Foxley Cl Droylsden M43 . . .99 E8
Lymm WA13 . . . . .117 A2
Foxley Gr BL3 . . . . .145 D6
Foxley Hall Mews WA13 . .117 A1
Foxley Wlk M12 . . . . .165 A5
Foxton St M24 . . . . .64 C7
Foxton Wlk 6 M23 . . . . . .121 A2
Foxwell Wlk 5 M8 . . . . . .156 B6
Foxwood Cl WN5 . . . . .53 E5
Foxwood Dr OL5 . . . . .68 D2
Foxwood Gdns M19 . . . . . .110 E5
Foy St WN4 . . . . .73 B3
Fram St Manchester M9 . . .157 F8
Salford M6 . . . . .154 E2
Framingham Rd M33 . . . . .108 C5
Framley Rd M20,M21 . . . . .109 F7
Frampton Cl M24 . . . . .65 B7
France St Hindley WN2 . . . . .56 D6
Westhoughton BL5 . . . . . .57 E6
Wigan WN5 . . . . .54 F7
Frances Ave SK8 . . . . .122 A6
Frances Pl M46 . . . . .58 A2
Frances St Bolton BL1 . . . .143 D2
Cheadle SK8 . . . . .122 E6
Denton M34 . . . . .113 B8
Dukinfield SK14 . . . . .101 C3
Irlam M44 . . . . .105 C5
Littleborough OL16 . . . . . .15 D4
Manchester M13 . . . . . . .163 B6
Oldham OL1 . . . . .49 B1
7 Stockport SK1,SK3 . . . .170 E8
Frances St W SK1 . . . . . . .101 C3
Francesca Wlk M18 . . . . . .165 C6
Francis Ave Eccles M30 . . . .79 D3
Walkden M28 . . . . .60 F2
Francis Rd Irlam M44 . . . . . .93 F1
Manchester M20 . . . . . . .110 C5
Francis St Eccles M30 . . . . .79 D3
Failsworth M35 . . . . .83 F7
Farnworth BL4 . . . . .42 D1
Hindley WN2 . . . . .56 E5
Leigh WN7 . . . . .75 E7
Manchester M3 . . . . .158 F3
Tyldesley M29 . . . . .77 D8
Francis Terr 3 SK16 . . . . . .166 C1
Frandley Wlk 4 M13 . . . . .163 B7
Frank Cowan Ct M7 . . . . . .158 D4
Frank Fold OL10 . . . . .29 B3
Frank Perkins Way M44 . . .105 F7
Frank St Bolton BL1 . . . . . .143 D2
Bury BL9 . . . . .140 F1
Failsworth M35 . . . . .83 E7
Hyde SK14 . . . . .167 E2
3 Manchester M1 . . . . . .163 A7
Salford M6 . . . . .154 D1
Frank Swift Wlk 5 M14 . . . .98 A3
Frankby Cl M27 . . . . .80 C7
Frankford Ave BL1 . . . . . . .142 C2
Frankford Sq BL1 . . . . . . .142 C2
Frankland Cl M11 . . . . .83 A7
Franklin Cl Oldham OL1 . . .153 E8
Reddish M34 . . . . .100 A2
Franklin Rd M43 . . . . .84 A1
Franklin St Eccles M30 . . . .79 D2
Oldham OL1 . . . . .153 E8
Rochdale OL16 . . . . .31 B5
Franklyn Ave M41 . . . . .94 E2
Franklyn Rd M18 . . . . .99 E6
Franton Rd M45 . . . . .62 F7
Franton Rd M11 . . . . .83 B2
Fraser Ave M33 . . . . .108 E3
Fraser Ho BL1 . . . . .143 D1
Fraser Pl M17 . . . . .96 D5
Fraser Rd Manchester M8 . .156 A1
Wigan WN5 . . . . .54 E7
Fraser St Ashton-u-L OL6 . . .31 B4
Shaw OL2 . . . . .149 A2
Swinton M27 . . . . .62 A1
Fraternitas Terr M43 . . . . . .83 E3

Frawley Ave WA12 . . . . .89 C5
Freckleton Ave M21 . . . . . .109 C4
Freckleton Dr BL8 . . . . .43 F8
Freckleton St WN1 . . . . . . .37 C2
Fred Longworth High Sch
M29 . . . . .58 E1
Fred Tilson Cl M14 . . . . .98 A3
Freda Wlk M11 . . . . .160 F1
Frederica Gdns WN2 . . . . . .56 A3
Frederick Ave OL2 . . . . . . .149 B5
Frederick Ct BL4 . . . . .60 E8
Frederick Rd M6,M7 . . . . . . .81 B4
Frederick St
  Ashton-in-M WN4 . . . . . . .73 A5
  Ashton-u-L OL6 . . . . .85 E2
  Denton M34 . . . . .100 F5
  Farnworth BL4 . . . . .60 D8
  Hindley WN2 . . . . .56 D5
  Ince-in-M WN3 . . . . .151 C6
  Littleborough OL15 . . . . . .16 A6
  Manchester M3 . . . . .158 E2
  Oldham OL8 . . . . .66 D4
  Oldham OL9 . . . . .152 B8
  Ramsbottom BL0 . . . . . . .138 B3
  Wigan WN1 . . . . .151 E8
Free La BB4 . . . . .1 A6
Freehold Com Prim Sch
  OL9 . . . . .152 C5
Freehold St OL11 . . . . .139 E5
Freeholds Rd OL12 . . . . .4 E6
Freeholds Terr OL12 . . . . .4 E6
Freeland Wlk M11 . . . . . . .165 C8
Freelands M29 . . . . .59 C1
Freeman Ave OL6 . . . . .85 D3
Freeman Rd SK16 . . . . .101 C7
Freeman Sq M15 . . . . .163 A6
Freemantle St SK3 . . . . . . .170 D8
Freesia Ave 9 M28 . . . . . . .59 F3
Freestone Cl BL8 . . . . .140 D3
Freetown M14 . . . . .98 A4
Freetown Cl M14 . . . . .98 A4
Freetrade St OL11 . . . . . . .139 E4
Freiston 5 OL12 . . . . .139 F8
Fremantle Ave M18 . . . . . . .99 D3
French Ave 5 Oldham OL1 .49 C1
  Stalybridge SK15 . . . . .86 C1
French Barn La M9 . . . . . . .64 C3
French Gr BL3 . . . . .42 D5
French St Ashton-u-L OL6 . .85 D4
  Stalybridge SK15 . . . . .86 C1
Frenchwood Ct WN2 . . . . . .38 C1
Frensham Wlk M23 . . . . . .120 F4
Fresca Rd OL1 . . . . .49 D4
Fresh Ct SK13 . . . . .115 F7
Freshfield SK8 . . . . .131 B8
Freshfield Ave
  Atherton M46 . . . . .58 C4
  Bolton BL3 . . . . .147 D2
  Bolton BL3 . . . . .147 F2
  Hyde SK14 . . . . .167 D1
  Prestwich M25 . . . . .63 C6
Freshfield Cl
  Failsworth M35 . . . . .84 A6
  Romiley SK6 . . . . .114 B1
Freshfield Gr BL3 . . . . .147 F2
Freshfield Rd Hindley WN2 .56 F5
  Manchester SK4 . . . . .110 F3
  Wigan WN3 . . . . .54 E3
Freshfield Wlk 11 M11 . . .83 C2
Freshfields M26 . . . . .43 D5
Freshford Wlk 2 M22 . . . .121 B1
Freshville St M1 . . . . .163 B8
Freshwater Dr M34 . . . . . .113 B8
Freshwater St 3 M18 . . . . .99 E6
Freshwinds Ct M6 . . . . .67 D4
Fresnel Cl SK14 . . . . .102 B6
Frew Cl M9 . . . . .65 B2
Frewland Ave SK3 . . . . . . .123 F4
Freya Gr M5 . . . . .161 C8
Friar's Cl SK9 . . . . .136 E8
Friar's Rd M33 . . . . .108 B4
Friarmere Rd OL3 . . . . .50 E5
Friars Cl Altrincham WA14 .119 B1
  Tyldesley M29 . . . . .59 D1
Friars Cres OL11 . . . . .30 F2
Friars Ct M5 . . . . .80 E2
Friars Prim Sch The M3 .158 D3
Friendship Ave M18 . . . . . . .99 E4
Frieston Rd WA14 . . . . . . .119 C4
Friezland Cl SK15 . . . . .86 E6
Friezland La OL3 . . . . .69 A4
Friezland Prim Sch OL3 .68 E5
Frimley Gdns M22 . . . . . . .121 D3
Frinton Ave M40 . . . . .65 D3
Frinton Cl M33 . . . . .107 F1
Frinton Rd BL3 . . . . .146 B3
Frith Rd M20 . . . . .110 C5
Frith St WN5 . . . . .150 A7
Frobisher Cl M13 . . . . .164 D5
Frobisher Pl SK5 . . . . .169 E4
Frobisher Rd OL15 . . . . .6 C1
Frodsham Ave SK4 . . . . . . .168 C3
Frodsham Cl WN6 . . . . .36 D3
Frodsham Rd M33 . . . . . . .108 E2
Frodsham St 9 M14 . . . . . .98 B3
Frodsham Way SK9 . . . . . .131 E4
Frodsley Wlk M12 . . . . . . .164 F6
Frog La Wigan WN1,WN6 . .150 B8
  Wigan WN6 . . . . .37 A1
Frogley St BL2 . . . . .25 B3
Frogmore Ave SK14 . . . . . .113 E2
Frome Ave Stockport SK2 .124 C5
  Urmston M41 . . . . .95 B1
Frome Cl M29 . . . . .77 C6
Frome Dr M8 . . . . .156 B7

Frome St OL4 . . . . .67 C6
Frost St Manchester M4 . . .160 D1
  Oldham OL8 . . . . .66 E4
Frostlands Rd 12 M16 . . . . .97 E4
Froxmer St M18 . . . . .165 C6
Fulbeck Ave WN3 . . . . .55 A2
Fulbeck Wlk M8 . . . . .155 E5
Fulbrook Dr SK8 . . . . .132 A6
Fulbrook Way M29 . . . . . . .59 C1
Fulford St 4 M16 . . . . .97 C4
Fulham Ave M40 . . . . .83 B5
Fulham St OL4 . . . . .67 C6
Full Pot La OL11 . . . . .29 E8
Fullerton Rd SK4 . . . . .168 B2
Fulmar Cl Poynton SK12 . . .133 A4
  Westhoughton BL5 . . . . . . .57 D6
Fulmar Dr Hazel Grove SK2 .124 F5
  Sale M33 . . . . .107 C2
Fulmar Gdns OL11 . . . . . . .29 F7
Fulmards Cl SK9 . . . . .137 C2
Fulmead Wlk 16 M8 . . . . . .155 F6
Fulmer Dr M4 . . . . .159 C2
Fulmere Ct M27 . . . . .79 D6
Fulneck Sq 2 M43 . . . . . . .100 A8
Fulshaw Ave SK9 . . . . .137 A6
Fulshaw CE Prim Sch
  SK9 . . . . .136 F6
Fulshaw Cross SK9 . . . . . .137 A5
Fulshaw Ct SK9 . . . . .137 A5
Fulshaw Pk SK9 . . . . .137 A5
Fulshaw Pk S SK9 . . . . . . .137 A4
Fulshaw Wlk 7 M13 . . . . .163 B7
Fulstone Mews SK2 . . . . . .124 B6
Fulthorpe Wlk 13 M9 . . . . .64 C5
Fulton Ct M15 . . . . .163 A5
Fulwell Ave M46 . . . . .76 E8
Fulwood Ave M9 . . . . .64 F4
Fulwood Cl BL8 . . . . .26 F1
Fulwood Rd WA3 . . . . .90 E7
Furbarn La OL11 . . . . .29 D8
Furbarn Rd OL11 . . . . .29 D8
Furlong Cl WN2 . . . . .73 F7
Furlong Rd M22 . . . . .121 B3
Furnace St
  Dukinfield SK14 . . . . .101 C4
  Dukinfield SK16 . . . . .166 B2
Furness Ave Ashton-u-L OL7 84 F5
  Bolton BL2 . . . . .25 B2
  Heywood OL10 . . . . .29 C3
  Littleborough OL15 . . . . . .16 A6
  Oldham OL8 . . . . .67 C3
  Whitefield M45 . . . . .44 E1
Furness Cl Glossop SK13 . .116 F8
  Milnrow OL16 . . . . .31 E6
  Poynton SK12 . . . . .133 D4
Furness Cres WN7 . . . . .57 D1
Furness Gr SK4 . . . . .168 A1
Furness Quay M5 . . . . .161 A7
Furness Rd Bolton BL1 . . . .144 B7
  Bramhall SK8 . . . . .132 C6
  Manchester M14 . . . . .98 C1
  Middleton M24 . . . . .47 A3
  Urmston M41 . . . . .95 D3
Furness Sq BL2 . . . . .25 B2
Furnival Cl M34 . . . . .100 A2
Furnival Rd M18 . . . . .165 C5
Furnival St Leigh WN7 . . . . .75 F7
  Reddish SK5 . . . . .99 F2
Furrow Com Prim Sch
  M24 . . . . .46 D2
Further Cl OL11 . . . . .13 D1
Further Heights Rd 1
  OL12 . . . . .14 F1
Further Hey Cl OL4 . . . . . . .67 F1
Further La SK14 . . . . .102 E3
Further Pits OL11 . . . . .30 C7
Furtherwood Rd OL1 . . . . . .48 C1
Furze Ave BL5 . . . . .57 F7
Furze La OL4 . . . . .49 D1
Furze Wlk M31 . . . . .106 A3
Furzegate OL16 . . . . .31 C3
Fushia Gr M7 . . . . .155 D6
Fyfield Wlk 8 M8 . . . . .156 B6
Fylde Ave Bolton BL2 . . . . . .42 F4
  Gatley SK8 . . . . .131 C8
Fylde Ct M32 . . . . .108 C8
Fylde Rd SK4 . . . . .168 A2
Fylde St BL4 . . . . .42 D2
Fylde St E BL4 . . . . .42 D2

G

Gabbot St PR7 . . . . .21 A7
Gable Ave SK9 . . . . .137 A7
Gable Ct M34 . . . . .100 F2
Gable Dr M24 . . . . .46 E1
Gable St Bolton BL2 . . . . . .25 D5
  Manchester M11 . . . . .164 F8
  Newton-le-W WA12 . . . . . .89 B3
Gables The M33 . . . . .108 B3
Gabriel Wlk 11 M16 . . . . . .97 F3
Gabriels Terr M24 . . . . .65 C7
Gabriels The OL2 . . . . .48 F7
Gadbury Ave M46 . . . . .58 B3
Gaddum Rd
  Altrincham WA14 . . . . . . .119 B1
  Manchester M20 . . . . .110 C3
Gadwell Cl M28 . . . . .78 D8
Gail Ave SK4 . . . . .169 D2
Gail Cl
  Alderley Edge SK9 . . . . . .137 B2
  Failsworth M35 . . . . .83 E5
Gainford Ave SK8 . . . . .122 B4
Gainford Gdns M40 . . . . . . .65 B1
Gainford Rd SK5 . . . . .99 F1
Gainford Wlk BL3 . . . . .147 E4

Gainsborough Ave
  Bolton BL3 . . . . .146 C3
  Manchester M20 . . . . .110 C5
  Marple SK6 . . . . .126 B8
  Oldham OL8 . . . . .66 E4
  Stretford M32 . . . . .96 F3
Gainsborough Cl
  Wigan WN3 . . . . .54 D3
  Wilmslow SK9 . . . . .137 D8
Gainsborough Dr
  Cheadle SK8 . . . . .122 F6
  Rochdale OL11 . . . . .30 C3
Gainsborough Rd
  Chadderton OL9 . . . . .47 E1
  Droylsden M34 . . . . .84 D1
  Ramsbottom BL0 . . . . .11 B1
Gainsborough St M7 . . . . .155 E7
Gainsborough Wlk
  Denton M34 . . . . .100 E1
  1 Dukinfield SK14 . . . . . .101 F3
Gair Rd SK5 . . . . .169 F4
Gair St SK14 . . . . .167 D4
Gairloch Ave M32 . . . . .96 B2
Gaitskell Cl M12 . . . . .160 E1
Galbraith Rd M20 . . . . .110 C3
Galbraith Way OL11 . . . . . . .29 E8
Gale Dr M24 . . . . .46 D2
Gale Rd M25 . . . . .62 F3
Gale St Heywood OL10 . . . . .29 B2
  Rochdale OL12 . . . . .14 F3
Gales Terr OL11 . . . . .139 E5
Galgate Cl Bury BL8 . . . . . . .26 F1
  Manchester M15 . . . . .162 E7
Galindo St BL2 . . . . .25 C4
Galland St BL2 . . . . .67 D7
Galleria The 10 BL1 . . . . . .145 F7
Galleries The 11 M1 . . . . .150 C8
Galloway Cl Bolton BL3 . . . .40 E5
  Heywood OL10 . . . . .45 F8
Galloway Dr M27 . . . . .61 F4
Galloway Rd M27 . . . . .79 D6
Gallowsclough Rd SK15 . .102 E6
Galsworthy Ave M8 . . . . . .156 A6
Galvin Rd M9 . . . . .64 B3
Galway St OL1 . . . . .153 F6
Galway Wlk M23 . . . . .120 F2
Galwey Gr WN1 . . . . .37 C4
Gamble St WN7 . . . . .76 A5
Gambleside Cl M28 . . . . . . .78 B8
Gambrel Bank Rd OL6 . . . . .85 B6
Gambrel Gr OL6 . . . . .85 B6
Game St OL4 . . . . .67 C6
Games Wlk 8 M22 . . . . . . .121 B1
Gamesley Cty Prim Sch
  SK13 . . . . .171 E2
Gamma Wlk M11 . . . . .83 B2
Gan Eden 13 M7 . . . . .63 E1
Gandy La OL12 . . . . .14 D4
Gantley Ave WN5 . . . . .53 D3
Gantley Cres WN5 . . . . .53 D3
Gantley Rd WN5 . . . . .53 D4
Gantock Wlk 10 M14 . . . . .98 C3
Ganton Ave M45 . . . . .62 D7
Garbrook Ave M9 . . . . .64 C5
Garden Ave Droylsden M43 .84 B2
  Stretford M32 . . . . .96 D3
Garden City BL0 . . . . .11 A2
Garden Cl OL15 . . . . .15 F2
Garden La
  Altrincham WA14 . . . . . . .119 D5
  Boothstown M28 . . . . .78 A4
  Manchester M3 . . . . .158 E2
  3 Manchester M3 . . . . . .158 F1
  17 Rochdale OL12 . . . . . . .14 D2
Garden Row Heywood OL10 29 C4
  Rochdale OL12 . . . . .14 D2
Garden St 11 Bacup OL13 . .3 C8
  Bury BL8 . . . . .26 F7
  Denton M34 . . . . .100 F6
  Eccles M30 . . . . .79 E1
  Farnworth BL4 . . . . .60 E8
  Heywood OL10 . . . . .29 C2
  6 Heywood OL10 . . . . .29 D2
  Hollingworth SK14 . . . . . .103 D5
  Leigh WN7 . . . . .75 F5
  Platt Bridge WN2 . . . . .56 B2
  Rochdale OL11 . . . . .139 E7
  Stockport SK4 . . . . .169 E1
Garden Terr OL2 . . . . .48 C7
Garden Wall Cl M5 . . . . . . .161 C8
Garden Way OL15 . . . . .15 F2
Garden Wlk
  Ashton-u-L OL6 . . . . .166 C4
  3 Denton M34 . . . . .101 A2
Gardens The Bolton BL1 . . .24 F6
  Salford M30 . . . . .80 A4
Gardner Grange SK5 . . . . .112 C4
Gardner Ho 8 M30 . . . . . . .79 E2
Gardner Rd M25 . . . . .62 F4
Gardner St
  Manchester M12 . . . . .165 B6
  Salford M6 . . . . .81 A3
Garfield Ave M19 . . . . .99 B1
Garfield Cl OL11 . . . . .13 C1
Garfield Gr BL3 . . . . .145 D5
Garfield St Bolton BL3 . . . .146 C3
  Stockport SK3 . . . . .112 A2
Garforth Ave M4 . . . . .159 C2
Garforth St OL9 . . . . .152 C8
Gargrave Ave BL1 . . . . .23 F2
Gargrave St Manchester M7 80 F8
  2 Oldham OL4 . . . . .67 B6
Garland Rd M22 . . . . .121 E3
Garlick St Hyde SK14 . . . . .167 D1
  Manchester M18 . . . . .99 D5

Garlick St continued
  Oldham OL9 . . . . .153 E6
Garnant Cl M9 . . . . .157 F7
Garner Ave WA15 . . . . .108 A1
Garner Cl WA14 . . . . .119 D2
Garner Dr Eccles M30 . . . . .79 C3
  Tyldesley M29 . . . . .77 B5
Garner's La SK3 . . . . .170 E5
Garnet St OL1 . . . . .67 B8
Garnett Cl SK14 . . . . .102 F3
Garnett Rd SK14 . . . . .102 F3
Garnett St Bolton BL1 . . . . .143 E3
  Ramsbottom BL0 . . . . .138 B5
  Stockport SK1 . . . . .169 F1
Garnett Way SK14 . . . . . . .102 F3
Garnham Wlk 10 M9 . . . . . .64 E5
Garratt Way M18 . . . . .165 C5
Garrett Hall Prim Sch
  M29 . . . . .77 D7
Garrett Hall Rd M28 . . . . . .77 D7
Garrett La M28,M29 . . . . . . .77 D7
Garrett Wlk SK3 . . . . .123 C8
Garron Wlk 1 M22 . . . . . .121 A2
Garrowmore Wlk 22 M9 . .64 E3
Garsdale La BL1 . . . . .40 D7
Garside Ave WA3 . . . . .90 D7
Garside Gr Bolton BL1 . . . .142 C2
  Wigan WN3 . . . . .54 E2
Garside Hey Rd BL8 . . . . . . .27 C6
Garside St Bolton BL1 . . . . .145 E7
  Denton M34 . . . . .100 F2
  Hyde SK14 . . . . .167 E1
Garstang Ave BL2 . . . . .42 F7
Garstang Dr BL8 . . . . .26 F1
Garston Ave M46 . . . . .58 B5
Garston Cl Leigh WN7 . . . . .57 C1
  Manchester SK4 . . . . .168 C3
Garston St BL9 . . . . .141 C4
Garswood Cres WN5 . . . . . .71 E4
Garswood Cty Prim Sch
  WN4 . . . . .72 C4
Garswood Dr BL8 . . . . .27 B6
Garswood Old Rd
  WA11,WN4 . . . . .71 E1
Garswood Rd Billinge WN5 .71 F1
  Bolton BL3 . . . . .147 E2
  Garswood WA11 . . . . .72 C3
  Manchester M14 . . . . .98 A2
Garswood St WA4 . . . . .73 B3
Garswood Sta WN4 . . . . . . .72 D3
Garth Ave WA15 . . . . .119 E6
  Stockport SK2 . . . . .124 C7
  Wythenshawe M22 . . . . . .121 D4
Garth The M5 . . . . .154 D2
Garthland Rd SK7 . . . . .124 F3
Garthmere Rd M46 . . . . . . .58 F5
Garthorne Cl M16 . . . . .97 D4
Garthorp Rd M23 . . . . .108 E1
Garthwaite Ave OL8 . . . . . . .66 A4
Gartland St M8 . . . . .156 C8
Garton Dr WA3 . . . . .74 E1
Garton Wlk 12 M9 . . . . . . .64 E5
Gartside Cl Ashton-u-L OL7 .84 E1
  Delph OL3 . . . . .50 E4
  Manchester M3 . . . . .158 E1
  Oldham OL4 . . . . .67 B5
Garwick Rd BL1 . . . . .142 B3
Garwood St M15 . . . . .162 F7
Gas St Adlington PR7 . . . . . .21 A6
  Ashton-u-L OL6 . . . . .166 B3
  Bolton BL1 . . . . .145 E7
  Farnworth BL4 . . . . .60 D8
  6 Heywood OL10 . . . . .29 D2
  Hollingworth SK14 . . . . . .103 D5
  Leigh WN7 . . . . .75 F5
  Platt Bridge WN2 . . . . .56 B2
  Rochdale OL11 . . . . .139 E7
  Stockport SK4 . . . . .169 E1
Gascoyne St M14 . . . . .98 B3
Gaskell Cl OL15 . . . . .16 A4
Gaskell Cty Prim Sch
  BL1 . . . . .145 E8
Gaskell Rd
  Altrincham WA14 . . . . . . .119 D6
  Eccles M30 . . . . .79 C1
Gaskell Rise OL1 . . . . .49 E5
Gaskell St Bolton BL1 . . . . .145 D8
  26 Dukinfield SK16 . . . . . .166 B1
  Failsworth M40 . . . . .83 D6
  Hindley WN2 . . . . .56 E7
  Swinton M27 . . . . .61 F2
  Wigan WN1 . . . . .151 D8
Gaskell's Brow WN4 . . . . . .72 E5
Gaskill St OL10 . . . . .29 A2
Gaston Wlk M9 . . . . .64 D5
Gatcombe Mews 1 SK9 . .137 A6
Gatcombe Sq M14 . . . . .98 D3
Gate Ctr The SK8 . . . . .112 E6
Gate Field Cl M26 . . . . .43 E3
Gate Keeper Fold OL7 . . . . .85 A7
Gate Rd M32 . . . . .96 A3
Gate St Dukinfield SK16 . . .101 A6
  Manchester M11 . . . . .165 C8
  Rochdale OL11 . . . . .139 F5
Gate Stirrup M28 . . . . .79 A5
Gateacre Wlk M23 . . . . . . .120 E8
Gategill Gr WN5 . . . . .53 D3
Gatehead Croft OL3 . . . . . . .50 F3
Gatehead Ho OL3 . . . . .50 F3
Gatehead Mews OL3 . . . . . .50 F3
Gatehead Rd OL3 . . . . .50 F3
Gatehouse Rd M28 . . . . . . .60 A4
Gatemere Cl M28 . . . . .78 B8
Gatesgarth Rd M24 . . . . . . .46 C2

Gateshead Cl M14 . . . . .98 B4
Gateside Wlk 6 M9 . . . . . . .64 E5
Gateway Cres OL9 . . . . .65 F3
Gateway Ind Est M1 . . . . . .159 B1
Gateway Rd M18 . . . . .165 C6
Gateways The M27 . . . . .61 F1
Gathill Cl SK8 . . . . .122 F1
Gathurst La WN5,WN6 . . . . .36 A4
Gathurst Rd Orrell WN5 . . . .35 F2
  Orrell WN5 . . . . .53 E8
Gathurst St M18 . . . . .99 E6
Gathurst Sta WN5 . . . . .36 A3
Gatley Ave M14 . . . . .98 A1
Gatley Brow OL1 . . . . .153 E8
Gatley Gn SK8 . . . . .122 A5
Gatley Prim Sch SK8 . . . .122 A5
Gatley Rd Cheadle SK8 . . . .122 C5
  Sale M33 . . . . .108 A3
Gatley Sta SK8 . . . . .122 B5
Gatling Ave M12 . . . . .99 B3
Gatwick Ave M23 . . . . .121 B6
Gavel Wlk M24 . . . . .46 E1
Gavin Ave M5 . . . . .81 A1
Gawsworth Ave M20 . . . . .110 C1
Gawsworth Cl
  Altrincham M23,WA15 . . . .120 C6
  Bramhall SK7 . . . . .132 E6
  Hadfield SK13 . . . . .104 A5
  Poynton SK12 . . . . .133 F2
  Shaw OL2 . . . . .48 F7
  Stockport SK3 . . . . .170 E5
Gawsworth Mews SK8 . . . .122 B5
Gawsworth Pl M12 . . . . . . .121 F1
Gawsworth Rd
  Golborne WA3 . . . . .73 F1
  Sale M33 . . . . .108 C1
Gawsworth Way
  15 Denton M34 . . . . .101 A1
  Handforth SK9 . . . . .131 E4
Gawthorpe Cl BL9 . . . . .45 A5
Gaydon Rd M33 . . . . .107 C4
Gayford Wlk 9 M9 . . . . . . .64 E5
Gaythorn St M3,M5 . . . . . . .81 C1
Gaythorne St BL1 . . . . .143 F3
Gayton Cl WN3 . . . . .54 D3
Gayton Wlk 7 M40 . . . . . . .65 D2
Gaywood Wlk M40 . . . . . . .156 C6
Gee Cross Fold SK14 . . . . .113 E7
Gee Cross Holy Trinity
  CE Prim Sch SK14 . . . . .113 F8
Gee La Eccles M30 . . . . .79 B3
  7 Oldham OL8 . . . . .66 B2
Gee St SK3 . . . . .170 D8
Geinsbury Cl OL8 . . . . .67 B4
Gelder Clough
  Residential Cvn Pk OL10 .29 C5
Gellert Pl BL5 . . . . .57 E6
Gellert Rd BL5 . . . . .57 E6
Gellfield La OL3 . . . . .51 D1
Gemini Rd M6 . . . . .81 C4
Gencoyne Dr BL1 . . . . .24 D6
Gendre Rd BL7 . . . . .24 B4
Geneva Rd SK7 . . . . .123 E3
Geneva Terr OL11 . . . . .30 C5
Geneva Wlk
  11 Manchester M8 . . . . . .156 A6
  Oldham OL9 . . . . .152 C6
Genista Gr M7 . . . . .155 D6
Geo Hampson's Bldgs
  WA3 . . . . .92 C8
Geoff Bent Wlk M40 . . . . . .83 B5
Geoffrey St Atherton BL5 . . .58 F8
  Bury BL9 . . . . .141 A4
  Ramsbottom BL0 . . . . .11 A4
George Barton St 28 BL2 . .25 B1
George Ct 10 SK16 . . . . . .166 B1
George H Carnall
  Sports Ctr M41 . . . . .95 C4
George La SK6 . . . . .113 A4
George Leigh St M4 . . . . . .159 B2
George Mann Cl M22 . . . . .121 C1
George Rd BL0 . . . . .138 B5
George Richards Way
  WA14 . . . . .119 C2
George Sq OL1 . . . . .153 E6
George St
  Alderley Edge SK9 . . . . . .137 A3
  Altrincham WA14 . . . . . . .119 D4
  Ashton-in-M WN4 . . . . . . .73 C4
  Ashton-u-L OL6 . . . . .166 C3
  3 Atherton M46 . . . . .58 D3
  4 Bacup OL13 . . . . .3 C8
  Bury BL9 . . . . .140 F2
  Chadderton OL9 . . . . .152 A7
  Denton M34 . . . . .101 A3
  Eccles M30 . . . . .79 C1
  Failsworth M35 . . . . .83 E8
  Farnworth BL4 . . . . .60 B7
  Glossop SK13 . . . . .116 C8
  Heywood OL10 . . . . .29 B3
  Hindley WN2 . . . . .56 E5
  Horwich BL6 . . . . .22 C3
  Ince-in-M WN2 . . . . .151 F7
  Irlam M44 . . . . .94 B3
  8 Littleborough OL15 . . . .16 B5
  Littleborough OL16 . . . . . .15 D3
  Manchester M1 . . . . .163 A8
  Manchester M25 . . . . .63 B1
  Milnrow OL16 . . . . .31 E7
  Mossley OL5 . . . . .68 C1
  Newton-le-W WA12 . . . . . .89 A4
  Oldham OL1 . . . . .153 E6
  Radcliffe M26 . . . . .43 F3
  Rochdale OL16 . . . . .31 A8
  Romiley SK6 . . . . .114 B2
  Shaw OL2 . . . . .149 C8
  5 Stalybridge SK15 . . . . . .86 A2
  Stockport SK1 . . . . .112 A2

George St *continued*
Urmston M41 95 E2
Westhoughton BL5 57 F8
Whitefield M45 44 E1
Whitworth OL12 14 C8
George St E SK1 124 B8
George St N M7 155 F8
George St S M7 155 F8
George St W SK1 124 B8
George Thomas Ct M9 157 D8
George Tomlinson Sch BL4 60 E6
George's Cl SK12 133 E3
George's La BL6 22 E5
George's Rd Sale M33 108 B3
Stockport SK4 169 D2
George's Rd E SK12 133 E3
George's Rd W SK12 133 E3
George's Row 2 BB4 2 F8
George's Terr WN5 53 D5
Georges La WN1 151 F8
Georgette Dr M3 158 E3
Georgian Ct 5 Leigh WN7 76 B4
12 Tyldesley M29 58 F1
Georgian Sq 2 WN2 56 A2
Georgiana St 2 Bury BL9 140 F1
3 Farnworth BL4 42 B2
Georgina Ct BL3 146 B3
Georgina St BL3 146 B3
Gerald Ave M8 156 A8
Gerald Rd M6,M7 81 B5
Gerard St WN4 73 B3
Germain Cl M9 64 C5
Gerrard Ave WA15 120 A8
Gerrard Cl WN2 38 D2
Gerrard Rd WN5 71 E5
Gerrard St Farnworth BL4 60 E8
Leigh WN7 75 F5
Rochdale OL11 31 A2
2 Salford M6 81 A3
Stalybridge SK15 86 B1
5 Westhoughton BL5 39 E1
Gerrards Cl M44 94 A2
Gerrards Gdns SK14 113 E7
Gerrards Hollow SK14 113 D7
Gerrardswood SK14 113 D7
Gertrude Cl M5 161 A8
Gertrude St OL12 4 E6
Gervis Cl M40 157 D5
Ghyll Gr Billinge WA11 71 B1
Walkden M28 60 E2
Giants Hall Rd WN6 36 E3
Gib Fold M46 58 D4
Gib La M23 121 C8
Gibb La SK6 126 E5
Gibb Rd M28 79 B7
Gibbon Ave M22 121 D2
Gibbon St Bolton BL3 145 D5
Droylsden M11 83 A2
Gibbon's Rd WN4 72 D3
Gibbs St M3 158 D1
Gibraltar La M34 113 B8
Gibraltar St Bolton BL3 145 D6
Oldham OL4 67 D5
Gibsmere Cl M23,WA15 120 D6
Gibson Ave M18 99 F6
Gibson Gr M28 60 A3
Gibson La M28 60 A3
Gibson Pl M4 159 A3
Gibson St Bolton BL2 25 C1
Leigh WN2 56 D1
Oldham OL4 67 C6
Rochdale OL16 31 C8
Gibson Terr OL7 166 A1
Gibson Way WA14 119 C8
Gibsons Rd SK4 168 B4
Gibwood Rd M22 121 C8
Gidlow Ave Adlington PR6 21 A7
Wigan WN6 37 A2
Gidlow La WN6 37 A2
Gidlow New Hos WN6 37 A4
Gidlow St 4 Hindley WN2 56 D6
Manchester M18 99 E6
Gifford Ave M9 64 F4
Gifford Pl WN2 56 F4
Gifford Wlk SK7 124 A2
Gigg La BL9 44 F8
Gilbert Rd WA15 119 E1
Gilbert St Eccles M30 95 B8
Hindley WN2 56 D5
Manchester M15 162 E7
Ramsbottom BL0 1 C1
Salford M6 154 F1
Walkden M28 60 D1
Gilbertbank SK6 113 B4
Gilbrook Way OL16 31 B2
Gilchrist Rd M44 105 F6
Gilda Brook Rd M30 80 A2
Gilda Cres M30 80 A3
Gilda Rd M28 77 F7
Gilded Hollins Prim Sch WN7 75 C1
Gilden Wlk 11 M9 64 E5
Gildenhall M35 84 A7
Gilderdale Cl OL2 149 B8
Gilderdale St 7 BL3 42 A4
Gildersdale Dr M9 64 C6
Gildridge Rd M16 97 E1
Giles St M12 99 A4
Gilesgate 3 M14 98 C3
Gill Ave WN6 36 B6
Gill St Manchester M9 64 F1
Stockport SK1 112 B3
Gillan Rd WN6 37 B3
Gillbent Rd SK8 132 A7
Gillbrook Rd M20 110 B2
Gillbrow Cres WN1 37 F1
Gillemere Gr OL2 149 C7
Gillers Gn M28 60 C3
Gillford Ave M9 157 F8
Gilliburns Wlk BL5 57 F5
Gillingham Rd M30 79 B2
Gillingham Sq M11 164 F8
Gillwood Dr SK6 112 F1
Gilman Cl M9 64 C2
Gilman St M9 64 C2
Gilmerton Dr 22 M40 83 C5
Gilmore Dr M25 63 B5
Gilmore St SK3 170 E7
Gilmour St M24 65 A8
Gilmour Terr M9 64 F1
Gilnow Cty Prim Sch BL1 144 C6
Gilnow Gdns BL1 144 C6
Gilnow Gr BL1 145 D6
Gilnow La BL3 145 D6
Gilnow Rd BL1 144 C6
Gilpin Pl WN2 55 F2
Gilpin Rd M41 95 F2
Gilpin Wlk M24 46 E1
Gilroy St WN1 151 D8
Giltbrook Ave M40 160 D4
Gilwell Dr M23 120 F4
Gilwood Gr M24 46 F4
Gin Croft La BL0 1 E4
Gingham Brow BL6 22 E4
Gingham Ct 7 M26 44 C4
Gingham Pk M26 43 E5
Gipsy La Stockport SK2 124 C6
Stockport SK2 124 D6
Girton Ave WN4 72 F4
Girton St Bolton BL2 42 D7
Manchester M7 158 E4
Girton Wlk M40 65 D1
Girvan Ave M40 65 D2
Girvan Cl BL3 146 C3
Girvan Cres WN4 72 D4
Girvan Wlk OL10 28 F1
Gisborn Dr M6 81 A5
Gisburn Ave Bolton BL1 23 E2
Golborne WA3 73 F2
Gisburn Dr BL8 26 E3
Gisburn Rd OL11 31 A3
Gisburne Ave M40 65 D2
Gissing Wlk M9 157 D6
Givendale Dr M8 64 A2
Givvons Fold 10 OL4 49 D1
Glabyn Ave BL6 39 F8
Gladden Hey Dr WN3 54 D1
Glade Brow OL4 68 A6
Glade St BL1 144 C7
Glade The Bolton BL1 143 D1
Shevington WN6 36 B6
Stockport SK4 168 A1
Gladeside Rd M22 121 C4
Gladewood Cl SK9 137 C8
Gladstone Cl
6 Bolton BL1 143 E2
Glossop SK13 116 D8
Gladstone Cres OL11 31 A3
Gladstone Ct
Farnworth BL4 42 C1
Manchester M15 97 E4
Manchester SK4 168 B3
Gladstone Gr SK4 168 A3
Gladstone Mews SK4 169 E3
Gladstone Pl BL4 42 C1
Gladstone Rd
Altrincham WA14 119 D6
Eccles M30 79 E2
Farnworth BL4 42 D1
Urmston M41 95 E2
Gladstone St Bolton BL1 143 E2
Bury BL9 141 B3
Glossop SK13 116 D8
Hadfield SK13 104 A4
Oldham OL4 67 B6
Pendlebury M27 80 B8
Stockport SK2 124 C4
Westhoughton BL5 39 E1
Gladstone Terrace Rd OL3 69 A4
Gladville Dr SK8 123 A6
Gladwyn Ave M20 109 E4
Gladys St 3 Farnworth BL4 42 D2
Manchester M16 97 C4
Glaisdale OL4 67 D6
Glaisdale Cl
Ashton-in-M WN4 73 C3
Bolton BL2 25 B2
Glaisdale St BL2 25 B2
Glaister La BL2 25 D1
Glamis Ave Droylsden M11 83 B3
Heywood OL10 46 F8
Stretford M32 96 A2
Glamis Cl WN7 76 D6
Glamorgan Pl OL9 152 C5
Glandon Dr SK8 132 C8
Glanford Ave M9 64 A3
Glanton Wlk M40 65 D1
Glanvor Rd SK3 123 C8
Glass St BL4 60 E7
Glassbrook St WN6 37 A1
Glasscroft Cl M14 97 F2
Glasshouse St 7 M4 159 C3
Glasson Wlk OL9 152 A6
Glastonbury 28 OL12 139 E8
Glastonbury Ave
Altrincham WA15 120 B2
Bramhall SK8 132 C6
Golborne WA3 91 C8
Glastonbury Dr SK12 133 D5
Glastonbury Gdns M26 43 E5
Glastonbury Rd
Tyldesley M29 77 B7
Urmston M32 95 F3
Glaswen Gr SK5 169 F4
Glaze Wlk M45 45 C2
Glazebrook Cl OL10 29 C1
Glazebrook La WA3 105 B5
Glazebrook Sta WA3 105 B5
Glazebury CE Prim Sch WA3 92 C7
Glazebury Dr
Westhoughton BL5 39 F2
Wythenshawe M23 121 B5
Glazedale Ave OL2 48 C5
Glaziers La WA3 91 D2
Gleave St 10 Bolton BL1 145 F8
Sale M33 108 B6
Gleaves Ave BL2 26 A4
Gleaves Rd M30 79 E1
Glebe Ave WN4 73 C2
Glebe Cl WN6 19 F1
Glebe End St WN6 150 B8
Glebe House M24 47 A2
Glebe House Sch OL16 139 E6
Glebe La OL1 49 E4
Glebe Rd Standish WN6 19 F1
Urmston M41 95 D2
Glebe St
Ashton-u-L OL6 166 C3
Bolton BL2 148 A6
Hindley WN2 57 C2
Leigh WN7 75 F6
Oldham OL9 66 A3
Radcliffe M26 44 B3
Shaw OL2 149 B7
Stockport SK1 112 A1
Westhoughton BL5 39 E1
Glebeland WA3 91 E2
Glebeland Rd BL3 144 B5
Glebelands Rd
Prestwich M25 63 B5
Sale M33 108 A6
Wythenshawe M23 120 F6
Gleden St Manchester M40 160 E2
Manchester M40 160 E3
Gledhall St SK15 86 A2
Gledhill Ave M5 161 B7
Gledhill Cl OL2 32 A1
Gledhill St M20 110 B7
Gledhill Way BL7 9 A1
Glegg St WN2 151 F8
Glemsford Cl
Failsworth M40 83 B6
Wigan WN3 55 B3
Glen Ave Bolton BL3 144 B5
Kearsley BL4 61 B6
Manchester M9 64 F1
Sale M33 108 A6
Swinton M27 79 D8
Worsley M28 79 A8
Glen Bott St BL1 143 D2
Glen Cl WA3 105 B2
Glen Cres OL13 3 A8
Glen Dr WN6 35 E8
Glen Gdns OL12 14 F2
Glen Gr Middleton M24 65 C7
Royton OL2 48 D5
Glen Maye M33 108 C4
Glen Rd Oldham OL4 67 C6
Rawtenstall BB4 2 F8
Glen Rise WA15 120 A5
Glen Royd 1 OL12 14 C1
Glen St Bacup OL13 3 E8
Ramsbottom BL0 138 B7
Salford M5 161 A7
Glen The Bolton BL1 40 E7
Middleton M24 65 B6
Glen Trad Est OL4 67 D6
Glen View
Littleborough OL15 16 C7
Royton OL2 48 D5
Glenacre Gdns M18 99 E3
Glenarm Wlk M22 121 E2
Glenart M30 79 E3
Glenavon Dr Rochdale OL12 14 D3
Shaw OL2 48 F8
Glenbarry Cl M13 163 B6
Glenbarry St M12 164 D8
Glenbeck Rd M45 44 E1
Glenboro Ave BL8 27 C2
Glenborough Ave OL13 3 C8
Glenbourne Pk SK7 132 D5
Glenbranter Ave WN2 56 A8
Glenbrook Gdns BL4 42 D2
Glenbrook Hill SK13 104 C2
Glenbrook Rd M9 64 A5
Glenburn St BL3 147 D3
Glenby Ave M22 121 F3
Glencar BL5 57 D7
Glencar Dr 8 M40 65 D2
Glencastle Rd M18 99 C4
Glencoe BL2 148 B7
Glencoe Cl OL10 28 F1
Glencoe Dr Bolton BL2 42 F6
Sale M33 107 C2
Glencoe Pl OL11 139 D7
Glencoe St 3 OL8 66 C2
Glencross Ave M21 97 A2
Glendale M27 62 B2
Glendale Ave
Ashton-in-M WN4 73 C4
Manchester M19 110 F6
Whitefield BL9 44 F3
Glendale Cl
Boothstown M28 77 F7
8 Heywood OL10 29 D2
Glendale Ct OL8 66 F4
Glendale Dr BL3 40 F6
Glendale Rd
Boothstown M28 77 F7
Salford M30 80 A3
Glenden Foot OL12 14 D2
Glendene Ave
Bramhall SK7 132 D5
Droylsden M43 84 C3
Glendevon Cl Bolton BL3 40 F5
Ince-in-M WN2 56 A8
Glendevon Pl M45 63 B7
Glendinning St M6 154 E2
Glendon Cres OL6 85 B7
Glendon Ct OL1 49 E4
Glendore M5 80 C2
Glendower Dr M40 156 C5
Gleneagles BL3 40 F3
Gleneagles Ave
10 Droylsden M11 83 C2
Heywood OL10 46 D8
Gleneagles Cl
Bramhall SK7 133 A7
Wilmslow SK9 137 D8
Gleneagles Rd Gatley SK8 122 C1
Urmston M41 94 F3
Gleneagles Way BL0 138 B5
Glenfield WA14 119 B4
Glenfield Cl OL4 67 D6
Glenfield Dr SK12 133 D3
Glenfield Rd SK4 169 D4
Glenfield Sq 2 BL4 42 B2
Glenfyne Rd M6 80 D5
Glengarth OL3 69 B7
Glengarth Dr BL1,BL6 40 C6
Glenham Ct 1 M15 97 E4
Glenhaven Ave M41 95 C2
Glenholme Rd SK7 132 D7
Glenhurst Rd M19 110 E5
Glenilla Ave M28 78 E7
Glenlea Dr M20 122 B8
Glenluce Wlk BL3 40 E5
Glenmaye Gr WN2 57 A5
Glenmere Cl M25 62 F6
Glenmere Rd M20 122 C8
Glenmoor Rd 2 SK1 112 A1
Glenmore Ave
Farnworth BL3,BL4 42 A2
Manchester M20 109 E4
Glenmore Bglws SK16 101 C7
Glenmore Cl Bolton BL3 40 E5
Rochdale OL11 29 E5
Glenmore Dr
Failsworth M35 84 B8
Manchester M8 156 B7
Glenmore Gr SK16 101 C8
Glenmore Rd BL0 10 F2
Glenmore St BL9 140 E1
Glenolden St M11 83 D2
Glenpark WN7 76 B6
Glenpark Wlk 5 M9 157 E7
Glenridding Cl OL1 49 A1
Glenridge Cl BL1 143 F2
Glenroy Wlk 15 M9 64 E5
Glensdale Dr M40 65 E1
Glenshee Dr BL3 40 F5
Glenside WN6 18 B2
Glenside Ave M18 99 D3
Glenside Dr Bolton BL3 147 F2
Romiley SK6 113 B5
Wilmslow SK9 137 C6
Glenside Gdns M35 84 B7
Glenside Gr M28 60 E3
Glent View SK15 86 A4
Glenthorn Gr M33 108 B3
Glenthorn Rd M9 64 D6
Glenthorne Dr OL7 166 A4
Glenthorne St 16 BL1 143 E1
Glentress Mews BL1 144 A8
Glentrool Mews BL1 144 A7
Glenvale Cl M26 44 B3
Glenville Way M34 101 A2
Glenville Wlk 13 SK15 86 A1
Glenwood Ave 2 SK14 101 D5
Glenwood Dr
Manchester M9 157 E7
Middleton M24 47 C1
Glenwood Gr SK2 124 B4
Glenwyn Ave M9 64 E4
Globe Cl M16 162 D5
Globe Ind Est M26 44 B3
Globe La Bolton BL7 8 D3
Dukinfield SK16 101 B7
Globe Lane Ind Est SK16 101 B6
Globe Lane Prim Sch SK16 101 B6
Globe Sq SK16 101 A7
Glodwick OL4 67 B5
Glodwick Inf Sch OL4 67 B5
Glodwick Rd OL4 67 B6
Glossop Brook Rd SK13 104 B1
Glossop Central Sta SK13 104 C1
Glossop Dale Com Coll
Glossop SK13 104 C2
Hadfield SK13 104 A4
Glossop Heritage Ctr SK13 104 C1
Glossop Rd
Charlesworth SK13 115 D7
Romiley SK14,SK6 114 D3
Rowarth SK13,SK22 116 C1
Glossop Way WN2 56 F4
Gloster St 8 BL2 148 A7
Gloucester Ave
Golborne WA3 90 B8
Heywood OL10 46 C8
Horwich BL6 22 D2
Littleborough OL12 15 D4
Manchester M19 111 B8
Marple SK6 125 F6
Whitefield M45 63 A8
Gloucester Cl OL6 85 D8
Gloucester Cres WN2 56 E6
Gloucester Ct BL6 22 D2
Gloucester Dr Diggle OL3 51 C4
Sale M33 107 D4
Gloucester Pl Atherton M46 58 D4
1 Salford M6 81 A3
Gloucester Rd
Droylsden M43 84 A3
Gatley SK8 131 C7
Hyde SK14 113 E8
Middleton M24 65 B6
Poynton SK12 133 D4
Reddish M34 100 A2
Salford M6 80 C4
Urmston M41 95 D1
Wigan WN5 54 C6
Gloucester Rise SK16 102 A7
Gloucester St Atherton M46 58 D3
1 Manchester M1 162 F7
Salford M5 161 C8
Salford M6 81 A4
Stockport SK3 170 D7
Gloucester St N OL9 152 C5
Gloucester Way SK13 116 F8
Glover Ave M8 156 B6
Glover Ct M7 155 F8
Glover Field M7 155 D6
Glover St Horwich BL6 22 B4
Leigh WN7 75 C8
Newton-le-W WA12 89 C3
Glyn Ave WA15 120 A2
Glyneath Cl M11 164 F8
Glyniss Cl SK3 170 F6
Glynn Gdns M20 109 D4
Glynne St BL4 60 C8
Glynrene Dr M27 61 C1
Glynwood Pk BL4 42 C1
GMB National Coll M16 97 D2
GMex Sta M1 162 F8
Goadsby St M4 159 A2
Goats Gate Terr M45 44 D2
Godbert Ave M21 109 C5
Goddard La Hadfield SK13 104 A6
Rowarth SK22 127 E7
Goddard Rd SK13 104 A4
Goddard St OL8 66 F4
Godfrey Ave M43 83 D3
Godfrey Ermen Meml CE Prim Sch M30 95 C8
Godfrey Range M18,M34 99 F4
Godfrey Rd M6 80 C5
Godlee Dr M27 79 E7
Godley Cl M11 165 C8
Godley Ct SK14 167 F2
Godley Hill SK14 102 B2
Godley Hill Rd SK14 102 B3
Godley Prim Sch SK14 167 F3
Godley St SK14 167 F4
Godley Sta SK14 102 A3
Godmond Hall Dr M28 77 F5
Godson St OL1 48 E1
Godward Rd SK22 127 B1
Godwin St M18 99 E6
Goit Pl OL16 139 F7
Golborne (All Saints) RC Prim Sch WA3 90 B8
Golborne Ave M20 109 F7
Golborne Cty Prim Sch WA3 90 A8
Golborne Dale Rd WA12 90 A5
Golborne Ent Pk WA3 74 A1
Golborne Gallery 9 WN1 150 C8
Golborne Ho 3 BL1 145 F8
Golborne Pl WN1 151 E8
Golborne Rd
Ashton-in-M WA3,WN4 73 E4
Golborne WA3 90 C8
Golborne St WA12 89 E4
Golbourne High Sch WA3 74 C1
Golbourne St Thomas' CE Jun & Inf Sch WA3 74 B1
Gold St M1 159 A1
Goldborne Ho OL2 149 B8
Goldbourne Dr OL2 149 B8
Goldbrook Cl 2 OL10 29 E1
Goldcraft Cl 4 OL10 29 E1
Goldcrest Cl
Boothstown M28 78 B7
Wythenshawe M22 121 F5
Golden St Eccles M30 79 D1
Shaw OL2 49 E8
Goldenhill Ave M11 83 C3
Goldenways WN1 37 C2
Goldfinch Dr BL9 141 C4
Goldfinch Way M43 84 C3
Goldie Ave M22 121 F2
Goldrill Ave BL2 42 F8
Goldrill Gdns BL2 42 F8
Goldsmith Ave Oldham OL1 49 E4
Salford M5 154 D2
Goldsmith Pl WN3 55 A4
Goldsmith Rd SK5 99 E1
Goldsmith St BL3 147 D4
Goldsmith Way 8 M34 113 A7
Goldstein Rd BL6 40 B4
Goldsworthy Rd M41 94 E2
Goldwick Wlk M23 108 E1
Golf Rd Altrincham WA15 119 F3
Sale M33 108 F4
Golfview Dr M30 79 D4
Gooch Dr WA12 89 D2
Gooch St BL6 22 C2
Good Shepherd Cl OL16 31 B8
Goodacre SK14 102 B6

Gooden St OL10 ....29 E1
Goodier St
  Manchester M40 .....160 F4
  Sale M33 ....108 A4
Goodier View SK14 ....101 F5
Goodiers Dr M5 ....161 B8
Goodison Cl B3 ....45 B3
Goodlad St BL8 ....27 B4
Goodman St M9 ....64 E1
Goodrich 3 OL11 ......139 E6
Goodridge Ave M22 ...121 C1
Goodrington Rd SK9 ..131 C8
Goodshaw Rd M28 .....78 C8
Goodwill Cl M27 ....79 F7
Goodwin Ct OL9 ....66 C3
Goodwin Sq M9 ....157 D7
Goodwin St BL1 ....148 A8
Goodwood Ave Sale M23 .120 D7
  Sale M33 ....107 C4
Goodwood Cl BL3 ......42 F3
Goodwood Cres WA15 .120 C6
Goodwood Ct M7 ......155 D6
Goodwood Dr Oldham OL1 .49 B1
  Pendlebury M27 ......80 B7
Goodwood Lo 14 M16 ..97 D3
Goodwood Rd SK6 ....125 E5
Goodworth Wlk M40 ...83 B7
Goole St M11 ....165 A8
Goose Cote Hill BL7 ....8 E1
Goose Gn WA14 ......119 D4
Goose La OL12 ....139 F8
Goosetrey Cl SK9 .....131 E1
Goostrey Ave M20 ....110 A8
Gorden St 11 OL13 .....3 C8
Gordon Ave Bolton BL3 .144 C5
  Garswood WN4 ....72 E4
  Hazel Grove SK7 ....124 D3
  Manchester M19 .....111 B8
  Oldham OL4 ....67 C6
  Oldham OL9 ....66 A3
Gordon Cl WN5 ....54 E8
Gordon Pl M20 ....110 B5
Gordon Rd Eccles M30 .79 D3
  Sale M33 ....108 B6
  Swinton M27 ....79 C6
Gordon St
  14 Ashton-u-L OL6 ....85 D4
  Bury BL9 ....140 E3
  Droylsden M18 ....99 E6
  Hyde SK14 ....167 E2
  Leigh WN7 ....75 F6
  Manchester M16 ....162 D5
  Manchester M7 .....158 D4
  Newhey OL16 ....32 B3
  Oldham OL4 ....68 A6
  Oldham OL9 ....66 A5
  9 Rochdale OL11 .....31 A5
  Shaw OL2 ....149 C7
  3 Stalybridge SK15 ..86 B1
  Stockport SK4 ....169 E3
  Wigan WN1 ....151 E7
Gordon Terr 2 SK15 ...86 A2
Gordon Way OL10 ......28 F1
Gordonstoun Cres WN5 .53 F7
Gore Ave Failsworth M35 .84 B7
  Salford M5 ....154 D2
Gore Cl BL9 ....141 C1
Gore Cres M5 ....154 D3
Gore Dr M5 ....154 D3
Gore La SK9 ....136 C3
Gore St Manchester M1 .159 B1
  Manchester M3 .....158 E1
  Salford M6 ....81 A3
  Wigan WN5 ....54 B6
Gore's La WA11 ....71 A5
Gorebrook Ct M12 .....99 A4
Goredale Ave M18 .....99 E4
Goring Ave M18 ....99 D6
Gorman St Wigan WN3 ..54 F5
Gorman Wlk WN3 .....54 F5
Gorrel St 4 OL11 ......31 A5
Gorrells Way OL11 .....30 D3
Gorrels Cl OL11 ....30 D3
Gorrels Way OL11 .....30 E3
Gorse Ave Droylsden M43 .84 C2
  Marple SK6 ....125 E6
  Mossley OL5 ....68 E1
  Oldham OL8 ....67 C3
  Stretford M32 ....96 F3
Gorse Bank BL9 ......141 C3
Gorse Bank
  Com Specl Sch OL9 ..65 F5
Gorse Bank Rd WA15 .129 C7
Gorse Cres M32 ....96 F3
Gorse Dr Stretford M32 .96 F3
  Walkden M38 ....59 F6
Gorse Gr BB4 ....1 A8
Gorse Hall Cl SK16 ...101 F7
Gorse Hall Dr SK15 ....85 F1
Gorse Hall Prim Sch SK15 86 A1
Gorse Hall Rd SK16 ..101 F7
Gorse Hill Prim Sch M32 .96 E4
Gorse La M32 ....96 F3
Gorse Rd Milnrow OL16 ..32 A6
  Swinton M27 ....79 E6
  Walkden M38 ....60 E2
Gorse Sq M31 ....105 D3
Gorse St Oldham OL9 ...66 A3
  Stretford M32 ....96 E3
Gorse The WA14 .....128 B8
Gorse Way SK13 .....116 F7
Gorse Wlk WN7 ....75 B5
Gorsefield Cl M26 .....44 A4
Gorsefield Dr 1 M27 ..79 F7

Gorsefield Hey SK9 ...137 E8
Gorsefield Prim Sch M26 .44 A4
Gorselands SK8 ......132 B5
Gorses Dr WN2 ....38 C6
Gorses Mount BL2 ....148 C5
Gorses Rd BL2,BL3 ....42 D5
Gorseway SK5 ....112 B4
Gorsey Ave M22 .....121 C4
Gorsey Bank Prim Sch
  SK9 ....136 F7
Gorsey Bank Rd SK3 .123 B8
Gorsey Brow Billinge WN5 .71 E5
  Mottram-in-L SK14 ..103 A1
  Romiley SK6 ....113 A2
  Stockport SK1 ......112 A1
Gorsey Brow Cl WN5 ..71 D5
Gorsey Clough Wlk BL8 ..26 F5
Gorsey Dr M22 ......121 C4
Gorsey Hey BL5 ....57 E7
Gorsey Hill St OL10 ...29 D1
Gorsey Intakes SK14 .115 A8
Gorsey La
  Altrincham WA14 ....119 B5
  Ashton-u-L OL6 ....85 F6
  Partington WA13 ....118 B7
Gorsey Mount St SK1 .112 A1
Gorsey Rd Wilmslow SK9 .136 F8
  Wythenshawe M22 ..121 C4
Gorsey Way OL6 ....85 E6
Gorseyfields M43 ....100 A8
Gorsley Bank OL15 ....16 C7
Gorston Wlk M22 ....130 C8
Gort Cl M45 ....45 A1
Gorton Brook Fst Sch
  M12 ....165 A6
Gorton Cres M34 ....100 C2
Gorton Cross Ctr M18 ..99 D5
Gorton Fold BL6 ....22 C3
Gorton Gr M28 ....60 C5
Gorton Ind Est M18 ..165 C6
Gorton La M12,M18 ..165 B6
Gorton Mount
  Jun & Inf Schs M18 ..99 C3
Gorton Parks M18 ...165 C6
Gorton Rd
  Manchester M11,M12 .164 F7
  Reddish M34 ....99 F5
Gorton St Ashton-u-L OL7 .84 F1
  Bolton BL2 ....148 A6
  Eccles M30 ....79 B1
  Farnworth BL4 ....60 B7
  Heywood OL10 ....29 C2
  Manchester M3 .....158 F2
  Manchester M40 ....159 C4
  Oldham OL9 ....152 B6
Gorton Sta M18 ....99 D6
Gortonvilla Wlk M12 .164 F6
Gosforth Cl Bury BL8 ..27 C5
Gosforth Wlk M23 ...108 F1
Goshen La BL9 ....49 A1
Goshen Sports Ctr BL9 .45 A6
Gosling Cl 3 M16 .....97 F3
Gosport Sq M7 ......155 D5
Gosport Wlk M8 .....156 C6
Goss Hall St OL4 ......67 C6
Gotha Wlk M13,M13 .163 C6
Gotherage Cl SK6 ....113 C2
Gotherage La SK6 ....113 C2
Gothic Cl SK6 ....113 F2
Gough St Heywood OL10 .29 E2
  Stockport SK3 ......169 D1
Gould St Denton M34 .100 C3
  Manchester M4 .....159 B3
  Oldham OL1 ....67 B8
Goulden Rd M20 .....110 A5
Goulden St
  Manchester M4 .....159 B2
  Salford M6 ....154 E2
Goulder Rd M18 ....99 E3
Gourham Dr SK8 .....122 F2
Govan St M22 ....109 E1
Gowan Dr M24 ....46 D1
Gowan Rd M16 ....97 E1
Gowanlock's St BL1 ..143 E2
Gower Ave SK7 ......124 C3
Gower Rd Hyde SK14 .167 D1
  Reddish SK4 ....169 D4
Gower St Ashton-u-L OL6 .166 C3
  Bolton BL1 ....145 D8
  Farnworth BL4 ....42 C1
  Leigh WN7 ....75 E4
  Oldham OL1 ....67 A7
  Swinton M27 ....62 A1
  Wigan WN5 ....150 A7
Gowerdale Rd SK5 ...112 C5
Gowers St OL16 ....31 B8
Gowran Pk 3 OL4 .....67 D6
Gowy Cl SK9 ....131 E1
Goya Rise OL1 ....49 D4
Goyt Ave SK6 ....125 F4
Goyt Cres Bredbury SK6 .112 F3
  Stockport SK1 ......112 B3
Goyt Hey Ave WN5 ....71 E5
Goyt Rd Disley SK12 .135 D5
  Marple SK6 ....125 F4
  Stockport SK1 ......112 B3
Goyt Valley Rd SK6 ..112 F3
Goyt Valley Wlk SK6 .112 F3
Goyt Wlk M45 ....45 B2
Grace St Horwich BL6 ..22 B3
  Leigh WN7 ....75 C5
  Rochdale OL12 ....15 A2
Grace Wlk M4 ....160 D1
Gracie Ave 2 OL1 .....67 B8
Gradwell St SK3 .....170 D8
Graeme St 6 M14,M16 .97 F3
Grafton Ave M30 ......80 A4

Grafton Ct
  Manchester M15 ....162 E5
  14 Rochdale OL16 ...31 B6
Grafton Mall 5 WA14 .119 D4
Grafton St Adlington PR7 .20 F6
  Altrincham WA14 ....119 D4
  Ashton-u-L OL6 ....85 D2
  Atherton M46 ....58 A1
  5 Bolton BL1 ....145 D8
  Bury BL9 ....44 F8
  Failsworth M35 ......84 A8
  Hyde SK14 ....167 D3
  Manchester M13 ....163 B6
  Newton-le-W WA12 ...89 B3
  Oldham OL4 ....49 E4
  Rochdale OL16 ....31 B6
  Stalybridge SK15 ....86 D3
  Stockport SK4 ......169 E3
Graham Ave WN6 ......18 C2
Graham Cres M44 ....105 C3
Graham Dr SK12 .....135 C6
Graham Rd Salford M6 ..80 C4
  Stockport SK1 ......124 C8
Graham St Abram WN2 ..56 A1
  Ashton-u-L OL7 ....84 F1
  Bolton BL1 ....145 F8
  Manchester M11 ....165 A8
Grain View WN5 ......161 A8
Grainger Ave M12 .....99 A3
Grains Rd Delph OL3,OL4 .50 C4
  Shaw OL1,OL2 ....49 D7
Gralam Cl M33 ....108 C1
Grammar School Rd
  Lymm WA13 ....117 A2
  Oldham OL8 ....153 D5
Grampian Cl OL9 .....152 A5
Grampian Way
  Golborne WA3 ....74 D1
  6 Platt Bridge WN2 ..56 B2
  Shaw OL2 ....149 A8
Granada Mews M16 ...97 C1
Granada Rd M34 .....100 A3
Granada TV Ctr M3 ..158 E1
Granary La M28 ....78 F3
Granary Way M33 ...107 F2
Granby Rd Cheadle SK8 .132 B8
  Sale WA15 ....108 A1
  Stockport SK2 ......124 B5
  Stretford M32 ....96 E1
  Swinton M27 ....79 C7
Granby Row M1 ......163 A8
Granby St Bury BL8 ...26 F4
  Oldham OL9 ....66 A3
Grand Union Way M30 .95 D8
Grandale St 5 M14 ...98 C3
Grandidge St OL11 ...139 E5
Granford Cl WA14 ...119 D7
Grange Ave
  Altrincham WA15 ...120 A2
  Cheadle SK8 ....122 F3
  Denton M34 ....101 B2
  Eccles M30 ....79 D4
  Little Lever BL3 ......43 C3
  Milnrow OL16 ....31 F4
  Oldham OL8 ....66 C4
  Reddish SK4 ....111 D5
  Sale WA15 ....120 B7
  Stretford M32 ....96 D2
  Swinton M27 ....61 D2
  Urmston M41 ....94 E2
  Wigan WN3 ....150 B5
Grange Cl Golborne WA3 .90 C6
  Hyde SK14 ....167 F1
Grange Com Sec Sch
  OL9 ....153 E7
Grange Cres M41 ......95 C1
Grange Ct
  Altrincham WA14 ....119 C1
  Oldham OL8 ....66 D4
Grange Dr Eccles M30 ..79 D4
  Manchester M9 ....64 F3
Grange Gr M45 ....62 F8
Grange La Delph OL3 ...50 F6
  Manchester M20 ....110 B2
Grange Mill Wlk M40 ..83 B7
Grange Park Ave
  Ashton-u-L OL6 ....85 F6
  Cheadle SK8 ....122 D5
  Wilmslow SK9 ......137 A8
Grange Park Rd Bolton BL7 25 C7
  Cheadle SK8 ....122 D5
Grange Pl M44 ....105 E5
Grange Rd
  Altrincham WA14 ....119 C1
  Ashton-in-M WN4 ....72 F6
  Bolton BL1 ....144 B5
  Bolton BL7 ....25 C8
  Boothstown M28 .....77 E7
  Bury BL8 ....27 B2
  Eccles M30 ....79 A4
  Farnworth BL4 ....42 A1
  Leigh WN2 ....56 E1
  Manchester M21 .....97 A2
  Middleton OL11 ......47 D6
  Sale M33 ....108 A4
  Sale WA15 ....120 B7
  Stockport SK7 ......123 F3
  Urmston M41 ....95 C1
  Whitworth OL12 ......4 D3
Grange Rd N SK14 ...167 F2
Grange Rd S SK14 ...102 A1
Grange Sch M14 ......98 D3
Grange St Failsworth M35 .83 D6
  Hindley WN2 ....57 A4
  Leigh WN7 ....75 E3
  Oldham OL9 ....153 E7
  Salford M6 ....154 E2

Grange The Hyde SK14 .167 F1
  Manchester M14 ......98 C2
  5 Oldham OL1 ....67 B8
  Westhoughton BL5 ...57 D8
Grange Wlk M24 ......46 E2
Grangeforth Rd M8 ..155 F8
Grangepark Rd M9 ....65 A3
Grangethorpe Dr M19 .110 F7
Grangethorpe Rd
  Manchester M14 ......98 C2
  Urmston M41 ....95 D1
Grangeway SK9 .....131 D4
Grangewood BL7 ......25 C7
Grangewood Dr M9 ..157 D7
Granite St 4 OL1 .....67 B8
Gransden Dr M8 .....156 C6
Granshaw St M40 ....160 E3
Gransmoor Ave M11 ..99 F7
Gransmoor Rd M11,M43 .99 F7
Grant Cl M9 ....64 D2
Grant Mews WN3 .....55 A3
Grant Rd WN3 ....55 A3
Grant St Farnworth BL4 .42 B2
  Rochdale OL11 ....30 D2
Grantchester Pl BL4 .147 F1
Grantchester Way BL2 ..25 E1
Grantham Cl BL1 ....143 E1
Grantham Dr BL8 ....140 D4
Grantham Gr WN2 ....37 F2
Grantham Rd SK4 ...168 C2
Grantham St
  Manchester M14 ......98 B3
  Oldham OL4 ....67 A5
Grantley St WN4 ......73 A5
Grants La BL0 ....138 C6
Grantwood M40 ....73 A5
Granville Ave
  Manchester M16 ......97 C2
  Manchester M7 .....155 E8
Granville Cl OL9 .....152 C7
Granville Ct
  Manchester M16 ......97 C3
  Newhey OL16 ....32 B3
Granville Gdns M20 .110 A2
Granville Rd
  Altrincham WA15 ...120 C6
  Bolton BL3 ....146 C3
  Cheadle SK3,SK8 ...123 C5
  Droylsden M34 ....84 B1
  Manchester M14 ....110 C8
  Urmston M41 ....95 E3
  Wilmslow SK9 ......136 F5
Granville St Adlington PR6 .21 A7
  Ashton-u-L OL6 ....85 D2
  Eccles M30 ....79 D3
  Farnworth BL4 ....42 D2
  Haslingden BB4 ....1 A7
  1 Hindley WN2 ....56 E5
  Leigh WN7 ....75 F7
  Oldham OL1 ....48 E1
  Oldham OL9 ....152 C8
  Walkden M28 ....60 D4
Granville Terr 7 OL6 ..85 D2
Granville Wlk OL9 ...152 C8
Grasdene Ave 2 M9 ..64 E3
Grasmere Ave
  Farnworth BL4 ....59 F7
  Heywood OL10 ....46 D8
  Hindley WN2 ....56 E4
  Ince-in-M WN2 ....56 B7
  Little Lever BL3 ......43 A4
  Orrell WN5 ....53 F8
  Orrell WN8 ....53 B7
  Reddish SK4 ....111 E6
  Swinton M27 ....61 C2
  Urmston M41 ....94 E1
  Whitefield M45 ....62 C7
Grasmere Cl SK15 ....86 A4
Grasmere Cres
  Bramhall SK7 ....132 E8
  Eccles M30 ....79 B4
  High Lane SK6 ......125 E1
Grasmere Dr WN4 .....73 B5
Grasmere Gr
  Ashton-u-L OL7 .....166 A4
  Ashton-u-L OL7 ......84 F4
Grasmere Ho 5 M28 ..60 E2
Grasmere Rd
  Alderley Edge SK9 ..137 A1
  Altrincham WA15 ...120 C6
  Gatley SK8 ....122 B3
  Haslingden BB4 ....1 C8
  Oldham OL4 ....67 C7
  Partington M31 .....105 E3
  Royton OL2 ....48 D6
  Sale M33 ....108 C2
  Stretford M32 ....96 D3
  Swinton M27 ....79 F6
  Wigan WN5 ....54 C7
Grasmere St Bolton BL1 .143 F2
  Leigh WN7 ....75 E5
  Manchester M12 ......99 B3
  10 Middleton OL11 ...14 F1
Grasmere Terr WN2 ...74 B8
Grasmere Wlk M24 ...46 F2
Grason Ave SK9 .....131 C1
Grass Mead M34 ....113 B8
Grasscroft SK5 ......112 C6
Grasscroft Ind Sch OL4 .68 C5
Grasscroft Rd Hindley WN2 .57 A4
  Stalybridge SK15 ....86 A1
Grassfield Ave M7 ....81 C6
Grassholme Dr SK2 ..125 C6
Grassingham Gdns M6 .154 F3
Grassington Ave M40 ..65 A1
Grassington Ct BL8 ...26 F4
Grassington Dr BL9 ...28 D1
Grassington Pl BL2 ...25 A1

Grassland Rise M38 ...59 E4
Grassmoor Cres SK13 .171 D2
Grathie Ct BL1 ....142 B1
Grathome Wlk BL3 ..147 E3
Gratrix Ave M5 ......161 B7
Gratrix La M33 ......108 F3
Gratrix St M18 ....99 E4
Gratten Ct M28 ....60 C4
Grave Oak La WN7 ...76 B3
Gravel Bank Rd SK6 .114 B8
Gravel La Manchester M3 .158 F2
  Wilmslow SK9 ......136 E5
Gravel Wlks 4 OL4 ...67 B7
Gravenmoor Dr M7 ..155 E6
Graver La Failsworth M40 .83 D5
  Failsworth M40 ......83 E4
Graves St M26 ....43 F6
Graveyard La WA16 .136 A5
Gray Cl Aspull WN2 ...38 A2
  Mottram-in-L SK14 ..102 F3
Gray St BL1 ....145 E8
Gray St N BL1 ....145 E8
Graymar Rd M38 ......60 A4
Graymarsh Dr SK12 .133 E2
Grayrigg Wlk M9 ....157 D7
Graysands Rd WA15 .119 F3
Grayson Ave M45 .....63 B8
Grayson Rd M38 ......60 B4
Grayson Way OL3 .....69 B6
Grayson's Cl WN1 .....37 C1
Grayston Ct SK6 ....126 B7
Graythorp Wlk 8 M14 .98 B3
Graythorpe Wlk 5 M5 .81 A1
Graythwaite Rd BL1 ..23 F7
Grazing Dr M44 ....94 B3
Greame St M14 ....98 A3
Great Acre WN1 ......37 D1
Great Ancoats St
  Manchester M1 .....159 B1
  Manchester M1,M4 ..160 D8
Great Arbor Way 12 M24 .46 F1
Great Bank Rd BL5 ....39 D3
Great Bent Cl OL12 ...15 D4
Great Bridgewater St
  M1,M3 ....162 F8
Great Cheetham St E
  M7,M8 ....155 E7
Great Cheetham St W
  M6,M7 ....81 C5
Great Clowes St M7 .155 D5
Great Ducie St M3 ...158 F3
Great Eaves Rd BL0 .138 C8
Great Egerton St SK1,SK4 169 E2
Great Flatt OL12 ......14 B1
Great Gable Cl OL1 ...67 A8
Great Gates Cl OL11 ..31 A4
Great Gates Rd OL11 ..31 A3
Great George St
  Manchester M3 .....158 D2
  Rochdale OL16 .....139 F7
  Wigan WN3 ....150 B7
Great Hall Cl M26 .....44 A4
Great Heaton Cl M24 ..64 C7
Great Holme BL3 ....147 F4
Great Howarth OL12 ..15 B4
Great Jackson St M15 .162 E7
Great John St M3 ...162 E8
Great Jones St M12 ..165 A6
Great Lee OL12 ....14 D3
Great Lee Wlk OL12 ..14 D2
Great Marlborough St
  M1 ....163 A7
Great Marld Cl BL1 ...23 F2
Great Mdw OL2 ....31 F1
Great Moor Prim Sch
  SK2 ....124 B4
Great Moor St Bolton BL1 .145 F6
  Stockport SK2 ......124 B5
Great Moss Rd M29 ...77 C2
Great Newton St M40 ..83 C5
Great Norbury St SK14 .167 D2
Great Portwood St SK1 .169 F2
Great Southern St M14 .98 B3
Great Stone Cl M26 ...43 D3
Great Stone Rd
  Manchester M16,M21,M32 .97 A3
  Stretford M16,M32 ...96 F3
Great Stones Cl BL7 ...8 E2
Great Underbank SK1 .169 F1
Great Western St M14 .98 B4
Greater Manchester
  Visitor Ctr (GMex)
  M1,M2,M3 ....162 F8
Greatfield Rd M22 ...121 B4
Greave SK6 ....113 C4
Greave Ave OL11 ......30 B7
Greave Fold SK6 ....113 C4
Greave Ho OL11 ......30 B8
Greave Prim Sch SK6 .113 D4
Greave Rd SK1,SK2 ..124 C8
Greaves Ave M35 .....83 C6
Greaves Cl WN6 ......35 F8
Greaves Rd SK9 .....136 E7
Greaves St Mossley OL5 .68 C2
  Oldham OL1 ....153 F6
  2 Oldham OL4 ....67 F6
  Shaw OL2 ....149 C7
Grebe Cl Poynton SK12 .133 B4
  Wigan WN3 ....54 B4
Grebe Wlk SK5 ......125 A4
Grecian Cres BL3 ...147 F4
Grecian St BL7 ....81 C5
Grecian St N M7 ......81 C5
Grecian Terr M7 ......81 C5
Gredle Cl M41 ....95 F2
Greek St Manchester M1 .163 B7
  Stockport SK1,SK3 ..170 E8

Green Acre BL5 57 F7
Green Ave Bolton BL3 42 B3
Swinton M27 79 F7
Tyldesley M29 77 A4
Walkden M38 59 E5
Green Bank Bacup OL13 3 D8
Bolton BL2 25 E3
Farnworth BL4 42 C1
Glossop SK13 115 F7
Reddish SK4 111 D7
Green Booth Cl SK16 101 F7
Green Bridge Cl OL11 30 F4
Green Bridge N BB4 2 E7
Green Bridge S BB4 2 E7
Green Brook Cl BL9 141 A4
Green Cl Gatley SK8 122 A6
Tyldesley M46 58 E1
Green Clough OL15 16 C8
Green Common La BL5 58 E7
Green Courts WA14 119 B3
Green Croft SK6 113 E3
Green Ct WN7 75 B1
Green Dr Altrincham WA15 120 A7
Bolton BL6 40 C7
Handforth SK9 131 D2
Manchester M19 98 F1
Green End M34 113 B8
Green End Jun Sch M19 110 F5
Green End Rd M19 110 E5
Green Fold M18 99 F6
Green Fold La BL5 57 E7
Green Fold Sch BL4 59 F8
Green Gables Cl SK8 122 B1
Green Grove Bank OL16 15 D3
Green Hall Cl M46 58 F5
Green Hall Mews SK9 137 B6
Green Hayes Ave WN1 37 C3
Green Hill OL15 16 A7
Green Hill Rd SK14 102 A3
Green Hill St SK3 170 D7
Green Hill Terr SK3 170 D7
Green La
Alderley Edge SK9 136 F1
Altrincham WA15 120 B4
Ashton-u-L OL6 85 B5
Bolton BL3 42 B2
Coppull PR7 20 A8
Delph OL3 50 F4
Disley SK12 135 D4
Eccles M30 79 C2
Failsworth M35 83 F4
Glossop SK13 115 F7
Golborne WA3 75 A2
Hadfield SK14 171 F4
Hazel Grove SK7 124 D3
Heywood OL10 29 F1
High Lane SK12 134 C4
Hindley WN2 57 B4
Hollingworth SK14 103 D6
Horwich BL6 22 B5
Hyde SK14 102 A1
Hyde SK14 102 A2
Irlam M44 105 E5
Kearsley BL4 61 A7
Leigh WN7 76 C6
Manchester M18 99 D6
Manchester SK4 168 B3
Middleton M24 47 C2
Middleton M24 65 D7
Oldham OL4 50 A2
Oldham OL8 66 E2
Orrell WN5 53 D3
[1] Rochdale OL12 139 E8
Romiley SK6 113 B2
Sale M33 107 E6
Standish WN6 36 E8
Stockport SK4 168 C2
Stockport SK4 169 D1
Whitefield M45 44 F1
Wilmslow SK9 137 B7
Green La N WA15 120 B5
Green Lane High Sch
WA15 120 B3
Green Lane Ind Est
Stockport SK4 168 C1
Stockport SK4 169 D2
Green Mdw Golborne WA3 90 E5
Marple SK6 125 F7
Rochdale OL12 15 D4
Green Mdws BL5 57 D8
Green Meadows Dr SK6 125 F8
Green Meadows Wlk
M22 121 E1
Green Pastures SK4 110 E1
Green Pine Rd BL6 39 D8
Green Rd M31 105 E3
Green Royde OL11 139 E5
Green St Adlington PR6 21 B8
[3] Alderley Edge SK9 137 A1
Bolton BL1 145 F7
Bury BL8 26 F4
Bury BL8 27 B4
[6] Eccles M30 79 B1
Eccles M30 95 B8
Edenfield BL0 1 E3
Farnworth BL4 42 C1
Hyde SK14 167 E1
Manchester M14 110 E7
Middleton M24 47 B1
Oldham OL8 153 D6
[2] Platt Bridge WN2 56 B2
Radcliffe M26 44 A3
Stockport SK3 170 F6
Stretford M32 108 C8
[8] Tyldesley M29 59 A1
Tyldesley M46 58 E1
Wigan WN3 150 C7
Green The Cheadle SK8 131 F8
Green The *continued*
Glossop SK13 116 A7
Handforth SK9 131 E3
Marple SK6 126 A3
Oldham OL8 67 A3
Partington M31 105 F4
Ramsbottom BL8 10 F1
Rochdale OL11 30 C3
Sale WA15 120 C7
Stalybridge SK15 86 E4
Stockport SK4 168 C2
Swinton M27 62 B2
Wigan WN5 54 B6
Wigan WN5 54 C7
Worsley M28 78 F5
Green Tree Gdns SK6 113 B2
Green View WA13 117 B5
Green Villa Pk SK9 136 E4
Green Way Bolton BL1 25 B4
[6] Mottram-in-L SK14 102 F2
Rochdale OL11 30 B1
Green Way Cl BL1 25 B4
Green Wlk
Altrincham WA14 119 B3
Altrincham WA15 120 A7
Gatley SK8 122 A6
Manchester M16 97 C2
[7] Mottram-in-L SK14 102 F2
Partington M31 105 E3
Stretford M32 96 B2
Green Wlks M25 63 C3
Greenacre WN1 37 D1
Greenacre Cl BL0 11 E7
Greenacre La M28 78 F4
Greenacres Edgworth BL7 9 E6
Lymm WA13 117 A4
Greenacres Cl WA3 91 B8
Greenacres Ct [5] OL12 15 D4
Greenacres Dr M19 110 E4
Greenacres Prim Sch OL4 67 C7
Greenacres Rd OL4 67 D7
Greenall St WN4 73 B5
Greenbank
Abram Brow WN2 74 B7
Hadfield SK13 103 F5
Hindley WN2 57 B3
Horwich BL6 22 D1
Whitworth OL12 14 C5
Greenbank Ave
Gatley SK8 122 A5
Manchester SK4 110 E2
Orrell WN5 53 D3
Swinton M27 79 D6
Uppermill OL3 51 C1
Greenbank Cres SK6 125 F5
Greenbank Dr OL15 15 F3
Greenbank Ind Est WN2 57 B3
Greenbank Rd Bolton BL3 144 B5
Bolton BL3 146 B4
Gatley SK8 122 A6
Radcliffe M26 44 A5
Rochdale OL12 14 F2
Rochdale OL12 15 A2
Romiley SK6 114 B1
Sale M33 107 E5
Salford M6 154 E3
Greenbank Sch
Cheadle SK8 123 A1
Rochdale OL12 14 F1
Greenbank Terr
Middleton M24 47 C1
Stockport SK4 169 E2
Greenbarn Way BL6 21 D1
Greenbeech Cl SK6 125 E7
Greenbooth Rd OL11,OL12 13 D2
Greenbridge La OL3 69 B5
Greenbrook St [6] BL9 141 A4
Greenbrow Par M23 121 A4
Greenbrow Prim Sch
M23 120 F3
Greenbrow Rd M23 121 A4
Greenburn Ave WA11 71 C1
Greenburn Dr BL2 25 E2
Greencourt Dr M38 59 F3
Greencourts Bsns Pk
M22 131 A8
Greencroft Mdw OL2 48 F5
Greencroft Rd M30 79 B4
Greendale M46 58 E4
Greendale Cres WN7 76 C4
Greendale Dr M9 64 E3
Greendale Gr M34 113 B8
Greenfeld Cty Prim Sch
OL3 69 B6
Greenfield Ave
Ashton-u-L OL6 85 C6
Eccles M30 95 A8
Ince-in-M WN2 151 F7
Urmston M41 95 D2
Greenfield Cl
Altrincham WA15 120 C6
Bury BL8 27 A1
Newton-le-W WA12 89 C4
Stockport SK3 170 E6
Westhoughton BL5 40 A1
Greenfield Ct OL10 29 D1
Greenfield La
Littleborough OL16 15 D3
Rochdale OL11 31 A4
Shaw OL2 149 B6
Greenfield Prim Sch
SK14 167 E2
Greenfield Rd
Adlington PR6 21 A8
Atherton M46 58 E5
Walkden M38 60 A4
Greenfield St Denton M34 100 D7
Hadfield SK13 104 A6
Greenfield St *continued*
Hyde SK14 167 D2
Rochdale OL11 31 A4
Greenfield Sta OL3 69 A6
Greenfield View WN5 71 D4
Greenfields WN6 37 A4
Greenfields Cl WN2 56 F6
Greenfields Cres WN4 73 B4
Greenfold Ave BL4 60 B7
Greenfold Way WN7 76 A3
Greenford Cl Cheadle SK8 123 B4
Orrell WN5 53 D6
Greenford Rd M8 156 A7
Greengate
Altrincham WA15 129 D7
Hyde SK14 113 D8
Manchester M3 158 F2
Middleton OL9,M24,M40 65 C5
Greengate Cl OL12 15 D3
Greengate E M40 65 D3
Greengate Ind Pk M24 65 C5
Greengate La Bolton BL2 42 F8
Prestwich M25 63 A4
Greengate Rd M34 101 A4
Greengate St OL4 67 B6
Greengate W M3 158 E3
Greenhalgh La PR6 21 B8
Greenhalgh Moss La BL8 27 B5
Greenhalgh St
Failsworth M35 83 C6
Stockport SK4 169 E2
Greenham Rd M23 108 F2
Greenhaven WN8 53 B7
Greenhead Fold SK6 113 A1
Greenhead Wlk BL3 147 E3
Greenheigh Wlk [1] M4 159 C1
Greenhey WN5 54 B7
Greenheys Bolton BL2 25 E3
Droylsden M43 84 A2
Greenheys Bsns Ctr M15 163 A5
Greenheys Cres BL8 10 F1
Greenheys La M15 163 A5
Greenheys La W M15 162 F5
Greenheys Rd M38 59 E6
Greenhill M25 63 A4
Greenhill Ave Bolton BL3 144 B5
Farnworth BL4 60 C6
Rochdale OL12 139 E8
Sale M33 108 A6
Shaw OL2 31 E1
Greenhill Comm Sch OL4 67 A6
Greenhill Cotts OL5 68 D2
Greenhill Cres WN5 71 F5
Greenhill La BL3 40 F4
Greenhill Pas [2] OL1 67 A6
Greenhill Prim Sch BL8 26 F1
Greenhill Rd
Altrincham WA15 120 C6
Billinge WN5 71 F5
Bury BL8 27 A1
Manchester M8 156 A8
Middleton M24 65 D7
Greenhill Terr
Middleton M24 65 C7
[6] Oldham OL1 67 A6
Greenhill Wlk SK12 135 D6
Greenholm Cl M40 65 D1
Greenhow St M43 99 F8
Greenhurst Cres OL8 67 A2
Greenhurst La OL6 85 E6
Greenhurst Rd OL6 85 D7
Greenhythe Rd SK8 131 C6
Greening Rd M19 99 B2
Greenland Ave WN6 19 E1
Greenland Cl M29 77 B6
Greenland La PR6 21 D5
Greenland Rd Bolton BL3 147 F2
Farnworth BL3,BL4 42 A2
Tyldesley M29 77 B6
Greenland St
Manchester M8 155 F7
[3] Salford M6 154 E2
Greenlands Cl [3] SK8 131 E8
Greenlaw Ct M16 161 C5
Greenlea Ave M18 99 D3
Greenlea Cl WN5 53 D5
Greenleach La M28 79 A7
Greenleaf Cl M28 77 F6
Greenleas BL6 40 C6
Greenlees St OL12 139 F8
Greenmount Cl BL8 10 F2
Greenmount Ct BL1 144 A8
Greenmount Dr
Heywood OL10 46 F7
Ramsbottom BL8 10 F2
Greenmount La BL1 144 A8
Greenmount Pk BL4 61 A7
Greenmount Prim Sch
BL8 10 F2
Greenoak M26 61 C6
Greenoak Dr Sale M33 108 C1
Walkden M28 60 C5
Greenock Cl BL3 40 E5
Greenock Dr OL10 28 F1
Greenough St
Atherton M46 58 A1
Wigan WN1 151 D8
Greenpark Cl BL8 10 F1
Greenpark Rd M22 109 D1
Greenpine Ind Pk BL6 39 D7
Greenrigg Cl WN6 36 F7
Greenroyd Ave BL2 25 E2
Greens Arms Rd BB3,BL7 8 E7
Greens La Bacup OL13 3 D7
Haslingden BB4 1 C7
Greens The OL12 4 C1
Greenshall La SK12 135 F5
Greenshank Cl Leigh WN7 76 B5
Greenshank Cl *continued*
Newton-le-W WA12 89 C4
Rochdale OL11 29 F7
Greenside Eccles M28 79 A5
Farnworth BL4 42 C1
Stockport SK4 168 A1
Greenside Ave
Kearsley BL4 60 F6
Oldham OL4 49 E2
Greenside Cl
Ramsbottom BL8 10 B3
Stalybridge SK16 102 A8
Greenside Cres M43 83 F2
Greenside Ct M30 79 D3
Greenside Dr
Altrincham WA14 119 E1
Bury BL8 26 F8
Irlam M44 93 F1
Greenside La M43 83 F3
Greenside Pl M34 113 B8
Greenside Prim Sch M43 83 F2
Greenside St Ainsworth BL2 26 C1
Manchester M11 165 C8
Greenside Way M24 65 C5
Greenslate Ave WN6 35 E8
Greenslate Ct WN5 53 E3
Greenslate Rd WN5 53 E3
Greensmith Way BL5 39 E3
Greenson Dr M24 64 E7
Greenstead Ave M8 156 A8
Greenstone Ave BL6 22 B3
Greenstone Dr M6 80 F5
Greensward Cl WN6 19 B1
Greensway Ctr OL2 149 B7
Greenthorn Wlk M15 162 F5
Greenthorne Ave SK4 111 D7
Greenthorne Cl BL7 9 E7
Greenvale Rochdale OL11 29 D8
Shevington WN6 35 F4
Greenvale Dr SK8 122 C6
Greenview Dr
Rochdale OL11 30 A8
Wythenshawe M20 122 C8
Greenwatch Cl [7] M30 79 C1
Greenway
Altrincham WA14 119 A5
Ashton-in-M WN4 73 A4
Bramhall SK7 132 D6
Horwich BL6 22 F3
Hyde SK14 167 D1
Middleton M9 64 F5
Romiley SK6 113 E1
Shaw OL2 31 F1
Wilmslow SK9 137 B6
Wythenshawe M22 121 E8
Greenway Ave [10] M19 99 B1
Greenway Cl Bury BL8 27 B3
Sale M33 107 E3
Greenway Dr OL5 68 C2
Greenway Mews BL0 11 C4
Greenway Rd Gatley SK8 131 C6
Sale WA15 119 F8
Greenways
[7] Ashton-u-L OL7 85 A6
Failsworth M40 65 D1
Leigh WN7 76 B6
Orrell WN5 53 D3
Standish WN6 37 A6
Greenwich Cl
Failsworth M40 83 D4
Rochdale OL11 29 F6
Greenwood Ave
Ashton-u-L OL6 85 C6
Horwich BL6 22 D1
Stockport SK2 124 C6
Swinton M27 62 B1
Walkden M28 60 C3
Wigan WN5 54 E7
Greenwood Bsns Ctr [10]
M5 81 A1
Greenwood Cl
Altrincham WA15 120 D5
Boothstown M28 77 E7
Culcheth WA3 91 F1
Greenwood Dr
Newton-le-W WA12 89 D2
Wilmslow SK9 137 D8
Greenwood Gdns SK6 112 F3
Greenwood La BL6 22 E1
Greenwood Prim Sch M30 79 E4
Greenwood Rd
Standish WN6 19 E2
Wythenshawe M22 121 C5
Greenwood St
[1] Altrincham WA14 119 D4
Farnworth BL4 60 D8
[2] Littleborough OL15 16 B5
Oldham OL4 67 C8
Oldham OL4 67 F5
Oldham OL8 66 F1
Rochdale OL16 139 F7
Salford M6 154 F4
Salford M6 81 A4
Greenwood Vale BL1 143 E3
Greenwood Vale S [7]
BL1 143 F3
Greenwoods La BL2 25 F4
Greer St M11 165 C8
Greg Mews SK9 131 B2
Greg St SK5 111 E5
Gregge St Heywood OL10 29 E1
Heywood OL10 46 E8
Gregory Ave Atherton M46 58 C5
Bolton BL2 42 E8
Romiley SK6 113 C1
Gregory Fold BB4 1 A7
Gregory St Dukinfield SK14 101 E5
Hindley WN2 56 C6
Gregory St *continued*
Leigh WN7 75 E4
Manchester M12 164 F6
Oldham OL8 66 C3
Westhoughton BL5 57 A7
Gregory Way SK5 111 F6
Gregorys Row WA3 75 A1
Gregson Field BL3 147 E4
Gregson Rd SK5 111 E6
Gregson St [4] OL1 153 F6
Grelly Wlk [2] M14 98 C3
Grenaby Ave WN2 57 B5
Grendale Ave
Hazel Grove SK7 124 E1
Stockport SK1 112 B1
Grendale Dr M16 161 C5
Grendon Ave OL8 66 E4
Grendon St BL3 146 C3
Grendon Wlk M12 165 A6
Grenfel Cl WN3 150 A5
Grenfell Rd M20 110 B3
Grenham Ave M15 162 D6
Grenville Rd SK7 124 D3
Grenville St
Dukinfield SK16 101 C8
Stalybridge SK15 86 D4
Stockport SK3 170 D8
Gresford Cl M21 109 A8
Gresham Cl M45 62 D7
Gresham Dr OL9 152 C7
Gresham St Bolton BL1 143 F3
Denton M34 100 F4
Gresham Wlk SK4 169 E3
Gresley Ave BL6 22 B3
Gresley Cl WN1 151 E8
Gresty Ave M22 121 F1
Greswell Prim Sch M34 100 E2
Greswell St M34 100 F4
Greta Ave SK8 131 C6
Greta Wlk WN2 56 A2
Gretna Rd M46 58 A1
Greton Cl M13 98 E4
Gretton Cl OL2 48 F4
Greville St M13 98 E4
Grey Cl SK6 113 A4
Grey Knotts M28 78 A5
Grey Mare La M11 83 A1
Grey Rd Altrincham WA14 119 C5
Ashton-in-M WN4 73 A4
Grey St Ashton-u-L OL6 166 C2
Denton M34 100 D3
Manchester M12 164 E6
Middleton M24 46 F1
Prestwich M25 63 C4
Radcliffe M26 44 B3
Stalybridge SK15 86 C1
Greyfriars WN4 72 F4
Greyfriars Ct M3 158 E3
Greyfriars Rd M22 121 B2
Greyhound Dr M6 81 C5
Greylag Cres M28 78 D8
Greylands Cl M33 107 F4
Greylands Rd M20 122 C8
Greymont Rd BL9 27 F6
Greysham Ct M16 97 E2
Greystoke Ave
Altrincham WA15 120 D5
Reddish M19 99 C1
Sale M33 108 B3
Greystoke Cres M45 44 E2
Greystoke Dr
Alderley Edge SK9 137 A2
Bolton BL1 24 E6
Middleton M24 46 D2
Greystoke La M35 83 D6
Greystoke St SK1 112 A1
Greystone Ave Aspull WN2 38 C5
Manchester M21 109 F8
Greystone Wlk SK4 111 D7
Greyswood Ave [2] M8 155 F6
Greytown Cl M6 80 F5
Greywood Ave BL9 141 B2
Grid La SK6 114 F1
Grierson St BL1 143 E3
Grierson Wlk [8] M16 97 E4
Griffe La BL9 45 D4
Griffin Cl BL9 141 B4
Griffin Ct M3 158 E2
Griffin Gr M19 111 A8
Griffin Rd M35 83 D6
Griffin St M7 81 C6
Griffiths Cl M7 158 D4
Griffiths St [10] M40 83 C5
Grime St BL0 11 A4
Grimeford La BL6,PR6 21 C5
Grimes Cotts [4] OL11 13 F1
Grimes St OL12 13 F1
Grimscott Cl [7] M9 64 F1
Grimshaw Ave M35 84 A8
Grimshaw Cl SK6 113 A4
Grimshaw La
Manchester M40 160 F4
Middleton M24 65 C7
Grimshaw St
Failsworth M35 83 E8
Golborne WA3 74 A1
Stockport SK1 112 A1
Grimstead Cl M23 120 E6
Grindall Ave M40 65 B2
Grindle Gn M30 95 C8
Grindleford Gdns [19]
SK13 171 E2
Grindleford Gr [20] SK13 171 E2
Grindleford Lea [21]
SK13 171 E2

Grindleford Wlk
22 Gamesley SK13 . . . .**171** E2
Manchester M21 . . . .**109** D5
Grindley Ave M21 . . . .**109** D5
Grindlow St M13 . . . .**164** E5
Grindlow Wlk WN3 . . . . . .**54** C2
Grindon Ave M7 . . . .**81** A7
Grindrod St 1 M26 . . . .**44** A4
Grindsbrook Ave BL8,M26 . .**43** F7
Grinton Ave M13 . . . .**98** F2
Grisbeck Way 3 OL1 . . . .**153** E7
Grisdale Dr M24 . . . .**46** E2
Grisdale Rd BL3 . . . .**144** C5
Grisedale Ave OL2 . . . .**48** C8
Grisedale Ct M9 . . . .**65** A4
Grisedale Rd OL11 . . . .**30** B4
Gristlehurst La BL9,OL10 . .**29** A5
Gritley Wlk 7 M22 . . . .**121** C1
Grizebeck Cl M18 . . . .**165** C6
Grizedale Cl Bolton BL1 . . . .**23** F2
Mossley SK15 . . . .**86** F7
Grizedale Dr WN2 . . . .**56** A7
Grizedale Rd SK6 . . . .**113** B4
Groby Ct WA14 . . . .**119** C4
Groby Pl WA14 . . . .**119** D5
Groby Rd Altrincham WA14 **119** C4
Denton M34 . . . .**100** E7
Manchester M21 . . . .**109** B8
Groby Rd N M34 . . . .**100** D8
Groby St Oldham OL8 . . . . . .**67** A3
Stalybridge SK15 . . . .**86** C1
Groom St M1 . . . .**163** B7
Grosvenor Ave
3 Golborne WA3 . . . .**90** D8
5 Whitefield M45 . . . .**44** E1
Grosvenor Cl Walkden M28 .**60** C5
Wilmslow SK9 . . . .**137** A4
Grosvenor Cres SK14 . . . .**101** C1
Grosvenor Ct
9 Ashton-u-L OL7 . . . .**166** A1
Cheadle SK8 . . . .**122** D6
9 Manchester M16 . . . .**97** E3
Manchester M7 . . . .**155** D8
Sale M33 . . . .**107** F5
Grosvenor Dr
Poynton SK12 . . . .**133** D3
Walkden M28 . . . .**60** C5
Grosvenor Gdns
Manchester M7 . . . .**158** D4
Newton-le-W WA12 . . . .**89** C2
9 Stalybridge SK15 . . . .**86** A1
Wythenshawe M22 . . . . . .**121** E6
Grosvenor Ho
1 Ashton-u-L OL7 . . . .**166** A1
Manchester M16 . . . .**97** E1
8 Stalybridge SK15 . . . .**86** A1
Grosvenor House Mews
M8 . . . .**63** E7
Grosvenor Pl 6 OL7 . . . .**166** A1
Grosvenor Rd
Altrincham WA14 . . . .**119** E5
Cheadle SK8 . . . .**123** C4
Eccles M30 . . . .**79** A3
Hyde SK14 . . . .**167** D1
Leigh WN7 . . . .**75** D6
Manchester M16 . . . .**97** D2
Manchester SK4 . . . .**168** B3
Marple SK6 . . . .**125** F7
Pendlebury M27 . . . .**80** D5
Sale M33 . . . .**107** F6
Urmston M41 . . . .**95** C2
Walkden M28 . . . .**60** C5
4 Whitefield M45 . . . .**44** E1
Grosvenor Rd
Cty Prim Sch M27 . . . .**80** B7
Grosvenor Sq
Manchester M7 . . . .**158** D4
5 Oldham OL3 . . . .**69** B8
Sale M33 . . . .**108** A4
Grosvenor St
Ashton-u-L OL7 . . . .**166** A1
Ashton-u-L OL7 . . . .**84** F1
Bolton BL2 . . . .**148** A6
Bury BL9 . . . .**44** F8
Denton M34 . . . .**100** D4
Hazel Grove SK7 . . . .**124** D3
Heywood OL10 . . . .**29** C1
Hindley WN2 . . . .**56** D5
Kearsley BL4 . . . .**60** F7
Little Lever BL3 . . . .**43** B4
Manchester M1 . . . .**163** B7
Prestwich M25 . . . .**63** C4
Radcliffe M26 . . . .**43** F4
Rochdale OL11 . . . .**30** C1
6 Stalybridge SK15 . . . .**86** A1
7 Stockport SK1 . . . .**170** F8
Stretford M32 . . . .**96** D2
Swinton M27 . . . .**61** F2
3 Wigan WN5 . . . .**54** F6
Grosvenor Way
Horwich BL6 . . . .**22** C3
Oldham OL1,OL2 . . . .**48** D2
Grotton Hollow OL4 . . . . . .**68** A6
Grotton Mdws OL4 . . . .**68** B5
Grouse St OL12 . . . .**14** F1
Grove OL15 . . . .**16** C8
Grove Arc SK9 . . . .**137** A2
Grove Ave
Adlington PR6 . . . .**21** A7
Failsworth M35 . . . .**83** E5
Wilmslow SK9 . . . .**137** B7
Grove Cl M14 . . . .**98** C2
Grove Cotts OL3 . . . .**69** B1
Grove Cres PR6 . . . .**21** A7
Grove Ct M33 . . . .**108** D4

Grove Hill M28 . . . .**77** F6
Grove La Altrincham WA15 .**120** A6
Altrincham WA15 . . . .**120** B3
Bramhall SK7,SK8 . . . .**132** A6
Manchester M20 . . . .**110** B3
Standish WN6 . . . .**36** F8
Grove Pk 6 M33 . . . .**107** F4
Grove Pl WN6 . . . .**36** F8
Grove Rd
Altrincham WA15 . . . .**119** E3
Middleton M24 . . . .**47** B2
Oldham OL3 . . . .**69** B7
Orrell WN8 . . . .**53** C8
Stalybridge SK16 . . . .**86** D4
Grove St Ashton-in-M WN4 .**73** A4
Ashton-u-L OL7 . . . .**84** E5
Bolton BL1 . . . .**143** D2
Bury BL9 . . . .**141** C3
Droylsden M43 . . . .**99** F8
Farnworth BL4 . . . .**60** E8
Heywood OL10 . . . .**29** E2
Leigh WN7 . . . .**76** B4
Manchester M7 . . . .**155** E6
Oldham OL1 . . . .**67** B7
Oldham OL3 . . . .**69** B5
Rochdale OL11 . . . .**139** E5
Stalybridge SK16 . . . .**85** D1
Wilmslow SK9 . . . .**137** B7
Grove Terr OL4 . . . .**67** C8
Grove The
Appley Bridge WN6 . . . .**18** C2
Bolton BL2 . . . .**148** B5
Bramhall SK8 . . . .**132** A6
Eccles M30 . . . .**79** F1
Golborne WA3 . . . .**74** D1
Hadfield SK13 . . . .**171** F4
Ince-in-M WN2 . . . .**151** F7
Little Lever BL3 . . . .**43** B3
Sale M33 . . . .**108** B3
Shaw OL2 . . . .**149** A6
Stockport SK2 . . . .**170** E7
Uppermill OL3 . . . .**50** F1
Urmston M41 . . . .**94** F1
Grove Way SK9 . . . .**137** B7
Grovehurst M27 . . . .**79** C6
Grovewood Cl OL7 . . . .**84** E5
Grovewood Dr WN6 . . . . . .**35** E8
Grundey St SK7 . . . .**124** E2
Grundy Ave M25 . . . .**62** F2
Grundy Rd BL4 . . . .**60** E7
Grundy St Bolton BL3 . . . .**147** D4
Golborne WA3 . . . .**90** A7
Heywood OL10 . . . .**46** E8
Manchester SK4 . . . .**110** C2
Walkden M28 . . . .**60** F2
Westhoughton BL5 . . . .**39** E1
Grundy's Cl M29 . . . .**77** C5
Grundys Bldgs M29 . . . . . .**77** A8
Guardian Angel's
RC Prim Sch BL8 . . . .**27** B3
Guardian Ct M33 . . . .**108** A5
Guernsey Cl M19 . . . .**111** A6
Guest Rd M25 . . . .**63** A6
Guest St WN7 . . . .**76** B5
Guide Bridge Mills
Ind Est OL7 . . . .**100** E8
Guide Bridge Sta M34 . . . .**100** F8
Guide La M34 . . . .**100** F7
Guide Post Sq M13 . . . . . .**164** D6
Guide St M5 . . . .**80** C1
Guido St Bolton BL1 . . . . . .**143** E2
Failsworth M35 . . . .**83** E7
Guild Ave M28 . . . .**60** D2
Guild St BL7 . . . .**25** B7
Guildford Ave SK8 . . . .**132** A6
Guildford Cl SK1 . . . .**124** B7
Guildford Cres WN6 . . . . . .**36** F3
Guildford Dr OL6 . . . .**85** C7
Guildford Gr M24 . . . .**47** C3
Guildford Rd Bolton BL1 . . .**142** B2
Dukinfield SK16 . . . .**102** A7
Manchester M19 . . . .**99** B2
Salford M6 . . . .**80** B4
Urmston M41 . . . .**95** E4
Guildford St OL16 . . . .**31** A7
Guildhall Cl M15 . . . .**163** A5
Guilford Rd M30 . . . .**79** B1
Guinness Circ M17 . . . .**96** A8
Guinness Ho 2 OL16 . . . . . .**31** B6
Guinness Rd M17 . . . .**96** A8
Guinness Road Trad Est
M17 . . . .**95** F7
Guiseley Cl BL9 . . . .**27** E8
Gull Cl SK12 . . . .**133** B3
Gullane Cl M40 . . . .**83** C7
Gulvain Pl OL9 . . . .**65** F8
Gun Rd SK13,SK6 . . . .**115** C2
Gun St M4 . . . .**159** B2
Gunson Ct 18 M40 . . . .**159** C3
Gunson St M40 . . . .**159** C3
Gunters Ave BL5 . . . .**57** F6
Gurner Ave M5 . . . .**161** B7
Gurney St M4 . . . .**160** D1
Gutter La BL0 . . . .**138** B7
Guy Fawkes St M5 . . . .**161** B7
Guy St M7 . . . .**155** F7
Guywood La SK6 . . . .**113** C3
Gwelo St M11 . . . .**83** A2
Gwenbury Ave SK1 . . . . . .**112** B1
Gwendor Ave M8,M9 . . . . . .**63** F2
Gwladys St SK15 . . . .**86** E6
Gwynant Pl M20 . . . .**110** C2
Gylden Cl SK14 . . . .**102** B5
Gypsy La OL11 . . . .**30** C3
Gypsy Wlk SK2 . . . .**124** C6
Gyte's La M19 . . . .**99** C2

H

Habergham Cl M28 . . . .**78** C7
Hackberry Cl WA14 . . . .**119** B8
Hacken Bridge Rd BL3 . . . . .**42** D4
Hacken La BL3 . . . .**42** C4
Hackford Cl Bolton BL1 . . . .**144** C8
Bury BL8 . . . .**27** D5
Hacking St Bury BL9 . . . . . .**141** A2
Manchester M7 . . . .**155** E6
Prestwich M25 . . . .**63** A4
Hackle St M11 . . . .**83** C2
Hackleton Cl M4 . . . .**160** D1
Hackness Rd M21 . . . .**108** F3
Hackney Ave M40 . . . .**83** C4
Hackney Cl M26 . . . .**44** A5
Hackwood Wlk 16 M8 . . . . .**155** F7
Hackworth Cl WN1 . . . .**151** E8
Hadbutt La M29 . . . .**76** F4
Haddan Gn 31 SK13 . . . . . .**171** D2
Haddan Lea 30 SK13 . . . . . .**171** D2
Haddington Dr M9 . . . .**64** E3
Haddon Ave M40 . . . .**65** F1
Haddon Cl
Alderley Edge SK9 . . . .**136** F2
High Lane SK6 . . . .**134** E6
Whitefield BL9 . . . .**45** A5
Haddon Gr
Altrincham WA15 . . . .**119** F7
Reddish SK5 . . . .**111** E7
Sale M33 . . . .**108** A4
Haddon Hall Rd M43 . . . .**83** E2
Haddon Ho M5 . . . .**154** D3
Haddon Mews SK13 . . . . . .**171** D2
Haddon Rd Eccles M30 . . . . .**95** D8
Gatley M33 . . . .**131** C7
Golborne WA3 . . . .**74** D2
Hazel Grove SK7 . . . .**124** E1
Manchester M21 . . . .**109** D5
Swinton M28 . . . .**79** C6
Wigan WN3 . . . .**54** E3
Haddon St
5 Ashton-in-M WN4 . . . .**72** F5
Rochdale OL11 . . . .**30** C1
Salford M6 . . . .**81** B5
Stretford M32 . . . .**96** D4
Haddon Way
17 Denton M34 . . . .**101** A1
Shaw OL2 . . . .**149** C6
Hadfield Ave OL6 . . . .**66** B4
Hadfield Cres OL6 . . . .**85** E5
Hadfield Cty Inf Sch
SK13 . . . .**103** F5
Hadfield Ind Est SK13 . . . .**103** F6
Hadfield Pl SK13 . . . .**116** C8
Hadfield Rd SK14 . . . .**171** F4
Hadfield Sq SK13 . . . .**116** C8
Hadfield St
Dukinfield SK16 . . . .**101** A7
Glossop SK13 . . . .**116** C8
Manchester M16 . . . .**161** C6
Manchester M7 . . . .**155** E6
Oldham OL8 . . . .**66** F7
Hadfield St Andrew's
CE Jun Sch SK14 . . . .**171** F4
Hadfield Sta SK13 . . . .**104** A5
Hadfields Ave SK14 . . . . . .**103** D5
Hadleigh Cl BL1 . . . .**25** A6
Hadley Ave M13 . . . .**98** E2
Hadley Cl SK8 . . . .**122** F1
Hadley St M6 . . . .**81** B5
Hadlow Gn SK5 . . . .**112** B6
Hadlow Wlk M40 . . . .**160** E3
Hadrian Ho M1 . . . .**153** F7
Hadwin St BL1 . . . .**143** F1
Hafton Rd M7 . . . .**81** B6
Hag Bank La SK12 . . . .**135** C2
Hag Fold Sta M46 . . . .**58** C5
Haggate OL2 . . . .**48** C3
Haggate Cres OL2 . . . .**48** C3
Hagley Rd M5 . . . .**161** A6
Hags The BL9 . . . .**45** A5
Hague Bar Prim Sch
SK22 . . . .**135** E8
Hague Bar Rd SK22 . . . . . .**135** F8
Hague Bush Cl WA3 . . . .**74** E1
Hague Ct 5 M20 . . . .**110** A5
Hague Fold Rd SK22 . . . . . .**135** F8
Hague Ho OL8 . . . .**153** F5
Hague Pl 3 SK15 . . . .**86** A2
Hague Rd Manchester M20 .**110** A5
Mottram-in-L SK13,SK14 . . .**103** B1
Hague St Ashton-u-L OL6 . . . .**85** D4
Glossop SK13 . . . .**116** D6
Manchester M10,M40 . . . . .**157** F5
Oldham OL4 . . . .**67** E8
Haig Ave M44 . . . .**105** C4
Haig Ct BL8 . . . .**27** B1
Haig Rd Aspull WN2 . . . .**38** B7
Bury BL8 . . . .**27** B1
Stretford M32 . . . .**96** D3
Haig St WN3 . . . .**150** B7
Haigh Ave SK4 . . . .**111** E5
Haigh Ctry Pk WN2 . . . .**37** F5
Haigh Hall BL0 . . . .**11** B4
Haigh La M24,OL9 . . . .**47** E1
Haigh Lawn WA14 . . . .**119** B3
Haigh Pk SK4 . . . .**111** E5
Haigh Rd WN2 . . . .**38** C5
Haigh St Bolton BL1 . . . . . .**145** F8
Rochdale OL11 . . . .**31** A6
Haigh View
Ince-in-M WN3 . . . .**151** E6
Wigan WN1 . . . .**37** D2
Hail St BL0 . . . .**11** A4
Haile Dr M28 . . . .**77** F6
Hailsham Cl BL8 . . . .**27** C7

Hailsham St M11 . . . .**160** F2
Hailwood St OL11 . . . .**30** E4
Halcyon Cl 6 OL12 . . . .**14** B2
Haldene Wlk M8 . . . .**155** F6
Haldon Rd M20 . . . .**110** D5
Hale Ave SK12 . . . .**133** D2
Hale Cl WN7 . . . .**76** B2
Hale Ct WA14 . . . .**119** D2
Hale Gr WA14 . . . .**72** F5
Hale Green Ct WA15 . . . . . .**120** A3
Hale La M35,M40 . . . .**83** E8
Hale Low Rd WA15 . . . .**119** F3
Hale Rd
Altrincham WA15,WA14 . . .**120** B1
Manchester SK4 . . . .**168** C3
Hale Prep Sch WA15 . . . . .**119** E3
Hale Sta WA14 . . . .**119** D2
Hale Wlk SK8 . . . .**123** A5
Halebank Ave M20 . . . .**109** F7
Hales Cl M43 . . . .**83** F3
Halesden Rd SK4 . . . .**111** D5
Halesfield WN2 . . . .**57** B2
Halesworth Wlk M40 . . . . . .**159** C4
Halewood Ave WA3 . . . .**73** F1
Haley Cl 6 SK5 . . . .**111** F8
Haley St M8 . . . .**156** B7
Half Acre M26 . . . .**43** F6
Half Acre Dr OL11 . . . .**30** B6
Half Acre La Blackrod BL6 . . .**21** C2
Rochdale OL11 . . . .**30** B6
Half Acre Mews OL11 . . . . . .**30** B6
Half Acre Rd OL11 . . . .**30** B6
Half Edge La M30 . . . .**79** F3
Half Moon La SK2 . . . .**124** E6
Half St Manchester M3 . . . .**158** E3
Middleton M24 . . . .**46** F1
Halfacre Rd M22 . . . .**121** C4
Halford Dr M40 . . . .**83** C8
Halfpenny Bridge Ind Est
OL11 . . . .**31** A6
Halifax Rd
Littleborough OL12 . . . .**15** C3
Littleborough OL15 . . . .**16** D7
Halifax St OL6 . . . .**166** B4
Haliwell St OL15 . . . .**16** C5
Hall Ave Altrincham WA15 .**119** F7
Manchester M14 . . . .**98** D3
Sale M33 . . . .**107** E6
Stalybridge SK15 . . . .**86** C5
Hall Bank M30 . . . .**79** C2
Hall Cl Mottram-in-L SK14 . .**103** A5
Shevington WN6 . . . .**36** B6
Hall Coppice The BL7 . . . . . .**8** E1
Hall Dr Middleton M24 . . . . . .**64** F7
Mottram-in-L SK14 . . . .**103** A5
Hall Farm Ave M41 . . . .**95** B3
Hall Farm Cl SK7 . . . .**125** A3
Hall Fold OL12 . . . .**14** C8
Hall Gdns OL12 . . . .**14** C2
Hall Gn WN8 . . . .**53** B7
Hall Gr Cheadle SK8 . . . . . .**122** C6
Manchester M14 . . . .**98** D3
Hall Green Cl
Dukinfield SK16 . . . .**166** C1
Orrell WN8 . . . .**53** B7
Hall Green Rd SK16 . . . . . .**166** C1
Hall House La WN7 . . . .**76** C4
Hall i' th' Wood La
Bolton BL1 . . . .**25** A4
Bolton BL1,BL2 . . . .**25** B3
Hall i'th'Wood (Mus) BL1 . .**25** A4
Hall La Appley Bridge WN6 . .**18** D2
Bolton BL3,BL4 . . . .**42** E3
Farnworth BL4 . . . .**42** D2
Horwich BL6 . . . .**39** E7
Orrell WN5 . . . .**53** F4
Partington M31 . . . .**105** F4
Pennington Green WN2 . . . . .**38** D2
Romiley SK6 . . . .**113** B6
Wigan WN1 . . . .**37** D4
Wigan WN3,WN5 . . . .**54** A4
Wythenshawe M23 . . . . . .**121** B6
Hall Lane Gr WN2 . . . .**56** D8
Hall Lee Dr BL5 . . . .**40** A1
Hall Mdw SK8 . . . .**122** E1
Hall Moss La SK7 . . . .**132** C4
Hall Moss Rd M9 . . . .**65** A3
Hall Pool Dr SK2 . . . .**124** E7
Hall Rd Altrincham WA14 . . .**119** C7
Ashton-u-L OL6 . . . .**85** C5
Bramhall SK7 . . . .**123** D1
Handforth SK9 . . . .**131** E3
Manchester M14 . . . .**98** D3
Wilmslow SK9 . . . .**137** A7
Hall St Ashton-in-M WN2 . . . .**73** E7
Ashton-u-L OL6 . . . .**85** E2
Bury BL8 . . . .**26** E4
Bury BL8 . . . .**27** C4
Cheadle SK8 . . . .**122** D6
Denton M34 . . . .**101** B3
Failsworth M35 . . . .**83** D6
1 Farnworth BL4 . . . .**42** D2
Heywood OL10 . . . .**29** E1
Ince-in-M WN2 . . . .**151** F8
Manchester M1,M2 . . . . . .**162** F8
Middleton M24 . . . .**65** A8
3 Oldham OL4 . . . .**67** B7
Radcliffe M26 . . . .**43** F6
Ramsbottom BL9 . . . .**11** C2
Royton OL2 . . . .**48** D4
Stockport SK1 . . . .**112** A1
Swinton M27 . . . .**61** F2
Whitworth OL12 . . . .**14** B8
Whitworth OL12 . . . .**14** C8
Wigan WN1 . . . .**151** D7
Hall Wood Ave WA11 . . . . . .**72** F1

Hall's Ct 3 SK13 . . . .**104** C1
Hallam Rd M40 . . . .**83** B5
Stockport SK2 . . . .**124** A6
Hallas Gr M23 . . . .**109** B1
Hallbottom St SK14 . . . .**101** F5
Hallbridge Gdns WN8 . . . . . .**53** B8
Hallcroft M31 . . . .**105** F4
Hallcroft Gdns OL16 . . . .**31** E6
Hallgate Westhoughton BL5 . .**57** E5
Wigan WN1 . . . .**150** C8
Hallgate Dr SK8 . . . .**122** A2
Hallgate Rd SK1 . . . .**124** B8
Halliday Ct 4 OL15 . . . .**15** E4
Halliday Rd M40 . . . .**83** B4
Halliford Rd M40 . . . .**83** A6
Hallington Cl BL3 . . . .**145** E5
Halliwell Ave OL8 . . . .**66** E3
Halliwell Ind Est BL1 . . . . .**143** D3
Halliwell La M8 . . . .**155** F7
Halliwell Rd Bolton BL1 . . . .**143** D2
Manchester M25 . . . .**62** F1
Halliwell St 14 Bolton BL1 . .**143** D2
Milnrow OL16 . . . .**31** E7
Oldham OL9 . . . .**66** A2
5 Rochdale OL12 . . . .**139** E8
Halliwell St W 17 M8 . . . . . .**155** F7
Halliwell Wlk M25 . . . .**62** F1
Hallkirk Wlk 4 M40 . . . .**65** D2
Hallows Ave M21 . . . .**109** C5
Hallows Farm Ave OL12 . . . .**14** D2
Hallroyd Brow OL1 . . . .**153** E8
Hallstead Ave M38 . . . .**59** E4
Hallstead Gr M38 . . . .**59** E4
Hallsville Rd M19 . . . .**99** C1
Hallsworth Rd M30 . . . .**79** A1
Hallwood Ave M6 . . . .**80** C5
Hallwood Rd
Wilmslow SK9 . . . .**131** D2
Wythenshawe M23 . . . . . .**121** A6
Hallworth Ave M34 . . . .**84** C1
Hallworth Rd M8 . . . .**156** B8
Hallworthy Cl WN7 . . . .**75** B1
Halmore Rd M40 . . . .**160** D2
Halsall Cl BL9 . . . .**27** F6
Halsall Dr BL3 . . . .**147** A3
Halsbury Cl M12 . . . .**164** E6
Halset Wlk SK7 . . . .**124** A2
Halsey Cl OL9 . . . .**65** E2
Halsey Wlk 19 M8 . . . .**155** F7
Halshaw La BL4 . . . .**60** F7
Halsmere Dr M9 . . . .**64** D3
Halstead Ave
Manchester M21 . . . .**109** A4
Salford M6 . . . .**80** E5
Halstead Dr M44 . . . .**94** B1
Halstead Gr Leigh WN7 . . . . .**76** B5
Wythenshawe SK8 . . . .**121** F5
Halstead St Bolton BL2 . . . .**148** A7
Bury BL9 . . . .**141** A4
Halstead Wlk BL9 . . . .**28** A5
Halstock Wlk M40 . . . .**157** D5
Halston Cl SK5 . . . .**169** F4
Halston St M15 . . . .**162** E6
Halstone Ave SK9 . . . .**136** E4
Halter Cl M26 . . . .**44** A5
Halton 12 OL10 . . . .**29** C2
Halton Bank M6 . . . .**154** F4
Halton Dr WA15 . . . .**108** B1
Halton Ho 4 M5 . . . .**154** F1
Halton Rd M11 . . . .**83** C2
Halton St Bolton BL2 . . . . . .**148** B7
Hyde SK14 . . . .**167** F3
Halvard Ave BL9 . . . .**27** F6
Halvard Ct BL9 . . . .**27** F6
Halvis Gr M16 . . . .**97** B3
Hambledon Cl BL3 . . . .**40** F5
Hambledon Cl M46 . . . .**58** C5
Hambleton Cl BL8 . . . .**26** F1
Hambleton Dr Sale M33 . . . .**107** C6
Wythenshawe M23 . . . . . .**121** A4
Hambleton Rd SK8 . . . .**131** C8
Hamblett St WN7 . . . .**75** B5
Hambridge Cl M8 . . . .**156** A7
Dukinfield SK14 . . . .**101** F5
Hamel St Bolton BL3 . . . . . .**147** E3
Dukinfield SK14 . . . .**101** F5
Hamer Cl OL7 . . . .**166** A1
Hamer Com Prim Sch
OL16 . . . .**15** B2
Hamer Dr M16 . . . .**162** D5
Hamer Hall Cres OL12 . . . . .**15** B1
Hamer Hill M9 . . . .**64** C3
Hamer La OL16 . . . .**15** B1
Hamer St Bolton BL2 . . . . . .**25** B1
Heywood OL10 . . . .**29** B2
Radcliffe M26 . . . .**44** C4
Ramsbottom BL0 . . . .**11** B2
Royton OL2 . . . .**48** B3
Hamer's Bldg OL10 . . . .**29** B2
Hamerton Rd M40 . . . .**159** C4
Hamilcar Ave M30 . . . .**79** E2
Hamilton Ave Eccles M30 . . .**79** E1
Irlam M44 . . . .**105** D4
Royton OL2 . . . .**48** B3
Hamilton Cl Bury BL8 . . . . . .**27** B3
Prestwich M25 . . . .**63** A3
Hamilton Cres SK4 . . . .**168** B3
Hamilton Ct Little Lever BL3 .**43** B3
Wigan WN5 . . . .**54** E8
Hamilton Gr M16 . . . .**162** D5
Hamilton Lo 6 M14 . . . .**98** C3
Hamilton Mews M30 . . . .**79** B3
Hamilton Rd
Garswood WN4 . . . .**72** C4
Hindley WN2 . . . .**56** F4
Manchester M13 . . . .**98** F3
Prestwich M25 . . . .**63** A3
Tyldesley M29 . . . .**77** D6

Hamilton Rd *continued*
Whitefield M45 .....62 E8
Hamilton Sq
Stockport SK4 .....169 E3
Wigan WN5 .....54 E8
Hamilton St Ashton-u-L OL7 .84 F1
Atherton M46 .....58 C2
Bolton BL1 .....24 E5
Bury BL9 .....140 F4
Chadderton OL9 .....152 A7
Eccles M30 .....79 B3
Leigh WN7 .....75 D6
Manchester M16 .....162 D5
Manchester M7 .....155 D7
Oldham OL4 .....67 B7
Stalybridge SK15 .....85 F2
Swinton M27 .....61 D1
Hamilton Way OL10 .....28 E1
Hamlet Dr M33 .....107 E6
Hamlet The BL6 .....40 B8
Hammer Terr BL9 .....11 C3
Hammerstone Rd M18 ..165 C6
Hammett Rd M21 .....109 A8
Hammond 13 OL10 .....29 C2
Hammond Ave Bacup OL13 ..3 D8
Reddish SK4 .....111 E5
Hamnet Cl BL1 .....25 A5
Hamnett St
Droylsden M11,M43 .....83 D1
Hyde SK14 .....167 D3
Hamon Rd WA15 .....119 E4
Hampden Cres M18 .....165 C5
Hampden Gr M30 .....79 D2
Hampden Pl WN5 .....36 D1
Hampden Rd
Prestwich M25 .....63 C4
Sale M33 .....108 A3
Shaw OL2 .....49 D6
Hampden St Heywood OL10 29 D1
Rochdale OL11 .....139 F6
Hampshire Cl
Brinnington SK5 .....112 C5
Bury BL9 .....45 A8
Glossop SK13 .....116 F8
Hampshire Ho SK5 .....112 C5
Hampshire Rd
Brinnington SK5 .....112 C5
Droylsden M43 .....84 A3
Oldham OL9 .....152 B5
Partington M31 .....105 D2
Hampshire St M7 .....155 E7
Hampshire Wlk 6 M8 ...156 B6
Hampson Ave WA3 .....91 F3
Hampson Cl
Ashton-in-M WN4 .....73 B2
5 Eccles M30 .....79 B1
Hampson Cres SK9 .....131 C4
Hampson Fold M26 .....43 F4
Hampson Mill La BL9 .....44 F5
Hampson Pl OL6 .....85 E6
Hampson Rd
Ashton-u-L OL6 .....85 E6
Stretford M32 .....96 C2
Hampson Sq 5 M26 .....44 A4
Hampson St Atherton M46 .58 C3
Droylsden M43 .....84 A2
Eccles M30 .....79 B1
Horwich BL6 .....22 B4
Manchester M3,M5 .....158 D1
Manchester M40 .....160 D4
Radcliffe M26 .....44 A3
Sale M33 .....108 D4
Stockport SK1 .....124 B8
Swinton M27 .....62 A1
Hampstead Ave M41 .....94 E1
Hampstead Dr SK2 .....124 C5
Hampstead La SK2 .....124 C5
Hampstead Rd WN6 .....19 D1
Hampton Gr Bury BL9 .....27 F6
Cheadle SK8 .....122 E2
Leigh WN7 .....76 E7
Sale WA14 .....107 F1
Hampton Mews 1 SK3 ...123 F4
Hampton Rd Bolton BL3 ...42 A3
Failsworth M35 .....84 B8
Irlam M44 .....105 D4
Stretford M21 .....96 F1
Urmston M41 .....95 D2
Hampton St OL8 .....66 D4
Hamsell Rd M13 .....163 C7
Hanborough Ct M29 .....76 F8
Hancock Cl M14 .....98 B3
Hancock St M32 .....108 D8
Hand La WN7 .....75 E1
Handel Ave M41 .....95 A2
Handel Mews M33 .....108 C4
Handel St Bolton BL1 .....143 D3
Whitworth OL12 .....14 B8
Handford Ho 5 M41 .....95 E2
Handforth Gr M13 .....98 E2
Handforth Hall Cty Prim Sch SK9 .....131 D4
Handforth Rd
Handforth SK9 .....131 E1
Reddish SK5 .....111 F5
Handforth Sta SK9 .....131 D3
Handley Ave M14 .....98 B1
Handley Cl SK3 .....123 C5
Handley Rd SK7 .....123 E3
Handley St Bury BL9 .....44 F8
Rochdale OL12 .....139 D8
Hands La OL11 .....30 A7
Handsworth St M12 .....164 D7
Hanging Birch M24 .....64 B7
Hanging Chadder La OL2 .48 C7
Hanging Ditch M4 .....158 F2
Hanging Lees Cl OL16 .....32 C4
Hani Ct M8 .....63 F1
Hankinson Cl M31 .....105 E2
Hankinson Way M6 .....81 A3
Hanley Cl Disley SK12 .....135 D5
Middleton M24 .....65 A5
Hanlith Mews M19 .....110 F8
Hanlon St Manchester M8 .156 A8
Manchester M8 .....63 F1
Hanmer St WN2 .....56 D5
Hannah Baldwin Cl M11 .164 F8
Hannah Lo M20 .....110 A4
Hannah St M12 .....99 A2
Hannerton Rd OL2 .....49 D7
Hannesburg Gdns M23 ..120 F4
Hannet Rd M22 .....121 D2
Hanover Bsns Pk WA14 ..119 B7
Hanover Cres M14 .....98 D4
Hanover Ct Bolton BL3 ...144 B5
Manchester M7 .....155 D7
Swinton M28 .....79 B6
Hanover Gdns M7 .....155 E8
Hanover Ho Bolton BL3 ...146 B2
10 Manchester M14 .....110 D8
Oldham OL8 .....153 D6
Hanover Rd
Altrincham WA14 .....119 B7
Hindley WN2 .....56 C6
Hanover St Bolton BL1 .....145 E7
Leigh WN7 .....76 A6
Littleborough OL15 .....16 A5
Manchester M4 .....159 A2
Mossley OL5 .....68 C1
Rochdale OL11 .....30 C2
Stalybridge SK15 .....85 F2
Hanover St N M34 .....100 E8
Hanover St S 4 M34 .....100 E8
Hanover Towers SK5 .....169 F3
Hansdon Cl M8 .....156 A6
Hansen Wlk 3 M22 .....121 C2
Hansham Wlk M23 .....108 E1
Hanslope Wlk 14 M9 .....157 E8
Hanson Cl M24 .....47 A1
Hanson Mews SK1 .....112 B2
Hanson Rd M40 .....83 B7
Hanson St Bury BL9 .....140 F4
Middleton M24 .....47 A1
Oldham OL4 .....67 C7
Hanstock Cl WN5 .....53 E5
Hanwell Cl WN7 .....75 E1
Hanworth Cl M13 .....163 B7
Hapsford Wlk M40 .....83 A5
Hapton Ave M32 .....96 D1
Hapton Pl SK4 .....169 E3
Hapton St M19 .....99 A1
Harbern Cl M30 .....79 D4
Harbern Dr WN7 .....57 D2
Harbord St M24 .....65 A8
Harboro Ct M33 .....107 F3
Harboro Gr M33 .....107 F4
Harboro Rd M33 .....107 E4
Harboro Way M33 .....107 F4
Harbour City Sta M5 .....96 F8
Harbour Farm Rd SK14 ..101 E5
Harbour La Edgworth BL7 ...9 D5
Milnrow OL16 .....31 F5
Harbour La N OL16 .....31 F6
Harbourne Ave M28 .....78 C8
Harbourne Cl M28 .....78 C8
Harburn Wlk M22 .....130 E8
Harbury Cl WN6 .....36 F2
Harbury Cres M22 .....121 C5
Harbury Wlk WN6 .....36 F2
Harcles Dr BL0 .....11 B2
Harcombe Rd M20 .....110 C6
Harcourt Ave M41 .....95 F1
Harcourt Cl M41 .....95 F1
Harcourt Ind Ctr M28 .....60 D5
Harcourt Mews 10 BL6 .....22 B4
Harcourt Rd
Altrincham WA14 .....119 D6
Sale M33 .....108 A6
Harcourt St Oldham OL1 ...67 B8
Reddish SK5 .....111 F8
Stretford M32 .....96 E3
Walkden M28 .....60 D5
Hard La OL12 .....15 A8
Hardacre St WN3 .....151 D6
Hardberry Pl SK2 .....124 E6
Hardcastle Ave M21 .....109 C6
Hardcastle Cl BL2 .....25 C6
Hardcastle Gdns BL2 .....25 C6
Hardcastle Rd SK3 .....170 D7
Hardcastle St Bolton BL1 .143 F2
Oldham OL1 .....153 F7
7 Oldham OL1 .....67 A7
Harden Dr BL2 .....25 D2
Harden Hills OL2 .....49 D8
Harden Pk SK9 .....137 A3
Hardfield Rd M24 .....65 B5
Hardfield St OL10 .....29 D2
Hardicker St M19 .....111 B7
Hardie Ave BL4 .....60 B7
Harding St Adlington PR6 ...21 B8
Dukinfield SK14 .....101 D5
Manchester M3 .....158 F2
Manchester M4 .....160 D1
Salford M6 .....81 A4
Stockport SK1 .....112 B1
Hardman Ave
Manchester M25 .....63 D2
Rawtenstall BB4 .....2 A8
Romiley SK6 .....113 A3
Hardman Cl Radcliffe M26 ..43 F6
Rawtenstall BB4 .....2 F7
Hardman Dr BB4 .....2 F7
Hardman Fold BL3 .....42 B2
Hardman Fold Sch M35 .....83 D7
Hardman La M35 .....83 E8
Hardman Rd SK5 .....111 F8
Hardman St Bury BL9 .....140 F4
Failsworth M35 .....83 D7
Farnworth BL4 .....60 E7
Heywood OL10 .....29 D2
Manchester M3 .....158 E1
Milnrow OL16 .....32 A5
Oldham OL9 .....66 B3
Radcliffe M26 .....43 F6
Stockport SK3 .....169 D1
Stockport SK3 .....170 D8
Wigan WN3 .....150 B6
Hardman Terr OL13 .....3 D8
Hardman's La BL7 .....24 F8
Hardman's Mews M45 .....62 F6
Hardman's Rd M45 .....62 F6
Hardmans BL7 .....24 F7
Hardon Gr M13 .....98 F2
Hardrow Cl WN3 .....55 B2
Hardrush Fold M35 .....84 A6
Hardshaw Cl M13 .....163 B6
Hardsough La BL0 .....1 D5
Hardwick Cl
High Lane SK6 .....134 F6
Little Lever BL3 .....43 B5
Hardwick Rd
Ashton-in-M WN4 .....73 A5
Partington M31 .....106 A3
Hardwick St OL7 .....84 F2
Hardwicke Rd SK12 .....133 F4
Hardwicke St OL11 .....30 E4
Hardy Ave M21 .....109 A8
Hardy Cl Rochdale OL11 .....30 F3
Westhoughton BL5 .....39 E3
Hardy Dr Altrincham WA15 .119 F7
Bramhall SK7 .....132 D7
Hardy Farm M21 .....109 B6
Hardy Gr Swinton M27 .....79 D5
Worsley M28 .....78 F8
Hardy La M21 .....109 B6
Hardy Mill Com Prim Sch BL2 .....25 F4
Hardy Mill Rd Bolton BL2 ..25 F4
Bolton BL2 .....26 A3
Hardy St Ashton-u-L OL6 ...85 E6
Eccles M30 .....79 B1
Oldham OL4 .....67 A6
Wigan WN6 .....37 A1
Hardybutts Wigan WN1 ...151 D8
Wigan WN1 .....151 E8
Hardywood Rd 4 M34 ...113 A7
Hare Dr BL9 .....45 B4
Hare Hill Prim Sch SK14 .102 C3
Hare Hill Rd
Hattersley SK14 .....102 C2
Littleborough OL15 .....16 B6
Hare Hill Wlk SK14 .....102 C3
Hare St 7 Manchester M4 .159 A2
Rochdale OL11 .....139 F5
Rochdale OL11 .....31 A6
Harebell Ave 10 M28 .....59 F3
Harebell Cl OL12 .....14 D3
Haredale Dr M8 .....156 B6
Harefield Ave OL11 .....139 F5
Harefield Dr Heywood OL10 29 F2
Manchester M20 .....110 A2
Wilmslow SK9 .....137 B5
Harefield Rd SK9 .....131 E4
Hareford Wlk M9 .....156 C6
Harehill Cl 5 M13 .....163 B7
Hareshill Rd OL10 .....46 C7
Harewood Ave
Rochdale OL11 .....13 D2
Sale M33 .....107 D3
Harewood Cl OL11 .....13 D2
Harewood Ct M33 .....108 C3
Harewood Dr
Rochdale OL11 .....13 C2
Royton OL2 .....48 C5
Harewood Gr SK5 .....111 E8
Harewood Rd Hindley WN2 .56 C5
Irlam M44 .....94 B2
Rochdale OL11 .....13 D2
Shaw OL2 .....49 D8
Harewood Way
Rochdale OL11 .....13 C2
Swinton M27 .....61 F2
Harewood Wlk 23 M34 ...101 A1
Harford Cl SK7 .....124 A1
Hargate Ave OL12 .....14 A2
Hargate Cl BL9 .....11 C2
Hargate Dr
Altrincham WA15 .....120 A1
Irlam M44 .....94 A3
Hargate Hill La SK13 .....115 E7
Hargrave Cl M9 .....64 C6
Hargreave's St M4 .....159 A3
Hargreaves Ho BL3 .....145 E6
Hargreaves Rd WA15 .....120 C6
Hargreaves St Bolton BL1 .143 E2
Oldham OL1 .....153 F7
Oldham OL9 .....152 C6
Rochdale OL11 .....30 C4
Harkerside Cl M21 .....109 C8
Harkness St M12 .....164 D7
Harland Dr
Ashton-in-M WN4 .....73 C3
Manchester M8 .....156 B7
Harland Way OL12 .....14 B2
Harlea Ave WN2 .....57 A3
Harlech Ave Hindley WN2 ..57 B4
Prestwich M25,M45 .....63 B7
Harlech Dr SK7 .....124 D1
Harlech St WN4 .....72 F5
Harleen Gr SK2 .....124 D7
Harley Ave Ainsworth BL2 ..26 D1
Bolton BL2 .....25 E3
Manchester M14 .....98 E3
Harley Ct M24 .....46 F1
Harley Hall Royal Northern Coll of Music M16 .....97 E1
Harley Rd Middleton M24 ...46 F1
Sale M33 .....108 C5
Harley St Ashton-u-L OL6 ..166 B3
Manchester M11 .....99 D8
Harling Rd M22 .....121 E7
Harlington Cl 8 M23 .....120 D7
Harlock Ct M6 .....81 B3
Harlow Dr M18 .....99 D3
Harlyn Ave SK7 .....132 F7
Harmer Cl M40 .....83 B5
Harmol Gr OL7 .....84 F6
Harmony St OL4 .....67 A6
Harmsworth Dr SK4 .....111 B5
Harmsworth St M6 .....154 E2
Harmuir Cl WN6 .....36 E4
Harold Ave
Ashton-in-M WN4 .....73 A5
Dukinfield SK16 .....101 D8
Reddish M18 .....99 F4
Harold Lees OL10 .....29 F3
Harold Priestnall Cl M40 ..83 B6
Harold St Aspull WN2 .....38 D5
Bolton BL1 .....143 D2
Failsworth M35 .....83 E7
Manchester M16 .....161 C6
Middleton M24 .....46 E1
Oldham OL9 .....153 D7
Prestwich M25 .....62 F4
Rochdale OL16 .....15 C2
Stockport SK1,SK2 .....124 B8
Haroldene St BL2 .....25 B2
Harp Ind Est OL11 .....30 D2
Harp Rd M17 .....96 A8
Harp St M11 .....99 E7
Harp Trad Est M17 .....96 A8
Harper Ct SK3 .....170 E7
Harper Fold Rd M26 .....43 E3
Harper Green Rd BL3,BL4 ..42 B1
Harper Green Sch BL4 .....42 B1
Harper Ho M19 .....98 F1
Harper Pl OL6 .....166 C3
Harper Rd M22 .....121 E7
Harper Sq OL2 .....149 C7
Harper St Farnworth BL4 ...42 B2
Hindley WN2 .....56 C4
Oldham OL8 .....66 E4
Rochdale OL11 .....139 E5
Stockport SK3 .....170 E7
Wigan WN1 .....151 E7
Harper's La BL1 .....142 B2
Harpford Cl BL2 .....43 A5
Harpford Dr BL2 .....43 A5
Harptree Gr WN7 .....75 D7
Harpur Mount Prim Sch M9 .....157 D8
Harpurhey Rd M8,M9 .....157 D8
Harridge Ave
Rochdale OL12 .....14 C3
Stalybridge SK15 .....86 D2
Harridge St OL12 .....14 C3
Harridge The OL12 .....14 C3
Harrier Cl Leigh WN7 .....76 B5
Worsley M28 .....78 D8
Harriet St Irlam M44 .....105 E5
Walkden M28 .....60 D3
Harriett St Manchester M4 159 C2
Rochdale OL16 .....31 A7
Harringay Rd M40 .....83 B5
Harrington Rd WA14 .....119 B5
Harrington St M18 .....99 E5
Harris Ave Reddish M34 ...100 B3
Urmston M41 .....95 D5
Harris Cl Heywood OL10 ....28 E1
Reddish M34 .....100 B3
Harris Dr Hyde SK14 .....102 A4
Whitefield BL9 .....45 B2
Harris Rd WN6 .....19 B3
Harris St Bolton BL3 .....145 E6
Manchester M8 .....158 E4
Harrison Ave M19 .....99 B2
Harrison Cl 1 OL12 .....13 F1
Harrison Cres BL6 .....21 C3
Harrison Rd PR7 .....21 A6
Harrison St Bacup OL13 .....4 B8
Eccles M30 .....95 B8
Hindley WN2 .....57 B3
Horwich BL6 .....22 B4
Hyde SK14 .....113 F8
Manchester M4 .....160 D1
Manchester M7 .....158 D4
1 Oldham OL1 .....153 F6
Ramsbottom BL0 .....138 C7
Stalybridge SK15 .....86 A2
Stockport SK1,SK2 .....170 F7
Walkden M38 .....60 A4
4 Wigan WN5 .....54 F6
Harrison Way WA12 .....89 C4
Harrison's Dr SK6 .....113 C5
Harrock La WN6 .....18 A5
Harrogate Ave M25 .....63 D2
Harrogate Cl M11 .....99 E7
Harrogate Dr SK5 .....111 E8
Harrogate Rd SK5 .....99 E1
Harrogate Sq BL8 .....26 F1
Harrogate St WN1 .....151 D7
Harrop Court Rd OL3 .....51 D5
Harrop Edge La OL3 .....51 B5
Harrop Edge Rd
SK14,SK15 .....102 E4
Harrop Fold OL8 .....67 A1
Harrop Green OL3 .....51 D5
Harrop Green La OL3 .....51 D5
Harrop Rd WA15 .....119 F2
Harrop St Bolton BL3 .....146 A4
Droylsden M18 .....99 F6
Harrop St *continued*
10 Stalybridge SK15 .....86 A2
Stockport SK1 .....124 A7
Walkden M28 .....60 B3
Harrow Ave
Manchester M19 .....111 A6
Oldham OL8 .....66 E3
Rochdale OL11 .....30 A6
Harrow Cl Bury BL9 .....44 F5
Orrell WN5 .....53 F8
Harrow Cres WN7 .....75 F3
Harrow Dr M33 .....108 A2
Harrow Mews OL2 .....149 B7
Harrow Pl WN3 .....55 F4
Harrow Rd Bolton BL1 .....144 B8
Sale M33 .....108 A2
Shevington WN5 .....36 D1
Harrow St Manchester M8 ..64 B1
Rochdale OL11 .....31 B2
Harrowby Ct BL4 .....60 B8
Harrowby Dr M40 .....157 D5
Harrowby Fold BL4 .....60 C8
Harrowby La BL4 .....60 C8
Harrowby Rd Bolton BL1 ....23 F2
Bolton BL3 .....146 A3
Swinton M27 .....79 E7
Harrowby St Farnworth BL4 60 C8
Wigan WN5 .....54 E6
Harrowdene Wlk 6 M9 ..157 D8
Harry Hall Gdns M7 .....81 C3
Harry Pigott Ave M40 .....83 A7
Harry Rd SK5 .....111 F8
Harry Rowley Cl 1 M22 .121 C2
Harry St Oldham OL2 .....48 E2
Oldham OL9 .....152 C6
Rochdale OL11 .....30 B3
Harry Thorneycroft Wlk
M11 .....164 E8
Harry's Ct 3 WN7 .....75 D5
Harrycroft Rd SK6 .....113 B5
Harrytown SK6 .....113 A2
Harrytown RC High Sch SK6 .....113 A2
Hart Ave Droylsden M43 ....84 B1
Sale M33 .....108 F3
Hart Ct OL5 .....68 B2
Hart Dr BL9 .....45 B4
Hart Hill Dr M5 .....154 D3
Hart Mill Cl OL5 .....68 B2
Hart Rd M14 .....98 B1
Hart St Altrincham WA14 ..119 E5
Droylsden M43 .....84 B1
Manchester M1 .....159 A1
Tyldesley M29 .....77 C8
Westhoughton BL5 .....57 B7
Hart's Houses BL6 .....22 D5
Harter St M1 .....163 A8
Hartfield Cl M13 .....163 C6
Hartfield Wlk BL2 .....148 C8
Hartford Ave
Heywood OL10 .....29 B3
Reddish SK4 .....111 D6
Wilmslow SK9 .....136 F5
Hartford Cl OL10 .....29 B3
Hartford Gdns WA15 .....120 D5
Hartford Rd Sale M33 .....107 D2
Urmston M41 .....95 E4
Westhoughton BL5 .....57 F6
Hartford Sq OL9 .....152 C6
Hartford St M34 .....100 E5
Harthill St M8 .....155 F5
Hartington Cl 4 M41 .....95 E2
Hartington Ct OL2 .....48 E4
Hartington Dr
Droylsden M11 .....83 B3
Hazel Grove SK7 .....133 E8
Standish WN6 .....36 F7
Hartington Rd
Altrincham WA14 .....119 D8
Bolton BL1 .....144 C8
Bramhall SK7 .....132 E6
Eccles M30 .....79 A3
Gatley SK8 .....131 D8
High Lane SK12,SK6 .....134 F7
Manchester M21 .....109 B8
Stockport SK2 .....124 D5
Hartington St M14 .....97 F3
Hartis Ave M7 .....155 E6
Hartland Ave M41 .....96 A2
Hartland Cl Poynton SK12 .133 D5
Stockport SK2 .....124 C8
Tyldesley M29 .....77 B8
Hartland St OL10 .....29 D2
Hartlebury OL11 .....139 E6
Hartlepool Cl M14 .....98 B3
Hartley Ave
Manchester M25 .....63 D3
Wigan WN1 .....151 E7
Hartley Gr Irlam M44 .....94 B4
Wigan WN5 .....54 B7
Hartley Hall Gdns M16 ....97 E1
Hartley La OL11 .....30 E3
Hartley Rd
Altrincham WA14 .....119 C5
Manchester M21 .....97 A1
Hartley St Heywood OL10 ...29 D2
Horwich BL6 .....22 B3
Littleborough OL12 .....15 C6
Littleborough OL15 .....16 A5
Manchester M40 .....157 F8
Milnrow OL16 .....31 D7
Rochdale OL12 .....14 B1
Stalybridge SK15 .....86 D3
Stockport SK3 .....170 D8
13 Wigan WN5 .....54 B6

Hartley Terr
Ince-in-M WN3 150 C7
Rochdale OL11 30 E3
Harton Ave M18 99 C3
Harton Cl OL2 149 A6
Harts Farm Mews WN7 75 F7
Hartshead Ave
Ashton-u-L OL6 85 C6
Stalybridge SK15 86 A3
Hartshead Cl M11 100 A7
Hartshead Cres M35 84 C6
Hartshead High Sch OL6 85 E7
Hartshead Rd OL6 85 C6
Hartshead St OL4 67 F5
Hartshead View SK14 167 F1
Hartsop Dr M24 46 C2
Hartswell Cl WA3 74 A2
Hartswood Cl M34 101 A4
Hartswood Rd M20 110 D6
Hartwell Cl Bolton BL2 25 C3
Manchester M11 164 F8
Hartwell Gr 2 SK3 123 F4
Harty Ho M30 79 E2
Harvard Cl SK6 113 C5
Harvard St 13 OL11 31 A4
Harvest Cl Salford M6 80 E5
Wythenshawe M33 109 A3
Harvey Cl M11 165 A8
Harvey Ct WN7 75 B1
Harvey La WA3 73 F1
Harvey St Bolton BL1 143 D3
Bury BL8 27 C3
Ince-in-M WN3 151 E6
Rochdale OL12 15 B2
Stockport SK1 169 F1
Harvin Gr M34 101 A2
Harwich Cl
Brinnington SK5 112 C6
1 Manchester M19 99 B1
Harwin Cl OL12 14 D3
Harwood Cres BL8 26 E7
Harwood Ct
Manchester SK4 110 E2
Salford M6 81 B4
Harwood Dr BL8 27 A1
Harwood Gdns OL10 29 D1
Harwood Gr 27 BL2 25 B1
Harwood Mdw BL2 25 F3
Harwood Meadows
Com Prim Sch BL2 25 F3
Harwood Park Prim Sch
OL10 29 D1
Harwood Rd Bury BL2,BL8 26 C6
Manchester M19 110 E6
Manchester SK4 110 E2
Harwood St
Littleborough OL15 15 F5
Stockport SK4 169 E3
Harwood Vale BL2 25 E3
Harwood Vale Ct BL2 25 E3
Harwood Wlk BL8 26 E7
Haseldine St WN4 72 F6
Haseley Cl Little Lever BL3 43 B5
Poynton SK12 133 E5
Haselhurst Wlk 7 M23 108 F2
Hasguard Cl BL1 40 F8
Haskoll St BL6 22 D1
Haslam Brow BL9 44 E8
Haslam Ct M7 63 D1
Haslam Hey Cl
Ainsworth BL2 26 C1
Bury BL8 26 F2
Haslam Park
Cty Prim Sch BL3 144 B5
Haslam Rd SK3 170 E6
Haslam St Bolton BL3 145 D5
Bury BL9 141 A4
Middleton M24 65 C7
Rochdale OL12 139 D8
Haslemere Ave WA15 129 C6
Haslemere Dr SK8 123 A1
Haslemere Ind Est
Ashton-in-M WN4 72 F8
Ashton-in-M WN4 73 A8
Haslemere Rd
Manchester M20 110 D6
Urmston M41 95 B1
Haslingden High Sch BB4 1 B8
Haslington Rd M22 121 E2
Hasper Ave M20 110 A7
Hassal St BL9 44 E5
Hassall Ave M20 109 F7
Hassall St 4 SK15 86 B1
Hassall Way 7 SK9 131 E5
Hassnes Cl WN3 55 B2
Hassop Ave M7 81 A7
Hassop Cl M11 160 E1
Hassop Rd SK5 100 A1
Hastings Ave
Manchester M21 109 A8
Prestwich M45 63 B7
Hastings Cl Bramhall SK8 123 C2
Prestwich M45 63 B7
Stockport SK1,SK2 124 B7
Hastings Dr M41 94 E3
Hastings Rd Bolton BL1 144 B8
Eccles M30 79 A4
Prestwich M25 63 C5
Hastings St OL11 139 F5
Hasty La Altrincham WA15 129 E8
Wythenshawe WA15 129 F8
Wythenshawe M90 130 A8
Hatchett Rd M22 121 E1
Hatchmere Cl WA15 120 D6
Hatchmere Rd SK8 122 F4
Hatfield Ave M19 110 F6
Hatfield Cl WN3 55 F4
Hatfield Rd BL1 142 C1
Hatford Cl M29 59 C1
Hathaway Cl SK8 131 B7
Hathaway Ct WN7 76 B6
Hathaway Dr BL1 25 A5
Hathaway Gdns SK6 112 F3
Hathaway Rd BL9 45 A3
Hathaway Wlk WN3 55 F4
Hatherleigh Wlk BL2 42 F6
Hatherley Rd M20 110 D6
Hatherlow SK6 113 A1
Hatherlow Hts SK6 113 A1
Hatherlow La SK7 124 D2
Hatherop Cl M30 79 B1
Hathersage Ave M5,M6 154 D3
Hathersage Cres SK13 171 E2
Hathersage Dr SK13 116 F8
Hathersage Rd M13 98 D4
Hathersage St OL9 152 C6
Hathersage Way 6 M34 113 A8
Hathershaw OL8 66 F3
Hathershaw
Com High Sch OL8 66 F2
Hathershaw La OL8 66 F3
Hatro Ct M41 96 A1
Hatter St M4 159 B2
Hattersley Ct SK14 102 D1
Hattersley Ctr The 2
SK14 102 E2
Hattersley High Sch
SK14 102 D2
Hattersley Rd E SK14 102 E2
Hattersley Rd W SK14 102 C2
Hattersley Sta SK14 102 C1
Hattersley Wlk SK14 102 C3
Hatton Ave Atherton M46 58 D5
Manchester M7 158 D3
Hatton Gr BL1 25 A5
Hatton St Adlington PR7 20 F6
Manchester M12 99 A3
Stockport SK1 169 E2
Hatton Terr 24 SK16 166 B1
Hattonfold M33 108 C1
Hattons Ct M32 96 C3
Hattons Rd M17 96 B6
Haugh Farm OL16 32 C4
Haugh Fold OL16 32 C4
Haugh Hill Rd OL4 49 E3
Haugh La OL16 32 C4
Haugh Sq OL16 32 C4
Haughton Cl SK6 113 A6
Haughton Dr M22 109 D1
Haughton Green Rd M34 113 B8
Haughton Hall Rd M34 101 A3
Haughton St Denton M34 100 F5
Hyde SK14 167 E1
Havana Cl M11 160 F1
Have Ct M6 154 F4
Haveley Hey Prim Sch
M22 121 C4
Haveley Rd M22 121 C5
Havelock Dr M7 158 D4
Havelock St OL8 153 F5
Haven Cl Hazel Grove SK7 124 C1
Radcliffe M26 43 D5
Uppermill OL4 68 D6
Haven Dr M43 83 E2
Haven La OL4 49 E3
Haven St M6 154 E1
Haven The
Altrincham WA15 119 F3
Little Lever BL3 43 B3
Havenbrook Gr BL0 11 A3
Havenscroft Ave M30 95 D8
Havenwood Rd WN1 37 B4
Havercroft Cl WN3 54 E3
Havercroft Pk BL1 40 D8
Haverfield Rd M9 64 E3
Haverford St M12 164 F6
Havergate Wlks SK2 124 F5
Haverhill Gr BL2 25 B2
Havers Rd M18 99 E5
Haversham Rd M8 63 E2
Haverton Dr M22 121 B2
Haverty Prec WA12 89 C1
Havisham Cl BL6 40 B4
Haw Clough La OL3 69 C6
Hawarde Cl WA12 89 A4
Hawarden Ave M16 97 C2
Hawarden Rd WA14 119 D6
Hawarden St BL1 24 E5
Hawdraw Gn SK2 124 E6
Hawes Ave Farnworth BL4 59 E8
Manchester M14 110 E7
Swinton M27 79 F6
Hawes Cl Bury BL8 27 B5
Stockport SK2 124 A6
Hawes Cres WN4 73 B5
Haweswater Ave
Ince-in-M WN2 56 B7
Tyldesley M29 77 B7
Haweswater Cl M34 100 A2
Haweswater Cres BL9 45 B5
Haweswater Dr M24 46 E2
Haweswater Mews 5 M24 46 E2
Hawfinch Gr M28 78 D8
Hawick Gr OL10 28 E1
Hawk Cl BL9 141 B4
Hawk Green Rd SK6 126 A3
Hawk Rd M44 94 A3
Hawk Yard La OL3 69 D5
Hawke St SK15 86 C1
Hawker Ave BL3 147 D3
Hawkeshead Rd M8 156 B6
Hawkhurst Rd M13 98 F3
Hawkhurst St Leigh WN7 76 B4
Hawkhurst St *continued*
Leigh WN7 76 C5
Hawkins St SK5 169 E4
Hawkins Way OL15 6 C1
Hawkley Ave WN3 54 F2
Hawkley Brook Trad Est
WN3 54 E2
Hawkley Hall High Sch
WN3 55 B3
Hawkridge Dr M23 108 F2
Hawkrigg Cl WN6 36 F7
Hawkshaw Cl WN2 38 A3
Hawkshaw Ct Salford M5 161 A8
9 Salford M5 81 A1
Hawkshaw La BL8 10 B5
Hawkshaw St BL6 22 B3
Hawkshead Dr Bolton BL3 146 A3
Middleton M24 46 E1
Royton OL2 48 D6
Hawkshead Rd
Glossop SK13 104 E3
Shaw OL2 149 A8
Hawksheath Cl BL7 8 E1
Hawksley St Horwich BL6 22 D2
Oldham OL8 66 C3
Hawksmoor Dr OL2 149 B8
Hawkstone Ave
Droylsden M43 83 E3
Whitefield M45 62 D7
Hawkstone Cl BL2 25 E3
Hawkswick Dr M23 109 A2
Hawkworth M29 77 B5
Hawkyard Farm OL3 69 D5
Hawley Dr WA15 129 B8
Hawley Gn OL12 14 D2
Hawley La WA15 129 B8
Hawley St M19 111 B8
Haworth Ave BL0 11 A2
Haworth Cl BL9 44 F6
Haworth Dr Bacup OL13 3 C8
Stretford M32 96 A3
Haworth Rd M18 99 D4
Haworth St Bury BL8 26 F4
Edgworth BL7 9 D5
Hindley WN2 56 D6
Oldham OL1 48 E1
Radcliffe M26 44 B3
Hawsworth Cl M15 163 B5
Hawthorn Ave
Altrincham WA15 119 F8
Bury BL8 27 C4
Downall Green WN4 72 D5
Eccles M30 79 D3
Edenfield BL0 1 D2
Hindley WN2 57 A4
Marple SK6 125 D6
Newton-le-W WA12 89 D3
Orrell WN5 53 F6
Radcliffe M26 44 B1
Ramsbottom BL0 11 A2
Standish WN1 37 B6
Urmston M41 95 F1
Walkden M28 60 E1
Wigan WN5 54 D6
Wilmslow SK9 137 A7
Hawthorn Bank Bolton BL2 25 E4
Hadfield SK14 171 F4
Hawthorn Cl
Altrincham WA15 119 F7
Billinge WN5 71 D5
Tyldesley M29 59 D1
Hawthorn Cres Bury BL8 26 F7
Shaw OL2 149 B6
Hawthorn Ct SK6 112 D3
Hawthorn Dr Irlam M44 105 D5
Manchester M19 110 F7
Pendlebury M27 80 C7
Salford M6 80 B4
Stalybridge SK15 101 F8
Hawthorn Gn SK9 137 A7
Hawthorn Gr
Bramhall SK7 132 C6
Hollingworth SK14 103 D6
Hyde SK14 167 D1
Manchester SK4 168 B3
Wilmslow SK9 137 B7
Hawthorn La Sale M33 107 D6
Stretford M21 108 F8
Wilmslow SK9 137 A7
Hawthorn Lo 8 SK3 123 F4
Hawthorn Pk SK9 137 A7
Hawthorn Rd
Altrincham WA15 119 E3
Droylsden M43 84 C2
Failsworth M40 65 F1
Gatley SK8 122 A5
Kearsley BL4 61 B5
Manchester SK4 110 F2
Oldham OL8 66 B1
Reddish M34 100 B4
Rochdale OL11 29 E6
Stretford M21,M32 108 E8
Westhoughton BL5 57 F7
Hawthorn Rd S M43 84 C2
Hawthorn St
Denton M34 100 E6
Manchester M18 99 E5
Wilmslow SK9 137 A6
Hawthorn Terr
Manchester SK4 168 B3
8 Mossley OL5 68 C2
Wilmslow SK9 137 A6
Hawthorn View SK9 137 A7
Hawthorn Wlk
Littleborough OL15 15 F5
3 Partington M31 105 E3
Wilmslow SK9 137 A7
Hawthornden 1 M20 110 A3
Hawthorne Ave
Farnworth BL4 60 B8
Fowley Common WA3 92 C5
Horwich BL6 22 E1
Hawthorne Cres OL8 66 F2
Hawthorne Dr M28 79 A7
Hawthorne Gr
Ashton-u-L OL7 84 F1
Bredbury SK6 112 E4
High Lane SK12 134 C4
Leigh WN7 75 E7
Oldham OL9 152 B8
Hawthorne La OL16 32 A4
Hawthorne Rd BL3 146 B4
Hawthorne St BL3 144 C5
Hawthorne View WA16 136 B2
Hawthorns Com Sch
M34 100 E5
Hawthorns The
6 Atherton M46 58 D3
Denton M34 100 D6
Hawthorpe Gr 7 OL3 69 B8
Haxby Rd M18 99 D3
Haxworth Wlk SK7 124 A2
Hay Croft SK8 131 E8
Hay Ho OL4 67 E8
Haybarn Rd M23 121 B7
Hayburn Rd SK2 124 C8
Haycock Cl SK15 102 E7
Hayden Ct
4 Glossop SK13 104 C1
Manchester M40 157 D5
Hayden Fold SK13 115 D7
Haydn Ave M14 98 B4
Haydock Ave M33 107 B2
Haydock Dr
Altrincham WA15 120 B5
Boothstown M28 78 B6
Hazel Grove SK7 124 F2
Haydock La
Ashton-in-M WA11 72 E1
Bolton BL7 25 A8
Bolton BL7 9 B1
Haydock Mews M7 155 D6
Haydock Park Gdns WA12 73 B1
Haydock Park
Race Course WA12 73 D1
Haydock St
Ashton-in-M WN4 73 B2
Bolton BL1 145 F8
Newton-le-W WA12 89 A3
Haydock Wlk OL9 152 C7
Haye's Rd M44 105 E5
Hayes Row WA3 75 A1
Hayes St Leigh WN7 75 A4
Leigh WN7 75 E7
Hayeswater Circ 7 M41 95 C3
Hayeswater Rd M41 95 C3
Hayfell Rd WN3 55 A1
Hayfield Ave Romiley SK6 113 A4
Tyldesley M29 77 C6
Hayfield Cl
Manchester M12 164 E7
Middleton M24 47 C3
Oldham OL4 49 F4
Ramsbottom BL8 10 F1
Hayfield Rd
New Mills SK22 127 E1
Romiley SK6 113 A4
Salford M6 80 B4
Hayfield St M33 108 B5
Hayfield Wlk
Altrincham WA15 120 C6
1 Denton M34 113 A8
Haygrove Wlk 10 M9 157 D8
Hayle Rd OL1 49 D4
Hayley St M12,M13 98 E4
Hayling Rd M33 107 E5
Haymaker Rise OL12 15 D6
Hayman Ave WN7 75 D2
Haymans Wlk M13 163 B7
Haymarket Cl M13 163 C5
Haymarket St BL9 140 E2
Haymarket The BL9 140 F2
Haymill Ave M38 60 A6
Haymond Cl M6 81 A5
Haynes St Bolton BL3 146 C3
Rochdale OL12 139 F8
Haysbrook Ave M28 60 A4
Haysbrook Cl OL7 85 A7
Hayside Way BL9 140 F1
Haythorp Ave M22 121 E3
Hayward Ave BL3 43 C3
Hayward Sch BL3 147 D2
Hayward Sports Ctr BL3 146 C2
Hayward St BL8 27 C3
Hayward Way SK14 102 F3
Haywards Cl SK13 104 C3
Haywood Cl WA3 74 E1
Haywood Gdns BL3 147 E4
Haywood Park View BL3 147 E4
Hazel Ave Ashton-u-L OL6 85 E6
Bury BL8 27 A5
Bury BL9 141 B3
Cheadle SK8 122 E5
Kearsley M26 61 A8
Manchester M16 97 D2
Newhey OL16 32 A3
Pendlebury M27 80 A7
Ramsbottom BL0 11 B1
Romiley SK6 113 D2
Sale M33 108 B3
Walkden M38 59 E5
Westhoughton BL5 57 F7
Wigan WN6 37 A3
Hazel Cl Droylsden M43 84 C2
Marple SK6 125 E4
Hazel Ct 12 M16 97 D3
Hazel Dr Gatley M22 131 A8
Poynton SK12 133 F3
Stockport SK2 124 D6
Hazel Gr Farnworth BL4 60 B8
Golborne WA3 90 B8
Leigh WN7 75 E7
Oldham OL9 152 B8
Radcliffe M26 61 F8
Salford M5 80 C2
Urmston M41 95 E2
Hazel Grove High Sch
SK7 133 C8
Hazel Grove Prim Sch
SK7 124 E3
Hazel Grove Sta SK7 124 D2
Hazel Hall La BL0 11 B1
Hazel La OL8 66 D2
Hazel Mount BL7 8 E2
Hazel Rd Altrincham WA14 119 D6
Atherton M46 58 C4
Cheadle SK8 123 B1
Middleton M24 47 B2
Stalybridge SK15 86 C3
Whitefield M45 63 B8
Hazel St Denton M34 100 E6
Hazel Grove SK7 124 E3
Ramsbottom BL0 11 A4
Hazel Terr M9 64 D4
Hazel View SK6 125 F3
Hazel Wlk M31 105 E3
Hazel-Dene Cl BL9 44 F7
Hazelbadge Cl SK12 133 C4
Hazelbadge Rd SK12 133 C4
Hazelbank Ave M20 110 B7
Hazelbottom Rd
Manchester M8 156 B7
Manchester M8 156 C7
Hazeldean Ct 16 SK9 131 E1
Hazeldene BL5 57 D5
Hazeldene Rd M40 65 E1
Hazelfields M28 79 C7
Hazelhurst Cl Bolton BL1 143 E2
Ramsbottom BL0 11 B4
Hazelhurst Dr M24 46 F4
Hazelhurst Fold M28 79 C7
Hazelhurst Prim Sch BL0 11 A4
Hazelhurst Rd
Ashton-u-L OL6 85 F6
Stalybridge SK15 86 A4
Swinton M27,M28 79 C7
Hazelmere Ave M30 79 C4
Hazelmere Cl M30 95 E8
Hazelmere Gdns WN2 56 E4
Hazelwell M33 108 B3
Hazelwood OL9 65 E8
Hazelwood Ave BL2 25 E3
Hazelwood Cl SK14 102 A2
Hazelwood Ct M41 95 D3
Hazelwood Dr Bury BL9 27 F7
Denton M34 100 F6
Hazelwood Rd
Altrincham WA15 119 E2
Bolton BL1 142 B2
Hazel Grove SK7 124 F3
Stockport SK2 124 A4
Wigan WN1 37 B4
Wilmslow SK9 137 D8
Hazlehurst Gr WN4 73 C4
Hazlemere BL4 61 A7
Headen Ave WN5 54 B5
Headingley Dr M16 97 A3
Headingley Rd M14 110 D7
Headingley Way BL3 147 D3
Headland Cl WA3 90 E6
Headlands Dr M25 63 A1
Headlands Rd SK7 123 F1
Headlands St OL12 14 E1
Heady Hill Ct OL10 29 A2
Heady Hill Rd OL10 29 A2
Heald Ave M14 98 B3
Heald Cl Altrincham WA14 119 C2
Littleborough OL15 16 A3
Rochdale OL12 14 C3
Heald Dr Altrincham WA14 119 C2
Rochdale OL12 14 C3
Heald Gr Gatley SK8 122 A1
Manchester M14 98 B4
Heald Green Sta M22 131 A8
Heald La OL15 16 A3
Heald Pl M14 98 B3
Heald Place Prim Sch
M14 98 B3
Heald Rd WA14 119 C2
Healds Gn OL1 47 F3
Healdwood Rd SK6 113 C4
Healey Ave Heywood OL10 29 E3
Rochdale OL12 14 D4
Healey Cl Manchester M7 81 C8
Wythenshawe M23 108 F2
Wythenshawe M23 109 A2
Healey Dell Cotts OL12 14 B4
Healey Dell
Nature Reserve OL12 14 B6
Healey Gr OL12 14 C5
Healey Hall Farm OL12 14 C4
Healey Hall Mews OL12 14 C4
Healey La OL12 14 E3
Healey Prim Sch OL12 14 E3
Healey St OL16 139 E6
Healey Stones OL12 14 E4
Healing St 8 OL11 31 A5
Heanor Ave M34 113 A8
Heap Bridge
Cty Prim Sch BL9 28 D1
Heap Brow BL9 28 D1
Heap Rd OL12 13 D2
Heap St Bolton BL3 147 E4
Heywood BL9 28 D1

Heap St *continued*
Oldham OL4 67 C7
Radcliffe M26 44 B3
Whitefield M45 62 F7
Heape St OL11 30 C1
Heapfold 4 OL12 14 B2
Heaplands BL8 10 F1
Heaps Farm Ct SK15 102 D7
Heapworth Ave BL0 138 B6
Heapy Cl BL8 26 F1
Heardman Ave 1 WN6 37 A1
Hearlesden Cres 5 BL3 144 C5
Heath Ave Manchester M7 81 C4
Ramsbottom BL0 11 B1
Urmston M41 95 E3
Heath Cl BL3 146 B2
Heath Cres SK2 170 F5
Heath Farm La M31 106 B3
Heath Gdns WN2 57 C3
Heath Hill Dr OL13 3 C8
Heath La Culcheth WA3 91 A1
Golborne WA3 90 F2
Leigh WN7 75 B5
Heath Rd
Altrincham WA14 119 D2
Ashton-in-M WN4 73 C2
Glossop SK13 104 D2
Littleborough OL12 15 C6
Sale WA15 119 F8
Stockport SK2,SK3 170 F6
Heath St Ashton-in-M WN4 73 C2
Golborne WA3 90 A8
Manchester M8 155 F7
Rochdale OL11 139 D6
Heath The Ashton-u-L OL7 85 A7
Middleton M24 65 B6
Heath View M7 81 A8
Heathbank Rd
Cheadle SK8 131 F8
Manchester M9 64 C5
Stockport SK3 123 B7
Heathbourne Rd OL13 3 C8
Heathcliffe Wlk 1 M13 163 C5
Heathcote Ave SK4 168 C3
Heathcote Gdns SK6 113 E1
Heathcote Rd M18 99 C4
Heather Ave Droylsden M43 84 C2
Irlam M44 105 D6
Shaw OL2 49 D8
Heather Bank Bury BL8 26 E7
Littleborough OL15 16 D6
Rawtenstall BB4 1 F8
Heather Bank Cl SK13 116 A7
Heather Brae WA12 89 A4
Heather Brow SK15 102 E7
Heather Cl Haslingden BB4 1 A8
Heywood OL10 46 D8
Horwich BL6 22 B4
Oldham OL4 49 E1
Heather Ct SK4 111 D5
Heather Gr
Ashton-in-M WN4 73 E4
Droylsden M43 100 B8
Hollingworth SK14 103 D6
Leigh WN7 75 E7
Wigan WN5 54 E6
Heather Lea M34 101 A2
Heather Rd WA14,WA15 119 E1
Heather St M11 83 B2
Heather Way Diggle OL3 51 C4
Marple SK6 125 E6
Heather Wlk M31 105 E3
Heatherdale Dr M8 156 A6
Heatherfield Bolton BL1 24 D5
Edgworth BL7 9 E6
Heatherfield Ct SK9 137 E8
Heatherlands OL12 4 D4
Heatherlea Cl WN8 53 C7
Heathers The SK2 124 B4
Heatherside Reddish SK5 100 A1
Stalybridge SK15 86 D2
Heatherside Ave OL5 68 E1
Heatherside Rd BL0 138 C7
Heatherway
Manchester M14 98 B4
Sale M33 107 D5
Heathfield Bolton BL2 25 F3
Farnworth BL4 42 E1
Wilmslow SK9 137 A5
Worsley M28 78 F5
Heathfield Ave Bacup OL13 3 C8
Denton M34 100 D1
Gatley SK8 122 B5
Manchester SK4 111 C5
Heathfield Cl M33 108 F4
Heathfield Dr Bolton BL3 146 B2
Pendlebury M27 80 A7
Tyldesley M29 59 D1
Heathfield Prim Sch BL3 146 A2
Heathfield Rd Bacup OL13 3 C8
Stockport SK2 170 F6
Whitefield BL9,M45 44 F3
Heathfield St M40 83 C5
Heathfields WA14 119 C3
Heathfields Rd OL3 69 C8
Heathfields Sq OL3 69 C8
Heathland Rd M25,M7 81 B8
Heathland Terr SK3 170 E7
Heathlands Dr M25 63 A1
Heathlea WN2 57 C2
Heathmoor Ave WA3 90 D6
Heathside Gr M28 60 E3
Heathside Park Rd SK3 122 F7
Heathside Rd Cheadle SK3 123 A7
Manchester M20 110 D6
Heathway Ave M11 83 D2
Heathwood OL3 69 C8
Heathwood Rd M19 110 E4
Heatley Cl Lymm WA13 117 A5
Reddish M34 100 B2
Heatley Rd OL16 31 D6
Heatley Way 5 SK9 131 D4
Heaton Ave Bolton BL1 23 F1
Bolton BL2 25 E5
Farnworth BL4 60 C8
Little Lever BL3 43 A4
Stockport SK7 123 E3
Heaton Chapel Sta SK4 111 C5
Heaton Cl Manchester SK4 168 A3
Orrell WN8 53 A7
Whitefield BL9 45 A5
Heaton Court Gdns BL1 40 E7
Heaton Ct Manchester SK4 168 B4
Prestwich M25 63 C3
Heaton Dr BL9 45 A5
Heaton Fold BL9 44 E8
Heaton Gr BL9 44 E7
Heaton Grange Dr BL1 144 A7
Heaton Hall M25 63 E5
Heaton La SK4 169 E1
Heaton Moor Rd SK4 168 B4
Heaton Mount BL1 23 F1
Heaton Park M25 63 E5
Heaton Park Prim Sch
M45 63 B6
Heaton Park Rd M9 64 B5
Heaton Park Rd W M9 64 A5
Heaton Park Sta M25 63 C4
Heaton Rd Bolton BL6 40 D6
Little Lever BL3 43 B5
Manchester M20 110 C6
Manchester SK4 168 C3
Heaton Sch SK4 111 B5
Heaton St Aspull WN2 38 D5
Denton M34 100 D3
Ince-in-M WN3 151 E6
Manchester M7 155 E7
Middleton M24 64 B7
Milnrow OL16 32 A5
Prestwich M25 63 C4
Standish WN6 19 E1
Wigan WN1 37 C2
Heaton Towers SK4 169 E2
Heatons Gr BL5 40 A2
Heaviley Gr Horwich BL6 22 A5
Stockport SK2 124 A6
Hebble Butt Cl OL16 31 E6
Hebble Cl BL2 25 B5
Hebburn Dr BL8 27 C5
Hebden Ave
Fowley Common WA3 92 B5
Romiley SK6 113 A4
Salford M5,M6 80 C3
Hebden Ct BL1 145 E8
Hebden Dr SK13 116 F8
Hebden Wlk M15 162 F5
Hebdon Cl WN4 73 A5
Heber Pl 10 OL15 16 B5
Heber St Ince-in-M WN2 151 F7
Radcliffe M26 44 A3
Hebron St OL2 49 A3
Hector Ave OL16 31 B8
Hector Rd Manchester M13 98 F3
Shevington WN5 36 D1
Heddles Ct WN7 75 E4
Heddon Cl SK4 110 E3
Heddon Wlk M8 156 C6
Hedge Rows OL12 4 C1
Hedgelands Wlk 4 M33 107 C5
Hedgemead 5 WN6 37 A1
Hedgerows The SK14 102 A3
Hedges St M35 84 A8
Hedley St BL1 142 C2
Hedley Wlk 8 M8 155 F7
Heeley St WN1 37 B2
Heginbottom Cres OL6 85 C5
Height Barn La OL13 4 A8
Heights Ave OL12 14 E2
Heights Cl OL12 14 E2
Heights La Chadderton OL1 47 F2
Delph OL3 50 E7
Rochdale OL12 14 E1
Heights The BL6 22 D1
Helen St Ashton-in-M WN4 73 A4
Eccles M30 95 B8
Farnworth BL4 60 D7
Golborne WA3 73 F1
Manchester M7 81 C5
Helena St M6 80 C5
Helensville Ave M6 80 F5
Helga St M40 160 D4
Helias Cl M28 59 F3
Hell Nook WA3 73 F1
Helmclough Way M28 78 B8
Helmet St M1,M12 163 C8
Helmsdale M28 60 C2
Helmsdale Ave BL3 40 F6
Helmsdale Cl BL0 11 A4
Helmshore Ave OL4 49 E3
Helmshore Ho OL2 149 B8
Helmshore Prim Sch BB4 1 A7
Helmshore Rd
Haslingden BB4 1 A7
Ramsbottom BL0,BL8,BB4 1 A3
Helmshore Way OL2 149 B8
Helmshore Wlk M13 163 B7
Helmsman Way WN3 150 B5
Helsby Cl OL4 68 A6
Helsby Gdns BL1 143 F4
Helsby Rd M33 108 E2
Helsby Way
4 Handforth SK9 131 D4
Wigan WN3 54 C2
Helsby Wlk M12 164 E8
Helston Cl Bramhall SK7 132 F7
Hattersley SK14 102 D1
Helston Cl *continued*
Irlam M44 94 B2
Helston Dr OL2 48 F4
Helston Gr SK8 131 C8
Helston St M40 160 F4
Helston Way M29 77 C8
Helston Wlk SK14 102 D1
Helton Wlk M24 46 C1
Helvellyn Dr M24 46 D2
Helvellyn Rd WN5 54 B7
Helvellyn Wlk 2 OL1 49 A1
Hembury Ave M19 110 F6
Hembury Cl M24 47 B2
Hemfield Ct WN2 56 C8
Hemfield Rd WN2 56 C8
Hemley Cl BL5 57 E6
Hemlock Ave OL8 66 E3
Hemming Dr M30 79 E1
Hemmington Dr M9 157 D7
Hemmons Rd M12 99 B3
Hempcroft Rd WA15 120 D5
Hempshaw La SK1,SK2 124 B7
Hemsby Cl BL3 146 A4
Hemsley St M9 64 E1
Hemsley St S M9 64 E1
Hemswell Cl M6 154 E4
Hemsworth Rd
Bolton BL1 145 D8
Manchester M18 99 D3
Hen Fold Rd M29 77 C7
Henbury Dr SK6 113 B6
Henbury La SK8 131 F6
Henbury Rd SK9 131 D4
Henbury St
Manchester M14 98 A3
Stockport SK2 124 C4
Henderson Ave 3 M27 61 F1
Henderson St
Littleborough OL15 16 A5
Manchester M19 111 B8
Rochdale OL12 15 B2
Henderville St OL15 16 A6
Hendham Cl SK7 124 A2
Hendham Dr WA14 119 B5
Hendham Vale M9 156 C6
Hendon Dr Bury BL9 44 F5
Cheadle SK3 123 A7
Hendon Gr WN7 75 F8
Hendon Rd Manchester M9 64 D4
Wigan WN5 54 E8
Hendon St WN7 75 F8
Hendriff Pl 4 OL12 14 F1
Henfield Wlk M22 121 C3
Hengist St Bolton BL2 148 C7
Manchester M18 99 D4
Henley Ave Cheadle SK8 122 F2
Irlam M44 105 E6
Manchester M16 97 B3
Henley Cl BL8 44 B8
Henley Dr
Altrincham WA15 119 F7
Ashton-u-L OL7 84 F4
Henley Gr BL3 147 D3
Henley Pl M19 111 A6
Henley St Aspull WN2 38 B6
Oldham OL1 153 D8
Oldham OL9 66 A4
9 Rochdale OL12 14 F1
Henley Terr OL11 139 E5
Henlow Wlk 9 M40 65 D2
Henniker Rd BL3 146 A2
Henniker St M27 79 E6
Hennon St BL1 143 D1
Henrietta St
Ashton-u-L OL6 166 B4
Bolton BL3 146 B4
Leigh WN7 75 F5
Manchester M16 161 C5
Henry Herman St BL3 146 A3
Henry Lee St BL3 146 C3
Henry Park St WN1 151 E7
Henry Sq OL6 166 A2
Henry St Bolton BL2 148 A6
Denton M34 113 B8
Droylsden M43 84 A1
Eccles M30 79 C1
Failsworth M35 83 F7
Glossop SK13 104 C1
Hyde SK14 167 D2
Ince-in-M WN3 55 E4
Leigh WN7 76 A3
Leigh WN7 76 A4
Littleborough OL12 15 C7
Littleborough OL15 15 F3
Manchester M16 161 C5
Manchester M4 159 B2
Middleton M24 64 F8
Prestwich M25 63 C5
Ramsbottom BL0 11 D7
Rochdale OL11 139 F6
Stockport SK1 124 B8
6 Tyldesley M29 59 A1
14 Westhoughton BL5 39 E1
Henshall La WA14 118 C6
Henshaw Ct M16 97 B4
Henshaw La OL9 65 F2
Henshaw St Oldham OL1 153 E7
Oldham OL1 153 F8
Stretford M32 96 D2
Henshaw Wlk 10 M13 163 B7
Henson Gr WA15 120 A4
Henthorn St Oldham OL1 67 A8
Shaw OL2 149 B6
Henton Wlk M40 159 C4
Henwick Hall Ave BL0 11 B4
Henwood Rd M20 110 C5
Hepley Rd SK12 134 A3
Hepple Cl SK4 110 F3
Hepple Wlk OL7 84 E5
Heppleton Rd M40 65 D2
Hepton St OL1 153 E8
Heptonstall Wlk M18 165 C5
Hepworth Cl WN3 73 E2
Hepworth St SK14 113 E7
Heraldic Ct M6 81 A4
Herbert St Bacup OL13 3 D8
Droylsden M43 83 F1
Dukinfield M34 101 A4
Horwich BL6 22 B4
Little Lever BL3 43 B3
Manchester M8 155 F5
Oldham OL4 49 D1
Oldham OL9 152 B7
Prestwich M25 62 F4
Radcliffe M26 43 F5
Stockport SK3 170 D7
Stretford M32 96 D2
Westhoughton BL5 39 E2
Wigan WN3 150 B7
Hereford Ave WA3 90 B8
Hereford Cl
Ashton-in-M WN4 73 C2
Ashton-u-L OL6 85 D7
Shaw OL2 48 F7
Hereford Cres BL3 43 A4
Hereford Ct SK5 112 C5
Hereford Dr Bury BL9 44 F8
Handforth SK9 131 E3
Manchester M25 63 C2
Swinton M27 79 F6
Hereford Gr M41 95 C2
Hereford Rd Bolton BL1 144 B8
Brinnington SK5 112 C5
Cheadle SK8 123 A4
Hindley WN2 56 F6
Salford M30 80 A5
Hereford St Bolton BL1 143 F2
Oldham OL9 152 C5
18 Rochdale OL11 31 A5
Sale M33 108 B4
Hereford Way
Middleton M24 47 C2
Stalybridge SK15 102 D7
Hereford Wlk
6 Denton M34 100 F1
Romiley SK6 113 A1
Herevale Grange M28 78 B7
Herevale Hall Dr BL0 11 B4
Heristone Ave M34 100 F3
Heritage Gdns M20 110 B2
Heritage Wharf OL7 166 A1
Herle Dr M22 121 C1
Hermitage Ave SK6 113 F2
Hermitage Cl WN6 35 E7
Hermitage Ct WA15 120 A3
Hermitage Gdns SK6 113 F2
Hermitage Rd
Altrincham WA15 120 A3
Manchester M8 64 A1
Hermon Ave OL8 66 E4
Herne St M11 165 A8
Heron Ave Dukinfield SK16 101 E7
Farnworth BL4 59 F7
Heron Ct Salford M6 80 B3
Stockport SK3 170 E7
Heron Dr Droylsden M34 84 C1
Irlam M44 94 A3
Poynton SK12 133 A3
Wigan WN3 54 E2
Heron Pl WN5 54 C8
Heron St Manchester M15 162 E5
Oldham OL8 66 D3
Stockport SK3 170 D7
Swinton M27 62 A1
Heron's Way BL2 148 A6
Herondale Cl M40 83 B5
Herries St OL6 85 D4
Herristone Rd M8 64 A2
Herrod Ave SK4 111 E5
Herschel St M40 83 A8
Hersey St M6 154 E2
Hersham Wlk 1 M9 157 E8
Hertford Dr M29 59 A3
Hertford Gr M44 105 C6
Hertford Rd M9 64 D1
Hertford St OL7 166 A1
Hertfordshire Park
Cl OL2 149 B8
Hesford Ave M9 157 F7
Hesketh Ave Bolton BL1 24 F5
Manchester M20 110 A3
Shaw OL2 149 B5
Hesketh Ct Atherton M46 58 C3
5 Manchester M20 110 A3
Hesketh Dr WN6 19 A2
Hesketh Fletcher
CE High Sch M46 58 C2
Hesketh Manor M46 58 C3
Hesketh Meadow La
Golborne WA3 90 F8
Golborne WA3 91 A8
Hesketh Rd Rochdale OL16 31 C7
Sale M33 107 F3
Hesketh St Atherton M46 58 D4
Leigh WN7 75 D5
Stockport SK4 169 E3
Wigan WN5 54 F7
Hesketh Wlk
5 Farnworth BL4 60 D8
Middleton M24 46 E2
Hesnall Cl WA3 92 C8
Hessel St M5 154 D1
Hester Wlk 2 M15 163 A5
Heston Ave M13 98 F2
Heston Dr M41 95 C3
Heswall Ave Culcheth WA3 91 E4
Heswall Ave *continued*
Manchester M20 110 B7
Heswall Dr BL8 26 F5
Heswall Rd SK5 99 F1
Heswall St BL2 42 F7
Hetherington Wlk M12 99 A4
Hethorn St M40 83 C5
Hetton Ave M13 98 E2
Heversham Ave OL2 49 D7
Heversham Wlk M18 165 C6
Hewart Cl M40 159 C4
Hewart Dr BL9 141 C3
Hewitt Ave M34 99 F3
Hewitt Bsns Pk WN5 53 E4
Hewitt St M15 162 F7
Hewlett Rd M21 97 A1
Hewlett St Bolton BL2 148 A7
Westhoughton BL5 57 B7
Wigan WN1 150 C8
Hexham Ave Bolton BL1 23 F1
Wigan WN3 54 F4
Hexham Cl Atherton M46 58 E4
Oldham OL9 152 C7
Sale M33 107 D3
Stockport SK2 124 E5
Hexham Rd M18 99 C3
Hexon Cl M6 154 E3
Hey Bottom La OL12 15 A6
Hey Cres OL4 67 F7
Hey Croft M45 62 C7
Hey Head Ave BB4 3 A8
Hey Head La OL15 6 B1
Hey Hill Cl OL2 149 A5
Hey House Mews BL8 10 F4
Hey Shoot La WA3 92 C5
Hey St Ince-in-M WN3 55 F3
Rochdale OL16 31 B8
Wigan WN6 150 B8
Hey Top OL3 69 D3
Hey Willow BL7 25 C6
Hey with Zion
CE/Methodist Prim Sch
OL4 67 E7
Heybrook Cl M45 63 C8
Heybrook Prim Sch OL12 15 A1
Heybrook Rd M23 121 B5
Heybrook St OL16 31 B8
Heybrook Wlk M45 63 C8
Heybury Cl M11 164 F8
Heycrofts View BL0 1 E3
Heyden Bank 24 SK13 171 D2
Heyden Fold 23 SK13 171 D2
Heyden Terr 22 SK13 171 D2
Heyes Ave WA15 120 B7
Heyes Dr WA15 120 B7
Heyes La
Alderley Edge SK9 137 B3
Sale WA15 120 B8
Heyes Leigh WA15 120 B7
Heyes Rd WN5 53 E6
Heyes St WN6 35 C7
Heyes Terr WA15 120 B8
Heyford Ave M40 65 D2
Heyford Rd WN5 54 D8
Heyheads New Rd SK15 86 E7
Heyland Rd M23 121 A6
Heyridge Dr M22 109 D1
Heyrod St Manchester M1 163 C8
Mossley SK15 86 D5
Heyrose Wlk 14 M15 162 D6
Heys Ave Romiley SK6 113 E3
Swinton M27 61 D2
Wythenshawe M23 109 A1
Heys Cl N M27 61 C2
Heys La Heywood OL10 29 A1
Romiley SK6 113 E3
Heys Prim Sch The OL6 85 D3
Heys Rd Ashton-u-L OL6 85 D3
Prestwich M25 63 B5
Heys St BL8 140 D2
Heys The Prestwich M25 63 B5
Reddish SK5 100 A1
Heys View M25 63 B4
Heysbank Rd SK12 135 D5
Heyscroft Rd
Manchester M20 110 C6
Manchester SK4 168 A2
Heysham Ave M20 109 F7
Heysham Rd WN5 54 B7
Heyshaw Wlk M23 108 F1
Heyside OL2 49 A3
Heyside Ave OL2 49 A3
Heyside Cl SK15 86 E6
Heywood Ave
Golborne WA3 74 B1
Oldham OL4 68 A8
Swinton M27 62 B2
Heywood Cl SK9 137 B2
Heywood Com High Sch
OL10 28 E1
Heywood Ct M25 64 A7
Heywood Distribution Pk
BL9,OL10 45 F8
Heywood Fold Rd OL4 67 F7
Heywood Gdns
Golborne WA3 74 B1
Prestwich M25 63 B4
Heywood Gr M33 108 B6
Heywood Hall Rd OL10 29 D3
Heywood Ho
Atherton M46 58 C3
Oldham OL8 153 F5
Salford M6 80 C3
Heywood La OL4 68 A7
Heywood Old Rd M24,OL10 46 B3

Heywood Rd
Alderley Edge SK9 137 B2
Prestwich M25 63 C7
Rochdale OL11 30 C1
Sale M33 108 B3
Heywood St Bolton BL1 145 F8
Bury BL9 141 A2
Failsworth M35 83 D7
Little Lever BL3 43 B3
Manchester M8 156 A6
Oldham OL4 67 E8
Swinton M27 79 E8
Heywood Sta OL10 29 E1
Heywood Way M6 154 F3
Heywood's Hollow BL1 143 F3
Heyworth Ave SK6 113 D3
Heyworth St 4 M5 154 E1
Hibbert Ave Denton M34 100 E5
Hyde SK14 167 E1
Hibbert Cres M35 84 A6
Hibbert La SK6 125 F5
Hibbert St Bolton BL1 143 F2
Manchester M14 98 C3
Oldham OL4 67 E7
Reddish SK4,SK5 111 E5
Hibernia St BL3 144 C5
Hibernia Way M32 96 A5
Hibson Ave OL12 13 E2
Hibson Cl OL12 15 C6
Hic Bibi La PR7 19 E6
Hicken Pl SK14 101 F5
Hickenfield Rd SK14 101 F5
Hickton Dr WA14 119 B6
Hieland Rd WN1 37 E2
Higginshaw La OL1,OL2 49 A2
Higginshaw Rd OL1 67 A8
Higginson Rd SK5 111 E8
Higginson St WN7 76 A5
Higgs Cl OL4 67 D7
High Ash Gr M34 100 D7
High Ave BL2 42 E7
High Bank
Altrincham WA14 119 D5
Atherton M46 59 A6
Bolton BL7 24 F7
Manchester M18 99 E5
High Bank Ave SK15 102 D7
High Bank Cl M44 105 D6
High Bank Cres M25 63 C3
High Bank Gr M25 63 C3
High Bank La BL6 40 B8
High Bank Rd
Droylsden M43 99 F8
Hyde SK14 167 F3
Pendlebury M27 80 B7
High Bank Side SK1 169 F1
High Bank St BL2 148 C7
High Barn Cl OL11 139 E5
High Barn Com Prim Sch OL2 48 E4
High Barn La OL12 4 C3
High Barn Rd
Middleton M24 65 A7
Royton OL2 48 F4
High Barn St OL2 48 E4
High Beeches BL3 43 B5
High Beeches Cres WN4 73 A6
High Bent Ave SK8 132 A6
High Birch Specl Sch OL11 30 B4
High Crest Ave SK8 121 F5
High Croft Cl SK16 102 A8
High Elm Dr WA15 129 C8
High Elm Rd WA15 129 D7
High Elms SK8 132 B5
High Field WA14 118 B2
High Gates M33 108 E5
High Grove Rd
Cheadle SK8 122 C5
Uppermill OL4 68 E5
High Hill Rd SK22 127 D1
High Hurst Cl M24 64 C7
High Knowls OL4 68 A4
High La Glossop SK13 115 E7
Manchester M21 109 B8
Romiley SK6 113 B4
High Lane Prim Sch SK6 134 F8
High Lawn Com Prim Sch BL1 24 E6
High Lea SK8 122 C5
High Lee Ho M33 108 D4
High Lee La OL4 50 B4
High Legh Rd M11 99 D8
High Level Rd OL11 31 A6
High Mdw 2 SK8 131 E8
High Mdws Bolton BL7 25 B8
Glossop SK13 116 B7
Romiley SK6 113 C3
High Moor Cres OL4 49 E1
High Moor La WN6 18 B4
High Moor View OL4 49 E1
High Mount BL2 25 E3
High Peak OL15 16 F5
High Peak Rd
Ashton-u-L OL6 86 A6
Whitworth OL12 14 C6
High Peak St M40 83 B6
High Pk WN6 36 C6
High Rid La BL6 23 B1
High St Altrincham WA14 119 D4
Aspull WN2 38 B3
Atherton M46 58 D3
Bolton BL3 147 E4
Bury BL8 26 F4
Cheadle SK8 122 D6

High St *continued*
Delph OL3 50 F5
Droylsden M43 84 B1
Edgworth BL7 9 C4
Golborne WA3 90 A8
Hazel Grove SK7 124 F2
Heywood OL10 29 B2
Horwich BL6 22 B4
Hyde SK14 167 F3
Ince-in-M WN3 151 E6
Leigh WN7 76 A5
Little Lever BL3 43 B3
5 Littleborough OL15 15 F5
Manchester M1,M4 159 A1
Manchester M4 159 A2
Middleton M24 47 A1
Middleton M24 47 A2
Mossley OL5 68 D2
Newton-le-W WA12 89 D4
Oldham OL1 153 F7
Oldham OL3 69 B8
Oldham OL4 67 E6
Rochdale OL12 139 F8
Royton OL2 48 D4
Shaw OL2 149 B6
Stalybridge SK15 85 F1
Stalybridge SK15 86 A1
Standish WN6 19 E1
Stockport SK1 169 F1
Tyldesley M29 58 F1
Tyldesley M29 77 B5
Walkden M28 60 D3
Wigan WN1 37 D2
High St E SK13 104 D1
High St W SK13 104 B1
High Stile La OL3 51 D2
High Stile St BL4 60 E7
High View St
Bolton BL1 24 E6
1 Bolton BL3 146 C4
High Wood Fold SK6 126 C8
Higham Cl OL2 149 A5
Higham La SK14 114 A7
Higham St SK8 123 A1
Higham View M6 81 A3
Highbank SK13 103 F7
Highbank Cres OL4 68 E5
Highbank Dr M20 122 B8
Highbank Private Hospl BL8 26 F4
Highbank Rd
Glossop SK13 116 F7
Newhey OL16 32 C4
Whitefield BL9 44 F3
Highbridge Cl BL2 43 A6
Highbrook Gr 14 BL1 143 E1
Highbury SK4 110 F2
Highbury Ave Irlam M44 94 A1
Urmston M41 94 E2
Highbury Cl BL5 57 D6
Highbury Rd
Manchester M16 97 E1
Reddish SK4 111 C6
Highbury Way OL2 48 D6
Highclere Ave M7,M8 155 F6
Highclere Rd M8 63 F2
Highcliffe Ct WN6 36 F7
Highcliffe Rd M9 64 A3
Highclove La M28 77 F5
Highcrest Gr M29 59 D1
Highcroft SK14 113 F6
Highcroft Ave M20 109 E4
Highcroft Rd SK6 113 C3
Highcroft Way OL12 14 F4
Highdales Rd M23 121 B5
Highdown Wlk 28 M9 157 E8
Higher Ainsworth Rd BL8,M26 43 E7
Higher Ardwick M12 163 C7
Higher Arthurs OL3 69 B6
Higher Bank Rd OL15 16 A3
Higher Barlow Row SK1 170 F8
Higher Barn BL6 22 F3
Higher Barn Rd SK14 171 F4
Higher Bents La SK6 113 A3
Higher Blue Bell Cotts BL5 39 C4
Higher Bridge St BL1 145 F8
Higher Bury St SK4 169 D2
Higher Calderbrook Rd OL15 6 C2
Higher Cambridge St M15 163 A6
Higher Carr La OL3 69 B7
Higher Chatham St M15 163 A6
Higher Cleggswood Ave OL15 16 A3
Higher Count Hill OL4 49 E2
Higher Croft Eccles M30 95 C8
Whitefield M45 62 C6
Higher Cross La OL3 69 C8
Higher Crossbank OL4 67 F8
Higher Damshead BL5 57 F8
Higher Darcy St BL2 148 C5
Higher Dean St M26 43 E3
Higher Dinting SK13 104 A2
Higher Downs WA14 119 C3
Higher Drake Mdw BL5 57 E5
Higher Dunscar BL7 8 E1
Higher Fold La BL0 11 E7
Higher Folds Prim Sch WN7 76 D7
Higher Fullwood OL1 49 D4
Higher Gamesley SK13 115 D8
Higher Gn Ashton-u-L OL6 166 C4
Salford M6 154 F4
Higher Green La M29 77 C6
Higher Henry St SK14 167 E1

Higher Hillgate SK1,SK2 170 F8
Higher House Cl OL9 66 A4
Higher La Aspull WN2 38 A4
Disley SK12 135 E1
Lymm WA13 117 B1
Orrell WN8 53 C7
Whitefield M45 62 E8
Higher Lane Cty Jun & Inf Sch M45 62 F7
Higher Lime Rd OL8 84 C8
Higher Lo OL11 13 D2
Higher Lomax La OL10 29 A3
Higher Lydgate Pk OL4 68 C6
Higher Market St BL4 60 E8
Higher Moulding BL9 28 E5
Higher Newtons OL5 68 D2
Higher Noon Sun SK22 127 F2
Higher Ormond St M13,M15 163 A6
Higher Oswald St 4 M4 159 A2
Higher Park OL2 32 C2
Higher Pit La BL8 43 E8
Higher Rd M41 95 E2
Higher Ridings BL7 24 F7
Higher Rise OL2 32 A1
Higher Row BL9 141 B3
Higher Shady La BL7 25 C7
Higher Shore Rd OL15 15 E7
Higher Southfield BL5 57 E7
Higher Summerseat BL0 11 B2
Higher Swan La BL3 147 D3
Higher Tame St SK15 86 B2
Higher Turf La OL4 50 B1
Higher Turf Pk OL2 48 E3
Higher Wharf St OL6,OL7 166 B2
Higher Wheat La OL16 31 C8
Higher Wood St M24 46 F1
Higher York St M13 163 B6
Highfield Sale M33 108 C3
Wigan WN3 54 D4
Highfield Ave Atherton M46 58 E5
Bolton BL2 26 A3
Boothstown M28,M29 77 F7
Bredbury SK6 112 F2
Golborne WA3 89 F8
Heywood OL10 29 A2
Leigh WN7 76 C3
Radcliffe M26 44 C1
Shevington WN6 36 A6
Wigan WN1 37 E1
Highfield Cl Adlington PR6 21 A7
Dukinfield SK14 101 F6
Stockport SK3 123 F4
Stretford M32 108 C8
Highfield Cres SK9 131 C1
Highfield Ct Farnworth BL4 60 B7
Mottram-in-L SK14 103 A4
Highfield Dr Eccles M30 79 D3
Farnworth BL4 60 A7
Middleton M24 64 F7
Mossley OL5 86 C8
Oldham OL2 48 E2
Pendlebury M27 80 C7
Standish WN6 36 F7
4 Urmston M41 95 C3
Highfield Est SK9 131 C1
Highfield Gdns
Hollingworth SK14 103 D5
Hyde SK14 167 F3
Highfield Glen OL6 85 F5
Highfield Gr WN2 38 F5
Highfield Grange Ave WN3 54 E2
Highfield Ho SK3 170 F5
Highfield La Golborne WA3 90 C5
Whitefield M45 44 F3
Highfield Park Rd SK6 112 F3
Highfield Parkway SK7 132 D4
Highfield Pk SK4 110 F2
Highfield Pl Prestwich M25 63 A5
Reddish M18 99 F4
Highfield Prim Sch M41 95 F2
Highfield Private Hospl OL11 139 E5
Highfield Range M18 99 F4
Highfield Rd Adlington PR6 21 A7
Altrincham WA15 120 A3
Altrincham WA15 120 B5
Blackrod BL6 21 E1
Bolton BL1 142 B2
Cheadle SK8 122 F1
Eccles M30 79 D4
Edenfield BL0 1 D3
Farnworth BL4 60 A8
Glossop SK13 116 D8
Hazel Grove SK7 125 A2
Hindley WN2 56 D7
10 Marple SK6 125 F6
Marple SK6 126 B6
Milnrow OL16 32 A6
Poynton SK12 133 A4
Prestwich M25 63 A5
Reddish M19 99 C1
Rochdale OL11 13 E1
6 Rochdale OL11 13 F1
Salford M6 154 F2
Stockport SK7 123 F3
Stretford M32 108 C8
Walkden M38 59 F5
Highfield Rd N PR6 21 A8
Highfield St Denton M34 100 E5
Denton M34 100 F6
Dukinfield SK16 166 B1
Kearsley BL4 61 A6
Manchester M7,M8 155 F7
Middleton M24 65 B8
Oldham OL9 153 D7
2 Stockport SK3 123 C8

Highfield St Mathews CE Prim Sch WN3 54 C4
Highfield St W SK16 166 B1
Highfield Terr
Ashton-u-L OL7 85 A7
Manchester M9 157 D8
Highfields Cty Prim Sch BL4 60 A8
Highgate BL3 40 C2
Highgate Ave M41 95 A4
Highgate Cres
Appley Bridge WN6 35 E7
Manchester M18 99 D3
Highgate Ctr 4 SK6 112 F3
Highgate Dr Royton OL2 48 C7
Walkden M38 59 E5
Highgate Ho 7 OL8 66 D2
Highgate La Walkden M38 59 E5
Whitworth OL12 14 C5
Highgate Rd
Altrincham WA14 119 B4
Orrell WN8 53 B7
Highgrove Cl BL1 143 F3
Highgrove Mews 2 SK9 137 A6
Highgrove The BL1 23 D1
Highland Ave SK6 113 A2
Highland Lo WN6 19 D1
Highland Rd Bolton BL7 25 C8
Horwich BL6 22 E1
Highland View 1 OL5 68 C2
Highland Wlk M35 83 D6
Highlands
Littleborough OL15 16 A3
Royton OL2 48 C3
Highlands Dr SK2 124 F6
Highlands Rd
Hazel Grove SK2 124 F6
Rochdale OL11 29 E5
Royton OL2 48 C3
Shaw OL2 149 A8
Highlands The 3 OL5 68 C1
Highmarsh Cres WA12 89 B4
Highmead St M18 99 D5
Highmead Wlk M16 162 D5
Highmeadow Orrell WN8 53 A6
Radcliffe M26 43 F1
Highmore Dr M9 64 E3
Highnam Wlk M22 121 A1
Highover Ho M20 109 F4
Highshore Dr M8 155 F7
Highstone Dr M8 156 C6
Highthorne Gn OL2 48 C8
Highview SK13 116 A7
Highview Wlk M9 64 E3
Highwood OL11 13 E1
Highwood Cl 3 Bolton BL2 25 F1
Glossop SK13 116 B8
Highwoods Cl WN4 73 B5
Highworth Cl BL3 145 E5
Highworth Dr M40 65 D2
Higifield Ave M33 108 C3
Higson Ave Bredbury SK6 112 F2
Eccles M30 95 C8
Manchester M21 109 B7
Hilary Ave Atherton M46 58 C5
Gatley SK8 131 D8
Golborne WA3 74 D1
Oldham OL8 84 F8
Hilary Cl SK4 169 D2
Hilary Gr BL4 60 D7
Hilary Rd M22 121 C1
Hilary St OL11 30 D1
Hilbre Ave OL1 48 D2
Hilbre Rd M19 110 F8
Hilbury Ave M9 64 D1
Hilda Ave Bury BL8 26 F6
Cheadle SK8 122 E5
Hilda Gr SK5 169 F4
Hilda Rd SK14 113 D7
Hilda St 6 Bolton BL3 42 A4
Heywood OL10 29 D3
Leigh WN7 75 D6
Oldham OL9 153 D7
Reddish SK5 169 F4
Hilden Ct M16 97 D4
Hilden St Bolton BL2 148 A6
4 Leigh WN7 75 F5
Hilditch Cl M23 121 B6
Hildyard St WN5 54 F6
Hiley Rd M30 79 A1
Hilgay Cl WN3 54 D3
Hill Cl WN6 35 E8
Hill Cot Rd BL1 24 F5
Hill Court Mews SK6 113 B2
Hill Cres Leigh WN7 75 C8
Manchester M9 64 A3
Hill Crest M46 58 F5
Hill Crest Ave Leigh WN7 75 C8
Manchester SK4 168 A2
Hill Dr SK9 131 E3
Hill End Rd OL3 50 F4
Hill Farm Cl OL8 67 B3
Hill House Fold La WN6 18 C5
Hill House La WN6 18 C5
Hill La Blackrod BL6 21 C2
Bolton BL2 148 A8
Manchester M9 64 D4
Hill Mount SK16 102 A8
Hill Rise Altrincham WA14 119 A5
Ramsbottom BL0 11 A4
Romiley SK6 113 B2
Hill Side BL1 40 F7
Hill St Altrincham WA14 119 C8
Ashton-u-L OL6,OL7 166 B2
Bury BL8 26 F4
Dukinfield SK16 166 B1
Heywood OL10 29 C2
Hindley WN2 56 D6

Hill St *continued*
Leigh WN7 75 E5
Manchester M20 110 B7
Manchester M7 155 D6
Middleton M24 47 A3
Oldham OL4 67 B7
Radcliffe M26 43 F4
Ramsbottom BL9 11 C3
Rochdale OL16 31 A7
Romiley SK6 113 B2
Shaw OL2 149 C6
Wigan WN6 37 B1
Hill Top Altrincham WA15 120 A1
Atherton M46 58 F5
Bolton BL1 143 D3
Little Lever BL3 43 A4
Romiley SK6 113 B3
Hill Top Ave Cheadle SK8 132 B8
Prestwich M25 63 B4
Wilmslow SK9 137 B8
Hill Top Com Prim Sch OL11 31 A1
Hill Top Com Specl Sch OL4 50 A4
Hill Top Ct SK8 123 B1
Hill Top Dr
Altrincham WA15 120 A1
Rochdale OL11 30 F2
Hill Top Fold 1 WN2 56 E6
Hill Top La OL3 50 C4
Hill Top Rd M28 60 D4
Hill View Delph OL3 50 F4
Stalybridge SK15 102 E6
Hill View Cl OL1 49 C2
Hill View Dr PR7 19 D8
Hill's Ct 3 BL8 27 B4
Hillam Cl M41 95 F1
Hillary Ave Ashton-u-L OL7 85 B5
Wigan WN5 54 D5
Hillary Rd SK14 102 A5
Hillbank WN6 37 A7
Hillbank Cl BL1 142 C3
Hillbank St OL11 47 D6
Hillbeck Cres WN4 72 D4
Hillbrae Ave WA11 71 A1
Hillbre Way Handforth SK9 131 E4
1 Wilmslow SK9 131 D4
Hillbrook Ave M40 65 B2
Hillbrook Rd
Bramhall SK7 132 D6
Stockport SK1,SK2 124 C6
Hillbrow Wlk 9 M8 155 F7
Hillbury Rd SK7 123 F1
Hillcote Wlk M18 165 B6
Hillcourt Rd
High Lane SK6 134 F7
Romiley SK6 113 C4
Hillcourt St M1 163 A7
Hillcrest Hyde SK14 113 F7
Middleton M24 46 F3
Platt Bridge WN2 56 B2
Salford M6 80 A3
Hillcrest Ave OL10 29 A3
Hillcrest Cres OL10 29 A3
Hillcrest Dr Denton M34 101 B1
Reddish M19 111 C7
Hillcrest Gram Sch SK3 170 F6
Hillcrest Rd Prestwich M25 62 F2
Rochdale OL11 30 D1
Stockport SK2 124 C7
Stockport SK7 123 F1
Tyldesley M29 77 D8
Hillcroft Oldham OL8 67 A1
Stockport SK2 124 E6
Hillcroft Cl M8 156 A8
Hillcroft Rd WA14 119 A5
Hilldale Ave M9 64 E4
Hilldean WN8 53 C8
Hillel Ho M15 163 A5
Hillend SK14 103 A1
Hillend La SK14 103 A1
Hillend Pl M23 109 A2
Hillend Rd M23 109 A2
Hillfield M5 154 D2
Hillfield Cl M13 164 D5
Hillfield Dr Bolton BL2 25 B1
Boothstown M28 78 A7
Hillfield Wlk 10 BL2 25 B1
Hillfoot Wlk 25 M15 162 D6
Hillgate Ave M5 161 B7
Hillgate St OL6 166 C4
Hillhead Wlk M8 156 A5
Hillhouse Ct OL12 30 B3
Hillier St M9 157 E8
Hillier St N M9 157 E8
Hillingdon Cl OL8 84 B8
Hillingdon Dr M9 65 B2
Hillingdon Rd
Stretford M32 96 E2
Whitefield M45 62 D7
Hillington Rd Sale M33 107 F5
Stockport SK3 123 C8
Hillkirk Dr OL12 14 C3
Hillkirk St M11 160 E1
Hillman Cl M40 157 D5
Hillock The Bolton BL2 25 D5
Tyldesley M29 77 B5
Hillreed WN6 36 F1
Hills La BL9 45 C2
Hillsborough Dr BL9 45 B2
Hillsdale Gr BL2 25 E3
Hillside WA13 117 E1
Hillside Ave
Ashton-in-M WN4 72 F8
Atherton M46 58 E4
Blackrod BL6 21 E1
Bolton BL7 25 C8
Diggle OL3 51 C3

Hillside Ave *continued*
Farnworth BL4 . . . . .60 C7
Horwich BL6 . . . . .22 C4
Manchester M7 . . . . .81 A8
Mossley SK15 . . . . .86 F6
Oldham OL4 . . . . .67 C7
Oldham OL4 . . . . .68 B5
Romiley SK14 . . . . .113 F6
Royton OL2 . . . . .48 E5
Shaw OL2 . . . . .49 D8
Walkden M28 . . . . .60 C4
Whitefield M45 . . . . .44 E2
Hillside Cl Billinge WN5 . . . .71 D5
Bolton BL2 . . . . .25 E5
Bolton BL3 . . . . .40 D2
Bramhall SK7 . . . . .133 A7
Disley SK12 . . . . .135 F6
Hadfield SK13 . . . . .171 E3
Manchester M40 . . . . .65 A1
Wigan WN3 . . . . .54 D3
Hillside Cres
Ashton-u-L OL6 . . . . .85 F5
Bury BL9 . . . . .27 F6
Horwich BL6 . . . . .22 C4
Hillside Ct BL1 . . . . .40 F7
Hillside Dr Middleton M24 . .47 B1
Pendlebury M27 . . . . .80 D6
Hillside Gr SK6 . . . . .114 B1
Hillside Rd
Altrincham WA15 . . . . .120 A3
Ramsbottom BL0 . . . . .138 A5
Romiley SK14,SK6 . . . . . . .113 D5
Stockport SK2 . . . . .124 D7
Hillside St 6 BL3 . . . . .145 D5
Hillside View Denton M34 . .113 A7
Milnrow OL16 . . . . .32 A6
Hillside Way OL12 . . . . .4 C1
Hillside Wlk OL12 . . . . .14 D4
Hillspring Rd OL4 . . . . .68 A6
Hillstone Ave OL12 . . . . . . .14 D4
Hillstone Cl BL8 . . . . .10 F2
Hilltop OL12 . . . . .14 D4
Hilltop Ave Manchester M9 . .64 D3
Whitefield M45 . . . . .63 B8
Hilltop Ct Manchester M14 . .98 D1
Manchester M8 . . . . .63 F2
Hilltop Dr Bury BL8 . . . . . . .26 E6
Haslingden BB4 . . . . .1 C7
Marple SK6 . . . . .125 C7
Oldham OL2 . . . . .48 E2
Hilltop Gr M45 . . . . .63 B8
Hilltop Rd SK13 . . . . .104 B2
Hillview Ct BL1 . . . . .143 E4
Hillview Rd Bolton BL1 . . . .143 E4
Reddish M34 . . . . .100 A1
Hillwood Ave M8 . . . . .63 F3
Hillwood Dr SK13 . . . . .116 F8
Hilly Croft BL7 . . . . .24 F8
Hillyard St 7 BL8 . . . . .27 C3
Hilmarton Cl BL2 . . . . .25 E5
Hilrose Ave M41 . . . . .95 F2
Hilson Ct M43 . . . . .84 A1
Hilton Arc OL1 . . . . .153 F7
Hilton Ave Horwich BL6 . . . .22 A3
Urmston M41 . . . . .95 D2
Hilton Bank M28 . . . . .60 B3
Hilton Cl WN7 . . . . .76 A5
Hilton Cres Ashton-u-L OL6 . .85 C5
Boothstown M28 . . . . .78 B6
Prestwich M25 . . . . .63 A2
Hilton Ct SK3 . . . . .170 E8
Hilton Dr Irlam M44 . . . . . .105 C5
Manchester M25 . . . . .63 B2
Hilton Fold La M24 . . . . . . .47 B1
Hilton Gr Poynton SK12 . . .133 D4
Walkden M28 . . . . .60 B3
Hilton La Prestwich M25 . . .63 A2
Walkden M28 . . . . .60 B2
Hilton Lo M25 . . . . .63 A2
Hilton Pl WN2 . . . . .38 C6
Hilton Rd Bury BL9 . . . . . .140 F2
Disley SK12 . . . . .135 B7
High Lane SK12 . . . . .134 C5
Stockport SK3 . . . . .123 F1
Hilton Sq M27 . . . . .62 A1
Hilton St
Ashton-in-M WN4 . . . . .73 C3
Bolton BL2 . . . . .148 C7
Bury BL9 . . . . .140 F4
Dukinfield SK14 . . . . .101 F5
Manchester M1 . . . . .159 B1
Manchester M1,M4 . . . . . . .159 B2
Manchester M7 . . . . .155 D5
Stockport SK3 . . . . .170 D8
Walkden M38 . . . . .60 A4
Wigan WN1 . . . . .37 D1
Hilton St N M7 . . . . .155 D6
Hilton Wlk M24 . . . . .64 C8
Hiltons Farm Cl M34 . . . . .100 E6
Himley Rd M11 . . . . .83 C3
Hincaster Wlk M18 . . . . . .165 C5
Hinchcombe Dr M38 . . . . . .60 A6
Hinchley Way M27 . . . . . . .61 F2
Hinckley St M11 . . . . .164 F8
Hind Hill St OL10 . . . . .29 D1
Hind Rd WN5 . . . . .54 D8
Hind St BL2 . . . . .148 C7
Hind's Head Ave WN6 . . . . .18 F6
Hindburn Cl M45 . . . . .45 B1
Hindburn Dr M28 . . . . .78 A8
Hindburn Wlk M45 . . . . . . .45 B1
Hinde St M40 . . . . .83 A8
Hindell Terr OL3 . . . . .50 F4
Hindhead Wlk M40 . . . . . . .83 D4
Hindle Dr OL2 . . . . .48 C3
Hindle St Bacup OL13 . . . . .3 F7
Radcliffe M26 . . . . .44 A3
Hindles Cl M46 . . . . .58 A1

Hindley All Saints
CE Prim Sch WN2 . . . . . . .56 E5
Hindley Ave M22 . . . . .121 B2
Hindley Borsdane Brook
Com Specl Sch WN2 . . . . .56 E4
Hindley Bsns Ctr 10 WN2 . .56 D5
Hindley Cl OL7 . . . . .84 F1
Hindley Green
Cty Prim Sch WN2 . . . . . .57 B3
Hindley Jun & Inf Sch
WN2 . . . . .56 E5
Hindley Mill La WN2 . . . . . .56 F7
Hindley Rd BL5,WN2 . . . . . .57 D5
Hindley St Ashton-u-L OL7 . .84 F1
Stockport SK1 . . . . .170 F8
Hindley Sta WN2 . . . . .56 D7
Hindley Tanfield Sch WN2 .56 E5
Hindley Wlk 1 WN1 . . . . . .150 C8
Hinds La Bury BL8 . . . . .27 C1
Bury BL8,BL9 . . . . .44 C7
Hindsford CE Prim Sch
M46 . . . . .58 E1
Hindsford Cl M23 . . . . .108 E1
Hindsford St M46 . . . . .58 F1
Hinkler Ave BL3 . . . . .147 E3
Hinstock Cres M18 . . . . . . .99 D5
Hinton 10 OL12 . . . . .139 E8
Hinton Cl OL11 . . . . .29 E6
Hinton Gr SK14 . . . . .114 A8
Hinton Mews SK1 . . . . .112 B1
Hinton St Manchester M4 . .159 B3
Oldham OL8 . . . . .153 F5
Hipley Cl SK6 . . . . .113 A5
Hirons La OL4 . . . . .68 A5
Hirst Ave M28 . . . . .60 C5
Hitchen Cl SK16 . . . . .101 F7
Hitchen Dr SK16 . . . . .101 F7
Hitchin Wlk M13 . . . . .164 D5
Hive St OL8 . . . . .66 B2
HM Prison Strangeways
M3,M8 . . . . .158 F4
HMS Bronington M17 . . . . . .96 E7
Hoad Wlk 3 M34 . . . . .113 A7
Hoade St WN2 . . . . .56 E7
Hob Hey La WA3 . . . . .91 D3
Hob Hill SK15 . . . . .85 F1
Hob Hill Mdws SK13 . . . . . .116 D7
Hob La BL7 . . . . .9 C7
Hob Mill Rise OL5 . . . . .68 E4
Hobart Cl SK7 . . . . .132 F4
Hobart St Bolton BL1 . . . . .143 D2
Manchester M18 . . . . .99 E5
Hobby Gr WN7 . . . . .76 B5
Hobson Cres M34 . . . . .100 E6
Hobson Ct M34 . . . . .100 E6
Hobson Moor Rd
SK14,SK15 . . . . .103 A7
Hobson St Droylsden M11 . .100 A7
Failsworth M35 . . . . .83 D6
Oldham OL1 . . . . .153 F6
Reddish SK5 . . . . .99 F2
Hockenhull Cl M22 . . . . . . .121 E2
Hockery View WN2 . . . . .56 C4
Hockley Cl SK12 . . . . .134 A3
Hockley Rd Poynton SK12 . .134 A3
8 Wythenshawe M23 . . . . .120 F6
Hodder Ave
Littleborough OL15 . . . . . . .15 F6
Platt Bridge WN2 . . . . .55 F2
Hodder Bank SK2 . . . . .124 E5
Hodder Cl WN5 . . . . .54 D7
Hodder Way M45 . . . . .63 C8
Hoddesdon St M8 . . . . .156 B7
Hodge Clough Inf Sch
OL1 . . . . .49 D3
Hodge Clough Jun Sch
OL1 . . . . .49 D3
Hodge Clough Rd OL1 . . . . .49 D3
Hodge La
Mottram-in-L SK14 . . . . . .114 F8
Salford M5,M6 . . . . .154 F1
Hodge Rd Oldham OL1 . . . . .49 D3
Walkden M28 . . . . .60 D2
Hodge St M9 . . . . .64 F1
Hodges St WN6 . . . . .37 A2
Hodgson Dr WA15 . . . . . . .120 A8
Hodgson St
Ashton-u-L OL6 . . . . .166 A2
Manchester M8 . . . . .155 F5
Hodnet Dr WN4 . . . . .73 C3
Hodnet Wlk M34 . . . . .100 E1
Hodnett Ave M41 . . . . .94 E1
Hodson Fold OL8 . . . . .67 A1
Hodson Rd M27 . . . . .61 E2
Hodson St Manchester M3 .158 F2
Wigan WN3 . . . . .150 C7
Hogarth Rd Marple SK6 . . .126 B8
Rochdale OL11 . . . . .30 F3
Hogarth Rise OL1 . . . . .49 D4
Hogarth Wlk M8 . . . . .156 C6
Hoghton Ave OL13 . . . . .4 A8
Holbeach Cl Bury BL8 . . . . .27 D5
Hindley WN2 . . . . .56 E4
Holbeck M29 . . . . .77 B5
Holbeck Ave OL12 . . . . .14 D4
Holbeck Gr M14 . . . . .98 E4
Holberton Cl M8 . . . . .155 E5
Holbeton Cl SK7 . . . . .124 A3
Holborn Ave
Failsworth M35 . . . . .84 B7
Leigh WN7 . . . . .75 F8
Radcliffe M26 . . . . .43 D4
Wigan WN3 . . . . .150 B5
Holborn Dr M8 . . . . .156 B5
Holborn Gdns OL11 . . . . . .139 D5
Holborn Sq OL11 . . . . .139 D5
Holborn St OL11 . . . . .139 D5
Holbrook Ave M38 . . . . .60 A6

Holbrook St M1 . . . . .163 A8
Holcombe Ave Bury BL8 . . . .27 B2
Golborne WA3 . . . . .90 C8
Holcombe Brook
Prim Sch BL0 . . . . .11 A2
Holcombe Cl
Altrincham WA14 . . . . .119 B6
Kearsley BL4 . . . . .61 A6
Oldham OL4 . . . . .68 A7
Salford M6 . . . . .81 A2
Holcombe Cres BL4 . . . . . . .61 A6
Holcombe Ct BL0 . . . . .10 F2
Holcombe Gdns M19 . . . . .110 E5
Holcombe Lee BL0 . . . . .11 A4
Holcombe Mews BL0 . . . . . .10 F3
Holcombe Old Rd BL8 . . . .138 A5
Holcombe Rd
Haslingden BB4 . . . . .1 A6
Little Lever BL3 . . . . .42 F3
Manchester M14 . . . . .110 E7
Ramsbottom BL8 . . . . .10 F2
Holcombe View Cl OL4 . . . . .49 D2
Holcombe Wlk SK4 . . . . . . .111 D7
Holcroft La WA3 . . . . .92 C2
Holden Ave Bolton BL1 . . . . .24 E6
Bury BL9 . . . . .28 E4
Ramsbottom BL0 . . . . .138 A5
Holden Brook Cl WN7 . . . . .76 B5
Holden Clough Dr OL7 . . . . .85 B7
Holden Clough Prim
& Com Sch OL6 . . . . .85 D7
Holden Fold La OL1,OL2 . . . .48 D3
Holden Lea BL5 . . . . .39 E3
Holden Rd Leigh WN7 . . . . .76 B5
Manchester M25,M7 . . . . . .63 D1
Holden St Adlington PR7 . . . .20 C7
Ashton-u-L OL6 . . . . .166 C4
Oldham OL8 . . . . .66 F3
Rochdale OL12 . . . . .15 A2
Holder Ave BL3 . . . . .43 B5
Holderness Dr OL1 . . . . . . .48 C2
Holdgate Cl M15 . . . . .162 E5
Holding St WN2 . . . . .56 D6
Holdsworth St M27 . . . . . . .79 D7
Hole House Fold SK6 . . . . .113 B2
Holebottom OL6 . . . . .85 C6
Holford Ave M14 . . . . .98 B2
Holford Ct M34 . . . . .100 F3
Holford St M6 . . . . .81 C4
Holford Way WA12 . . . . .89 F3
Holgate Dr WN5 . . . . .53 E6
Holgate Prim Sch WN5 . . . .53 E6
Holgate St OL4 . . . . .49 E1
Holhouse La BL8 . . . . .10 F2
Holiday La SK2 . . . . .124 F7
Holker Cl
Manchester M13 . . . . .164 D5
Poynton SK12 . . . . .133 F4
Holker Way 21 M34 . . . . . .101 A1
Holkham Cl 6 M4 . . . . . . .159 C2
Holland Ave SK15 . . . . .86 A2
Holland Cl OL3 . . . . .50 E4
Holland Ct Manchester M8 . .63 F2
Radcliffe M26 . . . . .44 C4
Stockport SK1 . . . . .124 A7
Holland Gr OL6 . . . . .85 B6
Holland Rd Bramhall SK7 . .132 E7
Dukinfield SK14 . . . . .101 F5
Manchester M8 . . . . .63 F2
Holland Rise 7 OL12 . . . . .139 E8
Holland St E M34 . . . . .100 A4
Holland St W M34 . . . . .100 D4
Denton M34 . . . . .100 D4
Heywood OL10 . . . . .29 D2
Littleborough OL16 . . . . . . .15 D4
Manchester M40 . . . . .160 D3
Radcliffe M26 . . . . .44 C4
Rochdale OL12 . . . . .139 E8
Salford M6 . . . . .81 A5
Holland Wlk M6 . . . . .81 A5
Hollies Ct M33 . . . . .108 B4
Hollies Dr SK6 . . . . .126 A5
Hollies La SK9 . . . . .137 F7
Hollies The
10 Atherton M46 . . . . .58 D3
Bolton BL2 . . . . .42 F8
Gatley SK8 . . . . .122 B5
Manchester M20 . . . . .109 F3
Manchester M8 . . . . .168 B3
Pendlebury M27 . . . . .80 B3
Salford M6 . . . . .80 B3
Wigan WN1 . . . . .37 D3
Hollin Ave BL5 . . . . .57 F7
Hollin Bank SK4 . . . . .111 D7
Hollin Cres OL3 . . . . .68 E5
Hollin Cross La SK13 . . . . .116 C8
Hollin Dr M24 . . . . .46 F4
Hollin Hey Cl WN5 . . . . .71 D3
Hollin Hey Rd BL1 . . . . .23 E3
Hollin House M24 . . . . .47 A3
Hollin La
Middleton M24,OL10 . . . . . .46 F4
Rochdale OL11 . . . . .29 E6
Styal SK9 . . . . .130 F5
Hollin Prim Sch M24 . . . . . .47 A3
Hollinbrook WN6 . . . . .36 F2
Holliney Ave M22 . . . . .121 F1
Holliney Rd M22 . . . . .121 F1
Hollington Way WN3 . . . . . . .54 C2
Hollingwood Cl WN4 . . . . . . .73 A3
Hollingworth Ave M40 . . . . .65 D2
Hollingworth Cl 4 SK1 . . .170 F8
Hollingworth Dr SK6 . . . . . .125 F3
Hollingworth High Sch
OL16 . . . . .32 A6
Hollingworth La OL14 . . . . . .6 B8

Hollingworth Lake Cntry Pk
Visitor Ctr OL15 . . . . .16 C3
Hollingworth Lake Cntry Pk
OL15 . . . . .16 B2
Hollingworth Lake
Water Sports Ctr OL15 . . .16 B3
Hollingworth Prim Sch
SK14 . . . . .103 C5
Hollingworth Rd
Bredbury SK6 . . . . .112 E4
Littleborough OL15 . . . . . . .16 B4
Hollingworth St OL9 . . . . . . .66 B3
Hollinhall St OL4 . . . . .67 C7
Hollinhey Terr SK14 . . . . . .103 C5
Hollinhurst Dr BL6 . . . . .40 C2
Hollinhurst Rd M26 . . . . . . .44 C1
Hollins Ave
40 Gamesley SK13 . . . . . .171 D2
Hyde SK14 . . . . .113 E4
Oldham OL4 . . . . .67 F8
Hollins Bank 35 SK13 . . . .171 D2
Hollins Brook Cl BL9 . . . . . .45 B5
Hollins Brow BL9 . . . . .44 F4
Hollins Cl
34 Gamesley SK13 . . . . . .171 D2
Garswood WN4 . . . . .72 D4
Tyldesley M29 . . . . .77 A8
Whitefield BL9 . . . . .45 B4
Hollins Cty Prim Sch WN2 57 A5
Hollins Fold 36 SK13 . . . . .171 D2
Hollins Gdns 39 SK13 . . . .171 D2
Hollins Gn M24 . . . . .47 A3
Hollins Gr
37 Gamesley SK13 . . . . . .171 D2
Sale M33 . . . . .108 A4
Hollins Green Rd SK6 . . . .125 F6
Hollins Grundy Prim Sch
BL9 . . . . .45 A5
Hollins Ind Pk SK13 . . . . . .104 B5
Hollins La Edenfield BL0 . . . .1 E2
Gamesley SK13 . . . . .171 D2
Marple SK6 . . . . .125 F6
Marple SK6 . . . . .126 C8
Mossley OL5 . . . . .68 D1
Oldham OL3 . . . . .69 B5
Whitefield BL9 . . . . .45 B4
Hollins Mews
Gamesley SK13 . . . . .171 D2
Whitefield BL9 . . . . .45 C4
Hollins Mount SK6 . . . . . . .126 B8
Hollins Rd Hindley WN2 . . . .57 A5
Oldham OL4 . . . . .67 F8
Oldham OL8 . . . . .66 D2
Hollins St Bolton BL2 . . . . .148 B6
6 Oldham OL4 . . . . .67 F6
Stalybridge SK15 . . . . .101 F8
Walsden OL14 . . . . .6 B8
Hollins Terr 2 SK6 . . . . . .125 F6
Hollins The 3 SK6 . . . . . .125 F6
Hollins Way 38 SK13 . . . . .171 D2
Hollins Wlk M22 . . . . .121 D2
Hollinscroft Ave WA15 . . . .120 D5
Hollinshead M7 . . . . .155 E6
Hollinsmoor Rd SK22 . . . . .127 D7
Hollinswood Rd
Bolton BL2 . . . . .148 B6
Boothstown M28 . . . . .78 B6
Hollinwood La M40,OL9 . . . .65 B2
Hollinwood Rd SK13 . . . . . .135 D6
Hollinwood Sta OL9 . . . . . . .66 A2
Hollow End SK5 . . . . .112 B7
Hollow Mdws M26 . . . . .61 C6
Hollow The SK8 . . . . .122 C1
Hollow Vale Dr SK5 . . . . . .112 A8
Hollow Vale Rd SK5 . . . . . . .99 F1
Holloway Dr M27,M28 . . . . .61 C1
Hollowbrook Way 4
OL12 . . . . .14 D2
Hollowell La BL6 . . . . .22 D1
Hollowfield OL11 . . . . .13 D1
Hollowgate M28 . . . . .79 B6
Hollows The SK8 . . . . .122 C1
Hollowspell OL12 . . . . .15 C3
Holly Ave Cheadle SK8 . . . .122 D5
Newton-le-W WA12 . . . . . . .89 D3
Urmston M41 . . . . .95 B2
Walkden M28 . . . . .60 E2
Holly Bank
Ashton-u-L OL6 . . . . .85 D2
Edgworth BL7 . . . . .9 B7
Failsworth M40 . . . . .83 C7
Hollingworth SK14 . . . . . . .103 D5
2 Royton OL2 . . . . .48 D4
Royton OL2 . . . . .48 D6
Sale M33 . . . . .108 C3
Holly Bank Cl M15 . . . . . . .161 C6
Holly Bank Ct SK8 . . . . . . .123 A1
Holly Bank Rd SK9 . . . . . . .131 B1
Holly Cl WA15 . . . . .120 A6
Holly Ct Hyde SK14 . . . . . .102 A2
Holly Dene Dr BL6 . . . . .40 B7
Holly Dr M33 . . . . .108 A4
Holly Fold M45 . . . . .44 F1
Holly Gr Bolton BL1 . . . . . .142 C1
Bolton BL6 . . . . .40 B7
Chadderton OL9 . . . . .152 B8
Denton M34 . . . . .101 A3
Dukinfield SK15 . . . . .101 E8
Farnworth BL4 . . . . .60 A8
Leigh WN7 . . . . .75 E7
Oldham OL4 . . . . .67 E7
Sale M33 . . . . .108 D4

Holly Grange
Altrincham WA14 . . . . .119 D2
Stockport SK7 . . . . .123 F3
Holly Heath Dr WN1 . . . . . . .37 B4
Holly Heys 4 M33 . . . . .108 D4
Holly House Dr M41 . . . . . . .94 F2
Holly La Oldham OL8 . . . . . .66 C2
Wythenshawe SK9 . . . . . . .130 E5
Holly Mill Cres BL1 . . . . . . .143 F4
Holly Mount BB4 . . . . .1 A7
Holly Mount RC Prim Sch
BL8 . . . . .10 D1
Holly Oak Gdns OL10 . . . . . .29 C1
Holly Rd Aspull WN2 . . . . . . .38 B5
Bramhall SK7 . . . . .132 E5
Golborne WA3 . . . . .90 C8
High Lane SK6 . . . . .134 F7
Lymm WA13 . . . . .117 B5
Poynton SK12 . . . . .133 E3
Reddish SK4 . . . . .111 C5
Swinton M27 . . . . .79 D6
Wigan WN5 . . . . .54 E6
Holly Rd N SK9 . . . . .137 B6
Holly Rd S SK9 . . . . .137 B5
Holly Royde Cl M20 . . . . . .110 B6
Holly St Bolton BL1 . . . . . .143 F4
Bury BL8 . . . . .26 F6
Bury BL9 . . . . .141 A2
Droylsden M43 . . . . .83 D2
Littleborough OL12 . . . . . . .15 C6
Manchester M11 . . . . .164 E8
Ramsbottom BL9 . . . . .11 C3
Stockport SK1 . . . . .112 B1
Wigan WN2 . . . . .37 F2
Holly Wlk M31 . . . . .105 D3
Hollybank Rise SK16 . . . . .101 F8
Hollybank St M26 . . . . .43 F3
Hollybank St M18 . . . . .99 E6
Hollycroft Ave Bolton BL2 . . .42 F5
Wythenshawe M22 . . . . . . .121 D6
Hollyedge Dr M25 . . . . .63 A2
Hollyhedge Ave M22 . . . . . .121 D5
Hollyhedge Court Rd
M22 . . . . .121 E5
Hollyhedge Ct M22 . . . . . . .121 E4
Hollyhedge Rd M22,M23 . . .121 C5
Hollyhey Dr M23 . . . . .109 C2
Hollyhouse Dr SK6 . . . . . . .113 A5
Hollyhurst M28 . . . . .79 B6
Hollymount M16 . . . . .97 B4
Hollymount Ave SK2 . . . . . .124 C5
Stockport SK2 . . . . .124 C5
Hollymount Dr Oldham OL4 .49 E3
Stockport SK2 . . . . .124 C5
Hollymount Gdns SK2 . . . .124 D5
Hollymount Rd SK2 . . . . . .124 D5
Hollythorn Ave SK8 . . . . . .132 C7
Hollythorn Mews SK8 . . . . .132 C7
Hollyway M22 . . . . .121 E8
Hollywood
Altrincham WA14 . . . . .119 D2
Bolton BL1 . . . . .142 B2
Hollywood Rd Bolton BL1 . .142 B2
Moorend SK6 . . . . .126 F8
Hollywood Towers SK3 . . . .170 D8
Hollywood Way SK3,SK4 . .169 D1
Holm Ct M6 . . . . .81 A3
Holmbrook M29 . . . . .59 C1
Holmcroft Rd M18 . . . . .99 D3
Holmdale Ave M19 . . . . . . .110 E5
Holme Ave Bury BL8 . . . . . . .27 C5
Wigan WN1 . . . . .37 C2
Holme Cres OL1 . . . . .48 C2
Holme Ct M7 . . . . .37 C2
Holme House St OL15 . . . . . .6 D1
Holme La Haslingden BB4 . . .1 A8
Rawtenstall BB4 . . . . .1 E8
Holme Park Way M35 . . . . . .84 B7
Holme Rd M20 . . . . .110 A3
Holme St Bacup OL13 . . . . . .3 D8
Hyde SK14 . . . . .167 D2
Holme Terr
Littleborough OL15 . . . . . . .6 D1
Rawtenstall BB4 . . . . .1 D8
Wigan WN1 . . . . .37 B3
Holme Vale BB4 . . . . .1 A6
Holmedale Ct M33 . . . . . . .108 C4
Holmefield M33 . . . . .108 B4
Holmepark Gdns M28 . . . . . .78 A5
Holmes Cotts BL1 . . . . .142 C3
Holmes House Ave WN3 . . . .54 D3
Holmes Rd OL12 . . . . .139 D7
Holmes St Bolton BL3 . . . . .42 A4
Cheadle SK8 . . . . .122 E4
Littleborough OL12 . . . . . . .15 C3
Rochdale OL12 . . . . .139 D7
Stockport SK2 . . . . .170 E7
Holmes Way M34 . . . . .112 F7
Holmeswood Cl SK9 . . . . . .137 C8
Holmeswood Pk BB4 . . . . . . .1 E8
Holmeswood Rd BL3 . . . . . .147 D2
Holmfield Ave
Manchester M25 . . . . .63 C3
Manchester M9 . . . . .157 F7
Holmfield Ave W M9 . . . . . .157 F7
Holmfield Cl SK4 . . . . .169 D3
Holmfield Dr SK8 . . . . .132 B8
Holmfield Gn BL3 . . . . .40 F4
Holmfirth St M13 . . . . .98 F4
Holmfoot Wlk 6 M9 . . . . . .157 D7
Holmlea Rd M43 . . . . .83 C2
Holmleigh Ave M9 . . . . .64 E1
Holmpark Rd M11 . . . . .99 F7
Holmrook WA14 . . . . .119 B5
Holmsfield Cl WN2 . . . . .38 A2

Holmside Gdns M19 . . . . . . .110 E4
Holmwood WA14 . . . . .119 A3
Holmwood Cl WN4 . . . . .73 A5
Holmwood Ct M20 . . . . .110 B4
Holmwood Rd M20 . . . . .110 B5
Holroyd St
  Manchester M11 . . . . .165 A8
  Rochdale OL16 . . . . .31 A7
Holset Dr WA14 . . . . .119 B5
Holst Ave M8 . . . . .156 A6
Holstein Ave OL12 . . . . .14 D4
Holt Ave WN5 . . . . .71 D4
Holt Cres WN5 . . . . .71 D4
Holt Ho M20 . . . . .110 B2
Holt La M35 . . . . .84 B7
Holt Lane Mews M35 . . . . . . .84 B7
Holt Mill Rd BB4 . . . . .2 D8
Holt St Altrincham WA14 . . . .119 C8
  Ashton-u-L M34 . . . . .100 E8
  Bolton BL3 . . . . .145 D5
  Eccles M30 . . . . .95 C8
  Hindley WN2 . . . . .56 C5
  Leigh WN7 . . . . .75 E7
  Littleborough OL15 . . . . .6 D2
  Manchester M10,M40 . . . . . .157 F5
  Milnrow OL16 . . . . .32 A5
  Oldham OL4 . . . . .67 C8
  Orrell WN5 . . . . .53 D5
  Ramsbottom BL0 . . . . .11 D6
  Rawtenstall BB4 . . . . .2 E8
  Shevington WN6 . . . . .36 F2
  Stockport SK1 . . . . .170 F8
  Swinton M27 . . . . .61 F2
  Tyldesley M29 . . . . .59 A1
  Whitworth OL12 . . . . .4 C1
  Wigan WN1 . . . . .151 F8
  Wigan WN3 . . . . .55 A4
Holt St W BL0 . . . . .138 B5
Holt Town M4,M40 . . . . .160 E2
Holt's La SK9 . . . . .130 F3
Holt's Terr OL12 . . . . .14 E2
Holtby St M9 . . . . .64 E1
Holthouse Rd BL8 . . . . .26 F5
Holtown Ind Est M40 . . . . . . .160 E2
Holts La OL4 . . . . .67 D4
Holtswell Cl WA3 . . . . .74 E1
Holtwood Wlk SK5 . . . . .112 C7
Holway Wlk M9 . . . . .156 C7
Holwick Rd M23 . . . . .108 F2
Holwood Dr M16 . . . . .109 E8
Holy Cross & All Saints
  RC Sch M30 . . . . .95 D8
Holy Cross Coll BL9 . . . . .44 E8
Holy Family RC Inf Sch
  WN2 . . . . .38 A2
Holy Family RC Prim Sch
  Boothstown M28 . . . . .77 E7
  Oldham OL8 . . . . .84 D8
  Platt Bridge WN2 . . . . .56 A1
  Rochdale OL11 . . . . .31 A2
  Sale M33 . . . . .108 E4
Holy Harbour St BL1 . . . . . .142 C2
Holy Inf & St Anthony
  RC Prim Sch BL1 . . . . . .143 E4
Holy Name RC Prim Sch
  M15 . . . . .163 A5
Holy Rosary RC Prim Sch
  OL8 . . . . .66 F2
Holy St OL16 . . . . .31 B2
Holy Trinity CE Dobcross
  Prim Sch OL3 . . . . .50 F2
Holy Trinity CE Prim Sch
  Ashton-u-L OL6 . . . . .166 A3
  Bury BL9 . . . . .140 F1
  Littleborough OL15 . . . . .16 B5
  Manchester M9 . . . . .157 E8
Holy Trinity Stacksteads
  CE Prim Sch OL13 . . . . .3 C8
Holybourne Wlk M23 . . . . . .120 D8
Holyhurst Wlk **22** BL1 . . . . . .143 E2
Holyoak St M40 . . . . .83 C6
Holyoake Rd M28 . . . . .60 E2
Holyoake St M43 . . . . .84 C2
Holyrood Cl Leigh WN7 . . . . . .76 E7
  Prestwich M25 . . . . .63 C6
Holyrood Ct M25 . . . . .63 C6
Holyrood Dr Prestwich M25 . .63 C6
  Swinton M27 . . . . .79 D7
Holyrood Gr M25 . . . . .63 C6
Holyrood Rd M25 . . . . .63 C5
Holyrood St Failsworth M40 . .83 E4
  Oldham OL1 . . . . .49 A1
Holywood St **1** M14 . . . . .98 B3
Home Dr M24 . . . . .64 F7
Home Farm Ave M14 . . . . . .102 F1
Homebury Dr M11 . . . . .83 B2
Homelands Cl M33 . . . . .107 F2
Homelands Rd M33 . . . . .107 F2
Homelaurel Ho M33 . . . . . . .108 B2
Homer Dr SK6 . . . . .126 B8
Homer St M26 . . . . .43 E3
Homerton Rd M40 . . . . .83 B4
Homestead M31 . . . . .106 A4
Homestead Cres M19 . . . . . .110 D3
Homestead Gdns OL12 . . . . . .15 C4
Homestead Rd SK12 . . . . . . .135 C6
Homestead The M33 . . . . . . .107 F5
Homewood Ave M22 . . . . . . .109 D1
Homewood Rd M22 . . . . .109 C1
Honduras St **1** OL4 . . . . .67 B7
Hondwith Cl **2** BL2 . . . . .25 C5
Honey St M8 . . . . .159 B4
Honeybourne Cl M29 . . . . . . .59 C1
Honeysuckle Ave WN6 . . . . . .36 F3

Honeysuckle Cl
  Romiley SK6 . . . . .113 A5
  Sale M23 . . . . .108 D1
Honeysuckle Dr SK15 . . . . . . .86 C2
Honeysuckle Way OL12 . . . . . .14 D3
Honeysuckle Wlk M33 . . . . . .107 D6
Honeywell La OL8 . . . . .66 F3
Honford Rd OL10 . . . . .46 B4
Hong Kong Ave M90 . . . . . . .130 A8
Honister Dr M24 . . . . .46 F2
Honister Rd
  Manchester M9 . . . . .157 F7
  Wigan WN3 . . . . .54 B6
Honister Way OL11 . . . . .30 B4
Honiton Ave M22 . . . . .102 D2
Honiton Cl Chadderton OL9 . .47 E1
  Heywood OL10 . . . . .46 C8
  Hindley WN7 . . . . .57 D2
Honiton Ct SK14 . . . . .102 D2
Honiton Dr BL2 . . . . .43 A6
Honiton Gr M26 . . . . .43 D4
Honiton Way M14 . . . . .119 B6
Honiton Wlk **3** SK14 . . . . . . .102 D2
Honor St M13 . . . . .98 F3
Hood Cl M29 . . . . .59 D1
Hood Gr WN7 . . . . .76 B3
Hood Sq OL4 . . . . .68 A5
Hood St M4 . . . . .159 B2
Hook St WN2 . . . . .151 F7
Hoole Cl SK8 . . . . .123 A5
Hooley Bridge Ind Est
  OL10 . . . . .29 C4
Hooley Range SK4 . . . . .168 B3
Hooper St
  Manchester M12 . . . . .164 D8
  9 Oldham OL4 . . . . .67 A6
  Stockport SK1,SK4 . . . . .169 E1
Hooten La WN7 . . . . .76 C3
Hooton St Bolton BL3 . . . . . .146 C3
  Manchester M40 . . . . .160 F3
Hooton Way **14** SK9 . . . . .131 D5
Hopcroft Cl M9 . . . . .64 B6
Hope Ave Bolton BL2 . . . . . . .148 B6
  Bolton BL2 . . . . .25 E5
  Handforth SK9 . . . . .131 C3
  Stretford M32 . . . . .96 B3
  Walkden M38 . . . . .60 C4
Hope Carr La WN7 . . . . .76 B2
Hope Carr Rd Leigh WN7 . . .76 A3
  Leigh WN7 . . . . .76 B3
Hope Carr Way WN7 . . . . . . .76 A3
Hope Cres WN6 . . . . .36 B6
Hope Ct **1** OL12 . . . . .139 F8
Hope Fold Ave M46 . . . . .58 B2
Hope Green Way SK10 . . . . .133 D2
Hope Hey La M38 . . . . .59 F5
Hope High Sch M6 . . . . .80 C4
Hope Hospl M6 . . . . .80 B3
Hope La Leigh WA3,WN7 . . . .76 E2
  Poynton SK10 . . . . .133 D1
  Poynton SK10 . . . . .133 E1
Hope Park Cl M25 . . . . .63 B3
Hope Park Rd M25 . . . . .63 B3
Hope Pl OL11 . . . . .30 C1
Hope Rd Manchester M14 . . . .98 D4
  Prestwich M25 . . . . .63 A2
  Sale M33 . . . . .108 B4
Hope St Adlington PR6 . . . . .21 B8
  Ashton-in-M WN4 . . . . .73 D5
  Ashton-u-L OL6 . . . . .85 D4
  Aspull WN2 . . . . .38 F3
  Blackrod BL6 . . . . .38 E8
  Denton M34 . . . . .100 F5
  Dukinfield SK16 . . . . .101 B8
  Eccles M30 . . . . .79 F2
  Glossop SK13 . . . . .104 E2
  Hazel Grove SK7 . . . . .124 D3
  Heywood OL10 . . . . .46 F8
  Hindley WN2 . . . . .56 F6
  Horwich BL6 . . . . .22 B4
  Ince-in-M WN3 . . . . .55 F4
  Leigh WN7 . . . . .75 F4
  Manchester M1 . . . . .159 A1
  Manchester M5 . . . . .81 C1
  Manchester M7 . . . . .155 D7
  Newton-le-W WA12 . . . . .89 B3
  Oldham OL1 . . . . .67 B7
  Pendlebury M27 . . . . .80 A8
  Ramsbottom BL0 . . . . .138 B5
  Rochdale OL12 . . . . .139 F8
  Shaw OL2 . . . . .149 B7
  Stockport SK4 . . . . .169 D1
  Swinton M27 . . . . .79 D7
  Tyldesley M29 . . . . .77 B5
  Walkden M38 . . . . .60 A4
  Wigan WN1 . . . . .150 C8
Hope St N BL6 . . . . .22 B5
Hope Terr Stockport SK3 . . .170 E8
  Dukinfield SK16 . . . . .101 B8
Hopecourt Cl M6 . . . . .80 B4
Hopedale Cl M11 . . . . .160 F1
Hopedale Rd SK5 . . . . .111 F6
Hopefield Rd WA13 . . . . .117 B4
Hopefield St BL3 . . . . .147 D4
Hopefold Dr M28 . . . . .60 E2
Hopelea St M20 . . . . .110 B7
Hopes Carr SK1 . . . . .169 F1
Hopgarth Wlk M40 . . . . .83 D5
Hopkin Ave OL1 . . . . .67 B8
Hopkin Mill OL4 . . . . .67 D4
Hopkin St OL1 . . . . .153 F7
Hopkins Bldgs OL5 . . . . .68 E3
Hopkins Field M4 . . . . .119 B1
Hopkins St Hyde SK14 . . . . .167 E4
  Manchester M12 . . . . .99 A3
Hopkinson Ave M34 . . . . . . .100 E5
Hopkinson Cl **4** OL3 . . . . . . .69 B8

Hopkinson Rd M9 . . . . .64 D5
Hoppet La M43 . . . . .84 C2
Hopton Ave M22 . . . . .121 F3
Hopton Ct M15 . . . . .163 A6
Hopwood Ave Eccles M30 . . .79 D3
  Heywood OL10 . . . . .46 D8
  Horwich BL6 . . . . .22 C4
Hopwood Cl
  6 Golborne WA3 . . . . .90 F8
  Whitefield M45 . . . . .44 F3
Hopwood Com Prim Sch
  OL10 . . . . .46 E8
Hopwood Ct Heywood OL10 .46 E8
  Middleton M24 . . . . .47 F4
Hopwood Hall Coll OL12 .139 E7
Hopwood Rd M24 . . . . .47 F4
Hopwood St Failsworth M40 .83 B6
  Manchester M3 . . . . .158 E2
  Pendlebury M27 . . . . .80 A8
Horace Barnes Cl M14 . . . . . .98 A3
Horace Gr SK4 . . . . .169 E4
Horace St BL1 . . . . .143 D2
Horatio St **4** M18 . . . . .99 F6
Horbury Ave M18 . . . . .99 D3
Horbury Dr BL8 . . . . .27 C2
Horden Wlk **9** OL2 . . . . .48 E4
Horeb St BL3 . . . . .145 D5
Horest La OL3 . . . . .50 B7
Horley Cl BL8 . . . . .27 C7
Hornbeam Cl
  Altrincham WA15 . . . . .120 E5
  Sale M33 . . . . .107 C5
Hornbeam Cres WN4 . . . . . . .73 B3
Hornbeam Ct M6 . . . . .81 A3
Hornbeam Rd M19 . . . . .99 B2
Hornby Ave M9 . . . . .64 E5
Hornby Dr BL3 . . . . .40 D3
Hornby Gr WN7 . . . . .76 D7
Hornby Rd M16,M32 . . . . .96 F4
Hornby St Bury BL9 . . . . .140 F4
  Heywood OL10 . . . . .29 D2
  Manchester M8 . . . . .158 F4
  Middleton M24 . . . . .65 A8
  Oldham OL8 . . . . .153 D5
  Wigan WN1 . . . . .37 C2
Horncastle Cl Bury BL8 . . . . .27 D5
  4 Golborne WA3 . . . . .90 F8
Horncastle Rd M40 . . . . .65 B1
Hornchurch Ct **2** M15 . . . . . .162 F6
Hornchurch St M15 . . . . .162 E6
Horncliffe Cl M43 . . . . .1 B8
Horncliffe View BB4 . . . . .1 B8
Horne Dr M4 . . . . .159 C2
Horne Gr Wigan WN3 . . . . . .150 A5
  Wigan WN3 . . . . .54 F5
Horne St BL9 . . . . .44 E8
Hornet Cl OL11 . . . . .31 A3
Hornsea Cl Bury BL8 . . . . .26 F2
  Chadderton OL9 . . . . .47 F1
Hornsea Rd SK2 . . . . .125 A5
Hornsea Wlk M11 . . . . .83 A1
Hornsey Gr WN3 . . . . .54 D3
Horridge Ave WA12 . . . . .89 C5
Horridge Fold BL7 . . . . .8 E3
Horridge Fold Ave BL5 . . . . . .40 F7
Horridge St BL8 . . . . .27 B4
Horrobin Fold BL7 . . . . .9 C2
Horrobin La Adlington PR6 . .21 C8
  Edgworth BL7 . . . . .9 C2
Horrocks Fold BL1 . . . . .24 C7
Horrocks Fold Ave BL1 . . . . .24 D6
Horrocks Rd BL7 . . . . .9 D6
Horrocks St Leigh WN7 . . . . .75 A4
  Radcliffe M26 . . . . .44 C4
  Tyldesley M29 . . . . .58 F1
  Tyldesley M46 . . . . .58 E1
Horsa St **10** BL2 . . . . .25 B1
Horsedge St OL1 . . . . .153 F7
Horsefield Ave OL12 . . . . .14 C6
Horsefield Cl M21 . . . . .109 E7
Horseforth La OL3 . . . . .69 A4
Horseshoe La
  Alderley Edge SK9 . . . . .137 A2
  Bolton BL7 . . . . .25 A8
  Oldham OL9 . . . . .65 F6
Horsfield St BL3 . . . . .144 A5
Horsfield Way SK6 . . . . .112 B5
Horsham Ave SK7 . . . . .124 C1
Horsham Cl Bury BL8 . . . . . . .27 C7
  Westhoughton BL5 . . . . .57 F6
Horsham Gr WN2 . . . . .37 F2
Horsham St M6 . . . . .154 E2
Horstead Wlk **8** M19 . . . . . . .99 A2
Horton Ave BL1 . . . . .24 E6
Horton Hill Prim Sch OL4 .67 B6
Horton Rd M14 . . . . .98 A4
Horton Sq OL2 . . . . .149 B6
Horton St Stockport SK1 . . .124 A7
  Wigan WN6 . . . . .36 E3
Hortree Rd M32 . . . . .96 E2
Horwich Bsns Pk 22 B2
Horwich L Ctr BL6 . . . . .22 C3
Horwich Parish
  CE Prim Sch BL6 . . . . .22 C4
Horwich Parkway Sta BL6 .39 C7
Horwood Cres M20 . . . . .110 D5
Hoscar Dr M19 . . . . .110 F7
Hoskers Nook BL5 . . . . .57 D7
Hoskers The BL5 . . . . .57 D6
Hoskins Cl M12 . . . . .165 A5
Hospital Ave M30 . . . . .79 E2
Hospital Cotts M25 . . . . .62 E7
Hospital Rd Bolton BL7 . . . . .25 A8
  Pendlebury M27 . . . . .79 F6
Hotel Rd M90 . . . . .130 C7
Hotel St Bolton BL1 . . . . .145 F7
  Newton-le-W WA12 . . . . .89 B3
Hothersall Rd **4** SK5 . . . . . . .111 F8

Hothersall St M7 . . . . .158 E3
Hotspur Cl M14 . . . . .110 A8
Hough Cl Oldham OL8 . . . . . .66 F3
  Oldham OL8 . . . . .67 A2
Hough End Ave M21 . . . . . . .109 C6
Hough End Ctr M21 . . . . . . .109 E7
Hough Fold Way BL2 . . . . . . .25 E4
Hough Gn WA15 . . . . .128 E5
Hough Hall Rd M40 . . . . .157 E8
Hough Hill Rd SK15 . . . . .102 B8
Hough La Bolton BL7 . . . . . . .24 F7
  Dukinfield SK14 . . . . .101 F6
  Middleton M24 . . . . .47 F4
  Tyldesley M29 . . . . .77 C8
  Wilmslow SK9 . . . . .137 D3
Hough Rd M20 . . . . .110 A7
Hough St Bolton BL3 . . . . . . .146 A4
  Tyldesley M29 . . . . .77 D8
Hough Wlk M7 . . . . .158 D3
Houghend Cres M21 . . . . . . .109 E8
Houghton Ave Oldham OL8 .66 D2
Houghton Cl
  Newton-le-W WA12 . . . . .89 B3
  Rochdale OL16 . . . . .31 C6
Houghton La
  Shevington WN6 . . . . .35 F6
  Swinton M27 . . . . .79 D5
Houghton Rd M8 . . . . .64 A1
Houghton St Bolton BL3 . . . .145 E5
  Bury BL9 . . . . .140 E1
  Leigh WN7 . . . . .75 F6
  Newton-le-W WA12 . . . . .89 B3
  Oldham OL2 . . . . .48 E2
  Pendlebury M27 . . . . .80 D6
Houghwood Grange WN4 . .72 F3
Houldsworth Ave M14 . . . . .119 E7
Houldsworth Mill Ind Est
  SK4,SK5 . . . . .111 E7
Houldsworth Sq **2** SK5 . . . .111 E7
Houldsworth St
  2 Radcliffe M26 . . . . .43 F5
  Reddish SK5 . . . . .111 E7
Houseley Ave OL9 . . . . .66 A3
Houseman Gr WN6 . . . . .37 A2
Housley Cl WN3 . . . . .150 A5
Houson St OL8 . . . . .153 F5
Houston Pk M5 . . . . .154 F1
Hove Cl BL8 . . . . .10 F1
Hove Dr M14 . . . . .110 E7
Hove St BL3 . . . . .144 C5
Hove St N **18** BL3 . . . . .144 C5
Hoveden St M8 . . . . .158 F4
Hovey Cl M8 . . . . .155 F7
Hovingham St M16 . . . . .31 B8
Hovington Gdns M19 . . . . . .110 E6
Hovis St M11 . . . . .165 C8
How Clough Cl M28 . . . . .60 F2
How Clough Dr M28 . . . . .60 F2
How Lea Dr BL9 . . . . .27 F6
Howard Ave Bolton BL3 . . . .146 A4
  Cheadle SK8 . . . . .123 A1
  Eccles M30 . . . . .79 D3
  Kearsley BL4 . . . . .60 F7
  Lymm WA13 . . . . .117 B4
  Reddish SK4 . . . . .111 C6
Howard Cl Glossop SK13 . . .104 B2
  Romiley SK6 . . . . .113 A2
Howard Ct OL6 . . . . .166 C3
Howard Dr WA15 . . . . .120 A1
Howard Hill BL9 . . . . .45 A5
Howard La M34 . . . . .100 E4
Howard Pl Hyde SK14 . . . . . .167 D2
  Rochdale OL16 . . . . .139 F8
Howard Rd Culcheth WA3 . . .92 A2
  Wythenshawe M22 . . . . .109 D1
Howard Spring Wlk M8 . . .155 F8
Howard St Ashton-u-L OL7 .166 A4
  Bolton BL1 . . . . .143 F1
  Denton M34 . . . . .100 E5
  Glossop SK13 . . . . .104 C1
  Manchester M8 . . . . .158 A4
  Oldham OL4 . . . . .49 E1
  Radcliffe M26 . . . . .44 B3
  Rochdale OL12 . . . . .139 F8
  Salford M5 . . . . .161 A8
  Shaw OL2 . . . . .149 A7
  Stalybridge SK15 . . . . .86 D4
  Stockport SK1 . . . . .169 F2
  Stretford M32 . . . . .96 D2
  Wigan WN5 . . . . .54 C5
Howard Way OL15 . . . . .6 C1
Howard's La OL5 . . . . .68 F1
Howards La WN5 . . . . .53 F7
Howarth Ave M28 . . . . .79 C7
Howarth Cl M11 . . . . .83 A1
Howarth Cross St OL16 . . . .15 B2
Howarth Ct
  8 Radcliffe M26 . . . . .44 B3
  Stockport SK2 . . . . .124 B5
Howarth Dr M44 . . . . .93 F1
Howarth Farm Way OL12 .15 C3
Howarth Gn OL12 . . . . .15 C3
Howarth Sq OL12 . . . . .15 C3
Howarth St Farnworth BL4 . .60 D7
  Leigh WN7 . . . . .76 B4
  Littleborough OL15 . . . . .16 B6
  Manchester M16 . . . . .97 C4
  Westhoughton BL5 . . . . .57 F8
Howarth Wlk **3** M26 . . . . . . .44 B3
Howbridge Cl M28 . . . . .78 C8
Howbro Dr OL7 . . . . .84 E5
Howbrook Wlk M15 . . . . . . .162 F6
Howcroft Cl BL1 . . . . .145 E8
Howcroft St BL3 . . . . .145 D5
Howden Cl SK5 . . . . .99 E2
Howden Dr WN3 . . . . .55 B4

Howden Rd Manchester M9 . .64 C5
  New Mills SK22 . . . . .127 C1
Howe Bridge Cl M46 . . . . . . .58 A1
Howe Dr BL0 . . . . .11 B2
Howe St Ashton-u-L OL7 . . . .100 F8
  Manchester M7 . . . . .155 D7
Howell Croft N **7** BL1 . . . . . .145 F7
Howell Croft S BL1 . . . . .145 F7
Howell's Yd **6** BL1 . . . . .145 F7
Howells Ave M33 . . . . .108 B5
Howgill St M11 . . . . .83 D1
Howsin Ave BL2 . . . . .25 B4
Howton Cl M12 . . . . .99 A4
Howty Cl SK9 . . . . .131 D1
Hoxton Cl SK6 . . . . .113 A4
Hoy Dr M41 . . . . .95 D5
Hoylake Cl Failsworth M40 . .83 D8
  Leigh WN7 . . . . .75 D2
Hoylake Rd Stockport SK3 . .123 B8
  Wythenshawe M33 . . . . .108 F2
Hoyland Cl M12 . . . . .164 F6
Hoyle Ave OL8 . . . . .153 E5
Hoyle St Bacup OL13 . . . . .3 E8
  3 Bolton BL1 . . . . .143 E4
  Manchester M12 . . . . .163 C8
  Radcliffe M26 . . . . .44 C1
  Whitworth OL12 . . . . .4 D3
Hoyle Street Ind Est M12 163 C7
Hoyle Wlk M13 . . . . .163 C6
Hoyle's Terr OL16 . . . . .31 E6
Hubert Worthington Ho
  SK9 . . . . .137 A1
Hucclecote Ave M22 . . . . . . .121 C3
Hucklow Ave M23 . . . . .121 A2
Hucklow Bank **27** SK13 . . . .171 D2
Hucklow Cl **28** SK13 . . . . . . .171 D2
Hucklow Fold **28** SK13 . . . . .171 D2
Hucklow Lanes **29** SK13 . . . .171 D2
Hudcar La BL9 . . . . .141 A4
Huddart Cl M5 . . . . .161 B8
Huddersfield Rd
  Diggle OL3 . . . . .51 C7
  Diggle OL3 . . . . .51 D5
  Newhey OL16,OL3 . . . . .32 D5
  Oldham OL1,OL4 . . . . .67 D8
  Stalybridge SK5,SK15 . . . . . .86 E4
Hudson Gr **9** WA3 . . . . .90 F8
Hudson Rd Bolton BL3 . . . . .146 B3
  Hyde SK14 . . . . .113 E7
Hudson St OL9 . . . . .66 A2
Hudsons Pas OL15 . . . . .16 C7
Hudsons Wlk OL11 . . . . .30 C7
Hudswell Cl M45 . . . . .62 E8
Hugh Lupus St BL1 . . . . .25 A5
Hugh Oldham Dr M7 . . . . . . .81 C6
Hugh St OL16 . . . . .31 A8
Hughendon Ct BL8 . . . . .26 F7
Hughes Ave BL6 . . . . .22 A4
Hughes Cl BL9 . . . . .141 A3
Hughes St Bolton BL1 . . . . . .142 C2
  Bolton BL1 . . . . .143 D2
  Manchester M11 . . . . .164 E8
Hughes Way M30 . . . . .79 A1
Hughley Cl OL2 . . . . .49 A4
Hughtrede St OL16 . . . . .31 B3
Hugo St Farnworth BL4 . . . . .42 B2
  Manchester M40 . . . . .83 A7
  Rochdale OL11 . . . . .30 D2
Hulbert St Bury BL8 . . . . .27 C1
  Middleton M24 . . . . .47 B1
Hull Mill La OL3 . . . . .50 F5
Hull Sq M3 . . . . .158 D2
Hullet Cl WN6 . . . . .35 E8
Hully St **7** SK15 . . . . .85 F2
Hulme Court Prep Sch
  OL8 . . . . .66 D4
Hulme Cl M15 . . . . .162 E7
Hulme Gr WN7 . . . . .75 C6
Hulme Gram Sch for Boys
  The OL8 . . . . .66 D4
Hulme Gram Sch for Girls
  The OL8 . . . . .66 D4
Hulme Hall Ave SK8 . . . . . . .132 B8
Hulme Hall Cl SK8 . . . . .123 A1
Hulme Hall Cres SK8 . . . . . .132 A8
Hulme Hall La M40 . . . . .160 E4
Hulme Hall Rd
  Cheadle SK8 . . . . .123 A1
  Manchester M15 . . . . .162 D7
Hulme Hall Schs SK8 . . . . .123 A1
Hulme Pl M5 . . . . .81 C2
Hulme Rd Bolton BL2 . . . . . . .25 E5
  Kearsley M26 . . . . .61 C7
  Leigh WN7 . . . . .75 C6
  Reddish M34 . . . . .100 B3
  Reddish M34 . . . . .111 B6
  Sale M33 . . . . .108 D3
Hulme St Ashton-u-L OL6 . . .85 D4
  Bolton BL1 . . . . .145 F8
  Bury BL8 . . . . .140 D3
  Manchester M1,M15 . . . . . .162 F7
  Manchester M15 . . . . .162 E7
  Manchester M3,M5 . . . . .81 C1
  Oldham OL8 . . . . .66 E4
  Stockport SK1 . . . . .124 B7
Hulme Wlk M15 . . . . .163 A6
Hulme's Terr BL2 . . . . .43 C8
Hulmes Rd M35,M40 . . . . . . .83 E5
Hulton Ave M28 . . . . .60 B3
Hulton Cl BL3 . . . . .146 A3
Hulton District Ctr M28 . . .60 A4
Hulton Dr Bolton BL3 . . . . . .146 A3
  Manchester M16 . . . . .97 C4
Hulton Hospl BL3 . . . . .146 A3
Hulton La Bolton BL3 . . . . . .146 A3
Hulton St Denton M34 . . . . . .100 E4
  Failsworth M35 . . . . .83 C4
  Salford M5 . . . . .161 A7

Humber Dr BL9 ....27 F7
Humber Pl WN5 ....54 C7
Humber Rd Milnrow OL16 .32 A6
  Tyldesley M29 ....77 C7
Humber St Manchester M8 156 B7
  Salford M5 ....154 D1
Humberstone Ave M15 .162 F6
Hume St Manchester M19 .111 B8
  Rochdale OL16 ....31 A5
Humphrey Booth Gdns
  M6 ....154 E3
Humphrey Cres M41 ....96 A2
Humphrey La M41 ....96 A2
Humphrey Park Sta M32 ..96 A3
Humphrey Pk M41 ....96 A2
Humphrey Rd M16 ....161 B5
Humphrey St
  Ince-in-M WN2 ....56 A7
  Manchester M8 ....155 F8
Humphries Ct M40 ....159 C4
Huncoat Ave SK4 ....111 D5
Huncote Dr M9 ....64 E1
Hunger Hill Ave M18 ....40 E2
Hungerford Wlk **5** M23 .120 D7
Hunmanby Ave M15 ....162 F7
Hunstanton Dr BL8 ....27 D5
Hunston Rd M33 ....107 F2
Hunt Ave OL7 ....85 B5
Hunt Fold Dr BL8 ....10 F1
Hunt La OL9 ....152 A7
Hunt Rd SK14 ....102 A5
Hunt St Atherton M46 ....58 D3
  Manchester M9 ....64 D1
  Wigan WN1 ....151 E7
Hunt's Bank
  Manchester M3 ....158 F2
  Westhoughton BL5 ....57 F6
Hunter Dr M26 ....44 A5
Hunter Rd WN5 ....36 E1
Hunter's La Oldham OL1 .153 F7
  Rochdale OL12,OL16 ....139 F5
Hunter's View SK9 ....131 C3
Hunters Chase WN5 ....53 E1
Hunters Cl
  6 Bredbury SK6 ....112 F3
  Wilmslow SK9 ....131 F1
Hunters Cl SK15 ....102 D8
Hunters Gn BL0 ....10 F3
Hunters Hill BL9 ....45 B2
Hunters Hill La OL3 ....51 C6
Hunters Glossop SK13 ..115 F8
Hunters Mews Sale M33 .108 A5
  Wilmslow SK9 ....131 F1
Hunterston Ave M30 ....80 A2
Huntingdon Ave OL9 ....152 B3
Huntingdon Cres SK5 ..112 C5
Huntingdon Way **7**
  M34 ....100 F1
Huntingdon Wlk **21** BL1 .143 E2
Huntington Ave M20 ....110 A7
Huntley Mount Rd BL9 .141 B3
Huntley Rd Cheadle SK3 .123 B7
  Manchester M8 ....63 C2
Huntley St BL9 ....141 B3
Huntly Chase SK9 ....137 C7
Huntroyde Ave **8** BL2 ....25 B1
Hunts Rd **2** M6 ....80 D5
Huntsham Cl WA14 ....119 B6
Huntsman Dr M44 ....105 F7
Huntsworth Wlk M13 ..164 F4
Hurdlow Ave M7 ....81 A7
Hurdlow Gn **14** SK13 ...171 D1
Hurdlow Lea **13** SK13 ..171 D1
Hurdlow Mews SK13 ....171 D1
Hurdlow Way **12** SK13 .171 D1
Hurdlow Wlk M9 ....157 D7
Hurdsfield Rd SK2 ....124 D4
Hurford Ave M18 ....99 D6
Hurlbote Cl SK9 ....131 D5
Hurley Dr SK8 ....122 E2
Hurlston Rd BL3 ....147 D2
Hurst Ave Bramhall SK8 ..132 C6
  Sale M33 ....107 C2
Hurst Bank Rd OL6 ....85 E4
Hurst Brook Cl OL6 ....166 C4
Hurst Cl BL5 ....58 F7
Hurst Cross OL6 ....85 E5
Hurst Ct Ashton-u-L OL6 ..85 E5
  Wythenshawe M23 ....120 F4
Hurst Gr OL6 ....85 E5
Hurst Green Cl BL3 ....43 F8
Hurst Hall Dr OL6 ....85 E5
Hurst Hill Cres OL6 ....85 D5
Hurst Inf Sch OL6 ....85 D5
Hurst Knoll Prim Sch
  OL6 ....166 C4
Hurst La WA3 ....92 C7
Hurst Lea Ct SK9 ....137 A2
Hurst Mdw OL16 ....31 C3
Hurst
  Methodist Jun Sch OL6 .85 D7
Hurst Mill La WA3 ....92 C8
Hurst Rd SK13 ....104 F1
Hurst St Bolton BL3 ....146 C3
  Bury BL9 ....141 A2
  Hindley WN2 ....56 C6
  Leigh WN7 ....76 B3
  Oldham OL9 ....153 D7
  Reddish SK5 ....111 E7
  Rochdale OL16 ....31 A5
  Walkden M28 ....60 D6
Hurst Wlk **4** M22 ....121 A2
Hurstbank Ave M19 ....110 D4
Hurstbourne Ave M11 ....83 B2
Hurstbrook Cl SK13 ....104 F1
Hurstbrook Dr M32 ....95 F2

Hurstclough Prim Sch
  SK14 ....102 E1
Hurstead **2** OL12 ....15 D4
Hurstead Gn **8** OL12 ....15 D4
Hurstead Rd OL16 ....31 F6
Hursted Rd OL16 ....31 F6
Hurstfield Ind Est
  SK4,SK5 ....111 E6
Hurstfield Rd M28 ....78 B8
Hurstfold Ave M19 ....110 D3
Hursthead Cty Jun Sch
  SK8 ....132 C7
Hursthead Inf Sch SK8 .132 C6
Hursthead Rd SK8 ....132 B7
Hursthead Wlk M13 ....163 B7
Hurstmead Terr M20 ....110 B2
Hurstvale Ave SK8 ....122 B1
Hurstville Rd M21 ....109 B6
Hurstway Dr **33** M9 ....64 E3
Hurstwood BL1 ....24 E5
Hurstwood Rd SK2 ....124 F6
Hus St **1** M43 ....100 A8
Husteads OL3 ....50 E1
Husteads La OL3 ....50 F1
Hutchins La OL4 ....49 D1
Hutchinson Rd OL11 ....13 D2
Hutchinson St
  4 Radcliffe M26 ....44 C4
  Rochdale OL11 ....30 C4
Hutchinson Way M26 ....44 A3
Huttock End La OL13 ....3 D8
Hutton Ave Ashton-u-L OL6 .85 E3
  Boothstown M28 ....77 F6
Hutton Cl WA3 ....91 E5
Hutton Lo M14 ....110 C7
Hutton St WN1 ....20 A1
Hutton Wlk **7** M13 ....163 C6
Huxley Ave M8 ....156 A6
Huxley Cl SK7 ....132 E7
Huxley Dr SK7 ....132 E7
Huxley Pl WN3 ....150 A5
Huxley St
  Altrincham WA14 ....119 D7
  Bolton BL1 ....142 C2
  6 Oldham OL4 ....67 C6
Huxton Gn SK7 ....124 A2
Huyton Dr PR6,PR7 ....21 A6
Huyton Terr PR6 ....21 B6
Hyacinth Cl SK3 ....170 D5
Hyatt Cres WN6 ....19 C3
Hyde Central Sta SK14 .101 C2
Hyde Cl WN3 ....150 A5
Hyde Dr M28 ....60 C2
Hyde Fold Cl M19 ....110 E6
Hyde Gr Manchester M13 .163 C5
  Sale M33 ....108 B4
  Walkden M28 ....60 C2
Hyde Ho SK4 ....111 C5
Hyde Hospl SK14 ....167 F1
Hyde North Sta SK14 ...101 C5
Hyde Pl M13 ....163 C5
Hyde Rd Denton M34 ....101 A3
  Manchester M12 ....164 E6
  Manchester M12,M18 ....99 D4
  Oldham M24 ....65 C6
  Romiley SK14,SK6 ....113 B5
  Walkden M28 ....60 C2
Hyde Sq M24 ....46 E1
Hyde St Bolton BL3 ....146 C3
  Droylsden M43 ....84 C4
  Dukinfield SK16 ....101 D8
  Manchester M16 ....162 D5
Hyde St Paul's
  RC Prim Sch SK14 ....167 F4
Hyde Tech Sch SK14 ....167 D4
Hyde's Cross M4 ....159 A2
Hyde-Clarendon
  Sixth Form Ctr SK14 ..167 E4
Hydes Terr SK15 ....86 B2
Hydon Brook Wlk OL11 ..30 C4
Hydrangea Cl **7** M33 ..107 C2
Hyldavale Ave SK8 ....122 B6
Hylton Dr Ashton-u-L OL7 ..84 F5
  Cheadle SK8 ....132 C8
Hyman Goldstone Wlk
  M8 ....155 F7
Hyndman Ct M5 ....154 D2
Hypatia St BL2 ....148 B7
Hythe Cl M14 ....98 C3
Hythe Rd SK3 ....123 B8
Hythe St BL3 ....146 A4
Hythe Wlk OL9 ....152 B6

Ibberton Wlk **8** M9 ....64 F1
Ibsley **20** OL12 ....139 E8
Ice House Cl **6** M28 ....59 F3
Iceland St M6 ....154 F2
Idonia St BL1 ....143 D3
Ifco Ctr M14 ....98 C3
Ilex Gr M7 ....155 D6
Ilford St M11 ....83 B2
Ilfracombe Rd SK2 ....124 D8
Ilfracombe St M40 ....83 D6
Ilk St M11 ....83 B2
Ilkeston Dr WN2 ....38 F3
Ilkeston Wlk
  5 Denton M34 ....113 A8
  4 Manchester M40 ....83 A6
Ilkley Cl Bolton BL2 ....148 C7
  Oldham OL9 ....152 B6
Ilkley Cres SK5 ....111 E8
Ilkley Dr M41 ....95 A4
Ilkley St M40 ....83 A8
Illingworth Ave SK15 ....86 C2
Illona Dr M7 ....81 A8

Ilminster OL11 ....139 E6
Ilminster Wlk **2** M9 ....64 E5
Ilthorpe Wlk **7** M40 ....83 A6
Imex Bsns Pk M13 ....98 F3
Imogen Ct M5 ....161 C8
Imperial Dr WN7 ....76 D6
Imperial Terr M33 ....108 A4
Ina Ave BL1 ....23 F7
Ince Cl Manchester M20 .110 B7
  Stockport SK4 ....169 E3
Ince Green La
  Ince-in-M WN2 ....56 A7
  Ince-in-M WN2,WN3 ....151 F6
Ince Hall Ave
  Ince-in-M WN2 ....56 A8
  Wigan WN2 ....151 F8
Ince St SK4 ....169 E3
Ince St Mary's
  CE Prim Sch WN3 ....55 F4
Ince Sta WN3 ....151 F6
Ince Wlk WN1 ....150 C8
Ince-in-Makerfield
  CE Prim Sch WN2 ....56 A7
Inchcape Dr M9 ....64 B4
Inchfield Cl OL11 ....29 E8
Inchfield Rd
  Manchester M40 ....65 B1
  Walsden OL14 ....6 A8
Inchley Rd M13 ....163 B7
Inchwood Mews OL4 ....49 E4
Incline Rd OL8 ....66 C2
Independent St BL3 ....43 A3
India St BL9 ....11 C3
Indigo St M6 ....80 F5
Indigo Wlk M6 ....80 F5
Industrial Cotts **10** BB4 ....2 F8
Industrial St Ramsbottom BL0 1 C1
  Westhoughton BL5 ....57 F7
Industry Rd **8** OL12 ....14 F1
Industry St
  14 Littleborough OL15 ....16 B5
  Oldham M9 ....66 A4
  Rochdale OL11 ....13 E1
  Whitworth OL12 ....4 D2
Infant St M25 ....63 C4
Infirmary St **11** BL1 ....145 F7
Ingersol Rd BL6 ....22 E1
Ingham Ave WA12 ....89 C1
Ingham Brow BL6 ....22 F4
Ingham St WA14 ....107 D1
Ingham St Bury BL9 ....141 A1
  Failsworth M40 ....83 E4
  Leigh WN7 ....75 E8
  5 Oldham OL1 ....67 A7
Inghams La OL15 ....16 B5
Inghamwood Cl M7 ....155 F7
Ingle Dr SK2 ....124 C7
Ingle Rd SK8 ....123 A6
Ingleby Ave M9 ....64 F4
Ingleby Cl Shaw OL2 ....149 A8
  Standish WN6 ....19 D2
  Westhoughton BL5 ....40 A3
Ingleby Ct M32 ....96 E1
Ingleby Way OL2 ....149 A8
Ingledene Ave M7 ....63 E1
Ingledene Ct **6** M7 ....63 E1
Ingledene Gr BL1 ....142 A2
Inglefield OL11 ....13 F1
Inglehead Cl M34 ....101 A2
Ingles Fold M28 ....78 B7
Inglesham Cl Leigh WN7 ..75 E1
  Wythenshawe M23 ....121 B6
Ingleton Ave M8 ....64 B2
Ingleton Cl Bolton BL2 ....25 D4
  Cheadle SK8 ....122 C6
  Newton-le-W WA12 ....89 B4
  Royton OL2 ....48 D5
Ingleton Dr WA11 ....71 B1
Ingleton Mews BL8 ....27 B4
Ingleton Rd SK3 ....123 C7
Inglewhite Ave WN1 ....37 C2
Inglewhite Cl BL9 ....44 D7
Inglewhite Cres **1** WN1 .37 C2
Inglewhite Pl **7** WN1 ....37 C2
Inglewood WA14 ....119 B3
Inglewood Ave WN1 ....151 E7
Inglewood Cl
  Ashton-u-L OL7 ....84 F5
  Bury BL9 ....141 C4
  Partington M31 ....105 F4
Inglewood Hollow SK15 .102 C8
Inglewood Rd M24 ....47 E1
Inglewood Wlk M13 ....163 C6
Inglis St OL15 ....16 B5
Ingoe Cl OL10 ....29 F3
Ingoldsby Ave M13 ....98 D4
Ingram Dr SK4 ....110 E3
Ingram St Platt Bridge WN2 .56 A3
  Shevington WN6 ....36 F2
Ings Ave WN2 ....14 B2
Ings La OL12 ....14 C2
Ink St OL16 ....139 F7
Inkerman St Hyde SK14 .167 D4
  Manchester M40 ....157 D6
  12 Rochdale OL12 ....14 F1
Inman St Bury BL9 ....44 E8
  Denton M34 ....100 F3
Innes St OL12 ....14 C1
Innes St M12 ....99 B3
Innis Ave M40 ....83 C5
Inst of Islamic H Ed BL7 .25 A8
Institute St BL1 ....148 A7
Instow Cl Chadderton OL9 .47 F1
  Manchester M13 ....164 D6
Intake Rd OL3 ....69 B3
International App M90 ..130 C7
Invar Rd M27 ....61 D1
Inver Wlk **10** M40 ....65 D2

Inverbeg Dr BL2 ....43 A7
Invergarry Wlk **19** M11 ..83 C1
Inverlael Ave BL1 ....144 B8
Inverness Ave M9 ....65 A4
Inverness Cl WN2 ....38 D5
Inverness Rd SK16 ....101 C7
Inward Dr WN6 ....36 A5
Inwood Wlk M8 ....156 C6
Inworth Wlk **10** M8 ....155 F7
Iona Pl BL2 ....25 C2
Iona Way M41 ....95 E5
Ionian Gdns **2** M7 ....81 C5
Ipswich St OL11 ....139 F5
Ipswich Way **10** M34 ..101 A1
Ipswich Wlk M12 ....164 E5
Iqbal Cl M12 ....165 A5
Irby Wlk SK8 ....123 A4
Ireby Cl M24 ....46 C2
Iredale Cres M26 ....36 F7
Iredine St **6** M11 ....83 C1
Irene Ave SK14 ....101 E5
Iris Ave Farnworth BL4 ....42 A1
  Kearsley BL4 ....60 F5
  Manchester M11 ....99 D8
Iris St Oldham OL8 ....66 F3
  Ramsbottom BL0 ....138 B6
Iris Wlk **7** M31 ....105 E2
Irk St M4 ....159 A3
Irk Vale Dr OL1,OL9 ....47 E1
Irk Wlk M45 ....45 B2
Irkdale St M8 ....156 C6
Irlam & Cadishead
  Com High Sch M44 ....105 E7
Irlam Ave M30 ....79 D1
Irlam Endowed Prim Sch
  M44 ....94 A2
Irlam Prim Sch M44 ....94 A1
Irlam Rd Sale M33 ....108 C4
  Urmston M41 ....94 D2
Irlam Sq M6 ....80 D5
Irlam St Bolton BL1 ....143 E3
  Manchester M40 ....157 E5
Irlam Sta M44 ....105 E7
Irlam Wharf Rd M44 ....106 A6
Irma St BL1 ....143 F3
Irmass Ind Est M17 ....96 D6
Iron St Denton M34 ....100 F3
  Horwich BL6 ....22 C2
  Manchester M40 ....160 E3
Irvin Dr M22,SK8 ....131 A8
Irvine Ave **6** M28 ....78 A6
Irvine St WN7 ....75 F6
Irving Cl SK2 ....124 A3
Irving Ho **1** BL1 ....143 E2
Irving St Bolton BL1 ....143 E2
  Oldham OL8 ....66 B2
Irwell Ave Eccles M30 ....79 C1
  Walkden M38 ....60 B4
Irwell Cl **4** M26 ....44 B2
Irwell Gr M30 ....79 F1
Irwell Ho **2** M15 ....162 D7
Irwell Pl Eccles M30 ....79 F1
  Salford M5 ....81 C2
  Wigan WN5 ....54 C6
Irwell Rd WN5 ....53 F7
Irwell St Bury BL9 ....140 E2
  Kearsley M26 ....61 A8
  Manchester M3 ....158 E1
  Manchester M7,M8 ....158 E4
  Radcliffe M26 ....44 B2
  Ramsbottom BL0 ....138 C6
  Salford M6 ....81 A6
Irwell Vale Rd BB4 ....1 C6
Irwell Vale Sta BL0 ....1 C5
Irwell Wlk OL8 ....66 C3
Irwin Dr SK9 ....131 C5
Irwin Rd WA14 ....119 D8
Irwin St M34 ....100 E3
Isa St BL0 ....11 A4
Isaac Cl M5 ....161 A8
Isaac St BL1 ....144 C8
Isabella Cl M16 ....97 C4
Isabella Sq WN1 ....151 E8
Isabella St OL12 ....15 A2
Isaiah St OL8 ....66 F4
Isca St M11 ....160 F1
Isel Wlk M24 ....46 D2
Isherwood Dr SK6 ....125 D6
Isherwood Fold BL7 ....9 D7
Isherwood Rd M31 ....106 F6
Isherwood St
  Heywood OL10 ....29 E1
  Leigh WN7 ....75 E8
  Rochdale OL11 ....31 A6
Isis St M7 ....81 A8
Islamic Acad M13 ....163 B6
Island Cotts BL9 ....11 C2
Island Row WN2 ....56 B7
Islington Rd SK2 ....124 C4
Islington St M3 ....158 D2
Islington Way M3 ....158 D1
Isobel Cl Eccles M30 ....79 B1
  1 Manchester M16 ....97 F4
Isobel Wlk BL3 ....145 D5
Ivanhoe Ave WA3 ....74 C1
Ivanhoe Ct BL3,BL4 ....42 C2
Ivanhoe St
  Farnworth BL3,BL4 ....42 C2
  Oldham OL1 ....49 C1
Iveagh Ct **19** OL16 ....31 B6
Ivor St Rochdale OL11 ....30 B3
Ivor St M11 ....30 B3
Ivy Ave WA12 ....89 C2
Ivy Bank Cl BL1 ....24 E5
Ivy Bank Rd BL1 ....24 E5
Ivy Cl Droylsden M43 ....83 F3
  Shaw OL2 ....149 B2
Ivy Cotts Denton M34 ....113 A7

Ivy Cotts continued
  Rawtenstall BB4 ....2 F8
Ivy Dr M24 ....64 F6
Ivy Gr Farnworth BL4 ....60 B8
  Kearsley BL4 ....60 F7
  Walkden M38 ....59 F4
Ivy House Rd WA3 ....74 D1
Ivy Rd Bolton BL1 ....142 B1
  Bury BL8 ....27 B2
  Golborne WA3 ....90 B8
  Poynton SK12 ....133 E3
  Westhoughton BL5 ....57 F7
Ivy St Ashton-in-M WN4 ....73 B3
  Bolton BL3 ....146 C4
  Eccles M30 ....79 D1
  Manchester M40 ....83 A8
  1 Rawtenstall BB4 ....2 F8
  Wigan WN1 ....150 B8
Ivy Wlk M31 ....105 D3
Ivybridge Cl M13 ....164 D5
Ivycroft SK13 ....171 E4
Ivydale Dr WN7 ....76 C5
Ivygreen Dr M5 ....67 F6
Ivygreen Rd M21 ....109 A8
Ivylea Rd M19 ....110 E4
Ivyleaf Sq M7 ....155 E6

J

Jack Brady Cl M23 ....120 E4
Jack La Droylsden M43 ....84 B2
  Droylsden M43 ....84 C2
  Urmston M41 ....95 E2
Jack McCann Ct **10** OL16 ..31 A8
Jack St **2** BL2 ....25 C1
Jack Taylor Ct OL12 ....15 B1
Jack's La BL5 ....57 A8
Jackdaw Rd BL8 ....10 F2
Jackie Brown Wlk M40 .157 D5
Jackman Ave OL10 ....46 D7
Jackroom Dr M4 ....159 C1
Jackson Ave Culcheth WA3 .91 E3
  3 Dukinfield SK16 ....101 D8
Jackson Cl OL8 ....153 E5
Jackson Cres M15 ....162 E7
Jackson Ct Manchester M21 96 F1
  Urmston M41 ....95 A4
Jackson Gdns M34 ....100 D2
Jackson Mews OL4 ....49 D1
Jackson Pit **1** OL1 ....153 E6
Jackson Pl OL16 ....31 B8
Jackson St Ashton-u-L OL6 166 B4
  Cheadle SK8 ....122 B4
  Failsworth M35 ....83 D6
  Farnworth BL4 ....60 D8
  Glossop SK13 ....116 C7
  Hadfield SK13 ....104 C5
  Hyde SK14 ....167 D2
  Ince-in-M WN2 ....56 A7
  Kearsley BL4 ....60 F7
  Littleborough OL12 ....15 C6
  Middleton M24 ....65 B8
  Mottram-in-L SK14 ....103 A3
  Oldham OL4 ....67 B7
  Oldham OL4 ....67 C6
  Radcliffe M26 ....44 B2
  Rochdale OL16 ....31 B6
  Sale M33 ....108 C3
  Stretford M32 ....96 C1
  Walkden M28 ....60 C4
  Whitefield M45 ....62 F7
Jackson's La SK7 ....133 C8
Jackson's Row M2 ....158 F1
Jacksons Edge Rd SK12 .135 B6
Jacob St WN2 ....56 D6
Jacobite Cl M7 ....63 C1
Jacobsen Ave SK14 ....167 F4
Jaffrey St WN7 ....75 E5
James Andrew St M24 ....47 B1
James Bentley Wlk **4**
  M40 ....83 C5
James Brindley Basin
  M1 ....159 C1
James Brindley
  Prim Sch M28 ....60 C1
James Butterworth Ct **6**
  OL16 ....31 B6
James Butterworth St **9**
  OL16 ....31 B6
James Cl SK16 ....101 E8
James Corbett Rd M5 ...154 D1
James Dr Hyde SK14 ....167 E1
  Hyde SK14 ....167 E2
James Henry Ave M5 ...161 B8
James Hill St **18** OL15 ...16 B5
James Leech St SK1,SK3 .170 E8
James Leigh St M1 ....163 A8
James Pl Coppull PR7 ....19 E8
  Standish WN6 ....19 D2
James Rd OL2 ....149 B7
James Sq M26 ....149 B7
James St Ashton-in-M WN2 .73 E7
  Bacup OL13 ....3 B7
  Bolton BL7 ....8 D3
  Bury BL9 ....141 A1
  Droylsden M43 ....84 B2
  Dukinfield M34 ....101 A4
  Dukinfield SK15,SK16 ....101 E8
  Failsworth M35 ....84 A4
  Glossop SK13 ....116 C8
  Heywood OL10 ....29 D3
  Horwich BL6 ....21 F3
  Ince-in-M WN3 ....151 D6
  Kearsley BL4 ....60 F8

James St continued
Little Lever BL3 . . . . .43 B3
Littleborough OL15 . . . . .15 E4
Manchester M3 . . . . .158 D1
3 Manchester M34 . . . . . .100 E8
Manchester M40 . . . . .160 A1
Prestwich M25 . . . . .63 A5
Radcliffe M26 . . . . .44 B2
Rochdale OL12 . . . . .44 B2
5 Rochdale OL12,OL16 . . . .31 A8
Romiley SK6 . . . . .113 A5
Sale M33 . . . . .108 D4
Shaw OL2 . . . . .149 A5
Stockport SK3 . . . . .170 E7
Tyldesley M29 . . . . .76 F8
Tyldesley M46 . . . . .58 E1
Westhoughton BL5 . . . . .39 E2
Whitworth OL12 . . . . .4 D2
James St S OL9 . . . . .152 A7
James's St OL4 . . . . .49 D1
Jameson St OL11 . . . . .30 B2
Jammy La OL9 . . . . .152 C6
Jane Barter Ho 1 BL4 . . .60 D8
Jane St Oldham OL9 . . . . .152 B6
Rochdale OL12 . . . . .139 E8
Whitworth OL12 . . . . .4 E6
Japan St M8 . . . . .155 F7
Jarmain St M12 . . . . .165 A7
Rochdale OL12 . . . . .14 F1
Jarvis St 11 Oldham OL4 . .67 A6
Rochdale OL12 . . . . .14 F1
Jasmine Ave M43 . . . . . . .84 C2
Jasmine Cl BL3 . . . . .108 E1
Jasmine Rd WN5 . . . . .54 D7
Jasmine Wlk M31 . . . . . . .105 F2
Jason St M4 . . . . .159 B3
Jasper Wlk 9 M16 . . . . . . .97 E4
Jauncey St BL3 . . . . .144 C5
Jaxons Ct WN1 . . . . .150 C8
Jayton Ave M20 . . . . .122 B8
Jean Ave WN7 . . . . .75 E2
Jean Cl M19 . . . . .99 A2
Jedburgh Ave BL1 . . . . . .144 B8
Jeff Joseph Sale Moor
Tech Coll M33 . . . . .108 D2
Jefferson Way OL12 . . . . . .14 F3
Jeffrey St M40 . . . . .56 A8
Jeffrey Wlk OL10 . . . . .29 A2
Jeffreys Dr SK16 . . . . .101 D8
Jehlum Cl M8 . . . . .156 B7
Jellicoe Ave M44 . . . . . . .105 E6
Jenkinson St Hindley WN2 .56 D6
Manchester M13,M15 . . . . .163 A6
Jenkyn Wlk 5 M11 . . . . . .160 F1
Jennet Hey WN4 . . . . .72 F6
Jennet's La WA3 . . . . .76 C1
Jennings Ave M5 . . . . . . .161 A8
Salford M5 . . . . .161 A8
Jennings St SK3 . . . . .170 D7
Jennison Cl M18 . . . . .165 B6
Jenny Beck Gr BL3 . . . . . .147 E4
Jenny La SK7 . . . . .132 E4
Jenny St OL8 . . . . .66 C2
Jepheys Pl 17 OL12 . . . . . .14 F1
Jepheys St OL12 . . . . .14 F1
Jepson St SK2 . . . . .124 A6
Jericho Rd BL9 . . . . .28 E4
Jermyn St OL12 . . . . .31 A8
Jerrold St 5 OL15 . . . . . . .16 B5
Jersey St M19 . . . . .110 F7
Jersey Rd SK5 . . . . .169 F4
Jersey St Ashton-u-L OL6 . .166 B4
Manchester M4 . . . . .159 C2
Jerusalem Pl M2 . . . . .162 F8
Jesmond Dr BL8 . . . . .27 C5
Jesmond Gr SK8 . . . . .132 B8
Jesmond Rd BL1 . . . . .142 B4
Jesmond Wlk M9 . . . . .64 D5
Jespersen St OL1 . . . . . . .153 F7
Jessamine Ave M7 . . . . . .158 D4
Jessel Cl M13 . . . . .163 C6
Jessica Way WN7 . . . . .75 B4
Jessie St Bolton BL3 . . . . .144 C5
Failsworth M40 . . . . .83 A6
Jessop Dr SK6 . . . . .125 F8
Jessop St M18 . . . . .99 D5
Jethro St Bolton BL2 . . . . .148 C8
Bolton BL2 . . . . .25 C4
Jetson St M18 . . . . .99 F6
Jevington Wlk 10 M13 . . .163 C6
Jimmy McMullen Wlk 6
M14 . . . . .98 A3
Jinnah Cl M11 . . . . .165 C8
Jo St M5 . . . . .81 A1
Joan St M40 . . . . .83 A7
Jobling St M11 . . . . .164 F8
Jocelyn St M40 . . . . .157 E5
Joddrell St M3 . . . . .158 E1
Joe Connolly Way BB4 . . . . .2 E8
Joel La SK14 . . . . .113 F7
Johannesburg Gdns M23 120 F4
John Ashworth St OL12 . . .15 B1
John Atkinson Ct M5 . . . .154 D2
John Ave SK8 . . . . .122 E5
John Beeley Ave M11 . . . . .99 D8
John Booth St OL4 . . . . . . .67 F5
John Boste Ct BL3 . . . . . . .42 C3
John Brown St 14 BL1 . . .145 F8
John Clynes Ave M40 . . . .159 C3
John Cross St BL3 . . . . . .147 E4
John Dalton St
Hadfield SK13 . . . . .103 E5
Manchester M2 . . . . .158 F1
John Foran Cl M40 . . . . . . .83 B6

John Gilbert Way M17 . . . .96 E5
John Henry St OL12 . . . . . .4 D4
John Heywood St M11 . . . .83 B2
John Kemble Ct OL11 . . . .30 D4
John Kennedy Gdn SK14 103 A3
John Kennedy Rd SK14 . .102 F3
John Knott St OL4 . . . . . . .67 F6
John Lee Fold M24 . . . . . . .47 A1
John Lloyd Ct M44 . . . . . .105 F8
John Nash Cres M15 . . . .162 E6
John Roberts Cl OL11 . . .139 E5
John Robinson Wlk 3
M40 . . . . .83 A7
John Shepley St SK14 . . . .167 E2
John Smeaton Ct 15 M1 .159 C1
John St Altrincham WA14 . .119 D4
Ashton-in-M WN4 . . . . .73 D5
Bolton BL7 . . . . .25 A7
Bury BL9 . . . . .140 F3
Denton M34 . . . . .100 F4
Droylsden M43 . . . . .83 F1
Eccles M30 . . . . .79 B1
Failsworth M35 . . . . .65 F1
Farnworth BL4 . . . . .60 E8
Glossop SK13 . . . . .116 C8
Golborne WA3 . . . . .90 A8
Hazel Grove SK7 . . . . .124 D3
Heywood OL10 . . . . .29 D2
Heywood OL10 . . . . .29 D3
Hindley WN2 . . . . .57 B3
Hyde SK14 . . . . .167 D3
Irlam M44 . . . . .105 E5
Leigh WN7 . . . . .75 F5
Little Lever BL3 . . . . .43 B3
Littleborough OL15 . . . . .16 A5
Littleborough OL16 . . . . .15 C3
Manchester M3 . . . . .158 E2
Manchester M4 . . . . .159 A2
Manchester M7 . . . . .158 D4
Marple SK6 . . . . .126 A5
Middleton M25 . . . . .63 E8
Oldham OL4 . . . . .68 A6
Oldham OL8 . . . . .153 E6
Pendlebury M27 . . . . .80 A8
Rochdale OL16,OL12 . . . . . . .31 A8
Romiley SK6 . . . . .113 A4
Romiley SK6 . . . . .113 C2
Romiley SK6 . . . . .114 B3
Royton OL2 . . . . .48 D4
Sale M33 . . . . .108 B5
Shaw OL2 . . . . .149 A5
Stalybridge SK15 . . . . .86 C5
Stockport SK1 . . . . .169 F1
7 Tyldesley M29 . . . . .59 A1
Walkden M28 . . . . .60 D4
Whitworth OL12 . . . . .4 D2
Wigan WN1 . . . . .151 D8
4 Wigan WN5 . . . . .54 D5
John St E OL7 . . . . .84 F1
John St W OL7 . . . . .100 F8
John William St
Droylsden M11 . . . . .83 D1
Eccles M30 . . . . .79 F2
John's Pl SK6 . . . . .113 C2
Johnny King Cl M40 . . . . .157 D5
Johns Cl M21 . . . . .109 B8
Johnson Ave Leigh WN2 . . .56 E1
Newton-le-W WA12 . . . . .89 B5
Oldham OL1 . . . . .49 E5
Johnson Cl WN7 . . . . .75 B4
Johnson Fold Ave BL1 . . .23 E2
Johnson Fold
Com Prim Sch BL1 . . . . . .23 F3
Johnson Gr M24 . . . . .64 E8
Johnson St Atherton M46 . .58 A1
Bolton BL1 . . . . .145 F6
Manchester M15 . . . . .162 D6
Manchester M3 . . . . .158 E2
Pendlebury M27 . . . . .80 D6
Radcliffe M26 . . . . .44 B1
Tyldesley M29 . . . . .59 A1
11 Wigan WN5 . . . . .54 B6
Johnson Terr 28 SK16 . . .166 B1
Johnson's Sq M40 . . . . . .160 D4
Johnsonbrook Rd
SK14,SK16 . . . . .101 D5
Johnston 21 OL12 . . . . . .139 E8
Johnston Ave OL15 . . . . . .15 F3
Johnstone St M32 . . . . . . .96 A3
Join Rd M33 . . . . .108 D4
Joiner St Manchester M4 . .159 A1
Manchester M5 . . . . .81 C1
Jolly Brows BL2 . . . . .25 D3
Jolly Tar La PR7 . . . . .20 B7
Jonas St Manchester M7 . .158 E3
Manchester M9 . . . . .157 E6
Jonathan Cl BB4 . . . . .1 A8
Jones Sq SK1 . . . . .124 A7
Jones St Bolton BL1 . . . . .145 F8
Hadfield SK13 . . . . .104 A5
Horwich BL6 . . . . .22 B4
Oldham OL1 . . . . .67 A8
Oldham OL2 . . . . .48 E2
Radcliffe M26 . . . . .44 B4
Rochdale OL16 . . . . .31 A6
Salford M6 . . . . .154 F2
Jonquil Dr M28 . . . . .59 F3
Jopson St M24 . . . . .47 B1
Jordan Ave OL2 . . . . .49 D8
Jordan St Glossop SK13 . .104 E1
Manchester M15 . . . . .162 E7
Joseph Eastham
High Sch M28 . . . . .60 B3
Joseph Jennings Ct OL7 . .85 A6
Joseph Johnson Mews
M22 . . . . .109 E1
Joseph St Eccles M30 . . . . .79 B1
Failsworth M35 . . . . .83 F8

Joseph St continued
1 Farnworth BL4 . . . . .42 D1
Marple SK6 . . . . .126 A6
Middleton M24 . . . . .46 F1
Radcliffe M26 . . . . .44 B2
3 Rochdale OL12 . . . . . . .14 D2
Josephine Dr M27 . . . . . . .80 A7
Joshua La M24 . . . . .65 D7
Josslyn Rd M5 . . . . .154 D3
Joule Cl M5 . . . . .161 A8
Joule St M9 . . . . .64 E1
Joules Ct 2 SK1 . . . . . . .170 F8
Jowett St Oldham OL1 . . . . .49 C1
Reddish SK5 . . . . .169 F4
Jowett's Wlk OL7 . . . . .84 F2
Jowkin La OL11 . . . . .29 D6
Joy Pl OL12 . . . . .14 F2
Joy St Ramsbottom BL0 . . .138 B6
Rochdale OL12 . . . . .14 F2
Joyce St M40 . . . . .83 B7
Joynson Ave M7 . . . . .158 D4
Joynson St M33 . . . . .108 B5
Jubilee OL2 . . . . .32 C2
Jubilee Ave Orrell WN5 . . . .53 D4
Radcliffe M26 . . . . .44 C1
Stalybridge SK16 . . . . .85 E1
Jubilee Cl M30 . . . . .79 D3
Jubilee Cotts M28 . . . . . . .60 C3
Jubilee Ct Manchester M16 .97 B4
Reddish SK5 . . . . .99 F2
Jubilee Ho BL1 . . . . .145 E6
Jubilee Rd M24 . . . . .47 B1
Jubilee St Bolton BL3 . . . .146 C3
Salford M6 . . . . .154 F2
Shaw OL2 . . . . .149 C6
Jubilee Terr M24 . . . . .47 B1
Jubilee Way BL9 . . . . .140 D2
Judith St OL12 . . . . .14 C3
Judson Ave M21 . . . . .109 C6
Judy St M9 . . . . .157 F8
Julia Mews 4 M46 . . . . . . .22 B4
Julia St Horwich BL6 . . . . . .22 B4
Manchester M3 . . . . .158 F3
Rochdale OL12 . . . . .139 E8
Julian Ho OL1 . . . . .153 F7
Julian St M19 . . . . .111 B8
Jumbles Ctry Pk BL7 . . . . .9 D2
Junction Alley OL16 . . . . .139 F7
Junction La WA12 . . . . .89 B3
Junction Rd Bolton BL3 . . .144 A5
Bolton BL3 . . . . .40 F1
Stockport SK1,SK2,SK3 . . . .170 F7
Junction Rd W BL6 . . . . . . .40 D5
Junction St
Dukinfield SK14 . . . . .101 C5
Middleton M24 . . . . .65 D6
Oldham OL8 . . . . .66 E4
Junction Terr WN3 . . . . . .151 E6
June Ave Leigh WN7 . . . . . .75 C6
Stockport SK4 . . . . .168 B2
June St OL7 . . . . .166 A2
Juniper Bank SK5 . . . . . . .112 A8
Juniper Cl Bolton BL1 . . . .143 E1
Oldham OL4 . . . . .49 F4
Sale M33 . . . . .107 F6
Sale M33 . . . . .108 A4
Juniper Dr Hindley WN2 . . .57 A3
Milnrow OL16 . . . . .31 D7
Jupiter Gr WN3 . . . . .54 E2
Jupiter Wlk M40 . . . . .83 A5
Jura Cl SK16 . . . . .101 D8
Jura Dr M41 . . . . .95 E5
Jura Gr OL10 . . . . .29 B1
Jurby Ave M9 . . . . .64 D4
Jury St Leigh WN7 . . . . .75 E7
Manchester M8 . . . . .158 F4
Justin Cl M13 . . . . .163 B7
Jutland Ave OL11 . . . . .30 C8
Jutland Gr BL5 . . . . .39 F1
Jutland St M1 . . . . .159 B1

K

Kale St M13 . . . . .163 B7
Kalima Gr M7 . . . . .155 F6
Kane Ct WA3 . . . . .75 A1
Kansas Ave M5 . . . . .96 E8
Kara St M6 . . . . .154 E2
Karen Rd WN1 . . . . .151 F8
Kaskenmoor Sch OL8 . . . . .66 B1
Kate St BL0 . . . . .138 B6
Kathan Cl OL16 . . . . .31 B7
Katherine Ct M16 . . . . . . .161 C5
Katherine Rd SK2 . . . . . . .124 C5
Katherine St OL6 . . . . .166 A2
Kathkin Ave M8 . . . . .64 B2
Kathleen Gr M14 . . . . .98 D2
Kathleen St OL12 . . . . . . .139 D7
Kay Ave SK6 . . . . .112 D3
Kay Brow Heywood OL10 . . .29 B2
Ramsbottom BL0 . . . . .138 C6
Kay Cl WN1 . . . . .151 D8
Kay Garden Sh Ctr BL9 . .140 E2
Kay St Atherton M46 . . . . . .58 D2
Bolton BL1 . . . . .145 F8
Bury BL9 . . . . .141 A3
Edgworth BL7 . . . . .9 C2
Heywood OL10 . . . . .29 C2
Little Lever BL3 . . . . .43 A3
Manchester M11 . . . . .164 F7
Manchester M6 . . . . .80 C4
Ramsbottom BL9 . . . . .11 C3
Rochdale OL11 . . . . .139 E5
Stalybridge SK15 . . . . .102 A8
16 Stalybridge SK15 . . . . .86 A1
Kay's Ave SK1 . . . . .112 B1

Kaye Ave WA3 . . . . .91 F3
Kayfields BL2 . . . . .25 E4
Kayley Ind Est OL7 . . . . . . .84 F3
Kays Gdns M3 . . . . .158 D2
Kays Wood Rd SK6 . . . . . .125 D6
Keadby Cl M30 . . . . .95 D8
Keal Dr M44 . . . . .94 B4
Kean Pl M30 . . . . .79 D1
Keane Cl M29 . . . . .58 F1
Keane St OL7 . . . . .166 A3
Kearsley Dr BL3 . . . . .42 B3
Kearsley Hall Rd M26 . . . . .61 C7
Kearsley Mount Sh Prec
BL4 . . . . .61 B6
Kearsley Rd Kearsley M26 . .61 D8
Manchester M8 . . . . .64 A2
Kearsley St Eccles M30 . . . .79 B2
Leigh WN7 . . . . .75 D5
Wigan WN6 . . . . .37 B1
Kearsley Sta BL4 . . . . .61 A7
Kearsley Vale M26 . . . . . . .61 B8
Kearsley West
Cty Prim Sch BL4 . . . . . . .60 E7
Kearton Dr M30,M5 . . . . . .80 A1
Keary Cl M18 . . . . .99 D6
Keaton Cl M6 . . . . .154 E4
Keats Ave Denton M34 . . . .113 A8
Droylsden M43 . . . . .84 A2
Longshaw WN5 . . . . .53 D1
Rochdale OL12 . . . . .14 A1
Wigan WN3 . . . . .150 B5
Keats Cl M46 . . . . .58 E5
Keats Cres M26 . . . . .43 E4
Keats Fold SK16 . . . . .102 B7
Keats Mews M23 . . . . .120 C8
Keats Rd Eccles M30 . . . . . .79 D1
Oldham OL1 . . . . .49 B1
Ramsbottom BL8 . . . . .10 F2
Keats St WN7 . . . . .75 D7
Keats Way 7 WN2 . . . . . . .56 B1
Keats Wlk 2 BL1 . . . . .143 E2
Keb La OL8 . . . . .85 A8
Keble Ave OL8 . . . . .66 E3
Keble Gr WN7 . . . . .75 C8
Keble St WN2 . . . . .151 F7
Kedington Cl 8 M40 . . . . .156 C5
Kedleston Ave M14 . . . . . . .98 E4
Kedleston Gn SK2 . . . . . . .124 D7
Kedleston Wlk M34 . . . . . .100 F1
Keele Cl SK2 . . . . .124 B6
Keele Wlk M40 . . . . .159 C3
Keeley Cl M40 . . . . .83 C4
Keepers Dr OL12 . . . . .13 E2
Keighley Ave M43 . . . . .84 A3
Keighley Cl BL8 . . . . .26 F2
Keighley St BL1 . . . . .142 C2
Keilder Mews BL1 . . . . . . .144 A7
Keilder Sq M5 . . . . .154 F1
Keith Dr SK3 . . . . .123 B7
Keith Wlk M40 . . . . .160 D3
Kelboro Ave M34 . . . . .100 D7
Kelbrook Ct SK2 . . . . .124 E5
Kelbrook Rd M11 . . . . .165 B8
Kelby Ave M23 . . . . .121 B7
Keld Cl BL8 . . . . .27 B5
Keld Wlk M18 . . . . .165 C5
Kelday Wlk M8 . . . . .156 C6
Kelfield Ave M23 . . . . .109 A2
Kelham Wlk M40 . . . . .65 C1
Kellaton Cl WN3 . . . . .151 E6
Kellbank Rd WN3 . . . . .54 E3
Kellbrook Cres
Manchester M7 . . . . .63 B1
Manchester M7 . . . . .81 A8
Kellet Wlk M11 . . . . .83 B2
Kellett Cl WN5 . . . . .36 D1
Kellett St 4 Bolton BL1 . . . .24 F6
Rochdale OL16 . . . . .31 B8
Kelling Wlk M15 . . . . .162 D7
Kells Gr WN3 . . . . .37 A2
Kelmarsh Cl 7 M11 . . . . . .99 D7
Kelsall Cres SK3 . . . . .170 D6
Kelsall Dr
Altrincham WA15 . . . . .120 C6
Droylsden M43 . . . . .83 F3
Kelsall Rd SK8 . . . . .123 A5
Kelsall St Manchester M12 .164 F6
Oldham OL9 . . . . .153 D6
Rochdale OL16 . . . . .139 F8
Sale M33 . . . . .108 B4
Kelsall Way 6 SK9 . . . . . .131 D5
Kelsey 10 OL10 . . . . .29 C2
Kelsey Wlk M9 . . . . .64 B5
Kelso Cl OL8 . . . . .66 F1
Kelson Ave OL7 . . . . .166 A4
Kelstern Ave M13 . . . . .98 E3
Kelstern Sq M13 . . . . .98 E3
Kelverlow St OL4 . . . . .67 C6
Kelvin Ave Middleton M24 . .64 B6
Sale M33 . . . . .108 B4
Kelvin Cl WN4 . . . . .72 D4
Kelvin Gr Manchester M8 . .156 A6
Wigan WN3 . . . . .54 F2
Kelvin St Ashton-u-L OL7 . .166 A2
Manchester M4 . . . . .159 A2
Kelvindale Dr WA15 . . . . . .120 C7
Kelvington Dr M9 . . . . .157 D6
Kelway Terr WN1 . . . . .37 D1
Kelwood Ave BL9 . . . . .28 D5
Kemball 3 M30 . . . . .79 F2
Kemble Ave M23 . . . . .109 C1
Kemble Cl BL6 . . . . .22 B5
Kemmel Ave M22 . . . . .121 E5
Kemnay Wlk 11 M11 . . . . . .83 C1
Kemp Ave OL11 . . . . .139 D5
Kemp Rd SK6 . . . . .126 C7
Kemp St Hyde SK14 . . . . . .167 E4

Kemp St continued
Middleton M24 . . . . .64 F6
Kempley Cl M12 . . . . .164 F6
Kempnough Hall Rd M28 .78 F7
Kempsey Cl OL9 . . . . .152 B7
Kempsey St OL9 . . . . .152 B7
Kempsey Wlk M40 . . . . .65 C1
Kempsford Cl M23 . . . . . . .121 B6
Kempster St M7 . . . . .158 D4
Kempston Gdns 28 BL1 . .143 E2
Kempton Ave
Little Lever BL3 . . . . .43 A2
Sale M33 . . . . .107 D3
Kempton Cl Droylsden M43 .84 C2
Hazel Grove SK7 . . . . .125 A1
Newton-le-W WA12 . . . . .89 D5
Kempton Rd M19 . . . . .111 A8
Kempton Way OL9 . . . . . . .152 C7
Kemsing Wlk 1 M5 . . . . . . .81 A1
Kenchester Ave M11 . . . . . .99 D8
Kendal Ave Ashton-u-L OL7 .84 F4
Denton M34 . . . . .101 A1
Dukinfield SK14 . . . . .101 C5
Rochdale OL12 . . . . .13 E2
Sale M33 . . . . .108 C3
Urmston M41 . . . . .94 E4
Kendal Cl
Altrincham WA15 . . . . .120 D5
Heywood OL10 . . . . .46 E8
Kendal Dr Bramhall SK7 . . .132 C5
Bury BL9 . . . . .44 D7
Gatley SK8 . . . . .122 C4
Shaw OL2 . . . . .49 D7
Kendal Gdns SK6 . . . . . . .113 B4
Kendal Gr Ashton-in-M WN4 .73 B4
Leigh WN7 . . . . .75 D5
Walkden M28 . . . . .60 F2
Whitefield M45 . . . . .62 F8
Kendal Rd Bolton BL1 . . . .144 C8
Boothstown M28 . . . . .77 E7
Hindley WN2 . . . . .56 E5
Ince-in-M WN3 . . . . .56 A7
Pendlebury M6 . . . . .80 C5
Ramsbottom BL0 . . . . .11 A2
Stretford M32 . . . . .96 D3
Kendal Rd W BL0 . . . . .10 F2
Kendal St WN6 . . . . .150 B8
Kendal Terr 4 SK16 . . . . .166 C1
Kendal Wlk M24 . . . . .46 E1
Kendall Rd M9 . . . . .63 F3
Kendon Gr M34 . . . . .100 E3
Kendrew Rd BL3 . . . . .146 A4
Kendrew Wlk M9 . . . . .64 E1
Kenford Dr WN3 . . . . .54 E2
Kenford Wlk M8 . . . . .155 F6
Kenhall Rd WN7 . . . . .76 C4
Kenilworth 1 OL11 . . . . . .139 E5
Kenilworth Ave
Chadderton OL9 . . . . .47 C1
Cheadle SK8 . . . . .123 A3
Handforth SK9 . . . . .131 D3
Manchester M20 . . . . .109 F5
Swinton M27 . . . . .62 B3
Whitefield M45 . . . . .63 A7
Kenilworth Cl Marple SK6 . .125 E4
Oldham OL4 . . . . .67 C5
Radcliffe M26 . . . . .43 F6
Kenilworth Dr
Hazel Grove SK7 . . . . .133 C4
Hindley WN2 . . . . .56 F4
Leigh WN7 . . . . .76 E7
Kenilworth Gdns WA12 . . . .89 C1
Kenilworth Gr M34 . . . . . .100 C8
Kenilworth Rd
Cheadle SK3 . . . . .122 F4
Golborne WA3 . . . . .90 E7
Royton OL11,OL16 . . . . .48 C8
Sale M33 . . . . .107 E4
Urmston M41 . . . . .94 C4
Kenilworth Sq BL1 . . . . . . .142 B1
Kenion Rd OL11 . . . . .30 B6
Kenion St OL16 . . . . .139 F7
Kenley Wlk M8 . . . . .156 C6
Kenmay Ave BL3 . . . . .40 F6
Kenmere Gr M40 . . . . .65 B1
Kenmor Ave BL8 . . . . .27 A1
Kenmore Cl M45 . . . . .63 B8
Kenmore Dr WA15 . . . . . . .120 B3
Kenmore Gr
Garswood WN4 . . . . .72 D4
Irlam M44 . . . . .105 D6
Kenmore Gr Sale M33 . . . .107 C1
Whitefield M45 . . . . .63 B8
Wythenshawe M22 . . . . . . .121 D7
Kenmore Way M45 . . . . . . .63 B8
Kennard Cl M9 . . . . .64 F1
Kennard Pl WA14 . . . . .119 E6
Kennedy Cl WN6 . . . . .36 F3
Kennedy Dr Little Lever BL3 .43 C3
Whitefield BL9 . . . . .45 B2
Kennedy Rd Salford M5 . . . .80 C2
Tyldesley M29 . . . . .77 D6
Kennedy St Bolton BL2 . . . .148 C7
Manchester M2 . . . . .158 F1
Oldham OL8 . . . . .153 E6
Kennedy Way Denton M34 100 D2
Stockport SK4 . . . . .168 C2
Kennerley Ct SK2 . . . . .124 A5
Kennerley Lo SK3 . . . . . . .170 F6
Kennerley Rd SK2 . . . . . . .124 A5
Kennerley's La SK9 . . . . . .137 A7
Kennet 15 OL10 . . . . .29 C2
Kennet Cl Handforth SK9 . .131 D2
Westhoughton BL5 . . . . .39 E1
Kennet Way OL7 . . . . .75 F7
Kenneth Ave WN7 . . . . .75 D6
Kenneth Collis Ct M22 . . .121 C3

Kenneth Gr WN7 75 D6
Kenneth Sq M7 155 E6
Kennett Rd M23 121 A3
Kenninghall Rd M22 121 D3
Kennington Ave M40 83 B4
Kennington Fold BL3 147 D3
Kenny Cl OL4 67 D5
Kenside Wlk 2 M16 97 F3
Kensington Ave
Ashton-u-L OL6 85 E4
Chadderton OL9 65 E8
2 Hyde SK14 167 E1
Manchester M14 98 D4
Radcliffe M26 43 D4
Royton OL2 48 C6
Kensington Cl
Milnrow OL16 32 A6
Ramsbottom BL8 11 A1
Kensington Ct Bolton BL1 145 E7
1 Hyde SK14 167 E1
Manchester M7 81 C8
Reddish M34 100 B4
Wilmslow SK9 137 A6
Kensington Dr Bury BL8 44 A8
Horwich BL6 22 D3
Leigh WN7 76 E7
Salford M5 154 D3
Kensington Gdns
Altrincham WA15 119 F1
Hyde SK14 167 F1
Kensington Gr
Reddish M34 100 B4
Sale WA14 119 E8
14 Stalybridge SK15 86 A1
Kensington Rd
Failsworth M35 84 B8
Manchester M21 97 B2
Oldham OL8 66 D4
Stockport SK3 123 B7
3 Wigan WN5 54 D5
Kensington St Bolton BL1 145 E7
Hyde SK14 167 E1
Manchester M14 98 A3
Rochdale OL11 30 E5
Kenslow Ave M8 63 F2
Kensworth Cl
6 Altrincham M23 120 D6
Bolton BL1 143 D1
Kensworth Dr BL1 143 D1
Kent Ave Cheadle SK8 123 C5
Droylsden M43 83 E1
Oldham OL9 152 B6
Platt Bridge WN2 56 A2
Kent Cl Diggle OL3 51 C4
Walkden M28 60 B2
Kent Ct Bolton BL1 145 E8
Manchester M14 98 C3
Kent Dr Bury BL9 45 A8
Kearsley BL4 61 B6
Kent Rd Atherton M46 58 C4
Failsworth M35 83 E6
Glossop SK13 104 D1
Irlam M44 105 C5
Partington M31 105 E2
Reddish M34 100 A2
Stockport SK3 123 B8
Tyldesley M29 59 A2
Kent Rd E M14 98 D3
Kent Rd W M14 98 D3
Kent St Bolton BL1 145 E8
Leigh WN7 76 E4
11 Manchester M2 158 F1
Manchester M7 158 D4
Oldham OL8 66 F4
Rochdale OL11 139 F6
Swinton M27 61 F2
Wigan WN1 151 D7
Kent Way WA12 89 C1
Kent Wlk Haslingden BB4 1 A8
Heywood OL10 29 A1
Heywood OL10 29 B2
Kentford Dr M40 159 C4
Kentford Gr 6 BL4 60 C8
Kentford Rd BL1 143 F1
Kentmere Ave
Billinge WA11 71 C1
Rochdale OL12 15 B3
Kentmere Cl SK8 122 B3
Kentmere Ct M9 65 B4
Kentmere Dr
Middleton M24 46 E3
Tyldesley M29 77 B7
Kentmere Gr BL4 59 F7
Kentmere Rd
Altrincham M23,WA15 120 D6
Bolton BL2 25 F1
Kentmore Cl SK4 110 E2
Kenton Ave M18 99 C3
Kenton Cl Bolton BL1 143 D1
Denton M34 100 D7
Kenton Rd Shaw OL2 149 A7
Shaw OL2 48 F7
Kenton St OL8 67 B5
Kentsford Dr BL3 43 B5
Kentstone Ave SK4 110 E3
Kentucky St OL4 67 C6
Kentwell Cl SK16 101 B7
Kenwick Dr M40 65 E2
Kenwood Ave
Altrincham WA15 119 F2
Bramhall SK7 132 D5
Gatley SK8 122 A6
Leigh WN7 76 C5
Manchester M19 110 F6
Kenwood Cl Leigh WN7 76 C4
Stretford M32 96 E2
Kenwood Ct M32 96 E1
Kenwood La M28 78 F5
Kenwood Rd Bolton BL1 142 B3
Oldham OL1 48 C1
Reddish M18,SK5 99 E2
Stretford M32 96 E1
Kenworthy Ave OL6 85 E5
Kenworthy Cl SK14 102 E2
Kenworthy Gdns OL3 51 B1
Kenworthy La M22 109 D1
Kenworthy St
Rochdale OL16 31 C7
Stalybridge SK15 102 A8
3 Stalybridge SK15 86 A1
Kenworthy Terr OL16 31 C7
Kenwright St M4 159 A2
Kenwyn St M40 160 E3
Kenyon Ave
Dukinfield SK16 101 E7
Oldham OL8 66 F3
Sale M33 108 E2
Kenyon Cl SK14 101 F5
Kenyon Fold OL11 29 E5
Kenyon Gr M38 59 E4
Kenyon La Culcheth WA3 91 A4
Golborne WA3 90 F3
Golborne WA3 90 F5
Manchester M40 83 A8
Middleton M24 65 C8
Prestwich M25 63 C4
Kenyon Rd Little Lever BL3 43 B5
Standish WN6 19 D2
Wigan WN1 37 C2
Kenyon St Bacup OL13 4 B8
Bury BL9 141 A3
Droylsden M18 99 F6
Dukinfield SK16 101 B8
Heywood OL10 29 C2
Leigh WN7 75 D8
Radcliffe M26 44 B3
Ramsbottom BL0 138 C6
Kenyon Terr M38 59 E3
Kenyon Way Bury BL8 26 F5
Walkden M38 59 E4
Keppel Rd M21 97 B1
Keppel St OL6 166 C3
Kepplecove Mdw M28 77 F5
Kepwick Dr M22 121 E1
Kerans Dr BL5 39 E1
Kerenhappuch St BL0 138 B6
Kerfield Wlk 13 M13 163 B7
Kerfoot Cl M22 121 E8
Kerfoot St WN7 76 C4
Kermishaw Nook M29 77 B6
Kermoor Ave BL1 24 E6
Kerne Gr M23 109 A1
Kerr St M9 64 D3
Kerrera Dr M5 154 D1
Kerridge Dr SK6 112 F4
Kerridge Wlk 1 M16 97 F3
Kerrier Cl M30 80 A2
Kerry Gr BL2 148 B8
Kerry Wlk M23 120 F3
Kersal Ave Pendlebury M27 80 C8
Walkden M38 60 B4
Kersal Bank M7 81 C8
Kersal Bar M7 63 C1
Kersal Cl Prestwich M25 63 A1
Prestwich M7 63 C1
Kersal Crag M25,M7 63 C1
Kersal Dr WA15 120 C7
Kersal Hall Ave M7 81 A8
Kersal High Sch M7 81 A8
Kersal Rd M25,M7 63 A1
Kersal Vale Ct M7 81 A8
Kersal Vale Rd M7,M25 80 F8
Kersal Way M7 81 B7
Kerscott Rd M23 108 F2
Kersh Ave M19 111 B8
Kershaw Ave
Little Lever BL3 43 A4
Prestwich M25 62 F2
Sale M33 108 E2
Kershaw Dr OL9 65 D3
Kershaw Gr M34 100 C8
Kershaw La M34 100 C8
Kershaw Rd M35 83 F7
Kershaw St Bolton BL2 25 C5
Bolton BL3 145 D5
Bury BL9 141 A2
Droylsden M43 83 F1
Dukinfield OL7 100 F8
Glossop SK13 116 C8
Heywood OL10 29 B2
2 Rochdale OL12 139 F8
Royton OL2 48 D5
Shaw OL2 149 B7
Tyldesley M29 59 A1
Wigan WN5 54 B6
Kershaw St E OL2 149 B7
Kershaw Way WA12 89 C5
Kershaw Wlk M12 164 D6
Kershope Gr M5 161 A8
Kersley St OL4 67 B6
Kerswell Wlk M40 83 A6
Kerwin Wlk M11 165 A8
Kerwood Dr OL2 48 E3
Kesteven Rd M9 157 D7
Keston Ave Droylsden M43 83 E1
Manchester M9 65 A3
Keston Cres SK5 112 B6
Keston Rd 4 OL1 49 C1
Kestor St BL2 148 B7
Kestrel Ave Droylsden M34 84 C1
Farnworth BL4 59 F7
Oldham OL4 67 C5
Swinton M27 62 B2
Walkden M38 60 A5
Kestrel Cl Marple SK6 126 A3
Prestwich M25 63 B6
Kestrel Dr Ashton-in-M WN4 73 C6
Bury BL9 141 B4
Irlam M44 94 A3
Kestrel Rd M17 95 F8
Kestrel St 3 BL1 148 A8
Kestrel Wlk M12 165 A6
Keswick Ave Ashton-u-L OL7 84 F5
Chadderton OL9 152 A7
Denton M34 100 D4
Dukinfield SK14 101 C4
Gatley SK8 122 B4
Oldham OL8 67 A3
Urmston M41 94 E1
Keswick Cl Irlam M44 105 D4
Manchester M13 164 D5
Middleton M24 46 D2
Stalybridge SK15 86 A4
Keswick Ct 3 M24 46 D2
Keswick Dr Bramhall SK7 132 C5
Bury BL9 44 D7
Keswick Gr M6 154 F2
Keswick Pl WN2 56 A7
Keswick Rd
Altrincham WA15 120 D6
High Lane SK6 134 E8
Reddish SK4 111 D7
Stretford M32 96 C3
Walkden M28 60 F2
Keswick St Bolton BL1 143 F2
Rochdale OL11 30 C2
Ketley Wlk 1 M22 121 F3
Kettering Rd M19 99 B2
Kettleshulme Way SK12 134 A3
Kettleshulme Wlk 4 SK9 131 E1
Kettlewell Wlk M18 165 C5
Ketton Cl M11 99 E7
Keverlow La OL8 67 C2
Kevin Ave OL2 48 E2
Kevin St M19 111 B8
Kew Ave SK14 167 E1
Kew Dr Cheadle SK8 122 E2
Urmston M41 95 A4
Kew Gdns M40 65 A1
Kew Rd Failsworth M35 84 A8
Oldham OL4 67 C6
Rochdale OL11 31 A3
Key Ct M34 113 A8
Key West Cl M11 160 F1
Keyhaven Wlk M40 157 D5
Keymer St M11 160 E2
Keynsham Rd M11 83 B3
Keystone Cl M6 154 E4
Keyworth Wlk M40 160 E4
Khartoum St
Droylsden M11 83 D2
Manchester M16 97 D4
Kibbles Brow BL7 25 B8
Kibboth Crew BL0 138 B7
Kibworth Cl M45 62 D8
Kibworth Wlk 7 M9 64 E5
Kid St 4 M24 46 F1
Kidacre Wlk 2 M40 83 A7
Kidd Rd SK13 116 E6
Kidderminster Way OL9 47 F1
Kidwall Wlk 9 M9 64 F1
Kiel Cl M30 95 E8
Kielder Hill M24 46 F4
Kilbride Ave BL2 42 F6
Kilbuck La WA11 89 A8
Kilburn Ave
Ashton-in-M WN4 73 D4
Manchester M9 64 D5
Kilburn Cl Gatley SK8 131 B7
Leigh WN7 57 D1
Kilburn Dr WN6 36 A7
Kilburn Gr WN3 54 D3
Kilburn Rd Orrell WN5 53 C5
Radcliffe M26 43 E4
Stockport SK3 123 C7
Kilburn St 7 OL1 49 D1
Kildale Cl BL3 40 E4
Kildare Cres OL11 30 F2
Kildare Grange WN2 56 C5
Kildare Rd
Manchester M21 109 D8
Swinton M27 79 E6
Kildare St Farnworth BL4 60 C7
Hindley WN2 56 C5
Wigan WN3,WN5 54 F6
Kildonan Dr BL3 40 F6
Killer St BL0 138 C6
Killington Cl WN3 55 B2
Killingworth Mews BL6 22 D1
Killon St BL9 141 A1
Kilmaine Dr BL3 40 E5
Kilmarsh Wlk 7 M8 155 F7
Kilmington Dr M8 155 F6
Kilmory Dr BL2 42 F6
Kiln Bank OL12 4 C2
Kiln Bank La OL12 4 C2
Kiln Brow BL7 25 C8
Kiln Croft SK6 112 F1
Kiln Croft La SK9 131 E4
Kiln Field BL7 24 F8
Kiln Hill Cl OL1 47 F2
Kiln Hill La OL1 47 F2
Kiln La Hadfield SK13 104 A5
Milnrow OL16 31 F6
Kiln St Little Lever BL3 43 A3
Ramsbottom BL0 138 B5
Kiln Terr 5 OL13 3 D8
Kiln Wlk OL12 14 E2
Kilnbrook Cl OL4 68 B4
Kilner Cl BL9 45 B4
Kilner Wlk M40 159 C4
Kilnerdeyne Terr OL16 139 E6
Kilnhurst Wlk 12 BL1 145 D8
Kilnside Dr M9 157 D7
Kilnsley Wlk M18 165 C5
Kilnwick Cl M18 99 B3
Kilphin The BL6 40 B8
Kilrush Ave M30 95 D8
Kilsby Cl Bolton BL6 40 D6
Farnworth BL4 42 C2
Kilsby Wlk M40 160 D4
Kilshaw St WN5 54 C5
Kilton Wlk M40 159 C4
Kilvert Dr M33 107 F5
Kilworth Ave M33 107 F3
Kilworth Dr BL6 40 D6
Kilworth St OL11 139 D5
Kimberley Ave SK6 113 C2
Kimberley Pl WN4 73 B3
Kimberley Rd BL1 24 E5
Kimberley St Bacup OL13 3 A7
Manchester M7 155 E7
Oldham OL8 66 C3
Stockport SK3 170 E7
Kimberley Wlk M15 162 D7
Kimberly St WN6 37 A1
Kimble Cl BL8 10 F2
Kimbolton Cl M12 165 A6
Kinburn Rd M19 110 D2
Kinbury Wlk M40 159 C4
Kincardine Rd M13 163 B6
Kincraig Cl Bolton BL3 40 E4
Droylsden M11 83 C1
Kinder Ave Ashton-u-L OL6 86 A6
Oldham OL4 67 D5
Kinder Cl SK13 116 A8
Kinder Ct SK3 170 E7
Kinder Dr SK6 126 A6
Kinder Fold SK15 102 D6
Kinder Gr Ashton-in-M WN4 72 F6
Romiley SK6 113 E2
Kinder Ho M5 154 D3
Kinder Mews OL3 69 B5
Kinder St Stalybridge SK15 86 A2
Stockport SK3 170 E7
Kinder Way Middleton M24 46 F2
Mottram-in-L SK14 102 F3
Kinders Cres OL3 69 B5
Kinders Fold OL15 15 F7
Kinders La OL3 69 B6
Kinderton Ave M20 110 B7
Kineton Wlk 12 M13 163 C6
King Albert St OL2 149 B7
King Charles Ct SK13 116 D7
King David High Sch M8 63 F1
King David
Jun & Inf Schs M8 63 F1
King Edward Ave SK13 104 D1
King Edward Rd SK14 113 E8
King Edward St Eccles M30 79 C2
4 Manchester M19 99 B1
Salford M5 161 B8
King Edward's Bldgs M7 155 F8
King George Cl WN4 73 B3
King George Rd
Ashton-in-M WA11 89 A7
Hyde SK14 113 E8
King La Oldham OL1 49 E4
Oldham OL1 49 E5
King Sq OL8 153 E6
King St Bolton BL1 145 E7
Bolton BL2 25 D5
5 Bolton BL7 24 F8
Delph OL3 50 F4
Denton M34 100 F3
Denton M34 100 F6
Droylsden M43 100 A8
Dukinfield SK16 101 C7
Eccles M30 79 F1
Failsworth M35 83 D6
Farnworth BL4 60 D8
Glossop SK13 116 C8
Heywood OL10 29 D1
Hindley WN2 56 D6
Hollingworth SK14 103 D5
Horwich BL6 22 A4
Hyde SK14 167 D3
Ince-in-M WN2 56 A7
Leigh WN7 75 F4
Manchester M2 158 F1
Manchester M3 158 E2
Manchester M7 155 E7
Middleton M24 47 A1
Mossley OL5 68 D1
Mottram-in-L SK14 115 A8
Newton-le-W WA12 89 B3
Oldham OL8 153 E6
Radcliffe M26 44 B2
Ramsbottom BL0 138 C6
Rawtenstall BB4 2 E8
Rochdale OL16 139 F7
Salford M6 80 D5
8 Stalybridge SK15 86 A2
Stretford M32 96 D1
Westhoughton BL5 39 F1
Whitworth OL12 4 D3
Wigan WN1 150 C7
King St E Rochdale OL11 139 F6
Stockport SK1 169 F2
King St S OL11 139 E5
King St W Manchester M3 158 F1
Stockport SK3 169 E1
Wigan WN1 150 C8
King William Ent Pk M5 161 A8
King William St Eccles M30 79 A3
Salford M5 161 A8
Tyldesley M29 76 F8
King's Ave WA3 90 F7
King's Cl Droylsden M18 99 F6
Stockport SK7 123 F2
King's Cres M46 76 E8
King's Dr Manchester SK4 168 A3
King's Dr *continued*
Marple SK6 125 E7
Middleton M24 64 D8
King's Gdns WN7 76 C5
King's Lynn Cl 5 M20 110 B3
King's Rd Ashton-in-M WN4 73 A5
Ashton-u-L OL6 85 E5
Manchester M25 63 C2
Oldham OL8 153 F5
Reddish M34 100 B6
Rochdale OL16 31 B5
Romiley SK6 113 A3
Wilmslow SK9 136 E8
King's Terr 14 SK16 166 B1
Kingcombe Wlk 12 M9 157 E8
Kingfisher Ave M34 84 C1
Kingfisher Cl M12 164 E5
Kingfisher Ct
Ashton-in-M WN4 73 B6
Rochdale OL12 15 C4
10 Wigan WN6 37 A1
Kingfisher Dr Bury BL9 141 B4
Farnworth BL4 59 F7
Kingfisher Mews SK6 126 A6
Kingfisher Rd SK2 124 F5
Kingham Dr M4 159 C2
Kingholm Gdns BL1 143 D1
Kingmoor Ave M26 44 B4
Kings Acre WA14 119 A1
Kings Ave Gatley SK8 122 A4
Manchester M8 156 B8
Whitefield M45 44 E2
Kings Cl Prestwich M25 63 C5
Wilmslow SK9 137 A6
Kings Cres M16 97 B3
Kings Ct Stockport SK5 169 F3
11 Tyldesley M29 58 F1
Kings Dr SK8 123 A3
Kings Gr Rochdale OL12 15 C4
Stretford M32 96 F3
Kings La M32 96 F3
Kings Rd Cheadle SK8 123 A3
Failsworth OL9 65 E3
Golborne WA3 90 A7
Hazel Grove SK7 124 E3
Irlam M44 105 E6
Manchester M16 97 B3
Manchester M21 109 D8
Sale M33 107 F4
Shaw OL2 149 A6
Stretford M32 96 E2
Kings Road Prim Sch M16 97 A3
Kings Terr M32 96 F3
Kings Wlk M43 100 A8
Kings'Wlk OL6 85 D5
Kingsbridge Ave
Ainsworth BL2 26 D1
Hattersley SK14 102 C2
Kingsbridge Cl SK6 125 E7
Kingsbridge Ct M9 157 D7
Kingsbridge Dr SK16 101 B7
Kingsbridge Rd
Manchester M9 157 D7
5 Oldham OL8 67 B5
Kingsbridge Wlk SK14 102 C2
Kingsbrook Ct M21 109 E8
Kingsbrook Rd M16,M21 109 E8
Kingsbury Ave BL1 142 A1
Kingsbury Ct BL1 142 A1
Kingsbury Ct Lo BL1 142 A1
Kingsbury Dr 13 SK9 131 D1
Kingsbury Rd M11 83 C2
Kingscliffe St M9 157 E8
Kingscourt Ave BL1 142 C2
Kingscroft Ct WN1 151 D7
Kingsdale Rd M18 100 A4
Kingsdown Cres WN1 37 C4
Kingsdown Dr BL1 143 F1
Kingsdown Gdns 8 BL1 143 F1
Kingsdown Rd
Abram Brow WN2 74 B7
Wythenshawe M22 121 C1
Kingsdown Wlk SK5 112 B5
Kingsfield Dr M20 110 C2
Kingsfield Way M29 77 B8
Kingsfold Ave M40 159 C4
Kingsfold Cl BL2 42 E6
Kingsford St M5 154 D2
Kingsgate BL1 145 E7
Kingsgate Rd M22 121 C1
Kingshill Ct WN6 36 F7
Kingshill Rd M21 109 A8
Kingsholme Rd M22 121 C2
Kingsland Cl M40 160 D3
Kingsland Rd Cheadle SK3 123 A7
Farnworth BL4 42 A1
Rochdale OL11 30 B3
Kingslea PR7 20 F8
Kingslea Rd M20 110 C5
Kingsleigh Rd SK4 110 F4
Kingsley Ave
Handforth SK9 131 C2
Manchester M7 81 B7
Manchester M9 157 F7
Stockport SK4 169 E4
Stretford M32 96 F3
Urmston M41 95 B2
Whitefield M45 63 B8
Wigan WN3 54 F3
Kingsley Cl
Ashton-u-L OL6 86 A5
Denton M34 100 D1
Kingsley Dr Cheadle SK8 123 A3
Oldham OL4 67 E7
Kingsley Gr M34 100 C8

Kingsley Rd
Altrincham WA15 . . . .**120** B7
Hindley WN2 . . . .**56** F5
Middleton M24 . . . .**47** B2
Oldham OL4 . . . .**67** C6
Swinton M27 . . . .**61** D1
Walkden M28 . . . .**60** C4
Wythenshawe M22 . . . .**121** D8
Kingsley St Bolton BL1 . . . .**143** D2
Bury BL8 . . . .**27** B2
Leigh WN7 . . . .**75** C7
Kingsmead Mews M9 . . . . . .**64** C5
Kingsmede WN1 . . . .**37** D3
Kingsmere Ave M19 . . . .**98** F1
Kingsmill Ave M19 . . . . . .**111** B8
Kingsmoor Fields SK13 . .**104** D3
Kingsmoor Rd SK13 . . . . .**104** D2
Kingsneath Ave M11 . . . . . .**83** B3
Kingsnorth Cl 5 BL1 . . . .**143** F1
Kingsnorth Rd M41 . . . .**94** E4
Kingsoak Cl WN1 . . . .**151** D8
Kingston Arc 6 SK14 . . . .**102** E2
Kingston Ave Bolton BL2 . .**25** C1
 Manchester M20 . . . .**110** B1
 5 Oldham OL1 . . . .**49** B1
 Oldham OL9 . . . .**66** A4
Kingston Cl
 Hattersley SK14 . . . .**102** E2
 Manchester M7 . . . .**155** D8
 Sale M33 . . . .**107** D2
 Shaw OL2 . . . .**149** B8
 Wigan WN3 . . . .**55** B3
Kingston Cres BB4 . . . .**1** A7
Kingston Ct
 14 Handforth SK9 . . . .**131** E1
 Manchester M20 . . . .**110** B1
Kingston Dr Royton OL2 . . .**48** C6
 Sale M33 . . . .**108** D5
 Urmston M41 . . . .**107** B8
Kingston Gdns SK14 . . . . .**101** B3
Kingston Gr M9 . . . .**64** F4
Kingston Hill SK8 . . . .**122** D4
Kingston Pl SK8 . . . .**122** E2
Kingston Rd Failsworth M35 **84** B7
 Handforth SK9 . . . .**131** D5
 Manchester M20 . . . .**110** B1
 Radcliffe BL9 . . . .**44** C6
Kingston St SK3 . . . .**169** D1
Kingsway
 Altrincham WA14 . . . .**119** D5
 Bredbury SK6 . . . .**112** E3
 Cheadle M20,SK8 . . . .**122** C6
 Dukinfield SK16 . . . .**101** E7
 Ince-in-M WN2 . . . .**151** F7
 Kearsley BL4 . . . .**60** F6
 Manchester M14,M19, M20 **110** D4
 Manchester M19 . . . .**98** F1
 Middleton M24 . . . .**65** B6
 Newton-le-W WA12 . . . .**89** C2
 Pendlebury M27 . . . .**80** C6
 Rochdale OL16 . . . .**31** C5
 Stockport SK7 . . . .**123** F2
 Stretford M32 . . . .**96** C1
 Walkden M28 . . . .**78** D8
 Wigan WN1 . . . .**37** D2
Kingsway Ave M19 . . . .**98** F1
Kingsway Bldgs M19 . . . . .**110** E5
Kingsway Cl OL8 . . . .**153** E5
Kingsway Cres M19 . . . . . .**110** E5
Kingsway Pk M41 . . . .**95** D4
Kingsway Prim Sch M41 .**95** E4
Kingsway Sec Sch The
 SK8 . . . .**122** C4
Kingsway W Ind Pk OL16 .**31** B5
Kingswood Gr SK5 . . . .**99** F1
Kingswood Rd Eccles M30 .**79** B4
 Manchester M14 . . . .**110** E8
 Middleton M24 . . . .**46** F3
 Prestwich M25 . . . .**62** F5
Kingthorpe Gdns BL3 . . . .**147** F4
Kingwood Ave BL1 . . . .**40** F8
Kingwood Cres WN5 . . . . . .**54** D6
Kinlet Rd WN3 . . . .**54** C4
Kinlett Wlk 11 M40 . . . .**65** D2
Kinley Cl M12 . . . .**164** F6
Kinloch Dr BL1 . . . .**144** B7
Kinloch St Droylsden M11 . .**83** A2
 Oldham OL8 . . . .**67** A4
Kinmel Ave SK5 . . . .**112** C4
Kinmel Wlk 4 M23 . . . . . .**120** F6
Kinmount Wlk M9 . . . .**157** D6
Kinnaird Cres SK1 . . . .**124** B8
Kinnaird Rd M20 . . . .**110** C5
Kinnerly Gr M28 . . . .**60** A1
Kinniside Cl WN3 . . . .**55** A2
Kinross Ave Garswood WN4 **72** C4
 Stockport SK2 . . . .**124** A3
Kinross Dr BL3 . . . .**40** F5
Kinross Rd M14 . . . .**98** E3
Kinsale Wlk M23 . . . .**120** F3
Kinsey Ave M23 . . . .**120** F7
Kinsley Dr M28 . . . .**60** C2
Kintbury St WN2 . . . .**73** F7
Kintore Ave SK7 . . . .**124** F3
Kintore Wlk 5 M40 . . . . . .**156** C5
Kintyre Ave M5 . . . .**154** E1
Kintyre Cl 5 M11 . . . .**83** C1
Kintyre Dr BL3 . . . .**40** E5
Kinver Cl BL3 . . . .**146** C3
Kinver Rd M40 . . . .**65** E3
Kipling Ave Denton M34 . .**113** A7
 Droylsden M43 . . . .**84** A3
 Wigan WN3 . . . .**55** A4
Kipling Cl SK2 . . . .**124** E7

Kipling Gr WN7 . . . .**75** D7
Kipling Rd OL1 . . . .**49** B2
Kipling St M7 . . . .**155** D6
Kippax St M14 . . . .**98** B3
Kirby Ave Atherton M46 . . . .**58** C5
 Failsworth OL9 . . . .**65** D3
 Swinton M27 . . . .**79** D5
Kirby Rd WN7 . . . .**75** E5
Kirby Wlk
 6 Manchester M4 . . . .**159** C2
 Shaw OL2 . . . .**149** B8
Kiribati Way WN7 . . . .**75** E6
Kirk Rd M19 . . . .**111** B7
Kirk St M18 . . . .**99** D5
Kirkbank St Oldham OL9 . .**153** D7
 Oldham OL9 . . . .**153** D8
Kirkbeck WN7 . . . .**76** C3
Kirkburn View BL8 . . . .**27** C5
Kirkby Ave Manchester M40 **83** D2
 Sale M33 . . . .**108** C2
Kirkby Cl BL9 . . . .**44** F7
Kirkby Dr M33 . . . .**108** D2
Kirkby Rd Bolton BL1 . . . . .**144** B8
 Culcheth WA3 . . . .**91** F3
Kirkdale Ave M40 . . . .**65** D2
Kirkdale Dr OL2 . . . .**48** C5
Kirkdale Gdns WN8 . . . .**53** A4
Kirkebrok Rd BL3 . . . .**146** A4
Kirkfell Dr High Lane SK6 .**134** E8
 Tyldesley M29 . . . .**77** B7
Kirkfell Wlk OL1 . . . .**48** F1
Kirkgate Cl 6 M40 . . . .**159** C3
Kirkhall La Bolton BL1 . . . .**144** C8
 Leigh WN7 . . . .**75** D2
Kirkhall Wkshp The BL1 .**144** C8
Kirkham Ave Golborne WA3 **90** B4
 Manchester M18 . . . .**99** D6
Kirkham Cl M34 . . . .**100** F3
Kirkham Rd Gatley SK8 . . .**131** C8
 Leigh WN7 . . . .**75** D2
Kirkham St Abram WN2 . . . .**74** B8
 Bolton BL2 . . . .**25** C1
 Oldham OL9 . . . .**153** E7
 Salford M5 . . . .**154** E1
 Walkden M38 . . . .**60** A5
Kirkhaven Sq M40 . . . .**160** E4
Kirkhill Wlk 12 M40 . . . . . .**65** D2
Kirkholt Wlk 11 M9 . . . .**64** E3
Kirkhope Dr BL1 . . . .**143** D1
Kirkhope Wlk BL1 . . . .**143** D1
Kirklands Bolton BL2 . . . . . .**25** D2
 Sale M33 . . . .**108** A2
Kirklee Ave OL9 . . . .**48** A1
Kirklee Rd OL11 . . . .**30** D2
Kirklees St Bury BL8 . . . . . .**26** F7
 Wigan WN1 . . . .**151** E8
Kirklees Wlk M45 . . . .**63** B8
Kirkless La WN2 . . . .**38** B1
Kirkless St WN2 . . . .**38** A3
Kirkless Villas WN2 . . . .**38** A3
Kirkley St SK14 . . . .**167** E1
Kirklinton Dr M9 . . . .**157** D6
Kirkman Ave M30 . . . .**95** C8
Kirkman Cl M18 . . . .**99** D4
Kirkman St BL9 . . . .**44** F3
Kirkmanshulme La
 M12,M18 . . . .**165** B5
Kirkpatrick St WN2 . . . .**57** B3
Kirkstall 27 OL12 . . . .**139** E8
Kirkstall Ave Heywood OL10 **29** C3
 Littleborough OL15 . . . .**16** A4
Kirkstall Cl SK12 . . . .**133** D4
Kirkstall Gdns M26 . . . .**43** E5
Kirkstall Rd Middleton M24 .**46** F3
 Urmston M41 . . . .**95** E3
Kirkstall Sq M13 . . . .**163** C6
Kirkstead Cl M11 . . . .**165** A8
Kirkstead Rd SK8 . . . .**132** C6
Kirkstile Cres WN3 . . . .**54** E2
Kirkstile Pl M27 . . . .**61** C8
Kirkstone Ave WN5 . . . .**54** C7
Kirkstone Ave M28 . . . .**60** F1
Kirkstone Cl OL1 . . . .**48** F1
Kirkstone Dr Middleton M24 **46** E2
 Royton OL2 . . . .**48** D6
Kirkstone Rd
 Dukinfield SK14 . . . .**101** C5
 Failsworth M40 . . . .**65** C2
Kirktown Wlk M11 . . . .**165** C8
Kirkwall Dr BL2 . . . .**148** B5
Kirkway Manchester M9 . . . .**65** A4
 Middleton M24 . . . .**65** A7
 Rochdale OL11 . . . .**30** F2
Kirkwood Dr M40 . . . .**159** C4
Kirtley Ave M30 . . . .**79** D3
Kirtlington Cl OL2 . . . .**149** A5
Kirton Lo M25 . . . .**63** C4
Kirton Wlk M9 . . . .**64** C5
Kitchen St 14 OL16 . . . .**31** A8
Kitchener Ave M44 . . . .**105** C4
Kitchener St Bolton BL3 . . . .**42** B3
 Bury BL8 . . . .**27** B1
Kite Gr WN7 . . . .**76** B5
Kitt Green Rd WN5 . . . .**54** C8
Kitt's Moss La SK7 . . . .**132** D6
Kitter St OL12 . . . .**15** C3
Kittiwake Cl M29 . . . .**77** A7
Kitty Wheeldon Gdns
 M33 . . . .**108** A5
Kiveton Cl M28 . . . .**60** C2
Kiveton Dr WN4 . . . .**73** C2
Knacks La OL12 . . . .**14** A5
Knaresborough Cl SK5 . . . .**99** E1
Knaresborough Rd
 WN2 . . . .**56** E4
Knarr Barn La OL3 . . . .**50** D3
Knarr La OL3 . . . .**50** E2

Kneller Wlk OL1 . . . .**49** D4
Knight Cres M24 . . . .**46** D3
Knight St Ashton-u-L OL7 . . .**84** F2
 Bolton BL1 . . . .**145** F8
 Bury BL8 . . . .**27** C2
 Hyde SK14 . . . .**167** E1
 Manchester M20 . . . .**110** B2
Knightley Wlk M40 . . . .**157** D5
Knights Cl M5 . . . .**80** A2
Knightsbridge SK1 . . . .**169** F2
Knightsbridge Cl
 12 Handforth SK9 . . . .**131** D1
 Manchester M7 . . . .**155** D8
Knightscliffe Cres WN6 . . . .**35** D6
Knightshill Cres WN6 . . . . . .**37** A1
Knightswood BL3 . . . .**40** F3
Kniveton Rd M12 . . . .**164** F6
Kniveton St SK14 . . . .**167** F3
Knob Hall Gdns M23 . . . . .**120** F3
Knole Ave SK12 . . . .**133** F4
Knoll St Manchester M7 . . . .**155** D7
 Rochdale OL11 . . . .**30** C2
Knoll The Mossley OL5 . . . . .**68** B1
 Shaw OL2 . . . .**149** C6
Knott Fold SK14 . . . .**167** D1
Knott Hill La OL3 . . . .**50** E3
Knott Hill St OL12 . . . .**4** E6
Knott La Bolton BL1 . . . .**23** F2
 Hyde SK14 . . . .**113** D8
Knott Lanes OL8 . . . .**84** F8
Knott's Hos Colborne WN7 . .**91** C8
 Golborne WN7 . . . .**91** B8
Knotts Brow BL7 . . . .**9** F4
Knowe Ave M22 . . . .**121** D1
Knowl Cl Ramsbottom BL0 . . .**11** C4
 Reddish M34 . . . .**100** B2
Knowl Hill Dr OL12 . . . .**13** C3
Knowl La OL12 . . . .**13** B5
Knowl Mdw BB4 . . . .**1** A6
Knowl Rd Milnrow OL16 . . . .**31** D6
 Shaw OL2 . . . .**149** C6
Knowl St Oldham OL8 . . . . . .**66** C2
 Stalybridge SK15 . . . .**86** B2
Knowl Syke St OL12 . . . .**15** C7
Knowl Top La OL3 . . . .**69** D7
Knowl View Bury BL8 . . . . . .**27** A6
 Littleborough OL15 . . . .**15** F2
Knowldale Way M12 . . . . . .**164** E5
Knowle Ave OL7 . . . .**166** A4
Knowle Dr M25 . . . .**63** A2
Knowle Gn SK9 . . . .**131** C3
Knowle Pk SK9 . . . .**131** C3
Knowle Rd SK6 . . . .**126** D6
Knowle Way 5 SK14 . . . . . .**102** E2
Knowles Ave WN3 . . . .**54** F4
Knowles Ct M6 . . . .**80** B3
Knowles Edge St BL1 . . . .**142** C2
Knowles Pl
 1 Manchester M15 . . . . . .**162** F6
Knowles St Bolton BL1 . . . . .**25** A1
 Ince-in-M WN3 . . . .**151** D6
 Radcliffe M26 . . . .**44** A4
Knowles The OL8 . . . .**66** C1
 Stretford M32 . . . .**96** D1
Knowls La OL4 . . . .**67** F5
Knowlsey Grange BL1 . . . . .**40** D7
Knowlsley OL4 . . . .**68** A7
Knowsley Ave
 Atherton M46 . . . .**58** C4
 Golborne WA3 . . . .**74** B1
 Oldham OL4 . . . .**68** A7
 Salford M5 . . . .**161** B8
 Urmston M41 . . . .**95** C4
Knowsley Cres
 Stockport SK1 . . . .**124** B8
 Whitworth OL12 . . . .**4** E6
Knowsley Dr Leigh WN7 . . . .**75** E2
 Oldham OL4 . . . .**68** A7
 Swinton M27 . . . .**79** D5
Knowsley Gn Oldham OL4 . . .**68** A7
 Salford M5 . . . .**161** B8
Knowsley Gr BL6 . . . .**22** D1
Knowsley Jun Sch OL4 . . . .**68** A7
Knowsley Park Way BB4 . . . .**1** B8
Knowsley Rd
 Ainsworth BL2 . . . .**26** C1
 Bolton BL1 . . . .**142** B2
 Haslingden BB4 . . . .**1** B8
 Hazel Grove SK7 . . . .**133** F8
 Stockport SK1 . . . .**124** B8
 Whitefield M45 . . . .**62** F8
 Wigan WN3 . . . .**37** A2
Knowsley Rd Ind Est
 BB4 . . . .**1** B8
Knowsley St Bolton BL1 . . .**145** F7
 Bury BL9 . . . .**140** E1
 Leigh WN7 . . . .**75** D5
 Manchester M8 . . . .**159** A4
 Rochdale OL12 . . . .**139** E8
Knowsley Terr OL4 . . . .**68** A7
Knutsford Ave
 Manchester M16 . . . .**97** D3
 Reddish SK4 . . . .**111** D7
 Sale M33 . . . .**108** E4
Knutsford Rd
 Manchester M18 . . . .**99** C4
 Wilmslow SK9,WA16 . . . . . .**136** D3
Knutsford St M6 . . . .**154** E2
Knutsford View WA15 . . . .**129** C8
Knutshaw Cres BL3 . . . .**40** E2
Knypersley Ave SK2 . . . . . .**124** C7
Kranj Way OL1 . . . .**153** F7
Krester Ct M20 . . . .**110** A5
Krokus Sq OL9 . . . .**152** A7
Kyle Rd SK7 . . . .**124** F1
Kylemore Ave BL3 . . . .**144** B5
Kynder St M34 . . . .**100** F3

L

Labrador Quay M5 . . . .**96** F7
Labtec St M27 . . . .**62** B1
Laburnum Ave
 Ashton-u-L OL6 . . . .**85** C6
 Atherton M46 . . . .**58** E3
 Bury BL8 . . . .**26** F7
 Droylsden M34 . . . .**84** C1
 Eccles M30 . . . .**95** A8
 Failsworth M35 . . . .**83** F6
 Hyde SK14 . . . .**113** D8
 Ince-in-M WN3 . . . .**151** F6
 Leigh WN7 . . . .**75** E8
 Oldham OL9 . . . .**48** C1
 Shaw OL2 . . . .**149** B6
 Stalybridge SK15,SK16 . . . .**101** F8
 Swinton M27 . . . .**79** E6
 Whitefield M45 . . . .**62** F7
Laburnum Cl 4 WA15 . . . .**120** B5
Laburnum Ct BL8 . . . .**26** F7
Laburnum Dr
 Whitefield BL9 . . . .**45** A1
 Wigan WN6 . . . .**37** A4
Laburnum Gr Horwich BL6 . .**22** E1
 Prestwich M25 . . . .**63** A5
 Tyldesley M29 . . . .**59** D1
Laburnum La
 Altrincham WA15 . . . .**128** E8
 Newhey OL16 . . . .**32** A3
Laburnum Pk BL2 . . . .**25** B5
Laburnum Rd
 Farnworth BL4 . . . .**60** B8
 Golborne WA3 . . . .**90** F7
 Haslingden BB4 . . . .**1** A7
 Irlam M44 . . . .**105** D5
 Manchester M18 . . . .**99** D4
 Middleton M24 . . . .**65** C8
 Oldham OL8 . . . .**84** C8
 Reddish M34 . . . .**99** F3
 Urmston M41 . . . .**95** B4
 Walkden M28 . . . .**60** E1
Laburnum St
 Ashton-in-M WN4 . . . .**73** B2
 Atherton M46 . . . .**58** E3
 7 Bolton BL1 . . . .**145** D8
 Salford M6 . . . .**154** F2
Laburnum Terr OL11 . . . .**30** E4
Laburnum Villas OL8 . . . . . .**67** A1
Laburnum Way
 Littleborough OL15 . . . .**15** F5
 Stockport SK3 . . . .**123** B8
Laburnum Wlk 1 M33 . . . .**107** C5
Lacey Ave SK9 . . . .**131** B1
Lacey Gn SK9 . . . .**131** C1
Lacey Gr SK9 . . . .**131** C1
Lacey Green
 Cty Prim Sch SK9 . . . . . .**131** B1
Lackford Dr M40 . . . .**159** C4
Lacrosse Ave OL8 . . . .**66** C4
Lacy Ct SK9 . . . .**131** B1
Lacy Gr M32 . . . .**96** D1
Lacy St Stockport SK1 . . . . .**170** F8
 Stretford M32 . . . .**96** D1
Lacy Wlk M12 . . . .**164** E8
Ladbrooke Cl OL6 . . . .**166** C4
Ladbrooke Rd OL6 . . . .**85** C5
Ladcastle Rd OL3 . . . .**69** A7
Ladhill La OL3 . . . .**69** B5
Ladies La WN2 . . . .**56** D6
Lady Barn House Sch
 SK8 . . . .**122** D3
Lady Bridge Brow BL1 . . . . .**40** F7
Lady Bridge La BL1,BL3 . . . .**40** F7
Lady Harriet Wlk M28 . . . . . .**60** C3
Lady Kelvin Rd WA14 . . . . .**119** C6
Lady La Culcheth WA3 . . . . . .**91** C1
 Wigan WN3 . . . .**54** E3
Lady Rd OL4 . . . .**67** E6
Ladybarn Ave WA3 . . . .**89** F7
Ladybarn Cres
 Bramhall SK7 . . . .**132** F6
 Manchester M14 . . . .**110** D7
Ladybarn Ho 1 M14 . . . . .**110** D8
Ladybarn La M14 . . . .**110** D8
Ladybarn Manor SK7 . . . . .**132** E8
Ladybarn Mews 2 M14 . .**110** D6
Ladybarn Prim sch M20 .**110** D6
Ladybarn Rd M14 . . . .**110** D8
Ladybower SK8 . . . .**123** C4
Ladybridge Ave M28 . . . . . .**78** C8
Ladybridge
 Com Prim Sch BL3 . . . .**40** F5
Ladybridge Prim Sch
 SK8 . . . .**123** B4
Ladybridge Rd SK8 . . . .**123** B3
Ladybridge Rise SK8 . . . . .**123** C3
Ladybrook Ave WA15 . . . . .**120** B8
Ladybrook Gr 6 SK9 . . . . .**137** A2
Ladybrook Prim Sch SK7 **132** F7
Ladybrook Rd SK7 . . . .**123** C1
Ladyfield St SK9 . . . .**137** B7
Ladyfield Terr SK9 . . . .**137** C7
Ladyhill View M28 . . . .**78** C8
Ladyhouse Cl OL16 . . . .**32** A5
Ladyhouse La OL16 . . . .**32** A5
Ladylands Ave 13 M11 . . . .**83** C2
Ladymere Dr M28 . . . .**78** B8
Ladys Cl SK12 . . . .**133** E4
Ladyshore Cl M6 . . . .**154** F1
Ladyshore Rd BL3 . . . .**43** C2
Ladysmith Ave
 Ashton-in-M WN4 . . . .**73** C1
 Bury BL9 . . . .**28** A5
Ladysmith Rd OL6 . . . .**85** D7
Ladysmith Rd
 Ashton-u-L OL6 . . . .**85** D7

Ladysmith Rd continued
 Manchester M20 . . . .**110** C3
 Stalybridge SK15 . . . .**86** A4
Ladysmith Sh Ctr OL6 . . . .**166** B3
Ladysmith St Oldham OL8 . .**66** C3
 Stockport SK3 . . . .**170** C3
Ladysmith The OL6 . . . .**85** F5
Ladythorn Ave SK6 . . . .**126** A5
Ladythorn Cres SK7 . . . . . .**132** F6
Ladythorn Ct M25 . . . .**63** A2
Ladythorn Gr SK7 . . . .**132** F6
Ladythorn Rd SK7 . . . .**132** E6
Ladythorne Ave M25 . . . . . .**63** A2
Ladythorne Dr M25 . . . .**63** A2
Ladywell Ave M38 . . . .**60** A5
Ladywell Cl SK7 . . . .**124** A2
Ladywell Gr M38 . . . .**60** A5
Lafford La Orrell WN8 . . . . . .**35** C2
 Orrell WN8 . . . .**53** C8
Lagos Cl M14 . . . .**98** A4
Laindon Rd M13,M14 . . . . . .**98** F1
Lainton Ct 8 SK3 . . . .**123** C8
Laithwaite Rd WN5 . . . .**54** E7
Lake Bank OL15 . . . .**16** A3
Lake Dr M24 . . . .**64** F7
Lake Rd Denton M34 . . . . . .**100** F4
 Stalybridge SK15 . . . .**85** F4
 Stretford M17 . . . .**96** C7
Lake Side Leigh WN7 . . . . . .**75** D6
 Littleborough OL15 . . . .**16** A2
Lake Side Cotts WN1 . . . . . .**20** C1
Lake St Bolton BL3 . . . .**145** F5
 Leigh WN7 . . . .**76** A6
 Stockport SK2 . . . .**124** C5
Lake View M9 . . . .**65** A2
Lake Wlk WN5 . . . .**54** B7
Lakeland Ave WN4 . . . .**73** C4
Lakeland Cres BL9 . . . .**44** E6
Lakeland Ct 11 M24 . . . . . .**46** D2
Lakeland Dr OL2 . . . .**48** C8
Lakelands Dr BL3 . . . .**40** F5
Lakenheath Cl 10 BL1 . . . . .**24** F6
Lakenheath Dr BL1 . . . .**25** A1
Lakes Dr WN5 . . . .**53** E6
Lakes Rd Dukinfield SK16 . .**101** C8
 Marple SK6 . . . .**126** B5
Lakes Terr M12 . . . .**56** A7
Lakeside Bury BL9 . . . .**44** F5
 Gatley SK8 . . . .**122** C3
 Hadfield SK13 . . . .**104** A6
 Prestwich M7 . . . .**63** D1
Lakeside Ave
 Ashton-u-L OL7 . . . .**84** F4
 Bolton BL3 . . . .**42** A2
 Orrell WN5 . . . .**53** E3
 Walkden M28 . . . .**60** D5
Lakeside Cl M18 . . . .**99** F4
Lakeside Dr SK12 . . . .**133** E5
Lakeside Gn SK2 . . . .**124** C6
Lakeside Way BL9 . . . .**140** F4
Lakin St M40 . . . .**83** A7
Laleham Gn SK7 . . . .**123** D3
Lamb Cl M12 . . . .**164** F5
Lamb La Ashley WA14 . . . . .**128** D4
 Manchester M3 . . . .**158** E2
Lamb St WN1 . . . .**37** C1
Lamb Wlk 8 M34 . . . .**113** A7
Lamberhead Ind Est WN5 .**54** B5
Lamberhead Rd WN5 . . . . . .**54** C6
Lambert Dr M33 . . . .**107** C6
Lambert St M7 . . . .**100** F8
Lamberton Dr M23 . . . .**120** E6
Lambeth Ave M35 . . . .**84** B8
Lambeth Cl BL6 . . . .**22** D3
Lambeth Gr SK6 . . . .**113** A5
Lambeth Rd Failsworth M40 **83** C4
 Reddish SK5 . . . .**111** F7
Lambeth St M46 . . . .**58** B3
Lambeth Terr OL11 . . . .**139** C5
Lambgates SK13 . . . .**104** A5
Lambley Cl WN7 . . . .**75** D8
Lambourn Cl Bolton BL3 . .**145** E5
 Poynton SK12 . . . .**133** D4
Lambourn Rd M41 . . . .**94** D4
Lambourne Cl M22 . . . .**130** D8
Lambourne Gr OL16 . . . .**31** D5
Lambrook Wlk M40 . . . .**83** D4
Lambs Fold SK4 . . . .**111** D5
Lambton Rd
 Manchester M21 . . . .**109** D8
 Swinton M28 . . . .**79** C7
Lambton St Bolton BL3 . . . .**146** C2
 Eccles M30 . . . .**79** B4
 Wigan WN5 . . . .**54** C5
Lamburn Ave M40 . . . .**65** D2
Lamerton Way SK9 . . . .**131** E2
Lamorna Cl M7 . . . .**81** B7
Lamport Cl M1 . . . .**163** B7
Lamport Ct M1 . . . .**163** B7
Lampson St M8 . . . .**158** E4
Lampton Cl WA14 . . . .**119** D7
Lamsholme Cl 7 M19 . . . . . .**99** A2
Lanark Ave M22 . . . .**121** E8
Lanark Cl Hazel Grove SK7 **125** A2
 Heywood OL10 . . . .**28** F1
Lanbury Dr M8 . . . .**155** F7
Lancashire Cotts OL5 . . . . . .**68** C4
Lancashire Cricket Club
 Mus M32 . . . .**96** C4
Lancashire Ct OL9 . . . .**152** C5
Lancashire Cty &
 Manchester Cricket Gd
 M16 . . . .**97** A4
Lancashire Fusiliers
 Regimental Mus BL8 . . . .**27** B1
Lancashire Hill
 SK1,SK4,SK5 . . . .**169** E3

Lancashire Rd M31 . . . . . .105 E2
Lancashire St M10,M40 .157 F5
Lancaster Ave
　Atherton M46 . . . . .58 E2
　Failsworth M35 . . . . .83 E7
　Golborne WA3 . . . . .90 C8
　Haslingden BB4 . . . . .1 D8
　Horwich BL6 . . . . .22 D2
　Middleton M24 . . . . .65 C7
　Ramsbottom BL0 . . . . . . .11 A4
　Stalybridge SK15 . . . . . . .86 A3
　Tyldesley M29 . . . . .59 A3
　Urmston M41 . . . . .95 E3
　Whitefield M45 . . . . .63 A7
Lancaster Cl Adlington PR6 .21 B7
　Bolton BL2 . . . . .148 A7
　Hazel Grove SK7 . . . . . . .133 D6
　Romiley SK6 . . . . .113 A1
Lancaster Ct
　Failsworth M40 . . . . .83 C4
　4 Leigh WN7 . . . . .76 B4
　8 Manchester M19 . . . . .110 F8
Lancaster Dr Bury BL9 . . . . .27 F8
　Little Lever BL3 . . . . .43 B4
　Manchester M25 . . . . . . .63 C2
Lancaster Ho Royton OL2 . .48 D5
　5 Stockport SK3 . . . . . . .170 E8
Lancaster Pl PR6 . . . . .21 A8
Lancaster Rd Denton M34 .100 H1
　Droylsden M43 . . . . .83 F3
　Handforth SK9 . . . . .131 E1
　Hindley WN2 . . . . .56 F5
　Irlam M44 . . . . .105 D5
　Manchester M20 . . . . . .110 A3
　Salford M6 . . . . .80 B4
　Shevington WN5 . . . . . . .36 D1
Lancaster Sq OL2 . . . . . . .48 D5
Lancaster St
　Ince-in-M WN3 . . . . .151 D6
　Mossley OL5 . . . . .68 B1
　Oldham OL9 . . . . .66 A3
　Radcliffe M26 . . . . .43 E3
　Stockport SK1 . . . . .112 A2
Lancaster Terr
　24 Bolton BL1 . . . . .143 E2
　Rochdale OL11 . . . . .13 D2
Lancaster Way BL5 . . . . . . .39 D2
Lancaster Wlk
　22 Bolton BL1 . . . . .143 E2
　Shevington WN5 . . . . . . .36 D1
Lancasterian Sch M20 . . .109 E4
Lance Wood Pl WN5 . . . .54 D6
Lancelot Rd M22 . . . . .121 F2
Lancelyn Dr SK9 . . . . .137 D8
Lanchester Dr BL3 . . . . . .145 D5
Lanchester St M40 . . . . . .160 E3
Lancing Ave M20 . . . . . . .110 D3
Lancing Wlk OL9 . . . . . . .152 A6
Land Gate OL12 . . . . .4 E5
Land Gate La WN4 . . . . . . .73 B8
Land La SK9 . . . . .137 C6
Land St WN6 . . . . .150 B8
Landcross Rd M14 . . . . . . .98 C1
Landedmans BL5 . . . . .58 A7
Landells Wlk M40 . . . . . . .83 A5
Lander Gr M9 . . . . .64 F3
Landgate Ind Est
　Ashton-in-M WN4 . . . . . . .72 F8
　Ashton-in-M WN4 . . . . . . .73 A8
Landkey Cl 1 M23 . . . . . .108 F2
Landor Cl WA3 . . . . .90 E8
Landor Ct M34 . . . . .99 F3
Landore Cl M26 . . . . .44 B4
Landos Ct 16 M40 . . . . . .159 C3
Landos Rd M40 . . . . .159 C3
Landrace Dr M28 . . . . .78 B6
Lands End Rd M24 . . . . . . .64 B7
Landsberg Rd M35 . . . . . . .84 B8
Landsberg Terr M35 . . . . . .84 B8
Landseer Dr SK6 . . . . . . .126 B7
Landseer St OL4 . . . . .67 A5
Landside WN7 . . . . .75 F2
Lane Brow OL4 . . . . .68 B5
Lane Dr OL4 . . . . .68 B5
Lane End Eccles M30 . . . . .79 F1
　Heywood OL10 . . . . .46 F8
Lane End Cl M35 . . . . .84 A6
Lane End Prim Sch SK8 .123 C2
Lane End Rd Bacup OL13 . . .4 A8
　Manchester M19,SK4 . . . .110 C4
Lane Ends Romiley SK6 . .113 D3
　5 Wigan WN5 . . . . .54 D5
Lane Head Ave WA3 . . . . .90 F8
Lane Head Rd
　Mossley OL4,OL5 . . . . .68 A3
　Oldham M4 . . . . .67 F4
Lane Mdw OL2 . . . . .149 A6
Lane The BL1 . . . . .40 D7
Lanegate SK14 . . . . .113 D8
Lanesfield Wlk M8 . . . . . .156 C6
Laneside Ave OL2 . . . . . . .49 D7
Laneside Dr SK7 . . . . .124 A1
Laneside Rd
　Manchester M20 . . . . . .122 C8
　Rowarth SK22 . . . . .127 E6
Laneside Wlk OL16 . . . . . .31 F7
Lanfield Dr M8 . . . . .155 F7
Langcliff Wlk 12 BL1 . . . .143 F2
Langcliffe Cl WA3 . . . . . . .91 E3
Langcliffe Wlk M18 . . . . .165 C5
Langcroft Dr 16 M40 . . . . .83 C5
Langdale Ave
　Golborne WA3 . . . . .74 C1
　Ince-in-M WN2 . . . . .56 B8
　Manchester M19 . . . . . . .111 B8
　Oldham OL8 . . . . .66 D4
　Royton OL11,OL16 . . . . . .48 C8

Langdale Ave continued
　Wigan WN1 . . . . .37 B3
Langdale Cl
　Altrincham WA15 . . . . . .119 E5
　Denton M34 . . . . .100 E1
　Gatley SK8 . . . . .122 C3
　High Lane SK6 . . . . .134 E8
Langdale Cres Abram WN2 .74 B8
　Wigan WN5 . . . . .54 B8
Langdale Ct M8 . . . . .156 B6
Langdale Dr Middleton M24 .46 F3
　Walkden M28 . . . . .60 F1
　Whitefield BL9 . . . . .45 A3
Langdale Rd Bramhall SK7 132 C5
　Hindley WN2 . . . . .56 E5
　Manchester M14 . . . . . . .98 D4
　Partington M31 . . . . .105 E4
　Reddish SK4 . . . . .111 C6
　Romiley SK6 . . . . .113 B4
　Sale M33 . . . . .107 E1
　Stretford M32 . . . . .96 C3
　Wigan WN5 . . . . .54 B7
Langdale St Bolton BL3 . .147 E3
　Farnworth BL4 . . . . .60 C7
　Leigh WN7 . . . . .75 E5
Langdale Terr SK15 . . . . . .86 A4
Langden Cl Culcheth WA3 .91 D4
　Shaw OL2 . . . . .149 A8
Langdon Cl BL1 . . . . .143 D1
Langdon Coll M7 . . . . .63 F1
Langfield WA3 . . . . .90 E7
Langfield Ave M16 . . . . . . .97 D3
Langfield Cres M43 . . . . . .84 C2
Langford Dr Irlam M44 . . . .94 A1
　Leigh WN7 . . . . .75 E2
Langford Rd
　Manchester M20 . . . . . . .110 A6
　Manchester SK4 . . . . . . .168 C4
Langford St M34 . . . . .100 F3
Langham Cl BL1 . . . . .25 A5
Langham Ct
　Manchester M20 . . . . . . .109 F4
　Stretford M32 . . . . .96 A4
Langham Gr WA15 . . . . . .120 B8
Langham Ho SK4 . . . . . . .168 B2
Langham Rd
　Altrincham WA14 . . . . . .119 C2
　Oldham OL8 . . . . .66 E4
　Salford M6 . . . . .154 F2
　Standish WN6 . . . . .19 D1
　Stockport SK4 . . . . .168 B1
Langham St OL7 . . . . .85 A5
Langholm Cl WN3 . . . . . . .54 D3
Langholm Dr BL2 . . . . .42 F6
Langholme Cl WN4 . . . . . .72 C4
Langholme Cl M15 . . . . . .162 D7
Langholme Pl M30 . . . . . . .79 B2
Langholme Way OL10 . . . .28 F1
Langland Cl
　Manchester M19 . . . . . . .99 D2
　Manchester M9 . . . . .64 E3
Langland Dr M30 . . . . .95 C7
Langley Ave
　Hazel Grove SK7 . . . . . .124 B1
　Middleton M24 . . . . .46 E4
　Newton-le-W WA12 . . . . .89 C1
　Oldham OL4 . . . . .68 B5
　Prestwich M25 . . . . .63 B6
Langley Cl Golborne WA3 . .74 C1
　Standish WN6 . . . . .19 E2
　Urmston M41 . . . . .95 E2
Langley Cres M25 . . . . . . .63 B6
Langley Ct Hadfield SK13 . .104 A5
　9 Manchester M9 . . . . . .157 E8
Langley Dr 3 Bolton BL3 . .144 C5
　Boothstown M28 . . . . . . .77 F6
　Glossop SK13 . . . . .116 F6
　Handforth SK9 . . . . .131 E3
Langley Gdns M25 . . . . . . .63 B6
Langley Gr M25 . . . . .63 B6
Langley Grange M25 . . . . .63 B6
Langley Hall Rd M25 . . . . .63 B6
Langley La M24,OL10 . . . . .46 D4
Langley Platt La
　M29,M46 . . . . .76 D8
Langley Prim Sch M24 . . . .46 E2
Langley Rd
　Manchester M14 . . . . . . .98 D1
　Manchester M6,M27 . . . . .80 F7
　Prestwich M25 . . . . .63 A5
　Sale M33 . . . . .107 E4
Langley Rd S M6,M27 . . . . .81 A5
Langley St WN5 . . . . .54 D6
Langness St 2 M11 . . . . . .83 C1
Lango St M16 . . . . .97 C4
Langport Ave M12 . . . . . .164 E6
Langroyd Wlk 11 M8 . . . .155 F7
Langset Ave 2 WN2 . . . . .56 D6
Langsett Ave
　24 Gamesley SK13 . . . . .171 D1
　Salford M6 . . . . .80 C3
Langsett Gr 22 SK13 . . . . .171 D1
Langsett Gn 23 SK13 . . . .171 D1
Langsett La SK13 . . . . . . .171 D1
Langsett Terr 21 SK13 . . .171 D1
Langshaw Rd BL3 . . . . . . .144 C6
Langshaw St
　Manchester M16 . . . . . . .97 C4
　Salford M5,M6 . . . . .154 F1
Langshaw Wlk BL3 . . . . . .144 C5
Langside Ave M9 . . . . .64 E4
Langside Dr BL3 . . . . .40 E4
Langston St M3 . . . . .158 F3
Langstone Cl BL6 . . . . .22 B3
Langthorne St M19 . . . . . .111 B8
Langthorne Wlk BL3 . . . .145 D5
Langton Ave WN6 . . . . . . .19 E1

Langton Cl
　Newton-le-W WA12 . . . . .89 A4
　Oldham M35 . . . . .84 C8
Langton Gn SK7 . . . . .124 A1
Langton Pl WN6 . . . . .19 E1
Langton St Heywood OL10 . .29 D3
　Middleton M24 . . . . .65 A8
　Salford M6 . . . . .154 F2
Langton Terr OL11 . . . . . . .30 E4
Langtree Cl M28 . . . . .78 B8
Langtree Cl 3 M16 . . . . . .97 D3
Langtree La WN6 . . . . .19 D3
Langworthy Ave M38 . . . . .60 B4
Langworthy Rd
　Manchester M40 . . . . . . .83 A7
　Salford M6 . . . . .154 F3
Langworthy Road Sch
　. . . . . .154 F3
Lanhill Dr M8 . . . . .156 C6
Lankro Way M30,M17 . . . . .79 F1
Lanreath Wlk 10 M8 . . . . .156 B6
Lansbury Pl 2 M16 . . . . . .97 D3
Lansbury St WN5 . . . . .54 A6
Lansdale Gdns M19 . . . . .110 E5
Lansdale St Eccles M30 . . .95 A8
　Walkden M28 . . . . .60 D5
Lansdown Cl SK7,SK8 . . . .132 C7
Lansdowne Ave
　Droylsden M34 . . . . .84 C4
　Romiley SK6 . . . . .113 D2
Lansdowne Ct 11 BL2 . . . .25 B1
Lansdowne Ct OL9 . . . . . .152 B6
Lansdowne Dr M28 . . . . . .60 C1
Lansdowne Ho M20 . . . . .110 B2
Lansdowne Rd
　Altrincham WA14 . . . . . .119 D6
　Atherton M46 . . . . .58 F5
　Bolton BL2 . . . . .25 B2
　Eccles M30 . . . . .79 D3
　Flixton M41 . . . . .106 E8
　Manchester M8 . . . . .64 A1
　Oldham OL9 . . . . .152 C6
　Sale M33 . . . . .108 A6
Lansdowne Rd N M41 . . . .94 E1
Lansdowne St OL11 . . . . . .30 C7
Lanstead Dr M40 . . . . . . .160 E2
Lantern View SK22 . . . . . .127 B1
Lapwing Cl
　Newton-le-W WA12 . . . . .89 C3
　Rochdale OL11 . . . . .29 C7
　Stalybridge SK15 . . . . . . .86 A4
Lapwing Ct 4 M20 . . . . . .110 A5
Lapwing La
　Brinnington SK5 . . . . . . .112 C6
　Manchester M20 . . . . . . .110 A5
Larch Ave Cheadle SK8 . . .123 A1
　Newton-le-W WA12 . . . . .89 C2
　Radcliffe M26 . . . . .44 B1
　Stretford M32 . . . . .96 D1
　Swinton M27 . . . . .79 C6
　Wigan WN5 . . . . .54 D6
Larch Cl Billinge WN5 . . . . .71 C5
　Failsworth M35 . . . . .83 F6
　Golborne WA3 . . . . .90 F6
　Marple SK6 . . . . .125 E5
　Poynton SK12 . . . . .133 F3
　Rawtenstall BB4 . . . . .1 F8
　Sale M33 . . . . .120 C8
Larch Gr Atherton M46 . . . .58 C4
　Oldham OL4 . . . . .67 E8
　Oldham OL9 . . . . .152 B8
　Swinton M27 . . . . .61 B2
Larch Rd Denton M34 . . . .101 A3
　Eccles M30 . . . . .79 A4
　Leigh WN7 . . . . .75 E8
　Partington M31 . . . . .105 E3
Larch St Bury M26 . . . . . .141 B2
　Oldham OL8,OL9 . . . . . . .153 D6
Larch Way SK13 . . . . .116 F8
Larches The OL5 . . . . .68 E1
Larchview Rd M24 . . . . . . .65 C4
Larchway Bramhall SK7 . .132 C7
　High Lane SK6 . . . . .134 F7
　Milnrow OL16 . . . . .31 D7
Larchwood Chadderton OL9 .65 E8
　Cheadle SK8 . . . . .122 D6
Larchwood Ave M9 . . . . . .157 F7
Larchwood Cl M33 . . . . . .107 C4
Larchwood Dr Wigan WN1 .37 B4
　Wilmslow SK9 . . . . .137 E8
Larchwood St BL1 . . . . . .143 F2
Larden Wlk 1 M8 . . . . . . .155 F6
Largs 7 M23 . . . . .120 F6
Lark Hill Farnworth BL4 . . . .60 E7
　Stalybridge SK15 . . . . . . .86 A4
Lark Hill Ct M24 . . . . .65 A8
Lark Hill La 3 . . . . .51 A4
Lark Hill Pl OL12 . . . . .14 E1
Lark Hill Prim Sch SK3 . .123 C8
Lark Hill Rd Stockport SK3 123 C8
　Uppermill OL3 . . . . .51 A3
Lark St Bolton BL1 . . . . . .145 F8
　Farnworth BL4 . . . . .60 D7
　Oldham OL1 . . . . .49 D3
Larkfield Ave Walkden M38 .59 F5
　Wigan WN1 . . . . .37 B4
Larkfield Cl Ashton-u-L OL7 .85 B7
　Ramsbottom BL8 . . . . . . .10 F1
Larkfield Gr Bolton BL2 . . .148 B8
　Walkden M38 . . . . .59 F5
Larkhill Ave WN6 . . . . .36 F6
Larkhill Cl WA15 . . . . .120 B6
Larkhill Rd SK8 . . . . .123 C5
Larkhill Wlk 2 M8 . . . . . . .156 B6
Larks Rise M43 . . . . .84 D3
Larkside Ave M28 . . . . . . .60 E3
Larkspur Cl WN7 . . . . .75 F3
Larkswood Dr SK2 . . . . . .124 F5

Larkwood Cl SK15 . . . . . . .86 E7
Larmuth Ave M21 . . . . . . .109 C6
Larne Ave Stockport SK3 . .123 B7
　Stretford M32 . . . . .96 C2
Larne St M11 . . . . .165 A8
Larwood Ave SK4 . . . . . . .168 B1
Lascar Ave M5 . . . . .161 A8
Lashbrook Cl M40 . . . . . . .160 D4
Lassell Fold SK14 . . . . . . .102 B6
Lassell St M11 . . . . .99 F7
Lassington Ave M11 . . . . . .99 D8
Last Drop Village The BL7 . .9 A1
Lastingham St M40 . . . . . .83 C6
Latchford Cl OL7 . . . . .166 A4
Latchmere Rd M14 . . . . . .110 C8
Latham Ave WA12 . . . . . . .89 C4
Latham Cl SK6 . . . . .112 F5
Latham Ho WA12 . . . . .89 B4
Latham La WN5 . . . . .54 A8
Latham Rd BL6 . . . . .21 C3
Latham St Bolton BL1 . . . .143 F2
　Droylsden M11 . . . . .99 F7
Lathbury Rd M40,M9 . . . .157 D6
Lathom Cl M33 . . . . .108 E3
Lathom Hall Ave OL4 . . . . .68 A7
Lathom Rd Irlam M44 . . . .105 F8
　Manchester M20 . . . . . . .110 D7
Lathom St 8 BL9 . . . . .141 A4
Latimer Cl 2 WN5 . . . . . . .53 F7
Latimer St OL4 . . . . .67 A6
Latrigg Cres M24 . . . . .46 C2
Latrobe St M43 . . . . .100 A8
Lauderdale Cres M13 . . . .163 C6
Launceston Dr SK7 . . . . . .132 E7
Launceston Rd
　Hindley WN2 . . . . .57 C3
　Radcliffe M26 . . . . .43 D5
Laundry St M6 . . . . .154 F4
Laura St BL9 . . . . .11 C2
Laureate's Pl OL4 . . . . . . .68 D1
Laurel Ave Chadderton OL9 .65 E8
　Cheadle SK8 . . . . .122 D5
　Manchester M14 . . . . . . .98 A2
　Newton-le-W WA12 . . . . .89 D3
Laurel Bank Hyde SK14 . . .113 E8
　Stalybridge SK15 . . . . . .102 B8
Laurel Bank Gdns M9 . . . . .64 D3
Laurel Cres WN2 . . . . .57 A3
Laurel Ct 18 OL4 . . . . .31 B6
Laurel Dr Altrincham WA15 120 B4
　Walkden M38 . . . . .60 A4
Laurel End La SK4 . . . . . .168 A3
Laurel Gn M34 . . . . .101 A2
Laurel Gr Ashton-in-M WN4 .73 B4
　Golborne WA3 . . . . .90 D8
　Leigh WN7 . . . . .75 E8
　Salford M5 . . . . .80 C2
Laurel Ho SK4 . . . . .168 B4
Laurel Rd SK4 . . . . .168 B4
Laurel St Bolton BL1 . . . . .144 C7
　Bury BL8 . . . . .26 F6
　Bury BL9 . . . . .141 B2
　Middleton M24 . . . . .65 D8
　Stockport SK4 . . . . .169 D2
　Wigan WN5 . . . . .54 F7
Laurel Way SK8 . . . . .132 C8
Laurel Wlk M31 . . . . .105 C8
Laurels Dr OL15 . . . . .15 F2
Laurels The OL5 . . . . .68 D1
Laurence Cl M12 . . . . .165 B6
Laurence Lowry Ct 2 M27 61 F1
Lauria Terr BL2 . . . . .26 D1
Laurie Pl 2 OL12 . . . . .14 F1
Laurieston Ct SK8 . . . . . .122 C5
Lausanne Rd
　Manchester M20 . . . . . . .110 B7
　Stockport SK7 . . . . .123 E3
Lavender Cl Sale M23 . . . .108 C1
　Sale M33 . . . . .107 C5
Lavender Hill BL4 . . . . .1 F8
Lavender Rd Farnworth BL4 42 A1
　Oldham OL4 . . . . .67 E4
　Wigan WN6 . . . . .36 F3
Lavender Wlk
　Downall Green WN4 . . . . .72 D5
　Partington M31 . . . . .105 E2
Lavenders Brow SK1 . . . .169 F1
Lavenham Ave M11 . . . . . .83 D1
Lavenham Cl
　Hazel Grove SK7 . . . . . .133 C8
　Whitefield M45 . . . . .44 F3
Laverton Cl BL9 . . . . .28 E1
Lavington Ave SK8 . . . . . .123 A6
Lavington Gr M18 . . . . .99 D4
Lavinia St M30 . . . . .79 B2
Lavister Ave M19 . . . . .110 D3
Law St Rochdale OL11 . . . . .30 C4
　Walsden OL14 . . . . .6 B7
Lawefield Cres M27 . . . . . .61 D4
Lawers Ave OL9 . . . . .152 A8
Lawflat OL12 . . . . .15 C5
Lawler Ave M5 . . . . .161 B6
Lawn Cl OL8 . . . . .67 C5
Lawn Dr Altrincham WA15 .119 E6
　Swinton M27 . . . . .79 E7
Lawn St BL1 . . . . .143 D1
Lawnbank Cl M24 . . . . .46 E1
Lawnfield Ct SK7 . . . . . . .123 D2
Lawnfold SK13 . . . . .171 E4
Lawngreen Ave M21 . . . . .109 A7
Lawnhurst Trad Est
　SK3,SK8 . . . . .123 B5
Lawns The
　Altrincham WA14 . . . . . .119 C3
　Hindley WN2 . . . . .56 C5
Lawnside Mews M20 . . . . .110 A5

Lan-Lea　221

Lawnswood OL11 . . . . .30 C3
Lawnswood Dr
　Pendlebury M27 . . . . .80 B6
　Tyldesley M29 . . . . .59 D1
Lawnswood Park Rd M27 .80 B6
Lawrence Cl OL12 . . . . . . .14 A1
Lawrence Ct WN2 . . . . . . .74 B8
Lawrence Pl SK12 . . . . . . .133 D2
Lawrence Rd
　Altrincham WA14 . . . . . .119 C6
　Hazel Grove SK7 . . . . . . .124 E3
　Urmston M41 . . . . .94 E2
Lawrence St Bury BL9 . . . .44 F4
　Stockport SK1 . . . . .169 E1
Lawrie Ave BL0 . . . . .138 B5
Lawson Ave Gatley SK8 . . .122 B5
　Leigh WN7 . . . . .57 E1
Lawson Cl Middleton M24 . .47 A4
　Swinton M28 . . . . .79 C7
Lawson Dr WA15 . . . . .120 A6
Lawson Gr M33 . . . . .108 A6
Lawson Rd Bolton BL1 . . . .142 C2
　Horwich BL6 . . . . .22 C4
Lawson St 2 Bolton BL1 . .143 E4
　Manchester M9 . . . . .64 C2
Lawson Wlk M34 . . . . .112 F8
Lawton Ave SK7 . . . . .132 E8
Lawton Cl Culcheth WA3 . . .91 E3
　Romiley SK6 . . . . .112 F1
Lawton Fold OL4 . . . . .68 B7
Lawton Moor Rd M23 . . . .109 A1
Lawton Rd SK4 . . . . .168 C4
Lawton Sq OL3 . . . . .50 F4
Lawton St Delph OL3 . . . . .50 F4
　Droylsden M43 . . . . .84 B2
　Hyde SK14 . . . . .167 E3
　Manchester M11 . . . . . . .99 D7
　Rochdale OL12 . . . . .15 A1
　1 Stalybridge SK15 . . . . .86 B1
Laxey Ave M46 . . . . .58 E2
Laxey Cres WN7 . . . . .75 C7
Laxey St M40 . . . . .83 B7
Laxfield Dr M41 . . . . .94 D3
Laxford Gr BL3 . . . . .40 E6
Layard St OL6 . . . . .166 A3
Laycock Ave Bolton BL2 . . .25 B3
　Stalybridge SK15 . . . . . . .86 E4
Laycock Cres 4 M35 . . . . .83 F7
Laycock Dr SK16 . . . . .102 A7
Laycock Gr M35 . . . . .83 F7
Laycock St OL16 . . . . .15 D3
Laycock Way M34 . . . . . . .112 F8
Layfield Cl BL8 . . . . .26 D7
Layland Ave WA3 . . . . .91 E4
Layland St WN3 . . . . .150 B8
Laystall St M1 . . . . .159 B1
Laythe Barn Cl OL16 . . . . .31 E6
Layton Ave SK14 . . . . .101 C2
Layton Cl SK1 . . . . .124 A8
Layton Dr Kearsley BL4 . . . .60 F6
　Romiley SK6 . . . . .113 C3
Layton St M40 . . . . .160 D2
Lazenby Cres WN4 . . . . . . .72 F3
Lazonby Ave WN2 . . . . . . .38 F3
Lazonby Wlk 7 M13 . . . . . .98 F4
Le Bas Ho M20 . . . . .109 F6
Le Gendre St 1 BL2 . . . . . .25 B2
Le Mans Cres BL1 . . . . . . .145 F7
Lea Ct Failsworth M35 . . . .83 E7
　Manchester SK4 . . . . . . .168 B4
Lea Dr M9 . . . . .64 F3
Lea Gate Cl Bolton BL2 . . . .25 D5
　Wigan WN3 . . . . .54 E3
Lea Mount Dr BL9 . . . . . . .28 D4
Lea Rd Gatley SK8 . . . . . .122 B1
　Manchester SK4 . . . . . . .168 C4
Lea St WN3 . . . . .150 A7
Lea Vale M38 . . . . .59 F4
Lea View Royton OL2 . . . . .48 C3
　Wigan WN3 . . . . .37 F1
Leabank St 5 M19 . . . . . . .99 A2
Leabrook Dr M40 . . . . .83 C8
Leaburn Dr M19 . . . . .110 E4
Leach Cl OL16 . . . . .15 C2
Leach St Bolton BL3 . . . . .145 E5
　4 Farnworth BL4 . . . . . . .42 E1
　Manchester M18 . . . . . . .165 B6
　Milnrow OL16 . . . . .31 F5
　Prestwich M25 . . . . .62 F4
　Rochdale OL16 . . . . .31 B6
　Shaw OL2 . . . . .149 C6
Leach Wlk OL4 . . . . .67 E8
Leaches Rd BL0 . . . . .11 D8
Leaconfield Dr M28 . . . . . .78 F7
Leacroft WN4 . . . . .72 F6
Leacroft Ave BL2 . . . . .42 D5
Leacroft Rd M21 . . . . .109 D5
Leadale Cl M9 . . . . .19 D1
Leadale Rise OL4 . . . . .68 A6
Leader Williams Rd M44 . .93 F1
Leader Williams Rd M44 . .93 F1
Leaf St Wigan WN1 . . . . . .151 E8
　Wigan WN5 . . . . .54 C6
Leaf St Bolton BL3 . . . . . .148 C5
　Manchester M15 . . . . . . .162 F6
　Reddish SK5 . . . . .111 E7
Leafield M29 . . . . .59 C1
Leafield Ave M20 . . . . . . .110 D4
Leafield Cl M26 . . . . .43 E3
Leafield Dr Boothstown M28 78 A6
　Cheadle SK8 . . . . .131 F6
Leafield Rd SK12 . . . . . . .135 C6
Leaford Ave M34 . . . . .100 D4
Leaford Cl M34 . . . . .100 D4
Leagate M41 . . . . .95 E1
League St OL16 . . . . .31 A5

Leah St 3 OL15 16 B5
Leaholme Cl M40 83 D5
Leak St M16 161 C6
Leal Holme Ave WN2 38 A3
Leam St OL6 85 D4
Leamington Ave Bury BL9 27 E8
Manchester M20 109 F4
Newton-le-W WA12 89 C1
Leamington Ct 3 SK5 111 E7
Leamington Rd Eccles M30 79 B3
Reddish SK5 111 E7
Urmston M41 95 C3
Leamington St
Manchester M11 99 D7
Oldham OL4 67 D8
Rochdale OL12 139 E8
Leamore Wlk 9 M9 64 E3
Leander Cl M9 64 E2
Leander Dr OL11 30 D1
Leas The WA15 120 C3
Leaside Ave OL1 48 B2
Leaside Cl OL12 14 D2
Leaside Dr M20 110 D5
Leaside Gr M28 60 E3
Leaside Way SK9 137 C6
Leaton Ave M23 121 A6
Leavengreave Ct OL12 4 D4
Leaway Ince-in-M WN2 151 F7
Littleborough OL12 15 C6
Lecester Rd M8 156 B6
Leckenby Cl 2 M28 78 A6
Leconfield Dr M9 64 E4
Leconfield Rd M30 78 F4
Lecturers Cl BL3 145 F5
Ledbrooke Cl M5 161 B8
Ledburn Cl M15 162 D6
Ledburn Ct M15 162 D6
Ledbury Ave M41 95 C3
Ledbury Cl M24 65 A6
Ledbury Rd M35 83 E4
Ledbury St Leigh WN7 75 F6
Leigh WN7 75 F7
Ledbury Wlk M9 64 C3
Leddy Wlk 1 M16 97 F4
Ledge Ley SK8 131 E8
Ledmore Gr WN4 72 D3
Ledsham Ave M9 64 A5
Ledson Rd M23 120 F5
Ledward La WA14 119 B2
Lee Ave Altrincham WA14 119 C7
Bolton BL3 147 D3
Lee Bank BL5 58 B8
Lee Cl M44 93 F2
Lee Cres M32 96 E2
Lee Ct M22 121 E8
Lee Dale Cl M34 101 A2
Lee Fold M29 77 C7
Lee Gate BL2 25 D5
Lee Gr BL4 59 F8
Lee Head SK13 115 C5
Lee Ho M22 121 E8
Lee La Abram WN2 74 B8
Horwich BL6 22 B4
Lee Mount SK13 116 C7
Lee Rd Bacup OL13 3 E8
Manchester M9 157 D8
Lee Side OL3 51 D4
Lee St Atherton M46 58 D2
Bury BL9 27 F8
Littleborough OL15 16 B6
Middleton M24 46 F3
Oldham OL3 69 B8
Oldham OL8 153 E5
Stockport SK1 169 F1
Lee Vale Dr SK13 115 D7
Lee's St OL13 4 C8
Leech Ave OL6 85 E5
Leech Brook Ave M34 100 E5
Leech Brook Cl M34 100 E6
Leech St Hyde SK14 167 F2
Stalybridge SK15 86 A1
Leedale St M12 99 A2
Leeds Cl BL9 45 B3
Leeds St WN3 150 B7
Leeds St Ind Est WN3 150 B7
Leefields Cl OL3 69 B8
Leegate Cl SK4 110 F4
Leegate Dr M9 64 F4
Leegate Gdns SK4 168 A4
Leegate Rd SK4 168 A4
Leegrange Rd M9 64 E1
Leek St M26 43 E3
Leemans Hill St BL8 27 A5
Lees Ave M34 100 E3
Lees Brook Pk OL4 67 D6
Lees Cotts BL7 9 C2
Lees Gr OL4 67 D5
Lees Hall Cres M14 110 D8
Lees Hall Ct 9 M14 110 D8
Lees La WN8 35 B6
Lees New Rd OL4,OL6 67 D2
Lees Park Ave M43 84 C2
Lees Park Way M43 84 C2
Lees Rd Adlington PR6 21 B8
Ashton-u-L OL6 85 D7
Bramhall SK7 132 D5
Oldham OL4 67 C6
Lees Row SK13 104 C5
Lees Sq OL6 166 C3
Lees St Ashton-u-L OL6 166 B4
Droylsden M43 84 B2
Manchester M11,M18 99 E6
Middleton M24 65 D7
2 Mossley OL5 68 C2
Oldham OL8 85 A8
Lees St *continued*
Shaw OL2 149 B7
6 Stalybridge SK15 86 A2
Swinton M27 61 F1
Lees St E OL2 149 C7
Leesfield OL6 166 B4
Leeside SK4 168 A1
Leestone Rd M22 121 E6
Leesway OL4 67 E5
Leesway Dr M34 101 A2
Leeswood Ave M21 109 C6
Leewood M27 61 D4
Leewood Ct SK4 168 B3
Left Bank M3 158 E1
Legh Ct M33 108 E3
Legh Dr Droylsden M34 84 B1
Romiley SK6 113 B6
Legh Rd High Lane SK12 135 A6
Manchester M7 155 D8
Sale M33 108 E3
Legh St Ashton-in-M WN4 73 B2
Eccles M30 79 C1
Golborne WA3 90 A8
Manchester M7 155 D7
Newton-le-W WA12 89 A3
Leghorn Wlk 14 M11 160 F1
Legion Gr M7 155 E6
Legwood Ct M41 95 C2
Leicester Ave Denton M34 100 F1
Droylsden M43 83 F3
Hindley WN2 56 F6
Horwich BL6 22 A3
Manchester M7 155 F8
Sale WA15 120 A8
Leicester Ct M7 63 F1
Leicester Dr SK13 116 F8
Leicester Rd
Altrincham WA15 119 F2
Failsworth M35 84 A6
Manchester M7 155 E7
Sale M33 108 B5
Tyldesley M29 59 A2
Whitefield M45 44 D1
Leicester St
Ashton-u-L OL7 166 B4
Oldham OL4 67 B6
Reddish SK5 99 F2
Rochdale OL11 31 A5
Leicester Wlk M7 155 E6
Leigh Arc 4 WN1 150 C8
Leigh Ave Marple SK6 125 E6
Swinton M27 79 D5
Leigh Bsns Pk WN7 76 B3
Leigh CE Inf Sch WN7 75 E5
Leigh CE Jun Sch WN7 75 F5
Leigh Cl BL8 26 E7
Leigh Commerce Pk WN7 76 B3
Leigh Common BL5 39 E1
Leigh Fold SK14 101 E5
Leigh Infmy WN7 76 A6
Leigh La BL8 27 B3
Leigh Prim Sch SK14 167 E2
Leigh Rd Altrincham WA15 119 E2
Atherton M46 58 B2
Hindley WN2 57 B2
Leigh WN7 75 F7
Westhoughton BL5 57 F7
Westhoughton BL5 57 F8
Wilmslow SK9 136 D5
Worsley M28 78 C6
Leigh St Aspull WN2 38 F3
Bury BL8 26 F4
Farnworth BL4 60 D8
Heywood OL10 29 C2
Hyde SK14 167 E2
Leigh WN2 57 B1
Leigh WN7 75 C5
Leigh WN7 75 F5
Milnrow OL16 31 D7
Westhoughton BL5 39 E1
Wigan WN1 151 D7
Leighbrook Rd M14 110 B8
Leighs Cotts WA15 120 C4
Leighton Ave Atherton M46 58 B3
Bolton BL1 144 B8
Littleborough OL15 15 F2
Leighton Dr Golborne WN7 75 B1
Marple SK6 126 C8
Leighton Rd M16 97 C4
Leighton St Atherton M46 58 B3
Manchester M40 83 A8
Leinster Rd M27 79 E7
Leinster St BL4 60 C7
Leith Ave M33 108 E4
Leith Rd M33 108 E4
Lemnos St OL1 67 A7
Lemon St M29 76 F8
Lemonpark Ind Est OL10 46 E8
Len Cox Wlk 3 M4 159 B2
Lena St Bury BL1 143 F2
Manchester M1 159 B1
Lench Rd BB4 2 D8
Lench St BB4 2 F8
Leng Rd M40 83 D5
Lenham Ave M30 79 B2
Lenham Cl SK5 112 B6
Lenham Gdns BL2 42 E6
Lenham Towers SK5 112 B6
Lenham Wlk M22 130 D8
Lennox Gdns BL3 40 F5
Lennox St OL6 166 C3
Lennox Wlk OL10 28 F1
Lenora St BL3 146 B4
Lenten Gr OL10 46 E7
Lenthall Wlk 20 M8 155 F7
Lentmead Dr M40 65 A1
Lenton Gdns M22 121 E5
Leominster Dr M22 121 F2
Leominster Rd M24 65 B6
Leonard Ct WN7 75 B4
Leonard St Bolton BL3 147 E3
Rochdale OL11 30 C1
Leonardin Cl OL2 48 F8
Leopold Ave M20 110 A5
Leopold St Rochdale OL11 139 D7
Wigan WN5 54 B5
Wigan WN5 54 C5
Lepp Cres BL8 27 C5
Leroy Dr M9 64 E2
Lerryn Dr SK7 123 D1
Lesley Rd M32 96 A1
Leslie Ave Oldham OL9 66 B3
Whitefield BL9 44 F3
Leslie Gr WA15 120 A6
Leslie Hough Way M6 81 B4
Leslie St Bolton BL2 25 B1
Manchester M14 98 B3
Lessingham Ave WN1 37 B3
Lester Rd M38 59 E5
Lester St M32 96 D2
Letchworth Ave 2 OL11 31 A5
Letchworth St M14 98 B3
Letcombe Cl WN7 75 F7
Letham St OL8 66 F2
Letitia St BL6 22 A3
Levedale Rd M9 64 E4
Leven Cl BL4 61 B5
Leven Wlk Whitefield M45 63 C8
2 Wythenshawe M23 121 A5
Levenhurst Rd M8 155 F7
Levens Cl SK8 122 B4
Levens Dr BL2 25 E1
Levens Pl Ince-in-M WN2 56 A8
Wigan WN5 54 C7
Levens Rd SK7 124 C2
Levens St Manchester M40 83 A7
Salford M6 81 B5
Levens Wlk Oldham OL9 152 A5
Wigan WN5 54 C7
Levenshulme High Sch
for Girls M19 111 A7
Levenshulme Rd M18 99 D4
Levenshulme Sta M19 99 A1
Levenshulme Terr 8 M19 99 A1
Levenshulme Trad Est
M19 99 C2
Lever Ave M27 62 B2
Lever Bridge Pl BL3 42 D5
Lever Cl 7 M29 58 F1
Lever Dr BL3 147 F4
Lever Edge La BL3 147 E3
Lever Edge Prim Sch
BL3 147 E2
Lever Gr BL2 148 A5
Lever Hall Rd BL2 42 D7
Lever Park Ave BL6 22 B5
Lever Park Sch BL6 22 C3
Lever St Bolton BL3 147 F4
Hazel Grove SK7 124 D3
Heywood OL10 29 D3
Little Lever BL3 43 A4
Manchester M1 159 B1
Middleton M24 47 A1
Radcliffe M26 43 F5
Ramsbottom BL0 138 C6
Tyldesley M29 58 F1
Westhoughton BL5 39 E3
Lever Wlk M24 64 F7
Leverett Cl WA14 119 A5
Leverhulme Ave BL3 42 A3
Levi St BL1 23 F1
Levington Dr OL8 85 A8
Lewes Ave M34 100 F1
Lewes Wlk OL9 152 B6
Lewis Ave Manchester M9 64 E1
Urmston M41 95 D5
Lewis Cl Adlington PR7 20 E6
Wigan WN3 150 A5
Lewis Dr OL10 28 F1
Lewis Rd Droylsden M43 83 E2
Reddish SK5 99 F1
Lewis St Eccles M30 79 D1
Heywood OL10 29 E3
Manchester M40 160 D3
Shaw OL2 149 B5
Lewis Street Prim Sch
M30 79 D1
Lewisham Ave M40 83 B4
Lewisham Cl OL2 48 C6
Lewtas St M30 79 E1
Lexton Ave M8 64 B2
Ley Cres M29 77 B6
Ley Dr OL10 46 E7
Ley Hey Ave SK6 125 F7
Ley Hey Ct SK6 125 F7
Ley Hey Rd SK6 125 F7
Ley La SK6 126 D8
Ley Rd M29 77 A7
Leybourne Ave M19 99 B2
Leybourne St BL1 143 E2
Leybrook Rd M22 121 C3
Leyburn Ave Royton OL2 48 D4
Stretford M32 96 C3
Urmston M41 95 A1
Leyburn Cl Whitefield M45 62 E8
Wigan WN1 151 F8
Wigan WN1 37 F1
Leyburn Gr
2 Farnworth BL4 42 D1
Romiley SK6 113 C2
Leyburn Ho 2 M13 98 E4
Leyburn Rd M40 65 C2
Leyburne Rd SK2 124 D6
Leycett Dr M23 109 A1
Leycroft St Manchester M1 159 B1
Manchester M1 163 B8
Leyden Wlk M23 121 A4
Leyfield Ave SK6 113 C2
Leyfield Rd OL16 31 E6
Leygate View SK22 127 B1
Leyland Ave Gatley SK8 122 B6
Hindley WN2 56 E3
Irlam M44 94 B4
Manchester M20 110 D3
Leyland Green Rd WN4 72 C5
Leyland Mill La WN1 37 C3
Leyland St Abram WN2 56 B1
Bury BL9 44 F4
Hindley WN2 56 C4
Stockport SK1 169 E1
Leylands La SK14 114 F7
Leys Rd WA14 119 E8
Leyton Ave M40 83 B7
Leyton Cl Farnworth BL4 147 F1
2 Wigan WN5 54 D5
Leyton Dr BL9 44 F5
Leyton St 2 OL12 15 A2
Leywell Dr OL1 49 D3
Libra St BL1 143 D2
Library La OL9 153 D8
Library St
Westhoughton BL5 57 F8
Wigan WN1 150 C8
Lichens Cres OL8 67 A3
Lichfield Ave
Altrincham WA15 120 C3
Ashton-u-L OL6 85 D8
Bolton BL2 25 B2
Golborne WA3 90 D8
Reddish SK5 111 E8
Tyldesley M29 77 C7
Lichfield Cl Farnworth BL4 60 A8
Radcliffe M26 43 D5
Lichfield Dr Bury BL8 140 D4
Chadderton OL9 48 A1
Manchester M25 63 C2
Manchester M8 156 B7
Swinton M27 79 F6
Lichfield Gr WN4 73 C2
Lichfield Rd Eccles M30 79 F4
Radcliffe M26 43 D5
Urmston M41 95 D3
Lichfield St Salford M6 81 B5
Wigan WN5 54 C5
Lichfield Terr OL16 31 C4
Lichfield Wlk SK6 113 A1
Lidbrook Wlk M12 164 E5
Liddington Hall Dr BL0 11 B4
Lidgate Cl WN3 54 D3
Lidgate Gr
7 Farnworth BL4 60 C8
4 Manchester M20 110 A3
Lidgett Cl M38 60 C5
Lidiard St M8 64 A1
Lido Ho OL4 68 A6
Liffey Ave M22 121 E3
Lifton Ave M40 160 E4
Light Alders La SK12 135 A6
Light Oaks Inf & Jun Sch
M6 80 B4
Light Oaks Rd
Fowley Common WA3 92 C6
Salford M6 80 C4
Lightborne Rd M33 107 E4
Lightbounds Rd BL1 23 F3
Lightbourne Ave 5 M27 79 F7
Lightbowne Rd M40 65 C2
Lightburn Ave OL15 15 E4
Lightburne Ave
Bolton BL1 144 B7
Leigh WN7 75 E3
Lightfoot Wlk 6 M11 160 F1
Lighthorne Ave SK3 122 F7
Lighthorne Gr SK3 122 F7
Lighthorne Rd SK3 122 F7
Lighthouse OL15 6 C1
Lightowlers La OL15 16 D7
Lightshaw La WA3 74 B4
Lightwood M28 78 B8
Lightwood Cl 7 BL4 42 E1
Lignum Ave OL9 152 B8
Lila St M9 157 F7
Lilac Ave Bury BL9 44 D7
Downall Green WN4 72 D5
Hyde SK14 113 D8
Leigh WN7 75 E7
Newhey OL16 32 A3
Pendlebury M27 80 A8
Wigan WN6 37 A3
Lilac Ct 5 M6 81 A2
Lilac Gdns WN3 55 F4
Lilac Gr Billinge WN5 71 D4
Manchester M40 65 A1
Oldham OL9 152 B8
Prestwich M25 63 A6
Lilac La OL8 66 D2
Lilac Rd Altrincham WA15 120 A3
Golborne WA3 74 A1
Rochdale OL11 30 F2
Lilac St SK2 170 F6
Lilac Terr 2 OL13 3 D8
Lilac View Cl OL2 49 D6
Lilac Wlk M31 105 E3
Lilburn Cl BL0 11 C4
Liley St OL16 31 A7
Lilford Cl M12 165 A6
Lilford St Atherton M46 58 B2
Leigh WN7 75 E4
Lilian Dr WN6 37 A3
Lilian St M16 97 C4
Lillian Gr SK5 111 F8
Lilly St Bolton BL1 145 D8
Hyde SK14 113 F8
Lilmore Ave M40 83 C6
Lilstock Wlk 10 M9 64 E3
Lily Ave Farnworth BL4 42 B1
Newton-le-W WA12 89 D2
Lily Cl SK3 170 D5
Lily Hill St M45 44 E2
Lily La Ashton-in-M WN2 73 F7
Manchester M40,M9 157 F8
Manchester M9,M40 83 A8
Platt Bridge WN2 56 A1
Lily Lane Jun & Inf Sch
M40 83 A8
Lily Lanes OL6 85 E8
Lily Pl WN4 73 C2
Lily St Ashton-in-M WN4 73 E5
Eccles M30 79 B1
Middleton M24 65 C8
Milnrow OL16 31 F6
Oldham OL1 48 E1
Royton OL2 48 F4
Lily Thomas Ct 3 M11 99 D7
Lima St BL9 141 B3
Limbert Circ M8 64 C1
Lime Ave Leigh WN7 75 E8
New Mills SK22 127 D1
Swinton M27 79 C6
Urmston M41 95 B2
Whitefield M45 62 F7
Lime Bank St M12 164 D8
Lime Cl Abram Brow WN2 74 C7
Dukinfield SK16 101 D6
Hollinfare WA3 105 A2
Salford M6 81 A3
Lime Cres M16 97 B4
Lime Ct M6 81 A3
Lime Gate OL8 66 C2
Lime Gdns Dukinfield SK16 101 B8
Middleton M24 64 E8
Lime Gn OL8 66 D1
Lime Gr Altrincham WA15 120 B7
Ashton-u-L OL6 85 C5
Bury BL9 27 F7
Cheadle SK8 122 D6
Denton M34 100 F4
Dukinfield SK15 101 E8
Golborne WA3 90 E6
Heywood OL10 29 C3
Hindley WN2 56 F3
Littleborough OL15 15 F6
Manchester M16 97 B4
Prestwich M25 63 A6
Ramsbottom BL0 11 D7
Royton OL2 48 D6
Walkden M28 60 D1
Lime Green Rd OL8 84 D8
Lime Kiln La SK6 126 A5
Lime La M35 84 C7
Lime Pl SK16 101 B8
Lime Rd M32 96 D1
Lime St Atherton M46 57 F3
Bredbury SK6 112 E4
Bury BL9 27 F6
Dukinfield SK16 101 B8
Eccles M30 79 D1
Farnworth BL4 60 E8
Oldham OL1 48 C1
Rochdale OL11 30 C4
Tyldesley M29 58 F1
Wigan WN1 151 D8
Lime Tree Cl M41 95 E1
Lime Tree Gr M35 84 B7
Lime Trees Prim Sch
M33 108 E3
Lime Vale WN3 55 F4
Lime Vale Rd WA11,WN5 71 C3
Lime Wlk
6 Handforth SK9 131 D1
8 Handforth SK9 131 D1
Partington M31 105 D3
Limebrook Cl M11 99 E7
Limeditch Rd M35 84 A8
Limefield Middleton M24 64 E8
Milnrow OL16 31 E7
Mossley OL5 68 B2
1 Wigan WN1 151 D8
Limefield Ave BL4 42 D1
Limefield Brow BL9 27 F7
Limefield Cl BL1 142 B4
Limefield Ct M7 63 D1
Limefield Rd Bolton BL1 142 B4
Bury BL9 27 F7
Manchester M7 63 D1
Radcliffe M26 43 E3
Limefield Terr M19 99 A1
Limehurst Ave
8 Ashton-u-L OL7 85 A6
Manchester M20 109 F8
Limehurst Prim Sch OL8 84 D8
Limehurst Rd OL7 85 A6
Limekiln La M12 164 D8
Limers Gate OL12 14 F5
Limerston Dr M40 83 A5
Limes Ave WN6 37 B6
Limes The Culcheth WA3 91 D4
Golborne WA3 90 D6
Mossley OL5 68 B1
Mossley OL5 68 E1
Standish WN6 37 A6
Limesdale Cl BL3 43 B5
Limeside Com Prim Sch
OL8 66 D1
Limeside Rd OL8 66 C1
Limestead Ave M8 156 A8
Limetree Wlk M11 160 F1
Limetrees Rd M24 64 F8
Limley Gr M21 109 C7
Linacre Ave BL3 147 E2
Linacre Way SK13 116 F7
Linbeck Gr WA3 74 E1

Linby St M15 162 E7
Lincoln Ave Denton M34 100 F1
Droylsden M43 84 A3
Gatley SK8 131 B7
Golborne WA3 74 D1
Irlam M44 105 C4
Little Lever BL3 43 A2
Manchester M19 99 B1
Urmston M32 95 F3
Lincoln Cl Ashton-u-L OL6 85 D8
Golborne WN7 91 C8
Rochdale OL11 31 A6
Tyldesley M29 59 A2
Lincoln Close Ind Est 2
OL11 31 A6
Lincoln Ct Failsworth M40 83 B4
12 Manchester M7 63 E1
Lincoln Dr
Altrincham WA15 120 B5
Ashton-in-M WN4 73 D2
Aspull WN2 38 D5
7 Bury BL9 44 F8
Littleborough OL15 16 A3
Manchester M25 63 C2
Lincoln Gn SK5 112 C6
Lincoln Gr Atherton M46 58 B3
Bolton BL2 25 F4
Manchester M13 163 C5
Sale M33 108 F4
Lincoln Leach Ct OL11 139 F5
Lincoln Mill (Ent Ctr)
BL3 144 C6
Lincoln Minshull Cl 12
M23 108 F2
Lincoln Pl WN5 36 C1
Lincoln Rd Bolton BL1 144 B8
Failsworth M35 84 A6
Handforth SK9 131 E1
Hindley WN2 56 E5
Middleton M24 65 C5
7 Swinton M27 79 E7
Lincoln Rise SK6 113 A1
Lincoln St Eccles M30 79 C1
Manchester M13 98 F4
Oldham OL9 152 C5
Rochdale OL11 31 A6
Lincoln Way SK13 116 F8
Lincoln Wlk OL10 29 A2
Lincombe Rd M22 130 D8
Lincroft Rd WN2 57 A3
Lind St M40 160 E2
Linda Dr SK7 124 D2
Lindale SK14 101 C5
Lindale Ave Bolton BL1 40 F8
Failsworth M40 65 D2
Oldham OL9 152 A6
Royton OL2 48 C8
Urmston M41 94 F3
Whitefield BL9 45 A3
Lindale Cl M28 77 E7
Lindale Dr M24 46 E3
Lindale Rd M28 77 E7
Lindale Rise OL2 49 D7
Lindbury Ave SK2 124 C7
Linden Ave
Altrincham WA15 119 E5
Ashton-in-M WN4 72 F5
Atherton M46 58 B2
Denton M34 100 D7
Little Lever BL3 43 A5
Oldham OL4 67 D8
Orrell WN5 53 E6
Pendlebury M6 80 E6
Ramsbottom BL0 11 D6
Sale M33 107 F4
Swinton M27 79 D7
Linden Cl Denton M34 101 A3
Edenfield BL0 1 D2
Lymm WA13 117 A4
Linden Ct WN5 53 E6
Linden Dr M5 161 A8
Linden Gr
Billinge WA11,WN5 71 C3
Bramhall SK7 132 D4
Leigh WN7 75 E7
Manchester M14 110 D8
Orrell WN5 53 E6
Stockport SK2 124 B4
Linden Lea Rawtenstall BB4 1 F8
Sale M33 108 B2
Linden Mews M28 77 F6
Linden Pk M19 111 A8
Linden Rd Boothstown M28 77 F6
Cheadle SK8 123 A3
Denton M34 101 A3
Hindley WN2 56 E7
Manchester M20 110 A4
Stalybridge SK15 102 D7
Linden Road Prim Sch
M34 101 A3
Linden St WN5 54 C5
Linden Way SK6 135 A7
Linden Wlk Bolton BL2 25 B5
Orrell WN5 53 E6
Lindenwood OL9 65 E8
Lindeth Ave M18 99 D4
Lindfield Dr BL1 143 E1
Lindfield Est N SK9 137 A6
Lindfield Est S SK9 136 F6
Lindfield Rd SK5 99 F1
Lindinis Ave M5,M6 81 B2
Lindisfarne 17 OL12 139 E8
Lindisfarne Ave WA3 91 C8
Lindisfarne Cl M33 108 B2
Lindisfarne Dr SK12 133 D4
Lindisfarne Pl BL2 25 C2
Lindisfarne Rd OL7 84 E5
Lindley Ave WN5 53 C5
Lindley Gr SK3 170 D5
Lindley St Kearsley BL4 61 B6
Little Lever BL3 43 B3
Lindleywood Rd M14 110 E8
Lindon Park Rd BB4 1 C7
Lindon Way M43 99 E8
Lindop Rd WA15 119 F1
Lindow Cl BL8 27 B6
Lindow Ct Bredbury SK6 112 D3
Sale M33 108 F3
Lindow Fold Dr SK9 136 D5
Lindow La SK9 136 E6
Lindow Par SK9 136 F6
Lindow Prim Sch SK9 136 D3
Lindow Rd M16 97 C2
Lindow St Leigh WN7 75 D6
Sale M33 108 F3
Lindrick Ave M45 62 D6
Lindrick Cl M40 83 C7
Lindrick Terr BL3 145 D5
Lindsay Ave Bramhall SK8 123 B1
Manchester M19 98 F1
Swinton M27 79 E7
Lindsay Cl OL4 49 D2
Lindsay Rd M19 110 F8
Lindsay St Horwich BL6 22 D1
Stalybridge SK15 86 B1
Lindsay Terr WN2 38 B5
Lindsell Rd WA14 119 C8
Lindsgate Dr WA15 120 B7
Lindside Wlk 13 M9 64 E3
Lindum Ave M16 97 C4
Lindum St M14 98 B3
Lindwall Cl M23 109 B2
Linear View WA12 89 C1
Linehan Cl SK4 110 D2
Lineholme OL1 48 C2
Linen Ct M3 158 D3
Lines Rd Droylsden M43 84 B1
Irlam M44 105 F8
Linfield Cl BL2 25 D4
Linfield St M11 83 B1
Linford Ave M40 65 C2
Ling Dr M46 58 D2
Lingard Cl M34 100 C8
Lingard La SK6 112 D5
Lingard Rd M22 109 D1
Lingard St Leigh WN7 76 B4
Reddish SK5 111 F8
Lingard Terr M34 100 C8
Lingards Dr M29 77 A4
Lingards La M29 77 A4
Lingcrest Rd M19 111 C7
Lingdale Rd SK8 122 F2
Lingdale Wlk M40 83 A7
Lingfield Ave
Hazel Grove SK7 124 F2
Sale M33 107 B2
Lingfield Cl Bury BL8 27 C7
Farnworth BL4 60 C7
Lingfield Cres WN6 36 E3
Lingfield Rd M11 83 C2
Lingfield Wlk OL9 152 C7
Lingholme Dr M24 46 C2
Lingmell Ave WA11 71 C1
Lingmell Cl Bolton BL1 40 F8
Middleton M24 46 D2
Urmston M41 95 A4
Lingmoor Cl Middleton M24 46 C2
Wigan WN3 55 A1
Lingmoor Dr M29 77 B7
Lingmoor Rd BL1 23 F1
Lingmoor Wlk M15 162 F5
Lings Wlk M22 121 E1
Linhope Cl SK4 110 E3
Link Ave M41 96 A1
Link La OL8 66 E2
Link Rd Oldham OL4 67 F7
Sale M33 107 D2
Link The Brinnington SK5 112 C6
Handforth SK9 131 D3
Shaw OL2 48 F8
Link Wlk M31 105 D2
Linkfield Dr M28 77 F6
Links Ave M35 83 F5
Links Cres M25 63 E2
Links Dr BL6 40 B7
Links Pl OL6 85 E6
Links Rd Bolton BL2 26 A3
Bolton BL6 40 B7
Heywood OL10 46 D8
Marple SK6 125 F4
Romiley SK6 113 D2
Wilmslow SK9 136 E4
Links Rise M41 95 A4
Links The M40 83 C7
Links View Manchester M25 63 A1
Rochdale OL11 30 B6
Links Way OL9 152 C8
Linksfield M34 100 F5
Linkside Ave OL2 48 D5
Linksview Ct M45 62 D7
Linksway Gatley SK8 122 A4
Manchester M25 63 D2
Pendlebury M27 80 A6
Linksway Cl SK4 111 A5
Linksway Dr BL9 45 B3
Linkway Ave WN4 73 E5
Linkway The BL6 39 D8
Linley Ave BL9 44 E5
Linley Cl WN6 36 C4
Linley Dr OL4 67 D4
Linley Gr BL0 11 A2
Linley Rd Cheadle SK8 132 B8
Sale M33 108 B5
Wigan WN5 54 E5
Linn St M8 64 A1
Linnell Dr OL11 29 E8
Linnet Cl Droylsden M34 84 C1
Hazel Grove SK2 124 F5
Manchester M12 98 F4
Newton-le-W WA12 89 C3
Linnet Dr Bury BL9 141 B4
Irlam M44 94 A3
Leigh WN7 76 B5
Linnet Hill OL11 30 C6
Linnet's Wood Mews M28 60 E3
Linney La OL2 149 C7
Linney Rd SK7 123 D2
Linney Sq WN1 151 E8
Linslade Gdns BL3 145 E5
Linslade Ho 10 M5 154 F1
Linslade Wlk 7 M9 157 D7
Linsley St M3 158 E2
Linstead Dr M8 155 F6
Linstock Way M46 58 B3
Linthorpe Wlk BL3 146 B4
Linton Ave Bury BL9 27 F5
Golborne WA3 73 F2
Reddish M34 100 A3
Linton Cl M4 164 D8
Linton Rd M33 108 C6
Linton Vale M26 61 B8
Linton Wlk M7 80 F8
Linwood Cl WN2 56 D4
Linwood Gr M12 99 A2
Linwood St M35,M40 83 C6
Lion Brow M9 64 D3
Lion Fold La M9 64 D3
Lion La BL6 21 C2
Lion St M9 64 D2
Lions Dr M27 80 A7
Liptrot St WN5 54 F7
Lisbon St 17 OL12 14 C1
Lisburn Ave
Manchester M16,M21 97 C1
Sale M33 108 A3
Lisburn Rd M40 83 A8
Lisburne Ave SK2 124 D7
Lisburne Cl SK2 124 D6
Lisburne La SK2 124 D6
Lisburne Sch SK2 124 E6
Liscard Ave M14 98 B1
Liscard St M46 58 B3
Lisetto Ave 1 OL4 67 B5
Liskeard Ave OL2 48 F4
Liskeard Cl OL16 15 C1
Liskeard Dr SK7 132 F7
Lisle St 3 OL12 31 A8
Lismore WA15 119 F2
Lismore Ave Bolton BL3 40 F5
Stockport SK3 123 B8
Lismore Rd SK16 101 D7
Lismore Way M41 95 E5
Lismore Wlk M22 130 E8
Lissadel St M6 81 B4
Lisson Gr WA15 119 E2
Lister Rd M24 64 B6
Lister St BL3 146 B3
Liston St SK16 101 F8
Litcham Cl M1 163 B7
Litchfield Cl OL3 33 C2
Litchfield Ct M24 64 C7
Litchfield Gr M28 79 A7
Litherland Ave M22 121 E2
Litherland Rd Bolton BL3 147 E2
Sale M33 108 E3
Little Ancoats St M1,M4 159 B2
Little Bank St 1 OL4 67 B6
Little Bollington
CE Prim Sch WA14 118 B2
Little Brook Rd M33 107 C1
Little Brow BL7 25 A7
Little Church St 3 WN5 54 B6
Little Clegg Rd OL15 15 F2
Little David St M1 163 A8
Little Ees La M33 107 F7
Little Egerton St SK1 169 E2
Little Factory St M29 58 F1
Little Flatt OL12 14 B1
Little Harwood Lee BL2 25 E3
Little Heath La WA14 118 D5
Little Heaton
CE Prim Sch M24 64 C7
Little Hey St OL2 49 B4
Little Holme St M4 160 D1
Little Holme Wlk BL3 147 F4
Little Howarth Way 1
OL12 15 C4
Little Hulton Com Sch
M28 60 A4
Little John St M3 158 E1
Little La WN3,WN5 54 E4
Little Lever Sch BL3 42 F3
Little Lever St
Manchester M1 159 B1
8 Manchester M1,M4 159 B2
Little London 5 WN1 37 C1
Little Mdws BL7 24 F7
Little Meadow Rd WA14 119 B1
Little Moor Clough BL7 8 E2
Little Moor La OL4 67 C8
Little Moss La M27 61 F2
Little Nelson St 1 M4 159 A3
Little Oak Cl OL4 67 E6
Little Pasture WN7 75 D7
Little Peter St M15 162 E7
Little Pitt St M1 159 B1
Little Quay St M3 158 E1
Little Scotland BL6 21 B2
Little St SK1 124 B8
Little Stones Rd BL7 8 E2
Little Town OL8 66 C4
Little Underbank SK1 169 F1
Littleborough
Com Prim Sch OL15 16 B7
Littleborough Sta OL15 16 B5
Littlebourne Wlk BL1 25 A6
Littlebrook Cl
Cheadle SK8 123 C4
Hadfield SK13 104 A4
Littledale St OL12 139 E8
Littlefields SK14 103 A4
Littlegate BL5 57 E5
Littlegreen Gdns M6 154 F3
Littleham Wlk M18 165 C5
Littlehaven Cl M12 164 E5
Littlehills Cl M24 46 E1
Littlemoor Cotts SK1 124 B8
Littlemoor Ho 1 OL4 67 C8
Littlemoor La OL3 51 B4
Littlemoor Prim Sch OL4 67 C8
Littlemoor Rd SK14 103 A2
Littlemoss Bsns Pk M43 84 C3
Littlemoss High Sch
for Boys M43 84 C4
Littlemoss Rd M43 84 C3
Littler Ave M21 109 C5
Littlers Point M17 96 D5
Littleton Gr WN6 19 E2
Littleton Rd M6,M7,M25 81 A6
Littlewood OL2 49 A4
Littlewood Ave 1 BL9 27 F5
Littlewood Rd M22 121 D4
Littlewood St M6 154 E2
Litton Bank 12 SK13 171 E1
Litton Fold 10 SK13 171 E1
Litton Gdns 11 SK13 171 E1
Litton Mews SK13 171 E1
Littondale Cl OL2 48 E5
Liverpool Cl SK5 111 E7
Liverpool Rd
Ashton-in-M WN4 73 A3
Eccles M30 79 C1
Eccles M30 95 A8
Garswood WA11,WN4 72 D2
Irlam M30,M44 94 D4
Irlam M44 &WA3 105 D4
Manchester M3 162 E8
Platt Bridge WN2 56 C3
Liverpool St
7 Reddish SK5 111 E7
Salford M6,M5 81 B1
Liverstudd Ave SK5 111 F8
Liverton Ct M9 64 B5
Livesey St
Manchester M19 111 B8
Manchester M4 159 C3
Oldham OL1 67 C8
Livingstone Ave 2 OL5 68 C1
Livingstone Pl M16 161 B5
Livingstone Prim Sch OL5 86 C8
Livingstone St
2 Ashton-in-M WN4 73 A5
Oldham OL4 67 E5
Oldham OL4 68 A6
Livsey La OL10 29 A2
Livsey St Rochdale OL16 31 A7
Whitefield M45 62 F8
Liza St WN7 75 E8
Lizard St M1 159 B1
Lizmar Terr
Manchester M40 83 A8
Manchester M40,M9 157 F8
Llanberis Rd SK8 122 E1
Llanfair Rd 7 SK3 123 C8
Lloyd Ave SK8 122 A6
Lloyd Ct M12 164 F6
Lloyd Gdns WA14 119 D3
Lloyd Rd M19 111 B7
Lloyd Sq 6 WA14 119 D4
Lloyd St
Altrincham WA14,WA15 119 D4
Heywood OL10 29 D1
Manchester M2 158 F1
Rochdale OL11 139 D5
Stockport SK4 169 D3
Whitworth OL12 4 C1
Lloyd St N M14,M15 163 A5
Lloyd St S M14 98 A2
Lloyd's Ct WA14 119 D4
Lobden Cres OL12 14 D8
Lobelia Ave BL4 42 A1
Lobelia Wlk 6 M31 105 E2
Lobley Cl OL12 15 B2
Local Board St WN2 151 F7
Loch St WN5 54 B6
Lochawe Cl OL10 29 A1
Lochinver Gr OL10 29 A1
Lochmaddy Cl SK7 124 F1
Lock Cl OL10 46 E8
Lock Flight Bldgs WN3 54 F2
Lock La Bolton BL3,BL6 40 D3
Partington M31 105 E3
Lock Rd WA14 119 C6
Locke Ind Est BL6 22 B3
Locker La WN4 73 F4
Lockerbie Pl WN3 54 E2
Lockett Bsns Pk WN4 73 C5
Lockett Gdns M3 158 D2
Lockett Rd WN4 73 C6
Lockett St Manchester M8 158 E4
Salford M6 81 A5
Lockhart Cl M12 165 A5
Lockhart St OL16 31 B5
Locking Gate Rise OL4 49 E1
Lockingate St OL6 85 B6
Locklands La M44 94 A2
Locks View WN1 151 F8
Lockside SK6 126 A6
Lockside View OL5 68 E3
Locksley Cl SK4 168 C2
Lockton Cl Manchester M1 163 B7
Reddish SK5 111 E6
Lockton Ct M1 163 B7
Lockwood St 7 M12 99 B3
Locomotion Ind Est BL6 22 B2
Lodden Wlk 21 M9 157 E8
Lodge Ave M41 95 E2
Lodge Bank SK13 104 A6
Lodge Bank Rd OL15 15 F3
Lodge Brow M26 44 B2
Lodge Cl Dukinfield SK16 101 E7
Lymm WA13 117 B4
Lodge Ct Manchester SK4 110 F2
Mottram-in-L SK14 103 A4
Wythenshawe M22 121 E5
Lodge Dr Culcheth WA3 91 F3
Tyldesley M29 77 B6
Lodge Farm Cl SK7 123 E2
Lodge Fold M43 84 B2
Lodge Gn SK16 101 E7
Lodge Gr M46 58 E1
Lodge La Atherton M46 58 D1
Delph OL3 50 E5
Dukinfield SK16 101 E8
Hyde SK14 167 D4
Leigh WN7 76 E4
Newton-le-W WA11,WA12,WN4
WA11,WA12,WN4 89 B8
Lodge Mill La BL0 2 A1
Lodge Rd Orrell WN5 53 E4
Radcliffe M26 44 B2
Tyldesley M46 58 E1
Lodge Rise M43 84 B2
Lodge St Ashton-u-L OL7 84 F1
Dukinfield SK14 101 E5
Littleborough OL12 15 C6
Littleborough OL15 16 B5
Manchester M40 157 E5
Middleton M24 47 A1
Ramsbottom BL0 11 E8
Ramsbottom BL0 138 C6
Lodge The SK13 104 A6
Lodgepole Cl M30 94 F8
Lodgeside Cl M43 84 B2
Loeminster Pl WN2 151 F7
Loen Cres BL1 142 C3
Logan St BL1 24 E5
Logan Wlk M22 121 E2
Loganberry Ave M6 81 A3
Logwood Ave Bury BL8 140 D3
Wigan WN5 54 E7
Logwood Ho WN5 54 E8
Logwood Pl WN5 54 E8
Loire Dr WN5 54 F8
Loisine Cl OL11 30 B3
Lomas Cl M19 110 E3
Lomas La BB4 1 F8
Lomas St Failsworth M35 66 A1
Middleton M24 47 B1
Stockport SK3 170 D7
Lomax St Bolton BL1 143 E2
Bury BL9 141 A3
7 Farnworth BL4 42 C2
Manchester M1,M4 159 C1
4 Platt Bridge WN2 56 B2
Radcliffe M26 44 A2
Ramsbottom BL8 10 F1
Rochdale OL12 14 F1
Whitefield M45 44 E2
Lomax's Bldgs BL2 145 F6
Lombard Cl SK6 112 F4
Lombard Gr M14 110 C8
Lombard St Atherton M46 58 B3
Oldham OL1 153 E7
Rochdale OL12 139 D8
Lombardy Ct 9 M6 81 A3
Lomond Ave
Altrincham WA15 120 A3
Stretford M32 96 D3
Lomond Cl SK2 124 A3
Lomond Dr BL8 27 B4
Lomond Pl BL3 40 E6
Lomond Rd M22,SK8 121 F2
Lomond Terr OL16 31 C4
London Cl WN5 54 E8
London Fields WN5 71 E5
London Pl SK1 169 F1
London Rd
Alderley Edge SK9 137 A1
Hazel Grove SK2,SK7 124 D3
Manchester M1 163 B8
Oldham OL1 49 B1
Poynton SK10,SK12 133 C1
London Rd N SK12 133 E5
London Rd S SK12 133 D3
London Sq SK1 169 F1
London St Bolton BL3 147 E4
Salford M6 81 B4
Whitefield M45 62 F7
Long Acres Dr OL12 4 D2
Long Croft La SK8 122 F1
Long Cswy Farnworth BL4 60 D7
Leigh M46 76 B8
Long Grain Pl SK2 124 D5
Long Hey WA15 120 A3
Long Heys or Back La
WN8 35 A6
Long Hill OL11 30 D4
Long La Bolton BL2,BL3 42 E6
Bury BL9 27 E7
Charlesworth SK13 115 C7
Hindley WN2 57 A4
Oldham OL9 65 F3
Uppermill OL3 51 A3
Westhoughton BL5 39 D2
Long Marl Dr SK9 131 F4
Long Mdw Bolton BL7 25 C7

Long Mdw continued
Dukinfield SK14 . . . . **101** F6
Long Meadow Pas SK14 . **167** D3
Long Millgate
Manchester M3,M4 . . . . **159** A2
Manchester M4 . . . . **158** F2
Long Row SK15 . . . . **86** F7
Long Rushes OL2 . . . . **48** F8
Long St Manchester M18 . . . **99** E6
Middleton M24 . . . . **47** A1
Swinton M27 . . . . **79** F7
Long Wlk M31 . . . . **105** D3
Longacre St M1,M4 . . . . **159** C1
Longacres La OL12 . . . . **4** D2
Longacres Rd WA15 . . . . **129** D2
Longbow Ct M7 . . . . **155** D5
Longbridge Rd M17 . . . . **96** A6
Longbrook WN6 . . . . **36** B7
Longbutt La WA13 . . . . **117** A2
Longclough Dr SK13 . . . . . . **116** A8
Longcrag Wlk 4 M15 . . . . . **163** A5
Longcroft M29 . . . . **76** E4
Longcroft Cotts BL9 . . . . **11** F1
Longcroft Dr WA14 . . . . **119** B4
Longcroft Gr
Droylsden M34 . . . . **100** B8
Wythenshawe M23 . . . . **120** F7
Longdale Cl OL2 . . . . **48** C4
Longdale Dr SK14 . . . . **103** A3
Longdale Gdns SK14 . . . . . . **103** A3
Longdell Wlk 4 M9 . . . . . **157** E8
Longden Ave OL4 . . . . **49** E3
Longden Ct SK7 . . . . **132** E5
Longden Rd
Ashton-in-M WN4 . . . . **73** A3
Manchester M19 . . . . **99** B2
Longden St 11 BL1 . . . . **144** C8
Longdendale High Sch
SK14 . . . . **103** C5
Longdendale Recn Ctr
SK14 . . . . **102** F3
Longdendale Rd WN6 . . . . . . **36** E8
Longfellow Ave BL3 . . . . **146** B3
Longfellow Cl WN3 . . . . **150** A5
Longfellow Cres OL1 . . . . **49** D4
Longfellow St M6 . . . . **81** C4
Longfellow Wlk 5 M34 . . . **113** A7
Longfield Ave
Altrincham WA15 . . . . **120** C6
Gatley SK8 . . . . **131** C7
Urmston M41 . . . . **95** C1
Longfield Cl SK14 . . . . **101** E6
Longfield Cres OL4 . . . . **67** D8
Longfield Dr M41 . . . . **95** B2
Longfield La 13 OL4 . . . . **49** D1
Longfield Pk OL2 . . . . **149** A6
Longfield Rd Bolton BL3 . . **146** B3
Rochdale OL11 . . . . **30** C8
Shaw OL2 . . . . **149** A6
Wythenshawe M23 . . . . **120** F8
Longfield Sh Ctr M25 . . . . . . **63** A5
Longfield St 3 WN2 . . . . **37** F2
Longford Ave Bolton BL1 . . **142** C2
Stretford M32 . . . . **96** E2
Longford Cl M32 . . . . **96** E3
Longford Cotts M32 . . . . **96** F2
Longford Gdns BL8 . . . . **147** E4
Longford Ho 4 M21 . . . . **96** F1
Longford Park Sch M32 . . . . **96** E1
Longford Pl M14 . . . . **98** C4
Longford Rd
Manchester M21 . . . . **97** A1
Reddish SK5 . . . . **99** F1
Stretford M32 . . . . **96** E3
Longford Rd W SK5 . . . . **99** E1
Longford St Heywood OL10 . **29** D2
Manchester M18 . . . . **99** D6
Longford Trad Est M32 . . . . **96** F2
Longham Cl Bramhall SK7 **123** D1
Manchester M11 . . . . **160** E1
Longhey Rd M22 . . . . **121** D5
Longhill Wlk 8 M40 . . . . **83** A6
Longhirst Cl BL1 . . . . **142** B3
Longhope Rd M22 . . . . **121** C2
Longhurst La SK6 . . . . **126** C6
Longhurst Rd Hindley WN2 . **57** A4
Manchester M9 . . . . **64** B5
Longlevens Rd M22 . . . . **121** C3
Longley Dr M28 . . . . **79** B6
Longley La M22 . . . . **121** E2
Longley Rd M28 . . . . **60** D2
Longley St Oldham OL1 . . . **153** F6
Shaw OL2 . . . . **149** B5
Longmead Ave
Ashton-in-M WN4 . . . . **73** C4
Hazel Grove SK7 . . . . **124** D1
Longmead Rd M6 . . . . **154** D4
Longmead Way M24 . . . . **47** B1
Longmeade Gdns SK9 . . . . **137** C6
Longmeadow SK8 . . . . **132** C7
Longmeadow Gr M34 . . . . . **100** E2
Longmere Ave M22 . . . . **121** D3
Longmoor Rd SK13 . . . . **116** A7
Longnor Gn 33 SK13 . . . . . . **171** D2
Longnor Mews SK13 . . . . . . **171** D2
Longnor Rd Gatley SK8 . . . **131** D8
Hazel Grove SK7 . . . . **133** C7
Longnor Way 32 SK13 . . . . **171** D2
Longport Ave M20 . . . . **110** A7
Longridge BL7 . . . . **25** C8
Longridge Ave
Stalybridge SK15 . . . . **86** A4
Standish WN6 . . . . **36** F8
Longridge Cres BL1 . . . . **23** F2
Longridge Dr Bury BL8 . . . . . **44** A8

Longridge Dr continued
Heywood OL10 . . . . **28** F2
Longridge Way WN6 . . . . **36** F8
Longshaw Ave
Longshaw WN5 . . . . **53** E1
Swinton M27 . . . . **61** F1
Longshaw Cl WN5 . . . . **53** E1
Longshaw Comm
Billinge WN5 . . . . **71** E8
Longshaw WN5 . . . . **71** E8
Longshaw Dr M28 . . . . **60** A4
Longshaw Ford Rd BL1 . . . . . **23** F7
Longshaw Old Rd WN5 . . . . . **53** E1
Longshoot Cl WN1 . . . . **37** D1
Longshut La SK1,SK2 . . . . . **170** F7
Longshut La W SK2 . . . . **170** F7
Longsides Rd WA15 . . . . **129** C3
Longsight BL2 . . . . **25** E5
Longsight Com Prim Sch
BL2 . . . . **25** E4
Longsight La Bolton BL2 . . . **25** D4
Cheadle SK8 . . . . **131** F6
Longsight Park Sch M12 . **164** E5
Longsight Rd
Manchester M18 . . . . **99** B3
Ramsbottom BL0,BL8 . . . . **11** A2
Sale M33 . . . . **108** E4
Urmston M41 . . . . **95** B3
Longson St SK5 . . . . **169** F3
Longthwaite Cl 2 M24 . . . . . **46** D2
Longton Ave Golborne WA3 . **90** C7
Manchester M20 . . . . **110** A5
Longton Rd Manchester M9 **64** C4
Pendlebury M6 . . . . **80** C5
Longton St Bury BL9 . . . . **44** F4
Hindley WN2 . . . . **56** C4
Longtown Gdns 7 BL1 . . . **143** D2
Longview Dr M27 . . . . **61** C1
Longwall Ave M28 . . . . **78** C8
Longwood Ave SK2 . . . . **124** B6
Longwood Cl SK6 . . . . **113** C3
Longwood Rd
Stretford M17 . . . . **96** B6
Wythenshawe M22 . . . . **121** C3
Longworth Ave BL6 . . . . **21** C3
Longworth Cl M41 . . . . **94** E1
Longworth Clough BL7 . . . . . . **8** D2
Longworth La BL7 . . . . **8** C2
Longworth Rd Bolton BL7 . . . **8** B3
Horwich BL6 . . . . **8** A3
Longworth St Bolton BL2 . . **148** C7
Manchester M3 . . . . **162** E8
Lonsdale Ave Leigh WN7 . . . **75** D2
Reddish SK5 . . . . **99** F3
Rochdale OL16 . . . . **31** B5
Swinton M27 . . . . **79** D5
Urmston M41 . . . . **95** B3
Lonsdale Gr 6 BL4 . . . . **60** C8
Lonsdale Rd Bolton BL1 . . **144** B8
Manchester M19 . . . . **99** B2
Oldham OL8 . . . . **66** B2
Lonsdale St Bury BL8 . . . . . . **27** C2
Failsworth M40 . . . . **83** C6
Lonsdale Wlk WN5 . . . . **54** B8
Loom St M4 . . . . **159** B2
Loonies Ct 1 SK1 . . . . **170** F8
Lord Ave Bacup OL13 . . . . **3** C8
2 Tyldesley M46 . . . . **58** F1
Lord Byron Sq M5 . . . . **154** F1
Lord Derby Rd SK14 . . . . . . **113** C4
Lord Gr 1 M46 . . . . **58** F1
Lord Kitchener Ct M33 . . . . **108** B5
Lord La M35 . . . . **83** F6
Lord Lane Mews M35 . . . . . . **83** F6
Lord Napier Dr M5 . . . . **161** B7
Lord North St M40 . . . . **160** F4
Lord St Ashton-in-M WN4 . . . **73** D4
Atherton M46 . . . . **58** B4
Bury BL9 . . . . **140** F2
Bury BL9 . . . . **141** C1
Farnworth BL4 . . . . **60** E8
Glossop SK13 . . . . **104** D1
Hindley WN2 . . . . **56** D4
Hollingworth SK14 . . . . **171** D4
Horwich BL6 . . . . **22** B4
Ince-in-M WN2 . . . . **56** A7
Leigh WN7 . . . . **75** F4
Little Lever BL3 . . . . **43** B3
Manchester M3,M4 . . . . **159** A3
Manchester M5,M7 . . . . **81** C4
Middleton M24 . . . . **47** A2
Newton-le-W WA12 . . . . **89** A3
Oldham OL1 . . . . **153** F7
Radcliffe M26 . . . . **44** A3
Reddish M34 . . . . **100** A4
Stalybridge SK15,SK16 . . . . **101** F8
Stockport SK1 . . . . **169** F1
Tyldesley M29 . . . . **76** F6
Tyldesley M46 . . . . **58** E1
Westhoughton BL5 . . . . **39** E1
Wigan WN1 . . . . **37** C1
Lord St S WN7 . . . . **76** A5
Lord Street Prim Sch BL6 . . **22** B4
Lord's Ave M5 . . . . **154** D2
Lord's St M44 . . . . **105** C6
Lord's Stile La BL7 . . . . **25** B7
Lords Coll BL2 . . . . **148** A6
Lordsfields Ave OL7 . . . . . . **166** B4
Lordship Cl M9 . . . . **64** F1
Lordsmead St M15 . . . . **162** D6
Lordy Cl WN6 . . . . **37** B7
Loreto Coll M15 . . . . **162** E5
Loreto Convent
Gram Sch WA14 . . . . **119** C5
Loreto Convent Prep Sch
WA14 . . . . **119** C5
Loretto Rd M41 . . . . **95** F1
Lorgill Cl SK3 . . . . **123** F4
Loring St M40 . . . . **83** C5

Lorland Rd SK3 . . . . **123** B7
Lorna Gr SK8 . . . . **121** F6
Lorna Rd SK8 . . . . **123** B2
Lorne Ave OL2 . . . . **48** B3
Lorne Gr Stockport SK3 . . . **170** G6
Urmston M41 . . . . **95** E2
Lorne Rd M14 . . . . **110** C8
Lorne St Bolton BL1 . . . . **145** F7
Eccles M30 . . . . **95** B8
Farnworth BL3,BL4 . . . . **42** C2
Heywood OL10 . . . . **29** D1
Manchester M13 . . . . **163** C5
Mossley OL5 . . . . **68** C1
Oldham OL4 . . . . **66** E4
Rochdale OL12 . . . . **15** B3
Wigan WN1 . . . . **151** E8
Lorne Way OL10 . . . . **28** F1
Lorraine Cl OL10 . . . . **46** E8
Lorraine Rd WA15 . . . . **120** B5
Lorton Cl Boothstown M28 . . **77** F6
Middleton M24 . . . . **46** C2
Lorton Gr BL2 . . . . **42** F8
Lostock Ave
Hazel Grove SK7 . . . . **124** B1
8 Manchester M19 . . . . **99** B1
Poynton SK12 . . . . **133** B4
Sale M33 . . . . **108** E4
Urmston M41 . . . . **95** B3
Lostock Cl Billinge WN5 . . . . **71** E5
Heywood OL10 . . . . **29** B3
Lostock Com Prim Sch
BL6 . . . . **40** C6
Lostock Ct Handforth SK9 . **131** D4
Urmston M32 . . . . **95** F4
Lostock Dr BL9 . . . . **27** F6
Lostock Gr M32 . . . . **96** B3
Lostock Hall
Cty Prim Sch SK12 . . . . . **133** B3
Lostock Hall Rd SK12 . . . . . **133** B3
Lostock High Sch M32 . . . . . **96** A3
Lostock Ind Est BL6 . . . . **39** E7
Lostock Junction La BL6 . . **40** C7
Lostock La BL5,BL6 . . . . **39** E6
Lostock Park Dr BL6 . . . . **40** A7
Lostock Park Sch BL6 . . . . . . **40** C5
Lostock Rd Poynton SK12 . **133** D2
Salford M5 . . . . **154** E2
Urmston M41 . . . . **95** D4
Westhoughton BL5 . . . . **39** C4
Lostock St M40 . . . . **160** D3
Lostock Sta BL6 . . . . **40** C6
Lostock Way SK9 . . . . **131** D4
Lostock Wlk Leigh WN7 . . . . **75** D6
Whitefield M45 . . . . **45** C1
Lothian Ave M30 . . . . **79** B3
Lottery Row BL1 . . . . **145** F7
Lottery St SK3 . . . . **169** D1
Lottie St M27 . . . . **80** A8
Loughborough Cl 2
M33 . . . . **107** D3
Loughfield M41 . . . . **95** A2
Loughrigg Ave
Billinge WA11 . . . . **71** B1
Royton OL2 . . . . **48** C8
Loughrigg Cl M29 . . . . **77** B7
Louis Ave BL9 . . . . **140** F4
Louis St BL0 . . . . **1** D5
Louisa St Bolton BL1 . . . . . . **143** E2
Manchester M11 . . . . **99** D8
Walkden M28 . . . . **60** D4
Louise Cl OL12 . . . . **15** C3
Louise Gdns Rochdale OL12 **15** C3
Westhoughton BL5 . . . . **57** F6
Louise St OL12 . . . . **15** C3
Louvaine Ave BL1 . . . . **23** F4
Louvoine Cl M18 . . . . **99** E5
Lovalle St BL1 . . . . **142** C1
Lovat Rd BL2 . . . . **43** A7
Love La Edenfield BL0 . . . . **1** E1
Stockport SK3 . . . . **169** E2
Loveless Ho M46 . . . . **58** D4
Lovell Ct M8 . . . . **63** F2
Lovell Dr SK14 . . . . **167** A4
Lovers La Atherton M46 . . . . **58** A1
Uppermill OL4 . . . . **68** D6
Lovett Wlk M22 . . . . **121** E8
Low Bank OL12 . . . . **15** C3
Low Bank Rd WN4 . . . . **72** F4
Low Crompton Rd OL2 . . . . . **48** E6
Low Gate La OL3 . . . . **34** A1
Low Gn M46 . . . . **58** F5
Low Grove La OL3 . . . . **68** C5
Low Hall Com Prim Sch
WN2 . . . . **56** A3
Low Hall Gdns WN2 . . . . **56** B3
Low Hill OL12 . . . . **15** C3
Low Lea Rd SK6 . . . . **126** B6
Low Mdws OL2 . . . . **48** D6
Low Wood Cl SK7 . . . . **123** C1
Low Wood Rd M34 . . . . **100** A4
Low's Pl 3 OL12 . . . . **15** A2
Lowcock St M7 . . . . **158** E4
Lowcroft Cres OL9 . . . . **65** F8
Lowcross Rd M40 . . . . **83** A6
Lowe Ave M46 . . . . **58** C5
Lowe Gn OL2 . . . . **48** E5
Lowe Mill La WN2 . . . . **56** D5
Lowe St Denton M34 . . . . **101** B3
Golborne WA3 . . . . **90** A8
Radcliffe M26 . . . . **43** F4
Stockport SK1 . . . . **169** F1
Lower Albion St M1 . . . . **163** B8
Lower Alma St SK16 . . . . . . **166** B1
Lower Bamford Cl 7 M24 **47** A2
Lower Bank SK13 . . . . **116** D8
Lower Bank Cl SK13 . . . . . . **171** F3
Lower Bank St BL9 . . . . **140** E2
Lower Barn Rd SK13 . . . . . . **171** E4

Lower Bennett St SK14 . . **101** C5
Lower Bents La SK6 . . . . . . **112** F4
Lower Blue Bell Cotts BL5 **39** C4
Lower Bridgeman St BL2 **148** A6
Lower Broadacre SK15 . . . **102** E6
Lower Brook La M28 . . . . . . **79** A5
Lower Brook St M1 . . . . **163** B8
Lower Broughton Rd
Manchester M7 . . . . **158** D4
Manchester M7 . . . . **81** C6
Lower Bury St SK4 . . . . **169** D2
Lower Byrom St M3 . . . . **162** E8
Lower Calderbrook OL15 . . . . **6** C1
Lower Carr La OL3 . . . . **69** B6
Lower Carrs SK1 . . . . **169** F1
Lower Chatham St M1 . . . . **163** A7
Lower Clowes BB4 . . . . **1** E8
Lower Clowes Rd BB4 . . . . **1** E8
Lower Count Hill OL4 . . . . . . **49** E2
Lower Crimble OL11 . . . . **29** F4
Lower Croft M45 . . . . **62** C6
Lower Crossbank OL4 . . . . . . **67** F8
Lower Darcy St BL2 . . . . **148** C5
Lower Dingle OL1 . . . . **49** C4
Lower Drake Fold BL5 . . . . . . **57** E5
Lower Edge Ave OL1 . . . . . . **153** E8
Lower Falinge OL12 . . . . **139** E8
Lower Fields SK1 . . . . **51** A1
Lower Fold Bolton BL2 . . . . . . **25** F4
Denton M34 . . . . **101** A2
Marple SK6 . . . . **126** B8
Lower Frenches Dr OL3 . . . . **69** A5
Lower Gates OL16 . . . . **139** F7
Lower Gn Ashton-u-L OL6 . **166** C4
Middleton M9 . . . . **64** F5
3 Rochdale OL12 . . . . **14** C1
Lower Goodwin Cl BL2 . . . . . **25** E2
Lower Green La M29 . . . . **77** C3
Lower Greenshall La
SK12 . . . . **135** F6
Lower Hague SK22 . . . . **135** E8
Lower Hardman St M3 . . . . **158** E1
Lower Hey La OL5 . . . . **68** C3
Lower Higham
Visitors Ctr SK14 . . . . **114** A8
Lower Hillgate SK1 . . . . **169** F1
Lower House Dr BL6 . . . . **40** C7
Lower House La OL12 . . . . . . **15** B7
Lower House Rd BL1 . . . . **67** B8
Lower House Wlk BL7 . . . . . . **25** A8
Lower Hyde Green Farm
SK15 . . . . **86** E4
Lower Jowkin La OL11 . . . . . **29** D7
Lower Kersall Prim Sch
M7 . . . . **81** B6
Lower Knoll Rd OL3 . . . . **51** C5
Lower La OL16 . . . . **31** D4
Lower Landemans BL5 . . . . . **57** F7
Lower Leigh Rd BL5 . . . . **57** F5
Lower Lime Rd OL8 . . . . **84** C8
Lower Longshoot WN1 . . . . **151** D8
Lower Lyndon Ave WN6 . . . . **36** A6
Lower Makinson Fold BL6 . . **22** D1
Lower Marlands BL7 . . . . **24** F8
Lower Mdw BL7 . . . . **9** C6
Lower Mead BL7 . . . . **8** F1
Lower Meadow Rd SK9 . . . . **131** E4
Lower Moat Cl SK4 . . . . **169** E3
Lower Monton Rd M30 . . . . . **79** D2
Lower Mosley St M1,M2 . . **162** F8
Lower Moss La
Manchester M15 . . . . **162** D7
Whitefield M45 . . . . **62** E6
Lower New Row M28 . . . . **60** A1
Lower Ormond St M15 . . . . **163** A7
Lower Park Cres SK12 . . . . **133** C6
Lower Park Prim Sch
SK12 . . . . **133** C4
Lower Park Rd
Manchester M14 . . . . **98** C3
Poynton SK12 . . . . **133** B5
Lower Rawson St BL4 . . . . . . **42** E1
Lower Rd BL0 . . . . **11** E8
Lower Seedley Rd M6 . . . . . **154** E3
Lower Sheriff St OL12 . . . . **139** E8
Lower Southfield BL5 . . . . **57** E7
Lower Sq SK13 . . . . **104** A4
Lower St Farnworth BL4 . . . . . **60** C7
15 Rochdale OL11 . . . . **31** A4
Lower St Stephen St 18
WN6 . . . . **37** A1
Lower Stones OL3 . . . . **50** E3
Lower Strines Rd SK6 . . . . . **126** A5
Lower Sutherland St M27 . . **79** E8
Lower Tenterfield OL11 . . . . . **13** D2
Lower Tong BL7 . . . . **24** F7
Lower Turf La OL4 . . . . **68** B8
Lower Tweedale St OL11 . . **139** F6
Lower Vickers St M40 . . . . . **160** D3
Lower Victoria St OL9 . . . . **152** B7
Lower Wharf St OL6 . . . . . . **166** C2
Lower Wheat End OL16 . . . . . **31** B8
Lower Woodhill Rd BL8 . . . **140** D3
Lowerbank M34 . . . . **100** F5
Lowercroft Prim Sch BL8 . . **26** F2
Lowerfield Dr SK2 . . . . **124** F5
Lowerfields OL8 . . . . **67** B4
Lowerfields Rise OL12 . . . . **149** B8
Lowerfold Cl OL12 . . . . **14** C4
Lowerfold Cres OL12 . . . . **14** C4
Lowerfold Dr OL12 . . . . **14** C4
Lowerfold Way OL12 . . . . **14** C4
Lowerford Ave OL2 . . . . **49** A4
Lowerlea SK12 . . . . **135** C6
Lowern Market St SK14 . . . **115** B8

Lowerplace
Com Prim Sch OL16 . . . . . . **31** B4
Lowerwood La 12 BL2 . . . . . **25** B1
Lowes Rd BL9 . . . . **28** A6
Lowes The WA14 . . . . **119** B1
Lowestead Rd 9 M11 . . . . . . **83** C2
Lowestoft St M14 . . . . **98** B2
Loweswater Ave M29 . . . . **77** A7
Loweswater Rd
Farnworth BL4 . . . . **59** E7
Gratley SK8 . . . . **122** B3
Loweswater Terr SK15 . . . . . . **86** A4
Lowfell Wlk M18 . . . . **99** D3
Lowfield Ave
Ashton-u-L OL6 . . . . **85** F5
Droylsden M43 . . . . **83** F3
Lowfield Gr SK2,SK3 . . . . . . **170** E7
Lowfield Rd SK2,SK3 . . . . . . **170** E7
Lowfield Wlk 7 M9 . . . . **64** E3
Lowhouse Cl OL16 . . . . **32** A7
Lowick Ave BL3 . . . . **42** A3
Lowick Cl SK7 . . . . **124** D2
Lowick Gn SK6 . . . . **112** F5
Lowland Gr OL7 . . . . **85** A6
Lowland Rd SK2 . . . . **124** B4
Lowlands Cl M24 . . . . **65** C5
Lowndes Cl SK2 . . . . **124** B7
Lowndes La SK1,SK2 . . . . . . **124** B7
Lowndes St BL1 . . . . **142** B1
Lowndes Wlk 6 M13 . . . . . . **163** C6
Lownorth Rd M22 . . . . **130** E8
Lowood Ave M41 . . . . **94** F4
Lowood Cl OL16 . . . . **31** F6
Lowood St WN7 . . . . **75** D5
Lowrey Wlk 11 M9 . . . . **157** E7
Lowry Ct SK14 . . . . **103** A4
Lowry Dr Marple SK6 . . . . . . **126** B8
Swinton M27 . . . . **61** F1
Lowry Gr SK14 . . . . **102** F3
Lowry High Sch M7 . . . . **155** D5
Lowry Ho Eccles M30 . . . . **79** E2
4 Manchester M14 . . . . **110** D8
Lowry The M5 . . . . **96** F7
Lowry Wlk BL1 . . . . **143** D1
Lows The OL4 . . . . **67** B5
Lowside Ave Bolton BL1 . . . . **40** C6
Romiley SK6 . . . . **113** C5
Lowside Dr OL4 . . . . **67** B5
Lowstern Cl BL7 . . . . **8** C1
Lowther Ave
Altrincham WA15 . . . . **120** A6
Culcheth WA3 . . . . **91** F4
Manchester M18 . . . . **99** B3
Royton OL2 . . . . **48** C8
Lowther Cl M25 . . . . **63** A3
Lowther Cres M24 . . . . **46** D1
Lowther Ct M25 . . . . **62** F3
Lowther Dr WN7 . . . . **76** E7
Lowther Gdns M41 . . . . **94** F4
Lowther Rd Manchester M8 **64** A1
Prestwich M25 . . . . **62** F3
Rochdale OL11 . . . . **30** E4
Lowther St BL3 . . . . **42** A3
Lowther Terr WN6 . . . . **35** C8
Lowthorpe St M14 . . . . **98** A2
Lowton Ave M9 . . . . **157** F7
Lowton Bsns Pk WA3 . . . . **91** A7
Lowton Gdns WA3 . . . . **90** B5
Lowton High Sch WA3 . . . . . . **91** B8
Lowton Jun & Inf Sch
WA3 . . . . **91** A7
Lowton Rd Golborne WA3 . . . **74** C1
Sale M33 . . . . **107** D2
Lowton St M26 . . . . **44** A4
Lowton St Mary's
CE Prim Sch WA3 . . . . **91** A8
Lowton West
Cty Prim Sch WA3 . . . . **90** D8
Loxford Ct M15 . . . . **162** F6
Loxford St M15 . . . . **162** F6
Loxham St BL4 . . . . **42** D2
Loxley Wlk M40 . . . . **160** E4
Loxton Cres WN3 . . . . **55** B3
Loynd St BL0 . . . . **11** D6
Lubeck St M9 . . . . **157** E8
Lucas Rd BL4 . . . . **60** A7
Lucas St Bury BL9 . . . . **141** A3
Oldham OL4 . . . . **67** B7
Lucas Wlk M11 . . . . **164** F8
Lucerne Cl OL9 . . . . **152** C6
Lucerne Rd SK7 . . . . **123** E3
Lucien Cl M12 . . . . **164** E5
Luciol Cl M29 . . . . **59** D1
Lucknow St OL11 . . . . **139** F5
Lucy St Bolton BL1 . . . . **142** A1
Manchester M15 . . . . **162** C5
Manchester M7 . . . . **155** D8
Stockport SK3 . . . . **170** E8
Ludford St M33 . . . . **107** F1
Ludgate Hill M4 . . . . **159** B3
Ludgate Rd Failsworth M40 **83** C4
Rochdale OL11 . . . . **31** A2
Ludgate St M4 . . . . **159** A4
Ludlow Ave Hindley WN2 . . . **57** A4
Swinton M27 . . . . **62** A2
Ludlow Dr WN7 . . . . **76** E7
Ludlow Pk 2 OL4 . . . . **67** D6
Ludlow Rd SK1,SK2 . . . . **124** C8
Ludlow St WN6 . . . . **19** D3
Ludovic Terr WN1 . . . . **37** C4
Ludwell Wlk 12 M8 . . . . **156** A6
Ludworth Prim Sch SK6 . . **126** B8
Lugano Rd SK7 . . . . **123** E3
Luke Kirby Ct M27 . . . . **61** F1
Luke Rd M43 . . . . **84** B1
Luke St Ashton-in-M WN4 . . . **73** D4

Luke St continued
17 Bacup OL13 ....3 C8
Luke Wlk M8 ....156 B6
Lullington Cl M22 ....121 C1
Lullington Rd M6 ....154 D4
Lulworth Ave M41 ....94 F2
Lulworth Cl BL8 ....27 C6
Lulworth Cres M35 ....84 B8
Lulworth Dr WN2 ....57 A4
Lulworth Gdns M23 ....120 F8
Lulworth Rd Bolton BL3 .146 A3
  Eccles M30 ....79 C3
  Middleton M24 ....47 A4
Lum Head Prim Sch SK8 122 B3
Lum St BL1 ....148 A8
Lumb Carr Ave BL0 ....11 A4
Lumb Carr Rd BL0,BL8 ....11 A4
Lumb Cl SK7 ....132 E6
Lumb Cotts BL0 ....1 B4
Lumb Flats BL0 ....1 B4
Lumb Holes La BB4 ....2 E7
Lumb La Bramhall SK7 ....132 E6
  Droylsden M34 ....100 C8
  Droylsden M34 ....84 C1
  Droylsden M34,M43,OL7 .84 D4
  Droylsden M43 ....84 C3
Lumber La M28 ....78 E8
Lumley Cl M14 ....98 B4
Lumn Hollow SK14 ....167 E2
Lumn Rd SK14 ....167 E2
Lumn St BL9 ....27 F8
Lumn's La M27 ....62 C1
Lumsden St BL3 ....145 E5
Lumwood BL1 ....142 B3
Luna St M4 ....159 B2
Lund Ave M26 ....62 B8
Lundale Wlk 18 M40 ....83 A3
Lundy Ave M21 ....109 C5
Lune Cl M45 ....45 A1
Lune Dr M45 ....63 A8
Lune Gr Heywood OL10 ....29 B3
  Leigh WN7 ....75 C5
Lune Rd WN2 ....56 A2
Lune St Oldham OL8 ....66 E4
  Tyldesley M29 ....76 F8
Lune Way SK5 ....111 F5
Lune Wlk Droylsden M43 .100 B8
  Whitefield M45 ....63 A8
Lunedale 7 WN2 ....56 B2
Lunedale Gn SK2 ....124 E6
Lunehurst 2 WA3 ....90 E8
Lunn Ave M18 ....99 F6
Lupin Ave BL4 ....42 A1
Lupton St Denton M34 ....100 F4
  Manchester M3 ....158 D2
Lurden Wlk OL9 ....66 B4
Lurgan Ave M33 ....108 C3
Lurdin La WN1,WN6 ....37 B7
Lutener Av WA14 ....119 C8
Luton Dr M23 ....121 A4
Luton Gr M46 ....58 B3
Luton Rd SK5 ....111 F8
Luton St Bolton BL3 ....42 A4
  3 Bury BL8 ....27 B1
Luxor Gr M34 ....99 F3
Luzley Brook Rd OL2 .149 A5
Luzley Rd OL5,OL6 ....86 B7
Lyceum Pas OL16 ....139 F7
Lyceum Pl M15 ....163 A7
Lychgate WN5 ....54 E5
Lychgate Ct OL4 ....67 E4
Lychgate Mews WA4 .110 E2
Lychwood 11 SK6 ....125 F6
Lydbrook Cl BL1 ....145 E6
Lydden Ave M11 ....83 D3
Lydford OL11 ....139 E6
Lydford Gdns BL2 ....42 F6
Lydford Gn WN6 ....36 F8
Lydford St M6 ....81 B4
Lydford Wlk M13 ....163 C6
Lydgate Ave BL2 ....42 F8
Lydgate Cl Denton M34 .101 B1
  Mossley SK15 ....86 E6
  Whitefield M45 ....45 A1
Lydgate Dr OL4 ....67 D5
Lydgate Fold OL4 ....67 C5
Lydgate Prim Sch OL4 ...68 C6
Lydgate Rd Droylsden M43 .83 E2
  Sale M33 ....108 C2
Lydgate The OL15 ....16 E6
Lydgate Wlk M45 ....45 A1
Lydiat La SK9 ....137 A1
Lydney Ave SK8 ....131 C7
Lydney Rd M41 ....94 D3
Lyefield Ave WN1 ....37 F1
Lyefield Wlk 24 OL16 ...31 B6
Lymbridge Dr BL6 ....21 D1
Lyme Ave SK9 ....131 A1
Lyme Clough Way M24 ...46 F4
Lyme Gr Altrincham WA14 .119 C4
  Droylsden M43 ....99 F8
  Marple SK6 ....125 F5
  Romiley SK6 ....113 D2
  Stockport SK2 ....170 F7
Lyme Hall SK12 ....135 C6
Lyme Park Cntry Pk SK12 .135 B2
Lyme Rd Disley SK12 .134 C3
  Hazel Grove SK7 ....124 E1
  High Lane SK12 ....135 B7
Lyme St Hazel Grove SK7 .124 D3
  Manchester SK4 ....110 F2
Lyme Terr 1 SK16 ....166 B1
Lymefield Dr M28 ....78 A7
Lymefield Gr SK2 ....124 B6
Lymefield Terr SK14 ....115 B7
  Wilmslow SK9 ....137 E8
Lymington Cl M24 ....65 B5

Lymington Dr M23 ....108 D1
Lymm Cl Stockport SK3 .170 D6
  Walkden M28 ....60 A3
Lymm High Sch WA13 .117 B3
Lymm Rd BL8 ....118 B1
Lymm Wlk SK8 ....123 A5
Lymn St WN2 ....56 B3
Lyn Gr OL10 ....29 A3
Lyncombe Cl SK8 ....132 B6
Lyndale Ave Reddish SK5 ..99 F3
  Swinton M27 ....79 D6
Lyndale Dr OL15 ....16 A6
Lyndene Ave M28 ....79 A8
Lyndene Ct OL10 ....29 C3
Lyndene Gdns SK8 ....122 B6
Lyndene Rd M22 ....121 D5
Lyndhurst Ave
  Ashton-u-L OL6 ....85 B5
  Bredbury SK6 ....112 F4
  Denton M34 ....100 E3
  Hazel Grove SK7 ....124 C1
  Irlam M44 ....94 B3
  Manchester M25 ....63 B3
  Middleton OL11 ....47 D8
  Oldham OL9 ....65 F5
  Sale M33 ....107 F3
  Urmston M41 ....95 C4
Lyndhurst Cl SK9 ....136 D5
Lyndhurst Com Prim Sch
  OL8 ....66 D3
Lyndhurst Dr WA15 ....120 A2
Lyndhurst Prim Sch
  SK16 ....166 C1
Lyndhurst Rd
  Manchester M20 ....110 B5
  Oldham OL8 ....66 D3
  Reddish SK5 ....99 E2
  Stretford M32 ....96 B3
Lyndhurst St M5,M6 ....154 E2
Lyndhurst View SK16 .166 C1
Lyndon Ave WN6 ....36 A7
Lyndon Cl Bury BL8 ....26 F6
  Oldham OL4 ....68 B8
Lyndon Croft OL8 ....66 C4
Lyndon Rd M44 ....93 F2
Lyne Ave SK13 ....116 A8
Lyne Edge Cres SK16 .101 F7
Lyne Edge Rd SK16 ....102 A7
Lyne View SK14 ....101 F6
Lyneham Wlk
  Manchester M7 ....155 F6
  10 Manchester M9 ....64 E5
Lyngard Cl SK9 ....131 E1
Lyngarth Ho 11 WA14 .119 E6
Lyngate Cl SK1 ....124 A8
Lynham Dr OL10 ....46 D8
Lynmouth Ave
  Manchester M20 ....110 A6
  Oldham OL8 ....66 F3
  10 Reddish SK5 ....111 E7
  Royton OL2 ....48 C3
  Urmston M41 ....107 B8
Lynmouth Cl
  Chadderton OL9 ....47 E1
  Radcliffe M26 ....44 C4
  Wigan WN6 ....37 A2
Lynmouth Ct M25 ....62 F3
Lynmouth Gr M25 ....62 F3
Lynn Ave M33 ....108 D6
Lynn Dr M43 ....83 E2
Lynn St OL9 ....66 E2
Lynne Cl SK13 ....116 F8
Lynnwood Dr OL11 ....30 B8
Lynnwood Rd M19 ....110 D2
Lynroyle Way OL11 ....30 D3
Lynside Wlk M22 ....130 E8
Lynsted Ave BL3 ....42 A3
Lynstock Way BL6 ....39 E6
Lynthorpe Ave M44 ....105 D6
Lynthorpe Rd M40 ....65 D2
Lynton Ave
  Hattersley SK14 ....102 C2
  Irlam M44 ....105 E6
  Oldham OL8 ....66 C2
  Rochdale OL11 ....30 B3
  Royton OL2 ....48 C3
  Swinton M27 ....61 F1
  Urmston M41 ....94 C2
  Wigan WN6 ....37 A3
Lynton Cl OL9 ....47 F1
Lynton Cres M28 ....78 D8
Lynton Dr High Lane SK6 .134 E8
  Manchester M19 ....110 F7
  Prestwich M25 ....63 C6
Lynton Gr WA15 ....119 F5
Lynton La SK9 ....137 A2
Lynton Lee M26 ....44 C4
Lynton Park Rd SK8 .131 F8
Lynton Rd Bolton BL3 .146 C2
  Cheadle SK8 ....122 C5
  Hindley WN2 ....56 F5
  Manchester M21 ....97 A1
  Manchester SK4 ....111 C5
  Swinton M27 ....61 F1
  Tyldesley M29 ....77 D8
Lynton St M14 ....98 B2
Lynton Wlk SK14 ....102 C2
Lyntonvale Ave SK8 ....122 B6
Lynway Dr M20 ....110 B5
Lynway Gr M24 ....47 B2
Lynwell Rd M30 ....79 D2
Lynwood Altrincham WA15 .129 A8
  Golborne WA3 ....90 E6
  Manchester M16 ....97 C2

Lynwood Cl OL7 ....85 A7
Lynwood Ct M8 ....63 F2
Lynwood Dr OL4 ....67 E8
Lynwood Gr Atherton M46 ..58 B3
  Bolton BL2 ....25 D4
  Droylsden M34 ....84 C1
  Reddish SK4 ....111 C6
  Sale M33 ....108 C5
Lyon Gr M28 ....79 A8
Lyon Ind Est WA14 ....119 B7
Lyon Rd Altrincham WA14 .119 C7
  Kearsley M26 ....60 E6
  Wigan WN6 ....37 A2
Lyon St Ashton-in-M WN4 ..72 F7
  Shaw OL2 ....149 B7
  Swinton M27 ....79 E7
  Wigan WN3 ....150 B7
Lyons Dr BL8 ....27 A1
Lyons Fold M33 ....108 B6
Lyons Rd M17 ....96 A4
Lysander Cl M14 ....110 B8
Lyth St M14 ....110 D7
Lytham Ave M21 ....109 C7
Lytham Cl OL6 ....85 E6
Lytham Dr Bramhall SK7 .133 A7
  Heywood OL10 ....29 C1
Lytham Rd
  Ashton-in-M WN4 ....72 F5
  Gatley SK8 ....122 B1
  Manchester M14,M19 ....98 F1
  Urmston M41 ....94 C2
Lytham St Rochdale OL12 ..14 E3
  Stockport SK3 ....170 F6
Lytherton Ave M44 ....105 D4
Lytton Ave M8 ....156 A6
Lytton Rd M43 ....84 A2
Lytton St BL1 ....143 D2

M

Mab's Cross Prim Sch
  WN1 ....37 D1
Mabel Ave Bolton BL3 ....42 A3
  Swinton M28 ....79 A7
Mabel Rd M35 ....66 A1
Mabel St 9 Bolton BL1 .144 C8
  Failsworth M40 ....83 D5
  2 Rochdale OL12 ....14 D2
  Westhoughton BL5 ....57 F6
  Wigan WN5 ....54 E6
Mabel's Brow BL4 ....60 E7
Maberry Ho WN6 ....35 D7
Mabfield Rd M14 ....98 C1
Mableden Cl SK8 ....131 D8
Mabs Ct OL4 ....67 D7
Macaulay St Rochdale OL11 30 D2
  Royton OL2 ....48 E4
Macaulay Way 7 M34 .113 A8
Macauley Cl SK16 ....102 A7
Macauley Pl WN3 ....54 F4
Macauley Rd
  Manchester M16 ....97 B2
  Reddish SK5 ....99 E1
Macclesfield St WN2 ....56 C5
Macclesfield Rd
  Alderley Edge SK9 ....137 B1
  Hazel Grove SK7 ....133 F8
  Wilmslow SK9 ....137 D6
Macdonald Ave
  Farnworth BL4 ....60 B7
  Wigan WN5 ....55 A3
Macdonald Rd M44 ....105 E8
Macdonald St Oldham OL8 .66 F4
  Wigan WN5 ....54 B6
Macefin Ave M21 ....109 D4
Macfarren St M12 ....99 A3
Macintosh Way OL1 ....153 F7
Mackenzie Ave WN3 ....55 A3
Mackenzie Gr BL1 ....24 D5
Mackenzie Ind Pk
  SK3,SK8 ....123 B6
Mackenzie Rd M7 ....81 B6
Mackenzie St Bolton BL1 .143 D4
  Manchester M12 ....99 A3
Mackenzie Wlk OL1 ....49 E5
Mackeson Dr OL6 ....85 E4
Mackeson Rd OL6 ....85 E4
Maclaren Dr M8 ....63 E1
Maclure Rd OL11 ....139 F6
Macnair Cl SK6 ....126 A5
Macnair Mews SK6 ....126 A5
Madams Wood Rd M28 ...60 A3
Maddison Rd M43 ....99 F8
Madeira Pl Eccles M30 ....79 B1
  Eccles M30 ....79 C2
Madeley Cl
  Altrincham WA14 ....128 E8
  Wigan WN3 ....54 E3
Madeley Dr OL9 ....152 B6
Madeley Gdns Bolton BL1 .143 E2
  Rochdale OL12 ....14 C1
Maden St M29 ....76 F6
Maden Wlk OL9 ....152 B8
Maden's Sq 9 OL15 ....16 B5
Madison Ave Cheadle SK8 123 A2
  Droylsden M34 ....100 C8
Madison Gdns M35 ....83 E7
Madison St M18 ....99 F6
Madras Rd SK3 ....123 C7
Maesbrook Dr M29 ....77 A8
Mafeking Ave M18 ....28 A5
Mafeking Pl WN4 ....73 C3
Mafeking Rd BL2 ....42 E7
Mafeking St OL8 ....66 C3
Magda Rd SK2 ....124 D5
Magdala St Heywood OL10 .46 E8
  Oldham OL1 ....153 E8

Magdalen Dr WN4 ....72 F4
Magenta Ave M44 ....105 E6
Magna Carta Ct M6,M27 ..80 B5
Magnolia Cl
  5 Partington M31 ....105 E2
  Sale M33 ....107 C6
Magnolia Ct 5 Sale M33 .107 C6
Magnolia Dr M8 ....156 A6
Magpie Cl M43 ....84 C3
Magpie La OL4 ....67 E4
Magpie Wlk 8 M11 ....160 F1
Maguire Ave M13 ....104 A6
Maher Gdns M15 ....162 E6
Mahogany Wlk 11 M33 .107 C5
Mahood St SK3 ....170 D7
Maida St M12 ....99 B2
Maiden Cl 5 OL7 ....85 A6
Maiden Mews 4 M27 ....79 F7
Maidford Cl
  Manchester M4 ....160 D1
  Stretford M32 ....96 C5
Maidstone Ave M21 ....97 A1
Maidstone Cl WN7 ....57 C2
Maidstone Mews 2 M21 .97 A1
Maidstone Rd SK4 ....110 D3
Maidstone Wlk M34 ....101 A1
Main Ave Manchester M19 .110 E7
  Stretford M17,M32 ....96 C5
Main La WA3 ....90 F3
Main Rd Oldham OL9 ....152 C7
  Swinton M27 ....62 C3
Main St Billinge WN5 ....71 E5
  Failsworth M35 ....83 F8
  Hyde SK14 ....167 D4
Maine Rd M14 ....98 A3
Mainhill Wlk M40 ....83 C5
Mainprice Cl M6 ....154 F4
Mains Ave WN2 ....73 F7
Mainwaring Dr SK9 ....137 D8
Mainwaring Terr M23 .109 A2
Mainway M24 ....64 F6
Mainway E M24 ....65 C6
Mainwood Rd WA15 ....120 C5
Maismore Rd M22 ....121 B1
Maitland Ave M21 ....109 D5
Maitland Cl Rochdale OL12 .15 C3
  Walsden OL14 ....6 A8
Maitland St Stockport SK1 .124 B7
  Walsden OL14 ....6 A8
Maizefield Cl M33 ....108 F4
Major St Manchester M1 .163 A8
  Milnrow OL16 ....31 F6
  Ramsbottom BL0 ....138 B6
  Wigan WN5 ....54 C6
Makants Cl M46 ....58 F5
Makepeace Wlk M8 ....63 E2
Makerfield Dr WA12 ....89 A5
Makerfield Way WN2 ....56 B7
Makin Ct OL10 ....29 D1
Makin St M1 ....163 A7
Makinson Arc 15 WN1 .150 C8
Makinson Ave Hindley WN2 56 E7
  Horwich BL6 ....22 E1
Makinson La BL6 ....22 F4
Makkah Cl M40 ....83 A5
Malaga Ave M90 ....130 B7
Malakoff St SK15 ....85 E1
Malbrook Wlk 3 M13 .163 C6
Malby St OL1 ....153 F8
Malcolm Ave M27 ....62 A3
Malcolm Dr M27 ....62 A2
Malcolm St OL11 ....30 D3
Malden Gr M23 ....121 A7
Maldon Cl
  Hazel Grove SK2 ....125 A6
  Wigan WN2 ....37 F2
Maldon Cres M27 ....79 F6
Maldon Dr M30 ....79 E4
Maldon St OL11 ....139 F5
Maldwyn Ave Bolton BL3 .146 C2
  Manchester M8 ....64 A2
Maleham St M7 ....155 E6
Malgam Dr M20 ....122 B8
Malham Ave WN3 ....55 A2
Malham Cl Leigh WN7 ....75 C5
  Royton OL2 ....48 D4
  Whitefield M45 ....63 A8
Malham Ct SK2 ....124 D6
Malham Gdns 6 BL3 .146 C3
Malika Pl WN4 ....72 E6
Malimson Bourne M7 .155 D6
Mall The Bury BL9 ....140 F2
  5 Eccles M30 ....79 F2
  Hyde SK14 ....167 D2
  Sale M33 ....108 B5
  Stalybridge SK15 ....102 E6
Mallaig Wlk M11 ....165 C8
Mallard Cl Dukinfield SK16 101 E7
  Hazel Grove SK2 ....125 A5
  1 Oldham OL8 ....66 D2
Mallard Cres SK12 ....133 A4
Mallard Dr BL6 ....22 A3
Mallard Gn WA14 ....119 B8
Mallard St M1 ....163 A7
Mallards Reach SK6 ....113 A2
Mallet Cres BL1 ....23 F2
Malley Wlk 18 M9 ....64 E3
Malling Rd M23 ....121 A4
Mallison St BL1 ....143 F3
Mallory Ave OL7 ....85 B5
Mallory Dr WN7 ....76 C5
Mallory Rd SK14 ....102 A4
Mallory Wlk M23 ....120 D8

Mallow Croft OL16 ....31 C4
Mallow St M15 ....162 E6
Mallow Wlk M31 ....105 F2
Mallowdale M28 ....78 B8
  7 Salford M6 ....81 A2
Mallowdale Cl BL1 ....40 D7
Mallowdale Rd SK2 ....124 E5
Mally Gdns OL5 ....86 D8
Malmesbury Cl SK12 ....133 D4
Malmesbury Rd SK8 ....132 B6
Malpas Ave WN1 ....37 E1
Malpas Cl Cheadle SK8 .123 A4
  Handforth SK9 ....131 E1
Malpas Dr WA14 ....107 E1
Malpas St Manchester M12 165 A6
  Oldham OL1 ....153 F7
Malpas Wlk M16 ....162 D5
Malsham Rd M23 ....108 F2
Malt St M15 ....162 D7
Malta Cl M24 ....65 D8
Malta St Manchester M4 .160 D1
  Oldham OL4 ....67 D6
Maltby Dr BL3 ....146 C3
Maltby Rd M23 ....120 F6
Malton Ave Bolton BL3 .146 A4
  Golborne WA3 ....90 E7
  Manchester M21 ....109 B8
  Whitefield M45 ....44 F2
Malton Cl Chadderton OL9 .47 F1
  Leigh WN7 ....75 C6
  1 Whitefield M45 ....44 F2
Malton Dr
  Altrincham WA14 ....119 A6
  Hazel Grove SK7 ....133 D7
Malton Rd Boothstown M28 .77 F7
  Manchester SK4 ....168 A4
Malton St OL8 ....153 D5
Malus Ct M6 ....81 A3
Malverley Dr WN7 ....76 C5
Malvern Ave Ashton-u-L OL6 85 C7
  Atherton M46 ....58 F5
  Bolton BL3 ....142 A1
  Bury BL9 ....27 F5
  Droylsden M43 ....84 C2
  Hindley WN2 ....57 A4
  Urmston M41 ....95 B2
  Wythenshawe SK8 ....121 F5
Malvern Cl
  Ashton-in-M WN4 ....73 B4
  2 Farnworth BL4 ....59 F8
  Horwich BL6 ....22 C5
  Milnrow OL16 ....32 A7
  Pendlebury M27 ....80 D6
  Prestwich M25 ....63 C5
  Royton OL2 ....48 C3
  Shaw OL2 ....48 F8
  Stockport SK4 ....169 D3
  Wigan WN3 ....54 C3
Malvern Cres WN3 ....55 F4
Malvern Dr
  Altrincham WA14 ....119 B5
  Pendlebury M27 ....80 D6
Malvern Gr
  Manchester M20 ....110 A6
  Salford M6 ....80 C3
  Walkden M28 ....60 D3
Malvern Rd M24 ....65 A5
Malvern Rise SK13 ....104 A5
Malvern Row 1 M15 ....162 D6
Malvern St
  Manchester M15 ....162 D6
  Oldham OL8 ....153 D5
  Standish WN6 ....19 D3
Malvern St E OL11 ....30 C7
Malvern St W OL11 ....30 C7
Malvern Terr WN7 ....75 F3
Malvern Way 1 ....1 A7
Manchester Utd FC
  (Old Trafford) M17 ....96 F5
Manby Rd M18 ....99 B4
Manby Sq M18 ....99 B4
Mancentral Trad Est M3 .158 D1
Manchester Airport
  M90 ....130 A7
Manchester Airport Sta
  M90 ....130 B7
Manchester Bsns Sch
  M15 ....163 A6
Manchester Cath (CE)
  M4 ....158 F2
Manchester Cath (RC)
  M3 ....158 D2
Manchester Chambers
  OL1 ....153 E7
Manchester City Coll
  (Wythenshawe Ctr)
  M23 ....120 F8
Manchester City FC
  (Maine Rd) M14 ....98 A3
Manchester Coll of Art
  & Tech M3 ....158 E1
Manchester Coll of Arts
  & Tech (Openshaw Ctr)
  M11 ....165 B7
Manchester Gram Sch
  M13 ....98 B2
Manchester High Sch
  for Girls M14 ....98 C1
Manchester Islamic
  High Sch for Girls M21 .109 A8
Manchester Jewish Mus
  M8 ....159 A4
Manchester Jewish Sch
  M25 ....63 B3
Manchester Jun Girls Sch
  M7 ....63 E1

Manchester Met Univ
Hollings Bldg M14 . . . .**98** D2
Manchester Met Univ
The Manchester M1 . . . . . .**163** B8
Manchester M1,M13,M15 . .**163** A7
Manchester M20 . . . .**110** B2
Manchester Met Univ
The (John Dalton Bldg)
M1,M15 . . . .**162** F7
Manchester Metropolitan
Univ, Elizabeth Gaskell
Campus M13,M14 . . . .**98** C4
Manchester Mus The
M13 . . . .**163** B6
Manchester New Rd
Middleton M24,M9 . . . .**64** F6
Partington M31 . . . .**105** F3
Manchester Northern
Hospl M8 . . . .**156** A7
Manchester Old Rd
Bury BL9 . . . .**140** E1
Middleton M24 . . . .**64** D7
Manchester Rd
Altrincham WA14 . . . .**119** D6
Ashton-u-L M34, M43, OL7 . .**84** E1
Blackrod BL6 . . . .**38** E8
Bolton BL3 . . . .**42** B4
Bury BL9 . . . .**140** E1
Bury BL9 . . . .**140** E2
Bury BL9,M45 . . . .**44** F5
Carrington M31 . . . .**106** B6
Cheadle M20,SK8 . . . .**122** D7
Denton M34 . . . .**100** E3
Diggle HD7,OL3 . . . .**52** A8
Droylsden M34 . . . .**100** B8
Dukinfield SK14 . . . .**101** C3
Handforth SK9 . . . .**131** C2
Haslingden BB4 . . . .**1** D7
Heywood OL10 . . . .**46** D7
Hollinfare WA3 . . . .**105** A2
Hollinfare WA3 . . . .**105** B3
Ince-in-M WN2,WN1 . . . . . .**56** A7
Kearsley BL4,M27 . . . .**61** D4
Leigh M29,WN7 . . . .**76** D4
Manchester M16,M21 . . . . . .**97** B1
Manchester M21 . . . .**109** A8
Mossley OL3,OL5,SK15 . . . . .**68** D3
Oldham OL8 . . . .**66** C3
Pendlebury M27 . . . .**80** B7
Ramsbottom BL0,BL9 . . . . . .**11** E4
Reddish M34 . . . .**100** B4
Rochdale OL11 . . . .**30** C4
Shaw OL2 . . . .**149** A5
Stockport SK4 . . . .**169** E4
Swinton M27,M28 . . . .**61** C2
Tintwistle SK13 . . . .**103** E7
Tintwistle SK13 . . . .**104** A7
Tyldesley M29 . . . .**77** C8
Walkden M28 . . . .**60** E2
Westhoughton BL5 . . . .**60** A4
Manchester Rd E M38 . . .**60** B4
Manchester Rd N M34 . .**100** D4
Manchester Rd S M34 . .**100** D3
Manchester Rd W M38 . . .**59** E5
Manchester Road
Cty Prim Sch M43 . . . .**83** E1
Manchester Royal Infmy
M13 . . . .**163** C5
Manchester St
Heywood OL10 . . . .**29** E1
Manchester M16 . . . .**161** C5
Oldham OL8,OL9 . . . .**153** D6
Manchester
Yeshivah Coll M8 . . . .**63** F1
Manchet St OL11 . . . .**30** B1
Mancroft Ave BL3 . . . . . .**147** D4
Mancroft Terr BL3 . . . . .**147** D4
Mancroft Wlk 1 M1 . . . .**163** B7
Mancunian Rd M34 . . . . .**113** A8
Mancunian Way
M1,M12,M15 . . . .**163** B7
Mandalay Gdns SK6 . . . .**125** D7
Mandarin Gn WA14 . . . . .**119** B8
Mandarin Wlk 3 M6 . . . . .**81** A3
Manderville Cl WN3 . . . . .**54** D2
Mandeville St M19 . . . . .**111** B8
Mandeville Terr BL8 . . . . .**10** B2
Mandley Ave M40 . . . .**65** D2
Mandley Cl BL3 . . . .**43** A5
Mandley Park Ave M7 . . .**155** E2
Mandley Park Sch M7 . . . .**155** D7
Mandon Cl M26 . . . .**43** E5
Manesty Cl M24 . . . .**46** C2
Manet Cl M7 . . . .**81** B8
Mangle St M1 . . . .**159** B1
Mango Pl M6 . . . .**81** A2
Manifold Dr SK6 . . . .**134** F6
Manifold St M6 . . . .**81** B5
Manilla Wlk 1 M11 . . . . .**160** F1
Manipur St M11 . . . .**164** F8
Manley Ave Golborne WA3 . .**73** F2
Kearsley M26 . . . .**61** E4
Manley Cl Leigh WN7 . . . . .**75** D8
Ramsbottom BL9 . . . .**11** C2
Manley Cres BL5 . . . .**40** B1
Manley Gr Bramhall SK7 . .**132** E6
Mottram-in-L SK14 . . . . . .**102** F3
Manley Park Inf Sch M16 .**97** C2
Manley Park Jun Sch M16 **97** C3
Manley Rd
Manchester M16,M21 . . . . . .**97** D1
Oldham OL8 . . . .**66** E4
Rochdale OL11 . . . .**30** C4
Sale M33 . . . .**107** F1
Manley St Ince-in-M WN3 . .**151** E6

Manchester M7 . . . .**155** D6
Manley Terr BL1 . . . .**143** E4
Manley Units M16 . . . .**97** E3
Manley Way SK14 . . . . . .**103** A3
Manning Ave WN6 . . . .**37** A2
Manningham Rd BL3 . . . . .**144** B5
Mannington Dr M9 . . . . . .**156** C7
Mannion Ho WN1 . . . .**151** D8
Mannock St OL8 . . . .**153** D6
Manns OL3 . . . .**68** F5
Manor Cl Golborne WA3 . . . .**90** C8
Little Lever BL3 . . . .**43** C3
Manchester M16 . . . .**97** D2
Sale M33 . . . .**107** D4
Urmston M41 . . . .**95** D1
Manor Cl Cheadle SK8 . . . .**123** C1
Denton M34 . . . .**101** B2
Garswood WN4 . . . .**72** C3
Oldham OL9 . . . .**152** C8
Uppermill OL4 . . . .**68** E5
Wilmslow SK9 . . . .**136** F8
Manor Cl Golborne WA3 . . . .**90** C8
Sale M33 . . . .**107** D4
Stretford M32 . . . .**96** B1
Manor Dr Manchester M21 **109** D4
Royton OL2 . . . .**48** E3
Manor Farm Cl OL7 . . . . .**84** F5
Manor Farm Rise OL4 . . .**67** D7
Manor Gate Rd BL2 . . . . . .**43** A8
Manor Gdns SK9 . . . .**137** D7
Manor Gr Aspull WN2 . . . . .**38** B5
Leigh WN7 . . . .**76** C3
Wigan WN6 . . . .**54** B8
Manor Green Prim Sch
M34 . . . .**113** A8
Manor Hill Rd SK6 . . . . . .**125** F7
Manor House Cl WA11 . . . .**71** B1
Manor La OL3 . . . .**51** E8
Manor Lo Bramhall SK8 . . .**123** C1
Pendlebury M27 . . . .**80** D8
Manor Park Rd SK13 . . . .**104** E1
Manor Pk M41 . . . .**95** D1
Manor Pl WN3 . . . .**151** F6
Manor Rd
Altrincham WA15 . . . .**119** E4
Bramhall SK7,SK8 . . . .**123** C1
Brinnington SK5 . . . .**112** C4
Denton M34 . . . .**101** B1
Droylsden M34 . . . .**100** B7
Droylsden M43 . . . .**83** F1
Dukinfield SK14 . . . .**101** F5
Hindley WN2 . . . .**56** F5
Horwich BL6 . . . .**22** D4
Manchester M19 . . . .**99** B2
Marple SK6 . . . .**125** F7
Middleton M24 . . . .**65** A6
Oldham OL4 . . . .**67** C4
Romiley SK6 . . . .**113** B5
Sale M33 . . . .**108** B5
Shaw OL2 . . . .**149** A6
Shevington WN6 . . . .**36** A4
Stretford M32 . . . .**96** B2
Swinton M27 . . . .**79** F6
Tyldesley M29 . . . .**77** C6
Wilmslow SK9 . . . .**136** E8
Manor St Bolton BL1 . . . .**145** F7
Bury BL9 . . . .**141** A2
Dukinfield M34 . . . .**100** F7
Farnworth BL4 . . . .**60** C7
Glossop SK13 . . . .**104** D1
Golborne WA3 . . . .**74** B1
Kearsley BL4 . . . .**61** B5
Manchester M12 . . . .**163** C7
Middleton M24 . . . .**47** A2
Mossley OL5 . . . .**68** C2
Oldham OL2 . . . .**49** A2
Ramsbottom BL0 . . . .**138** B7
Wigan WN5 . . . .**54** F6
Manor View SK6 . . . .**113** B5
Manor Wlk M34 . . . .**100** F7
Manordale Wlk M40 . . . .**156** C6
Manorfield Cl BL1 . . . . . .**142** A1
Manorial Dr M38 . . . .**59** E5
Mansart Cl WN4 . . . .**73** D3
Manse Ave WN6 . . . .**18** F5
Manse Gdns WA12 . . . . . .**89** D4
Manse The OL5 . . . .**86** C8
Mansell Way BL6 . . . .**39** E8
Mansfield Ave
Denton M34 . . . .**100** D5
Manchester M9 . . . .**64** A4
Ramsbottom BL0 . . . .**11** B2
Mansfield Cl Ashton-u-L OL7 **84** F1
Denton M34 . . . .**100** D5
Mansfield Cres M34 . . . .**100** D4
Mansfield Dr M9 . . . .**64** E4
Mansfield Gr BL1 . . . .**142** B1
Mansfield Grange OL11 . . .**30** C6
Mansfield Rd Hyde SK14 . .**167** F1
Manchester M9 . . . .**64** E4
Mossley OL5 . . . .**68** E1
7 Oldham OL8 . . . .**67** B5
Rochdale OL11 . . . .**29** E7
Urmston M41 . . . .**95** B1
Mansfield St Ashton-u-L OL7 **84** F1
Golborne WA3 . . . .**73** F1
Mansfield View OL5 . . . . .**68** E1
Mansford Dr M10,M40 . . .**157** F5
Manshaw Cres M34 . . . . .**100** A7
Manshaw Rd M11,M34 . . .**100** A7
Mansion Ave M45 . . . .**44** E3
Manson Ave M15 . . . .**162** D7
Manstead Wlk M40 . . . . .**160** E2
Manston Dr SK8 . . . .**123** A2
Manswood Dr M8 . . . .**156** A7

Mantell Wlk M40 . . . .**83** A5
Mantley La OL1,OL3 . . . . . .**50** A7
Manton Ave Manchester M9 **65** B2
Reddish M34 . . . .**100** A3
Manton Cl M7 . . . .**155** F6
Manvers St SK5 . . . .**169** E3
Manwaring St M35 . . . . . .**83** E8
Maple Ave
Altrincham WA15 . . . .**120** E5
Atherton WA46 . . . .**58** B4
Bolton BL1 . . . .**142** B1
Bury BL9 . . . .**141** B2
Cheadle SK8 . . . .**122** F2
Denton M34 . . . .**100** E3
Droylsden M34 . . . .**84** B1
Eccles M30 . . . .**79** A4
Golborne WA3 . . . .**90** F7
Hindley WN2 . . . .**56** F3
Horwich BL6 . . . .**22** E1
Ince-in-M WN2 . . . .**151** F6
Manchester M21 . . . .**109** B8
Marple SK6 . . . .**125** F4
Newton-le-W WA12 . . . .**89** D2
Poynton SK12 . . . .**133** F3
Stalybridge SK15 . . . .**101** F8
Stretford M32 . . . .**96** B1
Whitefield M45 . . . .**62** F6
Maple Cl Billinge WN5 . . . . .**71** D5
Kearsley BL4 . . . .**60** F5
Middleton M24 . . . .**65** D8
Oldham OL9 . . . .**48** B1
Sale M33 . . . .**107** C4
Salford M6 . . . .**154** F3
Shaw OL2 . . . .**48** F8
Stockport SK2 . . . .**124** B6
Maple Cres WN7 . . . .**75** F7
Maple Ct SK4 . . . .**168** C4
Maple Dr WN2 . . . .**74** B7
Maple Gr Bury BL8 . . . .**27** A5
Failsworth M35 . . . .**83** E5
Failsworth M40 . . . .**65** F7
Prestwich M25 . . . .**63** A6
Ramsbottom BL0 . . . .**11** D6
Walkden M28 . . . .**78** D8
Wigan WN6 . . . .**37** A3
Maple Lo M23 . . . .**120** C8
Maple Rd
Alderley Edge SK9 . . . .**137** B3
Bramhall SK7 . . . .**132** E6
Farnworth BL4 . . . .**60** A8
Oldham OL9 . . . .**48** B1
Partington M31 . . . .**105** E3
Sale M23 . . . .**108** C1
Swinton M27 . . . .**79** E6
Maple Rd W M23 . . . .**120** C8
Maple St Ashton-in-M WN4 . .**73** A6
Bolton BL2 . . . .**25** C5
Bolton BL3 . . . .**145** D5
Oldham OL8 . . . .**66** C5
Rochdale OL11 . . . .**139** D6
Walsden OL14 . . . .**6** A7
Maple Wlk M23 . . . .**120** C8
Maplecroft SK1 . . . .**124** B8
Mapledon Rd M9 . . . .**157** F8
Maplefield Dr M28 . . . .**78** B7
Maplewood Cl OL1 . . . . . .**48** C2
Maplewood Gdns BL1 . . .**143** F2
Maplewood Ho BL1 . . . . .**143** E1
Maplewood Rd SK9 . . . . .**137** E8
Mapley Ave M22 . . . .**121** D8
Maplin Cl M13 . . . .**163** C7
Maplin Dr SK2 . . . .**125** A5
Mapperton Wlk 6 M16 . . .**97** E3
Oldham OL1 . . . .**67** B8
Marble St Manchester M2 .**159** A1
Oldham OL1 . . . .**67** B8
Marbury Ave M14 . . . .**98** A5
Marbury Cl M41 . . . .**94** D3
Marbury Dr WA14 . . . . . .**107** E3
Marbury Gr WN6 . . . .**36** E8
Marbury Rd Handforth SK9 **131** B1
Reddish SK4 . . . .**111** D7
Marcer Rd M40 . . . .**160** D2
March Ave SK4 . . . .**168** B2
March Dr BL8 . . . .**27** D5
March St OL16 . . . .**31** A7
Marchbank M40 . . . .**38** A2
Marchbank Dr SK8 . . . . . .**122** C6
Marchioness St 6 M18 . . .**99** F6
Marchmont Cl M13 . . . . .**164** D6
Marchwood Ave M21 . . . . .**97** D1
Marcliff Gr SK4 . . . .**168** B2
Marcliffe Dr Reddish M19 . .**99** C1
Rochdale OL11 . . . .**30** B6
Marcliffe Ind Est SK7 . . . .**124** E1
Marcroft Pl 6 OL11 . . . . . .**31** A4
Marcus Garvey Ct M16 . . .**97** E2
Marcus Gr M14 . . . .**98** C3
Marcus St BL1 . . . .**142** B1
Mardale Ave
Manchester M20 . . . .**110** C5
Royton OL16,OL2 . . . .**48** C8
Swinton M27 . . . .**61** C2
Urmston M41 . . . .**94** F3
Mardale Cl Atherton M46 . .**58** C5
Bolton BL2 . . . .**25** F1
Prestwich M45 . . . .**63** C7
Stalybridge SK15 . . . .**86** A3
Mardale Dr 1 Bolton BL2 . .**25** F1
Gatley SK8 . . . .**122** B6
Middleton M24 . . . .**46** E1
Mardale Rd M27 . . . .**79** D6
Marden Rd M23 . . . .**121** A5
Mardyke OL12 . . . .**139** E8
Marfield Ave OL9 . . . .**152** A5
Marfield St M9 . . . .**64** E1
Marford Cl M22 . . . .**121** D6
Marford Cres M33 . . . . . .**107** F2
Margaret Ashton Cl M9 . .**157** F7

Margaret Ave
Rochdale OL16 . . . .**31** C7
Wigan WN6 . . . .**36** C4
Margaret Ho 5 OL6 . . . . .**166** A2
Margaret Rd Droylsden M43 **83** E2
Dukinfield M34 . . . .**101** A4
Margaret St
Ashton-u-L OL6 . . . .**166** A2
Ashton-u-L OL7 . . . .**166** A1
3 Bury BL9 . . . .**140** F1
Heywood OL10 . . . .**29** B2
Hindley WN2 . . . .**56** D6
Oldham OL8 . . . .**66** B2
Reddish SK5 . . . .**111** E7
Shaw OL2 . . . .**149** B6
Wigan WN6 . . . .**37** A1
Margaret Terr OL6 . . . . . .**166** A2
Margate Ave M40 . . . .**83** B5
Margate Rd SK5 . . . .**111** F7
Margrove Cl M35 . . . .**84** C7
Margrove Rd M6 . . . .**80** C4
Margroy Cl OL12 . . . .**15** A2
Marguerita Rd M40 . . . . . .**83** D4
Marham Cl
Dukinfield SK14 . . . .**101** D6
Manchester M21 . . . .**109** E6
Maria St BL1 . . . .**143** E2
Marie Cl M34 . . . .**100** F2
Marie St M7 . . . .**155** E7
Marigold St
Rochdale OL11 . . . .**139** F5
Wigan WN5 . . . .**54** D7
Marigold Terr M24 . . . . . .**65** D7
Mariman Dr M8 . . . .**64** A2
Marina Ave M34 . . . .**101** A1
Marina Cl SK9 . . . .**131** D5
Marina Cres M11 . . . .**83** B3
Marina Dr Marple SK6 . . . .**125** C7
Wigan WN5 . . . .**54** D5
Marina Rd Bredbury SK6 . .**112** E4
Droylsden M43 . . . .**84** B2
Marine Ave M31 . . . .**105** D3
Marion Pl WN2 . . . .**73** F8
Marion St Farnworth BL3 . . .**42** C2
Oldham OL8 . . . .**66** F3
Maritime Cl WA12 . . . .**89** C5
Maritime Cl 5 M33 . . . . .**107** F4
Marjorie Cl M18 . . . .**165** B6
Mark Ave M6 . . . .**81** B4
Mark Jones Wlk M40 . . . . .**83** B5
Mark La OL2 . . . .**49** D6
Mark St Bacup OL13 . . . . . .**3** C8
Boothstown M28 . . . .**77** F7
Oldham OL9 . . . .**153** D7
Rochdale OL12 . . . .**15** B1
Markenfield Dr OL2 . . . . . .**48** F7
Market App WN4 . . . .**73** B3
Market Ave OL6 . . . .**166** B3
Market Par BL9 . . . .**140** F2
Market Pl Adlington PR7 . . . .**21** A7
Ashton-u-L OL6 . . . .**166** B3
Bury BL9 . . . .**140** E2
Edenfield BL0 . . . .**1** D3
Farnworth BL4 . . . .**60** D8
Hyde SK14 . . . .**167** D2
Leigh WN7 . . . .**75** F5
Middleton M24 . . . .**47** A1
Mottram-in-L SK14 . . . . . .**103** A3
Oldham OL1 . . . .**153** E7
Ramsbottom BL0 . . . .**138** C7
Standish WN6 . . . .**19** E1
Stockport SK1 . . . .**169** F2
Wigan WN1 . . . .**150** C8
Market Pl The BL1 . . . .**145** E8
Market Prec BL4 . . . .**60** D8
Market Sq OL2 . . . .**48** D4
Market St Adlington PR7 . . .**21** A6
Altrincham WA14 . . . .**119** D4
Ashton-u-L OL6 . . . .**166** B3
Atherton M46 . . . .**58** C3
Bolton BL1 . . . .**145** F7
Bury BL8 . . . .**26** F6
Bury BL9 . . . .**140** F1
Bury BL9 . . . .**44** F8
Denton M34 . . . .**100** F3
Disley SK12 . . . .**135** D6
Droylsden M43 . . . .**84** B1
Edenfield BL0 . . . .**1** D4
Farnworth BL4 . . . .**42** D1
7 Glossop SK13 . . . .**104** C1
Heywood OL10 . . . .**29** C2
Hindley WN2 . . . .**56** D5
Hollingworth SK14 . . . .**103** D5
Hyde SK14 . . . .**167** D2
Kearsley M26 . . . .**61** B8
Leigh WN7 . . . .**75** F5
Little Lever BL3 . . . .**43** B3
Manchester M1 . . . .**159** A1
Manchester M4 . . . .**158** F2
Marple SK6 . . . .**125** F6
6 Middleton M24 . . . .**46** F1
Mossley OL5 . . . .**68** C1
Mottram-in-L SK14 . . . . . .**103** A4
Mottram-in-L SK14 . . . . . .**115** A8
Newton-le-W WA12 . . . .**89** A3
5 Rawtenstall BB4 . . . .**2** F8
Shaw OL2 . . . .**149** B6
Stalybridge SK15 . . . .**86** A2
Standish WN6 . . . .**19** E1
Swinton M27 . . . .**62** A1
Tyldesley M29 . . . .**58** F1
Westhoughton BL5 . . . .**57** F6
Whitworth OL12,OL13 . . . . . .**4** D4
Wigan WN1 . . . .**150** C8
Market Street Sta M1 . . .**159** A1
Market Way
Rochdale OL16 . . . .**139** F8

Market Way continued
Salford M6 . . . .**154** F3
Market Wlk M33 . . . .**108** A5
Marketgate WN1 . . . .**150** C8
Markfield Ave M13 . . . . . .**164** D5
Markham Cl M12 . . . .**164** E6
Markham St SK14 . . . . . .**101** D5
Markington St M14 . . . . . .**98** A3
Markland Ct M14 . . . .**150** A8
Markland Hill BL1 . . . .**40** E8
Markland Hill Cl BL1 . . . .**23** F1
Markland Hill
Com Prim Sch BL1 . . . . . .**40** F8
Markland Hill La BL1 . . . .**23** F1
Markland Hill 5 Bolton BL3 **145** F6
Hyde SK14 . . . .**167** E1
Ramsbottom BL0 . . . .**138** C6
Wigan WN1 . . . .**151** E8
Marklands Rd Horwich BL6 . .**22** E5
Marks St M26 . . . .**44** A3
Markwood OL3 . . . .**50** F4
Marl Gr WN5 . . . .**53** D4
Marland Ave Cheadle SK8 .**122** F2
Oldham OL8 . . . .**67** A1
Rochdale OL11 . . . .**30** B4
Marland Cl OL11 . . . .**30** B5
Marland Cres SK5 . . . . . .**111** E8
Marland Fold OL11 . . . . . .**30** B5
Marland Fold La OL8 . . . . .**66** F1
Marland Fold Sch OL8 . . . .**67** A1
Marland Gn OL11 . . . .**30** B4
Marland Hill
Com Prim Sch OL11 . . . . . .**30** C5
Marland Hill Rd OL11 . . . . .**30** C5
Marland Old Rd OL11 . . . . .**30** B4
Marland Sq 15 M29 . . . . . .**58** F1
Marlands Sq 15 M29 . . . . .**58** F1
Marlborough Ave
Alderley Edge SK9 . . . .**137** B2
Bramhall SK8 . . . .**123** C2
Ince-in-M WN3 . . . .**55** F4
Manchester M16 . . . .**97** C2
Marlborough Cl
Ashton-u-L OL7 . . . .**100** E8
Denton M34 . . . .**100** F3
Marple SK6 . . . .**125** D7
Ramsbottom BL0 . . . .**11** C3
Whitworth OL12 . . . .**14** C7
Marlborough Dr
Failsworth M35 . . . .**83** E6
Reddish SK4 . . . .**169** A4
Marlborough Gdns 3 BL4 .**59** F8
Marlborough Gr M43 . . . . .**84** C2
Marlborough Rd
Altrincham WA14 . . . .**119** D2
Atherton WA46 . . . .**58** F4
Hyde SK14 . . . .**113** E8
Irlam M44 . . . .**94** B3
Manchester M7 . . . .**155** F7
Manchester M7,M8 . . . . . .**155** F6
Oldham OL2 . . . .**48** E2
Sale M33 . . . .**108** B4
Stretford M30 . . . .**80** A4
Stretford M32 . . . .**96** C3
Urmston M41 . . . .**94** F2
Marlborough Rd
Prim Sch M7 . . . .**155** F6
Marlborough St
Ashton-u-L OL7 . . . .**166** A1
Bolton BL1 . . . .**145** D8
Heywood OL10 . . . .**46** E8
Oldham OL4 . . . .**67** A6
14 Rochdale OL12 . . . .**14** C1
Marlbrook Dr BL5 . . . .**57** E5
Marlbrook Wlk BL3 . . . . .**147** E4
Marlcroft Ave SK4 . . . . . .**168** B2
Marld Cres BL1 . . . .**23** F2
Marle Ave OL5 . . . .**68** E1
Marle Croft M45 . . . .**62** C6
Marle Rise OL5 . . . .**68** E1
Marled Hey BL7 . . . .**9** D5
Marler Rd SK14 . . . .**167** E4
Marley Cl WA15 . . . .**119** F7
Marley Dr M33 . . . .**108** A6
Marley Rd
Manchester M19 . . . .**111** B8
Poynton SK12 . . . .**133** E2
Marleyer Cl M40 . . . .**83** C7
Marleyer Rise SK6 . . . . . .**125** A8
Marlfield Rd
Altrincham WA15 . . . .**129** D7
Shaw OL2 . . . .**48** E8
Marlhill Cl SK2 . . . .**124** C5
Marlinford Dr M40 . . . .**83** C5
Marlor Ct OL10 . . . .**29** B2
Marlor St M34 . . . .**100** E4
Marlow Brow SK13 . . . . . .**104** A4
Marlow Cl 2 Bolton BL2 . . .**25** F1
Cheadle SK8 . . . .**122** F2
Urmston M41 . . . .**95** B4
Marlow Dr
Altrincham WA14 . . . .**118** F2
Handforth SK9 . . . .**131** C5
Irlam M44 . . . .**94** A3
Swinton M27 . . . .**79** E6
Marlow Ho 9 M5 . . . .**154** F1
Marlow Rd M9 . . . .**64** F1
Marlow St SK13 . . . .**104** A5
Marlowe Cl WN3 . . . .**150** A5
Marlowe Dr M20 . . . .**110** B4
Marlowe Wlk 16 M34 . . . .**113** A7
Marlowe Wlks SK6 . . . . . .**112** F2
Marlton Wlk M9 . . . .**64** E4
Marlwood Cl OL1 . . . .**48** C2
Marlwood Rd BL1 . . . .**23** F2
Marmion Dr M21 . . . .**74** E1
Marmion Dr M21 . . . .**109** A8

Marne Ave Ashton-u-L OL6 . .85 F5
Wythenshawe M22 . . . . . . .121 E5
Marne Cres OL11 . . . . .30 C7
Marnland Gr BL3 . . . . .40 E4
Marnock Cl WN2 . . . . .74 F8
Maroon Rd M22 . . . . .130 F7
Marple Ave BL1 . . . . .25 A4
Marple Cl Oldham OL8 . . . . .66 D2
Shevington Moor WN6 . . . . . .19 B2
Marple Ct SK1 . . . . .124 A7
Marple Gr M32 . . . . .96 C3
Marple Hall Dr SK6 . . . . . .125 C7
Marple Hall Sch SK6 . . . . .125 C7
Marple Old Rd SK2 . . . . . .125 A6
Marple Rd
Charlesworth SK13 . . . . . . .115 B5
Stockport SK2,SK6 . . . . . . .124 E6
Marple Sta SK6 . . . . .126 A7
Marquis Ave BL9 . . . . .140 E4
Marquis Dr SK8 . . . . .131 D7
Marquis St M19 . . . . .99 D1
Marrick Ave SK8 . . . . .122 C5
Marrick Cl WN3 . . . . .55 A2
Marriott St
Manchester M20 . . . . .110 B6
Stockport SK1 . . . . .170 F8
Marriott's Ct M1 . . . . .159 A1
Marron Pl M2 . . . . .162 F8
Marryat Ct M12 . . . . .164 F6
Mars Ave BL3 . . . . .146 C3
Mars St Edgworth BL7 . . . . . .9 E6
Oldham OL9 . . . . .152 C7
Marsden St Ashton-u-L OL7 .84 E6
Mossley OL5 . . . . .68 B1
Royton OL2 . . . . .48 C8
Marsden Dr WA15 . . . . . . .120 C6
Marsden Rd Bolton BL1 . . .145 E7
Romiley SK6 . . . . .113 C3
Marsden St
Boothstown M28 . . . . .77 F6
Bury BL9 . . . . .140 F3
Eccles M30 . . . . .79 C3
Hadfield SK13 . . . . .104 A4
Ince-in-M WN3 . . . . .55 F4
13 Manchester M2 . . . . . . .158 F1
Middleton M24 . . . . .65 C7
Walkden M28 . . . . .61 B2
Westhoughton BL5 . . . . .57 E8
Wigan WN1 . . . . .150 C8
Wigan WN5 . . . . .54 F6
Marsett Cl OL12 . . . . .14 A1
Marsett Wlk 9 M23 . . . . . .108 F2
Marsh Brook Fold BL5 . . . . .57 A7
Marsh Cl SK3 . . . . .170 D6
Marsh Fold La BL1 . . . . . . .144 C8
Marsh Gn WN5 . . . . .36 D1
Marsh Green Prim Sch
WN5 . . . . .54 D8
Marsh Hey Cl M38 . . . . .59 F6
Marsh La Ashley WA16 . . . .128 A4
Farnworth BL4 . . . . .60 A8
Little Lever BL3 . . . . .43 B4
Wigan WN1 . . . . .150 C8
Marsh Rd Little Lever BL3 . .43 B4
Walkden M38 . . . . .60 A4
Marsh Row WN2 . . . . .57 A4
Marsh St 12 Bolton BL1 . . .143 E2
Horwich BL6 . . . . .22 A4
Walkden M28 . . . . .60 F2
Westhoughton BL5 . . . . .39 E1
Wigan WN3 . . . . .55 A4
Marshall Ct
6 Ashton-u-L OL6 . . . . . . .85 D2
1 Oldham OL1 . . . . .153 E8
Marshall Rd M19 . . . . .99 A1
Marshall St Denton M34 . . .100 E4
Leigh WN7 . . . . .75 E4
Manchester M12 . . . . .163 C6
Manchester M4 . . . . .159 B2
Rochdale OL16 . . . . .31 C7
Marshall Stevens Way
M17 . . . . .96 B5
Marsham Cl
7 Manchester M13 . . . . . . .98 E4
Oldham OL4 . . . . .68 B5
Marsham Dr SK6 . . . . .126 A5
Marsham Rd
Hazel Grove SK7 . . . . .124 C1
Westhoughton BL5 . . . . .57 F6
Marshbank 16 BL5 . . . . . . .39 E1
Marshbrook Cl WN2 . . . . . . .57 A6
Marshdale Rd BL1 . . . . .40 F8
Marshfield Rd WA15 . . . . . .120 C6
Marshfield Wlk 13 M13 . . .163 C6
Marsland Ave WA15 . . . . . .120 B8
Marsland Cl M34 . . . . .100 B3
Marsland Green La M29 . .76 E3
Marsland Rd
Altrincham WA15 . . . . .120 B6
Marple SK6 . . . . .125 D7
Sale M33 . . . . .108 B3
Marsland St
Hazel Grove SK7 . . . . .124 D2
Stockport SK1 . . . . .169 F2
Marsland St N M7,M8 . . . .155 F7
Marsland St S M7,M8 . . . .155 F7
Marsland Terr SK1 . . . . . . .124 B8
Marslands OL3 . . . . .51 B3
Marston Cl Failsworth M35 .84 F6
Horwich BL6 . . . . .39 F8
Whitefield M45 . . . . .63 C8
Marston Dr M44 . . . . .94 B1
Marston Ho 8 M5 . . . . . . .154 F1
Marston Rd
Manchester M7 . . . . .155 E8
Stretford M32 . . . . .96 F2
Marston St M40 . . . . .157 D5

Marston Way SK14 . . . . . .102 F3
Marsworth Dr M4 . . . . .159 C2
Martens Rd M44 . . . . .105 E5
Martha St 8 Bolton BL3 . . .147 D4
Oldham OL1 . . . . .153 D8
Martha's Terr OL16 . . . . . . .15 C3
Marthall Dr M33 . . . . .108 E1
Marthall Way 8 SK9 . . . . .131 E5
Martham Dr SK2 . . . . .125 A6
Martin Ave Farnworth BL4 . .59 F7
Little Lever BL3 . . . . .43 C3
Newton-le-W WA12 . . . . . . .89 C5
8 Oldham OL4 . . . . .67 C6
Martin Cl Denton M34 . . . .100 F5
Marple SK2 . . . . .124 F5
Martin Dr M44 . . . . .94 A4
Martin Gr BL4 . . . . .60 F7
Martin Ho M14 . . . . .98 D3
Martin La OL12 . . . . .14 B1
Martin Rd M27 . . . . .62 B2
Martin St 8 Atherton M46 . .58 D3
Bury BL9 . . . . .28 D3
Dukinfield M34 . . . . .100 F7
Edgworth BL7 . . . . .9 D4
Hyde SK14 . . . . .167 E2
Salford M5 . . . . .154 E2
Martindale Cl OL2 . . . . .48 E5
Martindale Cres
Manchester M12 . . . . .164 E5
Middleton M24 . . . . .46 D3
Wigan WN5 . . . . .54 F6
Martindale Gdns BL1 . . . .143 E2
Martindale Rd WA11 . . . . . .71 C2
Martingale Cl M26 . . . . .44 A5
Martingale Way M43 . . . . . .84 D2
Martins Ct WN2 . . . . .57 A6
Martins Field OL12 . . . . . . .13 F1
Martinsclough BL6 . . . . .40 C6
Martinscroft Rd M23 . . . .121 B5
Martland Ave
Golborne WA3 . . . . .90 E7
Shevington WN6 . . . . .35 F5
Martland Cres WN6 . . . . . . .36 E3
Martland Mill La WN5 . . . . .36 D2
Martlesham Wlk 6 M4 . . .159 A2
Rochdale OL11 . . . . .29 F7
Martlet Ave Disley SK12 . .135 C6
Rochdale OL11 . . . . .29 F7
Martlet Cl M14 . . . . .98 B1
Martlew Dr M29 . . . . .58 F4
Martock Ave M22 . . . . .121 E3
Marton Ave Bolton BL2 . . .148 C8
Manchester M20 . . . . .110 C2
Marton Cl WA3 . . . . .91 E4
Marton Dr M46 . . . . .58 E4
Marton Gn SK3 . . . . .170 D5
Marton Gr SK4 . . . . .111 E6
Marton Grange M25 . . . . . .63 D3
Marton Pl M33 . . . . .108 A4
Marton St WN1 . . . . .37 C1
Marton Way 6 SK9 . . . . . .131 E5
Marus Ave WN3 . . . . .54 F3
Marus Bridge Prim Sch
WN3 . . . . .54 E2
Marvic Ct M13 . . . . .98 E3
Marwick Cl WN6 . . . . .19 D2
Marwood Cl
Altrincham WA14 . . . . .119 B6
Kearsley M26 . . . . .61 A8
Marwood Dr M23 . . . . .120 F3
Mary France St WN2 . . . . .162 E6
Mary Hulton Ct BL5 . . . . . . .58 A8
Mary St Cheadle SK8 . . . . .122 D6
Droylsden M43 . . . . .84 B1
Dukinfield M34 . . . . .101 A4
Dukinfield SK16 . . . . .166 B1
Farnworth BL4 . . . . .60 D7
Heywood OL10 . . . . .29 C2
Hyde SK14 . . . . .167 D3
Littleborough OL16 . . . . . . .15 D4
Manchester M3 . . . . .158 F3
Ramsbottom BL0 . . . . .138 B5
Stockport SK1 . . . . .112 A2
Tyldesley M29 . . . . .77 A8
Mary St E BL9 . . . . .22 B4
Mary St W BL6 . . . . .22 A4
Maryfield Cl WA3 . . . . .90 A7
Maryland Ave BL2 . . . . .42 D7
Marylebone Ct WN1 . . . . . .37 D3
Marylebone Pl WN1 . . . . . .37 D3
Marylon Dr M22 . . . . .121 E8
Masboro St M8 . . . . .155 F7
Masefield Ave Leigh WN7 . .75 D7
Prestwich M25 . . . . .62 F3
Radcliffe M26 . . . . .43 E4
Wigan WN5 . . . . .54 A6
Masefield Cl SK16 . . . . . . .102 B7
Masefield Com Prim Sch
BL3 . . . . .43 B4
Masefield Cres M43 . . . . . . .84 A1
Masefield Dr Farnworth BL4 60 B7
Stockport SK4 . . . . .168 A2
4 Wigan WN3 . . . . .54 F5
Masefield Gr SK5 . . . . .99 E1
Masefield Rd
Droylsden M43 . . . . .84 A1
Little Lever BL3 . . . . .43 B4
Oldham OL1 . . . . .49 B2
Mason Cl WN4 . . . . .73 D4
Mason Gdns BL3 . . . . .145 E6
Mason La M46 . . . . .58 E2
Mason Row 8 . . . . .8 E2
Mason St Abram WN2 . . . . .74 B8
Bolton BL7 . . . . .8 E1
Bury BL9 . . . . .141 A2
Heywood OL10 . . . . .29 B2
Horwich BL6 . . . . .22 B3
Manchester M3 . . . . .158 D1

Mason St continued
Manchester M4 . . . . .159 B2
Rochdale OL16 . . . . .139 F7
Wigan WN3 . . . . .150 B7
Mason Ind Est WN3 . . . . .150 B7
Masons Gr SK13 . . . . .104 A6
Massey Ave Ashton-u-L OL6 .85 C6
Failsworth M35 . . . . .84 B8
Massey Croft OL12 . . . . . . .14 C8
Massey Rd
Altrincham WA15 . . . . .119 E4
Sale M33 . . . . .108 E4
Massey St
4 Alderley Edge SK9 . . . . .137 A1
Bury BL9 . . . . .141 B3
Manchester M5 . . . . .81 C1
Stockport SK1 . . . . .169 F1
Massey Wlk M22 . . . . .121 F1
Massie St SK8 . . . . .122 D6
Matchmoor La BL6 . . . . . . .23 A4
Matham Wlk M15 . . . . .163 A7
Mather Ave Eccles M30 . . . .79 E2
Golborne WA3 . . . . .90 E6
Manchester M25 . . . . .63 C1
Whitefield M45 . . . . .44 F1
Mather Cl M45 . . . . .44 F1
Mather Fold Rd M28 . . . . . .60 B1
Mather La WN7 . . . . .76 A4
Mather Rd Bury BL9 . . . . . .27 F7
Eccles M30 . . . . .79 E2
Mather St 8 Atherton M46 . .58 D3
Bolton BL3 . . . . .145 E6
Failsworth M35 . . . . .83 E7
Farnworth BL4 . . . . .60 E8
Radcliffe M26 . . . . .44 A3
Mather Street Prim Sch
M35 . . . . .83 D7
Mather Way 4 M6 . . . . .81 A3
Matheson Dr WN5 . . . . .54 E8
Matisse Way M7 . . . . .81 B8
Matley Cl SK14 . . . . .102 B5
Matley Gn SK5 . . . . .112 C6
Matley La SK14,SK15 . . . .102 D6
Matley Park La SK15 . . . . .102 D6
Matlock Ave Ashton-u-L OL6 85 F6
Denton M34 . . . . .113 A8
Manchester M20 . . . . .109 F6
Manchester M7 . . . . .81 A7
Urmston M41 . . . . .94 F6
Matlock Bank 16 SK13 . . .171 E1
Matlock Cl Atherton M46 . . .58 D2
Farnworth BL4 . . . . .42 E1
Sale M33 . . . . .108 C4
Matlock Gdns 15 SK13 . . .171 E1
Matlock La 15 SK13 . . . . .171 E1
Matlock Mews WA14 . . . . .119 E5
Matlock Rd Gatley SK8 . . .131 C7
Reddish SK5 . . . . .100 A1
Stretford M32 . . . . .96 A3
Matlock St M30 . . . . .95 C8
Matson Wlk 3 M22 . . . . . .121 A2
Matt Busby Cl M27 . . . . . . .80 B7
Matterdale Terr SK15 . . . . . .86 A4
Matthew Cl SK13 . . . . .103 F7
Matthew Moss High Sch
OL11 . . . . .30 B4
Matthew Moss La OL11 . . . .30 B4
Matthew's St M12 . . . . . . .164 F7
Matthews Ave BL4 . . . . .60 F7
Matthews La M12,M19 . . . .99 F3
Matthias St M3 . . . . .158 D3
Mattison St M11 . . . . .99 E7
Maud St Bolton BL2 . . . . . . .25 C5
Rochdale OL12 . . . . .15 A2
Maudsley St BL9 . . . . .140 E1
Mauldeth Cl SK4 . . . . .168 A3
Mauldeth Rd
Manchester M14,M19,M20 .110 D7
Manchester M19,SK4 . . . . .110 F6
Manchester M4,M19 . . . . .168 A3
Mauldeth Rd W
Manchester M20 . . . . .110 B8
Manchester M20,M21 . . . .109 D8
Mauldeth Road
Prim Sch M20 . . . . .110 E7
Mauldeth Road Sta M20 . .110 E7
Maunby Gdns M38 . . . . . . .60 C3
Maureen Ave M8 . . . . .156 A8
Maureen St OL12 . . . . .15 A2
Maurice Cl SK16 . . . . .101 E8
Maurice Dr M6 . . . . .154 F4
Maurice Pariser Wlk M8 .155 F7
Maurice St M6 . . . . .154 F4
Maveen Gr SK2 . . . . .124 A4
Mavis Gr OL16 . . . . .32 A6
Mavis St OL11 . . . . .30 C1
Mawdsley Dr M8 . . . . .156 C8
Mawdsley St BL1 . . . . .145 F7
Max Woosnam Wlk 3
M14 . . . . .98 A3
Maxwell Ave SK2 . . . . .124 C5
Maxwell St Bolton BL1 . . .143 E4
Bury BL9 . . . . .141 B3
May Ave Abram Brow WN2 . .74 C7
Bramhall SK8 . . . . .132 B6
Leigh WN7 . . . . .75 D6
Stockport SK4 . . . . .168 C2
May Ct 13 M16 . . . . .97 D3
May Dr M19 . . . . .110 F6
May Pl M19 . . . . .111 B8
May Pl 9 OL11 . . . . .31 A4
May Rd Bramhall SK8 . . . .132 B6
Manchester M16 . . . . .97 D3
Pendlebury M27 . . . . .80 B6
May St Bolton BL2 . . . . . . .148 A7
Eccles M30 . . . . .79 C4

May St continued
Edgworth BL7 . . . . .9 E6
Failsworth M40 . . . . .83 C5
Golborne WA3 . . . . .74 B2
Heywood OL10 . . . . .46 E8
Leigh WN7 . . . . .75 C5
Oldham OL8 . . . . .66 C4
Radcliffe M26 . . . . .44 A3
May Tree Dr WN1 . . . . .37 B4
May Wlk 2 M31 . . . . .105 E3
Mayall St OL5 . . . . .68 C1
Mayall St E 8 OL4 . . . . . . .67 C7
Mayan Ave M3 . . . . .158 D2
Maybank St BL3 . . . . .145 D5
Maybank Ave M8 . . . . .64 A2
Maybreck Cl BL3 . . . . .144 C5
Maybrook Wlk 11 M9 . . . .157 D8
Mayburn Cl M24 . . . . .65 C5
Maybury St M18 . . . . .99 E6
Maycroft M24 . . . . .110 C5
Maycroft Ave M20 . . . . . . .110 C5
Maycroft Inf Sch SK5 . . . .112 C6
Maycroft Prim Sch SK5 . .112 C6
Mayer St SK2 . . . . .124 C7
Mayes Gdns M4 . . . . .160 D1
Mayes St M4 . . . . .159 A2
Mayfair Horwich BL6 . . . . . .22 D3
Manchester M7 . . . . .81 B8
Mayfair Ave Radcliffe M26 . .43 D4
Salford M6 . . . . .80 B3
Urmston M41 . . . . .95 B2
Whitefield M45 . . . . .62 F7
Mayfair Cl Haslingden BB4 . .1 A7
Poynton SK12 . . . . .133 E4
Stalybridge SK16 . . . . .101 F8
Stalybridge SK16 . . . . .102 A8
Mayfair Cotts WN1 . . . . . . .20 C1
Mayfair Cres M35 . . . . .84 B8
Mayfair Ct
Altrincham WA15 . . . . .120 B7
Manchester M20 . . . . .109 F4
Mayfair Dr Atherton M46 . . .58 F4
Irlam M44 . . . . .94 A2
Oldham OL2 . . . . .48 D2
Pennington Green WN2 . . . .38 D2
Sale M33 . . . . .107 E2
Wigan WN3 . . . . .54 F2
Mayfair Gdns OL11 . . . . . .139 D5
Mayfair Gr M35 . . . . .84 B8
Mayfair Rd M22 . . . . .121 E4
Mayfield Bolton BL2 . . . . . . .25 D5
Radcliffe M26 . . . . .43 B2
Mayfield Ave Adlington PR6 21 A7
Bolton BL3 . . . . .42 B3
7 Denton M34 . . . . .113 A7
Farnworth BL4 . . . . .60 C7
Oldham OL4 . . . . .68 A7
Reddish SK5 . . . . .111 F5
Sale M33 . . . . .108 E4
Stretford M32 . . . . .96 B1
Swinton M27 . . . . .79 C6
Walkden M28 . . . . .60 D3
Mayfield Cl
Altrincham WA15 . . . . .120 B6
Ramsbottom BL0 . . . . .11 A2
Mayfield Com Prim Sch
OL1 . . . . .49 B1
Mayfield Ct Wigan WN5 . . . .36 B1
Wigan WN5 . . . . .54 B8
Mayfield Dr WA3,WN7 . . . . .91 C8
Mayfield Gr Reddish SK5 . . .99 F3
Reddish SK5 . . . . .111 F5
Wilmslow SK9 . . . . .136 E5
Mayfield Ind Est M44 . . . . .94 C3
Mayfield Mans M16 . . . . . . .97 F3
Mayfield Rd
Altrincham WA15 . . . . .120 B6
Bramhall SK7 . . . . .132 E4
Manchester M16 . . . . .97 E3
Manchester M25 . . . . .63 C1
Oldham OL1 . . . . .49 B1
Orrell WN8 . . . . .53 B7
Ramsbottom BL0 . . . . .11 A2
Romiley SK6 . . . . .114 B1
Wigan WN5 . . . . .54 B8
Mayfield St
Ashton-in-M WN4 . . . . .73 A3
Atherton M46 . . . . .58 C2
Denton M34 . . . . .100 E5
Rochdale OL16 . . . . .15 B1
Mayfield Terr OL16 . . . . . . .15 B1
Mayflower Ave M5 . . . . . . .161 B8
Mayflower Cotts WN1 . . . . .37 C8
Mayford Rd M19 . . . . .99 B2
Maygate OL9 . . . . .153 D8
Mayhill Dr Salford M6 . . . . .80 A4
Worsley M28 . . . . .79 A8
Mayhurst Ave M21 . . . . . . .109 D3
Mayo St M12 . . . . .164 D8
Mayor St Bolton BL1 . . . . .145 D6
Bury BL8 . . . . .27 C3
Oldham OL9 . . . . .152 C7
Mayor's Rd WA15 . . . . .119 E4
Mayorlowe Ave SK5 . . . . . .112 C4
Maypole Ind Est WN2 . . . . .74 C7
Maypool Dr SK5 . . . . .111 F6
Maysmith Mews M7 . . . . . .155 D6
Mayton St M11 . . . . .165 B8
Mayville Dr M20 . . . . .110 B5
Maywood Ave M20 . . . . . . .122 B8
Maze St BL3 . . . . .42 D5
Mc Naught St 28 OL16 . . . .31 B6
McCall Wlk M11 . . . . .83 B2
McConnell Rd M40 . . . . .83 A7
McCormack Dr WN1 . . . . . .151 D8
McCready Dr M5 . . . . .161 B8
McDonna St BL1 . . . . .142 C7
Mcdonough Cl OL8 . . . . . . .67 A4

McEvoy St 6 BL1 . . . . .143 F2
McKean St BL3 . . . . .42 A4
Mckie Cl OL8 . . . . .67 A3
McLaren Ct M21 . . . . .97 A1
McLean Dr M44 . . . . .94 B4
Meachin Ave M21 . . . . .109 C5
Mead The Manchester M21 109 B7
Salford M5 . . . . .154 D2
Mead Way M34 . . . . .112 F8
Meade Cl M41 . . . . .95 C2
Meade Gr M13 . . . . .98 F3
Meade Hill Rd M25,M8 . . . .63 C3
Meade Hill Sch M8 . . . . . . .63 F4
Meade Manor M21 . . . . . . .109 B7
Meade The Bolton BL3 . . . .147 D8
Wilmslow SK9 . . . . .137 C8
Meadfoot Ave M25 . . . . . . .63 C3
Meadfoot Rd M18 . . . . .99 D6
Meadland Gr BL1 . . . . .143 F4
Meadow Ave
Altrincham WA15 . . . . .120 B3
Swinton M27 . . . . .62 B1
Meadow Bank
Altrincham WA15 . . . . .120 A7
Bredbury SK6 . . . . .112 F3
Glossop SK13 . . . . .115 F7
Hollingworth SK14 . . . . . . .103 D6
Manchester M21 . . . . .109 A4
Stockport SK4 . . . . .168 B2
Meadow Bank Cl OL4 . . . . .67 E4
Meadow Bank Ct M32 . . . . .96 B3
Meadow Brow SK9 . . . . . . .137 A2
Meadow Cl
Altrincham WA15 . . . . .120 B3
Denton M34 . . . . .113 A7
Heywood OL10 . . . . .29 C2
High Lane SK6 . . . . .134 F8
Leigh WN7 . . . . .75 E2
Little Lever BL3 . . . . .43 B2
Romiley SK6 . . . . .113 A5
Stretford M32 . . . . .96 E1
Uppermill OL5 . . . . .68 E3
Wilmslow SK9 . . . . .136 E4
Meadow Cotts OL12 . . . . . . .4 D3
Meadow Croft
Hazel Grove SK7 . . . . .124 E4
Whitefield M45 . . . . .62 C6
Meadow Ct
2 Altrincham WA15 . . . . . .120 D6
Salford M6 . . . . .80 B3
Stretford M21 . . . . .108 F8
7 Wigan WN6 . . . . .37 A1
Meadow Fold OL3 . . . . .69 C8
Meadow Head Ave OL12 . .14 D6
Meadow Ind Est SK1 . . . . .169 F3
Meadow La Bolton BL2 . . . .43 A7
Denton M34 . . . . .113 A7
Disley SK12 . . . . .135 D6
Dukinfield SK16 . . . . .101 D8
Oldham OL8 . . . . .66 E2
Worsley M28 . . . . .78 F5
Meadow Pit La WN2 . . . . . .37 F8
Meadow Pk BL0 . . . . .1 C4
Meadow Rd
Manchester M24 . . . . .64 C6
Manchester M7 . . . . .81 C3
Urmston M41 . . . . .95 D1
Meadow Rise
Glossop SK13 . . . . .115 F7
Shaw OL2 . . . . .32 A1
Meadow St Adlington PR7 . .21 A6
Hyde SK14 . . . . .167 E1
Stockport SK2 . . . . .124 C5
Meadow The BL6 . . . . .40 C7
Meadow View OL12 . . . . . . .14 A1
Meadow Way
Altrincham WA15 . . . . .120 B3
Blackrod BL6 . . . . .21 E1
Bury BL8 . . . . .26 E6
Coppull PR7 . . . . .19 D8
Edgworth BL7 . . . . .9 E6
Manchester M40 . . . . .65 A1
Wilmslow SK9 . . . . .136 E4
Meadow Wlk
Bredbury SK6 . . . . .112 F3
Farnworth BL4 . . . . .60 A8
Littleborough OL15 . . . . . . .15 F5
Meadowbank OL7 . . . . .85 B6
Meadowbank Ave M46 . . . . .58 E5
Meadowbank Cl M35 . . . . . .84 A6
Meadowbank
Cty Prim Sch M46 . . . . . . .58 D4
Meadowbank Gdns WA3 . . .92 C7
Meadowbank Rd BL3 . . . . .146 B3
Meadowbrook Cl
Bolton BL6 . . . . .40 B3
Bolton BL6 . . . . .141 C4
Meadowburn Nook M30 . . .79 B4
Meadowcroft
Ashton-in-M WN4 . . . . .72 F6
Mottram-in-L SK14 . . . . . . .103 A4
Radcliffe M26 . . . . .43 F5
Westhoughton BL5 . . . . .57 F7
Meadowcroft La
1 Oldham OL1 . . . . .49 B1
Rochdale OL11 . . . . .29 F6
Meadowfield Bolton BL6 . . .40 C7
Orrell WN8 . . . . .53 A7
Rochdale OL16 . . . . .31 B3
Meadowfield Cl SK13 . . . . .171 E4
Meadowfield Ct SK14 . . . . .167 D4
Meadowfield Dr M28 . . . . . .78 B6
Meadowgate Urmston M41 .95 D1
Worsley M28 . . . . .78 F8
Meadowgate Rd M6 . . . . . .80 C3

Meadows OL3 ....69 B7
Meadows M4 WN2 .....56 D5
Meadows La BL2 ....25 F3
Meadows Rd Cheadle SK8 .131 F8
  Gatley SK8 ....122 B1
  Reddish SK4 ....111 C6
  Sale M33 ....108 C6
Meadows St WN6 .....37 A1
Meadows The Irlam M44 .105 E6
  Middleton M24 ....65 B6
  Oldham OL4 ....68 A6
  Prestwich M25 ....63 C3
  Radcliffe M26 ....43 E5
  Romiley SK6 ....113 B4
  Whitworth OL12 ......4 C1
Meadowside
  Bramhall SK7 ....123 C2
  Newhey OL16 ....32 C3
Meadowside Ave
  Ashton-in-M WN4 ....73 A8
  Bolton BL2 ....148 C7
  Irlam M44 ....94 A2
  Walkden M28 ....60 E4
  Wythenshawe M22 ....121 E4
Meadowside Cl M26 ..44 A5
Meadowside Gr M28 ..60 E3
Meadowside Rd WN2 ..57 A4
Meadowvale Dr WN5 ..54 C6
Meads Gr Farnworth BL4 .59 E8
  Tyldesley M29 ....77 C6
Meads The OL9 ....152 A6
Meadscroft Dr SK9 ...136 F1
Meadway Bramhall SK7 .132 E5
  Bury BL9 ....44 F6
  Dukinfield SK16 .....101 E7
  Failsworth OL9 ......65 E2
  Golborne WA3 ....90 D8
  High Lane SK6 ....134 F8
  Ince-in-M WN2 ....151 F7
  Poynton SK12 ....133 B4
  Ramsbottom BL0 ......1 C1
  Rochdale OL11 ....30 C4
  Sale M33 ....107 E2
  Stalybridge SK15 ....102 E6
  Tyldesley M29 ....59 D1
Meadway Cl Horwich BL6 .22 D3
  Sale M33 ....107 E2
Meadway Rd SK8 .....123 B3
Meal St SK4 ....169 E3
Mealhouse Brow SK1 .169 F1
Mealhouse Ct M46 ...58 C3
Mealhouse La
  Atherton M46 ....58 C3
  Bolton BL1 ....145 F7
Meanley Rd M29,WN7 ..76 F7
Meanley St M29 ......59 A1
Meanwood Brow OL12 .14 C1
Meanwood Fold OL12 .139 D8
Meanwood Prim Sch
  OL12 ....14 C1
Measham Mews M1 ...163 A7
Meburn Wlk M14 .....98 B4
Mechinoh L'Yeshivah Sch
  M7 ....63 E1
Meddings Cl SK9 .....136 F1
Medina Cl SK8 ....123 B4
Medlar Way WN4 .....72 F5
Medley St OL12 ......14 C1
Medlock Cl BL4 ......60 B8
Medlock Cty Inf Sch M13 163 C7
Medlock Cty Prim Sch
  M13 ....163 C7
Medlock Dr OL8 ......85 A8
Medlock Ho M15 .....162 D7
Medlock Rd M35 .....84 B5
Medlock Sports Ctr M43 .84 B2
Medlock St Droylsden M43 .84 B2
  Manchester M15 .....162 E4
Medlock Vale M35 ....84 E6
Medlock Valley High Sch
  M11 ....160 E1
Medlock Valley
  Visitor Ctr OL6 .....67 C2
Medlock Way Oldham OL4 .67 B4
  Platt Bridge WN2 ....56 A2
  Whitefield M45 ......63 C8
Medowell Wlk M8 ....64 B2
Medway Cl
  Ashton-in-M WN4 ....72 F6
  Golborne WN7 ....91 C8
  Handforth SK9 ....131 D2
  Oldham OL8 ....66 C3
  Salford M5 ....154 D3
Medway Cres WA14 ..119 C6
Medway Dr Horwich BL6 .22 D3
  Kearsley BL4 ....61 B5
Medway Pl WN5 ......54 A2
Medway Rd Culcheth WA3 .92 A2
  Oldham OL8 ....66 C3
  Shaw OL2 ....149 B8
  Walkden M28 ....78 B8
Medway The OL10 ....29 B3
Medway Wlk
  Manchester M40 .....160 D3
  Wigan WN5 ....54 D1
Mee's Sq M30 ....95 D8
Meech St M11 ....165 C8
Meek St OL1,OL2 ....49 A2
Meerbrook Rd SK3 ..123 A8
Megfield BL5 ....57 E6
Melandra Castle Rd
  SK13 ....171 D2
Melandra Cres SK14 .102 E2
Melandra Rd SK13 ...171 E3
Melanie Cl SK13 ....116 A8

Melanie Dr SK5 .....111 F8
Melba St M11 ....99 E8
Melbecks Wlk M23 ..108 F2
Melbourne Ave
  Oldham OL9 ....152 B7
  Stretford M32 ......96 D2
  Wythenshawe M90 ...130 A8
Melbourne Cl Horwich BL6 .22 C3
  Rochdale OL11 ......31 B2
Melbourne Gr BL6 ...22 C3
Melbourne Mews M7 .155 E5
Melbourne Rd Bolton BL3 .144 B5
  Bramhall SK7 ....132 F5
  Rochdale OL11 ......31 A2
Melbourne St Denton M34 .100 E2
  Manchester M15 ....162 E7
  Manchester M7 .....155 E5
  Manchester M9 .....157 E8
  Oldham OL9 ....152 B7
  Pendlebury M27 ....80 B8
  Reddish SK5 ....111 F8
  Stalybridge SK15 ...86 A1
Melbourne St S OL6 .166 C4
Melbourne Wlk M5 ..161 B8
Melbury Ave M20 ...110 D4
Melbury Dr BL6 .....39 F8
Melbury Rd SK8 ....132 B6
Meldon Rd M13 .....98 E2
Meldreth Dr M12 ...98 F4
Meldrum St OL8 ....66 F4
Meldrum Wlk OL8 ...67 A4
Melford Ave M40 ...65 E1
Melford Dr
  Ashton-in-M WN4 ...73 A4
  Orrell WN5 ....53 D3
Melford Gr OL4 ....67 D6
Melford Rd SK7 ....124 F1
Melfort Ave M32 ...96 E1
Meliden Cres Bolton BL1 .142 B1
  Wythenshawe M22 ..121 E3
Melksham Cl M5,M6 .81 B2
  Oldham OL2 ....48 E2
Melland Ave M21 ...109 C5
Melland Rd M18 ....99 C3
Melland Sch M18 ...99 D2
Meller Rd M13 .....98 F2
Melling Ave
  Chadderton OL9 ....47 E1
  Reddish SK4 ....111 E6
Melling Cl WN7 ....75 F1
Melling Rd OL4 ....67 C6
Melling St Manchester M12 .99 A4
  Wigan WN5 ....54 E5
Melling Way WN3 ..54 D1
Mellings Ave WN5 ..53 E1
Mellington Ave M20 .122 C8
Mellodew Dr OL1 ...49 D4
Mellor Brook Dr WN2 .56 A2
Mellor Brow OL10 ..29 C2
Mellor Cl Ashton-u-L OL6 .85 E2
  Standish WN6 ......19 E2
Mellor Ct SK2 .....124 E6
Mellor Dr Bury BL9 .44 D7
  Walkden M28 ....60 C1
Mellor Gr BL1 .....142 B1
Mellor Prim Sch SK6 .126 C6
Mellor Rd Ashton-u-L OL6 .85 E3
  Ashton-u-L OL6 ....85 F4
  Cheadle SK8 ....123 B1
  New Mills SK22 ....127 C3
Mellor St Droylsden M43 .83 F1
  Eccles M30 ....79 D1
  Failsworth M35 ....83 D6
  Manchester M12 ...163 C8
  Manchester M40 ...160 D3
  Oldham OL4 ....67 C6
  Prestwich M25 ....62 F4
  Radcliffe M26 .....44 B2
  Rochdale OL11,OL12 .139 D7
  Royton OL2 ....48 D5
  Stretford M32 .....96 E4
Mellor Way OL9 ...66 B4
Mellors Rd M17 ...96 B7
Mellowstone Dr M21 .109 F8
Melloy Pl M8 ......159 A4
Melmerby Ct WN4 .72 F3
Melmerby Ct M5 ...154 F1
Melon Pl M6 ....81 B2
Melrose OL12 .....139 E8
Melrose Ave Bolton BL1 .142 A1
  Bury BL8 ....27 C3
  Cheadle SK3 ....122 F7
  Eccles M30 ....79 B4
  Heywood OL10 .....29 C3
  Leigh WN7 ....57 D1
  Littleborough OL15 .16 A7
  Manchester M20 ...110 C3
  Sale M33 ....108 B4
Melrose Cl M45 ...44 F2
Melrose Cres
  Altrincham WA15 ..120 B1
  Garswood WN4 ....72 C3
  High Lane SK12 ...134 D5
  Stockport SK3 .....123 D4
Melrose Ct
  Handforth SK9 ....131 E1
  Oldham OL9 ....66 A4
Melrose Dr WN3 ...54 D3
Melrose Gdns M26 .43 E5
Melrose Rd Little Lever BL3 .42 F3
  Radcliffe M26 .....43 E5
Melrose St Failsworth M40 .83 C5
  Oldham OL1 ....49 B1
  Ramsbottom BL9 ..11 B2
  Rochdale OL11 ....139 D7
Melsomby Rd M23 ..109 A2

Meltham Ave M20 ...110 A6
Meltham Cl SK4 ....110 E1
Meltham Pl BL3 ....147 D4
Meltham Rd SK4 ...110 E1
Melton Ave Reddish M34 .100 A3
  Urmston M41 ......94 D3
Melton Cl Heywood OL10 .29 B1
  Tyldesley M29 .....77 B8
  Walkden M28 ......60 C2
Melton Dr BL9 .....45 A5
Melton Rd M8 .....63 E1
Melton Row M26 ...43 F4
Melton St Heywood OL10 .29 B1
  Manchester M9 ....64 F1
  Radcliffe M26 .....43 F4
  Reddish SK5 ......169 F4
Melton Way M26 ...43 F4
Melverley Rd M9 ..64 A5
Melverley St WN3 .150 A7
Melville Cl M11 ...99 E7
Melville Ct M20 ...110 A2
Melville Rd Irlam M44 .105 C5
  Kearsley BL4 ......60 F6
  Stretford M32 .....96 B3
Melville St Ashton-u-L OL6 .166 B3
  Bolton BL3 ....42 A4
  Manchester M3 ...158 D2
  Oldham OL4 ....67 C5
  Rochdale OL11 ....30 D1
Melvin Ave M22 ...121 E4
Melyncourt Rd SK14 .102 E3
Memorial Rd M28 ...60 D2
Menai Gr SK8 .....123 A6
Menai Rd SK8 .....170 E6
Menai St BL3 ......146 B4
Mendip Av Wigan WN3 .54 C3
  Wythenshawe M22 .121 F4
Mendip Cl Bolton BL2 .43 A7
  Gatley SK8 ....131 B7
  Horwich BL6 ....22 C5
  Oldham OL9 ....152 A5
  Royton OL2 ....48 C3
  Stockport SK4 ....169 E3
Mendip Cres BL8 ..27 B3
Mendip Ct Platt Bridge WN2 56 B3
  Stockport SK4 ....169 E3
Mendip Dr Bolton BL2 .43 A6
  Milnrow OL16 .....32 A7
Mendip Rd OL8 ....66 D3
Mendips Cl OL2 ...48 F8
Menston Ave M40 .65 E1
Mentmore Rd OL16 .31 D8
Mentone Cres M22 .121 E4
Mentone Rd SK4 ..168 C3
Mentor St M13 ....98 F3
Menzies Ct M21 ...97 B1
Mercer Cres BB4 ...1 A8
Mercer La OL11 ...29 E8
Mercer Rd M18 ...99 D5
Mercer St Droylsden M43 .84 B2
  Manchester M19 ...99 B1
  Newton-le-W WA12 .89 D4
Mercer's Rd OL10 .46 D7
Merchants Cres WA3 .74 E1
Merchants Quay M5 .161 A6
Mercia St BL3 ......144 C5
Mercian Mall OL6 ..166 B3
Mercian Way SK3 ..170 E7
Mercury Bsns Pk M41 .95 F6
Mercury Way M41 ..95 F6
Mere Ave Droylsden M43 .99 B8
  Leigh WN7 ....75 D5
  Middleton M24 ....65 A6
  Salford M6 ....154 E2
Mere Bank Cl M28 .60 C3
Mere Cl Reddish M34 .100 B2
  Sale M33 ....108 F3
  Whitefield BL9 ....45 B5
Mere Dr Manchester M20 .110 B4
  Swinton M27 ......62 A2
Mere Fold M28 ....60 B3
Mere Gdns BL1 ...145 E8
Mere Gr WA11 ....71 B1
Mere Ho SK4 ......110 E1
Mere La OL11 .....139 F5
Mere Oaks Sch WN1 .37 B5
Mere Rd Ashton-in-M WN4 .73 C4
  Newton-le-W WA12 .89 F4
Mere Side SK15 ...85 F4
Mere St Leigh WN7 .75 D5
  Rochdale OL11 ....139 F6
  Wigan WN5 ....54 E5
Mere The Ashton-u-L OL6 .85 E6
  Cheadle SK8 ......123 A4
Mere Wlk BL1 .....145 E8
Merebank Cl OL11 .29 E8
Mereclough Ave M28 .60 F1
Meredew Ave M27 .79 E6
Meredith St Bolton BL3 .147 F3
  Manchester M14 ..110 D7
Merefield Ave OL11 .139 E5
Merefield Rd WA15 .120 C5
Merefield St OL11 .139 E5
Merefield Terr OL11 .139 E5
Merefold BL6 ......21 F3
Merehall Cl BL1 ..145 E8
Merehall Dr BL1 ..145 E8
Merehall St BL1 ..143 E1
Mereland Ave M20 .110 C4
Mereland Cl WN5 ..53 E6
Meremanor M28 ...60 F1
Merepool Cl SK6 ..125 C2
Mereside Cl SK8 ..122 F4
Mereside Gr M28 ..60 E3
Mereside Wlk M23 .162 D6
Merewood Ave M22 .121 D6

Meriden Cl M26 ....43 F6
Meriden Gr BL6 ...40 D6
Meridian Pl M20 ..110 A4
Merinall Cl OL16 ..31 C7
Meriton Rd SK9 ...131 D4
Meriton Wlk M18 .99 B4
Merlewood BL0 ...1 E3
Merlewood Ave
  Droylsden M34 ....84 B1
  Oldham OL8 ....69 B8
  Reddish M19 ......111 C5
Merlewood Dr
  Swinton M27 ......79 C6
  Tyldesley M29 ....77 B8
Merlin Cl Hazel Grove SK2 .125 A6
  Littleborough OL15 .16 A2
  Oldham OL8 ....85 A8
Merlin Gr BL1 .....142 B1
Merlin Rd Irlam M44 .94 A4
  Milnrow OL16 .....31 C7
Merlyn Ave Denton M34 .100 C2
  Manchester M20 ..110 C4
  Sale M33 ....108 C6
Merlyn Ct M20 ....110 C4
Merrick Ave M22 ..121 E4
Merrick St OL10 ..29 E1
Merridale The WA15 .129 A8
Merridge Wlk M8 .155 F6
Merrill St M11 ....160 D1
Merriman St M16 ..97 E4
Merrion St BL4 ....42 C2
Merrow Wlk M1 ...163 B7
Merrybent Cl SK2 .124 D4
Merrybower Rd M7 .155 E8
Merrydale Ave M30 .79 E4
Merryman Hall OL16 .15 B2
Mersey Bank Rd SK14 .171 F4
Mersey Cl Hindley WN2 .57 C3
  Whitefield M45 ....45 B1
Mersey Cres M20 ..109 D3
Mersey Dr Partington M31 .106 A4
  Whitefield M45 ....45 B1
Mersey Drive Com Sch
  M45 ....45 C2
Mersey Ind Est
  Manchester SK4 ...110 E1
  Oldham M35 ......66 B1
Mersey Mdws M20 .109 F3
Mersey Rd
  Manchester M20 ..109 F3
  Manchester SK4 ...110 F2
  Orrell WN5 ....53 F7
  Platt Bridge WN2 .55 F2
  Sale M33 ....108 B6
Mersey Rd N M35 .66 B1
Mersey Sq Stockport SK1 .169 E1
  Whitefield M45 ....45 B1
Mersey St Droylsden M11 .99 E7
  Leigh WN7 ....75 C5
  Stockport SK1 ....112 C4
Mersey Vale Prim Sch
  SK4 ....168 A1
Merseybank Ave M21 .109 D4
Merseyway SK1 ...169 E2
Merston Dr M20 ..122 C8
Merton Ave
  Hazel Grove SK7 ..133 F8
  Oldham OL8 ....66 D3
  Romiley SK6 ....113 A4
Merton Cl BL3 ....144 C5
Merton Dr M43 ...83 E1
Merton Gr
  Altrincham WA15 .120 B6
  Failsworth OL9 ...65 D3
  Tyldesley M29 ....77 C6
Merton Rd Prestwich M25 .63 C5
  Sale M33 ....108 A6
  Stockport SK3 ....123 B8
  Wigan WN3 ....54 C3
Merton St BL8 ....140 D3
Merton Wlk M9 ...157 E7
Merville Ave M40 ..64 F1
Mervyn Pl WN3 ...55 B4
Mervyn Rd M7 ....81 B6
Merwell Rd M41 ..94 E1
Merwood Ave SK8 .131 D8
Merwood Gr M14 .98 E4
Mesne Lea Gr M28 .78 E8
Mesne Lea Rd M28 .60 E1
Mesne Lea Sch M28 .60 E1
Mesnefield Rd M7 ..81 A8
Mesnes Ave WN3 ..150 A5
Mesnes Park Terr WN1 .37 C1
Mesnes Rd Wigan WN1 .150 C8
  Wigan WN1 ....37 C3
Mesnes Terr WN1 .37 C1
Metal Box Way BL5 .40 A2
Metcalf Mews OL3 .69 B8
Metcalf Terr BL2 ..26 D1
Metcalfe St M46 ..59 F4
Metfield Pl BL1 ...144 C8
Metfield Wlk M40 .65 D2
Methodist Cotts BL5 .39 D3
Methuen St M12 ...99 B3
Methwold St BL3 ..146 C4
Metron Rd SK12 ..133 B4
Metroplex Bsns Ctr M5 .96 D8
Mevagissey Wlk OL4 .67 C8
Mews The Bolton BL1 .144 B8
  Gatley SK8 ....122 B5
  Hindley WN2 ......56 D5
  Manchester M10,M40 .160 E3
  Prestwich M25 ....63 B3
  Sale M33 ....108 A5
  Whitefield M45 ...62 D8
  Wilmslow SK9 ....130 D4
  Worsley M28 ......78 E6
Meyer St SK2,SK3 .170 F6

Meynell Dr WN7 ...75 F2
Meyrick Rd M6 ....81 A3
Meyrick St WN5 ...54 F6
Miall St OL11 .....139 F6
Micawber Rd SK12 .133 E2
Michael Ct M19 ...110 D2
Michael St M24 ....64 F8
Michael Wife La
  Edenfield BL0 .....1 F2
  Edenfield BL0 .....1 F3
Michaels Hey Par M23 .120 C8
Michigan Ave M5 ..96 F8
Mickleby Wlk M40 .160 D3
Micklehurst All Saints'
  CE Prim Sch OL5 ..68 E1
Micklehurst Ave M20 .109 E4
Micklehurst Gn SK2 .124 E5
Micklehurst Rd OL5 .68 E1
Mickleton M38 ....58 E4
Midbrook Wlk M22 .121 B1
Middle Field OL11 .13 E1
Middle Gate OL8 ..66 E2
Middle Gn OL6 ....166 C4
Middle Hill OL12 ..14 F4
Middle Hillgate SK1 .170 F8
Middle Newgate OL15 .16 B8
Middle Rd M41 ....95 F6
Middle St OL12 ....4 D1
Middle Wood La OL15 .15 E6
Middlebourne St M6 .154 E2
Middlebrook Dr BL6 .40 D6
Middlefield OL8 ...85 A8
Middlefields SK8 ..123 B4
Middlegate M40 ...65 D3
Middleham St M14 .98 A2
Middlesex Dr BL9 .44 F8
Middlesex Rd
  Brinnington SK5 ..112 C6
  Manchester M9 ...64 D2
Middlesex Wlk OL9 .153 D6
Middlestone Dr M9 .157 D7
Middleton Ave M35 .83 F7
Middleton Central Ind Est
  M24 ....64 F8
Middleton Cl BL8 ..43 F7
Middleton Dr BL9,M45 .44 F3
Middleton Old Rd M9 .64 D2
Middleton Parish
  CE Prim Sch M24 ..46 F2
Middleton Rd
  Chadderton M24,OL9 .47 C1
  Heywood OL16 ....46 E7
  Manchester M7,M8,M9 .63 F3
  Middleton M24 ....64 A6
  Oldham OL9 ....152 C7
  Reddish SK5 ......99 F2
  Royton OL2 ....48 C3
Middleton Rd W OL9 .65 E8
Middleton Tech Sch M24 .65 C8
Middleton View M24 .65 B8
Middleton Way M24 .64 F8
Middleway OL4 ...68 B5
Middlewich Wlk M18 .165 C5
Middlewood WA3 .90 E8
Middlewood Ct OL9 .152 A8
Middlewood Dr SK4 .168 A1
Middlewood Gn OL9 .152 A8
Middlewood Rd
  High Lane SK12,SK7 .134 C7
  High Lane SK6 ....134 D7
  Poynton SK12 ....134 B4
Middlewood St M5 .158 E2
Middlewood Sta (Lower)
  SK6 ....134 D6
Middlewood Wlk M9 .157 D7
Midford Ave M20 ..79 B2
Midford Dr BL1 ...24 E7
Midford Wlk M8 ..156 A6
Midge Hall Dr OL11 .30 A6
Midge Hill OL5 ....68 D4
Midgley Ave M18 ..99 E6
Midgley Cres OL6 .85 E4
Midgley Dr OL16 ..31 C2
Midgley St M27 ...79 D6
Midgrove OL3 .....50 F3
Midgrove La OL3 ..50 F4
Midhurst Ave M40 .83 B4
Midhurst Cl Bolton BL1 .143 E1
  Cheadle SK8 ......131 F8
Midhurst St OL11 .139 F5
Midhurst Way OL9 .152 B6
Midland Cl WN7 ..75 C6
Midland Rd Reddish SK5 .99 F2
  Stockport SK7 ....123 E3
Midland St M12 ...164 D7
Midland Wlk SK7 .123 E3
Midlothian St M11 .83 B2
Midmoor Wlk M9 .64 E3
Midville Rd M11 ..83 C3
Midway SK8 ......132 B5
Midway St M12 ...99 A2
Milan St M7 ....155 E7
Milbourne Rd BL9 .27 F6
Milburn Ave M23 .109 B2
Milburn Dr BL2 ...42 F8
Milbury Dr OL15 ..16 A2
Milden Cl M20 ....110 C4
Mildred Ave
  Manchester M25 ..63 C1
  Oldham OL2 ....48 E2
  Oldham OL4 ....68 B5
Mildred St M7 ....81 C5
Mile End La SK2 ..124 B6
Mile La BL8 ....26 C1
Miles Ave OL13 ...3 D8
Miles La Appley Bridge WN6 .35 E6
  Shevington WN6 ..36 A6
Miles St Bolton BL1 .143 D2

Miles St *continued*
Farnworth BL4 . . . . .60 C8
Hyde SK14 . . . . .167 F1
Manchester M12 . . . . .165 A7
Oldham OL1 . . . . .67 B8
Milford Ave 2 OL8 . . . . . . .66 C2
Milford Brow OL4 . . . . .67 E7
Milford Cres OL15 . . . . . . .16 B6
Milford Dr M19 . . . . .111 C7
Milford Gr SK2 . . . . .124 C7
Milford Rd Bolton BL2 . . . .25 F4
Bolton BL3 . . . . .147 E3
4 Wigan WN2 . . . . .37 F2
Milford St Ince-in-M WN3 .151 E6
Manchester M9 . . . . .64 B4
6 Rochdale OL12 . . . . .14 F1
Salford M6 . . . . .154 E2
Milk St Hyde SK14 . . . . . . .167 D2
Manchester M12 . . . . .159 A1
3 Oldham OL4 . . . . .67 C7
Ramsbottom BL0 . . . . .138 B5
Rochdale OL11 . . . . .139 F6
Tyldesley M29 . . . . .59 A1
Wigan WN3 . . . . .150 C7
Milkstone Pl OL11 . . . . . . .139 F6
Milkstone Rd OL11 . . . . . . .139 F6
Milkwood Gr 2 M18 . . . . . .99 D4
Mill Bank
Appley Bridge WN6 . . . . . . .35 D7
Bolton M26 . . . . .44 B2
Mill Beck Gr BL3 . . . . .147 E4
Mill Brook Ind Est M23 . . .120 E6
Mill Brow Chadderton OL1 . .48 A2
Manchester M9 . . . . .64 C2
Mottram-in-L SK14 . . . . . . .115 A8
Oldham OL6,OL8 . . . . .67 C2
Worsley M28 . . . . .78 F6
Mill Brow Rd SK6 . . . . . . .126 E8
Mill Croft Bolton BL1 . . . . .145 D8
Shaw OL2 . . . . .149 C6
Mill Croft Cl OL12 . . . . . . .13 C2
Mill Ct M41 . . . . .95 E1
Mill Fold Rd M24 . . . . .64 F8
Mill Gate Oldham OL8 . . . . .66 D2
Rochdale OL16 . . . . .15 C2
Mill Green Spec Sch
WA2 . . . . .89 E3
Mill Green St M12 . . . . . . .164 D8
Mill Hill M38 . . . . .59 E6
Mill Hill Ave SK12 . . . . . . .133 D7
Mill Hill Gr SK14 . . . . .102 F2
Mill Hill Hollow SK12 . . . . .133 D7
Mill Hill St BL2 . . . . .148 A8
Mill Hill Way 3 SK14 . . . . .102 F2
Mill House Cl OL12 . . . . . . .15 D4
Mill House View WN8 . . . . .53 C7
Mill La Altrincham WA15 . .129 E4
Appley Bridge WN6 . . . . . . .35 D7
Ashton-u-L OL6 . . . . .166 B2
Aspull WN2 . . . . .38 F3
4 Bury BL8 . . . . .27 B4
Cheadle SK8 . . . . .122 D6
Cheadle SK8 . . . . .123 B3
Denton M34,SK14 . . . . .101 B2
Droylsden SK5 . . . . .99 F1
Failsworth M35 . . . . .83 C7
Hazel Grove SK6 . . . . .125 B4
Hazel Grove SK7 . . . . .133 F8
Horwich BL6 . . . . .22 D4
Leigh WN7 . . . . .76 B4
Lymm WA13 . . . . .117 C4
Mossley OL5 . . . . .68 C2
Newton-le-W WA12 . . . . . . .89 B3
Oldham OL9 . . . . .66 C4
Orrell WN8 . . . . .53 A8
Reddish SK5 . . . . .112 B8
Romiley SK6 . . . . .113 A5
Royton OL2 . . . . .48 C4
Uppermill OL4 . . . . .50 D1
Westhoughton BL5 . . . . .57 E5
Wythenshawe M22 . . . . .109 E1
Mill Mdw Ince-in-M WN1 . .151 D7
Newton-le-W WA12 . . . . . . .89 B3
Mill Rd Bury BL9 . . . . .27 F8
Orrell WN5 . . . . .53 D5
Mill St Adlington PR6 . . . . .21 B8
Altrincham WA14 . . . . .119 E5
Ashton-in-M WN4 . . . . .73 C2
Bolton BL1 . . . . .148 A8
9 Bolton BL7 . . . . .24 F1
Boothstown M28 . . . . .78 A6
Bury BL8 . . . . .26 F8
Dukinfield SK14 . . . . .101 E5
Failsworth M35 . . . . .83 D7
Farnworth BL4 . . . . .60 C8
Glossop SK13 . . . . .104 D1
Golborne WA3 . . . . .90 A8
Hazel Grove SK7 . . . . .124 D3
Hindley WN2 . . . . .56 D5
Leigh WN7 . . . . .76 A4
Manchester M11 . . . . .165 A8
Mossley OL5 . . . . .86 C8
Oldham OL3 . . . . .69 B8
Radcliffe M26 . . . . .44 B2
Ramsbottom BL0 . . . . .11 A4
Royton OL2 . . . . .48 D4
Salford M6 . . . . .81 A4
Stalybridge SK15 . . . . .86 C1
Tyldesley M46 . . . . .58 E1
Westhoughton BL5 . . . . .57 F8
Wigan WN3 . . . . .150 B7
Wilmslow SK9 . . . . .137 B7
Mill Yd BL9 . . . . .141 A3
Millais St M40 . . . . .83 A8
Millam Cl OL16 . . . . .15 C1
Millar Barn La BB4 . . . . . . .2 F8
Millard St OL9 . . . . .152 A7
Millard Wlk 4 M18 . . . . . . .99 D4

Millbank Ct OL10 . . . . .29 B2
Millbank St Heywood OL10 .29 B2
Manchester M1,M4 . . . . . . .159 C1
Millbeck Cres WN5 . . . . . . .54 D5
Millbeck Ct 4 M24 . . . . . . .46 D2
Millbeck Gr WA11 . . . . .71 B2
Millbeck Rd M24 . . . . .46 D2
Millbeck St 4 M15 . . . . . . .163 A6
Millbrae Gdns OL2 . . . . . . .48 F7
Millbrook SK14 . . . . .103 E6
Millbrook Ave
Atherton M46 . . . . .58 E5
Denton M34 . . . . .100 D1
Millbrook Bank OL11 . . . . .13 D1
Millbrook Cl OL2 . . . . .49 D6
Millbrook Gr 1 SK9 . . . . . .131 D1
Millbrook Ho BL4 . . . . .60 E8
Millbrook Prim Sch
Mossley SK15 . . . . .86 E5
Shevington WN6 . . . . .36 B6
Millbrook Rd M23 . . . . .121 A4
Millbrook St SK1 . . . . .170 F8
Millcrest Cl M28 . . . . .77 F5
Millcroft Ave WN5 . . . . .53 D5
Millcroft La OL3 . . . . .51 A7
Milldale Cl M46 . . . . .58 C3
Milldale Rd WN7 . . . . .75 B1
Miller Meadow Cl OL2 . .149 C8
Miller Rd OL8 . . . . .66 E3
Miller St Ashton-u-L OL6 . .166 C4
Blackrod BL6 . . . . .38 E7
Bolton BL1 . . . . .143 E4
Heywood OL10 . . . . .29 D2
Manchester M4 . . . . .159 A2
Radcliffe M26 . . . . .43 F6
Ramsbottom BL9 . . . . .11 C2
Miller's La Atherton M46 . .58 D1
Platt Bridge WN2 . . . . .56 A4
Millers Brook Cl OL10 . . . .29 D3
Millers Cl M23 . . . . .109 A3
Millers Ct M5 . . . . .80 A2
Millers La WA13 . . . . .117 B5
Millers St M30 . . . . .79 C2
Millersdale Ct SK13 . . . . . .104 F1
Millet Terr BL9 . . . . .28 E7
Millett St Bury BL9 . . . . . .140 D2
Ramsbottom BL0 . . . . .11 D7
Millfield Ct WA15 . . . . .119 F2
Millfield Dr M28 . . . . .78 B6
Millfield Gr OL16 . . . . .31 B6
Millfield La WN4,WA11 . . . .72 E1
Millfield Rd BL3 . . . . .43 A7
Millfield Wlk 2 M40 . . . . . .65 C2
Millfold OL12 . . . . .4 D2
Milford Ave M41 . . . . .94 E2
Milford Gdns M41 . . . . .94 E2
Millgate Bolton BL7 . . . . . . .8 D2
Delph OL3 . . . . .50 F4
Stockport SK1 . . . . .169 F2
Wigan WN1 . . . . .150 C8
Millgate La M20 . . . . .110 B1
Millgate Terr OL12 . . . . . . .4 E5
Millhall Cl M15 . . . . .162 E5
Millhead Ave M40 . . . . .160 E2
Millhouse Ave M23 . . . . . . .121 A4
Millhouse St BL0 . . . . .11 E8
Milling St M1 . . . . .162 F8
Millingford Ave WA3 . . . . . .73 F2
Millingford Gr WA3 . . . . . . .73 B3
Millingford Ind Est WA3 . . .90 A8
Millington Wlk 9 M15 . . . .162 D6
Millom Ave M23 . . . . .109 B1
Millom Dr BL9 . . . . .45 A2
Millom Pl SK8 . . . . .122 B3
Millow St M4 . . . . .159 A3
Millpool Wlk 1 M9 . . . . . . .157 D8
Millrise OL1 . . . . .153 E8
Mills Farm Cl OL8 . . . . . . .67 A1
Mills Hill Com Prim Sch
OL9 . . . . .65 E8
Mills Hill Rd M24 . . . . .65 D8
Mills Hill Sta M24 . . . . . . .47 D1
Mills St Heywood OL10 . . . .29 B2
Whitworth OL12 . . . . .4 D1
Millstone Cl SK12 . . . . .133 F5
Millstone Rd BL1 . . . . .23 F1
Millstream La M40 . . . . . . .83 E4
Milltown SK13 . . . . .104 D1
Milltown Cl 3 M26 . . . . . . .44 B2
Milltown St M26 . . . . .44 B3
Millwall Cl M18 . . . . .99 D5
Millway WA15 . . . . .129 C2
Millway Wlk 19 M40 . . . . . .83 C5
Millwell La 5 BL1 . . . . . . .145 F7
Millwood
Ashton-in-M WN4 . . . . .73 A5
4 Cheadle SK8 . . . . .131 E8
Millwood Ct BL9 . . . . .44 F6
Millwood Prim Sch BL9 . . .44 F6
Millwood Terr 3 SK14 . . . .167 D2
Millwright St M40 . . . . .83 C5
Milne Cl M12 . . . . .165 A6
Milne St Haslingden BL0 . . .1 C5
Oldham OL2 . . . . .49 A2
Oldham OL9 . . . . .152 B7
Oldham OL9 . . . . .152 C5
Oldham OL9 . . . . .48 C1
Rochdale OL11 . . . . .30 C2
Shaw OL2 . . . . .149 B6
Milner Ave
Altrincham WA14 . . . . .119 B7
Bury BL9 . . . . .27 F5
Milner St Manchester M16 . .97 D4
Pendlebury M27 . . . . .80 A4
Radcliffe M26 . . . . .43 E3
Whitworth OL12 . . . . .14 C8
Whitworth OL12 . . . . .4 C1

Milnes Ave WN7 . . . . .75 F2
Milngate Cl OL16 . . . . .31 C3
Milnholme BL1 . . . . .142 B3
Milnrow Cl M13 . . . . .163 B7
Milnrow Parish
CE Prim Sch OL16 . . . . . . .31 F6
Milnrow Rd
Littleborough OL15 . . . . . . .16 A2
Rochdale OL11,OL16 . . . . . .31 B7
Shaw OL16,OL2 . . . . .32 C2
Shaw OL2 . . . . .149 B7
Shaw OL2 . . . . .149 C8
Milnrow Sta OL16 . . . . .31 F5
Milnthorpe Rd BL2 . . . . . . .42 F8
Milnthorpe St M6 . . . . .81 B5
Milnthorpe Way M12 . . . . .164 E6
Milo St M9 . . . . .64 D3
Milsom Ave BL3 . . . . .146 C3
Milstead Wlk M40 . . . . .83 A5
Milston Wlk M8 . . . . .156 A6
Milton Ave Bolton BL3 . . . . .146 B4
Droylsden M43 . . . . .84 A1
Irlam M44 . . . . .105 E6
Little Lever BL3 . . . . .43 B4
Newton-le-W WA12 . . . . . . .89 B3
Salford M5 . . . . .154 D2
Stalybridge SK15 . . . . .86 E4
Milton Cl Atherton M46 . . . .58 D5
Dukinfield SK16 . . . . .102 B7
Haslingden BB4 . . . . .1 A7
Marple SK6 . . . . .125 F4
Stretford M32 . . . . .96 E3
Milton Cres Cheadle SK8 . .122 C5
Farnworth BL4 . . . . .60 B6
Milton Ct Bramhall SK7 . . . .132 F6
Manchester M19 . . . . .110 E4
5 Manchester M7 . . . . . . .63 E1
Milton Dr Oldham OL9 . . . .152 A6
Poynton SK12 . . . . .133 D4
Sale M33 . . . . .108 B6
Sale WA15 . . . . .108 A1
Milton Gr Longshaw WN5 . .53 D1
Manchester M16 . . . . .97 C2
Orrell WN5 . . . . .53 F6
Sale M33 . . . . .108 A6
Wigan WN1 . . . . .37 C3
Wigan WN5 . . . . .54 A6
Milton La Prim Sch M28 . .60 B3
Milton Lo M16 . . . . .97 C2
Milton Mount 1 M18 . . . . .99 D4
Milton Pl M6 . . . . .81 B3
Milton Rd Bramhall SK7 . . .132 E7
Coppull PR7 . . . . .19 E8
Droylsden M34 . . . . .84 D1
Golborne WA3 . . . . .90 D7
Prestwich M25 . . . . .63 C5
Radcliffe M26 . . . . .43 E4
Stretford M32 . . . . .96 E3
Swinton M27 . . . . .61 D1
Milton St Denton M34 . . . .100 E4
Eccles M30 . . . . .79 D2
Hyde SK14 . . . . .167 D4
Leigh WN7 . . . . .75 E5
Manchester M7 . . . . .158 E4
Middleton M24 . . . . .46 F1
Mossley OL5 . . . . .68 C2
Ramsbottom BL0 . . . . .138 B6
Rochdale OL16 . . . . .139 F7
Royton OL2 . . . . .48 E4
Milton St John's
CE Prim Sch OL5 . . . . .68 C4
Milton Street Day Hospl
OL2 . . . . .48 E4
Milton View OL5 . . . . .68 D2
Milverton Ave SK14 . . . . . .102 C2
Milverton Cl BL6 . . . . .40 D5
Milverton Dr SK7,SK8 . . . .132 B5
Milverton Rd M14 . . . . .98 D3
Milverton Wlk SK14 . . . . . .102 C2
Milwain Dr SK4 . . . . .111 C6
Milwain Rd
Manchester M19 . . . . .111 A8
Stretford M32 . . . . .96 C1
Mimosa Dr M27 . . . . .61 F2
Mincing St 2 M4 . . . . .159 A3
Minden Cl Bury BL8 . . . . . . .27 B2
Manchester M20 . . . . .110 D4
Minden Par BL9 . . . . .140 F2
Minden St M6 . . . . .80 E6
Mine Cl OL10 . . . . .29 D4
Minehead Ave
Hindley WN7 . . . . .57 D2
Manchester M20 . . . . .109 F6
Urmston M41 . . . . .107 B8
Minerva Rd
Ashton-u-L OL6,SK16 . . . . .166 C2
Farnworth BL4 . . . . .42 A2
Minford Cl M40 . . . . .83 B6
Minnie St Bolton BL3 . . . . .146 B3
Whitworth OL12 . . . . .4 D2
Minoan Gdns M7 . . . . .81 C5
Minor St Failsworth M35 . . .66 A1
Rochdale OL11 . . . . .30 C1
Minorca Ave M11 . . . . .83 D2
Minorca Cl OL11 . . . . .29 E8
Minorca St BL3 . . . . .147 E4
Minshull St M1 . . . . .159 A1
Minshull St S M1 . . . . .163 B8
Minsmere Cl 1 M8 . . . . . . .156 A6
Minsmere Wlks SK2 . . . . .124 F4
Minstead Cl SK14 . . . . . . .102 A1
Minstead Wlk M22 . . . . . . .121 B2
Minster Cl Bolton BL2 . . . . .25 C2
Dukinfield SK16 . . . . .101 D6
Minster Dr
Altrincham WA14 . . . . .128 A8
Cheadle SK8 . . . . .123 A5
Minster Gr M29 . . . . .77 B7

Minster Rd Bolton BL2 . . . .25 C2
Manchester M9 . . . . .157 F6
Minster Way OL9 . . . . .48 A1
Minsterley Par M22 . . . . . .121 C1
Minstrel Cl WN2 . . . . .74 B7
Mint St BL0 . . . . .1 C2
Minto St OL7 . . . . .166 A4
Minton St Failsworth M40 . .83 C8
Oldham OL4 . . . . .67 A5
Mintridge Cl 9 M11 . . . . . .99 E7
Mirabel St M3 . . . . .158 F3
Mirfield Ave
Manchester M9 . . . . .64 D4
Oldham OL8 . . . . .66 E4
Stockport SK4 . . . . .168 B2
Mirfield Cl WA3 . . . . .90 D7
Mirfield Dr Eccles M30 . . . .79 D4
Manchester M9 . . . . .64 D4
Urmston M41 . . . . .95 C4
Mirfield Rd M9 . . . . .64 D4
Miriam Gr WN7 . . . . .76 A4
Miriam St 8 Bolton BL3 . . .146 B4
Failsworth M35 . . . . .83 D5
Miry La Westhoughton BL5 . .57 E6
Wigan WN3,WN6 . . . . .150 B8
Missenden Ho 12 M5 . . . . .154 F1
Mission St OL10 . . . . .29 C2
Missouri Ave M5 . . . . .154 E1
Mistletoe Gr M3 . . . . .158 D3
Mistral Ct M30 . . . . .79 E3
Mitcham Ave M9 . . . . .65 A3
Mitchell Cl SK8 . . . . .121 F6
Mitchell Gdns M22 . . . . . . .121 E4
Mitchell Hey OL12 . . . . . . .139 E7
Mitchell Rd WN5 . . . . .71 E5
Mitchell St
Ashton-in-M WN4 . . . . .73 C2
Bury BL8 . . . . .27 C4
Eccles M30 . . . . .79 C3
Failsworth M40 . . . . .83 B5
Golborne WA3 . . . . .90 A8
Ince-in-M WN2 . . . . .56 A7
Leigh WN7 . . . . .75 E4
Littleborough OL16 . . . . . . .15 C3
Manchester M11 . . . . .164 F8
Middleton M24 . . . . .46 F1
Oldham OL1 . . . . .153 E8
Rochdale OL12 . . . . .139 D8
Wigan WN5 . . . . .54 E6
Mitchells Quay M35 . . . . . . .83 E7
Mitcheson Gdns M6 . . . . . .154 F3
Mitford Rd M14 . . . . .110 C7
Mitford St M32 . . . . .96 C1
Mitre Cl M12,M13 . . . . .98 F4
Mitre St Bolton BL1 . . . . . .143 E4
Failsworth M35 . . . . .83 F8
Mitton Cl Bury BL8 . . . . . . .26 F2
Culcheth WA3 . . . . .91 E5
Heywood OL10 . . . . .28 F2
Mizpah Gr BL8 . . . . .27 B2
Mizzy Rd OL12 . . . . .14 F1
Moadlock SK6 . . . . .113 C4
Moat Ave M22 . . . . .121 C5
Moat Gdns M22 . . . . .121 C4
Moat Hall Ave M30 . . . . . . .95 A8
Moat Hall Sports Ctr M30 .79 A1
Moat House St WN2 . . . . . .56 A7
Moat Rd M22 . . . . .121 C4
Moat Wlk SK5 . . . . .112 C7
Mobberley Cl M19 . . . . . . .110 E4
Mobberley Rd
Ashley WA14,WA15,WA16 . .128 E3
Bolton BL2 . . . . .42 E8
Wilmslow SK9 . . . . .130 D1
Mocha Par M7 . . . . .158 D3
Modbury Cl SK7 . . . . .124 A3
Modbury Wlk 14 M8 . . . . . .156 A6
Mode Hill La M45 . . . . .45 C1
Mode Wheel Circ M17 . . . .96 C7
Mode Wheel Rd M5 . . . . . .154 D1
Mode Wheel Rd S M5 . . . .154 D1
Mode Wheel Wkshp M5 . . .96 D8
Modwen Rd M5 . . . . .161 B6
Moelfre Dr SK8 . . . . .132 C7
Moffat Cl BL2 . . . . .42 F6
Moggie La SK10 . . . . .133 F1
Moisant St BL3 . . . . .147 D3
Mold St Bolton BL1 . . . . . .143 E3
Oldham OL1 . . . . .153 E8
Molesworth St OL16 . . . . . .31 A7
Mollets Wood M34 . . . . . . .101 A5
Mollington Rd M22 . . . . . .130 E8
Molyneux Rd Reddish M19 .99 C1
Westhoughton BL5 . . . . .40 B1
Molyneux St
Rochdale OL12 . . . . .139 D8
Wigan WN1 . . . . .151 D8
Mona Ave Cheadle SK8 . . . .122 D7
Stretford M32 . . . . .96 C3
Mona St Hyde SK14 . . . . . .167 E2
Salford M6 . . . . .81 A4
Wigan WN1 . . . . .150 B8
Monaco Dr M22 . . . . .109 D8
Monarch Cl Irlam M44 . . . .105 E6
Oldham OL2 . . . . .48 E2
Monart Rd M9 . . . . .64 E1
Moncrieffe St Bolton BL3 . .148 A6
Bolton BL4 . . . . .148 A5
Mond Rd M44 . . . . .94 B4
Monde Trad Est M17 . . . . .96 A6
Money Ash Rd WA15 . . . . .119 E3
Monfa Ave SK2 . . . . .124 A4
Monica Ave M8,M9 . . . . . . .63 F2
Monica Gr M19 . . . . .110 F8
Monica Terr WN4 . . . . .73 B2
Monks Cl Manchester M8 . .64 B2

Monks Cl *continued*
Milnrow OL16 . . . . .31 E6
Monks Ct M5 . . . . .80 B2
Monks Hall Gr M30 . . . . . . .79 F2
Monks La BL2 . . . . .25 D2
Monks' St SK13 . . . . .116 A3
Monksdale Ave M41 . . . . . .95 B2
Monkswood OL1 . . . . .153 E7
Monkton Ave M18 . . . . .99 C3
Monkwood Dr 3 M9 . . . . . .157 E8
Monmouth Ave Bury BL9 . . .27 F5
Sale M33 . . . . .107 F5
Monmouth Cres WN4 . . . . .73 D2
Monmouth Rd SK8 . . . . . . .123 B1
Monmouth St
2 Manchester M18 . . . . . .99 E6
Middleton M24 . . . . .65 C8
Oldham OL9 . . . . .152 C5
Rochdale OL11 . . . . .139 F6
Monroe Cl Salford M6 . . . . .154 E4
Wigan WN3 . . . . .55 A3
Mons Ave OL11 . . . . .30 C8
Monsal Ave Manchester M7 .81 A7
Stockport SK2 . . . . .124 D7
Monsall Cl BL9 . . . . .45 A2
Monsall Rd M40,M9 . . . . . .157 E6
Monsall St
Manchester M40 . . . . .157 D5
Oldham OL8 . . . . .66 E3
Montagu Rd SK2 . . . . .124 D8
Montagu St SK6 . . . . .114 B2
Montague Ho SK3 . . . . . . .170 D8
Montague Rd
Ashton-u-L OL6 . . . . .85 D3
Manchester M16 . . . . .161 A5
Sale M33 . . . . .108 B4
Montague St BL3 . . . . .146 B3
Montague Way SK15 . . . . . .86 A2
Montana Sq 4 M11 . . . . . . .99 E7
Monteagle St M9 . . . . .64 B4
Montford Rise WN2 . . . . . . .38 A2
Montford St M5 . . . . .96 F8
Montfort Cl BL5 . . . . .57 D6
Montgomery OL11 . . . . . . .139 E6
Montgomery Dr BL9 . . . . . .45 B2
Montgomery Ho OL8 . . . . . .66 B1
Montgomery Rd M13 . . . . . .98 F2
Montgomery St
Oldham OL8 . . . . .66 B1
Rochdale OL11 . . . . .30 C4
Montgomery Way BL3,M26 .43 C5
Monton Ave M30 . . . . .79 E3
Monton Bridge Ct M30 . . . .79 C4
Monton Gn M30 . . . . .79 D4
Monton Green Prim Sch
Eccles M30 . . . . .79 C4
Eccles M30 . . . . .79 E4
Monton Ho SK5 . . . . .112 B4
Monton La M30 . . . . .79 E2
Monton Mews 4 WN1 . . . . .37 B3
Monton Prep Sch M30 . . . .79 D3
Monton Rd
Brinnington SK5 . . . . .112 C4
Eccles M30 . . . . .79 D3
Monton St Bolton BL3 . . . .147 E3
Manchester M14 . . . . .98 A4
Radcliffe M26 . . . . .43 F3
Montondale M30 . . . . .79 C3
Montonfields Rd M30 . . . . .79 C3
Montonmill Gdns M30 . . . .79 C3
Montpellior Rd M22 . . . . . .121 D2
Montreal St
Abram Brow WN7 . . . . .74 C4
3 Manchester M19 . . . . . .99 B1
Oldham OL8 . . . . .66 F4
Montrey Cres WN4 . . . . . . .72 C3
Montrose 2 M30 . . . . .79 E2
Montrose Ave Bolton BL2 . .25 C1
Dukinfield SK16 . . . . .101 C7
2 Manchester M20 . . . . . .110 A5
Ramsbottom BL0 . . . . .11 A2
Stockport SK2 . . . . .124 A3
Stretford M32 . . . . .96 B2
Wigan WN5 . . . . .54 D7
Montrose Cres 3 M19 . . . . .99 A1
Montrose Dr BL7 . . . . .25 D2
Montrose Gdns OL2 . . . . . .48 F4
Montrose Sch WN5 . . . . . . .54 D7
Montrose St OL11 . . . . .30 C1
Montserrat Brow BL1 . . . . .23 D2
Montserrat Rd BL1 . . . . . . .23 E2
Monument Mansions 6
WN1 . . . . .37 C2
Monument Rd WN1 . . . . . . .37 D2
Monyash Ct 18 SK13 . . . . .171 D1
Monyash Gr 19 SK13 . . . . .171 D1
Monyash Lea 20 SK13 . . . .171 D1
Monyash Mews SK13 . . . . .171 D1
Monyash Pl 17 SK13 . . . . .171 D1
Monyash View WN2 . . . . . .56 F3
Monyash Way 16 SK13 . . . .171 E1
Moody St WN6 . . . . .19 E1
Moon Gr M14 . . . . .98 D3
Moon St OL9 . . . . .152 C7
Moor Allerton Sch M20 . . .109 F4
Moor Ave WN6 . . . . .35 D4
Moor Bank La OL16 . . . . . .31 E3
Moor Cl M26 . . . . .43 E5
Moor Cres OL3 . . . . .51 B3
Moor Edge Rd OL5,SK15 . .86 F8
Moor End M22 . . . . .121 D8
Moor End Ave M7 . . . . .81 C8
Moor End Ct M7 . . . . .81 C8
Moor End Rd SK6 . . . . . . .127 A5

Moor Gate BL2 ....25 D5
Moor Gate La OL15 ......15 E7
Moor Hill OL11 ....29 F8
Moor La Bolton BL1,BL3 ..145 E6
　Leigh WN7 ....75 E8
　Manchester M25,M7 .....81 B8
　Manchester M7 ....63 C1
　Uppermill OL3 ....51 C2
　Urmston M41 ....95 A3
　Wilmslow SK9 ....136 D5
　Wilmslow SK9 ....136 E5
　Woodford SK7 ....132 E3
　Wythenshawe M23 .....109 A2
Moor Lo SK4 ....168 B4
Moor Nook M33 ....108 D3
Moor Park Ave OL11 ....30 B2
Moor Park Rd M20 .....122 C8
Moor Platt M33 ....108 D3
Moor Platt CI BL6 ....22 F3
Moor Rd Haslingden BB4 ..1 A5
　Littleborough OL15 ......6 C1
　Orrell WN5 ....53 E6
　Ramsbottom BL8 ....138 A6
　Wythenshawe M23 .....120 E8
Moor Side La OL10 .....12 A7
Moor St Bury BL9 ......140 F3
　Eccles M30 ....79 B1
　Heywood OL10 ....29 B2
　Oldham OL1 ....67 B7
　Shaw OL2 ....149 A6
　Swinton M27 ....79 F7
Moor Top PI SK4 ....168 B3
Moor View Bacup OL13 ...3 B7
　Rawtenstall BB4 ....2 F6
Moor View CI OL12 .....13 F2
Moor Way BL8 ....10 C3
Moorbottom Rd BL8 .....10 C5
Moorby Ave M19 ....110 E4
Moorby St ⁊ OL1 ....67 A8
Moorby Wlk ⁊ 145 F5
Moorclose St M24 ....65 C8
Moorcock Ave M27 .....80 B8
Moorcot Ct M23 ....120 F7
Moorcroft Edenfield BL0 ...1 D2
　Rochdale OL11 ....30 F3
Moorcroft Dr M19 .....110 E4
Moorcroft Rd M23,M33 ..108 F1
Moorcroft Sq SK14 .....101 E6
Moorcroft St
　⁊ Droylsden M43 ....84 B1
　Oldham OL8 ....66 C2
Moordale Ave OL4 ......49 E1
Moordale St M20 ......110 A5
Moordown CI M8 ......156 B6
Moore Gr WA13 ....117 B5
Moore Ho M30 ....95 D8
Moore St Rochdale OL16 .139 F7
　Wigan WN1 ....37 E1
Moore St E WN1 ....37 E1
Moore Wlk ⁊⁊ M34 ....113 A7
Moore's Ct ⁊ BL1 .....144 C8
Mooredge Terr OL2 ......48 E2
Moores La WN6 ....19 D2
Moorfield Boothstown M28 ..77 F6
　Edgworth BL7 ....9 D6
　Manchester M7 ....63 C1
　Radcliffe M26 ....43 E4
　Worsley M28 ....78 F8
Moorfield Ave
　Denton M34 ....101 A2
　Littleborough OL15 .....16 A7
　Manchester M14 ....110 C7
　Stalybridge SK15 ......102 D7
Moorfield Chase BL4 ....60 D7
Moorfield CI ⁊ Eccles M30 79 D1
　Irlam M44 ....94 B3
　Swinton M27 ....79 D6
Moorfield Cres WA3 .....91 A7
Moorfield Dr
　Dukinfield SK14 ....101 E5
　Wilmslow SK9 ....136 E5
Moorfield Gr Bolton BL2 ..25 B7
　Manchester SK4 ....168 B4
　Sale M33 ....108 D3
Moorfield Hamlet OL2 ...48 F7
Moorfield Hts SK15 ......86 E7
Moorfield Inf Sch SK7 ...124 C1
Moorfield Jun Sch SK7 ..124 C1
Moorfield Mews OL2 ...149 B7
Moorfield Par M44 ......94 B3
Moorfield PI ⁊ OL12 ....14 F1
Moorfield Prec SK14 ...103 D5
Moorfield Prim Sch M44 ..94 A3
Moorfield Rd Irlam M44 ...94 B3
　⁊ Oldham OL8 ....66 B2
　Salford M6 ....80 D5
　Swinton M27 ....79 C6
Moorfield St
　Hollingworth SK14 ....103 D5
　⁊ Manchester M20 ...110 B7
　Platt Bridge WN2 ....56 B3
Moorfield Terr
　Hollingworth SK14 ....103 D5
　Mossley SK15 ....86 E7
Moorfield Wlk M41 .....95 D2
Moorgate BL9 ....141 A3
Moorgate Ave
　Manchester M20 ......109 F6
　Rochdale OL11 ....30 A7
Moorgate Ct BL2 ....25 B1
Moorgate Dr Mossley SK15 86 E6
　Tyldesley M29 ....77 C5
Moorgate Mews SK15 ...86 E7

Moorgate Prim Sch BL2 .148 B8
Moorgate Rd Bury BL8 ..43 F8
　Mossley SK15 ....86 E7
Moorgate St OL3 ....69 B8
Moorhead St M4 ....159 B8
Moorhey Rd M38 ....59 F6
Moorhey St OL4 ....67 B6
Moorhill Ct M7 ....63 C1
Moorhouse
　Com Prim Sch OL16 ....31 E6
Moorhouse Farm OL16 ..31 E6
Moorhouse Fold OL16 ...31 E6
Moorings CI WN1 ......151 F8
Moorings Rd M17 ....96 B8
Moorings The Disley SK12 135 E6
　Eccles M28 ....79 A5
　Uppermill OL5 ....68 E3
Moorland Ave
　Droylsden M43 ....83 E1
　Manchester M8 ....63 F2
　Milnrow OL16 ....32 A6
　Rochdale OL11 ....29 F8
　Sale M33 ....108 C3
　Uppermill OL3 ....50 F2
　Whitworth OL12 ....14 C7
Moorland Cres OL12 ....14 C7
Moorland Dr Cheadle SK8 .131 F8
　Horwich BL6 ....22 F3
　Walkden M38 ....60 A6
Moorland Gr BL1 ......142 A2
Moorland Rd
　Ashton-in-M WN4 ......73 E5
　Hindley WN2 ....56 C5
　Manchester M20 ......110 B3
　Mossley SK15 ....86 E5
　Stockport SK2 ....124 B4
Moorland St
　Littleborough OL15 .....16 C7
　Rochdale OL12 ....14 E1
Moorland Terr OL12 ....14 A1
Moorlands Ave Leigh WN7 .75 F3
　Urmston M41 ....95 B3
Moorlands Cres OL5 ....68 D1
Moorlands Dr OL5 ......68 E3
Moorlands Jun Sch M33 .108 E5
Moorlands St OL2 ......149 C7
Moorlands View
　Bolton BL3 ....146 A2
　Edenfield BL0 ....1 D5
Moorlea M35 ....83 F8
Moorsbrook Gr ⁊ SK9 .131 E1
Moorsholme Ave ⁊ M40 .83 A7
Moorside
　Littleborough OL15 .....16 D6
　Rochdale OL11 ....30 F3
Moorside & Wardley Sta
　M27 ....61 D1
Moorside Ave
　Ainsworth BL2 ....26 D1
　Bolton BL1 ....142 A1
　Droylsden M43 ....84 C2
　Farnworth BL4 ....60 B7
　Horwich BL6 ....22 C4
　Oldham OL4 ....49 F4
Moorside CI SK13 .....116 B7
Moorside Cres M43 ....84 C2
Moorside Ct
　Dukinfield M34 ....101 A4
　Sale M33 ....108 B4
Moorside High Sch M27 .79 D7
Moorside Ho WA15 ....120 C7
Moorside La M34 ......101 A4
Moorside Lo M27 ....79 D8
Moorside Prim Sch
　Droylsden M43 ....84 B1
　Swinton M27 ....79 D7
Moorside Rd Bury BL8 ..26 E5
　Manchester M25,M7 ...81 C8
　Manchester M8 ....64 A1
　Manchester SK4 ....168 A2
　Mossley OL5 ....68 E1
　Swinton M27 ....79 D8
　Urmston M41 ....94 E3
　Urmston M41 ....95 B3
Moorside St M43 ....84 C2
Moorside View OL2 ....149 C8
Moorside Wlk WN5 .....54 B8
Moorsley Dr M9 ....64 F4
Moorsview BL0 ....138 B6
Moorton Ave M19 .....110 F7
Moorton Pk M19 ......110 F7
Moortop CI M9 ....64 C6
Moorville Rd M6 ....80 C5
Moorway M9 ....136 D5
Moorway Dr M9 ....65 A4
Moorwood Dr Oldham OL8 .67 C4
　Sale M33 ....107 E3
Mora Ave OL9 ....48 B1
Mora St M9 ....157 F8
Moran CI SK9 ....131 E2
Moran Wlk ⁊ M15 .....162 F6
Morar Dr BL2 ....43 A7
Morar Rd SK16 ....101 D7
Moravian CI SK16 .....166 C1
Moravian Field ⁊ M43 .100 A8
Moray CI BL0 ....11 A4
Moray Rd OL9 ....66 A4
Morbourne CI M12 ....164 E6
Morden Ave
　Ashton-in-M WN4 ......73 B3
　⁊⁊ Droylsden M11 ....83 C2
Morecambe CI M40 ....83 B6
Morely St OL4 ....49 E1
Moresby Dr M20 ......122 B8
Moresby Rd WN7 ....75 D5
Moreton Ave
　Bramhall SK7 ....132 E5

Moreton Ave continued
　Sale M33 ....107 F3
　Stretford M32 ....96 D2
　Whitefield M45 ....44 F1
Moreton CI
　Dukinfield SK16 ......101 D6
　Golborne WA3 ....73 F1
Moreton Dr Bury BL8 ...27 B3
　Handforth SK9 ....131 E3
　Leigh WN7 ....75 E1
　Poynton SK12 ....133 F4
Moreton La SK2 ....124 C7
Moreton St OL9 ....65 F8
Moreton Wlk SK2 .....124 D7
Morgan PI SK5 ....169 F4
Morgan St OL15 ....16 B5
Morillon Rd M44 ....94 A4
Morland Rd M16 ....97 C4
Morley Ave
　Manchester M14 ......98 A1
　Swinton M27 ....79 E6
Morley Gn SK9 ....130 C1
Morley Rd M26 ....43 D4
Morley St Atherton M46 .58 C2
　Bolton BL3 ....145 D6
　Bury BL9 ....44 F8
　Glossop SK13 ....116 D8
　Rochdale OL16 ....15 B1
　Whitefield M45 ....62 F8
Morley Way OL3 ....69 B5
Morna Wlk M12 ....164 D8
Morningside CI
　Droylsden M43 ....100 A7
　⁊⁊ Rochdale OL12 ....14 D4
Morningside Dr M20 ..122 C8
Mornington Ave SK8 ..122 D3
Mornington Cres M14 .110 B8
Mornington Ct ⁊ OL1 .153 E8
Mornington High Sch
　WN2 ....56 F5
Mornington Rd
　Adlington PR6 ....21 B8
　Atherton M46 ....58 F6
　Bolton BL1 ....144 B8
　Cheadle SK8 ....122 D4
　Hindley WN2 ....56 F5
　Rochdale OL11 ....31 A3
　Sale M33 ....108 D5
Morpeth CI Ashton-u-L OL7 .84 E4
　Manchester M12 ......164 E5
Morpeth St M27 ....79 E6
Morrell Rd M22 ....121 E8
Morris Fold Dr BL6 .....40 C6
Morris Gn BL3 ....146 C2
Morris Gr M41 ....106 E8
Morris Green Bsns Pk
　BL3 ....146 C4
Morris Green La BL3 ..146 C3
Morris Green St BL3 ..146 C2
Morris Ho WN1 ....151 D8
Morris Rd WN8 ....53 A7
Morris St Bolton BL1 ..148 A7
　⁊ Hindley WN2 ....56 D5
　Ince-in-M WN3 ....55 E4
　Manchester M20 ......110 B7
　Oldham OL4 ....67 A5
　Radcliffe BL9 ....44 E5
　Tyldesley M29 ....58 F1
　Wigan WN1 ....151 D8
Morrison St BL3 ....147 E3
Morrison Wlk M40 .....83 A5
Morrowfield Ave M8 ..155 F7
Morse Rd M40 ....83 B5
Mort Fold M38 ....60 A5
Mort La M28,M29,M38 ..59 E2
Mort St Farnworth BL4 ..60 B8
　Hindley WN2 ....57 A5
　Horwich BL6 ....22 B4
　Leigh WN7 ....75 B5
　⁊ Tyldesley M29 ......58 F1
　Wigan WN6 ....37 A1
Mortar St Oldham OL4 ..67 C7
　Oldham OL4 ....67 C8
Mortfield Gdns BL1 ...145 D8
Mortfield La BL1 ......145 D8
Mortimer Ave M9 ......64 E4
Mortimer St OL1 ....67 A8
Mortlake CI M28 ....59 F3
Mortlake Dr M40 ....83 B5
Morton Ave WN3 ......150 B5
Morton CI WN3 ....54 C2
Morton St Failsworth M35 .83 C6
　Middleton M24 ....47 A1
　Radcliffe M26 ....44 B2
　Stockport SK4 ....169 E4
Morton Terr
　⁊⁊ Denton M34 ......101 A1
　Romiley SK6 ....113 B5
Mortons The BL5 ....39 E2
Morven Ave SK7 ......124 F3
Morven Dr M23 ....121 A5
Morven Gr BL2 ....42 F7
Morville Dr WN3 ....55 B4
Morville Rd M21 ....97 D1
Morville St M1 ....163 C8
Moschatel Wlk M31 ...106 A3
Moscow Rd SK3 ....170 D7
Moscow Rd E SK3 .....170 D7
Mosedale Ave WA11 ...71 B1
Mosedale CI
　Altrincham M23 ......120 E6
　Tyldesley M29 ....77 C6
Mosedale Rd M24 ......46 E2
Moseldene Rd SK2 ....124 D5
Moseley Ct WN7 ....91 F1
Moseley Grange SK8 ..122 F3
Moseley Rd Cheadle SK8 .122 F3

Moseley Rd continued
　Manchester M14 ......110 E8
Moseley St SK3 ....170 E8
Moses Gate Ctry Pk BL3 .42 D4
Moses Gate Sta BL4 ...42 C2
Moses Gate Wkshp ⁊ BL4 42 D2
Mosley Ave Bury BL9 ..27 F5
　Ramsbottom BL0 ......11 B2
Mosley CI WA15 ......119 F7
Mosley Common Rd
　Boothstown M28 ....78 A7
　Boothstown M28,M29 ..77 F7
Mosley Rd
　Altrincham WA15 ....120 B6
　Stretford M17 ....96 C6
Mosley St
　Manchester M1,M2 ...159 A1
　Radcliffe M26 ....43 F4
Mosley Street Sta M1 .159 A1
Moss Ave Leigh WN7 ...76 B5
　Orrell WN5 ....53 D3
　Rochdale OL16 ....31 C6
Moss Bank
　Bramhall SK7,SK8 ....132 C5
　Manchester M8 ....156 A8
Moss Bank Ave M43 ...84 C2
Moss Bank CI BL1 ....143 E4
Moss Bank Ct M43 ....84 C2
Moss Bank Gr M27 ....61 D2
Moss Bank Ho BL1 ...142 A3
Moss Bank Rd
　Billinge WA11 ....71 B2
　Swinton M27 ....61 D2
Moss Bank Way
　Bolton BL1 ....142 B3
　Bolton BL1 ....23 E1
Moss Bridge Rd OL16 ..31 C5
Moss Brook Rd M9 ...157 E7
Moss CI Haslingden BB4 ...1 A8
　Radcliffe M26 ....43 D5
Moss Colliery Rd M27 ..61 E4
Moss Croft ⁊ M41 ......94 E3
Moss Cty Prim Sch The
　BL3 ....42 F6
Moss Dr BL6 ....22 F3
Moss Farm CI M24 ....65 B6
Moss Field Com Sch OL10 29 C3
Moss Fold M29 ....77 C8
Moss Gate Rd OL2 .....32 A1
Moss Gn M31 ....106 F6
Moss Gr Lymm WA13 ..117 B4
　Shaw OL2 ....31 E1
　Standish WN6 ....36 E8
Moss Grange Ave M16 ..97 D4
Moss Grove Ct ⁊ M15 .97 E4
Moss Hall Rd BL9,OL10 ..45 F7
Moss Hey Dr M23 .....109 B1
Moss Hey Prim Sch SK7 .132 C5
Moss Hey St OL2 ......149 C6
Moss House La M28 ...78 A5
Moss House Terr M9 ...64 C1
Moss Ind Est Golborne WN7 75 B1
　Rochdale OL11 ....31 B5
Moss La Alderley Edge SK9 137 B1
　Altrincham WA14,WA15 .119 E4
　Altrincham WA15 ....119 F7
　Altrincham WA15 ....120 A5
　Appley Bridge WN6 ...18 E3
　Ashton-u-L OL7 ....84 E2
　Blackrod BL6 ....21 F2
　Bolton BL1 ....142 B3
　Bramhall SK7 ....132 D5
　Fowley Common WA3 ..92 D5
　Golborne WA3 ....90 B5
　Irlam M44 ....105 D5
　Kearsley BL4 ....61 B5
　Middleton M9 ....64 F5
　Mottram-in-L SK14 ...114 F8
　Partington M31 ......105 F3
　Partington M31,WA13,WA14
　　M31,WA13,WA14 ...106 A2
　Platt Bridge WN2 ......56 A3
　Rochdale OL16 ....31 A6
　Royton OL2 ....49 A3
　Sale M33 ....107 B3
　Sale M33 ....107 E4
　Swinton M27 ....61 D2
　Tyldesley M29 ....77 A1
　Urmston M41 ....95 A5
　Walkden M28 ....60 E4
　Whitefield M45 ....62 F8
　Wilmslow WA16 ......136 A4
　Wythenshawe SK9 ...130 E6
Moss La E M14,M16 ....98 A4
Moss La W M15,M16 ....97 E4
Moss Lea BL1 ....143 D4
Moss Lodge La OL7 ....84 E1
Moss Manor M33 .....107 E3
Moss Mdw BL5 ....39 E2
Moss Meadow Rd M6 ..80 C4
Moss Mill St OL16 ......31 B5
Moss Park Jun & Inf Sch
　M32 ....96 B2
Moss Park Rd M32 .....96 B2
Moss PI ⁊ BL9 ....44 A8
Moss Rd Alderley Edge SK9 137 C2
　Irlam M44 ....105 C7
　Irlam M44 ....93 B1
　Kearsley BL4 ....60 E5
　Orrell WN5 ....53 D3
　Sale M33 ....107 B3
　Stretford M32 ....96 C3
Moss Rose SK9 ....137 B2
Moss Row Bury BL9 ...140 F1
　Rochdale OL11 ....13 D1
Moss Shaw Way M26 ..43 D2
Moss Side
　Hollinfare WA3 ....105 A2

Moss Side La continued
　Rochdale OL16 ....31 C5
Moss Side Rd M44 ....105 E6
Moss Side St OL12 ......4 E5
Moss St Bury BL9 .....140 E2
　Droylsden M34 ....84 B1
　Droylsden M34 ....84 B2
　⁊ Farnworth BL4 ......42 E1
　⁊ Heywood OL10 .....29 C2
　Hollingworth SK14 ...103 D5
　Ince-in-M WN3 ....55 F3
　Manchester M7 ......155 D5
　Oldham OL4 ....67 E8
　Platt Bridge WN2 ......56 A3
　Ramsbottom BL9 ......11 D2
　Rochdale OL16 ....31 B6
　⁊⁊ Wigan WN5 ....54 B6
　Wigan WN6 ....37 A1
Moss St E OL6 ....166 B3
Moss St W OL7 ....84 F2
Moss Terr Ashton-u-L OL6 .166 A2
　Rochdale OL16 ....31 B6
　⁊ Wigan WN5 ....54 B5
　Wilmslow SK9 ....137 F8
Moss The M24 ....65 B6
Moss Vale Cres M32 ....95 F3
Moss Vale Rd M41 .....95 E2
Moss View Prim Sch
　M31 ....106 A3
Moss View Rd Bolton BL2 .42 E8
　Partington M31 ......106 A3
Moss Way M33 ....107 E4
Mossack Ave ⁊ M22 ..121 D1
Mossbank CI SK13 ....171 E4
Mossbank Gr OL10 ....29 C3
Mossbray Ave M19 ...110 D4
Mossbrook Ct M40 ...159 C4
Mossbrook Dr M38 ....59 E6
Mossclough Ct M9 ....157 E7
Mosscot Wlk M13 ....163 B7
Mossdale Ave BL1 ......40 D7
Mossdale Rd
　Ashton-in-M WN4 ......73 A8
　Sale M33 ....107 F1
　Wythenshawe M23 ...108 F1
Mossdown Rd OL2 .....49 A3
Mossfield CI Bury BL9 ..141 B4
　Stockport SK4 ....168 B2
Mossfield Ct BL1 .....145 E8
Mossfield Dr M9 ....65 A4
Mossfield Gr M30 ......94 C4
Mossfield Prim Sch M27 .61 F1
Mossfield Rd
　Altrincham WA15 ....120 A5
　Farnworth BL4 ....60 B8
　Kearsley BL4 ....60 F5
　Swinton M27 ....61 F2
Mossgrove Rd WA15 ..119 F6
Mossgrove St ⁊ OL8 ...66 D2
Mosshall CI M15 .....162 D6
Mossland CI OL10 ......46 D8
Mossland Gr BL3 ....40 D2
Mosslee Ave M8 ....63 F3
Mossley CE Prim Sch OL5 .68 B1
Mossley Hollins High Sch
　OL5 ....68 C1
Mossley Rd
　Ashton-u-L OL6 ......166 C3
　Ashton-u-L OL6 ....85 E5
　Ashton-u-L OL6 ....86 A7
　Uppermill OL4 ....68 D5
Mossley Sta OL5 ....68 C1
Mossmere Rd SK8 ....123 A4
Mossway M24,M9 ......64 F5
Mosswood Pk M20 ...122 B8
Mosswood Rd SK9 ....131 E3
Mossy Lea Fold WN6 ..19 A3
Mossy Lea Rd WN6 ....18 F5
Moston Bank Ave M9 .157 F7
Moston Brook High Sch
　M40 ....157 F6
Moston Fields Prim Sch
　M40 ....65 A1
Moston La Manchester M40 .65 B2
　Manchester M9,M40 .157 F8
Moston La E OL9,M40 ..65 E1
Moston Lane Prim Sch
　M40 ....157 F8
Moston Rd M24 ....65 D5
Moston St Manchester M7 .155 F7
　Reddish SK5 ....111 F8
Moston Sta M40 ....65 D2
Mostyn Ave Bury BL9 ..27 F5
　Cheadle SK8 ....122 C1
　Manchester M14 .....110 E8
Mostyn Rd SK7 ....124 C1
Mostyn St SK15,SK16 .101 C8
Motcombe Farm Rd SK8 .122 B1
Motcombe Gr SK8 ....122 A3
Motcombe Rd SK8 ....122 A2
Mother Street Prim Sch
　M35 ....83 D7
Motherwell Ave ⁊ M19 .99 A1
Mottershead Ave BL3 ..43 A4
Mottershead Rd M22 .121 C4
Mottram Ave M21 ....109 C5
Mottram CE Prim Sch
　SK14 ....103 A3
Mottram CI SK8 ......123 A5
Mottram Dr
　Altrincham WA15 ....120 A5
　Wigan WN3 ....150 B5
Mottram Fold SK1 ....170 F6
Mottram Mews ⁊ BL6 ..22 B4
Mottram Moor SK14 ..103 B6
Mottram Old Rd
　Hyde SK14 ....114 B8
　Stalybridge SK15 ....102 D7

Mottram Rd
Alderley Edge SK9 ... 137 D1
Hattersley SK14 ... 102 C3
Mottram-in-L SK14 ... 115 A8
Sale M33 ... 108 F3
Stalybridge SK14,SK15 ... 102 D7
Mottram St Horwich BL6 ... 22 B4
5 Stockport SK1 ... 170 F8
Mough La OL9 ... 65 E3
Mouldsworth Ave
Manchester M20 ... 110 A7
Reddish SK4 ... 111 D6
Moulton St M8 ... 158 E4
Moulton St Prec M8 ... 158 E4
Mouncey St M1 ... 163 A7
Mount Ave
Littleborough OL12 ... 15 E4
Littleborough OL15 ... 16 A7
Rawtenstall BB4 ... 2 F8
Mount Carmel Cres M5 ... 161 C7
Mount Carmel Ct M5 ... 161 C7
Mount Carmel RC Jun Sch M9 ... 64 D2
Mount Cl 4 OL7 ... 166 A1
Mount Cres WN5 ... 53 F6
Mount Dr Marple SK6 ... 125 F5
Urmston M41 ... 95 F2
Mount Fold M24 ... 65 B7
Mount Gr SK8 ... 121 F6
Mount La OL3 ... 50 E1
Mount Pleasant
Adlington PR6 ... 21 A8
16 Bacup OL13 ... 3 C8
Bolton BL3 ... 148 C5
Edgworth BL7 ... 9 D5
Hazel Grove SK7 ... 124 D3
Middleton M24 ... 64 C8
Middleton M25 ... 63 F8
Ramsbottom BL9 ... 11 F3
Wilmslow SK9 ... 137 B8
Mount Pleasant Rd
Denton M34 ... 100 F2
Farnworth BL4 ... 59 F8
Mount Pleasant St
Ashton-u-L OL6 ... 166 C3
Dukinfield M34 ... 100 F7
Horwich BL6 ... 22 D1
Oldham OL4 ... 67 B7
Mount Pleasant Trad Est OL6 ... 166 C4
Mount Pleasant Wlk M26 ... 44 A4
Mount Rd
Manchester M18,M19 ... 99 C3
Middleton M24 ... 65 A7
Prestwich M25 ... 63 C6
Romiley SK14 ... 114 A6
Stockport SK4 ... 168 C2
Mount Sion Rd M26 ... 43 E2
Mount Skip La M38 ... 60 A4
Mount St Bolton BL1 ... 143 E1
Denton M34 ... 101 B1
Eccles M30 ... 95 C8
Glossop SK13 ... 116 C8
Heywood OL10 ... 29 D1
Horwich BL6 ... 22 D2
Hyde SK14 ... 167 E2
Leigh WN7 ... 75 C4
Manchester M2 ... 162 F8
Manchester M3 ... 158 D3
Oldham OL2 ... 48 E3
Ramsbottom BL0 ... 138 B6
Rochdale OL11 ... 30 C1
Rochdale OL12 ... 139 E8
Swinton M27 ... 79 F7
Mount St Joseph Sch BL4 ... 42 A2
Mount St Joseph's Rd BL3 ... 144 B5
Mount Terr M43 ... 83 E3
Mount The
Altrincham WA14 ... 119 D5
Altrincham WA15 ... 129 C8
Ashton-u-L OL6 ... 85 D3
Brinnington SK5 ... 112 B4
Mount View
Ince-in-M WN3 ... 151 D5
Oldham OL3 ... 69 B8
Mount View Rd OL2 ... 49 D6
Mount Zion Rd BL9 ... 44 F5
Mountain Ash OL12 ... 14 B3
Mountain Ash Cl
Rochdale OL12 ... 14 B3
9 Sale M33 ... 107 C5
Mountain Ash Cotts OL3 ... 33 D1
Mountain Gr M28 ... 60 C4
Mountain Rd PR7 ... 19 E8
Mountain St
Failsworth M40 ... 83 D4
Mossley OL5 ... 68 C1
Stockport SK1 ... 112 A2
Walkden M28 ... 60 C4
Mountbatten Ave SK16 ... 101 F6
Mountbatten Cl BL9 ... 45 C2
Mountbatten St M18 ... 165 C5
Mountfield M25 ... 63 B4
Mountfield Ct WN5 ... 53 F7
Mountfield Rd
Bramhall SK7 ... 132 E5
Stockport SK3 ... 123 C7
Mountfield Wlk
5 Bolton BL1 ... 143 E1
11 Manchester M11 ... 160 F1
Mountford Ave M8 ... 63 F2
Mountheath Ind Pk M25 ... 63 B1
Mountmorres Cl BL5 ... 59 A7
Mountroyal Cl SK14 ... 102 A5
Mountside Cl OL12 ... 14 F2
Mountside Cres M25 ... 62 F4
Mousell St M8 ... 159 A4
Mouselow Cl SK13 ... 171 F3
Mow Halls La OL3 ... 51 A1
Mowat Ct M14 ... 110 D8
Mowbray Ave
Manchester M25 ... 63 C1
Sale M33 ... 108 C3
Mowbray St
Ashton-u-L OL7 ... 166 A2
Bolton BL1 ... 142 B1
5 Oldham OL1 ... 153 F6
Rochdale OL11 ... 30 B3
Stockport SK1 ... 170 F8
Mowbray Wlk 4 M24 ... 46 E2
Moxley Rd M8 ... 63 F1
Moxon Way WN4 ... 73 D4
Moyse Ave BL8 ... 26 F5
Mozart Cl M4 ... 159 C2
Mudhurst La SK12 ... 135 E3
Muirfield Ave SK6 ... 113 A4
Muirfield Cl Bolton BL3 ... 40 F3
Failsworth M40 ... 83 C7
Heywood OL10 ... 29 D1
Prestwich M25 ... 63 B5
Wilmslow SK9 ... 137 D8
Muirfield Dr M29 ... 77 C7
Muirhead Ct M6 ... 81 A5
Mulberry Ave WA3 ... 90 F7
Mulberry Cl Gatley SK8 ... 131 C7
Rochdale OL11 ... 139 E5
Wigan WN5 ... 54 D6
Mulberry Ct
Altrincham WA14 ... 119 D6
7 Salford M6 ... 81 A3
Mulberry Mews SK4 ... 169 E2
Mulberry Mount St SK3 ... 170 E8
Mulberry Rd M6 ... 81 A3
Mulberry St
2 Ashton-u-L OL6 ... 166 C3
Manchester M2 ... 158 F1
Mulberry Wlk
Droylsden M43 ... 99 E8
Sale M33 ... 107 D6
Mule St BL2 ... 148 A7
Mulgrave Rd M28 ... 79 A8
Mulgrave St Bolton BL3 ... 146 C2
Swinton M27 ... 61 D1
Mulgrove Wlk 29 M9 ... 64 E3
Mull Ave M12 ... 164 F5
Mullacre Rd M22 ... 121 D6
Mulliner St 1 BL1 ... 143 F1
Mullineux St M28 ... 60 D2
Mullins Ave WA12 ... 89 C5
Mullion Cl M19 ... 99 D2
Mullion Dr WA15 ... 119 E6
Mullion Wlk M8 ... 156 B6
Mulmount Cl OL8 ... 66 C3
Mumps OL1 ... 67 A7
Mumps Sta OL4 ... 67 A6
Munday St M4 ... 160 D1
Munford Wlk M40 ... 157 E5
Municipal Cl 2 OL10 ... 29 D2
Munn Rd M9 ... 64 C5
Munro Ave Orrell WN5 ... 53 E6
Wythenshawe M22 ... 121 F2
Munslow Wlk M9 ... 64 F3
Munster St M4 ... 159 A3
Muriel St Heywood OL10 ... 29 E2
Manchester M7 ... 155 D5
Rochdale OL16 ... 31 B5
Murieston Rd WA15 ... 119 E2
Murphy Cl WN3 ... 150 A5
Murray Rd BL9 ... 140 F2
Murray St Atherton M46 ... 58 B2
Manchester M4 ... 159 C2
Manchester M7 ... 155 D6
Murrayfield OL11 ... 29 E6
Murrow Wlk 3 M9 ... 157 D8
Murton Terr BL1 ... 143 F4
Mus of Science & Ind M3 ... 162 E8
Mus of Science & Ind (Air & Space Gal) M3 ... 162 E8
Musbury Ave SK8 ... 123 B2
Musden Ave BB4 ... 1 A7
Musden Wlk SK4 ... 111 D7
Museum of the Manchesters The OL6 ... 166 B3
Museum of Transport M8 ... 156 B6
Museum St M2 ... 162 F8
Musgrave Gdns BL1 ... 144 C8
Musgrave Rd Bolton BL1 ... 144 C8
Wythenshawe M22 ... 121 D3
Muslin St M5 ... 81 C1
Mustard La WA3 ... 91 B1
Muter Ave M22 ... 121 F2
Mutual St OL10 ... 29 E3
My St M5 ... 154 E1
Mycroft Cl WN7 ... 75 E8
Myerscroft Cl M40 ... 65 E1
Myrrh St BL1 ... 143 E2
Myrtle Ave
Ashton-in-M WN4 ... 72 F6
Leigh WN7 ... 75 E7
Newton-le-W WA12 ... 89 C2
Myrtle Bank M25 ... 63 A1
Myrtle Cl OL8 ... 153 E5
Myrtle Gdns BL9 ... 141 B2
Myrtle Gr Billinge WN5 ... 71 D4
Droylsden M43 ... 84 C2
Manchester M25 ... 63 B2
Reddish M34 ... 99 F3
Whitefield M45 ... 44 D2
Myrtle Pl M7 ... 81 C4
Myrtle Rd Middleton M24 ... 47 C2
Partington M31 ... 105 D3
Myrtle St Bolton BL1 ... 145 D8
Manchester M11 ... 164 F8
Myrtle St *continued*
3 Manchester M16 ... 97 C4
Stockport SK3 ... 123 B8
Wigan WN1 ... 150 B8
Myrtle St N BL9 ... 141 B2
Myrtle St S BL9 ... 141 B2
Myrtleleaf Gr M5 ... 154 D2
Mytham Com Prim Sch BL3 ... 43 B3
Mytham Gdns BL3 ... 43 B2
Mytham Rd BL3 ... 43 B2
Mythorn Wlk M40 ... 83 B5
Mythorne Ave M44 ... 105 C3
Mytton Rd BL1 ... 142 B4
Mytton St M15 ... 162 F5

N

Nabbs Fold BL8 ... 10 F3
Nabbs Way BL8 ... 11 A1
Naburn Cl SK5 ... 112 C6
Naburn St M13 ... 98 D4
Nada Lo M8 ... 63 F1
Nada Rd M8 ... 63 F1
Naden Wlk M45 ... 63 A8
Nadin St OL8 ... 66 E3
Nadine St M6 ... 154 E3
Nailgate OL16 ... 31 C2
Nailsworth Wlk 5 M13 ... 163 C5
Nairn Cl WN6 ... 19 D1
Nairn Wlk M40 ... 160 E3
Nall St Manchester M19 ... 111 B7
Milnrow OL16 ... 31 E6
Nameplate Cl M30 ... 79 B2
Nan Nook Rd M23 ... 108 F1
Nancy St M15 ... 162 D6
Nandywell BL3 ... 43 B3
Nangreave Rd SK1,SK2 ... 124 B6
Nangreave St M5 ... 158 D1
Nangreaves St WN7 ... 75 C5
Nansen Ave M30 ... 79 C3
Nansen Cl M32 ... 96 E4
Nansen Rd SK8 ... 122 A4
Nansen St
Manchester M11 ... 164 E8
Salford M6 ... 154 E2
Stretford M32 ... 96 E4
Nansmoss La SK9 ... 130 D1
Nantes Ct BL1 ... 143 D2
Nantwich Ave OL12 ... 14 F3
Nantwich Cl SK8 ... 123 A5
Nantwich Rd M14 ... 98 A1
Nantwich Way 6 SK9 ... 131 E5
Nantwich Wlk BL3 ... 147 E4
Napier Ct Manchester M15 ... 161 C6
Manchester SK4 ... 168 B3
Napier Gn M5 ... 161 B7
Napier Ho OL14 ... 6 A8
Napier Rd Eccles M30 ... 79 C3
Manchester M21 ... 109 B8
Manchester SK4 ... 168 B3
Napier St Hazel Grove SK7 ... 124 D3
Hyde SK14 ... 167 E1
Shaw OL2 ... 149 B8
Swinton M27 ... 79 D7
Napier St E OL8 ... 153 D5
Napier St W OL8 ... 153 D5
Naples Rd SK3 ... 123 B7
Naples St M4 ... 159 A3
Narbonne Ave M30 ... 80 A4
Narborough Cl WN2 ... 56 E4
Narbuth Dr M8 ... 155 F7
Narcissus Ave BB4 ... 1 A8
Narcissus Wlk 6 M28 ... 59 F3
Narrow La SK10 ... 134 A1
Narrows The WA14 ... 119 C4
Naseby Ave M9 ... 64 F4
Naseby Ct M25 ... 63 C5
Naseby Pl M25 ... 63 C5
Naseby Rd SK5 ... 99 F1
Naseby Wlk M45 ... 63 C8
Nash Rd M17 ... 95 F8
Nash St M15 ... 162 E6
Nasmyth Ave M34 ... 101 A4
Nasmyth Bsns Ctr M30 ... 79 C2
Nasmyth Rd M30 ... 95 C8
Nasmyth St Horwich BL6 ... 22 C3
Manchester M8 ... 156 C5
Nately Rd M16 ... 97 A2
Nathan Dr M3 ... 158 E2
Nathaniel Ct WN2 ... 56 B3
Nathans Rd M22 ... 121 C4
National Cycling Ctr M11 ... 83 A2
National Dr M5 ... 161 A8
Naunton Ave WN7 ... 75 C5
Naunton Rd M24 ... 65 B7
Naunton Wlk 24 M9 ... 157 E8
Naval St M4 ... 159 C2
Navenby Ave M16 ... 97 C4
Navenby Rd WN3 ... 55 A2
Navigation Cl WN7 ... 75 E4
Navigation Prim Sch WA14 ... 119 D6
Navigation Rd WA14,WA15 ... 119 D6
Navigation Road Sta WA14 ... 119 E6
Naylor Ave WA3 ... 90 B8
Naylor Ct 19 M40 ... 159 C3
Naylor St Atherton M46 ... 58 C2
Manchester M40 ... 160 D3
Oldham OL1 ... 153 E7
Naylorfarm Ave WN6 ... 35 F5
Nazarene Theological Coll The M20 ... 110 A3
Naze Ct 3 OL1 ... 153 E8
Naze Wlk SK5 ... 112 C6
Nazeby Wlk OL9 ... 152 C5
Neal Ave Ashton-u-L OL6 ... 85 D3
Gatley SK8 ... 122 A1
Neale Ave OL3 ... 69 B5
Neale Rd M21 ... 109 B7
Near Birches Par OL4 ... 67 E4
Near Hey Cl M26 ... 43 E3
Nearbrook Rd M22 ... 121 C4
Nearcroft Rd M23 ... 121 B7
Nearmaker Ave M22 ... 121 C4
Nearmaker Rd M22 ... 121 C4
Neary Way M41 ... 95 C5
Neasden Gr 6 BL3 ... 144 C5
Neath Ave M22 ... 121 D7
Neath Cl Poynton SK12 ... 133 D5
Prestwich M45 ... 63 C7
Neath Fold BL3 ... 147 D3
Neath St OL9 ... 153 D7
Nebo St BL3 ... 147 D4
Nebraska St BL1 ... 143 E1
Neden Cl M11 ... 165 B8
Needham Ave M21 ... 109 B8
Needwood Cl M40 ... 157 D5
Needwood Rd SK6 ... 113 C5
Neenton Sq M12 ... 165 A7
Neild Gdns WN7 ... 75 E4
Neild St Manchester M1 ... 163 B8
Oldham OL8 ... 66 F4
Neill St M7 ... 158 E4
Neilson Cl M24 ... 65 C7
Neilson Ct M23 ... 121 A6
Neilston Ave M40 ... 83 B7
Nel Pan La WN7 ... 75 D8
Nell Carrs BL0 ... 11 E8
Nell La M20,M21 ... 109 D6
Nell St BL1 ... 143 F4
Nellie St OL10 ... 29 B2
Nelson Ave Eccles M30 ... 79 D3
Poynton SK12 ... 134 A3
Nelson Cl SK12 ... 134 A3
Nelson Ct Manchester M15 ... 97 E4
Manchester M40 ... 160 D4
Nelson Dr Droylsden M43 ... 83 E2
Ince-in-M WN2 ... 56 A8
Irlam M44 ... 105 E6
Nelson Fold M27 ... 62 A1
Nelson Mandela Ct 11 M16 ... 97 E3
Nelson Rd M9 ... 64 D5
Nelson Sq BL1 ... 145 F7
Nelson St Atherton M46 ... 58 B3
Atherton M46 ... 58 B4
Bacup OL13 ... 4 C8
Bolton BL3 ... 148 A5
6 Bury BL9 ... 44 F8
Denton M34 ... 100 F4
Denton M34 ... 100 F6
Eccles M30 ... 79 D2
Farnworth BL4 ... 60 E8
Hazel Grove SK7 ... 124 F4
Heywood OL10 ... 29 D1
8 Hindley WN2 ... 56 D6
Horwich BL6 ... 22 D3
Hyde SK14 ... 167 E2
Little Lever BL3 ... 43 B3
7 Littleborough OL15 ... 16 B5
Manchester M13 ... 163 B5
Manchester M40 ... 160 E4
Manchester M7 ... 155 D5
Middleton M24 ... 65 C7
Newton-le-W WA12 ... 89 A3
Oldham OL4 ... 67 E5
Rochdale OL16 ... 139 F7
Salford M5 ... 154 E1
Stretford M32 ... 96 D1
Tyldesley M29 ... 77 B8
Walsden OL14 ... 6 A8
Nelson Way OL9 ... 66 B4
Nelstrop Cres SK4 ... 111 D6
Nelstrop Rd SK4 ... 111 D6
Nelstrop Rd N M19,SK4,SK5 ... 111 C8
Nelstrop Wlk SK4 ... 111 C6
Nepaul Rd M9 ... 64 E1
Neptune Gdns 11 M7 ... 81 C5
Nesbit St BL2 ... 25 B3
Nesfield Rd M23 ... 108 F2
Neston Ave Bolton BL1 ... 24 F5
Manchester M20 ... 110 A6
Sale M33 ... 108 E2
Neston Cl OL2 ... 49 D7
Neston Gr SK3 ... 170 D5
Neston Rd Bury BL8 ... 26 F5
Rochdale OL16 ... 31 C4
Neston St M11 ... 99 F7
Neston Way SK9 ... 131 D3
Neswick Wlk 4 M23 ... 108 F2
Nether Hey St OL8 ... 67 B4
Nether St Hyde SK14 ... 113 F8
Manchester M12 ... 163 C8
Netherbury Cl M18 ... 99 C3
Netherby Rd WN6 ... 37 A3
Nethercote Ave M23 ... 121 B6
Nethercott Ct M29 ... 58 E1
Nethercroft Ct
Altrincham WA14 ... 119 C5
Altrincham WA14 ... 119 C5
Nethercroft Rd WA15 ... 120 C5
Netherfield Cl OL8 ... 66 C4
Netherfield Rd BL3 ... 147 E2
Netherfields WN7 ... 75 D7
Netherhey La OL1 ... 48 C2
Netherhouse Rd OL2 ... 149 A7
Netherland St M5 ... 161 A8
Netherlees OL4 ... 67 D5
Netherley Rd PR7 ... 19 E8
Netherlow Ct SK14 ... 167 E2
Netherton Gr BL4 ... 42 B2
Netherton Rd M14 ... 98 A1
Nethervale Dr M9 ... 157 E7
Netherwood Ct WN6 ... 36 A6
Netherwood Rd M22 ... 121 C7
Netley Ave OL12 ... 14 F3
Netley Gdns M26 ... 43 E5
Netley Gr OL8 ... 67 C4
Netley Rd M23 ... 121 A4
Nettlebarn Rd M22 ... 121 C5
Nettleford Rd M16 ... 109 E8
Nettleton Gr M9 ... 64 F1
Nevada St 18 BL1 ... 143 E1
Nevendon Dr M23 ... 120 F4
Nevern Cl BL1 ... 40 F8
Nevile Ct M7 ... 81 B8
Nevile Rd M7 ... 81 B8
Nevill Rd SK7 ... 123 E2
Nevill Road Inf Sch SK7 ... 123 E2
Nevill Road Jun Sch SK7 ... 123 E2
Neville Cardus Wlk 12 M14 ... 98 C3
Neville Cl BL1 ... 145 E8
Neville Dr M44 ... 94 A4
Neville St Hazel Grove SK7 ... 124 D3
Newton-le-W WA12 ... 89 A3
Oldham OL9 ... 152 C7
Platt Bridge WN2 ... 56 A3
Nevin Ave SK8 ... 122 E1
Nevin Cl Bramhall SK7 ... 133 A7
5 Oldham OL8 ... 66 B2
Nevin Rd M40 ... 65 D1
Nevis Gr BL1 ... 24 D5
Nevis St OL11 ... 31 A2
Nevy Fold Ave BL6 ... 22 F3
New Allen St M4,M40 ... 159 C3
New Bailey St M3 ... 158 E1
New Bank St
1 Hadfield SK13 ... 104 A5
Hadfield SK13 ... 104 A5
Manchester M12 ... 164 F5
Tyldesley M29 ... 77 A8
New Barn BB4 ... 1 B6
New Barn Ave WN4 ... 73 C3
New Barn Inf Sch OL2 ... 149 A6
New Barn Jun Sch OL2 ... 149 A6
New Barn La Leigh WN7 ... 75 E2
Rawtenstall BB4 ... 2 A8
Rochdale OL11 ... 30 E4
New Barn Rd OL8 ... 67 A2
New Barn St Bolton BL1 ... 142 B1
11 Rochdale OL11 ... 31 A5
Shaw OL2 ... 149 A7
New Barton St M6 ... 80 C5
New Beech Rd SK4 ... 110 E2
New Bridge La SK1 ... 112 A2
New Bridge St M3 ... 158 F3
New Briggs Fold BL7 ... 8 E2
New Broad La OL16 ... 31 C3
New Broadcasting House (BBC) M1 ... 163 A7
New Brook Sch M20 ... 109 F5
New Brunswick St BL6 ... 22 B3
New Buildings Pl 4 OL16 ... 139 F8
New Cathedral St M1 ... 158 F2
New Chapel La BL6 ... 22 F2
New Church Coll M26 ... 44 C2
New Church Ct M45 ... 62 F7
New Church Rd BL1 ... 23 F2
New Church St M26 ... 44 B3
New City Rd M28 ... 78 A8
New Collier's Row BL1 ... 23 E6
New Court Dr BL7 ... 8 E3
New Croft High Sch M6 ... 154 F3
New Cross M4 ... 159 B2
New Cross St
Pendlebury M27 ... 80 A7
Salford M5 ... 80 C2
New Drake Gn BL5 ... 57 E5
New Earth St Mossley OL5 ... 68 D2
Oldham OL4 ... 67 C5
New Elizabeth St M8 ... 156 A5
New Ellesmere App M28 ... 60 D4
New Elm Rd M3 ... 162 D8
New Field Cl Radcliffe M26 ... 43 E3
Rochdale OL16 ... 31 B8
New Fold WN5 ... 53 C4
New Forest Rd M23 ... 120 C8
New Gate BL5 ... 146 A1
New George St 8 BL8 ... 27 C3
New Green BL2 ... 25 E6
New Hall Ave Eccles M30 ... 95 A8
Gatley SK8 ... 131 B7
Manchester M7 ... 155 D8
New Hall La Bolton BL1 ... 144 A8
Culcheth WA3 ... 91 E1
Culcheth WA3 ... 92 A2
New Hall Mews BL1 ... 23 D1
New Hall Pl BL1 ... 144 A8
New Hall Rd Bury BL9 ... 28 E4
Manchester M7 ... 155 D8
Sale M33 ... 108 F4
New Herbert St M6 ... 80 C5
New Hey Rd Cheadle SK8 ... 122 E6
Denshaw HD7 ... 34 F8
New Heys Way BL2 ... 25 D6
New Ho OL4 ... 68 C8
New Holder St BL1 ... 145 E7
New Islington M4 ... 159 C2
New Kings Head Yd M3 ... 158 F2
New La Bolton BL2 ... 25 E2
Eccles M30 ... 79 B1
Middleton M24 ... 47 A1
Royton OL2 ... 48 D4
New Lane Ct BL2 ... 25 E2

New Lawns SK5 . . . .**100** A1
New Lees St OL6 . . . .**85** D5
New Line OL13 . . . .**.4** B8
New Lodge WN1 . . . .**37** D2
New Lester Way M38 . . . . .**59** E4
New Market M2 . . . .**158** F1
New Market La M1,M2 . . .**159** A1
New Market St WN1 . . . .**150** C8
New Mdw BL6 . . . .**40** C7
New Miles La WN6 . . . . . .**35** F5
New Mill St OL15 . . . .**16** A5
New Mills Rd SK13 . . . . . .**115** B4
New Moor La SK7 . . . .**124** D3
New Moss Rd M44 . . . . . .**105** D6
New Moston Prim Sch
M40 . . . .**65** E2
New Mount St **5** M4 . . . .**159** A3
New Park Rd M5 . . . .**161** B7
New Quay St M3 . . . .**158** E1
New Radcliffe St OL1 . . .**153** E7
New Raven Ct BL3 . . . . . .**43** A3
New Rd Adlington PR6 . . .**21** D8
Aspull WN2 . . . .**38** A5
Littleborough OL15 . . . . . .**15** F5
Oldham OL8 . . . .**66** E4
Radcliffe M26 . . . .**44** B2
Tintwistle SK13 . . . .**104** A7
Whitworth OL12 . . . .**.4** B1
New Ridd Rise SK14 . . . .**113** D8
New Rock BL5 . . . .**57** F5
New Royd Ave OL4 . . . . . .**67** F8
New Smithfield Mkt M18 **165** C7
New Springs BL1 . . . .**142** B3
New St Altrincham WA14 . .**119** D4
Ashton-in-M WN4 . . . .**73** C4
Blackrod BL6 . . . .**21** D2
Bolton BL1 . . . .**145** E6
Bury BL8 . . . .**26** F6
Droylsden M43 . . . .**100** A8
Eccles M30 . . . .**79** C1
Littleborough OL15 . . . . . .**15** F4
Manchester M40 . . . .**160** E4
Milnrow OL16 . . . .**32** A5
Mottram-in-L SK14 . . . . .**115** A8
Oldham OL3 . . . .**69** B8
Oldham OL4 . . . .**67** E6
Platt Bridge WN2 . . . .**56** A2
Radcliffe M26 . . . .**44** B2
Rochdale OL12 . . . .**14** E2
Stalybridge SK15 . . . . . .**102** A8
Swinton M27 . . . .**62** A1
Wigan WN5 . . . .**54** B5
Wilmslow SK9 . . . .**136** E5
New Summerseat House
Specl Sch BL0 . . . .**11** B2
New Tame OL3 . . . .**50** C7
New Tempest Rd BL6 . . . .**40** C4
New Terr SK14 . . . .**101** F5
New Thomas St M6 . . . . . .**81** A4
New Tong Field BL7 . . . . .**24** F7
New Union St M4 . . . . . .**159** C2
New Vernon St **12** BL9 . . .**140** F4
New Viaduct St M11,M40 .**160** E4
New Vine St M15 . . . .**162** F6
New Wakefield St M1 . . .**163** A7
New Way OL12 . . . .**.4** C1
New Welcome St M15 . . .**162** F6
New York BL3 . . . .**40** F5
New York St OL10 . . . . . .**29** B2
New Zealand Rd SK1 . . . .**112** B2
Newall Gr WN7 . . . .**75** F6
Newall Green High Sch
M23 . . . .**120** F3
Newall Green Prim Sch
M23 . . . .**121** B4
Newall Rd M23 . . . .**120** F3
Newall St
Littleborough OL15 . . . . . .**16** B6
Oldham OL9 . . . .**66** B2
Walsden OL14 . . . .**.6** A8
Newark Ave
Little Lever M26 . . . .**43** C5
3 Manchester M14 . . . . . .**98** B3
Newark Park Way OL2 . . .**48** C6
Newark Rd Hindley WN2 . . .**56** C4
Reddish SK5 . . . .**111** F5
Rochdale OL12 . . . .**14** F3
Swinton M27 . . . .**62** B2
Newark Sq OL12 . . . .**14** F3
Newark St WN6 . . . .**36** F1
Newbank Chase OL9 . . . .**152** A8
Newbank Towers M3 . . . .**158** E3
Newbarn Cl OL2 . . . .**149** A7
Newbeck St **3** M4 . . . . . .**159** A2
Newberry Gr SK3 . . . . . .**170** D5
Newbold Moss OL16 . . . . .**31** B8
Newbold St Bury BL8 . . . .**27** C2
Rochdale OL16 . . . .**31** C7
Newboult Rd SK8 . . . . . .**122** E6
Newbourne Cl SK7 . . . . .**124** D3
Newbreak Cl **2** OL4 . . . . .**67** D8
Newbreak St **3** OL4 . . . . .**67** D8
Newbridge OL5 . . . .**86** D8
Newbridge Cl WN4 . . . . . .**72** D3
Newbridge Gdns BL2 . . . .**25** E4
Newbrook Ave M21 . . . . .**109** D4
Newbrook Rd BL5,M46 . . .**58** F6
Newburn Ave M9 . . . .**64** F4
Newburn Cl WN3 . . . .**54** E4
Newbury Ave M33 . . . . . .**107** C4
Newbury Cl SK8 . . . .**132** A6
Newbury Cl SK9 . . . .**137** A6
Newbury Dr Eccles M30 . . .**79** B3
Urmston M41 . . . .**95** C5
Newbury Gr OL10 . . . .**46** C8

Newbury Pl M7 . . . .**155** D7
Newbury Rd Gatley SK8 . .**131** C7
Little Lever BL3 . . . .**42** F3
Newbury Wlk Bolton BL1 .**143** E1
Manchester M9 . . . .**157** D6
Oldham OL9 . . . .**152** C7
Newby Dr
Altrincham WA14 . . . .**119** D6
Gatley SK8 . . . .**122** A6
Middleton M24 . . . .**46** F3
Sale M33 . . . .**108** E3
Newby Rd Bolton BL2 . . . .**25** F2
Hazel Grove SK7 . . . .**124** D2
Stockport SK4 . . . .**169** E2
Newby Road Ind Est SK7 **124** D2
Newby Sq WN5 . . . .**54** B5
Newcastle St **3** M15 . . . .**162** F8
Newcastle Wlk **2** M34 . . .**101** A1
Newchurch OL8 . . . .**85** A8
Newchurch Ct **6** M26 . . . .**44** B3
Newchurch Cty Prim Sch
WA3 . . . .**91** E2
Newchurch La WA3 . . . . . .**91** F2
Newchurch Rd OL13 . . . . . .**3** C8
Newchurch St
Manchester M11 . . . .**164** F8
Rochdale OL11 . . . .**30** D1
Newchurch Wlk **5** M26 . . .**44** B3
Newcliffe Rd M9 . . . .**64** F4
Newcombe Cl M11 . . . . . .**160** F1
Newcombe Ct **3** M33 . . . .**107** F4
Newcombe Dr M38 . . . . . .**59** F6
Newcombe Rd BL0 . . . . . .**11** B2
Newcombe St M3 . . . .**158** F3
Newcroft M35 . . . .**84** B6
Newcroft Cres M41 . . . . . .**95** F1
Newcroft Dr
Stockport SK3 . . . .**170** D6
Stretford M41 . . . .**96** A1
Newcroft Rd M41 . . . .**95** F1
Newdale Rd M12 . . . .**99** B2
Newearth Rd M28 . . . .**78** B8
Newenden Rd WN1 . . . . . .**37** B4
Newfield Cl WA3 . . . .**117** A5
Newfield Head La OL16 . . .**32** B5
Newfield View OL16 . . . . . .**32** A6
Newgate Rochdale OL16 . .**139** F7
Wilmslow SK9 . . . .**136** D7
Newgate Ave WN6 . . . . . .**35** E8
Newgate Dr M38 . . . .**60** A4
Newgate Rd M33 . . . .**107** C1
Newgate St M4 . . . .**159** A2
Newhall Ave BL3 . . . .**43** B6
Newhall Dr M23 . . . .**109** B2
Newham Ave M11 . . . .**83** B2
Newhart Gr M28 . . . .**60** C2
Newhaven Ave
Droylsden M11 . . . .**99** F7
Leigh WN7 . . . .**75** F8
Newhavens Bsns Pk M30 .**79** E1
Newhaven Cl
Bramhall SK8 . . . .**123** C2
Bury BL8 . . . .**27** C3
Newhaven Wlk **4** BL2 . . . .**25** B1
Newhey Ave M22 . . . . . .**121** D5
Newhey Com Prim Sch
OL16 . . . .**32** A4
Newhey Rd Milnrow OL16 . .**32** A5
Wythenshawe M22 . . . . .**121** D5
Newhey Sta OL16 . . . .**32** B3
Newholme Ct
Manchester M20 . . . .**110** C6
Stretford M32 . . . .**96** C2
Newholme Gdns M28 . . . . .**60** C3
Newholme Rd M20 . . . . .**109** F5
Newhouse Cl OL12 . . . . . .**15** C6
Newhouse Cres OL11 . . . . .**29** E8
Newhouse Rd OL10 . . . . . .**46** D8
Newhouse St OL12 . . . . . .**15** C6
Newick Wlk **6** M9 . . . .**64** E3
Newington Ave M8 . . . . . .**63** F3
Newington Ct WA14 . . . . .**119** B3
Newington Dr Bolton BL1 .**143** F1
Bury BL8 . . . .**27** A1
Newington Wlk **2** BL1 . . .**143** F1
Newland Ave WN5 . . . . . .**54** D5
Newland Dr BL5 . . . .**58** F8
Newland Mews WA3 . . . . .**91** A5
Newland St M8 . . . .**64** B1
Newlands M35 . . . .**83** E4
Newlands Ave Bolton BL2 . .**25** F1
Bramhall SK7 . . . .**132** F8
Cheadle SK8 . . . .**132** A4
Eccles M30 . . . .**94** F7
Irlam M44 . . . .**94** A2
Rochdale OL12 . . . .**14** F3
Tyldesley M29 . . . .**77** A6
Whitefield M45 . . . .**44** E1
Newlands Cl Cheadle SK8 .**132** A7
Rochdale OL12 . . . .**14** F3
Newlands Dr Blackrod BL6 .**38** E7
Golborne WA3 . . . .**90** D8
Hadfield SK14 . . . .**171** D4
Manchester M20 . . . .**122** C8
Pendlebury M27 . . . .**80** C4
Prestwich M25 . . . .**63** A5
Wilmslow SK9 . . . .**136** A5
Newlands Rd Cheadle SK8 **122** D6
Leigh WN7 . . . .**75** F3
Wythenshawe M23 . . . . .**120** F8
Newlands Wlk M24 . . . . . .**46** E3
Newlyn Ave SK15 . . . .**86** D3
Newlyn Cl SK7 . . . .**124** D1
Newlyn Dr Ashton-in-M WN4 **73** B1
Newlyn St M14 . . . .**98** B2

Newman Ave WN6 . . . .**37** A2
Newman Cl WN2 . . . .**56** C6
Newman St
Ashton-u-L OL6 . . . .**166** A3
Hyde SK14 . . . .**167** E3
Rochdale OL16 . . . .**15** C3
Wigan WN1 . . . .**37** E2
Newmarket Cl M33 . . . . .**107** B2
Newmarket Gr OL7 . . . . . .**84** E5
Newmarket Mews M7 . . .**155** D6
Newmarket Rd
Ashton-u-L OL7 . . . .**84** F5
Little Lever BL3 . . . .**43** A2
Newmill Wlk **2** M8 . . . . .**156** A6
Newport Ave SK5 . . . . . .**111** E7
Newport Mews BL4 . . . . . .**60** D7
Newport Rd Bolton BL3 . . .**42** A3
Denton M34 . . . .**113** B8
Manchester M21 . . . .**97** B1
Newport St Bolton BL1,BL3 **145** F6
Bury BL8 . . . .**27** A5
Farnworth BL4 . . . .**60** D7
Manchester M14 . . . .**98** B3
Middleton M24 . . . .**47** C1
Oldham OL8 . . . .**153** D5
Salford M6 . . . .**154** E2
Newquay Ave
Ainsworth BL2 . . . .**26** D1
Reddish SK5 . . . .**111** E7
Newquay Dr SK7 . . . .**132** F7
Newry Rd M30 . . . .**95** E8
Newry St BL1 . . . .**143** D3
Newry Wlk M9 . . . .**64** B3
Newsham Cl BL3 . . . .**145** D5
Newsham Wlk
2 Manchester M12 . . . . . .**99** B3
Shevington WN6 . . . .**36** F1
Newshaw La SK13 . . . . . .**171** F4
Newsholme Cl WA3 . . . . . .**91** F3
Newsholme St **4** OL12 . .**139** E8
Newstead Ave
Ashton-u-L OL6 . . . .**85** C7
Manchester M20 . . . .**110** D5
Newstead Cl SK12 . . . . . .**133** D5
Newstead Dr BL3 . . . . . .**146** A2
Newstead Gr SK6 . . . . . .**112** F3
Newstead Rd Urmston M41 .**95** E3
Wigan WN3 . . . .**54** F3
Newstead Terr WA15 . . . .**119** F7
Newton Ave
Manchester M12 . . . .**98** F4
Manchester M20 . . . .**110** A6
Newton Bank Sch WA12 . .**89** E4
Newton Bsns Pk SK14 . . .**102** A5
Newton Cl WN1 . . . .**37** D2
Newton Comm Hospl
WA12 . . . .**89** B2
Newton Cres M24 . . . .**46** D3
Newton Cty Prim Sch
WA12 . . . .**89** D3
Newton Dr BL8 . . . .**11** A1
Newton Gn SK14 . . . .**101** F5
Newton Hall Ct SK14 . . . .**101** C5
Newton Hall Rd SK14 . . . .**101** C5
Newton Heath
Upper Sch M40 . . . .**157** F5
Newton Ho M14 . . . .**110** D8
Newton La WA12 . . . .**89** E6
Newton Moor Ind Est
SK14 . . . .**101** E5
Newton Park Dr WA12 . . . .**89** F3
Newton Rd
Altrincham WA14 . . . .**119** E7
Billinge WN5,WA9,WN4 . . .**71** F6
Failsworth M35 . . . .**83** F5
Golborne WA12,WA3 . . . . .**90** D5
Golborne WA3,WN7 . . . . . .**91** A8
Handforth SK9 . . . .**131** A1
Manchester M24 . . . .**64** B6
Urmston M41 . . . .**95** C2
Newton St Ashton-u-L OL6 .**166** C3
Bolton BL1 . . . .**143** E2
Bury BL9 . . . .**27** F6
Droylsden M43 . . . .**84** C3
Failsworth M35 . . . .**83** C6
Hyde SK14 . . . .**167** D4
Leigh WN7 . . . .**75** F5
Manchester M1 . . . .**159** B1
Rochdale OL16 . . . .**31** A5
4 Stalybridge SK15 . . . . . .**85** F2
Stockport SK3 . . . .**170** E8
Stretford M32 . . . .**96** D1
Newton Sta SK14 . . . . . .**167** F4
Newton Terr
23 Bolton BL1 . . . .**143** E2
20 Dukinfield SK16 . . . . .**166** B1
Newton Westpark
Prim Sch WN7 . . . .**75** C8
Newton Wlk BL1 . . . .**143** E2
Newton Wood Rd SK16 . .**101** B6
Newton-le-Willows
Com High Sch WA12 . . . .**89** D5
Newton-le-Willows Sta
WA12 . . . .**89** D5
Newtondale Ave OL2 . . . . .**48** C4
Newtonhurst SK14 . . . . .**102** A5
Newtonmore Wlk M11 . . . .**83** B1
Newtown Ave M34 . . . . . .**100** F2
Newtown Cl
Manchester M11 . . . .**165** B8
Swinton M27 . . . .**61** F2
Newtown Ct
Manchester M40 . . . .**159** C4
Prestwich M25 . . . .**63** C4
Newtown St Prestwich M25 **63** C4

Newtown St continued
Shaw OL2 . . . .**149** B6
Newville Dr M20 . . . .**110** D5
Ney St OL7 . . . .**84** F6
Neyland Cl BL1 . . . .**40** F7
Niagara St SK2 . . . .**124** A6
Nicholas Croft M4 . . . . . .**159** A2
Nicholas Owen Cl M11 . .**165** C8
Nicholas Rd OL8 . . . .**66** E4
Nicholas St Bolton BL2 . .**148** A8
Manchester M1,M2 . . . . .**159** A1
Nicholas Varley Com Sch
M40 . . . .**160** E4
Nicholls St M12 . . . .**164** D7
Nichols St M6 . . . .**81** B3
Nicholson Cl SK14 . . . . . .**101** C5
Nicholson Sq SK16 . . . . .**101** B8
Nicholson St Oldham OL4 . .**67** E6
Rochdale OL11 . . . .**139** F5
Stockport SK4 . . . .**169** E2
Nickleby Rd SK12 . . . . . .**133** E3
Nicol Mere Dr WN4 . . . . . .**73** A5
Nicol Rd WN4 . . . .**73** B5
Nicola St BL7 . . . .**24** E8
Nicolas Rd M21 . . . .**97** A1
Nield Rd M34 . . . .**100** F3
Nield St OL5 . . . .**68** B2
Nield's Brow WA14 . . . . .**119** C2
Nields Way SK6 . . . .**126** C4
Nigel Rd M9 . . . .**157** F7
Nigher Moss Ave OL16 . . .**31** C6
Nightingale Cl SK9 . . . . .**131** B1
Nightingale Ct **11** WN6 . . .**37** A1
Nightingale Dr M34 . . . . . .**84** C1
Nightingale Gdns M23 . . .**109** A1
Nightingale Rd BL6 . . . . . .**21** C3
Nightingale St PR6 . . . . . .**21** A3
Nightingales Wlk **3** BL3 .**147** F3
Nile St Bolton BL3 . . . . . .**145** F5
Dukinfield OL7 . . . .**100** F8
Oldham OL1 . . . .**153** E8
Rochdale OL16 . . . .**31** A8
Nile Terr M7 . . . .**155** D5
Nimble Nook OL9 . . . . . .**152** A5
Nina Dr M40 . . . .**65** C3
Nine Acre Ct M5 . . . .**161** B7
Nine Acre Dr M5 . . . .**161** B7
Ninehouse La BL3 . . . . . .**147** F4
Ninfield Rd M23 . . . .**121** B4
Ninian Ct **2** M24 . . . .**46** F1
Ninian Gdns M28 . . . .**60** D3
Ninth Ave OL8 . . . .**66** D1
Nipper La WN5 . . . .**44** E2
Nisbet Ave M22 . . . .**121** E3
Niven St M12 . . . .**163** C7
Nixon Rd BL3 . . . .**146** C3
Nixon Rd S BL3 . . . .**146** C3
Nixon St Failsworth M35 . . .**83** E7
Rochdale OL11 . . . .**30** B3
Stockport SK3 . . . .**170** E8
No 11 Pass SK3 . . . .**109** F5
No 2 Pas SK3 . . . .**169** D1
Noahs Ark La WA16 . . . . .**136** A1
Noble Mdw OL12 . . . .**15** D4
Noble St Bolton BL3 . . . .**145** E5
7 Leigh WN7 . . . .**76** A5
Oldham OL8 . . . .**66** F4
Noel Dr M33 . . . .**108** D4
Noel St BL1 . . . .**145** E7
Nolan St M9 . . . .**157** E8
Nona St M6 . . . .**154** E3
Nook Farm Ave OL12 . . . .**14** F3
Nook Fields BL2 . . . .**25** E3
Nook La Ashton-u-L OL6 . . .**85** E6
Golborne WA3 . . . .**90** B8
Tyldesley M29 . . . .**77** D2
Nook The **1** OL12 . . . .**14** F3
Appley Bridge WN6 . . . . . .**35** E7
Bramhall SK7 . . . .**132** D5
Eccles M30 . . . .**79** A4
Noon Ct WA12 . . . .**89** B1
Noon Sun Cl OL3 . . . .**69** A4
Noon Sun St OL12 . . . .**14** F1
Norbet Wlk **8** M9 . . . . . .**157** E7
Norbreck Ave
Cheadle SK8 . . . .**123** A6
Manchester M21 . . . .**109** B7
Norbreck Cres WN6 . . . . . .**37** A5
Norbreck Gdns BL2 . . . .**148** C8
Norbreck St BL2 . . . .**148** C8
Norburn Rd M13 . . . .**98** F2
Norbury Ave Billinge WN5 . .**71** D6
Hyde SK14 . . . .**167** D2
Marple SK6 . . . .**125** E6
Sale M33 . . . .**107** F4
7 Salford M6 . . . .**80** D5
Uppermill OL3 . . . .**68** C6
Norbury Cl M40 . . . .**160** E4
Norbury Cres SK7 . . . . . .**124** D2
Norbury Dr SK6 . . . .**125** F6
Norbury Gr Bolton BL1 . . . .**25** A4
Hazel Grove SK7 . . . .**124** D2
Swinton M27 . . . .**61** F1
Norbury Ho **4** OL4 . . . . . .**67** E6
Norbury Hollow Rd SK7 .**134** B8
Norbury La OL8 . . . .**67** D3
Norbury Mews SK6 . . . . .**125** E6
Norbury St Leigh WN7 . . . .**75** D5
Manchester M7 . . . .**155** D6
Rochdale OL16 . . . .**31** A4
Stockport SK1 . . . .**169** F1
Norbury Way **9** SK9 . . . .**131** D2
Norcliffe Wlk M18 . . . .**99** B4
Norcot Wlk **15** M15 . . . . .**162** D6
Norcross Cl SK2 . . . .**124** D5

Nordale Pk OL12 . . . .**13** D2
Nordek Cl OL2 . . . .**48** D5
Nordek Dr OL2 . . . .**48** D5
Norden Ave M20 . . . .**110** A6
Norden Cl OL11 . . . .**13** C2
Norden Com Prim Sch
OL12 . . . .**13** F2
Norden Ct BL3 . . . .**147** E5
Norden Rd OL11 . . . .**29** E6
Norden Way OL11 . . . .**13** C2
Nordens Dr OL9 . . . .**47** F1
Nordens Rd OL9 . . . .**65** F8
Nordens St OL9 . . . .**152** A8
Noreen Ave M25 . . . .**63** C5
Norfield Cl SK16 . . . .**101** C8
Norfolk Ave Droylsden M43 .**83** F3
Heywood OL10 . . . .**29** C4
Manchester M18 . . . .**99** C4
Reddish M34 . . . .**99** F3
Reddish SK4 . . . .**111** C6
Whitefield M45 . . . .**63** A8
Norfolk Cl Hindley WN2 . . .**57** A6
Irlam M44 . . . .**105** C5
Little Lever BL3 . . . .**43** B4
Littleborough OL15 . . . .**6** C1
Shaw OL2 . . . .**48** F7
Norfolk Cres M35 . . . .**83** E6
Norfolk Dr BL4 . . . .**42** D1
Norfolk Gdns M41 . . . .**94** D3
Norfolk Ho
3 Manchester M7 . . . .**63** E1
1 Sale M33 . . . .**108** C4
Norfolk Rd Atherton M46 . .**58** C5
Longshaw WN5 . . . .**53** E1
Manchester M18 . . . .**99** C4
Norfolk St Glossop SK13 .**104** D5
Hyde SK14 . . . .**167** D2
10 Manchester M2 . . . . . .**158** F1
Manchester M2 . . . .**159** A1
Oldham OL9 . . . .**66** C4
Rochdale OL11 . . . .**139** F6
Salford M6 . . . .**81** A5
Walkden M28 . . . .**60** D6
9 Wigan WN5 . . . .**54** F6
Wigan WN6 . . . .**37** A2
Norfolk Way OL2 . . . .**48** D2
Norford Way OL11 . . . .**29** E7
Norgate St M20 . . . .**110** A6
Norlan Ave M34 . . . .**100** E7
Norleigh Rd M22 . . . .**121** D8
Norley Ave M32 . . . .**96** F3
Norley Cl OL1 . . . .**48** B2
Norley Dr Manchester M19 .**99** C2
Sale M33 . . . .**108** E4
Norley Hall Ave WN5 . . . . .**54** C6
Norley Rd Leigh WN7 . . . . .**75** B4
Wigan WN5 . . . .**54** C7
Norman Ave
Ashton-in-M WN4 . . . .**89** A7
Hazel Grove SK7 . . . .**124** C3
Newton-le-W WA12 . . . . . .**89** E3
Norman Cl M24 . . . .**47** C1
Norman Gr Manchester M12 **98** F4
Manchester M12 . . . .**99** A4
Reddish SK5 . . . .**111** E7
Norman House Prep Sch
M40 . . . .**65** D3
Norman Rd
Altrincham WA14 . . . .**119** C6
Ashton-u-L OL6 . . . .**85** C6
Manchester M14 . . . .**98** D2
Manchester M7 . . . .**155** E7
Manchester SK4 . . . .**168** B3
Rochdale OL11 . . . .**139** C6
Sale M33 . . . .**108** B3
Stalybridge SK15 . . . .**85** F2
Norman Rd W M9 . . . . . .**157** F7
Norman St **1** Bury BL9 . .**141** B4
Failsworth M35 . . . .**66** A1
Hyde SK14 . . . .**167** E2
Manchester M12 . . . .**165** B5
Middleton M24 . . . .**47** B1
Oldham OL1 . . . .**153** D8
Radcliffe M26 . . . .**44** B4
Norman Weall Ct **5** M24 . .**47** A2
Norman's Pl WA14 . . . . . .**119** D4
Normanby Chase WA14 . .**119** B4
Normanby Gr M27 . . . .**61** E4
Normanby Rd M28 . . . .**60** C1
Normanby St Bolton BL3 . .**146** C2
Manchester M14 . . . .**98** A4
Swinton M27 . . . .**61** E1
Wigan WN5 . . . .**54** B6
Normandale Ave BL1 . . . .**142** A1
Normandy Cres M26 . . . . .**43** F3
Normanton Ave M6 . . . . . .**80** C3
Normanton Cl WN6 . . . . . .**36** E4
Normanton Dr M9 . . . .**64** E4
Normanton Rd SK3,SK8 . .**123** A6
Normington St **1** OL4 . . . .**67** C7
Norreys Ave M41 . . . .**94** E3
Norreys St OL16 . . . .**31** A8
Norris Ave SK4 . . . .**168** C1
Norris Bank Prim Sch
SK4 . . . .**168** B3
Norris Bank Terr SK4 . . .**168** C1
Norris Hill Dr SK4 . . . . . .**168** C2
Norris Rd M33 . . . .**108** D2
Norris St Bolton BL3 . . . .**145** E5
Farnworth BL4 . . . .**60** D7
Little Lever BL3 . . . .**43** A3
Tyldesley M29 . . . .**77** A8
Norris Towers **1** SK1 . . . .**112** B2
North Ave Eccles M41 . . . .**95** E6
Farnworth BL4 . . . .**60** B8
Golborne WN7 . . . .**74** F4

North Ave continued
Leigh WN7 . . . .**76** C3
Manchester M19 . . . .**110** F7
Oldham OL3 . . . .**69** B5
Ramsbottom BL8 . . . .**10** F1
Stalybridge SK15 . . . .**86** A3
Whitefield BL9 . . . .**45** B4
North Back Rock BL9 . . .**140** F2
North Blackfield La M7 . .**81** C8
North Bolton
Sixth Form Coll BL1 . . .**142** C4
North Brook Rd SK13 . . .**171** E4
North Broughton St M3 .**158** E2
North Butts St WN7 . . . . .**76** B3
North Cestrian Gram Sch
WA14 . . . .**119** C5
North Chadderton
Comp Sch OL9 . . . .**152** A8
North Chadderton Sch
OL9 . . . .**48** A2
North Cheshire
Jewish Prim Sch SK8 . .**122** C2
North Circ M45 . . . .**63** A6
North Cl SK13 . . . .**103** F7
North Cres Droylsden M11 . .**83** D3
Failsworth M40 . . . .**65** D3
North Croft OL8 . . . .**67** A3
North Dean St M27 . . . . . .**62** A1
North Downs Rd SK8 . . . .**122** F3
North Dr Appley Bridge WN6 .**18** C2
Droylsden M34 . . . .**84** C1
Pendlebury M27 . . . .**80** B7
North Edge WN7 . . . .**76** B6
North End Rd SK15 . . . . . .**86** B2
North Gate OL8 . . . .**66** E2
North George St M3 . . . .**158** D2
North Gr Manchester M13 .**164** D5
Urmston M41 . . . .**95** C2
Walkden M28 . . . .**60** C3
North Grecian Street
Prim Sch M7 . . . .**81** C5
North Harvey St SK1 . . . .**169** F1
North Heaton Prim Sch
SK4 . . . .**111** C6
North Hill St M3 . . . .**158** D3
North La Rochdale OL12 . .**139** F8
Tyldesley M29 . . . .**77** A6
North Lonsdale St M32 . .**96** E4
North Manchester
General Hospl M8 . . . . . .**64** B1
North Manchester High
Sch for Boys (Lower)
M9 . . . .**65** B3
North Manchester
High Sch for Girls M40 . .**65** A1
North Mead M21 . . . .**109** B7
North Nook OL4 . . . .**67** F8
North Par Newhey OL16 . . .**32** C4
Sale M33 . . . .**108** D2
North Park Rd SK7 . . . . . .**123** E3
North Phoebe St M5 . . . .**161** B8
North Pl SK1 . . . .**169** F1
North Quarry Bsns Pk
WN6 . . . .**18** D2
North Rd Altrincham WA15 **129** A8
Atherton M46 . . . .**58** B5
Carrington M31 . . . .**106** E4
Droylsden M11 . . . .**83** C2
Droylsden M34 . . . .**84** D1
Glossop SK13 . . . .**104** C3
Prestwich M25 . . . .**62** F5
Stretford M17 . . . .**96** C5
Stretford M32 . . . .**96** B4
North Reddish
Jun & Inf Schs SK5 . . . .**99** F1
North Rise OL3 . . . .**69** B5
North St Ashton-in-M WN4 .**73** D5
Ashton-u-L OL6 . . . .**166** A2
Atherton M46 . . . .**58** E3
Heywood OL10 . . . .**29** B2
Leigh WN7 . . . .**76** A4
Manchester M8 . . . .**159** A4
Middleton M24 . . . .**47** A2
Radcliffe M26 . . . .**44** C4
Ramsbottom BL0 . . . .**1** C2
Rochdale OL16 . . . .**31** A8
Royton OL2 . . . .**48** D3
1 Royton OL2 . . . .**48** D4
Whitworth OL12 . . . .**4** C1
North Stage M5 . . . .**96** F8
North Star Dr M3 . . . . . .**158** D1
North Trafford
Coll of F Ed M32 . . . . . .**96** F4
North Vale Rd WA15 . . . .**119** F6
North Veiw M45 . . . .**44** E2
North View Mossley OL5 . .**68** E1
Ramsbottom BL0 . . . .**1** C2
Ramsbottom BL9 . . . .**11** B2
North View Cl OL4 . . . . . .**68** C5
North Walkden Prim Sch
M28 . . . .**60** C5
North Way Bolton BL1 . . . .**25** B4
Brinnington SK5 . . . .**112** A6
Hyde SK14 . . . .**167** E2
North Western St
Manchester M1,M12 . . . .**163** C8
Manchester M12 . . . .**164** D7
Manchester M19 . . . .**111** A8
North Woodley **6** M26 . . . .**44** C1
Northallerton Rd M7 . . . .**81** B6
Northampton Rd
Manchester M40 . . . .**157** F6
Manchester M40 . . . .**83** A6
Northampton Way **1**
M34 . . . .**101** A1
Northavon Cl M30 . . . .**80** A1
Northbank Gdns M19 . . .**110** E6

Northbank Ind Pk M44 . .**105** F7
Northbank Wlk M20 . . . .**109** D3
Northbourne St M6 . . . .**154** E2
Northbrook Ave M9 . . . . .**63** F4
Northcliffe Rd SK2 . . . . .**124** C8
Northcombe Rd SK3 . . . .**170** E5
Northcote Rd SK7 . . . . . .**132** F7
Northcroft WN1 . . . .**37** F1
Northdale Rd M9 . . . .**64** B5
Northden OL11 . . . .**29** F6
Northdown Ave
Manchester M15 . . . .**162** D6
Romiley SK6 . . . .**113** C5
Northdowns Rd OL2 . . . . .**48** F8
Northen Gr M20 . . . .**109** F4
Northenden Prim Sch
M22 . . . .**109** D1
Northenden Rd
Gatley SK8 . . . .**122** A6
Sale M33 . . . .**108** C4
Sale M33 . . . .**108** D4
Northenden View M20 . . .**110** B2
Northern Ave M27 . . . .**62** C3
Northfield Ave M40 . . . . . .**65** F4
Northfield Cl WN3 . . . .**74** C1
Northfield Dr SK9 . . . . . .**137** D8
Northfield Rd Bury BL9 . . .**27** F6
Failsworth M40 . . . .**65** F2
Northfield St BL3 . . . .**144** C5
Northfleet Rd M30 . . . . . .**94** F8
Northgate OL12 . . . .**14** C7
Northgate La OL1 . . . .**49** E3
Northgate Rd SK3 . . . . . .**123** C8
Northland Rd Bolton BL1 . .**24** F6
Manchester M9 . . . .**65** A3
Northlands M26 . . . .**43** E5
Northleach Cl BL8 . . . .**27** B3
Northleigh Dr M25 . . . . . .**63** D3
Northleigh Ho **1** M16 . . . .**97** B2
Northleigh Rd M16 . . . . . .**97** B3
Northmoor Rd M12 . . . . . .**99** A3
Northolme Gdns M19 . . . .**110** E5
Northolt Ave WN7 . . . .**75** F8
Northolt Cl M11 . . . .**83** D2
Northolt Dr BL3 . . . .**147** F4
Northolt Rd M23 . . . .**108** F1
Northridge Rd M9 . . . .**64** D6
Northside Ave M41 . . . . . .**94** F1
Northstead Ave M34 . . . . .**101** B2
Northumberland Ave
OL7 . . . .**166** B4
Northumberland Cl M16 .**161** C5
Northumberland Cres
M16 . . . .**161** C5
Northumberland Rd
Brinnington SK5 . . . .**112** B6
Manchester M16 . . . .**161** C5
Partington M31 . . . .**105** E2
Northumberland St
Manchester M7 . . . .**155** E7
Wigan WN1 . . . .**37** E1
Northumbria St **8** BL3 . .**144** F5
Northurst Dr M8 . . . .**63** F3
Northward Rd SK9 . . . . . .**136** F6
Northway
Altrincham WA14 . . . .**119** E6
Droylsden M43 . . . .**100** A8
4 Eccles M30 . . . .**79** F2
Wigan WN1 . . . .**37** C1
Northways WN6 . . . .**19** D2
Northwell St **2** WN7 . . . . .**75** E8
Northwold Cl WN3 . . . .**54** D3
Northwold Dr Bolton BL1 . .**40** E8
Manchester M9 . . . .**65** B3
Northwood BL2 . . . .**25** D4
Northwood Ave WA12 . . . .**89** F3
Northwood Cres BL3 . . . .**144** C5
Northwood Gr M33 . . . . . .**108** B4
Norton Ave
Manchester M12 . . . .**99** B3
Reddish M34 . . . .**100** A3
Sale M33 . . . .**107** D6
Urmston M41 . . . .**95** D4
Norton Gr SK4 . . . .**168** B1
Norton Grange M25 . . . . . .**63** F5
Norton Rd Boothstown M28 .**77** E7
Rochdale OL12 . . . .**14** F3
Norton St Bolton BL1 . . . .**143** F3
17 Manchester M1 . . . .**159** C1
Manchester M16 . . . .**97** D4
Manchester M3 . . . .**158** F2
Manchester M40 . . . .**160** E4
Manchester M7 . . . .**155** E7
Norview Dr M20 . . . .**122** B8
Norville Ave M40,M9 . . . . .**65** D3
Norway Gr SK5 . . . .**169** F4
Norway St Bolton BL1 . . . .**143** D2
Manchester M11 . . . .**164** E8
Salford M6 . . . .**154** E2
Stretford M32 . . . .**96** E3
Norweb Way WN7 . . . .**76** B3
Norwell Rd M22 . . . .**121** E5
Norwich Ave
Ashton-in-M WN4 . . . .**73** D3
Chadderton OL9 . . . .**48** A1
Denton M34 . . . .**100** F1
Golborne WA3 . . . .**90** D8
Rochdale OL11 . . . .**30** B7
Norwich Cl Ashton-u-L OL6 .**85** D7
Dukinfield SK16 . . . .**102** A7
Norwich Dr BL8 . . . .**140** D3
Norwich Rd M32 . . . .**95** F3
Norwich St OL11 . . . .**31** A5
Norwick Cl BL3 . . . .**40** E4
Norwood M25 . . . .**63** B2
Norwood Ave
Ashton-in-M WN4 . . . .**72** F6

Norwood Ave continued
Bramhall SK7 . . . .**132** D5
Cheadle SK8 . . . .**123** A3
Golborne WA3 . . . .**90** F7
High Lane SK6 . . . .**134** D7
Manchester M20 . . . .**110** D4
Manchester M7 . . . .**81** B8
Tyldesley M29 . . . .**77** B6
Wigan WN6 . . . .**37** A3
Norwood Cl Adlington PR6 . .**21** A8
Shaw OL2 . . . .**149** A8
Walkden M28 . . . .**78** E8
Norwood Cres OL2 . . . . . .**48** E2
Norwood Ct M32 . . . .**96** E1
Norwood Dr
Altrincham WA15 . . . .**120** D5
Swinton M27 . . . .**79** D7
Norwood Gr Bolton BL1 . . .**144** C8
Oldham OL2 . . . .**48** E2
Norwood Lo M7 . . . .**81** B8
Norwood Rd Gatley SK8 . . .**122** B6
Stockport SK2 . . . .**124** B4
Stretford M32 . . . .**96** E2
Noseby Ct M25 . . . .**63** C5
Nostell Rd WN4 . . . .**73** A5
Nottingham Ave SK5 . . . .**112** C6
Nottingham Cl SK5 . . . . .**112** C5
Nottingham Dr
Ashton-u-L OL6 . . . .**85** B7
Bolton BL1 . . . .**143** E1
Failsworth M35 . . . .**84** A6
Nottingham Pl WN1 . . . . . .**37** E1
Nottingham Way **3** M34 .**101** A1
Nowell Ct M24 . . . .**47** A3
Nowell House M24 . . . .**47** A3
Nowell Rd M24 . . . .**47** A3
Nudger Cl OL3 . . . .**50** F2
Nudger Gn OL3 . . . .**51** A2
Nuffield Rd M22 . . . .**121** E4
Nugent House Sch WN5 . . .**71** D4
Nugent Rd BL3 . . . .**147** E3
Nugget St OL4 . . . .**67** B6
Nuneaton Dr M40 . . . .**160** D3
Nuneham Ave M20 . . . . . .**110** C7
Nunfield Cl M40 . . . .**65** B2
Nunnery Rd BL3 . . . .**146** B4
Nunthorpe Dr M8 . . . .**156** C8
Nursery Ave WA15 . . . . . .**128** E8
Nursery Cl Glossop SK13 . .**116** C8
Sale M33 . . . .**108** D4
Stockport SK2 . . . .**124** D7
Nursery Dr SK12 . . . .**133** D4
Nursery La Cheadle SK3 . .**123** A7
Wilmslow SK9 . . . .**136** F5
Nursery Rd Cheadle SK8 . .**123** A1
Failsworth M35 . . . .**84** A7
Prestwich M25 . . . .**63** A6
Stockport SK4 . . . .**168** C2
Urmston M41 . . . .**95** A4
Nursery St Manchester M16 .**97** F3
Salford M6 . . . .**154** F3
Nuthatch Ave M28 . . . .**78** D8
Nuthurst Rd M40 . . . .**65** D1
Nutsford Vale M12,M18 . . .**99** B4
Nutt La M25 . . . .**63** E8
Nutt St WN1 . . . .**37** E2
Nuttall Ave M45 . . . .**62** F8
Nuttall Mews M45 . . . .**62** F8
Nuttall Ave Horwich BL6 . . .**22** A3
Little Lever BL3 . . . .**43** C3
Whitefield M45 . . . .**62** F8
Nuttall Cl BL0 . . . .**138** C5
Nuttall Hall Cotts BL0 . . .**11** D5
Nuttall Hall Rd BL0 . . . . . .**11** D5
Nuttall La BL0 . . . .**138** B5
Nuttall Mews M45 . . . .**62** F8
Nuttall Rd BL0 . . . .**11** D4
Nuttall Sq BL9 . . . .**44** F5
Nuttall St Atherton M46 . . . .**58** E3
Bury BL9 . . . .**141** A1
Irlam M44 . . . .**105** E6
Manchester M11 . . . .**165** A4
Manchester M16 . . . .**161** C5
Oldham OL8 . . . .**67** B4

O

O'Kane Ho **10** M30 . . . .**79** D1
Oadby Cl M12 . . . .**99** A4
Oak Ave Abram Brow WN2 . .**74** C7
Cheadle SK8 . . . .**123** A2
Golborne WA3 . . . .**90** B8
Hindley WN2 . . . .**57** A3
9 Horwich BL6 . . . .**22** E1
Irlam M44 . . . .**105** D5
Little Lever BL3 . . . .**43** B3
Manchester M21 . . . .**109** B8
Manchester SK4 . . . .**168** B2
Middleton M24 . . . .**65** A7
Newton-le-W WA12 . . . .**89** D3
Ramsbottom BL0 . . . .**11** A2
Reddish M18 . . . .**99** F4
Romiley SK6 . . . .**113** C2
Royton OL2 . . . .**48** D6
Standish WN6 . . . .**36** F8
Whitefield M45 . . . .**62** F7
Wilmslow SK9 . . . .**136** F5
Oak Bank Manchester M9 .**157** D8
Prestwich M25 . . . .**62** F1
Prestwich M25 . . . .**63** C5
Oak Bank Ave M9 . . . .**64** F1
Oak Bank Cl M45 . . . .**63** B8
Oak Brow Cotts SK9 . . . .**130** E6
Oak Cl Mottram-in-L SK14 . .**103** A4
Whitworth OL12 . . . .**4** D4
Wilmslow SK9 . . . .**136** F6
Oak Coppice BL1 . . . .**144** A7

Oak Cotts SK9 . . . .**130** E4
Oak Ct SK6 . . . .**113** A5
Oak Dr Bramhall SK7 . . . . .**132** C7
Manchester M14 . . . .**98** D1
Marple SK6 . . . .**125** D6
Reddish M34 . . . .**100** A4
Oak Gates BL7 . . . .**8** E1
Oak Gr Ashton-u-L OL6 . . . .**85** D6
Cheadle SK8 . . . .**122** E5
Eccles M30 . . . .**79** B1
Poynton SK12 . . . .**133** D4
Urmston M41 . . . .**95** E2
Oak Hill OL15 . . . .**15** F5
Oak Hill Cl WN1 . . . .**37** B4
Oak La Whitefield M45 . . . . .**63** B8
Wilmslow SK9 . . . .**136** F6
Oak Lea Ave SK9 . . . .**137** A5
Oak Lo SK3 . . . .**132** F7
Oak Mews SK9 . . . .**131** C1
Oak Rd Altrincham WA15 . . .**119** E3
Cheadle SK8 . . . .**122** E5
Failsworth M35 . . . .**83** F6
Manchester M20 . . . .**110** B5
Manchester M7 . . . .**81** C5
Oldham OL8 . . . .**66** D2
Partington M31 . . . .**105** D2
Sale M33 . . . .**108** D4
Oak St Atherton M46 . . . . . .**58** A1
Denton M34 . . . .**100** F6
Eccles M30 . . . .**79** D1
Glossop SK13 . . . .**104** C1
Hazel Grove SK7 . . . .**124** D3
Heywood OL10 . . . .**29** B3
Hyde SK14 . . . .**167** E4
Leigh WN7 . . . .**75** F3
Littleborough OL15 . . . .**16** C5
Manchester M4 . . . .**159** A2
2 Manchester M4 . . . .**159** B2
Middleton M24 . . . .**65** D7
Newhey OL16 . . . .**32** B4
3 Radcliffe M26 . . . .**44** C1
Ramsbottom BL0 . . . .**138** B5
Rochdale OL16 . . . .**139** F7
Shaw OL2 . . . .**149** C7
Stockport SK3 . . . .**123** B8
Swinton M27 . . . .**62** A1
Tyldesley M29 . . . .**59** A1
Whitworth OL12 . . . .**4** D5
Wigan WN1 . . . .**151** E2
Oak Terr OL15 . . . .**6** D2
Oak Tree Cl Atherton M46 . .**58** A1
Stockport SK2 . . . .**124** D8
Oak Tree Cres SK15 . . . . .**102** B8
Oak Tree Dr SK16 . . . .**101** F7
Oak View OL12 . . . .**4** D4
Oak View Rd OL3 . . . .**69** B5
Oak Wood View OL5 . . . . . .**86** C6
Oakbank WN2 . . . .**56** B3
Oakbank Ave OL9 . . . .**65** F8
Oakbank Dr BL1 . . . .**24** D6
Oakcliffe Rd OL12 . . . .**15** D4
Oakcroft SK15 . . . .**102** E8
Oakdale BL2 . . . .**25** E4
Oakdale Cl M45 . . . .**62** D8
Oakdale Ct
Altrincham WA14 . . . .**119** C5
Delph OL3 . . . .**50** E3
Stalybridge SK15 . . . .**86** B2
Oakdale Dr Gatley SK8 . . .**122** B2
Manchester M20 . . . .**110** C1
Tyldesley M29 . . . .**77** C6
Oakdale Sch SK16 . . . .**101** E6
Oakdene M27 . . . .**79** B6
Reddish SK4 . . . .**111** D5
Oakdene Ave Gatley SK8 . .**131** C7
Reddish SK4 . . . .**111** D5
Oakdene Cres SK6 . . . . . .**125** F7
Oakdene Gdns SK6 . . . . .**125** F7
Oakdene Rd Marple SK6 . . .**125** F7
Middleton M24 . . . .**65** C8
Sale WA15 . . . .**120** B8
Oakdene St M9 . . . .**157** F8
Oaken Bank Rd M24 . . . . . .**47** A5
Oaken Clough **3** OL7 . . . . .**85** A6
Oaken Clough Dr OL7 . . . .**85** A6
Oaken Clough Terr OL7 . . .**84** F6
Oaken St OL7 . . . .**85** A6
Oakenbottom Rd BL2 . . . . .**42** D7
Oakenclough **1** OL1 . . . . .**153** E7
Oakenclough Cl SK9 . . . . .**131** D2
Oakenclough Dr BL1 . . . . . .**23** E7
Oakenclough Prim Sch
SK9 . . . .**131** D1
Oakenden St WN4 . . . .**73** A6
Oakengates WN6 . . . .**19** F1
Oakenrod Hill OL11 . . . . . .**30** C6
Oakenrod Prim Sch
OL11 . . . .**139** D7
Oakenshaw Ave OL12 . . . . .**14** C6
Oakenshaw View OL12 . . . .**14** C6
Oaker Ave M20 . . . .**109** E4
Oaker Pl M20 . . . .**109** E4
Oakes St BL4 . . . .**60** F7
Oakes The SK13 . . . .**116** A7
Oakfield Dukinfield SK16 . . .**101** E6
Manchester M25 . . . .**63** D3
Sale M33 . . . .**108** A5
Oakfield Ave Atherton M46 .**58** C4
Cheadle SK8 . . . .**122** B6
Droylsden M43 . . . .**83** F1
Golborne WA3 . . . .**73** F1
Manchester M16 . . . .**97** A3
Manchester M16 . . . .**97** D3
Mossley SK15 . . . .**86** A6
Oakfield Cl
Alderley Edge SK9 . . . .**137** B3
Bramhall SK7 . . . .**132** E4
Horwich BL6 . . . .**22** F2
Oakfield Cres WN2 . . . .**38** C5

Nor–Oak **233**

Oakfield Ct WA15 . . . .**119** F6
Oakfield Dr M38 . . . .**59** E5
Oakfield Gr Farnworth BL4 . .**60** C6
Manchester M18 . . . .**99** D4
Oakfield Mews Sale M33 . .**108** A4
Stockport SK3 . . . .**170** F5
Oakfield Prim Sch SK14 . .**101** E5
Oakfield Rd
Alderley Edge SK9 . . . .**137** B2
Altrincham WA15 . . . .**119** E4
Dukinfield SK14 . . . .**101** E5
Hadfield SK13 . . . .**171** E3
Manchester M20 . . . .**110** A3
Poynton SK12 . . . .**133** F4
Stockport SK3 . . . .**170** F5
Oakfield St
Altrincham WA15 . . . .**119** E5
Manchester M8 . . . .**156** A6
Oakfield Terr OL11 . . . .**30** C8
Oakfield Trad Est WA15 . .**119** E5
Oakfold Ave OL6 . . . .**85** D6
Oakford Ave M40 . . . .**159** C3
Oakford Wlk BL3 . . . .**145** E8
Oakgrove Prim Sch SK8 . .**131** C7
Oakham Cl BL8 . . . .**27** C5
Oakham Mews M7 . . . .**63** D1
Oakham Rd M34 . . . .**101** A1
Oakhead WN7 . . . .**76** C3
Oakhill Cl BL2 . . . .**43** A7
Oakhill Ct M7 . . . .**155** E7
Oakhill Trad Est M28 . . . . .**60** C6
Oakhill Way M8 . . . .**155** F7
Oakhouse Dr M21 . . . .**109** B7
Oakhurst Chase SK9 . . . .**137** A2
Oakhurst Dr SK3,SK8 . . . .**123** B5
Oakhurst Gr BL2 . . . .**57** C7
Oakington Ave **10** M14 . . . .**98** D3
Oakland Ave
Manchester M19 . . . .**110** E4
Salford M6 . . . .**80** B4
Stockport SK2 . . . .**124** D6
Oakland Ct SK12 . . . .**133** D4
Oakland Gr BL1 . . . .**142** E3
Oakland Terr OL11 . . . .**30** C1
Oaklands BL1 . . . .**40** F7
Oaklands Ave
Cheadle SK8 . . . .**123** A2
Marple SK6 . . . .**126** C8
Oaklands Cl SK9 . . . .**131** E1
Oaklands Cty Inf Sch
SK9 . . . .**131** E1
Oaklands Dene SK14 . . . . .**102** A2
Oaklands Dr
Hazel Grove SK7 . . . .**124** E1
Hyde SK14 . . . .**102** A2
Prestwich M25 . . . .**63** B4
Sale M33 . . . .**108** A5
Oaklands Ho M14 . . . .**98** B1
Oaklands Hospl The M6 . .**80** B4
Oaklands Pk OL4 . . . .**67** C8
Oaklands Rd Edenfield BL0 . .**1** D2
Golborne WA3 . . . .**90** F7
Manchester M7 . . . .**81** A4
Oldham OL2 . . . .**48** E2
Swinton M27 . . . .**79** D6
Uppermill OL4 . . . .**68** F5
Oaklea **1** Manchester M16 . .**97** C3
Shevington Moor WN6 . . . . .**19** A2
Oaklea Rd M33 . . . .**107** E5
Oakleigh Manchester SK4 . .**168** B3
4 Stockport SK3 . . . .**123** F4
Oakleigh Ave
Altrincham WA15 . . . .**120** A7
Bolton BL2 . . . .**42** A2
1 Manchester M19 . . . . . .**110** F7
Oakleigh Cl OL10 . . . .**46** E7
Oakleigh Rd SK8 . . . .**131** E8
Oakley Ave WN5 . . . .**71** E6
Oakley Cl Failsworth M40 . . .**83** C5
Radcliffe M26 . . . .**62** A8
Oakley Dr WN5 . . . .**54** E6
Oakley Pk BL1 . . . .**40** F7
Oakley St OL15 . . . .**15** E4
Oakley Villas SK4 . . . .**168** B3
Oaklings The WN2 . . . .**57** A3
Oakmere Ave M30 . . . .**79** C4
Oakmere Cl M22 . . . .**121** D4
Oakmere Rd Cheadle SK8 . .**122** F4
Handforth SK9 . . . .**131** D5
Oakmoor Dr M7 . . . .**81** B8
Oakmoor Rd M23 . . . .**121** A6
Oakridge Wlk **3** M9 . . . . .**157** D7
Oaks Ave BL2 . . . .**25** C4
Oaks Cty Prim Sch The
BL1 . . . .**24** F6
Oaks La BL1,BL2 . . . .**25** B5
Oaks The Gatley SK8 . . . . .**122** A2
Hyde SK14 . . . .**102** A3
Oakshaw Dr OL12 . . . .**14** A1
Oakside Cl SK8 . . . .**122** E6
Oaktree Cl SK8 . . . .**122** D5
Oakville Dr M6 . . . .**80** A4
Oakville Terr **11** M40 . . . . .**64** F1
Oakway Manchester M20 . .**122** C8
Middleton M24 . . . .**46** F4
Oakwell Dr
Manchester M7,M8 . . . .**63** E1
Whitefield BL9 . . . .**45** B3
Oakwell Mans M7 . . . .**63** E1
Oakwood Chadderton OL9 . .**65** E7
Glossop SK13 . . . .**115** F8
Sale M33 . . . .**107** C4
Oakwood Ave
Ashton-in-M WN4 . . . .**73** A2
Denton M34 . . . .**100** E7

Oakwood Ave continued
Failsworth M40 . . . . .65 D1
Gatley SK8 . . . . .122 B5
Kearsley M27 . . . . .61 E4
Shevington WN6 . . . . .35 F5
Walkden M28 . . . . .60 F2
Wilmslow SK9 . . . . .136 E6
Oakwood Cl BL8 . . . . .27 B3
Oakwood Com Prim Sch
M31 . . . . .105 D3
Oakwood Ct WA14 . . . . .128 B8
Oakwood Dr Bolton BL1 . . . .40 F8
Leigh WN7 . . . . .75 E1
Salford M6 . . . . .80 B5
Walkden M28 . . . . .60 F2
Oakwood Est M5 . . . . .154 D1
Oakwood High Sch M21 . .109 C5
Oakwood High Sch
(Upper Sch) M21 . . . . . .109 C7
Oakwood La WA14 . . . . .119 B1
Oakwood Rd Disley SK12 . .135 D6
Romiley SK6 . . . . .113 C2
Oakworth Croft OL4 . . . . . .49 F4
Oakworth Dr BL1 . . . . .24 D5
Oakworth St M9 . . . . .64 C3
Oat St SK1 . . . . .124 A7
Oatlands Rd M22 . . . . .121 C2
Oban Ave OL1 . . . . .49 B1
Oban Cres SK3 . . . . .123 D4
Oban Dr Garswood WN4 . . .72 C4
Sale M33 . . . . .108 E3
Oban Gr BL1 . . . . .24 E5
Oban St BL1 . . . . .143 D3
Oban Way WN2 . . . . .38 D5
Oberlin St Oldham OL4 . . . .67 D7
Rochdale OL11 . . . . .139 D5
Oberon Cl M30 . . . . .79 D2
Occlestone Cl M33 . . . . . .108 E1
Ocean St WA14 . . . . .119 B6
Ocean Street Trad Est
WA14 . . . . .119 B7
Ocean Wlk M15 . . . . .162 F5
Ockendon Dr M9 . . . . .157 E7
Octavia Dr M40 . . . . .83 C4
Odell St M11 . . . . .165 B7
Odessa Ave M6 . . . . .80 B4
Odette St M18 . . . . .99 C4
Off Grove Rd SK15 . . . . . . .86 D4
Off Ridge Hill La [2] SK15 . .85 F2
Off Stamford St SK15 . . . . .86 D4
Offerton Dr SK2 . . . . .124 D6
Offerton Fold SK2 . . . . . . .124 C7
Offerton Gn SK2 . . . . .124 F6
Offerton Hall Prim Sch
SK2 . . . . .124 E6
Offerton High Sch SK2 . .124 E6
Offerton Ind Est SK1,SK2 .124 C7
Offerton La SK1,SK2 . . . . . .124 C8
Offerton Rd SK2,SK7 . . . . .125 A4
Offerton St Horwich BL6 . . .22 A3
Stockport SK1 . . . . .112 B2
Ogbourne Wlk [1] M13 . . .163 C6
Ogden Cl Haslingden BB4 . . .1 A7
Heywood OL10 . . . . .29 A2
Whitefield M45 . . . . .45 A1
Ogden Ct SK14 . . . . .167 E2
Ogden Dr BB4 . . . . .1 A7
Ogden Gdns SK16 . . . . .101 B8
Ogden Gr SK8 . . . . .122 E2
Ogden La Manchester M11 .99 D7
Newhey OL16 . . . . .32 D5
Ogden Rd Bramhall SK7 . .132 D5
Failsworth M35 . . . . .83 F6
Ogden Sq SK16 . . . . .101 B8
Ogden St
[4] Manchester M20 . . . . .110 B3
Middleton M24 . . . . .65 A8
Mottram-in-L SK14 . . . . . . .115 B8
[5] Oldham OL4 . . . . .67 D6
Oldham OL9 . . . . .152 C8
Prestwich M25 . . . . .63 C4
Rochdale OL11 . . . . .30 C2
Swinton M27 . . . . .79 F7
Ogden Wlk M45 . . . . .63 A8
Ogwen Dr M25 . . . . .63 B5
Ohio Ave M5 . . . . .96 F4
Okehampton Cl M26 . . . . . .43 C5
Okehampton Cres M33 . .107 D5
Okell Gr WN7 . . . . .75 D6
Okeover Rd M7 . . . . .155 D8
Olaf St [13] BL2 . . . . .25 B1
Old Bank Cl SK6 . . . . .113 A3
Old Bank St M2 . . . . .158 F1
Old Bank View OL1 . . . . . . .49 C4
Old Barn Pl BL7 . . . . .25 A8
Old Barton Rd M41 . . . . . . .95 C7
Old Bedions Sports Ctr
M20 . . . . .122 A8
Old Bent La OL12 . . . . .15 A7
Old Birley St M15 . . . . .162 F5
Old Boston WA11 . . . . .89 A7
Old Boston Trad Est WA11 89 B8
Old Broadway M20 . . . . . . .110 B5
Old Brook Cl OL2 . . . . .49 D8
Old Brow OL5 . . . . .68 C1
Old Brow La OL16 . . . . .15 C3
Old Brown Ct OL5 . . . . .86 C8
Old Chapel St SK3 . . . . . .170 D2
Old Church Mews [2]
SK16 . . . . .101 E8
Old Church St
Failsworth M40 . . . . .83 C6
Oldham OL1 . . . . .153 F7
Old Clay Dr OL12 . . . . .15 D4

Old Clough La
Walkden M28 . . . . .60 F1
Worsley M28 . . . . .78 F8
Old Colliery Yd WN4 . . . . . .72 C3
Old Croft Mews SK1 . . . . .124 B7
Old Crofts Bank M41 . . . . . .95 C3
Old Cross St OL6 . . . . .166 C3
Old Ctyd The M22 . . . . .121 F5
Old Dairy Mews SK14 . . .101 C5
Old Delph Rd OL11 . . . . .13 F1
Old Doctors St BL8 . . . . . . .26 F7
Old Eagley Mews BL1 . . . . .24 F6
Old Edge La OL2 . . . . .48 E2
Old Elm St M12,M13 . . . . .163 C6
Old Engine La BL0 . . . . .11 D6
Old Farm Cres M44 . . . . . . .99 F8
Old Farm Dr SK2 . . . . .124 F6
Old Fold Eccles M30 . . . . . .79 C4
[7] Oldham OL4 . . . . .67 D6
Old Fold Rd Aspull WN2 . . . .38 D5
Westhoughton BL5 . . . . .57 C7
Old Garden The WA15 . . . .120 B7
Old Gardens St [3] SK1 . . .170 F8
Old Gn BL2 . . . . .25 E6
Old Green BL8 . . . . .10 F1
Old Greenwood La BL6 . . . .22 D1
Old Ground St BL0 . . . . . . .138 C6
Old Hall Cl Bury BL8 . . . . . . .26 F7
Glossop SK13 . . . . .104 D2
Old Hall Clough BL6 . . . . . .40 C7
Old Hall Cres SK9 . . . . .131 E3
Old Hall Ct Sale M33 . . . . .108 E4
Whitefield M45 . . . . .62 C7
Old Hall Dr
Ashton-in-M WN4 . . . . .73 A2
Manchester M18 . . . . .99 D4
Stockport SK2 . . . . .124 E6
Old Hall Drive Prim Sch
M18 . . . . .99 D4
Old Hall Farm BL3 . . . . .42 E4
Old Hall La Bolton BL1,BL6 .23 C1
Manchester M13,M14,M19 . .98 E2
Manchester M25 . . . . .64 A6
Marple SK6 . . . . .126 C5
Mottram-in-L SK14 . . . . . . .103 A5
Westhoughton BL5 . . . . .57 E6
Whitefield M45 . . . . .62 C6
Woodford SK7 . . . . .132 D1
Worsley M28 . . . . .78 E7
Old Hall Mill La M46 . . . . . .76 A8
Old Hall Prim Sch BL8 . . . .27 B7
Old Hall Rd Failsworth M40 .83 B7
Gatley SK8 . . . . .122 A6
Manchester M7 . . . . .63 D1
Sale M33 . . . . .108 E4
Stretford M32 . . . . .96 A4
Whitefield M45 . . . . .62 C7
Old Hall Sq SK13 . . . . .104 A8
Old Hall St Dukinfield SK16 101 A7
Farnworth BL4 . . . . .60 E7
Ince-in-M WN3 . . . . .151 E6
Middleton M24 . . . . .47 A1
Old Hall St N BL1 . . . . .145 F7
Old Hey Wlk WA12 . . . . .89 C1
Old Heyes Rd WA15 . . . . . .120 B8
Old House Terrs OL6 . . . . . .85 E5
Old Kiln OL13 . . . . .3 D8
Old Kiln La Bolton BL1 . . . . .23 D1
Mossley OL4 . . . . .68 B4
Old La Bury OL9 . . . . .27 F8
Glossop SK13 . . . . .116 A7
Horwich BL6 . . . . .22 F2
Manchester M11 . . . . .99 D7
Oldham OL4 . . . . .68 A8
Oldham OL9 . . . . .66 B4
Shevington WN6 . . . . .36 B6
Uppermill OL3 . . . . .51 B2
Uppermill OL4 . . . . .68 C6
Walkden M38 . . . . .59 F6
Whitworth OL12,OL13 . . . . . . .4 E6
Wigan WN1 . . . . .37 B4
Old Lansdowne Rd M20 .110 A4
Old Lees St OL6 . . . . .85 D5
Old Lord's Cres BL6 . . . . . .22 B5
Old Manor Pk M46 . . . . .58 A2
Old Market Pl WA14 . . . . . .119 D5
Old Market St M9 . . . . .64 D2
Old Meadow Dr M34 . . . . .100 F5
Old Meadow La WA15 . . . .120 B3
Old Medlock St M3 . . . . . .162 E8
Old Mill Cl M27 . . . . .80 B8
Old Mill Ho OL4 . . . . .68 A5
Old Mill La
Hazel Grove SK7 . . . . .134 A8
Oldham OL4 . . . . .68 A5
Old Mill St M4 . . . . .159 C1
Old Mills Hill M24 . . . . .47 D1
Old Moat Jun & Inf Sch
M20 . . . . .110 A7
Old Moat La M20 . . . . .110 B7
Old Moss La WA3 . . . . .92 E6
Old Mount St M4 . . . . .159 B3
Old Nans La BL2 . . . . .25 F2
Old Nursery Fold BL2 . . . . .25 E4
Old Oak Cl BL3 . . . . .43 B5
Old Oak Dr M34 . . . . .101 A3
Old Oak St M20 . . . . .110 B3
Old Oak Cl M28 . . . . .60 E2
Old Orch The WA15 . . . . . .120 B8
Old Orchard SK9 . . . . .137 A7
Old Pack Horse Rd OL3 . .51 B6
Old Packhorse Rd OL15 . .16 F6
Old Parrin La M30 . . . . .79 B3
Old Pasture Cl SK2 . . . . . .124 E7
Old Pepper La WN6 . . . . . . .19 B2
Old Quarry La BL7 . . . . .8 F1

Old Rake BL6 . . . . .22 E5
Old Rd Ashton-in-M WN4 . . .73 A4
Ashton-u-L OL6 . . . . .86 A6
Bolton BL1 . . . . .143 E3
Cheadle SK8 . . . . .122 F6
Dukinfield SK16 . . . . .166 C1
Failsworth M35 . . . . .83 E8
Handforth SK9 . . . . .131 D3
Hyde SK14 . . . . .167 D4
Littleborough OL16 . . . . .15 E4
Manchester M9 . . . . .64 D2
Stalybridge SK15 . . . . .102 F5
Stalybridge SK15 . . . . .102 C8
Stockport SK4 . . . . .169 E3
Tintwistle SK13 . . . . .104 A7
Wilmslow SK9 . . . . .137 B8
Old Rectory Gdns SK8 . . .122 D5
Old River Cl M44 . . . . .94 A2
Old School Ct Eccles M30 . .79 D4
Manchester M9 . . . . .64 C2
Old School Dr M9 . . . . .64 C2
Old School House The
OL15 . . . . .15 F6
Old School La PR7 . . . . .20 E5
Old School Mews
[12] Bacup OL13 . . . . .3 C8
[1] Dukinfield SK15,SK16 . .101 E8
Old School Pl WN4 . . . . .73 A2
Old Shaw St M5 . . . . .161 B8
Old Sirs BL5 . . . . .57 F5
Old Sq [8] OL6 . . . . .166 C3
Old St Ashton-u-L OL6 . . . .166 B3
Mottram-in-L SK14 . . . . . . .115 A8
Oldham OL4 . . . . .67 D5
Stalybridge SK15 . . . . .86 A2
Old Station St [8] M30 . . . . .79 C1
Old Swan St BL7 . . . . .8 E2
Old Swan Cotts BL7 . . . . . . .8 E2
Old Thorn La OL3 . . . . .69 D6
Old Towns Cl BL8 . . . . .26 F7
Old Trafford Jun Sch
M16 . . . . .161 C5
Old Trafford Prim Sch
M15 . . . . .161 C6
Old Trafford Sta M16 . . . . .97 A4
Old Vicarage BL5 . . . . .57 E5
Old Vicarage Gdns M28 . . .60 D3
Old Vicarage Mews BL5 . . .57 E5
Old Vicarage Rd BL6 . . . . . .22 F3
Old Wargrave Rd WA12 . . .89 C3
Old Well Wlk M33 . . . . .107 C2
Old Wellington Rd M30 . . .79 C2
Old Wells Cl M38 . . . . .60 A6
Old Will's La BL6 . . . . .22 B6
Old Wool La SK8 . . . . .122 F4
Old York St M15 . . . . .162 E6
Oldbridge Dr WN2 . . . . .56 D6
Oldbrook Fold WA15 . . . . .120 B4
Oldbury Cl Heywood OL10 . .46 D7
Manchester M40 . . . . .160 D3
Oldcastle Ave M20 . . . . . .110 A8
Oldcott Cl M28 . . . . .77 F5
Oldcroft OL4 . . . . .68 A6
Oldershaw Dr M9 . . . . .157 D6
Oldfield Brow Prim Sch
WA14 . . . . .119 A5
Oldfield Cl BL5 . . . . .57 F8
Oldfield Dr WA15 . . . . .119 F6
Oldfield Gr M33 . . . . .108 C5
Oldfield La WA14 . . . . .118 F4
Oldfield Mews WA14 . . . . .119 C5
Oldfield Rd
Altrincham WA14 . . . . .119 B5
Manchester M30 . . . . .81 C1
Prestwich M25 . . . . .63 C7
Sale M33 . . . . .108 C5
Salford M5 . . . . .161 C8
Salford M5 . . . . .83 C8
Oldgate Wlk [17] M15 . . . . .162 D6
Oldham Art Gal & Mus
OL1 . . . . .153 F6
Oldham Athletic AFC
(Boundary Pk) OL1 . . . . .48 D2
Oldham Ave SK1 . . . . .112 B1
Oldham Coll OL9 . . . . .153 E7
Oldham Ct [15] M40 . . . . . .159 C3
Oldham Dr SK6 . . . . .113 A4
Oldham Rd Ashton-u-L OL7 .85 A5
Delph OL3,OL4 . . . . .50 D2
Failsworth M35,M40 . . . . . . .83 D6
Middleton M24 . . . . .65 A8
Rochdale OL11,OL16,OL2 . . .31 A3
Royton OL1,OL2 . . . . .48 E3
Shaw OL1,OL4 . . . . .50 B7
Shaw OL2 . . . . .149 B5
Uppermill OL4,OL3 . . . . .68 D6
Oldham Sixth Form Coll
OL8 . . . . .153 E6
Oldham St Denton M34 . . .100 C3
Droylsden M43 . . . . .84 B2
Hyde SK14 . . . . .167 A4
Manchester M1,M4 . . . . . . .159 B2
Manchester M5 . . . . .158 D1
[8] Reddish SK5 . . . . .111 E7
Oldham Study Ctr
& Natural History Mus
OL8 . . . . .153 D5
Oldham Way
OL1,OL4,OL8,OL9 . . . . . . .153 E6
Oldhams Com Prim Sch
BL1 . . . . .24 C5
Oldhams La BL1 . . . . .143 D4
Oldhams Terr BL1 . . . . .143 D4
Oldknow Rd SK6 . . . . .126 A6
Oldmill St OL12 . . . . .139 F8
Oldmoor Rd SK6 . . . . .112 E5
Oldstead Gr BL3 . . . . .40 F3
Oldstead Wlk M9 . . . . .157 D6

Oldway Wlk M40 . . . . .83 B5
Oldwood Inf Sch M22 . . . .121 B2
Oldwood Jun Sch M22 . . .121 B2
Oldwood Rd M23 . . . . .121 A3
Olga St BL1 . . . . .143 D2
Olivant St Bury BL9 . . . . . .140 E1
Bury BL9 . . . . .44 E8
Olive Bank BL8 . . . . .27 B4
Olive Gr WN6 . . . . .36 F3
Olive Rd WA15 . . . . .120 A8
Olive Shapley Ave M20 110 B3
Olive St Bacup OL13 . . . . . . .3 E8
Bolton BL3 . . . . .147 D4
Bury BL8 . . . . .140 D2
Failsworth M35 . . . . .83 E8
Heywood OL10 . . . . .29 E2
Radcliffe M26 . . . . .44 C3
Rochdale OL11 . . . . .30 C1
Olive Terr SK14 . . . . .115 A8
Olive Wlk [4] M33 . . . . .107 C6
Oliver Cl OL15 . . . . .15 F5
Oliver St Atherton M46 . . . . .58 D3
Manchester M11 . . . . .164 F8
Manchester M13 . . . . .163 A6
Oldham OL1 . . . . .153 F6
Stockport SK1,SK3 . . . . . . .170 F8
Olivia Ct M5 . . . . .161 C8
Olivia Gr M14 . . . . .98 D3
Ollerbarrow Rd WA15 . . . .119 E2
Ollerbrook Ct [11] BL1 . . . .143 F2
Ollersett Ave SK22 . . . . . .127 D1
Ollersett La SK22 . . . . .127 E1
Ollerton [16] OL12 . . . . .139 E8
Ollerton Ave
Manchester M16 . . . . .97 C3
Sale M33 . . . . .107 D5
Ollerton Cl WN2 . . . . .38 A2
Ollerton Dr M35 . . . . .83 F6
Ollerton Rd SK9 . . . . .131 E5
Ollerton St Adlington PR6 . .21 A3
Bolton BL1 . . . . .24 F6
Ollier Ave M12 . . . . .99 B2
Olney OL11 . . . . .139 E6
Olney Ave M22 . . . . .121 C6
Olney St M13 . . . . .98 D4
Olsberg Cl M26 . . . . .44 C4
Olwen Ave M12 . . . . .165 A5
Olwen Cres SK5 . . . . .111 F8
Olympia Ct [2] M44 . . . . . . .94 A2
Olympic Ct M5 . . . . .96 F8
Omer Ave M13 . . . . .98 F2
Omer Dr M19 . . . . .110 E7
Onchan Ave OL4 . . . . .67 B6
One Ash Cl OL12 . . . . .14 F2
One Oak Ct SK7 . . . . .123 C2
One Oak La SK9 . . . . .137 F7
Ongar Wlk M9 . . . . .64 B3
Onslow Ave M40 . . . . .65 E1
Onslow Rd SK3 . . . . .123 C8
Onslow St OL11 . . . . .30 C4
Onward St SK14 . . . . .167 D2
Oozewood Rd M24,OL2 . . . .48 B5
Opal Ct [5] M14 . . . . .110 D8
Opal Gdns M14 . . . . .98 D4
Opal Gr WN7 . . . . .75 E4
Opal St M19 . . . . .111 B8
Openshaw Fold Rd BL9 . . .44 D8
Openshaw La M44 . . . . . . .105 C6
Openshaw Pl BL4 . . . . .60 B8
Openshaw St BL9 . . . . .141 A1
Openshaw Wlk [15] M11 . . .83 C1
Oracle Ct M28 . . . . .60 D2
Oram St BL9 . . . . .141 A4
Orama Ave M6 . . . . .80 A4
Orange Hill Rd M25 . . . . . . .63 C5
Orange St M6 . . . . .81 A3
Orchard Ave Bolton BL1 . . .143 F3
Boothstown M28 . . . . .78 B7
Partington M31 . . . . .105 F4
Reddish M18 . . . . .99 E4
Orchard Brow WA3 . . . . . .105 A2
Orchard Cl Bramhall SK8 . .132 C2
Leigh WN7 . . . . .75 F7
Poynton SK12 . . . . .133 E3
Shevington WN6 . . . . .36 A7
Wilmslow SK9 . . . . .136 F5
Orchard Ct SK2 . . . . .124 D6
Orchard Dr
Altrincham WA15 . . . . .120 A3
Gamesley SK13 . . . . .171 E1
Handforth SK9 . . . . .131 E2
Orchard Gdns BL2 . . . . .25 F3
Orchard Gn SK9 . . . . .137 B1
Orchard Gr
Manchester M20 . . . . .109 F5
Shaw OL2 . . . . .149 A7
Orchard Ind Est M6 . . . . . . .81 A5
Orchard La WN7 . . . . .76 A7
Orchard Pl Poynton SK12 . .133 D4
Sale WA15 . . . . .120 B7
[3] Sale M33 . . . . .108 B5
Orchard Rd
Altrincham WA15 . . . . .119 E5
Failsworth M35 . . . . .83 F7
Lymm WA13 . . . . .117 B5
Romiley SK6 . . . . .114 B2
Orchard Rd E M22 . . . . . . .109 E2
Orchard Rd W M22 . . . . . .109 D2
Orchard Rise SK14 . . . . . .113 F7
Orchard St
Ashton-in-M WN4 . . . . .73 C3
Heywood OL10 . . . . .29 E3
Hyde SK14 . . . . .167 E2
Manchester M20 . . . . .109 F5
Salford M6 . . . . .81 A4
Stockport SK1 . . . . .169 E1
Wigan WN1 . . . . .151 D8

Orchard The Disley SK12 . .135 D6
Oldham OL4 . . . . .67 C3
[4] Westhoughton BL5 . . . . . .39 E1
Orchard Trad Est M6 . . . . . .80 F5
Orchard Vale SK3 . . . . .123 C6
Orchard Way BL8 . . . . .10 E1
Orchards The OL10 . . . . .29 E2
Orchid Ave BL4 . . . . .42 B1
Orchid Cl Irlam M44 . . . . . .105 E8
Oldham OL1 . . . . .48 E1
Orrell WN8 . . . . .53 B6
Orchid Dr BL9 . . . . .45 A7
Orchid St M9 . . . . .157 D7
Orchid Way OL12 . . . . .14 D3
Ordell Wlk [1] M9 . . . . .64 E3
Ordsall District Ctr M5 . . .161 B8
Ordsall Dr M5 . . . . .161 B7
Ordsall Hall (Mus) M5 . . .161 B7
Ordsall La M5 . . . . .161 B7
Oregon Ave OL1 . . . . .48 E1
Oregon Cl M13 . . . . .163 C6
Orford Ave SK12 . . . . .135 D6
Orford Cl SK6 . . . . .134 E7
Orford Rd Failsworth M40 . .83 C5
Prestwich M25 . . . . .63 B5
Organ St Hindley WN2 . . . . .57 B3
Leigh WN7 . . . . .75 E5
Oriel Ave OL8 . . . . .66 E3
Oriel Bank High Sch SK3 170 F5
Oriel Cl Oldham OL9 . . . . . .152 A5
Stockport SK2 . . . . .124 B6
Oriel Rd Ashton-in-M WN4 . .72 F3
Manchester M20 . . . . .110 A4
Oriel St Bolton BL3 . . . . . . .144 C5
Rochdale OL11 . . . . .139 F5
Orient Rd M6 . . . . .80 B4
Orient St M7,M8 . . . . .155 F7
Oriole Cl M28 . . . . .78 B8
Orion Bsns Pk SK3,SK8 . .123 B5
Orion Pl M7 . . . . .81 C4
Orkney Cl Radcliffe M26 . . . .44 A4
Wythenshawe M23 . . . . .121 A4
Orkney Dr M41 . . . . .95 D5
Orlanda Ave M6 . . . . .80 B4
Orlanda Dr M7 . . . . .155 F6
Orlando St BL3 . . . . .148 A5
Orleans Way OL1 . . . . .153 E7
Orley Wlk OL1 . . . . .49 D4
Orme Ave Middleton M24 . . .65 A7
Salford M6 . . . . .80 B4
Orme Cl Manchester M11 . .160 E1
Urmston M41 . . . . .95 F2
Orme St Alderley Edge SK9 137 A1
Oldham OL4 . . . . .67 A5
Ormerod Ave OL2 . . . . .48 E3
Ormerod Cl SK6 . . . . .113 A1
Ormerod St OL10 . . . . .29 E1
Ormond St Bolton BL3 . . . . .42 D5
Bury BL9 . . . . .141 A3
Ormonde Ave M6 . . . . .80 B4
Ormonde Ct OL6 . . . . .166 C4
Ormonde St OL6 . . . . .166 C4
Ormrod St Bolton BL2 . . . . .25 C4
Bolton BL3 . . . . .145 E6
Bury BL9 . . . . .141 A2
[10] Farnworth BL4 . . . . .60 C8
Ormrods The BL9 . . . . .28 F5
Orms Gill Pl SK2 . . . . .124 E6
Ormsby Ave M18 . . . . .99 B4
Ormsby Cl Standish WN6 . . .19 E2
Stockport SK3 . . . . .123 E4
Ormsgill St M15 . . . . .162 F6
Ormside Cl WN2 . . . . .57 C4
Ormskirk Ave M20 . . . . . . .109 F6
Ormskirk Cl BL8 . . . . .44 A8
Ormskirk Rd Orrell WN8 . . .53 A7
[2] Reddish SK5 . . . . .111 F6
Wigan WN5 . . . . .54 D6
Ormston Ave BL6 . . . . .22 C5
Ormston Gr WN7 . . . . .75 F7
Ornatus St BL1 . . . . .24 F5
Ornsey Wlk [12] M11 . . . . . .83 C1
Oronsay Gr M5 . . . . .154 E1
Orphanage St SK4 . . . . . . .169 E3
Orpington Dr BL8 . . . . .27 B1
Orpington Rd [2] M9 . . . . . .157 E7
Orpington St WN5 . . . . .54 C6
Orrel St M5,M6 . . . . .154 E2
Orrell Arc [3] WN1 . . . . . . .150 C8
Orrell Gdns WN5 . . . . .53 F6
Orrell Hall Cl WN5 . . . . .54 B8
Orrell Lamberhead Green
Cty Jun Sch WN5 . . . . . . .54 A7
Orrell Lamberhead Green
Cty Prim Sch WN5 . . . . . .54 B6
Orrell Newfold
Cty Prim Sch WN5 . . . . . .53 D4
Orrell Rd WN5 . . . . .53 E7
Orrell St Bury BL8 . . . . .140 D3
Manchester M11 . . . . .99 D8
Wigan WN1 . . . . .151 D7
Orrell Sta WN5 . . . . .53 E4
Orrell Water Pk WN5 . . . . . .53 E4
Orrishmere Prim Sch
SK8 . . . . .123 A3
Orrishmere Rd SK8 . . . . . .122 F3
Orron St OL15 . . . . .16 A5
Orsett Cl M40 . . . . .159 C3
Orthes Gr SK4 . . . . .111 D5
Orton Ave M23 . . . . .109 A1
Orton Rd M23 . . . . .109 A1
Orton Way WN4 . . . . .72 F3
Ortonbrook Prim Sch
M31 . . . . .105 E2
Orvietto Ave M6 . . . . .80 B4
Orville Dr M19 . . . . .111 B8
Orwell Ave Reddish M34 . .100 A3

Orwell Ave continued
Wythenshawe M22 . . . . . . .121 D6
Orwell Cl Bury BL8 . . . . . . .140 D4
Handforth SK9 . . . . .131 D2
Orwell Rd BL1 . . . . .142 B2
Osborne Cl BL8 . . . . .44 B8
Osborne Dr M27 . . . . .80 C7
Osborne Gr Bolton BL1 . . .142 C1
Gatley SK8 . . . . .122 A3
Leigh WN7 . . . . .76 D6
Osborne Ho M30 . . . . .79 C2
Osborne Pl SK13 . . . . . . .104 A5
Osborne Rd
Altrincham WA15 . . . . .119 E5
Ashton-in-M WN4 . . . . .73 A4
Denton M34 . . . . .100 F4
Golborne WA3 . . . . .90 E7
Hyde SK14 . . . . .167 D1
Manchester M19 . . . . .99 A1
8 Manchester M9 . . . . . . .157 E7
Oldham OL8 . . . . .153 D5
Salford M6 . . . . .80 A2
Stockport SK2 . . . . .170 F7
Osborne St Bredbury SK6 .112 D3
Heywood OL10 . . . . .29 D1
Manchester M20 . . . . .110 A3
Manchester M40 . . . . .159 C4
Oldham OL9 . . . . .152 C8
Rochdale OL11 . . . . .139 F5
Salford M6 . . . . .154 F2
Shaw OL2 . . . . .149 B6
Osborne Terr Bacup OL13 . . .3 D8
Sale M33 . . . . .108 A4
Osbourne Cl Farnworth BL4 42 D1
Wilmslow SK9 . . . . .137 D6
Osbourne Ct M46 . . . . . . .58 C3
Osbourne Pl 7 M14 . . . . .119 D4
Osbourne Wlk M26 . . . . . .43 E3
Oscar St Bolton BL1 . . . . .142 C2
Manchester M40 . . . . .83 A7
Oscott Ave M38 . . . . .60 A6
Oscroft Cl M8 . . . . .155 F6
Oscroft Wlk M14 . . . . . . .110 D7
Osmond St OL4 . . . . .67 C7
Osmund Ave BL2 . . . . . . .42 D7
Osprey Ave BL5 . . . . .57 D6
Osprey Cl Dukinfield SK16 .101 E7
Manchester M15 . . . . .162 E5
Osprey Ct M15 . . . . .162 E5
Osprey Dr Droylsden M43 . .84 C3
Irlam M44 . . . . .94 A3
Wilmslow SK9 . . . . .137 C8
Osprey Wlk M13 . . . . . . .163 C6
Ospreys The WN3 . . . . . . .54 C4
Ossington Ct M23 . . . . . . .109 A3
Ossington Wlk M23 . . . . . .109 A2
Ossory St M14 . . . . .98 B3
Osterley Rd M9 . . . . .65 A3
Ostlers Gate M43 . . . . . . .84 D2
Ostrich La M25 . . . . .63 C3
Oswald Cl M6 . . . . .81 A5
Oswald La M21 . . . . .97 B1
Oswald Rd M21 . . . . .97 A1
Oswald Road Prim Sch
M21 . . . . .97 A1
Oswald St Bolton BL3 . . . .146 C4
Manchester M4 . . . . .159 A3
Manchester M4 . . . . .160 D1
Oldham OL9 . . . . .153 A8
Reddish SK5 . . . . .99 F3
Rochdale OL16 . . . . .31 B8
Shaw OL2 . . . . .149 C8
Oswestry Cl BL8 . . . . .26 F8
Otago St 2 OL4 . . . . .49 C1
Othello Dr M30 . . . . .79 D2
Otley Ave M6 . . . . .80 C3
Otley Cl OL9 . . . . .152 B6
Otley Gr SK3 . . . . .123 D4
Otmoor Way OL2 . . . . .49 A4
Otranto Ave M6 . . . . .80 B4
Otter Dr Manchester M8 . . .155 E5
Whitefield BL9 . . . . .45 B4
Otterburn Pl SK2 . . . . . . .124 E6
Otterbury Cl BL8 . . . . .26 F2
Otterham Wlk M40 . . . . . . .83 D5
Otterspool Rd SK6 . . . . . .125 B8
Otterwood Sq WN5 . . . . . .36 C2
Ottery Wlk 5 M40 . . . . . . .65 D2
Ottowa Cl M23 . . . . .120 F4
Oughtrington Cres WA13 117 B4
Oughtrington La WA13 . . .117 A2
Oughtrington Prim Sch
WA13 . . . . .117 B4
Oughtrington View
WA13 . . . . .117 B4
Oulder Hill OL11 . . . . .30 B7
Oulder Hill Com Sch
OL11 . . . . .30 B7
Oulder Hill Dr OL11 . . . . . .30 B7
Oldfield Cl 22 OL16 . . . . . .31 B6
Oulton Ave M33 . . . . .108 E5
Oulton Cl 5 WN7 . . . . .76 A4
Oulton St BL1 . . . . .25 A5
Oulton Wlk M40 . . . . .160 D1
Oundle Cl M14 . . . . .98 C3
Our Lady & St Paul
RC Prim Sch OL10 . . . . . .28 F1
Our Lady &
the Lancashire Martyrs
RC Prim Sch M28 . . . . . . .60 A3
Our Lady Mount Carmel
RC High Sch M6 . . . . .80 C3
Our Lady of Grace
RC Prim Sch M25 . . . . . . .63 A6
Our Lady of Lourdes
RC Prim Sch Bury BL8 . . .27 C6
Farnworth BL4 . . . . .60 A8
Partington M31 . . . . .105 E3

Our Lady of Mount Carmel
Inf Sch M9 . . . . .64 D1
Our Lady of the Rosary
RC Prim Sch Leigh WN7 . .75 B5
Urmston M41 . . . . .95 C4
Our Lady's RC Comp Sch
OL2 . . . . .48 D3
Our Lady's RC High Sch
M9 . . . . .64 D5
Our Lady's RC Prim Sch
Aspull WN2 . . . . .38 C5
Manchester M16 . . . . .97 D3
Oldham OL4 . . . . .49 E3
Stockport SK3 . . . . .170 E8
Ouse St M5 . . . . .80 C1
Outham Mews OL3 . . . . . . .51 B1
Outram Cl SK6 . . . . .125 F4
Outram Rd SK14,SK16 . . .101 B6
Outram Sq M43 . . . . .100 A8
Outrington Dr M11 . . . . . .165 A8
Outterside St PR7 . . . . . . .21 A6
Outwood Ave M27 . . . . . . .61 D4
Outwood Dr SK8 . . . . .131 A8
Outwood Gr BL1 . . . . .24 E5
Outwood La M90 . . . . . . .130 C7
Outwood La W M90 . . . . . .130 B8
Outwood Prim Sch SK8 . .131 D7
Outwood Rd Gatley SK8 . . .131 A8
Radcliffe M26 . . . . .44 A1
Oval Dr SK16 . . . . .101 B7
Oval The Gatley SK8 . . . . .131 B8
Shevington WN6 . . . . .35 F5
Over Hos BL7 . . . . .9 B6
Over Town La
Rochdale OL12 . . . . .13 A3
Rochdale OL12 . . . . .13 C3
Overbeck Cl WN6 . . . . .37 A4
Overbridge Rd M7,M8 . . .158 E4
Overbrook Ave M40 . . . . . .156 C5
Overbrook Dr M25 . . . . . . .63 B3
Overcombe Wlk 1 M40 . .156 C5
Overdale 1 Marple SK6 . . .125 C6
Pendlebury M27 . . . . .80 A6
Overdale Cl OL1 . . . . .48 E1
Overdale Cres M41 . . . . . . .94 F2
Overdale Dr BL1 . . . . .144 A7
Overdale Rd
New Mills SK12 . . . . .135 F6
Romiley SK6 . . . . .125 A8
Wythenshawe M22 . . . . . . .121 D5
Overdell Dr OL12 . . . . .14 F2
Overdene Cl BL6 . . . . .40 C6
Overens St OL4 . . . . .67 B7
Overfield Way OL12 . . . . . .14 F2
Overgreen BL2 . . . . .25 E3
Overhill Dr SK9 . . . . .137 E7
Overhill La SK9 . . . . .137 E7
Overhill Rd Chadderton OL9 .65 F8
Wilmslow SK9 . . . . .137 D7
Overhill Way WN3 . . . . . . .54 D3
Overlea Dr M19 . . . . .110 E6
Overlinks Dr M6 . . . . .80 B5
Overshores Rd BL7 . . . . . . .9 B8
Overstone Dr M8 . . . . .155 F7
Overt St OL11 . . . . .139 F5
Overton Ave M22 . . . . . . .121 D5
Overton Cres
Hazel Grove SK7 . . . . .124 E4
Sale M33 . . . . .107 D1
Overton Rd M22 . . . . .121 D5
Overton St WN7 . . . . .75 E4
Overton Way 3 SK9 . . . . . .131 D5
Overwood Rd M22 . . . . . . .121 D8
Ovington Wlk 6 M40 . . . .156 C5
Owen Fold OL4 . . . . .67 F7
Owen St 2 Eccles M30 . . . .79 B1
2 Leigh WN7 . . . . .75 D5
Oldham OL1 . . . . .49 E3
Salford M6 . . . . .81 A5
Stockport SK3 . . . . .169 D1
Owen's Row BL6 . . . . .22 C3
Owenington Gr M38 . . . . . .60 A5
Owens Cl OL9 . . . . .65 E8
Owens Farm Dr SK2 . . . . .124 E7
Owler La OL9 . . . . .65 E8
Owlerbarrow Rd BL8 . . . . . .27 A3
Owlwood Cl M38 . . . . .59 E3
Owlwood Dr M38 . . . . .59 E3
Ox Gate BL2 . . . . .25 D5
Ox Hey Cl BL6 . . . . .39 E8
Ox Hey La Denshaw OL3 . . .33 A7
Horwich BL6 . . . . .39 F7
Ox St BL0 . . . . .138 B5
Oxbow Way M45 . . . . .63 A8
Oxbridge Cl 3 M33 . . . . . .107 D3
Oxburgh Rd WN3 . . . . .55 F4
Oxendale Dr M24 . . . . .46 D1
Oxendon Ave M11 . . . . .83 B3
Oxenhurst Gn SK2 . . . . . .124 E5
Oxford Ave Droylsden M43 . .83 F3
Rochdale OL11 . . . . .30 A6
Sale M33 . . . . .107 D4
Whitefield M45 . . . . .63 A8
Oxford Cl BL4 . . . . .59 F8
Oxford Ct Manchester M16 162 D5
Manchester M2 . . . . .162 F4
Wigan WN1 . . . . .37 D1
Oxford Dr Middleton M24 . . .47 C2
Romiley SK6 . . . . .113 C4
Oxford Gr Bolton BL1 . . . .142 C1
Irlam M44 . . . . .105 C6
Oxford Grove
Com Prim Sch BL1 . . . . . .142 C1
Oxford Ho OL9 . . . . .152 C7
Oxford Pl Manchester M14 . .98 C4
14 Rochdale OL11 . . . . . . .31 A5
Oxford Rd
Altrincham WA14 . . . . .119 D3

Oxford Rd continued
Atherton M46 . . . . .58 B5
Dukinfield SK16 . . . . .101 D8
Horwich BL6 . . . . .39 F8
Hyde SK14 . . . . .113 E8
Little Lever BL3 . . . . .42 F3
Manchester M1,M13 . . . . . .163 B6
Orrell WN5 . . . . .53 F8
Salford M6 . . . . .80 B4
Oxford Road Sta M1 . . . . .163 A7
Oxford St Adlington PR7 . . .21 A6
Bolton BL1 . . . . .145 F7
Bury BL9 . . . . .141 A1
Eccles M30 . . . . .79 E1
Hindley WN2 . . . . .56 F7
Leigh WN7 . . . . .75 F6
Manchester M1,M60,M2 . . .163 A8
Manchester M16 . . . . .162 D5
Newton-le-W WA12 . . . . . . .89 B3
Oldham OL9 . . . . .152 C5
Shaw OL2 . . . . .149 B7
Stalybridge SK15 . . . . .86 C1
Stalybridge SK15 . . . . .86 A4
Oxford St E OL7 . . . . .166 A1
Oxford St W OL7 . . . . .100 F8
Oxford Way Rochdale OL12 .14 E2
Stockport SK4 . . . . .169 D3
Oxford Wlk M34 . . . . .101 A1
Oxhill Wlk 17 M40 . . . . . . .65 D2
Oxhouse Rd WN5 . . . . .53 D4
Oxlea Gr BL5 . . . . .57 E7
Oxney Rd M14 . . . . .98 C4
Oxted Wlk 9 M8 . . . . .156 A6
Oxton Ave M22 . . . . .121 C4
Oxton St M11 . . . . .99 F7
Ozanam Ct M7 . . . . .155 D7

P

Pacific Rd WA14 . . . . .119 A6
Pacific Way M50 . . . . .96 C8
Pack Horse Yd OL16 . . . . .139 F7
Packer St 1 Bolton BL1 . . .142 C2
Rochdale OL16 . . . . .139 F7
Packwood Chase OL9 . . . . .65 F8
Padbury Cl M41 . . . . .94 D3
Padbury Ho 7 M6 . . . . . . .154 F1
Padbury Way BL2 . . . . .25 E1
Padbury Wlk M40 . . . . . . .157 F5
Padden Brook SK6 . . . . . .113 B2
Padden Brook
Mews SK6 . . . . .113 B2
Paddington Ave M40 . . . . . .83 B5
Paddington Cl M6 . . . . .81 A2
Paddison St 2 M27 . . . . . . .79 E7
Paddock Chase SK12 . . . .133 F6
Paddock Cl M46 . . . . .58 E5
Paddock Hill La WA16 . . . .136 A3
Paddock La Failsworth M35 .83 F5
Lymm WA13 . . . . .117 C2
Partington WA13,WA14 . . .118 B5
Paddock Rd SK14 . . . . . . .113 D8
Paddock Rise WN6 . . . . . . .36 E3
Paddock St M12 . . . . .163 C7
Paddock The
Altrincham WA15 . . . . .120 B4
Ashton-in-M WN4 . . . . .72 F6
Bramhall SK7 . . . . .123 D1
Cheadle SK8 . . . . .122 E5
Hadfield SK13 . . . . .103 F5
Handforth SK9 . . . . .131 D4
Hollingworth SK14 . . . . . . .103 E5
Lymm WA13 . . . . .117 C4
Ramsbottom BL0 . . . . .138 B7
Uppermill OL3 . . . . .68 F4
Worsley M28 . . . . .78 E7
Paddocks The SK3 . . . . . .124 A4
Paderborn Ct BL1 . . . . . . .145 E6
Padfield Cty Prim Sch
SK13 . . . . .104 B5
Padfield Gate SK13 . . . . . .116 D7
Padfield Main Rd SK13 . . .104 C5
Padiham Cl Bury BL9 . . . . . .44 D7
Leigh WN7 . . . . .76 A5
Padstow Cl SK14 . . . . .102 D3
Padstow Dr SK7 . . . . .132 F7
Padstow St M40 . . . . .160 E3
Padstow Wlk SK14 . . . . . . .102 D3
Padworth Wlk M23 . . . . . .120 D8
Pagan St OL16 . . . . .139 F8
Pagefield Cl 15 WN6 . . . . . .37 A1
Pagefield Ind Est WN6 . . . .36 F1
Pagefield St WN6 . . . . .37 A1
Paget St M40 . . . . .157 D5
Pagnall Ct OL9 . . . . .152 B5
Paignton Ave
Hattersley SK14 . . . . .102 D3
Manchester M19 . . . . .110 F8
Paignton Cl WN5 . . . . .71 E8
Paignton Dr M33 . . . . .107 D5
Paignton Gr SK5 . . . . .111 E7
Paignton Wlk SK14 . . . . . .102 C2
Pailin Dr M43 . . . . .84 C2
Pailton Cl BL6 . . . . .40 D6
Painswick Rd M22 . . . . . . .121 B1
Paiton St BL1 . . . . .144 C7
Palace Arc WN4 . . . . .73 B3
Palace Gdns OL1 . . . . .48 D2
Palace Gr WN7 . . . . .76 D6
Palace Rd Ashton-u-L OL6 . .85 C5
Sale M33 . . . . .108 A5
Palace St Bolton BL1 . . . . .145 E8
Bury BL9 . . . . .141 A2
Oldham OL9 . . . . .152 C7
Palatine Ave
Manchester M20 . . . . .110 B5
Rochdale OL11 . . . . .30 A8

Palatine Cl Irlam M44 . . . . .93 F1
Wigan WN3 . . . . .54 E4
Palatine Cres M20 . . . . . . .110 B5
Palatine Dr BL9 . . . . .27 E3
Palatine Ho 4 SK3 . . . . . .170 E8
Palatine Rd
Manchester M20 . . . . .110 B6
Rochdale OL11 . . . . .30 A8
Wythenshawe M20,M22 . . .109 E2
Palatine Sq WN7 . . . . .75 D5
Palatine St 4 Bolton BL1 . .145 F7
Denton M34 . . . . .100 E4
Ramsbottom BL0 . . . . .138 C6
Rochdale OL16 . . . . .31 C7
Palewood Cl WN1 . . . . .37 E1
Paley St BL1 . . . . .145 F7
Palfrey Pl M12 . . . . .163 C7
Palgrave Ave M40 . . . . . . .157 D5
Palin St WN2 . . . . .57 B3
Palin Wood Rd OL3 . . . . . . .50 F5
Pall Mall M2 . . . . .158 F1
Pallotine Wlk OL11 . . . . . .139 D5
Palm Ave M4 . . . . .72 C5
Palm Bsns Ctr OL9 . . . . . .152 B7
Palm Cl M33 . . . . .107 D5
Palm Gr Oldham OL9 . . . . .152 B8
Wigan WN5 . . . . .54 D6
Palm St Bolton BL1 . . . . . .143 F3
Droylsden M43 . . . . .83 E2
Manchester M13 . . . . .98 F3
Oldham OL4 . . . . .67 C8
Palma Ave M90 . . . . .130 B8
Palmer Ave SK8 . . . . .122 F6
Palmer Cl Manchester M8 . .64 B2
Oldham OL8 . . . . .66 F4
Palmer Gr WN7 . . . . .57 E1
Palmer St Dukinfield SK16 .166 B1
Manchester M7 . . . . .81 C5
Sale M33 . . . . .108 A4
Palmerston Ave M16 . . . . . .97 D2
Palmerston Cl
Ramsbottom BL0 . . . . .11 C4
Reddish M34 . . . . .100 B3
Palmerston Rd
Reddish M34 . . . . .100 B3
Stockport SK2 . . . . .124 B3
Palmerston St M12 . . . . . .160 E2
Pandora St M20 . . . . .110 A5
Panfield Rd M22 . . . . .121 D4
Pangbourne Ave M41 . . . . .95 E3
Pangbourne Cl SK3 . . . . . .123 C6
Pankhurst Wlk 11 M14 . . . .98 B3
Panmure St OL8 . . . . .66 F4
Pansy Rd BL4 . . . . .60 A8
Panton St BL6 . . . . .22 D1
Paper Mill Rd BL7 . . . . .25 A7
Parade Rd M90 . . . . .130 C2
Parade The
1 Alderley Edge SK9 . . . .137 A1
Romiley SK6 . . . . .113 A1
Swinton M27 . . . . .79 F8
2 Whitefield M45 . . . . . . .44 F2
Paradise St Dukinfield M34 100 F7
Hadfield SK13 . . . . .104 A5
Ramsbottom BL0 . . . . .138 C7
Parbold Ave M20 . . . . .110 A6
Parbrook Cl M40 . . . . .157 D5
Parbrook La WN4 . . . . .36 B7
Parchments The WA12 . . . .89 D4
Pardoners Ct M30,M5 . . . . .80 B2
Parham Wlk 4 M9 . . . . . . .64 E3
Paris Ave Salford M5 . . . . .161 B7
Wigan WN3 . . . . .54 C3
Paris St BL3 . . . . .146 B4
Parish Church
CE Jun Sch The OL1 . . . . .153 F8
Parish View M5 . . . . .161 B8
Park Ave Altrincham WA14 .119 E8
Altrincham WA15 . . . . .119 F1
Bolton BL1 . . . . .143 E4
Bramhall SK7 . . . . .132 D5
Chadderton OL9 . . . . .48 B1
Cheadle SK8 . . . . .122 F1
Cheadle SK8 . . . . .122 F1
Failsworth M35 . . . . .83 D8
Golborne WA3 . . . . .73 F2
Hyde SK14 . . . . .167 D4
Longshaw WN5 . . . . .53 E1
Manchester M16 . . . . .161 C5
Manchester M19 . . . . .99 A1
Manchester M7 . . . . .155 D8
Pendlebury M27 . . . . .80 A7
Poynton SK12 . . . . .133 E4
Prestwich M25 . . . . .63 B4
Ramsbottom BL0 . . . . .11 D6
Romiley SK6 . . . . .113 C2
Sale M33 . . . . .108 A6
Shevington WN6 . . . . .36 B7
Urmston M41 . . . . .95 C2
Whitefield M45 . . . . .62 D6
Wilmslow SK9 . . . . .137 C8
Park Ave N WA12 . . . . .89 C2
Park Ave S WA12 . . . . .89 C2
Park Bank M46 . . . . .58 F6
Park Bglws 4 SK6 . . . . . .125 F5
Park Bridge Rd
Oldham OL6 . . . . .67 B1
Oldham OL7,OL8 . . . . .85 A8
Park Brow Cl M21 . . . . . . .109 C7
Park Cl Chadderton OL9 . . .48 B1
Glossop SK13 . . . . .104 D2
Sale WA14 . . . . .119 F8
Stalybridge SK15 . . . . .85 F3
Whitefield M45 . . . . .62 F6
Park Cotts OL3 . . . . .68 E5
Park Court Mews SK8 . . . .122 E4
Park Cres Ashton-u-L OL6 . .85 E2
Bacup OL13 . . . . .3 F8

Orw–Par 235

Park Cres continued
Chadderton OL9 . . . . .47 F1
Glossop SK13 . . . . .104 B3
Handforth SK9 . . . . .131 B1
Manchester M14 . . . . .98 C3
Wigan WN1 . . . . .37 B1
Park Cres W BL1 . . . . .37 B1
Park Ct Manchester M25 . . .63 E2
Rochdale OL11 . . . . .139 F6
Sale M33 . . . . .108 A5
Wythenshawe M22 . . . . . . .121 D3
Park Dean Sch OL8 . . . . . . .67 B2
Park Dene Dr SK13 . . . . . .104 C2
Park Dr Altrincham WA15 . .119 F1
Altrincham WA15 . . . . .120 A7
Eccles M30 . . . . .79 D4
Hyde SK14 . . . . .167 D4
Manchester M16 . . . . .97 C2
Stockport SK4 . . . . .168 B2
Park Edge BL5 . . . . .58 A7
Park Field Rd OL4 . . . . .68 C6
Park Gate Ave M20 . . . . . .110 B6
Park Gate Cl SK6 . . . . .112 E5
Park Gates Ave SK8 . . . . .123 C1
Park Gates Dr SK8 . . . . . .123 C1
Park Gr Manchester M19 . . .99 A2
Manchester SK4 . . . . .168 B4
Radcliffe M26 . . . . .43 F4
Walkden M28 . . . . .78 D8
Park Hey Dr WN6 . . . . .35 E7
Park Hill Manchester M25 . .63 D2
21 Rochdale OL12 . . . . . . .14 F1
Park Hill Cl SK22 . . . . .127 C1
Park Hill Dr M45 . . . . .62 A8
Park Hill Rd WA15 . . . . . . .120 A1
Park Hill St BL1 . . . . .145 D8
Park Ho Manchester M19 . . .99 A1
Manchester M20 . . . . .110 A4
Sale WA15 . . . . .120 C7
Droylsden M43 . . . . .100 A8
Park House Bridge Rd M6 80 E6
Park Ind Est WN4 . . . . .72 E3
Park La Altrincham WA15 . .120 A1
Dukinfield SK16 . . . . .101 C8
Golborne WN2,WN7 . . . . . .74 D6
Horwich BL6 . . . . .22 D3
Leigh WN7 . . . . .76 C4
Little Bollington WA14 . . . .118 B2
Manchester M7 . . . . .155 D8
Oldham OL3 . . . . .69 C5
Oldham OL8 . . . . .66 F2
Pendlebury M27 . . . . .80 D6
Pendlebury M6 . . . . .80 C5
Poynton SK12 . . . . .133 F3
Radcliffe M26 . . . . .44 D4
Rochdale OL16 . . . . .139 F8
Royton OL2 . . . . .48 D4
Royton OL2 . . . . .48 D5
Royton OL2 . . . . .48 E5
Stockport SK1 . . . . .124 B8
Whitefield M45 . . . . .62 D7
Park La W M27 . . . . .80 D7
Park Lane Ct M7 . . . . .155 D8
Park Lane Inf Sch WN4 . . . .72 F7
Park Lo 1 WN4 . . . . .99 A1
Park Lodge Cl SK8 . . . . . .122 E6
Park Mdw BL5 . . . . .58 A8
Park Mews M16 . . . . .97 C2
Park Mount SK8 . . . . .122 A5
Park Par Ashton-u-L OL6 . .166 B2
Shaw OL2 . . . . .32 C1
Park Par Ind Est OL6 . . . . .166 A2
Park Pl Manchester M4 . . .159 A3
Manchester SK4 . . . . .110 F2
Prestwich M25 . . . . .63 C5
Salford M6 . . . . .80 A3
Park Range M14 . . . . .98 D3
Park Rd Adlington PR7 . . . . .20 F6
Altrincham WA14 . . . . .119 A2
Altrincham WA15 . . . . .119 F1
Altrincham WA15 . . . . .120 A7
Bolton BL1 . . . . .144 C7
Bramhall SK8 . . . . .123 C1
Bury BL9 . . . . .140 E4
Cheadle SK8 . . . . .122 E6
Denton M34 . . . . .100 E3
Droylsden M34 . . . . .100 D8
Eccles M30 . . . . .79 D4
Edgworth BL7 . . . . .9 E5
Golborne WA3 . . . . .90 A7
Hadfield SK13 . . . . .104 B4
High Lane SK12 . . . . .134 E6
Hindley WN2 . . . . .56 E3
Hyde SK14 . . . . .167 D4
Little Lever BL3 . . . . .42 F4
Longshaw WN5 . . . . .53 F1
Manchester M25,M7,M8 . . .63 E2
Manchester SK4 . . . . .111 B5
Middleton M24 . . . . .65 A8
Oldham OL4,OL8 . . . . .67 A5
Oldham OL8 . . . . .153 F5
Partington M31 . . . . .106 A3
Partington WA13 . . . . .117 C8
Ramsbottom BL0 . . . . .10 F3
Rochdale OL12 . . . . .15 A1
Romiley SK6 . . . . .113 C3
Sale M33 . . . . .108 A6
Sale WA15,WA14 . . . . .120 B7
Salford M6 . . . . .80 A3
Stalybridge SK15,SK16 . . . .85 D1
Standish WN6 . . . . .36 E8
Stretford M17,M32 . . . . . . .96 C3
Walkden M28 . . . . .60 D1
Westhoughton BL5 . . . . . . .58 A8
Wigan WN5 . . . . .54 B6

Park Rd *continued*
Wigan WN6 37 A1
Wilmslow SK9 136 F7
Wythenshawe SK8 121 F5
Park Rd N
Newton-le-W WA12 89 E4
Urmston M41 95 C2
Park Rd S
Newton-le-W WA12 89 D2
Urmston M41 95 C2
Park Rise SK6 113 C3
Park Road Prim Sch
Sale M33 108 A6
Sale WA14 119 E8
Park Row 3 Bolton BL1 24 F6
Manchester SK4 110 F2
Park Seventeen M45 44 F1
Park Side Ave OL2 149 C8
Park Sq Ashton-u-L OL6 85 E4
Manchester M16 97 A2
Park St Ashton-u-L OL7 166 A1
Ashton-u-L OL7 166 B2
Atherton M46 58 E4
Bolton BL1 145 D8
Bredbury SK6 112 F3
Denton M34 100 D3
Droylsden M43 84 C2
Farnworth BL4 42 D1
Heywood OL10 46 E8
Manchester M3 158 D1
Manchester M3 158 F3
Manchester M7 155 D8
Mossley OL5 86 C8
Oldham OL8 153 E5
Oldham OL8 153 E6
Pendlebury M27 80 A7
Prestwich M25 63 C4
Radcliffe M26 44 C4
Rochdale OL16 139 F6
Royton OL2 48 E4
Shaw OL2 149 C7
Stalybridge SK15 86 B1
Stockport SK1 169 F2
1 Tyldesley M29 59 A1
Wigan WN3 150 B6
Park Sta M40 83 A4
Park Terr Heywood OL10 29 D3
Mossley OL5 86 C8
Prestwich M45 62 D7
Westhoughton BL5 39 F1
Park The Oldham OL3 69 C5
Uppermill OL4 68 D6
Park View Abram WN2 56 B1
Abram WN2 74 B8
Ashton-in-M WN4 73 B2
2 Bolton BL1 24 F6
Bredbury SK6 112 C3
Chadderton OL9 48 B1
Cheadle SK3 122 F7
Droylsden M34 100 D8
Farnworth BL4 42 D1
Gatley SK8 122 A6
High Lane SK7 134 B8
Kearsley BL4 60 F7
Little Bollington WA14 118 B2
Littleborough OL15 16 B6
Manchester M14 110 E7
7 Manchester M21 96 F1
Manchester M9 156 C6
Newton-le-W WA12 89 E3
Stockport SK1 124 B7
Park View Ct
Poynton SK12 133 E4
Prestwich M25 63 B3
Romiley SK6 113 C2
Park View Prim Sch M25 63 B3
Park View Rd Bolton BL3 146 C4
Prestwich M25 63 B3
Park View Rise SK22 127 C1
Park Way Eccles M17,M41 96 A6
Eccles M32,M41 95 F5
Parkbridge Wlk M13 163 B6
Parkbrook Rd M23 121 B7
Parkdale Chadderton OL9 48 B1
Tyldesley M29 77 B5
Parkdale Ave Denton M34 100 D7
Manchester M18 165 C5
Parkdale Rd BL2 25 C1
Parkdene Cl BL2 25 D4
Parkend Dr WN7 75 D2
Parkend Rd M23 121 A5
Parker St Bury BL9 141 A2
Manchester M1 159 A1
Parkes Field Prim Sch
M27 80 A7
Parkfield Chadderton OL9 48 B1
1 Middleton M24 64 F8
Salford M5 154 D2
Shevington WN6 36 B7
Parkfield Ave
Farnworth BL4 60 C7
Manchester M14 98 B3
Manchester M25 63 D3
Marple SK6 125 F6
2 Oldham OL8 66 B2
Tyldesley M29 77 B6
Urmston M41 95 B1
Parkfield Cl Leigh WN7 76 A7
Tyldesley M29 77 B6
Parkfield Ct WA14 119 C4
Parkfield Dr Middleton M24 64 E8
Tyldesley M29 59 D1
Parkfield Ind Est M24 64 F8
Parkfield Lo M20 110 A4
Parkfield Prim Sch M24 46 E1
Parkfield Rd
Altrincham WA14 119 C4
Bolton BL3 147 F3
Cheadle SK8 122 F1
Parkfield Rd N M40 65 F1
Parkfield Rd S M20 110 A4
Parkfield St
Manchester M14 98 B3
Manchester M14 98 B4
Rochdale OL16 31 B2
Parkfields
Abram Brow WN2 74 C6
Stalybridge SK15 86 D3
Parkgate Altrincham WA14 119 B4
Bury BL8 26 F5
Chadderton OL9 48 B1
Parkgate Dr Bolton BL1 25 A5
Pendlebury M27 80 A7
Stockport SK2 124 B4
Parkgate Way
7 Handforth SK9 131 D4
Shaw OL2 49 D7
Parkhill Ave M8 64 B2
Parkhills Rd BL9 44 F8
Parkhouse St M11 165 B8
Parkhurst Ave M40 65 E1
Parkin Cl SK16 101 C8
Parkin St M12 99 A3
Parkinson St Bolton BL3 144 C5
Bury BL9 27 F5
Parklake Ave M7 155 E8
Parkland Ave SK22 127 C1
Parklands Royton OL2 48 C7
Sale M33 108 C5
Shaw OL2 49 D8
Whitefield M45 62 E8
Parklands Dr Aspull WN2 38 C6
Sale M33 107 D2
Parklands High Sch M22 121 C3
Parklands Rd M23 120 F7
Parklands The SK4 169 E4
Parklands Way SK12 133 E4
Parklea Ct 6 M7 63 E1
Parklee Cty Prim Sch M46 58 D2
Parkleigh Dr M40 65 E2
Parkmount Rd M9 64 E1
Parks Nook BL4 60 C7
Parks The WA12 73 B1
Parks Yd BL9 140 E2
Parkside High Lane SK6 134 D8
Hindley WN2 56 E6
Middleton M24 64 F6
Parkside Ave
Ashton-in-M WN4 72 F8
Eccles M30 79 C1
Failsworth M35 83 F5
Manchester M7 155 E8
Walkden M28 60 D1
Parkside Cl High Lane SK6 134 D8
Radcliffe M26 44 D4
Parkside Cres WN5 53 F6
Parkside Ind Est OL2 48 E4
Parkside La SK6 126 C6
Parkside Rd
Golborne WA12,WA2 90 B2
Manchester M14 98 A2
Sale M33 108 D3
Parkside St 6 BL2 25 C1
Parkside Wlk Bury BL9 140 F1
Stockport SK7 123 E3
Parkstead Dr M9 157 D6
Parkstone Ave
Droylsden M18 99 F6
Whitefield M45 62 D6
Parkstone Cl BL8 26 F2
Parkstone Dr M27 80 B6
Parkstone La M28 78 F4
Parkstone Rd M44 94 A3
Parksway Manchester M25 63 C2
Manchester M9 64 B6
Pendlebury M27 80 C6
Parkview Ct M32 96 E1
Parkview Pk WA13 117 D1
Parkville Rd
Manchester M20 110 C5
Prestwich M25 63 C6
Parkway Chadderton OL9 48 A1
Cheadle SK3 122 F7
New Mills SK22 127 C1
Rochdale OL11 30 B8
Shevington Moor WN6 19 A2
Stockport SK7 123 E2
Walkden M38 59 F4
Westhoughton BL5 57 D6
Wilmslow SK9 137 B6
Parkway Bsns Ctr M14 97 F2
Parkway Circ M17 96 A6
Parkway Four Ind Est M17 96 A6
Parkway Gr M38 59 E4
Parkway Ind Est M17 96 A6
Parkway Trad Est M32 96 A5
Parkwood BL7 8 D2
Parkwood Cl WN3 151 E6
Parkwood Dr BL5 58 F7
Parkwood Rd M23 121 C7
Parlane St M4 159 B3
Parliament Pl BL9 140 E1
Parliament St Bury BL9 140 E1
Ince-in-M WN3 151 D6
Orrell WN8 53 C7
Parndon Dr SK2 124 C7
Parnell Ave M22 121 D8
Parnell Cl M29 77 B5
Parnham Cl BL3 43 B5
Parr Cl BL4 60 B8
Parr Fold M45 45 B2
Parr Fold Ave M28 60 C1
Parr Ho OL8 153 F5
Parr La BL9,M45 45 B2
Parr St Droylsden M11 99 E7
Eccles M30 79 D1
Tyldesley M29 76 F8
Parrbrook Cl M45 45 A1
Parrbrook Wlk M45 45 B1
Parrenthorn High Sch
M25 63 D7
Parrenthorn Rd M25 63 C7
Parrfield Rd M28 79 A7
Parrin La M30 79 C3
Parrot St Bolton BL3 145 E5
Droylsden M11 83 C1
Parrs Ct M44 93 F2
Parrs Mount Mews SK4 110 F2
Parrs Wood Ave M20 110 C2
Parrs Wood High Sch
M20 110 D1
Parrs Wood La
M19,M20,SK4 110 D2
Parrs Wood Rd
Manchester M20 110 D4
Manchester M20 122 B8
Parry Mead SK6 113 A4
Parry Rd M12 99 A4
Parry Wlk 11 OL6 85 D4
Parslow Ave M8 156 A8
Parson's La BL9 140 F3
Parson's Wlk WN1 37 B1
Parsonage M3 158 F1
Parsonage Brow WN8 53 A8
Parsonage Cl Bury BL9 141 A3
Orrell WN8 53 A7
Salford M5 161 C8
Parsonage Ct
4 Manchester M20 110 B6
Manchester SK4 168 B4
Parsonage Dr M28 60 C2
Parsonage Gdns SK6 126 A4
Parsonage La M3 158 F2
Parsonage Rd
Kearsley M26 61 C7
Manchester M20 110 C7
Manchester SK4 168 C4
Urmston M41 94 E1
Walkden M28 60 C2
Parsonage St Bury BL9 141 A3
Hyde SK14 167 D1
Manchester M15 162 E5
Manchester M8 63 F1
Radcliffe M26 44 A3
Stockport SK4 169 E2
Parsonage Way
Cheadle SK8 123 B5
Leigh WN7 75 E6
Parsonage Wlk OL16 31 F7
Parsons Dr M24 46 F2
Parsons Field M27 81 A5
Parsons St OL9 152 C6
Part St BL5 39 E2
Parth St BL9 28 D1
Partington Ct
Farnworth BL4 42 C1
Glossop SK13 104 F1
Partington La M27 79 E7
Partington Pk SK13 104 C3
Partington Pl 2 M33 108 B5
Partington Prim Sch
M31 105 F3
Partington St Bolton BL3 146 C2
Eccles M30 79 D3
Failsworth M35 83 F7
Heywood OL10 29 A2
Manchester M10,M40 157 F5
4 Oldham OL1 67 A7
Rochdale OL11 30 B2
Swinton M28 79 C8
Wigan WN5 54 E8
Partridge Ave M23 121 C6
Partridge Cl Irlam M44 94 A4
Rochdale OL11 29 F7
Partridge Rd M35 84 C6
Partridge Rise M43 84 D3
Partridge St M32 96 F5
Partridge Way OL9 65 E8
Parvet Ave M43 83 F3
Pascal St M19 111 A8
Pass St OL9 153 D6
Pass The OL16 31 A8
Passmonds Cres
OL11,OL12 14 B1
Passmonds Way OL11 30 B8
Paston Rd M22 121 D7
Pasture Cl Ashton-in-M WN4 72 E6
Heywood OL10 29 B1
Pasture Field Rd M22 121 F1
Pasturefield Cl 1 M33 108 F3
Pasturegreen Way M44 94 B3
Pastures La OL4 68 B8
Patch Croft Rd M22 121 F1
Patch La SK7 132 D5
Patchett St
Manchester M12 164 F6
9 Tyldesley M29 59 A1
Pateley Sq 2 WN6 37 B3
Patey St M12 99 A3
Pathfield Wlk 8 M9 157 D8
Patience St 11 OL12 14 C1
Patmos St BL0 11 D6
Paton Ave BL3 42 A3
Paton Ct M7 81 C4
Paton Mews 5 BL3 42 A3
Paton St Manchester M1 159 B1
Rochdale OL12 14 D3
Patricia Dr M28 60 E2
Patrick Roddy Ct M18 165 C5
Patricroft Rd WN2 151 F6
Patricroft Sta M30 79 C2
Patten St M20 110 B6
Patterdale Ave
Ashton-u-L OL7 84 F5
Urmston M41 95 B4
Patterdale Cl Oldham OL1 49 A1
Rochdale OL11 30 B3
Stalybridge SK15 86 A3
Patterdale Dr Bury BL9 44 E7
Middleton M24 46 E2
Patterdale Pl WN2 56 A7
Patterdale Rd
Ashton-in-M WN4 73 A8
Ashton-u-L OL7 84 F5
Bolton BL2 25 F4
Leigh WN7 76 C4
Partington M31 105 E3
Romiley SK6 113 B4
Stockport SK1,SK2 124 B7
Wythenshawe M22 121 E8
Patterdale Wlk WA15 120 D5
Patterson Ave M21 97 A1
Patterson St Bolton BL3 146 A4
Denton M34 100 F4
Newton-le-W WA12 89 B3
Westhoughton BL5 57 B7
Pattishall Cl M4 160 D1
Pattison Cl OL12 14 D3
Patton Cl BL9 45 B2
Paul Ct 6 SK1 112 A1
Paul Row OL15 6 C1
Paulden Ave Oldham OL4 49 E1
Wythenshawe M23 121 B6
Paulden Dr M35 84 A7
Paulette St BL1 143 E2
Paulhan Rd M20 110 D4
Paulhan St BL3 147 E3
Pauline St WN2 57 B1
Pavilion Cl OL12 14 F2
Pavilion Dr OL6 85 D5
Pavilion Ho M20 110 A4
Pavilion Wlk M26 43 F3
Pavilions The M20 110 B4
Paxford Pl SK9 137 A5
Paythorne Cl WA3 91 F3
Paythorne Gn SK2 124 E5
Peabody St BL3 147 E4
Peace St Atherton M46 58 E3
Bolton BL3 145 D5
3 Failsworth M35 66 A1
Tyldesley M29 76 F7
Peacefield SK6 125 E5
Peacefield Prim Sch
SK6 125 E5
Peacehaven Ave 12 M11 83 C2
Peaceville Rd M19 98 F1
Peach Bank M24 65 A8
Peach Bank Ho M24 65 A8
Peach Rd OL4 49 D1
Peach St M25 63 C5
Peach Tree Cl M7 155 F6
Peach Tree Ct M6 81 A2
Peacock Ave Gatley SK8 131 B6
8 Salford M6 80 D5
Peacock Cl Hadfield SK13 171 E4
Manchester M18 165 C6
Peacock Fold WN7 75 D6
Peacock Gr M18 99 D4
Peacock Way 5 SK9 131 D5
Peak Ave M46 58 D5
Peak Bank SK6 113 B3
Peak Cl OL4 49 F4
Peak St Bolton BL1 143 D2
Manchester M1 159 B1
Oldham OL9 152 C6
Stockport SK1 112 A2
Peakdale Ave Gatley SK8 122 B1
Manchester M8 156 B8
Peakdale Rd Droylsden M43 83 E3
Hadfield SK13 171 E3
Marple SK6 126 A4
Peaknaze Cl Glossop SK13 116 B8
Pendlebury M27 80 B8
Pear Ave BL9 141 C3
Pear Cl M24 65 B6
Pear New Mill Ind Est
SK6 112 C2
Pear Tree Cl
Hadfield SK13 171 E4
Marple SK6 126 B8
Salford M6 81 A2
Pear Tree Ct 3 M6 81 A2
Pear Tree Dr SK15 86 B2
Pear Tree Gr M29 59 E1
Pear Tree Wlk 10 M33 107 C5
Pearl Ave M7 63 E1
Pearl Brook Ind Est BL6 22 B3
Pearl Mill Cl OL8 67 B4
Pearl St Denton M34 100 E3
Hazel Grove SK7 124 E4
Rochdale OL11 30 C8
Wigan WN6 37 B3
Pearl Way SK14 103 A2
Pearly Bank OL1 49 D4
Pearn Ave M19 110 F5
Pearn Rd M19 110 F5
Pearson Cl Milnrow OL16 31 F7
Partington M31 106 A3
Pearson Gr 7 OL4 67 E6
Pearson Ho M30 95 D8
Pearson Mews SK16 101 C6
Pearson St Bury BL9 141 B3
Dukinfield SK16 101 C6
Reddish SK5 169 F3
Rochdale OL16 31 C8
Peart Ave SK6 113 C6
Peart St M34 100 E3
Peartree Wlk M22 121 B4
Peary St M4 159 B3
Peaslake Cl SK6 113 D2
Peatfield Ave M27 61 E2
Peatfield Wlk M15 162 F5
Pebble Cl SK15 86 A4
Pebworth Cl M24,M9 64 F5
Peckford Dr M40 83 A5
Peckforton Cl SK8 122 A5
Peckforton Wlk 11 SK9 131 E1
Peckmill Cl SK9 131 E2
Pedder St BL1 142 C1
Pedler Brow La OL12 15 E6
Pedley Wlk M13 163 B7
Peebles Cl WN4 72 C4
Peebles Dr M40 83 D4
Peel Ave Altrincham WA14 119 D2
Ramsbottom BL0 138 A5
Peel Brow BL0 11 D6
Peel Brow Prim Sch BL0 11 D6
Peel Cl M46 58 E3
Peel Cnr M29 77 B8
Peel Cott St OL14 6 A8
Peel Cottage Rd OL14 6 A8
Peel Cross Rd M5 81 A1
Peel Ctr The
Stockport SK1 112 A2
Stockport SK1 169 F2
Peel Dr Sale M33 108 E4
Walkden M38 59 F4
Peel Gr Manchester M12 99 A4
Worsley M28 78 F8
Peel Green Rd M30 95 C8
Peel Hall Prim Sch
Walkden M38 59 F3
Wythenshawe M22 121 F3
Peel Hall Rd
Ramsbottom BL0,BL9 11 B2
Wythenshawe M22 121 F2
Peel La Heywood OL10 29 B3
Manchester M8 159 B4
Tyldesley M29 77 B4
Walkden M28,M38 59 F3
Peel Moat Ct SK4 111 B5
Peel Moat Rd SK4 111 B5
Peel Moat Sports Ctr
SK4 111 B5
Peel Mount
Ramsbottom BL0 11 A4
Salford M6 81 B3
Peel Park Cres M38 59 F4
Peel Rd WA15 119 E3
Peel Sq M18 99 D5
Peel St Adlington PR6 21 B8
Ashton-u-L OL6 166 B3
Denton M34 100 E4
Denton M34 100 E6
Droylsden M43 99 F8
Dukinfield SK16 166 C1
Eccles M30 79 F2
Failsworth M35 83 D6
Farnworth BL4 60 E8
Hadfield SK13 104 C5
Heywood OL10 29 B2
Hyde SK14 167 F1
Leigh WN7 75 E5
Littleborough OL15 16 B5
Newton-le-W WA12 89 A3
Oldham OL9 152 B7
Platt Bridge WN2 56 A2
1 Radcliffe M26 44 B2
Rochdale OL12 139 E8
Stalybridge SK15 85 F1
Stockport SK2 170 F6
Westhoughton BL5 39 E1
Peel Terr 13 SK16 166 B1
Peel Twr BL8 10 F5
Peel View BL8 27 A6
Peel Way BL9 140 E2
Peelgate Dr SK8 122 A2
Peels Ave OL4 68 A7
Peelwood Ave M38 60 A4
Peelwood Gr M46 58 E2
Peerglow Pk Est WA14 119 E8
Peers Cl M41 94 D4
Peers St BL8 27 C2
Pegamoid St BL2 25 B1
Pegasus Ct Rochdale OL11 30 C6
Sale M33 108 D5
Pegasus Sq M7 81 C3
Pegwell Dr M7,M8 155 E5
Pekin St OL6 166 C4
Pelham Pl M8 64 B2
Pelham St Ashton-u-L OL7 84 E1
Bolton BL3 146 C3
Oldham OL8 66 F2
Pellowe Rd OL8 66 E4
Pelton Ave M27 61 D2
Pelton Wlk M40 157 D5
Pemberlei Rd WN2 38 D2
Pemberton
Com High Sch WN5 54 C7
Pemberton Ho OL2 149 B8
Pemberton
Prim Sch WN5 54 C6
Pemberton Rd
Garswood WN3,WN5 72 A8
Wigan WN3,WN5 54 B2
Pemberton St Bolton BL1 143 E4
Manchester M16 97 C4
3 Rochdale OL11 30 C2
Walkden M38 60 B4
Pemberton Sta WN3 54 D4
Pemberton Way OL2 149 B8
Pembridge Fold M24 65 C8
Pembridge Rd M9 64 F4
Pembroke Ave Eccles M30 79 D2
Sale M33 107 F5
Pembroke Cl Horwich BL6 22 A4
Manchester M13 164 D6

Pembroke Ct
Bredbury SK6 . . . . .112 F2
Hazel Grove SK7 . . . . .124 E2
Pendlebury M27 . . . . .80 B8
14 Rochdale OL12 . . . . .14 F1
Pembroke Dr Bury BL9 . . . .44 E7
Oldham OL4 . . . . .49 E4
Pembroke Gr M44 . . . . . .105 C6
Pembroke Ho 3 SK3 . . . . .170 E8
Pembroke Rd Hindley WN2 .57 C3
Shevington WN5 . . . . .36 D1
Pembroke St Bolton BL1 . .145 D8
Littleborough OL15 . . . . . . .16 B6
Manchester M7 . . . . .155 E6
Oldham OL8 . . . . .153 D6
3 Salford M6 . . . . .154 E1
Pembroke Way 6 M34 . . .101 A1
Pembry Cl SK5 . . . . .112 F2
Pembury Cl M22 . . . . . . .121 C3
Penarth Rd Bolton BL3 . . .146 B4
Wythenshawe M22 . . . . . .121 D8
Penbury Rd WN1 . . . . . . .37 B5
Pencarrow Cl M20 . . . . . .109 F3
Pencombe Cl M12 . . . . . .165 A5
Pencroft Way M15 . . . . . .163 A5
Pendeen Cl M29 . . . . .77 A7
Pendennis 2 OL11 . . . . . .139 E6
Pendennis Ave BL6 . . . . . .40 D5
Pendennis Cl M26 . . . . . . .43 C5
Pendennis Cres WN2 . . . . .57 A3
Pendennis Rd SK4 . . . . . .168 C3
Pendle Ave BL1 . . . . .24 E6
Pendle Cl Bury BL8 . . . . . .27 B3
Oldham OL4 . . . . .67 D5
Wigan WN5 . . . . .54 D5
Pendle Ct BL1 . . . . .143 D3
Pendle Dr BL6 . . . . .22 C5
Pendle Gdns WA3 . . . . . . .91 E2
Pendle Gr OL2 . . . . .48 C3
Pendle Rd Denton M34 . . .100 F2
Golborne WA3 . . . . .74 C1
Pendle Wlk SK5 . . . . .112 A4
Pendlebury Cl M25 . . . . . .62 F2
Pendlebury Fold BL3 . . . . .40 D2
Pendlebury La WN1,WN2 . .37 D6
Pendlebury Rd Gatley SK8 122 B6
Swinton M27 . . . . .79 F8
Pendlebury St BL1 . . . . . .143 F3
Pendlebury Towers SK5 . .169 F3
Pendlecroft Ave M27 . . . . .80 C7
Pendlegreen Cl M11 . . . . .164 F8
Pendleton Coll M6 . . . . . . .154 D4
Pendleton Gn 8 M6 . . . . .154 F3
Pendleton Sta M6 . . . . .81 A4
Pendleton Way M6 . . . . . .154 F3
Pendleway M27 . . . . .62 A1
Pendragon Pl M35 . . . . . . .84 A7
Pendrell Wlk 32 M9 . . . . . .64 E3
Pendrell Wlk 4 M6 . . . . . .80 D5
Penelope Rd M6 . . . . .80 D5
Penerly Dr M9 . . . . .157 D6
Penfair Cl M11 . . . . .83 A1
Penfield Cl M1 . . . . .163 B7
Penfold Wlk M12 . . . . . . .164 F6
Pengarth Rd BL6 . . . . .22 C4
Pengham Wlk M23 . . . . . .109 A1
Pengwern Ave 2 BL3 . . . .146 B4
Penhale Mews SK7 . . . . . .132 F7
Penhall Wlk M40 . . . . .83 A5
Peninsula M7 . . . . .81 B7
Penistone Ave
Manchester M9 . . . . .65 A3
Rochdale OL16 . . . . .31 C6
Salford M6 . . . . .80 C3
Penketh Ave
Manchester M18 . . . . .99 B4
Tyldesley M29 . . . . .77 B6
Penketh St WN6 . . . . .37 B2
Penleach Ave WN7 . . . . . .76 B5
Penmere Gr M33 . . . . . . .107 E1
Penmoor Chase SK7 . . . . .124 B1
Penmore Cl OL2 . . . . .49 D7
Penn Gn SK8 . . . . .123 A1
Penn House Cl SK7 . . . . . .132 E8
Penn St Farnworth BL4 . . . .60 C8
Heywood OL10 . . . . .29 D1
Horwich BL6 . . . . .22 C3
Manchester M40 . . . . .157 F8
Oldham OL8 . . . . .153 D5
Rochdale OL16 . . . . .139 F8
Pennant Dr M25 . . . . .63 A5
Pennant St OL1 . . . . .67 B8
Pennant Street Ind Est
OL1 . . . . .67 B8
Pennell Dr 3 WN3 . . . . . . .54 F5
Pennell St M11 . . . . .83 D1
Pennine Ave Oldham OL9 .152 A5
Wigan WN3 . . . . .54 C2
Pennine Cl Bury BL8 . . . . .27 B3
Horwich BL6 . . . . .22 C5
Manchester M9 . . . . .64 F4
Pennine Ct 3 Oldham OL4 .67 A6
Stalybridge SK15 . . . . .86 D3
Swinton M27 . . . . .62 A1
Pennine Dr
Altrincham WA14 . . . . .119 B5
Ashton-u-L OL6 . . . . .85 E4
Littleborough OL12 . . . . . . .15 C6
Milnrow OL16 . . . . .32 A6
Pennine Gr Ashton-u-L OL6 .85 E6
Leigh WN7 . . . . .75 C8
Pennine La WA3 . . . . .74 C1
Pennine Prec OL16 . . . . . .31 B5
Pennine Rd Glossop SK13 .116 A8
Horwich BL6 . . . . .22 C5
Romiley SK6 . . . . .113 C6
Stockport SK7 . . . . .124 B1
Pennine Terr 2 SK16 . . . .166 C1
Pennine Vale OL2 . . . . . .149 C8

Pennine View Denton M34 100 E5
Littleborough OL15 . . . . .6 D2
Mossley OL5 . . . . .68 D1
Royton OL2 . . . . .48 E4
Stalybridge SK15 . . . . .86 C4
Pennine Wlk WN2 . . . . . . .56 B2
Pennington Ave WN7 . . . . .75 E3
Pennington Cl
Pennington Green WN2 . . . .38 E2
Walkden M38 . . . . .59 E4
Pennington Ct WN7 . . . . . .75 B1
Pennington Flash Ctry Pk
Golborne WA3 . . . . .74 F4
Leigh WN7 . . . . .74 F4
Pennington Gdns WN7 . . . .75 E3
Pennington Green La
WN2 . . . . .38 E2
Pennington La
Ince-in-M WN2 . . . . .56 A8
Standish WN2 . . . . .37 E8
Pennington Mews WN7 . . .75 E2
Pennington Rd Bolton BL3 147 F3
Leigh WN7 . . . . .75 F3
Pennington St Bury BL8 . . .26 F4
7 Hindley WN2 . . . . .56 D6
Manchester M12 . . . . .99 A2
Oldham OL9 . . . . .66 B3
1 Walkden M28 . . . . .60 C4
Penny Black Chambers
M28 . . . . .78 F5
Penny Bridge La M41 . . . . .95 A2
Penny Brook Fold SK7 . . .124 C3
Penny La Ashton-in-M WA11 89 A7
Stockport SK5 . . . . .169 F3
Penny Mdw OL6 . . . . .166 C3
Pennygate Cl WN2 . . . . . .56 D6
Pennyhurst St WN3 . . . . .150 B1
Pennymoor Dr WA3 . . . . .119 B6
Penrhos Ave Cheadle SK8 .121 F4
Penrhyn Ave Cheadle SK8 .121 F4
Middleton M24 . . . . .65 A7
Penrhyn Cres SK7 . . . . . .133 C8
Penrhyn Dr
Hazel Grove SK7 . . . . .124 D1
Prestwich M25 . . . . .63 B4
Penrhyn Gr M46 . . . . .58 C5
Penrhyn Rd SK3 . . . . .123 C8
Penrice Cl M26 . . . . .43 D5
Penrice Fold M28 . . . . .78 A7
Penrith Ave Ashton-u-L OL7 .84 F5
Bolton BL1 . . . . .142 A1
Droylsden M11 . . . . .83 B3
Oldham OL8 . . . . .66 C4
Prestwich M45 . . . . .63 B7
Reddish SK5 . . . . .99 F1
Sale M33 . . . . .108 C2
Walkden M28 . . . . .60 C4
Penrith Cl M31 . . . . .105 E4
Penrith Cres WN4 . . . . . . .73 B4
Penrith St OL11 . . . . .139 F5
Penrod Pl M6 . . . . .81 B4
Penrose Gdns M24 . . . . . .47 B1
Penrose St BL2 . . . . .148 C7
Penrose Wlk M24 . . . . . . .47 A4
Penroy Ave M20 . . . . .109 D3
Penroyson Cl M12 . . . . . .164 F6
Penry Ave M44 . . . . .105 E6
Penryn Ave Royton OL2 . . .48 C3
Sale M33 . . . . .108 C1
Penryn Ct M7 . . . . .63 D1
Pensarn Ave M14 . . . . . . .110 E8
Pensarn Gr SK5 . . . . .169 F4
Pensby Cl M27 . . . . .80 C7
Pensby Wlk M40 . . . . . . .157 D5
Pensford Cl BL2 . . . . .25 E6
Pensford Rd M23 . . . . . . .120 F3
Penshaw Ave WN3 . . . . . .55 B3
Penshurst Rd SK5 . . . . . .112 B6
Penshurst Wlk 20 M34 . . .101 A1
Penson St WN1 . . . . .37 D2
Penthorpe Dr OL2 . . . . . . .48 F3
Pentland Ave M40 . . . . . . .65 C2
Pentland Cl SK7 . . . . .124 B1
Pentland Terr BL1 . . . . . . .143 E1
Pentland Way SK14 . . . . . .102 B6
Pentlands Ave M7 . . . . . .155 D5
Penton Wlk 6 M16 . . . . . .97 F3
Pentwyn Gr M23 . . . . . . .121 B7
Penzance St M40 . . . . . . .160 E3
Peover Ave M33 . . . . .108 E4
Peover Rd SK9 . . . . .131 E5
Peover Wlk SK8 . . . . .123 A5
Pepler Ave M23 . . . . .109 B2
Peploe Wlk M23 . . . . .108 D1
Pepper Ct SK9 . . . . .137 A6
Pepper La WN6 . . . . .19 B3
Pepper Mill Bsns Pk
WN1 . . . . .151 D7
Pepper Mill La WN1 . . . . . .151 D7
Pepper Rd SK7 . . . . .124 B2
Pepper St WA16 . . . . .128 F1
Pepperhill Rd M16 . . . . . . .97 F4
Peppermint Cl OL16 . . . . . .32 C4
Pepys Pl WN3 . . . . .55 A4
Perch St 4 WN1 . . . . .37 E1
Perch Wlk 7 M4 . . . . .159 C1
Percival Cl M8 . . . . .155 F6
Percival Rd M43 . . . . .84 B1
Percival Wlk OL2 . . . . .48 E3
Percy Dr M5 . . . . .161 B7
Percy Rd M34 . . . . .100 E2
Percy St Bolton BL1 . . . . . .143 F2
Bury BL9 . . . . .141 B3
Farnworth BL4 . . . . .60 E7
Manchester M15 . . . . .162 D6
Oldham OL4 . . . . .67 C7
Ramsbottom BL0 . . . . .138 B5

Percy St continued
Rochdale OL16 . . . . .31 B5
Stalybridge SK16 . . . . .86 B2
Stockport SK1 . . . . .169 F2
Whitworth OL12 . . . . .4 E6
Peregrin Dr WN7 . . . . .76 B5
Peregrine Cres M43 . . . . . .84 C3
Peregrine Dr M44 . . . . . . .94 A3
Peregrine Rd SK2 . . . . . . .125 A4
Peregrine St M15,M16 . . . .162 F5
Periton Wlk 8 M9 . . . . . . .64 E3
Perivale Dr OL8 . . . . .67 B4
Perkins Ave M7 . . . . .155 E5
Pernham St OL4 . . . . .67 C7
Perrin St SK14 . . . . .167 D2
Perry Ave SK14 . . . . .102 A4
Perry Brook
Com Prim Sch WN4 . . . . . .73 A7
Perry Cl OL11 . . . . .139 D5
Perry Rd WA15 . . . . .120 B6
Perrybrook Wlk WN4 . . . . .73 D4
Perrygate Ave M20 . . . . . .110 A6
Perrymead M25 . . . . .63 C6
Perryn Pl WN6 . . . . .19 F1
Pershore 8 OL12 . . . . . . .139 E8
Pershore Rd M24 . . . . .47 A3
Perth 4 M30 . . . . .79 E2
Perth Ave Ince-in-M WN2 . .56 A8
Oldham OL9 . . . . .66 A4
Perth Cl SK7 . . . . .132 F5
Perth Rd OL11 . . . . .31 B2
Perth St Bolton BL3 . . . . .146 C3
Royton OL2 . . . . .49 A4
Swinton M27 . . . . .79 D7
Peru St M3 . . . . .158 D2
Peter Martin St 2 BL6 . . . .22 B4
Peter Moss Way M19 . . . . .99 C1
Peter St Altrincham WA14 .119 D3
Ashton-in-M WN4 . . . . .73 C3
Bury BL9 . . . . .140 F3
Denton M34 . . . . .101 A3
Eccles M30 . . . . .79 D1
Golborne WA3 . . . . .90 A8
Hadfield SK13 . . . . .104 A6
Hazel Grove SK7 . . . . .124 D3
Hindley WN2 . . . . .56 D5
Leigh WN7 . . . . .76 B4
Manchester M2,M3 . . . . . .162 F8
Oldham OL1 . . . . .153 F6
Stockport SK1 . . . . .112 A2
Wigan WN5 . . . . .54 B8
Peterborough Cl OL6 . . . . .85 B6
Peterborough Dr 10 BL1 . .143 F1
Peterborough St 1 M18 . . .99 F6
Peterborough Wlk BL1 . . . .143 E1
Peterchurch Wlk M11 . . . .165 C8
Peterhead Cl BL1 . . . . . . .143 D1
Peterhead Wlk 4 M5 . . . . .81 A1
Peterhouse Gdns SK6 . . . .113 C4
Peterhouse Wlk WN4 . . . . .72 A1
Peterloo Ct 6 M5 . . . . . . .154 E2
Peterloo Terr 8 M24 . . . . .47 A2
Peters Ct WA15 . . . . .120 D5
Petersburg Rd SK3 . . . . . .170 D6
Petersfield Dr M23 . . . . . .120 D7
Petersfield Gdns WA3 . . . .91 E4
Petersfield Wlk 1 BL1 . . . .145 E8
Peterswood Cl M22 . . . . . .121 B3
Petheridge Dr 3 M22 . . . .121 B1
Petrel Ave SK12 . . . . .133 B4
Petrel Cl Droylsden M43 . . .84 C3
Rochdale OL16 . . . . .29 F7
Stockport SK3 . . . . .170 D6
Petrie Ct M6 . . . . .81 B4
Petrie St OL12 . . . . .139 F8
Petrock Wlk 5 M40 . . . . . .83 C5
Petticoat La WN2 . . . . .56 B7
Petts Cres OL15 . . . . .16 A6
Petunia Wlk 8 M28 . . . . . .59 F3
Petworth Ave WN3 . . . . . . .54 D2
Petworth Cl M22 . . . . .121 E5
Petworth Rd OL9 . . . . . . .152 B6
Pevensey Ave M9 . . . . . . .65 A2
Pevensey Rd M6 . . . . .80 E5
Pevensey Wlk OL9 . . . . . .152 B6
Peveril Ave SK22 . . . . . . .127 C1
Peveril Cl M25,M45 . . . . . .63 C7
Peveril Cres M21 . . . . .97 A2
Peveril Ct SK13 . . . . .116 F8
Peveril Dr SK7 . . . . .133 F8
Peveril Rd
Altrincham WA14 . . . . .119 C7
Oldham OL1 . . . . .49 C1
Salford M5 . . . . .154 D2
Peveril St BL3 . . . . .146 C3
Peveril Terr SK14 . . . . . . .113 F8
Pewfist Gn BL5 . . . . .57 E6
Pewfist Spinney BL5 . . . . .57 D7
Pewfist The BL5 . . . . .57 E7
Pewsey Rd M22 . . . . .121 F3
Pexhill Ct SK4 . . . . .168 A2
Pexwood OL1 . . . . .47 E1
Pheasant Cl M28 . . . . .78 B6
Pheasant Dr M21 . . . . . . .109 D7
Pheasant Rise WA14 . . . . .119 C5
Phelan Cl M40 . . . . .156 C5
Phethean St Bolton BL2 . . .148 A7
Farnworth BL4 . . . . .42 C7
Philip Arnold Ct 2 BL4 . . . .60 C8
Philip Ave M34 . . . . .100 E5
Philip Cl 6 WN5 . . . . .54 D5
Philip Dr M33 . . . . .108 B2
Philip Howard Rd SK13 . . .116 C8
Philip St Bolton BL3 . . . . .145 D5
Eccles M30 . . . . .79 D1

Philip St continued
Oldham OL4 . . . . .67 C8
Rochdale OL12 . . . . .139 F5
Philips Ave BL4 . . . . .60 D7
Philips Dr M45 . . . . .62 D6
Philips High Sch M45 . . . . .62 E8
Philips Park Rd
Manchester M11 . . . . .160 D6
Whitefield M45 . . . . .62 D6
Whitefield M45 . . . . .62 F6
Phillimore St OL4 . . . . .67 E5
Phillip Way 1 SK14 . . . . . .102 E1
Phillips Pl WN7 . . . . .62 F7
Phillips St WN7 . . . . .75 E8
Phipps St M28 . . . . .60 C4
Phoebe St 5 Bolton BL3 . .146 C4
Salford M6 . . . . .161 B8
Phoenix Cl OL10 . . . . .29 F1
Phoenix Park Ind Est OL10 29 F1
Phoenix Pl OL4 . . . . .67 F7
Phoenix St Bolton BL1 . . . .148 A8
Bury BL9 . . . . .140 E2
Farnworth BL4 . . . . .60 D7
Littleborough OL15 . . . . . . .16 B6
Manchester M2 . . . . .159 A1
Oldham OL1 . . . . .153 F6
Oldham OL4 . . . . .67 F7
Rochdale OL12 . . . . .14 C1
Phoenix Way Eccles M41 . . .95 B4
Radcliffe M26 . . . . .44 A2
Phyllis St Middleton M24 . . .65 C7
Rochdale OL12 . . . . .14 B1
Picadilly WN5 . . . . .71 E5
Stockport SK1 . . . . .169 F1
Piccadilly Manchester M1 .159 B1
Piccadilly Gardens Sta
M1 . . . . .159 A1
Piccadilly Plaza M1 . . . . . .159 A1
Piccadilly Sta M1 . . . . .163 B8
Piccadilly Trad Est M1 . . . .163 C8
Piccadilly Village M1 . . . . .159 C1
Pickering Cl
Altrincham WA15 . . . . .120 C1
Bury BL8 . . . . .27 B5
Kearsley M26 . . . . .61 A8
Urmston M41 . . . . .95 B2
Pickford Ave BL3 . . . . .43 C3
Pickford Ct M15 . . . . .162 E5
Pickford La SK16 . . . . . . .101 C8
Pickford Mews SK16 . . . . .101 C8
Pickford St M4 . . . . .159 B2
Pickford Wlk OL2 . . . . .48 E3
Pickford's Brow SK1 . . . . .169 F1
Pickhill La OL3 . . . . .69 B8
Pickhill Mews 8 OL3 . . . . .69 B8
Pickley Gn WN7 . . . . .57 E1
Pickmere Ave M20 . . . . . .110 B8
Pickmere Cl
4 Droylsden M43 . . . . .84 B1
Stockport SK3 . . . . .123 C6
Wythenshawe M33 . . . . . .108 F2
Pickmere Ct 10 SK9 . . . . .131 D5
Pickmere Gdns SK8 . . . . .122 F4
Pickmere Mews 2 OL3 . . . .69 B8
Pickmere Rd SK9 . . . . . . .131 D5
Pickmere Terr 2 SK16 . . . .166 B1
Picksley St WN7 . . . . .76 B4
Pickthorn Cl WN2 . . . . .56 B3
Pickup St Ince-in-M WN2 . .151 F7
Rochdale OL16 . . . . .31 A7
Pickwick Rd SK12 . . . . . . .133 D3
Picton Cl M3 . . . . .158 E2
Picton Dr SK9 . . . . .131 E2
Picton Sch M33 . . . . .107 F4
Picton Sq 4 OL4 . . . . .67 A6
Picton St Ashton-u-L OL7 . .85 A6
Manchester M7 . . . . .158 D3
Picton Wlk 9 M16 . . . . . . .97 F3
Pierce St OL1 . . . . .49 C1
Piercy Ave M7 . . . . .158 D4
Piercy St Failsworth M35 . . .83 E7
Manchester M4 . . . . .160 D2
Pierpoint St WA3 . . . . .90 A7
Piethorne Cl OL16 . . . . . . .32 C4
Pigeon St M1 . . . . .159 B1
Piggott St BL4 . . . . .60 C7
Pigot St 2 WN5 . . . . .54 B6
Pike Ave Atherton M46 . . . .58 A2
Failsworth M35 . . . . .84 C6
Pike Fold La M9 . . . . .64 C3
Pike Fold Prim Sch M9 . . . . .64 C3
Pike Nook Wkshp BL3 . . . .145 D5
Pike Rd BL3 . . . . .147 D4
Pike St OL11 . . . . .139 F5
Pike View BL6 . . . . .22 D4
Pike View Cl OL4 . . . . .67 B5
Pike's La SK13 . . . . .116 B8
Pikehouse Cotts OL15 . . . .16 D7
Pikes Lane Prim Sch
BL3 . . . . .145 D6
Pilgrim Dr M11 . . . . .160 F1
Pilgrims Way WN6 . . . . . . .37 A7
Pilkington Dr M45 . . . . . . .45 C6
Pilkington Rd Kearsley BL4 .60 F6
Manchester M9 . . . . .65 A3
Radcliffe M26 . . . . .43 F4
Pilkington St Bolton BL3 . .145 E5
Hindley WN2 . . . . .56 D6
Middleton M24 . . . . .47 C1
Ramsbottom BL0 . . . . .138 B5
Pilkington Way M26 . . . . . .44 A2
Pilling Field BL7 . . . . .8 E1
Pilling St Bury BL8 . . . . . . .27 C3
Denton M34 . . . . .100 F3
Leigh WN7 . . . . .75 D5
Manchester M10,M40 . . . .157 F5
3 Rawtenstall BB4 . . . . . . .2 F8
Rochdale OL12 . . . . .139 D8

Pilling Wlk OL9 . . . . .152 A6
Pilning St BL3 . . . . .42 A4
Pilot Ind Est BL3 . . . . .42 B4
Pilot St BL9 . . . . .140 F1
Pilsley Cl WN5 . . . . .36 A1
Pilsworth Cotts BL9 . . . . . .45 C5
Pilsworth Rd
Heywood BL9,OL10 . . . . . . .45 C7
Heywood OL10 . . . . .46 A8
Pilsworth Way BL9 . . . . . . .45 A6
Pimblett St Golborne WA3 . .90 A7
Manchester M3 . . . . .158 F3
Pimbo La WN8 . . . . .53 A4
Pimhole Rd BL9 . . . . .141 A2
Pimlico Cl M7 . . . . .155 D6
Pimlott Gr Dukinfield SK14 101 D5
Prestwich M25 . . . . .62 F2
Pimlott Rd M33 . . . . .25 B3
Pimmcroft Way M33 . . . . .109 A3
Pin Mill Brow M12 . . . . . . .164 D8
Pincher Wlk M11 . . . . .83 C1
Pinder Wlk 4 M15 . . . . . . .162 F6
Pine Ave
Newton-le-W WA12 . . . . . . .89 D2
Whitefield M45 . . . . .62 F6
Pine Cl Denton M34 . . . . . .100 E6
Marple SK6 . . . . .125 E4
Pine Ct Manchester M20 . . .110 A4
Stockport SK7 . . . . .123 D2
Pine Gr Denton M34 . . . . . .101 A3
Eccles M30 . . . . .79 E4
Farnworth BL4 . . . . .60 B8
Golborne WA3 . . . . .90 C8
Manchester M13,M14 . . . . .98 E4
Prestwich M45 . . . . .63 A6
Royton OL2 . . . . .48 D6
Sale M33 . . . . .107 D6
Stalybridge SK16 . . . . . . .101 F8
Swinton M27 . . . . .79 D7
Westhoughton BL5 . . . . . . .57 E7
Worsley M28 . . . . .78 E8
Pine Lo SK7 . . . . .132 F7
Pine Mdw M26 . . . . .61 C6
Pine Rd Bramhall SK7 . . . .132 F8
Dukinfield SK15 . . . . .101 E8
Manchester M20 . . . . .110 B4
Poynton SK12 . . . . .133 F3
Wigan WN5 . . . . .54 E6
Pine St Ashton-u-L OL6 . . .166 B4
Bolton BL1 . . . . .143 F2
Bury BL9 . . . . .141 B2
Chadderton OL9 . . . . .152 A8
Dukinfield SK14 . . . . .101 D5
Heywood OL10 . . . . .29 D2
Littleborough OL15 . . . . . . .16 B5
Manchester M1 . . . . .159 A1
Middleton M24 . . . . .65 C7
Newhey OL16 . . . . .32 B4
Radcliffe M26 . . . . .44 B4
Rochdale OL16 . . . . .31 B7
Romiley SK6 . . . . .113 B5
5 Tyldesley M29 . . . . .59 A1
Pine St S BL3 . . . . .141 B3
Pine Tree Rd OL8 . . . . .66 D1
Pine View WN3 . . . . .54 B1
Pine Wlk 1 M31 . . . . .105 E3
Pineapple St SK7 . . . . . . .124 E2
Pinehurst Rd M40 . . . . . . .157 E5
Pines The WN7 . . . . .75 D7
Pinetop Cl M21 . . . . .109 D7
Pinetree St M18 . . . . .165 C5
Pinevale WN6 . . . . .37 A7
Pineway OL4 . . . . .67 F6
Pinewood
Altrincham WA14 . . . . .119 A2
Ashton-in-M WN4 . . . . .73 A2
Chadderton OL9 . . . . .65 E7
Sale M33 . . . . .107 D4
Pinewood Cres
Ince-in-M WN2 . . . . .151 F6
Orrell WN5 . . . . .53 E6
Ramsbottom BL0 . . . . .11 B2
Pinewood Ct
Altrincham WA14 . . . . .119 E1
Sale M33 . . . . .108 D5
Pinewood Rd
Manchester M21 . . . . .109 A7
Wilmslow SK9 . . . . .137 E8
Pinewoods The SK6 . . . . .113 B5
Pinfold Hadfield SK13 . . . .171 E4
Rochdale OL11 . . . . .139 E6
Pinfold Ave M9 . . . . .65 A2
Pinfold Cl
Altrincham WA15 . . . . .129 D7
Westhoughton BL5 . . . . . . .57 D5
Pinfold Ct 4 M32 . . . . .96 C1
Pinfold Dr Cheadle SK8 . . .123 A1
Prestwich M25 . . . . .62 F3
Pinfold La Romiley SK6 . . .113 E4
Whitefield M45 . . . . .62 F8
Wythenshaw M90,WA15 . . .129 F6
Pinfold Prim Sch SK14 . . . .102 E1
Pinfold Rd M28 . . . . .60 C1
Pinfold St WN7 . . . . .56 A7
Pingate Dr SK8 . . . . .132 A6
Pingate La SK8 . . . . .132 A6
Pingate La S SK8 . . . . . . .132 A6
Pingle La OL3 . . . . .50 E5
Pingot OL2 . . . . .32 D1
Pingot Ave M23 . . . . .109 B1

Pingot Ct 6 WN7 ....75 D5
Pingot La SK14 ....103 B1
Pingot Rd WN5 ....71 E5
Pingot The Irlam M44 ....94 B3
  Leigh WN7 ....75 D5
Pingott La 5 SK13 ....104 A5
Pink Bank La M12 ....99 A4
Pinnacle Dr BL7 ....8 E2
Pinner Pl M19 ....111 A6
Pinners Cl BL0 ....138 E7
Pinnington La M32 ....96 D2
Pinnington Rd M18 ....99 D6
Pintail Ave SK3 ....170 D6
Pintail Cl 5 OL12 ....14 B2
Pinwood Ct 15 SK9 ....131 E1
Pioneer Rd M27 ....62 D2
Pioneer St Droylsden M11 ....83 B2
  Horwich BL6 ....22 C4
  4 Littleborough OL15 ....16 B5
  Walsden OL14 ....6 A7
Pioneers St 4 BL1 ....31 A6
Pioneers Villa OL16 ....32 E4
Piper Hill High Sch M23 ..109 B2
Piperhill Ave M22 ....109 D2
Pipers Cl OL11 ....29 D8
Pipers The WA3 ....90 F8
Pipewell Ave M18 ....165 C5
Pipit Ave WA12 ....89 C3
Pipit Cl M34 ....84 C2
Pirie Wlk 4 M40 ....83 C6
Pit La OL16,OL2 ....31 D1
Pit St Denton M34 ....100 F3
  Oldham OL9 ....66 B4
Pitcairn Ho 12 M30 ....79 D1
Pitchcombe Rd M22 ....121 B2
Pitcombe Cl BL1 ....24 D7
Pitfield Gdns M23 ....120 F7
Pitfield La BL2 ....25 F4
Pitfield St BL2 ....148 B7
Pitman Cl M11 ....165 A8
Pitmore Wlk 3 M40 ....65 D2
Pits Farm Ave OL11 ....30 C7
Pitsford Rd M40 ....157 E5
Pitshouse OL12 ....13 E2
Pitshouse La OL12 ....13 E2
Pitt St Denton M34 ....100 F6
  Heywood OL10 ....29 C2
  Hyde SK14 ....167 D3
  Ince-in-M WN3 ....151 D6
  Oldham OL4 ....67 A5
  Radcliffe M26 ....43 E3
  Rochdale OL12 ....139 F8
  Stockport SK3 ....170 D8
  Wigan WN3 ....150 B7
Pitt St E OL4 ....67 B5
Pittbrook St M12 ....164 D7
Pixmore Ave BL1 ....25 B4
Place Rd WA14 ....119 C6
Plain Pit St SK14 ....101 C5
Plainsfield Cl M16 ....97 F4
Plane Ave WN5 ....54 E7
Plane Ct 4 M6 ....81 A2
Plane Rd M35 ....83 F5
Plane St OL4 ....67 C7
Plane Tree Cl SK6 ....125 D5
Plane Tree Gr WA11 ....89 A7
Plane Tree Rd M31 ....105 D3
Planet Way M34 ....100 E5
Planetree Rd WA15 ....120 A2
Planetree Wlk M23 ....120 C8
Plank La WN7 ....75 B4
Plant Cl M33 ....108 A5
Plant Hill High Sch M9 ..64 C4
Plant Hill Rd M9 ....64 D4
Plant St M1 ....159 B1
Plantagenet Wlk M40 ....83 D4
Plantation Ave M28 ....60 C4
Plantation Gr BL2 ....45 C4
Plantation Ind Est
  Ashton-u-L OL6 ....85 D2
  Dukinfield OL6 ....166 C2
Plantation Rd BL7 ....9 F7
Plantation St
  Ashton-u-L OL6 ....85 D2
  Bacup OL13 ....3 C8
  Manchester M18 ....99 E5
Plantation View BL9 ....11 C3
Plasden St M23 ....121 A5
Plate St OL1 ....153 F7
Plato St OL9 ....153 D7
Platt Ave OL6 ....85 C6
Platt Cl OL16 ....32 A5
Platt Croft WN7 ....76 C4
Platt Ct M14 ....98 C2
Platt Fold Rd WN7 ....76 A6
Platt Fold St WN7 ....76 A5
Platt Hall Art Gall &
  Gallery of English
  Costume M14 ....98 C2
Platt Hill Ave BL3 ....146 A4
Platt La Atherton BL5 ....58 B7
  Hindley WN2 ....56 D5
  Manchester M14 ....98 B2
  Standish WN1 ....20 B3
  Uppermill OL3 ....50 F2
  Wigan WN1 ....37 E1
Platt St Cheadle SK8 ....122 E6
  Dukinfield SK16 ....101 A4
  Hadfield SK13 ....104 B5
  Leigh WN7 ....75 F6
  8 Oldham OL4 ....67 F6
  Platt Bridge WN2 ....56 A2
Platt Wlk M34 ....100 E1
Plattbrook Cl M14 ....98 B1

Platting La OL11 ....31 A4
Platting Rd OL4 ....68 C7
Platts Dr M44 ....94 A4
Plattwood Wlk 18 M15 ..162 D6
Playfair Cl OL10 ....46 E7
Playfair St Bolton BL1 ....24 F6
  Manchester M14 ....98 A4
Pleachway SK4 ....110 F2
Pleasance Way WA12 ....89 D4
Pleasant Cl 8 OL11 ....30 C2
Pleasant Gdns BL1 ....145 E8
Pleasant Rd M30 ....79 E1
Pleasant St Bury BL8 ....26 F4
  Heywood OL10 ....29 C4
  Manchester M9 ....157 D7
  Rochdale OL11 ....30 C2
Pleasant Terr 16 OL16 ..166 C1
Pleasant View Bacup OL13 ..3 C7
  Radcliffe M26 ....62 B8
Pleasant Way SK7,SK8 ..132 C6
Pleasington Dr Bury BL8 ..26 E2
  Failsworth M40 ....65 C2
Plevna St BL2 ....148 A7
Plodder La BL4,BL5 ....59 D8
Plodder La Prim Sch BL4 .60 D8
Plough Cl M41 ....94 C1
Plough Fields M28 ....78 A5
Plough St 8 SK16 ....101 D8
Ploughbank Dr M21 ....109 D7
Ploughfields BL5 ....39 E3
Plover Cl
  Newton-le-W WA12 ....89 C3
  Rochdale OL11 ....29 F7
Plover Dr
  Altrincham WA14 ....119 B8
  Bury BL9 ....141 B4
  Irlam M44 ....94 A4
Plover Way WA3 ....90 E8
Plowden Ave BL3 ....146 C3
Plowden Rd M22 ....121 B2
Plowley Cl M20 ....110 B2
Plucksbridge Rd SK6 ..126 B3
Plum St OL8 ....153 D5
Plum Tree Ct 2 M5 ....81 A2
Plumbley Dr M16 ....97 C3
Plumbley St 11 M11 ....99 E7
Plumley Cl SK3 ....170 F5
Plumley Rd SK9 ....131 D5
Plummer Ave M21 ....109 B6
Plumpton Cl OL1,OL2 ....48 E1
Plumpton Dr BL9 ....27 E6
Plumpton Rd OL11 ....48 C8
Plumpton Wlk 6 M13 ....98 F4
Plunge Rd BL0 ....1 E3
Pluto Cl M6 ....81 C4
Plymouth Ave M13 ....164 E5
Plymouth Cl OL6 ....85 C7
Plymouth Dr Bramhall SK7 132 F7
  1 Farnworth BL4 ....59 F8
Plymouth Gr
  Manchester M13 ....164 D5
  Radcliffe M26 ....43 D5
  Standish WN6 ....37 A7
  Stockport SK3 ....123 B7
Plymouth Gr W M13 ....164 E5
Plymouth Grove Jun Sch
  M13 ....164 E5
Plymouth Rd M33 ....107 D5
Plymouth St OL8 ....66 F4
Plymouth View M13 ....163 C6
Plymtree Cl M8 ....63 E2
Pobgreen OL3 ....51 D1
Pochard Dr
  Altrincham WA14 ....119 B7
  Poynton SK12 ....133 A4
Pochin St M40 ....160 E3
Pocket Nook La WA3 ....91 B7
Pocket Nook Rd BL6 ....40 B3
Pocket Wkshp The BL3 ..144 C6
Pocklington Dr M23 ....120 F7
Podnor La SK6 ....127 F2
Podsmead Rd M22 ....121 B2
Poet's Nook WN7 ....75 E4
Poise Brook Dr SK2 ....124 F5
Poise Brook Rd SK2 ....124 F5
Poise Cl SK7 ....125 A3
Poke St 1 WN5 ....54 B6
Poland St
  1 Ashton-u-L M34 ....100 E8
  Manchester M4 ....159 C2
Poland Street Ind Est
  M4 ....159 C2
Polden Wlk 1 M9 ....64 F1
Polding St WN3 ....55 E4
Pole La Failsworth M35 ....83 F8
  Whitefield BL9,M45 ....45 C2
  Whitefield M45 ....45 D1
Pole Lane Ct BL9 ....45 C3
Pole St Ashton-u-L OL7 ..166 B4
  Bolton BL2 ....25 B1
  Standish WN6 ....19 E1
Poleacre La SK6 ....113 C6
Polebrook App M25 ....63 B6
Polefield Circ M25 ....63 B6
Polefield Gdns M25 ....63 B6
Polefield Gr M25 ....63 B6
Polefield Grange M25 ....63 B6
Polefield Hall Rd M25 ....63 B6
Polefield Rd
  Manchester M9 ....64 E2
  Prestwich M25 ....63 C6
Polegate Dr WN2 ....57 D2
Polesworth Cl M12 ....165 A6
Police St
  1 Altrincham WA14 ....119 D5
  Eccles M30 ....79 C2
  Manchester M2 ....158 F1

Pollard Ct 4 OL1 ....153 E8
Pollard Gr OL15 ....16 C8
Pollard Ho BL3 ....146 B2
Pollard Sq M31 ....106 A3
Pollard St M4 ....160 D1
Pollard St E M4,M40 ....160 D2
Pollards La BL9 ....11 C2
Polldean Ho SK8 ....122 D3
Pollen Cl M33 ....108 D2
Pollen Rd WA14 ....119 C6
Polletts Ave SK5 ....112 C6
Pollit Croft SK6 ....112 F1
Pollitt Ave OL6 ....85 C5
Pollitt Cl M12 ....164 F6
Pollitt St M26 ....44 C3
Pollitts Cl M30 ....79 B2
Polly Cl OL12 ....14 F3
Polonia Ct OL8 ....66 C3
Polperro Cl OL2 ....49 A4
Polperro Wlk SK14 ....102 D3
Polruan Rd M21 ....97 A2
Polruan Wlk SK14 ....102 E3
Polworth Rd M9 ....64 E1
Polygon Ave M12,M13 ..163 C6
Polygon Rd M8 ....63 F1
Polygon St M13 ....163 C7
Polygon The
  Manchester M7 ....81 C5
  Salford M30 ....80 A2
Pomfret St M6 ....80 C5
Pomona Cres M5 ....161 B7
Pomona St OL11 ....139 F5
Pomona Sta M5,M16 ....161 B6
Pomona Strand
  Salford M15 ....161 C7
  Salford M16,M5 ....161 B6
Pond St WA3 ....91 A8
Ponds Cl M21 ....97 B1
Pondwater Cl M28 ....60 A3
Pondwood Wlk 6 M16 ....97 E3
Ponsford Ave M9 ....65 A3
Ponsonby Rd M32 ....96 D3
Pontefract Cl M27 ....80 B7
Pool Bank St M24 ....64 B7
Pool Fold M5 ....84 A6
Pool House Rd SK12 ....134 D5
Pool Rd WA3 ....105 A3
Pool St Bolton BL1 ....145 E7
  Bolton BL1 ....145 E8
  Hindley WN2 ....56 D4
  Oldham OL8 ....66 F4
  Wigan WN3 ....150 B6
Pool Terr BL1 ....142 A2
Poolcroft M33 ....108 F3
Poole Cl SK7 ....123 D1
Pooley Cl M24 ....46 B1
Poolfield Cl M26 ....43 E3
Poolstock WN3 ....150 B6
Poolstock La WN3 ....55 A4
Poolton Rd M9 ....64 B4
Poot Hall OL12 ....14 F6
Pope John Paul II
  RC High Sch M9 ....81 A5
Pope Way 3 M34 ....113 A8
Poplar Ave
  Altrincham WA14 ....119 E6
  Bolton BL1 ....24 F5
  Bolton BL2 ....25 C6
  Bury BL9 ....141 B3
  Culcheth WA3 ....91 F3
  Downall Green WN4 ....72 D5
  Horwich BL6 ....22 E1
  Manchester M19 ....111 B7
  New Mills SK22 ....127 D1
  Newton-le-W WA12 ....89 D3
  Oldham M46 ....66 D2
  4 Rochdale OL16 ....14 C1
  Uppermill OL4 ....68 C4
  Wigan WN5 ....54 E6
  Wilmslow SK9 ....136 F5
Poplar Cl SK8 ....122 B5
Poplar Ct Dukinfield M34 ..100 F7
  Manchester M14 ....98 D1
Poplar Dr M25 ....63 A2
Poplar Gr Ashton-u-L OL7 ..85 C5
  Hindley WN2 ....57 B3
  Irlam M44 ....105 D6
  Manchester M18 ....99 D4
  Ramsbottom BL0 ....11 D7
  Sale M33 ....108 B3
  Stockport SK2 ....124 C4
  Tyldesley M29 ....77 A8
  Urmston M41 ....95 C2
  Westhoughton BL5 ....57 E8
Poplar Rd Dukinfield SK16 ..101 F7
  Eccles M30 ....79 E4
  Manchester M19 ....110 D3
  Stretford M32 ....108 C8
  Swinton M27 ....79 D7
  Walkden M28 ....60 E1
Poplar St Dukinfield M34 ..100 F7
  Failsworth M35 ....83 D6
  Golborne WA3 ....74 B1
  Leigh WN7 ....75 F4
  Manchester M11 ....164 E8
  Manchester SK4 ....110 F2
  Middleton M24 ....65 C6
  Tyldesley M29 ....59 A1
Poplar St Prim Sch M34 ..100 E6
Poplar Way SK6 ....135 A7
Poplar Wlk
  Chadderton OL9 ....152 B8
  Partington M31 ....105 D3
Poplars The Adlington PR7 ..20 F6
  Golborne WA3 ....74 B1
  Golborne WN7 ....91 C8
  Mossley OL5 ....68 E1

Poplin Dr M3 ....158 E3
Poppy Cl Chadderton OL9 ..65 E7
  Sale M33 ....108 C1
Poppythorn La M25 ....63 A5
Porchester Dr M26 ....43 C5
Porchfield Sq M3 ....162 E8
Porlock Ave
  Droylsden M34 ....100 C8
  Hattersley SK14 ....102 C2
Porlock Cl Platt Bridge WN2 ..56 A1
  Stockport SK1 ....124 C8
Porlock Rd Urmston M41 ..107 B8
  Wythenshawe M23 ....121 B6
Porlock Wlk SK14 ....102 C2
Porritt Cl OL11 ....29 E6
Porritt St Bury BL9 ....141 A4
  Bury BL9 ....141 A4
Porritt Way BL0 ....138 C7
Port Soderick Ave M5 ....81 A1
Port St Manchester M1 ..159 B1
  Oldham OL8 ....66 F4
  Stockport SK1 ....169 E2
Portal Ct M24 ....65 C8
Portal Gr M34 ....101 B1
Portal Wlk 9 M9 ....157 D8
Porter Ave WA12 ....89 C5
Porter St Bury BL9 ....140 F4
  Oldham OL9 ....152 C5
Porters Wood Cl WN5 ....54 B7
Portfield Cl BL1 ....40 F8
Portfield Wlk 18 M40 ....83 A6
Portgate Wlk M13 ....164 D5
Porthleven Cres M29 ....77 C8
Porthleven Dr M23 ....120 C6
Porthtowan Wlk SK14 ..102 E3
Portinscale Cl BL8 ....27 B3
Portland Basin Mus OL7 ..166 A1
Portland Cl Abram WN2 ..74 A8
  Hazel Grove SK7 ....124 B1
  Platt Bridge WN2 ....56 A1
Portland Cres M13 ....164 D5
Portland Ct M20 ....110 B3
Portland Gr SK4 ....168 B4
Portland Ho
  3 Ashton-u-L OL6 ....166 A2
  Salford M6 ....80 A3
  Marple SK6 ....125 E5
Portland Ind Est 18 BL9 ..141 A4
Portland Pl OL7 ....166 A2
Portland Rd
  Altrincham WA14 ....119 D3
  Manchester M13 ....98 F3
  New Mills SK22 ....127 D1
  Pendlebury M27 ....80 B7
  Salford M30 ....80 A4
  Walkden M28 ....60 C5
Portland St Bolton BL1 ..143 E4
  Bury BL9 ....141 A4
  6 Leigh WN7 ....75 F5
  Manchester M1 ....159 A1
  Manchester M1 ....163 A8
  Rochdale OL16 ....139 F8
  Wigan WN5 ....54 E6
Portland St N OL6 ....166 A3
Portland St S OL6,OL7 ..166 A2
Portland Terr OL6 ....166 A2
Portloe Rd SK8 ....131 B7
Portman Cl M16 ....97 E4
Portman St SK5 ....68 C1
Porton Wlk 1 M22 ....121 B1
Portrea Cl SK3 ....170 F5
Portree Cl M30 ....79 B2
Portrush Rd M22 ....121 B2
Portside Cl M29 ....78 B5
Portslade Wlk
  Wythenshawe M23 ....120 F4
  10 Wythenshawe M23 ..121 A5
Portsmouth Cl M7 ....155 D5
Portsmouth St M13 ....163 B5
Portstone Cl 10 M16 ....97 E4
Portugal Rd M27 ....63 B2
Portugal St Ashton-u-L OL7 ..84 F1
  Bolton BL2 ....148 B7
  Manchester M4 ....159 C4
  10 Manchester M4 ....159 C3
Portugal St E M1 ....163 C8
Portville Rd M19 ....99 A2
Portway M22 ....121 C1
Portwood Ind Est SK1 ..112 B2
Portwood Pl SK1 ....169 F2
Portwood Wlk 9 M9 ....157 D7
Posnett St SK3 ....123 C8
Post Office St WA14 ....119 D5
Post St SK13 ....104 B5
Postal St M1 ....159 B1
Postbridge Cl M13 ....163 C6
Pot Gn BL0 ....11 A3
Pot Hill OL6 ....166 C4
Pot Hill Sq OL6 ....166 C4
Potato Wharf M3 ....162 D8
Pott St M27 ....61 F2
Potter Ho OL6 ....153 F5
Potter St Bury BL9 ....141 A4
  Radcliffe M26 ....44 D4
Potterdale Cl OL1 ....49 A1
Potters La M9 ....157 F7
Pottery La M11,M12 ....165 A7
Pottery Rd WN3 ....150 B7
Pottery Terr WN3 ....150 B7
Pottinger St Ashton-u-L OL7 84 F1
  Dukinfield OL7 ....100 F8
Poulton Ave BL2 ....42 F7
Poulton Dr 7 WN4 ....72 F5
Poulton St M11 ....99 E7
Poundswick Cty Prim Sch
  M22 ....121 D3
Poundswick La M22 ....121 D3

Powell Ave SK14 ....167 E3
Powell Dr WN5 ....71 D3
  Bury BL8 ....27 B1
  Droylsden M11 ....83 D2
  Manchester M16 ....97 C4
  10 Wigan WN1 ....37 C1
Powicke Dr SK6 ....112 F1
Powicke Wlk SK6 ....113 A1
Powis Rd M41 ....94 C1
Pownall Ave Bramhall SK7 132 F7
  4 Manchester M20 ....110 A8
Pownall Ct SK9 ....136 E5
Pownall Green Prim Sch
  SK7 ....132 E7
Pownall Hall Sch SK9 ....136 F8
Pownall Rd
  Altrincham WA14 ....119 D3
  Cheadle SK8 ....123 A1
  Wilmslow SK9 ....136 F8
Pownall St
  Hazel Grove SK7 ....124 D3
  Leigh WN7 ....76 A5
Powys St M46 ....58 E1
Poynings Dr M22 ....121 C1
Poynt Chase M28 ....78 B6
Poynter St M40 ....65 C1
Poynter Wlk OL1 ....49 D4
Poynton High Sch SK12 ..133 F2
Poynton St Bury BL9 ....141 A1
  Manchester M15 ....162 F6
Poynton Sta SK12 ....133 A3
Poynton Worth Prim Sch
  SK12 ....133 F2
Praed Rd M17 ....96 C6
Pratt Wlk 21 M11 ....160 F1
Precinct The Cheadle SK8 ..123 A2
  Ramsbottom BL0 ....10 F3
  Rochdale OL11 ....29 E7
  Stockport SK2 ....124 D6
Preece Cl SK14 ....102 A4
Preesall Ave SK8 ....131 B8
Preesall Cl BL8 ....26 F1
Prefect Pl WN5 ....54 C8
Premier Rd M8 ....158 F4
Premier St M16 ....97 D4
Prentice Wlk M11 ....83 A1
Prenton St M11 ....99 E8
Prenton Way M8 ....26 F5
Presall St 2 BL2 ....148 B7
Presbury Ct 1 M20 ....110 A2
Presbyterian Fold 6 WN2 56 D6
Prescot Ave Atherton M46 ..58 E5
  Tyldesley M29 ....59 D1
Prescot Cl BL9 ....141 A1
Prescot Rd
  Altrincham WA15 ....119 F2
  Manchester M9 ....157 D7
Prescott Ave WA3 ....73 F2
Prescott La WN5 ....54 B8
Prescott St Bolton BL3 ..146 C4
  Golborne WN2 ....74 A1
  Hindley WN2 ....56 D5
  Leigh WN7 ....75 F6
  Rochdale OL16 ....15 C2
  Walkden M28 ....60 B3
  Wigan WN3,WN1,wn6 ..150 B8
Prescott Wlk M34 ....101 B1
Press St M11 ....99 D7
Prestage St
  Manchester M12 ....99 B2
  Manchester M16 ....97 D4
Prestbury Ave
  Altrincham WA15 ....119 E6
  Manchester M14 ....97 F1
  Wigan WN3 ....54 E2
Prestbury Cl Bury BL9 ....141 A1
  Stockport SK2 ....124 D4
Prestbury Dr
  Bredbury SK6 ....112 E3
  Oldham OL1 ....48 D1
Prestbury Rd Bolton BL1 ..25 A1
  Wilmslow SK10,SK9 ....137 E5
Prestfield Rd M45 ....63 A7
Prestolee Prim Sch M26 ..61 B8
Prestolee Rd Kearsley M26 43 B1
  Little Lever BL3 ....43 A1
Preston Ave Irlam M44 ....105 F4
  Salford M30 ....80 A3
Preston Cl M30 ....80 A3
Preston Rd
  Manchester M19 ....111 A4
  Standish PR7,WN6 ....19 D5
Preston St 2 Bolton BL3 ..42 B4
  Manchester M18 ....165 C6
  Middleton M24 ....65 A8
  Oldham OL4 ....67 A6
  18 Rochdale OL12 ....14 C1
Prestwich Ave
  Culcheth WA3 ....91 E3
  Leigh WN7 ....76 B5
Prestwich Cl SK2 ....124 B7
Prestwich Com High Sch
  M25 ....63 B6
Prestwich Forest Pk M25 ..62 E3
Prestwich Hills M25 ....63 A2
Prestwich Hospl M25 ....62 F5
Prestwich Ind Est M46 ....58 B3
Prestwich Park Rd S M25 ..63 A3
Prestwich Prep Sch M25 ..63 C5
Prestwich Sta M25 ....63 A5
Prestwick Wlk 1 M40 ....65 C2

Prestwood Cl BL1 . . . . .143 D1
Prestwood Dr BL1 . . . . .143 D1
Prestwood Rd
  Farnworth BL4 . . . . .42 A1
  Salford M6 . . . . .80 C4
Pretoria Rd
  Ashton-in-M WN4 . . . . .73 B4
  Bolton BL2 . . . . .42 E8
  Oldham OL8 . . . . .66 C3
Pretoria St **2** OL12 . . . . .14 C1
Price St Bury BL9 . . . . .141 A1
  Dukinfield SK16 . . . . .101 C8
  Farnworth BL4 . . . . .42 D1
  Manchester M4 . . . . .160 D1
Prichard St M32 . . . . .96 D2
Prickshaw OL12 . . . . .14 B6
Prickshaw La OL12 . . . . .14 B6
Pridmouth Rd M20 . . . . .110 C6
Priest Ave SK8 . . . . .122 A4
Priest St SK1 . . . . .170 F7
Priestley Rd M27,M28 . . . . . . .79 C8
Priestley Way OL2 . . . . .49 D7
Priestnall Ct SK4 . . . . .110 F3
Priestnall Rd SK4 . . . . .110 F3
Priestnall Rec Ctr SK4 . . . . . .110 F3
Priestnall Sch SK4 . . . . .110 F3
Priestners Way WN7 . . . . .75 E6
Priestwood Ave OL4 . . . . .49 F4
Primley Wlk **8** M9 . . . . .157 E8
Primrose Ave
  Farnworth BL4 . . . . .42 A1
  Hyde SK14 . . . . .113 D8
  Marple SK6 . . . . .125 E6
  Uppermill OL3 . . . . .51 C1
  Urmston M41 . . . . .95 D2
  Walkden M28 . . . . .60 B2
Primrose Bank
  Altrincham WA14 . . . . .119 C1
  1 Bacup OL13 . . . . .3 C8
  Bury BL8 . . . . .26 E7
  Oldham OL3 . . . . .69 B5
  Oldham OL8 . . . . .153 E5
  Walkden M28 . . . . .60 B2
Primrose Cl Bolton BL2 . . . . . .26 A4
Primrose Cotts WA14 . . .119 C1
Primrose Cres
  Glossop SK13 . . . . .116 B8
  Hyde SK14 . . . . .113 D8
Primrose Dr Bury BL9 . . . . . . .28 D4
Droylsden M43 . . . . .84 C3
Primrose Gr WN5 . . . . .54 E7
Primrose Hill SK13 . . . . .116 B8
Primrose La Glossop SK13 . . .116 B8
  New Mills SK6,SK22 . . . . . .127 A3
  Standish WN6 . . . . .19 D2
Primrose St **3** Bacup OL13 . . .3 C8
  Bolton BL1 . . . . .143 F4
  Farnworth BL4 . . . . .60 E7
  4 Leigh WN7 . . . . .75 D5
  Manchester M4 . . . . .159 B2
  Rochdale OL12 . . . . .139 D8
  Tyldesley M29 . . . . .59 A1
Primrose St N M29 . . . . .59 A1
Primrose St S M29 . . . . .77 A8
Primrose Terr
  Glossop SK13 . . . . .116 B8
  Urmston M41 . . . . .95 C6
Primrose View WN4 . . . . .73 C2
Primrose Wlk Marple SK6 .125 E6
  Oldham OL8 . . . . .153 E5
Primula Dr WA3 . . . . .90 D8
Primula St BL1 . . . . .24 F5
Prince Albert Ave **4** M19 . . .99 A2
Prince Charlie St OL1 . . . .67 C8
Prince Edward Ave
  Denton M34 . . . . .100 F2
  8 Oldham OL4 . . . . .67 C7
Prince George St **3** OL1 . .49 C1
Prince of Wales Bsns Pk
  OL1 . . . . .67 C8
Prince Rd SK12 . . . . .134 C5
Prince St Ashton-in-M WN4 . .73 A5
  Bacup OL13 . . . . .4 D7
  Bolton BL1 . . . . .145 E6
  Heywood OL10 . . . . .29 D2
  6 Oldham OL1 . . . . .67 A7
  Ramsbottom BL0 . . . . .138 C6
  Rochdale OL16 . . . . .31 B5
Prince Way OL2 . . . . .48 C6
Prince's Ave
  Little Lever BL3 . . . . .43 B4
  Manchester M20 . . . . .110 C4
  Romiley SK6 . . . . .113 A3
  Tyldesley M29 . . . . .77 B6
Prince's Bridge M3 . . . . .162 D8
Prince's Dr SK6 . . . . .125 E7
Prince's Pk SK6 . . . . .35 F4
Prince's Rd SK6 . . . . .113 A3
Prince's St SK1 . . . . .169 E2
Princedom St M9 . . . . .157 E8
Princes Ave M44 . . . . .94 C3
Princes Ct M20 . . . . .110 B5
Princes Dr M33 . . . . .108 D3
Princes Gdns WN7 . . . . .76 C5
Princes Rd
  Altrincham WA14 . . . . .119 D6
  Manchester SK4 . . . . .168 A4
  Sale M33 . . . . .108 D3
Princes St WA12 . . . . .89 B3
Princess Ave
  Ashton-in-M WA11 . . . . .89 A7
  Ashton-in-M WN4 . . . . .73 C3
  Atherton M46 . . . . .58 D5
  Cheadle SK8 . . . . .123 A3
  Denton M34 . . . . .100 E3
  Kearsley BL4 . . . . .60 F6
  Manchester M25 . . . . .63 C2

Princess Ave continued
  Rochdale OL12 . . . . .15 C4
Princess Christian Coll
  M14 . . . . .98 C1
Princess Cl
  Dukinfield SK16 . . . . .101 D8
  Heywood OL10 . . . . .29 D1
  Mossley OL5 . . . . .86 E8
Princess Ct M15 . . . . .162 D6
Princess Dr M24 . . . . .64 E8
Princess Gr BL4 . . . . .60 D8
Princess Par BL9 . . . . .140 F2
Princess Parkway
  Wythenshawe
  M20,M22,M23 . . . . .109 C2
  Wythenshawe M23 . . . . . . .121 C8
Princess Rd Adlington PR6 .21 B8
  Ashton-in-M WN4 . . . . .73 C3
  Bolton BL6 . . . . .40 B8
  Failsworth OL9 . . . . .65 E3
  Manchester M14,M16 . . . . . .97 F4
  Manchester
  M14,M20,M21,M15 . . . . . .109 E6
  Milnrow OL16 . . . . .31 D7
  Prestwich M25 . . . . .63 C4
  Shaw OL2 . . . . .149 A6
  Wilmslow SK9 . . . . .136 F5
Princess St
  Altrincham WA14 . . . . .119 C8
  Ashton-u-L OL6 . . . . .85 D4
  Bolton BL1 . . . . .145 F7
  Eccles M30 . . . . .79 C2
  Failsworth M35 . . . . .83 E7
  Glossop SK13 . . . . .116 C8
  Hindley WN2 . . . . .56 C5
  Hyde SK14 . . . . .167 E2
  5 Leigh WN7 . . . . .76 A5
  Manchester M1,M60,M2 . . .163 A8
  Manchester M15 . . . . .162 D6
  Oldham OL4 . . . . .67 E6
  Pendlebury M27 . . . . .80 A7
  Radcliffe M26 . . . . .43 E3
  Rochdale OL12 . . . . .14 F1
  Salford M6 . . . . .81 A4
  Whitworth OL12 . . . . .14 C8
  Wigan WN3 . . . . .150 C7
Princess Wlk SK7 . . . . .133 A7
Princethorpe Cl BL6 . . . . .40 D6
Prinknash Rd M22 . . . . .121 D1
Printer St Droylsden M11 . . .99 D8
  Oldham OL1 . . . . .153 F6
Printers Fold OL4 . . . . .103 D5
Printers La BL2,BL7 . . . . .25 C6
Printers Pk SK14 . . . . .103 E5
Printon Ave M9 . . . . .64 B3
Printshop La M46 . . . . .58 E1
Printworks La M19 . . . . .99 C1
Printworks Rd SK15 . . . . .86 C3
Prior St OL8 . . . . .67 B5
Priorsleigh SK4 . . . . .110 F2
Priory Ave Leigh WN7 . . . . . . .57 D1
  Manchester M21 . . . . .109 B8
  Manchester M7 . . . . .81 C6
Priory Cl Dukinfield SK16 . .101 D6
  Oldham OL8 . . . . .66 D3
  Sale M33 . . . . .108 D6
  1 Wigan WN5 . . . . .54 B5
Priory Ct Eccles M30 . . . . . . .79 E2
  Reddish SK5 . . . . .111 E8
Priory Gdns M20 . . . . .110 B4
  Oldham OL9 . . . . .66 A4
Priory Gr Manchester M7 . . . .81 C6
Priory La SK5 . . . . .111 E8
Priory Nook WN8 . . . . .53 C7
Priory Pl Bolton BL2 . . . . .25 C2
  Manchester M7 . . . . .81 C6
Priory Rd Altrincham WA14 .128 B8
  Ashton-in-M WN4 . . . . .72 F5
  Cheadle SK8 . . . . .123 A5
  Orrell WN8 . . . . .53 C7
  Sale M33 . . . . .108 D5
  Swinton M27 . . . . .79 E8
  Wilmslow SK9 . . . . .136 E8
Priory St M33 . . . . .108 A4
Priory St WA14 . . . . .119 C1
Priory The M7 . . . . .81 C6
Pritchard St M1 . . . . .163 A7
Private La BB4 . . . . .1 C8
Privet St OL4 . . . . .49 D1
Proctor Cl WN5 . . . . .36 E1
Proctor St BL8 . . . . .27 C1
Proctor Way M30 . . . . .94 F7
Prodesse Ct WN2 . . . . .56 D6
Proe's Ct WN1 . . . . .150 B8
Progress Ave M34 . . . . .100 F6
Progress St
  Ashton-u-L OL6 . . . . .166 A3
  Bolton BL1 . . . . .143 F1
  Hindley WN2 . . . . .56 D5
  Rochdale OL11 . . . . .30 C1
Promenade St OL10 . . . . .29 E2
Props Hall Dr M35 . . . . .83 E6
Props Prim Sch M35 . . .83 E6
Prospect Ave
  Farnworth BL4 . . . . .60 C7
  Irlam M44 . . . . .105 E6
Prospect Cotts WN2 . . . . .38 A6
Prospect Ct BL8 . . . . .26 F7
Prospect Dr
  Altrincham WA15 . . . . .129 D8
  Failsworth M35 . . . . .83 F5
Prospect Hill BL2 . . . . .25 F4
Prospect Ho M9 . . . . .157 E7
Prospect Ind Ctr **13** WN2 . .56 D5
Prospect Pl Ashton-u-L OL6 .85 D5
  Farnworth BL4 . . . . .60 C7

Prospect Pl continued
  Heywood OL10 . . . . .29 D3
Prospect Rd Ashton-u-L OL6 85 E5
  Dukinfield SK16 . . . . .101 D8
  Irlam M44 . . . . .105 E6
  Oldham OL9 . . . . .152 C7
  Standish WN6 . . . . .36 E7
Prospect St Bolton BL1 . . . . .143 F1
  Heywood OL10 . . . . .46 E8
  Hindley WN2 . . . . .56 D5
  Littleborough OL15 . . . . .16 B6
  Rochdale OL11 . . . . .30 E4
  Tyldesley M29 . . . . .58 F1
Prospect Terr Bacup OL13 . . . .3 D7
  Bury BL8 . . . . .140 D4
Prospect Vale SK8 . . . . .122 B1
Prospect Vale Prim Sch
  SK8 . . . . .122 B1
Prospect View M27 . . . . .80 A7
Prospect Villas **3** M9 . . . . .64 F1
Prosperity M29 . . . . .77 D8
Prosser Ave M46 . . . . .58 A2
Protector Way M44 . . . . .105 F8
Prout St M12 . . . . .99 A3
Providence Ho OL4 . . . . .67 E8
Providence St
  4 Ashton-u-L OL6 . . . . . . .85 D4
  Bolton BL3 . . . . .145 F5
  Dukinfield M34 . . . . .100 F7
  Manchester M4 . . . . .160 D1
  Walsden OL14 . . . . .6 A7
Provident Ave M19 . . . . .99 C1
Provident St OL2 . . . . .149 B7
Provident Way WA15 . . . . . . .120 A7
Provis Rd M21 . . . . .109 B7
Prubella Ave M34 . . . . .100 E5
Pryce Ave WN2 . . . . .151 F7
Pryce St BL1 . . . . .143 D1
Pryme St M15 . . . . .162 E7
Pudding La SK14 . . . . .102 C3
Puffin Ave SK12 . . . . .133 B4
Puffingate Cl SK15 . . . . .86 E7
Pugin Wlk M9 . . . . .157 D6
Pulborough Cl BL8 . . . . .27 B7
Pulford Ave M21 . . . . .109 D4
Pulford Rd M33 . . . . .108 D2
Pullman Cl M19 . . . . .111 B8
Pullman Dr M32 . . . . .95 F3
Pullman St OL11 . . . . .139 F5
Pulman Ct BL3 . . . . .148 A5
Pump House (Mus) The
  M3 . . . . .158 E1
Pump St **10** Hindley WN2 . . .56 D5
  Manchester M4,M12 . . . . . .160 E2
  9 Oldham OL9 . . . . .66 B2
Punch La BL3 . . . . .40 D2
Punch St BL3 . . . . .145 D6
Pungle The BL5 . . . . .57 D5
Purbeck Cl M22 . . . . .121 C1
  Horwich BL6 . . . . .39 F8
Purbeck Dr Bury BL8 . . . . . . .27 C6
Purbeck Way M29 . . . . .77 B7
Purcell Cl BL1 . . . . .143 D1
Purcell St M12 . . . . .99 A3
Purdon St BL9 . . . . .27 F6
Purdy Ho OL8 . . . . .153 E5
Puritan Wlk **7** M40 . . . . . .156 C5
Purley Ave M23 . . . . .109 B1
Purley Dr M44 . . . . .105 C5
Purple St BL1 . . . . .145 F7
Purslow Cl M12 . . . . .160 E1
Purton Wlk **9** M9 . . . . . . .157 E7
Putney Cl OL1 . . . . .48 E1
Puzzletree Ct SK2 . . . . .124 C7
Pye OL WA11 . . . . .89 B8
Pyegrove SK13 . . . . .104 F1
Pyegrove Rd SK13 . . . . .104 E1
Pyke St WN1 . . . . .37 D1
Pym St Eccles M30 . . . . .79 D2
  Heywood OL10 . . . . .29 D1
  Manchester M40 . . . . .157 F8
Pymgate Dr SK8 . . . . .122 A2
Pyramid Ct M7 . . . . .155 D6
Pyrus Cl M30 . . . . .94 F8
Pytha Fold Rd M20 . . . . .110 D5

Q

Quadrant The
  Droylsden M43 . . . . .83 F1
  Manchester M9 . . . . .65 A3
  Romiley SK6 . . . . .113 A2
  Stockport SK1 . . . . .112 B1
Quail Dr M44 . . . . .94 A3
Quail St OL4 . . . . .67 C6
Quainton Ho **5** M5 . . . . . . .154 F1
Quakerfields BL5 . . . . .57 D7
Quakers Field M8 . . . . .26 F8
Quakers Terr WN6 . . . . .19 D3
Quakers' Pl WN6 . . . . .19 E1
Quantock Cl
  7 Manchester M16 . . . . . . .97 E4
  Stockport SK4 . . . . .169 E2
  Wigan WN3 . . . . .54 C2
Quarlton Dr BL8 . . . . .10 B3
Quarmby Rd M18 . . . . .99 F4
Quarry Bank Mill SK9 . .130 F1
Quarry Bank Rd SK9 . . . .130 F3
Quarry Cl SK13 . . . . .104 D1
Quarry Clough SK15 . . . . . . .102 D8
Quarry Hill OL12 . . . . .14 E3
Quarry Hts **4** SK15 . . . . . . .101 F8
Quarry Pl WN1 . . . . .151 E8
Quarry Pond Rd M28 . . . . .59 F3
Quarry Rd Kearsley BL4 . . . . .61 A7
  New Mills SK22 . . . . .127 F2
  Romiley SK6 . . . . .113 B2

Quarry Rise Romiley SK6 . . . .113 B3
  Staly-B SK15,SK16 . . . . . . .101 F8
Quarry St Radcliffe M26 . . . . .44 B3
  Ramsbottom BL0 . . . . .11 D6
  Rochdale OL12 . . . . .14 E1
  Romiley SK6 . . . . .113 B5
  Stalybridge SK15 . . . . .85 F1
  Whitworth OL12 . . . . .4 E6
Quarry Wlk **17** M11 . . . . . . .160 F1
Quay St Heywood OL10 . . . . . .29 E1
  Manchester M2 . . . . .158 E1
  Manchester M3 . . . . .158 E2
Quay View M5 . . . . .161 A8
Quays The M5 . . . . .96 E7
Quayside WN7 . . . . .75 E4
Quayside Cl M28 . . . . .78 B5
Quebec Pl BL3 . . . . .145 D5
Quebec St
  Abram Brow WN2,WN7 . . . . .74 E5
  Bolton BL3 . . . . .145 D5
  Denton M34 . . . . .100 E4
  Oldham OL9 . . . . .153 D8
Queen Alexandra Cl M5 .161 C8
Queen Ann Rd BL9 . . . . .45 C4
Queen Ann Dr M28 . . . . .78 B7
Queen Anne Ct SK9 . . . . .137 C6
Queen Elizabeth Sch The
  M24 . . . . .46 F4
Queen Sq OL6 . . . . .85 D3
Queen St Ashton-u-L OL6 . . .166 C3
  5 Bacup OL13 . . . . .3 C8
  Bolton BL1 . . . . .145 E7
  Bury BL9 . . . . .27 A5
  Bury BL9 . . . . .141 A2
  Cheadle SK8 . . . . .122 F6
  Denton M34 . . . . .100 E4
  Denton M34 . . . . .100 F6
  Dukinfield SK16 . . . . .166 B1
  Eccles M30 . . . . .79 F1
  Failsworth M35 . . . . .83 E7
  Farnworth BL4 . . . . .60 D8
  Glossop SK13 . . . . .116 B8
  Golborne WA3 . . . . .90 B8
  Hadfield SK13 . . . . .104 A4
  Heywood OL10 . . . . .29 D2
  5 Hindley WN2 . . . . .56 D5
  Horwich BL6 . . . . .22 B3
  Hyde SK14 . . . . .167 E1
  Leigh WN7 . . . . .76 A5
  Littleborough OL15 . . . . .16 B5
  Manchester M2 . . . . .158 F1
  Manchester M3 . . . . .158 E2
  Marple SK6 . . . . .126 A4
  Middleton M24 . . . . .65 C8
  Mossley OL5 . . . . .68 C1
  Newton-le-W WA12 . . . . . . .89 B3
  Oldham OL1 . . . . .153 F6
  10 Oldham OL4 . . . . .67 F6
  Platt Bridge WN2 . . . . .56 A2
  Radcliffe M26 . . . . .44 C2
  Ramsbottom BL0 . . . . .138 B6
  Rochdale OL12 . . . . .139 F8
  Royton OL2 . . . . .48 D4
  Salford M6 . . . . .80 D5
  Shaw OL2 . . . . .149 B6
  Stalybridge SK15 . . . . .86 A2
  Stockport SK1 . . . . .112 A2
  Walkden M38 . . . . .60 B3
  Westhoughton BL5 . . . . .57 E8
  Wigan WN3 . . . . .150 C7
  Wigan WN5 . . . . .54 B6
Queen St Prim Sch BL4 . .60 D8
Queen St W M20 . . . . .110 B7
Queen Victoria St
  Eccles M30 . . . . .79 C2
  Rochdale OL11 . . . . .31 A4
Queen's Ave
  Ashton-in-M WN4 . . . . .73 B3
  Atherton M46 . . . . .58 C5
  Bolton BL7 . . . . .25 A7
  Glazebury WA3 . . . . .92 C7
  Little Lever BL3 . . . . .43 A4
  Romiley SK6 . . . . .113 A3
Queen's Cl M28 . . . . .60 D3
Queen's Ct
  Manchester M20 . . . . .110 A4
  3 Manchester M21 . . . . . . .97 B2
Queen's Dr Glossop SK13 . . .104 F1
  Manchester M25 . . . . .63 C2
  Manchester SK4 . . . . .168 A2
Queen's Gdns SK8 . . . . .122 F6
Queen's Gr M12 . . . . .99 A4
Queen's Park Rd OL10 . . . . . .29 D3
Queen's Rd
  Altrincham WA15 . . . . .119 F3
  Ashton-in-M WN4 . . . . .73 B4
  Ashton-u-L OL6 . . . . .85 D5
  Cheadle SK8 . . . . .122 F4
  Cheadle SK8 . . . . .123 A3
  Hazel Grove SK7 . . . . .124 E3
  12 Littleborough OL15 . . . . .16 B5
  Romiley SK6 . . . . .113 A3
  Urmston M41 . . . . .95 D1
  Wilmslow SK9 . . . . .137 A6
Queen's Terr **3** Bacup OL13 . .3 E8
  7 Dukinfield SK16 . . . . . . .166 B1
Queenhill Dr SK14 . . . . .102 A5
Queenhill Rd M22 . . . . .109 E1
Queens Ave
  Manchester M18 . . . . .165 B5
  Rochdale OL12 . . . . .15 C4
Queens Cl Boothstown M28 .77 F7
  Hyde SK14 . . . . .113 E7
  Manchester SK4 . . . . .168 A2
Queens Ct
  Manchester M40 . . . . .157 D5
  Manchester SK4 . . . . .168 A3

Queens Ct continued
  Urmston M41 . . . . .94 E2
Queens Dr Cheadle SK8 . . . .123 A2
  Golborne WA3 . . . . .90 C8
  Hyde SK14 . . . . .113 F7
  Newton-le-W WA12 . . . . . . .89 C5
  Rochdale OL11 . . . . .30 E3
Queens Gdns WN7 . . . . .76 C5
Queens Pl BL9 . . . . .11 C2
Queens Rd
  Ashton-in-M WA11 . . . . .89 A7
  Bolton BL3 . . . . .146 B4
  Chadderton OL9 . . . . .152 A7
  Manchester M40 . . . . .160 E4
  Manchester M8 . . . . .156 A5
  Manchester M8,M9 . . . . . . .156 C5
  Oldham OL8 . . . . .67 A5
  Orrell WN5 . . . . .53 C5
  Sale M33 . . . . .107 F5
Queens Road Prim Sch
  SK8 . . . . .123 A3
Queens Terr SK9 . . . . .131 D3
Queens View OL15 . . . . .16 A3
Queens Wlk M43 . . . . .84 A1
Queensbrook BL1 . . . . .145 E7
Queensbury Cl Bolton BL1 . .24 D5
  14 Handforth SK9 . . . . . . .131 D1
Queensbury Ct M40 . . . . . . .160 E3
Queensbury Par M40 . . . . . .160 E3
Queenscroft M30 . . . . .79 F3
Queensferry St M40 . . . . .83 C6
Queensgate Bolton BL1 . . . .144 C8
  Bramhall SK7 . . . . .132 E5
Queensgate Dr OL2 . . . . .48 C6
Queensgate Prim Sch
  SK7 . . . . .132 E4
Queensland Rd M18 . . . . . . .165 B5
Queenston Rd M20 . . . . .110 A4
Queensway
  Dukinfield SK16 . . . . .101 F7
  Gatley SK8 . . . . .131 C8
  Ince-in-M WN2 . . . . .56 A8
  Irlam M44 . . . . .93 F2
  Kearsley BL4 . . . . .60 F5
  Leigh WN7 . . . . .76 D6
  Manchester M19 . . . . .110 D2
  Mossley OL5 . . . . .86 D8
  Oldham OL3 . . . . .69 B6
  Poynton SK12 . . . . .133 D3
  Rochdale OL11 . . . . .30 E3
  Shevington WN6 . . . . .35 F4
  Swinton M27 . . . . .62 A2
  Urmston M41 . . . . .95 E4
  Walkden M28 . . . . .78 C8
  Wigan WN1 . . . . .37 B2
Queensway Com Prim Sch
  OL11 . . . . .30 F3
Quenby St M15 . . . . .162 D7
Quendon Ave M7 . . . . .158 E4
Quick Edge La OL4 . . . . .68 B4
Quick Rd OL4,OL5 . . . . .68 D4
Quick View OL5 . . . . .68 E3
Quickedge Rd OL4,OL5 . . . . .68 C3
Quickwood OL5 . . . . .68 D2
Quill Ct M44 . . . . .105 E6
Quilter Gr M9 . . . . .64 C2
Quinn St M11 . . . . .83 A1
Quinney Cres M16 . . . . .97 F4
Quinton **10** OL12 . . . . .139 E8
Quinton Wlk M13 . . . . .163 B6
Quintrell Brow BL7 . . . . .25 A8

R

Rabbit La SK14 . . . . .103 A6
Raby St M14,M16 . . . . .97 F4
Race The SK9 . . . . .131 D2
Racecourse Pk SK9 . . . . . . .136 F6
Racecourse Rd SK9 . . . . . . .136 E6
Racecourse Wlk M26 . . . . . . .43 F4
Racefield Hamlet OL2 . . . . . .48 A4
Racefield Rd WA14 . . . . .119 C4
Rachel Rosing Wlk M8 . . . . .155 F8
Rachel St M12 . . . . .163 C8
Rackhouse Prim Sch
  M23 . . . . .109 A1
Rackhouse Rd M23 . . . . .109 B1
Radbourne Cl M12 . . . . .165 A6
Radcliffe Ave WA3 . . . . .91 E3
Radcliffe Gr WN7 . . . . .75 F7
Radcliffe Hall
  CE/Meth Prim Sch M26 . .44 D4
Radcliffe High Sch M26 . . .43 E4
Radcliffe Inf Sch M26 . . . .43 E4
Radcliffe Jun Sch M26 . . . .43 E4
Radcliffe Moor Rd
  BL2,BL3,M26 . . . . .43 C5
Radcliffe New Rd
  M45,M26 . . . . .44 D2
Radcliffe Park Cres M6 . . . . .80 C5
Radcliffe Park Rd M6 . . . . . .80 C5
Radcliffe Rd Bolton BL2 . . . .148 B7
  Bolton BL2,BL3 . . . . .42 D5
  Bury BL9 . . . . .44 E7
  Oldham OL4 . . . . .49 D2
Radcliffe St Oldham OL1 . . . .153 F7
  Oldham OL1 . . . . .153 F8
  Oldham OL4 . . . . .68 A6
  Royton OL2 . . . . .48 E4
Radcliffe Sta M26 . . . . .44 B3
Radcliffe View M5 . . . . .161 B7
Radclyffe Com Sec Sch
  (Upper) The OL9 . . . . .65 F7

Radclyffe Prim Sch M5 . .161 A7
Radclyffe Sch (Lower)
　The OL9 . . . . .152 A6
Radclyffe St Middleton M24　47 A2
　Oldham OL9 . . . . .152 C8
Radclyffe Terr M24 . . . . . . .47 A2
Radelan Gr M26 . . . . .43 D4
Radford Cl SK2 . . . . .124 E7
Radford Dr Irlam M44 . . . . .94 A3
　2 Manchester M9 . . . . . .157 E8
Radford Ho SK2 . . . . .124 E7
Radford St M7 . . . . .81 C8
Radium St M4 . . . . .159 C2
Radlet Dr WA15 . . . . .120 A8
Radlett Wlk 9 M13 . . . . . .163 C5
Radley Cl Bolton BL1 . . . . .142 A1
　7 Sale M33 . . . . .107 D3
Radley St M43 . . . . .99 E8
Radley Wlk 12 M16 . . . . . .97 F3
Radnor Ave M34 . . . . .100 B3
Radnor Cl WN2 . . . . .57 A3
Radnor Dr WN7 . . . . .75 C5
Radnor St Manchester M15　.97 F4
　Manchester M18 . . . . . . .99 C4
　Oldham OL9 . . . . .152 C5
　Stretford M32 . . . . .96 D1
Radnormere Dr SK8 . . . . .123 A4
Radstock Cl Bolton BL1 . . . .24 E7
　Manchester M14 . . . . . . .98 B1
Radstock Rd M32 . . . . . . .96 C2
Radway M29 . . . . .59 C1
Rae St SK3 . . . . .123 C8
Raeburn Dr SK6 . . . . .126 B8
Raglan Ave
　Prestwich M25,M45 . . . . .63 B7
　Swinton M27 . . . . .62 B2
Raglan Cl M11 . . . . .160 F1
Raglan Dr WA14 . . . . .119 E8
Raglan Rd Sale M33 . . . . .108 A3
　Stretford M32 . . . . .96 B3
Raglan St Bolton BL1 . . . . .143 E4
　Denton M34 . . . . .101 C2
　Rochdale OL11 . . . . .30 C1
Raglan Wlk 5 M15 . . . . . .162 F6
Ragley Cl SK12 . . . . .133 F3
Raikes Clough Ind Est
　BL3 . . . . .42 C4
Raikes La OL3 . . . . .42 B4
Raikes Lane Ind Est BL3 . .42 C4
Raikes Rd BL3 . . . . .42 D5
Raikes Way BL3 . . . . .42 D5
Rail Pl 7 M15 . . . . .163 A6
Railgate OL13 . . . . .4 C8
Railside Terr M30 . . . . .80 A2
Railton Ave M16 . . . . .97 D3
Railton Terr M9 . . . . .157 F7
Railway App 4 OL11 . . . . .30 C2
Railway Bank SK14 . . . . . .101 C2
Railway Brow OL11 . . . . . .30 C1
Railway Cotts
　Bredbury SK6 . . . . .112 F4
　Hollinfare WA3 . . . . .105 B5
Railway Rd
　Adlington PR6,PR7 . . . . . .21 A7
　Golborne WA3 . . . . .74 B1
　Leigh WN7 . . . . .75 E5
　Oldham OL9 . . . . .153 D6
　Oldham OL9 . . . . .66 A2
　Stockport SK1,SK3 . . . . .170 E8
　Stretford M32 . . . . .96 F5
　Urmston M41 . . . . .95 E2
Railway St
　Altrincham WA14 . . . . . .119 D4
　Atherton M46 . . . . .58 B4
　Bacup OL13 . . . . .3 B8
　Dukinfield SK16 . . . . . . .166 B1
　Farnworth BL4 . . . . .42 E1
　Glossop SK13 . . . . .104 C1
　Hadfield SK13 . . . . .104 A5
　Heywood OL10 . . . . .29 E1
　Hindley WN2 . . . . .56 E7
　Littleborough OL15 . . . . .16 B5
　Manchester M18 . . . . . . .99 D6
　Newhey OL16 . . . . .32 B4
　Newton-le-W WA12 . . . . .89 B3
　Radcliffe M26 . . . . .44 A3
　Ramsbottom BL0 . . . . . .138 C6
　Ramsbottom BL9 . . . . . . .11 C2
　Rochdale OL16 . . . . .31 A6
　Stockport SK4 . . . . .169 E2
　Wigan WN6 . . . . .37 D1
Railway Street Ind Est
　M18 . . . . .99 D6
Railway Terr Bury BL8 . . . .27 C1
　Disley SK12 . . . . .135 D6
　Edgworth BL7 . . . . .9 B8
　5 Manchester M21 . . . . .97 B2
Railway View
　3 Oldham OL4 . . . . .67 F6
　Shaw OL2 . . . . .149 C8
Raimond St BL1 . . . . .142 C3
Rainbow Cl M21 . . . . .109 B7
Rainbow Dr M46 . . . . .58 D5
Raincliff Ave M13 . . . . . . .98 F2
Raines Crest OL16 . . . . . . .32 A6
Rainford Ave
　Altrincham WA15 . . . . . .120 A6
　Manchester M20 . . . . . .110 A8
Rainford Ho 2 BL1 . . . . . .145 F8
Rainford Rd WA11,WN5 . . .71 C5
Rainford St BL2 . . . . .25 C6
Rainforth St M13 . . . . .98 F3
Rainham Dr Bolton BL1 . . .143 E1
　Manchester M8 . . . . . . .156 A7
Rainham Gr 2 BL1 . . . . . .143 E1

Rainham Way
　Brinnington SK5 . . . . . . .112 B6
　Oldham OL9 . . . . .152 B6
Rainhill Wlk M40 . . . . .83 D4
Rainow Ave M43 . . . . .83 E1
Rainow Rd SK3 . . . . .123 C6
Rainow Way 10 SK9 . . . . .131 E1
Rainshaw St Bolton BL1 . . .143 F4
　1 Oldham OL4 . . . . .67 D8
　Royton OL2 . . . . .48 D4
Rainsough Ave M25 . . . . . .63 A1
Rainsough Brow M25 . . . . .62 F1
Rainsough Cl M25 . . . . . . .63 A1
Rainton Wlk 2 M40 . . . . . .65 D2
Rainwood OL9 . . . . .65 E8
Raithby Dr WN3 . . . . .55 A3
Raja Cl M8 . . . . .156 B7
Rake Cl OL11 . . . . .29 D8
Rake Fold BL3 . . . . .138 A6
Rake Head Barn La OL14 . .6 A8
Rake La OL3 . . . . .62 B2
Rake Terr OL15 . . . . .16 C6
Rakehead La OL13 . . . . .3 B8
Rakehead Wlk M15 . . . . . .162 F5
Rakewood Dr OL15 . . . . . .49 E4
Rakewood Rd OL15 . . . . . .16 C2
Raleigh Cl
　Manchester M20 . . . . . .110 A5
　Oldham OL1 . . . . .153 F8
Raleigh Gdns OL15 . . . . . . .6 C1
Raleigh St Reddish SK5 . . .169 E4
　Stretford M32 . . . . .96 E2
Ralli Courts M3 . . . . .158 E1
Ralph Ave SK14 . . . . .113 E7
Ralph Green St OL9 . . . . . .66 B3
Ralph Sherwin Ct OL12 . . .15 D4
Ralph St Bolton BL1 . . . . . .143 D2
　Droylsden M11 . . . . .83 D1
　Rochdale OL12 . . . . .15 A1
Ralphs La SK16 . . . . .101 C7
Ralston Cl M7 . . . . .155 F8
Ralstone Ave OL8 . . . . .66 F4
Ram St M38 . . . . .59 F5
Ramage Wlk M12 . . . . . . .160 E1
Ramillies Ave SK8 . . . . . . .123 C1
Ramillies Hall Sch SK8 . . .123 C2
Ramp Rd E M90 . . . . .130 C7
Ramp Rd S M90 . . . . .130 C7
Ramp Rd W M90 . . . . .130 B7
Ramsay Ave BL4 . . . . .60 B7
Ramsay Pl OL16 . . . . .31 A8
Ramsay St Bolton BL1 . . . .143 E4
　Rochdale OL16 . . . . .31 A8
Ramsay Terr 19 OL16 . . . . .31 A8
Ramsbottom
　Cottage Hospl BL0 . . . . .138 C5
Ramsbottom
　Heritage Ctr Mus BL0 . .138 C7
Ramsbottom La BL0 . . . . .138 C7
Ramsbottom Rd
　Horwich BL6 . . . . .22 C3
　Ramsbottom BL8,BL7 . . .10 A3
Ramsbottom Sta BL0 . . . .138 C6
Ramsbury Dr M40 . . . . . . .65 D2
Ramsdale Rd SK7 . . . . . . .132 E8
Ramsdale St OL9 . . . . .152 A7
Ramsden Cl Glossop SK13　104 D2
　Oldham OL1 . . . . .153 E7
　Wigan WN3 . . . . .150 A5
Ramsden Cres OL1 . . . . . .153 E8
Ramsden Fold M27 . . . . . . .61 F2
Ramsden La OL14 . . . . .5 F7
Ramsden Rd OL12 . . . . . . .15 C6
Ramsden St
　Ashton-u-L OL6 . . . . . . .166 B4
　Bolton BL3 . . . . .42 D5
　Oldham OL1 . . . . .153 E7
　Walsden OL14 . . . . .6 A7
Ramsden Wood Rd OL14 . .6 A7
Ramsey Ave M19 . . . . .99 D1
Ramsey Cl Ashton-in-M WN4 73 B2
　Atherton M46 . . . . .58 E2
Ramsey Gr BL8 . . . . .27 B2
Ramsey St 3 Leigh WN7 . .76 A4
　Manchester M40 . . . . . . .83 B7
　Oldham OL1 . . . . .67 B8
　Oldham OL9 . . . . .152 B5
Ramsgate Rd
　Failsworth M40 . . . . .83 C4
　Reddish SK5 . . . . .111 F7
Ramsgate St M7,M8 . . . . .155 E5
Ramsgill Cl M23 . . . . .108 F1
Ramsgreave Cl M9 . . . . . . .64 D7
Ramwell Gdns BL3 . . . . . .145 D5
Ramwells Brow BL7 . . . . . .25 A8
Ranbys Ave M9 . . . . .64 F4
Rand St 6 OL1 . . . . .49 D1
Randale Dr BL9 . . . . .45 A2
Randall Ave M9 . . . . .36 A5
Randall Cl WA12 . . . . .89 B4
Randall Wlk 22 M11 . . . . .160 F1
Randle St 1 WN2 . . . . . . .56 D6
Randlesham St M25 . . . . . .63 C4
Randolph Pl SK3 . . . . .170 E7
Randolph Rd BL4 . . . . .60 F7
Randolph St Bolton BL3 . . .145 D5
　Manchester M19 . . . . . . .99 B2
　Oldham OL8 . . . . .66 C2
Rands Clough Dr M28 . . . . .78 B6
Ranelagh Rd M27 . . . . .80 C7
Ranelagh St M11 . . . . .83 B2
Raneley Gr OL11 . . . . .31 A2
Ranford Rd M19 . . . . .111 A8
Range Dr SK6 . . . . .113 C6
Range Hall Ct 7 SK1 . . . . .112 A1

Range La OL3 . . . . .33 D1
Range Rd Dukinfield SK16 . .102 B7
　Manchester M16 . . . . . . .97 E3
　Stalybridge SK15 . . . . . .102 B8
　Stockport SK3 . . . . .170 E7
Range St Bolton BL3 . . . . . .147 D4
　Manchester M11 . . . . . .165 C8
Rangemore Ave M22 . . . . .121 D8
Ranicar Steet WN2 . . . . . . .57 C3
Rankine Terr BL3 . . . . .145 D5
Ranmore Ave
　Droylsden M11 . . . . .99 D8
　Garswood WN4 . . . . .72 A4
Rannoch Rd BL2 . . . . .43 A7
Ransfield Rd M21 . . . . .97 B1
Ranulph Ct 1 M6 . . . . .80 D5
Ranworth Ave SK4 . . . . . .110 F2
Ranworth Cl Bolton BL1 . . .25 A6
　Manchester M11 . . . . . .165 A8
Raper St OL4 . . . . .67 C8
Rapes Highway OL3 . . . . . .33 F5
Raphael St BL1 . . . . .143 D2
Rappax Rd WA15 . . . . . . .129 A8
Rasbottom St BL3 . . . . . . .145 E5
Raspberry La M44 . . . . . . .94 A5
Rassbottom Brow 5 SK15　.85 F2
Rassbottom Ind Est SK15　.85 F2
Rassbottom St SK15 . . . . . .85 F2
Rassey Cl WN6 . . . . .37 A7
Rastell Wlk 28 M9 . . . . . . .64 E3
Ratcliffe Ave M44 . . . . .94 A2
Ratcliffe Rd WN2 . . . . .38 C6
Ratcliffe St Leigh WN7 . . . .75 F6
　Manchester M19 . . . . . . .99 B1
　Tyldesley M29 . . . . .59 B1
　Wigan WN6 . . . . .37 A1
Ratcliffe Terr OL5 . . . . .86 C8
Rath Wlk 14 M40 . . . . .83 C5
Rathan Rd M41 . . . . .95 C4
Rathbone St OL16 . . . . .31 C7
Rathbourne Ave M9 . . . . . .64 D4
Rathen Ave WN2 . . . . .56 A8
Rathen Rd M20 . . . . .110 C5
Rathmel Rd M23 . . . . .108 F2
Rathmell Cl WA3 . . . . .91 E3
Rathmore Ave M40 . . . . . .157 E5
Rathvale Dr M22 . . . . .130 C8
Rattenbury Ct M6 . . . . .80 C5
Raveden Cl BL1 . . . . .142 C3
Raveley Ave M14 . . . . . . .110 D8
Ravelston Dr M9 . . . . .157 D7
Raven Ave Haslingden BB4　.1 A7
　Oldham OL9 . . . . .152 A5
Raven Cl M43 . . . . .84 C3
Raven Croft BB4 . . . . .1 B8
Raven Ct M15 . . . . .162 E5
Raven Dr M44 . . . . .94 A3
Raven Ho M6 . . . . .81 A5
Raven Pk BB4 . . . . .1 B8
Raven Rd Bolton BL3 . . . . .146 A4
　Sale M33 . . . . .108 B1
Raven St Bury BL9 . . . . . .140 F4
　Manchester M12 . . . . . .163 C8
　Rochdale OL11 . . . . .13 C1
Raven Terr 1 SK16 . . . . . .166 C1
Raven Way Salford M6 . . . .154 F3
　5 Salford M6 . . . . .81 A3
Ravendale Cl OL12 . . . . . . .14 A1
Ravenfield Gr 10 BL1 . . . . .145 D8
Ravenhead Cl 13 M14 . . . .110 D8
Ravenhead Dr WN8 . . . . . .53 A7
Ravenhead Sq SK15 . . . . . .86 E5
Ravenhurst 4 M7 . . . . .63 E1
Ravenhurst Dr BL1 . . . . . . .40 D6
Ravenna Ave M23 . . . . . . .120 D7
Ravenoak Ave M19 . . . . . .111 C8
Ravenoak Dr M35 . . . . .84 A8
Ravenoak Park Rd SK8 . . .132 B8
Ravenoak Rd Cheadle SK8　132 B8
　Stockport SK2 . . . . .124 A4
Ravens Cl M25,M8 . . . . . . .63 E2
Ravens Holme BL1 . . . . . . .40 E7
Ravens Wood BL1 . . . . . . .40 E7
Ravensbury Cty Prim Sch
　M11 . . . . .83 B2
Ravensbury St M11 . . . . . . .83 B2
Ravenscar Cres M22 . . . . .130 D8
Ravenscar Wlk BL4 . . . . . . .60 D7
Ravenscraig Rd M38 . . . . . .60 B6
Ravensdale Gdns M30 . . . . .79 E3
Ravensdale Rd BL1 . . . . . . .40 D7
Ravensdale St M14 . . . . . . .98 C3
Ravensfield Ind Est SK16　166 B1
Ravenside Pk OL9 . . . . . . .152 A5
Ravenside Ret Pk BL2 . . . .148 A6
Ravenstone Dr Diggle OL3　.51 C3
　Sale M33 . . . . .108 C5
Ravenstonedale Dr OL2 . . .48 E5
Ravensway M25,M8 . . . . . .63 D2
Ravenswood M20 . . . . . . .109 F4
Ravenswood Ave
　Stockport SK4 . . . . .168 A1
　Wigan WN3 . . . . .54 D3
Ravenswood Ct 5 SK3 . . .123 F4
Ravenswood Dr Bolton BL1　40 E7
　Cheadle SK8 . . . . .132 B8
　Hindley WN2 . . . . .56 E7
　Manchester M9 . . . . .64 E3
Ravenswood Rd
　Stretford M32 . . . . .96 F4
　Wilmslow SK9 . . . . .136 E4
Ravenwood OL9 . . . . .65 D7
Ravenwood Dr
　Altrincham WA15 . . . . . .129 D7
　Denton M34 . . . . .100 E6
Ravine Ave M9 . . . . .157 F3
Rawcliffe Ave BL2 . . . . .42 F7
Rawcliffe St M14 . . . . .98 B3

Rawdon Cl 9 M19 . . . . .99 B1
Rawkin Cl M15 . . . . .162 E5
Rawlinson St 1 BL6 . . . . . .22 B4
Rawlyn Rd BL1 . . . . .142 A2
Rawpool Gdns M23 . . . . . .121 A7
Rawson Ave BL4 . . . . .42 E1
Rawson Rd BL1 . . . . .142 C1
Rawson St BL4 . . . . .42 E1
Rawsons Rake BL0,BL8 . . .138 A6
Rawsthorne Av Bolton BL1　143 D2
　Tyldesley M29 . . . . .77 D8
Rawsthorne St Bolton BL1　143 E4
Rawstron St OL12 . . . . .4 C1
Rawthey Pl WN2 . . . . .55 F2
Rayburn Way M8 . . . . .156 A5
Raycroft Ave M9 . . . . .65 A2
Raydale Cl WA3 . . . . .74 E1
Rayden Cres BL5 . . . . .57 E6
Raydon Ave M40 . . . . .157 D5
Rayleigh Ave M11 . . . . .99 F7
Raymond Ave Bury BL9 . . . .27 C5
　Oldham OL9 . . . . .66 B4
Raymond Rd M23 . . . . . . .109 B2
Raymond St M27 . . . . .61 F1
Rayner Ave WN2 . . . . .56 E3
Rayner La M34,M43,OL7 . . .84 E2
Rayner St SK1 . . . . .124 B8
Rayners Cl SK15 . . . . .85 F1
Raynham Ave M20 . . . . . .110 B3
Raynham St OL6 . . . . .166 C3
Rayson Hill Dr M9 . . . . .64 C2
Rayson St M9 . . . . .64 C2
Reabrook Ave M12 . . . . . .164 F6
Reach The M28 . . . . .60 E2
Read Cl BL9 . . . . .44 D7
Read St SK14 . . . . .101 C3
Read St W SK14 . . . . .101 C3
Reade Ave M41 . . . . .94 F1
Reade Ho M41 . . . . .94 F1
Reading Cl M11 . . . . .165 C8
Reading Dr M33 . . . . .107 A4
Reading St M6 . . . . .81 B5
Reading Wlk 1 M34 . . . . .100 F1
Readitt Wlk M11 . . . . .83 B2
Reaney Wlk M12 . . . . .165 A6
Reather Wlk M40 . . . . .159 C3
Rebecca St M8 . . . . .156 A8
Recreation Ave WN4 . . . . . .73 D4
Recreation Dr WN5 . . . . . . .71 E5
Recreation Rd M35 . . . . . . .66 B1
Recreation St Bolton BL2 . . .25 E5
　Bolton BL3 . . . . .147 E4
　Prestwich M25 . . . . .63 C4
Rectory Ave Golborne WA3　.90 C8
　Manchester M8 . . . . .64 A1
　Prestwich M25 . . . . .63 B4
Rectory CE Prim Sch
　WN4 . . . . .72 D5
Rectory Cl Denton M34 . . .101 A2
　Radcliffe M26 . . . . .44 D4
Rectory Ct 3 SK6 . . . . . . .125 F5
Rectory Fields SK1 . . . . . .112 A1
Rectory Gdns
　Prestwich M25 . . . . .63 B4
　Westhoughton BL5 . . . . . .57 E5
Rectory Gn Prestwich M25　.63 B4
　Stockport SK1 . . . . .112 A1
Rectory Gr M25 . . . . .63 B3
Rectory La Bury BL9 . . . . . .28 C8
　Prestwich M25 . . . . .63 A4
　Radcliffe M26 . . . . .44 B3
　Standish WN1,WN6 . . . . .20 A1
Rectory Rd
　Downall Green WN4 . . . . .72 D5
　Manchester M8 . . . . .63 F1
Rectory St M24 . . . . .46 F1
Red Bank M4,M8 . . . . .159 A3
Red Bank Ave WA12 . . . . . .89 C1
Red Bank Rd M26 . . . . .43 F5
Red Barn Rd WN5 . . . . . . .71 C6
Red Bridge BL2 . . . . .26 A1
Red Brook St OL11 . . . . . .139 D7
Red Gables OL7 . . . . .166 A4
Red Hall St M4 . . . . .67 C6
Red Hill Way WN2 . . . . .56 D6
Red House La WA14 . . . . .118 C8
Red La Bolton BL2 . . . . .25 E1
　Disley SK12 . . . . .135 C5
　Rochdale OL12 . . . . .15 B2
Red Lane Com Prim Sch
　BL2 . . . . .25 F1
Red Lion St M4 . . . . .159 A2
Red Lumb St OL12 . . . . . . .13 A3
Red Pike Wlk 2 OL1 . . . . . .67 A8
Red Rock Brow WN1 . . . . . .37 C8
Red Rock La Kearsley M26　.61 E6
　Standish WN1,WN2 . . . . .37 D5
Red Rose Cres M19 . . . . . .111 C7
Red Rose Gdns M38 . . . . . .60 A4
Red Rose Ret Pk M5 . . . . .161 B8
Red Row SK7 . . . . .134 B8
Red St M46 . . . . .58 E3
Red Waters WN7 . . . . .76 A6
Redacre SK12 . . . . .133 F6
Redacre Rd M18 . . . . .99 C5
Redbourne Dr M41 . . . . . . .94 F4
Redbrick Ct 8 OL7 . . . . . .166 A1
Redbridge Gr M21 . . . . . . .109 A8
Redbrook Cl BL4 . . . . .42 E1
Redbrook Gr 2 SK9 . . . . . .131 D1
Redbrook Rd
　Altrincham WA15 . . . . . .120 D5
　Partington M31 . . . . . . .105 D2
　Wigan WN3 . . . . .151 G6

Redburn Rd M23 . . . . .121 B7
Redby St M11 . . . . .165 B7
Redcar Ave
　Manchester M20 . . . . . .110 B6
　Urmston M41 . . . . .95 A4
Redcar Cl SK7 . . . . .125 A1
Redcar Rd Bolton BL1 . . . .142 B4
　Little Lever BL3 . . . . .43 A3
　Pendlebury M27 . . . . . . .80 C7
Redcar St 12 OL12 . . . . . .139 E8
Redcliffe Ct M25 . . . . .63 B2
Redcliffe Rd M8 . . . . .98 C3
Redclyffe Rd Eccles M41 . . .95 D7
　Manchester M20 . . . . . .110 A5
Redcot Cl M45 . . . . .62 C7
Redcote St M40 . . . . .83 A8
Redcourt Ave M20 . . . . . .110 B6
Redcroft Gdns 2 M19 . . . .110 E4
Redcroft Rd M33 . . . . .107 E6
Redcross St
　Rochdale OL12 . . . . .139 F8
　Rochdale OL12 . . . . .14 F1
Redcross St N OL12 . . . . . .14 F1
Reddaway Cl M6 . . . . .81 A5
Reddish Cl BL2 . . . . .25 E6
Reddish La Lymm WA13 . . .117 A1
Reddish M18,M34 . . . . .99 E4
Reddish North Sta SK5 . . .99 F2
Reddish Rd SK5 . . . . .111 F6
Reddish South Sta SK5 . . .111 F7
Reddish Vale Ctry Pk
　SK5 . . . . .112 B7
Reddish Vale Sch SK5 . . . .111 F7
Reddy La WA14 . . . . .118 B1
Reddyshore Brow OL15 . . . .16 C5
Reddyshore Scout Gate
　OL14 . . . . .6 C5
Redesmere Cl
　Altrincham WA15 . . . . . .120 D6
　Droylsden M43 . . . . .84 B1
Redesmere Dr
　Alderley Edge SK9 . . . . .137 A1
　Cheadle SK8 . . . . .122 F4
Redesmere Pk M41 . . . . . .107 B8
Redesmere Rd SK9 . . . . . .131 D5
Redfearn Wood OL12 . . . . .14 B2
Redfern Ave M33 . . . . .108 E3
Redfern Cl SK13 . . . . .104 A6
Redfern Cotts OL11 . . . . . .13 D1
Redfern Ho SK6 . . . . .113 A2
Redfern St M4 . . . . .159 A2
Redfern Way OL11 . . . . . . .13 D1
Redfield Cl M11 . . . . .160 F1
Redford Cl WN7 . . . . .76 A5
Redford Dr SK7 . . . . .124 A2
Redford Rd M9 . . . . .63 F4
Redford St BL8 . . . . .27 C3
Redgate Hadfield SK13 . . .104 C4
　Hyde SK14 . . . . .113 D8
Redgate La
　Manchester M12 . . . . . .164 F5
　Manchester M12 . . . . . . .99 A4
Redgate Rd WN4 . . . . .73 B6
Redgate Way BL4 . . . . . . .147 F1
Redgrave Pas OL4 . . . . . . .67 D8
Redgrave Rise WN3 . . . . . .54 D3
Redgrave St OL4 . . . . .67 D8
Redgrave Wlk M19 . . . . . . .99 C1
Redhill Dr SK6 . . . . .112 E3
Redhill Gr BL1 . . . . .143 E1
Redhill St M4 . . . . .159 C2
Redhouse La Disley SK12 . .135 E7
　Romiley SK6 . . . . .113 A4
Redington Dr M28 . . . . .78 A5
Redisher Cl BL0 . . . . .10 F3
Redisher Croft BL0 . . . . . . .10 F3
Redisher La BL8 . . . . .10 E3
Redland Ave SK5 . . . . .111 F5
Redland Cl OL15 . . . . .16 B6
Redland Cres M21 . . . . . . .109 B6
Redland Ct WN2 . . . . .73 E7
Redlynch Wlk M8 . . . . .156 A7
Redmain Gr WA3 . . . . .90 E8
Redmayne Cl WA12 . . . . . . .89 B4
Redmere Gr M14 . . . . .110 C8
Redmire Mews SK16 . . . . .101 F7
Redmires Ct 7 M5 . . . . . . .81 A1
Redmond Cl M34 . . . . .100 E7
Rednal Wlk WN3 . . . . .150 B6
Redpol Ave WN7 . . . . .76 B5
Redpoll Cl M28 . . . . .78 B7
Redruth St M14 . . . . .98 B2
Redscar Wlk M24 . . . . .46 E1
Redshank Cl WA12 . . . . . . .89 C4
Redshank Gr WN7 . . . . .76 A6
Redshaw Ave BL2 . . . . .25 E5
Redshaw Cl M14 . . . . .98 D1
Redstart Cl 7 WA3 . . . . . . .90 E8
Redstart Gr M28 . . . . .78 D8
Redstock Cl BL5 . . . . .40 B1
Redstone Rd M19 . . . . . . .110 D3
Redthorn Ave 2 M19 . . . . .110 F7
Redvale Wlk M7 . . . . .155 E6
Redvales Rd BL9 . . . . .44 E7
Redvers St
　Manchester M11 . . . . . .164 E8
　Oldham OL1 . . . . .153 D8
Redwater Cl M28 . . . . .78 A6
Redwing Rd BL8 . . . . .10 F2
Redwood Chadderton OL9 . .65 D7
　Sale M33 . . . . .107 C4
　Shevington WN6 . . . . . . .36 B6
　Westhoughton BL5 . . . . . .57 D6
Redwood Ave Wigan WN5 . .54 A6
　Wigan WN6 . . . . .36 F3
Redwood Cl OL12 . . . . .14 B3

Redwood Dr Bredbury SK6 .112 F3
  Denton M34 . . . . .100 E6
  Manchester M8 . . . . .156 B5
  Rawtenstall BB4 . . . . .1 F8
Redwood Ho M22 . . . . . . .109 E1
Redwood La OL4 . . . . .67 E7
Redwood Park Gr OL16 . .31 D7
Redwood Rd OL3 . . . . .69 C7
Redwood St M6 . . . . .81 A4
Reece Ct 4 SK16 . . . . . . .101 E8
Reed Cres WN3 . . . . .55 A4
Reed Ct 2 OL1 . . . . .153 E8
Reed Hill OL16 . . . . .139 F8
Reed St Manchester M18 . . .99 D6
  9 Oldham OL1 . . . . .67 A7
Reedbank M26 . . . . .62 A8
Reedbank Cl BL1 . . . . .144 C8
Reedham Wlk
  Manchester M40 . . . . .160 D4
  Oldham OL9 . . . . .66 C4
Reedley Dr M28 . . . . .78 C8
Reedmace Cl M28 . . . . .60 E1
Reedshaw Bank SK2 . . . . .124 D5
Reedshaw Rd M9 . . . . .156 C6
Reedsmere Cl WN5 . . . . . . .54 F6
Reeman Cl SK6 . . . . .113 A4
Reeman Ct SK9 . . . . .131 B2
Reepham Cl WN3 . . . . .54 D3
Reeve Cl SK2 . . . . .124 F5
Reeve St WA3 . . . . .91 B8
Reeves Ct M5 . . . . .80 A2
Reeves Rd M21 . . . . .109 B7
Reeves St WN7 . . . . .75 F6
Reevey Ave SK7 . . . . .124 C2
Reform St OL12 . . . . .14 F1
Reform Wlk M11 . . . . .165 B8
Refuge St OL2 . . . . .149 B6
Regaby Gr WN2 . . . . .57 A5
Regal Cl M45 . . . . .63 B8
Regal Wlk 11 M40 . . . . . . .83 C6
Regan Ave M21 . . . . .109 D7
Regan St Bolton BL1 . . . . . .143 D3
  5 Radcliffe M26 . . . . .44 B2
Regatta Cl OL9 . . . . .66 A3
Regatta St M6 . . . . .80 F6
Regency Chambers BL9 . . .140 E2
Regency Cl Glossop SK13 .104 D1
  Manchester M40 . . . . .157 D5
  Oldham OL8 . . . . .66 D4
Regency Ct Cheadle SK8 . .123 A2
  Rochdale OL11 . . . . .29 F7
  Wigan WN1 . . . . .151 D8
Regency Gdns SK8 . . . . . .131 E8
Regency Lo M25 . . . . .63 A3
Regency Pk SK9 . . . . .136 F5
Regency Wharf WN7 . . . . .76 C4
Regent Ave
  Ashton-in-M WN4 . . . . .72 F5
  Manchester M14 . . . . .98 A2
  Walkden M38 . . . . .60 C4
Regent Bank SK9 . . . . . . .136 F5
Regent Cl Bramhall SK7 . . .132 D4
  Cheadle SK8 . . . . .123 C4
  Wilmslow SK9 . . . . .136 F5
Regent Cres Failsworth M35 83 E6
  Oldham OL1,OL2 . . . . .48 D2
Regent Ct
  Altrincham WA14 . . . . .119 D4
  Manchester M7 . . . . .63 D1
  Manchester M4 . . . . .111 C5
Regent Dr Bolton BL6 . . . . . .40 B7
  Denton M34 . . . . .100 D1
  Leigh WN7 . . . . .76 D7
Regent Ho M14 . . . . .98 D3
Regent Rd M14 . . . . .98 C4
  Altrincham WA14 . . . . .119 D4
  Bolton BL6 . . . . .40 B6
  Platt Bridge WN2 . . . . .56 A3
  Salford M15,M5 . . . . .161 C8
  Salford M5 . . . . .81 A1
  Stockport SK2 . . . . .124 A6
Regent Road Ind Est M5 162 D8
Regent Sq M5 . . . . .161 B8
Regent St Bury BL9 . . . . . .140 E2
  Eccles M30 . . . . .79 F2
  Failsworth M40 . . . . .83 E8
  Glossop SK13 . . . . .104 D1
  Hadfield SK13 . . . . .104 B5
  Heywood OL10 . . . . .29 B2
  3 Hindley WN2 . . . . .56 D5
  Littleborough OL15 . . . . . . .16 B5
  Middleton M24 . . . . .46 F2
  Newton-le-W WA12 . . . . . . .89 A3
  Oldham OL1 . . . . .67 A7
  Ramsbottom BL0 . . . . .11 A4
  Rochdale OL12,OL16 . . . . . .15 A1
  2 Rochdale OL16 . . . . .31 A8
  Shaw OL2 . . . . .149 B7
  Tyldesley M46 . . . . .58 E2
Regent Trad Est M5 . . . . .158 D1
Regent Wlk BL4 . . . . .60 D8
Regents Dr OL5 . . . . .86 D8
Regina Ave SK15 . . . . .86 A2
Regina Cres WN7 . . . . .76 E6
Regina Ct M6 . . . . .80 A3
Reginald Latham Ct M40 160 D3
Reginald St Bolton BL3 . . .146 A2
  2 Droylsden M11 . . . . .99 F7
  Eccles M30 . . . . .95 A8
  Swinton M27 . . . . .61 D1
Reid Cl M34 . . . . .113 A8
Reigate Cl BL8 . . . . .27 E1
Reigate Rd M41 . . . . .106 E8
Reilly St M15 . . . . .162 F6
Reins Lee Ave OL8 . . . . . . .67 A2
Reins Lee Rd OL7 . . . . .85 A6
Reliance St M40 . . . . .83 C6

Reliance Street Ent Pk
  M40 . . . . .83 C6
Reliance Street Trad Est
  M40 . . . . .83 C6
Rembrandt Wlk OL1 . . . . . .49 D4
Rena Cl SK4 . . . . .169 D3
Rena Ct SK4 . . . . .169 D3
Rendel Cl
  Newton-le-W WA12 . . . . . . .89 D2
  Stretford M32 . . . . .96 D2
Renfrew Cl WN3 . . . . .55 A3
Renfrew Dr BL3 . . . . .40 F3
Renfrew Rd WN2 . . . . .38 D5
Rennie Cl M32 . . . . .96 E2
Renshaw Ave M30 . . . . .79 D1
Renshaw Dr BL9 . . . . .141 C3
Renshaw St
  Altrincham WA14 . . . . .119 E5
  Eccles M30 . . . . .79 D1
Renton Rd Bolton BL3 . . . .146 B3
  Stretford M32 . . . . .96 E3
  Wythenshawe M22 . . . . . . .121 D4
Renwick Gr BL3 . . . . .146 C3
Renwick Sq WN4 . . . . .72 F3
Repton Ave Droylsden M43 .83 D3
  Failsworth M40 . . . . .65 E1
  Hyde SK14 . . . . .167 E3
  Ince-in-M WN3 . . . . .55 F4
  Oldham OL8 . . . . .66 D3
  Urmston M41 . . . . .94 D2
Repton Cl 6 M33 . . . . . . .107 D3
Reservoir Rd SK3 . . . . . . .170 D7
Reservoir St Aspull WN2 . . .38 F3
  Ince-in-M WN2 . . . . .56 A8
  Manchester M3 . . . . .158 E3
  Rochdale OL16 . . . . .15 C1
  Salford M6 . . . . .154 F2
Restormel Ave WN2 . . . . . .38 D5
Retford Ave OL16 . . . . .31 B4
Retford Cl BL8 . . . . .27 E5
Retford St OL4 . . . . .67 B5
Retiro St OL1 . . . . .153 E6
Retreat The SK6 . . . . .113 C1
Reuben St SK4 . . . . .169 E4
Revers St BL8 . . . . .140 D3
Reveton Gn SK7 . . . . .124 A2
Rex Bldgs SK9 . . . . .137 B6
Reynard Ct 5 M14 . . . . . . .98 E4
Reynard Rd M21 . . . . .109 B7
Reynard St SK14 . . . . .167 D3
Reynell Rd M13 . . . . .98 F2
Reynold St Ashton-u-L OL6 .85 E2
  Manchester M1 . . . . .163 A8
  Marple SK6 . . . . .126 B8
Reynolds Cl BL5 . . . . .58 F6
Reynolds Dr Atherton BL5 . .58 F7
  Manchester M18 . . . . .99 D6
  Marple SK6 . . . . .126 B8
Reynolds Mews SK6 . . . . .137 E8
Reynolds Rd M16 . . . . .97 C4
Rhine Cl BL8 . . . . .26 F7
Rhine Dr M8 . . . . .155 E5
Rhiwlas Dr BL9 . . . . .44 F8
Rhode Hos SK6 . . . . .125 F3
Rhode St BL8 . . . . .26 F6
Rhodes Ave Haslingden BB4 . .1 A7
  Oldham OL4 . . . . .67 F5
  Uppermill OL3 . . . . .51 C1
Rhodes Bank OL1 . . . . .67 A6
Rhodes Cres OL11 . . . . . . .30 C3
Rhodes Dr BL9 . . . . .45 A2
Rhodes Hill OL4 . . . . .67 F5
Rhodes St Dukinfield SK14 .101 C3
  Hadfield SK13 . . . . .104 B5
  Oldham OL1 . . . . .67 A4
  Oldham OL4 . . . . .67 F7
  Rochdale OL12 . . . . .15 B3
  Royton OL2 . . . . .49 A3
Rhodes St N SK14 . . . . . . .101 C3
Rhodeswood Dr SK13 . . . .104 A6
Rhos Ave Cheadle SK8 . . . .122 E1
  Manchester M14 . . . . .110 E8
  Middleton M24 . . . . .65 A7
Rhos Dr SK7 . . . . .124 D1
Rhosleigh Ave BL1 . . . . . .143 E4
Rialto Gdns M7 . . . . .155 E6
Ribbesford Rd WN3 . . . . . .54 C4
Ribble Ave Bolton BL2 . . . . .42 E7
  Chadderton OL9 . . . . .47 F1
  Littleborough OL15 . . . . . . .15 F6
Ribble Cl WA3 . . . . .91 F2
Ribble Cres WN5 . . . . .71 C3
Ribble Dr Boothstown M28 . .77 F6
  Bury BL9 . . . . .27 F8
  Kearsley BL4 . . . . .61 B5
  Whitefield M45 . . . . .45 A1
  Wigan WN5 . . . . .54 C7
Ribble Drive
  Com Prim Sch M45 . . . . . . .45 A1
Ribble Gr Heywood OL10 . . .29 A3
  Leigh WN7 . . . . .75 C5
Ribble Rd Oldham OL8 . . . . .66 C3
  Platt Bridge WN2 . . . . .56 A2
  Shevington Moor WN6 . . . . .19 B2
Ribble St Bacup OL13 . . . . . .4 A8
  Rochdale OL11 . . . . .30 C4
Ribble Wlk M43 . . . . .100 A8
Ribblesdale Cl OL10 . . . . . .46 E7
Ribblesdale Dr M40 . . . . . .156 C5
Ribblesdale Rd BL3 . . . . . .147 D4
Ribbleton Cl BL8 . . . . .26 F1
Ribchester Dr BL9 . . . . .44 D7
Ribchester Gdns WA3 . . . . .91 A4
Ribchester Gr BL2 . . . . .25 E1
Riber Bank SK13 . . . . .171 E1
Riber Cl 28 SK13 . . . . .171 E1
Riber Fold 27 SK13 . . . . . .171 E1

Riber Gn 26 SK13 . . . . . . .171 E1
Ribston St M15 . . . . .162 E6
Rice St M3 . . . . .162 E8
Richard Burch St 3 BL9 .140 F3
Richard Gwyn Cl BL5 . . . . .57 D6
Richard Reynolds Ct
  M44 . . . . .105 E6
Richard St Failsworth M35 . .83 F7
  Ince-in-M WN3 . . . . .151 D6
  Radcliffe M26 . . . . .43 F3
  Ramsbottom BL0 . . . . .11 E7
  Rochdale OL11 . . . . .139 F6
  Stockport SK1 . . . . .169 F2
Richards Rd WN6 . . . . .19 B3
Richardson Cl M45 . . . . . . .44 F1
Richardson Rd M30 . . . . . . .79 E2
Richardson St
  8 Manchester M11 . . . . . . .99 E7
  Stockport SK1 . . . . .124 A7
Richbell Cl M44 . . . . .105 F7
Richborough Cl M7 . . . . . . .155 E5
Richelieu St BL3 . . . . .42 A4
Richmond Ave
  Handforth SK9 . . . . .131 D4
  Manchester M25 . . . . .63 C1
  Oldham OL9 . . . . .66 A4
  Royton OL2 . . . . .48 D4
  Urmston M41 . . . . .95 E2
Richmond Cl Bury BL8 . . . . .26 F6
  Culcheth WA3 . . . . .91 D4
  Dukinfield SK16 . . . . .101 D6
  Hadfield SK13 . . . . .104 A5
  Lymm WA13 . . . . .117 B4
  Mossley OL5 . . . . .86 E8
  Rochdale OL16 . . . . .31 C3
  Sale M33 . . . . .108 F3
  Shaw OL2 . . . . .149 B5
  Stalybridge SK15 . . . . .86 A1
  Standish WN1 . . . . .37 B7
  Whitefield M45 . . . . .62 D7
Richmond Cres OL5 . . . . . .86 E8
Richmond Ct
  Altrincham WA14 . . . . .119 B2
  Cheadle SK8 . . . . .122 C5
  1 Manchester M13 . . . . . . .98 E4
  Stockport SK2 . . . . .124 D5
Richmond Dr Leigh WN7 . . .76 D7
  Lymm WA13 . . . . .117 B4
  Swinton M28 . . . . .79 C8
Richmond Gdns Bolton BL3 42 B3
  Newton-le-W WA12 . . . . . . .89 C2
Richmond Gn WA14 . . . . .119 B2
Richmond Gr Cheadle SK8 122 F1
  Eccles M30 . . . . .79 E3
  Farnworth BL4 . . . . .42 A1
  Leigh WN7 . . . . .76 E6
  Manchester M13 . . . . .98 E4
Richmond Gr E M12 . . . . .164 E5
Richmond Hill Hyde SK14 .167 F1
  Wigan WN5 . . . . .54 C6
Richmond Hill Rd SK8 . . . .122 C6
Richmond Ho 7 SK15 . . . . .86 A1
Richmond Inf Sch OL9 . . . .153 D6
Richmond Jun Sch OL9 . . .153 D6
Richmond Pk M14 . . . . .98 D1
Richmond Rd
  Altrincham WA14 . . . . .119 C2
  Altrincham WA14 . . . . .119 D5
  Ashton-in-M WN4 . . . . .72 F5
  Boothstown M28 . . . . .77 E7
  Dukinfield SK16 . . . . .101 D6
  Eccles M17 . . . . .96 A7
  Failsworth M35 . . . . .84 B8
  Hindley WN2 . . . . .57 A3
  Manchester M14 . . . . .110 D8
  Manchester SK4 . . . . .110 F2
  Reddish M34 . . . . .100 A3
  Romiley SK6 . . . . .113 C3
Richmond St
  Ashton-u-L OL7 . . . . .84 F3
  Atherton M46 . . . . .58 C2
  Bury BL9 . . . . .44 E8
  Denton M34 . . . . .100 F6
  Droylsden M43 . . . . .84 C2
  Horwich BL6 . . . . .22 B3
  Hyde SK14 . . . . .167 E2
  Manchester M1 . . . . .163 A8
  Manchester M3 . . . . .158 A3
  Stalybridge SK15 . . . . .86 C2
  Wigan WN1 . . . . .150 B8
  Wigan WN3 . . . . .150 A5
Richmond Terr SK6 . . . . . .126 B1
Richmond Wlk
  Oldham OL9 . . . . .153 D6
  Radcliffe M26 . . . . .43 E6
Ricroft Rd SK6 . . . . .114 B3
Ridding Ave M22 . . . . .121 E3
Ridding Cl SK2 . . . . .124 D6
Riddings Ct WA15 . . . . . . .119 F8
Riddings Rd
  Altrincham WA14 . . . . .119 F2
  Sale M33, WA15 . . . . .108 A1
  Sale M33 . . . . .120 A8
Riddle Ct M5 . . . . .80 C2
Ridge Ave
  Altrincham WA15 . . . . .129 D6
  Marple SK6 . . . . .126 A4
  Standish WN1 . . . . .37 B7
Ridge Cl Hadfield SK14 . . . .171 E3
  Romiley SK6 . . . . .113 F2
Ridge Cres Marple SK6 . . . .126 A3
  Whitefield M45 . . . . .63 B8
Ridge Danyers Coll
  Cheadle SK8 . . . . .122 F3
  Marple SK6 . . . . .125 E5
  Marple SK6 . . . . .125 F5
Ridge End Fold SK6 . . . . . .126 A2
Ridge Gr M9 . . . . .63 B8

Ridge Hill La SK15 . . . . . . .86 A3
Ridge La OL3 . . . . .51 D5
Ridge Pk SK7 . . . . .132 D6
Ridge Rd SK6 . . . . .126 A3
Ridge The SK6 . . . . .126 A3
Ridge Wlk M9 . . . . .64 D3
Ridgecroft OL7 . . . . .85 B6
Ridgedale Ctr 3 SK6 . . . .125 F6
Ridgedales The OL1 . . . . . .49 E4
Ridgefield M2 . . . . .158 F1
Ridgefield St M35 . . . . .83 E6
Ridgegreen M28 . . . . .78 A5
Ridgemont SK4 . . . . .168 B2
Ridgemont Wlk 10 M23 . . .108 F2
Ridgeway Golborne WA3 . . .90 D7
  Swinton M27 . . . . .62 B2
  Wilmslow SK9 . . . . .137 F7
Ridgeway Gates 3 BL1 . . .145 F7
Ridgeway Rd WA15 . . . . . .120 C5
Ridgeway The SK12 . . . . . .135 C6
Ridgewell Ave 4 WA3 . . . . .90 D8
Ridgewood Ave
  Manchester M40 . . . . .157 D5
  Oldham OL9 . . . . .65 E8
Ridgmont Cl BL6 . . . . .22 F3
Ridgmont Dr
  Boothstown M28 . . . . .77 F6
  Horwich BL6 . . . . .22 F3
Ridgmont Rd SK7 . . . . .132 E5
Ridgway Gr M43 . . . . .84 D3
Ridgway Rd M27 . . . . .160 D2
Ridgway The SK6 . . . . .113 A1
Riding M27 . . . . .77 D7
Riding Fold M43 . . . . .84 D3
Riding Fold La M28 . . . . . . .79 A5
Riding Gate BL2 . . . . .25 E6
Riding Gate Mews BL2 . . . .25 E6
Riding Head La BL0 . . . . . . .11 F8
Riding La WN4 . . . . .73 F5
Riding St M3 . . . . .158 E1
Ridings Ct SK8 . . . . .51 A2
Ridings Rd SK13 . . . . .103 F5
Ridings St
  Manchester M10,M40 . . . . .157 D5
  Manchester M11 . . . . .165 B8
Ridings Way OL9 . . . . .152 B6
Ridley Dr WA14 . . . . .107 E1
Ridley Gr M33 . . . . .108 F3
Ridley St OL4 . . . . .67 A6
Ridley Wlk M15 . . . . .163 A5
Ridling La SK14 . . . . .167 E2
Ridsdale Ave M20 . . . . . . .110 A6
Ridsdale Way M6 . . . . .81 A5
Ridyard St Platt Bridge WN2 56 B3
  Walkden M38 . . . . .60 C4
  Wigan WN5 . . . . .54 E7
Riefield BL1 . . . . .142 B3
Rifle Rd M21, M33 . . . . . . .108 F5
Rifle St OL1 . . . . .153 F8
Riga Rd M14 . . . . .98 C1
Riga St M4 . . . . .159 A2
Rigby Ave Blackrod BL6 . . . .21 C2
  Radcliffe M26 . . . . .44 C5
Rigby Ct Bolton BL3 . . . . . .147 F4
Rigby Gr M38 . . . . .59 E4
Rigby La BL2 . . . . .25 C5
Rigby St Altrincham WA14 .119 D3
  Ashton-in-M WN4 . . . . .73 A3
  Bolton BL3 . . . . .147 F4
  Golborne WA3 . . . . .90 A8
  Hindley WN2 . . . . .56 D6
  Manchester M7 . . . . .155 D6
Rigby Wlk M7 . . . . .155 E6
Rigby's Yd 5 WN5 . . . . . . .54 B6
Rigel Pl M7 . . . . .81 C3
Rigel St M4 . . . . .159 C3
Rigton Cl M12 . . . . .165 A5
Riley Cl M33 . . . . .107 B1
Riley Ct 3 BL1 . . . . .143 F1
Riley La WN2 . . . . .38 B7
Riley Sq WN1 . . . . .151 D8
Riley St M46 . . . . .58 A1
Riley Wood Cl SK6 . . . . . .112 F1
Rilldene Wlk OL11 . . . . .29 D8
Rilston Ave WA3 . . . . .91 D3
Rimington Ave WA3 . . . . . .74 C1
Rimington Cl WA3 . . . . .91 E3
Rimington Fold M24 . . . . . .46 D3
Rimmer Cl M11 . . . . .160 E1
Rimmington Cl M9 . . . . .65 A2
Rimsdale Cl SK8 . . . . .122 A3
Rimsdale Wlk BL3 . . . . .40 E5
Rimworth Dr M40 . . . . .159 C4
Rindle Rd M29 . . . . .93 C8
Ring Lows La OL12 . . . . . . .14 A4
Ring-o-Bells La SK12 . . . . .135 D6
Ringcroft Gdns M40 . . . . . .65 B1
Ringfield Cl M16 . . . . .97 E4
Ringford Wlk M40 . . . . . . .157 E5
Ringley Ave WA3 . . . . .73 F1
Ringley Chase M45 . . . . . . .62 E8
Ringley Cl M45 . . . . .62 D8
Ringley Dr M45 . . . . .62 D7
Ringley Gr BL1 . . . . .24 E5
Ringley Hey M45 . . . . .62 D8
Ringley Mdws M26 . . . . . . .61 C7
Ringley Old Brow M26 . . . .61 C7
Ringley Pk M45 . . . . .62 D8
Ringley Rd Kearsley M26 . . .61 C8
  Kearsley M26 . . . . .61 C8
  Whitefield M45 . . . . .62 C7
Ringley Rd W M26 . . . . . . .61 D8
Ringley St M9 . . . . .157 D8
Ringlow Ave M27 . . . . .79 C7
Ringlow Park Rd M27 . . . .79 C7
Ringmer Dr 4 M22 . . . . . .121 C1
Ringmere Ct 7 OL1 . . . . .153 E8

Ringmore Rd SK7 . . . . . . .124 A2
Rings Cl M35 . . . . .83 F6
Ringstead Cl SK9 . . . . .131 D1
Ringstead Dr
  Manchester M40 . . . . .159 C3
  9 Handforth SK9 . . . . .131 D1
Ringstone M25 . . . . .63 A3
Ringway Ave WN7 . . . . .75 F8
Ringway Gr M33 . . . . .108 E2
Ringway Rd M22,M90 . . . .130 D7
Ringway Rd W M22,M90 . .130 D8
Ringway Trad Est M22 . . .130 E8
Ringwood Ave
  Droylsden M34 . . . . .84 C1
  Hazel Grove SK7 . . . . .124 B1
  Hyde SK14 . . . . .102 A1
  Manchester M12 . . . . .99 B3
  Radcliffe M26 . . . . .44 B1
  Ramsbottom BL0 . . . . .11 A4
Ringwood Way OL9 . . . . . .152 C8
Rink St M14 . . . . .110 D7
Ripley Ave Bramhall SK8 . .132 B5
  Stockport SK2 . . . . .124 B4
Ripley Cl Hazel Grove SK7 .133 E8
  Manchester M4 . . . . .164 D8
Ripley Cres M41 . . . . .94 F5
Ripley Dr Leigh WN7 . . . . . .75 F6
  Wigan WN3 . . . . .54 C4
Ripley St BL2 . . . . .25 B4
Ripley Way M34 . . . . .112 F8
Ripon Ave Bolton BL1 . . . . .23 F1
  Golborne WA3 . . . . .90 D8
  1 Wigan WN6 . . . . .37 B3
Ripon Cl Altrincham WA15 .120 C1
  Little Lever BL3 . . . . .42 F3
  Newton-le-W WA12 . . . . . . .89 C5
  Oldham OL9 . . . . .152 B6
  Radcliffe BL9 . . . . .44 D5
  5 Whitefield M45 . . . . .44 F2
Ripon Cres M32 . . . . .95 F3
Ripon Dr Ashton-in-M WN4 .73 D2
  Bolton BL1 . . . . .23 F1
Ripon Gr M33 . . . . .107 F6
Ripon Hall Ave BL0 . . . . . . .11 A4
Ripon Ho M14 . . . . .98 E4
Ripon Rd M32 . . . . .95 F3
Ripon St Ashton-u-L OL6 . .166 C3
  Manchester M15 . . . . .163 A5
  Oldham OL1 . . . . .153 D8
Ripon Wlk SK6 . . . . .113 A1
Rippenden Ave M21 . . . . . .97 A2
Rippingham Rd M20 . . . . . .110 B3
Rippleton Rd M22 . . . . . . .121 E4
Ripponden Rd
  Denshaw OL3 . . . . .33 D3
  Oldham OL1,OL4 . . . . .49 E3
Ripponden St 11 OL1 . . . . .49 C1
Ripton Wlk M9 . . . . .64 B4
Rise The Oldham OL4 . . . . . .67 F7
  Wigan WN6 . . . . .36 C3
Rises The SK13 . . . . .103 F5
Rishton Ave BL3 . . . . .147 F2
Rishton La BL3 . . . . .147 F3
Rishworth Cl SK2 . . . . .124 D5
Rishworth Dr M40 . . . . .83 E8
Rishworth Rise OL2 . . . . . .32 A1
Rising La OL8 . . . . .66 E2
Rising Lane Cl OL8 . . . . . . .66 E2
Risley St M9 . . . . .64 D1
Risley St OL1 . . . . .153 F8
Rissington Ave M23 . . . . . .121 B6
Rita Ave 4 M14 . . . . .98 B3
Ritson Cl M18 . . . . .165 B6
Riva Rd M19 . . . . .110 D2
River La M31 . . . . .105 F4
River Pl Manchester M15 . .162 F7
  Milnrow OL16 . . . . .31 F6
River St Bolton BL2 . . . . . .148 A6
  Heywood OL10 . . . . .29 D3
  Manchester M12 . . . . .163 C8
  Manchester M15 . . . . .162 F7
  Radcliffe M26 . . . . .44 B2
  Ramsbottom BL0 . . . . .138 C6
  Rochdale OL16 . . . . .139 F7
  Stockport SK1 . . . . .112 B3
  Wilmslow SK9 . . . . .137 B8
River View SK5 . . . . .112 A7
River View Cl M25 . . . . . . .62 F2
River Way WN1 . . . . .150 C8
Riverbank OL3 . . . . .50 F1
Riverbank Dr BL8 . . . . .140 D3
Riverbank Lawns M3 . . . . .158 E3
Riverbank The M26 . . . . . . .61 A8
Riverbank Tower M7 . . . . .158 E3
Riverbank Way SK13 . . . . .116 F7
Riverbank Wlk M20 . . . . . .109 E4
Riverdale Cl WN6 . . . . .36 D4
Riverdale Rd M9 . . . . .64 B3
Rivermead OL16 . . . . .32 B3
Rivermead Ave WA15 . . . .129 C7
Rivermead Cl M34 . . . . . . .113 A7
Rivermead Rd M34 . . . . . .113 B7
Rivermead Way M45 . . . . . .63 A8
Riverpark Rd M40 . . . . .83 A3
Rivers La M41 . . . . .95 C5
Rivers St WN5 . . . . .53 E6
Riversdale Dr OL8 . . . . .67 A1
Riversdale Rd SK8 . . . . . . .122 C5
Riversdale View SK6 . . . . .113 A5
Riversdole Ct M25 . . . . . . .63 A3
Rivershill M9 . . . . .108 A6
Rivershill Dr OL10 . . . . .29 B1
Rivershill Gdns WA15 . . . .129 D6
Riverside Bolton BL1 . . . . . .25 A2

Riverside *continued*
Chadderton OL1 47 E1
Dukinfield SK16 166 C1
Manchester M7 158 D3
Riverside Ave Irlam M44 94 B1
Manchester M21 109 D3
Wigan WN1 37 D1
Riverside Bsns Pk SK9 137 B7
Riverside Cl SK13 104 D1
Riverside Ct
Manchester M20 109 F3
Whitworth OL12 4 D4
Riverside Dr Kearsley M26 61 B8
Ramsbottom BL9 11 B2
Rochdale OL16 15 C2
Urmston M41 107 B8
Riverside Mews M15 162 E7
Riverside Rd M26 44 D4
Riverside Wlk BB4 1 A7
Riversleigh Cl BL1 23 F3
Riversmeade Bolton BL7 25 C7
Leigh WN7 76 A6
Riverstone Bridge OL15 16 B5
Riverstone Dr M23 120 D7
Riverton Rd M20 122 B8
Riverview Cotts SK13 116 C7
Riverview Ct M7 81 C8
Riviera Ct OL12 13 C2
Rivington M6 80 C4
Rivington & Blackrod Coll Horwich Campus BL6 22 D2
Rivington & Blackrod High Sch BL6 22 B6
Rivington & Blackrod High Sch (Annexe) BL6 22 B4
Rivington Ave
Adlington PR6 21 B7
Golborne WA3 74 C1
Pendlebury M27 80 C8
Platt Bridge WN2 56 B3
Wigan WN1 37 B2
Rivington Cres M27 80 C7
Rivington Ct M45 62 C7
Rivington Ctry Pk BL6 22 A8
Rivington Dr
Bickershaw WN2 74 F8
Bury BL8 27 A1
Orrell WN8 53 C7
Shaw OL2 49 D7
Rivington Gr
Droylsden M34 100 C8
Irlam M44 105 D6
Rivington Hall Cl BL0 11 C4
Rivington La Adlington PR6 21 D6
Horwich BL6 22 A7
Rivington Pl PR7 19 D6
Rivington Rd
Altrincham WA15 119 F2
Oldham OL4 68 A7
Salford M6 80 C4
Rivington St Atherton M46 58 B2
Blackrod BL6 21 D2
Oldham OL1 48 F1
Rochdale OL12 14 F1
Rivington Way WN6 36 F8
Rivington Wlk M12 164 F5
Rix St BL1 143 E2
Rixson St OL4 49 D2
Rixton Ct M16 97 B3
Rixton Dr M29 77 B8
RL Hughes Cty Prim Sch WN4 73 A3
Roach Ct M40 159 C4
Roach Gn WN1 37 E1
Roach Pl OL16 31 A8
Roach St Bury BL9 141 C2
Bury BL9 44 F4
Roach Vale OL16 15 C2
Roaches Mews OL5 68 D3
Roaches Way OL5 68 E3
Roachill Cl WA14 119 B5
Roachwood Cl OL9 65 E7
Road La OL12 14 D4
Roading Brook Rd BL2 26 B3
Roads Ford Ave OL16 31 F7
Roadside Ct WA3 90 C8
Roaring Gate La WA15 120 E2
Rob La WA12 89 E5
Robe Wlk 5 M18 99 D6
Robert Hall St M5 161 B8
Robert Lawrence Ct M41 95 A1
Robert Malcolm Cl M40 157 D5
Robert Owen Gdns M22 121 D8
Robert Owen St M43 84 C2
Robert Salt Ct WA14 119 E6
Robert Saville Ct OL11 30 C6
Robert St Bolton BL2 25 E5
Bury BL8 27 C3
Dukinfield SK14 101 C3
Dukinfield SK16 101 B8
6 Failsworth M35 66 A1
Heywood OL10 46 E8
Manchester M10,M40 157 F5
Manchester M3 158 F3
Manchester M8 158 F4
Oldham OL8 66 B3
Platt Bridge WN2 56 A3
Prestwich M25 63 C4
Radcliffe M26 44 A4
Ramsbottom BL0 1 C1
15 Rochdale OL16 31 A8
Sale M33 108 E4
Tyldesley M46 58 E1
Roberts Ave M14 98 B4
Roberts St M30 79 D1
Robertscroft Cl M22 121 C3
Robertshaw Ave M21 109 B6
Robertshaw St WN7 75 E7
Robertson St M26 44 A4
Robeson Way M22,SK8 121 F6
Robin Cl BL4 59 F7
Robin Croft SK6 112 D3
Robin Dr M44 94 A3
Robin Hill Dr WN6 19 B2
Robin Hill La WN6 19 C3
Robin Hood La WN6 18 B3
Robin Hood St M8 155 F8
Robin Park Rd WN5 54 F7
Robin Rd BL9 11 B2
Robin St OL1 153 E8
Robin's La Billinge WA11 71 A8
Bramhall SK7 132 D7
Robinia Cl M30 94 F8
Robins Cl Bramhall SK7 132 E7
Droylsden M43 84 C3
Robins La WA3 91 D2
Robinsbay Rd M22 130 E8
Robinson St
Ashton-u-L OL6 166 B4
Dukinfield SK15 101 E8
15 Horwich BL6 22 B4
Hyde SK14 167 F3
Leigh WN7 76 A4
Oldham OL9 152 B6
Rochdale OL16 31 A7
Stockport SK3 170 D7
13 Tyldesley M29 59 A1
Robinsway WA14 119 C1
Robinswood Rd M22 121 D2
Robinwood Lo SK13 171 E1
Robson Ave M41 95 E7
Robson Pl WN2 74 B8
Robson St Oldham OL1 153 F6
Oldham OL1 67 A6
Robson Way 3 WA3 90 F8
Roby Mill WN8 35 B3
Roby Mill CE Prim Sch WN8 35 B3
Roby Rd M30 95 C8
Roby St M1 159 B1
Roby Well Way WN5 71 D5
Roch Ave OL10 29 A2
Roch Cl M45 45 B1
Roch Cres M45 45 C1
Roch Mills Cres OL11 30 C5
Roch Mills Gdns OL11 139 D5
Roch Pl WN2 55 F2
Roch St OL16 15 B1
Roch Valley Way OL11 30 C5
Roch Way M45 45 B1
Roch Wlk M45 45 B1
Rochbury Cl OL11 29 F6
Rochdale AFC (Spotland Stadium) OL11 30 C8
Rochdale Ho M15 162 E7
Rochdale Ind Ctr OL11 139 D6
Rochdale Infmy OL12 14 F1
Rochdale La Heywood OL10 29 D2
Royton OL2 48 D5
Rochdale Old Rd BL9 28 D4
Rochdale Pioneers Mus OL12 139 F8
Rochdale Rd Bacup OL13 4 B8
Bury BL9 141 B2
Denshaw OL3 33 C3
Edenfield BL0 1 F2
Heywood OL10 29 D2
Littleborough HX6,OL15 7 E1
Manchester M40,M8,M9 157 D6
Manchester M9 64 D3
Middleton M24 &OL11 47 C4
Milnrow OL16 31 E7
Oldham OL1 153 E8
Oldham OL1 48 E1
Ramsbottom BL0,BL9 12 B7
Royton OL2 48 D6
Shaw OL2 149 B7
Shaw OL2,OL16 48 F8
Walsden OL14,OL15 6 B6
Rochdale Rd E OL10 29 F3
Rochdale Sta OL11 139 F6
Roche Gdns SK8 132 B6
Roche Rd OL3 50 E5
Rochester Ave Bolton BL2 25 E1
Manchester M25 63 C2
Walkden M28 60 C1
Rochester Cl
Ashton-u-L OL6 85 C7
Dukinfield SK16 102 A7
Golborne WA3 90 A8
Rochester Dr WA14 107 E1
Rochester Gr SK7 124 E3
Rochester Rd M41 95 D4
Rochester Way OL9 152 B6
Rochford Ave
Whitefield M45 62 D7
Wythenshawe M22 130 D8
Rochford Cl M45 62 D7
Rochford Ho M34 100 E6
Rochford Rd M30 94 F8
Rock Ave BL1 142 C2
Rock Fold BL7 8 F1
Rock Gdns SK14 113 E7
Rock Nook OL15 6 D1
Rock Rd Boothstown M28 78 B2
Urmston M41 95 F2
Rock St Ashton-u-L OL7 85 A5
Droylsden M11 99 E8
Golborne WA3 74 A2
3 Heywood OL10 29 E1
Horwich BL6 22 B3
Hyde SK14 113 E7
Rock St *continued*
Manchester M7 155 D6
Oldham OL1 153 F7
Radcliffe M26 44 B2
Ramsbottom BL0 11 E7
Rock Terr Bolton BL7 8 F1
Mossley OL5 68 D3
Rock The Bury BL9 140 E2
Bury BL9 140 F3
Rockall Wlk M11 160 F1
Rockbourne Cl WN2 56 D4
Rockcliffe Villas OL13 3 E8
Rockdove Ave M15 162 F7
Rocket Way M3 158 D1
Rockfield Dr 5 M9 157 E8
Rockhampton St M18 99 E5
Rockhaven Ave BL6 22 C4
Rockhouse Cl M30 95 C8
Rockingham Cl
Manchester M12 164 D6
Shaw OL2 48 E8
Rockland Wlk 6 M40 65 C2
Rockley Gdns M6 81 B4
Rocklyn Ave M40 65 C2
Rocklynes SK6 113 B2
Rockmead Dr M9 64 E3
Rocky Bank Terr WN3 151 E5
Rocky La M27,M30 79 D4
Roda St M9 157 F7
Rodborough Rd M23 121 A3
Rodeheath Cl SK9 137 D7
Rodenhurst Dr 14 M40 83 A7
Rodepool Cl SK9 131 D2
Rodgers Cl BL5 57 E6
Rodgers Way BL5 57 E6
Rodmell Ave M40 157 D5
Rodmell Cl BL7 24 F7
Rodmill Ct M14 98 C1
Rodmill Dr SK8 122 A4
Rodney Ct 8 M4 159 C3
Rodney Dr SK6 113 A5
Rodney St Ashton-u-L OL6 85 D4
Atherton M46 58 C2
Manchester M3 158 D1
Manchester M4 159 C2
Rochdale OL11 30 B2
Wigan WN1 150 C7
Roe Cross Gn SK14 102 F5
Roe Cross Ind Est SK14 103 A5
Roe Cross Rd SK14,SK15 102 F5
Roe Gn M28 79 A8
Roe Green Ave M28 79 A8
Roe La OL4 67 D5
Roe St Manchester M4 159 C3
Rochdale OL12 14 C1
Roeacre St OL10 29 E2
Roebuck La Oldham OL4 50 A3
Sale M33 108 A4
Roebuck St WN2 57 C3
Roeburn Wlk M45 63 C8
Roecliffe Ct WN3 150 B6
Roedean Gdns M41 94 D2
Roefield Terr OL12 30 C8
Rogate Dr M23 121 A5
Roger Byrne Cl M40 83 B5
Roger Cl SK6 112 F2
Roger Hay SK8 123 A2
Roger St M8 159 A3
Rogerstead BL3 144 C6
Rogerton Cl WN7 76 B4
Rokeby Ave Golborne WA3 74 D1
Stretford M32 96 D1
Rokeden WA12 89 D4
Roker Ave M13 98 F2
Roker Ind Est OL1 67 B7
Roker Park Ave M34 100 D7
Roland Rd 2 Bolton BL3 146 C4
Reddish SK5 111 F7
Rolla St M3 158 E2
Rollesby Cl BL8 27 D5
Rolleston Ave M40 160 D2
Rollins La SK6 114 A1
Rolls Cres M15 162 E5
Rollswood Dr M40 83 A6
Roman Cl
Newton-le-W WA12 89 C2
Wigan WN3 54 F4
Roman Ct M7 155 D5
Roman Rd Ashton-in-M WN4 73 A5
Manchester M25 63 A1
Oldham M35,OL8 66 B1
Royton OL2 48 E3
Stockport SK4 169 E2
Roman St Manchester M4 159 A2
Mossley OL5 68 D3
Radcliffe M26 43 E3
Rome Rd M40 159 C3
Romer Ave M40 65 E1
Romer St BL2 148 C7
Romford Ave
Dukinfield M34 101 A4
Leigh WN7 75 F6
Romford Cl OL8 153 E5
Romford Pl WN2 56 E5
Romford Rd M33 107 E6
Romford St WN2 56 E5
Romford Wlk M9 64 A3
Romiley Cres BL2 42 D8
Romiley dr Bolton BL2 148 B8
Bolton BL2 42 D8
Romiley Prec SK6 113 C2
Romiley Prim Sch SK6 113 C2
Romiley Sq WN6 36 E8
Romiley St Salford M6 80 D5
Stockport SK1 112 B3
Romiley Sta SK6 113 C2
Romley Rd M41 95 D4
Romney Ave OL11 30 F2
Romney Rd BL1 23 E2
Romney St Ashton-u-L OL6 166 C3
Manchester M40 83 A8
Salford M6 81 B5
Romney Towers SK5 112 B6
Romney Way
Brinnington SK5 112 B6
Wigan WN1 37 B3
Romney Wlk OL9 152 B6
Romsey 9 OL12 139 E8
Romsey Ave M24 46 F3
Romsey Dr SK8 132 C6
Romsey Gdns M23 121 A6
Romsey Gr WN3 54 D2
Romsley Cl M12 165 A6
Romsley Dr BL3 146 C3
Rona Wlk M12 164 F5
Ronald St
Droylsden M11,M43 83 D1
Oldham OL4 67 C7
Rochdale OL11 30 C1
Ronaldsay Gdns M5 154 E1
Rondin Cl M12 164 E7
Rondin Rd M12 164 E8
Ronnis Mount OL7 85 A7
Ronton Wlk M8 156 C8
Roocroft Ct BL1 143 D1
Roocroft Sq BL6 21 C2
Rooden Ct M25 63 C4
Roods La OL11 13 C1
Rook St Manchester M15 162 E5
Oldham OL4 67 C5
Ramsbottom BL0 138 C6
Rooke St M30 95 A8
Rookery Ave
Appley Bridge WN6 35 E8
Ashton-in-M WN4 73 B2
Droylsden M18 99 F6
Rookery Cl SK15 102 E7
Rookery The WA12 89 D4
Rookerypool Cl SK9 131 D2
Rookfield M33 108 C5
Rookfield Ave M33 108 C5
Rookley Wlk 11 M14 98 C3
Rookswood Dr OL11 30 B3
Rookway M24 65 A7
Rookwood OL1,OL9 47 E1
Rookwood Ave M23 120 F7
Rookwood Hill SK7 123 E1
Rooley Moor Rd
Bacup OL12,OL13 3 C4
Rochdale OL12 14 A3
Rochdale OL12 14 C1
Rooley St OL11,OL12 14 C1
Roosevelt Rd BL4 60 F7
Rooth St SK4 169 D2
Rope St OL12 139 F8
Rope Wlk M3 158 E3
Ropefield Way OL12 14 E3
Ropley Wlk 4 M9 64 F1
Rosa Gr M7 155 D6
Rosalind Ct M5 161 C8
Rosamond Dr M3 158 D2
Rosamond St BL3 146 C4
Rosamond St W M13,M15 163 A6
Rosary Rd OL8 67 A1
Roscoe Ave WA12 89 E3
Roscoe Ct BL5 57 F7
Roscoe Lowe Brow PR6 21 D7
Roscoe Pk Est WA14 119 E8
Roscoe Rd Irlam M44 105 F8
Irlam M44 93 E1
Roscoe St Oldham OL1 67 A6
Stockport SK3 170 D8
Wigan WN1 151 E7
Roscow Ave BL2 42 E8
Roscow Fold Prim Sch BL2 42 E8
Roscow Rd BL4 61 A7
Rose Acre M28 78 B7
Rose Ave Abram Brow WN2 74 B7
Farnworth BL4 42 C1
Irlam M44 93 F1
Littleborough OL15 15 F3
Rochdale OL11 13 D2
Wigan WN6 37 A4
Rose Bank Cl
Hollingworth SK14 103 D5
Wigan WN1 37 B4
Rose Bridge High Sch WN1 151 F8
Rose Cottage Rd
M14,M20 110 B8
Rose Cotts 11 M14 110 D8
Rose Cres M44 93 F1
Rose Ct WN1 151 F8
Rose Gr Bury BL8 27 A2
Kearsley BL4 60 F7
Rose Hey La M35 83 E4
Rose Hill Bolton BL2 148 A5
Delph OL3 50 F4
Denton M34 100 E3
Ramsbottom BL0 138 B6
Stalybridge SK15 102 A8
Rose Hill Ave
Failsworth M40 83 B4
Wigan WN5 54 C6
Rose Hill Cl Ashton-u-L OL6 85 F5
Bolton BL7 25 A7
Rose Hill Cres OL6 85 F5
Rose Hill Dr BL7 25 A7
Rose Hill Rd OL6 85 F5
Rose Hill St OL10 29 B2
Rose Hill Sta SK6 125 E6
Rose Hill View WN4 72 F7
Rose La SK6 125 E6
Rose Lea BL2 25 E4
Rose Leigh M41 95 D2
Rose Mount M24 46 F2
Rose St Bolton BL2 148 A5
Hindley WN2 56 D5
Middleton M24 65 C8
Oldham OL9 66 A3
Reddish SK5 169 F3
Wigan WN1 151 F8
Rose Terr SK15 86 A1
Rose Thorns Cl M24 46 F4
Rose Vale SK8 122 B1
Rose Wlk Marple SK6 125 E6
5 Partington M31 105 E3
Rose Wood M34 100 D3
Roseacre Cl BL2 148 C8
Roseacre Dr SK8 122 C1
Rosebank Bolton BL6 40 C7
Edenfield BL0 1 D1
Rosebank Cl BL2 26 C1
Rosebank Rd
Failsworth M40 83 B4
Irlam M44 105 C4
Roseberry Ave 4 OL1 49 B1
Roseberry Cl BL0 11 C3
Roseberry Rd WN4 73 A5
Roseberry St Bolton BL3 146 C4
Oldham OL8 153 D6
Rosebery St
Manchester M14 97 F3
Stockport SK2 124 D4
Westhoughton BL5 57 F8
Rosebridge Ct WN1 151 E7
Rosebridge Way WN1 151 F7
Rosebury Ave WN7 76 B5
Rosecroft Cl SK3 123 E4
Rosecroft Sch M20 110 B3
Rosedale Ave Atherton M46 58 D3
Bolton BL1 24 E5
Golborne WA3 90 C7
Rosedale Cl OL1 49 B1
Rosedale Ct M34 100 E3
Rosedale Dr WN7 76 C5
Rosedale Rd
Manchester M14 98 A2
Reddish SK4 169 D4
Rosedale Way SK16 101 C6
Rosefield Cl SK3 170 E5
Rosefield Cres OL16 31 C7
Rosegarth Ave M20 109 D4
Rosegate Cl M16 97 F3
Rosehay Ave M34 100 F2
Rosehill Cl M6 154 F2
Rosehill Ct Oldham OL4 67 E8
Salford M6 154 F2
Rosehill Rd M27 61 F2
Roseland Ave M20 110 B4
Roseland Dr M25 63 C6
Roselands Ave M33 107 F2
Roseleigh Ave M19 110 F7
Rosemary Cres WN1 37 D2
Rosemary Dr Hyde SK14 113 D7
Littleborough OL15 15 F6
Newton-le-W WA12 89 F3
Rosemary Gr M7 155 D8
Rosemary La Atherton BL5 59 B6
Stockport SK1 112 A1
Rosemary Wlk M31 105 F2
Rosemead Ct 5 SK5 111 F6
Rosemount SK14 101 D5
Rosemount Cres SK14 101 D5
Rosen Sq OL9 152 B7
Roseneath SK7 123 D1
Roseneath Ave M19 99 C1
Roseneath Gr BL3 147 D3
Roseneath Rd Bolton BL3 147 D3
Urmston M41 95 C2
Rosette Wlk 3 M27 79 F7
Rosevale Ave M19 110 E5
Roseway SK7 123 F2
Rosewell Cl M40 160 D4
Rosewood Rochdale OL11 13 E1
Westhoughton BL5 57 D6
Rosewood Ave Bury BL8 27 A6
Droylsden M43 84 C3
Stockport SK4 168 A1
Rosewood Cl
Abram Brow WN2 74 B7
Dukinfield SK16 101 D6
Rosewood Cres OL9 48 B1
Rosewood Gdns
4 Sale M33 108 F3
Wythenshawe SK8 121 F6
Rosewood Wlk M23 120 C8
Rosford Ave M14 98 B2
Rosgill Cl SK4 110 E2
Rosgill Wlk M18 165 C5
Rosina Cl WN4 72 F6
Rosina St M11 99 F7
Rosley Rd WN3 55 B3
Roslin Gdns BL1 142 C3
Roslin St M11 83 D2
Roslyn Ave M41 94 E1
Roslyn Rd SK3 170 E5
Ross Ave Manchester M19 98 F1
Oldham OL9 65 F4
Stockport SK3 170 E5
Whitefield M45 62 F6
Ross Cl Billinge WN5 71 E6
Wigan WN2 37 F2
Ross Dr M27 61 E4
Ross Gr M41 95 C2
Ross Lave La M34 100 C1
Ross St OL8 153 D5
Rossall Ave
5 Radcliffe M26 44 C1
Stretford M32 96 C3
Rossall Cl BL2 148 C8
Rossall Cres WN7 76 A3
Rossall Dr SK7 132 E6

Rossall Rd Bolton BL2 . . . . . .148 C8
Rochdale OL12 . . . . .15 A2
Rossall St **1** BL2 . . . . .148 C8
Rossall Way M6 . . . . .81 A3
Rossdale Gr WN6 . . . . .37 A7
Rossenclough Rd SK9 . . . . .131 D1
Rossendale Ave **6** M9 . . . . . .64 F1
Rossendale Cl OL2 . . . . .49 D7
Rossendale Rd SK8 . . . . . . .131 C8
Rossendale Sch BL0 . . . . . . .12 A7
Rossendale Way OL2 . . . . . .149 B8
Rossett Ave Sale WA15 . . . . .120 A8
1 Wythenshawe M22 . . . . .130 D8
Rossett Cl WN3 . . . . .54 D2
Rossett Dr M41 . . . . .95 A4
Rossetti Wlk **2** M34 . . . . . . .113 A7
Rosshill Wlk **28** M15 . . . . . .162 D6
Rossington St M40 . . . . .83 D5
Rossini St BL1 . . . . .143 D3
Rosslare Rd M22 . . . . .121 D2
Rosslove Wlk SK5 . . . . .112 C7
Rosslyn Gr WA15 . . . . .120 A6
Rosslyn Rd Cheadle SK8 . . . .122 D1
Manchester M16 . . . . .97 A2
Manchester M40 . . . . .65 A1
Rossmere Ave OL11 . . . . . . .30 C6
Rossmill La WA15 . . . . .129 B7
Rostherne Ave
Golborne WA3 . . . . .90 D8
High Lane SK6 . . . . .134 E8
Manchester M14 . . . . .98 A1
Manchester M16 . . . . .97 C3
Rostherne Ct WA14 . . . . . . .119 D3
Rostherne Gdns BL3 . . . . . .146 B4
Rostherne Rd Sale M33 . . . . .108 F3
Stockport SK3 . . . . .170 E5
Wilmslow SK9 . . . . .136 F4
Rostherne St
1 Altrincham WA14 . . . . . .119 D3
1 Salford M6 . . . . .154 E1
Rosthernmere Rd SK8 . . . . .122 F4
Rosthwaite Cl
Middleton M24 . . . . .46 C1
Wigan WN3 . . . . .55 A2
Rosthwaite Gr WA11 . . . . . . .71 D1
Roston Ct M7 . . . . .155 E8
Roston Rd M7 . . . . .155 E8
Rostrevor Rd SK3 . . . . .170 E5
Rostron Ave M12 . . . . .164 E6
Rostron Rd BL0 . . . . .138 B6
Rostron St **6** M19 . . . . .99 B1
Rothay Cl BL2 . . . . .25 F1
Rothay Dr Middleton M24 . . . .46 E3
Reddish SK5 . . . . .111 F8
Rothay St WN7 . . . . .76 B4
Rothbury Ave OL7 . . . . .84 E5
Rothbury Cl BL8 . . . . .26 F2
Rothbury Ct BL3 . . . . .146 B3
Rotherby Rd M22 . . . . .121 E5
Rotherdale Ave WA15 . . . . . .120 D5
Rotherhead Cl BL6 . . . . .21 F2
Rothermere Wlk **5** M23 . . . .120 E7
Rotherwood Ave M32 . . . . . . .96 E3
Rotherwood Rd SK9 . . . . . . .136 D6
Rothesay Ave SK16 . . . . . . .101 C7
Rothesay Cres M33 . . . . . . .107 C2
Rothesay Rd Bolton BL3 . . . .146 B3
Manchester M8 . . . . .63 E2
Oldham OL1 . . . . .49 C1
Pendlebury M27 . . . . .80 C7
Rothesay Terr OL16 . . . . . . .31 C4
Rothiemay Rd M41 . . . . .94 E2
Rothley Ave M22 . . . . .121 D5
Rothman Cl M40 . . . . .83 C6
Rothwell Cres M38 . . . . .59 E5
Rothwell La M38 . . . . .59 E5
Rothwell Rd Adlington PR6 . . .21 B7
Golborne WA3 . . . . .74 C1
Rothwell St Bolton BL3 . . . . .145 E5
Failsworth M35 . . . . .83 F7
Failsworth M40 . . . . .83 C6
Ramsbottom BL0 . . . . .138 B6
Rochdale OL12 . . . . .15 B1
Royton OL2 . . . . .48 D3
Walkden M28 . . . . .60 F3
Rottingdene Dr **3** M22 . . . . .121 C1
Rough Hill La BL9 . . . . .28 E4
Roughey Gdns M22 . . . . . . .121 D4
Roughlea Ave WA3 . . . . .91 D4
Roughlee Ave M27 . . . . .79 D7
Roughtown Rd OL5 . . . . .68 D2
Round Hey OL5 . . . . .86 C8
Round Hill Cl SK13 . . . . . . .171 F3
Round House Ave WN1 . . . . . .37 E1
Round Thorn Rd M24 . . . . . . .65 B7
Roundcroft SK6 . . . . .113 C3
Roundham Wlk **27** M9 . . . . .157 E8
Roundhey SK8 . . . . .131 C8
Roundhill Way OL4 . . . . .49 E1
Roundmoor Rd WN6 . . . . . . .37 A7
Roundthorn Bsns Pk
M23 . . . . .120 E5
Roundthorn Ct **8** BL1 . . . . . .143 F1
Roundthorn Ind Est M23 .120 E6
Roundthorn La SK7 . . . . .57 F2
Roundthorn Prim Sch
OL4 . . . . .67 C5
Roundthorn Rd
Oldham OL4 . . . . .67 C5
Wythenshawe M23 . . . . . . .120 F6
Roundthorn Wlk **9** M23 .120 F6
Roundthorne Ind Est
M23 . . . . .120 E4
Roundway SK7 . . . . .132 D6
Roundwood High
Sch M22 . . . . .121 D7
Roundwood Rd M22 . . . . . . .121 D7
Rousdon Cl M40 . . . . .157 D5

Rouse Cl M11 . . . . .160 F1
Rouse St OL11 . . . . .30 C4
Routledge Wlk M9 . . . . .157 E8
Rowan Ave Golborne WA3 . . .90 F7
2 Horwich BL6 . . . . .22 C1
Manchester M16 . . . . .97 D3
Sale M33 . . . . .108 C2
Urmston M41 . . . . .95 D3
Wigan WN6 . . . . .36 F3
Rowan Cl Failsworth M35 . . . .83 F6
Rochdale OL12 . . . . .14 B3
6 Salford M6 . . . . .81 A2
Rowan Cres M16 . . . . .101 F7
Rowan Ct Hyde SK14 . . . . . .167 E1
Wilmslow SK9 . . . . .137 B7
Rowan Dr SK8 . . . . .132 C8
Rowan Lo SK7 . . . . .132 F7
Rowan Pl M25 . . . . .63 B3
Rowan St SK14 . . . . .167 F1
Rowan Tree Dr M33 . . . . . . .108 B1
Rowan Tree Rd OL8 . . . . .66 D1
Rowan Wlk Hadfield SK13 .171 E4
Partington M31 . . . . .105 E2
Rowanhill WN1 . . . . .37 D1
Rowans St BL8 . . . . .27 C4
Rowans The Bolton BL1 . . . . .40 F7
Mossley OL5 . . . . .68 C1
Rowanside Dr SK14 . . . . . . .137 E8
Rowanswood Dr SK14 . . . . .102 A3
Rowanwood OL9 . . . . .65 E7
Rowany Cl M25 . . . . .63 B3
Rowarth Ave Denton M34 .113 A8
10 Gamesley SK13 . . . . . .171 D2
Rowarth Bank **5** SK13 . . . . .171 D2
Rowarth Cl **6** SK13 . . . . . . .171 D2
Rowarth Fold **9** SK13 . . . . .171 D2
Rowarth Rd
Wythenshawe M23 . . . . . . .120 F2
Wythenshawe M23 . . . . . . .121 A2
Rowarth Way **8** SK13 . . . . .171 D2
Rowbotham St SK14 . . . . . . .113 E8
Rowbottom Sq WN1 . . . . . . .150 C8
Rowbottom Wlk OL8 . . . . . .153 E5
Rowcon Cl M34 . . . . .100 E6
Rowdell Wlk M23 . . . . .109 B2
Rowden Rd OL4 . . . . .67 E4
Rowe Gn M34 . . . . .100 F2
Rowell Sq M3 . . . . .158 D2
Rowell St M3 . . . . .158 D2
Rowena St BL3 . . . . .42 C2
Rowendale St M1,M15 . . . . .162 F8
Rowfield Dr M23 . . . . .120 F3
Rowland Ave M41 . . . . .95 E3
Rowland Ct **17** OL16 . . . . . . .31 B6
Rowland St Atherton M46 . . . .58 D7
16 Rochdale OL16 . . . . .31 B6
Rowland St S M46 . . . . .58 D2
Rowland Way OL4 . . . . .67 E4
Rowlands Rd BL9 . . . . .11 D2
Rowlandsway M22 . . . . .121 D2
Rowley Rd SK7 . . . . .133 E8
Rowley St OL6 . . . . .85 D6
Rowood Ave
Manchester M8 . . . . .156 B6
Reddish SK5 . . . . .99 F2
Rowrah Cres M24 . . . . .46 C4
Rowsley Ave Bolton BL1 . . . .142 A1
Manchester M20 . . . . .109 E4
Rowsley Cl **25** SK13 . . . . . .171 D2
Rowsley Gn **29** SK13 . . . . . .171 D2
Rowsley Gr
30 Gamesley SK13 . . . . . .171 E2
Reddish SK5 . . . . .111 E7
Rowsley Mews SK13 . . . . . .171 E2
Rowsley Rd Eccles M30 . . . . .95 C8
Stretford M32 . . . . .96 A3
Rowsley St
Manchester M11 . . . . .160 F1
Salford M6 . . . . .81 B5
Rowsley Wlk **28** SK13 . . . . .171 E2
Rowson Dr M44 . . . . .105 D6
Rowton Rise WN1 . . . . .37 B8
Rowton St BL2 . . . . .25 B3
Roxalina St BL3 . . . . .147 E4
Roxburgh St **6** M18 . . . . . . .99 D5
Roxbury Ave OL4 . . . . .67 D5
Roxby Cl M28 . . . . .60 B3
Roxby Dr **18** M40 . . . . .65 D2
Roxholme Wlk M22 . . . . . . .130 C8
Roxton Cl BL6 . . . . .22 B5
Roxton Rd SK4 . . . . .111 C6
Roxwell Wlk **8** M9 . . . . . . .157 D8
Roy Grainger Ct **10** M16 . . . .97 E3
Roy Ho OL2 . . . . .48 D6
Roy St Bolton BL3 . . . . .146 B4
Royton OL2 . . . . .48 D4
Royal Arc **5** WN1 . . . . .150 C8
Royal Ave Bury BL9 . . . . .27 F5
Droylsden M43 . . . . .84 B2
Heywood OL10 . . . . .29 D1
Manchester M21 . . . . .109 A8
Urmston M41 . . . . .95 D2
Royal Bolton Hospl BL4 . .147 F1
Royal Dr WN7 . . . . .76 E6
Royal Eye Hospl M13 . . . . .163 B5
Royal Gdns WA14 . . . . .118 F2
Royal George Cotts OL3 . .68 E5
Royal George St SK1,SK3 .170 F8
Royal Manchester
Children's Hospl M27 . . . .80 C7
Royal Northern Coll
of Music
M13 . . . . .163 A6
Royal Oak Prim Sch M23 121 A7
Royal Oak Rd M23 . . . . .121 A7
Royal Oak Yd SK1 . . . . .169 F1

Royal Oldham Hospl The
OL1 . . . . .48 D1
Royal Rd SK12 . . . . .135 D5
Royal School
for the Deaf The SK8 . . .131 D6
Royal St OL16 . . . . .15 C8
Royalthorn Ave M22 . . . . . . .121 D6
Royalthorn Dr M22 . . . . . . .121 C6
Royalthorn Rd M22 . . . . . . .121 D6
Royce Ave WA15 . . . . .119 E5
Royce Ct **22** M15 . . . . .162 D6
Royce Prim Sch M15 . . . . . .162 E5
Royce Rd M15 . . . . .162 E6
Royce Trad Est M17 . . . . . . .95 F7
Royd St OL8 . . . . .66 C4
Roydale St M40 . . . . .160 E3
Royden Ave Irlam M44 . . . . .105 F8
Manchester M9 . . . . .64 D5
Wigan WN3 . . . . .55 A2
Royden Cres WN5 . . . . .71 E5
Royden Rd WN5 . . . . .71 E5
Roydes St M24 . . . . .47 B2
Royds Cl M13 . . . . .164 D5
Royds Pl **15** OL16 . . . . .31 A5
Royds Rd OL13 . . . . .3 A7
Royds St Bury BL8 . . . . .26 F7
Bury BL8 . . . . .28 D4
Littleborough OL15 . . . . . . .16 C5
Milnrow OL16 . . . . .32 A5
Rochdale OL16 . . . . .31 B5
Royds St W OL11,OL16 . . . . .31 A5
Royland Ave BL3 . . . . .42 A3
Royland Ct BL3 . . . . .147 F3
Royle Ave SK13 . . . . .104 D1
Royle Barn Rd OL11 . . . . . . .30 C3
Royle Cl Oldham OL8 . . . . . . .66 F3
Stockport SK2 . . . . .124 A5
Royle Green Rd M22 . . . . . . .121 D8
Royle Pennine Trad Est
OL11 . . . . .30 D3
Royle Rd OL11 . . . . .30 D3
Royle St Denton M34 . . . . . .100 F5
Manchester M14 . . . . .110 D7
Salford M6 . . . . .154 F1
Stockport SK1 . . . . .170 F7
Walkden M28 . . . . .60 D2
Roylelands Bglws OL11 . . .30 C3
Royley OL2 . . . . .48 C3
Royley Carr Flats SK6 . . . . .113 A3
Royley Cres OL2 . . . . .48 C3
Royley House OL2 . . . . .48 C3
Royley Rd OL8 . . . . .66 E4
Royley Way OL2 . . . . .48 C3
Roynton Rd BL6 . . . . .22 B7
Royon Dr SK3 . . . . .123 B7
Royston Ave Bolton BL2 . . . .148 C8
Manchester M16 . . . . .97 D3
Reddish SK4 . . . . .100 A3
Royston Cl
2 Golborne WA3 . . . . .90 E8
Ramsbottom BL8 . . . . .10 F1
Royston Ct **5** M16 . . . . .97 D3
Royston Rd
Manchester M16 . . . . .97 B3
Urmston M41 . . . . .95 E3
Royton & Crompton
Com Sec Sch OL2 . . . .49 A4
Royton Ave M33 . . . . .108 E2
Royton Hall Wlk OL2 . . . . . .48 E4
Rozel Sq M3 . . . . .162 E8
Ruabon Cres WN2 . . . . .57 A4
Ruabon Rd M20 . . . . .110 C2
Rubens Cl SK6 . . . . .126 C8
Ruby Gr WN7 . . . . .75 E4
Ruby St Bolton BL3 . . . . . . .143 F3
Denton M34 . . . . .100 E3
Manchester M15 . . . . .163 A6
Ramsbottom BL9 . . . . .11 C3
Rudcroft Cl M13 . . . . .163 B6
Rudd St M40 . . . . .83 A7
Rudding St OL2 . . . . .49 A2
Ruddpark Rd M22 . . . . .121 D1
Rudford Gdns BL3 . . . . .147 F4
Rudgwick Dr BL8 . . . . .27 C7
Rudheath Ave M20 . . . . .110 A7
Rudman Dr M5 . . . . .161 C8
Rudman St OL12 . . . . .14 E2
Rudolph St BL3 . . . . .147 F3
Rudston Ave M40 . . . . .65 B2
Rudyard Ave Middleton M24 .47 C3
Standish WN6 . . . . .19 E2
Rudyard Gr Reddish SK4 . . . .111 D6
Sale M33 . . . . .107 E2
Rudyard Rd OL11 . . . . .30 F2
Rudyard St M7 . . . . .155 D6
Rufford Ave Hyde SK14 . . . .167 F2
Rochdale OL11 . . . . .30 D4
Rufford Cl Ashton-u-L OL6 . . .85 C7
Shaw OL2 . . . . .48 F7
Whitefield BL9 . . . . .45 A2
Rufford Dr Bolton BL3 . . . . .147 D2
Whitefield M45 . . . . .44 F2
Rufford Gr BL3 . . . . .147 D2
Rufford Pl Reddish M18 . . . . .99 F4
Tyldesley M29 . . . . .76 F4
Rufford Rd M16 . . . . .97 D3
Rufford St **4** WN4 . . . . .72 F5
Rufus St M14 . . . . .110 E7
Rugby Dr Orrell WN5 . . . . . . .53 F8
Rugby Rd Leigh WN7 . . . . . . .75 F3
Rochdale OL12,OL16 . . . . . .15 A1
Salford M6 . . . . .80 A3
Rugby Rd Ind Est OL16 . . .15 A1
Rugby St M7,M8 . . . . .158 E4
Rugeley St M6 . . . . .81 B5

Ruins La BL2 . . . . .25 E4
Ruislip Ave M40 . . . . .157 E5
Ruislip Cl OL8 . . . . .67 B4
Rumbles La OL3 . . . . .50 F4
Rumbold St **18** M18 . . . . . . .99 E6
Rumworth Rd BL6 . . . . .40 C6
Rumworth St BL3 . . . . .147 D4
Runcorn St M15 . . . . .161 C2
Runger La M90,WA15 . . . . . .129 F8
Runhall Cl M12 . . . . .165 A6
Running Hill Farm OL3 . . .51 D2
Running Hill Gate OL3 . . . .51 D1
Running Hill La OL3 . . . . .51 D1
Runnymede Cl SK3 . . . . . . .123 C6
Runnymede Ct Bolton BL3 .145 D5
Royton OL2 . . . . .48 E4
Stockport SK3 . . . . .123 C6
Runshaw Ave WN6 . . . . .35 E8
Rupert St Bolton BL3 . . . . . .147 F3
Failsworth M40 . . . . .83 E4
Radcliffe M26 . . . . .44 B1
Reddish SK5 . . . . .111 E7
Rochdale OL12 . . . . .14 C1
Wigan WN1 . . . . .151 E7
Rupert Terr **5** SK5 . . . . . . .111 E7
Ruscombe Fold M24 . . . . . . .46 D3
Rush Acre Cl M26 . . . . .43 E3
Rush Bank OL2 . . . . .48 F8
Rush Gr OL3 . . . . .69 B7
Rush Hill Rd OL3 . . . . .69 B7
Rush Mount Shaw OL2 . . . .149 A8
Shaw OL2 . . . . .48 F8
Rush St SK16 . . . . .101 F8
Rushall Wlk M23 . . . . .120 F2
Rushbrooke Ave **1** M11 . . . .83 C2
Rushbury Dr OL2 . . . . .49 A4
Rushcroft Com Prim Sch
OL2 . . . . .149 B8
Rushcroft Ct M9 . . . . .65 A2
Rushcroft Rd OL2 . . . . .48 F8
Rushden Rd M19 . . . . .99 B2
Rushdene WN3 . . . . .55 B4
Rushen St **4** M11 . . . . .83 C1
Rushes The SK14 . . . . .171 F4
Rushey Ave M22 . . . . .121 C6
Rushey Cl WA15 . . . . .129 D7
Rushey Field BL7 . . . . .24 D1
Rushey Fold **24** BL1 . . . . . .143 F4
Rushey Fold La BL1 . . . . . . .143 F4
Rushey Rd M22 . . . . .121 C6
Rusheylea Cl BL1 . . . . .142 C2
Rushfield Dr M13 . . . . .98 F3
Rushfield Rd SK8 . . . . .132 A6
Rushford Ave M19 . . . . .99 A2
Rushford Ct **1** M19 . . . . .99 A2
Rushford Gr BL1 . . . . .143 F4
Rushford St M12 . . . . .99 A3
Rushgreen Rd WA13 . . . . . .117 A4
Rushill Terr OL3 . . . . .69 B7
Rushlake Dr BL1 . . . . .143 E1
Rushley Ave M7 . . . . .81 B7
Rushmere OL6 . . . . .85 E6
Rushmere Ave M19 . . . . .99 B1
Rushmere Dr BL8 . . . . .27 C5
Rushmere Wlk M16 . . . . . . .162 D5
Rushmoor Ave WN4 . . . . . . .73 E4
Rushmoor Cl M44 . . . . .94 A2
Rusholme Gdns **3** M14 . . . .98 C2
Rusholme Gr M14 . . . . .98 C3
Rusholme Pl M14 . . . . .98 C4
Rushside Rd SK8 . . . . .132 A6
Rushton Ave Leigh WN7 . . . . .75 D8
Newton-le-W WA12 . . . . . . .89 B4
Rushton Cl SK6 . . . . .113 C3
Rushton Dr Marple SK6 . . . . .125 F5
Romiley SK6 . . . . .113 C3
Stockport SK7 . . . . .123 D3
Rushton Gdns SK7 . . . . . . .123 D2
Rushton Gr
Manchester M11 . . . . .99 E7
Oldham OL4 . . . . .49 E3
Rushton Rd Bolton BL1 . . . .142 B1
Cheadle SK8 . . . . .132 A6
Stockport SK3 . . . . .123 B7
Rushton St **20** Bacup OL13 . . .3 C8
Manchester M20 . . . . .110 B2
Walkden M28 . . . . .60 D2
Rushwick Ave M40 . . . . .157 E5
Rushworth Bldgs OL13 . . .3 C8
Rushworth Ct SK4 . . . . .111 C5
Rushy Hill View OL12 . . . . . .14 C1
Rushy View WA12 . . . . .89 A4
Rushycroft SK14 . . . . .103 A4
Ruskin Ave Denton M34 . . . .100 C7
Droylsden M34 . . . . .100 C7
Kearsley BL4 . . . . .60 F7
Manchester M14 . . . . .98 B4
Newton-le-W WA12 . . . . . . .89 B4
Oldham OL9 . . . . .65 F3
Wigan WN3 . . . . .54 F3
Ruskin Cres Abram WN2 . . . .56 B1
Prestwich M25 . . . . .62 F3
Ruskin Gdns SK6 . . . . .113 A3
Ruskin Gr SK6 . . . . .113 A3
Ruskin Rd Droylsden M43 . . . .84 B4
Little Lever BL3 . . . . .43 B4
Manchester M16 . . . . .97 C3
Prestwich M25 . . . . .62 F3
Reddish SK5 . . . . .99 E1
Rochdale OL11 . . . . .30 F2
Ruskin St Oldham OL1 . . . . .153 D8
Radcliffe M26 . . . . .44 C4
Ruskington Dr M9 . . . . .157 D7
Rusland Ct Manchester M9 . . .65 A3
Sale M33 . . . . .108 A5
Rusland Dr BL2 . . . . .25 E2

Rusland Wlk **8** M22 . . . . . .121 C2
Russel St OL11 . . . . .139 E5
Russeldene Rd WN3 . . . . . . .54 E3
Russell Ave High Lane SK6 .134 E7
Manchester M16 . . . . .97 D2
Sale M33 . . . . .108 D5
Russell Cl BL1 . . . . .144 C8
Russell Ct Farnworth BL4 . . . .60 E7
Manchester M16 . . . . .97 C3
Walkden M38 . . . . .60 C3
Russell Dr M44 . . . . .94 A2
Russell Gdns SK4 . . . . .168 B1
Russell Rd Manchester M16 . .97 D3
Partington M31 . . . . .106 A3
Salford M6 . . . . .80 B5
Russell Scott Prim Sch
M34 . . . . .100 E4
Russell St
6 Ashton-u-L OL6 . . . . . . .85 D4
Atherton M46 . . . . .58 C3
Bolton BL1 . . . . .145 D8
5 Bury BL9 . . . . .140 E4
Denton M34 . . . . .100 F3
Dukinfield SK16 . . . . .101 C8
Eccles M30 . . . . .79 F2
Farnworth BL4 . . . . .60 E7
Heywood OL10 . . . . .29 E1
Hindley WN2 . . . . .57 C2
Hyde SK14 . . . . .167 D3
Ince-in-M WN2 . . . . .56 A8
Manchester M16 . . . . .97 F3
Manchester M8 . . . . .158 F4
Mossley OL5 . . . . .68 C1
Oldham OL9 . . . . .152 B7
Prestwich M25 . . . . .63 C4
Stockport SK2 . . . . .124 A6
Walkden M38 . . . . .60 C3
Russet Rd M9 . . . . .64 D1
Russet Wlk BL1 . . . . .143 E4
Rustons Wlk **2** M40 . . . . . . .65 E1
Ruth Ave M40 . . . . .65 E1
Ruth St Bolton BL1 . . . . .145 E8
10 Bury BL9 . . . . .140 E4
Edenfield BL0 . . . . .1 D2
Manchester M18 . . . . .99 D3
Oldham OL1 . . . . .153 F8
Whitworth OL12 . . . . .4 D1
Ruthen La M16 . . . . .97 A4
Rutherford Ave **2** M14 . . . . .98 B3
Rutherford Cl SK14 . . . . . . .167 D2
Rutherford Dr BL5 . . . . .58 F7
Rutherford Way SK14 . . . . . .167 D2
Rutherglade Cl M40 . . . . . . .156 C6
Rutherglen Dr BL3 . . . . .40 F6
Rutherglen Wlk M40 . . . .157 E5
Ruthin Ave Cheadle SK8 . . . .122 E2
Manchester M9 . . . . .64 C5
Middleton M24 . . . . .65 A6
Ruthin Cl Oldham OL8 . . . . . .66 B2
Salford M6 . . . . .81 A2
Ruthin Ct M6 . . . . .81 A2
Rutland OL11 . . . . .139 E6
Rutland Ave Atherton M46 . . .58 F5
Denton M34 . . . . .101 B2
Golborne WA3 . . . . .90 D7
Manchester M16 . . . . .97 A3
Manchester M20 . . . . .110 A6
Swinton M27 . . . . .61 F2
Urmston M41 . . . . .95 A4
Rutland Cl
5 Ashton-u-L OL6 . . . . . . .85 D2
Gatley SK8 . . . . .122 B6
Little Lever BL3 . . . . .43 B4
Rutland Cres SK5 . . . . .112 C6
Rutland Ct SK2 . . . . .124 A5
Rutland Dr
Ashton-in-M WN4 . . . . .73 C4
Bury BL9 . . . . .45 A8
Manchester M7 . . . . .63 D1
Rutland Gr Bolton BL1 . . . . .142 C1
Farnworth BL4 . . . . .60 C7
Rutland La M33 . . . . .108 F4
Rutland Rd
Altrincham WA14 . . . . .119 D6
Droylsden M43 . . . . .83 E2
Eccles M30 . . . . .79 F3
Hazel Grove SK7 . . . . .133 E8
Hindley WN2 . . . . .56 F6
Irlam M44 . . . . .105 D5
Partington M31 . . . . .105 E2
Tyldesley M29 . . . . .58 F2
Walkden M28 . . . . .60 D1
Rutland St Ashton-u-L OL6 . .85 D2
Bolton BL3 . . . . .147 D4
Droylsden M43 . . . . .100 B8
Dukinfield SK14 . . . . .101 D5
Failsworth M35 . . . . .83 F8
Heywood OL10 . . . . .29 D3
Leigh WN7 . . . . .76 E4
4 Manchester M18 . . . . . . .99 E6
Oldham OL9 . . . . .152 C6
Swinton M27 . . . . .61 E1
Rutland Way OL2 . . . . .149 C7
Rutland Wlk BL4 . . . . .1 A8
Rutter's La SK7 . . . . .124 C2
Ryall Ave M5 . . . . .161 B8
Ryall Ave S M5 . . . . .161 B8
Ryan St M11 . . . . .99 E7
Ryburn Sq OL11 . . . . .29 E6
Rydal Ave Chadderton OL9 . . .47 F1
Droylsden M43 . . . . .83 E1
Dukinfield SK14 . . . . .101 C5
Eccles M30 . . . . .79 B4
Hazel Grove SK7 . . . . .124 C3
High Lane SK6 . . . . .134 E8

Rydal Ave continued
Hindley WN2 . . . . **56** E5
Middleton M24 . . . . **64** F6
Orrell WN5 . . . . **53** F7
Royton OL2 . . . . **48** C8
Sale M33 . . . . **107** F5
Urmston M41 . . . . **107** A8
Rydal Cl Ashton-in-M WN4 . . **73** C4
Blackrod BL6 . . . . **21** C3
Bury BL9 . . . . **44** E7
Gatley SK8 . . . . **122** B4
Reddish M34 . . . . **100** B2
Tyldesley M29 . . . . **77** A7
Rydal Cres Swinton M27 . . **60** E1
Walkden M28 . . . . **60** E1
Rydal Dr WA15 . . . . **129** D8
Rydal Gr Ashton-u-L OL7 . . **166** A4
Farnworth BL4 . . . . **59** F7
Heywood OL10 . . . . **46** D8
Whitefield M45 . . . . **63** A8
Rydal Ho ❹ M28 . . . . **60** E2
Rydal Mount SK5 . . . . **99** F2
Rydal Pl Abram WN2 . . . . . . **74** B8
Ince-in-M WN2 . . . . **56** B8
Rydal Rd Bolton BL1 . . . . . **144** A8
Haslingden BB4 . . . . **1** C8
Little Lever BL3 . . . . **43** A3
Stretford M32 . . . . **96** D3
Rydal St Leigh WN7 . . . . . . **75** E5
Newton-le-W WA12 . . . . **89** C3
Rydal Wlk Stalybridge SK15 **86** A3
Wigan WN5 . . . . **54** C7
Ryde Ave Denton M34 . . . **113** B8
Manchester SK4 . . . . **168** B2
Ryde St Bolton BL3 . . . . . . **146** A4
Wigan WN5 . . . . **54** E6
Ryder Ave WA14 . . . . **119** E7
Ryder Brow M18 . . . . **99** D4
Ryder Brow Sta M18 . . . . **99** D4
Ryder Gr WN7 . . . . **76** C2
Ryder St Bolton BL1 . . . . . **142** C2
Heywood OL10 . . . . **29** D2
Manchester M40 . . . . **160** D4
Ryderbrow Rd M18 . . . . . . **99** D4
Rydings La OL12 . . . . **15** A5
Rydings Rd OL12 . . . . **15** B4
Rydings Specl Sch OL12 . . . **15** B4
Rydley St BL2 . . . . **148** B6
Rye Bank Rd M16 . . . . **97** B3
Rye Croft M45 . . . . **62** C7
Rye Croft Ave M6 . . . . **80** C3
Rye Hill BL5 . . . . **57** F8
Rye St OL10 . . . . **29** D2
Rye Wlk Chadderton OL9 . . **152** A6
Manchester M13 . . . . **163** C5
Ryebank Gr OL6 . . . . **85** D5
Ryebank Mews ❸ M21 . . . . **96** F1
Ryebank Rd M21 . . . . **96** F1
Ryeburn Ave M22 . . . . **121** D3
Ryeburn Dr BL2 . . . . **25** B5
Ryeburn Wlk M41 . . . . **94** F4
Ryeburne St OL4 . . . . **67** C7
Ryecroft Ave Bury BL8 . . . . **26** F6
Golborne WA3 . . . . **74** E1
Heywood OL10 . . . . **29** E2
Ryecroft Cl OL9 . . . . **65** F3
Ryecroft Dr BL5 . . . . **39** D3
Ryecroft Gr M23 . . . . **121** A7
Ryecroft Ho ❷ OL7 . . . . . . **166** A1
Ryecroft La Dukinfield M34 **100** F7
Worsley M28 . . . . **78** F4
Ryecroft Rd M32 . . . . **96** C1
Ryecroft St OL7 . . . . **84** F1
Ryecroft View M34 . . . . . . **100** C8
Ryedale Ave M40 . . . . **157** D5
Ryedale Cl SK4 . . . . **168** B3
Ryefield M6 . . . . **80** D6
Ryefield Cl WA15 . . . . **120** C5
Ryefield Rd M33 . . . . **107** C2
Ryefield St BL1 . . . . **25** A1
Ryefields ❹ OL12 . . . . **15** D4
Ryefields Dr OL3 . . . . **51** B1
Ryeford Cl WN3 . . . . **151** F6
Ryeland Cl OL16 . . . . **31** B4
Ryelands BL5 . . . . **57** F8
Ryelands Ct BL5 . . . . **57** F8
Rygate Wlk ❸ M8 . . . . . . **155** F6
Rylance Ave WN3 . . . . **54** D1
Rylance St M11 . . . . **164** E8
Ryland Cl SK5 . . . . **99** F1
Rylands Ave WN6 . . . . **37** A2
Rylands Ct ❽ M15 . . . . . . **162** D6
Rylands Ho ❼ M14 . . . . . . **110** D8
Rylands St M18 . . . . **99** E6
Rylane Wlk M40 . . . . **157** D5
Rylatt Ct M33 . . . . **107** F5
Ryley Ave BL3 . . . . **144** B5
Ryley St ❹ BL3 . . . . **144** C6
Ryleys La SK9 . . . . **136** F1
Ryleys Sch The SK9 . . . . **136** F1
Rylstone Ave M21 . . . . . . **109** D3
Ryther Gr M9 . . . . **64** B5
Ryton Ave M18 . . . . **99** C3
Ryton Cl WN3 . . . . **150** B6

S

Sabden Brook Dr WN2 . . . **55** F2
Sabden Cl Bury BL9 . . . . . . **27** F7
Heywood OL10 . . . . **29** A2
Manchester M40 . . . . **160** E3
Sabden Rd BL1 . . . . **23** E2
Sabrina St M7 . . . . **81** A4
Sack St ❹ SK14 . . . . **101** D5

Sackville Cl OL2 . . . . **32** A1
Sackville St
Ashton-u-L OL6 . . . . **166** B3
❷ Bolton BL2 . . . . **148** C7
Manchester M1 . . . . **163** A8
Manchester M3 . . . . **158** E2
❻ Manchester M11 . . . . **30** C2
Sacred Heart RC Inf Sch
M18 . . . . **99** D4
Sacred Heart RC Jun Sch
M18 . . . . **99** D4
Sacred Heart
RC Prim Sch Hindley WN2 . **57** B3
Leigh WN7 . . . . **75** E5
Oldham OL1 . . . . **49** C2
Rochdale OL16 . . . . **31** C6
Westhoughton BL5 . . . . **39** F1
Wigan WN6 . . . . **36** F2
Wythenshawe M23 . . . . . . **120** F6
Saddle Ct ❻ WN5 . . . . **54** F6
Saddle Gr M43 . . . . **84** D3
Saddle St BL2 . . . . **25** D3
Saddleback Cl ❸ M28 . . . **78** B6
Saddleback Cres WN5 . . . **54** B6
Saddleback Rd WN5 . . . . . **54** B7
Saddlewood Ave M19 . . . . **110** D2
Saddleworth Bsns Pk OL3 **50** F4
Saddleworth Mus OL3 . . . . **69** B8
Saddleworth Prep Sch
OL4 . . . . **68** C8
Saddleworth Sch OL3 . . . . **51** B1
Sadie Ave M32 . . . . **96** A4
Sadler St Bolton BL3 . . . . . . **42** A4
Middleton M24 . . . . **46** F1
❷ Middleton M24 . . . . **47** A1
Saffron Cl WA3 . . . . **90** E8
Saffron Dr OL4 . . . . **49** D2
Saffron Wlk
Partington M31 . . . . **105** F2
❽ Wythenshawe M22 . . . . **121** D1
Sagar Cl M8 . . . . **158** F4
Sagars Rd Handforth SK9 . **131** B4
Handforth SK9 . . . . **131** C3
St Aelred's RC High Sch
WA12 . . . . **89** D4
St Agnes CE Prim Sch
Manchester M13 . . . . **98** F3
Oldham OL4 . . . . **68** A4
St Agnes Rd M13 . . . . **98** F2
St Agnes St SK5 . . . . **99** F3
St Aidan's Cl Billinge WN5 . **71** E6
Rochdale OL11 . . . . **139** D5
St Aidan's Gr M7 . . . . **81** B6
St Aidan's RC Prim Sch
WN3 . . . . **54** D7
St Aidans RC Prim Sch
M23 . . . . **109** B1
St Aiden's Cl M26 . . . . **44** A1
St Alban's Ave SK4 . . . . . . **111** C5
St Alban's Ct OL11 . . . . . . **139** E6
St Alban's St OL16 . . . . . . **139** E6
St Alban's Terr
Manchester M8 . . . . **155** F5
Rochdale OL11 . . . . **139** E6
St Albans Ave
Ashton-u-L OL6 . . . . **85** C7
Failsworth M40 . . . . **83** B5
St Albans Cl
Ashton-in-M WA11 . . . . **89** A7
Oldham OL8 . . . . **66** F4
St Albans Cres WA14 . . . . **119** C8
St Albans RC High Sch
M18 . . . . **99** D2
St Aldates SK6 . . . . **112** F2
St Aldwyn's Rd M20 . . . . . **110** B5
St Alphonsus
RC Prim Sch M16 . . . . **162** D5
St Ambrose Barlow
RC High Sch M27 . . . . **79** F7
St Ambrose Barlow
RC Prim Sch M29 . . . . **77** A5
St Ambrose Coll WA15 . . . . **129** B8
St Ambrose Gdns M6 . . . . **154** F2
St Ambrose RC Prim Sch
Manchester M21 . . . . **109** D4
Stockport SK3 . . . . **170** E5
St Ambrose Rd
Oldham OL1 . . . . **49** C1
Tyldesley M29 . . . . **77** A5
St Andrew's Ave
Altrincham WA15 . . . . **119** F7
Droylsden M43 . . . . **83** C4
St Andrew's CE Prim Sch
Boothstown M28 . . . . **78** A6
Eccles M30 . . . . **79** E1
Littleborough OL12 . . . . **15** E4
Manchester M19 . . . . **111** B8
Radcliffe M26 . . . . **43** F6
Ramsbottom BL0 . . . . **138** B5
Shevington WN6 . . . . **36** F2
St Andrew's Cl
Ramsbottom BL0 . . . . **138** C5
Romiley SK6 . . . . **113** B1
St Andrew's Cres WN2 . . . . **56** D5
St Andrew's Dr
Heywood OL10 . . . . **29** D1
Shevington WN6 . . . . **36** F2
St Andrew's RC Prim Sch
BL2 . . . . **42** E8
St Andrew's Rd
Radcliffe M26 . . . . **43** F6
Stretford M32 . . . . **96** B2
St Andrew's Sq M1 . . . . . . **163** C8
St Andrew's St
Manchester M1 . . . . **163** C8
Radcliffe M26 . . . . **43** F6
St Andrew's View M26 . . . . **43** F6
St Andrews Ave M30 . . . . . . **79** E1

St Andrews Cl
Manchester SK4 . . . . **168** B4
Sale M33 . . . . **107** C1
St Andrews Ct
Altrincham WA15 . . . . **119** F3
Stockport SK1 . . . . **112** A1
St Andrews Dr
Heywood OL10 . . . . **46** D8
Leigh WN7 . . . . **76** C5
St Andrews
Meth Prim Sch M28 . . . . . . **60** B3
St Andrews Over Hulton
CE Prim Sch BL5 . . . . **59** A8
St Andrews Rd Bolton BL6 . **40** B7
Gatley SK8 . . . . **122** C4
Manchester SK4 . . . . **168** B4
St Ann St Bolton BL1 . . . . . **143** E1
Manchester M2 . . . . **158** F1
St Ann's Pas M2 . . . . **158** F1
St Ann's RC Inf Sch M32 . **96** D2
St Ann's RC Jun Sch M32 . **96** D2
St Ann's RC Prim Sch
OL6 . . . . **166** A3
St Ann's Rd
Hazel Grove SK7 . . . . **124** C1
Prestwich M25 . . . . **63** A3
Rochdale OL16 . . . . **31** D8
St Ann's Rd N SK8 . . . . . . **122** B2
St Ann's Rd S SK8 . . . . . . **131** C8
St Ann's Sq Gatley SK8 . . . **131** C8
Manchester M2 . . . . **158** F1
St Ann's St M27 . . . . **79** E8
St Anne's Ave Oldham OL2 . **48** E3
Salford M6 . . . . **154** E3
Tyldesley M46 . . . . **58** E1
St Anne's CE Prim Sch
Oldham OL2 . . . . **48** E3
Sale M33 . . . . **108** D4
Shevington WN6 . . . . **35** F5
St Anne's Cres OL4 . . . . . . **68** D5
St Anne's Ct Denton M34 . **100** E6
Sale M33 . . . . **108** D4
Shevington WN6 . . . . **35** F5
St Anne's Dr
Dukinfield M34 . . . . **101** A4
Shevington WN6 . . . . **36** A5
St Anne's Gdns OL10 . . . . . **29** F2
St Anne's Hospl WA14 . . . **119** C3
St Anne's Prim Sch M34 . **101** A4
St Anne's RC Prim Sch
Droylsden M34 . . . . **100** A7
Manchester M4 . . . . **160** D1
Manchester M8 . . . . **156** A8
Oldham OL4 . . . . **67** C7
St Anne's Rd M34 . . . . **101** A4
St Anne's St Bury BL9 . . . . **140** F4
Manchester M10,M40 . . . . **157** F5
St Annes Mdw BL8 . . . . **26** F7
St Annes RC High Sch
SK4 . . . . **169** D4
St Annes Rd Denton M34 . **100** F6
Horwich BL6 . . . . **22** C4
Manchester M21 . . . . **109** B7
St Annes Sq OL3 . . . . **50** F4
St Annes St SK14 . . . . **115** A8
St Anns Cl M25 . . . . **63** A3
St Anns St M33 . . . . **108** F3
St Anselm's RC Prim Sch
M41 . . . . **4** D2
St Anthony's
RC Prim Sch M22 . . . . **121** D1
St Antony's RC High Sch
M41 . . . . **95** F2
St Asaph's Dr M7 . . . . **155** F8
St Asaphs Dr OL6 . . . . **85** B6
St Aubin's Rd BL2 . . . . **148** B6
St Aubyn's Rd WN1 . . . . . . **37** C4
St Augustine of
Canterbury RC Sec Sch
M8 . . . . **66** D3
St Augustine St
Bolton BL1 . . . . **143** D2
Manchester M40 . . . . **157** E5
St Augustine's CE Prim
Sch Manchester M40 . . . . **157** E5
Pendlebury M27 . . . . **80** B8
St Augustine's Ave ❷❻ BL2 . **25** B1
St Augustine's Rd SK3 . . . **123** B8
St Austell Ave M29 . . . . **77** C8
St Austell Dr Gatley SK8 . . **131** B8
Ramsbottom BL8 . . . . **10** F2
St Austell Ho M16 . . . . **97** E1
St Austell Rd M16 . . . . **97** E1
St Austell's Dr M27 . . . . **80** C7
St Austells Dr M25 . . . . **63** B5
St Barnabas
CE Prim Sch M11 . . . . **165** B8
St Barnabas Sq M11 . . . . . **165** B8
St Barnabas's Dr OL15 . . . . **16** A6
St Bartholomew St ❹
BL3 . . . . **42** A4
St Bartholomew's
CE Prim Sch OL12 . . . . **14** C8
St Bartholomew's Dr M5 **161** C8
St Bede CE Prim Sch
BL3 . . . . **146** C2
St Bede's Ave BL3 . . . . . . **146** B2
St Bede's Coll
Development Trust M16 . . **97** E3
St Bees Cl Gatley SK8 . . . . **122** B3
Manchester M14 . . . . **98** A4
St Bees Rd BL2 . . . . **25** C2
St Bees Wlk ❾ M24 . . . . . . **46** E2
St Benedict's
RC Prim Sch SK9 . . . . **131** E3
St Benedict's Sq M12 . . . . **164** F6
St Benedicts
RC Prim Sch WN2 . . . . **56** C6

St Bernadett's
RC Prim Sch WN6 . . . . **36** A6
St Bernadette's RC
Prim Sch Brinnington SK5 **112** B4
Whitefield M45 . . . . **44** F2
St Bernard RC Prim Sch
BL3 . . . . **40** D7
St Bernard's Ave ❶
M6,M7 . . . . **81** C5
St Bernard's Cl M6 . . . . **81** B5
St Bernard's RC Prim Sch
M19 . . . . **110** F6
St Boniface RC Prim Sch
M7 . . . . **81** C6
St Boniface Rd M7 . . . . **81** C4
St Brannock's Rd M21 . . . . **97** C1
St Brannocks Rd M21 . . . . . **97** C1
St Brannocks Rd SK8 . . . . **132** B7
St Brelades Dr M7 . . . . **155** F8
St Brendan's
RC Prim Sch BL2 . . . . **25** C4
St Brendan's Rd M20 . . . . **110** B7
St Brendan's Rd N M20 . . **110** B7
St Bride St M16 . . . . **162** D5
St Brides Cl BL6 . . . . **22** A4
St Brides Way M16 . . . . . . **162** D5
St Brigid's RC Prim Sch
(Jun & Inf) M11 . . . . **165** A8
St Catherine's
CE Prim Sch Horwich BL6 . **22** B3
Wigan WN1 . . . . **151** B1
St Catherine's RC
Prim Sch Golborne WA3 . . . **90** E7
Manchester M20 . . . . **110** C3
St Catherine's Rd M20 . . . **110** B7
St Catherines Prep Sch
SK6 . . . . **126** B7
St Chad's Ave SK6 . . . . . . **113** C2
St Chad's CE Jun Sch BL9 **44** F8
St Chad's CE
Saddleworth Prim Sch
OL3 . . . . **51** C1
St Chad's Cl OL16 . . . . **139** F7
St Chad's Gr SK6 . . . . **113** C2
St Chad's Rd M20 . . . . **110** D7
St Chad's St M4,M8 . . . . . **159** A4
St Chads Cres Oldham OL3 . **69** D8
Oldham OL8 . . . . **66** D1
St Chads RC Prim Sch
M8 . . . . **156** A1
St Charles Cl SK13 . . . . . . **103** F5
St Charles RC Prim Sch
SK13 . . . . **103** E8
St Charles's Rd M27 . . . . . . **79** D8
St Christopher's Ave OL6 . **85** E6
St Christopher's Dr SK6 . **113** A2
St Christopher's RC
Prim Sch Ashton-u-L OL6 . **85** E6
Romiley SK6 . . . . **113** A2
St Christopher's Rd OL6 . **85** E6
St Christophers Cl M20 . . **109** F6
St Chrysostoms
CE Prim Sch M13 . . . . **164** D5
St Clair Rd BL8 . . . . **10** F3
St Clare Terr BL6 . . . . **39** F8
St Clare's RC Inf Sch M9 . **64** C5
St Clare's RC Jun Sch M9 **64** C5
St Clement's (Egerton)
CE Prim Sch M5 . . . . **161** B7
St Clement's
CE Prim Sch M11 . . . . **99** E7
St Clement's Ct
❷ Irlam M44 . . . . **94** B3
Oldham OL8 . . . . **153** F5
Prestwich M25 . . . . **63** C4
Wigan WN3 . . . . **150** A5
St Clement's Dr M5 . . . . . . **161** B7
St Clement's Rd
Manchester M21 . . . . **109** A8
Wigan WN1 . . . . **37** C4
St Clement's St WN3 . . . . . **55** F4
St Clements Fold M41 . . . . **95** E2
St Columbo's
RC Prim Sch BL2 . . . . **25** B4
St Cuthbert's
RC High Sch OL16 . . . . **31** B1
St Cuthbert's
RC Prim Sch M20 . . . . **110** C6
St Cuthberts Fold OL8 . . . . **67** A1
St Damian's RC High Sch
OL6 . . . . **85** E7
St David's Ave SK6 . . . . . . **113** B2
St David's CE Prim Sch
WN2 . . . . **38** B7
St David's Cl OL6 . . . . **85** D7
St David's Cres WN2 . . . . . . **38** B5
St David's Ct M8 . . . . **156** A5
St David's Rd SK7 . . . . **124** C1
St David's Wlk M32 . . . . . . **96** A2
St Davids Cl M33 . . . . **108** A3
St Davids Rd SK8 . . . . **123** A6
St Domingo St OL9 . . . . . . **153** E6
St Dominics Mews BL3 . . **146** C3
St Dominics Way M24 . . . . **65** A7
St Dunstan's RC Prim Sch
M40 . . . . **83** A8
St Dunston Wlk ❶❹ M40 . . **83** A6
St Edmund Arrowsmith
RC High Sch WN4 . . . . **73** A2
St Edmund Hall Cl BL0 . . . . **11** C4
St Edmund St BL1 . . . . **145** E7
St Edmund's RC Sch M38 . **60** B4
St Edmund's Rd M40 . . . . **157** E6
St Edmunds RC Prim Sch
M40 . . . . **157** E6

St Edward's RC Prim Sch
Manchester M14 . . . . **98** B2
Oldham OL4 . . . . **67** C7
Wigan WN5 . . . . **54** F7
St Edwards CE Prim Sch
OL11 . . . . **30** C2
St Elisabeth's
CE Prim Sch SK5 . . . . **111** E8
St Elisabeth's Way SK5 . . **111** E8
St Elizabeth Pk M34 . . . . . **100** D3
St Elizabeth's
RC Prim Sch M22 . . . . **121** E2
St Elizabeth's Rd WN2 . . . . **38** B5
St Elmo Ave SK2 . . . . **124** D7
St Elmo Pk SK12 . . . . **134** C4
St Ethelbert's Ave BL3 . . **144** B5
St Ethelbert's
RC Prim Sch BL3 . . . . **144** B5
St Francis' RC Prim Sch
M12 . . . . **165** B6
St Gabriel Cl WN8 . . . . **35** C3
St Gabriel's CE Prim Sch
M24 . . . . **65** D7
St Gabriel's Cl OL11 . . . . . . **30** D1
St Gabriel's RC High Sch
BL9 . . . . **140** D1
Leigh WN7 . . . . **76** C1
Rochdale OL11 . . . . **30** D1
St George's Ave M15 . . . . **162** D5
St George's Ave
Sale WA15 . . . . **120** A8
Westhoughton BL5 . . . . **57** E6
St George's CE Inf Sch
Atherton M46 . . . . **58** B4
Stockport SK2 . . . . **170** F1
St George's CE Jun Sch
SK2 . . . . **170** F1
St George's
CE Prim Sch Hyde SK14 . **167** D1
Salford M6 . . . . **81** A5
Tyldesley M29 . . . . **76** F8
St George's Cres
Sale WA15 . . . . **120** A8
Salford M6 . . . . **80** A3
Walkden M28 . . . . **60** D2
St George's Ct
Altrincham WA14 . . . . **119** B7
❶❻ Bolton BL1 . . . . **145** E8
❽ Bolton BL1 . . . . **145** E8
Eccles M30 . . . . **79** F1
❸ Stretford M32 . . . . **96** C1
Whitefield BL9 . . . . **45** C3
St George's Dr M40 . . . . . . **83** B7
St George's Gdns M34 . . . **101** A1
St George's Pl
Atherton M46 . . . . **58** B4
Salford M6 . . . . **81** A5
St George's
RC High Sch M28 . . . . **60** C2
St George's Rd
Bolton BL1 . . . . **145** E8
Carrington M31 . . . . **106** D6
Droylsden M43 . . . . **83** C4
Manchester M14 . . . . **110** E7
Rochdale OL11 . . . . **29** C4
St George's Sq
❼ Bolton BL1 . . . . **145** E8
Failsworth OL9 . . . . **65** C5
St George's St Bolton BL1 . **145** E8
Stalybridge SK15 . . . . **86** A3
Tyldesley M29 . . . . **76** F8
St George's Terr BB4 . . . . . . **3** A6
St George's Way M6 . . . . . . **81** A5
St Georges CE Prim Sch
BL5 . . . . **57** D7
St Georges St Hyde SK14 **167** E2
Manchester M15 . . . . **162** D6
Tyldesley WN7 . . . . **76** F8
St Georges Dr SK14 . . . . . **167** D1
St Georges Rd
Stretford M32 . . . . **96** C1
Whitefield BL9 . . . . **45** C4
St Germain St BL4 . . . . **60** C8
St Gilbert's RC Prim Sch
M30 . . . . **79** B2
St Giles Dr SK14 . . . . **167** F2
St Gregory's RC High Sch
M11 . . . . **99** E8
St Gregory's RC Prim Sch
BL4 . . . . **60** E8
St Gregorys Cl BL4 . . . . **60** E8
St Helen's Coll
Newton Campus WA12 . . . . **89** B4
St Helena Rd BL1 . . . . **145** E7
St Helens CE Prim Sch
WA3 . . . . **105** B2
St Helens Rd WA3 . . . . **105** B3
St Helens Rd
Bolton BL3,BL5 . . . . **146** B3
Golborne WN7 . . . . **75** C1
Leigh WN7 . . . . **75** E2
St Helier St M19 . . . . **110** F5
St Helier's Dr M7,M8 . . . . . **155** F8
St Heliers St BL3 . . . . **147** D4
St Herberts Ct OL9 . . . . . . **152** B7
St Herberts RC Prim Sch
OL9 . . . . **152** A7
St Hilda's CE Prim Sch
Manchester M16 . . . . **97** B2
Oldham OL1 . . . . **153** D8
Prestwich M25 . . . . **63** C4
St Hilda's Cl M22 . . . . **109** C1
St Hilda's Dr OL1 . . . . **153** D8
St Hilda's Rd Denton M34 . **100** F5
Manchester M16 . . . . **161** C5
Wythenshawe M22 . . . . . . **109** D1
St Hilda's View M34 . . . . . **100** E5

St Hugh of Lincoln
  RC Prim Sch M32 ....95 F3
St Hugh's CE Prim Sch
  OL4 ....67 E3
St Hugh's Cl WA14 .....119 E8
St Hugh's RC Prim Sch
  WA15 ....119 F8
St Ignatius Prim Sch
  M13 ....163 C6
St Ignatius Wlk M5 ....161 B8
St Ives Ave SK8 ....123 A6
St Ives Cres M33 ....108 A1
St Ives Rd M14 ....98 B2
St Jame's Cl OL16,OL2 ...48 C8
St James Ave BL2 ....42 E7
St James CE Prim Sch
  Farnworth BL4 ....60 C7
  Littleborough OL12 ......15 C6
  Manchester M14 ....98 D2
St James CE Sch OL2 ..149 B7
St James Cl Glossop SK13 116 C7
  Salford M6 ....80 B3
St James Cres WN2 ......74 F8
St James Ct
  Altrincham WA15 ....119 E4
  Cheadle SK8 ....131 F6
  Manchester M20 ....122 B8
  4 Oldham OL4 ....67 C8
  Standish WN6 ....19 D2
St James Dr M33 ....108 A3
St James Gr WN3 ....150 B6
St James Lo SK3 ....124 A4
St James Rd M14 ....111 B5
St James St Ashton-u-L OL6 85 D2
  Eccles M30 ....79 E2
  Farnworth BL4 ....60 B7
  Heywood OL10 ....29 C2
  Manchester M1 ....163 A8
  Milnrow OL16 ....31 F6
  Shaw OL2 ....149 B7
  Westhoughton BL5 ......57 F5
St James' Ave BL8 ......27 B4
St James' CE Prim Sch
  Ashton-u-L OL6 ....166 C1
  Manchester M18 ....99 D5
  Wigan WN3 ....54 F5
St James' Ct
  1 Hattersley SK14 ....102 D2
  Salford M6 ....80 B3
St James' Dr SK9 ....137 A6
St James' Gr 8 OL10 ...29 C2
St James' RC High Sch
  SK8 ....131 F6
St James' RC Prim Sch
  Hattersley SK14 ....102 D2
  Orrell WN5 ....53 D4
St James' Rd WN5 ....53 D4
St James' St BB4 ....2 E8
St James' Way SK8 .....131 F6
St James's CE Sch BL4 ..60 A8
St James's Gr WA14 ....107 F1
St James's RC Prim Sch
  M6 ....154 F3
St James's Rd M7 ......155 E6
St James's Sq 8 M2 ...158 F1
St James's St 6 OL1 ...67 B7
St James's Terr OL10 ...29 C2
St John Bosco
  RC Prim Sch M9 ....65 A3
St John Fisher
  & St Thomas More
  RC Prim Sch M22 ......121 D4
St John Fisher
  RC High Sch WN6 ......36 F2
St John Fisher
  RC Prim Sch Denton M34 101 B1
  Middleton M24 ....47 B3
St John Rigby
  RC Sixth Form Coll WN5 .35 F2
St John Southworth
  RC Prim Sch WN4 ....73 D4
St John St Atherton M46 ..58 D3
  Dukinfield SK16 ....101 E8
  1 Eccles M30 ....79 D1
  Horwich BL6 ....22 B3
  Irlam M44 ....94 A2
  Manchester M3 ....162 E8
  Newton-le-W WA12 .....89 A3
  6 Oldham OL4 ....67 E6
  Oldham OL4 ....67 F6
  Pendlebury M27 ....80 D6
  Walkden M28 ....60 D4
  Wigan WN5 ....54 B6
St John the Baptist
  CE Sch WN2 ....37 F3
St John the Evangelist
  RC Prim Sch BL7 ....24 F8
St John Vianney
  Lower Sch SK4 ....168 B2
St John Vianney
  Upper Sch M16 ....97 B2
St John with St Michael
  CE Prim Sch OL12 ....4 E5
St John's (Wingates)
  CE Prim Sch BL5 ....39 E3
St John's Ave
  Droylsden M43 ....84 B2
  Westhoughton BL5 ......39 D3
St John's CE Inf Sch
  Failsworth M35 ....83 F8
  Leigh WN7 ....75 F6
St John's CE Jun Sch M35 84 A7
St John's CE Mosley
  Common Prim Sch M28 ..77 F7
St John's CE Prim Sch
  BL9 ....140 F4
St John's CE Prim Sch
  Coppull PR7 ....19 D6

St John's CE Prim Sch continued
  Dukinfield SK16 ....101 E8
  Farnworth BL4 ....60 E8
  Hindley WN2 ....57 B3
  Manchester M13 ....98 E4
  Manchester SK4 ....110 C2
  Middleton M24 ....47 E6
  Radcliffe M26 ....44 B1
  Wigan WN5 ....54 B6
St John's Cl
  Dukinfield SK16 ....101 E8
  Romiley SK6 ....113 B2
St John's Ct 5 Abram WN2 56 B1
  Altrincham WA14 ....119 D3
  Hyde SK14 ....167 F3
  Manchester M7 ....155 D6
  Radcliffe M26 ....44 C2
  4 Rochdale OL16 ....31 B6
St John's Dr Hyde SK14 ..167 F3
  8 Rochdale OL16 ....31 B6
St John's Gdns OL5 .....68 D2
St John's Ind Est OL4 ...67 C6
St John's Pl SK4 ....110 C2
St John's RC Prim Sch
  Manchester M21 ....97 A1
  Rochdale OL11 ....139 F6
St John's Rd
  Altrincham WA14 ....119 D3
  Aspull WN2 ....38 B5
  Bolton BL6 ....40 B4
  Boothstown M28,M29 ...77 E7
  Denton M34 ....100 F5
  Hazel Grove SK7 ....124 B1
  Manchester M13 ....98 F4
  Manchester M16 ....97 C4
  Manchester SK4 ....110 C2
  Wilmslow SK9 ....136 E3
St John's St Abram WN2 ..74 B8
  Farnworth BL4 ....60 B4
  Manchester M7 ....155 D6
  Oldham OL9 ....152 C6
  Radcliffe M26 ....44 B2
  Rawtenstall BB4 ....2 C6
St John's Wlk OL9 .....152 C6
St John's CE Prim Sch
  Rochdale OL12 ....15 B4
  Salford M6 ....80 C6
St Johns Ct OL4 ....67 F7
St Johns Sq M3 ....158 D2
St Johns Wlk SK3 ......123 B8
St Johns Wood BL6 .....40 B4
St Joseph & St Bede
  RC Prim Sch BL9 ....141 B4
St Joseph St 12 BL1 ...143 D2
St Joseph's Con Ctr WN8 .35 B2
St Joseph's Dr
  Rochdale OL16 ....31 B4
  Salford M5 ....161 B8
St Joseph's
  RC High Sch OL10 ....29 C1
St Joseph's RC Inf Sch
  SK5 ....111 E8
St Joseph's RC Jun Sch
  Manchester M13 ....98 E4
  Reddish SK5 ....111 E8
St Joseph's RC Prim Sch
  Adlington PR6 ....21 B3
  Bacup OL13 ....3 D8
  Bolton BL1 ....142 C1
  Heywood OL10 ....29 C1
  Irlam M44 ....94 A3
  Leigh WN7 ....76 A4
  Mossley OL5 ....68 C1
  Ramsbottom BL0 ....138 B6
  Sale M33 ....108 B4
  Salford M5 ....161 B8
  Shaw OL2 ....149 B5
  Walkden M28 ....60 A5
St Joseph's RC Sch
  Horwich BL6 ....22 C1
  Stockport SK1 ....169 F1
St Joseph's Wrightington
  RC Prim Sch WN6 ....19 A3
St Josephs Ave M45 ....63 C7
St Jude's Jun & Inf Schs
  WN3 ....54 F5
St Katherines Dr BL6 ...21 C3
St Kentigern's
  RC Prim Sch M14 ....98 A1
St Kilda Ave BL4 ....60 E6
St Kilda's Ave M43 .....83 F3
St Kilda's Dr M7 ....155 F8
St Lawrence Quay M5 ...96 F7
St Lawrence Rd M34 ...101 A3
St Leonard's Ave BL6 ...22 F1
St Leonard's Ct 4 M33 .107 F4
St Leonard's Rd M8 ....111 D5
St Leonard's Sq 8 M24 ..47 A1
St Leonard's St M24 ....47 A1
St Leonards Dr WA15 ..119 F6
St Lesmo Ct SK3 ......123 C7
St Lesmo Rd SK3 ......123 C7
St Lewis RC Prim Sch
  WA3 ....91 B1
St Luke St OL11 ....139 F5
St Luke with All Saints
  CE Prim Sch M5 ....154 D1
St Luke's Ave WA3 .....90 D8
St Luke's CE Prim Sch
  Glossop SK13 ....104 C1
  Golborne WA3 ....90 E7
  Heywood OL10 ....29 D3
  Manchester M12 ....164 E5
St Luke's Cres SK16 ...101 C8
St Luke's Dr SK14 ......53 E4
St Luke's RC Prim Sch
  M6 ....80 C5
St Luke's Rd M5,M6 ...154 E2

St Lukes CE Prim Sch
  OL9 ....152 A7
St Lukes Ct Bolton BL1 .144 C8
  Chadderton OL9 ....152 A7
St Lukes Wlk 15 M40 ...83 A6
St Malachy's
  RC Prim Sch M40 ......156 C5
St Malo Rd WN1 ....37 C4
St Margaret Mary's
  RC Prim Sch M40 ....65 D3
St Margaret Ward
  RC Prim Sch M33 ......107 C2
St Margaret's Ave M19 .110 F6
St Margaret's CE
  Prim Sch Heywood OL10 ..29 A1
  Manchester M16 ....97 D2
  Oldham OL4 ....66 B2
  Prestwich M25 ....63 D7
St Margaret's Cl
  Altrincham WA14 ....119 C4
  Bolton BL1 ....144 B8
  Prestwich M25 ....63 C6
St Margaret's Gdns OL8 .66 C3
St Margaret's Rd
  Altrincham WA14 ....119 C4
  Bolton BL1 ....144 B8
  Cheadle SK8 ....123 A6
  Failsworth M24,M40 ....65 D3
  Prestwich M25 ....63 C6
St Margarets
  RC Prim Sch SK13 .....115 D8
St Marie's RC Prim Sch
  BL9 ....140 F1
St Maries RC Prim Sch
  WN6 ....19 E2
St Mark St SK16 ....166 B1
St Mark's Ave
  Altrincham WA14 ....119 A5
  Royton OL2 ....49 A4
  Wigan WN5 ....54 F7
St Mark's CE Prim Sch
  Bury BL9 ....141 A4
  Manchester M40 ....160 D3
  Romiley SK6 ....113 A4
  Worsley M28 ....78 F6
St Mark's Cl OL2 ....49 A4
St Mark's Cres M28 .....60 D1
St Mark's Ct OL9 ......152 B8
St Mark's La M7,M8 ....155 F8
St Mark's St 11 BL9 ...140 F4
  Reddish M19 ....99 C1
  Romiley SK6 ....113 A4
St Mark's View BL3 ....145 F5
St Mark's Wlk BL3 .....147 E4
St Marks CE Prim Sch
  WN5 ....54 F6
St Martin's Ave SK4 ...168 C2
St Martin's CE Prim Sch
  OL8 ....67 B2
St Martin's Cl
  Droylsden M43 ....83 F3
  Hyde SK14 ....167 F2
St Martin's Dr M7,M8 ..155 F8
St Martin's Rd
  Marple SK6 ....126 A6
  Oldham OL8 ....67 B2
St Martin's Sch M33 ...107 E5
St Martin's St 11 OL11 ..30 D1
St Martins Rd M33 ....107 E6
St Mary & St John
  RC Prim Sch WN1 ....37 D1
St Mary's Ave Billinge WN5 71 C4
  Bolton BL3 ....144 B5
  Denton M34 ....113 A8
St Mary's CE Prim Sch
  Bolton BL3 ....146 A4
  Droylsden M43 ....84 B1
  Failsworth M40 ....65 C1
  Irlam M44 ....105 C5
  Manchester M16 ....97 E4
  Oldham OL3 ....69 C4
  Prestwich M25 ....63 A4
  Ramsbottom BL8 ....10 C2
  Reddish SK5 ....112 A6
  Rochdale OL11 ....31 A4
  Sale M33 ....108 A4
  Shaw OL2 ....48 F8
  Urmston M41 ....95 B4
St Mary's Cl Aspull WN2 ..38 B5
  Atherton M46 ....58 E2
  Rochdale OL16 ....31 B4
  Stockport SK1 ....112 A1
St Mary's Crest OL5 ....69 C5
St Mary's Ct Failsworth M40 83 B8
  Manchester M8 ....63 F1
  Prestwich M25 ....63 F1
St Mary's Dr Cheadle SK8 122 F6
  Oldham OL3 ....69 C5
  Reddish SK5 ....111 F6
St Mary's Gate
  Manchester M3 ....158 F2
  Oldham OL3 ....69 B8
  Rochdale OL12,OL16 ...139 E8
  Shaw OL2 ....149 B7
St Mary's Hall Rd M8 ...63 F1
St Mary's Hospl M13 ....98 C4
St Mary's Parsonage M3 158 F1
St Mary's Pl BL9 ......140 E2
St Mary's Prim Sch M35 .83 E6
St Mary's RC High Sch
  M29 ....77 A4
St Mary's RC Inf Sch
  WA12 ....89 C4
St Mary's RC Jun Sch
  WA12 ....89 B3

St Mary's RC Prim Sch
  Ashton-u-L OL6 ....85 D4
  Denton M34 ....100 E3
  Dukinfield SK16 ....101 E6
  Glossop SK13 ....116 D8
  Horwich BL6 ....22 B4
  Horwich BL6 ....22 C1
  Littleborough OL15 .....16 A5
  Manchester M19 ....111 A8
  Marple SK6 ....126 B7
  Middleton M24 ....46 E2
  Radcliffe M26 ....44 A4
  Stockport SK4 ....169 E2
  Swinton M27 ....79 F8
St Mary's RC Sch M30 ..79 E1
St Mary's Rd
  Altrincham WA14 ....119 C3
  Aspull WN2 ....38 C5
  Disley SK12 ....135 D5
  Dukinfield SK16 ....101 F5
  11 Eccles M30 ....79 F2
  Failsworth M40 ....83 B7
  1 Glossop SK13 ....104 C1
  Glossop SK13 ....116 C8
  Prestwich M25 ....63 B4
  Sale M33 ....107 F5
  Walkden M28 ....60 C5
St Mary's St
  Manchester M15 ....162 E5
  Manchester M3 ....158 F1
St Mary's Way
  2 Leigh WN7 ....75 F5
  Oldham OL1 ....153 F7
  Stockport SK1 ....112 A2
St Marys Cl M25 ....63 A4
St Marys St OL1 ....153 F8
St Matthew's
  CE Prim Sch Bolton BL1 .143 E1
  Little Lever BL3 ....43 A3
  Stockport SK3 ....170 E8
St Matthew's Ct SK24 ..47 F2
St Matthew's Cl WN3 ...54 C4
St Matthew's Dr OL1 ...48 A2
St Matthew's RC High Sch
  Failsworth M40 ....65 C2
  Manchester M9 ....64 F1
St Matthew's Rd SK3 ..170 E8
St Matthew's Terr 8 BL1 143 E1
St Matthew's Terr SK3 .170 D8
St Matthew's Wlk BL1 .143 E1
St Matthews
  CE Prim Sch M28 ......108 C8
St Matthews Ct 9 M32 ..96 C1
St Mawes Ct M26 ....43 C5
St Maxentius CE Prim Sch
  BL2 ....25 D5
St Michael's Ave
  Atherton M46 ....58 A1
  Bolton BL3 ....42 B2
  Bramhall SK7 ....132 E8
St Michael's Bamford
  CE Prim Sch OL10 ....29 D5
St Michael's CE Prim Sch
  Atherton M46 ....58 A2
  Bolton BL3 ....42 B3
  Middleton M24 ....65 A5
  Urmston M41 ....94 F1
St Michael's Ct Eccles M30 95 A8
  8 Wigan WN1 ....37 C2
St Michael's RC Prim Sch
  M45 ....45 B1
St Michael's Rd SK14 ..102 A2
St Michael's Sq
  6 Ashton-u-L OL6 .....166 C3
  3 Manchester M4 .....159 A3
St Michaels Cl BL8 ......43 F8
St Michaels Ct M33 ....107 E6
St Michaels Gdns M45 ..45 B1
St Modwen Rd M32 .....96 A5
St Monica's RC High Sch
  M25 ....63 C3
St Monica's RC Sch M41 .94 E2
St Nathaniel's
  CE Prim Sch WN2 ....56 B3
St Nicholas Rd WA3 .....75 A1
St Osmund's Dr BL2 ....42 E7
St Osmund's Gr BL2 ....42 E7
St Osmund's RC Prim Sch
  BL2 ....42 E7
St Oswald's RC Prim Sch
  Ashton-in-M WN4 ....73 B3
  Coppull PR7 ....19 D6
St Oswald's Rd M19 ....99 B2
St Oswalds Rd WN4 ....73 A2
St Ouen Ctr M28 ....60 D1
St Patrick St WN1 ......151 D6
St Patrick's RC High Sch
  M30 ....79 B2
St Patrick's RC Prim Sch
  Manchester M4,M40 ...159 C3
  Rochdale OL16 ....15 A1
  Wigan WN1 ....37 B3
St Patricks RC Prim Sch
  OL8 ....153 D6
St Patricks Way WN1 ..151 D7
St Paul's Ave WN3 ......54 F4
St Paul's
  Catholic High Sch M23 121 B4
St Paul's CE Prim Sch
  Adlington PR6 ....21 A7
  Bolton BL1 ....143 F3
  Brinnington SK5 ....112 B4
  Bury BL9 ....141 B4
  Manchester M20 ....110 B6
  Ramsbottom BL0 ....138 C6
  Royton OL2 ....48 C3
  Stalybridge SK15 ....86 C2
  Walkden M28 ....60 F2

St Paul's CE Prim Sch continued
  Wigan WN3 ....54 F3
St Paul's Cl PR6 ....21 A8
St Paul's Ct M26 ....44 A1
St Paul's Gdns SK14 ...167 E3
St Paul's Hill SK14 .....102 A2
St Paul's Rd SK14 ......167 F2
St Paul's Pl 1 BL1 .....142 C3
St Paul's Rd
  Manchester M20 ....110 C6
  Manchester M25 ....63 C1
  Manchester SK4 ....168 A4
St Paul's St Bury BL9 ..141 A3
  Hyde SK14 ....167 E3
  Ramsbottom BL0 ....138 C6
  Stalybridge SK15 ....86 C2
  Stockport SK1 ....112 A3
St Paul's Villas BL9 ...141 A3
St Pauls CE Prim Sch
  Salford M5 ....81 B1
  Walkden M28 ....60 E3
St Pauls Cl SK15 ....86 C2
St Pauls Ct Prestwich M7 .63 C1
  Walkden M28 ....60 D2
St Pauls Peel
  CE Prim Sch M38 ....59 E5
St Pauls Rd M28 ....60 E2
St Pauls Trad Est SK15 ..86 C2
St Peter & St Paul's
  Prim Sch BL3 ....145 E5
St Peter Smithills Dean
  CE Prim Sch 142 B4
St Peter's Ave BL1 .....142 A2
St Peter's CE Prim Sch
  Ashton-in-M WN4 ....72 F6
  Ashton-u-L OL7 ....166 A1
  Bury BL9 ....44 F4
  Farnworth BL4 ....60 D7
  Hindley WN2 ....56 C5
  Newton-le-W WA12 .....89 C4
  Rochdale OL16 ....31 B5
  Swinton M27 ....79 E8
St Peter's Cl SK14 .....117 A4
St Peter's Ct M32 ....96 E3
St Peter's Dr SK14 ....167 F2
St Peter's Gate OL14 ....6 B8
St Peter's RC High Sch
  WN5 ....53 F7
St Peter's RC Prim Sch
  Hazel Grove SK7 ....124 D1
  Middleton M24 ....65 A7
  Stalybridge SK15 ....86 A1
  Wythenshawe M22 .....121 A3
St Peter's Rd Bury BL9 ..44 F6
  Swinton M27 ....79 E8
St Peter's Sq
  Manchester M1,M2 .....162 F8
  Stockport SK1 ....169 F1
  Stockport SK Sta M2 ..162 F8
St Peter's St
  6 Ashton-u-L OL6 .....166 A2
  Rochdale OL16 ....31 B6
St Peter's Terr BL4 .....60 D7
St Peter's Way
  Bolton BL1,BL2,BL3,BL4 .42 B4
St Peters CE Jun Sch
  WN7 ....75 C5
St Petersgate SK1 .....169 F1
St Philip Howard RC Sch
  SK13 ....116 B8
St Philip's Ave BL3 ....147 D4
St Philip's CE Prim Sch
  M46 ....58 E3
St Philip's Pl M3 ......158 D2
St Philip's RC Prim Sch
  Manchester M7 ....63 C1
  Stockport SK2 ....124 E6
St Philip's Rd M18 .....99 D4
St Philips CE Prim Sch
  Manchester M15 ....162 F6
  Manchester M3 ....158 D1
St Philips Sq M3 ....158 D1
St Phillip's Dr OL1,OL2 ..48 E1
St Raphael's RC Prim Sch
  SK15 ....86 E4
St Richard's
  RC Jun & Inf Sch M46 ..58 C4
St Richard's RC Prim Sch
  M12 ....99 B3
St Robert's RC Prim Sch
  M13 ....98 F3
St Saviour's
  Com Prim Sch OL13 .....4 A8
St Saviour's Cty Prim
  Sch OL13 ....3 F8
St Saviour's RC Prim Sch SK2 124 C5
St Saviours CE Prim Sch
  M26 ....61 C7
St Sebastian's
  RC Prim Sch M6 ....81 A5
St Simon St M3 ....158 E3
St Simon's Cl
  SK7 ....124 C3
St Simons Cl SK2 ......124 C8
St Stephen & All Martyrs
  CE Inf Sch OL1 ....153 F8
St Stephen & All Martyrs'
  CE Prim Sch
  BL4 ....148 C5
St Stephen CE Prim Sch
  BL4 ....61 A6
St Stephen St
  Manchester M3 ....158 E2

St Stephen St continued
  6 Oldham OL1 . . . .**67** A8
St Stephen's Ave
  Denton M34 . . . .**100** E8
  Wigan WN1 . . . .**37** E2
St Stephen's
  CE Prim Sch Bury BL8 . . .**27** B1
  Hazel Grove SK2 . . . .**124** F4
  Tyldesley M29 . . . .**77** B6
  Wigan WN1 . . . .**37** E2
St Stephen's Cl
  Bolton BL2 . . . .**148** C5
  Manchester M13 . . . .**164** D5
St Stephen's Gdns
  Kearsley BL4 . . . .**61** A6
  10 Middleton M24 . . . . . .**47** A2
St Stephen's RC Prim Sch
  M43 . . . .**84** A2
St Stephen's Rd WN6 . . . .**19** C1
St Stephens Cl M29 . . . . . .**77** A5
St Stephens View M43 . . . .**84** A2
St Teresa's RC Prim Sch
  Irlam M44 . . . .**105** E8
  Little Lever BL3 . . . .**43** A3
  Manchester M16 . . . .**97** A3
  Orrell WN8 . . . .**35** B1
St Teresa's Rd M16 . . . .**97** A3
St Thomas (Chequerbent)
  CE Prim Sch BL5 . . . .**40** B1
St Thomas Aquinas
  RC High Sch M16 . . . .**97** E1
St Thomas Aquinus
  RC High Sch
  (Upper Sch) M21 . . . . . .**109** D7
St Thomas
  CE Jun & Inf Sch WN4 . . . .**73** C3
St Thomas CE Leesfield
  Prim Sch OL4 . . . .**67** E5
St Thomas CE Moorside
  Prim Sch OL1 . . . .**49** E4
St Thomas CE Prim Sch
  Leigh WN7 . . . .**76** A4
  Newhey OL16 . . . .**32** B4
St Thomas CE BB4 . . . .**1** A7
St Thomas Ct 1 BL9 . . . . .**141** A2
St Thomas Hospl SK3 . . . .**170** E8
St Thomas More
  RC High Sch Denton M34 **100** F2
  Wigan WN5 . . . .**54** F7
St Thomas More
  RC Prim Sch M24 . . . .**65** A5
St Thomas of Canterbury
  RC Prim Sch
  Bolton BL1 . . . .**144** A8
  Manchester M7 . . . .**155** E6
St Thomas Par OL4 . . . . . .**67** E6
St Thomas St
  Bolton BL1 . . . .**143** D2
  Wigan WN3 . . . .**150** C7
St Thomas St N OL8 . . . . .**153** D5
St Thomas St S OL8 . . . . .**153** E5
St Thomas the Martyr
  CE Prim Sch WN8 . . . .**53** B7
St Thomas'
  CE Parochial Sch SK4 . . .**111** C6
St Thomas' CE Prim Sch
  BL9 . . . .**141** B1
St Thomas' Cl M26 . . . .**44** A3
St Thomas' Cty Prim Sch
  M8 . . . .**156** C6
St Thomas' Pl M8 . . . .**159** A4
St Thomas'CE Prim Sch
  SK1 . . . .**170** F8
St Thomas's CE Prim Sch
  Bolton BL1 . . . .**143** D2
  Oldham OL8 . . . .**153** D5
St Thomas's Circ CE **153** D5
St Thomas's Ct WN8 . . . . .**53** C7
St Thomas's Pl SK1 . . . . . .**170** F8
St Veronica's
  RC Prim Sch BB4 . . . .**1** B7
St Vincent de Paul
  RC High Sch M14 . . . .**98** D3
St Vincent St
  Altrincham WA14,WA15 . . .**119** E4
  Manchester M4 . . . .**159** C2
St Vincent's RC Inf Sch
  WA15 . . . .**119** E5
St Vincent's RC Jun Sch
  WA15 . . . .**119** E5
St Vincent's RC Prim Sch
  OL12 . . . .**14** A1
St Werburgh's Rd
  M21,M16 . . . .**109** C8
St Wilfred's CE Jun
  & Inf Schs WN6 . . . .**19** F1
St Wilfred's CE Prim Sch
  M40 . . . .**83** D5
St Wilfred's Dr OL12 . . . . . .**14** D4
St Wilfrid's RC Prim Sch
  M15 . . . .**162** E6
St Wilfrid's Rd WN6 . . . . . .**19** F1
St Wilfrid's Way WN6 . . . . .**19** E1
St Wilfrids CE Prim Sch
  M22 . . . .**121** E8
St Wilfrids St M15 . . . . . .**162** E6
St William's RC Prim Sch
  WN2 . . . .**151** F7
St Williams Ave BL3 . . . .**147** E3
St Williams' RC Prim Sch
  BL3 . . . .**147** E3
St Willibrord's
  RC Prim Sch M11 . . . .**83** C3
St Winifred's
  RC Prim Sch SK4 . . . .**168** A2

SS Aidan & Oswald's
  RC Prim Sch OL2 . . . .**48** E3
SS Peter & John
  RC Prim Sch M3 . . . .**158** D2
SS Simon & Jude's
  CE Prim Sch BL3 . . . .**42** A3
Saintsbridge Rd M22 . . . .**121** C2
Salcombe Ave BL2 . . . .**26** D1
Salcombe Cl Sale M33 . . . .**107** E5
  Wigan WN1 . . . .**37** E2
Salcombe Gr BL2 . . . .**42** F6
Salcombe Rd
  Droylsden M11,M43 . . . . . .**99** D8
  Stockport SK2 . . . .**124** C8
Salcot Wlk 3 M40 . . . . . .**159** C3
Sale Gram Sch M33 . . . . . .**108** C3
Sale Heys Rd M33 . . . .**107** F3
Sale La M29 . . . .**77** D8
Sale Rd M23 . . . .**109** B2
Sale St OL15 . . . .**16** B6
Sale Sta M33 . . . .**108** B4
Sale Water Pk M33 . . . . . .**108** E7
Sale West Cty Sec Sch
  M33 . . . .**107** D5
Salem Gr OL4 . . . .**67** D6
Sales's La BL2 . . . .**12** B3
Salesbury Way WN3 . . . . . .**55** A3
Salford App M3 . . . .**158** F2
Salford Art Gall & Mus
  M6 . . . .**81** C2
Salford Central Sta M3 . .**158** E1
Salford Coll
  (Wardley Campus) M27 . .**61** C2
Salford Coll
  (Worsley Campus) M28 . .**60** D1
Salford Crescent Sta M6 . .**81** B2
Salford Foyer M6 . . . .**154** F3
Salford Quays M5 . . . .**96** F7
Salford Quays Sta M5 . . . .**161** A7
Salford Rd BL5 . . . .**59** C7
Salford St Bury BL9 . . . . . .**141** A4
  Oldham OL4 . . . .**67** C5
Salik Gdns OL11 . . . .**139** F5
Salisbury Ave
  Heywood OL10 . . . .**46** C8
  Hindley WN2 . . . .**56** E6
Salisbury Cres OL6 . . . .**85** D7
Salisbury Dr
  Dukinfield SK16 . . . .**102** A7
  Manchester M25 . . . .**63** C2
Salisbury House M3 . . . . .**158** E2
Salisbury Rd
  Altrincham WA14 . . . .**119** D7
  1 Ashton-in-M WN4 . . . . .**73** A5
  Horwich BL6 . . . .**22** F1
  Manchester M21 . . . .**97** C1
  Oldham OL4 . . . .**67** B6
  Radcliffe M26 . . . .**43** E5
  Salford M30 . . . .**80** A4
  Swinton M27 . . . .**79** E7
  Urmston M41 . . . .**95** D4
  Whitefield M45 . . . .**62** F8
Salisbury St Bolton BL3 . . .**145** D6
  Golborne WA3 . . . .**90** A8
  Hadfield SK13 . . . .**104** A5
  Manchester M14 . . . .**98** A4
  Middleton M24 . . . .**47** B1
  Reddish SK5 . . . .**111** F8
  Shaw OL2 . . . .**48** F8
Salisbury Terr BL3 . . . .**43** C3
Salisbury Way M29 . . . .**77** B8
Salix Ct M6 . . . .**81** A3
Salkeld Ave WN4 . . . .**72** F3
Salkeld St OL11 . . . .**139** F5
Salley St OL15 . . . .**6** C2
Sallowfields WN5 . . . .**53** D5
Salmon Fields OL2 . . . .**48** F3
Salmon St Manchester M4 **159** A2
  1 Wigan WN1 . . . .**37** B1
Salmsbury Hall Cl BL0 . . . .**11** C4
Salop St Bolton BL2 . . . . . .**148** A6
  Salford M6 . . . .**81** A4
Saltash Ct M22 . . . .**121** D1
Saltburn Wlk 28 M9 . . . . .**157** E8
Saltdene Rd 2 M22 . . . . . .**121** C1
Salter Rake Gate OL14 . . . . .**6** B8
Saltergate BL3 . . . .**40** F4
Saltergate Mews M5 . . . . . .**81** A1
Salters Ct M46 . . . .**58** D3
Saltersbrook Gr 12 SK9 . . .**131** E1
Salterton Dr Bolton BL3 . .**146** A2
  Bolton BL5 . . . .**40** F2
Salterton Wlk 17 M40 . . . . .**83** A7
Salteye Rd M30 . . . .**79** A1
Saltford Ave M4 . . . .**159** C2
Saltford Ct M4 . . . .**160** D2
Salthill Ave OL10 . . . .**46** E7
Salthill Dr M22 . . . .**121** E2
Saltire Gdns M7 . . . .**155** E8
Saltney Ave M20 . . . .**109** F7
Saltram Cl BL3,M26 . . . .**43** C5
Saltram Rd WN3 . . . .**54** C4
Saltrush Rd M22 . . . .**121** D1
Salts Dr OL15 . . . .**16** A6
Salts St OL2 . . . .**149** B7
Saltwood Dr BL1 . . . .**143** F1
Salutation St 7 M15 . . . . .**162** F6
Salvin Cl WN4 . . . .**73** D3
Salvin Wlk 27 M9 . . . .**64** E3
Sam Cowan Cl M14 . . . .**98** A3
Sam Rd OL3 . . . .**51** C5
Sam Swire St M15 . . . . . .**162** F5
Samian Gdns M7 . . . .**81** C5
Samlesbury Cl
  Manchester M20 . . . .**109** F3
  Shaw OL2 . . . .**48** F7
Sammy Cookson Cl M14 . . .**98** A3
Samouth Cl M40 . . . .**160** D3

Sampson Sq M14 . . . .**98** A4
Samson St OL16 . . . .**31** C8
Samuel La OL2 . . . .**48** E8
Samuel Laycock
  Specl Sch SK15 . . . .**85** F4
Samuel Ogden St M1 . . . .**163** A8
Samuel St Bury BL9 . . . . . .**141** A3
  Failsworth M35 . . . .**83** F8
  Hollingworth SK14 . . . . . .**103** C4
  Manchester M19 . . . .**111** B8
  Middleton M24 . . . .**47** A2
  Rochdale OL10 . . . .**30** C2
  Stockport SK4 . . . .**169** D3
  Tyldesley M46 . . . .**58** F1
Samwoods Ho WN4 . . . .**73** A5
Sanby Ave M18 . . . .**99** C4
Sanby Rd M18 . . . .**99** C4
Sanctuary Cl M15 . . . .**163** B5
Sanctuary The M15 . . . . . .**162** E6
Sand Banks BL1 . . . .**24** F6
Sand Beds La BL0,BB4 . . . . .**2** B5
Sand Hole La
  Rochdale OL11 . . . .**29** E5
  Rochdale OL11 . . . .**30** F1
Sand Hole Rd BL4 . . . .**61** A6
Sand St Manchester M40 . .**159** C4
  Stalybridge SK15 . . . .**101** F8
Sandacre Rd M23 . . . .**121** B7
Sandal Ct M40 . . . .**160** E3
Sandal St M40 . . . .**160** E3
Sandalwood BL3 . . . .**57** D6
Sandalwood Dr WN6 . . . . . .**36** F3
Sandbach Ave M14 . . . . . .**109** F8
Sandbach Rd Reddish SK5 . .**99** E2
  Sale M33 . . . .**108** F3
Sandbank Wlk SK8 . . . . . .**123** A4
Sandbank Gdns OL12 . . . . . .**4** C2
Sandbed La Delph OL3 . . . . .**51** A5
  Mossley OL5 . . . .**68** C2
Sandbrook Gdns WN5 . . . . .**53** C5
Sandbrook Rd WN5 . . . .**53** C5
Sandbrook Way M34 . . . . .**101** A5
Sandby Dr SK6 . . . .**126** B8
Sanderling Cl BL5 . . . .**57** D6
Sanderling Dr WN7 . . . .**76** A4
Sanderling Rd
  Hazel Grove SK2 . . . .**125** A4
  Newton-le-W WA12 . . . . . .**89** C4
Sanderson Ave M40 . . . . . .**157** E5
Sanderson Cl M28 . . . .**79** B7
Sanderson Ct M40 . . . .**157** E5
Sanderson La PR7 . . . .**18** A8
Sanderson St Bury BL9 . . . .**141** A3
  Leigh WN7 . . . .**75** D5
  Manchester M40 . . . .**157** E5
Sanderson's Croft WN7 . . . .**76** C4
Sanderstead Dr M9 . . . .**64** E3
Sandfield Cl 3 WA3 . . . .**90** E8
Sandfield Cres WA3 . . . .**92** C7
Sandfield Dr BL6 . . . .**40** C6
Sandfield Rd OL16 . . . .**31** B5
Sandfold SK5 . . . .**99** E2
Sandford Ave 3 M18 . . . . . .**99** D6
Sandford Cl BL2 . . . .**25** F4
Sandford Rd Orrell WN5 . . . .**53** C5
  Sale M33 . . . .**108** F3
Sandford St M26 . . . .**44** D4
Sandford Station La SK5 . .**99** D2
Sandgate Ave
  Droylsden M11 . . . .**83** D2
  Kearsley M26 . . . .**61** C7
Sandgate Cl WN7 . . . .**75** F6
Sandgate Dr M41 . . . .**95** D4
Sandgate Rd Oldham OL9 . .**152** B6
  Prestwich M45 . . . .**63** B7
Sandham St BL3 . . . .**147** F4
Sandham Wlk BL3 . . . .**147** F4
Sandheys M34 . . . .**100** F5
Sandheys Gr M18 . . . .**99** E4
Sandhill Cl BL3 . . . .**147** F4
Sandhill La SK6 . . . .**114** E1
Sandhill St SK14 . . . .**167** F4
Sandhill Wlk M22 . . . .**121** B2
Sandhurst Ave M20 . . . . . .**110** A6
Sandhurst Cl BL8 . . . .**27** B3
Sandhurst Ct BL2 . . . .**42** E6
Sandhurst Dr
  Farnworth BL2 . . . .**42** E6
  Wilmslow SK9 . . . .**137** C8
Sandhurst Rd
  Manchester M20 . . . .**110** C2
  Stockport SK2 . . . .**124** B5
Sandhutton Rd M9 . . . .**64** D1
Sandiacre WN6 . . . .**36** E8
Sandilands Prim Sch
  M33 . . . .**120** D8
Sandilands Rd M23 . . . . . .**120** D7
Sandilea Ct M7 . . . .**63** A1
Sandleigh Ave
  Altrincham WA15 . . . .**119** F3
  Brinnington SK5 . . . .**112** B4
  Cheadle SK8 . . . .**123** A6
  Manchester M20 . . . .**110** B5
Sandleigh Dr WA15 . . . . . .**119** F3
Sandimoss Ct 1 M33 . . . . .**107** F4
Sandiway Bredbury SK6 . . .**112** F3
  Glossop SK13 . . . .**116** F7
  Heywood OL10 . . . .**29** C2
  Irlam M44 . . . .**94** A2
  Stockport SK7 . . . .**123** E2
Sandiway Cl SK6 . . . .**125** F8
Sandiway Dr M20 . . . .**110** A3
Sandiway Pl WA14 . . . .**119** D4
Sandiway Rd
  Altrincham WA14 . . . .**119** D6
  Handforth SK9 . . . .**131** D5
  Sale M33 . . . .**107** F4
Sandling Dr WA3 . . . .**74** A2

Sandmere Wlk 25 M9 . . . . . .**64** E3
Sandon St BL3 . . . .**147** D4
Sandown Ave M5,M6 . . . . .**154** E2
Sandown Cl Culcheth WA3 . .**91** F4
  6 Oldham OL1 . . . .**49** A1
  Wilmslow SK9 . . . .**137** D8
Sandown Cres
  Little Lever BL3 . . . .**43** A2
  Manchester M18 . . . .**99** D3
Sandown Dr
  Altrincham WA15 . . . .**129** D6
  Denton M34 . . . .**113** B8
  Sale M33 . . . .**107** E3
Sandown Gdns M41 . . . .**95** A2
Sandown Rd Bolton BL2 . . . .**25** E3
  Hazel Grove SK7 . . . .**125** A2
  Stockport SK3 . . . .**123** B8
  Whitefield BL9 . . . .**44** F3
  Whitefield BL9 . . . .**45** A2
  Wigan WN6 . . . .**36** B3
Sandown St M18 . . . .**99** F6
Sandpiper Cl
  Dukinfield SK16 . . . .**101** E7
  Farnworth BL4 . . . .**59** F7
  Newton-le-W WA12 . . . . . .**89** C4
  Rochdale OL11 . . . .**29** F7
Sandpiper Dr SK3 . . . .**170** E6
Sandpiper Rd WN3 . . . .**54** B4
Sandra Dr WA12 . . . .**89** C3
Sandray Cl BL3 . . . .**40** F5
Sandray Gr M5 . . . .**154** E1
Sandridge Cl BL4 . . . .**60** E8
Sandridge Wlk M12 . . . . . .**164** E6
Sandringham Ave
  Denton M34 . . . .**100** D6
  Reddish M34 . . . .**100** A3
  Stalybridge SK15 . . . .**86** A3
Sandringham Cl
  Adlington PR7 . . . .**20** C5
  Altrincham WA14 . . . .**118** F1
  Wigan WN5 . . . .**54** E5
Sandringham Ct 5 SK9 . . .**137** A6
Sandringham Dr
  Dukinfield SK16 . . . .**101** F7
  Leigh WN7 . . . .**76** E7
  Milnrow OL16 . . . .**32** A6
  Poynton SK12 . . . .**133** D3
  Ramsbottom BL8 . . . .**11** A3
  Stockport SK4 . . . .**168** A1
Sandringham Grange M25 **63** A3
Sandringham Rd
  Boothstown M28 . . . .**78** A6
  Bredbury SK6 . . . .**112** D3
  Cheadle SK8 . . . .**123** A3
  Hazel Grove SK7 . . . .**124** F2
  Hindley WN2 . . . .**56** E4
  Horwich BL6 . . . .**22** E2
  Hyde SK14 . . . .**113** E4
Sandringham St M18 . . . . . .**99** C4
Sandringham Way
  Royton OL2 . . . .**48** C6
  4 Wilmslow SK9 . . . .**137** A6
Sands Ave M24,OL9 . . . .**47** D1
Sands Cl SK14 . . . .**102** D1
Sands Wlk SK14 . . . .**102** D1
Sandsend Cl M8 . . . .**155** C5
Sandsend Rd M41 . . . .**95** C3
Sandstone Rd
  Milnrow OL16 . . . .**31** F7
  Wigan WN3 . . . .**54** E2
Sandstone Way M21 . . . . .**109** D6
Sandway WN6 . . . .**36** F2
Sandwell Dr M33 . . . .**108** B6
Sandwich Rd M30 . . . .**79** F3
Sandwich St M28 . . . .**60** D2
Sandwick Cres BL3 . . . . . .**145** D5
Sandwith Cl WN3 . . . .**55** B2
Sandwood Ave BL3 . . . .**40** E6
Sandy Acre OL5 . . . .**86** C8
Sandy Bank OL2 . . . .**48** F8
Sandy Bank Ave SK14 . . . .**102** D1
Sandy Bank Ct SK14 . . . . .**102** D1
Sandy Bank Rd
  Edgworth BL7 . . . .**9** D5
  Manchester M8 . . . .**155** F8
Sandy Bank Wlk SK14 . . . .**102** D1
Sandy Brow M9 . . . .**64** D2
Sandy Brow La WA3 . . . . . .**90** E2
Sandy Cl BL9 . . . .**44** F4
Sandy Ct WN7 . . . .**75** A1
Sandy Gr Dukinfield SK16 . .**101** D8
  Salford M6 . . . .**154** E3
  Swinton M27 . . . .**79** F8
Sandy Haven Cl SK14 . . . .**102** D1
Sandy Haven Wlk SK14 . . .**102** D1
Sandy La Adlington PR7 . . . .**20** F6
  Altrincham WA14 . . . .**120** E7
  Charlesworth SK13 . . . . . .**115** A4
  Culcheth WA3 . . . .**91** A1
  Droylsden M43 . . . .**84** C1
  Dukinfield SK16 . . . .**101** D8
  Golborne WA3 . . . .**75** A1
  Golborne WA3 . . . .**89** F8
  Irlam M44 . . . .**94** A2
  Lymm WA13 . . . .**117** B4
  Manchester M21 . . . .**109** C8
  Middleton M24 . . . .**65** C8
  Orrell WN5 . . . .**53** D4
  Prestwich M25 . . . .**63** A2
  Reddish SK4,SK5 . . . .**169** E3
  Rochdale OL11 . . . .**30** C7
  Romiley SK6 . . . .**113** D3
  Royton OL2 . . . .**48** D4
  Salford M6 . . . .**154** E3
  Stretford M32 . . . .**96** C1
  Tyldesley M29 . . . .**77** A4
  Tyldesley M29 . . . .**77** B1
  Uppermill OL3 . . . .**51** B2

Sandy La continued
  Wilmslow SK9 . . . .**136** E8
Sandy Meade M25 . . . .**63** A3
Sandy Pk WN2 . . . .**57** A6
Sandy Way WN2 . . . .**56** F6
Sandy Wlk 4 OL2 . . . .**48** C3
Sandyacre Cl BL5 . . . .**59** A6
Sandybank SK13 . . . .**171** E4
Sandybrook Cl BL8 . . . .**26** F6
Sandycroft Ave 1 WN1 . . . .**37** C1
Sandygate Cl M27 . . . .**79** E7
Sandyhill Rd M9 . . . .**64** B3
Sandyhills BL3 . . . .**147** E4
Sandylands Dr M25 . . . .**63** A1
Sandyshot Wlk 4 M22 . . . .**121** F3
Sandyway M25 . . . .**63** A3
Sandywell Cl M11 . . . .**99** D7
Sandywell St M11 . . . .**99** D8
Sanfold La M19 . . . .**99** C2
Sangster Ct M5 . . . .**161** A8
Sankey Gr M9 . . . .**64** B3
Sankey St Bury BL9 . . . . . .**140** D2
  Golborne WA3 . . . .**90** A8
  Newton-le-W WA12 . . . . . .**89** A3
Sankey Valley Ind Est
  WA12 . . . .**89** A2
Santiago St M14 . . . .**98** B3
Santley St M12 . . . .**99** A3
Santon Ave M14 . . . .**110** E8
Santon Dr WA3 . . . .**90** E8
Sapling Gr M33 . . . .**107** D2
Sapling Rd Bolton BL3 . . . .**146** C2
  Swinton M27 . . . .**79** D5
Sarah Butterworth Ct 11
  OL16 . . . .**31** B6
Sarah Butterworth St 9
  OL16 . . . .**31** B6
Sarah St Bacup OL13 . . . .**4** C8
  1 Eccles M30 . . . .**79** B1
  Edenfield BL0 . . . .**1** E3
  Hindley WN2 . . . .**57** B2
  Manchester M11 . . . .**164** F8
  Middleton M24 . . . .**64** F8
  2 Oldham OL8 . . . .**66** D2
  5 Rochdale OL11 . . . .**31** A6
  Shaw OL2 . . . .**149** A5
Sargent Dr M16 . . . .**97** E4
Sargent Rd SK6 . . . .**112** D2
Sark Rd M21 . . . .**97** A2
Sarn Ave M22 . . . .**121** D4
Sarnesfield Cl M12 . . . .**99** A4
Sarnia Ct M7 . . . .**155** D7
Sarsfield Ave 1 WA3 . . . . . .**90** D8
Satinwood Cl WN4 . . . .**72** F2
Saturn Gr M6 . . . .**81** C4
Saunton Ave BL2 . . . .**25** F3
Saunton Rd M11 . . . .**99** D8
Sautridge Cl OL11 . . . .**47** D7
Savernake Rd SK6 . . . .**113** C5
Savick Ave BL2 . . . .**42** F7
Saville Rd Gatley SK8 . . . . .**122** B6
  Radcliffe BL8 . . . .**43** F7
Saville St Bolton BL2 . . . . .**148** A6
  Middleton M24 . . . .**65** C7
Savio Way M24 . . . .**65** A7
Saviour CE Prim Sch
  M40 . . . .**156** C5
Saviours Terr BL3 . . . .**144** C5
Savoy Ct M45 . . . .**44** E2
Savoy Dr OL2 . . . .**48** C2
Savoy St Oldham OL4 . . . . . .**67** B5
  Rochdale OL11 . . . .**30** C3
Saw St BL1 . . . .**143** E2
Sawley Ave Golborne WA3 . .**74** D1
  Littleborough OL15 . . . .**16** A7
  Oldham OL4 . . . .**67** D4
  Shevington WN6 . . . .**36** F2
  Whitefield M45 . . . .**44** F2
Sawley Cl WA3 . . . .**92** A2
Sawley Dr SK8 . . . .**132** C6
Sawley Rd M40 . . . .**160** E4
Sawpit St WA13,WA14 . . . .**118** A6
Sawston Wlk M40 . . . .**65** C3
Sawyer Brow SK14 . . . .**167** F4
Sawyer St Bury SK18 . . . . . .**27** B4
  5 Rochdale OL12 . . . .**14** F1
Saxbrook Wlk 3 M22 . . . . .**121** F3
Saxby Ave BL7 . . . .**24** F8
Saxby St M6 . . . .**80** C5
Saxelby Dr M8 . . . .**156** B7
Saxfield Dr M23 . . . .**121** C6
Saxholme Wlk 5 M22 . . . . .**121** C2
Saxon Ave Dukinfield SK16 **101** C8
  Manchester M8 . . . .**64** A2
Saxon Cl BL8 . . . .**27** B2
Saxon Dr Chadderton OL9 . . .**65** E8
  Denton M34 . . . .**100** F4
  Droylsden M43 . . . .**84** B2
Saxon Hall L Ctr OL16 . . . . .**31** C8
Saxon Ho 8 M16 . . . .**97** D3
Saxon Rd OL5 . . . .**68** D3
Saxon St Denton M34 . . . . .**100** F3
  Droylsden M43 . . . .**84** B2
  Manchester M40 . . . .**160** A3
  Middleton M24 . . . .**65** B8
  Oldham OL4 . . . .**67** C7
  Radcliffe M26 . . . .**43** F3
Saxonholme Rd OL11 . . . . . .**47** C7
Saxthorpe Cl Sale M33 . . . .**107** D5
  Wigan WN3 . . . .**54** F2
Saxthorpe Wlk M12 . . . . . .**164** E6
Saxwood Ave M9 . . . .**64** D1
Saxwood Cl OL12 . . . .**13** F1
Scafell Ave OL7 . . . .**84** F4
Scafell Cl High Lane SK6 . .**134** E8
  Oldham OL1 . . . .**48** F1
Scafell Dr WN5 . . . .**54** B6
Scafell Gr WN2 . . . .**56** B2

Scalby Wlk **2** M22 . . . . . .121 D1
Scale St M5 . . . . .81 A1
Scarborough St M40 . . . . .83 A8
Scarcroft Rd M12 . . . . . . .165 A5
Scardale Ave BL1 . . . . . . .142 A1
Scarfield Dr OL11 . . . . .13 E1
Scargill Cl M14 . . . . .110 C8
Scargill Rd BL3 . . . . .146 A4
Scarisbrick Ave M20 . . . . .110 D3
Scarisbrick Rd M19 . . . . . .110 F8
Scarisbrick St **3** WN1 . . . .37 C1
Scarr Ave M26 . . . . .44 C2
Scarr Dr OL12 . . . . .14 F3
Scarr La OL2 . . . . .49 D7
Scarsdale Rd M14 . . . . .98 E4
Scarsdale St M6 . . . . .81 B3
Scarthwood Cl BL2 . . . . . . .25 E5
Scawfell Ave BL2 . . . . .25 E2
Scawton Wlk M9 . . . . .64 B5
Sceptre Cl WA12 . . . . .89 A3
Schofield Gdns WN7 . . . . . .75 E3
Schofield Hall Rd OL15 . . . .16 C1
Schofield La M46 . . . . .57 F3
Schofield Rd
  Droylsden M43 . . . . .84 B1
  Eccles M30 . . . . .79 A1
Schofield St Droylsden M11 83 C2
  Failsworth M35 . . . . .83 F8
  Haslingden BB4 . . . . .1 A6
  Heywood OL10 . . . . .29 D1
  Leigh WN7 . . . . .75 E4
  Littleborough OL15 . . . . . .16 C6
  Littleborough OL15 . . . . . . .6 D2
  Manchester M3 . . . . .158 D1
  Milnrow OL16 . . . . .32 A5
  Oldham OL8 . . . . .66 F3
  Radcliffe M26 . . . . .44 B4
  Rawtenstall BB4 . . . . .2 E8
  Rochdale OL11 . . . . .31 A4
  Royton OL2 . . . . .48 D5
Scholars Dr M20 . . . . .110 A7
Scholars Way **18** M24 . . . .46 F1
Scholefield La WN1 . . . . . .151 E8
Scholes WN1 . . . . .151 D8
Scholes Bank BL6 . . . . .22 A5
Scholes Cl M7 . . . . .155 F8
Scholes Dr M40 . . . . .65 E2
Scholes La M25 . . . . .63 C3
Scholes St Bury BL8 . . . . . .27 C3
  Failsworth M35 . . . . .66 A1
  11 Oldham OL1 . . . . .67 A7
  Oldham OL9 . . . . .66 A4
  Pendlebury M27 . . . . .80 A8
  Rochdale OL11 . . . . .30 C1
Scholes Wlk M25 . . . . .63 B3
Scholey St BL2 . . . . .148 A5
Scholfield Ave M41 . . . . . . .95 F1
School Ave Ashton-u-L OL6 .85 D6
  Stretford M32 . . . . .96 F3
  Wigan WN1 . . . . .37 E1
School Brow Billinge WN5 . .71 E5
  Bury BL9 . . . . .140 E3
  Bury BL9 . . . . .140 F2
  Romiley SK6 . . . . .113 A2
  Worsley M28 . . . . .78 F6
School Cl SK12 . . . . .133 F3
School Court No 1 M4 . . . .159 B3
School Cres WN5 . . . . .86 A4
School Ct Bolton BL7 . . . . . . .8 E7
  Manchester M4 . . . . .159 C2
  Ramsbottom BL0 . . . . .1 D2
  Stockport SK3 . . . . .170 F6
School Dr WN5 . . . . .71 E5
School Gr
  Manchester M20 . . . . . . .110 D6
  Prestwich M25 . . . . .63 A2
School Gr W M20 . . . . . . .110 C6
School Hill BL1 . . . . .145 E8
School House Flats **1**
  OL8 . . . . .66 C2
School La Aspull WN2 . . . . .37 E7
  Bury BL9 . . . . .27 E8
  Carrington M31 . . . . .106 E6
  Cheadle SK8 . . . . .132 A8
  Edgworth BL7 . . . . .9 D8
  Garswood WN4 . . . . .72 C3
  Hollinfare WA3 . . . . .105 A2
  Hyde SK14 . . . . .113 E7
  Irlam M44 . . . . .105 D5
  Irlam M44 . . . . .93 F2
  Manchester M19,M20 . . . .110 C3
  Manchester M9 . . . . .64 C2
  Mossley SK15 . . . . .86 E7
  Orrell WN5,WN8 . . . . .53 C7
  Orrell WN8 . . . . .35 B3
  Partington WA14 . . . . . . .118 D5
  Poynton SK12 . . . . .133 F4
  Reddish SK4 . . . . .111 C5
  Rochdale OL11 . . . . .29 C8
  Rochdale OL16 . . . . .139 F7
  Romiley SK6 . . . . .114 B4
  Standish WN6 . . . . .19 D1
  Wigan WN1 . . . . .151 D8
School Mews
  Bramhall SK7 . . . . .132 E4
  Newhey OL16 . . . . .32 B4
School Rd
  Altrincham WA15 . . . . . . .119 F3
  Eccles M30 . . . . .95 C8
  Failsworth M35 . . . . .83 F7
  Handforth SK9 . . . . .131 D4
  Oldham OL8 . . . . .66 B2
  Sale M33 . . . . .108 A5
  Sale M33 . . . . .108 B5
  Stretford M32 . . . . .96 C2
School St Ashton-in-M WN4 .73 D5
  Atherton M46 . . . . .58 B2
  Bacup OL13 . . . . .3 B8

School St continued
  Bolton BL7 . . . . .24 F7
  Bury BL9 . . . . .141 B1
  Eccles M30 . . . . .79 B3
  Golborne WA3 . . . . .90 A8
  Hazel Grove SK7 . . . . . . .124 E2
  Heywood OL10 . . . . .29 C2
  Horwich BL6 . . . . .22 C3
  Ince-in-M WN2 . . . . .151 F1
  Leigh WN7 . . . . .75 E8
  Little Lever BL3 . . . . .43 B3
  Littleborough OL15 . . . . . .15 E5
  Manchester M4 . . . . .159 B3
  Manchester M7 . . . . .158 E4
  Newton-le-W WA12 . . . . . .89 B3
  Oldham OL3 . . . . .69 B8
  Oldham OL4 . . . . .68 A6
  Oldham OL8 . . . . .153 D5
  Radcliffe M26 . . . . .44 A3
  Ramsbottom BL0 . . . . . . .138 B5
  Rochdale OL12 . . . . .139 F8
  Tyldesley M29 . . . . .76 F7
  Tyldesley M29 . . . . .76 F7
  Westhoughton BL5 . . . . . . .57 E8
  Wigan WN1 . . . . .151 D8
School Street Ind Est
  SK7 . . . . .124 E2
School Terr Golborne WA3 . .90 A8
  Whitworth OL12 . . . . .4 D1
School View BL7 . . . . .9 D8
School Way WN5 . . . . .54 C6
School Wlk M16 . . . . .162 D5
Schoolhouse M17 . . . . .96 D5
Schools Hill SK8 . . . . .122 D3
Schools Rd M18 . . . . .99 E5
Schoolside La M24 . . . . . . .64 C7
Schwabe St M24 . . . . .64 C8
Scobell St BL8 . . . . .27 E4
Scoles Prec WN1 . . . . .151 D8
Score St M11 . . . . .83 A1
Scorton Ave BL2 . . . . .42 F7
Scorton St **15** BL1 . . . . . .144 C8
Scorton Wlk **23** M40 . . . . .65 D2
Scot La Aspull BL6,WN2 . . . .38 E6
  Shevington WN5,WN6 . . . . .36 E1
  Wigan WN5 . . . . .54 F7
Scot Lane End
  CE Prim Sch BL6 . . . . .38 D2
Scot Lane Prim Sch WN5 . .54 F7
Scotforth Cl M15 . . . . .162 E7
Scotia Wlk **1** WA3 . . . . . . .90 F8
Scotland M4 . . . . .159 A3
Scotland Hall Rd M40 . . . . .83 C4
Scotland La BL9 . . . . .28 D8
Scotland Pl BL0 . . . . .138 C6
Scotland St
  Ashton-u-L OL6 . . . . .166 C2
  Failsworth M40 . . . . .83 C5
Scott Ave Bury BL9 . . . . . . .44 F6
  Eccles M30 . . . . .79 C3
  Hindley WN2 . . . . .56 E6
  Manchester M21 . . . . .97 B2
Scott Cl SK5 . . . . .169 F4
Scott Dr SK6 . . . . .126 B8
Scott Gate M34 . . . . .100 F7
Scott Ho Manchester M19 . .99 A2
  Walsden OL14 . . . . .6 A8
Scott House
  (Childrens Orthopaedic)
  Hospl OL11 . . . . .29 D8
Scott Rd Denton M34 . . . . .100 E1
  Droylsden M43 . . . . .84 A1
  Golborne WA3 . . . . .74 D2
  Prestwich M25 . . . . .62 F3
Scott St Kearsley M26 . . . . .61 D7
  Leigh WN7 . . . . .75 D5
  Oldham OL8 . . . . .153 F5
  Salford M6 . . . . .81 C4
  Tyldesley M29 . . . . .77 C4
  Walsden OL14 . . . . .6 A8
  Westhoughton BL5 . . . . . . .39 E2
  Wigan WN1 . . . . .37 B1
Scott Wlk WA12 . . . . .89 C1
Scottfield OL8 . . . . .153 F5
Scottfield Rd OL8 . . . . . . .153 F5
Scottia Rd M30 . . . . .95 C8
Scotts Ind Est OL16 . . . . . .31 A6
Scout Dr M23 . . . . .120 F4
Scout Rd Bolton BL1,BL7 . . .24 B7
  Edenfield BL0 . . . . .2 A2
Scout View BL8 . . . . .27 A6
Scovell St M7 . . . . .155 D6
Scowcroft La OL2 . . . . .149 A6
Scowcroft St **21** BL2 . . . . .25 B1
Scroggins La M31 . . . . . . .105 F4
Scropton St M40 . . . . .157 D6
Seabright Wlk **12** M11 . . .160 F1
Seabrook Cres M41 . . . . . . .95 D4
Seabrook Rd M40 . . . . .83 C4
Seacombe Ave M14 . . . . . . .98 A1
Seacombe Gr SK3 . . . . . . .123 B8
Seaford Rd Bolton BL2 . . . . .25 E6
  Salford M6 . . . . .81 B4
Seaford Wlk
  Manchester M9 . . . . .64 C3
  Oldham OL9 . . . . .152 B6
Seaforth Ave M46 . . . . .58 C4
Seaforth Rd BL1 . . . . .24 E5
Seaham Dr BL8 . . . . .27 C5
Seaham Wlk **5** M14 . . . . . .98 B3
Seal Rd SK7 . . . . .133 A2
Sealand Cl M33 . . . . .108 E2
Sealand Dr M30 . . . . .95 A8
Sealand Ho M25 . . . . .63 C5
Sealand Rd M23 . . . . .108 F2
Sealand Way **2** SK9 . . . . .131 D4
Seale Ave M34 . . . . .100 D7
Sealey Wlk M40 . . . . .160 E4

Seaman Way WN2 . . . . .56 A6
Seamon's Dr WA14 . . . . . .119 A6
Seamon's Rd WA14 . . . . . .119 A6
Seamons Wlk WA14 . . . . . .119 B5
Searby Rd M18 . . . . .99 B4
Searness Rd M24 . . . . .46 D2
Seascale Ave M11 . . . . .83 B3
Seascale Cres WN1 . . . . . . .37 C3
Seascales Wlk **6** M24 . . . .46 E2
Seathwaite M38 . . . . .77 A7
Seathwaite Cl M29 . . . . .77 A6
Seathwaite Rd BL4 . . . . . . .59 F7
Seathwaite Wlk M18 . . . . .165 C5
Seatoller Ct OL2 . . . . .48 E4
Seatoller Dr M24 . . . . .46 C1
Seatoller Pl WN5 . . . . .54 B7
Seaton Cl SK7 . . . . .124 D1
Seaton Mews OL7 . . . . .84 F4
Seaton Rd BL1 . . . . .142 C2
Seaton Way M14 . . . . .98 A4
Sebastopol Wlk **2** M4 . . .159 C2
Second Ave Atherton M46 . .58 D4
  Bolton BL1 . . . . .144 B7
  Bury BL9 . . . . .28 D4
  Droylsden M11 . . . . .83 D2
  Little Lever BL3 . . . . .42 F4
  Mossley SK15 . . . . .86 E5
  Oldham OL8 . . . . .66 D1
  Poynton SK12 . . . . .133 D1
  Stretford M17 . . . . .96 D5
  Swinton M27 . . . . .79 D5
  Tyldesley M29 . . . . .77 B4
  Wigan WN6 . . . . .37 A2
Second St BL1 . . . . .23 F4
Section St **6** BL3 . . . . . . .145 F6
Sedan Cl M5 . . . . .81 A1
Sedburgh Cl M33 . . . . .107 D3
Sedbury Cl M23 . . . . .108 F1
Seddon Ave
  Manchester M18 . . . . .99 D6
  Radcliffe BL9,M26 . . . . . . .44 D5
Seddon Cl M46 . . . . .58 C3
Seddon Gdns M26 . . . . .61 A8
Seddon House Dr WN6 . . . .36 E3
Seddon La M26 . . . . .61 A8
Seddon Rd M16 . . . . .161 C1
Seddon St Little Lever BL3 . .43 B3
  Manchester M12 . . . . .99 B2
  Radcliffe M26 . . . . .44 A3
  Walkden M38 . . . . .59 F5
  Westhoughton BL5 . . . . . . .39 E3
Seddons Ave BL8 . . . . .44 A8
Sedge Cl SK5 . . . . .112 A8
Sedgeborough Rd M16 . . . .97 E3
Sedgefield Cl M5,M6 . . . . . .81 A2
Sedgefield Dr Bolton BL1 . .142 B3
  Wigan WN6 . . . . .36 E3
Sedgefield Pk **1** OL4 . . . . .67 D6
Sedgefield Rd M26 . . . . . . .62 A8
Sedgefield Wlk **8** M23 . . .108 F2
Sedgeford Cl SK9 . . . . .131 D1
Sedgeford Rd M40 . . . . . . .157 D5
Sedgemoor Cl SK8 . . . . . . .123 B2
Sedgemoor Vale BL2 . . . . . .25 F2
Sedgemoor Way OL1 . . . . .153 E7
Sedgley Ave
  Manchester M25 . . . . .63 C2
  Prestwich M25 . . . . .62 F5
  Rochdale OL16 . . . . .31 B4
Sedgley Cl M24 . . . . .65 C7
Sedgley Dr BL5 . . . . .57 E5
Sedgley Park
  Com Prim Sch M25 . . . . . .63 D2
Sedgley Park Rd M25 . . . . .63 C2
Sedgley Park Trad Est
  M25 . . . . .63 B1
Sedgley Rd M8 . . . . .156 A8
Sedgley St M24 . . . . .65 C7
Sedgwick Cl M46 . . . . .58 E3
Sedwyn St **7** WN1 . . . . . . .37 E1
Seed St BL1 . . . . .144 C7
Seedfield Rd BL9 . . . . .27 F5
Seedley Ave M38 . . . . .60 B4
Seedley Park Rd M6 . . . . . .154 E2
Seedley Prim Sch M6 . . . . .154 E2
Seedley Rd M6 . . . . .154 F3
Seedley St M14 . . . . .98 B3
Seedley Terr M6 . . . . .154 E3
Seedley View Rd M6 . . . . . .154 E2
Seel St M5 . . . . .68 B1
Sefton Ave Atherton M46 . . .58 C5
  Orrell WN5 . . . . .53 D5
Sefton Cl Manchester M13 .163 B6
  Middleton M24 . . . . .64 E8
  Orrell WN5 . . . . .53 D5
Sefton Cres M33 . . . . .108 B6
Sefton Ct **8** BL1 . . . . . . .145 E8
Sefton Dr Bury BL9 . . . . . . .28 A6
  Eccles M28 . . . . .79 A6
  Handforth SK9 . . . . .131 C2
  Swinton M27 . . . . .79 D6
Sefton Fold Dr WN5 . . . . . .71 D5
Sefton Fold Gdns WN5 . . . .71 D5
Sefton La BL6 . . . . .22 D1
Sefton Rd Ashton-in-M WN4 .73 D5
  Bolton BL1 . . . . .142 B2
  Manchester M21 . . . . . . .109 B8
  Middleton M24 . . . . .64 E8
  Orrell WN5 . . . . .53 D5
  Sale M33 . . . . .108 B5
  Swinton M27 . . . . .61 F1
  Wigan WN3 . . . . .54 F4
Sefton St Bury BL9 . . . . . . .27 F6
  Glossop SK13 . . . . .116 C8
  Heywood OL10 . . . . .29 E1
  Leigh WN7 . . . . .75 F5
  Manchester M8 . . . . .156 A8
  Oldham OL1 . . . . .66 B2

Sefton St continued
  Radcliffe M26 . . . . .44 C1
  Rochdale OL16 . . . . .139 F5
  Whitefield M45 . . . . .62 F7
Sefton View WN5 . . . . .53 D5
Selborne Rd M21 . . . . .97 B1
Selborne Cl Bolton BL5 . . . .40 A1
  Reddish SK5 . . . . .99 E2
Selbourne St WN7 . . . . .75 F7
Selby Ave Chadderton OL9 . .47 F1
  Whitefield M45 . . . . .44 F2
Selby Cl Milnrow OL16 . . . . .31 E6
  Poynton SK12 . . . . .133 D5
  Radcliffe BL9 . . . . .44 D5
  Stretford M32 . . . . .96 A3
Selby Dr Salford M6 . . . . . . .80 B3
  Urmston M41 . . . . .94 F5
  Urmston M41 . . . . .95 A5
  Wigan WN3 . . . . .54 C4
Selby Gdns SK8 . . . . .132 C6
Selby Rd Middleton M24 . . . .46 F3
  Stretford M32 . . . . .96 A3
Selby St Manchester M11 . .165 A8
  Reddish SK4 . . . . .169 D4
  Rochdale OL16 . . . . .31 B8
Selby Wlk BL8 . . . . .26 F1
Selden St OL8 . . . . .153 D5
Selham Wlk M13 . . . . .163 C7
Selhurst Ave M11 . . . . .83 C2
Selkirk Ave Garswood WN4 . .72 D4
  Oldham OL8 . . . . .66 D4
Selkirk Gr WN5 . . . . .54 C8
Selkirk Pl OL10 . . . . .29 A1
Selkirk Rd Bolton BL1 . . . . .24 D5
  Oldham OL9 . . . . .66 A4
Sellars Sq M43 . . . . .100 A8
Sellers Way OL9 . . . . .66 A3
Selsby Ave M30 . . . . .79 B2
Selsey Ave Cheadle SK3 . . .122 F7
  Sale M33 . . . . .107 F3
Selsey Dr M20 . . . . .122 C8
Selside WN3 . . . . .55 B2
Selside Wlk M14 . . . . .110 C8
Selstead Rd M22 . . . . .121 C1
Selston Rd M9 . . . . .64 B4
Selwood Wlk **8** M9 . . . . . .157 D7
Selworth Ave M33 . . . . . . .108 E4
Selworth Cl **5** WA15 . . . . .119 E6
Selworthy Rd M16 . . . . .97 E4
Selwyn Ave
  Manchester M9 . . . . .157 D8
  Manchester M9 . . . . .64 D1
Selwyn Cl
  Newton-le-W WA12 . . . . . .89 B5
  Oldham OL8 . . . . .153 E5
Selwyn Dr SK8 . . . . .132 C7
Selwyn St Bolton BL2 . . . . .148 A6
  Leigh WN7 . . . . .75 F6
  Oldham OL8 . . . . .153 E5
Senecar Cl WN2 . . . . .38 B2
Senior Ave M14 . . . . .110 E7
Senior Rd Eccles M30 . . . . .94 F8
  Eccles M30 . . . . .95 A8
Senior St M3 . . . . .158 E3
Sennicar La Aspull WN2 . . . .37 E6
  Wigan WN1 . . . . .37 C5
Sepal Cl SK5 . . . . .100 A1
Sephton Ave WA3 . . . . .91 E3
Sephton St WN3 . . . . .151 F6
Sepia Gr M24 . . . . .46 F1
Sequoia St M9 . . . . .157 E8
Sergeants La M45 . . . . .62 C7
Serin Cl Hazel Grove SK2 . .124 F5
  Newton-le-W WA12 . . . . . .89 C3
Service St SK3 . . . . .123 B8
Set St SK15 . . . . .85 F1
Settle Cl BL8 . . . . .26 F2
Settle St Bolton BL3 . . . . . .147 E3
  Little Lever BL3 . . . . .43 C3
Settstones La OL3 . . . . .51 D1
Seven Acres La OL12 . . . . . .13 E2
Seven Oaks WN7 . . . . .76 A6
Seven Stars Rd WN3 . . . . .150 A7
Seven Stiles Dr SK6 . . . . . .125 E7
Sevenacres OL3 . . . . .50 F5
Sevenoaks Ave
  Manchester SK4 . . . . .111 A5
  Urmston M41 . . . . .95 D4
Sevenoaks Dr Bolton BL3 . .147 E3
  Pendlebury M27 . . . . .80 A6
Sevenoaks Rd SK8 . . . . . . .122 B6
Sevenoaks Wlk **3** M13 . . .163 C5
Sevenside Trad Est M17 . . . .96 B5
Seventh Ave OL8 . . . . .66 D1
Severn Cl
  Altrincham WA14 . . . . . . .119 C6
  Billinge WN5 . . . . .71 D3
  Bury BL9 . . . . .27 F7
Severn Dr Bramhall SK7 . . .132 C6
  Hindley WN2 . . . . .57 C3
  Milnrow OL16 . . . . .32 A5
Severn Rd Ashton-in-M WN4 73 E5
  Chadderton OL9 . . . . .65 F8
  Culcheth WA3 . . . . .91 F2
  Heywood OL10 . . . . .29 A3
  Oldham OL8 . . . . .66 C1
Severn St WN7 . . . . .76 B4
Severn Way Kearsley BL4 . . .61 B6
  Reddish SK5 . . . . .111 F5
Seville St Oldham OL2 . . . . .48 E2
  Shaw OL2 . . . . .149 A5
Seville's Bldgs OL5 . . . . . . .68 C2
Sewerby St M16 . . . . .97 F4
Sexa St M11 . . . . .99 D8
Sexton St Heywood OL10 . . .29 C2
  Tintwistle SK13 . . . . .103 F7

Sca-Sha 247

Seymour Ave M11 . . . . .83 D2
Seymour Cl M16 . . . . .161 C5
Seymour Ct
  Manchester M7 . . . . .155 F8
  Manchester SK4 . . . . .110 E2
  2 Radcliffe M26 . . . . . . .44 B3
Seymour Dr BL2 . . . . .25 C6
Seymour Gr
  Altrincham WA15 . . . . . . .120 A5
  Farnworth BL4 . . . . .42 A1
  Manchester M16 . . . . .97 B4
  Marple SK6 . . . . .125 E6
  Rochdale OL16 . . . . .31 B3
  Sale M33 . . . . .108 B4
Seymour Ho **16** SK9 . . . . .131 E1
Seymour Park Jun Sch
  M16 . . . . .97 B4
Seymour Park Prim Sch
  M16 . . . . .97 B4
Seymour Rd Bolton BL1 . . .143 F3
  Cheadle SK8 . . . . .132 A8
  Manchester M7,M8 . . . . . .63 F1
  Stockport SK2 . . . . .124 B5
Seymour Rd S M11 . . . . . . .83 D2
Seymour Road Inf Sch
  M11 . . . . .83 D1
Seymour Road Jun Sch
  M11 . . . . .83 D1
Seymour St Bolton BL2 . . . .25 C4
  Denton M34 . . . . .100 D4
  Heywood OL10 . . . . .29 C5
  Manchester M18 . . . . .99 D6
  Radcliffe M26 . . . . .44 B3
Seymour Wlk **4** M26 . . . . .44 B3
Shackleton Ct M40 . . . . . . .83 C4
Shackleton Gr BL1 . . . . .23 E2
Shackleton St M30 . . . . . . .79 C3
Shackliffe Rd M40 . . . . .65 B2
Shaddock Ave OL12 . . . . . . .13 F1
Shade Ave OL4 . . . . .67 F5
Shade Terr SK6 . . . . .134 F7
Shadowmoss Rd M22 . . . .130 E8
Shadows La OL3 . . . . .68 E4
Shadows Mews OL5 . . . . . . .68 E4
Shadwell Gr WN7 . . . . .75 C8
Shadwell St E OL10 . . . . . . .29 E3
Shadwell St W OL10 . . . . . .29 D3
Shadworth Cl OL5 . . . . .68 E4
Shady La Altrincham M23 . .120 D7
  Bolton BL7 . . . . .25 B7
Shady Oak Rd SK2 . . . . . . .124 F6
Shaftesbury Ave
  Altrincham M23,WA15 . . . .120 C6
  Bramhall SK8 . . . . .123 C1
  Eccles M30 . . . . .95 C8
  Horwich BL6 . . . . .39 F8
  Littleborough OL15 . . . . . .15 F3
Shaftesbury Cl BL6 . . . . . . .39 F8
Shaftesbury Dr OL12 . . . . . .15 D6
Shaftesbury Gdns M41 . . . . .94 D2
Shaftesbury Ho **4** M6 . . .154 F3
Shaftesbury Rd
  Cheadle SK3 . . . . .123 B6
  Manchester M8 . . . . .156 A7
  Swinton M27 . . . . .79 F7
Shafton Wlk **22** M40 . . . . .65 D2
Shaftsbury Cl **20** BL1 . . . .143 E1
Shaftsbury Ct **1** WA15 . . .120 A5
Shaftsbury Dr OL10 . . . . . . .46 C8
Shaftsbury Rd WN5 . . . . . . .54 A8
Shaftsbury St WN6 . . . . . . .36 F3
Shakerley CE Prim Sch
  M29 . . . . .59 A2
Shakerley La M29 . . . . .58 F4
Shakerley Rd M29 . . . . .58 F1
Shakespeare Ave Bury BL9 .44 F6
  Denton M34 . . . . .112 F8
  Radcliffe M26 . . . . .43 E4
  Stalybridge SK15 . . . . .86 E4
Shakespeare Cl OL15 . . . . . .6 C1
Shakespeare Cres
  Droylsden M43 . . . . .84 A2
  Eccles M30 . . . . .79 D2
Shakespeare Dr SK8 . . . . . .122 F6
Shakespeare Gr WN3 . . . . . .55 A4
Shakespeare Rd
  Bredbury SK6 . . . . .112 F2
  Droylsden M43 . . . . .84 A2
  Oldham OL1 . . . . .49 C2
  Prestwich M25 . . . . .62 F3
  Swinton M27 . . . . .79 E8
Shakespeare Wlk M13 . . . .163 C6
Shakleton Ave **19** M9 . . . .65 A3
Shalbourne Rd M28 . . . . . . .60 C3
Shaldon Dr M40 . . . . .83 E4
Shalfleet Cl BL2 . . . . .25 E5
Shalford Dr M22 . . . . .130 D8
Shandon Ave M22 . . . . . . .109 D1
Shanklin Ave M41 . . . . .95 C2
Shanklin Cl Denton M34 . . .113 B8
  Manchester M21 . . . . .97 A1
Shanklin Ho M21 . . . . .97 A1
Shanklin Wlk BL3 . . . . .148 C5
Shanley Ct OL9 . . . . .152 B8
Shannon Cl OL10 . . . . .29 A3
Shannon Rd M22 . . . . .121 E4
Shap Ave WA15 . . . . .120 D5
Shap Cres M28 . . . . .60 F1
Shap Dr M28 . . . . .60 F1
Shap Gate WN5 . . . . .54 B7
Shapwick Cl **6** M9 . . . . . .157 D8
Sharcott Wlk **3** M16 . . . . .97 F4
Shardlow Cl M40 . . . . .160 D4
Shared St WN1 . . . . .151 D7

Shargate Cl SK9 ....131 C1
Sharman St BL3 ....148 B5
Sharnbrook Wlk
 9 Bolton BL2 ....25 B1
 4 Manchester M8 ....63 E2
Sharnford Cl M12 ......165 A6
Sharnford Sq M12 ......165 A6
Sharon Ave OL4 ....68 E5
Sharon Cl OL7 ....84 E1
Sharon Sq WN2 ....73 F8
Sharp St Bury BL8 ......27 B4
 Ince-in-M WN3 ....151 E6
 Manchester M4 ....159 B3
 Middleton M24 ....65 A8
 Prestwich M25 ....63 A4
 Walkden M28 ....60 C3
Sharples Ave BL1 ....24 E6
Sharples Com Prim Sch
 BL1 ....25 A5
Sharples Com Sec Sch
 BL1 ....24 F5
Sharples Dr BL8 ....27 A3
Sharples Gn BL7 ....9 D6
Sharples Hall **9** BL1 ...24 F6
Sharples Hall Dr BL1 ...24 F6
Sharples Hall Fold BL1 ..24 F5
Sharples Hall Mews BL1 ..24 F6
Sharples Hall St OL4 ....67 D8
Sharples Mdw BL7 ....9 D6
Sharples Pk BL1 ....143 D4
Sharples St SK4 ....169 E3
Sharraw Wlk M9 ....157 E7
Sharrington Dr M23 ....120 E6
Sharrow Wlk M9 ....157 D7
Sharston Ind Area M22 ..121 E7
Sharston Rd M22 ......121 E7
Shaving La M28 ....60 D1
Shaw & Crompton Sta
 OL2 ....149 C6
Shaw Ave SK14 ....113 F8
Shaw Hall Ave SK14 ....102 B5
Shaw Hall Bank Rd OL3 ..68 F5
Shaw Hall Cl OL3 ....68 F5
Shaw Head Dr M35 ......83 F6
Shaw Heath SK2,SK3 ...170 E7
Shaw Ho Atherton M46 ..58 D4
 Farnworth BL4 ....60 D7
Shaw La Hadfield SK13 ..171 F3
 Littleborough OL15,OL16 ..16 A1
Shaw Moor Ave SK15 ....86 C1
Shaw Rd Horwich BL6 ...22 B5
 Manchester SK4 ......168 B4
 Newhey OL16 ....32 B3
 Oldham OL1 ....67 A8
 Royton OL16 ....31 B1
 Royton OL2 ....48 F4
Shaw Rd S SK3 ....170 E6
Shaw St Ashton-in-M WN4 ..73 B5
 Ashton-u-L OL6 ....85 D3
 Bolton BL3 ....145 E5
 Bury BL9 ....141 B3
 Culcheth WA3 ....92 A3
 Farnworth BL4 ....42 D2
 Glossop SK13 ....116 C8
 Manchester M3 ....158 F3
 Mottram-in-L SK14 ....103 A4
 Oldham OL1 ....153 F8
 Oldham OL3 ....69 B6
 Oldham OL4 ....68 A6
 Rochdale OL12 ....15 B2
 Royton OL2 ....48 E4
 Wigan WN1 ....37 C1
Shaw Terr **5** SK16 ....166 C1
Shaw The SK13 ....171 F3
Shaw's Rd WA14 ....119 D4
Shawbrook Ave M28 ....78 B8
Shawbrook Rd M19 ....111 A5
Shawbury Cl BL6 ....21 D1
Shawbury Gr M33 ......107 F2
Shawbury Rd M23 .....121 B4
Shawbury St M24 ....65 C7
Shawclough Cl OL12 ....14 D3
Shawclough
 Com Prim Sch OL12 ....14 E3
Shawclough Dr OL12 ....14 D3
Shawclough Rd OL12 ...14 C3
Shawclough Way OL12 ..14 D3
Shawcroft Cl OL2 .....149 A5
Shawcross Fold SK1 ...169 F2
Shawcross La M22 .....121 E8
Shawcross St Hyde SK14 ..113 F8
 Salford M6 ....154 F1
 Stockport SK1 ....124 A8
Shawdene Rd M22 .....121 D8
Shawe Hall Ave M41 ...107 A8
Shawe Hall Cres M41 ..107 A8
Shawe Rd M41 ....95 A2
Shawe View M41 ....95 A2
Shawes Dr PR6 ....21 C7
Shawfield Cl M14 ......110 A8
Shawfield Ct SK2 .....124 D5
Shawfield La Rochdale OL12 13 F2
 Rochdale OL12 ....14 A2
Shawfield Rd SK13 ....171 F3
Shawfields SK15 ....86 D3
Shawfold OL2 ....149 B7
Shawford Cres M40 ....65 C2
Shawford Rd M40 ......65 C2
Shawgreen Cl M15 ....162 D6
Shawgrove Sch M20 ...109 F5
Shawheath Cl M15 ....162 D6
Shawhill Wlk M40 ....160 E2
Shawlea Ave M19 .....110 E6
Shaws Fold SK9 ....130 F3
Shaws La OL3 ....69 C7

Shay Ave WA15 ....120 E1
Shay La WA15 ....120 D1
Shayfield Ave
 Chadderton OL9 ....65 E8
 Wythenshawe M22 ....121 D5
Shayfield Dr M22 .....121 D6
Shayfield Rd M22 .....121 D5
Sheader Dr M5 ....80 C2
Sheaf Field Wlk M26 ...44 A4
Sheard Ave OL6 ....85 D6
Sheardhall Ave SK12 ..135 E5
Shearer Way M6,M27 ...80 E7
Shearing Ave OL12 .....13 F1
Shearsby Cl M15 ......162 E5
Shearwater Ave M29 ...77 A8
Shearwater Dr
 Walkden M28 ....60 C3
 Westhoughton BL5 .....57 D6
Shearwater Gdns M30 ..95 A8
Shearwater Rd SK2 ...125 A5
Shed St OL12 ....4 D1
Sheddings The BL3 .....42 A4
Sheep Gap OL12 ....14 B1
Sheep Gate Dr BL8 ....26 E5
Sheepfoot La
 Manchester M25,M8 ...63 C3
 Oldham OL1 ....48 D1
Sheerness St M18 ......99 D5
Sheffield Rd Glossop SK13 104 F1
 Hyde SK14 ....102 A3
 Hyde SK14 ....167 F4
Sheffield St
 Manchester M1 ....163 C8
 Stockport SK4 ....169 E3
Shefford Cl M11 ......164 F8
Shefford Cres WN3 .....54 C2
Sheiling Ct WA14 .....119 C4
Sheilings The WA3 .....90 F8
Shelbourne Ave BL1 ...142 B1
Shelden Mews SK13 ...171 D1
Shelderton Cl **5** M40 ..83 A7
Sheldon Ave Standish WN6 .19 E2
 Urmston M41 ....95 B2
Sheldon Cl Farnworth BL4 .42 B2
 8 Gamesley SK13 ....171 D1
 Partington M31 ....105 E3
Sheldon Ct OL7 ....85 B5
Sheldon Fold **9** SK13 ..171 D1
Sheldon Pl **3** SK13 ...171 D1
Sheldon Rd Disley SK12 134 C2
 Hazel Grove SK7 .....133 E8
Sheldon St M11 ....83 B2
Sheldrake Cl SK16 ....101 E7
Sheldrake Rd WA14 ...119 B8
Sheldwich Cl WN7 .....75 D7
Shelfield OL11 ....13 F1
Shelfield Cl OL11 ......13 F1
Shelfield La OL11 ......13 F1
Shelford Ave M18 ......99 B4
Shellbrook Gr **3** SK9 ..131 D1
Shelley Ave M24 ....47 B3
Shelley Cl PR7 ....19 F8
Shelley Ct SK8 ....123 A1
 Wigan WN5 ....54 A6
Shelley Dr Abram WN2 ..56 B1
 Dukinfield SK14 ......101 D5
 Stalybridge SK15 ......86 E4
Shelley Rd **9** Oldham OL1 ..49 C1
 Oldham OL9 ....65 F3
 Prestwich M25 ....62 F3
 Reddish SK5 ....99 E1
 Swinton M27 ....79 E8
 Walkden M38 ....60 A5
Shelley Rise SK16 .....102 B7
Shelley St Failsworth M40 .83 C8
 Leigh WN7 ....75 D7
Shelley Way M34 .....112 F8
Shelley Wlk Atherton M46 .58 D5
 9 Bolton BL1 ....143 D1
Shellingford Cl WN6 ...35 D7
Shelmerdine Cl **1** SK14 .102 F2
Shelmerdine Gdns M6 ..80 C4
Shelton Ave M33 ......107 D4
Shena Simon Coll M1 ..163 A8
Shenfield Wlk M40 ....160 D3
Shenhurst Cl SK9 .....136 E4
Shenton Park Ave M33 ..107 C2
Shenton St SK14 ......101 C4
Shentonfield Rd M22 ..121 E6
Shepherd Cross St
 Ind Est BL1 ....143 D2
Shepherd Ct **1** OL16 ...31 B6
Shepherd St Bury BL8 ..26 F8
 Bury BL9 ....140 F1
 3 Bury BL9 ....141 A1
 Heywood OL10 ....29 C2
 Manchester M9 ....64 E1
 Rochdale OL11 ....13 D1
 Rochdale OL12 ....139 F8
 Royton OL2 ....48 E3
 Royton OL2 ....48 E4
Shepherd Wlk M34 ....112 F8
Shepherd's Brow WA14 .119 A3
Shepherd's Dr BL6 .....23 A3
Shepherds Cl Blackrod BL6 .21 C3
 Ramsbottom BL8 ....10 F1
Shepherds Gn OL3 .....69 D5
Shepherds Way OL16 ...31 F5
Shepley Ave BL3 .....144 C5
Shepley Cl
 2 Dukinfield SK16 ...101 D8
 Hazel Grove SK7 .....133 D8
Shepley Dr SK7 ....124 E1
Shepley La Marple SK6 .125 F3
 Marple SK6 ....125 F4

Shepley North Ind Est
 M34 ....101 A7
Shepley Rd M34,SK16 ..100 F6
Shepley South Ind Est
 M34 ....101 A6
Shepley St Dukinfield M34 .100 F7
 Failsworth M35 ....66 A1
 Glossop SK13 ....104 F2
 Hadfield SK13 ....171 E3
 Hyde SK14 ....167 E2
 Manchester M1 ....163 B8
 4 Oldham OL4 ....67 E6
 11 Stalybridge SK15 ...86 A2
Shepton Ave M40 ......56 A1
Shepton Cl BL1 ....24 D7
Shepton Dr M23 ......121 A2
Sheraton Cl WN5 ......36 B1
Sheraton Rd OL8 ......66 E4
Sherborne Ave WN2 ...57 A5
Sherborne Rd
 Cheadle SK3 ....123 A7
 Middleton M24 ....47 A3
 Urmston M41 ....95 E3
 Wigan WN5 ....54 A8
Sherborne St M3,M8 ...158 F4
Sherborne St W M3,M7 .158 F4
Sherborne Trad Est M8 ..156 A5
Sherbourne Cl
 Bramhall SK8 ....132 B6
 Oldham OL8 ....67 C4
 Radcliffe M26 ....43 D5
Sherbourne Ct M25 ....63 A4
Sherbourne Dr OL10 ...29 A3
Sherbourne Pl WN3 ...151 E5
Sherbourne Rd BL1 ...142 A1
Sherbourne St M25 ....63 A4
Sherbrook Cl M33 ....107 F3
Sherbrook Rise SK9 ..137 C6
Sherbrooke Ave OL3 ...51 C1
Sherbrooke Rd SK12 ..135 D6
Sherdley Cl M8 ....64 A1
Sherdley Rd M8 ....64 A1
Sherford Cl SK7 ......124 A2
Sheri Dr WA12 ....89 E2
Sheridan Ave WA3 .....90 D7
Sheridan Ct M40 .....157 E5
Sheridan Way
 Chadderton OL9 ....65 E8
 Denton M34 ....112 F8
Sheriff St Bolton BL2 ..25 B1
 Milnrow OL16 ....32 A5
 Rochdale OL12 ....139 E8
 Rochdale OL12 ....14 E1
Sheriffs Dr M29 ....59 D1
Sheringham Dr Bury BL8 .27 D5
 Hyde SK14 ....102 A3
 Swinton M27 ....79 F6
Sheringham Pl BL3 ...145 D5
Sheringham Rd M14 ..110 D7
Sherlock St M14 ......110 D7
Sherratt St M4 ....159 B2
Sherrington St M12 ...99 A3
Sherway Dr WA15 ....120 C6
Sherwell Rd M9 ....64 B3
Sherwin Way OL11 .....30 D1
Sherwood Ave
 Ashton-in-M WN4 .....73 C4
 Bury BL8 ....43 F8
 Cheadle SK8 ....122 F2
 Droylsden M43 ....84 C2
 Manchester M14 .....110 C8
 Manchester M7 ....81 B7
 Sale M33 ....108 D5
 Stockport SK4 ....168 A1
 Tyldesley M29 ....77 A6
Sherwood Bsns Pk OL11 ..30 D2
Sherwood Cl
 Ashton-u-L OL6 ....85 C7
 Bury BL8 ....26 C7
 Marple SK6 ....125 F4
 Salford M5 ....154 D3
Sherwood Cres
 Platt Bridge WN2 ......56 A2
 Wigan WN5 ....54 D7
Sherwood Dr
 Pendlebury M27 ....80 B7
 Wigan WN5 ....54 D6
Sherwood Fold SK13 ..115 D7
Sherwood Gr Leigh WN7 .76 B3
 Wigan WN5 ....54 D6
Sherwood Ind Pk OL11 ..30 D2
Sherwood Rd
 Reddish M34 ....100 B3
 Romiley SK6 ....113 B5
Sherwood St Bolton BL1 .143 F3
 Manchester M14 .....110 C8
 Oldham OL1 ....153 D8
 Rochdale OL11 ....30 D2
Sherwood Way OL2 ....48 E8
Shetland Rd M40 .....160 D3
Shetland Way
 Radcliffe M26 ....44 A5
 Urmston M41 ....95 D5
Shevington
 Com Prim Sch WN6 ....35 F6
Shevington Gdns M23 .109 B1
Shevington High Sch
 WN6 ....36 B7
Shevington La WN6 ....35 F8
Shevington Moor WN6 ..19 A2
Shevington Vale Prim Sch
 WN6 ....35 E8
Shiel St M28 ....60 D3
Shield Cl OL8 ....153 E6
Shield Dr M28 ....79 C8
Shield St SK3 ....170 E8
Shieldborn Dr M9 ....157 E7

Shields View M5 ......161 B7
Shiers Dr SK8 ....122 E4
Shiffnall St BL2 ......148 A6
Shildon Cl WN2 ....37 F2
Shilford Dr M4 ....159 C3
Shillingford Rd BL4 ...60 C8
Shillingstone Cl BL2 ..26 A3
Shillington Cl **1** M28 ..59 F3
Shiloh La OL1 ....50 B3
Shiloh Rd SK6 ....127 B6
Shilton Gdns BL3 ....145 E5
Shilton St BL0 ....138 B5
Shilton Wlk **21** M40 ...65 D2
Ship Canal Ho M15 ...162 E8
Ship La OL3,OL4 ....50 B5
Ship Yd WN1 ....150 C8
Shipgates BL1 ....145 F7
Shipham Cl WN7 ......75 D8
Shipla Cl OL9 ....153 E7
Shipley Ave M6 ....80 C3
Shipley View M14 .....94 F5
Shipper Bottom La BL0 ..11 D5
Shippey St M14 ......110 D7
Shipston Cl BL3 ....27 B3
Shipton St BL1 ....142 B1
Shirburn **8** OL11 ....139 E6
Shire Gdns M26 ....43 D4
Shire Hill Hospl SK13 ..104 E3
Shire Way SK13 ......104 E3
Shirebrook Dr
 Glossop SK13 ....116 F8
 Radcliffe M26 ....44 B4
Shireburn Ave BL2 ...148 C8
Shiredale Cl SK8 .....123 B4
Shiredale Dr M9 .....157 D7
Shiregreen M40 ......156 C5
Shirehills M25 ....63 D3
Shireoak Rd M20 .....110 D7
Shires Cl WN2 ....56 E4
Shires The Droylsden M43 .84 D3
 Radcliffe M26 ....44 A5
Shirley Ave Droylsden M34 100 C8
 Droylsden M34 ....99 F3
 Dukinfield SK14 ......101 D5
 Eccles M30 ....95 C8
 Failsworth OL9 ....65 E2
 Gatley SK8 ....131 C6
 Manchester M7 ....81 A7
 Marple SK6 ....125 E6
 Pendlebury M27 ....80 C7
 Stretford M32 ....96 F3
Shirley Cl SK7 ....124 C2
Shirley Ct M33 ....108 C4
Shirley Gr SK3 ....170 E6
Shirley Rd M8 ....156 A7
Shirley St OL11 ....30 C2
Shoecroft Ave M34 ...100 E2
Shoemaker Gdns WN2 ..38 C5
Sholver Hill Cl OL1 ....49 E4
Sholver La OL1 ....49 D4
Shone Ave M22 ......121 F2
Shore Ave OL2 ....32 C1
Shore Fold OL15 ....15 F6
Shore Hill OL15 ....16 C6
Shore Lea OL15 ....15 F6
Shore Mount OL15 ....15 F6
Shore Rd OL15 ....15 F7
Shore St Milnrow OL16 ..31 F6
 Oldham OL1 ....67 A7
Shoreditch Cl SK4 ...111 B5
Shorefield Cl OL16 ....31 F7
Shorefield Mount BL7 ..24 E8
Shoreham Cl **5** M16 ..97 E4
Shoreham Wlk OL9 ...152 A6
Shoreswood BL1 ......24 D5
Shorland St M27 ......79 C7
Shorrocks St BL8 .....26 F3
Short Ave M43 ....99 F8
Short St Bacup OL13 ...3 B8
 Golborne WA3 ....74 B1
 Hazel Grove SK7 .....124 D3
 Heywood OL10 ....29 B1
 Manchester M1 ....159 A1
 Manchester M7 ....158 E3
 Stockport SK4 ....169 E3
 3 Tyldesley M46 ......58 F1
 12 Wigan WN5 ....54 B6
Short St E SK4 ....169 E3
Shortcroft St M15 ....162 F7
Shortland Cres M19 ..110 D3
Shortland Pl WN2 .....75 A8
Shortlands Ave BL9 ...44 F8
Shortwood Cl **17** M40 .83 A6
Shottery Wlks SK6 ...112 F3
Shotton Wlk **4** M14 ..98 C3
Shrewsbury Cl WN2 ...56 F6
Shrewsbury St M16 ..162 D5
Shrewsbury Gdns SK8 .132 C5
Shrewsbury Rd
 Bolton BL1 ....144 B8
 Droylsden M43 ....84 C3
 Prestwich M25 ....63 A3
 Sale M33 ....108 A2
Shrewsbury St
 Glossop SK13 ....104 C1
 Manchester M16 .....162 D5
 Oldham OL4 ....67 A6
Shrewsbury Way **7** M34 .101 A1
Shrigley Cl SK9 ......131 D1
Shrigley Rd SK10,SK12 .134 C2
Shrigley Rd N SK12 ..134 D3
Shrivenham Wlk M23 ..120 F7
Shropshire Ave SK5 ..112 C6
Shropshire Dr SK13 ..116 F8
Shropshire Rd M35 ...84 A6
Shropshire Sq M12 ...164 F6
Shrowbridge Wlk M12 .165 A6
Shrub St BL3 ....146 C2

Shudehill M4 ....159 A4
Shudehill Rd M28 ......60 A1
Shurdington Rd BL5,M46 .58 F6
Shurmer St BL3 ......146 C4
Shutt La OL3 ....50 F2
Shuttle Hillock Rd WN2 ..74 F7
Shuttle St **6** Eccles M30 ..79 F2
 Hindley WN2 ....56 E6
 Radcliffe M26 ....44 C1
 Tyldesley M29 ....59 A1
Shuttleworth Cl M21 ..109 A4
Shutts La SK15 ......102 D8
Siam St M11 ....164 F8
Sibley Ave WN4 ....73 D4
Sibley Rd SK4 ....168 B3
Sibley St M18 ....99 D5
Siblies Wlk **7** M22 ..121 B1
Sibson Ct **3** M21 ....97 A1
Sibson Rd Manchester M21 .97 A1
 Sale M33 ....108 B3
Sickle St
 Manchester M1,M2 ...159 A1
 Oldham OL4 ....67 A5
Sidbrook St WN2 ......56 C5
Sidbury Rd M21 ......109 C8
Sidcup Rd M23 ......120 F5
Siddal Moor Sports Coll
 OL10 ....46 D7
Siddall St Heywood OL10 ..46 E8
 Manchester M12 ....99 A2
 Oldham OL1 ....153 F8
 2 Radcliffe M26 ....44 A4
 Shaw OL2 ....149 B7
Siddeley St WN7 ......75 D5
Siddington Ave
 Manchester M20 .....110 A7
 Stockport SK3 ....170 D6
Siddington Rd
 Handforth SK9 ....131 D5
 Poynton SK12 ....133 F2
Siddow Comm WN7 ...76 A4
Side Ave WA14 ......119 C1
Side St Droylsden M11 ..83 B2
 Oldham OL8 ....66 C2
Sidebotham St SK6 ...112 F4
Sidebottom St
 Droylsden M43 ....83 F1
 Oldham OL4 ....67 E8
 Stalybridge SK15 ......86 A2
Sidford Cl BL3 ....42 D5
Siding St OL13 ....3 C8
Sidings The Bacup OL13 ..4 B8
 Eccles M30 ....79 A5
Sidley Ave M9 ....64 F4
Sidley Pl SK14 ......167 F3
Sidley St SK14 ......167 F3
Sidmouth Ave M41 ....94 E3
Sidmouth Dr M9 ......64 D2
Sidmouth Gr Cheadle SK8 .131 F7
 Wigan WN3 ....54 E3
Sidmouth Rd M33 ....107 D5
Sidmouth St Denton M34 .100 D7
 Oldham OL9 ....152 B5
Sidney Rd M9 ....64 D1
Sidney St Bolton BL3 ..145 F5
 Leigh WN7 ....76 A5
 Manchester M1 ......163 A7
 Manchester M3 ......158 D2
 6 Manchester M3 ....158 F1
Sidwell Wlk M4 ......160 D1
Siemens Rd Irlam M44 ..105 E5
 Manchester M20 .....109 E5
Siemens St BL6 ....22 C2
Sienna Cl M44 ....105 E6
Sighthill Wlk M9 ....157 D8
Signal Cl M30 ....79 B2
Signet Wlk M8 ......156 B5
Silas St OL6 ....85 D5
Silburn Way M24,M9 ..64 D7
Silbury Wlk M8 ......155 F5
Silchester Dr M40 ....157 D6
Silchester Way BL2 ...25 E1
Silchester Wlk **3** OL1 .153 F7
Silcock St WA3 ....74 A1
Silfield Cl M11 ....160 E1
Silk Mill Rd SK9 .....137 E1
Silk St Eccles M30 ....79 F1
 Failsworth M40 ....83 C6
 Glossop SK13 ....104 E1
 Leigh WN7 ....75 F5
 Manchester M3 ....158 D3
 Manchester M4 ....159 C2
 Middleton M24 ....64 F8
 Rochdale OL11 ....30 D4
 Westhoughton BL5 .....39 E1
Silkhey Gr M28 ....60 D1
Silkin Cl M13 ....163 B7
Silkin Ct M13 ....163 B7
Silkstone St M11 .....165 C7
Sillavan Way M3 .....158 E2
Sillitoe Dr WN6 ....37 A1
Silsbury Gr WN6 ......37 A8
Silsden Ave Golborne WA3 .91 B8
 Manchester M9 ....64 E5
Silsden Wlk M7 ....80 F8
Silton St M9 ....157 F8
Silver Birch Gr
 Ashton-in-M WN4 .....73 A5
 Pendlebury M27 ....80 B6
Silver Birch Mews SK16 .101 E7
Silver Cl SK16 ....101 B7
Silver Ct **3** M45 .....44 E1
Silver Hill OL16 ....31 F7
Silver Hill Rd SK14 ...167 E1
Silver Jubilee Wlk **4** M4 159 B2
Silver Spring SK14 ...113 F8
Silver St Bury BL9 ...140 E2
 Irlam M44 ....94 B4

Silver St *continued*
Manchester M1 .... 159 A1
Manchester M1 .... 163 A8
Oldham OL1 .... 153 E6
5 Platt Bridge WN2 .... 56 B2
Ramsbottom BL0 .... 138 C6
Rochdale OL12 .... 139 D8
Walsden OL14 .... 6 A7
Whitefield M45 .... 44 E1
Silver Terr WN1 .... 151 D7
Silverbirch Cl M33 .... 107 D2
Silverbirch Way 3 M35 .... 83 F7
Silvercroft St M15 .... 162 E7
Silverdale
Altrincham WA14 .... 119 C4
5 Bredbury SK6 .... 112 F3
Swinton M27 .... 62 A2
Wigan WN1 .... 37 C2
Silverdale Ave
Denton M34 .... 101 A2
Ince-in-M WN2 .... 56 A8
Irlam M44 .... 94 B3
Manchester M25 .... 63 E2
Oldham OL9 .... 152 A6
Walkden M38 .... 60 A5
Silverdale Cl SK6 .... 134 E8
Silverdale Ct WN1 .... 151 D8
Silverdale Dr Oldham OL4 .... 67 F6
Wilmslow SK9 .... 137 A4
Silverdale Prim Sch M27 .... 62 B1
Silverdale Rd Bolton BL1 .... 144 C7
Farnworth BL4 .... 42 A1
Gatley SK8 .... 122 B4
Hindley WN2 .... 56 F5
Manchester M21 .... 97 C1
Manchester SK4 .... 168 C4
Newton-le-W WA12 .... 89 B4
Wigan WN5 .... 54 B8
Silverdale St M11 .... 99 F8
Silverlea Dr M9 .... 64 C2
Silvermere OL6 .... 85 E6
Silverstone Dr M40 .... 83 D4
Silverthorne Cl 12 SK15 .... 86 A1
Silverton Cl SK14 .... 102 E2
Silverton Gr Bolton BL1 .... 143 F4
Middleton M24 .... 46 D4
Silverton Ho M6 .... 80 A3
Silverwell La BL1,BL2 .... 145 F7
Silverwell St Bolton BL1 .... 145 F7
Failsworth M40 .... 83 D5
Horwich BL6 .... 22 B4
Silverwood OL9 .... 65 E7
Silverwood Ave M21 .... 109 B8
Silvester St BL6 .... 21 D2
Silvington Way WN2 .... 38 A2
Simeon St
Manchester M4 .... 159 B3
Milnrow OL16 .... 31 F6
Walsden OL14 .... 6 A8
Simfield Cl WN6 .... 19 D1
Simister Dr BL9 .... 45 A2
Simister Gn M25 .... 63 E8
Simister La
Middleton M24,M25 .... 46 A1
Middleton M25 .... 63 E8
Simister Rd M35 .... 83 F7
Simister St 10 M9 .... 157 E8
Simm's Sq WN2 .... 38 D4
Simmondley Cty Prim Sch SK13 .... 116 A8
Simmondley Gr SK13 .... 116 A8
Simmondley La SK13 .... 116 A8
Simmondley New Rd SK13 .... 116 A7
Simms Cl M3 .... 158 D2
Simon Cl M33 .... 108 A3
Simon Freeman Cl M19,SK4 .... 111 C6
Simon La M24 .... 46 A2
Simonbury Cl BL8 .... 26 F2
Simons Cl SK13 .... 116 A7
Simons Wlk SK13 .... 116 A8
Simonsway M22,M23,SK8 .... 121 D2
Simpkin St Abram WN2 .... 56 B1
Abram WN2 .... 74 C8
Simpson Ave M27 .... 62 C2
Simpson Gr M28 .... 78 A6
Simpson Hill Cl OL10 .... 29 F3
Simpson Rd M28 .... 78 A6
Simpson Sq OL9 .... 66 C3
Simpson St Droylsden M11 .... 83 A1
Hyde SK14 .... 167 D2
Manchester M4 .... 159 B3
Oldham OL9 .... 66 B4
Wilmslow SK9 .... 136 F6
Sinclair Pl WN5 .... 54 E8
Sinclair St OL11 .... 30 D3
Sinderland La
Partington WA14 .... 106 D1
Partington WA14 .... 118 E8
Sinderland Rd
Altrincham WA14 .... 119 C8
Partington M31,WA14 .... 106 C2
Sindsley Ct M27 .... 61 D1
Sindsley Gr BL3 .... 147 E3
Sindsley Rd M27 .... 61 D2
Singapore Ave M90 .... 130 A8
Singleton Ave Bolton BL2 .... 42 F7
Horwich BL6 .... 22 C5
Singleton Cl M7 .... 63 C1
Singleton Gr BL5 .... 40 B1
Singleton Lo M7 .... 63 D1
Singleton Rd
Manchester M7,M8 .... 63 D1
Manchester SK4 .... 168 B4
Singleton St M26 .... 43 D4
Sion St M26 .... 44 A2
Sir Matt Busby Way M17 .... 96 F5
Sir Richard Fairey Rd SK4 .... 111 B7
Sirdar St M11 .... 99 F8
Sirius Pl M7 .... 158 D3
Siskin Cl Leigh WN7 .... 76 B5
Newton-le-W WA12 .... 89 C3
Siskin Rd SK2 .... 124 F5
Sisley Cl M7 .... 81 B8
Sisson St M35 .... 83 E7
Sisters' St M43 .... 100 A8
Sitch La SK22 .... 127 F3
Sittingbourne Rd WN1 .... 37 C4
Sixpools Gr 6 M28 .... 78 C8
Sixth Ave Bolton BL1 .... 144 B7
Bury BL9 .... 28 D4
Little Lever BL3 .... 42 F4
Oldham OL8 .... 66 C1
Sixth St M17 .... 96 D5
Size House Pl 7 WN7 .... 76 A4
Size St OL12 .... 4 D1
Skagen BL1 .... 143 E1
Skagen Ct BL1 .... 143 E1
Skaife Rd M33 .... 108 E4
Skarratt Cl M12 .... 164 F6
Skegness Cl BL8 .... 27 D5
Skellorn Green La SK10 .... 133 F1
Skelton Gr Bolton BL2 .... 42 F8
Manchester M13 .... 98 F2
Skelton Rd
Altrincham WA14 .... 119 E7
Stretford M32 .... 96 D3
Skelton St WN4 .... 72 F6
Skelwith Ave BL3 .... 147 F2
Skelwith Cl M41 .... 95 A4
Skerry Cl M13 .... 163 B7
Skerton Rd M16 .... 97 B4
Skiddaw Pl WN5 .... 54 C6
Skilgate Wlk 10 M40 .... 83 C6
Skip Pl M3,M4 .... 159 A3
Skipton Ave
Chadderton OL9 .... 47 F1
Failsworth M40 .... 65 D1
Hindley WN2 .... 57 A4
Skipton Cl Bury BL8 .... 26 F2
Hazel Grove SK7 .... 133 C8
Reddish SK5 .... 111 E8
Skipton Dr M41 .... 94 F5
Skipton St Bolton BL2 .... 148 C8
Oldham OL8 .... 67 B4
Skipton Wlk BL2 .... 148 C7
Skull House La WN6 .... 35 D8
Skye Cl OL10 .... 28 F1
Skye Croft SK6 .... 113 D3
Skye Rd M41 .... 95 D5
Skye Wlk M23 .... 121 A4
Skyes Cres WN3 .... 54 C1
Skyes Ct 8 OL16 .... 31 B6
Slack Fold La BL4 .... 147 D1
Slack Gate OL12 .... 14 F8
Slack Gate La OL3 .... 50 D8
Slack Hall OL4 .... 67 F8
Slack La Bolton BL2 .... 25 E7
Delph OL3 .... 50 D6
Swinton M27 .... 62 A1
Westhoughton BL5 .... 39 F3
Slack Rd M9 .... 64 D1
Slack St Hyde SK14 .... 167 F4
Rochdale OL16 .... 139 F7
Slackcote OL3 .... 50 C7
Slackcote La OL3 .... 50 C7
Slackey Brow BL4 .... 61 C6
Slackey Fold WN2 .... 57 B1
Slade Gr M13 .... 98 F3
Slade Hall Rd M12 .... 99 A2
Slade La M13,M19 .... 98 F2
Slade Mount M19 .... 110 F8
Slade St BL3 .... 43 A3
Sladen Fold OL15 .... 16 D8
Sladen St OL12 .... 14 F1
Slades View Cl OL3 .... 51 C5
Slag La Golborne WA3 .... 74 F2
Golborne WA3 .... 90 D8
Slaidburn Ave BL2 .... 42 F6
Slaidburn Cl Milnrow OL16 .... 31 F5
Wigan WN3 .... 55 A3
Slaidburn Cres WA3 .... 73 F2
Slaidburn Dr BL8 .... 26 F3
Slaithwaite Dr 5 M11 .... 83 C2
Slant Cl SK13 .... 116 E8
Slate Ave 10 M4 .... 159 C1
Slate La Ashton-u-L OL7 .... 84 E1
Droylsden M34 .... 100 C8
Droylsden OL7 .... 100 E8
Slate Wharf M15 .... 162 D7
Slateacre Rd SK14 .... 113 F7
Slatelands Ave SK13 .... 116 B8
Slatelands Rd SK13 .... 116 B8
Slater Ave BL6 .... 22 C4
Slater La Bolton BL1 .... 148 A8
Bolton BL1 .... 25 A1
Slater St Bolton BL1 .... 143 F1
Eccles M30 .... 79 B2
Failsworth M35 .... 65 F1
Farnworth BL4 .... 60 D8
Oldham OL8,OL9 .... 153 E6
Slater St N WN7 .... 75 D5
Slater Way 2 SK14 .... 102 F2
Slater's Nook 10 BL5 .... 39 E1
Slaterfield BL3 .... 145 E5
Slaunt Bank OL12 .... 13 D2
Slawson Way OL10 .... 29 F3
Sleaford Cl Bury BL8 .... 27 D5
Manchester M40 .... 160 D3
Sledbrook St WN5 .... 54 C5
Sleddale Cl SK2 .... 124 D5
Sledmere Cl Bolton BL1 .... 143 F2
Droylsden M11 .... 83 A1
Sledmoor Rd M23 .... 108 F1
Slimbridge Cl BL2 .... 26 A1
Sloane Ave OL4 .... 67 F8
Sloane St
5 Ashton-u-L OL6 .... 166 C3
Bolton BL3 .... 146 B3
Droylsden M11 .... 83 A2
Slough Ind Est M5 .... 161 C8
Smallbridge Cl 5 M28 .... 78 C8
Smallbridge Prim Sch OL12 .... 15 B3
Smallbrook La WN7 .... 57 E3
Smallbrook Rd OL2 .... 32 C1
Smalldale Ave M16 .... 97 F3
Smalley St Rochdale OL11 .... 30 C2
Standish WN6 .... 19 E1
Smallfield Dr M9 .... 157 D8
Smallridge Cl M40 .... 160 D3
Smallshaw Cl WN4 .... 73 A2
Smallshaw La OL6 .... 85 C5
Smallshaw Rd OL12 .... 14 A4
Smallshaw Sq OL6 .... 85 B5
Smallwood St M40 .... 83 C6
Smart St M12 .... 99 A3
Smeaton Cl M32 .... 96 E2
Smeaton St Horwich BL6 .... 22 C2
Manchester M8 .... 156 C6
Smedley Ave Bolton BL3 .... 42 A3
Manchester M8 .... 156 C6
Smedley La
Manchester M8 .... 156 B6
Manchester M8,M9 .... 156 B7
Smedley Rd M40,M8 .... 156 C6
Smedley St M8 .... 156 B6
Smethurst Hall Pk WN5 .... 53 C2
Smethurst Hall Rd BL9 .... 28 F4
Smethurst La
Bolton BL3,BL4 .... 146 B2
Wigan WN5 .... 54 C5
Smethurst Rd WN5 .... 53 C2
Smethurst St 7 Bury BL8 .... 27 C4
Heywood OL10 .... 29 B2
Manchester M9 .... 64 D1
Middleton M24 .... 65 D7
Wigan WN5 .... 54 C5
Smith Ave WN5 .... 54 B8
Smith Brow BL6 .... 21 C3
Smith Fold La M28 .... 60 A3
Smith Hill OL16 .... 32 A6
Smith La Ashley WA16 .... 128 E1
Bolton BL7 .... 8 F1
Smith St Adlington PR7 .... 20 F6
Ashton-u-L OL7 .... 84 F1
Aspull WN2 .... 38 C5
Atherton M46 .... 58 C3
Bury BL9 .... 141 A3
Cheadle SK8 .... 122 F6
Denton M34 .... 100 F2
Dukinfield SK14 .... 101 D5
Dukinfield SK16 .... 101 A8
7 Heywood OL10 .... 29 D2
Leigh WN7 .... 76 A5
6 Littleborough OL15 .... 16 B5
Manchester M16 .... 161 C6
Mossley OL5 .... 68 B2
Oldham OL4 .... 67 E8
Ramsbottom BL0 .... 138 B5
Rochdale OL16 .... 139 F7
Walkden M28 .... 60 D3
Smith's La WN2 .... 75 B8
Smith's Pl 11 M46 .... 58 D3
Smith's Rd BL3 .... 42 D3
Smithies Ave M24 .... 47 A2
Smithies St OL10 .... 29 E2
Smithill's Hall (Mus) BL1 .... 142 B4
Smithills Croft Rd BL1 .... 142 B3
Smithills Dean Rd BL1 .... 142 B4
Smithills Dr BL1 .... 23 F2
Smithills Hall Cl BL0 .... 138 C5
Smithills Sch BL1 .... 142 C4
Smiths Lawn SK9 .... 137 A5
Smithwood Ave WN2 .... 56 F6
Smithy Bridge Prim Sch OL15 .... 15 F3
Smithy Bridge Rd OL15,OL16 .... 15 F3
Smithy Bridge Sta OL15 .... 15 F3
Smithy Brow WN6 .... 18 C8
Smithy Cl SK13 .... 104 D1
Smithy Croft BL7 .... 24 F8
Smithy Fold Glossop SK13 .... 104 D1
Rochdale OL12 .... 14 C1
Smithy Fold Rd 3 SK14 .... 167 E1
Smithy Gn Cheadle SK8 .... 132 A8
Newhey OL16 .... 32 E4
Romiley SK6 .... 113 B5
Smithy Gr OL6 .... 166 C4
Smithy Hill BL3 .... 146 A4
Smithy La
Altrincham WA14 .... 118 D3
Flixton SK6 .... 114 F1
Hyde SK14 .... 167 E1
4 Manchester M3 .... 158 F1
Oldham OL3 .... 69 B8
Partington M31 .... 105 F3
Smithy Nook OL15 .... 6 C1
Smithy St Hazel Grove SK7 .... 124 D3
Leigh WN7 .... 75 F4
Ramsbottom BL0 .... 138 C6
Westhoughton BL5 .... 39 E3
Smock La WN4 .... 72 C4
Smyrna St Heywood OL10 .... 29 C1
7 Oldham OL4 .... 67 C6
Radcliffe M26 .... 43 F4
Salford M5 .... 154 E1
Smyrna Wlk M26 .... 43 F4
Snape St M26 .... 43 F6
Snapebrook Wlk 6 SK9 .... 131 E1
Snell St M4 .... 160 D1
Snipe Ave OL11 .... 29 F7
Snipe Cl SK12 .... 133 A4
Snipe Rd OL8 .... 67 B2
Snipe Ret Pk OL7 .... 100 D8
Snipe St BL3 .... 147 F4
Snipe Way OL7 .... 100 D8
Snow Hill Rd BL3 .... 42 D5
Snowberry Wlk M31 .... 105 E3
Snowden Ave
Urmston M41 .... 107 B8
Wigan WN3 .... 55 A4
Snowden St Bolton BL1 .... 145 E8
Heywood OL10 .... 46 E8
1 Oldham OL8 .... 66 F4
Snowden Wlk 4 M40 .... 65 C2
Snowdon Dr BL6 .... 22 C5
Snowdon Rd M30 .... 80 A3
Snowdon St OL11 .... 31 A2
Snowdrop Cl BB4 .... 1 A8
Snowdrop Wlk M7 .... 155 D6
Snowshill Dr WN3 .... 54 C4
Snydale Cl BL5 .... 40 B2
Snydale Way BL3,BL5 .... 40 C1
Soane Cl WN4 .... 73 D3
Soap St M4 .... 159 A2
Society St OL2 .... 149 B7
Sofa St BL1 .... 142 B1
Soham Cl WN2 .... 56 E4
Soho St Bolton BL3 .... 145 F6
Oldham OL4 .... 67 B7
Wigan WN5 .... 54 F7
Sole St WN1 .... 37 E1
Solent Ave M8 .... 64 A2
Solent Dr BL3 .... 42 D5
Solness St BL9 .... 27 F6
Solway Cl Ashton-in-M WN4 .... 73 A4
Bolton BL3 .... 147 D3
Kearsley M27 .... 61 E4
Oldham OL8 .... 153 E5
Solway Rd M22 .... 121 E4
Somerby Dr M22 .... 121 C1
Somerdale Ave BL1 .... 144 A7
Somerfield Rd M9 .... 64 D1
Somerford Ave M20 .... 110 A8
Somerford Rd SK5 .... 99 F2
Somerford Way 3 SK9 .... 131 E5
Somers Rd SK5 .... 99 F1
Somers Wlk M9 .... 64 B3
Somersby Dr BL7 .... 24 F8
Somersby Wlk BL3 .... 145 F5
Somerset Ave Shaw OL2 .... 48 F7
Tyldesley M29 .... 58 F3
Somerset Cl
Brinnington SK5 .... 112 C4
Irlam M44 .... 105 D6
Somerset Dr BL9 .... 44 F8
Somerset Gr OL11 .... 30 A8
Somerset Pl M33 .... 108 B6
Somerset Rd
Altrincham WA14 .... 119 D6
Atherton M46 .... 58 C5
Bolton BL1 .... 144 B8
Droylsden M43 .... 84 A3
Failsworth M35 .... 83 E6
Salford M30 .... 80 A4
Wigan WN5 .... 54 C7
Somerset St OL4 .... 67 C6
Somerset Wlk BB4 .... 1 B8
Somerton Ave Sale M33 .... 108 C3
Wythenshawe M22 .... 121 C3
Somerton Ct M9 .... 65 A3
Somerton Rd BL2 .... 43 A6
Somerville Gdns WA15 .... 119 F7
Somerville Rd WN1 .... 37 C3
Somerville Sq BL1 .... 142 C3
Somerville St BL1 .... 142 C3
Somerwood Wlk M12 .... 164 F6
Sommerville Ct M7 .... 155 D8
Sonning Dr BL3 .... 146 A2
Sonning Wlk M8 .... 156 B6
Sopwith Dr M14 .... 98 B1
Sorby Rd M44 .... 106 A7
Sorrel Bank M6 .... 154 F4
Sorrel Dr OL15 .... 15 F6
Sorrel St M15 .... 162 E6
Sorrel Way OL4 .... 49 E2
Sorrell Bank SK5 .... 100 A1
Sorton St M1 .... 163 A7
Soudan Rd SK2 .... 124 A6
Soudan St M24 .... 47 C1
Sougher's La WN4 .... 72 F7
Sougher's Lane End WN4 .... 72 E6
Sound The OL3 .... 50 F4
Souracre Fold SK15 .... 86 B3
South Acre Dr SK9 .... 131 D3
South Ave Eccles M41 .... 95 E6
Golborne WN7 .... 74 F4
Heywood OL10 .... 29 B2
Kearsley BL4 .... 60 F6
Leigh WN7 .... 76 C3
Manchester M19 .... 110 F7
Oldham OL3 .... 69 B6
Swinton M27 .... 79 D5
Whitefield M45 .... 44 E1
South Back Rock 1 BL9 .... 140 F2
South Bank Cl SK9 .... 137 B2
South Bank Rd BL9 .... 140 E1
South Bolton Sixth Form Coll BL3 .... 146 C2
South Chadderton Com Sec Sch OL9 .... 65 F3
South Cl Tintwistle SK13 .... 103 F7
Whitefield BL9 .... 45 A3
Wilmslow SK9 .... 136 F6
South Cliffe St 1 M11 .... 99 F7
South Cres Droylsden M11 .... 83 D2
Failsworth M40 .... 65 D3
South Croft OL8 .... 67 B3
South Cross St Bury BL9 .... 140 F2
Bury BL9 .... 141 A1
South Croston St M16 .... 97 D4
South Ct OL16 .... 31 A8
South Downs Dr WA14 .... 119 D1
South Downs Rd WA14 .... 119 D1
South Dr Altrincham WA15 .... 120 A7
Appley Bridge WN6 .... 18 C2
Bolton BL2 .... 25 E3
Gatley SK8 .... 122 A4
Manchester M21 .... 109 B6
South Failsworth Cty Prim Sch M35 .... 83 F5
South Field Ind Est M17 .... 96 C6
South Gr
Alderley Edge SK9 .... 137 A1
Manchester M13 .... 164 D5
Sale M33 .... 108 B3
Walkden M28 .... 60 C2
South Hall St M5 .... 161 C8
South Hey WN7 .... 75 C5
South Hill OL4 .... 67 F5
South Hill St OL4 .... 67 A6
South King St Eccles M30 .... 79 B2
Manchester M2 .... 158 F1
South La M29 .... 77 A5
South Lancashire Ind Est WN4 .... 73 B6
South Langworthy Rd
Salford M5 .... 154 F1
Salford M5 .... 96 E8
South Lonsdale St M32 .... 96 E3
South Manchester High Sch M22 .... 121 D3
South Marlow St SK13 .... 104 A4
South Mead SK12 .... 133 B5
South Meade
Altrincham WA15 .... 120 A7
Manchester M21 .... 109 B7
Manchester M25 .... 63 D2
Swinton M27 .... 79 E6
South Meadway SK6 .... 134 F7
South Mesnefield Rd M7 .... 81 A8
South Oak La SK9 .... 136 F5
South Par Rochdale OL16 .... 139 F7
Stockport SK7 .... 123 F2
South Park Dr SK12 .... 133 E5
South Park Rd SK8 .... 122 B6
South Pine St BL9 .... 141 B2
South Pl 11 OL16 .... 31 A8
South Pump St M1 .... 163 B8
South Radford St M7 .... 81 A7
South Rd Altrincham WA14 .... 119 C2
Altrincham WA14 .... 128 E8
Manchester M20 .... 110 B2
Stretford M17,M32 .... 96 C4
Stretford M32 .... 96 B4
Swinton M27 .... 62 D2
South Ridge M34 .... 100 F5
South Row M25 .... 62 F1
South Royd St BL8 .... 26 F7
South Side SK14 .... 113 F8
South St Alderley Edge SK9 .... 137 A1
Ashton-u-L OL7 .... 100 E8
Bolton BL3 .... 147 E3
Heywood OL10 .... 29 B2
Manchester M11 .... 165 C7
Manchester M12 .... 164 E5
Oldham OL8 .... 66 B2
Ramsbottom BL0 .... 11 D6
Rochdale OL16 .... 31 A8
Tyldesley M46 .... 58 E1
South Terr Bury BL9 .... 44 D7
Ramsbottom BL0 .... 1 C2
South Terrace Ct 12 OL16 .... 31 A5
South Trafford Coll WA14 .... 119 D8
South Vale Cres WA15 .... 119 F5
South View Atherton M46 .... 58 C3
2 Manchester M14 .... 98 C2
Mossley SK15 .... 86 F6
Reddish SK5 .... 99 F3
Rochdale OL11 .... 29 E6
Romiley SK6 .... 113 C6
South View Gdns SK8 .... 122 C3
South View Rd OL12 .... 15 E3
South View St BL2 .... 148 C7
South View Terr OL16 .... 15 E4
South Way OL8 .... 66 E2
South William St M3 .... 158 D1
Southall St M3,M8 .... 158 F4
Southam St M7,M8 .... 155 F7
Southampton Cl M7 .... 155 D5
Southbank Rd M19 .... 110 D5
Southbourne Ave M41 .... 95 F2
Southbourne St M6 .... 154 E2
Southbrook Ave M9 .... 63 F3
Southbrook Cl SK13 .... 171 E4
Southbrook Gr BL3 .... 147 F3
Southchurch Par M40 .... 159 C4
Southcliffe Rd 3 SK5 .... 111 F6
Southcombe Wlk M15 .... 97 F4
Southcourt WN7 .... 76 B6
Southcross Rd M18 .... 99 D3
Southdene Ave M20 .... 109 E4
Southdown Cl
Rochdale OL11 .... 30 C5
Stockport SK4 .... 169 E2
Southdown Cres
Cheadle SK8 .... 131 F8
Manchester M9 .... 65 A2
Southdown Dr M28 .... 77 F6
Southdowns Cl Shaw OL2 .... 149 A8
Shaw OL2 .... 48 F8
Southend Ave M15 .... 162 D6

Southend St BL3 . . . . .146 C3
Southern App M27 . . . . . . .62 C2
Southern Cl Denton M34 . . .112 F8
Stockport SK7 . . . . .123 F1
Southern Cres SK7 . . . . . .123 F1
Southern Ho 4 BL1 . . . . . .143 D1
Southern Rd M33 . . . . .108 A6
Southern St
Manchester M3 . . . . .162 E8
Salford M6 . . . . .154 E4
Walkden M28 . . . . .60 D5
Wigan WN5 . . . . .54 D5
Southern's Fold WN2 . . . . . .38 A3
Southernby Cl 9 M13 . . . . .98 F4
Southery Ave WN3 . . . . . . .54 D3
Southey Cl OL15 . . . . .15 F2
Southey Ct 12 M34 . . . . . . .113 A8
Southey Wlk 6 M34 . . . . . .113 A7
Southfield WN2 . . . . .56 B2
Southfield Ave BL9 . . . . . . .27 F5
Southfield Cl
Dukinfield SK16 . . . . .101 D6
Handforth SK9 . . . . .131 C3
Southfield Dr BL5 . . . . .57 E7
Southfield Rd BL0 . . . . .11 A2
Southfield St 15 BL3 . . . . . .42 A4
Southfields Ave 2 M11 . . .83 C2
Southfields Dr WA15 . . . . .120 B7
Southgarth Rd M6 . . . . . . .154 E3
Southgate Bolton BL2 . . . . .25 E4
Manchester M21 . . . . .109 B7
Manchester M3 . . . . .158 F1
Manchester SK4 . . . . .111 C5
Uppermill OL3 . . . . .51 A2
Urmston M41 . . . . .107 B8
Whitworth OL12 . . . . .14 C7
Southgate Ave M40 . . . . . . .83 A4
Southgate Ct M33 . . . . . . .108 C5
Southgate Ind Pk OL10 . . .29 E1
Southgate Rd
Failsworth OL9 . . . . .65 E3
Whitefield BL9 . . . . .44 F3
Southgate St OL1 . . . . .153 E6
Southgate Way 11 OL7 . . .166 A1
Southgrove Ave BL1 . . . . . .24 E6
Southlands Ave Eccles M30 95 A8
Standish WN6 . . . . .36 E8
Southlawn SK9 . . . . .137 A5
Southlea Rd M19,M20 . . . .110 D5
Southleigh Dr BL2 . . . . .43 A6
Southlink OL4 . . . . .67 A6
Southlink Bsns Pk OL4 . . .67 A6
Southlink Wkshp OL4 . . . . .67 A6
Southmere Cl M40 . . . . . . .65 C3
Southmill St M2 . . . . .162 F8
Southmoor Rd M23 . . . . . .120 F6
Southmoor Wlk BL3 . . . . . .145 E5
Southover BL5 . . . . .57 E6
Southpoint SK4 . . . . .168 A2
Southpool Cl SK7 . . . . .124 A2
Southsea St M11 . . . . .99 D7
Southside SK6 . . . . .112 E6
Southview Rd SK13 . . . . . .116 F7
Southview Wlk OL4 . . . . . . .49 E1
Southward Rd WA11 . . . . . .89 A7
Southwark Dr SK16 . . . . . .101 D6
Southway
Altrincham WA14 . . . . .119 E6
Ashton-u-L OL7 . . . . .85 B6
Droylsden M43 . . . . .100 A8
7 Eccles M30 . . . . .79 F4
Failsworth OL9 . . . . .65 F2
Southwell Cl
18 Bolton BL1 . . . . .145 D8
Golborne WA3 . . . . .90 C8
Romiley SK6 . . . . .113 A1
Southwell Ct 6 M32 . . . . . .96 C1
Southwell St M9 . . . . .157 E7
Southwick Rd M23 . . . . . . .109 A2
Southwold Cl M19 . . . . .99 C1
Southwood Cl BL3 . . . . . . .147 F3
Southwood Dr M9 . . . . .64 A5
Southwood Rd SK2 . . . . . .124 B4
Southworth Ct M3 . . . . . . .158 D2
Southworth Rd WA12 . . . . .89 F4
Southyard St M19 . . . . . . .111 B8
Sovereign Ent Pk M5 . . . . .161 A7
Sovereign Fold Rd WN7 . . .57 A7
Sovereign Rd WN1 . . . . . . .151 D7
Sovereign St M6 . . . . .81 A4
Sowerby Cl BL8 . . . . .26 F2
Sowerby Wlk M9 . . . . .64 B4
Spa Cl SK5 . . . . .111 E8
Spa Cres M38 . . . . .60 A6
Spa Gr M38 . . . . .60 A6
Spa La Oldham OL4 . . . . . . .67 E5
Walkden M38 . . . . .60 A6
Spa Rd Atherton M46 . . . . . .58 D5
Bolton BL1 . . . . .145 D7
Spa St M13,M15 . . . . .163 B5
Spadden Wlk M45 . . . . .45 C1
Spalding Dr M23 . . . . .121 A2
Spark Rd M23 . . . . .120 F7
Sparkford Ave M23 . . . . . .108 D1
Sparkle St M1 . . . . .163 B8
Sparrow Cl SK5 . . . . .99 E2
Sparrow Hill
Appley Bridge WN6,WN8 . . .18 A2
Rochdale OL16 . . . . .139 F7
Sparrow Hill
Com Prim Sch OL16 . . . .139 E7
Sparrow Hill Com Prim
Sch (Annexe) OL11 . . . . .139 F6
Sparrow St OL2 . . . . .48 E2

Sparrowfield Cl SK15 . . . . .86 E7
Sparta Ave M28 . . . . .60 D2
Sparta Wlk M11 . . . . .165 A8
Sparth Bottoms Rd OL11 139 D6
Sparth Ct SK4 . . . . .169 D3
Sparth Hall SK4 . . . . .169 D3
Sparth La SK4 . . . . .169 D3
Sparthfield Ave OL11 . . . . .139 E5
Sparthfield Rd SK4 . . . . . . .169 D3
Spath Holme 2 M20 . . . . .110 A3
Spath La SK8 . . . . .131 F5
Spath La E SK8 . . . . .132 A5
Spath Rd M20 . . . . .110 A3
Spath Wlk SK8 . . . . .132 B5
Spathfield Ct SK4 . . . . .169 D3
Spaw St M3 . . . . .158 E2
Spawell Cl WA3 . . . . .90 E8
Speakman Ave Leigh WN7 .76 E5
Newton-le-W WA12 . . . . . . .89 C5
Speakmans Dr WN6 . . . . . .35 C6
Spean Wlk 8 M11 . . . . .83 C1
Spear St M1,M4 . . . . .159 B2
Spectator St M4 . . . . .160 D2
Specton Wlk 5 M12 . . . . . .99 B3
Speedwell Cl SK13 . . . . . .103 F7
Speedwell Cl
11 Golborne WA3 . . . . .90 E8
Tintwistle SK13 . . . . .103 F7
Speke Wlk M34 . . . . .100 E1
Spelding Dr WN6 . . . . .36 E4
Spen Fold Bury BL8 . . . . . . .44 A8
Littleborough OL15 . . . . . . .16 A4
Spencer Ave
11 Dukinfield SK14 . . . . . . .101 D5
Little Lever BL3 . . . . .43 C3
Manchester M16 . . . . .97 C2
Whitefield M45 . . . . .44 E2
Spencer La OL11 . . . . .29 E5
Spencer Rd WN1 . . . . .37 C3
Spencer Rd W WN6 . . . . . . .37 A3
Spencer St Bury BL8 . . . . . .27 C3
Dukinfield SK16 . . . . .101 C8
Eccles M30 . . . . .79 C1
Littleborough OL15 . . . . . . .16 C6
Mossley OL5 . . . . .68 B1
Oldham OL1 . . . . .67 A8
Oldham OL9 . . . . .66 C4
Radcliffe M26 . . . . .44 C4
Ramsbottom BL0 . . . . .138 B5
Reddish SK5 . . . . .111 F8
Spencer's La WN5 . . . . .53 D7
Spender Ave M8 . . . . .156 A6
Spendmore La PR7 . . . . . . .19 D8
Spenleach La BL8 . . . . .10 D3
Spenlow M27 . . . . .76 C3
Spenlow Cl SK12 . . . . .133 E1
Spennithorne Rd M41 . . . . .95 B2
Spenser Ave Denton M34 . .113 A8
Radcliffe M26 . . . . .43 E4
Spenwood Rd OL15 . . . . . . .15 F5
Spey Cl Altrincham WA14 . .119 C6
Standish WN6 . . . . .19 D1
Spey Ho SK5 . . . . .99 F2
Speyside Cl M45 . . . . .63 A8
Spilsby Sq WN3 . . . . .55 A2
Spindle Ave SK15 . . . . .86 C3
Spindle Croft BL4 . . . . .60 D8
Spindle Ct OL2 . . . . .48 E4
Spindle Hillock WN4 . . . . . .72 E4
Spindle Point Prim Sch
BL4 . . . . .61 B5
Spindle Wlk BL5 . . . . .39 F2
Spindlepoint Dr 4 M28 . . . .78 C8
Spindles Sh Ctr The OL1 .153 E6
Spindles The OL5 . . . . .86 B8
Spindlewood Cl SK15 . . . . .86 D2
Spindlewood Rd WN3 . . . . .151 F6
Spinks St OL4 . . . . .67 B5
Spinnerbottom SK22 . . . . .127 F2
Spinnerette Cl WN7 . . . . . . .76 A5
Spinners Gdns OL12 . . . . . .15 C4
Spinners Gn OL12 . . . . .14 F2
Spinners La SK12 . . . . .133 C4
Spinners Mews BL1 . . . . . .145 E8
Spinners Way OL4 . . . . .49 E4
Spinney Cl Glossop SK13 . .104 C2
Handforth SK9 . . . . .131 C3
Spinney Dr Bury BL9 . . . . . .27 E6
Sale M33 . . . . .107 C2
Spinney Gr M34 . . . . .100 F5
Spinney Nook BL2 . . . . .25 D2
Spinney Rd M23 . . . . .121 B7
Spinney The Bolton BL1 . . .144 B7
Cheadle SK8 . . . . .122 E3
Edgworth BL7 . . . . .9 C2
Oldham OL4 . . . . .68 A8
Rochdale OL12 . . . . .14 D3
Urmston M41 . . . . .95 A2
Whitefield M45 . . . . .62 C7
Wigan WN5 . . . . .54 E5
Spinning Gate Sh Ctr WN7 75 F4
Spinning Jenny Way WN7 .75 F4
Spinning Jenny Wlk 5
M4 . . . . .159 C2
Spinning Mdw BL1 . . . . . . .145 D8
Spinningdale M38 . . . . .59 D6
Spinningfield BL8 . . . . .11 B3
Spinningfield Way OL10 . . .46 D7
Spinningfields BL1 . . . . . . .145 D8
Spinnings The BL9 . . . . .11 C3
Spion Kop WN4 . . . . .73 A3
Spire Hollin SK13 . . . . .104 C3
Spire Wlk M12 . . . . .164 D8
Spiredale Dr M9 . . . . .64 A4
Spirewood Gdns SK6 . . . . .113 A2
Spod Rd OL12 . . . . .14 D1
Spodden Cotts OL12 . . . . . . .4 D2

Spodden Fold OL12 . . . . . . .14 C8
Spodden St OL12 . . . . .139 D8
Spodegreen La WA14 . . . . .118 C1
Spokeshave Way OL16 . . . .15 C2
Spooner Rd M30 . . . . .79 C1
Sportside Ave M28 . . . . . . .60 E4
Sportside Cl M28 . . . . .60 E4
Sportside Gr M28 . . . . .60 E4
Sportsman St WN7 . . . . . . .75 D5
Sportsmans Dr OL8 . . . . . . .67 A3
Spotland Bridge Ind Ctr
OL11 . . . . .139 D8
Spotland Prim Sch OL12 139 D8
Spotland Rd OL12 . . . . .139 D8
Spotland Tops OL12 . . . . . .14 B1
Spreadbury St 7 M40 . . . . .83 A7
Spring Ave Hyde SK14 . . . .113 F8
Whitefield M45 . . . . .44 E2
Spring Bank
Altrincham WA14 . . . . .119 D3
Appley Bridge WN6 . . . . . . .35 C8
Rochdale OL12 . . . . .14 D4
Salford M6 . . . . .154 E3
Stalybridge SK15 . . . . .102 B8
Stalybridge SK15 . . . . .86 B1
Spring Bank Ave
Ashton-u-L OL6 . . . . .85 B6
Denton M34 . . . . .100 D7
Spring Bank La
Rochdale OL11 . . . . .29 E8
Stalybridge SK15 . . . . .86 C5
Spring Bank Pl SK1 . . . . . .170 E8
Spring Bank Rd SK22 . . . .127 C1
Spring Bank St OL8 . . . . . . .66 C4
Spring Bank Terr M34 . . . .100 C7
Spring Bottom 5 F7
Spring Bridge Rd M16 . . . . .97 F1
Spring Cl Bury BL8 . . . . .26 E6
Oldham OL4 . . . . .67 D5
Ramsbottom BL0 . . . . .138 B6
Spring Clough M28 . . . . . . .79 B6
Spring Clough Ave M28 . . . .60 F2
Spring Clough Dr
Oldham OL8 . . . . .67 C4
Walkden M28 . . . . .60 F2
Spring Cotts 6 OL5 . . . . . . .68 C2
Spring Gardens St 4 BB4 . .2 F8
Spring Gdns
Altrincham WA15 . . . . .120 C5
11 Atherton M46 . . . . .58 D3
Bolton BL2 . . . . .25 F4
Hadfield SK13 . . . . .104 A5
Hazel Grove SK7 . . . . .124 D3
12 Horwich BL6 . . . . .22 B4
Hyde SK14 . . . . .167 A4
Manchester M1,M2 . . . . . .159 A1
Middleton M24 . . . . .47 A1
Rawtenstall BB4 . . . . .2 F6
8 Royton OL2 . . . . .48 D4
Salford M6 . . . . .154 F3
Stockport SK1 . . . . .112 A1
Spring Gr Oldham OL3 . . . . .69 B5
Wigan WN1 . . . . .151 D7
Spring Grove M45 . . . . .44 E2
Spring Hall Rise OL4 . . . . . .49 F4
Spring Hill Ct 5 OL4 . . . . . .67 D8
Spring Hill High Sch OL16 31 B5
Spring La Lymm WA13 . . . .117 F3
Oldham OL4 . . . . .67 D5
Radcliffe M26 . . . . .44 B3
Spring Meadow La OL3 . . . .69 C8
Spring Mill Cl 4 BL3 . . . . .147 E4
Spring Mill Wlk OL16 . . . . .15 C2
Spring Pl OL12 . . . . .4 D3
Spring Rd
Altrincham WA14 . . . . .119 D2
Orrell WN5 . . . . .53 F8
Poynton SK12 . . . . .133 F2
Wigan WN5 . . . . .36 A1
Spring Rise Glossop SK13 .115 F7
Shaw OL2 . . . . .32 A3
Spring Side Rawtenstall BB4 .2 F6
Whitworth OL12 . . . . .4 D4
Spring Side Cotts BL7 . . . . .8 A2
Spring St Bolton BL3 . . . . .145 F5
Bury BL8 . . . . .26 F4
Bury BL8 . . . . .26 F7
Bury BL9 . . . . .140 F1
Farnworth BL4 . . . . .42 D1
Glossop SK13 . . . . .104 B1
Hollingworth SK14 . . . . . . .103 C5
Horwich BL6 . . . . .22 B4
Ince-in-M WN3 . . . . .55 E4
Manchester M12 . . . . .99 A2
Mossley OL5 . . . . .68 C2
Mottram-in-L SK14 . . . . . . .115 A8
Oldham OL3 . . . . .69 B8
Oldham OL4 . . . . .67 C8
Oldham OL4 . . . . .68 A6
Ramsbottom BL0 . . . . .11 D7
Ramsbottom BL0 . . . . .138 B6
Stalybridge SK15 . . . . .86 A2
Wigan WN1 . . . . .151 D7
Wilmslow SK9 . . . . .137 A7
Spring Terr 4 Bacup OL13 . .3 D8
Bury BL8 . . . . .26 F7
Chadderton OL9 . . . . .152 A7
Newhey OL16 . . . . .32 B3
Rochdale OL11 . . . . .14 A1
Spring Vale
Hazel Grove SK7 . . . . .124 C2
Middleton M24 . . . . .47 B1
Prestwich M25 . . . . .63 A4
Spring Vale Dr BL8 . . . . . . .26 E6
Spring Vale St BL8 . . . . .26 F6
Spring Vale Terr OL15 . . . . .16 B5
Spring Vale Way OL2 . . . . .149 A5

Spring Wood St BL0 . . . . . .138 B7
Springbank
Chadderton OL9 . . . . .152 A7
Hadfield SK13 . . . . .103 F5
Springbank Cl SK6 . . . . . . .113 C6
Springbank Ct
Manchester M8 . . . . .63 F7
Romiley SK6 . . . . .113 B5
Springbank Ind Est WN2 . .56 B3
Springbank Rd SK6 . . . . . .113 C6
Springbourne WN6 . . . . . . .36 F2
Springburn Cl 1 M28 . . . . .78 A6
Springdale Gdns M20 . . . .110 A3
Springfield
Charlesworth SK13 . . . . . . .115 C6
Kearsley M26 . . . . .61 C6
1 Urmston M41 . . . . .95 C2
Springfield Ave
Golborne WA3 . . . . .89 F8
Hazel Grove SK7 . . . . .124 D3
Littleborough OL15 . . . . . . .16 A7
Lymm WA13 . . . . .117 B5
Reddish SK5 . . . . .111 E7
Springfield Cl
Failsworth M35 . . . . .83 F8
Hadfield SK13 . . . . .171 E4
6 Heywood OL10 . . . . .29 E1
Springfield Dr SK9 . . . . . . .136 D5
Springfield Gdns BL4 . . . . . .61 A6
Springfield La Irlam M44 . . .93 F2
Littleborough OL15 . . . . . . .15 D3
Manchester M3 . . . . .158 E3
Royton OL2 . . . . .48 C7
Springfield Prim
Sch M33 . . . . .108 B4
Springfield Rd
Adlington PR6 . . . . .21 A8
Altrincham WA14 . . . . .119 D5
Atherton M46 . . . . .58 E4
Bolton BL1 . . . . .24 E7
Coppull PR7 . . . . .19 E8
Droylsden M43 . . . . .83 F3
Farnworth BL4 . . . . .42 A1
Gatley SK8 . . . . .122 B5
Hindley WN2 . . . . .56 C6
Horwich BL6 . . . . .22 D1
Kearsley BL4 . . . . .60 F6
Middleton M24 . . . . .47 A1
Ramsbottom BL0 . . . . .11 A2
Sale M33 . . . . .108 B4
Wigan WN6 . . . . .37 D2
Springfield Rd N PR7 . . . . .19 E8
Springfield St
Ashton-u-L OL6 . . . . .85 E5
18 Bolton BL3 . . . . .42 A4
Denton M34 . . . . .100 F4
Heywood OL10 . . . . .29 A2
Wigan WN1 . . . . .37 D2
Springhead Ave
Manchester M20 . . . . .110 A7
Oldham OL4 . . . . .68 A5
Springhead Inf Sch OL4 . .68 A6
Springhill Ave OL13 . . . . . . .3 D8
Springhill Villas OL13 . . . . .3 D8
Springlawn BL1 . . . . .40 F8
Springlees Ct 7 OL4 . . . . . .67 F6
Springmeadow SK13 . . . . .115 C6
Springmount WA3 . . . . .90 E7
Springpool WN3 . . . . .54 B2
Springs Brow PR7 . . . . .19 D5
Springs La SK15 . . . . .85 F3
Springs Rd M24,OL9 . . . . . .65 C6
Springs The
Altrincham WA14 . . . . .119 B2
Rochdale OL11 . . . . .29 E7
Springside SK4 . . . . .111 D7
Springside Ave M28 . . . . . . .60 E3
Springside Cl M28 . . . . .60 E3
Springside Cotts BL8 . . . . . .27 C7
Springside Gr M28 . . . . .60 E3
Springside Prim Sch BL9 . .27 E7
Springside Rd BL8 . . . . .27 E8
Springside View BL8 . . . . . .27 C7
Springside Wlk 23 M15 . . .162 D6
Springvale Cl OL7 . . . . .84 F5
Springvale Ct M24 . . . . .65 B8
Springville Ave M9 . . . . . . .157 F7
Springwater Ave BL0 . . . . . .11 A3
Springwater Cl BL2 . . . . . . .25 E3
Springwater La M45 . . . . . . .44 E2
Springwell Cl 1 M6 . . . . . .154 E2
Springwell Gdns SK14 . . . .102 E1
Springwell Way 2 SK14 . . .102 E1
Springwood Delph OL3 . . . .50 E5
Glossop SK13 . . . . .115 C6
Springwood Ave
Chadderton OL9 . . . . .47 E1
Pendlebury M27 . . . . .80 B6
Springwood Cres SK6 . . . .113 E2
Springwood Hall OL7 . . . . . .85 A7
Springwood Hall Rd OL8 . . .67 A2
Springwood La SK6 . . . . . .113 E3
Springwood Prim
Sch SK6 . . . . .113 E3
Springwood Way OL7 . . . . . .85 A6
Sprodley Dr WN6 . . . . .18 B2
Spruce Ave BL9 . . . . .141 B2
Spruce Cl WA3 . . . . .90 F7
Spruce Ct 1 M6 . . . . .81 B2
Spruce Lo SK8 . . . . .122 D6
Spruce Rd WN6 . . . . .36 F3
Spruce St Manchester M15 162 E4
Ramsbottom BL0 . . . . .138 B5
Rochdale OL16 . . . . .31 B6
Spruce Wlk 6 Sale M33 . . .107 C6
Walsden OL14 . . . . .6 A8

Sprucewood OL9 . . . . .65 D8
Spur The OL8 . . . . .67 A3
Spur Wlk M8 . . . . .155 F7
Spurley Hey High
Sch M18 . . . . .99 C3
Spurn La OL3 . . . . .51 E4
Square Rd OL14 . . . . .6 A8
Square St BL0 . . . . .138 C6
Square The
Altrincham WA15 . . . . .129 C4
Bury BL9 . . . . .140 F2
Hyde SK14 . . . . .167 D2
Stockport SK4 . . . . .168 C3
Swinton M27 . . . . .79 E5
Uppermill OL3 . . . . .51 A2
Square View OL14 . . . . .6 B8
Squire Rd M8 . . . . .155 F7
Squires Ct M5 . . . . .80 A2
Squires La M46 . . . . .76 E8
Squirrel Dr WA14 . . . . .119 C8
Squirrel La BL6 . . . . .22 A4
Squirrel's Jump SK9 . . . . . .137 C1
Stable Fold M26 . . . . .44 A4
Stable St OL9 . . . . .66 A2
Stablefold Eccles M28 . . . . .79 A5
Mossley OL5 . . . . .86 C8
Stableford Ave M30 . . . . . . .79 C4
Stables The Droylsden M43 .84 D3
Prestwich M25 . . . . .63 C3
Stablings The SK9 . . . . . . .137 A5
Stack La OL13 . . . . .4 B8
Stadium Way WN5 . . . . .36 E1
Stafford Cl SK13 . . . . .116 F8
Stafford Ct 2 OL16 . . . . . . .15 E4
Stafford Rd Eccles M30 . . . .79 E3
Failsworth M35 . . . . .84 A5
Swinton M27 . . . . .79 F8
Walkden M28 . . . . .60 C1
Stafford St Bury BL8 . . . . . .140 D4
Hindley WN2 . . . . .56 C5
Ince-in-M WN3 . . . . .55 E4
Leigh WN7 . . . . .76 D4
New Mills SK22 . . . . .127 C1
Oldham OL9 . . . . .66 C4
Stafford View M5 . . . . .161 B7
Stafford Way 12 M34 . . . . .101 A1
Stag Hill Cl SK14 . . . . .119 B6
Stag Pasture Rd OL8 . . . . . .66 D1
Stage La WA13 . . . . .117 C4
Stainburn Cl WN6 . . . . .35 E6
Stainburn Rd M11 . . . . .165 B6
Stainburne Rd SK2 . . . . . . .124 D6
Staindale OL4 . . . . .67 D6
Stainer St M12 . . . . .99 A3
Stainforth Cl BL8 . . . . .26 F3
Stainforth St M11 . . . . .164 F8
Stainmoor Ct SK2 . . . . .124 D6
Stainmore Ave OL6 . . . . . . .85 D7
Stainsbury St BL3 . . . . .146 C4
Stainton Ave M18 . . . . .99 E4
Stainton Cl M26 . . . . .43 F5
Stainton Dr M24 . . . . .46 D3
Stainton Rd M26 . . . . .43 F5
Stairgate WN1 . . . . .150 C8
Staithes Rd M22 . . . . .130 D8
Stakehill Ind Est M24 . . . . . .47 D4
Stakehill La M24 . . . . .47 E5
Staley Cl SK15 . . . . .86 C2
Staley Hall Cres SK15 . . . . .86 C3
Staley Rd OL5 . . . . .86 E8
Staley St Oldham OL4 . . . . . .67 B6
18 Oldham OL4 . . . . .67 F6
Stalham Cl M40 . . . . .160 D3
Stalmine Ave SK8 . . . . .131 B8
Staly Hall Rd SK15 . . . . .86 C2
Stalybridge Ridge Hill City
Inf Sch SK15 . . . . .85 F3
Stalybridge Ridge Hill
Jun Sch SK15 . . . . .85 F3
Stalybridge Sta SK15 . . . . .85 F2
Stalyhill Dr SK15 . . . . .102 E7
Stalyhill Inf Sch SK15 . . . .102 E7
Stalyhill Jun Sch SK15 . . .102 D7
Stamford Arc 7 OL6 . . . . . .166 C3
Stamford Ave
Altrincham WA14 . . . . .119 A5
Ashton-u-L SK15 . . . . .85 E2
Stamford Cl SK15 . . . . .85 E2
Stamford Ct 3
Ashton-u-L OL6 . . . . .85 D2
Manchester M13 . . . . .98 F3
Stamford Dr
Failsworth M35 . . . . .84 B6
Stalybridge SK15 . . . . .85 F2
Stamford Gr SK15 . . . . .85 F2
Stamford
Grange 1 WA14 . . . . . . .119 C4
Stamford High Sch OL6 . . .85 E4
Stamford New Rd WA14 . . .119 D4
Stamford Park Inf
Sch WA15 . . . . .119 E3
Stamford Park Jun
Sch WA15 . . . . .119 E3
Stamford Park Rd WA15 . .119 E3
Stamford Pl M33 . . . . .108 C4
Stamford Rd
Alderley Edge SK9 . . . . . . .137 B1
Altrincham WA14 . . . . .119 C2
Carrington M31 . . . . .106 D7
Denton M34 . . . . .100 E6
Handforth SK9 . . . . .131 A1
Little Bollington WA14 . . . . .118 B2
Manchester M7 . . . . .81 B6
Oldham OL4 . . . . .67 F7
Urmston M41 . . . . .95 B2

Stamford Sq
3 Altrincham WA14 ......119 D5
Ashton-u-L OL6 ....85 D2
Stamford St
Altrincham WA14 ....119 D5
Atherton M46 ....58 E4
Heywood OL10 ....29 E1
Manchester M16 ....161 C5
Manchester M16 ....97 D4
Mossley OL5 ....68 B1
10 Oldham OL4 ....67 E6
Rochdale OL16 ....31 B6
Sale M33 ....108 A6
Stalybridge OL6,SK15 ..85 F2
Stalybridge SK15 ......86 A2
Stalybridge SK15 ......86 D4
Swinton M27 ....62 A1
Stamford St Central OL6 .166 B2
Stamford St E OL6 .....85 D2
Stamford St W OL6 ....166 A2
Stamford Way 2 WA14 .119 D5
Stampstone St OL1 .....67 B8
Stan Jolly Wlk M11 ...165 C8
Stanage Ave M9 ....64 F4
Stanbank St SK4 ......169 E4
Stanbourne Dr BL1 ....143 F4
Stanbridge Ct SK4 ....169 E2
Stanbrook St M19 .....111 C8
Stanbury Cl BL9 ....28 D1
Stanbury Dr SK16 .....101 D8
Stanbury Wlk M40 .....160 D3
Stancliffe Gr WN2 .....38 C6
Stancliffe Rd M22 ....121 E5
Stancross Rd M23 .....120 C4
Stand Ave M45 ....44 E1
Stand Cl M45 ....62 C8
Stand La M26,M45 ......44 C1
Stand Rise M26 ....62 B8
Standedge Foot Rd OL3 .51 D8
Standedge Rd OL3 ......51 C5
Standedge Wlk SK15 ....86 E6
Standell Wlk M9 ....64 C1
Standfield Ctr 8 M28 ..78 A6
Standfield Dr M28 .....78 A7
Standish Ave WN5 ......71 E5
Standish Com High Sch
WN6 ....19 C2
Standish Gallery 16 WN1 .150 C8
Standish Rd M14 ......110 C8
Standish St M29 ....77 A8
Standish Wlk M34 .....100 E1
Standish Wood La WN6 ..36 E5
Standishgate WN1 .....150 C8
Standmoor Rd M45 .....62 D7
Standon Wlk 20 M40 ...65 D7
Standring Ave BL8 .....44 A8
Stanedge Cl BL0 ....11 C4
Stanedge Gr WN3 ....55 B2
Stanford Cl M26 ....61 C7
Stanford Hall Cres BL0 .11 B4
Stanhope Ave Denton M34 .100 E1
Prestwich M25 ....63 A5
Stanhope Cl Denton M34 .100 E1
Wilmslow SK9 ....137 D8
Stanhope Ct M25 ....63 A5
Stanhope Rd
Altrincham WA14 ......119 A2
Salford M6 ....80 E5
Stanhope St Ashton-u-L OL6 85 D4
Denton M34 ....100 E5
Leigh WN7 ....75 D6
Manchester M19 ....99 B1
Mossley OL5 ....86 C8
Reddish SK5 ....111 E7
Rochdale OL11 ....139 F5
Stanhope Way M35 .....83 E8
Stanhorne Ave M8 .....64 A2
Stanier Ave M30 ....79 D3
Stanier Pl BL6 ....22 C2
Stanion Gr SK16 ......101 D8
Stanlaw M30 ....79 E1
Stanley Ave
Hazel Grove SK7 ......124 D3
Hyde SK14 ....167 E4
Manchester M14 ....98 D3
Marple SK6 ....125 D7
Stanley Ave N M25 .....63 A6
Stanley Ave S M25 .....63 A6
Stanley Cl
Manchester M16 ....161 C5
Westhoughton BL5 ......57 F7
Whitefield M45 ....44 F1
Stanley Ct M16 ....161 C5
Stanley Dr
Altrincham WA15 ......120 A5
Gatley SK8,SK9 ....131 D6
Leigh WN7 ....75 D8
Whitefield M45 ....62 F6
Stanley Gr Horwich BL6 ..22 D1
Manchester M12 ....98 F4
Manchester M12,M18 ....99 B4
Manchester M21 ....109 A8
Manchester M34 ....168 B4
Urmston M41 ....95 D2
Stanley Green Ind Est
SK8 ....131 E5
Stanley Green Ret Pk
SK8 ....131 F6
Stanley Grove Jun
& Inf Sch M12 ....99 A4
Stanley Hall La SK12 .135 C6
Stanley Ho M16 ....97 E2
Stanley La WN2 ....38 C7
Stanley Mews BL2 ......42 D7
Stanley Mount M33 ....108 A3
Stanley Park Wlk BL2 .148 C8
Stanley Pl Rochdale OL12 .139 E8
Wigan WN1 ....151 E8

Stanley Rd Aspull WN2 .38 C6
Bolton BL1 ....142 B1
Eccles M30 ....95 C8
Farnworth BL4 ....59 E8
Handforth SK8,SK9 ....131 E6
Manchester M16 ....161 C5
Manchester M16 ....97 E2
Manchester M27 ....155 E8
Manchester SK4 ....168 B3
Oldham OL9 ....66 B4
Orrell WN8 ....53 B7
Pendlebury M27 ....80 A8
Platt Bridge WN2 ......56 A3
Radcliffe M26 ....43 E6
Reddish M34 ....100 B3
Walkden M28 ....60 D2
Whitefield M45 ....44 F1
Stanley Road Jun
& Inf Sch OL9 ....66 B4
Stanley Sq SK15 ....85 F1
Stanley St Atherton M46 .58 C3
Heywood OL10 ....29 D2
Manchester M10,M40 ..157 F5
Manchester M11 ....99 E7
Manchester M3 ....158 E1
Manchester M8 ....159 A4
Manchester M9 ....157 E8
Newton-le-W WA12 ......89 A3
Oldham OL4 ....67 E5
Oldham OL4 ....68 A6
Oldham OL9 ....152 B8
Prestwich M25 ....63 C4
Ramsbottom BL0 ....138 B5
Rochdale OL12 ....139 E8
3 Stalybridge SK15 ....85 F1
Stockport SK1 ....112 A2
Tyldesley M29 ....59 A1
Whitefield M45 ....44 F1
Wigan WN5 ....54 F6
Stanley St S BL3 .....145 E6
Stanmoor Dr WN2 ......38 D6
Stanmore Ave M32 .....96 B2
Stanmore Dr BL3 .....144 C5
Stannary Rd M30 ....79 A1
Stanney Cl OL16 ....31 E5
Stanney Rd OL16 ....31 B8
Stanneybrook Cl OL16 ..31 B8
Stanneylands Cl SK9 ..131 C2
Stanneylands Dr SK9 ..131 B2
Stanneylands Rd SK9 ..131 B2
Stanrose Cl BL7 ....8 E1
Stansbury Pl SK2 .....124 E6
Stansby Gdns M12 ....164 E6
Stansfield Cl M17 .....76 C2
Stansfield Dr OL11 ....13 F1
Stansfield Hall OL15 ...6 C1
Stansfield Hall CE/Free
Church Prim Sch OL15 .16 D8
Stansfield Rd
Failsworth M35 ....84 A8
Hyde SK14 ....167 E4
Rawtenstall BB4 ....2 E8
Stansfield Road Jun
& Inf Schs M35 ....84 A8
Stansfield St 2 Bacup OL13 .3 C8
Droylsden M11 ....99 D8
Failsworth M40 ....83 D4
Oldham OL1 ....153 E8
Oldham OL9 ....152 B5
Stanstead Cl WN2 ......37 F2
Stansted Wlk M23 ....108 D1
Stanton Ave
Manchester M20 ....109 E4
Manchester M7 ....81 B7
Stanton Cl WN3 ....55 B3
Stanton St M32 ....96 D4
Stanton Gdns
Manchester M20 ....109 E4
Stockport SK4 ....168 B1
Stanton St Droylsden M11 .83 C2
Oldham OL9 ....66 B3
Stretford M32 ....96 D4
Stanway Ave BL3 .....145 D6
Stanway Cl 6 Bolton BL3 .145 D6
Middleton M24 ....65 B6
Stanway Dr WA15 .....119 F3
Stanway Rd M45 ....63 B8
Stanway St
Manchester M9 ....157 E8
Stretford M32 ....96 D4
Stanwell Rd Failsworth M40 65 C1
Swinton M27 ....79 F7
Stanwick Ave M9 ......64 A4
Stanworth Ave BL2 .....42 E6
Stanworth Cl 8 M16 ...97 E3
Stanyard Ct M5 ......161 A8
Stanycliffe La M24 ....47 B3
Stanyforth St SK13 ...104 A4
Stapleford Cl Atherton BL5 .59 A6
Sale M33 ....108 A6
Stapleford Gr BL8 .....27 A2
Stapleford Wlk M34 ...100 E1
Staplehurst Cl WN7 ....57 C2
Staplehurst Rd M40 ....83 A4
Staplers Wlk 9 M14 ...98 C3
Stapleton Ave BL1 .....40 E6
Stapleton Rd M6 ....80 C5
Stapleton St WN2 ......56 A2
Star Bank OL13 ....3 D7
Star Gr M7 ....155 E6
Star Ind Est OL8 .....153 F5
Star La M13 ....21 F3
Starbeck Cl BL8 ....26 E7
Starcliffe St BL3,BL4 ..42 D2
Starcross Wlk M40 .....83 B6

Starfield Ave OL15 .....15 F2
Starkey St OL10 ....29 D3
Starkie Rd BL2 ....25 B1
Starkie St M28 ....79 A8
Starkies BL9 ....44 E7
Starling Cl M43 ....84 D3
Starling Dr BL4 ....59 F7
Starling Rd BL8 ....43 E8
Starmoor Dr M8 ......156 A6
Starmount Cl BL2 ......43 B6
Starring La OL15 ......15 E5
Starring Rd OL15 ......15 E5
Starring Way OL15 .....15 F5
Startham Ave WN5 .....71 D3
Starting Chair OL4 ....68 C8
Statford Ave M30 ......95 C8
Statham Cl M34 ......101 A3
Statham Fold SK14 ...102 A4
Statham St M6 ....81 B2
Statham Wlk 2 M13 ...163 B7
Station App
Manchester M1 ....163 A8
Manchester M1 ....163 B8
Manchester M20 ......110 C1
Station Approach
Bsns Ctr OL11 ....139 F6
Station Ave Leigh WN2 .56 D1
Orrell WN5 ....53 D5
Station Bridge M41 ....95 D2
Station Cl 1 SK14 ....167 D2
Station Cotts SK8 ....123 B2
Station La OL4 ....68 B1
Station Mews WN4 .....72 D3
Station Rd Adlington PR7 .21 A6
Blackrod BL6 ....21 E1
Cheadle SK8 ....123 B1
Diggle SK3 ....51 D5
Eccles M30 ....79 D1
Edgworth BL7 ....9 C4
Garswood WN4 ....72 C3
Hadfield SK13 ....104 A5
Handforth SK9 ....131 A4
Handforth SK9 ....131 D3
Haslingden BB4 ....1 A7
Hyde SK14 ....102 B2
Irlam M44 ....105 E7
Kearsley BL4 ....61 A7
Manchester M8 ....64 A1
Manchester M4 ....110 E1
Marple SK6 ....125 F6
Marple SK6,SK22 .....126 D1
Milnrow OL16 ....31 F5
Mossley OL5 ....68 D1
Oldham OL4 ....69 B8
Oldham OL4 ....68 A5
Partington WA14 .....118 B5
Ramsbottom BL8 ....10 F1
Reddish SK5 ....99 E2
Rochdale OL11 ....139 F6
Romiley SK6 ....113 B5
Stockport SK1 ....170 E8
Stockport SK3 ....170 E8
Stretford M32 ....96 D3
Swinton M27 ....61 F1
Urmston M41 ....95 D2
Whitworth OL12 ....14 C5
Whitworth OL12 ....4 D3
Wigan WN1 ....150 C8
Wilmslow SK9 ....137 B7
Station St Bolton BL3 .145 F6
Dukinfield SK16 ......166 B1
Glossop SK13 ....104 D1
Hazel Grove SK7 .....124 D2
Oldham OL4 ....67 F6
Station View 11 M19 ...99 A1
Stationers Entry OL16 .139 F7
Staton Ave BL2 ......148 C8
Staton St M11 ....165 C8
Statter St BL9 ....45 A4
Staveleigh Mall OL6 ..166 B3
Staveley Ave Bolton BL1 .24 E6
Stalybridge SK15 ......86 A3
Staveley Cl Middleton M24 .46 E2
Shaw OL2 ....49 D6
Stavely Wlk 8 OL12 ...48 E4
Staverton Cl M13 ....163 C7
Stavesacre WN7 ....75 F3
Staveton Cl SK7 .....124 A3
Staverdale 11 OL12 ..139 E8
Stayley Dr SK15 ....86 C2
Stayley Rd OL5 ....86 D8
Stead St BL8 ....138 C6
Steadway OL3 ....69 C5
Stedman Cl M11 ......160 E1
Steele Gdns BL2 ....42 E5
Steeles Ave SK14 ....167 E3
Steeple Dr M5 ....161 A8
Steeple View OL2 .....48 D4
Stein Ave WA3 ....90 E8
Stelfox Ave
Manchester M14 ....98 A1
Sale WA15 ....120 C7
Stelfox La M34 ....100 E7
Stelfox St M30 ....95 B8
Stella Maris RC Jun Sch
M40 ....110 E2
Stella St M9 ....64 B4
Stelling St M18 ....99 D5
Stenbury Cl M14 ....98 C3
Stenner La M20 ......110 B1
Stenson Sq 1 M11 .....99 D7
Stephen Cl 7 BL8 .....27 C2
Stephen Lowry Wlk 1
M40 ....83 A7
Stephen St Bury BL8 ..27 C2
Manchester M3 ....158 F4

Stephen St continued
Platt Bridge WN2 ......56 A2
Stockport SK1 ....124 B8
Urmston M41 ....95 E2
Stephen St S BL2 ......27 C1
Stephen Wlk SK1 .....124 B8
Stephen's Way WN3 ....54 E5
Stephens Rd
Manchester M20 ....110 D6
Stalybridge SK15 ......85 F4
Stephens St BL2 ....42 D8
Stephens Terr M20 ...110 B3
Stephenson Ave M43 ...84 A1
Stephenson Rd
Newton-le-W WA12 .....89 D2
Stretford M32 ....96 E3
Stephenson Sq OL12 ...15 C3
Stephenson St Abram WN2 .74 B8
Failsworth M35 ....66 A1
Horwich BL6 ....22 D2
4 Oldham OL4 ....67 D8
Stepping Hill Hospl SK2 .124 C4
Steps Mdw OL12 ....15 D4
Sterling St M30 ....79 E2
Sterling Pl OL10 ......28 F1
Stern Ave M5 ....161 A8
Sterndale Ave WN6 ....19 E2
Sterndale Rd
Boothstown M28 ....77 F6
Romiley SK6 ....113 B1
Stockport SK3 ....170 E5
Sterratt St BL1 ......145 D6
Stetchworth Dr M28 ...78 B7
Steven Ct M21 ....109 C8
Stevens St SK9 ......137 A1
Stevenson Cl WN3 ....150 B5
Stevenson Dr OL1 .....49 E4
Stevenson Pl M1 .....159 B1
Stevenson Rd M27 .....61 E1
Stevenson Sq M1 ....159 B1
Stevenson St
Manchester M3 ....158 D1
Walkden M28 ....60 B3
Stewart Ave BL4 ....60 B7
Stewart Rd WN3 ....55 A3
Stewart St Ashton-u-L OL7 .84 F2
Bolton BL1 ....143 E2
Bury BL8 ....27 B3
Bury BL8 ....27 C4
Newhey OL16 ....32 B3
Stewerton Cl WA3 .....73 E2
Steynton Cl BL1 ....40 F8
Stile Cl M41 ....94 C2
Stiles Ave SK6 ....125 F7
Stiles Cl SK13 ....103 E5
Stilton Dr M11 ......165 A8
Stirling Ave
Hazel Grove SK7 .....124 D1
Ince-in-M WN2 ....56 A8
Manchester M20 ......109 F8
6 Marple SK6 ....125 F5
Stirling Cl Leigh WN7 .76 D6
Stockport SK3 ....123 C6
Stirling Dr Garswood WN4 .72 D4
Stalybridge SK15 ......86 A3
Stirling Gr M45 ....63 A8
Stirling Rd Bolton BL1 .24 E5
Hindley WN2 ....56 F4
Oldham OL9 ....65 F4
Stirling St Oldham OL9 .152 C2
Wigan WN1 ....37 C2
Stirrup Brook Gr M28 ..77 F5
Stitch La SK4 ....169 D3
Stitch-Mi-Lane BL2 ....25 F2
Stiups La OL16 ....31 B4
Stobart Ave M25 ....63 C2
Stock Gr OL16 ....31 F7
Stock La OL9 ....152 B6
Stock St BL8 ....27 E5
Stockburn Dr M35 .....84 C7
Stockdale Ave SK3 ...170 F5
Stockdale Gr BL2 ......25 F1
Stockdale Rd M9 ......64 E4
Stockfield Mount OL9 .152 B6
Stockfield Rd OL9 ....152 B7
Stockholm Rd SK3 ....170 E6
Stockholm St M11 .....83 B2
Stockland Cl M13 ....163 B7
Stockley Ave BL2 ......25 E2
Stockley Dr WN6 ....35 E8
Stockley Wlk 20 M15 .162 D6
Stockport Air Raid
Shelters Mus SK1 ....169 E1
Stockport Coll
of F & H Ed SK1 ....170 F8
Stockport Gram Sch
SK2 ....124 A5
Stockport Hat Mus SK4 .169 E1
Stockport Infmy SK3 ..170 F4
Stockport Rd
Altrincham M23,WA15 .120 B6
Altrincham WA15 ......119 F5
Cheadle SK3 ....123 A3
Cheadle SK8 ....122 E6
Denton M34 ....100 F2
Dukinfield OL7 ....100 F8
Hattersley SK14 .....102 E2
Hyde SK14 ....113 D7
Manchester M12,M13,M19 .99 D7
Marple SK6 ....125 E6
Mossley OL5 ....68 C2
Romiley SK6 ....113 B2
Uppermill OL4 ....68 C5
Stockport Rd E SK6 ..112 F4
Stockport Rd W SK6 ..112 D3
Stockport Sch SK2 ....124 B5
Stockport Sta SK3 ...170 E8

Stockport Trad Est
Stockport SK3 ....168 B1
Stockport SK4 ....123 B8
Stocks Gdns SK15 ......86 C1
Stocks La SK15 ....86 C1
Stocks Park Dr BL6 ....22 C3
Stocks St
Manchester M4,M8 ....159 A4
Rochdale OL16 ....30 B2
Stocks St E M4,M8 ...159 A4
Stocks The SK13 .....104 A7
Stocksfield Dr
3 Manchester M9 ......64 E3
Walkden M28 ....59 F5
Stocksgate OL12 ....14 B2
Stockton Ave 4 SK3 ..123 B8
Stockton Dr BL8 ....27 B5
Stockton Pk OL4 ....67 D6
Stockton Rd
Manchester M21 ......109 A8
Wilmslow SK9 ....136 F4
Stockton St Farnworth BL4 .42 C2
Littleborough OL15 ...16 A5
1 Manchester M16 .....97 E4
3 Swinton M27 ....79 E7
Stockwell Cl WN3 ......54 D3
Stockwood Wlk M9 ...157 D7
Stoke Abbott Cl SK7 ..132 E7
Stoke St OL16 ....31 B6
Stokes St M11 ....83 D1
Stokesay Cl Bury BL9 ..44 F5
Royton OL2 ....49 A4
Stokesay Dr SK7 .....124 C1
Stokesay Rd M33 .....107 C5
Stokesley Wlk BL3 ...147 E3
Stokoe Ave WA14 .....119 A6
Stonall Ave M15 .....162 D7
Stone Breaks Rd OL4 ..68 B7
Stone Cl BL0 ....11 A4
Stone Cross La N WA3 ..90 C7
Stone Cross La S WA3 ..90 C6
Stone Cross Park WA3 ..90 B7
Stone Gdns WN7 ....76 A5
Stone Hall La WN8 .....35 A5
Stone Haven WN3 ......54 D2
Stone Hill La OL12 ....14 A2
Stone Hill Rd BL4 .....60 D6
Stone House Rd WN5 ...36 D2
Stone Mead SK6 ......113 E3
Stone Mead Ave WA15 .129 C7
Stone Pale M45 ....62 F7
Stone Pit Cl WA3 ......74 F1
Stone Pit La WA3 ......90 F2
Stone Pits BL0 ....1 E3
Stone Pl M14 ....98 C3
Stone Row SK6 ....126 A6
Stone St Bolton BL2 ...25 B1
Manchester M3 ....162 E8
Milnrow OL16 ....31 F5
Rawtenstall BB4 ....2 F8
Stoneacre BL6 ....39 F8
Stoneacre Ct M27 .....79 F7
Stoneacre Rd M22 ....121 C2
Stonebeck Rd M23 ....120 F5
Stonebridge Cl BL6 ....40 C6
Stonechat Cl
Boothstown M28 ....78 B8
Droylsden M43 ....84 C3
10 Golborne WA3 ......90 E8
Stonechurch BL3 .....145 D5
Stonecliffe Ave SK15 ..86 A2
Stonecliffe Terr SK15 ..86 A3
Stoneclough Rd BL4,M26 .61 A7
Stonecroft 2 OL1 ....153 E7
Stonecroft Cl M20 ...110 A4
Stonecrop WN6 ....18 D2
Stonedelph Cl BL2 .....26 D1
Stonefield M29 ....59 C1
Stonefield Dr M8 .....155 F5
Stonefield St OL16 ....31 F5
Stoneflat Ct OL12 ....139 D8
Stonehaven BL3 ....40 F3
Stonehead St M9 .....157 F7
Stonehewer St M26 ....44 B2
Stonehill Cres OL12 ...14 A3
Stonehill Dr OL12 .....14 B3
Stonehill Rd OL12 .....14 B3
Stonehouse BL2 ....25 B7
Stonehouse Wlk 3 M23 .120 E7
Stonehurst Cl M12 ...165 A6
Stonelands Way OL4 ...68 A4
Stoneleigh Ave M33 ..107 C5
Stoneleigh
Com Prim Sch OL1 ....49 B2
Stoneleigh Dr M26 .....61 B7
Stoneleigh Rd OL4 .....68 A7
Stoneleigh St OL1 .....67 B8
Stonelow Cl M15 .....162 F6
Stonely Dr OL14 ....6 A7
Stonemead Cl BL3 ....147 F4
Stonemead Ct SK15 ...169 F3
Stonepail Cl SK8 .....121 F5
Stonepail Rd SK8 ....122 A5
Stoner Rd PR7 ....20 F7
Stoneridge SK13 .....103 F5
Stones Bank Rd BL7 ....8 B5
Stonesby Cl M16 ....97 D4
Stonesdale Cl OL2 .....48 E5
Stonesteads Dr BL7 ...25 A8
Stonesteads Way BL7 ..25 A8
Stonewood Dr OL5 .....68 D2
Stonewood Dr OL4 .....50 F4
Stonethwaite Cl WN3 ..55 A2
Stoney Bank M26 ......61 C7
Stoney Brow WN8 ......35 B1

Stoney Knoll M7 . . . . .155 D6
Stoney La Adlington PR7 . . 20 E4
Delph OL3 . . . . .50 D7
Wilmslow SK9 . . . . .136 F5
Stoneycroft Ave BL6 . . . . . .22 D4
Stoneycroft Cl BL6 . . . . . . .22 D5
Stoneyfield SK15 . . . . .86 A4
Stoneyfield Cl M16 . . . . . . .97 F2
Stoneygate La WN6 . . . . . .18 B2
Stoneygate Wlk M11 . . . . . .99 D7
Stoneyhurst Cres WA3 . . . .91 D5
Stoneyroyd OL12 . . . . .4 D1
Stoneyside Ave M28 . . . . . .60 E4
Stoneyside Gr M28 . . . . . . .60 E4
Stoneyvale Ct OL11 . . . . . . .30 F4
Stonie Heyes Ave OL12 . . .15 B2
Stonyhurst Rd M33 . . . . . .108 D4
Ince-in-M WN3 . . . . .151 D6
Stopes Rd BL3,M26 . . . . . . .43 C3
Stopford Ave OL15 . . . . . . .15 E4
Stopford St Droylsden M11 .99 F7
Ince-in-M WN2 . . . . .151 F7
Stockport SK3 . . . . .170 D8
Stopford Wlk M34 . . . . . . .100 F3
Stopforth St WN6 . . . . .37 A1
Stopley Wlk M11 . . . . .165 A8
Store St Ashton-u-L OL7 . . .85 A6
Horwich BL6 . . . . .22 C4
Manchester M1,M4 . . . . . .159 C1
Manchester M11 . . . . .165 B7
Radcliffe M26 . . . . .44 D4
Rochdale OL11 . . . . .13 E1
Shaw OL2 . . . . .149 C8
Stockport SK3 . . . . .124 C4
Stores St M25 . . . . .63 C4
Storeton Cl M22 . . . . .121 E2
Stortford Dr M23 . . . . .109 B2
Storth Bank SK13 . . . . . . .115 F7
Storth Meadow Rd SK13 . .115 F7
Stothard Rd M32 . . . . .96 C1
Stott Dr M41 . . . . .94 D1
Stott Ho OL8 . . . . .153 E5
Stott La Bolton BL2 . . . . . . .25 B1
Eccles M6,M5 . . . . .80 B2
Middleton M24,OL10 . . . . . .46 F5
Stott Milne St OL9 . . . . . . .152 B5
Stott St Failsworth OL9 . . . .65 E3
Swinton M27 . . . . .79 D6
Stott St Failsworth M35 . . . .83 D6
7 Littleborough OL16 . . . . .15 D4
Milnrow OL16 . . . . .31 F4
Rochdale OL12 . . . . .14 F1
Stott's La M35 . . . . .83 D6
Stottfield OL2 . . . . .48 B3
Stour Cl WA14 . . . . .119 C6
Stour Rd M29 . . . . .77 B7
Stourbridge Ave M38 . . . . .60 A6
Stourport Cl SK6 . . . . .113 A1
Stourport St OL1 . . . . .67 A8
Stout St WN7 . . . . .75 C4
Stovell Ave M12 . . . . .99 A2
Stovell Rd M40 . . . . .83 A8
Stow Cl BL8 . . . . .27 D5
Stow Gdns M20 . . . . .110 A6
Stowell Ct BL1 . . . . .143 E1
Stowell Ho **7** M5 . . . . . . .154 E1
Stowell St Bolton BL1 . . . . .143 E1
Salford M5 . . . . .154 E1
Stowell Tech Ctr M5 . . . . . .96 F8
Stowfield Cl M9 . . . . .64 B4
Stracey St M40 . . . . .160 E3
Stradbroke Cl
Golborne WA3 . . . . .91 A7
Manchester M18 . . . . .165 C5
Strain Ave M9 . . . . .64 D4
Straits The M29 . . . . .77 C6
Strand Ave WN4 . . . . .73 B4
Strand Ct M32 . . . . .108 C8
Strand The
Ashton-in-M WN4 . . . . .73 B4
Horwich BL6 . . . . .22 D3
Rochdale OL11 . . . . .30 F2
Strand Way OL1,OL2 . . . . . .48 D2
Strang St BL0 . . . . .138 C6
Strange Rd WN4 . . . . .72 D3
Strange St WN7 . . . . .75 B4
Strangford St M26 . . . . .43 D4
Stranraer Rd WN5 . . . . .36 D1
Stranton Dr M28 . . . . .79 C8
Stratfield Ave M23 . . . . . . .108 D1
Stratford Ave Bolton BL1 . .142 A1
Bury BL9 . . . . .27 E8
Manchester M20 . . . . .109 F5
Oldham OL8 . . . . .66 F3
Rochdale OL11 . . . . .139 E5
Stratford Cl BL4 . . . . .147 F1
Stratford Gdns SK6 . . . . . .112 F3
Stratford Rd M24 . . . . .65 B5
Stratford Sq SK8 . . . . .131 C7
Stratford St WN6 . . . . .37 A1
Strathaven Pl OL10 . . . . . . .28 F1
Strathblane Cl **3** M20 . . . .110 B7
Strathfield Dr **8** M11 . . . . .83 C2
Strathmere Ave M32 . . . . . .96 D3
Strathmore Ave
Ashton-in-M WN4 . . . . .73 A5
Denton M34 . . . . .101 B2
4 Manchester M16 . . . . . .97 B2
Strathmore Cl BL0 . . . . . . .11 C4
Strathmore Rd BL2 . . . . . . .25 E1
Stratton Dr WN2 . . . . .55 F1
Stratton Gr BL6 . . . . .22 B5
Stratton Rd
Manchester M16 . . . . .97 B2

Stratton Rd *continued*
Stockport SK2 . . . . .124 C8
Swinton M27 . . . . .61 F1
Strawberry Bank M6 . . . . . .81 B3
Strawberry La WA14 . . . . .119 B7
Strawberry Hill M6 . . . . . . .81 B3
Strawberry Hill Rd BL2 . . .148 B5
Strawberry La
Uppermill OL5 . . . . .68 C4
Wilmslow SK9 . . . . .136 E6
Strawberry Rd M6 . . . . .81 B3
Stray St M11 . . . . .99 E8
Stream Terr SK1 . . . . .112 B1
Streamside OL15 . . . . .120 B4
Street Bridge Rd OL1,OL2 . .48 A2
Street La BL8 . . . . .43 F8
Street Lodge OL11 . . . . . . .30 B1
Streetgate M38 . . . . .59 F5
Streethouse La OL3 . . . . . . .50 F1
Stretford Gram Sch M32 . . .96 E1
Stretford High Sch M32 . . . .96 F4
Stretford Ho **7** M32 . . . . . .96 C1
Stretford Meml Hosp
M16 . . . . .97 B3
Stretford Motorway Est
M32 . . . . .96 A5
Stretford Rd
Manchester M15,M16 . . . . .161 C5
Urmston M41 . . . . .95 E1
Stretford Sta M32 . . . . .96 D1
Stretton Ave Billinge WN5 . .71 C5
Golborne WA3 . . . . .90 E7
Manchester M20 . . . . .110 C3
Sale M33 . . . . .107 E4
Stretford M32 . . . . .96 A3
Stretton Cl
Manchester M40 . . . . .157 D5
Standish WN6 . . . . .36 E8
Stretton Rd Bolton BL3 . . .146 B4
Ramsbottom BL0 . . . . .11 A2
Stretton Way **3** SK9 . . . .131 D5
Striding Edge Wlk **1** OL1 .49 A1
Strines Cl WN2 . . . . .56 D6
Strines Ct SK14 . . . . .167 E4
Strines Rd Marple SK6 . . . .126 B3
New Mills SK6 . . . . .135 D8
Strines St OL14 . . . . .6 A7
Strines Sta SK22 . . . . .126 D1
Stringer Ave M40 . . . . .102 F2
Stringer Cl SK14 . . . . .102 F2
Stringer St Leigh WN7 . . . .75 F5
Stockport SK1 . . . . .112 A2
Stringer Way SK14 . . . . . . .102 F2
Stroma Gdns M41 . . . . .95 C5
Stromness Gr OL10 . . . . . . .28 F1
Strong St M7 . . . . .158 E4
Strongstry Rd BL0 . . . . .1 C2
Strontian Wlk **9** M11 . . . .83 C1
Stroud Ave M30 . . . . .79 B3
Stroud Cl Middleton M24 . . .65 A5
Wigan WN2 . . . . .37 F2
Stuart Ave Bacup OL13 . . . . .3 D8
Hindley WN2 . . . . .57 C3
Irlam M44 . . . . .93 F2
Stuart Cres WN5 . . . . .71 E5
Stuart Dr SK6 . . . . .125 C7
Stuart Hampson Ct **1**
M31 . . . . .105 F3
Stuart Ho M43 . . . . .100 A8
Stuart Rd Bredbury SK6 . . .112 D6
Stretford M32 . . . . .96 D3
Stuart St Droylsden M11 . . .83 A2
Manchester M11 . . . . .160 F2
Middleton M24 . . . . .65 C8
Oldham OL8 . . . . .153 E5
Rochdale OL16 . . . . .31 A6
Rochdale OL16 . . . . .31 B6
Wigan WN1 . . . . .151 D8
Stuart St E M11 . . . . .83 A2
Stuart Wlk M24 . . . . .64 F7
Stubbins Cl M23 . . . . .108 E1
Stubbins La BL0 . . . . .138 C8
Stubbins Prim Sch BL0 . . . .1 D1
Stubbins St BL0 . . . . .1 C1
Stubbins Vale Rd BL0 . . . . . .1 C1
Stubbins Vale Terr BL0 . . . . .1 B1
Stubbs M7 . . . . .81 B8
Stubbylee La OL13 . . . . .3 F8
Stubley Gdns OL15 . . . . . . .16 A5
Stubley La OL15 . . . . .15 F4
Stubley Mill Rd
Littleborough OL15 . . . . . . .15 F4
Littleborough OL15 . . . . . . .15 F4
Studford Wlk **3** M15 . . . .163 A5
Studland Rd M22 . . . . .121 F3
Studley Cl OL2 . . . . .49 A4
Studley Ct M29 . . . . .58 F1
Sturton Ave WN3 . . . . .54 E3
Styal Ave Reddish SK5 . . . .111 F6
Stretford M32 . . . . .96 A3
Styal Ctry Pk SK9 . . . . . . .130 E3
Styal Cty Prim Sch SK9 . .130 E4
Styal Gn SK9 . . . . .130 F3
Styal Gr SK8 . . . . .122 A3
Styal Rd
Gatley M22,SK8,& SK9 . . . .122 A3
Wilmslow SK9 . . . . .137 B8
Wythenshawe M22 . . . . . .130 F7
Styal St BL1 . . . . .144 B8
Styal Sta SK9 . . . . .131 A4
Styal View SK9 . . . . .131 B2
Styhead Dr M24 . . . . .46 D3
Style St M4 . . . . .159 A3
Styperson Way SK12 . . . . .133 E2
Sudbrook Cl WA3 . . . . .90 E8
Sudbury Cl
Manchester M16 . . . . .161 C5

Sudbury Cl *continued*
Wigan WN3 . . . . .55 B2
Sudbury Dr Bolton BL6 . . . .40 C6
Gatley SK8 . . . . .131 C8
Sudbury Rd SK7 . . . . .133 E8
Sudden St OL11 . . . . .30 C1
Sudell St M4,M40 . . . . .159 B3
Sudell Street Ind Est M4 . .159 B3
Sudley Rd OL11 . . . . .139 D5
Sudlow St OL16 . . . . .15 B2
Sudren St BL8 . . . . .26 F3
Sue Patterson Wlk M40 . .156 C5
Suez St WA12 . . . . .89 B3
Suffield St M24 . . . . .65 A8
Suffield Wlk **1** M22 . . . . .121 D1
Suffolk Ave M43 . . . . .84 A3
Suffolk Cl Little Lever BL3 . .43 B5
Standish WN1 . . . . .37 B8
Suffolk Dr Brinnington SK5 .112 C6
Handforth SK9 . . . . .131 C1
Suffolk Gr WN7 . . . . .75 C5
Suffolk Rd WA14 . . . . .119 B5
Suffolk St Oldham OL9 . . . . .66 B4
Rochdale OL11 . . . . .139 F6
Salford M6 . . . . .81 A5
Sugar La OL3 . . . . .51 A2
Sugden Sports Ctr M1 . . . .163 A7
Sugden St OL6 . . . . .85 D3
Sulby Ave M32 . . . . .96 E2
Sulby St Kearsley M26 . . . .61 B7
Manchester M40 . . . . .83 A8
Sulgrave Ave SK12 . . . . . .133 F4
Sullivan St M12 . . . . .99 A3
Sullivan Way WN1 . . . . .37 D1
Sultan St BL9 . . . . .44 F8
Sulway Cl M27 . . . . .80 A7
Sumac St M11 . . . . .83 D2
Sumbland Ho M27 . . . . .62 B2
Summer Ave M41 . . . . .95 E2
Summer Castle
Rochdale OL16 . . . . .139 F7
Rochdale OL16 . . . . .31 A7
Summer Pl **1** M14 . . . . . .98 C2
Summer St Horwich BL6 . . .22 B4
Rochdale OL16 . . . . .31 A7
Summerbottom SK14 . . . .115 A8
Summercroft OL9 . . . . .66 B4
Summerdale Dr BL0 . . . . . .11 B2
Summerfield Ave M43 . . . . .83 E3
Summerfield Ct **2** M21 . . .96 F1
Summerfield Dr
Middleton M24 . . . . .47 C1
Tyldesley M29 . . . . .77 B8
Summerfield Pl SK9 . . . . . .137 A5
Summerfield Rd
Bolton BL3 . . . . .42 B4
Worsley M28 . . . . .79 A8
Wythenshawe M22 . . . . . .121 C2
Summerfields PR7 . . . . . . .19 F7
Summerfields Ctr SK9 . . . .131 D1
Summerfields View OL8 . . .67 C3
Summerlea SK8 . . . . .132 B8
Summers Ave SK15 . . . . . . .86 C2
Summers St OL9 . . . . .152 C7
Summersales Ind Est
WN3 . . . . .54 C4
Summerseat Cl
Oldham OL4 . . . . .68 A7
Salford M5 . . . . .161 A8
Summerseat La BL0 . . . . . .11 A2
Summerseat
Meth Prim Sch BL9 . . . . .11 D2
Summerseat Sta BL9 . . . . .11 C2
Summersgill Cl OL10 . . . . . .29 E1
Summershades La OL4 . . . .68 D6
Summershades Rise OL4 . .68 D6
Summerton Ho **3** M5 . . . . .81 A1
Summerville Ave M9 . . . . .157 F7
Summerville Prim Sch
M6 . . . . .80 D5
Summerville Rd M6 . . . . . .80 D5
Summit Cl BL9 . . . . .28 F4
Summit St OL10 . . . . .28 F3
Sumner Ave BL2 . . . . .26 D1
Sumner Rd M6 . . . . .80 D5
Sumner St Aspull WN2 . . . .38 D5
Atherton M46 . . . . .58 C3
Bolton BL3 . . . . .146 B2
Glossop SK13 . . . . .116 C8
Shaw OL2 . . . . .149 B5
Sumner Way M41 . . . . .95 D2
Sumners Pl SK13 . . . . .104 B1
Sun Gate OL15 . . . . .15 F1
Sun Inn Mews OL3 . . . . . . .33 D3
Sun St Mossley OL5 . . . . . . .68 C1
Ramsbottom BL0 . . . . .138 B7
Sun Vale Ave OL14 . . . . .6 B7
Sunadale Cl BL3 . . . . .144 B5
Sunbank Cl OL12 . . . . .14 D2
Sunbank La WA15 . . . . . . .129 E6
Sunbeam St WA12 . . . . .89 C3
Sunbeam Wlk **10** M11 . . .160 F1
Sunbury Cl Handforth SK9 .131 E2
Stalybridge SK16 . . . . .101 F8
Sunbury Dr M40 . . . . .83 D4
Sundance Ct M5 . . . . .96 E8
Sunderland Ave OL6 . . . . .166 C4
Sunderland Pl WN5 . . . . . . .36 D1
Sunderton Wlk M12 . . . . . .164 E6
Sundew Pl M24 . . . . .65 D7
Sundial Cl SK14 . . . . .102 D3
Sundial Rd SK2 . . . . .124 D7
Sundial Wlk SK14 . . . . . . .102 D3
Sundridge Cl BL3 . . . . .146 A3
Sunfield OL16 . . . . .6 C3
Sunfield Ave OL4 . . . . .49 E4
Sunfield Cres OL2 . . . . .48 E3
Sunfield Dr OL2 . . . . .48 F3

Sunfield Est OL3 . . . . .51 C4
Sunfield La OL3 . . . . .51 C4
Sunfield Rd OL1 . . . . .153 E8
Sunfield Way OL4 . . . . .67 C2
Sunflower Mdw M44 . . . . . .94 B3
Sunhill Cl OL16 . . . . .31 B2
Sunk La M24 . . . . .65 A7
Sunlaws St SK13 . . . . .116 B8
Sunleigh Rd WN2 . . . . .56 E6
Sunlight Rd BL1 . . . . .144 C7
Sunning Hill
Cty Prim Sch BL3 . . . . . .147 D4
Sunning Hill St **18** BL3 . .147 D5
Sunningdale Ave
Droylsden M11 . . . . .83 B2
Radcliffe M26 . . . . .43 D4
Sale M33 . . . . .108 E3
Whitefield M45 . . . . .62 C7
Sunningdale Ct Bury BL8 . .44 A8
Dukinfield SK14 . . . . .101 F5
Sunningdale Ct
Reddish M34 . . . . .100 B4
Sale M33 . . . . .108 E3
Sunningdale Dr
Bramhall SK7 . . . . .133 A7
Glossop SK13 . . . . .104 E1
Heywood OL10 . . . . .46 D8
Irlam M44 . . . . .93 F3
Prestwich M25 . . . . .63 B5
Salford M6 . . . . .80 B5
Sunningdale Gr WN7 . . . . . .76 D7
Sunningdale Rd
Denton M34 . . . . .101 B1
Urmston M41 . . . . .95 B1
Sunningdale Wlk **1** BL3 .145 D5
Sunninghey Ct SK9 . . . . . .136 F2
Sunny Ave BL9 . . . . .27 F5
Sunny Bank Kearsley M26 . .61 A8
Oldham OL4 . . . . .67 C5
Wilmslow SK9 . . . . .136 D4
Wilmslow SK9 . . . . .137 B6
Sunny Bank Ave M43 . . . . .83 F1
Sunny Bank Cl BB4 . . . . .1 A6
Sunny Bank Prim Sch BL9 45 A3
Sunny Bank Rd
Altrincham WA14 . . . . .128 C3
Droylsden M43 . . . . .83 F1
Haslingden BB4 . . . . .1 A6
Manchester M13 . . . . .98 E3
Whitefield BL9 . . . . .45 A3
Sunny Banks SK13 . . . . . .116 B8
Sunny Bower St BL8 . . . . . .26 F6
Sunny Brow Rd
Manchester M18 . . . . .99 C4
Middleton M24 . . . . .64 E8
Sunny Dr Orrell WN5 . . . . . .53 F6
Prestwich M25 . . . . .62 F4
Sunny Garth BL5 . . . . .57 E8
Sunny Lea Mews SK9 . . . .137 A6
Sunny Side M32 . . . . .96 F3
Sunnybank Ave Eccles M30 .79 F3
Manchester SK4 . . . . .110 F4
Sunnybank Cl WA12 . . . . . .89 C4
Sunnybank Rd Bolton BL1 .142 C2
Tyldesley M29 . . . . .77 B6
Sunnyfield Rd
Manchester SK4 . . . . .110 F3
Prestwich M25,M45 . . . . . .63 C7
Sunnyfields WN3 . . . . .54 C2
Sunnylea Ave M19 . . . . . . .110 E5
Sunnymead Ave BL1 . . . . .143 F4
Sunnymede Vale BL0 . . . . .11 A3
Sunnyside OL7 . . . . .84 F5
Sunnyside Ave M43 . . . . . . .83 E4
Sunnyside Cres **8** OL6 . . .85 D2
Sunnyside Ct
Droylsden M43 . . . . .83 F3
Manchester M20 . . . . .110 C3
Sunnyside Gr OL6 . . . . .85 D2
Sunnyside Rd
Ashton-in-M WN4 . . . . .72 F7
Bolton BL1 . . . . .142 C2
Droylsden M43 . . . . .84 A3
Sunnywood Dr BL8 . . . . . . .27 A6
Sunnywood La BL8 . . . . . . .27 A6
Sunset Ave M22 . . . . .109 C2
Sunwell Terr SK6 . . . . .125 F3
Surbiton Rd M40 . . . . .83 B4
Surma Cl Oldham OL9 . . . .153 D7
Rochdale OL16 . . . . .31 B5
Surrey Ave Droylsden M43 . .83 F3
Leigh WN7 . . . . .76 E4
Shaw OL2 . . . . .48 F7
Surrey Cl BL3 . . . . .43 B4
Surrey Dr BL9 . . . . .44 F8
Surrey Park Cl OL12 . . . . .149 B8
Surrey Rd M9 . . . . .64 D2
Surrey St Ashton-u-L OL6 . .85 D5
Glossop SK13 . . . . .104 C1
Manchester M9 . . . . .64 C2
Oldham OL9 . . . . .152 C5
Surrey Way SK5 . . . . .112 C4
Surtees Rd M23 . . . . .109 A2
Sussex Ave Heywood OL10 . .28 E1
Manchester M20 . . . . .110 B4
Sussex Cl Hindley WN2 . . . .57 A5
Oldham OL9 . . . . .152 B6
Standish WN1 . . . . .20 B1
Swinton M27 . . . . .62 A2
Sussex Dr Bury BL9 . . . . . . .44 F8
Droylsden M43 . . . . .84 A3
Haslingden BB4 . . . . .1 B8
Sussex Pl SK14 . . . . .101 F5
Sussex Rd Irlam M44 . . . . .105 C6
Partington M31 . . . . .105 C2
Stockport SK3 . . . . .123 B8
Sussex St Leigh WN7 . . . . . .76 E4
12 Manchester M2 . . . . .158 F1

Sussex St *continued*
Manchester M7 . . . . .158 D4
Rochdale OL11 . . . . .139 F6
Sutch La WA13 . . . . .117 A3
Sutcliffe Ave M12 . . . . .99 B2
Sutcliffe St Ashton-u-L OL7 .84 F1
Bacup OL13 . . . . .4 C8
Bolton BL1 . . . . .143 E2
Littleborough OL15 . . . . . . .16 B6
Middleton M24 . . . . .65 C8
Oldham OL8 . . . . .153 E5
Royton OL2 . . . . .49 A3
Sutcliffes Pl **3** OL11 . . . . .31 A4
Sutherland Cl OL8 . . . . .66 F1
Sutherland Gr BL4 . . . . .60 C8
Sutherland Rd Bolton BL1 142 A1
Heywood OL10 . . . . .28 F1
Manchester M16 . . . . .97 A3
Wigan WN3 . . . . .55 A3
Sutherland St
Ashton-u-L OL6 . . . . .85 E3
Eccles M30 . . . . .79 B3
3 Farnworth BL4 . . . . . . .60 C8
Hindley WN2 . . . . .56 C5
Swinton M27 . . . . .61 E1
1 Wigan WN5 . . . . .54 F6
Suthers St Oldham OL9 . . .152 C6
Radcliffe M26 . . . . .44 C1
Sutton Ave WA3 . . . . .91 F4
Sutton Dr M43 . . . . .83 E3
Sutton Ho **8** M6 . . . . . . .154 F3
Sutton La PR6 . . . . .21 B8
Sutton Manor **1** M21 . . . .97 A1
Sutton Rd
Alderley Edge SK9 . . . . . . .136 F2
Bolton BL3 . . . . .40 F4
Manchester M18 . . . . .99 C3
Manchester SK4 . . . . .168 C3
Poynton SK12 . . . . .134 A2
Sutton Way Hadfield SK13 .104 A3
1 Handforth SK9 . . . . . .131 E5
Salford M6 . . . . .154 F3
Swailes St **3** OL4 . . . . . . .67 B6
Swain St SK12 . . . . .14 E1
Swaindrod La OL15 . . . . . . .16 F7
Swaine St SK3 . . . . .169 E3
Swainsthorpe Dr **15** M9 .157 E8
Swale Cl SK9 . . . . .131 E2
Swale Dr WA14 . . . . .119 C6
Swalecliff Ave M23 . . . . . .108 D1
Swaledale Cl OL2 . . . . .48 E5
Swallow Bank Dr OL11 . . . .30 B3
Swallow Cl SK15 . . . . .86 F7
Swallow Ct SK1 . . . . .169 E4
Swallow Dr Bury BL9 . . . . .141 B4
Irlam M44 . . . . .94 A3
Rochdale OL11 . . . . .29 F7
Swallow La SK15 . . . . .86 F6
Swallow St
Manchester M11 . . . . .160 F1
Manchester M12 . . . . .99 A2
Oldham OL8 . . . . .66 D2
Stockport SK1 . . . . .170 F7
Swallowfield WN7 . . . . .76 A5
Swan Cl SK12 . . . . .133 B4
Swan Ct OL2 . . . . .149 B6
Swan La Bolton BL3 . . . . . .147 D4
Hindley WN2 . . . . .57 B4
Swan Meadow Rd WN3 . .150 B3
Swan Rd Ramsbottom BL8 . .10 F2
Sale WA15 . . . . .108 A1
Swan St Ashton-u-L OL6 . . .166 S2
Manchester M4 . . . . .159 B2
Radcliffe M26 . . . . .44 B2
Wilmslow SK9 . . . . .137 B7
Swanage Ave Sale M23 . . .108 D1
Stockport SK2 . . . . .124 D6
Swanage Cl BL8 . . . . .27 C6
Swanage Rd M30 . . . . .79 B3
Swanbourne Gdns SK3 . . .123 C6
Swanfield Wlk WA3 . . . . . . .73 F2
Swanhill Cl **2** M18 . . . . . .99 F6
Swanley Ave M40 . . . . .157 E5
Swann Gr SK8 . . . . .123 B1
Swann La SK8 . . . . .123 B1
Swann St WN3 . . . . .150 B7
Swansea St OL8 . . . . .67 B4
Swanton Wlk **17** M8 . . . . .155 F6
Swanbrick Dr M25 . . . . .62 F2
Swayfield Ave M13 . . . . . . .98 F3
Swaylands Dr M33 . . . . . . .108 B1
Sweet Briar Cl OL12 . . . . . .14 E2
Sweet Briar La OL12 . . . . . .14 E2
Sweetbriar Cl OL2 . . . . . . .149 B7
Sweetloves Gr BL1 . . . . . . .24 E5
Sweetloves La BL1 . . . . . . .24 E5
Sweetnam Dr M11 . . . . .83 B2
Swettenham Rd SK9 . . . . .131 D5
Swift Cl SK6 . . . . .113 C5
Swift Rd Oldham OL1 . . . . .49 E5
Rochdale OL11 . . . . .29 F7
Swift St Ashton-u-L OL6 . . . .85 D5
Wigan WN5 . . . . .150 A7
Swift Wlk **2** M40 . . . . .83 C5
Swiftsure Ave M3 . . . . .158 D1
Swinbourne Gr M20 . . . . . .110 C7
Swinburn St WN5 . . . . .53 D1
Swinburn St **2** M9 . . . . . .64 F1
Swinburne Ave M43 . . . . . . .84 A3
Swinburne Gn SK5 . . . . . . .99 D1
Swinburne Way **12** M34 . .113 A7
Swindell's St M11 . . . . .99 E7
Swindells St SK14 . . . . . . .101 E5
Swindon Cl M18 . . . . .99 D5
Swinfield Ave M21 . . . . . . .108 F8
Swinford Gr OL2 . . . . .149 A5
Swinford Wlk **14** M9 . . . . .64 C3

Swinley Chase SK9 ....131 F1
Swinley La WN1 ....37 C2
Swinley Rd WN1 ....37 C2
Swinley St WN1 ....37 C2
Swinside WN1 ....37 F1
Swinside CI M24 ....46 C2
Swinside Rd BL2 ....42 F8
Swinstead Ave M40 ....157 E5
Swinton Cres M45 ......45 A1
Swinton Gr M13 ....163 C5
Swinton Hall Rd M27 ...80 A8
Swinton High Sch The
M27 ....61 F1
Swinton Park Rd M6 ....80 B5
Swinton St Bolton BL2 ..42 E7
Oldham OL4 ....67 C5
Swinton Sta M27 ....61 F1
Swiss Hill SK9 ....137 B1
Swithembe St BL6 ......22 A4
Swithin Rd M22 ....130 E5
Swythamley CI SK3 ....123 A8
Swythamley Rd SK3 ...123 A8
Sybil St OL15 ....16 A6

Sycamore Ave
Altrincham WA14 .....119 A5
Denton M34 ....100 F2
Golborne WA3 ....74 A1
Heywood OL10 ....46 E8
Hindley WN2 ....56 F3
Newhey OL16 ....32 A3
Newton-le-W WA12 ....89 C3
Oldham OL4 ....67 D8
Oldham OL5 ....65 F3
Radcliffe M26 ....61 F8
Tyldesley M29 ....59 D1
Wigan WN6 ....36 F3

Sycamore CI
Ashton-u-L OL6 ....85 E2
Handforth SK9 ....131 B2
Littleborough OL15 ...15 F5
Manchester M20 ......110 C2
New Mills SK22 ......127 E1
Stalybridge SK16 ....101 F8
Sycamore Cotts OL3 ...50 F1
Sycamore Cres
Ashton-u-L OL6 ....85 C5
Hollinfare WA3 ......105 B2
Sycamore Ct
11 Manchester M16 ...97 D3
Manchester M40 .....160 E3
8 Salford M6 ....81 A3
Sycamore Dr Radcliffe M26 44 A5
Wigan WN3 ....54 C2
Sycamore Gr M35 ......84 B7
Sycamore Lo SK7 .....132 F7
Sycamore PI M45 ......62 F6
Sycamore Rd Atherton M46 58 A4
Bury BL8 ....26 F5
Eccles M30 ....79 A4
New Mills SK22 .....127 F6
Partington M31 .....105 E3
Romiley SK6 ....113 A4
Sycamore St Sale M33 108 E4
Stockport SK3 ......123 B8
Sycamore Wlk
Cheadle SK8 ....122 D6
1 Horwich BL6 ....22 E1
Sycamores The
Hadfield SK13 ......171 F3
Kearsley M26 ....61 B6
Mossley OL5 ....68 C1
Oldham OL4 ....67 E8
Stalybridge SK15 ...102 B8
Sydall St M34 ....100 F3
Syddal CI SK7 ......132 D5
Syddal Cres SK7 ....132 D4
Syddal Gn SK7 ......132 D5
Syddal Park Prep Sch
SK7 ....132 D5
Syddal Park Sch SK7 132 D5
Syddal Rd SK7 ......132 D5
Syddall Ave SK8 ....131 D8
Syddall St SK14 ....167 D2
Sydenham St 2 OL1 ...49 B1
Sydenham Terr OL12 ..14 D3
Syderstone CI WN2 ...56 E4
Sydney Ave Eccles M30 79 D2
Leigh WN7 ....75 D2
Wythenshawe M90 ..130 A8
Sydney Gdns OL15 .....6 C1
Sydney Jones Ct M40 .65 C1
Sydney Rd SK7 ......132 F5
Sydney St Failsworth M35 83 E7
Mossley OL5 ....86 D8
Platt Bridge WN2 ....56 A3
Salford M6 ....154 E2
Stockport SK2 .....124 C7
Stretford M32 ....96 D2
Swinton M27 ....79 D7
Syke OL12 ....14 F4
Syke Rd Littleborough OL15 16 C2
Rochdale OL12 ......15 A3
Sykes Ave BL9 ....45 B4
Sykes CI OL3 ....69 B5
Sykes Mdw SK8 .....170 D6
Sykes St Bury BL9 ..141 A4
Hyde SK14 ....167 F1
Newhey OL16 ....32 A4
Reddish SK5 ....111 F8
7 Rochdale OL16 ....31 B6
Sykes Wlk 2 SK5 ...111 F8
Sylvan Ave Failsworth M35 83 E5
Manchester M16 .....97 D3
Sale M33 ....108 C3
Sale WA15 ....119 F8
Urmston M41 ....95 D3
Wilmslow SK9 .....136 F5
Sylvan CI M24 ......46 D2

Sylvan Gr WA14 .....119 D5
Sylvan St OL9 ......152 C7
Sylvandale Ave M19 ..99 A1
Sylvester Ave SK1,SK2 124 B7
Sylvester CI SK14 ..102 E2
Sylvester Way
1 Denton M34 ......113 A7
8 Hattersley SK14 .102 E2
Sylvia Gr 9 SK5 ....111 E7
Symms St M6 ....81 B4
Symond Rd M9 ....64 E5
Symons Rd M33 .....108 B5
Symons St M7 ......155 E7
Syndall Ave M12 ...164 D6
Syndall St M12 ....164 D6
Synergy Ho M15 ...163 A5
Syresham St 1 WN2 .56 B2

T

Taberner CI WN6 ....19 F1
Taberner St 3 WN2 .56 B2
Tabley Av M14 ......98 B2
Tabley Gdns
3 Droylsden M43 ...84 B1
Marple SK6 ....126 A4
Tabley Gr Manchester M13 98 E4
Reddish SK5 ....111 E7
Sale WA15 ....120 A8
Tabley Mere Gdns SK8 122 F3
Handforth SK9 ....131 D5
Sale M33 ....108 A4
Tabley St Dukinfield SK16 101 E8
Mossley OL5 ....86 D8
Salford M6 ....81 B5
Tabor St M24 ....46 F2
Tackler CI M27 ....79 F7
Tadcaster Wlk OL1 153 F7
Taddington PI 17 SK13 171 E1
Tadlow Wlk 2 M40 .159 C3
Tadman Gr WA14 ...119 A6
Tadmor CI M38 .....59 F4
Tagore CI M13 .....98 E4
Tahir CI M8 ....156 B7
Tait Mews SK4 ....110 F2
Talavera St M7 ...155 D5
Talbenny CI BL1 ...40 F8
Talbot Ave BL3 ....43 A4
Talbot CI Oldham OL4 67 C8
Rawtenstall BB4 ....1 E8
Talbot Ct BL1 ....143 F4
Talbot Gr BL9 .....28 A6
Talbot PI M16 ....161 B5
Talbot Rd
Alderley Edge SK9 137 B1
Altrincham WA14 ..119 B2
Dukinfield SK16 ..101 F5
Glossop SK13 .....104 C2
Manchester M14 ...110 E7
Sale M33 ....108 E4
Stretford M16,M32,M15 96 F3
Talbot St Ashton-u-L OL6 166 A3
Eccles M30 ....79 E1
Glossop SK13 .....104 C1
Golborne WA3 ......90 A8
Hazel Grove SK7 ..124 E4
Middleton M24 .....47 A2
Rochdale OL11 ....139 F6
Stockport SK1,SK4 169 E1
Talford Gr M20 ...110 A5
Talgarth Rd M40 ..159 C4
Talkin Dr M24 .....46 E3
Tall Trees M33 ....63 D1
Tall Trees CI OL2 .48 C4
Tall Trees PI SK2 124 C6
Talland Wlk M13 .164 D5
Tallarn CI M20 ...110 C2
Tallis St M12 .....99 A3
Talman Gr WN4 ....73 D3
Talmine Ave M40 .157 E5
Tamar CI BL5 ......61 B5
Tamar Ct 5 M15 ..162 D6
Tamar Dr M23 ....121 A4
Tamar Way OL10 ...29 A3
Tamarin CI M27 ...61 C1
Tame Barn CI OL16 32 A6
Tame Ct SK15 .....86 C3
Tame La OL3 ....50 D7
Tame St Denton M34 100 F4
Dukinfield M34 ...100 F7
Manchester M4 ...160 D1
Oldham OL3 ....69 B8
Stalybridge SK15,SK16 85 E1
Uppermill OL5 .....68 E3
Tame Valley Prim Sch
SK5 ....112 C7
Tame View SK15 ...68 C2
Tame Water Villas OL3 50 F1
Tamebank OL5 .....68 D3
Tamer Gr WN7 .....75 C8
Tamerton Dr M8 ..156 A6
Tameside Coll
(The Hyde Ctr) SK14 113 D7
Tameside Coll of Tech
Ashton-u-L OL6 ...166 B2
Ashton-u-L OL6 ....85 D3
Hyde SK14 ....167 E2
Tameside Ct
Dukinfield SK16 ..101 B8
5 Hattersley SK14 102 E2
Tameside General Hospl
OL6 ....85 E4
Tameside
Tamworth Ave
Prestwich M45 .....63 B7

Tamworth Ave continued
Salford M5 ....161 B8
Tamworth Ave W M5 161 A8
Tamworth CI
Hazel Grove SK7 .133 D8
Manchester M15 ..162 E5
Tamworth Ct M15 162 E5
Tamworth Dr Bury BL8 27 C5
Wigan WN2 ....37 F2
Tamworth Gn SK1 112 B2
Tamworth St
Manchester M15 ..97 E4
Newton-le-W WA12 89 A3
Oldham OL9 ......152 C5
Stockport SK1 ...112 B2
Tamworth Wlk M5 161 B8
Tan House Dr WN3 54 C2
Tan House La WN3 54 C2
Tan Pit Cotts WN8 35 C4
Tan Pits CI M29 ..77 C7
Tan Yard Brow M18 99 E5
Tandis Ct M6 .....80 A4
Tandle Hill Ctry Pk OL2 48 A6
Tandle Hill Rd OL2 48 B6
Tandlewood Mews 8
M40 ....83 C5
Tandlewood Pk OL2 48 B6
Tanfield Dr M26 ..61 B7
Tanfield Rd M20 122 B8
Tang The SK6 ...113 B1
Tangmere CI M40 .65 C3
Tangmere Ct M16 .97 D3
Tanhill CI SK2 ..124 E6
Tanhill La OL8 ...67 A2
Tanhouse Ave M29 77 D7
Tanhouse Rd M41 .94 D3
Tanner Brook CI BL3 147 E4
Tanner St SK14 ..167 D3
Tanner's La WA3 ..90 B8
Tanners Croft BL0 138 B6
Tanners Fold OL8 67 A2
Tanners Gn 7 M6 154 F3
Tanners St Droylsden M18 99 E5
Ramsbottom BL0 138 B6
Tannery Way WA14 119 E7
Tannock Rd SK7 .124 F1
Tanpit Wlk 4 M22 121 C2
Tanpits Rd BL9 ..140 E3
Tansey Gr M7 ....155 F7
Tansley Ave PR7 ..19 D8
Tansley CI BL6 ...22 C2
Tansley Rd M8 ....64 B2
Tansley Sq WN5 ..54 D5
Tanworth Wlk 22 BL1 143 E2
Tanyard Dr M29 .129 C6
Tanyard Gn SK5 .111 F5
Tanyard La WA15 129 A5
Tape St BL0 ....138 B6
Taper St BL0 ...138 B6
Tapley Ave SK12 133 E2
Taplin Dr M18 ..165 C5
Taplow Gr SK8 ..122 F2
Taplow Wlk M14 ..98 E3
Tarbet Dr BL2 ...42 F7
Tarbet Rd SK16 .101 C7
Tarbolton Cres WA15 120 C3
Tarbrook Gr 1 SK9 131 D2
Tariff St M1 ....159 B1
Tarland Wlk 11 M11 83 C1
Tarleton Ave M46 58 B5
Tarleton CI BL8 ..26 F1
Tarleton PI BL3 146 A3
Tarleton Wlk M13 164 D6
Tarn CI WN4 .....73 B5
Tarn Dr BL9 .....44 E6
Tarn Gr M28 .....60 F1
Tarnbrook CI M45 63 C8
Tarnbrook Dr WN2 38 B5
Tarnbrook Wlk M15 163 A5
Tarnrigg CI WN3 .54 E3
Tarns The SK8 ..122 B3
Tarnside
Hazel Grove SK2 124 F6
Littleborough OL16 15 C3
Tarnside Fold SK13 116 A7
Tarnside Rd WN5 .53 E6
Tarnway WA3 .....90 F7
Tarporley Ave M14 110 A8
Tarporley CI SK3 170 D5
Tarporley Wlk SK9 131 E2
Tarran Gr M34 ..101 B1
Tarran PI WA14 .119 E6
Tarrant CI M14 ..54 D2
Tarrington CI M12 165 A5
Tartan St M11 ...83 B2
Tarves Wlk M11 .83 B1
Tarvin
Manchester M20 110 A7
Reddish SK4 ....111 D7
Tarvin CI WA3 ...90 E7
Tarvin Dr SK6 ..112 E4
Tarvin Rd M32 ...96 E3
Tarvin Way 1 SK9 131 D5
Tarvin Wlk BL1 .143 E2
Tarvington CI M40 156 C6
Tasle Alley M2 .158 F1
Tatchbury Rd M35 84 A7
Tate St OL8 .....67 B5
Tatham CI 3 M13 98 F3
Tatham Gr WN3 ..54 D1
Tatham St OL16 ..31 A7
Tatland Dr M22 .121 F3
Tatlock CI OL5 ..71 C5
Tattenhall Wlk 12 M14 110 D8
Tattersall Ave BL1 23 E2
Tattersall St OL9 153 D6
Tatton CI Cheadle SK8 123 A4

Tatton CI continued
Hazel Grove SK7 .124 F4
Tatton Ct
4 Handforth SK9 131 E5
8 Manchester M14 110 D8
Manchester SK4 .168 C4
Tatton Dr WN4 ...72 F4
Tatton Fold M22 109 E1
Tatton Gdns SK6 113 D5
Tatton Gr M20 ..110 B6
Tatton Mere Dr M43 84 B1
Tatton PI Manchester M13 98 E4
Sale M33 ....108 B5
Tatton Rd Denton M34 101 A1
Handforth SK9 ...131 E5
Sale M33 ....108 B5
Tatton Rd N SK4 111 C5
Tatton Rd S SK4 168 C4
Tatton St Hyde SK14 113 E2
Manchester M15 .162 D7
Salford M5 ......161 B8
Stalybridge SK15 86 B1
Stockport SK1 ..169 F1
Tatton Terr 5 SK16 166 B1
Tatton View 6 M20 110 B6
Tattonmere Gdns SK8 123 A4
Taunton Ave
Ashton-u-L OL7 ..166 A4
Brinnington SK5 .112 C5
Eccles M30 ......79 B3
Hindley WN2 .....57 D7
Rochdale OL11 ...30 B7
Urmston M41 ...107 B8
Taunton Brook La OL7 84 E5
Taunton CI Bolton BL1 142 C1
Hazel Grove SK7 125 A2
Taunton Dr BL4 .147 F1
Taunton Gn OL7 .84 F5
Taunton Gr M25,M45 63 A6
Taunton Hall CI OL7 84 F5
Taunton Lawns OL7 85 A5
Taunton PI OL7 .84 F5
Taunton Rd
Ashton-u-L OL7 ..166 A4
Chadderton OL9 ..48 A1
Sale M33 ....107 D4
Taunton Wlk 13 M34 101 A1
Taurus St OL4 ...67 C8
Tavern Court Ave M35 84 B7
Tavern Ct M35 ...84 B7
Tavery CI 7 M4 .159 C2
Tavistock CI SK14 102 E2
Tavistock Dr OL9 47 F1
Tavistock Rd Bolton BL1 145 D4
Hindley WN2 .....57 A4
Rochdale OL11 ...30 F2
Sale M33 ....107 D5
Tavistock Sq M9 157 D7
Tavistock St M46 58 B4
Tawton Ave SK14 102 E3
Taxi Rd M90 ....130 B7
Tay CI OL8 .....153 E5
Tayfield Rd M22 121 C2
Taylor Ave OL11 .29 F8
Taylor Bldgs BL4 61 B6
Taylor Gr WN2 ...57 C3
Taylor Green Way OL4 67 F7
Taylor Ho M8 ....27 C5
Taylor Holme Ind Est OL13 3 B8
Taylor Ind Est WA3 91 F1
Taylor La
Altrincham WA14 119 A5
Eccles M41 ......95 E7
Hindley WN2 .....57 C7
Taylor Rd
Altrincham WA14 119 A5
Eccles M41 ......95 E7
Hindley WN2 .....57 C7
Taylor St 8 Bolton BL3 145 F6
Bury BL9 ....141 A3
Chadderton OL9 152 A7
Denton M34 ....100 F4
Droylsden M43 ...84 A1
Golborne WN3 ...74 C1
Heywood OL10 ...29 C2
Hollingworth SK14 171 D4
Horwich BL6 ....22 B3
Hyde SK14 .....167 F3
Leigh WN7 ......75 D8
Manchester M14 98 C2
Manchester M18 165 C6
Middleton M24 ..65 A8
Oldham OL1 .....67 C8
1 Oldham OL4 ...67 E6
Prestwich M25 ..63 C4
Radcliffe M26 ..44 A3
Rochdale OL12 ..14 F1
Royton OL2 .....48 D5
Stalybridge SK15 86 B1
Whitworth OL12 .14 D8
Wigan WN3 ....150 B8
Taylor Terr 18 SK16 166 B1
Taylor's La Bolton BL2 43 B7
Ince-in-M WN3 ..55 F3
Taylor's Rd M32 .96 E3
Taylors PI 18 OL12 14 F1
Taylorson St M5 161 B7
Taylorson St S M5 161 A6
Tayton CI M29 ..59 C1
Taywood Rd BL3 .40 D2
Teak Dr BL4 ....61 D4
Teak St BL9 ...141 B2
Teal Ave SK12 .133 A4
Teal CI Altrincham WA14 119 B8
Hazel Grove SK2 124 C5
Wigan WN3 .....54 B4
Teal Ct OL11 ...29 F7
Teal St BL3 ...147 F4
Tealby Ave M16 .97 C4
Tealby Ct M21 ..97 C1

Swi–Ten 253

Tealby Rd M18 ...99 B4
Teasdale CI OL9 .65 E3
Tebbutt St M4 ..159 B3
Ted Jackson Wlk M11 164 F8
Tedburn Wlk 5 M40 159 E5
Tedder CI BL9 ...45 B2
Tedder Dr M22 .130 F7
Teddington Rd M40 65 C1
Teer St M4 .....160 D2
Tees St OL16 ....31 B6
Tees Wlk OL8 ..153 E5
Teesdale Ave M41 95 A4
Teesdale CI SK2 124 E6
Teesdale Dr WN7 76 C5
Teesdale Wlk 20 M9 64 E3
Teignmouth Ave M40 159 C4
Teignmouth St M40 159 C4
Telfer Ave M13 .98 E2
Telfer Rd M13 ..98 E2
Telford CI M34 100 E7
Telford Cres WN7 75 D8
Telford Mews 1 OL3 69 B8
Telford Rd SK6 126 A4
Telford Sch M9 .64 C4
Telford St Atherton M46 58 A2
Horwich BL2 ....22 D2
Manchester M8 156 C5
Telford Way OL11 31 A2
Telford Wlk M16 97 D4
Tell St OL12 ...139 D7
Tellers CI M46 ..58 D3
Tellson CI M6 ..80 D6
Tellson Cres M6 80 D6
Telryn Wlk M8 156 C8
Temperance Sq SK14 103 A4
Temperance St
Bolton BL3 ....145 E5
Manchester M1,M12 163 C8
Manchester M12 164 D7
Mottram-in-L SK14 115 A8
Tempest Chase BL6 40 C4
Tempest Rd
Alderley Edge SK9 137 C1
Bolton BL6 .....40 C4
Tempest St BL3 146 B4
Temple Ave SK13 104 C5
Temple CI OL4 ..67 E8
Temple Dr Bolton BL1 142 C3
Pendlebury M27 .80 B7
Temple Inf & Jun Sch
M8 ....156 A6
Temple La OL15 ..6 D1
Temple Moor Inf Sch
M33 ....108 E4
Temple Rd Bolton BL1 142 C3
Sale M33 ......108 D4
Temple Sq M8 .156 B6
Temple St Hadfield SK13 104 C5
Heywood OL10 ..29 D2
Middleton M24 ..47 B1
Oldham OL1 ....67 B7
Templecombe Dr BL1 24 E7
Templegate CI WN6 19 F2
Templeton CI
Altrincham WA14 119 B6
Westhoughton BL5 57 E8
Templeton Rd WN2 56 B2
Temsbury Wlk M40 157 E5
Ten Acre Ct M45 62 D7
Ten Acre Dr M45 62 D7
Ten Acres La M40 83 A4
Ten Foot CI SK13 104 B2
Ten Ho OL8 .....67 C2
Tenax Circ M17 .96 B8
Tenax Rd M17 ..96 B7
Tenbury CI M6 .154 F3
Tenbury Dr
Ashton-in-M WN4 73 A4
Middleton M24 ..65 A5
Tenby Ave Bolton BL1 142 A1
Manchester M20 110 B6
Stretford M32 ...96 E4
Tenby Ct M15 ..161 C6
Tenby Dr Cheadle SK8 123 B1
Pendlebury M27 .80 D5
Tenby Gr 6 OL12 14 C1
Tenby Rd Oldham OL8 66 B2
Stockport SK3 ..123 B7
Tenby St OL12 ..14 C1
Tenement La SK7,SK8 123 C3
Tenement St WN2 56 B1
Teneriffe St M7 155 D5
Tenham Wlk 28 M9 64 E3
Tennis St Bolton BL1 143 D3
Manchester M16 97 B4
Tennyson Ave Bury BL9 44 F6
Denton M34 ....113 A7
Dukinfield SK16 102 B7
Leigh WN7 ......75 C8
Radcliffe M26 ..43 E4
Tennyson CI SK4 168 B2
Tennyson Dr
Longshaw WN5 ..53 D1
Wigan WN1 ......37 C3
Tennyson Gdns M25 62 F3
Tennyson Rd Cheadle SK8 122 F6
Droylsden M43 ..84 A2
Farnworth BL4 ..60 B6
Middleton M24 ..47 B2
Reddish SK5 ....99 D1
Swinton M27 ....79 D6
Tennyson St Bolton BL1 143 D1
Manchester M13 163 C5
Oldham OL1 .....49 C1
1 Rochdale OL11 31 A5

Tennyson St continued
Salford M6 . . . .**81** C4
Tennyson Wlk 3 BL1 . . . .**143** E2
Atherton M46 . . . .**58** C5
Tensing Ave Ashton-u-L OL7 .**85** B5
Tensing St OL8 . . . .**85** A8
Tenter Dr WN6 . . . .**37** B7
Tentercroft Oldham OL1 . .**153** E7
Rochdale OL12 . . . .**139** E7
Tenterden St BL9 . . . .**140** D2
Tenterden Wlk M22 . . . . .**121** C3
Tenterfield St 6 BB4 . . . . .**2** F8
Tenterheads BB4 . . . .**2** F7
Tenterhill La OL11 . . . . . .**13** D2
Tenters St BL9 . . . .**140** D2
Tenth St M17 . . . .**96** D6
Terence St M40 . . . .**83** D5
Terling Wlk M40 . . . .**157** E5
Terminal Rd E M90 . . . . .**130** C7
Terminal Rd N M90 . . . . .**130** B7
Terminal Rd S M90 . . . . . .**130** B7
Tern Ave BL4 . . . .**59** F8
Tern Cl Altrincham WA14 . .**119** B8
Dukinfield SK16 . . . .**101** E7
Rochdale OL11 . . . .**29** F7
Tern Dr SK7 . . . .**133** B4
Ternhill Ct BL4 . . . .**60** D8
Terrace St OL4 . . . .**67** B7
Terrace The M25 . . . .**63** B3
Terrington M21 . . . .**109** E7
Tetbury Dr BL2 . . . .**43** A8
Tetbury Rd M22 . . . .**121** B1
Tetlow Gr M30 . . . .**79** C1
Tetlow La M7,M8 . . . .**155** E8
Tetlow St Dukinfield SK14 .**101** E5
Failsworth M40 . . . .**83** D5
Middleton M24 . . . .**65** A8
Oldham OL9 . . . .**153** D6
Tetsworth Wlk 16 M40 . . . .**65** D2
Teviot St 8 M13 . . . .**98** E4
Tewkesbury Ave
Altrincham WA15 . . . .**120** C3
Ashton-u-L OL6 . . . .**85** C7
Chadderton OL9 . . . .**48** A2
Droylsden M43 . . . .**84** A3
Middleton M24 . . . .**46** F3
Urmston M41 . . . .**95** D4
Tewkesbury Cl
Bramhall SK8 . . . .**132** B6
Poynton SK12 . . . .**133** D4
Tewkesbury Dr M25 . . . . . .**63** C2
Tewkesbury Rd
Cheadle SK3 . . . .**123** B6
Golborne WA3 . . . .**90** B8
Manchester M40 . . . .**160** D3
Texas St OL6 . . . .**166** C2
Textile St M12 . . . .**165** A7
Textilose Rd M17 . . . .**96** B5
Teynham Wlk 5 M22 . . . .**121** C1
Thackeray Cl M8 . . . .**156** A6
Thackeray Gr M43 . . . .**84** A2
Thackeray Pl WN3 . . . . . .**150** A5
Thackeray Rd OL1 . . . .**49** C1
Thames Ave WN7 . . . .**75** F1
Thames Cl Bury BL9 . . . . . .**27** F7
Manchester M11 . . . .**165** B8
Thames Ct 2 M15 . . . . . .**162** D6
Thames Dr WN5 . . . .**53** F7
Thames Ind Est M12 . . . . .**164** D7
Thames Rd Culcheth WA3 . .**92** A2
Milnrow OL16 . . . .**32** B6
Thames St OL1 . . . .**67** A8
Thames Steet OL16 . . . . . .**31** B6
Thames Trad Ctr M44 . . . .**105** F7
Thanet Cl M7 . . . .**155** E5
Thanet Gr WN7 . . . .**76** A5
Thankerton Ave M34 . . . . .**84** D1
Thatch Leach OL9 . . . .**65** F5
Thatch Leach La M45 . . . . .**63** A7
Thatcher WA14 . . . .**119** C1
Thatcher St OL8 . . . .**67** A4
Thaxmead Dr M40 . . . . . .**83** D4
Thaxted Cl SK2 . . . .**125** A5
Thaxted Dr SK2 . . . .**125** A5
Thaxted Pl BL1 . . . .**144** C8
Thaxted Wlk M22 . . . . . .**130** C8
Theatre St OL1 . . . .**153** F7
Thekla St OL9 . . . .**153** D8
Thelma St BL0 . . . .**138** B6
Thelwall Ave Bolton BL2 . . .**42** D8
Manchester M14 . . . .**110** A8
Thelwall Cl
3 Altrincham WA15 . . . . .**119** E6
Leigh WN7 . . . .**75** E6
Thelwall Ct M14 . . . .**110** A8
Thelwall Rd M33 . . . .**108** E3
Theobald Rd WA14 . . . . . .**119** D1
Theta Cl M11 . . . .**83** B2
Thetford 12 OL12 . . . . . .**139** E8
Thetford Cl Bury BL8 . . . . .**27** D5
Hindley WN2 . . . .**56** E4
Thetford Dr M8 . . . .**156** B7
Thicketford Brow BL2 . . . .**25** D1
Thicketford Cl BL2 . . . . . .**25** C2
Thicketford Rd BL2 . . . . . .**25** C1
Thicknesse Ave WN6 . . . . .**36** F3
Thimble Cl OL12 . . . .**15** D4
Thimbles The OL12 . . . . . .**15** D4
Third Ave Bolton BL1 . . . .**144** B7
Bury BL9 . . . .**28** D4
Droylsden M11 . . . .**83** C3
Little Lever BL3 . . . .**42** E6
Mossley SK15 . . . .**86** E6
Oldham OL8 . . . .**66** D1
Poynton SK12 . . . .**133** D1

Third Ave continued
Stretford M17 . . . .**96** D6
Swinton M27 . . . .**79** E5
Tyldesley M29 . . . .**77** B4
Wigan WN6 . . . .**37** A2
Third St BL1 . . . .**23** F4
Thirkhill Pl 2 M30 . . . . . .**79** F2
Thirlby Dr M22 . . . .**121** D1
Thirlemere Rd SK1 . . . . . .**124** B7
Thirlmere Ave Abram WN2 .**74** B8
Ashton-in-M WN4 . . . . . .**73** C4
Ashton-u-L OL7 . . . .**84** F4
Haslingden BB4 . . . .**1** C8
Horwich BL6 . . . .**22** C2
Ince-in-M WN2 . . . .**56** B7
1 Orrell WN5 . . . .**53** F7
Orrell WN8 . . . .**53** B7
Pendlebury M27 . . . .**80** A7
Standish WN6 . . . .**37** A7
Stretford M32 . . . .**96** C3
Tyldesley M29 . . . .**77** A7
Thirlmere Cl Adlington PR6 .**21** B8
Alderley Edge SK9 . . . . . .**136** F1
Stalybridge SK15 . . . .**86** A4
Thirlmere Dr Bury BL9 . . . .**44** E7
Middleton M24 . . . .**46** E2
Walkden M38 . . . .**60** A5
Thirlmere Gr
Farnworth BL4 . . . .**59** E8
Royton OL2 . . . .**48** D6
Thirlmere Mews M24 . . . . .**46** E2
Thirlmere Rd Atherton BL5 .**58** F7
Blackrod BL6 . . . .**21** C3
Golborne WA3 . . . .**74** C1
Hindley WN2 . . . .**56** E5
Partington M31 . . . .**105** E4
Rochdale OL11 . . . .**30** B4
Urmston M41 . . . .**94** E3
Wigan WN5 . . . .**54** C7
Wythenshawe M22 . . . . . .**121** B1
Thirlmere St WN7 . . . .**75** E5
Thirlspot Cl BL1 . . . .**24** E6
Thirlstone Ave OL4 . . . . . .**49** F4
Thirsfield Dr 6 M11 . . . . .**83** C2
Thirsk Ave Chadderton OL9 .**47** F1
Sale M33 . . . .**107** C3
Thirsk Cl BL8 . . . .**27** B5
Thirsk Mews M7 . . . .**155** D6
Thirsk Rd BL3 . . . .**43** A2
Thirsk St M12 . . . .**163** C7
Thorn Grove Prim Sch
SK8 . . . .**132** A7
Thorn Lea Atherton M46 . . .**58** E2
Bolton BL2 . . . .**25** D4
Thorn Lea Cl BL1 . . . .**40** F7
Thorn Rd Bramhall SK7 . . .**132** E5
Oldham OL8 . . . .**67** C3
Swinton M27 . . . .**79** E6
Thorn St Bolton BL1 . . . . .**143** F2
Hindley WN2 . . . .**56** D4
Ramsbottom BL9 . . . .**11** C3
Thorn View BL9 . . . .**141** C5
Thorn Well BL5 . . . .**57** E7
Thorn Wlk M31 . . . .**105** E2
Thornaby Wlk M9 . . . . . .**157** D6
Thornage Dr M40 . . . .**159** C4
Thornbank BL3 . . . .**144** C6
Thornbank Cl OL10 . . . . . .**46** E7
Thornbeck Dr BL1 . . . .**23** F1
Thornbeck Rd BL1 . . . .**23** F1
Thornbridge Ave M21 . . . .**109** B8
Thornbury 9 OL11 . . . . . .**139** E6
Thornbury Ave
Golborne WA3 . . . .**90** E7
Hattersley SK14 . . . .**102** E2
Thornbury Cl
3 Bolton BL1 . . . .**145** E8
Bramhall SK8 . . . .**123** C1
Thornbury Rd M32 . . . . . .**96** E4
Thornbury Way M18 . . . . .**165** C5
Thornbush Cl WA3 . . . .**74** E1
Thornbush Way OL16 . . . . .**31** C8
Thornby Wlk 8 M23 . . . .**121** A5
Thorncliff Ave OL8 . . . . . .**66** E3
Thorncliffe Ave
Dukinfield SK16 . . . .**101** C7
Royton OL2 . . . .**48** C6
Thorncliffe Gr M19 . . . . . .**99** C1
Thorncliffe Pk OL2 . . . . . .**48** C6
Thorncliffe Rd Bolton BL1 . .**24** E5
Hadfield SK14 . . . .**171** F4
Thorncombe Rd 1 M16 . . .**97** E3
Thorncross Cl M15 . . . . . .**161** C7
Thorndale Cl OL2 . . . .**48** C5
Thorndale Gr WA15 . . . . .**120** A5
Thornden Rd M40 . . . . . .**160** D4
Thorne Ave M41 . . . .**95** A3
Thorne Ho M14 . . . .**98** D2
Thorne St BL4 . . . .**42** C1
Thornecliffewood SK14 . .**103** D5
Thorneside M34 . . . .**100** F5
Thorney Dr SK7,SK8 . . . . .**132** C6
Thorney Hill Cl OL4 . . . . . .**67** A6
Thorneycroft WN7 . . . . . .**76** C5
Thorneycroft Ave M21 . . . .**109** C5
Thorneycroft Cl WA15 . . . .**120** B5
Thorneycroft Rd WA15 . . .**120** B5
Thorneyholme Cl BL6 . . . . .**40** C6
Thorneylea OL12 . . . .**4** D1
Thornfield Ave 8 BB4 . . . . .**2** F8
Thornfield Cl WA3 . . . .**90** C8
Thornfield Cres M38 . . . . .**59** F5
Thornfield Ct SK4 . . . . . .**168** A3
Thornfield Dr 4 M27 . . . . .**79** E7
Thornfield Gr
Cheadle SK8 . . . .**123** A2
Walkden M38 . . . .**59** F5
Thornfield Hey SK9 . . . . .**137** E8
Thornfield Rd Bury BL8 . . . .**26** E7
Manchester M19 . . . .**110** E5

Thompson Rd continued
Eccles M17 . . . .**95** E8
Reddish M34 . . . .**100** B3
Thompson St
Ashton-in-M WN4 . . . . . .**73** D4
Bolton BL3 . . . .**145** F5
Horwich BL6 . . . .**22** A3
Leigh WN7 . . . .**75** B5
Manchester M10,M40 . . . .**157** F5
Manchester M3 . . . .**158** F3
Manchester M4 . . . .**159** B2
Wigan WN1 . . . .**37** E1
Wigan WN3 . . . .**55** A4
Thomson Rd M18 . . . .**99** C4
Thomson St
Manchester M13 . . . .**163** C6
Stockport SK3 . . . .**170** E8
Thor Gr M5 . . . .**161** C8
Thoralby Cl M12 . . . .**165** A5
Thorburn Dr OL12 . . . .**14** B7
Thorburn Ho WN5 . . . .**54** C7
Thorburn La WN5 . . . .**54** D8
Thorburn Rd WN5 . . . .**54** D6
Thoresby Cl
Little Lever M26 . . . .**43** C5
Wigan WN3 . . . .**54** E3
Thoresway Rd
Manchester M13 . . . .**98** E3
Wilmslow SK9 . . . .**136** F5
Thorgill Wlk 10 M40 . . . . .**83** A7
Thoriby Rd WA3 . . . .**91** F3
Thorley Cl OL9 . . . .**65** E2
Thorley Dr
Altrincham WA15 . . . . . .**120** B5
Urmston M41 . . . .**95** D2
Thorley La
Altrincham WA15 . . . . . .**120** B4
Wythenshawe M22,WA15 . .**121** A1
Thorley Mews SK7 . . . . . .**132** F7
Thorley St M35 . . . .**83** F8
Thorn Ave M35 . . . .**83** F6
Thorn Cl OL10 . . . .**29** B3
Thorn Ct 2 M6 . . . .**81** B2
Thorn Dr M22 . . . .**131** A8
Thorn Gr Altrincham WA15 .**119** E3
Bramhall SK8 . . . .**132** A7
Manchester M14 . . . .**110** D8
Sale M33 . . . .**108** B4

Thornfield Rd continued
Manchester SK4 . . . .**168** A3
Thornfield Sch SK4 . . . . .**168** A3
Thornfield St M5 . . . .**154** D1
Thornfield Terr OL6 . . . . .**166** C2
Thornford Wlk 14 M40 . . . .**65** D2
Thorngate Rd M8 . . . .**156** A5
Thorngrove Ave 1 M23 . . .**120** D7
Thorngrove Dr SK9 . . . . . .**137** C6
Thorngrove Hill SK9 . . . . .**137** C6
Thorngrove Ho 4 M23 . . .**120** D7
Thorngrove Rd SK9 . . . . . .**137** C6
Thornham Cl BL8 . . . .**27** C6
Thornham Ct OL16 . . . .**48** C8
Thornham Dr BL1 . . . .**25** A6
Thornham La
Middleton M24,OL11,OL2 . . .**47** E6
Royton OL16,OL2 . . . .**48** C8
Thornham New Rd
OL11,OL16 . . . .**47** E8
Thornham Old Rd OL2 . . . .**48** B7
Thornham Rd Sale M33 . . .**108** D7
Shaw OL2 . . . .**48** E8
Thornham St James'
CE Prim Sch OL2 . . . . . .**48** C8
Thornhill Cl Bolton BL1 . . .**142** C3
Reddish M34 . . . .**100** A2
Thornhill Dr M28 . . . .**60** E1
Thornhill Rd Droylsden M43 .**84** B2
Garswood WN4 . . . .**72** C4
Manchester SK4 . . . .**110** F2
Ramsbottom BL0 . . . .**11** A1
Thornholme Cl M18 . . . . . .**99** B3
Thornholme Rd SK6 . . . . .**125** F4
Thorniley Brow M4 . . . . .**159** A2
Thornlea M43 . . . .**83** E8
Thornlea Ave Oldham OL8 . .**66** C1
Swinton M27 . . . .**79** D6
Thornlea Dr OL12 . . . .**14** B2
Thornlee Ct OL4 . . . .**68** B5
Thornleigh Rd M14 . . . . . .**98** B1
Thornleigh Salesian Coll
BL1 . . . .**143** D4
Thornley Ave BL1 . . . .**142** C2
Thornley Cl OL4 . . . .**68** A5
Thornley Cres Oldham OL4 . .**68** A5
Romiley SK6 . . . .**113** A4
Thornley La OL4 . . . .**68** A5
Thornley La N M34,SK5 . . . .**99** F3
Thornley La S M34,SK5 . . .**100** A2
Thornley Mews BL1 . . . . .**142** C2
Thornley Park Rd OL4 . . . .**68** A5
Thornley Rd
Dukinfield M34 . . . .**101** A4
Prestwich M25 . . . .**63** C7
Thornley St Hyde SK14 . . .**167** E1
Middleton M24 . . . .**47** B1
Radcliffe M26 . . . .**44** B2
Thornmere Cl M27 . . . .**61** C2
Thorns Ave BL1 . . . .**143** D3
Thorns Cl BL1 . . . .**143** D3
Thorns Clough OL3 . . . . . .**51** C5
Thorns Rd BL1 . . . .**143** D3
Thorns The M21 . . . .**109** B7
Thorns Villa Gdns M28 . . . .**78** A5
Thornsett SK22 . . . .**127** E2
Thornsett Cl 11 M9 . . . . .**157** E8
Thornsett Cty Prim Sch
SK22 . . . .**127** E3
Thornsgreen Rd M22 . . . .**130** D8
Thornton Ave Bolton BL1 . . .**23** F1
Droylsden M34 . . . .**100** C8
Urmston M41 . . . .**95** A2
Thornton Cl
Ashton-in-M WN4 . . . . . .**72** F4
Boothstown M28 . . . .**77** E7
Farnworth BL4 . . . .**60** B7
Golborne WA3 . . . .**75** A1
Leigh WN7 . . . .**75** F1
Little Lever BL3 . . . .**43** C3
Thornton Cres M25 . . . . . .**62** F5
Thornton Ct M16 . . . .**161** C5
Thornton Dr SK9 . . . .**131** D3
Thornton Gate SK8 . . . . .**122** A6
Thornton Pl SK4 . . . .**168** B4
Thornton Rd
Boothstown M28 . . . .**77** E7
Gatley SK8 . . . .**131** C8
Manchester M14 . . . .**110** D8
Thornton St N M40 . . . . .**157** D5
Thornton St
Manchester M40 . . . .**160** D4
Oldham OL4 . . . .**153** F5
Rochdale OL11 . . . .**139** F5
Thorntree Cl M9 . . . .**157** E7
Thorntree Pl 2 OL12 . . . .**139** E8
Thornvale WN2 . . . .**74** C7
Thornway Boothstown M28 . .**78** A8
Bramhall SK7,SK8 . . . . . .**132** C7
High Lane SK6 . . . .**134** F7
Thornwood Ave M18 . . . . .**99** E4
Thornycroft Sch OL8 . . . . .**66** D4
Thornydyke Ave BL1 . . . . .**24** E5
Thorold Gr M33 . . . .**108** E4
Thorp Ave BL9 . . . .**44** D5
Thorp Com Prim Sch OL2 .**48** C5
Thorp Rd Manchester M40 . .**83** A6
Royton OL2 . . . .**48** D4
Thorp St Eccles M30 . . . . .**95** B8
Whitefield M45 . . . .**44** E1
Thorp View OL2 . . . .**48** C6
Thorpe Ave M27 . . . .**61** E1
Thorpe Cl Denton M34 . . . .**100** F4
Oldham OL4 . . . .**68** A8
Thorpe Gr SK4 . . . .**111** D6
Thorpe Hall Gr SK14 . . . . .**101** F6
Thorpe La Denton M34 . . . .**100** F5
Oldham OL4 . . . .**68** A8

Thorpe St Bolton BL1 . . . .**143** D2
Glossop SK13 . . . .**104** E2
Manchester M16 . . . .**97** C4
Middleton M24 . . . .**64** C7
Ramsbottom BL0 . . . .**138** B5
Walkden M28 . . . .**60** D4
Thorpe View M5 . . . .**161** C7
Thorpebrook Rd M40 . . . . .**83** A6
Thorpeness Sq M18 . . . . . .**99** D6
Thorsby Ave SK14 . . . . . .**167** F2
Thorsby Cl Bolton BL7 . . . .**24** F8
Droylsden M18 . . . .**99** E5
Thorsby Rd WA15 . . . . . .**119** E5
Thorsby Way 18 M34 . . . .**101** A1
Thorverton Sq M40 . . . . . .**83** C8
Thrapston Ave M34 . . . . . .**84** D1
Threaphurst La SK7 . . . . .**125** C1
Threapwood Rd M22 . . . .**121** E1
Three Acre Ave OL2 . . . . . .**49** A4
Three Acres Dr SK5 . . . . .**111** E5
Three Lane Ends OL10 . . . .**45** F7
Three Sisters Rd WN4 . . . .**73** B8
Three Sisters Recn Area
WN4 . . . .**73** C7
Threlkeld Cl M24 . . . .**46** C1
Threlkeld Rd Bolton BL1 . . .**24** D6
Middleton M24 . . . .**46** C1
Thresher Cl 3 M33 . . . . .**108** F3
Threshfield Cl BL9 . . . .**27** F7
Threshfield Dr WA15 . . . .**120** C7
Throstle Bank St SK14 . . .**101** C4
Throstle Cl 3 OL2 . . . . . .**48** D4
Throstle Gr Bury BL8 . . . . .**27** C5
Marple SK6 . . . .**125** E5
Throstle Hall Ct 1 M24 . . .**46** F1
Throstle Nest Ave WN6 . . .**37** A2
Throstle St OL14 . . . .**6** B6
Throstles Cl M43 . . . .**84** C3
Thrum Fold OL12 . . . .**14** D3
Thrum Hall La
Rochdale OL12 . . . .**14** D3
Rochdale OL12 . . . .**14** E3
Thrush Ave BL4 . . . .**59** F8
Thrush Dr BL9 . . . .**141** B4
Thrush Ho M6 . . . .**81** A5
Thrush St OL12 . . . .**14** C1
Thruxton Cl 4 M16 . . . . . .**97** E3
Thurland Rd OL4 . . . .**67** C6
Thurland St OL9 . . . .**65** E8
Thurlby Ave M9 . . . .**64** E5
Thurlby Cl WN4 . . . .**73** C1
Thurlby St M13 . . . .**98** D4
Thurleigh Rd M20 . . . . . .**110** B3
Thurlestone Ave BL2 . . . . .**26** C1
Thurlestone Dr
Stockport SK7 . . . .**124** B2
3 Urmston M41 . . . .**95** C3
Thurlestone Rd WA14 . . .**119** B6
Thurloe St M14 . . . .**98** C3
Thurlow WA3 . . . .**90** E7
Thurlow St Salford M5 . . . .**154** F1
Stretford M5 . . . .**96** F8
Thurlston Cres M8 . . . . . .**156** B7
Thurlwood Ave M20 . . . . .**110** A7
Thurnham St BL3 . . . .**146** C3
Thurnley Wlk M8 . . . .**155** F5
Thursby Ave M20 . . . .**110** A6
Thursby Ho WN5 . . . .**54** C7
Thursby Wlk M24 . . . .**46** C2
Thursfield St M6 . . . .**81** B5
Thursford Gr BL6 . . . .**21** D1
Thurstan St WN3 . . . .**55** E4
Thurstane St BL1 . . . .**142** C2
Thurston Ave WN3 . . . . . .**55** B3
Thurston Cl BL9 . . . .**45** A2
Thurston Clough
Rd** OL3,OL4 . . . .**50** D2
Thurston Gn SK9 . . . .**137** A3
Thurstons OL3 . . . .**51** D6
Thynne St Bolton BL3 . . . .**145** F5
Farnworth BL4 . . . .**42** C2
Tib La M2 . . . .**158** F1
Tib St Denton M34 . . . . . .**101** A2
Manchester M1,M4 . . . . . .**159** A2
Ramsbottom BL0 . . . .**138** B5
Tiber Ave OL8 . . . .**66** C1
Tideswell Ave
Manchester M40 . . . .**160** D3
Wigan WN5 . . . .**36** A1
Tideswell Bank 8 SK13 . .**171** E1
Tideswell Cl SK8 . . . .**131** D8
Tideswell Rd
Droylsden M43 . . . .**83** E3
Hazel Grove SK7 . . . .**133** E8
Tideswell Way M34 . . . . .**113** A4
Tideswell Wlk 7 SK13 . . .**171** E1
Tideway Cl M7 . . . .**80** F8
Tidworth Ave M4 . . . .**160** D2
Tiefield Wlk M21 . . . .**109** E6
Tiernan Lo 14 WN6 . . . . . .**37** A1
Tiflis St OL12 . . . .**139** E8
Tig Fold Rd BL4 . . . .**59** E8
Tilbury Gr WN6 . . . .**35** D7
Tilbury St OL1 . . . .**153** E8
Tilbury Wlk M40 . . . .**160** D3
Tilby Cl M41 . . . .**94** E2
Tildsley St BL3 . . . .**147** E4
Tile St BL9 . . . .**140** F3
Tilehurst Ct M7 . . . .**81** B7
Tilgate Wlk 17 M9 . . . . . .**64** E3
Tillard Ave SK3 . . . .**123** B8
Tillhey Rd M22 . . . .**121** D2
Tillington Cl BL1 . . . .**143** E3
Tilney Ave M32 . . . .**96** E1
Tilshead Wlk M13 . . . . . .**163** C6
Tilson Rd M23 . . . .**120** F5
Tilstock Wlk M23 . . . .**120** E8
Tilston Wlk 5 SK9 . . . . . .**131** E1

Tilton St OL1 . . . . . 49 C1
Timberbottom BL2 . . . . . 25 C4
Timbercliffe OL15 . . . . . 6 D1
Timberhurst BL9 . . . . . 28 D2
Timbersbrook Gr 5 SK9 . 131 D2
Times Ret Pk OL10 . . . . . 29 C2
Times St M24 . . . . . 65 B8
Timothy Cl M6 . . . . . 80 B3
Timperley Cl OL8 . . . . . 67 B2
Timperley Fold OL6 . . . . . 85 C6
Timperley Heyes Lane Prim Sch WA15 . . . . . 120 B8
Timperley La WN7 . . . . . 76 B2
Timperley Rd OL6 . . . . . 85 C6
Timperley St M11 . . . . . 165 C8
Timperley Sta WA15 . . . . . 119 F8
Timpson Rd M23 . . . . . 120 E7
Timsbury Cl BL2 . . . . . 42 F5
Timson St 2 M35 . . . . . 83 F7
Tin St BL3 . . . . . 145 E5
Tindall St Eccles M30 . . . . . 95 B8
Reddish SK5 . . . . . 99 F3
Tindle St M28 . . . . . 60 F3
Tinkersfield WN7 . . . . . 75 D7
Tinline St BL9 . . . . . 141 A2
Tinningham Cl 7 M11 . . . 99 E7
Tinsdale Wlk M24 . . . . . 46 C1
Tinshill Cl M12 . . . . . 165 A5
Tinsley Cl M40 . . . . . 160 E2
Tinsley Gr BL2 . . . . . 148 B8
Tintagel Ct Bolton M26 . . . 43 C5
Stalybridge SK15 . . . . . 85 F2
Tintagel Rd WN2 . . . . . 57 A4
Tintagel Wlk SK14 . . . . . 102 E3
Tintern Ave
Ashton-in-M WN4 . . . . . 73 D3
Bolton BL2 . . . . . 25 B2
Heywood OL10 . . . . . 29 C4
Littleborough OL15 . . . . . 16 A7
Manchester M20 . . . . . 109 F5
Rochdale OL12 . . . . . 14 E2
Tyldesley M29 . . . . . 77 C7
Urmston M41 . . . . . 107 A8
Whitefield M45 . . . . . 44 F1
Tintern Cl SK12 . . . . . 133 D5
Tintern Ct M20 . . . . . 109 F5
Tintern Dr WA15 . . . . . 120 C2
Tintern Gr SK1 . . . . . 112 B1
Tintern Pl OL10 . . . . . 29 C4
Tintern Rd Bramhall SK8 . . 132 B6
Middleton M24 . . . . . 47 A4
Tintern St M14 . . . . . 98 B2
Tintwistle CE Prim Sch SK13 . . . . . 104 A7
Tinwald Pl WN1 . . . . . 37 F1
Tipperary St SK15 . . . . . 86 E5
Tipping St
Altrincham WA14 . . . . . 119 D3
Wigan WN3 . . . . . 150 B6
Tipton Cl Cheadle SK8 . . . 123 B4
Radcliffe M26 . . . . . 43 D5
Tipton Dr M23 . . . . . 109 B2
Tiptree Wlk 13 M9 . . . . . 157 E8
Tiree Cl SK7 . . . . . 124 F1
Tirza Ave M19 . . . . . 110 F8
Tissington Bank 15 SK13 . 171 D1
Tissington Terr 16 SK13 . . 171 D1
Titanian Rise OL1 . . . . . 49 D5
Titchfield Rd OL8 . . . . . 67 C4
Tithe Barn Cl OL12 . . . . . 15 D4
Tithe Barn Cres BL1 . . . . . 25 B4
Tithe Barn Ct SK4 . . . . . 110 F4
Tithe Barn Prim Sch SK4 168 A3
Tithe Barn Rd
Garswood WN4 . . . . . 72 C2
Manchester SK4 . . . . . 110 F4
Tithe Barn St 6 BL5 . . . . . 39 E1
Tithebarn Rd
Altrincham WA15 . . . . . 129 C8
Garswood WN4 . . . . . 72 D2
Tithebarn St 3 Bury BL9 . 140 F2
Orrell WN8 . . . . . 53 B7
Radcliffe M26 . . . . . 44 D4
Titian Rise OL1 . . . . . 49 D3
Titterington Ave M21 . . . . . 97 B2
Tiverton Ave Hindley WN7 . 57 D2
Sale M33 . . . . . 107 F3
Tiverton Cl Little Lever M26 43 C5
Tyldesley M29 . . . . . 77 D7
Tiverton Dr M33 . . . . . 107 F3
Tiverton Ho M6 . . . . . 80 A3
Tiverton Pl OL7 . . . . . 85 A5
Tiverton Rd M41 . . . . . 95 E3
Tiverton Wlk BL1 . . . . . 142 C1
Tiviot Dale SK1 . . . . . 169 F2
Tiviot Way SK1,SK4,SK5 . . 169 F3
Tivoli St M3 . . . . . 158 E1
Tixall Wlk 3 M8 . . . . . 63 E2
Toad La OL12 . . . . . 139 F8
Tobermory Cl M11 . . . . . 83 D1
Tobermory Rd SK8 . . . . . 122 C1
Todd St Bury BL9 . . . . . 140 F4
Glossop SK13 . . . . . 116 D8
Heywood OL10 . . . . . 29 A2
Manchester M3 . . . . . 159 A2
Manchester M7 . . . . . 155 D6
Rochdale OL16 . . . . . 31 A7
Todd's Pl M9 . . . . . 64 C1
Toddington La WN2 . . . . . 38 B8
Todmorden Rd OL15 . . . . . 16 C7
Toft Rd M18 . . . . . 99 C4
Toft Way SK9 . . . . . 131 E4
Toledo St M11 . . . . . 83 D1
Toll Bar Bsns Pk OL13 . . . . . 3 C8
Toll Bar St M12 . . . . . 164 E6
Toll Gate Cl M13 . . . . . 98 E4
Toll Green Cl WN2 . . . . . 56 D7
Toll St Platt Bridge WN2 . . . 56 A1
Toll St *continued*
Radcliffe M26 . . . . . 43 D4
Tolland La WA15 . . . . . 128 F8
Tollard Ave M40 . . . . . 157 D5
Tollard Cl SK8 . . . . . 132 B6
Tollbar St SK1 . . . . . 170 F8
Tollemache Cl SK14 . . . . . 103 A5
Tollemache Rd SK14 . . . 103 A5
Tollesbury Cl M40 . . . . . 160 D4
Tollgate Way OL16 . . . . . 31 C8
Tolworth Dr M8 . . . . . 156 B7
Tom Lomas Wlk M11 . . . . . 83 B2
Tom Shepley St SK14 . . . 167 E2
Tomcroft La M34 . . . . . 100 D2
Tomlin Sq 7 BL2 . . . . . 148 C7
Tomlinson Cl OL8 . . . . . 153 E5
Tomlinson St Horwich BL6 . 22 B3
Manchester M40 . . . . . 65 C3
Rochdale OL11 . . . . . 30 C4
Tommy Browell Cl 9 M14 . 98 A3
Tommy Johnson Wlk 7 M14 . . . . . 98 A3
Tommy Taylor Cl 1 M40 . . 83 C5
Tomwood Rise SK13 . . . . . 115 C6
Tonacliffe Cty Prim Sch OL12 . . . . . 14 C6
Tonacliffe Rd OL12 . . . . . 14 C6
Tonacliffe Terr OL12 . . . . . 14 C7
Tonacliffe Way OL12 . . . . . 14 C6
Tonbridge Cl BL8 . . . . . 27 C7
Tonbridge Pl 5 BL2 . . . . . 25 B1
Tonbridge Rd
Manchester M19 . . . . . 111 B8
Reddish SK5 . . . . . 111 F8
Tong End OL12 . . . . . 4 C2
Tong Head Ave BL1 . . . . . 25 B4
Tong La Bacup OL13 . . . . . 4 C8
Whitworth OL12 . . . . . 4 D1
Tong Rd BL3 . . . . . 43 A5
Tong St BL4 . . . . . 61 C5
Tonge Bridge Way BL2 . . 148 B8
Tonge Cl M45 . . . . . 45 B1
Tonge Clough BL7 . . . . . 24 F8
Tonge Ct M24 . . . . . 65 B8
Tonge Fold Rd BL2 . . . . . 148 C7
Tonge Gn SK15 . . . . . 120 E6
Tonge Hall Cl M24 . . . . . 65 B8
Tonge Moor Com Prim Sch BL2 . . . . . 25 B1
Tonge Moor Rd BL2 . . . . . 25 B2
Tonge Old Rd BL2 . . . . . 148 C7
Tonge Park Ave BL2 . . . . . 25 C1
Tonge Roughs M24 . . . . . 65 D8
Tonge St Heywood OL10 . . . 29 D2
Manchester M12 . . . . . 164 D7
Oldham M24 . . . . . 65 E6
Rochdale OL11,OL16 . . . . . 31 A6
Tongfields BL7 . . . . . 24 F8
Tongley Wlk 15 M40 . . . . . 65 D2
Tonman St M3 . . . . . 162 E8
Tontine WN5 . . . . . 53 C5
Tontine Rd WN5,WN8 . . . . . 53 C6
Toogood La WN6 . . . . . 18 D6
Tooley Ho M30 . . . . . 95 D8
Toon Cres BL8 . . . . . 27 C6
Tootal Dr M5,M6 . . . . . 80 C3
Tootal Drive Prim Sch M6 80 C3
Tootal Gr M5 . . . . . 80 C2
Tootal Rd M5 . . . . . 154 D2
Toothill Cl WN4 . . . . . 73 B5
Top o' th' Brow Com Prim Sch BL2 . . . . . 25 E2
Top o' th' Gn OL9 . . . . . 66 C4
Top o' th' La BL2 . . . . . 42 D5
Top o' th' Meadows La OL4 . . . . . 50 A1
Top O'Th' Close Rd OL14 . . . 6 C6
Top Of Heap OL10 . . . . . 28 F2
Top of Wallsuches BL6 . . . . . 22 F4
Top Schwabe St M24 . . . . . 64 C8
Top St Middleton M24 . . . . . 46 F1
Oldham OL4 . . . . . 67 D8
Walsden OL14 . . . . . 5 F7
Topcliffe St WN2 . . . . . 56 F6
Topcroft Cl M22 . . . . . 121 E8
Topfield Rd M22 . . . . . 121 C4
Topham St Bury BL9 . . . . . 141 A1
Bury BL9 . . . . . 45 A8
Topley St M40 . . . . . 157 D6
Topp St BL4 . . . . . 60 E7
Topp Way BL1 . . . . . 145 E8
Topping Fold Rd BL9 . . . . . 141 C3
Topping St Bolton BL1 . . . . . 143 E1
Bury BL9 . . . . . 141 A3
Toppings Gn BL7 . . . . . 25 A7
Toppings The SK6 . . . . . 113 A3
Topsham Wlk M40 . . . . . 83 D5
Tor Ave BL8 . . . . . 10 F2
Tor End Rd BB4 . . . . . 1 A6
Tor View Sch Valley Site BB4 . . . . . 1 D8
Torah St M8 . . . . . 159 A4
Torbay Cl 1 BL3 . . . . . 144 C5
Torbay Dr SK2 . . . . . 124 B7
Torbay Rd
Manchester M21 . . . . . 109 C8
Urmston M41 . . . . . 95 E1
Torcross Rd M9 . . . . . 64 B5
Torkington Ave M27 . . . . . 61 F1
Torkington La SK6,SK7 . . 125 E3
Torkington Prim Sch SK7 . . . . . 125 A2
Torkington Rd Gatley SK8 . 122 B5
Hazel Grove SK7 . . . . . 124 F2
Hazel Grove SK7 . . . . . 125 B3
Wilmslow SK9 . . . . . 137 D6
Torkington St SK3 . . . . . 170 D8
Torksey Wlk M9 . . . . . 64 C5
Torness Wlk M11 . . . . . 83 B1
Toronto Ave M90 . . . . . 130 B7
Toronto Rd SK2 . . . . . 124 A6
Toronto St BL2 . . . . . 42 E8
Torpoint Wlk M40 . . . . . 65 C1
Torquay Cl 2 M13 . . . . . 163 C5
Torquay Dr WN5 . . . . . 71 E8
Torquay Gr SK2 . . . . . 124 B4
Torra Barn Cl BL7 . . . . . 8 E3
Torrax Cl M6 . . . . . 80 B6
Torre Cl M24 . . . . . 47 A3
Torrens St M6 . . . . . 80 D5
Torridon Cl WN6 . . . . . 37 B7
Torridon Rd BL2 . . . . . 42 F7
Torridon Wlk 1 M22 . . . . . 121 C1
Torrin Cl SK3 . . . . . 170 F5
Torrington Ave
Bolton BL1 . . . . . 143 E3
Manchester M9 . . . . . 65 A2
Torrington Dr SK14 . . . . . 102 E2
Torrington Rd M27 . . . . . 80 B6
Torrington St OL10 . . . . . 46 E8
Torrisdale Cl BL3 . . . . . 144 B5
Torside Cl WN2 . . . . . 56 D6
Torside Way SK13 . . . . . 104 A5
Torver Cl WN3 . . . . . 55 A2
Torver Dr Bolton BL2 . . . . . 42 F8
Middleton M24 . . . . . 46 D2
Torver Wlk M22 . . . . . 121 B2
Torwood Rd OL9 . . . . . 47 E1
Totland Cl M12 . . . . . 99 B3
Totley Ave 35 SK13 . . . . . 171 D1
Totley Cl 32 SK13 . . . . . 171 D1
Totley Gdns 30 SK13 . . . . . 171 D1
Totley Gn 33 SK13 . . . . . 171 D1
Totley Lanes 34 SK13 . . . . . 171 D1
Totley Mews SK13 . . . . . 171 D1
Totley Pl 31 SK13 . . . . . 171 D1
Totnes Ave Chadderton OL9 . 47 F1
Stockport SK7 . . . . . 124 A2
Totnes Rd
Manchester M21 . . . . . 109 C8
Sale M33 . . . . . 107 D5
Totridge Cl SK2 . . . . . 124 D5
Tottenham Dr M23 . . . . . 120 E7
Tottington Ave OL4 . . . . . 67 F7
Tottington High Sch BL8 . . 26 F6
Tottington La M25 . . . . . 62 F5
Tottington Prim Sch BL8 . . 26 F5
Tottington Rd Bolton BL2 . . 25 E6
Bolton BL7,BL8 . . . . . 9 F2
Bury BL8 . . . . . 27 C4
Tottington St 18 M11 . . . . . 83 C2
Totton Ho BL1 . . . . . 144 C7
Totton Rd M35 . . . . . 83 F7
Touchet Hall Rd M24 . . . . . 47 D4
Toulston Rd WN6 . . . . . 36 F2
Tours Ave M23 . . . . . 109 A2
Towcester Cl M4 . . . . . 160 D1
Tower Ave BL0 . . . . . 138 A5
Tower Ct BL7 . . . . . 9 C4
Tower Gr WN7 . . . . . 76 D6
Tower Grange M7 . . . . . 155 D8
Tower Hill Rd WN8 . . . . . 53 B6
Tower Nook WN8 . . . . . 53 A5
Tower Sq M13 . . . . . 163 C6
Tower St Edgworth BL7 . . . . . 9 C4
Heywood OL10 . . . . . 29 C2
Hyde SK14 . . . . . 167 D1
Radcliffe M26 . . . . . 44 D4
Stalybridge SK16 . . . . . 85 D1
Tower View BL6 . . . . . 21 C3
Towers Ave BL3 . . . . . 146 A4
Towers Cl SK12 . . . . . 133 F5
Towers Rd SK12 . . . . . 133 F5
Towers St 2 OL4 . . . . . 49 D1
Towey Cl M18 . . . . . 99 D6
Town Fields Cl BL9 . . . . . 140 F1
Town Fold SK6 . . . . . 126 B7
Town Gate Dr M41 . . . . . 94 C2
Town Hall La 14 M2 . . . . . 158 F1
Town Hall Sq OL16 . . . . . 139 F7
Town House Rd OL15 . . . . . 16 B6
Town La
Charlesworth SK13 . . . . . 115 D6
Coppull PR7 . . . . . 19 B8
Denton M34 . . . . . 100 E2
Dukinfield SK16 . . . . . 101 C8
Town Mill Brow OL12 . . . . . 139 E7
Town Sq M33 . . . . . 108 B4
Town Sq Sh Ctr OL1 . . . . . 153 F6
Town St SK6 . . . . . 126 B7
Town's View SK15 . . . . . 86 B1
Towncliffe Wlk 18 M15 . . 162 D6
Towncroft M34 . . . . . 101 A4
Towncroft Ave M24 . . . . . 46 F2
Towncroft La BL1 . . . . . 40 E8
Townend St SK14 . . . . . 167 E2
Townfield M41 . . . . . 95 B1
Townfield Ave WN4 . . . . . 73 B2
Townfield Gdns WA14 . . . . . 119 D5
Townfield La WA13 . . . . . 117 B7
Townfield Rd WA14 . . . . . 119 D5
Townfield St 9 OL4 . . . . . 67 B7
Townfield Wlk 10 M15 . . . 162 D6
Townfields WN4 . . . . . 73 A3
Townley Fold SK14 . . . . . 102 B6
Townley Rd OL16 . . . . . 32 A6
Townley St
Manchester M11 . . . . . 164 F8
Manchester M8 . . . . . 155 F5
Middleton M24 . . . . . 65 A8
Townrow St OL10 . . . . . 29 E2
Townscliffe La SK6 . . . . . 126 C6
Townsend Rd M27 . . . . . 61 F1
Townsend St BB4 . . . . . 2 F8
Townsfield Rd BL5 . . . . . 57 F7
Townside Row BL9 . . . . . 140 F1
Townsley Gr OL6 . . . . . 85 E5
Townson Dr WN7 . . . . . 75 F1
Towton St M9 . . . . . 157 E8
Towyn Ave M5 . . . . . 81 A2
Toxhead Cl BL6 . . . . . 22 A3
Toxteth St M11 . . . . . 99 F7
Tracey St M8 . . . . . 64 A1
Tracks La WN5 . . . . . 53 D3
Tracy Dr WA12 . . . . . 89 E3
Traders Ave M41 . . . . . 95 E6
Trafalgar Ave Denton M34 100 C7
Poynton SK12 . . . . . 134 A3
Trafalgar Bsns Pk M7,M8 158 E4
Trafalgar Cl SK12 . . . . . 134 A3
Trafalgar Ct M16 . . . . . 97 E2
Trafalgar Gr M7 . . . . . 155 D5
Trafalgar Ho M34 . . . . . 100 C7
Trafalgar Pl M20 . . . . . 110 A4
Trafalgar Rd Hindley WN2 . . 56 D5
Sale M33 . . . . . 108 C6
Salford M6 . . . . . 80 A3
Wigan WN1 . . . . . 37 C1
Trafalgar Sq OL7 . . . . . 84 F1
Trafalgar St Ashton-u-L OL7 . 84 F1
Manchester M7 . . . . . 155 E5
Oldham OL1 . . . . . 153 E8
Rochdale OL16 . . . . . 31 A8
Trafalgar Wlk
Manchester M11 . . . . . 165 B8
Manchester M15 . . . . . 162 E5
Trafford Ave M41 . . . . . 95 E3
Trafford Bank Rd M16 . . 161 C5
Trafford Bar Sta M16 . . . 161 B5
Trafford Ct 7 M15 . . . . . 162 D6
Trafford Ctr The M41 . . . . . 95 D6
Trafford Dr Sale WA15 . . . . . 120 B8
Walkden M38 . . . . . 60 B5
Trafford General Hospl M41 . . . . . 95 A3
Trafford Gr Farnworth BL4 . . 42 E1
Stretford M32 . . . . . 96 D1
Trafford Mans 2 M16 . . . . . 97 B2
Trafford Park Rd M17 . . . . . 96 D6
Trafford Park Sta M32 . . . 96 C3
Trafford Pl M15 . . . . . 162 D6
Trafford Rd
Alderley Edge SK9 . . . . . 137 B1
Eccles M30 . . . . . 79 D1
Eccles M30 . . . . . 95 D8
Handforth SK9 . . . . . 131 B1
Hindley WN2 . . . . . 56 C5
Salford M5 &M16,M17 . . . 161 A7
Trafford Ret Pk M41 . . . . . 95 C5
Trafford St Farnworth BL4 . . 42 D1
Manchester M1,M3 . . . . . 162 F8
Oldham OL8 . . . . . 153 E5
Rochdale OL11 . . . . . 139 E5
Trafford Wharf Rd M17 . . . 96 E6
Tragan Cl SK2 . . . . . 124 D6
Tragan Dr SK2 . . . . . 124 D6
Trail St M6 . . . . . 154 E2
Trajan Ho OL1 . . . . . 153 F7
Tram St Manchester M11 . . 165 C8
Platt Bridge WN2 . . . . . 56 A1
Tramore Wlk M22 . . . . . 121 E2
Tramway Rd M44 . . . . . 105 F7
Tranby Cl M22 . . . . . 121 F4
Tranmere Cl M18 . . . . . 165 B5
Tranmere Dr SK9 . . . . . 131 E2
Tranmere Rd 1 SK3 . . . . . 123 B8
Transpennine Trad Est OL11 . . . . . 30 D3
Transvaal St M11 . . . . . 83 D1
Travers St BL6 . . . . . 22 D1
Travis Brow SK4 . . . . . 169 D1
Travis Ct OL2 . . . . . 48 E4
Travis Ho OL14 . . . . . 6 A7
Travis St Hyde SK14 . . . . . 167 E2
Manchester M1 . . . . . 163 C8
Newhey OL16 . . . . . 32 B4
Shaw OL2 . . . . . 149 C7
Trawden Ave BL1 . . . . . 142 C2
Trawden Dr BL9 . . . . . 27 E8
Trawden Gn SK2 . . . . . 124 D4
Traylen Way OL12 . . . . . 14 A1
Trecastell Cl WN1 . . . . . 37 F1
Tredcroft St SK13 . . . . . 116 B8
Tredgold St BL6 . . . . . 22 C2
Tree Ave M43 . . . . . 84 A3
Tree Cl OL4 . . . . . 67 D8
Tree House Ave 2 OL7 . . . 85 A6
Tree Tops BL7 . . . . . 25 C6
Tree Wlk M32 . . . . . 96 C1
Treelands Wlk M5 . . . . . 161 B6
Treen Rd M29 . . . . . 77 C8
Treetop Cl OL3 . . . . . 50 F1
Treetops Ave BL0 . . . . . 11 A3
Trefoil Way OL15 . . . . . 15 F6
Tregaer Fold M24 . . . . . 65 C8
Tregaron Gr WN2 . . . . . 57 A3
Tremain Wlk 10 M9 . . . . . 157 D7
Trenam Pl M5 . . . . . 81 B2
Trenant Rd M6 . . . . . 154 D4
Trenchard Ct M11,M43 . . . 83 D2
Trenchard Dr M22 . . . . . 130 F7
Trencherbone M26 . . . . . 43 E5
Trengrove St 7 OL12 . . . . . 14 C1
Trent Ave Chadderton OL9 . . 65 E8
Heywood OL10 . . . . . 29 A3
Milnrow OL16 . . . . . 32 A6
Trent Bridge Wlk M16 . . . . . 97 A3
Trent Cl Bramhall SK7 . . . . . 132 C6
Brinnington SK5 . . . . . 112 C5
Trent Ct Manchester M15 . . 162 D6
Stockport SK3 . . . . . 170 D7
Trent Dr Bury BL9 . . . . . 27 F8
Hindley WN2 . . . . . 57 C3
Walkden M28 . . . . . 60 B2
Trent Gr WN7 . . . . . 75 C4
Trent Rd Ashton-in-M WN4 . . 73 E5
Billinge WN5 . . . . . 71 D3
Shaw OL2 . . . . . 149 A8
Wigan WN5 . . . . . 54 C7
Trent St OL16 . . . . . 31 B6
Trent Way BL4 . . . . . 61 B5
Trentham Ave
Farnworth BL4 . . . . . 42 C1
Manchester SK4 . . . . . 110 F4
Trentham Cl BL4 . . . . . 42 C1
Trentham Gr M40 . . . . . 65 A1
Trentham Lawns M6 . . . . . 81 B4
Trentham Rd M16 . . . . . 97 A3
Trentham St Farnworth BL4 42 C1
Salford M15 . . . . . 161 C7
Swinton M27 . . . . . 61 E1
Tresco Ave M32 . . . . . 96 E1
Trescott Mews WN6 . . . . . 36 F8
Trevarrick Ct Horwich BL6 . . 22 E2
2 Oldham OL4 . . . . . 67 C8
Trevelyan Dr WN5 . . . . . 53 D1
Trevelyan St M30 . . . . . 80 A2
Trevor Ave Bolton BL3 . . . 147 D3
Sale M33 . . . . . 107 F2
Trevor Dr M40 . . . . . 65 E2
Trevor Gr SK1 . . . . . 124 A8
Trevor Rd Eccles M30 . . . . . 79 B3
Swinton M27 . . . . . 79 E6
Urmston M41 . . . . . 94 F3
Urmston M41 . . . . . 95 A2
Trevor St Manchester M11 . . 99 E7
Rochdale OL11 . . . . . 30 B3
Triangle The WA15 . . . . . 120 B7
Tribune Ave WA14 . . . . . 119 B7
Trident Rd M30 . . . . . 94 F7
Trillo Ave BL2 . . . . . 148 B6
Trimdon Cl M11 . . . . . 83 B2
Trimingham Dr BL8 . . . . . 27 D5
Trimley Ave M40 . . . . . 157 E5
Tring Wlk M9 . . . . . 64 B3
Trinity Ave M33 . . . . . 108 D4
Trinity Bldgs OL5 . . . . . 68 D2
Trinity CE High Sch M15 . 163 A6
Trinity Cl SK16 . . . . . 101 E8
Trinity Cres M28 . . . . . 60 E3
Trinity Ct M3 . . . . . 158 D2
Trinity Gdns
Ashton-in-M WN4 . . . . . 72 F4
Manchester M3 . . . . . 158 D2
Stockport SK3 . . . . . 123 F3
Trinity Gn BL0 . . . . . 11 B2
Trinity Ho OL1 . . . . . 153 E8
Trinity Rd M33 . . . . . 108 D4
Trinity Ret Pk BL2 . . . . . 148 A6
Trinity Sch SK15 . . . . . 85 F1
Trinity St 15 Bacup OL13 . . . 3 C8
Bolton BL3 . . . . . 145 F6
Bury BL9 . . . . . 140 F1
Marple SK6 . . . . . 125 F6
2 Middleton M24 . . . . . 64 F8
Oldham OL1 . . . . . 153 E8
Rochdale OL12 . . . . . 13 E2
Stalybridge SK15 . . . . . 86 A1
Trinity Way M3 . . . . . 158 E2
Trinity Wlk 13 M14 . . . . . 98 B3
Trippier Rd M30 . . . . . 94 F8
Tripps Mews M20 . . . . . 109 F4
Triscombe Way M16 . . . . . 97 E3
Tristam Cl M13 . . . . . 163 C7
Trojan Gdns 7 M7 . . . . . 81 C5
Trongate Wlk 15 M9 . . . . . 157 E7
Troon Cl Bolton BL3 . . . . . 40 F3
Bramhall SK7 . . . . . 133 A7
Troon Dr SK8 . . . . . 122 C1
Troon Rd M23 . . . . . 120 F6
Trough Gate OL8 . . . . . 66 D2
Troutbeck Ave M4 . . . . . 160 D2
Troutbeck Cl BL8 . . . . . 10 B2
Troutbeck Dr
Ramsbottom BL0 . . . . . 138 C7
Tyldesley M29 . . . . . 77 A7
Troutbeck Gr WA11 . . . . . 71 B2
Troutbeck Rd
Altrincham WA15 . . . . . 120 D5
Ashton-in-M WN4 . . . . . 73 C5
Gatley SK8 . . . . . 122 B3
Troutbeck Rise WN5 . . . . . 54 B6
Troutbeck Way OL11 . . . . . 30 B4
Troutbeck Wlk 5 OL2 . . . . . 48 E4
Trowbridge Dr M40 . . . . . 65 C1
Trowbridge Rd M34 . . . . . 101 A1
Trows La OL11 . . . . . 30 D1
Trowtree Ave M12 . . . . . 164 E6
Troy Wlk M5 . . . . . 161 B7
Troydale Dr M40 . . . . . 83 B6
Trumpet St M1 . . . . . 162 F8
Truro Ave Ashton-u-L OL6 . . 85 D7
Brinnington SK5 . . . . . 112 C5
Stretford M32 . . . . . 96 E2
Truro Cl Bramhall SK7 . . . . . 132 F7
Bury BL8 . . . . . 140 D3
Truro Dr M33 . . . . . 107 D4
Truro Rd Chadderton OL9 . . 48 A1
Tyldesley M29 . . . . . 77 C8
Truro Wlk M34 . . . . . 100 F1
Trust Rd M18 . . . . . 99 C3
Tucker's Hill Brow WN2 . . 21 B1
Tudbury Way M3 . . . . . 158 D2
Tudor Ave Bolton BL1 . . . . . 144 B7
Failsworth OL9 . . . . . 65 D3
Farnworth BL4 . . . . . 60 B7
Manchester M9 . . . . . 64 E1
Stalybridge SK15 . . . . . 86 D3
Tudor Cl OL5 . . . . . 68 E1

Tudor Ct Bolton BL1 . . . . . .**145** E8
Manchester M16 . . . .**161** C5
Manchester M25 . . . .**63** C3
Rochdale OL12 . . . .**15** B1
Tudor Gn SK9 . . . .**131** E1
Tudor Gr Middleton M24 . . . .**46** D3
Wigan WN3 . . . .**54** E2
Tudor Hall St OL11 . . . .**30** C2
Tudor Hey SK5 . . . .**111** E7
Tudor Ind Est SK16 . . . . . .**101** A7
Tudor Rd Altrincham WA14 **119** B7
Handforth SK9 . . . .**131** E1
Tudor St 9 Bolton BL3 . . . . .**146** C4
Middleton M24 . . . .**65** B8
Oldham OL8 . . . .**153** D5
Oldham OL8 . . . .**153** E5
Shaw OL2 . . . .**149** B7
Tuer St M13 . . . .**163** A6
Tuffley Rd M23 . . . .**121** A3
Tufton Wlk M9 . . . .**157** D7
Tugford Cl M16 . . . .**97** E4
Tuley St M11 . . . .**164** F7
Tulip Ave Farnworth BL4 . . .**42** A1
Kearsley BL4 . . . .**60** F5
Tulip Cl Chadderton OL9 . . . .**65** E7
Sale M33 . . . .**107** C4
Stockport SK3 . . . .**170** D5
Tulip Dr Altrincham WA15 . .**119** F6
Wigan WN6 . . . .**36** F3
Tulip Gr OL12 . . . .**14** E3
Tulip Rd M31 . . . .**105** E2
Tulketh Street Ind Est
  M40 . . . .**83** A8
Tulle Ct M25 . . . .**63** A4
Tully St M7 . . . .**155** E7
Tully St S M7 . . . .**155** E6
Tulpen Sq OL9 . . . .**152** B7
Tulworth Rd SK12 . . . .**133** D4
Tumblewood Dr SK8 . . . . . .**122** E4
Tumbling Bank Terr OL4 . . .**67** F5
Tumbling Wlk M9 . . . .**64** D3
Tunbridge Sq M5 . . . .**81** A2
Tunicliffe's New Row
  WN7 . . . .**75** C5
Tunley La WN6 . . . .**18** E5
Tunley Moss WN6 . . . .**18** E4
Tuns Rd OL8 . . . .**67** B2
Tunshill Gr OL16 . . . .**32** A6
Tunshill La OL16 . . . .**32** C7
Tunshill Rd M23, M33 . . . . .**108** E1
Tunstall La WN5 . . . .**54** D5
Tunstall Rd OL4 . . . .**67** C6
Tunstall St
  2 Manchester M11 . . . .**99** E7
  Stockport SK4 . . . .**169** E2
Tunstead Ave M20 . . . .**109** F6
Tunstead La Bacup OL13 . . . . .**3** B8
Oldham OL13 . . . .**69** D5
Tunstead Mill Terr 3 OL13 . .**3** B8
Tunstead Rd OL13 . . . .**3** C8
Turbory Wlk OL16 . . . .**31** D6
Turf Cl OL2 . . . .**48** E3
Turf Hill Rd OL16 . . . .**31** C4
Turf House Cl OL15 . . . .**15** F7
Turf La Oldham OL9 . . . .**66** A3
Royton OL2 . . . .**48** F3
Turf Lea Rd SK6 . . . .**126** B1
Turf Park Rd OL2 . . . .**48** F3
Turf Pit La OL4 . . . .**49** F4
Turf St M26 . . . .**43** F3
Turf Terr OL15 . . . .**16** A6
Turfland Ave OL2 . . . .**48** F3
Turfton Rd OL2 . . . .**48** F3
Turk St 6 BL1 . . . .**144** C8
Turks Rd M26 . . . .**43** E5
Turley St M8 . . . .**156** B6
Turn Moss Rd M21,M32 . . . .**96** F1
Turn Rd BL0 . . . .**11** E8
Turn St OL6 . . . .**85** D4
Turnberry BL3 . . . .**40** F3
Turnberry Cl M29 . . . .**77** C8
Turnberry Dr SK9 . . . .**137** D8
Turnberry Rd SK8 . . . .**122** C1
Turnberry Wlk M8 . . . .**156** C8
Turnbull Ave M25 . . . .**63** C7
Turnbull Rd
  Manchester M13 . . . .**98** F2
  Reddish M18 . . . .**99** F4
Turnbury Cl M33 . . . .**108** B6
Turnbury Rd M22 . . . .**121** E5
Turncliff Cres SK6 . . . .**125** D7
Turncroft La SK1 . . . .**112** B1
Turncroft Way M28 . . . .**77** F7
Turnditch Cl WN6 . . . .**37** A4
Turnell Way M28 . . . .**79** A5
Turner Ave Failsworth M35 . .**83** E6
Irlam M44 . . . .**94** A3
Leigh WN2 . . . .**56** E1
Turner Bridge Rd BL2 . . . .**148** C8
Turner Dr M41 . . . .**95** F2
Turner Gdns SK14 . . . .**167** E4
Turner La Ashton-u-L OL6 . .**166** B4
Bredbury SK6 . . . .**112** F6
Hyde SK14 . . . .**167** F4
Turner Rd SK6 . . . .**125** F5
Turner St Ashton-u-L OL6 . .**166** B4
  3 Bacup OL13 . . . .**3** C8
  Bolton BL1 . . . .**148** A8
  Denton M34 . . . .**100** E5
  Droylsden M11 . . . .**83** C1
  Hindley WN2 . . . .**56** D7
  Leigh WN7 . . . .**76** A4
  Manchester M16 . . . .**161** C6
  Manchester M18 . . . .**99** D5
  Manchester M4 . . . .**159** A2

Turner St continued
  Manchester M7 . . . .**155** E7
  Oldham OL4 . . . .**67** E8
  Rochdale OL12 . . . .**14** E1
  Westhoughton BL5 . . . .**57** E5
  Wigan WN1 . . . .**37** D1
Turner's Pl OL12 . . . .**14** E3
Turnerford Cl BL7 . . . .**8** E1
Turnfield Cl OL16 . . . .**15** D3
Turnfield Ho SK8 . . . .**122** D3
Turnfield Rd SK8 . . . .**122** D3
Turnhill Rd OL16 . . . .**31** B3
Turnill Dr WN4 . . . .**73** B2
Turnlee Cl SK13 . . . .**116** C7
Turnlee Dr SK13 . . . .**116** C7
Turnlee Rd SK13 . . . .**116** C7
Turnough Rd OL16 . . . .**31** F7
Turnpike Cl OL3 . . . .**51** C5
Turnpike Ct 7 M16 . . . .**97** D3
Turnpike Gn 1 M6 . . . .**154** F3
Turnpike The SK6 . . . .**125** D7
Turnpike Wlk M11 . . . .**160** F1
Turnstone Ave WA12 . . . . .**89** C4
Turnstone Cl WN7 . . . .**76** A6
Turnstone Rd
  3 Bolton BL2 . . . .**148** A6
  Hazel Grove SK2 . . . .**125** A5
Turret Hall Dr 1 WA3 . . . . .**90** E8
Turriff Gr WN2 . . . .**56** A8
Turton Ave BL3 . . . .**43** A4
Turton Cl Bury BL8 . . . .**44** A8
  Heywood OL10 . . . .**29** A2
Turton High Sch SK15 . . . . .**25** B7
Turton Ho 1 BL1 . . . .**148** A8
Turton Hts BL2 . . . .**25** B6
Turton La M25 . . . .**62** F5
Turton Rd Bolton BL2,BL7 . . .**25** C5
  Bury BL8 . . . .**26** D8
Turton St Bolton BL1 . . . . . .**148** A8
  Golborne WA3 . . . .**90** A8
  Manchester M11 . . . .**99** D7
Turton Tower BL7 . . . .**9** C3
Turves Rd SK8 . . . .**122** F1
Turville Ho SK9 . . . .**131** D2
Turvin Rd HX6,OL15 . . . .**7** D2
Tuscan Rd M20 . . . .**122** B8
Tuscany View M7 . . . .**81** B8
Tutbury St M4 . . . .**160** D1
Tutor Bank Dr WA12 . . . . . .**89** D3
Tuxford Wlk M40 . . . .**157** D5
Tweed Cl Altrincham WA14 **119** C6
  Oldham OL8 . . . .**153** E5
Tweed St WN7 . . . .**76** B4
Tweedale Ave M9 . . . .**64** C4
Tweedale St OL11 . . . .**139** E6
Tweedale Way OL9 . . . .**66** A1
Tweedle Hill Rd M9 . . . .**64** C4
Tweedsdale Cl M45 . . . .**45** B1
Tweenbrook Ave M23 . . . . .**121** A3
Twelve Apostles
  RC Prim Sch WN7 . . . .**75** D8
Twelve Yards Rd
  Irlam M30 . . . .**94** B6
  Irlam M44 . . . .**93** D4
Twigworth Rd M22 . . . .**121** C2
Twillbrook Dr M3 . . . .**158** E3
Twin St OL10 . . . .**29** E1
Twinegate OL12 . . . .**14** E3
Twining Brook Rd SK8 . . . .**123** B4
Twining Rd M17 . . . .**95** E8
Twinnies Ct SK9 . . . .**131** B1
Twinnies Rd SK9 . . . .**131** B1
Twirl Hill Rd OL6 . . . .**85** E8
Twiss Green Cty Prim Sch
  WA3 . . . .**91** E4
Twiss Green Dr WA3 . . . . . .**91** E4
Twiss Green La WA3 . . . . . .**91** E4
Twisse Rd BL2 . . . .**42** F7
Twist Ave WA3 . . . .**90** C8
Twist La WN7 . . . .**75** E5
Two Acre Dr OL2 . . . .**48** F7
Two Acre La OL4 . . . .**50** B3
Two Bridges Rd OL16 . . . . . .**32** C3
Two Brooks La BL8 . . . .**10** B2
Two Porches Specl Sch
  M46 . . . .**58** D4
Two Trees Com High Sch
  M34 . . . .**101** A1
Two Trees La M34 . . . .**101** A1
Twoacre Ave M22 . . . .**121** C5
Twyford Cl M20 . . . .**109** F3
Tybyrne Cl M28 . . . .**77** F7
Tydden St OL8 . . . .**66** F3
Tydeman Wlk OL16 . . . .**32** A5
Tydesley Arc 1 WN1 . . . . . .**150** C8
Tyersall Cl M30 . . . .**79** E4
Tyldesley Cty Prim Sch
  M29 . . . .**76** F8
Tyldesley Highfield Sch
  M28 . . . .**77** F7
Tyldesley Old Rd M46 . . . . .**58** E2
Tyldesley Pas 5 M29 . . . . . .**58** F1
Tyldesley Prim Sch M29 . . . .**77** F7
Tyldesley Rd M46 . . . .**58** E2
Tyldesley St M14 . . . .**98** A3
Tyler St SK9 . . . .**137** A1
Tyler Wlk 2 WA3 . . . .**90** F8
Tymm St M40 . . . .**83** C8
Tyndall Ave M40 . . . .**65** A1
Tyndall St OL4 . . . .**67** C6
Tyne Ct M28 . . . .**60** C3
Tyne St 10 OL4 . . . .**67** C7
Tynedale Cl SK5 . . . .**111** F5
Tynesbank M28 . . . .**60** C3
Tynesbank Cotts M28 . . . . . .**60** C3
Tyntesfield Cty Prim Sch
  M33 . . . .**107** E1
Tynwald St OL4 . . . .**67** C7

Tynwell Wlk 2 M40 . . . . . .**156** C5
Tyrer Ave WN3 . . . .**54** F5
Tyrer Rd WA12 . . . .**89** C1
Tyrol Wlk M11 . . . .**164** F8
Tyrone Cl M23 . . . .**120** D8
Tyrone Dr OL11 . . . .**29** F5
Tyrrel Rd SK5 . . . .**99** F1
Tyrrell Gr SK14 . . . .**102** A1
Tysoe Gdns M3 . . . .**158** D2
Tyson St M8 . . . .**155** F8
Tytherington Dr M19 . . . . . .**99** D1

U

Uganda St BL3 . . . .**146** C2
Ukraine Rd M7 . . . .**81** B6
Uldale Dr M24 . . . .**46** E1
Ullesthorpe 18 OL12 . . . . .**139** E8
Ulleswater Cl BL3 . . . .**42** F3
Ulleswater St BL1 . . . .**143** F2
Ullock Wlk M24 . . . .**46** D2
Ullswater Ave
  Ashton-in-M WN4 . . . .**73** B5
  Ashton-u-L OL7 . . . .**166** A4
  Orrell WN5 . . . .**53** F7
  Rochdale OL12 . . . .**14** C1
  Royton OL2 . . . .**48** D7
Ullswater Ct WA3 . . . .**74** C1
Ullswater Dr Bury BL9 . . . . . .**44** E7
  Farnworth BL4 . . . .**59** E7
  Ince-in-M WN2 . . . .**56** B7
  Middleton M24 . . . .**46** F2
Ullswater Gr OL10 . . . .**46** D8
Ullswater Rd Golborne WA3 . .**74** F1
  Handforth SK9 . . . .**131** C4
  Stockport SK1 . . . .**124** B7
  Tyldesley M29 . . . .**77** B6
  Urmston M41 . . . .**94** E3
  Wythenshawe M22 . . . .**121** C2
Ullswater St WN7 . . . .**75** E5
Ullswater Terr SK15 . . . .**86** A4
Ullswater Wlk 28 M9 . . . . . .**64** E3
Ulster Ave OL11 . . . .**139** E5
Ulundi St M26 . . . .**44** A3
Ulverston Ave
  Manchester M20 . . . .**109** F7
  Oldham OL9 . . . .**152** A6
Ulverston Rd WN3 . . . .**54** F3
Umberton Rd BL5 . . . .**58** F7
Uncouth Rd OL16 . . . .**31** E7
Under La Oldham OL4,OL5 . . .**68** B4
  Oldham OL9 . . . .**66** B3
Underhill SK6 . . . .**113** C2
Underhill Rd OL1 . . . .**48** E1
Underhill Wlk M40 . . . .**83** B4
Underwood OL12 . . . .**139** E7
Underwood Cl M18 . . . .**99** F6
Underwood Rd
  Alderley Edge SK9 . . . .**137** C1
  Hattersley SK14 . . . .**102** D2
Underwood St SK16 . . . . . .**101** B8
Underwood Villas OL15 . . . .**15** E4
Underwood Way OL2 . . . .**49** D8
Underwood Wlk 2 SK14 . . .**102** D2
Undsworth Ct 5 OL10 . . . . . .**29** D2
Unicorn St M30 . . . .**95** B8
Union Arc BL9 . . . .**140** F2
Union Bldgs BL3 . . . .**145** F6
Union Ct 18 OL13 . . . .**3** C8
Union Rd Ashton-u-L OL6 . . .**166** C4
  Bolton BL1,BL2 . . . .**25** A1
  Littleborough OL12 . . . .**15** E4
  Marple SK6 . . . .**125** F6
Union St Ashton-u-L OL6 . . .**166** C3
  Bacup OL13 . . . .**3** C8
  Bolton BL1 . . . .**145** F8
  Bolton BL7 . . . .**8** D2
  Bury BL9 . . . .**140** F2
  Glossop SK13 . . . .**116** C8
  Hyde SK14 . . . .**167** E2
  Ince-in-M WN2 . . . .**56** A8
  Leigh WN7 . . . .**75** F5
  Manchester M12 . . . .**163** C7
  Manchester M14 . . . .**98** B3
  Manchester M18 . . . .**99** E6
  Manchester M4 . . . .**159** A2
  Middleton M24 . . . .**47** A1
  Oldham OL1 . . . .**153** F6
  Oldham OL1 . . . .**64** A7
  Oldham OL4 . . . .**67** E6
  Oldham OL9 . . . .**66** B4
  Ramsbottom BL0 . . . .**138** C6
  Rochdale OL12,OL16 . . . . .**139** F8
  Royton OL2 . . . .**48** D3
  Salford M6 . . . .**81** A4
  Stockport SK1 . . . .**170** F8
  Swinton M27 . . . .**62** A1
  Swinton M27 . . . .**79** E8
  Tyldesley M29 . . . .**58** F1
  Whitworth OL12 . . . .**14** C8
Union St W OL8 . . . .**153** E6
Union Terr M7 . . . .**155** F8
United Rd M17 . . . .**96** F5
United Trad Est M17 . . . .**96** F5
Unity Cl OL10 . . . .**29** B1
Unity Cres OL10 . . . .**29** B1
Unity Dr M7 . . . .**155** F6
Unity St Heywood OL10 . . . . .**29** B1
  Walsden OL14 . . . .**6** A1
Unity Way SK1 . . . .**124** A8
Unity Wlk SK13 . . . .**116** C7
Univ of Manchester (Lab)
  M30 . . . .**94** D6
Univ of Manchester
  Inst of Science & Tech
  M1 . . . .**163** B8

Univ of Manchester The
  Manchester M15 . . . .**163** A5
  M13 . . . .**163** B6
Univ of Salford
  Manchester M3 . . . .**158** D2
  Salford M6 . . . .**81** B3
University Rd
  Salford M5,M6 . . . .**81** B2
  Salford M5,M6 . . . .**81** B3
University Rd W M5,M6 . . . .**81** B2
Unsworth Ave
  Golborne WA3 . . . .**74** E1
  Tyldesley M29 . . . .**77** B8
Unsworth Prim Sch BL9 . . . . .**45** A2
Unsworth St Bacup OL13 . . . . .**3** D7
  2 Hindley WN2 . . . .**56** D4
  Leigh WN7 . . . .**75** E7
  Radcliffe M26 . . . .**43** F4
  Tyldesley M29 . . . .**59** B1
Unsworth Terr WN2 . . . .**56** C5
Unsworth Way OL1 . . . .**153** E8
Unwin Ave M18 . . . .**99** D4
Up Holland High Sch
  WN5 . . . .**53** C4
Upavon Ct M8 . . . .**155** F6
Upavon Rd M22 . . . .**121** F3
Upcast La SK9 . . . .**136** E3
Upholland Rd WN5 . . . .**53** D2
Upland Dr Ashton-in-M WN4 **73** D4
  Walkden M38 . . . .**59** F6
Upland Rd OL8 . . . .**66** E4
Uplands M24 . . . .**65** A7
Uplands Ave M26 . . . .**44** C2
Uplands Rd Flixton M41 . . . .**106** E8
  Glossop SK13 . . . .**116** D8
  Romiley SK14 . . . .**114** A6
Uplands The OL5 . . . .**68** D1
Upper Brook St
  Manchester M13 . . . .**163** B6
  Stockport SK1 . . . .**170** A1
Upper Broom Way BL5 . . . . .**40** A2
Upper Camp St M7 . . . .**155** D5
Upper Chorlton Rd M16 . . . . .**97** C3
Upper Cliff Hill OL2 . . . .**32** C1
Upper Conran St M9 . . . . . .**157** E8
Upper Cyrus St M40 . . . . . .**160** E2
Upper Dicconson St WN1 . . .**37** C1
Upper Downs WA14 . . . .**119** C3
Upper George St
  23 Rochdale OL12 . . . .**14** F1
  Tyldesley M29 . . . .**77** A8
Upper Gloucester St M6 . . . .**81** A3
Upper Hayes Cl OL16 . . . . . .**31** C8
Upper Helena St M40 . . . . .**160** E2
Upper Hibbert La SK6 . . . . .**125** F4
Upper Kent Rd M14 . . . .**98** E3
Upper Kirby St M4 . . . .**159** C1
Upper Lees Dr BL5 . . . .**40** A1
Upper Lloyd St M14 . . . .**98** A3
Upper Mead BL7 . . . .**8** F1
Upper Medlock St M15 . . . .**162** F6
Upper Monsall St M40 . . . . .**157** E6
Upper Moss La M15 . . . . . .**162** E6
Upper Park Rd
  Manchester M14 . . . .**98** C4
  Manchester M7 . . . .**63** E1
Upper Passmonds Gr
  OL11 . . . .**30** B8
Upper St Stephen St
  WN6 . . . .**150** B8
Upper Stone Dr OL16 . . . . . .**31** D6
Upper West Gr M13 . . . . . .**164** D5
Upper Wharf St M3,M5 . . . . .**81** C1
Upper Wilton St M25 . . . .**63** C4
Uppermill Dr M19 . . . .**110** E3
Uppingham Dr BL0 . . . .**138** B7
Upton OL11 . . . .**139** E6
Upton Ave Cheadle SK8 . . . .**132** A8
  Manchester SK4 . . . .**110** E4
Upton Cl Golborne WA3 . . . . .**90** D8
  Middleton M24 . . . .**65** A5
Upton Dr WA14 . . . .**119** E8
Upton La M29 . . . .**77** C8
Upton Rd M46 . . . .**58** E4
Upton St M1 . . . .**159** B1
Upton Way Bury BL8 . . . .**26** F5
  12 Handforth SK9 . . . .**131** D5
Upton Wlk 10 OL7 . . . .**166** A1
Upwood Rd WA3 . . . .**90** D7
Upwood Wlk 31 M9 . . . .**64** E3
Urban Ave WA15 . . . .**119** E4
Urban Dr WA15 . . . .**119** E4
Urban Rd Altrincham WA15 **119** E4
  Sale M33 . . . .**108** A4
Urmston St OL8 . . . .**66** F3
Urmston Ave WA12 . . . .**89** B1
Urmston Gram Sch M41 . . . . .**95** C2
Urmston Inf Sch M41 . . . .**95** C2
Urmston Jun Sch M41 . . . . . .**95** C2
Urmston La M32,M41 . . . . . .**96** B1
Urmston Pk M41 . . . .**95** E2
Urmston St WN7 . . . .**75** D5
Urmston Sta M41 . . . .**95** D2
Urwick Rd SK6 . . . .**113** B2
Usk Cl WN5 . . . .**63** C7
Uttley St Bolton BL1 . . . . . .**143** D2
  Rochdale OL11 . . . .**30** C4
Uvedale Ho 11 M40 . . . .**79** D1
Uxbridge Ave 18 M11 . . . . . .**83** C2
Uxbridge St OL6 . . . .**166** A3

V

Vaal St OL8 . . . .**66** C3
Valance Cl M12 . . . .**165** A6
Valdene Cl BL4 . . . .**60** D7
Valdene Dr Farnworth BL4 . . .**60** D7

Valdene Dr continued
  Walkden M28 . . . .**78** D8
Vale Ave Bury BL9 . . . .**44** D7
  Horwich BL6 . . . .**22** A3
  Hyde SK14 . . . .**102** A3
  Kearsley M26 . . . .**61** C7
  Sale M33 . . . .**108** E5
  Swinton M27 . . . .**62** A1
  Urmston M41 . . . .**94** E1
Vale Cl Appley Bridge WN6 . . .**35** E8
  Hazel Grove SK4 . . . .**124** E4
  Manchester SK4 . . . .**110** F2
  Romiley SK6 . . . .**113** F2
Vale Coppice Horwich BL6 . . .**22** A3
  Ramsbottom BL0 . . . .**11** C3
Vale Cotts Horwich BL6 . . . . .**21** F2
  Littleborough OL15 . . . .**16** A5
Vale Cres SK8 . . . .**122** E3
Vale Dr Oldham OL9 . . . .**153** D6
  Prestwich M25 . . . .**63** A3
Vale Edge M26 . . . .**44** A5
Vale Head SK9 . . . .**131** D2
Vale House Dr SK13 . . . . . .**104** A5
Vale La M35 . . . .**84** A4
Vale Park Ind Est M8 . . . . . .**156** C7
Vale Rd Altrincham WA14 . .**119** B1
  Altrincham WA15 . . . .**120** B5
  Droylsden M43 . . . .**84** B3
  Manchester SK4 . . . .**110** F1
  Mossley SK15 . . . .**86** E6
  Romiley SK6 . . . .**125** B8
  Shaw OL2 . . . .**49** D6
  Wilmslow SK9 . . . .**136** E8
Vale Side OL5 . . . .**86** C3
Vale St Ashton-u-L OL7 . . . . .**85** A6
  Bolton BL2 . . . .**43** A7
  Droylsden M11 . . . .**83** C2
  Heywood OL10 . . . .**29** E2
  Middleton M24 . . . .**65** B8
Vale The Appley Bridge WN6 .**35** D8
  Mossley OL5 . . . .**86** C8
Vale Top Ave M9 . . . .**157** F7
Vale View BL7 . . . .**24** F7
Valencia Rd M7 . . . .**81** B6
Valentia Rd M9 . . . .**64** D4
Valentine St Failsworth M35 **83** E7
  Oldham OL4 . . . .**67** C6
Valentines Rd M46 . . . .**58** A4
Valerie Wlk 4 M15 . . . .**162** F7
Valetta Cl M14 . . . .**110** B8
Valewood Ave SK4 . . . .**168** A1
Valiant Rd WN5 . . . .**54** D8
Valiant Wlk 1 M40 . . . .**65** E1
Valletts La BL1 . . . .**142** C1
Valletts S BL1 . . . .**142** C1
Valley Ave BL8 . . . .**27** B4
Valley Cl Cheadle SK8 . . . . .**122** E3
  Mossley OL5 . . . .**68** B2
Valley Cotts OL3 . . . .**69** C4
Valley Dr SK9 . . . .**131** C3
Valley Gdns SK14 . . . .**114** E8
Valley Gr M34 . . . .**101** B2
Valley New Rd OL2 . . . .**48** E3
Valley Rd Bramhall SK7 . . . .**123** F1
  Bredbury SK6 . . . .**112** D4
  Cheadle SK8 . . . .**122** E3
  Glossop SK13 . . . .**115** F8
  Hattersley SK14 . . . .**114** E8
  Middleton M24 . . . .**47** B2
  Oldham OL2 . . . .**48** E3
  Stockport SK4 . . . .**168** A1
  Urmston M41 . . . .**94** D4
  Wigan WN5 . . . .**54** D5
Valley Rd S M41 . . . .**94** C2
Valley Rise OL2 . . . .**32** A1
Valley Sch SK7 . . . .**132** C3
Valley The M46 . . . .**58** E3
Valley View Bolton BL7 . . . . . .**25** A4
  Hyde SK14 . . . .**102** A4
  Newton-le-W WA12 . . . .**89** B1
  Whitworth OL12 . . . .**4** D4
Valley Way SK15 . . . .**86** C1
Valley Wlk M11 . . . .**160** F1
Valpy Ave BL2 . . . .**25** B3
Vanbrugh Gr WN5 . . . .**36** B1
Vancouver Quay M5 . . . .**96** F7
Vandyke Ave M6 . . . .**80** B3
Vandyke St 3 OL12 . . . .**13** F1
Vane St M30 . . . .**79** D2
Vanguard Cl M30 . . . .**94** F7
Vannes Gr SK14 . . . .**102** F3
Vantomme St BL1 . . . .**143** E4
Varden Gr SK3 . . . .**170** D5
Varden Rd SK12 . . . .**133** E3
Vardon Dr SK9 . . . .**137** D6
Varey St M18 . . . .**99** D5
Varley Rd BL3 . . . .**146** A4
Varley St M40 . . . .**160** D3
Varna St M11 . . . .**99** D7
Varna Street Prim Sch
  M11 . . . .**99** D6
Vauban Dr M6 . . . .**80** B3
Vaudrey Dr Cheadle SK8 . . .**123** A2
  Hazel Grove SK7 . . . .**124** E4
  Sale WA15 . . . .**120** A8
Vaudrey La M34 . . . .**101** A2
Vaudrey Rd SK6 . . . .**113** A5
Vaudrey St 15 SK15 . . . .**86** A1
Vaughan Ave M40 . . . .**83** A8
Vaughan Gr OL4 . . . .**67** C6
Vaughan Ind Est M12 . . . . . .**164** F7
Vaughan Rd
  Manchester M21 . . . .**109** D8
  Manchester SK4 . . . .**169** D3
Vaughan St Eccles M30 . . . . .**79** B3
  Manchester M12 . . . .**164** F7
  Royton OL2 . . . .**48** E3
Vauxhall Ct M40 . . . .**159** C4

Vauxhall Ind Est SK5 ....111 E6
Vauxhall Rd WN1 ....151 D8
Vauxhall St M40 ....159 B4
Vauze Ave BL6 ....21 D1
Vauze House Cl BL6 .....21 D2
Vavasour Ct 5 OL16 ....31 B6
Vavasour St OL16 ....31 B6
Vawdrey Dr 6 M23 .....108 F2
Vaynor 18 OL12 ....139 E8
Vega St M8 ....158 E4
Vela Wlk M6 ....81 C3
Velmere Ave M9 ....64 A5
Velour Cl M3 ....158 D2
Velvet Ct M1 ....163 A8
Vendale Ave M27 ....79 D6
Venesta Ave M6 ....80 B4
Venetia St M40 ....83 C5
Venice St Bolton BL3 ..146 C4
Manchester M1 ....163 A8
Venlow Gdns SK8 ....123 B1
Ventnor Ave Bolton BL1 .143 F3
Manchester M19 ....111 C8
Sale M33 ....108 B6
Whitefield BL9 ....45 A3
Ventnor Cl M34 ....113 B8
Ventnor Rd
Manchester M20 ....110 C3
Manchester M14 ....168 A2
Ventnor St Manchester M9 157 E8
Rochdale OL11 ....139 F5
Salford M6 ....81 B4
Ventor St M9 ....157 D8
Ventura Cl M34 ....98 A1
Ventura Ct SK22 ....127 D1
Venture Scout Way M8 .155 F6
Venture Way SK12 .....133 F3
Venwood Rd M25 ....62 F2
Verbena Ave BL4 ....42 A1
Verbena Cl M31 ....105 F3
Verda St WN2 ....74 B8
Verdant La Eccles M30 ..94 F8
Eccles M30 ....95 A8
Verdon St M4 ....159 A3
Verdun Ave M6 ....80 B3
Verdun Cres OL11 ....30 C8
Verdun Rd M30 ....79 B4
Verdure Ave Bolton BL1 .40 E8
Sale M33 ....108 C1
Verdure Ct M35 ....84 B7
Vere St M5 ....154 F1
Verity Cl Manchester M20 .110 C6
Royton OL2 ....48 D3
Verity Wlk M9 ....64 B3
Vermont St BL1 ....145 D8
Verne Ave M27 ....79 E8
Verne Dr OL1 ....49 E5
Verney Rd OL2 ....48 E2
Vernham Wlk BL3 ......147 E4
Vernon Ave Eccles M30 ..79 F2
Stockport SK1 ....112 B2
Stretford M32 ....96 D1
Vernon Cl Cheadle SK8 .122 E1
Poynton SK12 ....133 D2
Vernon Ct M7 ....63 C1
Vernon Dr Marple SK6 ..125 D7
Prestwich M25 ....63 A2
Vernon Gr M33 ....108 E3
Vernon Jun & Inf Schs
The SK12 ....133 E3
Vernon Park Prim Sch
SK1 ....112 A1
Vernon Pk WA15 ....120 A7
Vernon Rd Bredbury SK6 .112 E3
Droylsden M43 ....83 E2
Manchester M7 ....63 C1
Poynton SK12 ....133 E2
Ramsbottom BL0 ....11 A1
Vernon St Ashton-u-L OL6 .166 C4
Bolton BL1 ....145 E8
Bury BL9 ....140 F4
Farnworth BL4 ....42 E1
Hazel Grove SK7 ....124 D3
Hyde SK14 ....167 E2
Leigh WN7 ....75 F5
Manchester M16 ....162 D5
Manchester M7 ....155 D5
Mossley OL5 ....68 C2
Stockport SK1 ....169 E1
Vernon View 3 SK6 ....112 F3
Vernon Wlk 5 Bolton BL1 .145 E8
Stockport SK1 ....169 E1
Verona Dr M40 ....83 C4
Veronica Rd M20 ....110 C3
Verrill Ave M23 ....109 C1
Verwood Wlk 9 M23 ....121 A5
Vesper St M35 ....84 A8
Vesta St Manchester M4 .159 C2
Ramsbottom BL0 ....138 B6
Vestris Dr M6 ....80 B3
Vetch Cl WA3 ....105 B5
Viaduct St
Manchester M12 ....164 E8
Manchester M3 ....158 F2
Newton-le-W WA12 .....89 A3
Stockport SK3 ....169 E1
Vicar's Dr OL16 ....139 F6
Vicar's Gate OL16 .....139 F7
Vicarage Ave SK8 .....132 B7
Vicarage Cl Adlington PR6 .21 A8
Dukinfield SK16 ....101 E8
Oldham OL4 ....67 F7
Platt Bridge WN2 ....56 A2
Salford M6 ....80 B3
Vicarage Cres OL6 .....85 D5
Vicarage Ct 3 M23 ....120 D6
Vicarage Dr
Dukinfield SK16 ....101 E8

Vicarage Dr continued
Littleborough OL12,OL16 ..15 C3
Vicarage Gdns SK14 ...167 F2
Vicarage Gr M30 ....79 F2
Vicarage La
Altrincham WA14 ......119 C1
Middleton M24 ....65 D7
Poynton SK12 ....133 E5
Shevington WN6 ....36 A5
Vicarage Rd Abram WN2 ..73 B2
Ashton-in-M WN4 ....73 B2
Ashton-u-L OL7 ....85 B5
Blackrod BL6 ....21 D2
Golborne WN2 ....74 B1
Irlam M44 ....94 A2
Orrell WN5 ....53 D4
Stockport SK3 ....170 E6
Swinton M27 ....79 E8
Urmston M41 ....95 B4
Walkden M28 ....60 C4
Vicarage Rd N OL11 ....30 D1
Vicarage Rd S OL11 ....30 C1
Vicarage Rd W BL6 .....21 C2
Vicarage Sq WN7 ....75 F5
Vicarage St Bolton BL3 .145 D5
Oldham OL8 ....66 C3
1 Radcliffe M26 ....44 A3
Shaw OL2 ....149 B7
Vicarage View OL11 ....30 D1
Vicarage Way OL2 .....149 A6
Vicars Hall Gdns M28 ..77 F5
Vicars Hall La M28 ....77 F4
Vicars Rd M21 ....109 A8
Vicars St M30 ....79 F2
Viceroy St OL10 ....110 B2
Vicker Cl M27 ....61 F2
Vicker Gr M20 ....109 F5
Vickerman St BL1 .....143 D2
Vickers Row BL4 ....60 B8
Vickers St Bolton BL3 .145 E5
Victor Ave BL9 ....140 E4
Victor Cl WN5 ....54 D8
Victor Mann St M11 ...100 A7
Victor St Heywood OL10 ..46 E8
Manchester M3 ....158 D2
Manchester M40 ....159 C4
Victoria Ave
Altrincham WA15 ......119 F7
7 Bredbury SK6 ......112 F3
Cheadle SK8 ....123 A2
Eccles M30 ....79 F3
Hadfield SK13 ....104 A5
Hazel Grove SK7 ......124 E3
Leigh WN2 ....56 E1
Manchester M19 ......111 A8
Manchester M20 ......110 A3
Manchester M9 ....64 C5
Pendlebury M27 ....80 A8
Whitefield M45 ....63 A8
Wigan WN6 ....37 A1
Victoria Ave E M24,M40,M9 65 B4
Victoria Avenue Prim Sch
M9 ....64 D5
Victoria Bridge St M3 .158 F2
Victoria Cl Aspull WN2 ..38 B6
5 Boothstown M28 ....78 A6
Bramhall SK7 ....132 D6
Stockport SK3 ....170 E7
Victoria Cres Eccles M30 .79 F3
Standish WN6 ....36 E8
Victoria Ct
5 Ashton-u-L OL7 ....166 A1
Farnworth BL4 ....42 C2
Horwich BL6 ....22 C3
Manchester M11 ......165 C8
7 Manchester M20 ...110 A3
Stretford M32 ....96 C1
Victoria Dr M33 ......108 E3
Victoria Gdns Hyde SK14 .167 F4
Shaw OL2 ....149 B7
Victoria Gr Bolton BL1 .142 C1
Manchester M14 ......110 C7
Reddish SK4 ....111 D5
Victoria Grange M20 ..110 A4
Victoria Ho
Manchester M11 ......165 C8
Salford M6 ....80 A4
Victoria Ind Est The M4 .160 D1
Victoria La Swinton M27 ..79 D8
Whitefield BL9 ....62 F7
Victoria Lo M7 ....81 C5
Victoria Mews
1 Dukinfield SK16 ...101 C6
Whitefield BL9 ....45 B2
Victoria Mkt SK15 .....86 A1
Victoria Par Rawtenstall BB4 .2 E8
Urmston M41 ....95 D2
Victoria Park Jun Sch
M32 ....96 D2
Victoria Pk SK1 ....124 B8
Victoria Rd
Altrincham WA14 .....119 D3
Altrincham WA15 .....120 A6
Bolton BL1 ....40 D8
Dukinfield SK16 ......101 C6
Eccles M30 ....79 E3
Garswood WN4 ....72 D4
Horwich BL6 ....22 C2
Irlam M44 ....93 F1
Kearsley BL4 ....61 A6
Manchester M16 ....97 D2
Manchester M19 ......111 F1
Manchester M14 ......110 B8
Newton-le-W WA12 .....89 C3
Platt Bridge WN2 ......56 A2
Sale M33 ....108 D3
Salford M6 ....80 A4

Victoria Rd continued
Stockport SK1 ....112 B1
Stretford M32 ....96 D2
Urmston M41 ....95 B2
Wilmslow SK9 ....137 A6
Wythenshawe M22 .....121 D8
Victoria Sq Bolton BL1 .145 F7
Manchester M4 ....159 B2
Walkden M28 ....60 D3
Victoria St
Altrincham WA14 .....119 C5
Ashton-u-L OL7 ......166 A1
Bacup OL13 ....3 D8
Blackrod BL6 ....21 D2
Boothstown M28 ....78 A6
Bury BL8 ....140 D2
Bury BL8 ....140 D3
Bury BL8 ....26 E7
Denton M34 ....100 F3
Dukinfield SK14 ......102 A5
Dukinfield SK16 ......101 D8
Failsworth M35 ....83 D6
4 Farnworth BL4 .....42 B2
Glossop SK13 ....116 C8
Heywood OL10 ....29 C1
Leigh WN7 ....75 E6
Littleborough OL15 ...16 B5
Manchester M11 ......165 C8
Manchester M3 ....158 F2
Middleton M24 ....65 A8
Oldham OL4 ....67 A6
Oldham OL4 ....67 E6
Oldham OL8 ....84 F8
Oldham OL9 ....152 C8
Platt Bridge WN2 ......56 A2
1 Radcliffe M26 .....44 A3
Ramsbottom BL0 ......138 B6
Rawtenstall BB4 ......2 E8
22 Rochdale OL12 ...14 F1
Shaw OL2 ....149 B7
1 Stalybridge SK15 ..85 F2
Stalybridge SK15 .....86 D4
Westhoughton BL5 ....57 F8
Whitworth OL12 ....14 C8
Wigan WN5 ....54 F6
Victoria St E OL7 ....166 A2
Victoria Sta M3 ......159 A2
Victoria Station App M3 .159 A2
Victoria Terr
Bickershaw WN2 ....74 F8
Heywood OL10 ....29 C4
Manchester M12 ....98 F4
Milnrow OL16 ....32 A5
Victoria Way
Bramhall SK7 ....132 D6
Leigh WN7 ....75 E7
Royton OL2 ....48 C6
Victory Gr M34 ....100 C7
Victory Rd Irlam M44 ..105 C4
Little Lever BL3 ....43 B4
Victory St Bolton BL1 .144 C8
Manchester M14 ....98 C3
Vienna Rd SK3 ....170 D6
Vienna Rd E SK3 .....170 E6
View St BL3 ....145 E5
Viewfield Wlk 16 M9 .157 E7
Viewlands Dr SK9 ....131 D2
Vigo Ave BL3 ....146 B3
Vigo St Heywood OL10 ..29 E1
Oldham OL4 ....67 D5
1 Wigan WN2 ....37 F2
Viking Cl M11 ....160 F1
Viking St Bolton BL3 ..42 A4
Rochdale OL16 ....30 C8
Villa Ave WN6 ....37 A4
Villa Rd OL8 ....66 F4
Village Circ M17 ......96 D6
Village Ct Stretford M17 ..96 C6
Wilmslow SK9 ....131 D1
Village Gn 9 OL3 .....69 B8
Village Gn M7 ....81 C5
Village The M41 ......106 F8
Village View 2 WN7 ...76 B4
Village Way SK9 .....131 D1
Village Way
(Ashburton Rd E) M17 .96 C6
Village Wlk 18 M11 ...83 C1
Villdale Ave SK2 .....124 C3
Villiers Ct M45 ....63 A6
Villiers Dr OL8 ....153 E5
Villiers St Ashton-u-L OL6 .85 D2
Bury SK14 ....141 A3
Hyde SK14 ....167 F2
Salford M6 ....154 F4
Vinca Gr M7 ....155 D6
Vincent Ave Eccles M30 ..79 D4
Manchester M21 ....97 A1
Oldham OL4 ....67 C8
Vincent Ct BL3 ......147 E3
Vincent St Bolton BL1 .145 D6
Hyde SK14 ....113 F8
Littleborough OL15 ...16 A6
Manchester M11 ......165 C8
Manchester M7 ....155 E7
Middleton M24 ....47 A2
17 Rochdale OL16 ...31 A5
Vincent Way WN5 .....54 D8
Vine Ave M27 ....80 B8
Vine Cl Sale M33 .....107 C5
Shaw OL2 ....149 B7
Vine Ct Rochdale OL16 ..31 B6
Stretford M32 ....96 D1
Vine Fold M40 ....65 D1
Vine Gr Stockport SK2 .124 C6
Wigan WN3 ....150 C7
Vine Pl OL11 ....139 F5

Vine St Eccles M30 ....79 C1
Hazel Grove SK7 .....124 E3
Hindley WN2 ....56 D6
Manchester M11,M18 ..99 E6
Manchester M7 ....81 C8
Oldham OL9 ....66 B3
Prestwich M25 ....63 C5
Ramsbottom BL0 ....11 A4
Wigan WN1 ....37 D1
Vinery Gr M34 ....100 E3
Vineyard Cl OL12 ......15 C7
Vineyard St OL4 ....67 B7
Viola Cl WN6 ....19 D2
Viola St Bolton BL1 ..143 E3
Droylsden M11 ....83 D2
Violet Ave BL4 ....42 A1
Violet St M22 ....121 D3
Violet Hill Ct OL4 ....67 E8
Violet St Ashton-in-M WN4 .73 B2
Ince-in-M WN3 ....151 E6
Stockport SK2 ....170 F6
Violet Way M24 ....65 D7
Vip Centre Ind Est OL1 .49 C1
Virgil St M15 ....162 D6
Virginia Chase SK8 ..131 F8
Virginia St 3 BL2 ...25 B4
Virginia St Bolton BL3 .146 B4
Rochdale OL11 ....30 E4
Virginia Way WN5 ....54 C8
Viscount Dr Gatley SK8 .131 D7
Wythenshaw M90 .....129 F7
Viscount Rd WN5 .....54 C8
Viscount St M14 ......98 C3
Vista Ave WA12 ....89 A4
Vista Rd WA11,WA12 ..89 A6
Vista The M44 ....105 C4
Vista Way WA12 ......89 A4
Vivian Pl 9 M14 ....98 E4
Vivian St OL11 ......139 E5
Vixen Cl M21 ....109 E7
Voewood Ho SK1 ....124 B8
Voltaire Ave M6 ......80 B3
Vorlich Dr OL9 ....65 F8
Vulcan Cl WA12 ......89 C1
Vulcan Dr WN1 ......151 D7
Vulcan Ind Est WA12 ..89 D1
Vulcan Rd WN5 ....54 D8
Vulcan St OL1 ....49 B1
Vyner Gr M33 ....107 F6

W

Wadcroft Wlk 19 M9 .157 E8
Waddicor Ave OL6 ....85 E6
Waddington Cl Bury BL8 .26 E2
Golborne WA3 ....90 F8
Waddington Fold OL16 .31 C2
Waddington Rd BL1 ..142 A1
Waddington St M9 ...152 C8
Wade Bank BL5 ....57 F8
Wade Hill La OL3 .....68 E8
Wade Ho 8 M30 ......79 D1
Wade Row OL3 ....69 B8
Wade St 7 Bolton BL3 .147 F3
Middleton M24 ....65 D6
Wade Wlk M11 ....165 A8
Wadebridge Ave M23 .120 D7
Wadebridge Cl 3 BL2 .25 B1
Wadebrook Gr 4 SK9 .131 D1
Wadeford Cl M4 ......159 C3
Wadesmill Wlk M13 ..163 B7
Wadeson Rd M13 ....163 C7
Wadham Gdns SK6 ...113 C5
Wadham Way WA15 ..119 F1
Wadhurst Wlk 4 M13 .163 C5
Wadlow Cl M3 ....158 E3
Wadsworth Cl SK9 ...131 E3
Wadsworth Ind Pk BL3 .147 E4
Wadsworth Mews M43 ..83 F1
Waggon Rd Bolton BL2 .42 D8
Mossley OL5 ....86 C8
Waggoners Ct 2 M27 ..79 F7
Wagner St BL1 ....143 D3
Wagstaffe Dr M35 ....83 F7
Wagstaffe St M24 .....47 A2
Wagtail Cl M28 ....78 D8
Wain Cl M30 ....79 B2
Wain Stones Gn SK2 .124 E7
Waincliffe Ave M20,M21 .109 D4
Wainfleet Cl WN3 ....54 E2
Waingap Cres OL12 ..14 D8
Waingap Rise
Rochdale OL12 ....113 A1
Whitworth OL12 ......14 D7
Wainman St M6,M7 ...81 B5
Wainscot Cl M29 ......77 B7
Wainwright Ave M34 ..99 F3
Wainwright Rd WA14 .119 C5
Wainwright St
Oldham OL8 ....153 D5
Stalybridge SK16 .....85 D1
Waithlands Rd OL16 ..31 B6
Wakefield Cres
Romiley SK6 ....113 A1
Standish WN6 ....37 A6
Wakefield Dr Kearsley M27 .61 D4
Oldham OL1 ....48 C1
Wakefield Rd SK15 ...86 B3
Wakefield St Golborne WA3 90 A7
2 Manchester M1 ...163 A2
Wakefield Wlk M34 ..101 A1
Wakeling Rd M34 ....112 E8
Walcot Pl WN3 ....54 F2

Walcott Cl M13 ......164 E5
Wald Ave M14 ....110 E4
Waldeck St 1 BL1 ...145 D8
Waldeck Wlk 2 M9 ..64 E3
Walden 18 OL10 .....29 C2
Walden Ave OL4 ......49 D2
Walden Cl Hindley WN2 ..56 F4
Manchester M14 ......110 A8
Walden Cres SK7 ....124 C3
Waldon Ave SK8 ....122 D5
Waldon Cl BL3 ......146 C4
Waldorf Cl WN3 ......54 D2
Wales St OL1 ....49 C1
Walford Rd WN4 ......73 C3
Walford St M16 ....97 E4
Walk Mill Cl OL12 ....15 D4
Walk The Atherton M46 .58 D3
Rochdale OL16 ....139 F7
Walkdale Brow SK13 .116 B7
Walkden Ave WN1 .....37 B2
Walkden Ave E WN1 ..37 C2
Walkden High Sch M28 .60 E1
Walkden Market Pl M28 .60 D3
Walkden Rd Walkden M28 .60 D1
Worsley M28 ....78 E7
Walkden Sta M28 .....60 D2
Walkdene Dr M28 .....60 B3
Walkdens Ave M46 ...58 A2
Walker Ave Bolton BL4 .147 F3
Failsworth M35 ....84 B6
Prestwich M25,M45 ...63 A6
Stalybridge SK15 .....86 C2
Walker Cl Hyde SK14 .167 F2
Kearsley BL4 ....61 A6
Walker Fold SK14 ....167 F2
Walker Fold Rd BL1 ..23 D4
Walker Gn M28 ....79 B5
Walker Ho M30 ....79 D1
Walker La SK14 ......167 F2
Walker Rd Eccles M30 ..79 A4
Failsworth OL9 ....65 F2
Irlam M44 ....93 F1
Manchester M9 ....64 E1
Walker St Bolton BL1 .145 D6
3 Bury BL9 ....44 E1
Denton M34 ....100 E4
Hadfield SK13 ....104 A4
Heywood OL10 ....29 C1
Middleton M24 ....64 C7
Oldham OL8 ....153 D6
4 Radcliffe M26 .....44 C1
Rochdale OL16 ....31 A7
Stockport SK1 ....169 E1
Westhoughton BL5 ....57 E8
Walker's Croft M3 ...158 F2
Walker's La OL4 ......68 A6
Walker's Rd OL8 .....66 C2
Walkers Cl OL3 ....69 D8
Oldham OL4 ....68 A6
Walkers Ct Farnworth BL4 .60 D8
Walkers Dr WN7 ......76 A5
Walkerwood Dr SK15 ..86 D2
Walkmill Cl OL3 ......50 F1
Walkway The BL3 .....40 F5
Wall Hill Rd OL3 .....50 E2
Wall St Oldham OL8 ..153 F5
Salford M6 ....154 F2
Shevington WN6 ....36 F1
Wall Way M18 ....99 E4
Wallace Ave M14 .....98 D3
Wallace La WN1 ......37 E1
Wallace St 2 OL8 ....66 F4
Wallasey Ave M14 ....98 A1
Wallbank Dr OL12 ....14 C7
Wallbank Rd SK7 ....124 A1
Wallbrook Ave WN5 ..53 D1
Wallbrook Cres M38 ..60 B6
Wallbrook Gr BL4 ....42 B2
Walled Gdn The M27 ..79 D6
Waller Ave M14 ......110 C8
Walley St BL1 ....143 E3
Wallgarth Cl WN3 ....54 E2
Wallgate WN3 ....150 B7
Wallgate WN1 ....150 C8
Wallhead Rd OL16 ...31 D7
Wallingford Rd
Handforth SK9 ....131 C5
Urmston M41 ....95 F3
Wallis St Failsworth M40 .83 C5
Oldham OL9 ....66 A4
Wallness La M6 ....81 C3
Walls St WN2 ....57 C2
Wallshaw Pl OL1 .....67 A7
Wallshaw St OL1 .....67 A7
Wallsuches BL6 ....22 F4
Wallwork Cl OL11 ...13 E1
Wallwork Rd M29 .....77 D6
Wallwork St Droylsden M11 .99 E8
Radcliffe M26 ....44 A4
Reddish SK5 ....99 F2
Wallworth Ave M18 ..99 D5
Wallworth Terr SK9 .136 E8
Wally Sq M7 ....155 E6
Walmer Dr SK7 ......124 A1
Walmer Rd WN2 ....57 C2
Walmer St Manchester M14 98 C3
Manchester M18 ....99 E6
Walmer St E M14 .....98 C3
Walmersley Cl 8 SK6 .125 F6
Walmersley Old Rd BL9 .27 F7
Walmersley Rd Bury BL9 .27 F6
Failsworth M40 ....65 E1
Walmesley Ave WN3 .150 C6
Walmesley Dr WN2 ...56 B7
Walmesley Rd WN7 ...75 E5

Walmesley St WN1 . . . . . .151 D7
Walmley Gr BL3 . . . . .146 C3
Walmsley Ave OL15 . . . . . .15 F3
Walmsley CE Prim Sch BL7 8 E1
Walmsley Gr M41 . . . . .95 D2
Walmsley St **1** Bury BL8 . . .27 B4
 Newton-le-W WA12 . . . . . .89 D4
 Reddish SK5 . . . . .169 F3
 Stalybridge SK15 . . . . . . .102 A8
Walney Rd Wigan WN3 . . . .54 D2
 Wythenshawe M22 . . . . . .121 D4
Walnut Ave Bury BL9 . . . . .141 C3
 Oldham OL4 . . . . .67 D8
 Wigan WN1 . . . . .37 D2
Walnut Cl Hyde SK14 . . . . .102 A2
 Kearsley M27 . . . . .61 D4
 Wilmslow SK9 . . . . .137 E8
Walnut Gr Leigh WN7 . . . . .75 F8
 Sale M33 . . . . .108 A4
Walnut Rd Eccles M30 . . . . .79 A4
 Partington M31 . . . . .105 D3
Walnut St Bolton BL1 . . . . .143 F2
 2 Manchester M18 . . . . . .99 D5
Walnut Tree Rd SK3 . . . . .123 A8
Walnut Wlk **2** M32 . . . . . .96 C1
Walpole Ave WN3 . . . . .54 F3
Walpole St OL16 . . . . .31 A7
Walsall St M6 . . . . .81 A5
Walsden Est OL14 . . . . .6 B7
Walsden St M11 . . . . .83 C2
Walsh Ave M9 . . . . .64 D2
Walsh Cl WA12 . . . . .89 C5
Walsh Fold BL7 . . . . .9 A4
Walsh Ho M46 . . . . .58 D4
Walsh St Horwich BL6 . . . . .22 B4
 Oldham OL9 . . . . .152 B6
Walshaw Brook Cl BL8 . . . .26 F4
Walshaw Dr M27 . . . . .79 F7
Walshaw La BL8 . . . . .26 F4
Walshaw Rd BL8 . . . . .27 B4
Walshe St BL3 . . . . .140 D2
Walsingham Ave
 Manchester M20 . . . . .109 F4
 Middleton M24 . . . . .65 A5
Walter Scott Ave WN1 . . . .37 B5
Walter Scott St **3** OL1 . . .67 B8
Walter St Ashton-in-M WN4 .73 D4
 Droylsden M18 . . . . .99 E6
 Leigh WN7 . . . . .75 B5
 Manchester M16 . . . . .97 C4
 Manchester M9 . . . . .157 D8
 3 Oldham OL1 . . . . .153 F6
 Prestwich M25 . . . . .62 F4
 Radcliffe M26 . . . . .43 F6
 Walkden M28 . . . . .60 D2
 Wigan WN5 . . . . .54 D6
Walters Dr OL8 . . . . .67 A3
Walters Green Cres WA3 .74 A2
Waltham Ave
 Glazebury WA3 . . . . .92 C7
 Shevington WN6 . . . . .36 F2
Waltham Dr SK8 . . . . .132 B6
Waltham Gdns M26 . . . . . . .43 E5
Waltham Rd M16 . . . . .97 E1
Waltham St OL4 . . . . .67 C4
Walthew House La WN5 . .36 B1
Walthew La
 Platt Bridge WN2 . . . . .56 A2
 Wigan WN5 . . . . .36 D2
Walton Cl Heywood OL10 . .46 D8
 Middleton M24 . . . . .46 C1
Walton Ct BL3 . . . . .147 F4
Walton Dr Bury BL9 . . . . . . .27 E8
 Marple SK6 . . . . .125 D7
Walton Hall Dr M19 . . . . . .99 D1
Walton Ho M35 . . . . .83 F8
Walton Pl BL4 . . . . .60 E7
Walton Rd
 Altrincham WA14 . . . . . . .119 B5
 Culcheth WA3 . . . . .91 F3
 Manchester M9 . . . . .64 D5
 Sale M33 . . . . .107 F2
Walton Way M34 . . . . .101 B1
Walworth Cl M26 . . . . .61 C7
Walwyn Cl M32 . . . . .96 E1
Wanborough Cl WN7 . . . . .75 F7
Wandsworth Ave M11 . . . . .83 D2
Wanley Wlk **2** M9 . . . . . .64 E3
Wansbeck Cl M32 . . . . .96 E1
Wansbeck Lo M32 . . . . .96 E1
Wansfell Wlk M4 . . . . .160 D2
Wansford St M14 . . . . .98 A3
Wanstead Ave M9 . . . . .65 B3
Wapping St BL1 . . . . .143 D2
War Office Rd OL11 . . . . . . .29 E6
Warbeck Cl Hindley WN2 . . .56 E3
 Reddish SK5 . . . . .100 A2
Warbeck Rd M40 . . . . .65 D2
Warbreck Gr M33 . . . . .108 D3
Warburton Bridge Rd
 WA13,WA3 . . . . .105 A1
Warburton Cl
 Altrincham WA15 . . . . . . .129 D6
 Lymm WA13 . . . . .117 A4
 Romiley SK6 . . . . .113 A1
Warburton Dr WA15 . . . . .129 D6
Warburton La
 Partington M31 . . . . .105 F4

Warburton La continued
 Partington M31,WA13 . . . .105 E2
Warburton Pl **12** M46 . . . . .58 D3
Warburton Rd SK9 . . . . . . .131 D4
Warburton St Bolton BL1 . .143 F2
 Eccles M30 . . . . .79 E1
 3 Manchester M20 . . . . . .110 B3
 Salford M5 . . . . .161 B6
Warburton View WA3 . . . .105 A2
Warcock Rd OL4 . . . . .67 C7
Ward La Diggle OL3 . . . . . . .51 D3
 Disley SK12 . . . . .135 F4
Ward Rd M43 . . . . .84 B1
Ward St Bredbury SK6 . . . .112 F3
 Hindley WN2 . . . . .56 E7
 Hyde SK14 . . . . .167 E2
 1 Manchester M20 . . . . . .110 B3
 Manchester M40 . . . . .157 F8
 Manchester M9 . . . . .64 C2
 Oldham OL1 . . . . .153 D8
 Oldham OL9 . . . . .152 C7
 Stockport SK1 . . . . .124 A7
Warde St M15 . . . . .162 E6
Warden La M40 . . . . .83 B6
Warden St M40 . . . . .83 B6
Wardend Cl M38 . . . . .60 A6
Wardens Bank BL5 . . . . . . .57 E5
Wardle Brook Ave SK14 . .102 D3
Wardle Brook Wlk SK14 . .102 D3
Wardle Cl Radcliffe M26 . . . .43 E5
 Stretford M32 . . . . .96 E2
Wardle Ct M33 . . . . .108 C4
Wardle Edge OL12 . . . . . . .15 B4
Wardle Fold OL12 . . . . .15 C4
Wardle Gdns OL12 . . . . .15 C3
Wardle High Sch OL12 . . . .15 D5
Wardle Rd Rochdale OL12 . . .15 C4
 Sale M33 . . . . .108 C4
Wardle St Bacup OL13 . . . . . .3 D8
 Bolton BL2 . . . . .148 C5
 Littleborough OL15 . . . . . . .16 A6
 Manchester M40 . . . . .160 E3
Wardley Ave
 Manchester M16 . . . . .109 E8
 Manchester M16 . . . . .97 E1
 Walkden M28 . . . . .60 B3
Wardley CE Prim Sch
 M27 . . . . .61 E2
Wardley Gr BL1 . . . . .144 A7
Wardley Hall La M28 . . . . . .79 A8
Wardley Hall Rd M27,M28 . .61 B1
Wardley Ho M6 . . . . .80 C4
Wardley Ind Est
 Swinton M28 . . . . .61 C1
 Swinton M28 . . . . .79 C8
Wardley Rd M29 . . . . .77 D8
Wardley Sq M29 . . . . .77 D8
Wardley St Swinton M27 . . .79 F8
 Wigan WN5 . . . . .54 B6
Wardlow Ave
 25 Gamesley SK13 . . . . . .171 D1
 Wigan WN5 . . . . .36 A1
Wardlow Fold **25** SK13 . . .171 D1
Wardlow Gdns **27** SK13 . . .171 D1
Wardlow Gr **28** SK13 . . . . .171 D1
Wardlow Mews SK13 . . . . .171 D1
Wardlow St BL3 . . . . .146 B4
Wardlow Wlk **26** SK13 . . . .171 D1
Wardour St Atherton M46 . . .58 C2
 Atherton M46 . . . . .58 D2
Wards Pl **3** WN7 . . . . .76 B4
Wardsend Wlk **13** M15 . . .162 D6
Ware Cl WN4 . . . . .73 D4
Wareham Gr M30 . . . . .79 C3
Wareham St M8 . . . . .64 B1
Wareing St M29 . . . . .76 F8
Wareing Way BL3 . . . . .145 E6
Wareings Yd **5** OL11 . . . . .31 A4
Warfield Wlk **30** M9 . . . . . .64 E3
Warford Ave SK12 . . . . . . .134 A2
Warford La WA16 . . . . .136 B1
Warford St M4 . . . . .159 B4
Warford Terr WA16 . . . . . .136 B2
Wargrave CE Prim Sch
 WA12 . . . . .89 C1
Wargrave House Sch
 WA12 . . . . .89 D1
Wargrave Mews WA12 . . . .89 C1
Wargrave Rd WA12 . . . . . . .89 C2
Warham St SK9 . . . . .137 B7
Warke The M28 . . . . .78 F6
Warlands End Gate OL14 . . .6 D5
Warley Cl SK8 . . . . .122 E6
Warley Gr SK16 . . . . .101 C8
Warley Rd M16 . . . . .97 A3
Warley St OL15 . . . . .16 B5
Warlingham Cl BL8 . . . . . . .27 B1
Warlow Crest OL3 . . . . .69 A4
Warlow Dr Leigh WN7 . . . . .57 D1
 Oldham OL3 . . . . .69 A4
Warmbly Gdns OL8 . . . . . . .66 D1
Warmington Dr M12 . . . . .164 E6
Warminster Gr WN3 . . . . . .54 D2
Warmley Rd M23 . . . . .120 D8
Warncliffe St **7** WN5 . . . . .54 D5
Warne Ave M43 . . . . .84 C2
Warner Wlk **9** M11 . . . . . .160 F1
Warnford Cl M40 . . . . .83 D4
Warnford St **3** WN1 . . . . . .37 C2
Warp Wlk **3** M4 . . . . .159 C1
Warre St OL6 . . . . .166 B3
Warren Ave SK8 . . . . .122 D5
Warren Bank M9 . . . . .64 D3
Warren Bruce Rd M17 . . . . .96 D6
Warren Cl Atherton M46 . . . .58 E5
 Denton M34 . . . . .100 D2
 Poynton SK12 . . . . .133 B4
 Stockport SK7 . . . . .123 D2

Warren Dr
 Altrincham WA15 . . . . . . .129 D7
 Newton-le-W WA12 . . . . . .89 F4
 Swinton M27 . . . . .79 D5
Warren Hey SK9 . . . . .137 E8
Warren La OL8 . . . . .67 A4
Warren Lea Poynton SK12 .133 C5
 Romiley SK6 . . . . .114 B2
Warren Rd Cheadle SK8 . . .123 B2
 Stockport SK3 . . . . .170 E6
 Stretford M17 . . . . .96 B6
 Walkden M28 . . . . .60 E3
Warren St **2** Bury BL8 . . . .27 B1
 Manchester M7 . . . . .155 F8
 Manchester M9 . . . . .64 C2
 Stockport SK1 . . . . .169 F2
Warren Wood Prim Sch
 SK2 . . . . .125 A6
Warrener St M33 . . . . .108 D4
Warrington La
 Broomedge WA13 . . . . . . .117 E2
 Wigan WN1 . . . . .151 D7
Warrington Rd
 Abram Brow WA3,WN2 . . . .74 B7
 Ashton-in-M WN4 . . . . . . .73 B2
 Fowley Common WA3,WN7 . .92 C5
 Golborne WA12 . . . . .90 A6
 Ince-in-M WN2,WN3,WN5 . .55 E5
 Leigh WN7 . . . . .76 B3
 Platt Bridge WN2 . . . . .56 A1
 Wigan WN3,WN5 . . . . .54 F3
Warrington St
 Ashton-u-L OL6 . . . . .166 B3
 9 Oldham OL4 . . . . .67 E6
 Stalybridge SK15 . . . . .86 B1
Warsall Rd M22 . . . . .121 E7
Warslow Dr M33 . . . . .108 E1
Warsop Ave M22 . . . . .121 E5
Warstead Wlk **8** M13 . . . .163 C5
Warth Fold Rd BL9,M26 . . . .44 C6
Warth La BB4 . . . . .2 D8
Warth Rd BL9 . . . . .44 D7
Warthenbury Wlk M13 . . . .98 E3
Warton Cl Bramhall SK7 . . .133 A7
 Bury BL8 . . . . .26 F1
Warton Dr M23 . . . . .121 A5
Warwick Ave
 Ashton-in-M WN4 . . . . . . .73 D2
 Denton M34 . . . . .100 F1
 Manchester M20 . . . . .109 F4
 Newton-le-W WA12 . . . . . .89 E2
 Prestwich M45 . . . . .63 B7
 Swinton M27 . . . . .61 D2
Warwick Cl **4** Bury BL8 . . . .27 B4
 Cheadle SK8 . . . . .123 A4
 Dukinfield SK16 . . . . .101 C6
 Glossop SK13 . . . . .116 F8
 Manchester SK4 . . . . .169 D4
 Middleton M24 . . . . .65 A5
 Prestwich M45 . . . . .63 A7
 Ramsbottom BL8 . . . . .11 A1
 Shaw OL2 . . . . .48 F7
Warwick Ct
 Manchester M16 . . . . .97 A3
 Manchester SK4 . . . . .169 D4
Warwick Dr
 Altrincham WA15 . . . . . . .119 F1
 Hazel Grove SK7 . . . . .124 D1
 Hindley WN2 . . . . .56 F6
 Sale M33 . . . . .108 D4
 Urmston M41 . . . . .95 B3
Warwick Gdns BL3 . . . . . .146 B2
Warwick Gr M46 . . . . .100 C8
Warwick Ho **2** Sale M33 . .108 C4
 2 Manchester M19 . . . . . .99 A2
Warwick Mall SK8 . . . . . . .122 D6
Warwick Rd
 Altrincham WA15 . . . . . . .119 E1
 Ashton-u-L OL6 . . . . .85 C5
 Aspull WN2 . . . . .38 C5
 Atherton M46 . . . . .58 C5
 Failsworth M35 . . . . .84 A5
 Irlam M44 . . . . .105 D5
 Manchester M16,M17 . . . . .97 A4
 Manchester M21 . . . . .97 B1
 Manchester SK4 . . . . .168 C3
 Middleton M24 . . . . .65 B6
 Radcliffe M26 . . . . .43 F6
 Romiley SK6 . . . . .113 A2
 Tyldesley M29 . . . . .59 A2
 Walkden M28 . . . . .60 C1
Warwick Rd S M16 . . . . . . .97 A3
Warwick St Adlington PR7 . . .20 F6
 Bolton BL1 . . . . .143 E4
 Leigh WN7 . . . . .76 E3
 Manchester M1,M4 . . . . . .159 B2
 Manchester M15 . . . . .162 F5
 Oldham OL9 . . . . .152 C5
 Oldham OL9 . . . . .66 C4
 Prestwich M25 . . . . .62 F4
 Rochdale OL12 . . . . .15 B2
 Swinton M27 . . . . .61 F1
Warwick Terr **15** SK16 . . .166 B1
Wasdale Ave Bolton BL2 . . .25 F1
 Urmston M41 . . . . .95 B3
Wasdale Dr Gatley SK8 . . . .122 B8
 Middleton M24 . . . . .46 E2
Wasdale Rd WN4 . . . . .73 D4
Wasdale St OL11 . . . . .30 C1
Wasdale Terr SK15 . . . . . . .86 A4
Wasdale Wlk **3** OL1 . . . . . .67 A8
Wash Brook OL9 . . . . .66 B4
Wash Fold BL8 . . . . .27 B5
Wash La Bury BL9 . . . . .141 B2
 Leigh WN7 . . . . .76 C5
Wash Terr BL8 . . . . .27 B5

Washacre BL5 . . . . .57 F7
Washacre Cl BL5 . . . . .57 F7
Washacre Cty Prim Sch
 BL5 . . . . .57 F7
Washbrook Ave M28 . . . . . .60 B1
Washbrook Ct OL9 . . . . .66 B4
Washbrook Dr M32 . . . . . . .96 B2
Washburn Cl BL5 . . . . .39 F2
Washford Dr M23 . . . . .120 D8
Washington Ct **6** BL9 . . . .140 F3
Washington St
 3 Bolton BL3 . . . . .144 C6
 Oldham OL9 . . . . .152 C7
Washway Rd Sale M33 . . . .107 F2
 Sale M33 . . . . .108 A4
Washwood Cl M38 . . . . .60 B6
Wasnidge Wlk M15 . . . . . .162 F5
Wasp Ave OL11 . . . . .31 A3
Wastdale Ave BL9 . . . . .45 A3
Wastdale Rd M23 . . . . .121 A4
Waste St **2** OL1 . . . . .67 A7
Wastwater St **5** OL1 . . . . .49 A1
Watburn Rd SK22 . . . . .127 D1
Watchgate Cl M24 . . . . .46 D3
Water Dr WN6 . . . . .37 E7
Water Gate OL3 . . . . .69 B8
Water Grove Rd SK16 . . . .101 F7
Water La Droylsden M43 . . . .83 E1
 Edenfield BL0 . . . . .1 D2
 Farnworth BL4 . . . . .60 E7
 Hollingworth SK14 . . . . . .103 D5
 Milnrow OL16 . . . . .32 A5
 Radcliffe M26 . . . . .43 F3
 Wilmslow SK9 . . . . .137 A7
Water Lane St
 Radcliffe M26 . . . . .43 F3
 4 Radcliffe M26 . . . . .44 A4
Water Rd SK15 . . . . .85 F2
Water Ski Ctr OL12 . . . . .4 C2
Water St Adlington PR7 . . . .21 A6
 Ashton-u-L OL6 . . . . .166 B3
 Atherton M46 . . . . .58 D3
 Bolton BL1 . . . . .145 F7
 Bolton BL7 . . . . .8 D2
 Denton M34 . . . . .100 F7
 Glossop SK13 . . . . .104 E2
 Hyde SK14 . . . . .167 D2
 Manchester M12 . . . . .163 C8
 Manchester M3 . . . . .158 E1
 Manchester M3 . . . . .162 D8
 Manchester M9 . . . . .157 D8
 Newton-le-W WA12 . . . . . .89 C4
 Radcliffe M26 . . . . .44 A3
 Ramsbottom BL0 . . . . . . .138 B5
 Rochdale OL16 . . . . .31 A7
 Royton OL2 . . . . .49 A4
 Stalybridge SK15 . . . . .86 A2
 Stockport SK1 . . . . .169 F3
 Whitworth OL12 . . . . .14 C8
 Wigan WN1 . . . . .150 C8
Water"s Reach SK6 . . . . . .134 E7
Water's Edge BL4 . . . . .42 A2
Water's Nook Rd BL5 . . . . .58 A8
Water's Reach M17 . . . . . . .96 F6
Waterbarn La OL13 . . . . .3 B8
Waterbeck Cl WN1 . . . . . . .37 F1
Waterbridge M28 . . . . .79 A5
Watercroft OL11 . . . . .13 D1
Waterdale Cl M28 . . . . .78 B6
Waterdale Dr M45 . . . . .63 A8
Waterfield Cl BL9 . . . . .27 F7
Waterfield Way M35 . . . . . .84 A6
Waterfold La BL9 . . . . .141 C1
Waterfoot Cotts SK14 . . . .103 A4
Waterfoot Cty Prim Sch
 BB4 . . . . .2 F8
Waterford Ave
 Manchester M20 . . . . .109 D3
 Romiley SK6 . . . . .113 F2
Waterford Pl SK8 . . . . .131 B8
Waterfront Quay M5 . . . . .161 A7
Watergate M34 . . . . .100 C8
Watergate Dr BL5 . . . . .59 C7
Watergate La BL4,BL5 . . . . .59 C7
Watergate Milne Ct **6**
 OL4 . . . . .67 D8
Waterhouse Cl OL12 . . . . . .15 C6
Waterhouse Rd M18 . . . . . .99 E4
Waterhouse St OL12 . . . . .139 F8
Waterloo Ct Bury BL9 . . . . .44 E8
 3 Manchester M20 . . . . . .110 A5
 4 Stalybridge SK15 . . . . . .86 A2
Waterloo Gdns OL6 . . . . . . .85 E5
Waterloo Ind Pk BL1 . . . . .25 A1
Waterloo Pk Sch SK1 . . . .112 A1
Waterloo Prim Sch OL7 . . .85 A5
Waterloo Rd
 Ashton-u-L OL6 . . . . .85 B5
 Bramhall SK7 . . . . .132 F8
 Manchester M8 . . . . .155 F6
 Manchester M8,M9 . . . . . . .64 C1
 Poynton SK12 . . . . .134 A2
 Romiley SK6 . . . . .113 E2
 Stalybridge SK15 . . . . .86 A2
 Stockport SK1 . . . . .169 F1
Waterloo St Ashton-u-L OL6 .85 D4
 Bolton BL1 . . . . .143 F1
 Bury BL8 . . . . .140 D2
 Manchester M1 . . . . .163 A8
 Manchester M8 . . . . .156 C8
 Oldham OL4 . . . . .67 A6
 3 Wigan WN6 . . . . .37 A1
Waterman View OL16 . . . . .31 C8
Watermans Cl Horwich BL6 22 C4
 Manchester M9 . . . . .157 F8
Watermead Cl SK3 . . . . . . .123 E4
Watermede WN5 . . . . .53 E3

Watermeetings La SK6 . .113 F1
Watermill Cl OL16 . . . . .31 D6
Watermill Ct OL7 . . . . .85 A5
Waterpark Rd M7 . . . . .155 E8
Waters Edge SK6 . . . . .126 B3
Waters Meeting Rd
 Bolton BL1 . . . . .143 F1
 Bolton BL1 . . . . .143 F3
 Bolton BL1 . . . . .25 A2
Waters Reach
 Poynton SK12 . . . . .133 F5
 Wigan WN1 . . . . .151 F8
Watersedge Cl SK8 . . . . . .123 B3
Watersfield Cl SK8 . . . . . . .131 F8
Watersheddings
 Com Prim Sch OL1 . . . . . .49 C1
Watersheddings St **9**
 OL4 . . . . .49 D1
Watersheddings Way **11**
 OL4 . . . . .49 D1
Waterside Hadfield SK13 . .104 A6
 Hattersley SK14 . . . . .102 D2
 Marple SK6 . . . . .125 F5
 Stretford M17 . . . . .96 F6
Waterside Ave **5** SK6 . . .125 F5
Waterside Cl
 Hattersley SK14 . . . . .102 D2
 Manchester M21 . . . . .109 D4
 Radcliffe M26 . . . . .44 D4
Waterside Cotts OL3 . . . . . .69 C4
Waterside Ct SK14 . . . . . . .102 D2
Waterside Dr WN3 . . . . . . .150 B7
Waterside La OL16 . . . . .31 D5
Waterside Rd Disley SK12 .135 F7
 Ramsbottom BL9 . . . . .11 C3
Waterside Trad Est **1**
 WN7 . . . . .76 B4
Waterside Wlk **4** SK14 . .102 D2
Waterslea M30 . . . . .79 C2
Waterslea Dr BL1 . . . . .40 F3
Watersmead Cl BL1 . . . . . .143 F2
Watersmead St BL1 . . . . . .143 F3
Watersmeet M32 . . . . .96 D4
Waterson Ave M40 . . . . .83 A7
Waterton Ave OL5 . . . . .68 B2
Waterton La OL5 . . . . .68 B2
Waterview Cl OL16 . . . . . . .32 A5
Waterview Pk WN4 . . . . . . .75 E4
Waterworks Rd OL4 . . . . . . .49 C1
Watfield Wlk **5** M9 . . . . . .157 D7
Watford Ave M14 . . . . .98 B2
Watford Bridge Ind Est
 SK22 . . . . .127 D1
Watford Bridge Rd SK22 .127 D1
Watford Cl **16** BL1 . . . . . . .143 E2
Watford La SK22 . . . . .127 C2
Watford Rd
 Manchester M19 . . . . .111 A6
 New Mills SK22 . . . . .127 C2
Watkin Ave SK13 . . . . .171 E4
Watkin Cl M13 . . . . .163 C6
 Hyde SK14 . . . . .102 A5
 Manchester M3 . . . . .158 D3
 Rochdale OL16 . . . . .31 B4
 Wigan WN1 . . . . .150 C8
Watkins Dr M25,M8 . . . . . . .63 F3
Watling St Bolton BL8 . . . . .26 B7
 Bury BL8 . . . . .26 F1
Watlington Cl OL1 . . . . .49 D3
Watson Ave
 Ashton-in-M WN4 . . . . . . .73 C3
 Golborne WA3 . . . . .73 F1
Watson Gdns OL12 . . . . . . .14 C2
Watson Rd BL4 . . . . .59 F8
Watson Sq SK1 . . . . .169 F1
Watson St Denton M34 . . . .101 B3
 Eccles M30 . . . . .79 C2
 Manchester M2,M3 . . . . . .162 F8
 Oldham OL4 . . . . .67 C8
 Radcliffe M26 . . . . .44 A4
 Swinton M27 . . . . .79 F8
Watts St Horwich BL6 . . . . .22 C4
 Manchester M19 . . . . .111 B8
 Oldham OL8 . . . . .66 D2
 Oldham OL9 . . . . .152 B7
 Rochdale OL12 . . . . .139 F4
 1 Rochdale OL12 . . . . . . .31 A8
Waugh Ave M35 . . . . .83 F7
Wavell Dr M45 . . . . .45 A1
Wavell Rd M22 . . . . .121 D2
Waveney Dr
 Altrincham WA14 . . . . . . .119 C6
 Handforth SK9 . . . . .131 D2
Waveney Rd Shaw OL2 . . . .149 A8
 Wythenshawe M22 . . . . . .121 E4
Waverley **17** Heywood OL10 .29 C2
 23 Rochdale OL12 . . . . . .139 E8
Waverley Ave Kearsley BL4 .60 C6
 Stretford M32 . . . . .96 F3
Waverley Cres M43 . . . . . . .84 A3
Waverley Ct WN3 . . . . .54 D3
Waverley Dr SK8 . . . . .132 B7
Waverley Gr WN7 . . . . .76 D6
Waverley Rd Bolton BL1 . . .143 E3
 Golborne WA3 . . . . .74 D1
 Hindley WN2 . . . . .56 C5
 Hyde SK14 . . . . .113 D8
 Manchester M9 . . . . .157 F7
 Middleton M24 . . . . .47 A3
 Pendlebury M27 . . . . .80 C7
 Sale M33 . . . . .108 C6
 Stockport SK3 . . . . .123 C7
 Walkden M28 . . . . .60 C1
Waverley Rd W M9 . . . . . . .157 F7
Waverley Sq BL4 . . . . .60 C6
Waverley St Oldham OL1 . . .49 C1
 Rochdale OL11 . . . . .30 C1

Waverton Ave SK4 ....111 D7
Waverton Rd M14 ....98 A1
Wavertree Ave M46 ....58 C4
Wavertree Ct 6 BL1 ....145 E8
Wavertree Rd M9 ....64 C4
Waybridge Ind Pk
Stretford M17 ....96 C7
Stretford M5 ....96 D8
Wayfarers Dr WA12 ....89 E2
Wayfarers Way M27 ....79 F7
Wayfaring BL5 ....39 F2
Wayford Wlk M9 ....156 C7
Wayland Rd M18 ....99 E4
Wayland Rd S M18 ....99 D3
Wayne Cl M43 ....84 C4
Wayne St M11 ....99 E8
Wayoh Croft BL7 ....9 D6
Wayside Dr SK12 ....133 C4
Wayside Gdns SK7 ....125 A2
Wayside Gr M28 ....60 E4
Weald Cl M13 ....163 C6
Wealdstone Gr BL2 ....25 B2
Weardale Rd M9 ....64 B5
Wearhead Cl Golborne WA3 89 F7
Golborne WA3 ....90 A7
Wearhead Row M5 ....154 F1
Wearish La BL5 ....57 C6
Weaste Ave M38 ....60 B4
Weaste Dr M5 ....154 D3
Weaste La M5,M6 ....154 D3
Weaste Rd M5 ....154 D2
Weaste Trad Est M6 ....154 D2
Weatherall St N M7 ....155 F7
Weatherley Cl OL8 ....67 A1
Weatherley Dr SK6 ....125 D6
Weaver Ave M28 ....60 A2
Weaver Cl WA14 ....119 C1
Weaver Ct M15 ....162 D6
Weaver Dr BL9 ....27 F8
Weaver Gr WN7 ....75 C4
Weaver Ho 5 M7 ....81 C5
Weaver Rd WA3 ....92 A2
Weaver Wlk 5 M11 ....99 D7
Weaverham Cl 2 M13 ....98 F3
Weaverham Way SK9 ....131 E4
Weaverham Wlk M33 ....108 E3
Weavers Ct Bolton BL3 ....145 E5
11 Middleton M24 ....46 F1
Mottram-in-L SK14 ....103 A4
Weavers Gn BL4 ....60 D8
Weavers La SK7 ....132 D6
Weavers Rd M24 ....46 F1
Webb Gr SK14 ....102 F1
Webb La SK1 ....124 A8
Webb St Bury BL8 ....140 D3
Horwich BL6 ....22 C3
Webb Wlk SK14 ....102 F1
Webdale Dr M40 ....83 A7
Weber Dr BL3 ....145 D5
Webster Gr M25 ....62 F2
Webster Jun Sch M15 ....98 A4
Webster St Bolton BL3 ....148 B5
3 Mossley OL5 ....68 C2
Oldham OL8 ....153 F5
Webster's St WN2 ....56 A3
Wedgewood Dr WN6 ....36 D3
Wedgewood St M40 ....160 F4
Wedgwood Rd M27 ....62 C2
Wedhurst St OL4 ....67 C7
Wedlock St OL1 ....67 A7
Wedneshough SK14 ....103 C5
Weedall Ave M5 ....161 A6
Weeder Sq OL2 ....49 E8
Weedon Ave WA12 ....89 B5
Weedon St OL16 ....31 B8
Weeton Ave BL2 ....42 F7
Weft Wlk 5 M4 ....159 C1
Weighbridge Ct M44 ....94 C3
Weint The WA3 ....105 B3
Weir Rd OL16 ....31 E7
Weir St Failsworth M35 ....83 E7
Manchester M15 ....162 E5
Welbeck Ave
Failsworth OL9 ....65 D3
Littleborough OL15 ....16 A6
Newton-le-W WA12 ....89 D2
Urmston M41 ....95 F3
Welbeck Cl Milnrow OL16 ....31 D6
Whitefield M45 ....44 F2
Welbeck Gr M7 ....155 E7
Welbeck Ho 4 OL6 ....166 A2
Welbeck Rd
Ashton-in-M WN4 ....73 C4
Bolton BL1 ....144 A8
Eccles M30 ....79 E4
Hyde SK14 ....167 F2
1 Reddish SK5 ....111 F8
Rochdale OL16 ....31 B4
Swinton M28 ....79 B6
Wigan WN3 ....54 E3
Welbeck St M18 ....99 E6
Welbeck St N OL6 ....166 A2
Welbeck St S OL6,OL7 ....166 A2
Welbeck Terr OL6 ....166 A2
Welburn Ave M22 ....121 E3
Welburn St OL11 ....139 F5
Welbury Rd M23 ....108 F1
Welby St M13 ....98 D4
Welch Hill St WN7 ....75 E4
Welch Rd SK14 ....167 F4
Welcomb Cl SK6 ....112 F4
Welcomb St M11 ....165 B7
Welcomb Wlk M45 ....62 F7
Welcome Par OL8 ....67 D3
Welcroft St SK1 ....170 F8
Weld Rd M20 ....110 D7
Weldon Ave BL3 ....146 A2
Weldon Cres SK3 ....123 E4
Weldon Dr M9 ....64 D5
Weldon Gr WN1 ....37 E2
Weldon Rd WA14 ....119 D6
Welfold Ho 3 OL4 ....67 B5
Welford Ave WA3 ....90 C7
Welford Cl SK9 ....137 E8
Welford Gn SK5 ....111 F5
Welford Rd M9 ....63 F3
Welford St M6 ....81 B4
Welkin Rd SK6 ....112 C3
Welkin Rd Ind Est SK6 ....112 C3
Well Ct WN6 ....19 E1
Well Gate SK13 ....104 E2
Well Gr M45 ....44 E2
Well Green Prim Sch
WA15 ....120 C2
Well i' th' La OL11 ....31 A4
Well La M45 ....44 F2
Well Mdw SK14 ....167 D4
Well Mead SK6 ....112 E3
Well Meadow La OL3 ....69 C8
Well Row SK14 ....115 A8
Well St Ainsworth BL2 ....26 C1
Bolton BL1 ....148 A7
Heywood OL10 ....29 E1
Manchester M4 ....159 A2
6 Rochdale OL11 ....31 A5
Tyldesley M29 ....77 A8
Well St N BL0 ....1 C2
Well St W BL0 ....138 B5
Well-i-Hole Rd OL3 ....68 F4
Wellacre Ave M41 ....94 D2
Wellacre High Sch M41 ....94 D2
Wellacre Inf Sch M41 ....94 D2
Wellacre Jun Sch M41 ....94 D2
Welland Ave OL10 ....29 A3
Welland Cl M15 ....162 D6
Welland Ct 4 M15 ....162 D6
Welland Rd
Ashton-in-M WN4 ....73 E5
Handforth SK9 ....131 E2
Shaw OL2 ....149 A8
Welland St Droylsden M11 ....99 D8
Reddish SK5 ....99 F1
Welland The BL5 ....57 E8
Wellbank SK15 ....102 D8
Wellbank Ave OL6 ....85 E6
Wellbank Cl OL8 ....67 A4
Wellbank St BL8 ....26 F6
Wellbank View OL12 ....13 F2
Wellbeck Rd WN4 ....73 C4
Wellbrooke Cl WN4 ....73 C3
Wellbrow Terr OL12 ....14 D2
Wellbrow Wlk 16 M9 ....64 E3
Wellburn Cl BL5 ....40 F2
Wellcross Rd WN8 ....53 B6
Wellens Way M24 ....64 C7
Weller Ave
Manchester M21 ....109 D7
Poynton SK12 ....133 D2
Weller Cl SK12 ....133 D2
Weller Gdns M21 ....109 D7
Wellesbourne Dr M23 ....120 F7
Wellesley Ave M18 ....99 D6
Wellesley Cl
Newton-le-W WA12 ....89 B5
Wigan WN5 ....54 E8
Wellfield SK6 ....113 C4
Wellfield Cl BL9 ....44 E6
Wellfield Gdns WA15 ....120 C3
Wellfield Inf Sch M33 ....107 F6
Wellfield Jun Sch M33 ....107 F6
Wellfield La WA15 ....120 C3
Wellfield Pl 5 OL11 ....31 A5
Wellfield Rd Bolton BL3 ....144 C5
Culcheth WA3 ....91 F4
Hindley WN2 ....57 A4
Manchester M8 ....156 A8
Stockport SK2 ....124 C6
Wigan WN6 ....37 A3
Wythenshawe M23 ....121 A7
Wellfield St OL11 ....31 A5
Wellgate Ave M19 ....111 B8
Wellgreen Cl WA15 ....120 C3
Wellgreen Lo WA15 ....120 C3
Wellham Rd WN3 ....55 B3
Wellhead Cl M15 ....162 F5
Wellhouse Dr M40 ....65 C3
Welling Rd M40 ....83 E8
Welling St 20 BL2 ....25 B1
Wellington Ave M16 ....97 D2
Wellington Cl
Newton-le-W WA12 ....89 A3
Sale M33 ....108 C4
Wellington Clough 4 OL7 ....85 A6
Wellington Cres M16 ....97 C3
Wellington Ct Bury BL8 ....26 F6
6 Bury BL8 ....27 B1
Oldham OL8 ....66 D4
Wellington Ctr OL6 ....166 C2
Wellington Gdns Bury BL8 ....27 B1
Newton-le-W WA12 ....89 A3
Wellington Gr
Ince-in-M WN3 ....151 D5
Manchester M15 ....162 D6
Stockport SK2 ....170 F7
Wellington Lo OL15 ....16 B6
Wellington Mill SK4 ....169 E1
Wellington Par SK16 ....166 B1
Wellington Pl
Altrincham WA14 ....119 D4
13 Rochdale OL16 ....31 A8
Wellington Rd
Altrincham WA15 ....119 F6
Ashton-u-L OL6 ....166 B3
Atherton M46 ....58 F5
Bury BL9 ....140 F1
Eccles M30 ....79 F2
Wellington Rd continued
Edgworth BL7 ....9 D4
High Lane SK7 ....134 B8
Manchester M14,M20 ....110 C8
Manchester M16 ....97 E2
Manchester M8 ....156 B8
Oldham OL3 ....69 B6
Oldham OL8 ....153 E5
Swinton M27 ....79 F8
Wellington Rd N
M19,SK3,SK4 ....169 D3
Wellington Rd S SK1,SK2 ....170 F8
Wellington Sch The
WA15 ....119 F6
Wellington Sq 5 BL8 ....27 B1
Wellington St
Ashton-u-L OL6 ....166 B2
Bolton BL3 ....145 E6
Bury BL8 ....140 D1
Chadderton OL9 ....152 B8
Denton M34 ....100 F6
Dukinfield SK14 ....101 C3
2 Failsworth M35 ....66 A1
Farnworth BL4 ....60 D8
Hazel Grove SK7 ....124 F3
1 Littleborough OL15 ....16 B5
Manchester M18 ....99 D5
Manchester M3 ....158 D2
Milnrow OL16 ....32 A6
Newton-le-W WA12 ....89 A3
Oldham OL4,OL8 ....153 F6
5 Radcliffe M26 ....44 C4
19 Rochdale OL12 ....14 F1
Stockport SK1 ....169 F1
Stretford M32 ....96 C1
Westhoughton BL5 ....39 E2
Wigan WN1 ....151 D8
Wellington St E M7 ....155 E7
Wellington St W M7 ....155 D6
Wellington Terr
13 Dukinfield SK16 ....166 B1
Salford M5 ....154 D2
Wellington Wlk BL3 ....145 E6
Wellmead Cl M8 ....155 F5
Wellock St M10,M40 ....157 F5
Wellpark Wlk 21 M40 ....83 C5
Wells Ave Billinge WN5 ....71 D6
Chadderton OL9 ....48 A1
Manchester M25 ....63 C2
Wells Cl Droylsden M43 ....99 F8
Gatley SK8 ....131 C7
Middleton M24 ....64 C7
Tyldesley M29 ....77 C8
Wells Ct SK16 ....101 C6
Wells Dr Dukinfield SK16 ....101 C6
Manchester SK4 ....110 E2
Wigan WN2 ....37 F2
Wells Pl WN1 ....151 E8
Wells Rd OL1 ....49 E5
Wells St BL9 ....140 E1
Wellside Wlk 8 M8 ....156 A6
Wellstock La M38 ....59 F6
Wellwood Dr 11 M40 ....83 A7
Wellyhole St OL4 ....67 D6
Welney Rd M16 ....97 B3
Welshpool Cl M23 ....109 B2
Welshpool Way 9 M34 ....101 A1
Welton Ave M20 ....110 C2
Welton Cl Leigh WN7 ....76 C5
Wilmslow SK9 ....136 F4
Welton Dr SK9 ....136 E4
Welton Gr SK9 ....136 E4
Welwyn Cl M41 ....95 B5
Welwyn Dr M6 ....80 A5
Welwyn Wlk M40 ....160 D2
Wem St OL9 ....66 A4
Wembley Gr M14 ....110 C8
Wembley Rd M18 ....99 C3
Wembury St M9 ....157 E8
Wembury St N M9 ....157 E8
Wembury Wlk SK14 ....102 E3
Wemsley Gr 29 BL2 ....25 B1
Wemyss Ave SK5 ....99 F1
Wendlebury Cl WN7 ....75 E1
Wendlebury Gn OL2 ....149 A5
Wendon Rd M23 ....121 B5
Wendover Dr BL3 ....40 E5
Wendover Rd Sale M23 ....120 D8
Urmston M41 ....95 C1
Wenfield Dr M9 ....65 B3
Wenlock Ave OL6 ....85 B5
Wenlock Cl
Hazel Grove SK2 ....125 A6
Horwich BL6 ....22 C6
Wenlock Ct M12 ....164 F6
Wenlock Gr 4 WN2 ....56 D4
Wenlock Rd Hindley WN2 ....56 D5
Leigh WN7 ....75 E2
Sale M33 ....108 A2
Wenlock St
9 Hindley WN2 ....56 D5
Swinton M27 ....79 D8
Wenlock Way M12 ....164 F6
Wenning Cl M45 ....45 C1
Wenning Wlk 3 WN2 ....56 A2
Wensley Ct M7 ....63 A1
Wensley Dr
Hazel Grove SK7 ....133 D7
Manchester M20 ....110 B5
Wensley Rd Cheadle SK8 ....122 C6
Golborne WA3 ....90 E7
Manchester M7 ....63 A1
Reddish SK5 ....169 F4
Wensley Way OL16 ....31 C6
Wensleydale Ave SK8 ....122 C6
Wensleydale Cl Royton OL2 48 C5
Whitefield BL9 ....45 A3
Wythenshawe M23 ....120 F3
Wensleydale Rd WN7 ....76 C5
Wentbridge Rd BL1 ....145 D8
Wentworth Ave
Altrincham WA15 ....120 A6
Bury BL8 ....27 B4
Farnworth BL4 ....60 C7
Heywood OL10 ....46 D8
Irlam M44 ....94 A3
8 Manchester M18 ....99 E6
Salford M6 ....80 C3
Whitefield M45 ....62 D7
Wentworth Cl Marple SK6 ....125 F8
Middleton M24 ....64 E8
Radcliffe M26 ....43 D4
Wentworth Ct M35 ....83 F6
Wentworth Dr
Bramhall SK7 ....133 A7
Sale M33 ....107 F5
Wentworth High Sch M30 ....79 F4
Wentworth Rd Reddish SK5 99 F1
Salford M30 ....80 A4
Swinton M27 ....79 D6
Wentworth Wlk 2 SK14 ....101 F5
Wenworth Ave M41 ....95 B1
Werneth Ave Hyde SK14 ....113 F8
Manchester M14 ....98 B2
Werneth Cl Denton M34 ....100 F2
Hazel Grove SK7 ....124 E4
Werneth Cres OL8 ....66 C4
Werneth Ct SK14 ....167 E1
Werneth Hall Rd OL8 ....153 D5
Werneth Hollow SK6 ....113 B6
Werneth Inf Sch OL8 ....153 E5
Werneth Jun Sch OL8 ....153 E5
Werneth Low Ctry Pk
SK14 ....114 A7
Werneth Low Rd
SK14,SK6 ....113 E5
Werneth Prep Sch OL8 ....153 D5
Werneth Rd Glossop SK13 116 A7
Hyde SK14 ....167 F2
Romiley SK6 ....113 C5
Werneth Rise SK14 ....113 F7
Werneth Sch SK6 ....113 A2
Werneth St Denton M34 ....100 F5
Stockport SK1 ....112 B3
Werneth Sta OL9 ....153 D6
Werneth Wlk M34 ....100 F2
Wescoe Cl WN5 ....53 E5
Wesley Cl Rochdale OL12 ....15 C3
Westhoughton BL5 ....39 E2
Wesley Ct Bury BL8 ....26 E7
Manchester SK4 ....110 F2
Walkden M28 ....60 D4
Westhoughton BL5 ....39 E2
Wesley Dr Ashton-u-L OL6 ....85 D6
Worsley M28 ....78 F8
Wesley Gn M5 ....161 B8
Wesley Methodist
Prim Sch M26 ....43 F5
Wesley Mews 4 BL2 ....148 B7
Wesley Sq M41 ....95 A2
Wesley St Atherton M46 ....58 E3
Bolton BL3 ....145 E5
Bolton BL7 ....25 A8
Bury BL8 ....26 F7
Eccles M30 ....79 C2
Failsworth M35 ....66 A1
Farnworth BL4 ....60 E7
Glossop SK13 ....104 E2
Hadfield SK13 ....104 A5
Hazel Grove SK7 ....124 E3
Heywood OL10 ....29 C2
Manchester M11 ....165 A8
Milnrow OL16 ....31 E6
1 Rochdale OL12 ....15 B3
Royton OL2 ....48 E3
Stockport SK1 ....169 F1
Stretford M32 ....96 E3
Swinton M27 ....79 F8
Westhoughton BL5 ....39 E2
Wigan WN5 ....54 D5
Wesleys The 4 BL4 ....59 F8
Wessenden Bank E SK2 ....124 D5
Wessenden Bank W SK2 ....124 D5
Wessex Cl WN1 ....20 B1
Wessex Park Cl OL2 ....149 B8
Wessex Rd WN5 ....36 D1
Wessington Bank 12
SK13 ....171 E2
Wessington Fold 14 SK13 171 E2
Wessington Gn 13 SK13 ....171 E2
Wessington Mews SK13 ....171 E2
West Ashton St M5 ....154 F1
West Ave Altrincham WA14 119 A5
Droylsden M18 ....99 E5
Failsworth M40 ....65 D1
Farnworth BL4 ....60 B8
Gatley SK8 ....122 C1
Golborne WA3 ....74 B1
Leigh WN7 ....76 C3
Littleborough OL12 ....15 C3
Manchester M19 ....110 F7
Stalybridge SK15 ....86 A3
Walkden M28 ....60 C3
Whitefield M45 ....44 E2
West Bank M11 ....100 A7
West Bank St Salford M5 ....161 C8
Tyldesley M46 ....58 E1
West Bridgewater St WN7 75 F4
West Canteen Rd M17,M32 96 C4
West Central Dr M27 ....80 B7
West Charles St M5 ....81 B1
West Church St 9 OL10 ....29 C2
West Cl M46 ....58 E1
West Cotts OL3 ....68 F5
West Craven St M5 ....161 B7
West Cres M24 ....64 F7
West Croft Ind Est M24 ....64 C7
West Crown Ave M5 ....161 B8
West Dean St M5 ....81 C1
West Downs Rd SK8 ....122 F3
West Dr Bury BL9 ....27 E5
Droylsden M43 ....83 F1
Gatley SK8 ....122 A4
Pendlebury M27 ....80 B7
Pendlebury M6 ....80 E6
Tintwistle SK13 ....103 F7
West Duke St M5 ....158 D1
West Egerton St M5 ....81 B1
West End SK14 ....114 F8
West End Ave SK8 ....122 A6
West End Prim Sch OL7 ....84 F2
West End St OL9 ....153 D7
West Gdns 1 OL13 ....3 B8
West Gn M24 ....64 B7
West Gr Manchester M13 ....164 D5
1 Mossley OL5 ....68 C1
Sale M33 ....108 B3
Westhoughton BL5 ....57 E6
West High St M5 ....81 A2
West Hill OL11 ....139 E6
West Hill Cl SK15 ....85 F2
West Hill Sch SK15 ....85 F2
West Hope St M5 ....81 B1
West King St M3 ....158 E2
West Lea M34 ....101 A2
West Liverpool Street
Prim Sch M6 ....154 F2
West Marwood St M7 ....155 E6
West Mdw SK5 ....100 A1
West Meade Bolton BL3 ....147 D2
Manchester M21 ....109 A7
Manchester M25 ....63 D2
Swinton M27 ....79 E6
West Mosley St M2 ....159 A1
West Mount Orrell WN5 ....53 F6
Wigan WN1 ....37 D2
West Oak Pl SK8 ....122 F1
West Over SK6 ....113 A1
West Par M33 ....107 C3
West Park Ave
Denton M34 ....101 B2
Poynton SK12 ....133 A4
West Park Rd
Stockport SK1 ....112 B2
Stockport SK7 ....123 D2
West Park St M5 ....161 B7
West Pk SK14 ....113 E6
West Pl M19 ....110 F7
West Point Lo 1 M19 ....110 F8
West Rd Altrincham WA14 ....119 C2
Eccles M41 ....95 E6
Prestwich M25 ....62 F5
Stretford M32 ....96 A4
West Row M25 ....62 F1
West St Alderley Edge SK9 ....137 A1
Ashton-u-L OL6 ....166 B3
Bolton BL1 ....144 C7
Droylsden M11 ....83 B2
Dukinfield SK14 ....101 D5
Dukinfield SK16 ....166 B1
Failsworth M35 ....83 F7
Farnworth BL4 ....42 E1
Heywood OL10 ....29 D2
Hindley WN2 ....57 B3
Ince-in-M WN2 ....56 A8
Littleborough OL15 ....16 C5
Middleton M24 ....47 A2
Milnrow OL16 ....31 D7
Oldham OL1 ....153 E7
Oldham OL4 ....67 E5
Oldham OL9 ....153 D6
2 Radcliffe M26 ....44 A3
Ramsbottom BL0 ....138 B5
Rawtenstall BB4 ....2 E8
Rochdale OL16 ....31 A8
Stalybridge SK15 ....85 F2
Stockport SK3 ....169 D1
Tintwistle SK13 ....103 F7
Tyldesley M46 ....58 E1
Wigan WN6 ....37 B1
West Starkey St OL10 ....29 C3
West Towers St M6 ....154 F1
West Vale M26 ....44 A5
West Vale Rd WA15 ....119 F6
West View Bacup OL13 ....3 B8
Denton M34 ....100 E7
Haslingden BB4 ....1 A7
Littleborough OL15 ....16 C5
Ramsbottom BL0 ....1 C2
West View Ct M22 ....121 F8
West View Gr M45 ....44 D1
West View Rd M22 ....121 E8
West Way Bolton BL1 ....25 B3
Walkden M38 ....60 A5
West Wlk BL7 ....8 D2
West Works Rd M17,M32 ....96 C5
Westage Gdns M23 ....121 A7
Westbank Rd Bolton BL6 ....40 D6
Manchester M20 ....110 D5
Westbourne BB4 ....1 A8
Westbourne Ave
Bolton BL3 ....42 B3
Kearsley M27 ....61 D5
Leigh WN7 ....75 E7
Leigh WN7 ....75 F7
Whitefield M45 ....44 D1
Westbourne Dr OL7 ....166 A4
Westbourne Gr
Manchester M20 ....110 A6
Manchester M9 ....157 D8
Reddish SK5 ....111 F8

Westbourne Gr continued
Sale M33 ....108 A4
Westbourne Pk M41 ....95 D2
Westbourne Range
M18,M34 ....99 F4
Westbourne Rd
Denton M34 ....100 E2
Eccles M30 ....79 B4
Manchester M14 ....110 D8
Urmston M41 ....95 D2
Westbourne St OL9 ....153 D7
Westbridge Mews WN1 ..150 C7
Westbrook Ct BL2 .....148 A6
Westbrook Rd
Stretford M17 ....96 D7
Swinton M27 ....79 E7
Westbrook Sq M12 ....165 A6
Westbrook St BL2 .....148 A6
Westbrook Wlk 3 M8 ..110 A8
Wigan WN3 ....54 D2
Westbury Ave Sale M33 ..107 C1
Westbury Cl Bury BL8 ..27 A1
Westhoughton BL5 ......40 A1
Westbury Dr SK6 ......125 E6
Westbury Rd M8 ....64 B1
Westbury St
Ashton-u-L OL6 ....166 C3
Dukinfield SK14 ....101 C5
Westbury Street Ind Est
SK14 ....101 C5
Westbury Way OL1,OL2 ..48 D2
Westby Cl SK7 ....133 A7
Westby Gr BL2 ....148 C8
Westcliffe Ho 3 OL12 ..15 D4
Westcliffe Rd BL1 .....24 F6
Westcombe Dr BL8 .....27 C5
Westcott Ave M20 .....110 A6
Westcott Cl BL2 ....25 E5
Westcott Ct M15 ......162 D7
Westcott Dr WN3 ......54 C4
Westcott Gr OL2 ......149 A5
Westcourt Rd Bolton BL3 ..147 D3
Sale M33 ....108 A6
Westcraig Ave M40 ....65 C3
Westcroft Rd M19,M20 ..110 D4
Westdale Gdns M19 ....111 A5
Westdean Cres M19 ....110 F5
Westend Ave PR7 ......19 D8
Westend St BL4 ....60 B8
Wester Hill Rd OL8 ....67 A1
Westerdale 1 OL4 .....67 C6
Westerdale M29 ....77 B8
Westerdale Dr Bolton BL3 144 A5
Royton OL2 ....48 C5
Westerham Ave M5 ....81 A1
Westerham Cl BL8 .....27 C7
Westerling Way M16 ...97 E3
Western Ave M27 ......62 D2
Western Circ M19 .....110 F6
Western Ct OL13 ......3 C8
Western Rd Bacup OL13 ..3 C8
Urmston M41 ....94 E1
Western St Manchester M18 99 E6
Salford M6 ....154 E3
Westerton Ct BL3 .....145 D5
Westfield
Altrincham WA14 ......119 C3
Salford M6 ....154 E4
Westfield Ave
Ashton-in-M WN4 .....73 A4
Middleton M24 ....65 A7
Westfield Cl OL11 .....13 F1
Westfield Dr Romiley SK6 .113 C5
Uppermill OL4 ....68 E5
Westfield Gr Denton M34 ..100 E5
Cheadle SK8 ....131 F8
Droylsden M43 ....83 E2
Manchester M21 ....97 B1
Tyldesley M46 ....58 E1
Westfield Rd Bolton BL3 ..146 B2
Cheadle SK8 ....131 F8
Droylsden M43 ....83 E2
Manchester M21 ....97 B1
Tyldesley M46 ....58 E1
Westfield St
Manchester M7 ....63 D1
Oldham OL1,OL9 ......48 C1
Oldham OL9 ....152 C8
Westfields WA15 ......128 F8
Westgate Altrincham WA15 119 E2
Sale M33 ....108 A4
Urmston M41 ....95 B1
Whitworth OL12 ....14 B7
Wilmslow SK9 ....137 A5
Westgate Ave Bolton BL1 .144 C7
Bury BL9 ....140 E1
Manchester M9 ....64 C2
Ramsbottom BL0 ......11 A2
Westgate Cl OL12 .....14 B7
Westgate Dr Orrell WN5 ..53 D5
Swinton M27 ....79 F6
Tyldesley M29 ....77 C6
Westgate Ho 4 OL8 ...66 D2
Westgate Rd M6 ......80 C4
Westgate St OL7 ......166 A1
Westgrove Ave BL1 ....24 E6
Westhead Ave WA3 ....74 E1
Westhide Wlk 5 M9 ....64 F1
Westholm SK4 ....111 B7
Westholme St SK9 ....137 A4
Westholme Rd
Manchester M20 ....110 B5
Prestwich M25 ....63 C7
Westhorne Fold 1 M8 ..63 E2
Westhoughton
Com Prim Sch BL5 .....39 F1
Westhoughton High Sch
BL5 ....57 F8

Westhoughton Parochial
CE Prim Sch BL5 ......57 E8
Westhoughton Rd PR6,PR7 20 F8
Westhoughton Sta BL5 ..39 E2
Westhulme Ave OL1 ....48 D1
Westhulme St OL1 .....48 D1
Westhulme Way OL1 ...48 C1
Westinghouse Cl WN6 ..150 A8
Westinghouse Rd M17 ..96 B5
Westlake Gr WN2 ......57 B4
Westlake St M11 ......165 C7
Westland Ave Bolton BL1 .142 A1
Farnworth BL4 ....60 C6
Stockport SK1 ....112 B1
Westland Dr M9 ....64 D4
Westlands M45 ....62 F6
Westlands The M27 ....80 C6
Westlea Dr M18 ......99 D3
Westleigh Br BL5 .....40 A3
Westleigh High Sch WN7 57 F1
Westleigh La WN7 .....57 D1
Westleigh Meth Prim Sch
WN7 ....75 D8
Westleigh St M9 ......64 F1
Westleigh St Paul's
CE Prim Sch WN7 .....75 E8
Westleigh View WN7 ...75 E8
Westlock WN3 ....150 C6
Westmarsh Cl 4 BL1 ..143 E1
Westmead WN6 ....36 E8
Westmead Dr
Manchester M8 ....155 E5
Sale WA15 ....120 B7
Westmeade Rd M28 ...60 C5
Westmere Dr M9 .....156 C6
Westminster Ave
Ashton-u-L OL6 ....85 D7
Farnworth BL4 ....60 C8
Manchester M16 ......97 C2
Radcliffe M26 ....43 D4
Reddish SK5 ....111 E7
Royton OL2 ....48 C6
Whitefield M45 ....62 F8
Westminster Cl
Marple SK6 ....125 D7
Sale M33 ....107 D3
Shaw OL2 ....149 B8
Westminster Dr
Bramhall SK8 ....132 B6
Leigh WN7 ....76 E7
Wilmslow SK9 ....137 A4
Westminster Ho M3 ...158 E3
Westminster Rd
Altrincham WA15 .....120 A2
Bolton BL1 ....24 E5
Eccles M30 ....79 F4
Failsworth M35 ....84 B8
Urmston M41 ....95 E4
Walkden M28 ....60 D2
Westminster St Bury BL9 .140 E1
Farnworth BL4 ....60 C8
5 Manchester M19 ....99 B1
Oldham OL1 ....67 B8
Rochdale OL11 ....139 D5
Salford M15 ....161 C7
Swinton M27 ....61 E1
Wigan WN5 ....54 F6
Westminster Way SK16 .101 D6
Westminster Wlk 4 BL4 ..60 C8
Westmoor Gables SK4 ..168 A4
Westmoorland St 3 WN1 .37 E1
Westmoreland Cl
Altrincham WA14 .....128 B8
Bury BL9 ....44 E6
Westmorland Ave
Ashton-u-L OL7 ......166 B4
Dukinfield SK16 ......101 E8
Westmorland Cl SK5 ..112 C6
Westmorland Dr
Brinnington SK5 ......112 C6
Littleborough OL12 ....15 D6
Westmorland Rd
Manchester M20 ......110 A2
Partington M31 ....105 E2
Sale M33 ....108 C2
Salford M30 ....80 A4
Tyldesley M29 ....59 A2
Urmston M41 ....95 C1
Westmorland Wlk 2 OL2 .48 E4
Westmount Cl M40 ....156 C6
Weston Ave Failsworth M40 65 E4
Kearsley M27 ....61 F4
Rochdale OL16 ....31 B4
Urmston M41 ....95 B1
Weston Ct M14 ......98 D2
Weston Dr Denton M34 ..101 A3
Stockport SK8 ....123 D4
Weston Gr Reddish SK4 ..111 C6
Wythenshawe M22 ....121 E8
Weston Pk N9 ....36 D3
Weston Rd 3 Irlam M44 ..94 A2
Wilmslow SK9 ....137 E6
Weston St Atherton M46 ..58 E4
Bolton BL3 ....42 A4
Manchester M4 ......160 D2
Milnrow OL16 ....31 E6
Reddish SK5 ....169 E4
Westonby Ct WN4 ....73 D3
Westover Rd M41 ....95 C3
Westover St M27 .....61 F1
Westpark M15 ....144 C7
Westpoint Ent Pk M17 ..95 F7
Westray Cres M5 ....154 E1
Westray St M9 ....98 E3
Westrees WN7 ....76 A7
Westville Gdns M19 ...110 E5
Westward Ho OL16 ...31 F6

Westward Rd SK9 .....136 F6
Westway Droylsden M43 .100 A8
Manchester M9 ....64 B6
Oldham OL4 ....67 E5
Shaw OL2 ....149 B6
Westwell Gdns 4 BL1 ..143 F1
Westwell Gr 3 WN7 ...75 E8
Westwell St WN7 .....75 E8
Westwick Terr 17 BL1 ..143 E2
Westwood WA14 .....119 B4
Westwood Ave
Altrincham WA15 .....119 F7
Failsworth M40 ....65 E1
Manchester M7 ......155 E8
Urmston M41 ....95 F1
Walkden M28 ....60 A3
Westwood Bsns Ctr OL9 .153 D6
Westwood
Com Prim Sch OL9 ....153 D7
Westwood Cotts 8 M16 ..97 F4
Westwood Cres M30 ..79 B4
Westwood Dr Oldham OL9 153 D7
Pendlebury M27 ......80 C6
Sale M33 ....108 B3
Westwood Ind Est OL9 .152 C7
Westwood La WN3 ....151 D5
Westwood Lo WA15 ...119 F2
Westwood Park
Com Prim Sch M30 ....79 B3
Westwood Rd Bolton BL1 .144 C8
Gatley SK8 ....131 B8
Stockport SK2 ....124 B4
Stretford M32 ....96 B2
Wigan WN3 ....150 C6
Westwood Terr WN3 ..151 E5
Westwood Trad Est SK6 .125 E5
Westworth OL11 BL1 ..145 C8
Wet Gate La WA13 ...117 E4
Wetheral Cl WN2 .....57 C3
Wetheral Dr BL3 .....147 E3
Wetherall St M19 .....99 B1
Wetherby Cl WA12 ....89 C5
Wetherby Dr
Hazel Grove SK7 .....125 A2
Royton OL2 ....48 D5
Wetherby St M11 .....99 E7
Wexford Wlk M22 ....121 E2
Wexham Gdns WN2 ...56 A3
Wey Gates Dr WA15 ..129 C7
Weybourne Ave M9 ...65 A2
Weybourne Dr
Bredbury SK6 ....112 F4
Wigan WN3 ....54 E3
Weybourne Gr BL2 ...25 B4
Weybridge Cl 4 BL1 ..145 E8
Weybridge Rd M4 ....159 C2
Weybrook Rd M19,SK4 .111 C7
Weycroft Cl BL2 ......43 A6
Weyhill Rd M23 ....121 A5
Weylands Gr M6 .....80 B5
Weymouth Dr WN2 ...57 A4
Weymouth Rd
Ashton-u-L OL6 ......85 F6
Eccles M30 ....79 B3
Weymouth St BL1 ....143 E2
Weythorne Dr Bolton BL1 .143 F4
Bury BL9 ....11 D3
Whalley Ave Bolton BL1 ..23 F3
Glazebury WA3 ....92 C7
Littleborough OL15 ...16 A6
Manchester M16 ......97 D3
Manchester M19 ......99 B2
Manchester M21 ......109 C7
Sale M33 ....108 C5
Urmston M41 ....95 E3
Whalley Cl
Altrincham WA15 .....119 F8
Milnrow OL16 ....31 D6
Whitefield M45 ....44 F1
Wigan WN3 ....55 A2
Whalley Dr BL8 ......26 F2
Whalley Gdns OL12 ...14 B1
Whalley Gr Ashton-u-L OL6 .85 C7
Leigh WN7 ....57 D1
Manchester M16 ......97 D2
Whalley Range
High Sch M14 ....109 F8
Whalley Range High Sch
for Girls M20 ....110 A7
Whalley Rd
Altrincham WA15 .....120 A2
Heywood OL10 ....29 A2
Manchester M16 ......97 D3
Middleton M24 ....46 F3
Ramsbottom BL0 .....11 E7
Rochdale OL12 ....14 B1
Stockport SK2 ....124 C7
Whitefield M45 ....44 F1
Whalley St M40 ......160 D2
Wham Bar Dr OL10 ...29 A2
Wham Bottom La OL12 ..14 D4
Wham La OL3 ....33 D1
Wham St OL10 ....29 B2
Wharf Cotts OL5 .....68 D1
Wharf End M17 ......161 A6
Wharf Rd
Altrincham WA14 .....119 D7
Sale M33 ....108 C5
Wharf St Dukinfield SK16 .166 C1
Oldham OL9 ....66 B3
Stockport SK4,SK5 ...169 E3
Wharf The OL3 ....51 B2
Wharfdale 2 WN7 ....76 A4
Wharfedale BL5 ......39 F2
Wharfedale Ave M40 ..65 A1
Wharfedale Rd SK5 ..111 E8
Wharfside Ave M30 ...95 D8

Wharfside Bsns Ctr M17 ..96 F6
Wharfside Way
(Trafford Park Rd) M17 ..96 E6
Wharmton Rise OL4 ...68 E6
Wharmton School Cotts
OL3 ....50 F1
Wharmton View
Oldham OL3 ....69 A6
Uppermill OL5 ....68 E3
Wharncliffe Cl SK13 ..171 E4
Wharncliffe St 6 WN2 ..56 D5
Wharton Ave M21 ....109 D7
Wharton La M38 .....59 E5
Wharton Lo M30 .....79 E3
Wharton Prim Sch M38 ..59 E5
Wheat Cl M13 ....163 C5
Wheat Croft SK3 .....170 F5
Wheatcroft SK13 .....171 E4
Wheater's Cres M7 ...158 D4
Wheater's St M7 .....158 D4
Wheater's Terr M7 ...158 D4
Wheatfield SK15 .....102 E7
Wheatfield Cl Bury BL9 ..27 F7
Romiley SK6 ....113 A4
Wheatfield Cres OL2 ..48 C3
Wheatfield Ho OL2 ...48 D3
Wheatfield St BL2 ...148 A6
Wheathill St M19 ....31 A4
Wheatlea Ind Est WN3 ..54 F1
Wheatlea Rd WN3 ....54 F2
Wheatley Ave WA12 ..89 C5
Wheatley Rd M27 ....61 D2
Wheatley Wlk M12 ...165 A6
Wheatsheaf Ctr The
OL16 ....139 F8
Wheatsheaf Ind Est M27 .62 B1
Wheatsheaf Wlk WN6 ..19 D1
Wheeldale Cl OL4 ....67 D6
Wheeldale Cl BL1 ....143 E2
Wheeldon St M14 ....98 A3
Wheelock Cl SK9 .....131 D1
Wheelton Cl BL8 .....27 A1
Wheelwright Cl
Marple SK6 ....125 F8
Rochdale OL11 ....30 B4
Wheelwright Dr OL16 ..15 C3
Whelan Ave BL9 .....44 E7
Whelan Cl BL9 ....44 E7
Wheler St M11,M43 ...99 E8
Whelley WN1,WN2 ...37 E2
Whelley Hospl (General)
WN1 ....37 E2
Whernside Ave
Ashton-u-L OL6 ......85 C7
Manchester M40 .....65 A1
Whernside Cl SK4 ....169 E3
Whetmorhurst Rd SK6 .126 E4
Whetstone Hill Cl OL1 ..49 B2
Whetstone Hill La
6 Oldham OL1 ......49 C1
Oldham OL1 ....49 C1
Whetstone Hill Rd OL1 ..49 B1
Whewell Ave BL9 ....44 E5
Whewell St 14 M29 ..59 A1
Whickham Cl M14 ....98 A3
Whiley St M13 ....98 F4
Whimberry Cl M5 ....161 C7
Whimbrel Ave WA12 ..89 C3
Whimbrel Rd
Hazel Grove SK2 .....125 A5
Tyldesley M29 ....77 C7
Whinberry Rd WA14 ..119 B7
Whinberry Way OL4 ..49 F4
Whinchat Ave WA12 ..89 C4
Whinchat Cl Golborne WA3 90 F7
Hazel Grove SK2 .....125 A4
Whinfell Dr M24 .....46 C1
Whinfield Cl WN6 ....150 A8
Whingroves Wlk 3 M40 .83 A6
Whinmoor Wlk M40 ...83 B7
Whins Ave BL4 ......59 E8
Whins Crest BL6 .....40 C7
Whinslee Ct BL6 .....40 C7
Whinslee Dr BL6 .....40 C7
Whinstone Way OL1,OL9 .47 E1
Whipp St OL10 ......29 B3
Whirley Cl SK4 ......111 D5
Whistlecroft Ct WN3 ..151 F6
Whistley St WN2 ....56 B3
Whiston Dr BL2 ......148 C6
Whiston Rd
Manchester M8 ......156 B8
Manchester M8 ......64 B1
Whit La Manchester M6 ..80 F6
Salford M6 ....81 A5
Whitaker St M24 ....64 F8
Whitbrook Way M24 ..47 C5
Whitburn Ave M13 ...98 E3
Whitburn Cl Bolton BL3 ..40 E4
Garswood WN4 ......72 D4
Whitburn Dr SK3 ....27 C5
Whitburn Rd M23 ....121 A4
Whitby Ave Heywood OL10 .29 C3
Manchester M14 .....110 E8
Manchester M16 ......97 D3
Salford M6 ....80 C3
Urmston M41 ....95 E2
Whitby Cl Bury BL8 ...26 F2
Cheadle SK8 ....122 C6
Poynton SK12 ....133 D4
Whitby Rd
Manchester M14 .....110 E8
Oldham OL4 ....67 C4
Whitby St Middleton M24 ..47 C1
Rochdale OL11 ....31 A5
Whitchurch Dr M16 ..162 D5
Whitchurch Gdns 8 BL1 .143 E2

Whitchurch Rd M20 ..110 A7
Whitchurch St M3 ...158 E3
White Bank Ave SK5 ..112 C4
White Bank Rd OL8 ..66 E1
White Birk Cl BL8 ...10 F2
White Brook La
Oldham OL3 ....69 C8
Oldham OL3 ....69 C6
White Broom WA13 ..117 B4
White Carr La BL9 ...12 A1
White City Ret Pk M16 ..161 A5
White City Way M16 ..161 A5
White Hart Mdw 2
M24 ....47 A2
White Hart St SK14 ..167 D4
White Hill Cl OL12 ...14 D4
White Horse Gr BL6 ..22 C5
White Horse Gr BL5 ..40 A2
White Horse Mdws OL1 ..31 C2
White House Ave M8 ..63 F4
White House Cl OL10 ..46 D7
White Lady Cl 2 M28 ..59 F3
White Lion Brow BL1 ..145 E7
White Lodge Dr WN4 ..73 D4
White Moss Ave M21 ..109 D8
White Moss Gdns M9 ..65 A2
White Moss Rd M9 ...64 E3
White Moss Rd E M9 ..65 A4
White Rd SK22 ......127 C2
White Slack Gate OL14 ..6 A6
White St Bury BL8 ...27 C1
Leigh WN7 ....76 C4
Manchester M15 ....162 D6
Salford M6 ....154 E1
5 Wigan WN5 ......54 B6
White Swallows Rd M27 .80 B6
White Swan Ind Est 5
OL1 ....67 C8
Whiteacre WN6 ......19 A3
Whiteacre Rd OL6 ...85 D4
Whiteacre Wlk M15 ..162 E6
Whiteacres M27 .....79 D7
Whitebeam Cl
Altrincham WA15 .....120 E5
Newhey OL16 ....32 A3
Salford M6 ....81 A3
Whitebeam St M6 ....81 A3
Whitebeam Wlk Sale M33 107 A3
Westhoughton BL5 ...39 F2
Whitebeck Cl M9 ....65 A4
Whitecar Ave M40 ...65 E1
Whitecarr La M23,WA15 .120 C3
Whitechapel Cl BL2 ..42 E7
Whitechapel St M20 ..110 B3
Whitecliff M14 ....98 C3
Whitecroft Ave
Golborne WA3 ....74 E1
Shaw OL2 ....49 D7
Whitecroft Dr BL8 ...26 F2
Whitecroft Gdns 3 M19 .110 E4
Whitecroft Rd Bolton BL1 .142 A1
Marple SK6 ....126 C1
Wigan WN3 ....55 B2
Whitecroft 12 OL1 ..49 C1
Whitefield Lymm WA13 ..117 A4
Manchester SK4 .....169 D3
Pendlebury M6 ....80 D6
Whitefield Ave
Newton-le-W WA12 ...89 E2
Rochdale OL11 ....29 F5
Whitefield Cl
Golborne WA3 ....90 A8
Lymm WA13 ....117 A5
Whitefield Com Prim Sch
M45 ....63 B4
Whitefield Ct WA3 ...91 F2
Whitefield Gr WA13 ..117 A4
Whitefield Prep Sch Ltd
M45 ....44 E1
Whitefield Rd
Bredbury SK6 ....112 E4
Bury BL9 ....44 D7
Sale M33 ....108 A5
Whitefield Sta M45 ...44 E1
Whitefriar Ct M3 ....158 E3
Whitefriars Wlk 2 M22 .130 E8
Whitegate Bolton BL3 ..40 C2
Littleborough OL15 ...15 E4
Whitegate Ave
Culcheth WA3 ....91 F2
Oldham OL9 ....65 F4
Whitegate Cl M40 ....65 E1
Whitegate Dr Bolton BL1 .143 F4
Salford M5 ....154 D2
Swinton M27 ....62 B2
Whitegate End
Com Prim Sch OL9 ...65 E3
Whitegate La OL9 ...66 A4
Whitegate Pk M41 ...94 E2
Whitegate Rd OL9 ...65 E3
Whitegates SK8 .....122 D5
Whitegates Cl WA15 ..120 B5
Whitegates La OL4 ...50 D2
Whitegates Rd
Cheadle SK8 ....122 D5
Middleton M24 ....47 C4
Whitehall Ave WN6 ..35 E4
Whitehall Cl SK9 ....137 A5
Whitehall La Blackrod BL6 .21 D3
Bolton BL1 ....24 D4
Oldham OL4 ....49 F4
Whitehall Rd
Manchester M20 .....110 C3
Sale M33 ....108 B3
Whitehall St
Ince-in-M WN3 ......151 E4
Oldham OL1 ....153 F8

Whitehall St *continued*
Rochdale OL12 .139 F8
Rochdale OL12 .14 F1
Whitehaven Gdns M20 .110 A2
Whitehaven Pl SK14 .101 C5
Whitehaven Rd SK7 .132 C5
Whitehead Cres Bury BL8 .27 C5
Kearsley M26 .61 C7
Whitehead Rd
Stretford M21 .108 F8
Swinton M27 .62 B2
Whitehead St
Dukinfield M34 .100 F7
Middleton M24 .47 C1
Middleton OL16 .31 E6
Newhey OL16 .32 D4
Shaw OL2 .48 F8
Walkden M28 .60 D4
Whitehill Cotts BL7 .24 D6
Whitehill Dr M40 .83 A7
Whitehill Ind Est SK4,SK5 111 E5
Whitehill Prim Sch SK4 .169 E4
Whitehill St SK4,SK5 .111 E5
Whitehill St W SK4 .169 E4
Whiteholme Ave M21 .109 D4
Whitehouse Ave 4 OL4 .67 C6
Whitehouse Dr
Altrincham WA15 .129 B8
Wythenshawe M23 .121 A5
Whitehouse La WA14 .118 D8
Whitehurst Rd SK4 .110 F4
Whitekirk Cl M13 .163 B6
Whitelake Ave M41 .94 F2
Whitelake View M41 .94 F3
Whiteland Ave BL3 .144 C5
Whitelands Rd
Ashton-u-L OL6,SK15 .85 D2
Stalybridge OL6,SK16 .166 C2
Whitelands Terr OL6 .166 C2
Whitelea Dr SK3 .170 D5
Whitelees Rd OL15 .16 A5
Whitelegge St BL8 .27 B4
Whiteley Dr M24 .65 C7
Whiteley Pl WA14 .119 D6
Whiteley St Droylsden M11 .83 C2
Oldham OL9 .66 B4
Whiteley's Pl 6 OL12 .139 E8
Whitelow Rd
Manchester M21 .109 A8
Manchester SK4 .168 A3
Ramsbottom BL0 .11 E5
Whitemoss OL12 .14 B2
Whiteoak Cl SK6 .125 E7
Whiteoak Ct M14 .110 C8
Whiteoak Rd M14 .110 C8
Whiteoak View BL3 .42 A4
Whiteside Ave Hindley WN2 56 E7
2 Wigan WN6 .37 A1
Whiteside Cl M5 .154 D2
Whiteside Fold OL12 .14 A1
Whitesmead Cl SK12 .135 D5
Whitestone Cl BL6 .40 D6
Whitestone Ho 10 OL1 .153 E8
Whitestone Wlk M13 .164 D5
Whitethorn Ave
1 Manchester M16 .97 D3
3 Manchester M19 .110 F7
Whitethorn Cl SK6 .125 E7
Whitewater Dr M7 .80 F8
Whiteway St M9 .157 E7
Whitewell Cl Bury BL9 .44 D7
Rochdale OL16 .31 C8
Whitewillow Cl M35 .84 A6
Whitewood Cl WN4 .73 A6
Whitfield Ave SK13 .116 C7
Whitfield Brows OL15 .16 C7
Whitfield CE Prim Sch SK13 .116 B8
Whitfield Cres OL16 .32 B3
Whitfield Cross SK13 .116 D7
Whitfield Dr OL16 .31 E5
Whitfield Pk SK13 .116 C7
Whitfield Rise OL2 .32 A1
Whitfield St Leigh WN7 .76 C4
Manchester M3 .159 A4
Whitford Wlk M40 .160 D3
Whiting Gr BL3 .40 E6
Whitland Ave BL1 .40 F8
Whitland Dr OL8 .66 B2
Whitle Rd SK22 .127 C1
Whitledge Gn WN4 .73 A5
Whitledge Rd WN4 .73 A5
Whitley Cres
Abram Brow WN2 .74 B7
Wigan WN1 .37 C4
Whitley Gdns WA15 .120 C7
Whitley Pl WA15 .120 C7
Whitley Rd
Manchester M40 .159 C4
Manchester SK4 .168 B3
Orrell WN8 .35 D3
Whitley St BL4 .42 D2
Whitlow Ave
Altrincham WA14 .119 B8
Golborne WA3 .73 F1
Whitman St M40,M9 .157 F8
Whitmore Rd M14 .98 B1
Whitnall Cl M16 .97 E4
Whitnall St SK14 .101 D5
Whitsand Rd M22 .121 E5
Whitsbury Ave
Hindley WN2 .56 D4
Manchester M18 .99 D3
Whitstable Cl OL9 .152 B6
Whitstable Rd M40 .65 C1
Whitsters Hollow BL1 .142 B3
Whitsundale BL5 .39 F2
Whitswood Cl 2 M16 .97 E3
Whittaker Dr OL15 .15 F2
Whittaker La
Littleborough OL15 .16 E4
Prestwich M25 .63 C4
Rochdale OL11 .13 D1
Whittaker Moss Prim Sch OL11 .13 E1
Whittaker St
Ashton-u-L OL6 .85 D5
Manchester M40 .83 A8
Radcliffe M26 .44 B4
Rochdale OL11 .13 E1
Whittingham Dr BL0 .11 C3
Whittingham Gr OL1 .153 D8
Whittington St OL7 .166 A1
Whittle Bank Rd SK22 .127 B2
Whittle Ct WN3 .54 E2
Whittle Dr Shaw OL2 .49 D8
Walkden M28 .60 D5
Whittle Gr Bolton BL1 .142 B1
Walkden M28 .60 E3
Whittle Hill BL7 .8 E3
Whittle La OL10 .46 B4
Whittle St Bury BL8 .27 C3
Littleborough OL15 .15 F5
Manchester M4 .159 B2
Swinton M27 .79 E7
Walkden M28 .60 E3
Whittle's Croft M1 .159 B1
Whittle's Terr 1 BL5 .39 E1
Whittlebrook Gr OL10 .46 E7
Whittles Ave M34 .101 A2
Whittles St OL13 .4 B8
Whittles Terr OL16 .32 C4
Whittles Wlk M34 .101 A2
Whitton Mews 5 BL6 .22 B4
Whitwell Bank 4 SK13 .171 D2
Whitwell Cl
3 Gamesley SK13 .171 D2
Standish WN6 .19 D2
Whitwell Fold 1 SK13 .171 D2
Whitwell Gdns BL6 .22 B5
Whitwell Gn 4 SK13 .171 E2
Whitwell Lea 2 SK13 .171 D2
Whitwell Way M18 .165 C5
Whitwell Wlk 6 M13 .98 E4
Whitworth Art Gall M15 .98 B4
Whitworth Cl OL6 .166 C4
Whitworth High Sch OL12 14 C8
Whitworth La M14 .98 D1
Whitworth Park Mans M14 .98 A4
Whitworth Park Sch M14 .98 A4
Whitworth Rake OL12 .14 D8
Whitworth Rd OL12 .14 F2
Whitworth Sq OL12 .14 D8
Whitworth St Horwich BL6 .22 C2
Manchester M1 .163 A8
Manchester M11 .165 B7
Milnrow OL16 .31 F6
Rochdale OL16 .15 C2
Whitworth St E M11 .165 C7
Whitworth St W M1,M3,M15 .162 F8
Whixhall Ave M12 .164 E6
Whoolden St BL4 .42 C1
Whowell Fold BL1 .142 C3
Whowell St BL3 .145 E6
Wibbersley Pk M41 .94 F2
Wibsey Cotts OL3 .33 D2
Wichbrook Rd 13 M28 .59 F3
Wicheaves Cres
11 Walkden M28 .59 F3
Walkden M28 .60 A3
Wicheries The M28 .59 F3
Wicken Bank OL10 .46 E7
Wicken St SK2 .124 C7
Wickenby Dr M33 .108 A4
Wickentree Holt OL12 .14 A1
Wickentree La M35 .66 A1
Wicker La WA15 .129 C8
Wicket Gr M27 .61 E4
Wickham Terr 11 M24 .47 A2
Wickliffe St 10 BL1 .145 E8
Wicklow Ave SK3 .123 B7
Wicklow Dr M22 .121 E2
Widcombe Dr BL2,BL3 .42 F5
Widdop St OL9 .153 D7
Widdow's St WN7 .76 B4
Widdrington Rd WN1 .37 D2
Widecombe Cl M41 .95 B4
Widford Wlk BL6 .21 E1
Widgeon Cl
Manchester M14 .110 B8
Poynton SK12 .133 B4
Widgeon Rd WA14 .119 B8
Widnes St M11 .165 C7
Wiend WN1 .150 C8
Wigan & Leigh Coll (Annexe) WN1 .150 B8
Wigan & Leigh Coll (Leigh Campus) Leigh WN7 .75 E3
Leigh WN7 .75 E5
Wigan & Leigh Coll (Linacre Bldg) WN1 .37 B1
Wigan & Leigh Coll (Mesnes Bldg) WN1 .37 C1
Wigan & Leigh Coll (Pagefield Bldg) WN1 .37 B2
Wigan & Leigh Coll (Parsons Wlk) WN1 .150 B8
Wigan (North Western) Sta WN3 .150 C7
Wigan Athletic FC & Wigan Warriors RLFC (JJB Stad) WN5 .54 F8
Wigan Gallery 2 WN1 .150 C8
Wigan Hope Sch WN3 .54 F2
Wigan Infmy WN1 .37 C2
Wigan La
Adlington PR7,WN1 .20 D7
Wigan WN1 .37 C4
Wigan Lower Rd WN6 .36 C3
Wigan Pier WN3 .150 B7
Wigan Rd Ashton-in-M WN4 .73 A5
Aspull WN2 .38 B4
Atherton M46 .58 B3
Billinge WN5 .71 F7
Bolton BL3 .144 B5
Bolton BL3 .40 E3
Golborne WA3 .74 B3
Leigh WN7 .75 D7
Shevington WN6 .36 B5
Standish WN6 .37 A6
Westhoughton BL5 .57 C7
Wigan Sq WN1 .150 C8
Wigan St WN2 .56 A1
Wiggins Wlk 13 M14 .98 C3
Wightman Ave WA12 .89 C5
Wighurst Wlk 6 M22 .121 D1
Wigley St M12 .164 E7
Wigmore Rd M8 .156 B7
Wigmore St 15 OL6 .85 D4
Wigsby Ave M40 .65 C2
Wigsey La WA13 .117 A7
Wigshaw Cl WN7 .75 F1
Wigshaw La WA3 .91 D2
Wigwam Cl SK12 .133 C4
Wike St BL8 .140 D3
Wilberforce Cl M15 .162 F5
Wilbraham Prim Sch M14 98 A1
Wilbraham Rd
Manchester M14 .98 B1
Manchester M14,M16,M21 .97 C1
Manchester M21 .109 B8
Walkden M28 .60 E3
Wilbraham Regency Ct M21 .97 A1
Wilbraham St Leigh WN7 .75 C5
Westhoughton BL5 .57 E8
Wilby Ave BL3 .43 B5
Wilby Cl BL8 .27 D5
Wilby St M8 .156 B6
Wilcock Rd WA11 .89 B8
Wilcock St Manchester M16 97 E4
Wigan WN3 .150 A7
Wilcockson Ho 4 BL4 .60 D8
Wilcott Dr Sale M33 .107 E5
Wilmslow SK9 .136 F4
Wilcott Rd SK8 .122 A5
Wild Arum Cl 8 WA3 .90 E8
Wild Clough SK14 .167 F1
Wild Ho OL8 .153 F5
Wild St Bredbury SK6 .112 F3
Dukinfield SK16 .101 D8
Hazel Grove SK7 .124 D2
Heywood OL10 .29 E2
Oldham OL1 .67 A7
Oldham OL4 .67 E6
Radcliffe M26 .44 D4
Shaw OL2 .149 C6
Stockport SK2 .124 A6
Wild's Pas WN7 .75 F4
Wild's Sq 5 OL5 .68 C2
Wildbank Chase SK15 .102 E7
Wildbank Prim Sch SK15 .86 D2
Wildbrook Cl M38 .59 E3
Wildbrook Cres OL8 .67 A2
Wildbrook Gr M38 .59 E3
Wildbrook Rd M38 .59 E3
Wildcroft Ave M40 .65 A1
Wilde St M34 .100 F3
Wilders Moor Rd 3 M28 .78 C8
Wilderswood Ave BL6 .22 C4
Wilderswood Cl M20 .110 C5
Wilderswood Ct BL6 .22 D4
Wildhouse La OL16 .31 F8
Wilding St WN3 .151 E6
Wildman La BL4 .59 F8
Wildmoor Ave OL4 .67 E4
Wilds Pl BL0 .138 B5
Wildwood Cl BL0 .11 A4
Wilford Ave M33 .108 A2
Wilfred Dr BL9 .141 B4
Wilfred Rd Eccles M30 .95 A8
Walkden M28 .60 D2
Wilfred St Bolton BL7 .25 A7
Manchester M3,M7 .158 E4
Manchester M40 .83 A8
Oldham OL4 .67 B6
Wigan WN5 .54 F7
Wilfrid St M27 .61 F1
Wilfrid's Pl WN6 .19 F1
Wilham Ave 7 M30 .79 D1
Wilkes St OL1 .49 D3
Wilkesley Ave WN6 .36 D8
Wilkin Croft SK8 .122 E1
Wilkins La SK9 .130 E5
Wilkinson Ave BL3 .43 A5
Wilkinson Rd Bolton BL1 .24 D5
Stockport SK4 .169 E2
Wilkinson St
Ashton-u-L OL6 .166 A2
Leigh WN7 .75 E5
3 Sale M33 .108 D4
Wilks Ave M22 .121 F3
Will Griffith Wlk M11 .164 E8
Willan Ent Ctr M17 .96 C6
Willan Ind Est M5 .154 F1
Willan Rd Eccles M30 .79 E2
Manchester M9 .64 C4
Willand Cl BL2 .43 A6
Willand Dr BL2 .43 A6
Willard Ave WN5 .53 D3
Willard St SK7 .124 D3
Willaston Cl M21 .109 A7
Willaston Way 8 SK9 .131 D5
Willbutts La OL11 .30 C8
Willdale Cl M11 .83 A2
Willdor Gr SK3 .123 B6
Willenhall Rd M23 .109 C2
Willerby Rd M7,M8 .155 E5
Willesden Ave M13 .98 E3
William Chadwick Cl 1 M40 .159 C3
William Cl M41 .95 C2
William Coates Ct 6 M16 .97 D3
William Ford Ho SK14 .103 A4
William Greenwood Cl OL10 .29 C2
William Henry St 2 OL11 .31 A4
William Hulme's Gram Sch M16 .97 F1
William Hulme's Gram Sch Prep Dept M21 .97 C1
William Jessop Ct 13 M1 .159 C1
William Kay Cl M16 .97 E4
William Lister Cl M40 .83 D4
William Murray Ct 4 M4 159 C2
William St Ashton-u-L OL7 .166 A1
Ashton-u-L OL7 .84 F2
Bacup OL13 .4 C8
Failsworth M35 .66 A1
Hindley WN2 .56 E5
Horwich BL6 .22 A3
Ince-in-M WN3 .151 D6
8 Leigh WN7 .76 A5
Leigh WN7 .76 A5
Littleborough OL15 .16 A5
Littleborough OL16 .15 D4
5 Manchester M1 .163 A7
Manchester M12 .164 D8
Manchester M20 .110 B3
Manchester M3 .158 E2
Middleton M24 .65 B8
Radcliffe M26 .44 B4
Ramsbottom BL0 .1 C1
Rochdale OL11 .139 F6
Whitworth OL12 .4 C1
William Wlk 2 WA14 .119 D3
Williams Ave WA12 .89 C5
Williams Cres OL9 .65 F3
Williams Rd Failsworth M40 83 C7
Manchester M18 .165 C5
Williams St Little Lever BL3 .43 B3
Manchester M18 .165 C5
Williamson Ave
Radcliffe M26 .43 F6
Romiley SK6 .113 A4
Williamson La M43 .100 B8
Williamson St
Ashton-u-L OL6 .166 B3
Manchester M4 .159 B3
Reddish SK5 .111 F7
Williamson's Yd 6 OL1 .67 B7
Willingdon Cl BL8 .27 C7
Willingdon Dr M25 .63 B5
Willis Rd SK3 .170 E6
Willis St BL3 .146 C4
Williton Wlk 6 M22 .121 F3
Willock St M7 .155 F6
Willoughby Ave M20 .110 C4
Willoughby Cl M33 .108 A5
Willow Ave Cheadle SK8 .122 F2
Middleton M24 .65 C8
Newton-le-W WA12 .89 E4
Reddish SK5 .169 F4
Tyldesley M29 .77 A6
Urmston M41 .95 E2
Willow Bank
Altrincham WA15 .120 A6
Bramhall SK8 .132 A6
Manchester M14 .110 C8
1 Manchester M9 .157 E7
Oldham OL4 .67 E8
Willow Bank Ct M20 .122 B8
Willow Bank Est WA12 .89 F4
Willow Cl Adlington PR6 .21 B8
Bolton BL3 .146 B4
Dukinfield SK16 .101 F7
Poynton SK12 .133 E3
Willow Cres WN7 .75 E8
Willow Ct Gatley SK8 .122 A6
Manchester M14 .110 C8
Manchester M14 .98 D1
Marple SK6 .125 F5
Sale M33 .108 E5
Willow Dr Handforth SK9 .131 D3
Hindley WN2 .56 F3
Sale M33 .107 E2
Willow Fold M43 .100 B8
Willow Gr Ashton-in-M WN4 .73 E5
Chadderton OL9 .152 B8
Denton M34 .100 E3
Golborne WA3 .74 A1
Manchester M18 .99 E4
Marple SK6 .125 F5
Willow Hill Rd M8 .64 A1
Willow Lo 1 WN2 .56 B1
Willow Pk M14 .110 C8
Willow Rd Eccles M30 .79 A4
High Lane SK6 .134 F7
Newton-le-W WA12 .89 E4
Oldham OL3 .69 C7
Partington M31 .105 E2
Prestwich M25,M45 .63 A6
Wigan WN6 .37 A3
Willow Rise OL15 .15 F3
Willow St 2 Abram WN2 .56 B1
Atherton M46 .58 C4
Bury BL9 .141 B3
Droylsden M11 .83 A1
Heywood OL10 .29 D2
Willow St *continued*
Manchester M8 .158 E4
Oldham OL1 .67 A7
Rawtenstall BB4 .2 E8
Swinton M27 .79 D5
Swinton M28 .79 C7
Willow Tree Cl WN1 .37 B4
Willow Tree Ct
1 Eccles M30 .79 C1
Sale M33 .108 B3
Willow Tree Mews SK8 .122 B1
Willow Tree Rd WA14 .119 D3
Willow Way Bramhall SK7 .132 D7
Manchester M20 .110 C3
Willow Wlk M43 .84 C2
Willow Wood Cl OL6 .85 E3
Willowbank M26 .61 F8
Willowbank Ave BL2 .148 B6
Willowbrook Ave M40 .83 A7
Willowbrook Dr WN6 .36 B7
Willowcroft Ave WN2 .38 F3
Willowdale WA12 .89 E3
Willowdale Ave SK8 .122 B2
Willowdene Cl Bolton BL7 .24 F8
3 Manchester M40 .156 C5
Willowfield Gr WN4 .73 A2
Willowfield Rd OL4 .49 D2
Willowmead Way OL12 .14 A2
Willowmoss Cl M28 .60 E1
Willows Cotts OL16 .31 E6
Willows Dr M35 .83 F5
Willows End SK15 .86 D3
Willows La Bolton BL3 .146 C4
Milnrow OL16 .31 E6
Willows Prim Sch WA15 .120 A6
Willows Rd M5 .154 D2
Willows The
5 Atherton M46 .58 D3
Coppull PR7 .19 E8
Little Lever BL3 .43 A5
Manchester M21 .109 A7
Manchester SK4 .168 A3
Mossley OL5 .68 E1
Partington M31 .105 F3
Sale M33 .107 D2
Whitworth OL12 .14 C5
Wilma Ave M9 .64 C4
Wilmans Wlk SK13 .104 A6
Wilmcote Cl BL6 .40 D6
Wilmcote Gdns 2 SK6 .112 F3
Wilmcote Rd M40 .159 C4
Wilmers OL15 .6 D2
Wilmington Rd M32 .96 B2
Wilmot Dr WA3 .89 F7
Wilmot St BL1 .142 C3
Wilmott St
Manchester M15 .162 F7
Manchester M15 .163 A6
Wilmslow Ave BL1 .24 E5
Wilmslow Grange Cty Prim Sch SK9 .131 C4
Wilmslow High Sch SK9 .137 B6
Wilmslow Old Rd M90 .130 A6
Wilmslow Park Rd SK9 .137 D7
Wilmslow Prep Sch SK9 .137 B7
Wilmslow Rd
Alderley Edge SK9 .137 A2
Cheadle SK8 .122 D3
Cheadle SK8 .122 D5
Gatley SK8,SK9 .131 C6
Handforth SK9 .131 D4
Manchester M14 .98 C2
Manchester M14,M20 .110 B5
Manchester M20 .110 C1
Woodford SK7 .132 C1
Wythenshaw M90,WA15,SK9 M90,WA15,SK9 .129 F5
Wilmslow Sta SK9 .137 C7
Wilmur Ave
Manchester M7 .155 E6
Whitefield M45 .63 A7
Wilpshire Ave 8 M12 .99 B3
Wilsford Cl WA3 .74 B1
Wilshaw Gr OL7 .85 B6
Wilshaw La OL7 .85 A5
Wilson Ave Heywood OL10 .29 A2
Swinton M27 .62 B2
Wigan WN6 .37 B2
Wilson Cres OL6 .85 E4
Wilson Fold Ave BL6 .39 F8
Wilson Rd Manchester M9 .64 D1
Manchester SK4 .168 B4
Wilson St 7 Bolton BL3 .145 F6
Bury BL9 .141 A1
Farnworth BL4 .60 E8
Horwich BL6 .22 A4
Hyde SK14 .167 E2
Manchester M11 .165 A8
Manchester M12,M13 .163 C6
Oldham OL3 .69 A6
Oldham OL8 .66 E4
Radcliffe M26 .43 F4
Rochdale OL12 .139 F8
1 Sale M33 .108 B5
Stretford M32 .96 E4
Wilson Way OL1 .153 F8
Wilson's Terr SK13 .116 B8
Wilsons Pk M40 .157 E5
Wilsthorpe Cl M19 .111 C7
Wilton Ave Gatley SK8 .131 C7
Manchester M16 .97 A3
Manchester M25 .63 D2
Pendlebury M27 .80 C7
Wigan WN2 .37 F2
Wilton Cotts WA3 .75 A2

Wilton Cres SK9 . . . .**136** F2
Wilton Ct Middleton M25 . . .**63** E8
Reddish M34 . . . .**100** A4
Wilton Dr
Altrincham WA15 . . . .**129** C2
Whitefield BL9 . . . .**45** A5
Wilton Gdns M26 . . . .**44** C5
Wilton Gr Heywood OL10 . . .**29** D1
Reddish M34 . . . .**100** A4
Wilton La WA3 . . . .**91** B5
Wilton Paddock M34 . . . . .**100** A4
Wilton Pl M3 . . . .**158** D2
Wilton Rd Bolton BL1 . . . . .**24** E5
Manchester M21 . . . .**109** B8
Manchester M8 . . . .**64** A2
Salford M6 . . . .**80** B4
Shevington WN6 . . . .**36** A6
Wilton St Ashton-in-M WN4 . .**73** A6
Bolton BL1 . . . .**143** F3
Denton M34 . . . .**100** E4
Heywood OL10 . . . .**29** C2
Manchester M13 . . . .**163** B6
Middleton M24 . . . .**64** B7
Oldham OL9 . . . .**66** B3
Prestwich M25 . . . .**63** C4
Reddish SK5 . . . .**99** F2
Whitefield M45 . . . .**62** F7
Wigan WN1 . . . .**151** D7
Wilton Terr OL12 . . . .**139** E8
Wiltshire Ave SK5 . . . . . .**112** C4
Wiltshire Cl BL9 . . . .**45** A8
Wiltshire Dr Glossop SK13 **116** F8
Haslingden BB4 . . . .**1** B8
Wiltshire Pl WN5 . . . .**54** C6
Wiltshire Rd
Failsworth M35 . . . .**84** A6
Oldham OL9 . . . .**152** B5
Partington M31 . . . .**105** E2
Wiltshire St M7 . . . .**155** E6
Wimberry Hill Rd BL5 . . . .**39** D3
Wimbledon Dr
Rochdale OL11 . . . .**139** D5
Stockport SK3 . . . .**123** C7
Wimbledon Rd M35 . . . . . .**84** B8
Wimborne Ave
Chadderton OL9 . . . .**48** A1
Urmston M41 . . . .**95** D3
Wimborne Cl Cheadle SK8 **123** C4
Horwich BL6 . . . .**22** F1
Wimborne Rd WN5 . . . . . .**54** A8
Wimpenny Ho OL8 . . . . . .**153** E5
Wimpole St
Ashton-u-L OL6 . . . .**166** C3
4 Oldham OL1 . . . .**49** A1
Wimpory St M11 . . . .**99** D7
Winbolt St SK2 . . . .**124** C4
Winby St **1** OL11 . . . .**31** A4
Wincanton Ave M23 . . . . .**120** D8
Wincanton Dr BL1 . . . .**24** D7
Wincanton Pk OL4 . . . .**67** D6
Wince Cl M24 . . . .**65** C6
Wincham Cl **21** M15 . . . . .**162** D6
Wincham Rd M33 . . . .**107** E2
Winchcombe Cl WN7 . . . . .**75** E1
Winchester Ave
Ashton-in-M WN4 . . . .**73** A3
Ashton-u-L OL6 . . . .**85** D8
Chadderton OL9 . . . .**47** F1
Denton M34 . . . .**100** F1
Heywood OL10 . . . .**46** C8
Manchester M25 . . . .**63** C2
Tyldesley M29 . . . .**77** C7
Winchester Cl Bury BL8 . . . .**27** C7
4 Orrell WN5 . . . .**53** F7
Rochdale OL11 . . . .**30** A7
Wilmslow SK9 . . . .**136** E5
Winchester Dr Sale M33 . .**107** D4
Stockport SK4 . . . .**168** B2
Winchester Gr WN3 . . . . .**151** D6
Winchester Pk M20 . . . . . .**109** F3
Winchester Rd
Altrincham WA15 . . . .**120** C1
Ashton-in-M WA11 . . . .**72** E1
Dukinfield SK16 . . . .**102** A7
Longshaw WN5 . . . .**53** D7
Radcliffe M26 . . . .**43** D5
Salford M30 . . . .**80** A4
Salford M6 . . . .**80** C4
Urmston M41 . . . .**95** E3
Winchester Way BL2 . . . . .**25** D1
Wincle Ave SK12 . . . .**134** A2
Wincombe St M14 . . . .**98** B2
Windale M28 . . . .**60** B3
Windcroft Cl M11 . . . .**165** A8
Winder Dr M4 . . . .**159** C2
Winder St BL1 . . . .**145** F8
Windermere Ave
Atherton M46 . . . .**58** D5
Little Lever BL3 . . . .**43** A4
Pendlebury M27 . . . .**80** A7
Reddish M34 . . . .**100** B2
Sale M33 . . . .**108** D2
Windermere Cl
Manchester M11 . . . .**165** A8
Prestwich M25 . . . .**62** F5
Stretford M32 . . . .**96** C3
Windermere Cres OL7 . . . .**84** F4
Windermere Dr
Adlington PR6 . . . .**21** B8
Alderley Edge SK9 . . . . . .**136** F1
Bury BL9 . . . .**44** E7
Ramsbottom BL0 . . . .**138** C7
Windermere Gr WN7 . . . . .**75** E6
Windermere Ho **3** M28 . . .**60** E2
Windermere Mews M24 . .**46** E3

Windermere Rd
Abram WN2 . . . .**74** B8
Dukinfield SK14 . . . .**101** C5
Farnworth BL4 . . . .**59** E7
Handforth SK9 . . . .**131** C4
High Lane SK6 . . . .**134** E8
Hindley WN2 . . . .**56** E5
Ince-in-M WN3 . . . .**56** B7
Leigh WN7 . . . .**75** E5
Middleton M24 . . . .**46** D3
Orrell WN5 . . . .**53** F8
Royton OL2 . . . .**48** D6
Stalybridge SK15 . . . .**86** A4
Stockport SK1,SK2 . . . . . .**124** B7
Urmston M41 . . . .**95** C1
Windermere St
Bolton BL1 . . . .**143** F2
5 Wigan WN1 . . . .**37** E1
Windermere Wlk **6** OL4 . .**67** C7
Winders Way M6 . . . .**81** B4
Windfields Cl SK8 . . . . . .**123** B3
Windham St OL16 . . . .**15** C3
Windle Ave M9 . . . .**63** F3
Windle Ct SK2 . . . .**124** E5
Windlehurst Dr M28 . . . . . .**78** B7
Windlehurst Old Rd SK6 .**125** F2
Windlehurst Rd SK6 . . . . .**125** E2
Windleshaw St WN3 . . . . .**151** E6
Windley St BL2 . . . .**148** A8
Windmill Ave M5 . . . .**161** B7
Windmill Cl Reddish M34 . .**100** B2
Walkden M28 . . . .**60** C5
Wigan WN1 . . . .**151** D8
Windmill Ct **21** OL16 . . . . .**31** B6
Windmill Hts WN8 . . . .**53** A8
Windmill La Denton M34 . .**100** C2
Reddish SK5 . . . .**100** A1
Tyldesley M29 . . . .**76** F4
Windmill Lane Ind Est
M34 . . . .**100** C2
Windmill Rd Sale M33 . . . .**108** F3
Walkden M28 . . . .**60** C5
Windmill St
Manchester M2 . . . .**162** F8
20 Middleton M24 . . . . . .**31** B6
Windover Cl BL5 . . . .**59** A7
Windover St **1** BL3 . . . . .**146** A4
Windrush Ave BL0 . . . .**11** A2
Windrush Dr
Manchester M9 . . . .**157** D7
Westhoughton BL5 . . . .**39** F1
Windrush The OL12 . . . . . .**14** C4
Windsor Ave Adlington PR7 . .**20** F6
Failsworth M35 . . . .**84** B8
Gatley SK8 . . . .**122** A5
Heywood OL10 . . . .**29** B2
Irlam M44 . . . .**94** B3
Little Lever BL3 . . . .**43** A3
Newton-le-W WA12 . . . . . .**89** D2
Oldham OL9 . . . .**66** A4
Sale M33 . . . .**108** B6
Swinton M27 . . . .**62** A2
Tyldesley M29 . . . .**77** A6
Urmston M41 . . . .**94** F2
Walkden M38 . . . .**60** B5
Whitefield M45 . . . .**63** A4
Wilmslow SK9 . . . .**136** E5
Windsor Cl Poynton SK12 .**133** D4
Ramsbottom BL8 . . . .**11** A1
Windsor Comm High Sch
The M5 . . . .**81** A2
Windsor Cres Aspull WN2 . .**38** D5
Manchester M25,M8 . . . . . .**63** E3
Windsor Ct Bolton BL3 . . . .**147** D2
Sale M33 . . . .**107** F5
Windsor Dr
Ashton-in-M WA11 . . . .**89** A7
Ashton-u-L OL7 . . . .**84** F4
Bury BL8 . . . .**44** B8
Droylsden M34 . . . .**84** D1
Dukinfield SK16 . . . .**101** F7
Horwich BL6 . . . .**22** F7
Marple SK6 . . . .**125** E5
Sale WA14 . . . .**119** F8
Stalybridge SK15 . . . .**86** A3
Windsor Gr Ashton-u-L OL6 .**85** C7
Bolton BL1 . . . .**142** C1
Cheadle SK8 . . . .**131** F8
Hindley WN2 . . . .**57** B3
Kearsley M26 . . . .**61** B7
Romiley SK6 . . . .**113** E2
Windsor Rd
Ashton-in-M WN4 . . . .**73** C1
Billinge WN5 . . . .**71** F5
Bolton BL7 . . . .**25** A7
Bredbury SK6 . . . .**112** C3
Droylsden M43 . . . .**83** E1
Failsworth M40 . . . .**83** E4
Golborne WA3 . . . .**90** C8
Hazel Grove SK7 . . . .**124** F2
Hyde SK14 . . . .**113** E7
Leigh WN7 . . . .**76** E6
Manchester M19 . . . .**99** A1
Manchester M25 . . . .**63** E3
Manchester M9 . . . .**157** E7
Oldham OL8 . . . .**66** D4
Orrell WN8 . . . .**53** A8
Reddish M34 . . . .**100** A3
Windsor St Failsworth M35 .**84** A8
Failsworth M40 . . . .**83** E4
Manchester M18 . . . .**99** C4
Rochdale OL11 . . . .**31** A5
Salford M5 . . . .**81** B1
Stockport SK1 . . . .**124** B3
Tyldesley M46 . . . .**58** E2
Wigan WN1 . . . .**37** D1
Windsor Terr Milnrow OL16 .**31** E6

Windsor Terr continued
Rochdale OL16 . . . .**31** C7
Windsor Wlk SK2 . . . .**170** F6
Windy Bank Ave WA3 . . . . .**90** E8
Windy Harbour La BL7 . . . .**25** B8
Windybank M9 . . . .**64** C5
Windyhill Dr BL3 . . . .**146** A3
Winfell Dr M40 . . . .**160** D3
Winfield Ave M20 . . . .**110** D6
Winfield Dr M18 . . . .**99** D6
Winfield Gr SK6 . . . .**114** B1
Winfield St M9 . . . .**157** E8
Winford St M9 . . . .**157** E8
Wingate Ave BL8 . . . .**27** B2
Wingate Dr
Altrincham WA15 . . . .**120** B5
Manchester M20 . . . .**110** C2
Whitefield M45 . . . .**44** E1
Wingate Rd
Manchester SK4 . . . .**168** C4
Walkden M28 . . . .**60** B4
Wingate St OL11 . . . .**13** E1
Wingates Gr BL5 . . . .**39** D3
Wingates Ind Est BL5 . . . . .**39** D2
Wingates La BL5 . . . .**39** E5
Wingates Rd WN1 . . . .**37** C4
Wingates Sq BL5 . . . .**39** E3
Wingfield Ave SK9 . . . . . .**136** E6
Wingfield Cl WN6 . . . .**37** A4
Wingfield Dr
Pendlebury M27 . . . .**80** A6
Wilmslow SK9 . . . .**136** E6
Wingfield Gr SK13 . . . . . .**116** F7
Wingfield St M32 . . . .**96** D4
Wingfield Villas OL15 . . . . .**16** C7
Wingrove Ho **3** M6 . . . . .**154** F2
Wings Gr OL10 . . . .**46** D7
Winhill Rd SK22 . . . .**127** C1
Winifred Ave BL9 . . . .**28** F4
Winifred Rd Failsworth M40 **83** B7
Farnworth BL4 . . . .**42** A1
Manchester M20 . . . .**110** B3
Stockport SK2 . . . .**124** A4
Urmston M41 . . . .**95** D2
Winifred St **2** Eccles M30 .**79** B1
Hyde SK14 . . . .**113** E7
Ince-in-M WN3 . . . .**151** E6
Ramsbottom BL0 . . . .**138** B5
Rochdale OL12 . . . .**14** B1
Winmarith Dr WA15 . . . . .**129** D7
Winmarleigh Cl BL8 . . . . . .**26** F1
Winmarleigh Gdns WN7 . .**75** E3
Winnall Wlk **3** M40 . . . . . .**83** C6
Winnard St WA3 . . . .**74** B2
Winnats Cl SK13 . . . .**116** F8
Winnie St M40 . . . .**83** A8
Winning Hill Cl M18 . . . . . .**99** D4
Winnington Gn SK2 . . . . . .**124** D6
Winnington Rd SK6 . . . . . .**125** F7
Winnipeg Quay M5 . . . . . .**96** F7
Winnows The M34 . . . . . .**100** D3
Winscar Rd WN2 . . . .**56** D6
Winscombe Dr M40 . . . . .**159** C4
Winser St M1 . . . .**163** A8
Winsfield Rd SK7 . . . .**133** E8
Winsford Dr OL11 . . . .**29** F5
Winsford Gr BL3 . . . .**40** F5
Winsford Rd M14 . . . .**98** A1
Winsford Wlk M33 . . . . . .**108** E3
Winskill Rd M44 . . . .**106** A8
Winslade Cl Oldham OL4 . . .**49** D1
Stockport SK7 . . . .**124** A2
Winsley Rd M23 . . . .**108** F2
Winslow Ave SK14 . . . . . .**103** A4
Winslow Pl M19 . . . .**110** F6
Winslow Rd BL3 . . . .**40** D3
Winslow St M11 . . . .**165** A8
Winsmoor Dr WN2 . . . . . .**56** E4
Winson Cl BL3 . . . .**147** E4
Winstanley Cl **6** M6 . . . . .**80** D5
Winstanley Coll WN5 . . . . . .**53** F3
Winstanley Pl WN1 . . . . . .**151** E6
Winstanley Prim Sch WN3 **54** C2
Winstanley Rd
Ashton-in-M WN2 . . . .**73** F8
Garswood WN4 &WN5 . . . . .**72** B6
Garswood WN5 . . . .**72** A8
Manchester M40 . . . .**160** D3
Orrell WN5 . . . .**53** F3
Sale M33 . . . .**108** C5
Winstanley St WN5 . . . . . .**54** F6
Winster Ave
Manchester M20 . . . .**109** E4
Manchester M7 . . . .**81** B6
Stretford M32 . . . .**96** A3
Winster Cl Bolton BL2 . . . . .**25** F1
Whitefield M45 . . . .**63** B8
Winster Dr Bolton BL2 . . . . .**25** F1
3 Middleton M24 . . . . . .**46** E2
Platt Bridge WN2 . . . .**55** F2
Winster Gn M30 . . . .**95** B8
Winster Gr SK2 . . . .**124** A6
Winster Mews **17** SK13 . .**171** E2
Winster Rd M30 . . . .**95** B8
Winston Ave
Little Lever BL3 . . . .**43** C3
Newton-le-W WA12 . . . . . .**89** C3
Rochdale OL16 . . . .**29** E6
Winston Cl Marple SK6 . . . .**125** D7
Radcliffe M26 . . . .**43** F5
Winston Rd
Manchester M40,M9 . . . . .**157** F8
Manchester M9 . . . .**64** F1
Sale M33 . . . .**107** F5
Winswell Cl M11 . . . .**83** B2
Winter Hey La BL6 . . . .**22** B3
Winter St BL1 . . . .**143** D3
Winterbottom Gr SK14 . . .**102** F2

Winterbottom St OL9 . . . .**153** D7
Winterbottom Wlk **4**
SK14 . . . .**102** F2
Winterburn Ave Bolton BL2 **25** B6
Manchester M21 . . . .**109** D4
Winterburn Gn SK2 . . . . . .**124** E5
Winterdyne St M9 . . . . . .**157** E7
Winterfield Dr BL3 . . . . . .**146** A3
Winterford Ave M13 . . . . .**164** D5
Winterford Rd
Manchester M7,M8 . . . . . .**155** F7
Mossley OL5 . . . .**68** E1
Wintergreen Wlk **3** M31 .**105** F3
Wintermans Rd M21 . . . . .**109** E7
Winterslow Ave M23 . . . . .**108** D1
Winterton Cl BL5 . . . .**40** A1
Winterton Rd SK5 . . . . . .**100** A1
Winthrop Ave M40 . . . .**65** D1
Winton Ave Denton M34 . . .**100** D7
Failsworth M40 . . . .**65** D1
Wigan WN5 . . . .**54** D5
Winton Cl SK7 . . . .**123** D1
Winton Ct WA14 . . . .**119** C2
Winton Gn BL6 . . . .**22** F1
Winton Gr BL3 . . . .**40** E4
Winton Rd
Altrincham WA14 . . . .**119** C2
Golborne WA3 . . . .**90** E6
Pendlebury M6 . . . .**80** D5
Winward St Bolton BL3 . . .**146** B3
Leigh WN7 . . . .**75** B5
13 Westhoughton BL5 . . . .**39** E1
Winwick La WA3 . . . .**90** E3
Winwick Rd WA12 . . . .**89** F1
Winwood Dr M24 . . . .**47** B1
Winwood Fold M24 . . . .**46** F4
Winwood Rd M20 . . . .**122** C8
Wirral Cl Culcheth WA3 . . . .**91** E4
Swinton M27 . . . .**62** A2
Wirral Cres SK3 . . . .**123** A8
Wirral Dr WN3 . . . .**54** C2
Wisbech Dr M23 . . . .**108** F1
Wisbeck Rd BL2 . . . .**148** C8
Wiseley St M11 . . . .**164** E8
Wiseman Terr M25 . . . .**63** C4
Wishaw Sq M21 . . . .**109** E7
Wisley Cl SK5 . . . .**112** A8
Wistaria Rd M18 . . . .**99** D5
Withall Ho **2** WN1 . . . . . .**151** D8
Witham Ave M22 . . . .**121** E5
Witham Cl Heywood OL10 . . .**29** A3
Standish WN6 . . . .**19** D1
Witham St OL6 . . . .**85** E4
Withenfield Rd M23 . . . . .**120** F8
Withens Gn SK2 . . . .**124** E6
Withern **18** OL10 . . . .**29** C2
Withington Ave WA3 . . . . . .**92** A4
Withington Dr M29 . . . .**77** C7
Withington Girls Sch
M14 . . . .**110** C8
Withington Gn M24 . . . .**47** A4
Withington Hospl M20 . . . .**109** F6
Withington La WN2 . . . .**38** C2
Withington Rd
Manchester M16,M21 . . . .**109** D8
Manchester M16,M21 . . . . .**97** D2
Withington St
Heywood OL10 . . . .**46** E8
Salford M6 . . . .**81** B2
Withins Ave M26 . . . .**44** C5
Withins Cl BL2 . . . .**42** E8
Withins Dr BL2 . . . .**42** E8
Withins Gr BL2 . . . .**42** E8
Withins La Bolton BL2 . . . . .**42** E8
Radcliffe M26 . . . .**44** C5
Withins Rd Culcheth WA3 . . .**91** F3
Oldham OL8 . . . .**66** B2
Withins Sch BL2 . . . .**25** E2
Withins Sports Ctr BL2 . . . .**25** E2
Withins St M26 . . . .**44** C4
Withnell Cl WN6 . . . .**37** A2
Withnell Dr BL8 . . . .**27** A1
Withnell Rd M19 . . . .**110** D3
Withy Gr M4 . . . .**159** A2
Withy Tree Gr **1** M34 . . . .**101** A2
Withycombe Pl M6 . . . .**81** A5
Withypool Dr SK2 . . . .**124** C5
Witley Dr M33 . . . .**107** D6
Witley Rd OL16 . . . .**31** B7
Witney Cl **18** BL1 . . . .**143** E2
Wittenbury Rd SK4 . . . . . .**168** B2
Wittenham Ho SK9 . . . . . .**131** D2
Witterage Cl M12 . . . .**164** F6
Witton Wlk M8 . . . .**155** F6
Woburn Ave Bolton BL2 . . . .**25** C3
Leigh WN7 . . . .**57** D1
Newton-le-W WA12 . . . . . .**89** D2
Woburn Cl Manchester M16 **97** F3
Milnrow OL16 . . . .**31** E6
Woburn Ct SK12 . . . .**133** F4
Woburn Dr
Altrincham WA15 . . . .**120** B2
Bury BL9 . . . .**44** F5
Woburn Rd M16 . . . .**97** A2
Woden St M5 . . . .**161** C7
Woden's Ave M5 . . . .**161** C7
Woking Rd SK8 . . . .**132** A7
Woking Terr M41 . . . .**131** E1
Wolfenden Cty Prim Sch
BL1 . . . .**143** E2
Wolfenden Gn BB4 . . . .**2** F8
Wolfenden St BL1 . . . .**143** E2
Wolfenden Terr **28** BL1 . . .**143** E2
Wolford Dr M29 . . . .**59** C1

Wolfreton Cres M27 . . . . . .**62** A3
Wolfson Sq WN4 . . . .**72** F4
Wollaton Wlk M34 . . . . . .**100** E1
Wolmer St WN4 . . . .**73** A4
Wolseley Ho M33 . . . .**108** C6
Wolseley Pl M20 . . . .**110** B5
Wolseley Rd M33 . . . .**108** C6
Wolseley St **1** Bury BL8 . . . .**27** B1
Newhey OL16 . . . .**32** B4
Wolsey Cl Ashton-in-M WN4 . .**73** A5
Radcliffe M26 . . . .**44** A3
Wolsey Dr WA14 . . . .**119** A1
Wolsey St Heywood OL10 . . .**29** C1
Radcliffe M26 . . . .**44** A3
Wolstenholme Ave BL9 . . . .**27** F6
Wolstenholme Coalpit La
OL11,OL12 . . . .**13** B2
Wolstenholme La
OL11,OL12 . . . .**13** C2
Wolstenvale Cl M24 . . . . . .**47** B1
Wolver Cl M38 . . . .**60** B6
Wolverton Ave OL8 . . . .**66** D3
Wolverton Dr SK9 . . . .**131** D1
Wolvesey OL11 . . . .**139** E6
Wolveton St M11 . . . .**164** F7
Wood Bank Rd OL15 . . . . . .**16** A3
Wood Bank Terr OL5 . . . . . .**68** D2
Wood Brook La OL4 . . . . . .**68** B7
Wood Brook Rd OL4 . . . . . .**68** B7
Wood Cottage Cl **4** M28 . . .**59** F3
Wood Cotts SK6 . . . .**113** A6
Wood Cres OL4 . . . .**67** E3
Wood Edge Cl BL4 . . . .**42** C2
Wood End SK7 . . . .**123** D2
Wood Fold BL7 . . . .**25** C6
Wood Gdns SK9 . . . .**137** B2
Wood Gr Denton M34 . . . . .**100** F4
Whitefield M45 . . . .**44** F3
Wood Hey Cl M26 . . . .**43** D3
Wood Hey Gr
2 Denton M34 . . . .**101** A2
Rochdale OL12 . . . .**14** F4
Wood La Altrincham WA15 . .**120** B5
Altrincham WA16 . . . .**129** B1
Altrincham WA16 . . . .**129** D1
Ashton-u-L OL6,OL7 . . . . . .**85** B5
Marple SK6 . . . .**125** E5
Middleton M24 . . . .**65** B7
Partington M31 . . . .**105** D3
Wrightington Bar WN6 . . . . .**18** E8
Wood La N SK10 . . . .**134** B1
Wood Lea Bank **8** BB4 . . . .**2** F1
Wood Lea Rd BB4 . . . .**2** C4
Wood Mount WA15 . . . . . .**120** B5
Wood Rd Manchester M16 . . .**97** D3
Sale WA15 . . . .**108** B1
Wood Rd N M16 . . . .**97** C3
Wood Road La Bury SK6 . . . .**27** B8
Ramsbottom BL9 . . . .**11** C1
Wood Sorrel Way WA3 . . . . .**90** E8
Wood Sq Droylsden M43 . . .**100** A8
Oldham OL3 . . . .**69** B6
Wood St Altrincham WA14 . .**119** D4
Ashton-u-L OL6 . . . .**166** B2
Atherton M46 . . . .**58** B4
Bolton BL1 . . . .**145** F7
Bury BL8 . . . .**27** C3
Cheadle SK8 . . . .**122** D6
Denton M34 . . . .**100** F4
Dukinfield SK16 . . . .**101** C6
Eccles M30 . . . .**79** F1
Glossop SK13 . . . .**116** C8
Golborne WA3 . . . .**90** B8
Hindley WN2 . . . .**57** B3
Hollingworth SK14 . . . . . .**103** D5
Horwich BL6 . . . .**22** C3
Hyde SK14 . . . .**167** E2
Littleborough OL15 . . . .**16** B5
Manchester M11 . . . .**165** B8
Manchester M3 . . . .**158** F1
Middleton M24 . . . .**64** F8
Newhey OL16 . . . .**32** C4
Oldham OL1 . . . .**67** B8
Radcliffe M26 . . . .**61** E8
Ramsbottom BL0 . . . .**138** B5
Rochdale OL16 . . . .**31** A6
Shaw OL2 . . . .**48** F8
6 Stalybridge SK15 . . . . .**85** F2
Stockport SK3 . . . .**169** D1
Tyldesley M29 . . . .**77** B8
Westhoughton BL5 . . . .**57** E8
Wigan WN3 . . . .**150** C2
Wigan WN5 . . . .**54** F7
Wood Terr BL2 . . . .**26** D1
Wood Top Ave OL11 . . . . . .**29** F5
Wood Top Cl SK2 . . . .**124** E7
Wood View Heywood OL10 . .**29** C4
Shevington WN6 . . . .**36** B5
Wythenshawe M22 . . . . . .**109** D1
Wood's Hospl SK13 . . . . . .**104** C3
Wood's La WN4 . . . .**73** C5
Wood's St WN3 . . . .**150** C7
Woodacres Ct SK9 . . . . . .**136** F6
Woodall Cl M33 . . . .**108** D4
Woodark Cl OL4 . . . .**67** F5
Woodbank Bolton BL2 . . . . .**25** D2
Stockport SK1 . . . .**112** B1
Woodbank Ave
Bredbury SK6 . . . .**112** E3
Stockport SK1 . . . .**124** C8
Woodbank Ct M41 . . . .**95** B3
Woodbank Dr BL8 . . . .**27** C4
Woodbank Works Ind Est
SK1 . . . .**112** B1
Woodbine Ave M44 . . . . . .**105** D4
Woodbine Cres SK2 . . . . .**170** F7
Woodbine Rd Bolton BL3 . .**146** C3

Woodbine Rd *continued*
Lymm WA13 117 B4
Woodbine St OL16 31 A5
Woodbine St E OL16 31 B5
Woodbine Terr 1 M44 94 A2
Woodbourne Ct M33 108 B2
Woodbourne Rd
Manchester SK4 111 C6
Sale M33 108 A2
Woodbray Ave M19 110 E5
Woodbridge Ave M34 100 E7
Woodbridge Gdns OL12 14 C2
Woodbridge Gr M23 109 A1
Woodbridge Rd M41 94 D3
Woodbrook Ave
Hyde SK14 167 F2
Oldham OL4 68 B7
Woodbrook Dr WN3 54 D4
Woodbrook Rd SK9 137 C1
Woodburn Dr BL1 142 B3
Woodburn Rd M22 121 D8
Woodburn Row M29 77 C3
Woodbury Cres SK16 101 B7
Woodbury Rd SK3 123 B7
Woodchurch WN1 37 F1
Woodchurch Cl 3 BL1 143 E1
Woodchurch Wlk
Oldham OL9 152 B6
5 Sale M33 108 F3
Woodcock Cl
Droylsden M43 84 C3
Rochdale OL11 29 F7
Woodcock Dr WN2 56 B2
Woodcock Gr SK13 104 E1
Woodcock Ho WN1 151 D8
Woodcock Sq 10 WN1 150 C8
Woodcote Ave SK7 123 C2
Woodcote Rd
Sale M14,M31 107 A2
Sale WA14 107 D1
Woodcote View SK9 131 F1
Woodcote Wlk M8 156 C8
Woodcott Bank BL1 143 E4
Woodcott Gr 3 SK9 131 E1
Woodcourt WN3 150 B6
Woodcroft
Appley Bridge WN6 35 E6
Stockport SK2 124 D6
Woodcroft Ave M19 110 E4
Wooddagger Cl WN2 56 F5
Woodeaton Cl OL2 49 A4
Wooded Cl BL9 27 F5
Woodedge WN4 73 A3
Woodend OL2 149 C8
Woodend Ct SK14 167 D1
Woodend Ctr Ind Pk OL5 68 D2
Woodend Dr SK15 102 D6
Woodend La
Altrincham WA16 129 E1
Hyde SK14 167 D1
Littleborough OL12 15 D6
Stalybridge SK15 102 D6
Woodend Mills OL4 67 F5
Woodend Rd
Stockport SK3 123 F4
Wythenshawe M22 121 D4
Woodend St Oldham OL1 48 E1
Oldham OL4 67 F5
Woodend View OL5 68 D2
Woodfield M22 121 D3
Woodfield Ave Hyde SK14 113 D8
Rochdale OL12 14 E2
Romiley SK6 113 A4
Woodfield Cl
Hadfield SK13 103 F5
Oldham OL8 66 C4
Woodfield Cres
Ashton-in-M WN4 73 A2
Bredbury SK6 112 F2
Woodfield Ct SK2 124 A4
Woodfield Dr M28 78 B6
Woodfield Gr Eccles M30 79 C1
Farnworth BL4 60 C6
Sale M33 108 A6
Woodfield Mews SK14 113 D8
Woodfield Prim Sch WN1 37 C4
Woodfield Rd
Altrincham WA14 119 C6
Bramhall SK8 132 B7
Manchester M24 64 E6
Manchester M8 64 A1
Salford M6 154 D4
Woodfield St Aspull WN2 38 A3
Bolton BL3 42 A3
Woodfield Terr OL10 29 E3
Woodfields Ret Pk BL9 140 F3
Woodfold Ave M19 99 A2
Woodfold Prim Sch WN6 36 D8
Woodford Rd M35 84 A7
Woodford Ave
Dukinfield M34 101 A4
Eccles M30 79 B2
Golborne WA3 90 D7
Shaw OL2 49 D7
Woodford Ct
Droylsden M43 100 B8
3 Hindley WN2 56 E6
Woodford Dr M27 61 E2
Woodford Gdns M20 110 A2
Woodford Gr BL3 146 C4
Woodford Rd
Bramhall SK12 133 B6
Bramhall SK7 132 E4
Woodford St
4 Hindley WN2 56 E6
8 Wigan WN5 54 B6
Woodgarth WN7 75 C5
Woodgarth Ave M40 83 D5
Woodgarth Dr M27 79 E6
Woodgarth La M28 78 F5
Woodgate Ave Bury BL9 28 D4
Rochdale OL11 30 A6
Woodgate Cl SK6 112 F3
Woodgate Dr M25 63 C6
Woodgate Hill Rd
Bury BL9 141 C4
Bury BL9 28 D4
Woodgate Rd M16 97 E1
Woodgate St BL3 42 A3
Woodgrange Cl 2 M6 154 E2
Woodgreen Cl 1 WN2 56 D4
Woodgreen Dr M26 62 A8
Woodhall Ave
Manchester M20 110 A7
Whitefield M45 62 D6
Woodhall Cl Bolton BL2 25 C3
Bury BL8 27 D5
Woodford SK7 132 E3
Woodhall Cres SK5 112 A4
Woodhall Rd SK5 169 F4
Woodhall St M35 83 F8
Woodhalt Rd M8 156 A8
Woodham Rd M23 108 F1
Woodham Wlk BL3 145 D5
Woodhead Cl Oldham OL4 67 E7
Ramsbottom BL0 11 C4
Woodhead Dr WA15 119 F1
Woodhead Gr WN3 55 B2
Woodhead Rd
Altrincham WA15 119 F1
Glossop SK13 104 D4
Tintwistle SK13 104 B8
Woodhead St 6 M16 97 E4
Woodhey Ct M33 107 E1
Woodhey High Sch BL0 11 A3
Woodhey Rd BL0 11 A3
Woodheys SK4 110 F3
Woodheys Dr M33 107 D1
Woodheys Prim Sch M33 107 E2
Woodheys Rd OL15 16 A2
Woodheys St 1 M5 154 F1
Woodhill M24 46 F2
Woodhill Cl
Manchester M12 99 B4
Middleton M24 46 F2
Woodhill Dr M25 63 B3
Woodhill Fold BL8 140 D3
Woodhill Gr M25 63 B3
Woodhill Ho 3 M6 154 F3
Woodhill Rd Bury BL8 140 D3
Bury BL8 140 D4
Woodhill St BL8 140 D4
Woodhouse Ct M41 95 A4
Woodhouse Dr WN6 36 E2
Woodhouse Farm Cotts
OL12 13 D2
Woodhouse Knowl OL3 50 F4
Woodhouse La
Partington WA14 118 C4
Rochdale OL12 13 E3
Sale M33 107 C2
Sale M33 107 D2
Wigan WN6 36 E3
Wigan WN6 36 F2
Wigan WN6 37 A1
Wythenshawe M22 121 D4
Wythenshawe M22 130 D8
Wythenshawe M90 130 D7
Woodhouse La E WA15 108 A1
Woodhouse Park
Prim Sch M22 130 D8
Woodhouse Prim Sch
M41 95 A4
Woodhouse Rd Shaw OL2 32 C1
Urmston M41 94 F4
Urmston M41 95 A4
Wythenshawe M22 130 D8
Woodhouse St
Atherton M46 58 D2
Manchester M10,M40 157 F5
Manchester M18 99 E5
Woodhouses Prim Sch
M35 84 C6
Woodhurst Dr WN6 19 D1
Wooding Cl M31 106 A4
Woodlake Ave M21 109 C4
Woodland Ave Bolton BL3 42 B2
Hazel Grove SK7 124 E1
Hindley WN2 57 A3
Lymm WA13 117 A2
Newton-le-W WA12 89 F3
Reddish M18 99 E4
Woodland Cres M25 63 B2
Woodland Dr
Ashton-in-M WN4 73 B5
Lymm WA13 117 A2
Standish WN6 19 E2
Woodland Gr Bolton BL7 8 D2
Wigan WN1 37 D2
Woodland Pk OL2 48 B6
Woodland Rd
Heywood OL10 29 E3
Manchester M19 111 A7
Reddish M18 99 E4
Rochdale OL12 14 C2
Tyldesley M29 77 B7
Woodland St
Heywood OL10 29 D2
Manchester M12 165 B5
Rochdale OL12 15 A2
Woodland View BL7 25 B8
Woodland Way M24 64 F6
Woodlands Failsworth M35 83 E4
5 Urmston M41 95 C3
Woodlands Ave
Cheadle SK8 123 A2
Woodlands Ave *continued*
Eccles M30 95 A8
Ince-in-M WN3 151 F6
Irlam M44 94 A3
Leigh WN7 75 F3
Rochdale OL11 30 A6
Romiley SK6 113 A5
Stretford M32 96 D2
Swinton M27 79 D6
Urmston M41 94 C2
Whitefield M45 44 E1
Woodlands Cl
Cheadle SK8 132 A8
Mottram-in-L SK14 102 F1
Stalybridge SK15 102 D7
Tintwistle SK13 103 F6
Worsley M28 78 E7
Woodlands Ct
Altrincham WA15 119 E5
Stockport SK2 124 D8
Woodlands Dr
Atherton M46 58 F5
Romiley SK6 113 A5
Sale M23, M33 108 C1
Shevington WN6 35 F4
Stockport SK2 124 D8
Woodlands Gr Bury BL8 27 B3
Mottram-in-L SK14 102 F1
Woodlands Hospl M38 59 F4
Woodlands Ind Est WA12 89 C6
Woodlands La WA15 119 E5
Woodlands Park Rd SK2 124 D8
Woodlands Parkway
WA15 119 E6
Woodlands Rd
Altrincham WA14,WA15 119 E5
Ashton-u-L OL6 85 E6
Edenfield BL0 1 D2
Handforth SK9 131 E3
High Lane SK12 135 A6
Manchester M21 97 E1
Manchester M8 156 B7
Manchester SK4 110 E2
Milnrow OL16 31 F5
Sale M33 108 C4
Stalybridge SK15 102 D7
Wilmslow SK9 130 F1
Worsley M28 78 F7
Woodlands Road Sta M8 156 B7
Woodlands St M8 156 A8
Woodlands The Bolton BL6 40 C8
Bury BL8 140 D4
Heywood OL10 46 E8
Pendlebury M27 80 B7
Wigan WN1 37 D3
Woodlands View
Ramsbottom BL0 138 C6
Rochdale OL16 31 C8
Woodlark Cl M3 158 D1
Woodlawn Ct M16 97 C3
Woodlea Oldham OL9 65 D7
Worsley M28 78 E8
Woodlea Ave M19 110 E6
Woodlea Rd SK13 116 B7
Woodleigh WA14 119 A5
Woodleigh Ct SK9 137 A2
Woodleigh Dr M43 84 C4
Woodleigh Rd OL4 68 A7
Woodleigh St M9 64 F1
Woodles M30 79 C4
Woodley Ave M26 44 B1
Woodley Cl SK2 124 D7
Woodley Gr WN7 75 D5
Woodley Inf Sch SK6 113 C5
Woodley Jun Sch SK6 113 C5
Woodley Prec SK6 113 A5
Woodley St BL9 44 F8
Woodley Sta SK6 113 B6
Woodliffe St M16 161 C5
Woodlinn Wlk M9 157 D7
Woodman Dr BL9 27 E6
Woodman St SK1 169 E2
Woodmeadow Ct 9 OL5 68 C2
Woodmere Dr M9 64 E3
Woodmount Cl SK6 113 F2
Woodnook Rd WN6 35 E8
Woodpark Cl OL8 67 A3
Woodpecker Pl M28 78 D8
Woodridge Dr BL2 25 B1
Woodridings WA14 119 B3
Woodrow Way M44 105 F8
Woodrow Wlk M12 164 F6
Woodroyd Cl SK7 123 D1
Woodroyd Dr BL9 141 C3
Woodruff Wlk 7 M31 105 F3
Woodruffe Gdns SK6 125 A8
Woodrush Rd WN6 36 D3
Woods Ct Middleton M24 64 C7
Newton-le-W WA12 89 A3
Woods Gr SK8 132 B7
Woods La Bramhall SK8 132 B7
Uppermill OL3 51 A2
Woods Lea BL1 40 F7
Woods Rd Aspull WN2 38 C4
Irlam M44 105 F8
Woods The
4 Altrincham WA14 119 E6
Oldham OL4 68 B6
Rochdale OL11 30 C3
Woodseats La SK13 115 B6
Woodsend Circ M41 94 D3
Woodsend Crescent Rd
M41 94 D2
Woodsend Gn M41 94 D3
Woodsend Prim Sch M41 94 D3
Woodsend Rd M41 94 E3
Woodsend Rd S M41 94 E1
Woodshaw Gr 2 M28 78 C8
Woodside Manchester SK4 110 F1
Newhey OL16 32 C5
Shaw OL2 49 D8
Woodside Ave
Ashton-in-M WN4 73 A8
Manchester M19 110 F5
Walkden M28 60 F2
Woodside Cl WN8 53 C8
Woodside
Com Specl Schs BL1 40 E7
Woodside Ct M16 97 E2
Woodside Dr
High Lane SK6 134 F7
Hyde SK14 167 E1
Ramsbottom BL0 138 A5
Salford M6 80 C3
Woodside La SK12 133 E4
Woodside Mews SK7 123 C2
Woodside Pl BL2 148 C5
Woodside Rd Lymm WA13 117 B1
Manchester M16 97 B2
Woodside Sq BL2 148 C5
Woodside St SK15 86 E6
Woodsley Rd BL1 23 F2
Woodsmoor La SK2,SK3 124 A4
Woodsmoor Rd M27 79 D7
Woodsmoor Sta SK2 124 B4
Woodstock Ave
Bramhall SK8 132 A7
Newton-le-W WA12 89 D2
Reddish SK5 111 F5
Woodstock Cl
Heywood OL10 29 E2
Leigh WN7 75 E1
Woodstock Cres SK6 113 A5
Woodstock Dr Bolton BL1 142 A1
Bury BL8 26 D7
Eccles M28 79 A6
Pendlebury M27 80 B6
Woodstock Gn SK5 112 A5
Woodstock Rd
Altrincham WA14 119 C8
Failsworth M40 65 C1
Manchester M16 97 B3
Romiley SK6 113 A5
Woodstock St Oldham OL4 153 F6
12 Rochdale OL12 14 C1
Woodthorpe Cl M25 63 D2
Woodthorpe Dr SK8 123 A2
Woodthorpe Grange M25 63 D2
Woodvale
Altrincham WA14 119 C2
Middleton M24 47 A4
Woodvale Ave Aspull WN2 38 F3
Atherton M46 58 B5
Bolton BL3 147 D2
Woodvale Dr Bolton BL3 147 D2
Golborne WA3 74 E1
Woodvale Gdns BL3 147 D2
Woodvale Gr BL3 147 D2
Woodvale Wlk 18 M11 160 F1
Woodview Ave M19 110 F5
Woodville Dr Marple SK6 125 E4
Sale M33 108 A5
Stalybridge SK15 86 D3
Woodville Gr SK5 111 F6
Woodville Rd
Altrincham WA14 119 C3
Ince-in-M WN3 55 F4
Sale M33 108 A5
Woodville Terr 10 M40 64 F1
Woodward Cl BL9 27 F5
Woodward Ct M4 160 D2
Woodward Pl M4 159 C2
Woodward Rd M25 62 F2
Woodward St M4 159 C2
Woodwards Rd BL5 57 F6
Woodwise La M23 108 E1
Woodyates St WN5 54 F6
Wool Rd OL3 51 B2
Woolden Rd M44,WA3 105 B8
Woolden St Eccles M30 79 B3
8 Wigan WN5 54 F6
Woolfall Cl M12 164 F6
Woolfold Trad Est BL8 27 C3
Woollacot St 2 OL1 153 F6
Woollam Pl M3 162 D8
Woolley Ave SK12 133 D2
Woolley Bridge Rd SK13 103 E5
Woolley Cl SK14 171 D4
Woolley La
Hollingworth SK14 103 D6
Hollingworth SK14 171 D4
Woolley Mill La SK13 103 E7
Woolley St M8 159 A4
Woolley Terr 3 SK16 166 B1
Woolpack Gn 2 M6 154 F3
Woolston Dr M29 77 C8
Woolston Ho M6 80 C4
Woolton Cl
Ashton-in-M WN4 72 F5
3 Failsworth M40 65 C2
Wootton St SK14 167 D4
Worcester Ave
Brinnington SK5 112 C5
Denton M34 101 A1
Golborne WA3 90 B8
Hindley WN2 56 F6
Worcester Cl
Ashton-u-L OL6 85 D8
Romiley SK6 113 A1
Salford M6 80 C4
Whitefield BL9 45 A8
Worcester Gr SK13 116 F8
Worcester Rd
Cheadle SK8 123 A4
Little Lever BL3 42 F3
Middleton M24 64 F5
Worcester Rd *continued*
Sale M33 107 D3
Salford M6 80 C4
Swinton M27 61 D2
Worcester St
19 Bolton BL1 143 E1
Bury BL8 140 D4
Manchester M7 155 E6
Oldham OL9 152 B5
Rochdale OL11 30 E4
Wordsworth Ave
Atherton M46 58 E5
Bury BL9 44 F6
Droylsden M43 84 A2
Farnworth BL4 60 B7
Leigh WN7 75 D7
Longshaw WN5 53 D1
Manchester M8 156 A6
Orrell WN5 53 F6
Radcliffe M26 43 E4
Wigan WN1 37 C3
Wordsworth Cl SK16 102 A7
Wordsworth Cres
Ashton-u-L OL7 84 E5
Littleborough OL15 15 F2
Wordsworth Gdns M25 62 F3
Wordsworth Rd
Denton M34 113 A7
Manchester M16 97 B3
Middleton M24 47 B2
6 Oldham OL1 49 B1
Reddish SK5 99 D1
Swinton M27 61 E1
Walkden M38 60 B5
Wordsworth St
Bolton BL1 143 D2
Salford M6 81 C4
Wordsworth Trad Est
BL1 143 D2
Wordsworth Way OL11 29 E6
Workesleigh St 9 M40 83 C5
World Freight Terminal
M17 96 E5
World Way M90 130 B8
Worrall St Failsworth M40 83 A6
1 Rochdale OL12 14 D2
Salford M5 161 C7
Stockport SK3 170 E7
Worrell Cl M26 43 F4
Worsbrough Ave M28 60 C2
Worsefold St M40 83 A8
Worsel St BL3 146 C4
Worsley Ave
Manchester M40 65 A1
Walkden M28 60 A2
Worsley Brow M28 78 F6
Worsley Bsns Pk M28 77 E8
Worsley Cl WN5 54 C5
Worsley Cres SK2 124 B7
Worsley Ct 4 M14 98 C2
Worsley Gn WN5 54 B5
Worsley Gr
Manchester M19 99 A1
Walkden M28 60 A2
Worsley Mesnes
Com Prim Sch WN3 55 A4
Worsley Mesnes Dr WN3 150 A5
Worsley Pl Rochdale OL16 31 B7
Shaw OL2 149 A6
Worsley Rd Bolton BL3 146 A4
Eccles M30 79 B3
Farnworth BL4 60 D7
Swinton M27,M28 79 C6
Worsley Rd N M28 60 D5
Worsley St Bolton BL3 145 E5
Bury BL8 26 E7
Golborne WA3 90 A8
Manchester M15 162 D7
Manchester M3 158 E2
Manchester M3 162 E8
Oldham OL8 67 B5
Pendlebury M27 80 A7
Rochdale OL16 31 B7
Swinton M27 61 F2
Wigan WN5 54 B5
Worsley Terr WN1 37 C1
Worston Ave BL1 23 F3
Worth's La M34 113 A7
Worthing Cl SK2 124 D6
Worthing Gr M46 58 B3
Worthing St M14 98 B2
Worthington Ave
Heywood OL10 46 E7
9 Partington M31 105 F3
Worthington Cl
Ashton-u-L OL7 85 A5
7 Hattersley SK14 102 E2
Worthington Ct M33 108 E4
Worthington Dr M7 63 D1
Worthington Fold M46 58 B3
Worthington Prim Sch
M33 108 F4
Worthington Rd
Denton M34 101 B1
Sale M33 108 F4
Worthington St
Ashton-u-L OL7 85 A5
4 Bolton BL3 146 C3
Failsworth M40 83 C8
Hindley WN2 56 D6
Manchester M16 97 C4
Stalybridge SK15 85 F1
Worthington Way WN3 54 F2
Wortley Ave M6 80 C3
Wortley Gr M40 65 B2

Wotton Dr WN4 . . . . .73 D4
Wragby Cl BL8 . . . . .27 D5
Wrath Cl BL2 . . . . .25 B5
Wraxhall Cres WN7 . . . . . .75 D7
Wray Pl OL16 . . . . .31 C6
Wray St WN1 . . . . .151 E8
Wraysbury Wlk 15 M40 . . . .83 A7
Wrayton Lo M33 . . . . .108 B3
Wrekin Ave M23 . . . . .121 A3
Wren Ave M27 . . . . .62 B2
Wren Cl Droylsden M34 . . . .84 C1
Farnworth BL4 . . . . .59 F8
Hazel Grove SK2 . . . . . . .124 F5
Wigan WN5 . . . . .36 B1
Wren Dr Bury BL9 . . . . . . .141 B4
Irlam M44 . . . . .94 A4
Wren Gdns M24 . . . . .46 F1
Wren Gn OL16 . . . . .31 B6
Wren Nest Rd SK13 . . . . . .104 B1
Wren Nest Terr SK13 . . . . .104 C1
Wren St OL4 . . . . .67 C6
Wren's Nest Ave OL2 . . . . .149 C8
Wrenbury Ave M20 . . . . . .109 F7
Wrenbury Cl 6 WN5 . . . . . .54 B5
Wrenbury Cres SK3 . . . . .123 C6
Wrenbury Dr 5 Bolton BL7 .24 F6
Cheadle SK8 . . . . .122 E6
Rochdale OL16 . . . . .31 C3
Wrenbury Wlk M33 . . . . . .108 E3
Wrenswood Dr M28 . . . . . .78 C8
Wrexham Cl OL8 . . . . .66 B2
Wrigglesworth Cl BL8 . . . .26 F3
Wright Robinson Cl M11 .164 E8
Wright.Robinson
High Sch M18 . . . . .99 F6
Wright St Abram Brow WN2 .74 B7
Ashton-in-M WN4 . . . . . . .73 A6
Ashton-u-L M34 . . . . .100 E8
18 Ashton-u-L OL6 . . . . . .85 D4
Failsworth M35 . . . . .83 F8
Horwich BL6 . . . . .22 B4
Manchester M16 . . . . . . .161 C6
12 Oldham OL1 . . . . .67 A7
Oldham OL9 . . . . .152 B5
Platt Bridge WN2 . . . . . . .56 A3
Radcliffe M26 . . . . .43 F3
6 Wigan WN1 . . . . .37 E1
Wright St W 8 BL6 . . . . . . .22 B4
Wright Tree Villas M44 . . .105 E5
Wrightington Hospl WN6 .18 D2
Wrightington Mossy Lea
Prim Sch WN6 . . . . .18 F6
Wrightington St WN1 . . . . .37 C1
Wrights Bank N SK2 . . . . .124 E5
Wrights Bank S SK2 . . . . .124 E5
Wrigley Cres M35 . . . . . . .83 F7
Wrigley Fold M24 . . . . . . .46 D3
Wrigley Head M35 . . . . . . .83 F8
Wrigley Head Cres M35 . .83 F8
Wrigley Pl OL15 . . . . .15 F3
Wrigley Sq 9 OL4 . . . . . . .67 F6
Wrigley St Ashton-u-L OL6 .166 B4
Oldham OL4 . . . . .67 B7
Oldham OL4 . . . . .67 F6
Oldham OL4 . . . . .68 B8
Wrington Cl WN7 . . . . .75 D8
Wroe St Manchester M3 . .158 D2
11 Oldham OL4 . . . . .67 F6
Swinton M27 . . . . .61 F3
Wroe Terr M27 . . . . .61 F3
Wrotham Cl 2 M5 . . . . . . .81 A1
Wroxeter Wlk M12 . . . . . .164 F6
Wroxham Ave
Reddish M34 . . . . .100 A3
Urmston M41 . . . . .95 B3
Wroxham Cl BL8 . . . . .27 D5

Wroxham Rd M9 . . . . .64 B3
Wuerdle Cl OL16 . . . . .15 E4
Wuerdle Farm Way 3
OL16 . . . . .15 E4
Wuerdle Pl OL16 . . . . .15 E4
Wuerdle St 1 OL16 . . . . . .15 E4
Wyatt Ave M5 . . . . .161 C7
Wyatt Gr M7 . . . . .73 D3
Wyatt St Dukinfield SK16 . .101 C8
Stockport SK4 . . . . .169 E2
Wybersley Rd SK6 . . . . . .135 A8
Wych Fold SK14 . . . . .113 E7
Wych St OL6 . . . . .166 B2
Wychbury St M5,M6 . . . . .154 E2
Wychelm Rd M31 . . . . . . .105 F3
Wycherley Rd OL12 . . . . . .14 B2
Wychwood WA14 . . . . . . .119 B1
Wychwood Cl M24 . . . . . . .65 B7
Wycliffe Ave SK9 . . . . . . .137 A4
Wycliffe Ct M41 . . . . .95 C2
Wycliffe Rd M41 . . . . .95 C2
Wycliffe St Eccles M30 . . . .79 C2
Stockport SK4 . . . . .169 D2
Wycombe Ave M18 . . . . . . .99 E6
Wycombe Cl M41 . . . . .95 C5
Wycombe Dr M29 . . . . .77 B7
Wye Ave M35 . . . . .83 F7
Wye St OL8 . . . . .153 D5
Wyecroft Cl SK6 . . . . .113 B5
Wyke Pk OL4 . . . . .67 D6
Wykeham Cl WN3 . . . . . . .151 F6
Wykeham Gr OL12 . . . . . . .14 B1
Wykeham Mews BL1 . . . . .144 A7
Wykeham St M14 . . . . .98 A3
Wylam Wlk 4 M12 . . . . . . .99 B3
Wylde The BL9 . . . . .140 E2
Wynard Ave WN1 . . . . . . .37 D1
Wynchgate Rd SK7 . . . . . .125 A3
Wyndale Dr M35 . . . . .83 F5
Wyndale Rd OL8 . . . . .66 F3
Wyndcliff Dr M41 . . . . .94 E1
Wyndham Ave Bolton BL3 .146 A3
Swinton M27 . . . . .61 F3
Wyndham Cl SK7 . . . . . . .132 E7
Wyne Cl SK7 . . . . .125 A3
Wynfield Ave M22 . . . . . . .130 F7
Wynford Sq M5 . . . . .154 F1
Wyngate Rd
Altrincham WA15 . . . . . . .128 F8
Cheadle SK8 . . . . .122 F1
Wynne Ave M27 . . . . .62 A3
Wynne Cl Denton M34 . . . .100 F1
Manchester M11 . . . . . . .164 F8
Wynne Gr M34 . . . . .100 F1
Wynne St Bolton BL1 . . . .143 E2
Salford M6 . . . . .81 B3
Tyldesley M29 . . . . .58 F1
Walkden M38 . . . . .60 A4
Wynnstay Gr M14 . . . . . . .110 C8
Wynnstay Rd M33 . . . . . .108 B5
Wynton Cl WN7 . . . . .75 E2
Wynyard Cl M33 . . . . .108 D2
Wynyard Rd M22 . . . . . . .121 C3
Wyre Ave WN2 . . . . .56 A2
Wyre Cl M45 . . . . .45 B1
Wyre Dr M28 . . . . .78 B7
Wyre St Manchester M1 . .163 B8
Mossley OL5 . . . . .68 B1
Wyresdale Rd BL1 . . . . . .144 C8
Wyrevale Gr WN4 . . . . . . .73 C3
Wythall Ave M38 . . . . .60 A6
Wythburn Ave Bolton BL1 .142 A1
Manchester M8 . . . . .156 C6
Urmston M41 . . . . .95 B3
Wythburn Rd
Middleton M24 . . . . .46 E3
Stockport SK1 . . . . .124 B7
Wythburn St M5,M6 . . . . .154 E2
Wythens Rd SK8 . . . . .131 B8

Wythenshawe Ctr M22 . .121 D2
Wythenshawe Hall
(Art Gal & Mus) M23 . .121 B8
Wythenshawe Hospl M23 120 F5
Wythenshawe Rd
Sale M33 . . . . .108 F4
Wythenshawe M23 . . . . . .109 B1
Wythop Gdns
Salford M5 . . . . .161 A8
Salford M5 . . . . .81 A1
Wyvern Ave SK5 . . . . .111 E5
Wyverne Rd M21 . . . . . . .109 D8
Wyville Cl SK7 . . . . .125 A3
Wyville Dr Manchester M9 . .64 B6
Salford M6 . . . . .154 F3
Swinton M27 . . . . .79 E6

X

Xaverian Coll M14 . . . . . . .98 C3

Y

Yale St BL7 . . . . .9 D4
Yarburgh St M16 . . . . .97 E3
Yardley Ave M32 . . . . .96 A2
Yardley Cl M32 . . . . .96 A2
Yare St 7 BB4 . . . . .2 F8
Yarmouth Dr M23 . . . . . . .109 B1
Yarn Croft M29 . . . . .77 B8
Yarn Wlk 9 M4 . . . . .159 C1
Yarnton Cl OL2 . . . . .149 A5
Yarrow Cl OL11 . . . . .139 F5
Yarrow Gr BL6 . . . . .22 B4
Yarrow Pl BL1 . . . . .143 E1
Yarrow St WN2 . . . . .56 C4
Yarrow Wlk M45 . . . . .45 C1
Yarwell 25 OL12 . . . . .139 E8
Yarwood Ave M23 . . . . . . .120 F7
Yarwood Cl OL10 . . . . .29 E3
Yarwood St
Altrincham WA14 . . . . . . .119 D3
Bury BL9 . . . . .141 A2
Yasmin Gdns OL1 . . . . . . .48 D1
Yates Dr M28 . . . . .60 A3
Yates Gr WN6 . . . . .36 F4
Yates St Bolton BL2 . . . . . .25 A1
Leigh WN7 . . . . .75 E7
Middleton M24 . . . . .64 C7
Oldham OL1 . . . . .49 B1
Stockport SK1 . . . . .112 B3
Yattendon Ave M23 . . . . .120 D8
Yea Fold OL15 . . . . .15 E3
Yeadon Rd M18 . . . . .99 D3
Yealand Ave SK4 . . . . . . .169 D3
Yealand Cl OL11 . . . . .30 B6
Yealand Gr WN2 . . . . .57 A5
Yeardsley Cl SK7 . . . . . . .123 E3
Yellow Brook Cl WN2 . . . . .38 C6
Yellow Lodge Dr BL5 . . . . .40 B1
Yeoford Dr WA14 . . . . . . .119 B6
Yeoman Cl SK7 . . . . .124 D3
Yeoman Wlk M11 . . . . . . .160 F1
Yeoman's Cl OL16 . . . . . . .31 F7
Yeomanry Ct 3 M16 . . . . .97 D3
Yeovil Wlk 10 M16 . . . . . . .97 F3
Yesoiday HaTorah Sch
M25 . . . . .63 B2
Yew Cl BL3 . . . . .146 B4
Yew Cres OL4 . . . . .67 D8
Yew Ct OL12 . . . . .15 B2
Yew Dale Gdns OL11 . . . . .30 B4
Yew Gr WN6 . . . . .36 F4
Yew St Bury BL9 . . . . .141 C3
Denton M34 . . . . .100 F5

Yew St continued
Heywood OL10 . . . . .29 B2
Manchester M15 . . . . . . .162 E5
Manchester M7 . . . . .81 C6
Stockport SK4 . . . . .168 C1
Yew Tree Ave
Cheadle SK7 . . . . .125 A1
Hazel Grove SK7 . . . . . . .124 F1
Manchester M14 . . . . .98 A2
7 Manchester M19 . . . . . .99 A1
Newton-le-W WA12 . . . . . .89 A4
Wythenshawe M22 . . . . . .109 D1
Yew Tree Cl Ashton-u-L OL7 .85 A6
Marple SK6 . . . . .125 E5
Wilmslow SK9 . . . . .137 D7
Yew Tree Com Prim Sch
SK16 . . . . .101 E6
Yew Tree Cres M14 . . . . . .98 B1
Yew Tree Ct OL14 . . . . .6 A8
Yew Tree Dr Bolton BL6 . . .40 B6
Bredbury SK6 . . . . .112 D3
Chadderton OL9 . . . . .65 D7
Prestwich M25 . . . . .63 B4
Sale M33 . . . . .108 A4
Urmston M41 . . . . .94 F4
Wythenshawe M23 . . . . . .109 D1
Yew Tree Farm Trad Est
WA11 . . . . .89 A8
Yew Tree Gr Gatley SK8 . .122 A3
Rawtenstall BB4 . . . . .1 F8
Yew Tree Inf Sch OL9 . . . .66 A4
Yew Tree Jun Sch OL9 . . .66 A4
Yew Tree La Bolton BL1 . . .25 A4
Dukinfield SK16 . . . . .101 F7
Yew Tree Park Rd SK8 . .132 B6
Yew Tree Rd Denton M34 .100 E1
Manchester M14 . . . . .98 B2
Poynton SK10 . . . . .134 B1
Stockport SK3 . . . . .123 F3
Yew Tree Way WA3 . . . . . .90 B7
Yew Wlk 1 M31 . . . . .105 E2
Yewbarrow Cl M29 . . . . . . .77 B7
Yewbarrow Rd 1 OL1 . . . .67 A8
Yewdale Shevington WN6 . .36 B6
Swinton M27 . . . . .62 B1
Yewdale Ave
Billinge WA11 . . . . .71 B1
Bolton BL2 . . . . .25 F2
Yewdale Cres 3 WN1 . . . . .37 B3
Yewdale Dr M24 . . . . .46 E1
Yewdale Gdns BL2 . . . . . . .25 F2
Yewdale Rd
Ashton-in-M WN4 . . . . . . .73 A7
Stockport SK1 . . . . .124 B7
Yewlands Ave M9 . . . . . . .64 D5
Yewtree Ave M46 . . . . .58 C4
Yewtree La Poynton SK12 .133 F3
Wythenshawe M23 . . . . . .109 B2
York Ave Culcheth WA3 . . .91 F2
Haslingden BB4 . . . . .1 B8
Little Lever BL3 . . . . .43 A3
Manchester M16 . . . . .97 C2
Manchester M25 . . . . .63 D2
Oldham OL8 . . . . .66 D4
Rochdale OL11 . . . . .30 A6
Sale M33 . . . . .108 B5
Swinton M27 . . . . .61 D2
Tyldesley M29 . . . . .59 A2
Urmston M41 . . . . .95 E3
York Cl Cheadle SK8 . . . . .123 A5
Denton M34 . . . . .100 F4
York Cres SK9 . . . . .137 D8
York Dr Altrincham WA14 . .119 D1
Hazel Grove SK7 . . . . . . .125 A2
Ramsbottom BL0 . . . . . . .11 A4
Wythenshaw M90 . . . . . . .129 F7
York Pl Adlington PR6 . . . .21 A8
Ashton-u-L OL6 . . . . .166 A4
Manchester M13 . . . . .98 C4

York Rd Altrincham WA14 . .119 C1
Ashton-in-M WN4 . . . . . . .73 B3
Chadderton OL9 . . . . .65 F8
Denton M34 . . . . .100 F4
Droylsden M43 . . . . .83 F3
Hindley WN2 . . . . .56 F6
Hyde SK14 . . . . .113 E8
Irlam M44 . . . . .105 D5
Manchester M21 . . . . . . .109 A8
Manchester SK4 . . . . .111 B5
Sale M33 . . . . .108 A5
York Rd E M24 . . . . .65 C5
York Rd S WN4 . . . . .73 C2
York Rd W M24 . . . . .65 C5
York Sq 6 OL2 . . . . .48 D4
York St Altrincham WA15 . .119 E3
Ashton-u-L M34 . . . . .100 E8
Atherton M46 . . . . .58 D3
Bury BL9 . . . . .141 A2
Farnworth BL4 . . . . .60 E8
Glossop SK13 . . . . .104 E1
Golborne WA3 . . . . .74 A1
Heywood OL10 . . . . .29 D2
Leigh WN7 . . . . .76 D4
Manchester M1 . . . . .163 A8
Manchester M1,M13 . . . .163 A7
Manchester M1,M2 . . . . .159 A1
Manchester M15 . . . . . . .162 E7
Manchester M19 . . . . . . .111 A8
Manchester M20 . . . . . . .110 B3
Manchester M9 . . . . .157 E8
Oldham OL9 . . . . .153 E6
Radcliffe BL9 . . . . .44 D5
Rochdale OL16 . . . . .31 B6
Stockport SK3 . . . . .170 E8
Whitefield M45 . . . . .62 F8
Wigan WN3 . . . . .150 B8
York Terr 19 Bolton BL1 . .143 E2
Glossop SK13 . . . . .116 C8
Sale M33 . . . . .108 A4
Yorkdale Rd OL4 . . . . .67 D6
Yorkshire Rd M31 . . . . . . .105 E2
Yorkshire St
Ashton-u-L OL6 . . . . .166 B3
Manchester M3 . . . . .158 E2
Oldham OL1 . . . . .153 F7
Rochdale OL12,OL16 . . . . .31 A8
Rochdale OL16 . . . . .139 F8
Yorkshire Terr OL5 . . . . . .68 C1
Yorkshire Way SK13 . . . . .116 C8
Youd St WN7 . . . . .75 F5
Youlgreave Cres SK13 . . .171 D1
Young St Farnworth BL4 . . .60 E7
Leigh WN7 . . . . .76 E4
Manchester M3 . . . . .158 E1
Radcliffe M26 . . . . .43 F5
Ramsbottom BL0 . . . . . . .138 B6
Yulan Dr M33 . . . . .107 C4
Yule St SK3 . . . . .170 D8
Yvonne Cl WN4 . . . . .73 D5

Z

Zama St BL0 . . . . .11 A4
Zealand St OL4 . . . . .67 C8
Zebra St M7 . . . . .155 F7
Zedburgh 22 OL12 . . . . . .139 E8
Zeta St M9 . . . . .157 F7
Zetland Ave BL3 . . . . .146 B2
Zetland Ave N BL3 . . . . . .146 B2
Zetland Rd M21 . . . . .109 B8
Zetland St SK16 . . . . .166 C1
Zinnia Dr M44 . . . . .105 E8
Zion Cres M15 . . . . .162 E6
Zion Terr OL12 . . . . .13 E2
Zulu St BL2 . . . . .148 B7
Zurich Gdns SK7 . . . . .123 E3
Zyburn Ct M6 . . . . .80 A3